AMERICAN DEMOCRACY

SECOND EDITION

AMERICAN DEMOCRACY

SECOND EDITION

Lewis Lipsitz

University of North Carolina, Chapel Hill

David M. Speak

Georgia Southern College

St. Martin's Press

New York

Senior Editor: Don Reisman
Development Editor: Bob Weber
Director of Editing: Richard Steins
Project Editor: Bruce Glassman
Production Supervisor: Christine Pearson
Copyeditor: Diana Drew

Book design: Barbara Bert/North 7 Atelier, Ltd.
Cover design: Tom McKeveney
Cover illustration: © Pete Turner/The Image Bank
Picture Editor: June Lundborg Whitworth
Color essays: Caliber Design Planning, Inc.

Library of Congress Catalog Card Number: 88–60538

Manufactured in the United States of America.
32109
fedcba

For information, write to: St. Martin's Press, Inc., 175 Fifth Avenue, New York, NY 10010

ISBN: 0–312–01316–7

For Max Blatt, who first taught me to love political debate.

For Lucho Quiros, Chilean democrat, who chose exile over compliance with tyranny.

L. L.

For Beverly, Julia, Emily, and Margaret.

For Sofia, a child in a slum community in El Salvador, who lives with flea bites every day; and for her mother, who (for now?) can do nothing about them.

D. S.

PREFACE

When we began our careers as university professors, we tended, like many of our colleagues, to put little faith in textbooks. It seemed to us that textbooks typically were dull, overloaded with irrelevant information, and eminently forgettable. For a textbook to clearly articulate opinions and interpretations seemed to be a contradiction in terms; punches had to be pulled, values and commitments disguised, issues evaded or drained of controversy. The few exceptions to these rules only illustrated how extensive the problem was.

It is with considerable irony, then, that we call your attention to our own U.S. politics text. What excuses can we find, now that we have committed the deed and have added one more title to a genre we ourselves distrusted?

American Democracy, we tell ourselves, is different. Although it, too, canvasses the nuts and bolts of U.S. government and politics, it does so to achieve something more. Its details amass to explore the concept of democracy—specifically, to examine how democratic principles and ideals fare within the U.S. political process. By describing American politics within this framework, we encourage readers to form judgments about how successful our democracy has been.

In short, this book links theory and practice in the hope that we will stimulate and provoke both students and professors. It is a skeptical book. We are not satisfied, by a long shot, with the current state of democratic politics in the United States.

Two centuries have brought us a long way toward remedying many obviously undemocratic aspects of our system, but many challenges remain—in the distribution of economic and political power, in foreign policy, in how political influence is exercised, in the working of our presidency and Congress, in the vast gaps between public information and understanding. We are not inclined to dampen our concerns about these things by accepting that the real world can never live up to supposedly utopian ideas; nor do we think anyone—least of all the young—should simply be satisfied with what we've got, more or less. Such "realism," in our opinion, is a bad compromise with history. It denies how much effort must continuously be activated if democracy—in this or any nation—is to survive and, more important, to prosper. And so our book is a critical one, designed to entice readers into asking difficult and sometimes uncomfortable questions.

We hope that the questions we raise are interesting ones and, above all, that *American Democracy* will not bore its readers. If this text is to have a meaning more enduring than its service in a one-semester required course, it is that readers remain aware throughout the book of our underlying purpose—understanding and judging democratic politics.

We don't mind saying that we care deeply about the subjects discussed here. Having lived in the United States and having participated in the turmoil of the sixties, having spent our adult lives teaching about politics, we readily acknowledge that we have wondered about, fought over, and tried to influence many of these issues. Yet it is our caring, not our political positions, that we hope to communicate to readers. By adding our textbook to the pile, we seek not agreement but a sharing of concern and a desire to think things through.

Acknowledgments

We appreciate the helpful suggestions—some solicited, some not—from many instructors who used the First Edition of *American Democracy*; the Second Edition no doubt benefits from their reports of classroom experiences with students of all kinds. We are especially grateful for the close examination the text received from Sue Davis, University of Delaware, Newark; Carol Lynn Tebben, University of Wisconsin, Parkside; R. Lawson Veasey, University of Central Arkansas; Ken Wald, University of Florida, Gainesville; and John Wettergreen, San Jose State.

More personally, we want to thank Doris Elkin for her help in preparing the manuscript for the Second Edition; Dan Levin for assistance in gathering and preparing data and other material; Bob Weber, a sagacious and generous development editor; and Lane Van Tassell, Jurg Steiner, Dick Richardson, and Thad Beyle for their encouragement. The efforts of two people on the First Edition keep us in their debt: Pam Mason, whose vital editorial assistance, research, and capacity for organization are still evident in the book; and Jinny Joyner, whose editorial skills and judgment shaped that first manuscript into publishable form. Finally, special thanks are reserved for Mary Clarke, who helped the senior author keep his perspective during work on the Second Edition.

Lou Lipsitz, Chapel Hill, North Carolina
Dave Speak, Statesboro, Georgia

CONTENTS

Introduction DEMOCRACY 1
The Real and the Ideal

COLOR ESSAY: **Continental Drift: New Americans in an Old Story**

COMPARATIVE PERSPECTIVE: **Which Nations Are Democracies?** 8

COMPARATIVE PERSPECTIVE: **The Consociational Model of Democracy** 18

Plessy v. *Ferguson* 20

Support for an Undemocratic Regime: Ferdinand Marcos 22

Various Definitions of Democracy 3
Majoritarian Democracy 3 • Liberal Democracy 4 • Egalitarian Democracy 6 • A Comprehensive View 6
Ideal and Real Democracies 7
Problems in Democratic Life 10
Uneven Distribution of Power 10 • Failure to Exercise Rights 12 • The Relationship between Government and Citizen 15
Is Democracy the Best System? 17
Struggles to Realize Democratic Ideals 19
Restricting Democracy 19 • Extending Democracy 23
The Plan of This Book 26

PART **I** FOUNDATIONS

1 AMERICAN POLITICAL CULTURE 31
Liberty and Its Limits

COMPARATIVE PERSPECTIVE: **Political Culture, Old and New** 33

COMPARATIVE PERSPECTIVE: **A Look at the National Characteristics of Sweden** 36

Judge Ginsburg and the Regulation of Morals 39

What Is Political Culture? 32
Political Culture and Democracy 32 • Cohesiveness in Political Culture 32
The Liberal Tradition 34
Economic, Social, and Political Values 35 • The Legacy of Liberalism 37

ix

Immigration Law Reform 42

The Melting Pot Today 43

Political Assassination
in America 46

Two Types of Liberalism 38
*Conservatism: Traditional Liberalism 38 • The New
Liberalism 39 • The Failure of Radicalism 40*
Limits of Liberalism 41
*Intolerance and Discrimination 41 • Violence and the Rule of
Law 44 • Making the World Safe for Democracy—or for
Us? 47 • Religion and Morality in Politics 49*

2   REVOLUTION AND CONSTITUTION   53
The American Way

COLOR ESSAY: **Debating the
Constitution: Political Roads
Not Taken**

"Half a Revolution" 56

**Thomas Paine: Radical Democrat,
Pamphleteer Supreme 59**

COMPARATIVE PERSPECTIVE: **The
French Revolution and Its
Aftermath 62**

What Is a Constitution? 64

Jefferson and Slavery 66

**Chronology of the
Constitution 70**

COMPARATIVE PERSPECTIVE:
**Americans Write Another
Constitution 75**

SUPPLEMENT: **Assessing the
Constitution Today 76**

COMPARATIVE PERSPECTIVE:
**Constitutional Democratic
Systems 77**

Background of the Revolution 54
*The Socioeconomic Environment 54 • The Political
Environment 55 • Imperial Authority and American Defiance 56*
The Revolutionary War 58
Independence Sparks Ferment 61
The Postrevolutionary Era 61 • The Articles of Confederation 61
The Constitutional Convention 63
*A Stronger National Government 63 • The Slavery
Issue 65 • Fragmentation of Power 65 • Four Key
Issues 69 • Ratification 71*
Amending the Constitution 73
An Enduring Political Legacy 74
Is the Constitution Outdated? 76

3   AMERICAN FEDERALISM   85
Can Democracy Be Divided Fifty Ways?

Limits on Government Power 89

The Northwest Ordinance
of 1787 91

Federal-State Relations after
McCulloch v. *Maryland* 95

State Taxes: The Burden
Varies 103

COMPARATIVE PERSPECTIVE:
Federalism in West Germany 106

Federalism: An Overview 86
*Division of Powers 88 • Limitations on Government
Actions 89 • Interstate Obligations 90 • Statehood and
the Alternatives 90*
The Evolution of Federalism 92
*Three Crises of State and Nation 92 • The Role of the
Courts 95 • "New Federalisms" 96*
Responsibilities of the States 100
*Education 100 • Transportation 101 • Health and
Welfare 101 • Criminal Justice 101 • Other Responsibilities 101*

Tensions in the Federal System   102
*Regional Rivalries   102 • Issues That Strain
Federalism   104 • Infrastructure—Whose Problem?   105*
Federal Intervention   107
*Reapportionment   107 • The Voting Rights Act   107 • The
Drinking Age   108*
When Intervention Fails   109

---

4   THE EVOLUTION OF RIGHTS AND LIBERTIES   114
Democracy with a Human Face

The Alien and Sedition Acts
of 1798   121

COMPARATIVE PERSPECTIVE: **Political
Extremism in Australia and West
Germany   124**

Highlights of Civil Rights
Progress   133

The Ludlow Massacre of 1913   147

The Harassment of Martin Luther
King, Jr.   150

The Bill of Rights and Constitutional Protections   116
*Federalism and Civil Liberties   117 • Freedom of
Speech   119 • Freedom of Religion   124 • The Rights of
the Accused   128 • Abortion   130*
Civil Rights   132
*The Right to Vote   132 • Blacks and Equal Rights   132 • Affirmative
Action and Black Progress   139 • Women and Equal Rights   144*
Basic Social Rights   145
*Pure Food and Drugs   145 • Trade Unions and Collective
Bargaining   147*
Government Repression   148

---

5   THE AMERICAN POLITICAL ECONOMY   154
Inequality and Democratic Politics

The TVA: An Experiment in
Socialism   157

COMPARATIVE PERSPECTIVE: **Income
Distribution in Selected
Nations   162**

Capitalism and Socialism   155
Capitalism   155 • Socialism   157 • Mixed Systems   158
The U.S. Political Economy   160
*Distribution of Income   162 • Distribution of Wealth and
Ownership   164 • Poverty   166*
Public Policy and the Political Economy   168
*Government Spending, Taxation, and Regulation   169 • Government
and Inequality   172*

PART **II**   POLITICS

6   PUBLIC SENTIMENT AND
ELECTORAL TRENDS   179
Majority Rule in Practice

COMPARATIVE PERSPECTIVE: **National
Pride and Military Service   182**

Rallying around the President   201

Majority Rule: An Overview   180
Political Socialization   181
*Childhood   182 • The Role of the School   185 • College
and Politics   186*
Public Opinion   187

Classifying Presidential
Elections 210

COMPARATIVE PERSPECTIVE: **Fewer
Voters, but More Voting 212**

*Gauging Public Opinion 188 • Public Opinion and
Democracy 190 • Efficacy and Alienation 194*
Understanding Public Sentiment 196
*Liberalism and Conservatism 196 • Contemporary Trends in U.S.
Politics 196 • Liberal and Conservative Views on Specific
Issues 197 • An Emerging Post-Materialist Dimension 202
Influences on Public Sentiment 202*
Electoral Trends 204
*Social Bases of Voting Patterns 204 • The 1950s—Ideology in
Decline 206 • The 1960s—the Reemergence of Ideology 207 • The
Elections of 1984 and 1986 208*
Nonparticipation 210
Barriers to Voting 211 • Who Votes? 213
Opinion and Policy 215

7 *POLITICAL PARTIES*   *221*
    Do They Offer a Choice?

COLOR ESSAY: **Campaign '88: Politics
as Usual?**

COMPARATIVE PERSPECTIVE: **Why
Margaret Thatcher Won a
"Majority" in 1987 226**

COMPARATIVE PERSPECTIVE: **The
Disciplined Parties of
Great Britain 234**

COMPARATIVE PERSPECTIVE: **A New
Party in West Germany 242**

Characteristics of Political Parties 222
*Three Facets of Political Parties 222 • Functions of Political
Parties 223 • Two-Party and Multiparty Systems 224*
The U.S. Party System 226
*Origins of Contemporary Parties 227 • The System of
1896 228 • The New Deal Coalition 229 • Since the New
Deal 230 • Dilemmas and Contributions of Third Parties 231 • Party
Organization 232 • Party Reforms After 1968 236 • Do the Political
Parties Differ? 240*
Current Issues 241
*The Decline of Parties 241 • Realignment: Who Has the
Majority? 243 • Party Responsibility and Party Reform 244*

8 *CAMPAIGNS, MONEY, AND THE MEDIA*   *248*
    Packaging Politics

COMPARATIVE PERSPECTIVE: **The
Election Game in Great
Britain 258**

COMPARATIVE PERSPECTIVE: **Foreign
Media 266**

**The Scripting of the
President 270**

The Lincoln-Douglas Debates 275

Campaigning: Beyond the Razzle-Dazzle 249
Political Campaigns 250
*Nonpresidential Campaigns 250 • Presidential Campaigns 252
The Electoral College 257*
Campaign Financing 259
*Reform Efforts 261 • The Consequences of Reform 262
Further Reforms 264*
Politics and the Media 265
Gathering the News 267 • Framing the Issues 267
Media and Campaigns 268
*The Media's Impact on Elections 268 • Image-making 271
Televised Presidential Debates 273 • Media and "Horse Races" 276*

9 INTEREST-GROUP POLITICS 282
Democracy to the Highest Bidder?

COMPARATIVE PERSPECTIVE: **British Trade Unions** 288

COMPARATIVE PERSPECTIVE: **Guns and Public Policy** 296

A Theorem on Special Interests 299

Interest-Group Dynamics 284
Functions of Interest Groups 285 • Problems with Interest Groups 286

Major Interest Groups 287
Business 287 • Labor 288 • The Defense Lobby 290 • Public Interest Groups 292 • Single-Issue Groups 294

How Lobbying Works 297
Overall Strategies 298 • Influence-Seeking through the Courts 301 • Insider and Outsider Strategies 301 • The New Lobbying 304

Regulation and the Public Interest 304
Regulatory Efforts 304 • Government and Interest Groups 305

10 MASS POLITICS AND PROTEST 309
A Threat? Or a Necessity?

The Invisible Empire 314

COMPARATIVE PERSPECTIVE: **Gandhi: The Essence of Nonviolence** 317

COMPARATIVE PERSPECTIVE: **The Referendum in Switzerland** 323

SUPPLEMENT: **From Martin Luther King's Letter from Birmingham Jail** 325

Extraordinary Politics 310
The Whys of Protest 312 • Extraordinary Politics and Government Action 313

Protest and Disobedience 315
Law and Disobedience 316 • Civil Disobedience: A Compromise 319

How Protest Works 319
Consciousness-Raising 320 • Activating Others 320 • Contexts for Effective Protest 320 • Limitations of Protest Tactics 320

Protest through the Ballot 322

PART **III** *INSTITUTIONS*

11 THE CONGRESS 333
The Heart of Democracy?

COLOR ESSAY: **The Enigma of Leadership: What *Is* the Right Stuff for Democracy?**

COMPARATIVE PERSPECTIVE: **The British Parliament** 339

The Rider: A Key Part of the Legislative Process 347

Basebuilding: One Way to Stay in Office 353

Voices from the U.S. Congress 356

The Filibuster: The Senate's Sacred Cow 358

Congress: An Overview 334
The Nature of Representation 334 • Functions of Congress 335

The Structure of Congress 337
The Hierarchy of Congress 338 • Legislative Committees 341 • How a Bill Becomes a Law 345

Members of Congress 349
Personal Characteristics 349 • Professional Concerns 350 • Influences on Voting Patterns 352 • Congressional Ethics 355

Tradition and Reform 357

Congress and the President 359
The Legislative Veto 361 • Congress and Secrets 361 • Congress and the War Powers Act 362 • Congress and the Budget 364

12 THE AMERICAN PRESIDENT   369
Unique, Necessary, and Dangerous

COMPARATIVE PERSPECTIVE: **The Head of State in West Germany 372**

Ronald Reagan: Revolutionary President? 378

The Presidential Pen, the Congressional Eraser 385

Congress Manipulated: The Gulf of Tonkin Resolution 387

COMPARATIVE PERSPECTIVE: **Political Crisis and Transition in France, 1958 392**

SUPPLEMENT: **U.S. Presidential Elections, 1789–1988 396**

The Unique President 370
Pressing Against the Limits of Power 371 • *Paradoxes of the Office 375*

The Necessary President 376
The Executive Office 380 • *The Cabinet 381* • *The Rest of the Bureaucracy 383* • *Relations with Congress 383*

The Dangerous President 386
The Vietnam War 388 • *The Watergate Affair 388* • *The Iran-Contra Affair 389*

Transition of Power 391
Modes of Succession 392 • *The Vice-Presidency 393*

13 THE BUREAUCRACY   400
Servant or Master?

COMPARATIVE PERSPECTIVE: **British and French Bureaucracies 407**

Reduce Speed: Bureaucracy at Work 416

Seven Propositions about Government Regulation 419

The Structure of the National Bureaucracy 403
Cabinet Departments 405 • *Independent Agencies 405* • *Regulatory Commissions 406*

Bureaucracy and the Political Process 406
Bureaucratic Discretion 409 • *Bureaucratic Expertise 410* • *Mobilization of Support 410*

Bureaucracy Evaluated 411
Is It Too Unresponsive? 411 • *Is There Too Much of It? 413* • *Are There Too Many Rules? 415* • *The Scorecard 420*

14 THE FEDERAL JUDICIARY   423
Nonelected Defenders of Democracy

COMPARATIVE PERSPECTIVE: **Court Systems in Sweden and Great Britain 432**

Marbury v. *Madison* **434**

Judge Garrity: Educator or Judicial Imperialist? 441

The U.S. Legal System 425
State Court Systems 426 • *The Federal Court System 427* • *The Flow of Litigation 427* • *The Decision-Making Process 429* • *Recruitment of Judges 430*

Powers and Restraints 431
Judicial Review 431 • *Self-Restraints on Power 432* • *Legislative Reaction 434* • *Noncompliance 435*

Major Periods in Supreme Court History 436
Focus on the Distribution of Power 436 • *Concern for Individual Rights 437* • *The Warren Court (1953–1969) 437* • *The Post-Warren Era 438*

The Dilemma of an Expanded Legal System 440

PART **IV** *PUBLIC POLICY*

15 *CREATING PUBLIC POLICY*   *447*
Power and Agendas

How Issues Reach the Political Agenda 448
Processing Issues 450
Competing Agendas 450 • Dealing with Issues 451
Policy Formulation and Implementation 452
Proposals for Action 452 • Implementation 453
Policy Evaluation 454
Who Rules and Why It Matters 454
Elitist and Pluralist Views 454 • The Boundaries of Policy Making 456

16 *MANAGEMENT OF THE ECONOMY*   *458*
In Whose Interest?

The Great Depression, City and Country 463

COMPARATIVE PERSPECTIVE: Industrial Policy 480

Economics and Democracy 459
History of Economic Management 459
Mercantilism 460 • Laissez Faire and the Growth of Regulation 460 • Controlled Capitalism 461 • The Recent Past 462
Tools of Economic Intervention 465
Fiscal Policy 465 • Monetary Policy 468
The Politics of Economics 469
Fiscal Policy in the 1960s 469 • Paul Volcker, the Fed, and Monetarism 470 • Reagan and Supply-Side Economics 471
Emerging Problems 474
Tax Equity and Tax Expenditures 474 • Federal Budget Deficits 475 • The Transformation of the Work Force 476 • The Decline in Industrial Power 477

17 *THE WELFARE STATE*   *484*
Benefiting the Poor and the Nonpoor

COLOR ESSAY: Life in the Margin: Poverty Now

Appalachian Development: Success or Failure? 487

COMPARATIVE PERSPECTIVE: A Cure for British Health Care? 495

COMPARATIVE PERSPECTIVE: Child Care Programs: Sweden v. the United States 501

The U.S. Welfare State 485
Income Security Programs 489
Social Security 489 • AFDC 491 • Job Programs 492 • Other Income Security Programs 493
Health Care Programs 494
Medicare 494 • Other Health Care Programs 496
Nutrition and Housing Programs 498
Food Stamps 498 • Other Nutrition Programs 500 • Housing Programs 502
Evaluating the Welfare State 503
The Conservative Approach 503 • The Liberal Critique 504 • Reflections on Policy 505

18 CIVIL LIBERTIES, CIVIL AND SOCIAL RIGHTS   *510*
Is Justice Being Done?

Freedom to Visit 516
OSHA and Cotton Dust 529

Civil Liberties in a Pluralistic Society 511
Gay Rights 512 • The Treatment of Immigrants 514
Government Intrusion into Personal Space 516
Obscenity 516 • The FBI and Domestic
Surveillance 518 • Mandatory Testing 519
Treatment as Equals 521
Rights of the Disabled 521 • Government Actions on Gender
Discrimination 523
Black America—Progress and Decline 525
Social Rights 526

19 FOREIGN AND DEFENSE POLICIES   *533*
What Values Are We Defending?

COLOR ESSAY: **A Race with No
Winners: Nuclear Arms and
National Security**

**The Reagan Doctrine and
Low-Intensity Warfare** 541

**Nuclear War: No Place to
Hide** 549

Human Rights Policy 558

A Historical Perspective 534
Isolation and Expansion 534
The Making of Foreign Policy 535
The President and the Executive Branch 535 • Influences on
Foreign Policy 538
Relations with the Soviet Union 540
Origins of the Cold War 540 • Containment 542 • Peaceful
Coexistence 542 • Regional Conflicts 543 • Crises and
Detente 545 • The 1980s: A Decade of Shifting
Patterns 546 • Current Issues 547
The Arms Race 548
Nuclear Strategy 548 • Arms Control Talks 549 • Reduced
Expectations in a Dangerous World 552 • Costs 552
The Third World 553
Movements for Social Change 553 • Economics: Rich and Poor 557

20 ENERGY AND ENVIRONMENT   *564*
Fulfilling or Polluting the American Dream?

The Ozone Layer 570
COMPARATIVE PERSPECTIVE: The
Europeans Deal with Toxic
Wastes 576
The Tellico Dam: A Triumph of
Bad Sense 585

Environmental Impacts 565
The Environment: From Exploitation to Protection 565
Environmental Problems and Government Responses 568
Air Pollution 569 • Water Pollution 573 • Toxic Chemicals 574
The Politics of Environmental Issues 578
Group Strategies 578 • The Reagan Record on the Environment 578
Energy: Its Sources and Problems 579
Energy Production and Consumption 580 • Alternative
Solutions 583 • The Politics of Energy Issues 586

Epilogue
On Improving American Democracy   591

Appendix A
The Declaration of Independence   599

Appendix B
The Constitution of the United States   601

Appendix C
Glossary of Terms   619

Index   629

AMERICAN DEMOCRACY
SECOND EDITION

DEMOCRACY

The Real and the Ideal

CHAPTER OUTLINE

Various Definitions of Democracy
Ideal and Real Democracies
Problems in Democratic Life
Is Democracy the Best System?
Struggles to Realize Democratic Ideals
The Plan of This Book

Tom Hollyman/Photo Researchers

Most Americans are used to thinking of their country as a "democracy." In fact, public opinion research has shown that Americans are particularly proud that they live in a democratic country. There is no point in debating whether or not the United States is a democracy—as if there were only two categories that nations could fit into, the democratic and the undemocratic. In the ordinary sense in which the term is used, the United States clearly is a democratic nation. However, here is a more difficult, more subtle, more interesting question: Just *how democratic* are we?

To put this question into perspective, imagine a society with a written constitution that grants everyone the right to vote, holds free elections, proclaims its belief in free speech, a free press, the rights of political parties to organize and advance their views, and so on. Superficially, such a nation might seem democratic. But we would have to look beyond the constitution to find out if, in fact, that was the case. For example, we might, on closer examination, discover that this nation was actually ruled by a small group of wealthy landowners who ignored the constitutional provisions whenever it was convenient to do so. Most of the inhabitants might be relatively poor peasants who depended on the landowners for employment. Anyone voicing serious dissent might be jailed or otherwise intimidated.

We draw several conclusions from this hypothetical case. To begin with, the written word is not enough: Democratic provisions in a constitution may or may not be honored in practice. Second, we see that great differences in wealth and power can undermine the drive for democracy. Where very few control most of the wealth and have inordinate access to power, democracy is usually drained of its meaning.

Consider another case: a country that gradually moves toward greater degrees of democracy. Early in this nation's history, only some citizens are granted the right to vote. Over decades, after considerable agitation and struggle, others are permitted to join the vote as well. Finally, after almost two hundred years, suffrage is opened to all. Nonetheless, many citizens remain ignorant about politics, and almost half of those who could vote simply do not bother to do so, even in the most important elections. How democratic would we say such a nation was?

The nation just described, of course, is the United States—in which women and blacks not only were excluded from suffrage for many years, but were also denied full legal protections for voting rights until 1920 and 1965, respectively. In our society today, many citizens remain politically uninformed and inactive, with only 50 percent of eligible voters likely to turn out even in presidential elections.

Democracy is a matter of degree and quality. The question of whether or not a country is democratic can be viewed from many perspectives:

> Are the political rights of every citizen effectively protected (and exercised)?
>
> Is the level of public knowledge high? Is public discussion informed and useful?
>
> Do most people, and especially most leaders, support the democratic idea?
>
> Do some people or groups have power and influence in great disproportion to their numbers?
>
> Does the government honor its stated principles in dealing with the people? Does it violate its own laws?
>
> Are political institutions honest, leaders trustworthy?
>
> Does the government often use violence against citizens? Is political life characterized by a high level of coercion?
>
> Does each citizen have a realistic chance of attaining and maintaining basic security, a reasonable standard of living, and opportunities for education and some amenities?
>
> Are some groups discriminated against and/or excluded from full participation in social and political life?
>
> Do violent confrontations between groups occur outside the political arena?
>
> Do nongovernmental institutions, such as churches, unions, and social organizations, encourage democratic attitudes and practices?

Some of these questions are fairly easy to answer. For example, it is not hard to see that the degree of democracy in the United States was once sharply diminished by the systematic denial of basic political rights to blacks. Other questions are tougher to handle. Exactly how much "influence" is too much influence? Just how great a degree of equality can we reasonably aim for in the power and political leverage exercised by various groups?

TABLE 1
Survey of Satisfaction with the Way Democracy Works (Percent)

Country	Very satisfied	Fairly satisfied	Not very satisfied	Not at all satisfied	Don't know	Index*
Belgium	4	43	33	15	5	2.39
Denmark	20	50	19	5	6	2.89
Federal Republic of Germany	11	61	21	5	2	2.78
France	4	34	38	14	10	2.32
Greece	18	39	24	13	6	2.67
Ireland	6	38	30	20	6	2.33
Italy	3	25	45	26	1	2.04
Luxembourg	11	57	24	5	3	2.75
Netherlands	7	51	30	9	3	2.57
United Kingdom	12	48	27	10	3	2.63
European Community (weighted average)	8	43	32	13	4	2.48

*Higher scores reflect relative satisfaction and lower scores relative dissatisfaction. Point system for the index: very satisfied = 4; not at all satisfied = 1.

SOURCE: Jurg Steiner, *European Democracies* (New York: Longman, 1986), Chap. 16.

After all, won't some individuals and some groups always wield greater power than others in even the most democratic polity?

These are the basic issues addressed in this book. Because this is a text on U.S. politics, it covers many topics, from constitutional history to current debate about nuclear weapons. But the connecting thread, knitting the chapters loosely together, is the idea of "democracy": We will try to understand the strengths and weaknesses of U.S. politics from a democratic perspective. In each chapter, the reader will be asked to weigh the democratic issues involved, to decide just how democratic our society is, or might be. **Table 1** reports a survey of how satisfied Europeans are with the way democracy works in their countries. Overall, the Danes, West Germans, Greeks, and British express the highest levels of satisfaction with democracy, while the Italians, French, Irish, and Belgians show lower levels of satisfaction. Given a similar sort of question, Americans scored more like the Danes than like the Italians, with 72 percent saying that our political system was "basically sound" despite needing some improvements.

Before discussing specific issues, however, we must decide just what constitutes democracy. To do so, we will now explore the various ways of

viewing democracy and then try to come up with an overall definition to serve as a yardstick as we examine the U.S. political system. Along the way we must inevitably make distinctions between democratic ideals and democracy in practice.

Various Definitions of Democracy

Confusion often arises in discussion about democracy. Frequently, this stems from the different premises people have in mind when they use the term. Most people fail to specify their underlying premises, and as a result, we often incorporate into our sense of democracy disparate elements that may or may not relate to it. To avoid such confusion, we must identify the key ideas central to democracy, and then clarify precisely how the term will be used in this book.

Majoritarian Democracy

The most basic and straightforward notion of democracy is that of simple majority rule. This means that a majority of the people give their consent to specific policies or leaders. They can do so either directly or through representatives selected to rule in the name of the people. But does **majoritarian democracy** give rise to a reasonably workable, equitable, and fair political system? Will a majority, for example, decide to outlaw certain religions or political factions? Will it take away the property of those few who hold great wealth? Will it be able to run the government in a coherent and sensible fashion? These are questions that a simple definition of majoritarian democracy cannot answer. Yet they are the very questions that have been asked about majoritarian democracy since its beginnings in ancient Greece.

It was in Athens that the issues associated with majority rule first became highly charged. Democracy in ancient Athens took the form of a legislative assembly selected by lot, which meant that any citizen might be called on to serve. In addition, there were popular courts, whose members also were selected by lot. Basic issues of public policy were debated in the assembly, with the citizens listening, participating, and finally voting to decide the issues. Defenders of majority rule in Athens saw this system as a device for allowing the populace to have a voice in political decision making. Any other arrangement, they argued, would tend to place power exclusively in the hands of the rich or the well-born—as had often been the case in Athens before the democratic reforms. For democrats* the Athenian political system demonstrated that a random selection of the people could assemble and attend to the public's business in a reasonable fashion. Some also argued that the Athenian experience showed that people who participate in making and enforcing the laws are likely to be more law-abiding. Democracy, that is, made for a more committed citizenry.

Critics of majoritarian democracy had no shortage of arguments either. They maintained that democracy could degenerate into sheer mob rule under which no one is safe. Property could be seized by the majority. Unpopular ideas could be suppressed. A popular assembly or jury might be easily swayed by emotion. Worst of all, the critics

*The term *democrat*, with a small *d*, refers to those who support "democratic" ideas and practices. The term *Democrat*, with a capital *D*, refers to supporters of the Democratic party of the United States.

charged, majoritarianism recognized no moral limits to its authority. A majority was empowered to do *anything*. The democrats replied that despite these problems, the majority was likely to rule more wisely than would any self-selected group of rich or powerful individuals.

Many of these same arguments have surfaced again and again throughout Western history. Can the people make decisions? Are experts needed to rule? Will majorities violate the rights of minorities? Or is it more likely that a ruling minority will violate the rights of a majority?

Liberal Democracy

A second, somewhat more complex view of democracy, and the one most familiar to Americans, is what has become known as **liberal democracy.** This concept combines majority rule with respect for civil liberties and protection of individual rights. In general, when people in the Western world today speak of democratic government, this is what they have in mind.

The concept of liberal democracy first came into political thought about three hundred years ago, when a great debate raged in Europe over the powers of kings and the rights of citizens. The monarchs of the seventeenth and eighteenth centuries claimed they ruled by "divine right," but the early liberal democrats envisioned a different kind of political society. Besides arguing for a society based on the consent of those governed, they also began to talk about basic human rights, equality among citizens, and the right to protest and rebel against oppressive governments.

These critics of monarchy were in no sense egalitarians, however. Many of them wanted a government based only on the consent of a small, prosperous middle class; very few were willing to advocate a society based on the consent of *all*. The notion that every person should have a voice in shaping the destiny of political life was so radical then it was barely conceivable. Many of the struggles over democracy in the last two centuries have focused directly on this issue: *Whose* consent is to be sought by a government based on the consent of the governed?

These modern democratic ideas developed in concert with a new socioeconomic system known

Voters wait in long lines to cast their ballots in the 1982 elections in El Salvador. The turnout was high, and a government elected. The U.S. government hailed the elections as a sign of El Salvador's developing democratic character. Elections are of course a necessary element in democracy, but they should not be seen as sufficient evidence that democracy exists. *(James Nachtwey/Black Star)*

as **capitalism.** The rising middle classes of the seventeenth and eighteenth centuries wanted to gain full freedom to buy and sell, to accumulate wealth, and generally to conduct business without government interference. Many observers have argued that democracy became possible only because of the rise of capitalism, which emphasized individual rights and individual potential. Capitalists struggled to limit government power, defending the individual's rights to carve out a sphere of private life exempt from government interference. It must be noted, however, that though these efforts contributed to an atmosphere in which democratic ideas could take hold, the simultaneous development of a capitalist economic system and a democratic political system also created problems and tensions that persist to this day (and form the basis of a third view of democracy, to be discussed shortly).

Today the two tenets underlying democracy are **majority rule** and the protection of **basic rights** for all citizens. Majority rule takes shape mainly through regular elections, though the exact type and timing of elections vary considerably from one nation to another. In the United States the timing of elections is fixed by law—every four years, for example, for the presidency. In Great Britain, a prime minister can call an election at any time within a five-year term.

Sometimes majorities are easy to recognize, as when a referendum (a specific issue on the ballot) must be approved or defeated. But in democratic elections, the clarity of majority opinion, and therefore the strength of majority rule, varies according to how clearly the issues are drawn between the competing parties and candidates. On occasion, a numerical majority is actually made up of a series of minorities, each supporting a particular candidate or party for different reasons. Sometimes parties and candidates deliberately blur the issues to gain more votes. All these factors make it difficult to determine just what majority rule means in any one case. Nonetheless, rule by majorities is a crucial element in democratic life today.

Equally crucial is the protection of basic rights. Citizens must have the right to organize groups, to form and join political parties, to acquire information, to protest in various ways, and to express and exchange opinions publicly. Without such rights, public opinion easily could be manipulated, authority abused, and elections made meaningless. And though elections are usually the most significant means of shaping public policy, they are not the only means. U.S. citizens, for instance, can try to influence political parties to nominate candidates holding particular views and also seek change through the courts. They can protest in the streets. They can lobby in Washington. They can peacefully refuse to obey certain laws.

Democracy must protect another set of basic rights as well—the rights fundamental to a decent social and political order. Such protections include prohibitions against the arbitrary exercise of government authority. In the United States, for example, the government is required to follow **due process of law** in dealing with its citizens: People cannot be arrested without reason or confined indefinitely without trial, property cannot be confiscated without cause, cruel and unusual punishments cannot be imposed. In the struggle against the monarchies of the late eighteenth century, democrats fought to ensure that citizens were not subject to such arbitrary government action.

Finally, the concept of **equal protection of the laws** is critical to democratic life. Equal protection means that no individual or group can be denied the rights and privileges granted to others. The question of who should be given equal protection has been one of the most fiercely contested issues in democratic nations over the last two centuries.

The early adherents of democracy focused most of their attention on curbing the arbitrary exercise of government power, and tended to ignore the power wielded by nongovernment institutions such as churches, businesses, and private groups. Also, their conception of rights was relatively limited: They sought primarily to protect rights already in existence. Later proponents of democratic rights took a more far-reaching approach, one in which the government played a much more creative role. For example, many of us would argue that every citizen has the right to an education. Guaranteeing such a right involves positive government action and community decision making, rather than simply the protection of a right already possessed by the citizen. In other words, the views on civil liberties and rights held by our nation's founders were significantly more restricted than those held widely today.

Egalitarian Democracy

A third view of democracy holds that it is not enough to specify and protect liberties and rights; an attempt must also be made to provide for basic social and economic equality. **Egalitarian democracy** finds the spirit of democracy violated in societies in which a few enjoy lives of affluence while many live in poverty. Such a democrat advocates a significant redistribution of wealth and calls for the equalization of educational opportunities and vigorous enforcement of laws protecting people from exploitation. For the egalitarian democrat, democracy attains its full meaning only in a society of relative equality.

Such views were first advanced about one hundred years ago by critics of the capitalist system, who maintained that real democracy could not work as long as large social and economic inequalities persisted in society. Giving each person a vote would hardly provide for genuine equality of influence, they argued. How could the average worker hope to compete politically with a wealthy and powerful industrialist? It might take an organization of thousands of workers to wield as much real political clout as a single steel company owner. These critics called for radical changes in the patterns of ownership in democratic societies; in their view, greater social and economic equality were preconditions for real rule by the people. Otherwise, they contended, there would be only partial rule by the people and partial rule by those possessing great economic power.

A Comprehensive View

The concept of **democracy** explored in this book incorporates the basic elements of all three interpretations: that democracy (1) must be founded on majority rule as expressed through meaningful, competitive elections, (2) must include effective protections for individual rights and liberties; and (3) must strive to achieve a significant degree of equality among citizens. Beyond these elements, however, the idea of democracy presented here encompasses several other factors: citizen participation that is extensive and informed, government that is honest and does not use unwarranted force to impose order, and foreign policies that serve democratic purposes as much as possible.

Using this rather detailed conception of democracy we will be examining the government, politics, and policies of the United States today. As a yardstick definition it sets a high standard, and in this text we will be probing democracy to explore the myriad possibilities inherent in it. To be sure, many of them have *not* been achieved, in the United States or anywhere else; some may not even be within reach. Of course, this definition, like the others just described, is itself controversial and subject to many interpretations—but then, that is what political discourse is all about.

Ideal and Real Democracies

We can construct the ideal circumstances for a democratic society. To begin, imagine a rather small, homogeneous community, with limited and generally acceptable inequalities. The citizens are active, informed participants in the political process. They attend town meetings. They talk and debate, weighing important issues with genuine inquisitiveness. They are fiercely committed to the democratic process and to the ideals of democratic life. They are fair-minded and tolerant, accepting and even encouraging dissent. Children are reared in families that stress equality among parents and respect for the young, and they learn early in life that they are personally secure.

No gross differences in wealth, power, and respect separate the citizens. There are no juxtapositions of conspicuous wealth and acute deprivation, no slums located two blocks from expensive condominiums. There are no color or gender barriers, prejudice and group hatred having long since dissolved in the soothing waters of common citizenship. These democratic citizens take their social and political responsibilities seriously; they inculcate respect for the law, but a respect that is not idolatrous. They recognize that democratic commitments sometimes allow for disobedience to law.

The government of this ideal democracy is highly responsive. Citizens' views are frequently consulted. Political debate, during campaigns, for example, is reasonable and civil. Candidates do not make personal assaults on each other, or attempt to obscure the issues, or pander to the baser emotions of the public; a democratic public would reject such tactics quickly and thoroughly. Political

Our political system provides for one person/one vote, but our economic system leads to a world in which some command far more resources than others. An egalitarian democrat would ask, How much inequality can democracy tolerate and still remain meaningful? *(Fredrik D. Bodin/Stock, Boston)*

leaders are selected from among the most qualified citizens. Leaders and those led relate to each other in an atmosphere of mutual instruction. Leaders attempt to put the difficult issues of political life before the electorate as clearly and fully as they can. The public, for its part, tries to comprehend these matters, and its response helps to inform the directions of future policy. When disputes occasionally go beyond the usual bounds of public discussion and threaten to burst into bitter controversy, the disputants either find ways of com-

COMPARATIVE PERSPECTIVE

Which Nations Are Democracies?

Political scientists have never entirely agreed on the definition of a democratic political process, but there has been enough agreement to establish some general criteria. Usually, democracies are defined as nations in which:

The government states that it derives its mandate to govern from the people.

Leaders are chosen through competitive elections, in which at least two political parties have a meaningful chance to win.

Alternative sources of information are available.

Balloting is secret, and votes are not coerced.

Citizens and leaders enjoy freedom of speech, press, assembly, and organization.

Majorities win elections and can carry through their public policy choices.

Some investigators also include additional requirements, for example, that each vote counts equally, or that force is not employed against any political group. Following is one way to classify contemporary nations:

Nations with democratic regimes for at least five years, 1958–1976

Australia	Finland
Austria	West Germany
Belgium	Iceland
Canada	Israel
Costa Rica	Italy
Denmark	Japan
Luxembourg	Switzerland
Netherlands	United Kingdom
New Zealand	United States
Norway	Venezuela[a]
Sweden	

Democratic regimes temporarily limited or suspended

France (1958)	Sri Lanka[c] (1971–76)
India (1975–76)	Turkey (1960–61, 1971–72)
Jamaica[b] (1976)	

Democratic regimes definitely replaced

Chile (1973–)	Philippines (1972–86)
Greece (1967–74)	Uruguay (1973–85)

To the first list we could now add Trinidad-Tobago, and some today would also add Colombia, the Dominican Republic, Malaysia, and Cyprus.

SOURCES: Bingham Powell, *Contemporary Democracies: Participation, Stability, and Violence* (Cambridge, Mass.: 1982) and Robert Dahl, *Polyarchy: Participation and Opposition* (New Haven: Yale University Press, 1971).
[a]A democratic regime was established in 1959, although emergencies and terrorism limited freedoms in the early 1960s.
[b]Became independent in 1962. A state of emergency was declared in 1976, but elections were held late that year, and the emergency later was lifted.
[c]Following guerrilla attacks in 1971, the government restricted freedom of press and assembly, which made the country's status doubtful until 1977.

promising or take their disputes before a court system that aids them in reconciling their differences.

Such an ideal democracy was imagined by early democratic theorists such as the French-Swiss political philosopher Jean-Jacques Rousseau (1712–1778), who felt that political democracy was possible *only* in a small and homogeneous society. This ideal world, of course, has little in common with the reality of contemporary life. However, we now recognize that a minimum level of political democracy can exist under many different conditions, some of them far from the ideal scenario just described. We know, for example, that most citizens are not very well-informed about political matters, and that large numbers never participate in political life even in the most minimal ways. We know that great disparities in wealth, power, and respect exist in democratic societies, and that these differences sharply affect the functioning of democracy. We know that political debate is often deliberately confusing, that leaders sometimes mislead or fail to lead, that politicians can be dishonest, that many of the best potential political leaders never seek or attain office. We also know that many of the people who live in democratic societies are not particularly democratic. Some hold deep-seated prejudices toward certain groups, others would prefer a political system that aided only themselves and groups they support and that even caused harm to others. Many people in democratic societies, in other words, do not hold democratic attitudes.

What conclusion can we draw from this failure of reality to approximate the ideal? On the one hand, we could be amazed that political democracy exists at all, and even prospers, despite many adverse conditions. On the other hand, we could react with concern, arguing that some contemporary societies have forfeited their claims as democracies.

Many students of politics have adopted the first of these positions, taking what might be charac-

terized as a **minimalist view of democracy.** This view was summed up by Winston Churchill, the British prime minister during World War II and in the 1950s, who stated that democracy was the worst political system, except for all the rest. Churchill, like many others, saw the democratic process as a way of avoiding the greater evils inherent in other political forms. At least in a democracy, minimalists argue, it is possible to get rid of a bad government through periodic competitive elections.

What about the low level of public information in the average electorate (see **Table 2**)? Although this may be unfortunate, they argue, it is probably unrealistic for believers in democracy to think that most people do not take such an interest, for too many citizens participating too actively might cause too much political conflict. In this view, our hopes for democracy must be scaled down. All in all, minimalists tell us, current democracies are doing rather well.

Under the minimalist approach, then, a democracy is any government that has relatively open political debate and competition and also holds periodic elections. Under a maximalist perspective, however, democracy can achieve far more. It is the

---

TABLE 2
Public Information and Understanding

"Thinking of the important national and international issues facing the country, how well do you think you understand these issues? How about local issues . . .?"

	United States		United Kingdom		West Germany		Italy		Mexico	
	Nat'l	Local	Nat'l	Local	Nat'l	Local	Nat'l	Local	Nat'l	Local
Very well	7	21	8	18	13	25	7	15	1	5
Moderately well	38	44	36	36	35	37	20	23	7	13
Not so well	37	23	36	25	24	18	24	19	46	49
Not at all	14	10	15	14	15	7	33	27	43	31
Depends, don't know, etc.	4	2	5	6	13	13	16	16	3	1
Total (%)	100	100	100	99	100	100	100	100	100	99

SOURCE: Kenneth Prewitt and Sidney Verba, *An Introduction to American Government* (New York: Harper & Row, 1974), p. 84.

maximalist view of democracy that undergirds the organization and approach of this text. We will assume that democracy encompasses much more than open elections, that elections are a necessary, but not sufficient, condition for democratic life. In examining U.S. democratic institutions we will hold maximalist standards, to see where the problems and tensions lie and what possibilities for improvement can be found.

Examining levels of democratic achievement leads to another difficult and complex issue: Are there cut-off points or plateaus that tell us whether or not a nation is democratic? Although we can specify various criteria for determining whether a country is a democracy, no one has devised a definitive, agreed-on formula for going about this. Political scientists have tried various ways of defining "democratic" nations. But in the end, democracy is always a matter of degree, and judgments about the degree of democracy are inherently controversial. In the next section, we will explore some of the typical problems and struggles of democratic life before we plunge directly into the murky, crowded sea of American politics.

Problems in Democratic Life

To better understand the obstacles to creating a more democratic society, we now turn to some of the most common and fundamental problems in contemporary democracies, including our own. These include (1) the uneven distribution of power, (2) failures to respect democratic rights, and (3) citizen-government conflict that threatens the democratic process.

Uneven Distribution of Power

In *Animal Farm*, the celebrated satirical novel by George Orwell, the farm animals, after revolting and taking control of the farm, proclaim that "all animals are equal." Somewhat later, one faction (the pigs) takes increasing control. The rest of the animals wake up one morning to find their slogan, printed on the barnyard wall, altered to "all animals are created equal, but some are more equal

than others." That, in fact, is what we find when we look closely at democratic politics: Particular individuals and groups enjoy great advantages in political life. Some of these advantages can pose serious threats to democratic politics. Here we look briefly at three such advantages: (1) those generated by concentrations of wealth and economic power; (2) those accruing from ease of political influence; and (3) those that develop out of oligarchy, when democratic competition for leadership is curtailed.

ECONOMIC POWER Some socialists are fond of saying that economic power more or less equals political power. While this may not always be true, it is a good approximation. In every democratic society, those who are financially better off usually have much more political access and influence than their numbers might suggest. For one thing, they can use their money for political purposes. A wealthy campaign contributor is likely to exercise a level of influence hundreds and perhaps thousands of times greater than the average voter. Although money is not everything in politics, it *is* a vital element; the unequal distribution of financial resources tends to skew democracy in the direction of the more affluent.

At another level, many of the major social decisions made in democratic societies fall outside democratic control. Important economic decisions made by corporations affect the lives of tens of thousands and yet are rarely based on democratic consultation. Business decisions made by a few individuals can shut down plants, alter work processes, flood the market with new products. That is, of course, how capitalism is supposed to work; but it also means that a relatively small number of people wield enormous economic power and make significant economic decisions. Yet these individuals are usually far removed from any sort of democratic control. Inevitably, those in politics are highly attentive to the interests and ideas of the business community, since business decisions affect the entire economic climate and may be a major source of trouble or success for political leaders.

In the latter part of the nineteenth century, a groundswell of popular opposition to economically powerful interests erupted into a series of

The fear of financial desperation in old age once haunted most citizens of industrial societies. Social security systems were created to help deal with this problem. But, in the United States, at least, social security payments, though helpful, often do not provide a reasonable standard of living. Vast inequalities of wealth persist from birth to death. *(Mark Antman/Image Works)*

pitched political clashes. Small farmers organized to battle the railroads. Factory workers organized to fight for better wages and decent working conditions. Much of U.S. politics around the turn of the century focused on the issue of economic power, which was then growing more and more concentrated in the hands of a few. Increasingly, government sought to limit and regulate concentrations of private economic power through legislation such as the Sherman Antitrust Act, which was enacted in 1890 to limit monopolies. Social movements also stirred government reforms on such key social and economic matters as child labor and the purity of food and drugs. In the twentieth century, the government gradually expanded its influence in these areas.

Great inequalities of wealth affect democratic life in yet another way. Often, money can help purchase the sorts of basic rights that should be open to all. For example, in theory the United States guarantees every person a fair trial and decent legal assistance. But in practice, we know that money helps a great deal in obtaining the best legal representation. The same holds true in the areas of education and health care. In our society money makes many important options available, and may

even make the difference between having real choices and having no choices.

To return to the fundamental point: Great inequalities of wealth and great concentrations of economic power both pose serious threats to the relative equality that is one of the basic premises of democratic life. Of course, there are countervailing forces that limit the power of wealth. Sometimes sheer numbers can prevail over the power of money; sometimes powerful organizations such as trade unions can weigh in on the other side of the scale; sometimes the wealthy are divided among themselves. But as long as some have a great deal more than others, democrats have to worry that politics may serve moneyed interests at the expense of majority interests.

SPECIAL INTERESTS In democratic societies, many groups organize and lobby for favorable policies from the government. Oil companies, for example, hire professional lobbyists to influence Congress, and the American Medical Association makes heavy campaign contributions to candidates the association feels will advance its interests in matters of health policy. The more powerful and well-organized such **interest groups** are, the greater the influence they exert over government affairs. Over the years, interest groups often develop very friendly relationships with the legislators and bureaucrats responsible for overseeing their particular interests, and as a result, seem to be systematically favored by government policy. Once established, such strong alliances are difficult to dislodge. Well-organized segments of society come to enjoy subsidies, protective tariffs, or other benefits. Truckers benefit from one sort of special arrangement, dairy farmers another, tobacco growers another, and sugar producers yet another.

Amid all this special-interest policy making, who is looking out for the public interest, for the needs and long-term good of the public at large? When no one is watching out for such interests, democracy suffers, and political life becomes a way of gaining wealth, power, and advantage for the few at the expense of the general public. Just how serious a problem this can be we will see in Chapter 8, which focuses on the role of interest groups in American politics.

OLIGARCHY   We can define **oligarchy** as "rule by the few." By definition, oligarchy and democracy are incompatible. When leadership becomes entrenched and unresponsive, democracy suffers. The problems posed by oligarchies within democracies were first addressed extensively in Robert Michels' 1915 study *Political Parties*. Michels saw a tension between the democratic impulses that prompt the formation of political parties and the pressures toward bureaucratization that seem inevitably to remove initiative from the rank-and-file and place it in the hands of a governing elite better situated to exercise continuous power.

Accusations of oligarchy have been made many times in U.S. history. In the late nineteenth century, for example, popular movements decried economic oligarchy, maintaining that industrialists were able to manipulate the economic and political systems to their advantage at the expense of the ordinary citizen. President Franklin Roosevelt joined in a similar attack on vested economic interests during the 1930s. In 1968, many Democratic party members complained that oligarchy in the party limited the role of popular sentiment in the nominating process. Finally, both trade unions and corporations have been justly accused of oligarchic practices by which leaders are able to perpetuate themselves. (One aside: Even in a democracy, certain institutions are not usually expected to be organized in a democratic manner. Corporations, for example, are not run by majority rule except in very exceptional circumstances, when stockholders organize to press their interests. Churches, too, are often oligarchical. When nondemocratic forms of decision making are justified, and why, are provocative questions that can only be touched on peripherally in this book.)

Unresponsive political or economic oligarchies often find themselves locked in bitter and protracted conflicts with those they seek to lead or control. These conflicts are costly for both sides and often fruitless for those challenging the status quo. Democracies must continually strive to reach some balance between effective leadership and mass influence.

Failure to Exercise Rights

According to many theorists, the quality of democratic life in large part depends on (1) the willingness of the polity to embrace democratic attitudes; (2) the degree of alienation among the people; and (3) the level of public awareness and public understanding of the issues facing the government. If the masses have undemocratic sentiments, if there is a strong animus against democratic institutions, if many are drawn to authoritarian movements, then democracy will be severely tested.

The same holds true if large numbers of people are hostile to the major political institutions, if they feel alienated by politics as it is usually conducted. Finally, if the mass of the population is uninformed, if the average citizen cannot or does not understand what political life and political issues are all about, decisions will be made by the few, without considering the views of the real majority. Let us now look more closely at each of these matters.

ANTIDEMOCRATIC ATTITUDES   We cannot be sure exactly what most German citizens were thinking in 1933, when the National Socialist German Workers party (the Nazis) received 40 percent of

Text continues following the color essay.

Continental Drift

New Americans in an Old Story

The United States has always been a "nation of nations," a country of people with diverse ethnic backgrounds and nationalities. We traditionally have taken pride in this diversity and have even come to think of the United States as a melting pot in which all color and cultural differences mingle and eventually merge into a common blend. Over the past quarter-century, however, the idea of the melting pot has been challenged, partly because historical reality has contradicted the optimistic view that color and culture are not sometimes serious barriers to success, and partly because the notion of a melting pot is antithetical to the celebration and preservation of distinct cultural heritages. Assimilation—becoming part of society by abandoning one's past and adapting the characteristics of the dominant group—is no longer the unquestioned goal of individuals entering America. Instead, the idea of cultural pluralism has become fashionable, reflecting our increased understanding of the importance of cultural and ethnic differences and our desire to use them to the advantage of the entire society.

The politics of groups has become a constant theme of American democracy in our times. Starting with the black civil rights movement in the 1960s, a variety of groups with shared cultures or ethnicity have emerged to underscore the fact that the United States is a pluralistic society. Their challenges to

SUPERSTOCK

SUPERSTOCK

existing political and social systems often arose from inequities in the country's past policies. But political balances also were challenged by a gradual, ongoing, and subtle demographic transformation of the United States itself—a kind of "continental drift" away from our early historic European attachments toward increasing ties with Latin America to the south and with the Pacific Basin to the west.

The glue that binds these connections has been the increasing immigration of Asians and Hispanics. From 1920, when Asian immigrants were only 4 percent of the total, to the mid-1980s, when they made up nearly half (48 percent) of legal immigrants, Asians have steadily increased as a percentage of the population. During the same period immigrants from Latin America also increased sharply—to about 40 percent of the total. Immigration thus accounts for the rapid increase in the *proportion* of the population that has Asian or Latin roots. While the white population grew about 6 percent in the 1980s and the black population expanded by about 11 percent, there was an increase of about 52 percent in the category which the Census Bureau calls "other races"

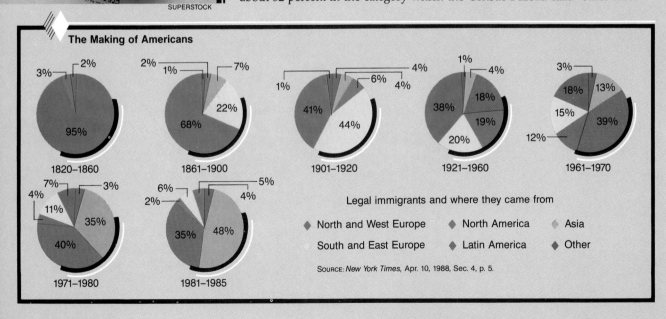

The Making of Americans

1820–1860: 3%, 2%, 95%

1861–1900: 2%, 1%, 7%, 22%, 68%

1901–1920: 1%, 6%, 4%, 4%, 41%, 44%

1921–1960: 1%, 4%, 18%, 19%, 20%, 38%

1961–1970: 3%, 18%, 13%, 15%, 39%, 12%

1971–1980: 7%, 3%, 4%, 11%, 35%, 40%

1981–1985: 6%, 2%, 5%, 4%, 35%, 48%

Legal immigrants and where they came from

◆ North and West Europe   ◆ North America   ◆ Asia

◆ South and East Europe   ◆ Latin America   ◆ Other

SOURCE: *New York Times*, Apr. 10, 1988, Sec. 4, p. 5.

(including principally Asians, Native Americans, Alaska Natives, and Pacific Islanders).[1] Reflecting the potential political significance of this new immigration pattern, in the mid-1980s the federal government introduced the term *Hispanic* as a uniform category in its data gathering (former census data included most Hispanics under "white"). Thus it has been difficult to chart the increase in the Hispanic portion of the population, but one private research firm estimated that it grew 29.4 percent from 1980 to 1987.[2]

Recent immigrants are not evenly distributed, of course, and so some areas of the country display enormous diversity, while others remain largely homogeneous. Southern Florida has experienced an influx of Spanish-speaking people from Cuba and from Central and South America. Southern California, similarly, has been enriched by large numbers of people from Southeast Asia, besides its traditionally significant Hispanic population from Central America.

Education may be the most complex and controversial issue facing our diverse society. As an agent of socialization—of integrating young people into the social and political mainstream—education has equalized the opportunities for all who have had access to it. But in a society that now celebrates cultural diversity, how much should the dominant culture impose its values on children? Should instruction be in English, or in the language of the home? Does an emphasis on cultural heritage and native, non-English languages prevent children from acquiring the skills needed to succeed in American society? In 1988, there were 2.7 million immigrant children in public schools—about 6 percent—and a study funded by the Ford Foundation concluded that these children were not served well by rigid placement practices, a lack of bilingual education, insensitivity and harassment from other children, and fear of deportation.[3]

Consider the challenges facing the Los Angeles County schools, a system of 600,000 students among whom *eighty-two* languages are spoken (163,000 students speak little or no English). Of those not fluent in English, 90 percent speak Spanish, 2 percent Korean, 1.5 percent Cantonese, 1 percent Vietnamese, and smaller percentages speak the other seventy-seven languages. In 1988 the school board adopted a master plan for bilingual education that calls for teaching most courses in students' own languages until they learn English; the school system also offers intensive English language courses for non-English speakers.[4] This plan steers a middle course between the two extremes.

Some have argued that English is the "official" language of the

Where New Americans Settled in 1987

Top 10 Areas of Residence	
Location	**Number**
New York City	97,510
Los Angeles–Long Beach	64,453
Miami–Hialeah	37,887
Chicago	20,297
San Francisco	16,234
Anaheim–Santa Ana, Calif.	12,998
San Diego	12,706
Houston	11,399
San Jose	11,152

SOURCE: *The Washington Post National Weekly Edition*, Aug. 1–7, 1988, p. 31.

United States, and that public education ought to be conducted exclusively in English. Opponents of this view, however, maintain that U.S. society is multilingual, like Canada and Switzerland, and that students should be encouraged to speak their native languages in bilingual or multilingual classrooms.

The debate about bilingual education has generated much heat, partly because it touches on matters so close to our identities as individuals. Americans have always been proud of their individualism, even though evidence of conformity abounds throughout our history. While many advocate bilingual education as a means of maintaining cultural pluralism, others see it as an insidious means of maintaining an economic underclass, on the assumption that non-English speakers will be at a disadvantage looking for a job or in any economic activity. Whatever the merits of these arguments, bilingual education is not inexpensive. In its first year the Los Angeles plan will cost an additional $20 million beyond the $93 million already being spent on bilingual education—in a total city budget of $3.2 billion.

Private businesses often adapt to changing conditions more quickly than government does, and Spanish-language TV broadcasting offers an example of how marketers have responded to new immigration patterns and the challenges of cultural pluralism. By the late 1980s two large broadcasting networks—Univision and Telemundo—were competing for the Spanish-speaking audience. In 1988 their advertising revenues were about $275 million, up more than 230 percent from 1984. These networks produce their own shows and news programming, and Univision broadcast live from both 1988 national conventions. Since after-tax income in Hispanic households has grown rapidly

(topping $150 billion in 1987), it was inevitable that this new market would be discovered by commercial television—that most-American hybrid of entertainment and hucksterism.[5]

No matter how American democracy responds to the challenges of cultural pluralism, the importance of the issues was clearly symbolized at both national conventions in 1988. In accepting the Democratic nomination, Michael Dukakis translated a portion of his speech into Spanish; and George Bush's Mexican-born daughter-

in-law announced her state delegation's vote at the Republican convention. These images speak eloquently of a diverse and still-maturing American society.

[1]*Current Population Reports,* Series P-25, Bureau of the Census, 1988.
[2]Richard W. Stevenson, "Spanish-Language TV Grows Up," *New York Times,* July 7, 1988, p. 25.
[3]"Study Says Schools Fall Short in Education of Immigrants," *New York Times,* Apr. 27, 1988, p. 14.
[4]"Bilingual Plan Backed in Los Angeles," *New York Times,* May 10, 1988, p. 8.
[5]Stevenson, *loc. cit.*

the vote in the last relatively open election held in that country before World War II. No Gallup or Harris polls were conducted; the opinions of the "average" person were not tapped for posterity. Yet it does not seem too far-fetched to guess that large numbers of Germans no longer had strong ties to democratic politics, if they had ever had such ties. Democratic politics was new in the Germany of that day: Only after World War I was a fully democratic political system installed. At a time when German democracy was just beginning to put down roots, many aspects of German society remained resolutely undemocratic. Strong patterns of military tradition and inherited aristocracy persisted. The Nazis represented perhaps the most extreme of the antidemocratic elements: Their ideology was not just critical of democracy, but entirely alien to it.

Many factors conspired to give the Nazis their chance at political power in 1933, including a worldwide economic crisis, but there seems little doubt that many Germans had a shaky allegiance, at best, to democratic institutions and practices. The great majority of them embraced authoritarian leadership and were willing to accept violence and prejudice as integral parts of political and social life.

We cannot afford to be too smug about this, however, or to think that our country could never be like Germany in the early 1930s. Fascist movements, in fact, arose in almost every European country, as well as in the United States, between the wars. The attitudes we associate with Nazism, such as anti-Semitism and racism, were common throughout the West. After World War II, however, negative attitudes toward Jews declined significantly, as did notions about the inferiority of blacks. Perhaps we were simply lucky to have avoided our own version of fascism, or perhaps the strength of our democratic attitudes and institutions have protected us. But even recent data about American attitudes toward freedom of expression are disturbing. In 1954, for example, only 37 percent of the population thought that an atheist should be allowed to make a public speech, and only 33 percent approved of a socialist's teaching in college (see **Table 3**, page 14). By 1987 things had improved measurably, but even then more than half the population objected to atheist teach-

Joseph Goebbels, Hitler's minister of propaganda, emerges from a polling station in the 1933 German elections. The Nazi Party won a plurality of the vote that year; then, their power secure, they permitted no further political competition in Germany. (*National Archives*)

ers, and more than 40 percent would ban homosexuals' books from libraries.

Why do such attitudes matter? Why does it matter if millions of Americans are anti-Semitic or racist, or have very weak allegiance to democratic ideas? It matters because the sort of equal treatment in social and political life that democracy requires is impossible where prejudice is widespread. And in a time of crisis and conflict, such antidemocratic attitudes may surface and lead to widespread violations of civil liberties or violence against certain groups. This too threatens democratic life, as we will see in Chapter 1.

ALIENATION Experts have offered many definitions of **alienation**. Some authorities have equated it with the sense of being an outsider. Others have associated it with powerlessness, futility, or meaninglessness. But even though a vast literature in sociology is devoted to exploring and understand-

TABLE 3
Support for Freedom of Expression in Specific Situations

	Percent tolerant		
	1954	*1977*	*1987*
Allow speech by:			
Atheist	37	62	70
Socialist	59	—	—
Communist	27	56	61
Racist	—	59	62
Militarist	—	51	58
Homosexual	—	62	70
Oppose removing from library books written by:			
Atheist	35	59	67
Socialist	53	—	—
Communist	27	55	59
Racist	—	61	65
Militarist	—	55	60
Homosexual	—	55	59
Allow to teach in college:			
Atheist	12	39	49
Socialist	33	—	—
Communist	6	39	49
Racist	—	41	45
Militarist	—	34	41
Homosexual	—	49	59

SOURCE: Michael Corbett, *Political Tolerance in America* (New York: Longman, 1982), p. 36 and NORC General Social Survey, 1987 (courtesy of the Institute for Social Science Research, University of North Carolina, Chapel Hill).

ing the phenomenon, it is usually not hard to spot alienation when one sees it. Alienated people are turned off; they've given up on something. Alienated people feel that nobody cares, that things have turned against them, that the world is dishonest, that they and people like them are too weak to change things. The extremes of alienation are either total hostility and cynicism or passive withdrawal, complete apathy.

In recent years many Americans have suffered from fairly serious bouts of political alienation (see **Table 4**). How does this concern democratic politics? If large numbers of people are alienated, then politics suffers. First, many people withdraw from

political life, reducing the effectiveness and breadth of democracy. Alienation is often expressed in nonvoting, and it comes as something of a shock to many Americans to learn that we have among the lowest levels of voter registration and voter turnout among democratic nations (see **Table 5**, page 16). It should be noted that several nations with high turnout rates—Australia, Belgium, and Italy—have laws that make voting compulsory. But this is not true of the others.

Alienated people may also pose a threat to democracy because of the hostility they have built up toward politics. In either case, the circle of meaningful participants in political life is narrowed.

Alienation presents a more complicated problem as well. A skeptic might suggest that some degree of alienation is to be expected in any political process, even the most democratic. Some people will always be put off because the political situation is not going their way. In the 1970s and 1980s, for example, many men were alienated by legislative and corporate initiatives to give women equal pay and professional advancement, making up for years of past discrimination. Perhaps this type of alienation is the price we have to pay for democratic change. The questions we need to ask are: Who is alienated? Why are they alienated? and How widespread and deep is the alienation? The answers to these questions will help us determine whether alienation is the sign of a defective democracy or the price of needed change.

IGNORANCE   Ignorance is a different matter. In theory, democracy requires an informed and politically aware citizenry. But is democracy working when more than half of all citizens feel they do not have a good grasp of national issues? The question in **Table 6** (page 16), about U.S. policy in Nicaragua, shows how long it took for a majority of the public to understand the basics about a policy that was a source of major public controversy throughout the 1980s.

Just how much can we expect the public to understand about political life? Isn't large-scale public ignorance to be expected in any large, complicated modern society? How many of us are prepared to put in the time and energy required to master the intricacies of the intermediate-range nuclear-

The feelings of powerlessness, of not counting in the political process, can lead to alienation and despair. But people can also rebel against their powerlessness and demand a place in the political system. For American blacks in the 1960s, the use of the ballot was a key to overcoming decades of powerlessness. (© *Bruce Davidson/Magnum*)

arms–control agreement, to explore the alternatives in the energy crisis, to assess the results of toxic waste dumping, or to grasp the consequences of passage of an equal rights amendment to the Constitution? Clearly, many such matters are beyond the scope of the average citizen. What, then, can a reasonable democrat hope for?

At a minimum, we can expect the public to grasp—in a general sense—the major alternatives

available on important questions of the day. Even if the average person cannot argue at length about the arms race or about supply-side economics, he or she usually can understand the basic issues involved, provided that (1) plentiful, accurate, and many-sided information about those issues is available and (2) the person cares enough to seek that information. When one of these factors is missing, widespread public ignorance results and the quality of democratic life suffers.

TABLE 4
One Measure of Alienation

"Would you say the government is pretty much run by a few big interests looking out for themselves or that it is run for the benefit of all people?"

	1964	1970	1976	1982
Few big interests	29%	50%	66%	61%
Benefit of all	64%	41%	24%	29%
Don't know	7%	9%	10%	10%

Based on data from *Public Opinion*.

The Relationship between Government and Citizen

The democratic ideal requires a relatively open, honest, and responsive relationship between citizens and government. But this relationship is often precarious. The power exercised by the citizenry might not be sufficient to keep the government responsive and under control. The power of political office might lead to corruption or give rise to imperial attitudes more appropriate to a monarchy. Citizens might also abuse the relationship,

TABLE 5
Voter Turnout and Registration in Selected Democracies (Percent)

Country	Average turnout	Average registered
Australia	86	91
Austria	88	96
Belgium	88	95
Canada	68	93
Denmark	85	98
Finland	82	100
France (presidential election)	78	91
West Germany	85	94
Ireland	77	100
Israel	80	100
Italy	94	100
Japan	72	100
Netherlands	82	98
New Zealand	83	95
Norway	82	100
Sweden	88	97
Switzerland	44	85
United Kingdom	75	100
United States (presidential election)	54	61
Spain	78	100

SOURCE: G. Bingham Powell, "American Voting in Comparative Perspective," *American Political Science Review*, March 1986, p. 43.

TABLE 6
The Nicaragua Question

"Do you happen to know which side the United States is backing in Nicaragua, the rebels or the government?"

	August 1983	March 1985	August 1987
Government	24%	23%	20%
Rebels	29%	37%	54%
Don't know	47%	39%	24%

SOURCE: *Public Opinion*, September/October 1987, p. 23. Reprinted by permission.

for example, by evading their responsibilities as voters or by disobeying reasonable and necessary laws.

Every society must also cope with conflict among the citizenry and between citizens and the government. Crime, disorder, and social and political combat challenge every society as well. In a democratic society, citizens expect such conflicts to be dealt with in a manner consistent with democratic norms. Let us now look a bit more closely at the issues of honesty and conflict, assessing how well contemporary societies live up to democratic standards.

HONESTY AND TRUST   In our society, citizens and governments relate at many levels. In elections, candidates appeal to citizens for votes. Once in office, legislators and executives make and enforce laws that affect the lives of citizens. Yet the most common way citizens encounter government authority is in the form of the school board official, the social worker, the police officer, the Social Security bureaucrat, the building inspector—that is, at the local level. Though we are usually taught to trust and respect such authority figures as teachers and police officers, at times encounters with these authorities breed a sense of grievance. In the ghetto, police are frequently feared or hated. Bureaucrats tend to be criticized for their tiresome attention to routine, or for their insensitivity. And yet these and other government employees play essential roles in our lives.

The citizen-government encounter, then, is many-sided. Consider, for example, just one of the levels at which citizen and government relate: that of executive leadership. Political executives, such as the U.S. president, play a critical role in modern societies. What presidents say and don't say, what they decide and how they make decisions, and how they communicate their ideas to the public at large have significant consequences for democratic life. At this level, democratic ideals furnish us with rather straightforward standards for judgment. Most obviously, we should expect a high level of integrity in a chief executive, as well as a determined effort to be honest and open with the public. Where such honesty and integrity are lacking, democratic practice is jeopardized. For example, while publicly vowing never to deal with terrorists, the Reagan administration in the mid-1980s secretly traded arms to Iran—an acknowledged instigator of terrorism—in exchange for American hostages being held in Lebanon by Iranian-sponsored terrorists. When this plan became known, the president's approval rating in the polls plunged to an all-time low.

HANDLING CONFLICTS In May 1970, at the height of political protest over the Vietnam War, four students were shot to death and many others wounded by National Guard troops at Kent State University in Ohio. This tragedy underlined a key issue for democracies: how government authority should be used to deal with conflict and protest.

Throughout much of our history, in fact, deadly force has been used both by citizens and governments to settle disputes. But ours is no longer a frontier society; we are a long way from the Wild West.

Again, the sense of democratic norms is quite clear: We cannot use force, especially deadly force, easily and often, if our society truly values individual life. A democrat wants to see such coercion reduced to a minimum. Widespread use of police power inevitably indicates a failure for democratic life. And if force is absolutely necessary, it should be used with considerable care. A troubled conscience over the use of police power is a good sign in a democratic society. Anytime democratic leaders find the killing or coercing of some citizens easily acceptable, that nation's democratic ideals are in deep trouble.

Is Democracy the Best System?

For most of recorded history, democracy was not regarded very highly by most thinkers. Yet democratic practices have proved themselves rather effective over the last two centuries; the concept of government by consent of the governed has shown its staying power. Few people would now argue for absolute monarchy or for the rule of a hereditary landed aristocracy—political practices that once were extremely common and widely accepted.

Still, throughout the world, and even in democratic nations, arguments about the limitations of democracy persist. Advocates of authoritarian regimes argue that a particular ruler or group of rulers is best suited to make decisions for the nation as a whole, and that strong leadership is required to prevent chaos. Often, we hear this argument made to justify military or other dictatorships; for years, such contentions were common throughout Latin America.

The communists often advance a different argument. They defend their rule by maintaining that only their political party with its particular theories truly understands how history works and which policies should be adopted. The communists' arguments often have a strongly moral tinge; dissenters are not only incorrect but immoral. This does not encourage a friendly attitude toward criticism and dissent: You are either with us or against us. As Fidel Castro put it in describing his views on the right to criticize: "Within the Revolution, everything; outside it, nothing." Of course, it was Castro and his supporters who defined what "within the Revolution" meant!

Others assert that democracy is a good idea but should not be pushed too far. In this view, similar to the position held by many of the American Founders, government needs to be "of the people" and "for the people" but not necessarily "by the people." Since the people, as a whole, will never be very well-informed, intelligent, farsighted, or morally enlightened, the more astute, thoughtful, and experienced members of the community must assume a dominant role in political leadership. The people need good, enlightened leaders—individuals who are in many ways "better" than the average citizen. Democracy will work, then, when a dose of elitism infuses the system with the leadership and intelligence it needs. And, oddly enough, political elites and activists often do show more respect for the norms of democracy than average citizens do, at least concerning many basic questions of civil liberties.

Another version of the argument for limited democracy was heard in the aftermath of the agitated 1960s and was articulated by Samuel Huntington, who quoted John Adams: "Democracy never lasts long. It soon wastes, exhausts and murders itself. There was never a democracy yet that did not commit suicide." The point is that the dynamics of democracy itself may run counter to other values,

COMPARATIVE PERSPECTIVE

The Consociational Model of Democracy

In recent years, some political scientists have concluded that many democratic nations in Western Europe do not really operate according to the norms of majoritarian democracy but have evolved into a somewhat different system. Austria, Belgium, the Netherlands, and Switzerland all seem to have systems based on compromise and coalition rather than on the majoritarian winner-take-all pattern followed in the United States. Known as *consociational democracy*, this system follows certain unwritten rules to preserve stability and avoid conflict.

Each of these nations has clearly identifiable subgroups. Austria has long been divided politically and culturally between socialists and Catholics; Belgium has the French-speaking and Flemish-speaking; the Netherlands has several religious and social-class subcultures; and Switzerland is made up of French, German, and Italian speakers.

In each nation, political patterns have developed to accommodate the interests of subgroups. Leaders of the various groups engage in extensive negotiations to avoid disagreements and splits that might lead to social conflict. Rather than settling issues by majority rule, they seek compromise.

The Swiss, for example, created the Federal Council, a seven-member executive office equivalent to our presidency. Elected by the parliament, the council allows all major political parties a share in government: Each of the three major parties is allocated two seats, and an important smaller party has one. The three linguistic groups are also guaranteed representation. Naturally, such a spirit of compromise extends into public policy.

To take another example, the Netherlands has institutionalized its form of coalition government. Rather than seeking a narrow majority of votes to win power, each party seeks to be a member of one large governing coalition. This pattern has been characterized as "accommodationist" for its effort to allocate a reasonable share of resources to each important group.

Of course, all democratic politics involves some compromise and accommodation. The significant point about consociational systems is that they have established norms of accommodation as part of their political processes, thus depending less on majority rule than America does today.

SOURCES: Arend Lijphart, *The Politics of Accommodation: Pluralism and Democracy in the Netherlands* (Berkeley: University of California, 1968); Val R. Lorwin, "Segmented Pluralism: Ideological Cleavages and Political Cohesion in the Smaller European Democracies," *Comparative Politics,* January 1971, pp. 141–75; Jeffrey Obler, "Assimilation and the Moderation of Linguistic Conflict in Brussels," *Administration,* Winter 1974, pp. 400–432; Jeffrey Obler, Jurg Steiner, and Guido Diereckx, "Decision-making in Smaller Democracies: The Consociational Burden," *Comparative Politics Series,* vol. 6 (Beverly Hills, Cal.: Sage, 1977), pp. 13–14, 21–33.

such as stability, efficiency, or effective government.

Although this text takes an opposing view, the argument is an important one and should be taken into account. We will return to these issues later. For now, consider that democracy in America, as well as elsewhere, has a good deal to say for itself after more than two centuries. Democratic practices, once widely imagined to be impractical and utopian, have shown they can work and have yielded substantial measures of popular enlightenment, respect for individual rights, and concern for the common good. Though far from perfect, democratic systems can claim numerous accomplishments. Keep this at the forefront as we examine and attempt to appraise our American version of the democratic idea.

Struggles to Realize Democratic Ideals

The preceding discussion of democratic ideals and practices may have seemed somewhat abstract. We turn now to a few exemplary cases of the struggle to realize democratic ideals in the highly imperfect real world. These cases are brief, but their significance ought to be clear. From them we can draw many lessons useful in examining the operation of American government today.

Restricting Democracy

We look now at two cases where democracy was curtailed: (1) the failure of Reconstruction after the Civil War, leading to the growth of segregation in the American South; and (2) American involvement in overthrowing the democratically elected socialist government in Chile in 1973.

SEGREGATION IN THE UNITED STATES Most of us were taught at a young age that the Civil War was fought to free the slaves and to realize the democratic ideal of equality for all. Perhaps a bit later we learned that the situation was more complicated, that democratic ideals were only a part of the story. In any event, the North won, and in the Thirteenth, Fourteenth, and Fifteenth amendments to the Constitution (the Civil War amendments), slavery was abolished and, seemingly, all U.S. citizens were guaranteed equal rights and equal protection under the law.

For over a decade after the Civil War, Northern troops occupied the South, and lengthy and intense political struggles were waged over how government in the South was to be reconstructed. Some people favored radical measures to secure full equality for freed slaves, and for a time in the 1870s there was some progress toward racial equality. Many blacks were elected to state and local offices, and whites and blacks mixed together on

Oklahoma City, 1939. Segregated drinking fountains were but one part of an elaborate system of racial separation imposed and maintained by law and custom throughout the American South. The races were supposedly accorded separate but equal treatment, but in fact black facilities were generally far inferior to those provided for whites. *(The Bettmann Archive)*

public transportation, in schools, and on juries. But others wished to turn back the clock and return as far as possible to a situation in which whites held the upper hand. In the end, the latter view prevailed. A bloody and terrible war had been fought, at least in part, to gain some measure of equality for blacks; these gains were substantially wiped out and a new system of white supremacy was restored by the 1880s.

A series of U.S. Supreme Court decisions also helped to restrict the meaning of the constitutional amendments passed after the Civil War. In 1877 the Court found that a state could not prohibit segregation in transportation, and in 1883 it sharply limited the application of the clause in the Fourteenth Amendment mandating equal protection of the laws for all citizens. And in 1890 it upheld a Mississippi state law that *required* segregation in transportation.

Plessy v. Ferguson

In 1890 the Louisiana legislature passed a law for the "comfort of passengers" that "all railway companies . . . carrying passengers in their coaches in this State, shall provide equal but separate accommodations for the white and colored races." Until this time the races had traveled together in second-class railway cars, though it was generally "whites only" in first-class cars.

The law evoked a strong protest from the large and vocal black community in New Orleans, leading to a deliberate test of its constitutionality. On June 7, 1892, Homer Adolph Plessy, a man seven-eighths white and one-eighth black, boarded an East Louisiana Railway train in New Orleans and took a seat in a car reserved for whites. When he refused to move to the colored car, he was arrested and brought before Judge John H. Ferguson of the Criminal District Court of the Parish in New Orleans, who ruled against him. The case was appealed to the State Supreme Court, and then to the U.S. Supreme Court, which handed down its decision in 1896.

The issue was whether Plessy had been denied his privileges, immunities, and equal protection of the law under the Fourteenth Amendment. Writing for the Court majority, Justice Henry

Brown declared that the Louisiana statute did *not* deprive blacks of equal protection of the laws, provided they were given accommodations equal to whites, thus establishing the precedent for "separate but equal." He also stated that the Fourteenth Amendment was not intended to abolish distinctions based upon color, or to enforce social equality, citing many examples of already established segregation in support of his argument. In a complicated, convoluted, and, subsequently, much denigrated opinion, Brown declared: "If the civil and political rights of both races be equal one cannot be inferior to the other civilly or politically. If one race be inferior to the other socially, the Constitution of the United States cannot put them upon the same plane."

In his famous and eloquent dissent Justice John Marshall Harlan spoke for the deeper conscience and ideals of the country, writing: "In view of the Constitution, in the eye of the law, there is in this country no superior, dominant, ruling class of citizens. There is no caste here. Our Constitution is color-blind, and neither knows nor tolerates classes among its citizens. In respect of civil rights, all citizens are equal before the law."

Then, in the famous case of *Plessy* v. *Ferguson* (1896), the Court established a constitutional standard for segregation—not overturned until 1954—declaring that "separate but equal" treatment of the races was legitimate under the Constitution. Being treated as a separate group, the Court majority argued, did not imply inferiority. Such a doctrine blatantly and deliberately flouted the spirit of the law: *Separate* did, in fact, mean "inferior."

As the rest of the country acquiesced, one Southern state after another established remarkably comprehensive systems of separation of the races. First, blacks were gradually denied the right to vote through various subterfuges, including the white primary (nominating elections restricted to white voters), literacy tests, and the "grandfather" test (one could not vote unless one's grandfather had voted, which effectively excluded all blacks). Social segregation followed—on street cars, in theaters, at water fountains, in boarding houses, rest rooms, and waiting rooms, at sporting and other recreational events, in mental institutions, orphanages, prisons, and hospitals, on jobs, in housing, in churches, and finally in funeral homes, morgues, and cemeteries. The breadth of the new system of segregation can be judged by the extremes to which it sometimes was carried: A 1909 curfew law in Mobile, Alabama, required blacks to be off the streets by 10:00 P.M.; a 1915

Oklahoma law required segregated telephone booths; laws in North Carolina and Florida required the separate storage of school textbooks.

A racist ideology elaborated on the new system. Many psychologists and biologists at the turn of the century held that the black race was inherently inferior to the white race in intelligence and morals. In the meantime, white violence against blacks increased, with the Ku Klux Klan growing more active. What evolved out of the Civil War and Reconstruction periods turned out to be, from the standpoint of the democratic spirit, about the worst possible outcome short of a return to slavery. This despite the many voices raised in favor of other options, even among Southern whites. Many Southern conservatives, while taking a paternalistic view of race relations, did not intend to create a system of total separation of the races. Unfortunately, over the final twenty years of the nineteenth century, the South systematically eliminated many legal rights for black people. Formal segregation became the law of the land, and once installed lasted a long time. This testifies to the failure of democratic leadership to live up to its own ideals.

UNDERMINING DEMOCRACY IN CHILE Our failure to live up to democratic ideals often has consequences outside our country. Such was the case in Chile in the early 1970s. Salvador Allende, elected president of Chile in 1970, was a socialist and the leader of a coalition of various left-wing political groups. He had run for president several times before and was a familiar figure in Chilean politics. The 1970 race for the presidency was a three-way affair, and Allende was able to win with only 36 percent of the total vote. By Chilean tradition, an absolute majority of the votes cast was not necessary for election; the candidate with a plurality could be declared the winner by the Chilean Senate.

President Richard Nixon and his advisor (and later secretary of state) Henry Kissinger regarded Allende's election as a serious threat to U.S. influence in the hemisphere. Several U.S. corporations—including the International Telephone and Telegraph Company and the Anaconda and Kennicott copper-mining companies—had significant holdings there. Also, U.S. political leaders feared the spread of communism into Chile. They were not prepared to tolerate another Cuba, which under Fidel Castro had embraced communism in the early 1960s.

Even before Allende took office, the U.S. government apparently was thinking about ways to undermine his regime. Then, during his three years in power, Allende faced several serious threats from our government. Not only did the United States supply money and other resources to political groups in Chile hostile to the Allende government, but the U.S. government made it difficult for Chile to obtain financial assistance from international funding agencies. In light of recent evidence, it also seems probable that Americans aided the Chilean military forces that overthrew Allende's government in 1973. In the midst of that military coup Allende lost his life. (The ruling junta said that he committed suicide.)

It may be that domestic opposition would have led to Allende's overthrow in any case, but we cannot be sure. Chile had a strong democratic tradition, and so if the United States had not thrown its weight so strongly against Allende, his experiment in democracy and socialism might well have survived, at least until the next presidential election, in 1976. Although U.S. policy was not the only factor involved, it may well have been a critical one in determining the fate of Chilean democracy. After the coup, there was virtually no remnant of democratic politics in Chile, and the next decade saw the military regime of that nation become one of the world's major violators of human rights.

The Carter administration, stimulated by congressional initiatives, looked closely at human rights problems in Chile and in 1977 banned all U.S. bilateral aid to that country. The Reagan administration, on the other hand, pursued a far friendlier approach at first. Regarding Chile as an ally, the administration adopted a course of "quiet diplomacy" to persuade the Chileans to move toward greater democracy. But little if any progress was forthcoming, and Chile remained high on the list of human rights violators. Finally, in 1986, the United States took the lead in drafting a United Nations resolution condemning Chile, after ab-

Support for an Undemocratic Regime: Ferdinand Marcos

The reign of Ferdinand Marcos over the Pacific island nation of the Philippines illustrates longterm U.S. support for a dictator because American security interests were at stake. During Marcos's twenty-year rule five U.S. presidents tolerated, and in some cases applauded, his administration, even though his efforts to run the country for his own personal profit were glaringly obvious. Marcos left the Philippines in early 1986 with a fortune estimated to be well over $2 billion; during his administration, the percentage of Filipinos living in poverty soared from 28 percent to 70 percent.

After Marcos came to power in fair elections in 1965, he began building a political machine that would keep him in power regardless of the country's constitution. He won reelection in 1969 through vote buying, fraud, and coercion. In 1972, realizing that he could not be reelected again because of a limit on the number of terms which presidents could serve, Marcos declared martial law, which was not lifted until Pope John Paul II visited the country in 1981. During this period, many civil liberties were suspended, and Marcos's political opponents were suppressed and occasionally tortured; many fled to the United States. In 1983, one of the opposition leaders, Benigno Aquino, returned to the Philippines, only to be shot at the airport; the army, under Marcos's command, was blamed for his killing.

U.S. support for the Marcos regime was consistent and wide-ranging, and Marcos relied on U.S. presidents for endorsement of many of his policies. Lyndon Johnson called Marcos his "right arm in Asia," and even as late at 1982 Ronald Reagan referred to him as an "old and good" friend of the United States. This special relationship meant that many in the Philippines associated Marcos with the United States; during the 1970s demonstrators often called for an end to "The U.S.–Marcos Dictatorship." Not until widespread protest of fraud in the 1986 elections and the growth of the New People's Army, a communist guerrilla force, did the United States withdraw its support for Marcos. As widespread rebellion grew, led by opposition candidate Corazon Aquino, widow of the slain Benigno Aquino, Marcos repeatedly called important officials in Washington to seek continued support. Finally, he left the presidential residence in a U.S. Marine helicopter, escaping to asylum in Hawaii.

Marcos keenly understood that any U.S. administration would rate the value of its military bases in the Philippines above concern for democratic politics in that nation. U.S. leaders tended to follow the path of least resistance in dealing with Marcos until he faced a full-fledged crisis. Even then, it is striking that Marcos retained considerable U.S. support almost until the very end. As one observer put it: ". . . A chauffer service for failed dictators should not be confused with a foreign policy."

SOURCE: Richard J. Kessler, "Marcos and the Americans," *Foreign Policy*, Summer 1986, pp. 40–57.

staining or voting against such resolutions for six years. Foreign policy advisors within the Reagan administration had grown worried that leftist opposition in Chile might become stronger because of the intransigence of the Pinochet government. Yet the administration persisted in sending ambivalent messages to Chile. The U.S. Defense Department maintained a cordial relationship with the Chilean military, and the United States voted for more than $2 billion in loans to Chile through international financial institutions, between 1980 and 1986, although it did abstain on a few votes. Critics have questioned why the Reagan administration was willing to put so much pressure on the Sandinistas in Nicaragua, but so little, comparatively, on the Pinochet government in Chile.*

*Based on Pamela Constable and Arturo Valenzuela, "Is Chile Next?" *Foreign Policy*, Summer 1986, pp. 58–75.

Some U.S. leaders are quick to see a threat to U.S. interests whenever a self-proclaimed socialist advocates rapid or radical social change. This attitude confuses the issue of defending democracy with that of defending capitalism and watching out for our economic interests. This problem is especially acute when it comes to Latin America, our geographic backyard.

The lessons of U.S. involvement in Chile are clear: (1) that in zealously opposing communism, the United States can destroy democratic political movements, and (2) that we must distinguish democracy from capitalism, and the interests of U.S. society from the interests of particular U.S. corporations. Otherwise, we may mistakenly come to view all radical change as anti-American.

Extending Democracy

Two examples of drives to expand democracy are the movement to gain women's suffrage and the protest to stop the war in Vietnam.

THE FIGHT FOR WOMEN'S SUFFRAGE   The Grimke sisters of Charleston, South Carolina, were a formidable pair. Long before the issues of women's suffrage and women's rights gained significant support on the public agenda in the United States, the Grimkes were articulating concepts very close to those we have become familiar with in recent decades:

> Human beings have *rights*, because they are *moral* beings: the rights of all men grow out of the moral nature, and as all men have the same moral nature, they have essentially the same rights. . . . Now, if rights are founded in the nature of our moral being, then the mere circumstance of sex does not give to man higher rights and responsibilities, than to a woman.   *Angelina Grimke, 1836*

> In most families it is considered a matter of far more consequence to call a girl off from making a pie, or a pudding, than to interrupt her whilst engaged in her studies.   *Sarah Grimke, 1838*

The Grimkes were among the more radical and forward-looking of the early advocates of women's rights. Like many other campaigners for women's

equality, they participated in the antislavery movement. To many women the position of black slaves paralleled the position of women: Both were excluded from full participation in democratic society because of physical attributes.

The Grimkes began their campaigning against slavery and for women's suffrage in the 1830s. More than eighty years of prolonged political and social struggle were to pass before the basic democratic right to vote was granted to American women. The story of the battle for suffrage testifies to the tenacity of opposition to democratic rights and, even more, to the tenacity required to overcome such opposition. Looking back, it seems remarkable that the issue was controversial at all. Why, after all, shouldn't women have the right to vote? But in asking the question this way, we fail to understand how deeply rooted were the sentiments that stood in the way of female equality.

Until the late nineteenth century, most men—and most women, as well—believed that women had a proper "place" in society, and that place did not include full-fledged participation as citizens. Former president Grover Cleveland voiced this position in 1905: "Sensible and responsible women do not want the vote. The relative positions assumed by men and women in the working out of our civilization were assigned long ago by a higher intelligence than ours." Political life was not entirely out of bounds to women—for example, some women participated in political campaigns in the early part of the nineteenth century—but equal participation was regarded as a violation of the natural order of things. Women were to play a domestic role, maintaining the home and rearing children.

By roughly 1830, universal suffrage for white males had been achieved in the United States—the first such achievement in the world. A few men and a few women spoke of the need to extend voting rights to women, but the dominant view of the day was that women could not be equal participants. In 1848 the first feminist convention was held in Seneca Falls, New York, and many date the struggle for suffrage from that meeting. The convention issued a "Declaration of Sentiments," one of the most significant documents in the history of feminism, that not only called for suffrage but also set forth an entire women's-rights ideol-

The power of an idea whose time has come! The demand for woman's suffrage had been around for more than half a century in American politics, but it required painstaking work over generations to make the reality happen. Woodrow Wilson helped push the necessary constitutional amendment. *(The Bettmann Archive)*

ogy of the sort that emerged fully only in the twentieth century. It was clear to some women even then that the struggle for equality between the sexes went far beyond the right to vote.

But that right itself proved difficult to obtain. The passage of the Civil War amendments raised some hopes, but then Supreme Court rulings narrowed the scope of these amendments. In 1878, a constitutional amendment to give women the right to vote was introduced for the first time in the Senate. Eleven years later, it reached the floor of the Senate, but was voted down. Meanwhile, the suffrage movement split into moderate and radical branches, and for a time the movement fell into decline. Yet as social attitudes began to change, some states moved to grant women the vote. The first to do so were in the West—Wyoming, Utah, Colorado, and Idaho. And by the turn of the century, more women had the time and energy necessary to join the movement. Families had grown smaller, and child rearing took up less time. Women were graduating from universities in larger numbers, considerably swelling the pool of leadership for a women's movement.

Women began to organize on a state-by-state basis and to campaign for suffrage reform within the states. Between 1910 and 1913, they succeeded in Washington and California. Then Illinois granted women the right to vote in presidential elections. At the same time, however, the opposition to women's suffrage was also growing. A formal association was created in 1911 to defeat the suffrage effort. This opposition drew support from many sources: textile manufacturers, who feared that women would favor stricter child labor legislation and thus limit the use of children in their factories; brewers and distillers, who feared that women would help pass laws prohibiting the sale of alcohol; and many Southerners, who felt women's suffrage would endanger white supremacy. And the traditional arguments continued about the appropriate "place" for women. For a long time political leaders played almost no role in the voting rights struggle. In 1912 the Progressive Party became the first major political party to endorse the vote for women, but the opposition was still strong enough to bring about the overwhelming defeat of a constitutional amendment in the Senate in 1914.

Women's organizations kept the pressure on at both state and national levels. In 1916, both the Democratic and Republican parties endorsed the idea of the individual states granting suffrage to women. Two years later, women's votes contributed significantly to President Woodrow Wilson's reelection in those states in which they could vote for president. Wilson then advised a delegation of Democrats to support the constitutional amendment. In January 1918, the House did so, 274–136, but the Senate rejected the measure by two votes. A new Congress passed the amendment in June 1919, and after fierce battles in state legislatures, the necessary three-fourths of the states ratified it by August 1920. It had been seventy-two years since the Seneca Falls convention, and eighty-four since Angelina Grimke had spoken of rights growing out of men's and women's status as equal moral beings.

The ideals on which U.S. political life was founded pointed toward women's suffrage from the start. But cultural assumptions pointed in the other direction—toward a subordinate and unequal role for women in politics and society. To extend democratic rights to half the population required decades of gradual social change plus the determined efforts of women's-rights advocates. And the struggles over women's rights continue, as more recent political battles over the equal rights amendment, abortion, parental leave, and many other issues indicate. How equal are women in our society? Should equality extend to every area of life? If so, how should it be extended? It is instructive to keep in mind how long it took to provide the most basic democratic right to 50 percent of the people.

PROTEST DURING THE VIETNAM WAR   One of the most useful roles a minority can play in democratic politics is that of critic, gadfly, questioner. The minority can keep alive debate and discussion that the majority would rather not hear. Such was the constructive role of political protest during the Vietnam War. Thanks to the determined democratic activities of millions of Americans, debate on the war deepened, and real communication among citizens increased. This was debate that our government did not wish to hear, and did much in its power to curtail.

During the 1960s most Americans were willing to take the president's word that we had to fight in Vietnam. The chief executive is usually granted the benefit of the doubt, especially when it comes to foreign policy emergencies. But a few challenged the president's stand. Particularly in universities and among the young, a spirit of questioning and rebellion arose. Protests were held on

One of many rallies held to protest the Vietnam War. As the war continued, more and more Americans of all backgrounds voiced their opposition to U.S. involvement. The antiwar movement raised many moral questions about American goals in Vietnam, the means employed to reach them, and the price paid to do so. *(Elliott Erwitt/Magnum)*

college campuses, and antiwar rallies were staged in Washington, D.C. The government was challenged to defend its case. The dissenters claimed that they were leading public debate on the real meaning of U.S. involvement in Vietnam—debate that the Congress should have engaged in, but had not, that the president should have listened to, but sought to avoid at every turn.

The dissenters did not have an immediate effect, and U.S. involvement in the war lasted until 1973. Millions were killed and wounded (over 50,000 Americans died), two other countries (Laos and Cambodia) were drawn into the fighting, and there were consequences at home and elsewhere that no one could have anticipated. But as more and more citizens expressed opposition to the war, government leaders began to feel the pressure. In 1968 an astounding grass-roots presidential campaign for peace candidate Eugene McCarthy helped persuade Lyndon Johnson to bow out of the presidential race altogether.

If the Vietnam War taught us many sobering lessons, it also gave rise to encouraging signs for democracy. Many Americans proved to be willing to raise difficult and painful questions about the behavior of their own government, and some risked jail or exile to express the conviction that the war was immoral. These were notable victories for the democratic spirit, regardless of what one might conclude about the wisdom of our involvement in Vietnam.

The Plan of This Book

This text is built around the questions and problems of democratic theory as outlined in this Introduction. In each chapter we will take up a different aspect of U.S. politics and relate it to the elements of democratic theory. In Part I we investigate the *foundations* of American democracy. For example, Chapter 1 focuses on U.S. political culture. The key questions are: Just how democratic is our political culture? And which aspects of that culture point in a democratic direction, and which do not?

Next, Chapters 2 and 3 examine basic political arrangements in the United States, specifically, the Constitution and the federal system. Do these arrangements facilitate or thwart democracy? Does the Constitution, for example, frustrate or enhance majority rule? Do the states do enough to protect democratic rights? Is a government that is "closer to the people" (such as local government) likely to be more democratic than state or national government?

Chapter 4 turns to basic questions of civil rights and liberties. How has U.S. society fared in these areas? We have already briefly glimpsed the struggles to grant full democratic rights to blacks and women, but what about other issues: free speech,

freedom of religion, due process of law, and so on?

Chapter 5 investigates the U.S. political economy. Here we return to the issues of democracy's relationship to capitalism and socialism, but more specifically exploring the distribution of wealth and income, the scope of poverty, the way government affects the distribution of material goods. Do the rich exercise excessive influence? Is democracy thwarted by the unequal distribution of resources?

In Part II we go beyond the foundations of government and dig more deeply into political *processes*. Here we look at political attitudes, voting, and political participation (Chapter 6); political parties (Chapter 7); campaigns and the media (Chapter 8); interest groups (Chapter 9); and mass political action (Chapter 10). All these chapters explore the issues of democratic representation. In each, the fundamental questions are: How are opinions shaped and acted on in our political life? How effective is the democratic process? For example, are political parties clearly related to popular attitudes? Do the media generate enlightenment? Is mass action constructive and sensible?

In Part III (Chapters 11 to 14) we turn to the fundamental political *institutions* of American national government—the Congress, the presidency, the federal bureaucracy, and the court system. How well do each of these institutions meet the needs of democratic politics? More specifically, are they responsive to popular sentiment, honest, protective of democratic rights and liberties, concerned in word *and* deed with creating a more decent society? These general questions break down into particular ones addressed to each institution. For example, we will ask whether presidential power has grown too great in some areas, or, conversely, whether presidential power is great enough to allow the chief executive to function effectively. In the case of Congress, we will be especially concerned with the power of "special interests." Is Congress really a democratic body, or is it too strongly influenced by the well-organized few?

Finally, Part IV (Chapters 15 to 20) is concerned with the four major areas of public *policy making*—economic policy, policies concerning civil rights and civil liberties, foreign and defense policies, and energy and environmental policies. The discussion of economic policy is divided into two parts. First Chapter 16 describes the overall management of the economy, including the relationship between government and business, the handling of inflation and unemployment, and the structure of the tax system. *In whose interest,* we will ask, is the economy managed? Chapter 17 then explores how economic policy affects the development of the welfare state—all the social programs designed to deal with the stresses and insecurities of economic life. This is one of the most controversial aspects of U.S. politics. What should a democrat ask of the welfare state? And how well does our welfare state meet these demands?

Chapter 18 is concerned with civil liberties and civil rights and considers several contemporary controversies. The thrust of the chapter is a consideration of how well civil rights and civil liberties are being protected. What does democratic theory tell us about ways of handling today's controversies?

Chapter 19 covers foreign and defense policy and focuses on the democratic issues involved: What forces shape foreign and defense policy? Who has the greatest influence over policy? What role does public opinion play, and how is it shaped? Does the United States further democratic goals through its foreign policy? Here we will consider recent wars, the arms race, Soviet-American relations, and other issues.

Finally, Chapter 20 focuses on the dilemmas posed for U.S. society by energy shortages and environmental damage. From the standpoint of democratic theory, several issues are significant: How are key decisions made in the areas of energy and the environment? Who benefits most from these decisions? What do the complex trade-offs involved in energy/environment problems mean for the common citizen?

In sum, this is a book that raises questions, offers opinions, and encourages you to think about the meanings, problems, and possibilities of democratic life. That is as it should be. Democracy is premised on the participation of citizens, and in America it has evolved into such an opportunity for participation that we all must learn to grapple with discrepancies between ideal and real political life.

GLOSSARY TERMS

majoritarian democracy
liberal democracy
capitalism
majority rule
basic rights
due process of law
equal protection of the laws
egalitarian democracy
minimalist view of democracy
maximalist view of democracy
interest group
oligarchy
alienation
Plessy v. *Ferguson*

SELECTED READINGS

VARIOUS DEFINITIONS OF DEMOCRACY

Discussions of **Greek political ideas** and practices can be found in Walter Agard, *What Democracy Meant to the Greeks* (Madison: University of Wisconsin Press, 1960); T. R. Glover, *Democracy in the Ancient World* (New York: Cooper Square, 1966).

There are many commentaries on the epic **seventeenth- and eighteenth-century** political struggles. See G. P. Gooch, *English Democratic Ideas in the Seventeenth Century* (New York: Harper, 1959); Carl L. Becker, *The Heavenly City of the Eighteenth Century Philosophers* (New Haven, Conn.: Yale University Press, 1932); Harry K. Girvetz, *The Evolution of Liberalism* (New York: Collier, 1963).

Certain **definitions of democracy** are quite broad, whereas some include many detailed sets of requirements. For discussion and examples, see Carl Cohen, *Democracy* (Athens, Ga.: University of Georgia Press, 1971), and H. B. Mayo, *An Introduction to Democratic Theory* (New York: Oxford, 1960). S. M. Lipset emphasizes the significance of competitive elections in *Political Man: The Social Bases of Politics* (Garden City, N.Y.: Doubleday, 1960; Johns Hopkins, 1981).

There have been three centuries of discussion on the subject of **egalitarian democracy.** For a sampling of interesting approaches, see C. B. MacPherson, *The Political Theory of Possessive Individualism: Hobbes to Locke* (Oxford:

Clarendon Press, 1962) and *Democratic Theory: Essays in Retrieval* (Oxford: Clarendon Press, 1973); R. H. Tawney, *Equality* (London: G. Allen & Unwin, 1964); G. B. Shaw, *The Intelligent Woman's Guide to Socialism and Capitalism* (Garden City, N.Y.: Garden City Publishing Co., 1928; Transaction Books, 1984).

IDEAL AND REAL DEMOCRACIES

The **philosophy of Rousseau** has been interpreted in several ways. See, for example, J. L. Talmon, *The Origins of Totalitarian Democracy* (New York: Praeger, 1960; Westview, 1985), and Maurice Cranston, "Rousseau and the Ideology of Liberation," *Wilson Quarterly*, January 1, 1983.

For a description of a modern **utopian democracy,** see Melford E. Spiro, *Kibbutz: Venture in Utopia* (Cambridge, Mass.: Harvard, 1975).

For discussions of **democratic theory** from several perspectives, see J. Cohen and J. Rogers, *On Democracy: Toward a Transformation of American Society* (Middlesex, England: Penguin, 1983); Amy Gutmann, *Liberal Equality* (Cambridge, England: Cambridge University Press, 1980); Elaine Spitz, *Majority Rule* (Chatham, N.J.: Chatham House, 1984); Giovanni Sartori, *Democratic Theory* (Westport, Conn.: Greenwood, 1973); Elias Berg, *Democracy and the Majority Principle* (Stockholm: Scandinavian University Books, 1965).

PROBLEMS IN DEMOCRATIC LIFE

Oligarchy and the problems of influence are among the most vigorously debated topics in modern politics. For a sampling of views, see Robert Michels, *Political Parties* (New York: Free Press, 1966); Michael Parenti, *Democracy for the Few*, 5th ed. (New York: St. Martin's 1988); John Plamenatz, *Democracy and Illusion* (New York: Longman, 1978), Chapter 3.

The literature on **alienation** is vast. A good starting point is R. S. Gilmour and R. B. Lamb, *Political Alienation in Contemporary America* (New York: St. Martin's, 1975).

STRUGGLES TO REALIZE DEMOCRATIC IDEALS

For a good overview of **race and Jim Crow laws,** see Eric Foner, *Reconstruction: America's Unfinished Revolution, 1863–1877* (New York: Harper & Row, 1988).

Among the more interesting sources on **women's suffrage** are Aileen S. Kraditor, ed., *Up from the Pedestal* (Chicago: Quadrangle Books, 1968); William L. O'Neill, *Everyone Was Brave* (Chicago: Quadrangle Books, 1969); Eleanor Flexner, *Century of Struggle: The Woman's Rights Movement in the United States*, rev. ed. (New York: Belknap Press, 1975).

The **protest movements** of the 1960s generated many thoughtful writings. For a sampling of different perspectives see Milton Viorst, *Fire in the Streets: America in the Nineteen Sixties* (New York: Touchstone Books, 1981); David Dellinger, *More Power Than We Knew: The People's Movement Towards Democracy* (New York: Doubleday, 1975); Lewis Feuer, *The Conflict of Generations* (New York: Basic Books, 1969); Stanley Rothman and Robert Lichter, *Roots of Radicalism: Jews, Christians and the New Left* (New York: Oxford, 1982).

For more extensive discussion of the U.S. role in **Chile,** see Seymour Hersh, *The Price of Power: Kissinger in the Nixon White House* (New York: Summit, 1983); Jorge Valacion, *Chile: An Attempt at Historic Compromise* (Chicago: Banner Press, 1979); Paul Sigmund, *The Overthrow of Allende and the Politics of Chile, 1964–1976* (Pittsburgh: University of Pittsburgh Press, 1977); J. Samuel Valenzuela and Arturo Valenzuela, *Military Rule in Chile* (Baltimore: Johns Hopkins, 1987).

PART 1

FOUNDATIONS

1 *AMERICAN POLITICAL CULTURE*

2 *REVOLUTION AND CONSTITUTION*

3 *AMERICAN FEDERALISM*

4 *THE EVOLUTION OF RIGHTS AND LIBERTIES*

5 *THE AMERICAN POLITICAL ECONOMY*

AMERICAN POLITICAL CULTURE

Liberty and Its Limits

CHAPTER OUTLINE

What Is Political Culture?
The Liberal Tradition
Two Types of Liberalism
Limits of Liberalism

Dan Cornish/Esto

The American political experience seems at first glance simple and straightforward enough. In the traditional view of grammar school textbooks, the United States was created as a full-fledged democracy, born in a revolution that rallied around the call for liberty and equality. Since that time, according to this version of history, the nation has gone on to greater and greater heights as a democratic society and as a defender of democracy elsewhere in the world. A closer look at our political history, however, reveals a far more ambiguous and troubling picture. The American experiment with government by the people was certainly innovative and has had worldwide significance. But there have been many rough moments in the evolution of U.S. democracy, from its beginnings to the present day. The very meaning of democracy has sometimes been called into question, and many battles have been waged over the concept of making democracy more meaningful.

One key factor in determining how democracy evolves is the character of a society's political culture. Let us now turn to that issue in connection with democracy in America.

What Is Political Culture?

A society's **political culture** arises from its members' attitudes toward the processes and institutions of politics. Such attitudes reflect conceptions about how politics works or ought to work, about the proper role of government, about one's fellow citizens and their place in the political process, about the rules of the political game. Political culture usually encompasses deeply rooted preconceptions about political life, which, in turn, shape political attitudes and behavior.[1] We will now explore the concept of political culture by examining (1) the interplay between political culture and democratic values and (2) the role of consensus in political culture.

Political Culture and Democracy

Is it possible to characterize the kind of political culture that is compatible with democracy? It is easy, after all, to cite attitudes hostile to democratic government. If, for example, citizens feel they play no legitimate role in their nation's politics; if a nation's leaders distrust its citizens and one another; if force is accepted as a necessary means of political action; if dissent and opposition are considered unacceptable—such feelings are unlikely to spawn a democratic form of government. But while it may be easy to point out undemocratic aspects of political culture, it is not so simple to describe the sort of political milieu likely to support democracy. We can, however, specify certain elements that any democratic society would have to include in its cultural repertoire: for example, belief in citizen participation, in the legitimacy of dissent and opposition, and in the meaningfulness of public debate and elections; reasonable respect for law and democratic principles; and tolerance toward other social groups.[2]

In describing the kind of society likely to develop and maintain a democratic political culture, some political scientists have cited high levels of education, affluence, and a large middle class as crucial elements.[3] Yet it is difficult to argue that any or all of these factors actually promote democracy. Democracies have developed under many conditions, and the vagaries of history sometimes help to shape political life in ways that could never be anticipated. At the end of World War II, for example, democracy was actually imposed on West Germany and Japan, two rabidly antidemocratic, fascist societies. Many authorities argued, not surprisingly, that the cultures of these nations were inherently inhospitable to democratic practices. Yet democracy has not only survived, but actually thrived, in both nations.

Cohesiveness in Political Culture

Consensus, more than any other element, distinguishes stable political cultures. Where political culture lacks consensus, political life is likely to be conflict-ridden, marked by disagreement over fundamentals.[4] In U.S. society, certain basic elements of the political culture, such as the near-sacred status of the Constitution, are virtually unchallengeable. Other facets of U.S. political culture, such as the interplay between religion and politics, have

---

COMPARATIVE PERSPECTIVE

Political Culture, Old and New

America, you are luckier
Than this old continent of ours;
You have no ruined castles
And no volcanic earth.
You do not suffer
In hours of intensity
From futile memories
And pointless battles.
  Concentrate on the present joyfully!
And when your children write books
May a good destiny keep them
From knight, robber, and ghost-stories.

Johann Wolfgang von Goethe (1749–1832)
Robert Bly, trans.

Early in the nineteenth century, the German poet Goethe expressed this poignant hope for the newly created United States. Unlike Europe, Goethe proclaims, America will not have to live under the shadow of a long and painful history. Note that Goethe's characterization of European history draws on the imagery of feudalism (knights and castles). Like many other observers before and since, he believed that it was the absence of a feudal history that made America different.

---

long sparked intense controversy. Our political culture, like most others, encompasses contradictory values, as well as conflicts between the values people proclaim and the values reflected in how they actually behave.

But if conflicts and contradictions characterize much of the style and dynamics of U.S. politics, some key areas of basic agreement, or consensus, mark U.S. political culture as well. Many observers of U.S. history have remarked on the strong consensus on political attitudes achieved in a society made up of so many disparate ethnic and racial groups. Ethnic diversity alone, obviously, does not rule out the development of a cohesive political culture. British colonists, who comprised 60 percent of the original colonial population, established the political processes, dominant language, and social and economic norms of interaction to which subsequent immigrant groups adjusted.

On one occasion in U.S. history the political consensus broke down and the issue had to be settled by war. This was, of course, the Civil War, which erupted out of the clash of differing concepts of citizenship and basic rights, as well as dis-

agreements over how political power should be exercised. The legacy of that conflict still shapes our political life today.

Overall, U.S. political culture has remained sufficiently cohesive to permit orderly government to carry on in spite of the many conflicts and contradictions in our society and political life. In fact, looking back over the last thirty years, it may seem remarkable that our political processes have been able to survive, relatively unchanged, in the face of assassinations, domestic violence, a bitterly opposed and costly war, and the resignation of a president. Whether this is a testimony to the resilience of our political culture, or to its irrelevance, is a question we will consider at the conclusion of this text.

We will now look at the pattern of our political culture, exploring the many ways it has supported and strengthened our democratic behavior. We will examine the fundamental values that have shaped U.S. political life, beginning with the liberal democratic tradition that informs much of our political culture. Then we will turn to the limita-

July 4, 1961. One of the chief bonds in any political culture is the spirit of belonging to the nation. In many American communities, this spirit remains a powerful force. This picture shows citizens of a neighborhood on Chicago's west side. *(National Archives)*

tions of that same political culture, to analyze some cultural and political patterns that have thwarted the evolution of democracy in the United States.

The Liberal Tradition

The United States was conceived in the tradition of eighteenth-century **liberalism,** a social and political set of values that decisively shaped our democratic politics.[5] The cornerstones of this political value system were a belief in government based on the consent of the governed and a belief that certain rights are guaranteed to all persons simply because they are human beings. These rights, as enunciated so eloquently by Thomas Jefferson in the Declaration of Independence, included "life, liberty and the pursuit of happiness." Government, according to eighteenth-century lib-

erals, gains legitimacy by protecting these rights. And when a government violates the rights of its citizens, those citizens have a right to rebel— which is exactly what some of the colonists did.

Liberals placed great emphasis on the liberty of the individual. The concept of the free individual actually evolved over the course of several centuries. In the Renaissance era (roughly, 1350–1600), as the tenets of classical humanism were revived and reinterpreted, intellectuals and artists celebrated what they saw as the uniqueness of human potential and the virtually unlimited possibilities of human creativity.[6] To the Renaissance celebration of humanism was added, beginning in the early 1500s, the Protestant Reformation's emphasis on the primacy of the individual conscience and the solitary relation of the individual to God.[7] Paralleling those developments, an economic movement called capitalism—based on private property and individual initiative—advocated freedom for every individual to buy and sell, to invest and gamble, to work and to relocate, as that person saw fit. Finally, seventeenth-century political philosophers such as John Locke applied the concept of the free individual to the political realm, arguing that government existed only to safeguard the **natural rights** of individuals.[8] These rights are considered essential human guarantees (such as freedom) that a government cannot curtail or eliminate arbitrarily and remain just.

The ideal society of free individuals envisioned by the liberal thinkers of the seventeenth and eighteenth centuries was a society based entirely on merit and open to all, in which each person was free to pursue any course of action, so long as it did not impinge on the freedom or rights of others. In such an open society, you had only yourself to blame if you failed to take advantage of life's opportunities. In the fledgling United States, a nation consisting primarily of small, individually owned farms and located on the edge of a vast, unexplored continent, these liberal ideas set down particularly tenacious roots.

Economic, Social, and Political Values

Given the tenets of the liberal creed, it is easy to see why the United States acted as a magnet for immigrants. Although some immigrants were refugees from political or religious persecution, most came to the United States to find a better life, lured by the liberal promise that even the lowest-born person could, through hard work, climb the ladder of success. The United States, with no hereditary nobility and seemingly no social or political restrictions on individual initiative, drew great waves of immigrants looking for a chance to better themselves.[9]

Along with Americans' faith in individual responsibility went a belief in the small business or individually owned farm as the appropriate vehicle for economic success. Throughout the nation's history, Americans generally have believed that although bigger may be better in some matters, too much bigness was a dangerous thing. Recurrently in U.S. political history, **populist,** or grass-roots, movements have arisen to defend the interests of

How many of us can trace our ancestors to people like these? Facing an uncertain future—but one they themselves chose—they arrived on American shores not knowing the language and usually with little idea of what kind of world they would find. *(Louis Hine/ The Bettmann Archive)*

the common citizen against institutions or power elites perceived as too big and oppressive. In the 1890s the Populist party attacked the big corporations and the railroads. More recently, populist movements have focused their attacks on so-called big government.[10]

Populist agitation, however, has rarely been directed against the capitalist system itself—only against perceived abuses of it. True to their liberal democratic heritage, most Americans continue to believe that capitalism is the best economic system. Private ownership has remained popular, although most people now accept the idea that sometimes business must be regulated for the public good.

Together with these economic values, eighteenth-century liberalism encompassed political and social values predicated on a considerable degree of equality among citizens. Because all indi-

COMPARATIVE PERSPECTIVE

A Look at the National Characteristics of Sweden

In *Sweden: Prototype of Modern Society* the social scientist Richard Tomasson compares Swedish and American values, including attitudes toward democracy, freedom, progress, achievement, work, material comfort, and efficiency. Tomasson concludes that Swedish and American values are similar in many ways, but he notes the following important differences.

Abhorrence of violence   There are extremely strong inhibitions on violence and the manifestation of aggression in Swedish culture. While it is now almost commonplace to see nudity and sexual intercourse in Swedish films, it is not usual to see violence. Most of the violence in the mass media (and much is censored) is in American films and television programs. . . .

Even when Swedes have been drinking heavily at parties, it is rare for any physical aggressiveness to be shown. It may be that the abhorrence of violence is greater in Sweden than in other Scandinavian countries, though in all of them it is clearly greater than in America. . . . In any case, if data on willful murder and sex offenses can be used as indicators of how much violence is inhibited in a society, then Sweden is certainly an extreme case. The disdain for violence in Sweden might be likened to the abhorrence of pornography in a puritanical society.

Democracy   Democracy is ideologically the most absolute of all modern values in Sweden. It is an ultimate appeal. That is ipso facto good which is democratic. In Sweden, democracy means the right of individuals to choose their leaders in the nation and in organizations, but, at the ideological level, it is frequently confounded with egalitarianism and equality of opportunity. While this is also the case in America, democracy seems to be a more pervasive value in Swedish than American culture. In Sweden it is believed that all organizations should be "democratic," and anything that is "not democratic" is liable to suspicion. In recent years there has been much concern with industrial democracy, the bringing of workers into the decision-making process. A common viewpoint is that democracy has been achieved in the political realm, in education, in most of the great organizations, but still not yet in the realm of work. It is clear that there is greater democracy in organizations in Sweden, notably in unions and in political parties, than in America.

Equality   This is a most complex value area and one with many ramifications. Yet in the aggregate it is probably as strong and pervasive a Swedish value as it is an American value, although it takes different forms than in American culture. Swedish egalitarianism is shaped by opposition to the traditions of the old hierarchical society, vestiges of which remain in the form of differential terms of address and titles. There is greater respect for authority and for expert opinion and less celebration of the views of "the common man" than one finds in American culture. Yet there is a greater concern in Sweden with economic equality, with the greater privileges of salaried as compared with wage workers, with realizing equality of opportunity in education, as well as with the greater emphasis on sexual equality.

SOURCE: Richard F. Tomasson, *Sweden: Prototype of Modern Society* (New York: Random House, 1970).

viduals are born with certain rights, all are entitled to have those rights protected by society and government. Each person should be equal before the law—a person cannot claim superiority before a judge, for example, simply by virtue of belonging to a richer or more privileged class. In addition, each person is entitled to basic political rights, starting with the right to participate meaningfully in political life.

Eighteenth-century liberals were also suspicious of the power of governments in general. Government power, they felt, could be abused all too easily, subverting the rights of the individual—through excessive taxation, for example. As a safeguard, liberals argued for a contractual arrangement between government and the governed. Government, they said, should be limited to specific functions, and the governed should be guaranteed certain rights; if any of those rights are violated, moreover, individuals have cause for disobedience or even rebellion.

To summarize, the values that eighteenth-century liberalism contributed to the U.S. democratic tradition included:

Individualism   A belief in the central value of the individual, whose rights government is created to defend. Each individual is responsible for his (or, by logical extension, her) own fate.

Liberty   Each person should have the maximum freedom possible, compatible with equal freedom for others.

Equality   All are entitled to equal legal and political rights.

An Open Society   Each person should be judged on individual merits and be free to enter various occupations and pursuits.

Rule of Law   Government must be nonarbitrary, exercising power through equitable laws that are fairly administered.

Limits on Government   Since power can easily corrupt, governments must be watched closely and hedged with restrictions lest they infringe on citizens' rights. A written constitution helps to set such limits.

As noble as these tenets of eighteenth-century liberalism sounded in theory, however, applying them to concrete situations proved extremely difficult. For example, early liberals had grave doubts about whether everyone ought to have the right to vote. Both in England and America many liberals were wary of the potential power of "the many" that political equality might create. They feared what was sometimes called the **tyranny of the majority,** or, less politely, mob rule. The U.S. Constitution, significantly, left the issue of voting rights up to the individual states, many of which stipulated that only those who owned a certain amount of property could vote. Still, for white males the right to vote was achieved earlier in the United States (by 1830) than it was anywhere else in the world.

Interestingly, the liberal values on which the United States was founded actually made it a purer liberal society than the European societies that gave birth to liberalism. In Europe, liberals were forced to do combat with the defenders of monarchy, of which there were few in the new United States. Of course, there was (and remains) tremendous disagreement over what "democratic liberalism" actually means, but the United States has never experienced the struggles over the very *form* of government that have been fairly commonplace in European history.[11] Compared with Europe, then, the United States was from the start more egalitarian, despite the vast differences in wealth that have always existed here.

Of course, many Americans throughout history have neither supported nor acted on these core liberal values, preferring beliefs and practices often at great variance with the liberal tradition. Nevertheless, liberalism is the American creed. We may not honor it, but it haunts our consciences. It represents our collective ideal, even if it is not always reflected in our collective practice.

The Legacy of Liberalism

The strength of the liberal tradition in the United States has helped democratic government survive here for more than two centuries. Apart from the Civil War, there has been no serious challenge to the legitimacy of democratic government and constitutional authority in our political history. As the nation's conscience, the liberal tradition has kept alive the hope of equal treatment and basic civil rights for all. Despite long periods of religious, racial, and political intolerance, respect for civil liberties has gradually increased throughout our history. Legal equality for American blacks, long believed to be a virtual impossibility, was achieved after a long struggle. The fundamental liberal commitment to political equality served as a goad in that struggle.[12]

Liberalism has also sustained a considerable distrust of government, which continues to show itself in grass-roots resistance to government intrusions, in tax revolts, and in attacks on the growth of government budgets at all levels. The liberal belief in equality before the law also served as the basis of the Watergate investigations of the early 1970s, leading to the first resignation of a president in U.S. history.

Finally, Americans embrace liberalism's deep commitment to the individual. The capitalist economic system, whose central premise is private ownership of the means of production, mirrors this emphasis on individual accomplishment. Despite many modifications in this economic system and much greater government involvement in economic life, most Americans still consider capitalism essential to the American way of life.

Two Types of Liberalism

U.S. political debate today revolves around two seemingly opposing viewpoints, usually labeled liberalism and conservatism. But ironically, eighteenth-century liberal ideas and assumptions stand at the core of both views. Regardless of the labels "liberal" and "conservative," U.S. political life basically operates within the framework and norms established at the founding of the nation. We will now examine how the beliefs of today's conservatives and liberals both derive from the same liberal tradition, and how that tradition has hampered the growth of radical groups in the U.S. political arena.

Conservatism: Traditional Liberalism

By and large, most U.S. **conservatives** are traditional liberals who have kept faith with liberalism as it was propounded two hundred years ago.[13]

The optimistic, activist president: Conservative Ronald Reagan and liberal Franklin Roosevelt both had a large agenda and exuded a positive attitude about achieving their goals, which, of course, were wildly different. *(Art Stein/Photo Researchers)*

Conservative politicians such as President Ronald Reagan and Senator Jesse Helms emphasize the individualist, antigovernment tenets of the liberal tradition. They continue to believe in the strength of U.S. capitalism, as represented by **free enterprise**—allowing supply and demand to regulate the marketplace without government interference. Out of a belief in individual responsibility, they generally disapprove of government programs to aid the disadvantaged. Because of their commitment to capitalism, they prefer to leave dollars in private hands, rather than redistributing wealth through social programs. They want less economic regulation by government and see virtue in what Reagan has called the "magic of the marketplace"—that is, the creation of wealth through individual initiative and free enterprise in business and finance, unfettered by government restrictions.

Occasionally, powerful forces on the political right (the Ku Klux Klan, for instance) have championed ideals contrary to the liberal creed, but such fringe elements have never entered the main-

Judge Ginsburg and the Regulation of Morals

In late 1987, after his nomination of Robert Bork to the Supreme Court had been rejected by the Senate, Ronald Reagan submitted the nomination of Douglas Ginsburg, a relatively young and not well-known federal appellate judge. This nomination turned out to be an embarrassment for the administration on several counts, but the chief source of discomfort emerged when it quickly became known that Judge Ginsburg had used marijuana in the late 1970s while he was a professor of law at Harvard. Although his use of the drug was occasional and recreational—and although Ginsburg characterized it as a "mistake" he regretted—many conservatives found the situation hard to accept. Within Congress and the administration, officials demanded that the nomination be withdrawn. After all, some conservative critics argued, how could even a *former* drug user be regarded as appropriate for a position on the High Court? And hadn't administration officials and the president himself spoken out repeatedly against drug use of any kind? In addition, the Justice Department itself has strict rules disqualifying prospective appointees for lesser positions who admit to past drug use of any sort.

President Reagan attempted to make light of Ginsburg's marijuana use, calling it a youthful indiscretion. But his relaxed attitude did not persuade other conservatives, and the pressure was sufficient for Ginsburg to ask that his nomination be withdrawn. It was a case where conservatives' efforts to legislate morality had come home to roost, awkwardly, on one of their own. In the aftermath of this episode some asked just how many members of the American legal profession under age forty had *not* experimented with marijuana or other drugs. If all of them were disqualified for judicial appointments, who would be left to staff the nation's courts?

stream of conservatism. Today's conservatives usually think of themselves as upholding the truest traditions of the nation, and they are fond of citing the words of the Founders on such issues as the danger of too much government power and the importance of the individual. Unlike most conservatives in Europe, U.S. conservatives are not usually comfortable with paternalistic government—with using the power of the state to protect or assist individuals.

The New Liberalism

The Great Depression of the 1930s prompted a major shift in U.S. politics. At that time millions were out of work, banks were failing, many stocks were practically worthless, much of the population was afraid and in want. President Franklin D. Roosevelt said he saw "one third of the nation ill-housed, ill-clothed and ill-fed." The U.S. economic system had failed, and there was widespread agreement on the need for a restructuring of the economy, in which government would gain far more power over economic affairs and make a firm commitment to the well-being of the common citizen. President Roosevelt's solution was a wide range of social and economic initiatives called the **New Deal,** which involved government regulations and subsidies in the economic sphere and welfare programs in the social sector.

FDR's New Deal was the crystallization of the "new" liberalism, an activist creed committed to the improvement of the average person's conditions of life, and particularly to elimination of the worst forms of poverty and deprivation.[14] Politicians committed to the new liberalism, such as former vice-president Walter Mondale and Senator Edward Kennedy, are not satisfied with letting the economy run according to is own laws, preferring to direct economic activity toward larger social interests. In general, this means initiating social programs aimed at aiding the unemployed, improving health care and housing for low-income people,

People either loved or hated Franklin Roosevelt, but no one could ignore him. His politics probably had more enduring influence on our political system than any other 20th-century figure. *(FDR Library, Hyde Park/Photo Researchers)*

raising educational opportunities for all, and so on.

The new liberals, like the conservatives, are not entirely consistent in their views and policies. Despite their commitment to social change, liberals often favor balanced budgets and reduced government spending. Conservatives, for their part, frequently defend government subsidies to groups such as farmers, while maintaining a general opposition to government spending. Conservatives also are the chief champions of government involvement in matters of personal morality such as abortion, pornography, and homosexuality.

When it comes to an activist government, then, conservatives usually prefer action in the realm of personal life, while opposing regulation of business. Liberals tend to take the opposite view—that morals are a matter of personal choice, whereas economic matters have general social significance and therefore legitimately fall within the areas that government may regulate.

The Failure of Radicalism

One consequence of the strength of the U.S. liberal tradition has been the relative failure of radical movements to gain national power. The United States is, in fact, the only industrial democracy without a significant **socialist** political party. The socialist ideology usually favors collective and government ownership over individual or private ownership (see further discussion in Chapter 5). In comparison with the United States, socialists have played a key part in the national politics of European democracies since the nineteenth century, and in recent years **democratic socialist parties** have held power in France, Spain, Great Britain, West Germany, Sweden, Denmark, Norway, Finland, Austria, Greece, the Netherlands, and Portugal. Even in Canada, where the political left has not been a major force nationally until recently, the socialist New Democratic Party has elected provincial governments in British Columbia, Saskatchewan, and Manitoba.

Many arguments have been advanced to explain this weakness of the American left.[15] Some argue that the United States is simply too rich a country: General affluence has made socialism less appealing to the masses. Others contend that the country's many ethnic, racial, religious, and regional divisions have made organizing a party based on social class very difficult. Most observers believe, however, that one of the central factors has been the strength of the liberal tradition. The American emphasis on individualism, with its ideology of opportunity and success, together with this nation's relative equality and lack of feudal heritage, has prevented radical ideas from catching on. European socialists, on the other hand, have benefited from the greater class consciousness and solidarity of the working class, as well as a more closed social system than in the United States. It has even proved more difficult to organize trade unions here, and union membership today is much lower in the United States than in most other democratic nations.

This is not to say, however, that socialists have seen no success at all in the United States. Many socialist mayors and legislators were elected around World War I, for example, and California came close to electing a socialist governor during the Depression. More recently, we saw something of a left-wing revival in the 1960s. It is also important to note that many programs advocated by socialists have, in fact, become accepted U.S. policies, from social security and unemployment insurance to the many efforts to protect consumers or the very idea of government responsibility for the performance of the economy. Nonetheless, the failure of a socialist party to become a significant part of the political spectrum has had many important political consequences, among them the relative weakness of the American **welfare state** (a point we return to in Chapters 5 and 17).

Looking to the other side of the American political spectrum, we see that the far right, including such antidemocratic groups as the Ku Klux Klan, has also failed to gain national power. Outright racist groups have had much greater success at the state and local levels. The Klan, for example, exerted some influence in several states during the 1920s, but never succeeded at anything more than a march in the nation's capital.

Both the far left and the far right, then, have played a less significant role in our history than they have in many other democratic nations. Shaped by our own brand of liberalism, the American political spectrum has remained narrower than that of most other democratic nations.

Limits of Liberalism

As we have seen, our nation's liberal heritage has in many ways supported democratic values and practices. Yet, we have often failed to live up to the standards of this heritage. Americans are proud to recite the tenets of the liberal faith, but we sometimes find it difficult to put our beliefs into practice. Too often, the doors of the "open society" have been shut to some citizens. Respect for law has not prevented bouts of violence. Our attempts to spread democracy to the world have become ensnared in national self-interest. Religious beliefs, supposedly matters of individual concern, have occasionally been thrust into the political arena.

This is not to imply that liberal values are not upheld much of the time. The United States justly deserves its reputation as the "land of opportunity," and many Americans are respectful of the rights of others and generous in sharing their resources. This section focuses on our lapses—areas where contradictions and problems persist in our culture.

Intolerance and Discrimination

"Fellow immigrants," President Franklin Roosevelt once began an address to the Daughters of the American Revolution, a group sometimes noted for its snobbish celebration of special hereditary connections. Roosevelt's irony was well placed. Except for the American Indians, whose journey here came centuries earlier, we are *all* immigrants. Social and economic distinctions often boil down to who got here first and made the most of it.

Despite assimilation by the various immigrants who settled here, however, enough lumps have remained in the so-called melting pot that politicians frequently find it advantageous to pitch their campaigns to specific ethnic groups.[16] Particular ethnic groups have even taken firm hold on local politics in certain areas. Still, only in the latter half of the twentieth century have the members of some ethnic groups been able to attain high elective office. The first Catholic president, John F. Kennedy, was elected in 1960, and it will probably be quite some time before a black or Hispanic president is elected.

Throughout U.S. history, foreigners, minority groups, and many who just seemed different have been subject to both personal intolerance and official discrimination. Discrimination has taken many forms: in employment, in college quotas established to limit the entrance of certain groups, in restrictions on where people can live. Social humiliation, harrassment, and even murder have sometimes greeted new Americans. In the middle of the nineteenth century the Nativist party accused newly arrived Catholic immigrants of plotting to take over the nation in the name of the papacy. This was to be the first of many such ac-

Immigration Law Reform

On November 6, 1986, Ronald Reagan signed into law the Immigration Reform and Control Act, a measure that represented a delicate compromise on a number of controversial, interconnected issues. The law was designed to reduce the flow of illegal immigrants (mainly from Mexico) while also addressing an anomaly in prior regulations: While it had been illegal to enter the country without proper papers and illegal to work here, it was not a violation for employers to hire "undocumented" workers.

At its core, the new law covered three points. First, it created the possibility of amnesty and eventual citizenship for immigrants who could prove they had resided in the United States continuously since before January 1982. Second, it created new penalties for employers who knowingly hired illegals after the law was signed. And third, it established special provisions to ensure sufficient agricultural laborers for western growers who had relied on illegal immigrants in the past.

The law's effects were mixed. The Immigration and Naturalization Service (INS) claimed a 34 percent drop in apprehensions along the 2,000-mile border with Mexico, and there were signs that many employers were more careful to stay within the new federal law. But some employers, determined to continue using cheap labor, accepted false proof of legal residence, reasoning that penalties were relatively minor and detection was unlikely.

As for the important amnesty provisions, almost 2 million illegal immigrants applied (of whom 92 percent were accepted) before the opportunity ran out in May 1988. This number fell somewhat short of expectations, and there were many complications in connection with amnesty. For example, how would the INS treat members of the same family who had arrived in the United States at different times? The agency refused to establish a uniform policy but stated that it would keep spouses together on a humanitarian, case-by-case basis, and that it would not deport children of single-parent families. Legislation introduced in the Senate, which would have granted full amnesty to families, was defeated; its opponents argued that it would discriminate against legal aliens who properly waited for their chance to enter the country or gain citizenship.

Although the 1986 law did strike some compromises after years of sharp disagreements, it did not end debate. Exclusionists argue that too many immigrants diminish the quality of life—for example, by enlarging the pool of cheap labor, we could make it even harder for poor Americans to find work. Some also fear that large numbers of immigrants will alter the balance of political power in certain areas. At times, a racist undertone colors anti-immigrant sentiments, and hostility has boiled over into conflict.

Inclusionists, on the other hand, favor expanded immigration and argue that tightly controlled borders violate America's traditions. The country thrives on immigrants who are anxious to work and succeed. Recently there was a backlog of 2 million applicants for the 270,000 places available each year for prospective immigrants, whose wait to enter the country can be from five to ten years. At present, Europeans account for 14 percent of immigrants; Asians number about 47 percent; and Hispanics total 40 percent. The proportion of immigrants in the entire U.S. population is now 6 percent, considerably lower than in the past.

Recent attitudes toward immigration are indicated in the following table:

The number of illegal immigrants is too high.	56%
U.S. should keep its doors open to new immigrants.	27%
Strictly limit the number of immigrants.	67%
Immigrants generally end up on welfare.	59%
Immigrants add to the crime problem.	54%
Immigrants are productive once they get established.	67%
Immigrants are basically good, honest people.	58%

SOURCES: *Congressional Quarterly Almanac 1986*, pp. 61–63; Morton M. Kondracke, "Moral Borders," *The New Republic*, Nov. 23, 1987; James Fallows, "Viva Bilingualism," *The New Republic*, Nov. 24, 1987; *Time* magazine, Special Issue: Immigrants, July 8, 1985; Dianna Solis and Pauline Yoshihashi, "Spotty Record," *Wall Street Journal*, Nov. 6, 1987, pp. 1, 18.

The Melting Pot Today

The last census, in 1980, counted more than 226 million Americans, and it will be a few years before we know how much the population has grown since then. (In March 1986 the Bureau of the Census put the total population at 240 million.) Even though the following figures will soon change somewhat, they give a good sense of the variety of people to be found in America's "melting pot."

Of the population counted in the last census, more than 118 million traced their origins to a single foreign nation, and almost 70 million others listed multiple foreign origins. Those of English ancestry led the list, with those of German origin a very close second and Irish-Americans a relatively close third. (Some experts speculate that the figures on English ancestry may be low because the English were assimilated so long ago.) About 38 million people polled by the census classified themselves as "Americans."

The ancestry groups reported by 100,000 or more Americans included:

English, 49,598,035
German, 49,224,146
Irish, 40,165,702
Afro-American, 20,964,729
French, 12,892,246
Italian, 12,183,692
Scottish, 10,048,816
Polish, 8,228,037
Mexican, 7,692,619
American Indian, 6,715,819
Dutch, 6,304,499
Swedish, 4,345,392
Norwegian, 3,453,839
Russian, 2,781,432
Spanish-Hispanic, 2,686,680
Czech, 1,892,456
Hungarian, 1,776,902
Welsh, 1,664,598
Danish, 1,518,273
Puerto Rican, 1,443,862
Portuguese, 1,024,351
Swiss, 981,543
Greek, 959,856
Austrian, 948,558
Chinese, 894,453
Filipino, 795,255
Japanese, 791,275

French-Canadian, 780,488
Slovak, 776,806
Lithuanian, 742,776
Ukrainian, 730,056
Finnish, 615,872
Cuban, 597,702
Canadian, 456,212
Korean, 376,676
Belgian, 360,277
Yugoslavian, 360,174
Romanian, 315,258
Asian Indian, 311,953
Lebanese, 294,895
Jamaican, 253,268
Croatian, 252,970
Vietnamese, 215,184
Armenian, 212,621
African, 203,791
Hawaiian, 202,052
Dominican, 170,698
Colombian, 156,276
Slovene, 126,663
Iranian, 122,890
Syrian, 106,638
Serbian, 100,941

SOURCE: U.S. Bureau of the Census.

cusations and efforts to restrict the entry of "foreigners" to the United States. Again and again religious, ethnic, and racial hatreds have flared, necessitating a continuous struggle to keep our society open.[17]

Many immigrant groups have had to contend with blatant discrimination by fellow Americans. In early 1942, close to one hundred thousand U.S. citizens were rounded up, forced to leave their homes, and taken to detention camps in remote

Hayward, California, 1942. The Mochida family awaits evacuation to an internment camp. Almost 100,000 Japanese-Americans were confined to camps in remote areas during World War II. Though the courts upheld the Japanese internment as a justifiable wartime measure, many concluded after the war that it was a policy based more on panic and racism than reason. In 1988 Congress passed legislation awarding $20,000 to each surviving victim of the internment. *(Dorothea Lange/National Archives)*

areas, where they were confined for three years. The only "crime" committed by these people was being of Japanese descent at a time when hatred of the Japanese, who had just attacked Pearl Harbor, was at fever pitch. The government justified its actions on the ground that Japanese-Americans posed a security threat to the country, even though there was no specific evidence that more than a handful had offered or intended to offer aid to the Japanese cause. The vast majority of Japanese-Americans were loyal to U.S. institutions, and yet the U.S. government, with the blessing of the Supreme Court, interned them without trial.[18]

Looking back from the vantage point of more than forty years, we can only be ashamed of what was done. Although the internment camps were not the concentration camps of the Nazis, Japanese-Americans nonetheless were innocent victims of hysteria and prejudice. Recognizing the harm done, Congress in the 1980s moved to compensate victims for their losses. Yet serious tensions over differences in ethnicity, religion, race, and other group characteristics—which periodically flare into the open—remain a problem for democratic politics.

Violence and the Rule of Law

Americans historically have displayed considerable respect for law and legal procedures. Faith in the Constitution, in the Supreme Court, and in the court system in general has helped to keep social and political conflicts within accepted boundaries. In fact, Americans seem overly fond of legal procedures and tend to litigate endlessly about all sorts of matters. Even one hundred years ago, foreign observers noted that Americans would take each other to court at the drop of a hat. Respect for law and the use of law to settle disputes seem ingrained in our heritage, fitting the liberal tradition's preference for an agreed-on legal framework as the basis of government.

Yet there is also a contrary tradition in the United States—the tradition of the gun. The use of force, by both government and individuals, has played a central role in the nation's growth and in the shaping of our folkways. Settlers fought with Indians, waged a war of independence, feuded over land. The Wild West remains legendary, its heroic figures still popularized in books, on television, and in films.[19] To survive in much of the

Deadly violence is becoming a commonplace in American society. We take it for granted, almost, that Americans will kill one another by the thousands each year. The right to own and use a gun (or an attack dog) to defend one's property is highly prized by many. Most Americans are not aware that other democracies have far lower levels of violence. How have they accomplished it?
(Archive Pictures)

United States in the nineteenth century, the gun was as necessary as the plow, the ax, or the Bible. The frontier often had no enforceable legal authority, so individuals relied on themselves and their friends to maintain social stability. Americans were also wary of granting to the central government the exclusive right to police. Even today, policing remains a predominantly local function in our country. The Constitution expressly provides for the citizen's right to bear arms, which, as the colonists considered it, was necessary for a citizen militia.

Private violence has taken many forms in the United States. Between 1885 and 1916, for example, more than 3,000 blacks were lynched and thousands of others brutalized.[20] Throughout the late nineteenth and early twentieth centuries, industrialists often hired private armies to combat strikes by workers. And there is a long tradition of vigilantes pursuing criminals and others who were thought to threaten communities. Examples of *public* violence are not lacking, either. Police forces, the army, and the National Guard have frequently been used against various perceived threats—Indians, union organizers, protestors, and others.

We do not have to go back very far in history to find striking evidence of the persistence of the violent streak in U.S. society. Five of the last nine presidents have been targets for assassins. The two most prominent black leaders of the 1960s,

Martin Luther King, Jr., and Malcolm X, were assassinated. Senator Robert Kennedy was killed and Governor George Wallace crippled by assailants. Also in the 1960s, rioting and arson erupted in black ghettoes throughout the country, and police and National Guard units often met this violence with deadly force. Fatalities were common.

Compared with contemporary Europe, the United States is a particularly violent country. Police are far more likely to kill citizens in this country, both in normal times and in times of disorder, than they are in the European democracies.[21] Perhaps because Europeans have experienced the violence of which totalitarian governments are capable, they are more sensitive about government use of force. A more important factor, however, may be that far more Americans are armed. Because tens of millions of guns circulate freely in U.S. society, the police here constantly face the possibility of deadly threat—something European police rarely have to confront. The large number of guns available has helped make U.S. homicide rates the highest among democratic countries (see **Table 1–1**, page 47). Yet various European nations have bred their own brands of violence. Organized terrorism has become all too common in Italy, France, and West Germany, as has violence among soccer fans in England.

Many issues related to violence have not been solved in our society. Gun ownership is one: Who should be permitted to own guns? And what kind

Political Assassination in America

Four of the eight attempts to assassinate American presidents have succeeded, and there also have been four attacks on presidential hopefuls. Abraham Lincoln, of course, was the first victim, shot by John Wilkes Booth in 1865. James Garfield, the twentieth president, was shot by Charles Guiteau on a railroad train in July 1881, only four months after taking office. William McKinley was standing in a receiving line at the Pan American Exposition in Buffalo, New York, when he was shot by Leon Czolgosz, a mill worker, in 1901. More than forty years passed before the next attempt, in 1948, when Puerto Rican nationalists Oscar Collazo and Griselio Torresola attempted to storm Blair House and kill Harry Truman, who was residing there while the White House was being renovated. Fifteen years later, in November 1963, John Kennedy was killed in Dallas, Texas, and Lee Harvey Oswald was charged with the assassination. Next, there were two attempts on the life of Gerald Ford, both in California in 1975, and both by women, Lynette Fromme and Sara Jane Moore. Finally, John Hinckley attempted to assassinate Ronald Reagan outside a hotel in Washington in 1981.

Among presidential contenders, Theodore Roosevelt was shot during the 1912 campaign, but survived. In 1933, an Italian immigrant construction worker, Giuseppe Zangara, fired at the new president-elect, Franklin Roosevelt, missing him but killing Anton Cermak, the mayor of Chicago. In June 1968, Robert Kennedy was shot by Sirhan Sirhan, immediately after winning the California presidential primary, and George Wallace was shot and left paralyzed by Arthur Bremer while campaigning in a shopping center in Maryland in 1972.

According to one study, the United States ranks thirtieth among eighty-nine nations in assassinations and attempts between 1918 and 1968, but fifth among eighty-four nations since 1945. Note that most American assassination attempts have been the work of lone assassins, not of larger political conspiracies. Yet the possibility of conspiracy sometimes raises nagging doubts, particularly in the case of John Kennedy. Many simply did not believe that a lone gunman, shooting from a considerable distance, could have done it. Conspiracy theories were rampant after Kennedy's death, especially since the accused assassin was himself killed just days after being taken into custody. To investigate matters and calm the public mind, President Johnson turned to Chief Justice Earl Warren. Other members of the Warren Commission were Representatives Gerald Ford and Hale Boggs; Senators Richard Russell and John Sherman Cooper; John J. McCloy, a government advisor; and Allen Dulles, former chief of the CIA.

The Warren Commission's report was issued ten months later and upheld the lone gunman theory. Lee Harvey Oswald had acted alone; there was no conspiracy. This was what many people had hoped to hear, but the inquiry failed to quiet some doubts. Although the investigation unearthed a considerable amount of fascinating detail—especially about Oswald's background—many felt that it failed to pursue other leads and possibilities. Some were never convinced, for example, that Oswald (not much of a marksman) could have shot so accurately and so quickly from such a distance with such a cheap weapon. (In tests, experts could not duplicate this feat.) The commission's report failed to resolve other issues as well. In the years that followed, theories abounded about what had happened in Dallas, but more recently the controversy appears to have subsided.

SOURCES: Jarol B. Manheim, *Déjà Vu: American Political Problems in Historical Perspective* (New York: St. Martin's Press, 1976), pp. 37–39; William O'Neill, *Coming Apart* (Chicago: Quadrangle Books, 1971), pp. 88–103.

1945. It was two for two for the United States—two world wars and two victories. Throughout Europe, Americans were welcomed as liberators: We had fought against tyranny, and we had won. The political consequences, however, proved difficult to handle and to predict. *(Robert Capa/Magnum)*

of guns should be allowed? Relations between police and citizens have also been controversial matters in some communities: How can such relations be made cooperative rather than confrontational?

Finally, a penchant for violence has often found its way into foreign and military policy making.[22] It has been argued that an excessive reliance on firepower in Vietnam raised the stakes of U.S. involvement there.

TABLE 1–1
Violent Crime Rates in Selected Nations

	Murder	Rape	Assault
United States	9.60	29.1	241.5
Netherlands	7.15	—	—
Finland	4.88	6.4	196.9
West Germany	4.47	—	—
Sweden	3.36	10.3	15.9
France	2.70	3.1	58.0
England	2.24	—	—
Denmark	2.03	9.5	85.5
Japan	1.74	2.5	25.2
Spain	0.67	—	—
Norway	0.50	3.4	12.3

SOURCES: Interpol Crime Statistics; *Facts on File.* All data are per 100,000 population.

Making the World Safe for Democracy—or for Us?

I have always believed that this anointed land was set apart in an uncommon way, that a divine plan placed this great continent here between the oceans to be found by people from every corner of the earth who had a special love of faith and freedom.   *Ronald Reagan, 1982*

It would be hard to find a more extreme statement of the allegedly special place in the world occupied by the United States. Although many U.S. leaders have been hard-headed, practical people who understood that the United States is very much like other nations, throughout history there has also been a strong missionary element in U.S. government policy.

Every country occasionally demonstrates a well-developed self-appreciation, but Americans early on displayed an especially lofty view of their role in the world and of the purity of their motives. From the founding of the nation to the present day, Americans have tended to decry other nations for seeking power or imperial domination, while asserting that their country was seeking only to spread democracy throughout the world. According to the Founders, we were to act as an example for humankind. As George Washington put it in his first inaugural address, "The preservation of the sacred fire of liberty and the destiny of the republican model of government are justly considered . . . staked on the experiment intrusted to the hands of the American people."

And the American example did spread. One Latin American country after another modeled its constitution after our own. And as recently as 1946, a radical nationalist quoted Thomas Jefferson when making a plea for his country's independence. That leader was Ho Chi Minh, the Vietnamese communist.

The United States has also been famous for its altruism and its generosity toward others. We opened our doors to the refugees of the world. Magazine ads ask us to "save the children" in faraway lands, or to send food to drought-stricken countries. When disaster strikes, U.S. aid is often the first to be sent. We train Peace Corps volunteers to assist development around the globe. We like to think of ourselves as an idealistic people trying to spread the gospel of democracy and capitalism to the rest of the world. Along with Washington and Jefferson, we want the United States to light the way for others, to help make the world, in President Woodrow Wilson's phrase, "safe for democracy."[23]

But there is another side to U.S. relations with the world—that of a powerful player. Throughout most of the nineteenth century the United States steered clear of entanglements abroad, largely because there was more than enough to do at home. The nation expanded internally, spreading across the continent, fighting constant battles against Indian peoples, as well as waging a war with Mexico.

Our treatment of the Indian nations certainly provided no model of democratic (or ethical) practice. The American Indians, by and large, were mistreated, betrayed, and often virtually exterminated.[24] Some U.S. leaders of the time proclaimed that it was our "manifest destiny," our God-given task, to expand across the continent, to put to use the vast resources available in North America. In their view, Native Americans stood in the way of this grand design.

By the end of the nineteenth century, the United States was ready to emerge as a world power. After intervening in Cuba and in the Philippines during the Spanish-American War (1898), purportedly to help end unjust Spanish rule, U.S. military forces actually helped to suppress the independence movements they were supposedly assisting.[25] And throughout the twentieth century, our government repeatedly intervened in Latin America to support U.S. interests and to stop radical social movements regarded as threats to our security.

After fighting World War II against the antidemocratic forces of Nazism and fascism, many Americans expected the postwar world to be one in which democratic forces would generally prevail. But the onset of the global rivalry, or **Cold War,** between the United States and the Soviet Union divided the world into communist and Western spheres of influence. Since 1945 U.S. foreign policy has been torn between adopting a primary stance as either an anticommunist or a prodemocratic power. As anticommunists, our policy makers could justify supporting many undemocratic regimes, such as those of Francisco Franco in Spain, Anastasio Somoza in Nicaragua, Ferdinand Marcos in the Philippines, and the Shah of Iran. Under a foreign policy oriented more toward democratic values, we would have kept our distance from such dictators.

Debate over the direction of our foreign policy continues today. The key questions are: What role should our commitment to democratic values play in shaping U.S. foreign policy? Should the United States concentrate on protecting its own security and power, or on protecting democratic values? If the latter, how are those values best protected?

Expanding westward across the continent, Anglo-American armies and settlers systematically destroyed the villages, possessions, and cultures of Native Americans.
(The Bettmann Archive)

Religion and Morality in Politics

In recent years many influential political leaders, including President Reagan, have advocated a vigorous injection of religion into public life. The most prominent example of this trend has been the widespread support for a constitutional amendment allowing prayer in public schools. To supporters of this amendment and similar measures, religious values can help define and shape public policies.

Controversy over the proper place of religion in political life is not new to U.S. politics. From the founding of the nation, many people have argued that a democratic society must be based on strong religious values. Proponents of various secular crusades—such as drives to outlaw the sale of alcohol and to regulate matters of personal morality, including forms of marriage and sexual preferences and conduct—have frequently solicited the support of religious groups. And religious values have been invoked by our leaders in support of U.S. foreign policies. Some students of U.S. political life argue that we have fashioned a "civic religion," in which church-related values are combined with a reverence for secular political forms and practices.[26]

Of course, the United States is not the only nation to mix religion and politics in sometimes volatile ways. Battles have been waged over the appropriate political role of organized religion in most democratic nations over the last two centuries. In modern-day France and Italy, the Roman Catholic church has repeatedly thrust itself into political controversy, especially on such issues as divorce, abortion, and aid to church-sponsored schools. And Pope John Paul II has attempted to influence governments worldwide by publicly voicing strong views on the new reproductive technologies.

From time to time, religious groups have also taken action in the sphere of American foreign policy, striving to impose particular religious or humanitarian values in geopolitically sensitive regions. During the 1980s, for example, many American churches carried on active campaigns in Central America—some to gain converts, some to assist various social and political movements or communities. Some conservative Protestant churches, for example, provided and campaigned for aid to the contras, rebels who were attempting to destabilize the Sandinista government of Nicaragua. On the other hand, church people from a variety of faiths attempted to assist development projects within Nicaragua as well. In addition, religious ideas, such as the concept of "liberation

Abortion has become one of the most divisive "moral" issues in politics, and there seems to be no ground for compromise. Is it a question of personal morality, for each pregnant woman to decide, or a matter for society to decide through legislation? *(David Burnett/Woodfin Camp & Associates)*

theology''—a policy developed by Catholic clerics in Latin America whereby parish priests actively promote the cause of political liberation rather than endorsing the status quo—have often had important political significance. In the United States itself, some churches protected exiles from Central America, hiding them and moving them from one part of the country to another. This struggle to provide ''sanctuary'' was sometimes prosecuted by the federal government on the ground that the exiles were in the country illegally. The churches spearheading the sanctuary movement maintained that the lives of these refugees would be in danger if they were forced to return home—to El Salvador, for instance.

Throughout U.S. history, Americans have argued over whether religion should be part of politics. Although the nation has tended to move in a more secular direction, Americans have remained overwhelmingly proreligion in attitude. This apparent contradiction leaves many significant conflicts and questions unresolved. Where should religious values end and public policy begin? Our liberal tradition calls for tolerance and acceptance of a diversity of values and approaches. Yet some contend that morality can and should be enforced, that public authorities ought to legislate what is good and right for us all. As a predominantly religious people and, at the same time, a liberal society, how do we decide?

Conclusions

Many of our core political values support democratic practices. As a predominantly ''liberal'' society, we officially and unequivocally favor individual rights, tolerance, equal opportunity, the rule of law, and democratic political institutions. On the other hand, Americans have experienced great difficulties in living up to the high standards of democracy. Many groups have been the objects of discrimination and exploitation. We have often reached for the gun to settle disputes, abandoning the rule of law. In foreign relations, the United States has acted both as a defender of democracy and as an imperial world power. Playing both these roles has often left Americans and their leaders confused about just what the nation is supposed to stand for. Finally, some Americans wish to impose their ideas of morality on others, in the name of preserving values essential to democracy. Others maintain that imposing one person's morality on another violates the basic spirit of liberalism.

In short, U.S. political culture is a mix; some elements tend to support democratic practices, others are hostile to them. The conflicts in U.S. history over equal treatment, tolerance, rule of law, and the direction of foreign policy reveal a dynamic tension that resonates to this day.

GLOSSARY TERMS

political culture

liberalism

natural rights

populist

tyranny of the majority

conservatives

free enterprise

New Deal

socialist

democratic socialist parties

welfare state

Cold War

NOTES

[1] Jarol B. Mannheim, *The Politics Within: A Primer in Attitudes and Behavior*, 2d ed. (New York: Longman, 1982), chap. 4.

[2] William F. Stone, *The Psychology of Politics* (New York: Free Press, 1974), chap. 7; and Seymour Martin Lipset, "Values, Social Character and the Democratic Polity," in *The First New Nation: The United States in Comparative and Historical Perspective* (New York: Basic Books, 1963), pp. 274–285.

[3] Seymour Martin Lipset, *Political Man* (Garden City, N.Y.: Doubleday, 1970), chap. 2.

[4] Mannheim, pp. 61–64.

[5] Louis Hartz, *The Liberal Tradition in America* (New York: Harcourt, 1964); and Alexis de Tocqueville, *Democracy in America* (New York: Harper & Row, 1966).

[6] Erich Fromm, *Escape from Freedom* (New York: Avon, 1965), chap. 2.

[7] *Ibid.*, chap. 3; and Erik H. Erikson, *Young Man Luther* (New York: Norton, 1958).

[8] John Locke, *Second Treatise on Civil Government* (New York: Appleton, 1937), chaps. 1–7; and Harry K. Girvetz, *The Evolution of Liberalism* (New York: Collier, 1963), chaps. 4 and 5.

[9] Thomas Archdeacon, *Becoming American: An Ethnic History* (New York: Macmillan, 1983).

[10] Lawrence Goodwyn, *The Populist Movement: A Short History of the Agrarian Revolt in America* (New York: Oxford University Press, 1978).

[11] Seymour Martin Lipset, "Values and Democratic Stability," in *The First New Nation*, pp. 207–247.

[12] Gunnar Myrdal, *An American Dilemma* (New York: Harper & Row, 1962).

[13] Girvetz, chap. 15.

[14] John Dewey, *Liberalism and Social Action* (New York: Capricorn Books, 1963).

[15] John H. M. Laslett and Seymour M. Lipset, eds., *Failure of a Dream: Essays on the History of American Socialism* (Garden City, N.Y.: Doubleday, 1974).

[16] Daniel P. Moynihan and Nathan Glazer, *Beyond the Melting Pot* (Cambridge, Mass.: MIT Press, 1963).

[17] Terry Eastland and William J. Bennett, *Counting by Race: Equality from the Founding Fathers to Baake and Weber* (New York: Basic Books, 1979); Stanley Feldstein, *The Poisoned Tongue: A Documentary History of American Racism and Prejudice* (New York: Morrow, 1972).

[18] Peter Irons, *Justice at War* (New York: Oxford University Press, 1983).

[19] Joe B. Frantz, "The Frontier Tradition: An Invitation to Violence," in Hugh David Graham and Ted Robert Gurr, eds., *The History of Violence in America* (New York: Praeger, 1969), pp. 127–153.

[20] J. F. Kirkham, S. Levy and W. J. Crotty, eds., *Assassination and Political Violence: Staff Report to the National Commission on the Causes and Prevention of Violence* (Washington, D.C.: U.S. Government Printing Office, 1969), pp. 171–177.

[21] George E. Berkley, *The Democratic Policeman* (New York: Ballantine, 1976).

[22] Theodore Draper, *Abuse of Power* (New York: Viking, 1967), chap. 8.

[23] Reinhold Niebuhr and Alan Heimert, *A Nation So Conceived* (New York: Scribners, 1963).

[24] Richard Drinnon, *Facing West: The Metaphysics of Indian-Hating and Empire-Building* (New York: New American Library, 1980).

[25] Frederick Merk, *Manifest Destiny and Mission in American History* (New York: Vintage, 1966); Albert K. Weinberg, *Manifest Destiny* (Baltimore: Johns Hopkins, 1970).

[26] Robert Bellah, *The Broken Covenant: American Civil Religion in a Time of Trial* (New York: Harper & Row, 1976); and Ernest Tuveson, *Redeemer Nation: The Idea of America's Millennial Role* (Chicago: University of Chicago Press, 1980).

SELECTED READINGS

For general discussions of **democracy and its preconditions,** see Robert Dahl, *Polyarchy: Participation and Opposition* (New Haven: Yale University Press, 1971); Peter Berger, *Pyramids of Sacrifice: Political Ethics and Social Change* (New York: Doubleday, 1976).

WHAT IS POLITICAL CULTURE?

Insights into **political culture** can be found in Donald Devine, *The Political Culture of the United States* (Boston: Little Brown, 1972); Walter Rosenbaum, *Political Culture* (New York: Praeger, 1975); Gabriel Almond and G. Bingham Powell, Jr., *Comparative Politics: A Developmental Approach* (Boston: Little Brown, 1966).

THE LIBERAL TRADITION

For illuminating discussions of the **liberal tradition** in the United States, see Louis Hartz, *The Founding of New Societies* (New York: Harcourt, 1969); Vernon Parrington, *Main Currents in American Thought* (University of Oklahoma Press, 1987); E. Fawcett and T. Thomas, *The American Condition* (New York: Harper & Row, 1982); John Patrick Diggins, *The Lost Soul of American Politics: Virtue, Self-Interest, and the Foundations of Liberalism* (University of Chicago Press, 1986).

TWO TYPES OF LIBERALISM

The **economic values** of liberalism are treated in Max Weber, *The Protestant Ethic and the Spirit of Capitalism* (New York, Scribner, 1958); R. H. Tawney, *Religion and the Rise of Capitalism* (New York: New American Library, 1947); Michael Novak, *The American Vision* (Washington, D.C.: ABI, 1982).

U.S. **conservatism** has been a notoriously difficult subject to pin down. For an assortment of approaches, see Russell Kirk, ed., *The Portable Conservative Reader* (New York: Penguin, 1982); George Will, *The Pursuit of Happiness and Other Sobering Thoughts* (New York: Harper & Row, 1979); Garry Wills, *Confessions of a Conservative* (Garden City, N.Y.: Doubleday, 1979).

There are many interpretations of the failure of **socialism** in the United States. For one intriguing interpretation see Michael Harrington, *Socialism* (New York: Saturday Review Press, 1972), chap. 6.

LIMITS OF LIBERALISM

For one general treatment of **intolerance** in the United States, see Richard Hofstadter, *The Paranoid Style in American Politics: And Other Essays* (University of Chicago Press, 1979). On current **immigration** issues, see Nathan Glazer, ed., *Clamor at the Gates* (San Francisco, ICS Press, 1985).

For discussions of **violence** in the United States, see especially Richard M. Brown, *Strain of Violence: Historical Studies of American Violence and Vigilantism* (New York: Oxford, 1975); Monica D. Blumenthal et al., *Justifying Violence: Attitudes of American Men* (Ann Arbor, Mich.: Institute for Social Research, 1972); Charles E. Silberman, *Criminal Violence, Criminal Justice* (New York: Random House, 1980); and H. D. Graham and T. R. Gurr, eds., *Violence in America: Historical and Comparative Perspectives* (Beverly Hills: Sage, 1979).

Among the more provocative discussions of U.S. **foreign policy** are William Appleman Williams, *The Tragedy of American Diplomacy* (New York: Norton, 1988); Robert Dallek, *The American Style of Foreign Policy: Cultural Politics and Foreign Affairs* (New York: Knopf, 1983); William Blanchard, *Aggression: American Style* (Santa Monica: Goodyear, 1978); Lester D. Langley, *The United States and the Caribbean in the Twentieth Century* (Athens, Ga.: University of Georgia Press, 1985).

For perspectives on **morality and politics,** see Joseph R. Gusfield, *Symbolic Crusade: Status Politics and the American Temperance Movement,* 2d ed. (Urbana, Ill.: University of Illinois Press, 1963); Alan Crawford, *Thunder on the Right: The "New Right" and the Politics of Resentment* (New York: Pantheon, 1980); Martin Marty, *Righteous Empire* (New York: Dial, 1970); Richard Pierard, *The Unequal Yoke: Evangelical Christianity and Political Conservatism* (Philadelphia: Lippincott, 1970); Jerry Falwell, *Listen, America* (Garden City, N.Y.: Doubleday, 1970).

2

REVOLUTION AND CONSTITUTION

The American Way

CHAPTER OUTLINE

Background of the Revolution
The Revolutionary War
Independence Sparks Ferment
The Constitutional Convention
Amending the Constitution
An Enduring Political Legacy

Holiday/Photo Researchers

Today the U.S. Constitution is often viewed as if it were of heavenly manufacture. We tend to forget the struggles embodied in it, the compromises struck to forge it. Often, we also forget that many of the integral figures in the American Revolution were not very happy with the Constitution, and that the battles over its ratification were bitter and very closely contested.

What did the American Revolution and the Constitution have to do with democracy? Did the revolutionaries espouse truly democratic ideals? Did they envision a government by consent, a society of equal rights and liberties? What political and social realities did the Constitution reflect? As we come to understand the colonial situation and the mentality of the American revolutionaries, we will gain a clearer view of the implications of our constitutional heritage for contemporary politics. We will then be in a position to address the question of whether the Constitution still responds to the demands of modern democratic life.

Background of the Revolution

What kind of society was colonial America? How was its economy structured, its wealth distributed? What political ideals were widely shared, and what role did those ideals play in conflicts between the colonies and Great Britain? We now explore (1) the socioeconomic environment that fostered the Revolutionary spirit; (2) the political environment that gave the Revolution momentum; and (3) the exercise of British imperial authority that provoked ever-greater American defiance.

The Socioeconomic Environment

In the 1770s the thirteen American colonies comprised a rapidly growing society of some 2.5 million inhabitants, 60 percent of whom were English in origin. The principal ethnic minorities were Scots, Irish, Welsh, and Germans, plus a significant number of black slaves (28 percent of the Southern population). Americans were a young people: Half the population was under 16, and much of the rest under 40. The population was doubling every twenty years.

Trading was a vital component of the colonial economy. The southern colonies carried on a large volume of direct trade with England, exporting tobacco, rice, and indigo—despite British taxes on American tobacco that consumed an estimated 75 percent of all profits. The middle, or "bread," colonies, including New York, New Jersey, Pennsylvania, and Delaware, traded principally in grain and flour. Pennsylvania was the fastest-growing colony, and Philadelphia, with a population of 40,000, was America's largest municipality. Only four urban centers other than Philadelphia could properly be called cities: New York; Charleston, S.C.; Boston; and Newport, R.I. Notably, all these cities were Atlantic ports, where news and traffic from abroad arrived first. Apart from these few urban centers, the colonies were overwhelmingly rural. Only 10 percent of the population lived in towns of more than 2,000 inhabitants. And despite the importance of trading activities, America was primarily a society of farmers and farm workers.

Colonial society was not fundamentally egalitarian. In many colonies, a small number of aristocratic families exercised great political and social power. Throughout America property ownership had grown increasingly concentrated in the hands of a few. In 1771, 5 percent of Boston families held almost half the total taxable wealth, and in Philadelphia 10 percent of the population held 46 percent of the total.[1]

In contrast, an estimated 20 to 30 percent of the colonial population, excluding slaves, was impoverished. In major cities, food shortages occasionally sparked riots; in rural areas, discontent with the working conditions of tenant farmers led to popular upheavals. Some of the poverty-stricken formed the core of urban mobs that helped foment revolutionary agitation, and many served in the Continental Army.

Between these extremes of wealth and poverty, however, was a fairly prosperous middle class encompassing 50 to 70 percent of the population. The presence of so large a middle class, combined with the "leveling" tendencies at work in colonial society, gave the colonies a degree of equality unknown in Europe. Social and class distinctions did not carry the weight they did across the Atlantic, and, as a result, the colonists displayed a spirit of independent-mindedness, a defiance of authority,

Independence Hall in Philadel-phia, 1776: Americans prepare for their epic act of separation, de-claring their independence. It was not possible then to realize that their decision would serve as a model for anticolonial revolutions for two centuries. Yet Jefferson's words found a way to convey the universality of the issues at stake. *(National Archives)*

and a desire for economic self-betterment unheard of in Europe.

Considerable religious diversity also marked the colonies, and in some areas religious intolerance took hold: In Rhode Island, for example, only Trin-itarian Protestants could become full citizens. Yet tolerance of religious differences became the rule rather than the exception, and lively religious dia-logues formed a staple of intellectual life.

The Political Environment

By the 1770s, most of the colonial governments had been functioning for over a century. Eight of the thirteen were royal colonies, whose governors were appointed by the British king. Connecticut and Rhode Island had charters granted in the sev-enteenth century allowing for self-government and thus elected their own governors. Maryland, Pennsylvania, and Delaware were so-called pro-prietary colonies, owned by families—the Penns in Pennsylvania and Delaware, the Calverts in Maryland. All colonial governors had broad pow-ers, including an absolute veto over acts of the legislatures and the power to appoint all judges and militia officers. In most colonies, the governor also appointed the members of the upper house of the legislature.

Every colony except Pennsylvania had a legis-lature with an upper and a lower house. The upper houses, which generally acted only as advisory bodies, were made up of the wealthier and more conservative citizens. In contrast, elections for the lower houses of colonial legislatures were remark-ably democratic by the standards of the day. Al-though the franchise was limited in many areas by property qualifications, in practice most white males were permitted to vote for legislators. It was in the lower houses that opposition to British tax-ation was most vociferous in the 1770s.

The colonies shared the British political tradi-tion, based to a significant degree on the rule of law and the principle of constitutionalism. Accord-ingly, the powers exercised by colonial govern-ments were generally limited by written charters. Because more colonists could participate more fully in local politics, they may actually have en-joyed greater political and civil rights than did most English citizens.

As heirs to the liberal tradition, most colonial political leaders believed that underlying consti-tutions and laws were fundamental rights, viola-tions of which entitled citizens to seek redress from the government. If the government did not honor these rights, liberal theory held, citizens could legitimately overthrow that government. Governments, in other words, could and should

"Half a Revolution"

How "revolutionary" was the American Revolution? To many historians and political scientists, the American colonists' revolt was only half a revolution. To see what they could mean, we must consider what the American rebels did and did not set out to accomplish.

The colonists did fight an anticolonial war, seeking independence and self-rule. And some principles on which they based their new government were genuinely innovative, including government by consent of the governed and guarantees of basic rights and liberties for all citizens. Certainly, they set out to create something new in political history.

But there also were things they did *not* do. The American Revolution did not uproot government, as did the French Revolution a decade later. Rather, the Americans only extended and perfected familiar political traditions. Their new government, although a genuine advance toward democratic politics, did not radically break with the past political life of the colonies. Moreover, the revolution did not overturn the social order. Power and property remained more or less intact afterward. Indeed, because America did not have an entrenched hereditary aristocratic class, there was no such class to overthrow.

To take a modern view, the American Revolution also differed profoundly from the radical social upheavals of our own century. For example, in the Russian and Chinese revolutions, private ownership of property was a principal target, whereas in colonial America the desire to defend property rights was what *sparked* the revolution and was of paramount importance to the colonists. Although there were many sources of friction between rich and poor in revolutionary America, the colonists had no thought of instituting government ownership of the means of production, or of taking radical steps toward equalizing opportunities for everyone.

Our revolutionary heritage, therefore, is political rather than social in nature. The revolutionaries sought a political framework that would free people from oppressive government and ensure political rights, not one that would equalize the conditions of life. But if it was not a "total revolution," the American Revolution and the Constitution that followed it did provide a living example of how a huge, diverse nation could achieve independence and be governed more or less by consent. This is still an extraordinary achievement—truly a pioneering venture in political history.

be held accountable for their actions and the ways in which they upheld the basic interests of citizens.

Imperial Authority and American Defiance

In the early 1760s, the British Empire was growing prodigiously. Having defeated France and Spain in the **Seven Years' War** (1756–1763; known in the colonies as the French and Indian War), the British had removed the threats formerly posed to their possessions in the New World by the French in Canada and the Spanish in Florida. As a result, the American colonists were feeling less dependent than ever before on the mother country. At the same time, however, the costs of empire had begun to weigh more and more heavily on the British treasury. Rather than going along with the colonists' desire for more autonomy, especially in economic matters, the British Crown sought greater authority over colonial affairs—in particular, the authority to impose direct taxes to defray the costs of defending and expanding the Empire.

In both financial and military terms, American participation in the Seven Years' War had fallen far short of expectations by the mother country, which considered that defeating the French and Spanish directly benefited the colonies. As one measure of the colonies' indifference to British concerns, only three of the thirteen contributed full quotas of troops to the war. In several ways, moreover, disobedience to the Crown and nonenforcement of British rules had become common in America. Various acts of Parliament imposing duties on American goods were largely circumvented or ignored by the colonists. In addition, a thriving trade between the French West Indies and American merchants was carried on contrary to British law.

Disobedience turned into defiance when the British Parliament in March 1765 passed the Stamp Act, which required "that Americans pay their own protection and defense out of revenues from the sale of stamped paper to be used on some fifty items, including newspapers, pamphlets, playing cards, wills, land deeds, marriage licenses, college diplomas, bills of sale, port clearance papers, and so on." Those who violated the act could be tried and penalized without benefit of jury. The Stamp Act had been conceived by George Grenville, First Lord of the Treasury under King George III. Grenville argued that the act was needed not merely to increase revenues, but also to assert Parliament's absolute sovereignty over the colonies. When the Americans argued that because they were not represented in Parliament, Parliament did not have the right to levy taxes on them, Grenville invoked the doctrine of virtual representation. According to this doctrine, a favorite argument of the day, each member of Parliament had a responsibility to the entire Empire, and therefore even the American colonists in some sense were represented in Parliament.

The Stamp Act was one in a series of serious miscalculations by British authorities. Intent on asserting control over the colonies, they underestimated the growing colonial spirit of independence and failed to recognize that each new attempt to exert control only aggravated the situation. Without the Stamp Act, and similar actions that followed, the British might have been able to capitalize on the relative calm that followed the Seven Years' War. Instead, many colonists came to view the Crown with increasing suspicion and to decry London's alleged exploitation of the colonies.

Colonial reaction to the Stamp Act was harsh—and very effective. Several months after the act

Many historians have remarked about the political folly of George III and the British government, whose high-handedness provoked the Revolutionary War and thereby lost the American colonies. In fact, many in England opposed these policies from the start. *(National Archives)*

was passed, the first organized resistance took place in Boston. The so-called Sons of Liberty, a radical group composed of artisans, apprentices, day laborers, and merchant seamen, hanged effigies of Andrew Oliver, the king's agent for stamp distribution in Massachusetts, and Lord Bute, a close friend of the king's. The effigies were hanged from what came to be known as the Liberty Tree. To make their points, the Sons of Liberty never shied away from using force. One group of defiant colonists, carrying the effigies, destroyed a warehouse belonging to Oliver, and then burned the effigies in a huge bonfire on a hillside near his home. Several protestors even ransacked Oliver's home, making off with his extensive wine collection. The following day Oliver resigned, and no one would take his place. None of the Sons of Liberty was ever brought to trial.

Disguised as Indians, rebellious colonists tossed heavily taxed British tea into Boston harbor. *(National Archives)*

A year after passing the Stamp Act, Parliament repealed it, only to enact the so-called Townshend duties, which taxed colonial imports of paint, tea, lead, and paper. Again the colonists protested, and eventually all the duties except one—on tea—were repealed. After a few years of relative calm between British authorities and American colonials, Parliament in 1773 granted the East India Company the exclusive right to sell tea to American local dealers. The mandate, which shut out American merchants from the tea trade, prompted the famous Boston Tea Party, in which protestors disguised as Indians dumped tea from British ships into Boston harbor. In response, the British closed the port of Boston—a drastic economic penalty for a city that depended so heavily on trading. In addition, the charter of the colony of Massachusetts was virtually withdrawn, and elections and town meetings were forbidden.

These actions provoked yet wider defiance of British authority. Groups of concerned citizens met in several colonies and sent delegates to the First Continental Congress. Convened in Philadelphia in 1774, the Congress promptly called for a boycott of British goods. Armed conflict broke out in Massachusetts the following year, when the British commander in Boston sent troops to seize weapons stored by the colonists in Concord. In 1775, the Second Continental Congress, although hesitating to make a final break with Britain, decided to raise an army and began making overtures to France for assistance. Shortly thereafter, the more radical American political leaders finally persuaded the moderates that the colonies needed full independence, and Congress commissioned Thomas Jefferson to write a formal Declaration of Independence. The radicals won over their more cautious peers with the help of a slim pamphlet, Tom Paine's *Common Sense*, which electrified colonial America when it appeared in January 1776. In *Common Sense*, Paine placed America's struggle in a larger perspective, viewing it as part of all humanity's drive for free government. For Paine the American cause exemplified the universal struggle between liberty and tyranny; the patriots' cause embodied much more than specific grievances against the British Crown.

When the Second Continental Congress reconvened in June 1776, Thomas Jefferson presented a draft of the Declaration of Independence. It was amended and approved by the Congress on July 4, 1776, two days after an official resolution of independence from Great Britain had been passed. Jefferson's declaration had been called the single most influential piece of American political writing. Its complete text appears in Appendix A at the end of this book.

The Revolutionary War

The war itself was an unexpectedly protracted and, in military terms, oddly inconclusive affair.

Thomas Paine: Radical Democrat, Pamphleteer Supreme

The radical ideas and eloquent pamphlets of Thomas Paine influenced political life in three countries during his lifetime (1737–1809). His most famous pamphlet, *Common Sense* (1776), helped stiffen American resistance to the British monarchy, and during the Revolution his series of papers *The American Crisis* did much to sustain American patriotism. It was Paine who characterized the war years as "the times that try men's souls." And after the war, Paine's writings also stimulated political reform in England.

Paine's power as a pamphleteer was grounded on intellectual courage: He dared to take popular ideas to logical, if radical, conclusions. In *Common Sense* he not only attacked the ruling British king but also rejected any form of monarchy and called for government based exclusively on the expressed will of the people. And in *The Rights of Man* (1791–1792), a defense of the French Revolution, he anticipated modern socialist ideas by portraying government as an instrument of the rich to exploit the poor; he called for pension systems, unemployment projects, public education, and aid to the poor—all to be paid for by progressive taxes.

Prosecuted for treason in Great Britain, Paine fled to France in 1792 and was made a member of the governing National Convention. He also published a widely read attack against formal religions, *The Age of Reason* (1794–1795). Returning to the United States in 1802, he met considerable resentment generated by his allegedly atheistic ideas (an untrue charge) and by his denunciation of George Washington in *Letter to Washington* (1796). When he died, he was an outcast in his adopted country, in whose formation he had played so significant a role.

COMMON SENSE;

ADDRESSED TO THE

INHABITANTS

OF

AMERICA,

On the following interesting

SUBJECTS.

I. Of the Origin and Design of Government in general, with concise Remarks on the English Constitution.

II. Of Monarchy and Hereditary Succession.

III. Thoughts on the present State of American Affairs.

IV. Of the present Ability of America, with some miscellaneous Reflections.

A NEW EDITION, with several Additions in the Body of the Work. To which is added an APPENDIX; together with an Address to the People called QUAKERS.

N. B. The New Addition here given increases the Work upwards of one Third.

Man knows no Master save creating HEAVEN, Or those whom Choice and common Good ordain. THOMSON.

(The Bettmann Archive)

The British had every reason to believe they could easily subdue the colonials. Their army was highly experienced and well trained, and their navy was the world's largest. By 1778, there were almost fifty thousand British troops in North America, along with thirty thousand German mercenaries.

The Americans, starting from scratch, eventually created a Continental Army of five thousand, supplemented by state militia units. Their officers were inexperienced, although George Washington had gained some actual combat experience in the French and Indian War.

"The first blow for liberty": the battle of Lexington. There was no reason for the great British empire to doubt its ability to subdue the unruly colonists. Yet it has often proved very difficult to wage successful wars against resistant populations—as the French discovered in Indochina in the 1950s and the Soviets learned in Afghanistan in the 1980s. *(National Archives)*

The British, however, suffered from serious disadvantages: The war had to be waged three thousand miles from the British Isles; the vast and mostly wild American terrain was difficult to conquer in any sense; and there was no single nerve center of revolutionary activity whose destruction would ensure a decisive British military victory. Moreover, even if the British had won the war militarily, they would have had to face the daunting task of restoring imperial domination over the defiant colonials. Finally, many observers criticized the British for waging the war indecisively, vacillating between ill-thought-out attempts to gain a pivotal military victory and efforts to achieve a reconciliation with the revolutionaries.

The American war for independence also became an international contest. France supplied large quantities of munitions to the Americans, and both France and Spain eventually declared war on Great Britain. Other nations, including Sweden, Russia, and Prussia, moved to protect their shipping from British blockades of the colonies. In the end, French support was crucial to the success of the revolutionary effort, with elements of the French fleet and army helping to make the decisive American victory at Yorktown (1781) possible.

The revolutionaries also had to overcome formidable difficulties. Keeping an army in the field was a constant problem for the new nation. Not only was labor in short supply, but popular support often flagged. Desertions from the Continental Army were numerous, and many farmers who did serve refused to extend their tours of duty when planting or harvest seasons arrived. Cash incentives were required to maintain more than a token force in the field. In January 1777, Congress offered twenty dollars, new clothing, and one hundred acres of land in exchange for a pledge to serve for the duration of the war. Nevertheless, there was no rush to enlist. States were given quotas to fill before each new campaign, and often slaves, indentured servants, and propertyless day laborers were paid to take the place of the middle-class farmers who would otherwise have had to serve. The revolutionary ideal was a militia based on a universal obligation to serve; the reality was an army made up largely of the poor and others who responded principally to financial incentives.

Of even greater concern to the revolutionaries, however, was active or passive opposition to the war within the colonies. It has been estimated that up to 20 percent of the white population remained actively loyal to the Crown and that close to 50 percent remained neutral in the struggle.[2] More and more colonials became less and less enthusiastic as the war dragged on.

In the end, however, British public opinion deserted the war faster than American public opinion. After the French-American victory at Yorktown, the British abandoned their attempt to crush the rebellion, even though they still held the dominant position militarily. The Americans defeated the British not by gaining a clear-cut military victory, but simply by persevering and refusing to lose the war.

Independence Sparks Ferment

In the Treaty of Paris, signed September 3, 1783, the British government formally recognized the independence of its former colonies. Few treaties have had such profound and far-reaching political ramifications. Both in the new United States of America and in Europe, political life was irrevocably changed.

The newly won American independence prompted a spurt of political activity. Organizations pressed various causes, and the states developed powerful legislatures that often bent to the wishes of these special interests. On the national level, leaders struggled to consolidate the thirteen states into one nation without creating a strong central authority. At all costs, they did not want to risk the abuses of power inherent in a centralized system like the British monarchy. But the first national government, based on the Articles of Confederation, was a political failure. Let us now examine this turning point in American history.

The Postrevolutionary Era

In the United States new political enthusiasms—some noble in vision, some narrow in scope—emerged following the war. Demands for equality—even when it came to slavery—marked much of political discourse. In 1774 the Continental Congress had urged abolition of the slave trade, and in 1775 the world's first antislavery society was formed by Quakers in Philadelphia. After the war, some Northern states granted freedom to slaves who had served in the Continental Army, and most Northern states moved to end slavery within their borders. By 1830, the Northern black population of 125,000 included only 3,000 slaves.

At the same time, a new parochialism was becoming evident in state legislatures—what James Madison described as a "spirit of locality." During and after the Revolution, legislatures increasingly became embroiled in conflicts between various narrow interests. Few legislators were looking out for the interests of the community as a whole. Critics of the actions of the Vermont legislature, for example, complained that laws were altered, altered again, made better, made worse—but were always in flux. Many of the new laws favored particular individuals or groups. Pressure group politics was already a force in U.S. political life.

Before the Revolution, many had seen the legislature as the basis for the people's sovereignty, the bulwark against executive excess. In the war's aftermath, however, fear of legislative excesses grew. As Jefferson put it, "173 despots would surely be as oppressive as one." Many people began to worry about how to ensure that fundamental law would not be tampered with, and, thus, "liberty" kept safe.

In Europe, meanwhile, the American Revolution was having a profound impact. The very idea that a people could declare their independence and base it on the ideal of equal rights for all seemed to show that liberty was not just an abstract concept. As each American state wrote its own constitution, and these were translated into French, the American example certainly prompted French revolutionaries to draw up a declaration of human rights and draft a new constitution. Latin American nations also looked to this example in the early nineteenth century, when they fought to free themselves from Spanish domination.

Finally, the new United States was widely seen abroad as the place where ordinary people could enjoy legal rights and could participate fully in political life. This perception, as well as the young nation's reputation as a land of limitless economic opportunity, made the United States attractive to immigrants and provided a model for change.

The Articles of Confederation

Soon after declaring independence, American political leaders turned to the task of establishing a new government. In 1781, shortly before the war ended, the last of the thirteen states ratified the

The French Revolution and Its Aftermath

The French and American revolutions seem to have had much in common. Both originated in rebellions against monarchical governments; and both sought constitutional rule, government by consent, and the affirmation of the basic rights of citizens. There the similarities end, however. In comparison with events in France, the American revolution and its aftermath were mild and orderly indeed.

The French Revolution began in 1789 in a rebellion within the Estates-General, an assembly summoned by King Louis XVI. The Estates-General comprised three estates, or classes, based on the status system of feudal society: the clergy; the nobles; and the Third Estate, consisting of everyone else. Once in session, the Estates-General quickly became a forum for reformist and even revolutionary sentiment, and a struggle for control developed between the nobles and the Third Estate. Violence broke out in many parts of the country. A mob in Paris stormed the Bastille (a state prison), murdered its governor after ninety-eight of the insurgents had been killed, and went on to murder the mayor. In the countryside, too, peasants began to rebel against the landed aristocracy.

The Third Estate separated from the Estates-General and declared itself a National Assembly. In effect, by enacting many reform measures, the Third Estate abolished the feudal system. In Au-gust 1789, it issued the Declaration of the Rights of Man and Citizen. A new government, in which the king would have only the power to suspend legislation by veto, was formed in 1791, but the king refused to participate in it. Counterrevolutionary forces, both foreign and indigenous, began to threaten the revolution, and war broke out in 1792 between France and its monarchist neighbors.

While fighting foreign foes, the revolutionary regime began a domestic reign of terror against real and suspected opponents of the government. During this period (1793–1794), an estimated forty thousand people (including the king) were executed, and thousands of others were driven into exile.

From 1795 to 1799 France was a constitutional republic in which all literate citizens had the right to vote. But war pressures and a lack of popular support weakened the republican government, and Napoleon Bonaparte seized power in 1799. He ruled under a form of benevolent despotism until his armies were finally defeated by foreign powers in 1815. Napoleon suppressed the democratic impulses of the original revolution, establishing, in effect, a new monarchy. For several decades the government alternated between more democratic and more royalist regimes. Not until 1870 was a genuine republic established that was destined to last for a substantial period.

nation's first written constitution—the **Articles of Confederation.** The government that the Articles created was a political failure, however. To understand the reasons for its failure is to understand why the subsequent (and present) Constitution has succeeded so well.

The principal political impulse behind the Articles was fear of a strong central authority; its authors wanted to ensure that the new national government was not endowed with the excessive power possessed by the British monarch. In doing so, they created a national government that could function effectively only with the unanimous consent of the states. The only national political body under the Articles was a one-house Continental Congress, in which each state had one vote. There was no independent chief executive and no national court system. Congress had the power to create executive departments and to approve treaties, but it could not print money, levy taxes on the citizens of the states, or regulate interstate commerce.

Political realities soon exposed the weaknesses of this government. Controversies raging among the states simply could not be settled without a national court system and a stronger national government. Many feared that Great Britain would foment and take advantage of interstate rivalries. Further, the central government had so few powers that the focus of blame for social and political problems shifted to state governments. For instance, because only the states could print money, those who felt the squeeze of tight money in the postwar depression looked to the states for help. In Massachusetts, debt-ridden farmers who were facing foreclosure demanded that the state legislature issue more paper money. When the legislature refused, the farmers, led by Daniel Shays, took up arms in August 1786. Their first protests were directed against local courts, which they prevented from conducting business. Later, the rebels also forced the state supreme court to adjourn. Only after both state militia and federal troops were called out against Shays and his supporters was the rebellion crushed in early 1787. However, most participants, including Shays, were pardoned by the state legislature.

Shays's Rebellion succeeded, at least in part. Largely because of this uprising, the Massachusetts legislature in 1787 decided not to impose new taxes, lowered court fees, and exempted household goods, clothing, and the tools of one's trade from the debt process (preventing them from being seized to pay off debts). But even of greater importance, Shays's Rebellion spotlighted the need for a strong national government. And it convinced many political leaders, particularly the more conservative, that a new constitution had to be created with power lodged more fully in the national government, including the power to issue currency.

The Constitutional Convention

The movement toward what was to become known as the Constitutional Convention was anything but swift and unanimous. Alexander Hamilton, a young New York lawyer and former delegate to the Continental Congress, took the lead in efforts to strengthen the national government. At the Annapolis Convention (1786), in which the states met to discuss interstate trade, he called for a national convention to amend the Articles. After Shays's Rebellion, five state legislatures appointed delegates to the proposed convention. The Continental Congress issued a tentative call for a convention as well, but carefully insisted that any revisions of the Articles would require both its approval and the approval of *all* state legislatures. When the convention finally did convene in Philadelphia in 1787, some delegates arrived with instructions to go no further than amendment of the Articles.

On May 14, 1787, the day appointed for the convention to begin, only the delegates of Virginia and Pennsylvania were present. By May 25, nine state delegations had arrived, and work on "revision" of the Articles began. State legislatures in twelve states named a total of seventy-three delegates, of whom fifty-five actually attended the convention and thirty-nine eventually signed the new Constitution. The thirteenth state, Rhode Island, decided not to participate.

Of the fifty-five delegates who met at Philadelphia, thirty-three were lawyers, forty-four had been members of the Continental Congress, twenty-seven had been officers in the Revolutionary War, twenty-five had been to college, twenty-one were rich (and another thirteen were affluent), and nineteen were slaveowners.[3] Among the many relatively young delegates were the very influential Alexander Hamilton, who was thirty-two, and James Madison, who was thirty-six. The patriarch of the group was Benjamin Franklin, at eighty-one.

The following sections explore the controversies surrounding (1) proposals and compromises that shaped the new national government; (2) the framers' handling of the pivotal slavery issue; (3) the fragmentation of power that checked both the majority and the elected and appointed officials; (4) some key issues that determined much of the nation's future; and (5) the struggle for ratification.

A Stronger National Government

From the start, the Convention sought to broaden its mandate to revise the Articles of Confederation.

What Is a Constitution?

The usual definition of a "constitution" hints of orderly things—systems and principles by which a harmonious whole (whether nation, state, or corporation) is governed. But political scientists sometimes view constitutions from another angle, arguing that they are a society's list of rules to regulate the inevitable *discord* which political competition engenders. That is, a constitution attempts to keep political struggles within tolerable limits.

When society's rules break down or can't be adapted, conflicts get out of hand, and the costs are usually high (the American Civil War being a vivid example). Since some rules of political struggle are deemed fundamental, they often are formulated into documents or bodies of law—into "constitutions." Sometimes one specific document results, as in America and contemporary Japan. But sometimes the political "constitution" develops over time, embodies many laws and traditions, and is not formulated into a single document; such is the case in Great Britain.

Not only do constitutions regulate a society's conflict and express its basic political values, but they also structure the rules of the game in a way that benefits some groups more than others. They embody not only "timeless" principles but also grubby political compromises to resolve the power conflicts of the time in which they are written. The U.S. Constitution, as this chapter illustrates, is no exception; it would be a far different document if it were written today. In fact, two-thirds of the world's 160 constitutions were written since 1970, and it is intriguing to ponder how they might fare over two centuries.

Albert Blaustein, an expert on constitution writing, offers the following thoughts about how constitutions work and fail. Are constitutions worth the paper they are written on? As Blaustein sees it, ours is:

Virtually every successful constitution is a constitution of compromise. It aims at achieving equilibrium.

All constitutions have to be autochthonous. That's a key word meaning "arise from the self." It must spring from the soil. It must be *the* constitution to represent the needs of these people. . . .

No one drawing up a constitution for America today would fail to include a right to privacy. I would also include the right to leave and to return. . . . The American method of selecting the President . . . if nobody has a majority is not very good. . . . Also I wouldn't have elections on the first Tuesday after the first Monday. I'd have them on Sunday.

I think [the Framers of the Constitution] would be very proud of how we turned out. I really do. I think our Constitution has met the test of time. When Mr. Nixon left power, the only person with a gun was a policeman directing traffic.

New proposals presented to the Convention called for a thoroughly altered national government, one with greatly strengthened powers. The delegates readily accepted the idea of a national judiciary and a stronger executive branch. There was considerable debate, however, over the nature of the new legislative structure. Benjamin Franklin favored a one-house **(unicameral)** arrangement. But most delegates supported the idea of a two-house **(bicameral)** Congress, an arrangement adopted by most state governments.

The earliest comprehensive proposal submitted for consideration at the Convention was the **Virginia Plan,** set forth by the delegation from that state. Under this plan, a strong national government would include a bicameral legislature: a lower house, elected by the voters, and an upper house, chosen by the members of the lower house. Either tax contributions or population would serve as the basis for proportional representation in both houses. Most of the larger states supported the Virginia Plan.

The smaller states responded with the **New Jersey Plan,** submitted by William Paterson of that based on population and from which all fiscal measures would originate. Although delegates from the larger states initially opposed the compromise, they soon realized it was the price they would have to pay for a strengthened national government. In any case, with the struggle for ratification by the states still to come, it was simply good politics to assuage the smaller states' fear that their interests would be neglected in a powerful national government based on proportional representation.

The Slavery Issue

The other great compromise of the Constitutional Convention concerned slavery. The southern (slaveholding) states sought to include slaves in the population counts used to determine representation in the House of Representatives—without, of course, giving them the right to vote. The South feared that without such additional representation, a northern majority might dominate the new Union. Southern recalcitrance on this matter led to the infamous compromise that each slave would be counted as three-fifths of a person. This was perhaps a pragmatic solution in the context of the time, since outlawing slavery was not yet practical. Yet the compromise starkly revealed the vulnerability of the new nation. In the end, only a war could settle the slavery issue.

The framers of the Constitution also had to deal with the question of the slave trade. In another compromise, the slave trade was allowed to continue until at least 1808, at which time Congress would be permitted to legislate against it. Commerce in human beings was subsequently prohibited by Congress as of January 1, 1808, although for many years thereafter a thriving smuggling business persisted.

Fragmentation of Power

Many delegates at the Convention were concerned about potential abuses of power by popular majorities. Was it possible to create a government based on the will of the people but not susceptible to tyranny of the majority? Doubts about relying

Benjamin Franklin, the patriarch of his country. Had he had his way, the wild turkey would be our national symbol, and our legislature would have only one house, as in many parliamentary systems today. *(National Archives)*

state. Paterson's plan called for a national government empowered to levy taxes and to regulate interstate commerce and, significantly, a national Supreme Court with the power to review state court rulings. On the key question of legislative structure, this plan established a one-house legislature in which each state would have one vote, as had been the case under the Articles.

Debate over the relative merits of the Virginia and New Jersey plans deadlocked the convention for weeks. The problem was finally resolved through the **Connecticut Compromise,** proposed by a special committee in which the Connecticut delegation played a pivotal role. The key element of the compromise was the concept of a two-house legislature consisting of an upper house in which the states would be represented equally and a lower house in which representation would be

Jefferson and Slavery

For many it comes as a shock to learn that the eloquent author of the Declaration of Independence—who spoke of all men being created equal and being endowed with certain inalienable rights—was himself a slaveholder for his entire adult life. Yet the contradictions in Jefferson's attitudes and actions concerning slavery reflect the difficulties which that issue posed at the time the Constitution was written and beyond.

As may have been true for many colonial Americans, Jefferson's first memory was that of being carried on a pillow by a slave. He remained intimately associated with slavery until his death, and the work of slaves helped make possible his architectural and cultural achievements. Yet Jefferson resolved early in life that slavery was abominable and that its eradication would be a prime achievement of the Revolution. In 1774 he delivered his first attack on slavery in print. His pamphlet *A Summary View of the Rights of British America* indicted the slave trade and declared that King George III was guilty of preventing the colonists from abolishing it. Jefferson expanded this attack on the king's role in maintaining slavery when he wrote the original draft of the Declaration of Independence. By blaming the British for slavery, he was able to escape the charge that the colonists themselves—though espousing equality and rights—did not really mean to include everyone in their new political community. Unfortunately for Jefferson, the Continental Congress removed his passage about slavery from the Declaration! Though Jefferson blamed northern slave traders for this excision, it was clear that very few Southerners were willing to commit themselves to abolishing slavery if independence were achieved. Thus the Declaration asserts the right of white Americans not to be enslaved by the Crown, but it implicitly refuses to apply the same principles to black slaves who might rebel against masters.

Jefferson did not free the slaves at Monticello until his death in 1826. Although he opposed slavery all his life—and philosophized about its evils—he never actively combatted it. An optimist about the eventual eradication of slavery, Jefferson believed that the slaves *would* be emancipated and that they might return to Africa or perhaps go to Haiti.

One student of Jefferson's life argues that, although our third president abhorred slavery, he unconsciously shared the racial prejudice on which it was based. In his autobiography Jefferson wrote: "The two races, equally free, cannot live in the same government. Nature, habit, opinion have drawn indelible lines of distinction between them." Even as he articulated the great revolutionary ideas of liberty and equality, Jefferson was a pragmatist—and a product of his own time and place.

SOURCE: John Chester Miller, *The Wolf by the Ears: Thomas Jefferson and Slavery* (New York: New American Library, 1977).

on the wisdom of "the people" were raised by, among others, Alexander Hamilton, who stated: "The voice of the people has been said to be the voice of God; and however generally this maxim has been quoted and believed, it is not true in fact. The people are turbulent and changing; they seldom judge or determine right." Fearing mass democracy on the one hand, and tyrannical monarchy or oligarchy on the other, the framers created a complex system of government designed to ensure the dispersal of power.

The electoral system they devised provided for a limited democracy. The people were given a direct voice in government through elections of the members of the lower house of Congress; members of the upper house, by contrast, were to be chosen by state legislatures. (This system remained in effect until the ratification in 1913 of the Seventeenth Amendment, which mandated direct popular election of senators.) The framers also sought to insulate the presidency from the popular vote by stipulating that the president be chosen by

Thomas Jefferson, gifted experimenter, architect, cultivator of plants, musician, and energetic writer and thinker. He was also a slaveholder who freed his slaves only upon his death. This irony—or hypocrisy?—embodies something of the nation's tragic history. *(National Archives)*

Alexander Hamilton saw the nation's vast potential as a manufacturer and argued for a strong central government to create the conditions for prosperity. As one author of *The Federalist Papers,* he helped to lay the groundwork for national development. *(National Archives)*

a group of electors (the **electoral college**) selected by the states in the general election. In Hamilton's view, this system of elections would prevent one class of voters from dominating another. Finally, the framers left the matter of voting requirements up to the individual states, which further diluted the power of the masses.

Convention delegates also feared excessive concentrations of power *within* the government. Their deliberations on this issue reflected the ideas and influence of James Madison, whose views were set forth in 1787–1788 in an impressive series of essays, written together with Alexander Hamilton and John Jay, and known collectively as *The Federalist Papers.* As a student of history and political philosophy, Madison was aware that republican government—government based on the will of the people—was most likely to succeed in small societies whose members shared common values and in which wealth was distributed relatively equally. But the United States was a sprawling society in which different interests abounded and wealth was distributed unevenly. For republican government to succeed in a large society with many conflicting interests, Madison argued, the political system must be fragmented so that power could be exercised effectively without encouraging excessive concentrations of it. In this way, he felt, rash or tyrannical actions by powerful interests could be blocked and the necessary measure of political unity preserved.

In *The Federalist,* No. 51, Madison contended that "you must first enable the government to control the governed; and in the next place, oblige it

Some historians regard James Madison as one of this nation's most original political thinkers. His defense of the U.S. Constitution in *The Federalist Papers* ranks as some of the most significant discussion ever of power, rights, and consent in a democratic context. Madison recognized how easily power can be abused and suggested ways of counteracting such abuse. *(National Archives)*

to control itself." He went on to point out that if the responsibility for decision making could be sufficiently fragmented, the rights of minorities could be protected while minority factions could be prevented from thwarting the properly expressed sentiments of the majority. Madison's ideas were implemented in the constitutional system of **separation of powers** and **checks and balances.**

First, powers were divided between the states and the national government (a matter we will explore fully in Chapter 3). Next, governing power within the central government was divided among the executive, legislative, and judicial branches (see **Figure 2–1**). Within the legislature, power was

further divided between two houses. In addition to this separation of powers, the decision-making process was fragmented by a delicate system of checks and balances. For example, the president, through the veto power, could intervene in the legislative process; the Senate was granted the power to confirm or reject appointments made by the president to the Supreme Court and the cabinet; and Congress was given the power to impeach and convict the president, the vice-president, and the members of the federal judiciary.

To the original checks and balances laid out in the Constitution have been added many other refinements in a kind of unwritten constitution—traditions, laws, and procedures that have evolved through political necessity. Consider, for example, the wide range of government officials and agencies, and nongovernment organizations, that shape economic policy today:

1. The president, whose broad economic powers include the ability to freeze wages and prices.

2. The Federal Reserve Board, which regulates the supply of money and credit.

3. Bureaucratic agencies, such as the Defense Department, with its enormous budget, and the Agriculture Department, which regulates farm-support prices and quotas.

4. Congress, which regulates every sector of the national economy.

5. The courts, whose power of legislative review and interpretation affects economic decisions.

6. States and cities, which enjoy economic powers outside federal control.

7. Private organizations—interest groups, corporations, and labor unions—whose views help shape the economy.

In every policy area, similar forces interact in constantly shifting arrangements.

Madison could not possibly have anticipated the extent to which the constitutional system of checks and balances would evolve and change. Nor could he have anticipated the development of certain elements of modern politics that have skewed some constitutional checks on power. Whereas in Madison's time political parties were not a significant force, today parties link officials of the various branches of government. Soon after

FIGURE 2–1
The Separation of Powers in U.S. Government

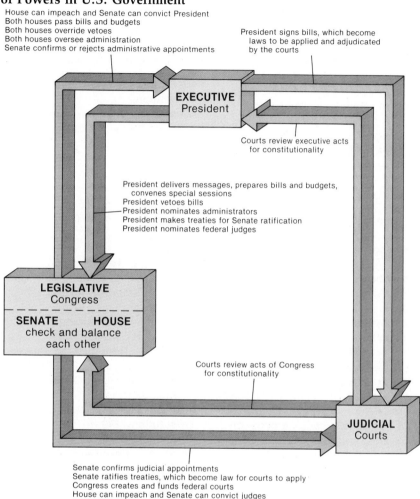

House can impeach and Senate can convict President
Both houses pass bills and budgets
Both houses override vetoes
Both houses oversee administration
Senate confirms or rejects administrative appointments

President signs bills, which become laws to be applied and adjudicated by the courts

EXECUTIVE
President

Courts review executive acts for constitutionality

President delivers messages, prepares bills and budgets, convenes special sessions
President vetoes bills
President nominates administrators
President makes treaties for Senate ratification
President nominates federal judges

LEGISLATIVE
Congress

SENATE   **HOUSE**
check and balance
each other

Courts review acts of Congress for constitutionality

JUDICIAL
Courts

Senate confirms judicial appointments
Senate ratifies treaties, which become law for courts to apply
Congress creates and funds federal courts
House can impeach and Senate can convict judges

the Constitution was written, the Supreme Court claimed the right to declare legislative acts unconstitutional (a power not explicitly stated in the Constitution), and thus vastly increased the powers of the federal judiciary. Presidents have gained the power to issue executive orders in some matters, bypassing congressional approval on particular pieces of legislation. Within Congress, legislative programs must move through an elaborate thicket of decision points, subject to potential ambushes by any number of interest groups. As political scientist Robert Dahl has stated: "The making of government decisions is not a majestic march of great majorities united upon certain mat-

ters of basic policy. It is the steady appeasement of relatively small groups."[4]

Four Key Issues

Among the many issues discussed at the Constitutional Convention, four merit further discussion here: (1) the regulation of commerce, (2) the establishment of voting rights, (3) the election of the president, and (4) the guarantee of civil liberties. How the framers dealt (or failed to deal) with these issues left a powerful imprint on American political life.

Chronology of the Constitution

1786

September 11–14   Annapolis Convention.

September 20   Congress receives Annapolis Convention report recommending that states elect delegates to a convention at Philadelphia in May 1787.

1787

February 21   Congress calls Constitutional Convention.

March 14   Rhode Island refuses to elect delegates.

May 14   Convention meets; quorum not present.

May 25   Convention begins with quorum of seven states.

July 13   Congress adopts Northwest Ordinance.

August 6   Committee of Detail submits draft constitution to Convention.

September 12   Committee of Style submits draft constitution to Convention.

September 17   Constitution signed and Convention adjourns.

September 20   Congress reads Constitution.

September 26–28   Congress debates Constitution.

September 28   Congress transmits Constitution to the states.

September 28–29   Pennsylvania calls state convention.

October 17   Connecticut calls state convention.

October 25   Massachusetts calls state convention.

October 26   Georgia calls state convention.

October 31   Virginia calls state convention.

November 1   New Jersey calls state convention.

November 10   Delaware calls state convention.

November 27   Maryland calls state convention.

December 6   North Carolina calls state convention.

December 7   Delaware Convention ratifies Constitution, 30 to 0.

December 12   Pennsylvania Convention ratifies Constitution, 46 to 23.

December 14   New Hampshire calls state convention.

December 18   New Jersey Convention ratifies Constitution, 38 to 0.

December 31   Georgia Convention ratifies Constitution, 26 to 0.

1788

January 9   Connecticut Convention ratifies Constitution, 128 to 40.

January 19   South Carolina calls state convention.

February 1   New York calls state convention.

February 6   Massachusetts Convention ratifies Constitution, 187 to 168, and proposes amendments.

March 1   Rhode Island calls statewide referendum on Constitution.

March 24   Rhode Island referendum: voters reject Constitution, 2,711 to 239.

April 26   Maryland Convention ratifies Constitution, 63 to 11.

May 23   South Carolina Convention ratifies Constitution, 149 to 73, and proposes amendments.

June 21   New Hampshire Convention ratifies Constitution, 57 to 47, and proposes amendments.

June 25   Virginia Convention ratifies Constitution, 89 to 79, and proposes amendments.

July 2   New Hampshire ratification read in Congress; Congress appoints committee to report an act for putting the Constitution into operation.

July 26   New York Convention Circular Letter calls for second constitutional convention.

July 26   New York Convention ratifies Constitution, 30 to 27, and proposes amendments.

August 2   North Carolina Convention proposes amendments and refuses to ratify until amendments are submitted to Congress and to a second constitutional convention.

September 13   Congress sets dates for election of President and meeting of new government under the Constitution.

November 20   Virginia requests Congress under the Constitution to call a second constitutional convention.

1789

June 8   Madison introduces Bill of Rights in Congress.
September 26   Congress adopts twelve amendments to Constitution to be submitted to the states.
November 21   Second North Carolina Convention ratifies Constitution, 194 to 77, and proposes amendments.

1790

January 17   Rhode Island calls state convention.
May 29   Rhode Island Convention ratifies Constitution, 34 to 32, and proposes amendments.

1791

December 15   Virginia is the tenth state to ratify, and the Bill of Rights becomes part of the Constitution.

SOURCE: Michael Kammen, ed., *The Origins of the American Constitution: A Documentary History* (New York: Penguin, 1986), pp. xxvii–xxix.

THE REGULATION OF COMMERCE   This was one of the problems that had led to the Constitutional Convention in the first place, and the framers decided to grant regulatory power to the national government. Specifically, the Constitution gives the federal government the power to regulate interstate commerce. This has vastly expanded national regulatory power in general, especially in the twentieth century. (This topic is discussed in Chapters 15 and 19.)

THE ESTABLISHMENT OF VOTING RIGHTS   The Constitution left this issue to the states; the framers thus sidestepped the thorny issues of property qualifications and the voting rights of nonwhites. Their inaction gave rise to prolonged battles over voting rights, particularly in the South. (The voting-rights issue is discussed in detail in Chapters 4 and 17.)

THE ELECTION OF THE PRESIDENT   As a result of various political compromises at the Convention, the electoral college—a somewhat peculiar and complex mechanism—became the method of choosing the U.S. president. State electors make up the electoral college, and each state has a number of electors equal to its total number of senators and representatives. Thus the only truly national political figures are elected by a mechanism rooted in the states. The electoral college has had vast

implications for political strategy because presidential candidates must win electoral, rather than popular, votes.

THE GUARANTEE OF CIVIL LIBERTIES   The Constitution omitted any mention of civil rights and liberties; these were added after ratification, in the first ten amendments (the Bill of Rights). Though these amendments ensured that citizens were protected against infringements by the national government, they provided no protection against civil rights violations by state governments. Consequently, civil rights advocates have had to pursue a complicated and lengthy process of securing rights from the individual states. (This process is discussed further in Chaper 4.)

Ratification

The struggle over ratification of the proposed Constitution was bitter and the outcome very close. The delegates to the Constitutional Convention opted to entrust the ratification process to conventions elected by the people in each state. In this way, they circumvented the state legislatures, where opposition to the Constitution was strong, and gained direct access to widespread popular support for the new Constitution. The delegates also specified that once two-thirds of the states had

FIGURE 2–2
Ratification of the U.S. Constitution

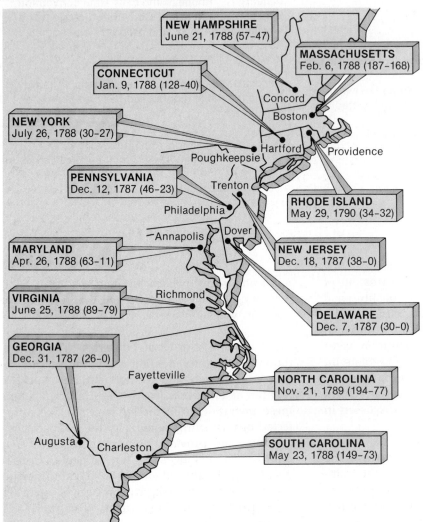

NEW HAMPSHIRE
June 21, 1788 (57–47)

MASSACHUSETTS
Feb. 6, 1788 (187–168)

CONNECTICUT
Jan. 9, 1788 (128–40)

NEW YORK
July 26, 1788 (30–27)

PENNSYLVANIA
Dec. 12, 1787 (46–23)

RHODE ISLAND
May 29, 1790 (34–32)

MARYLAND
Apr. 26, 1788 (63–11)

NEW JERSEY
Dec. 18, 1787 (38–0)

VIRGINIA
June 25, 1788 (89–79)

DELAWARE
Dec. 7, 1787 (30–0)

GEORGIA
Dec. 31, 1787 (26–0)

NORTH CAROLINA
Nov. 21, 1789 (194–77)

SOUTH CAROLINA
May 23, 1788 (149–73)

Concord
Boston
Hartford
Providence
Poughkeepsie
Trenton
Philadelphia
Annapolis
Dover
Richmond
Fayetteville
Augusta
Charleston

voted for ratification, the Constitution would be in force.

Supporters of the Constitution called themselves **Federalists,** and opponents became known as **Antifederalists.** Rural areas of the nation, populated by farmers and poorer people who feared the growth of centralized power, tended to oppose the new Constitution. Those living in cities and coastal areas generally supported it. Many crosscurrents affected the political struggle, however, and no one factor can explain the outcome.

Critics of the new Constitution immediately scored two powerful points against it. First, they cited the omission of a **Bill of Rights.** If some state constitutions included protections against government infringements on liberty, opponents argued, why shouldn't the national constitution incorporate such protections? The Federalists were forced to yield on this point, and it was agreed that a Bill of Rights would be added once the Constitution was ratified. The Antifederalists also decried what they viewed as an ill-considered rush toward ratification. New political arrangements of such import, they contended, demanded lengthy and

Much did not run smoothly in the new republic. This print shows a brawl in Congress between Federalist Roger Griswold and Republican Matthew Lyon. Early disputes revolved around U.S. policy toward revolutionary France and laws dealing with freedom of speech. Still, the fledgling nation held together for seventy-three years before being torn apart by the Civil War. *(The Bettmann Archive)*

thorough deliberation. While they recognized the merit in this argument, the Federalists knew that quick action was necessary to prevent their opponents from becoming fully organized. The Federalists also carried out a brilliant public relations campaign centered on *The Federalist Papers.*

The strategy adopted by the Federalists worked well. Within a year, nine states had ratified the Constitution, making it legal. But the votes for ratification were close in several states, and two crucial states, Virginia and New York, gave their approval only after the Constitution had been adopted. Rhode Island was the thirteenth state to ratify (1790), after refusing seven times to even call a ratification convention. (See **Figure 2–2.**)

Amending the Constitution

Thomas Jefferson was one of several framers of the Constitution who worried about the tendency of governments to break down or lose touch with the people over time. Therefore he proposed that a new constitutional convention be called in each succeeding generation, noting, ''We might as well require a man to wear still the coat which fitted

him as a boy, as a civilized society to remain ever under the regimen of their barbarous ancestors.'' Although the framers did not incorporate this idea into the Constitution, they did provide for a means of amending the Constitution as the need arose.

In order to be adopted, an **amendment** must first be proposed and then ratified. Each of these steps can be accomplished in either of two ways. For *proposal,* either two-thirds of the members of each house of Congress must approve the amendment, or two-thirds of the state legislatures must petition Congress to call a national constitutional convention. Only the first of these methods has ever been employed. In the 1960s, however, opponents of the Supreme Court's rulings on reapportionment came within one state legislature of petitioning Congress to call a national constitutional convention, and in the 1980s more than half the state legislatures had petitioned for a constitutional convention to consider an amendment requiring a balanced federal budget. To call such a convention, unprecedented complications would have to be dealt with.[5] Who would determine if the states had presented valid petitions? Could the convention be limited to the one issue named in the petition? If the convention were to exceed its original mandate (as the Constitutional Convention did), would political and social chaos follow? Opponents of the proposed convention argue that it might radically change the structure of our government.

Congress can deflect the threat of petition by the states by passing its own version of the proposed constitutional amendment and sending that version to the state legislatures for approval. When petitions calling for the direct election of U.S. senators began accumulating early in this century, for example, Congress recognized the strength of public sentiment and proposed the Seventeenth Amendment. One key unanswered question looms large, however: When two-thirds of the states have petitioned Congress for a national convention, must Congress comply? Article V of the Constitution states that Congress *shall* call a convention—not that it *must*.

The two methods of *ratifying* a constitutional amendment are approval by three-fourths of the state legislatures, or approval by three-fourths of ratifying conventions called by the states. Congress determines which method is to be used in each case. Ratifying conventions have been called only once—to approve the Twenty-first Amendment repealing Prohibition (which had been mandated by the Eighteenth Amendment). Congress chose that method because state legislatures were expected to be less likely to vote for repeal.

Ratification by state legislatures has its own complications. Congress has stipulated that the ratification process be limited to a period of seven years. In 1978, however, the ratification period was extended for the Equal Rights Amendment, amid considerable debate. Several state legislatures then rescinded prior ratifications of the ERA, but such actions were never put to a legal test. The dominant legal interpretation is that states cannot rescind their approval, although they can always ratify an amendment they had previously rejected.

Democratic theory and practice in this country demand that the amending procedures be both sufficiently flexible and sufficiently representative of majority sentiment. In two hundred years, only twenty-six amendments have been added to the Constitution, ten of which were adopted together as the Bill of Rights. Sometimes the amending process has been used in an effort to have the last word in the constitutional system—to overrule even the Supreme Court. At other times, it has been employed in attempts to hold back social change. In yet other cases, like the proposed Equal Rights Amendment, it has been the last resort when changes could not be obtained other ways. Though it is difficult to judge the overall impact of amending initiatives on our government system, it is probably fortunate that the Constitution has not been amended more frequently, and thus become laden with prohibitions and complications that would make governing extremely difficult. Still, democratic commitments do require that a polity based on a written constitution have some method of amendment which responds to majority impulses.

An Enduring Political Legacy

The world is strewn with scraps of paper called constitutions. Many are subterfuges for coups, caudillos, and corruption. But the U.S. Constitution is rare in its continuing capacity to prescribe rules of governance two centuries after its formulation.

Yet all constitutions are essentially political documents conceived in power politics and shaped by compromises. Like the U.S. Constitution, however, every successful constitution eventually becomes as much symbol as document. Written interpretations of it resemble analyses of the scriptures; it comes to prescribe civic virtue and to legitimize good behavior; and an elaborate code of laws and customs builds up around it, presumably shaped by the needs of the day. It is easy to forget that a constitution originally arises as a political document.

For many years the U.S. Constitution was considered an act of divine intervention in human affairs.[6] Those who (like the Founders) doubted that God acted so directly accepted the slightly different view that the Constitution represented a victory for "straight-thinking" over "narrow-mindedness," for visionaries over parochials, for the public interest over that of the individual.[7] According to this view, the framers discerned the weaknesses of the Articles of Confederation and made thoroughly rational and nonpolitical judg-

Americans Write Another Constitution

Americans have been directly responsible for formulating at least one constitution other than their own. In 1946 the Government Section of the Supreme Commander for the Allied Powers in Japan wrote a new constitution for that nation in six days. Adopted shortly thereafter by the parliament, that constitution has remained Japan's governing document and has never been amended.

This highly unusual procedure arose out of a singular set of circumstances. Following World War II, Japan was occupied by the United States, which was determined to prevent the return of Japan's fascist policies. General Douglas MacArthur was charged, in effect, with the democratization of Japanese society—a task that required drastic alterations in the so-called Meiji constitution, under which Japan had been governed since 1889.

The most elemental difference between the old and new Japanese constitutions lay in the status of the emperor. Under the old constitution the emperor, as sovereign, was the acknowledged source of all authority. Although he could act only through cabinet ministers, the concept that power resided in the person of the emperor symbolically denied the people's sovereignty. The new constitution transformed the emperor from sovereign to figurehead, a "symbol of the state" whose position derives "from the will of the people."

A second revolutionary feature of the new constitution was an extensive listing of inalienable, God-given rights that may not be abridged. The rights spelled out in the 1946 constitution cover not only the areas of speech, religion, and due process of law, but also such matters as employ-

ment (the right to choose an occupation); emigration; academic freedom; complete equality of the sexes; collective bargaining; and the right of each person to "minimum standards of wholesome and cultured living." In practice, many of these rights have not yet been realized fully, but it is interesting that so many social and political rights which are not included in the U.S. Constitution were incorporated into a modern constitution written by Americans.

The political structure created by the 1946 constitution is a parliamentary system much closer to Great Britain's than to ours. As in the U.S. Constitution, however, there is provision for an independent federal judiciary with the power to review legislation.

The most unusual and controversial element in the 1946 constitution is the "renunciation of war" clause, by which Japan formally eschewed the use or threat of force in international relations. In fact, the constitution seems to rule out the maintenance of *any* armed forces. Contemporary Japan, however, has developed quite extensive "security forces."

One student of Japanese politics has summarized the 1946 constitution as follows: "It introduces rights, institutions and practices into Japanese politics that undoubtedly go far beyond anything the Japanese themselves might realistically have been expected to establish. In fact, on the basis of the text alone, it is a considerably more democratic document than is the Constitution of the United States."*

---

*Robert E. Ward, *Japan's Political System*, 2nd ed. (Englewood Cliffs, N.J.: Prentice-Hall, 1978), p. 145.

ments about the best ways to change our political system. For generations, this interpretation of the Constitution's genesis was almost universally accepted.

In 1913, the historian Charles Beard, in *An Economic Interpretation of the Constitution*, made the shocking argument that the Constitution was a *political* document which had been constructed with political interests in mind.[8] Beard pointed out that the framers were for the most part rich and well-born, that most of them considered the preservation of property as the principal object of government, and that many of them shared John Jay's view that "the people who own the country ought to govern it." According to Beard, the wealthy framers, following the dictates of self-interest, developed the Constitution's checks and balances to prevent the unpropertied majority from making unpalatable demands on the propertied minority.

Although historical evidence does not fully support Beard's conclusions, most historians acknowledge that economic interests were very much at issue in the framing and ratification of the Constitution. Among James Madison's fundamental assumptions, in fact, were the notions that economic factors motivated human behavior to a great degree and that political conflict grew out of economic differences between classes of people.

However one judges the framers, it is remarkable that the institutional framework they created has endured. Although the U.S. political system has gradually shifted in a more democratic direction over the years—through the direct election of senators, the expansion of the right to vote, the emergence of mass-based political parties, and the transformation of the electoral college from a group with real power to little more than a rubber stamp—the constitutional system still reflects the framer's fears of majority tyranny and the excesses of popular control.

Is the Constitution Outdated?

Since at least the beginning of the twentieth century, political observers have been calling the constitutional system outdated. Most critics have charged that the system's built-in tensions between the various branches and levels of government thwart government effectiveness. In our form of government, unlike parliamentary democracies, one branch of government is pitted against another: Instead of unity, we seek division. But division of power, however laudable as a check on excessive concentration of power, can also lead to a government of stalemate. In this scenario, nothing can be accomplished except in crisis conditions, and Congress and the executive are locked in a perpetual standoff that makes for irresponsible policy making, or no policy making at all.

The economic and political crises of the twentieth century have greatly strained the constitutional structure. Presidents, in particular, have been forced into many political innovations in order to keep the ship of state afloat. Many observers argue that presidential power in this century has grown enormously to counteract the stalemate built into the system.

Ultimately, we cannot help but see the Constitution as impressive and enduring, but also deeply flawed. It marked a giant step forward for democratic ideas in its own time, but it also left many basic questions of democracy unanswered and incorporated some blatantly undemocratic concepts. We will take up the implications of these crosscurrents more fully in Chapter 4, when we address civil rights and civil liberties, and in Chapters 11 to 15, which focus on government institutions.

Supplement: Assessing the Constitution Today

The following thoughtful commentaries on the Constitution illustrate some key arguments in the continuing debate about the validity of this 200-year-old document now and in the future. In considering how well the Constitution addresses our deepest civic concerns today, keep in mind how vastly different our socioeconomic and geopolitical environment is now, compared with when the Constitution was written. The complete text of the Constitution and its amendments appears in Appendix B, at the end of the book.

THE CONSTITUTION AND NATIONAL SECURITY

In the period since the end of the Second World War, people have repeatedly wondered whether our Constitution, an eighteenth-century document, adopted at a time when the United States was a negligible power in the world and was separated from other countries by days or weeks of ocean travel, is an ade-

SOURCE: "Talk of the Town," *The New Yorker*, Dec. 22, 1986, pp. 23–24.

Text continues following the color essay.

Political Roads Not Taken

History is always written by the winners of any conflict. In the late 1780s, after a period of vigorous debate, the U.S. Constitution—under which we are still governed—was adopted. In hindsight, the Articles of Confederation seem fatally flawed, destined to be replaced by a strong central government with a vigorous executive. But how inevitable was the outcome of the Constitutional Convention? The record shows that different choices *could* have been made. Our current Constitution was by no means the product of harmonious agreement.

On the contrary, sharp disagreements divided even those participants whose ideas ultimately prevailed. Central figures changed their minds; most remained dissatisfied with one part or another of the compromises that emerged. Some prominent members, including Edmund Randolph, who introduced the famous Virginia Plan, eventually refused to sign. James Madison, called the Father of the Constitution, vigorously opposed major features of the final document, including equal representation for states in the Senate, a cornerstone of the Great Compromise. From the very beginning our governmental structure was a pieced-together response to specific conditions of the times. The genius of the Constitution is that it has survived, prospered, and *improved*, primarily because it effected a healthy compromise between narrow self-interest and grand idealism. Distinctions between these motives are often difficult to discern, but both were part of the great debate which forged the organic law that has guided our nation for two centuries.

Economic Troubles

One reason offered in the 1780s for a fundamental change in the Articles of Confederation was that the new nation's economy was suffering and perhaps even failing. We may easily—and improperly—assume that the constitutional debates about economic and social factors were based on accurate information about contemporary circumstances. At best, such information was fragmentary and was likely to have been drawn from personal experience. Was the economy failing in the 1780s? Even now historians disagree. Economic activity

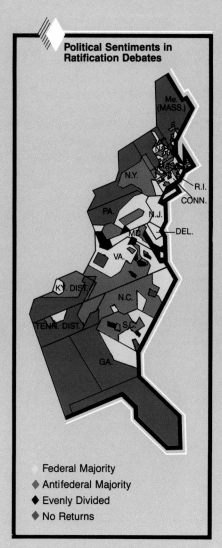

Political Sentiments in Ratification Debates

◇ Federal Majority
◆ Antifederal Majority
◆ Evenly Divided
◆ No Returns

Ratification of the Constitution

State	Date	Vote
Connecticut	Jan. 9, 1788	128–40
Delaware	Dec. 7, 1787	30–0
Georgia	Dec. 31, 1787	26–0
Maryland	Apr. 26, 1788	63–11
Massachusetts	Feb. 6, 1788	187–168
New Hampshire	June 21, 1788	57–47
New Jersey	Dec. 18, 1787	38–0
New York	July 26, 1788	30–27
North Carolina	Nov. 21, 1789	194–77
Pennsylvania	Dec. 12, 1787	46–23
Rhode Island	May 29, 1790	34–32
South Carolina	May 23, 1788	149–73
Virginia	June 25, 1788	89–79

Philadelphia, Pennsylvania

Edmund Jennings Randolph (1753–1813)

was certainly uneven throughout the country. Consider the following account of a French traveler in 1788—just as the ratification debates raged:

> With what pleasure did I contemplate this town which first shook off the English yoke! How I delighted to wander up and down that long street, whose simple houses of wood border the magnificent channel of Boston, and whose full stores offer me all the productions of the continent which I had quitted! How I enjoyed the activity of the merchants, the artisans, and the sailors! Everything in this street bears the marks of a town still in its infancy, but which, even in its infancy, enjoys a great prosperity. . . .
>
> Since the peace, the [citizens of Pennsylvania] have returned to their commerce with great activity. The capitals which diffidence had for a long time locked up in their coffers, are now drawn out to give a spring to industry, and encourage commercial speculations. The Delaware sees floating the flags of all nations; and enterprises are there formed for all parts of the world. Manufactories are rising in the town and in the country; and industry and emulation increase with great rapidity.[1]

Were there serious economic difficulties, or were the observations of the French visitor accurate? Did economic troubles arise in part because of the structure of government under the Articles of Confederation? Could they be remedied by a new Constitution?

Slavery

Slavery was another issue that greatly influenced the constitutional debates. Until the census of 1790—the first after the new government was in place—the number of slaves in various parts of the country was only roughly known. Everyone knew that the distribution of slaves was quite uneven, even within states that still allowed slave trade. (Six of the original thirteen states had outlawed the importation of slaves, but five of these still permitted the *holding* of slaves.) No serious effort to eliminate slavery was undertaken when the Constitution was written, but the issue was important in determining representation in the Congress and in considering taxation. The only direct references to slavery in the Constitution are in Article I, Section 2, the infamous compromise that counts "three-fifths of all other persons" for purposes of representation, and in Section 9, which prevents Congress from prohibiting the "migration or importation of such persons as any of the States now existing shall think proper to admit" until 1807. The word *slavery* does not appear in the Constitution until the Thirteenth Amendment ratified in 1865. But slavery certainly was a subject in the secret debates at the convention. Gouverneur Morris (later a diplomat and U.S. senator) was a staunch abolitionist throughout his life. On August 8 he spoke to the convention about slavery:

Upon what principle is it that slaves shall be computed in representation? Are they men? Then make them Citizens and let them vote. Are they property? Why then is no other prop-

THE GRANGER COLLECTION

erty included? The Houses of this city [Philadelphia] are worth more than all the wretched slaves which cover the rice swamps of South Carolina. The admission of slaves into Representation when fairly explained comes to this: that the inhabitant of Georgia and South Carolina who goes to the Coast of Africa, and in defiance of the most sacred laws of humanity tears away his fellow creatures from their dearest connection & damns them to the most cruel bondages, shall have more votes in a Government instituted for protection of the rights of mankind, than the Citizen of Pennsylvania or New Jersey who views with a laudable horror, so nefarious a practice. [2]

Gouverneur Morris (1752–1816)
CULVER PICTURES

Morris's passionate abolitionism was not shared by most delegates, however, and this "losing" point of view would have to wait another eighty years to be translated into law.

Representation

The question of representation in Congress confronted the writers of the Constitution with two major disputes: first, how much influence to give to the people directly and, second, how to apportion power among the states.

Samuel Adams (1722–1803)

An Exact Prospect of CHARLESTOWN. the Metropo

Charleston, South Carolina

Samuel Adams, the Revolutionary War leader, did not participate in the Philadelphia convention, but his democratic views were certainly well-known. His great confidence in the people is reflected in this letter of 1790:

> Where is this [natural] aristocracy found? Among men of all ranks and conditions. The cottager may beget a wise son; the noble, a fool. The one is capable of great improvement; the other is not. Education is within the power of men and societies of men. . . . Education leads youth to the study of human nature, society, and universal history, from whence they may draw all the principles of political architecture which ought to be regarded. All men are interested in truth; education, by showing them the end of all its consequences, would induce at least the greatest numbers to enlist on its side. The man of good understanding, who has been well educated, and improves these advantages as far as his circumstances will allow, in promoting the happiness of mankind, in my opinion. . . is indeed "well-born."[3]

But Adams's strong faith in the people was hardly the dominant sentiment. Elbridge Gerry, one of the most active participants in debate, came closer to the general feeling: "The evils we experience flow from the excess of democracy."[4] The Constitution provided for direct election only to the House of Representatives; other mechanisms preserved the choice of senators, presidents, and judges for the political elite. Colonel George Mason, who took part in the convention but ultimately refused to sign the document, said,"It would be as unnatural to refer the choice of a proper chief Magistrate to the people, as it would, to refer a trial of colours to a blind man."[5]

Perhaps the most difficult question to resolve was the matter of apportioning representation in Congress. Was property (including slaves) to be rep-

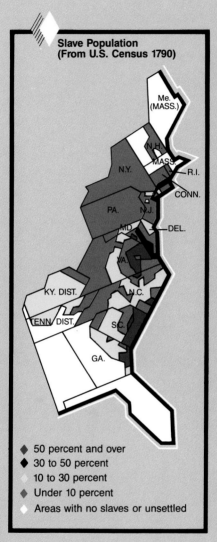

Slave Population (From U.S. Census 1790)

- ◆ 50 percent and over
- ◆ 30 to 50 percent
- ◇ 10 to 30 percent
- ◆ Under 10 percent
- ◇ Areas with no slaves or unsettled

Province of SOUTH CAROLINA.

resented? Or were people the only real object of representation? Pierce Butler, a wealthy Irish planter from South Carolina, stoutly championed the claims of property:

> *The labor of a slave in South Carolina is as productive & valuable as that of a freeman in Massachusetts. As wealth is the great means of defense and utility to the Nation they are equally valuable to it with freemen. Consequently, an equal representation ought to be allowed for them in a Government which is instituted principally for the protection of property, and is itself supported by property.*[6]

James Wilson, a lawyer and later a Supreme Court justice, stoutly defended the opposite principle:

> *Can we forget for whom we are forming a Government? Is it for men, or for the imaginary beings called States? Will our honest Constituents be satisfied with metaphysical distinctions?. . .The rule of suffrage [based strictly on population] ought on every principle be the same in the 2nd branch as in the 1st branch. If the Government is not laid on this foundation, it can be neither solid nor lasting. Any other principle will be local, confined and temporary. . . .We talk of States till we forget what they are composed of.*[7]

Wilson's point—which he was able to insert in the language of the Constitution—was that sovereignty resides in the people. But the convention responded to this conflict of principles with a mixed scheme that could be justified only by the need to keep all parties on board.

A Bill of Rights

The Bill of Rights, perhaps the most sacred portion of the Constitution in popular lore, also raised fierce debate. Jefferson, among others, strongly favored its inclusion. Madison originally opposed but eventually agreed to champion one in the new Congress. Hugh Henry Brackenridge, a prominent lawyer in antifederalist Pittsburgh, lampooned the need for a Bill of Rights:

> *The want of a bill of rights is the greatest evil. There was no occasion for a bill of wrongs; for there will be wrongs enough. But oh! a bill of rights! what is the nature of a bill of rights? "It is a schedule or inventory of those powers which congress do not possess." But if it be clearly ascertained what powers they have, what need of a catalogue of those powers they have not? Ah! there is the mistake. A minister preaching, undertook, first, to shew what was in his text; second, what was not in it. When it is specified what powers are given, why not also what powers are not given?*
>
> *I would submit it to any candid man, if in this constitution there be the least provision for the privilege of shaving the beard? or is there any mode laid down to take the measure of a pair of breeches? Whence is it then, that men of learning seem so much to approve, while the ignorant are against it? The cause is perfectly apparent, viz. that reason is an erring guide, while instinct, which is the governing principle of the untaught, is certain. Put a pig in a poke, carry it half a day's journey through the woods and by-ways; let it out, and it will run home without deviation. Could Dr. Franklin do this? What reason have we then to suppose his judgment, or that of Washington, could be equal to that of Mr. Smilie [a fervid antifederalist] in state affairs?*[8]

The convention decided that no Bill of Rights was needed but reversed itself during the ratification debates. Madison then promised to offer the Bill of Rights as amendments to the Constitution once it was ratified.

Secrecy

One of the earliest decisions taken by convention was that the proceedings be secret in order to allow a full, frank discussion of issues without concern for public alarm. That decision itself was controversial. Jefferson complained from Paris, in his position as American Minister to France, about "so abominable a precedent."[9] The *Pennsylvania Minority* wrote about "gilded chains" forged in *"the secret conclave."*

"Signing of the Constitution of the United States," by Howard Chandler Christy

New York City, July 26, 1788

The decision to keep the proceedings secret was strictly enforced. Although some fragmentary reports were offered by delegates who left in protest or dismay, no full accounting of the convention was available until Dolley Madison released her husband's careful notes decades later. The secrecy probably did allow for more vigorous debates. It also contributed to our reverence for the participants and product of that convention. The slogan "intention of the Framers" is still used as a trump card in debates about constitutional matters, as though the Framers spoke with a single, divinely guided voice.

After two centuries it is useful to recall the contentious, tentative nature of the debates in the convention and afterward. Reflection reveals that the real strength of our constitutional foundation is that it was erected by fallible human beings acting in the real world of everyday politics, as all patriots must, and as all Americans *can*.

The last signer of the Constitution died on June 28, 1836. He was eating breakfast and began to have trouble swallowing. When his niece asked what was wrong, the old man replied, "Nothing more than a change of mind." These last words spoken by one of the Framers are an evocative description of the debates that created American democracy.[10]

[1]Jean Pierre Brissot de Warville, quoted in Albert Bushnell Hart, *American History Told by Contemporaries*, vol. 3 (New York: The MacMillan Co., 1896), pp. 31–37.
[2]Quotations from the convention debates are taken from James Madison's *Notes on the Federal Convention*. The edition primarily used in developing this section has an introduction by Adrienne Koch and was published by Ohio University Press in 1966.
[3]Hart, *op. cit.*, p. 96.
[4]Quoted in Ezra Bowen, "Constitutional Convention, 1787," *Smithsonian*, Sept. 5, 1987, p. 36.
[5]Madison's notes, July 17.
[6]Madison's notes, July 11.
[7]Madison's notes, June 30.
[8]Quoted in Hart, *op. cit.*, pp. 238–239.
[9]Bowen, *op. cit.* p. 37.
[10]Timothy Foote, "After more than two centuries, this may be Mr. Madison's year," *Smithsonian*, Sept. 5, 1987, p. 88.

Two centuries after the constitutional debates, Americans still have reason to celebrate.

UPI/BETTMANN NEWSPHOTOS

COMPARATIVE PERSPECTIVE

Constitutional Democratic Systems

The political arrangements that were established by the U.S. Constitution and developed over two centuries have created a particular sort of democratic system, which Americans tend to think of as the only proper one—or certainly as the appropriate model for others to follow. Yet, although many democracies have modeled their constitutional arrangements on ours, American political structures are not necessarily the most typical—or even the best—arrangements for a democracy. Consider the following aspects of how our system compares with other working democracies.

1.   The United States has a chief executive who is elected separately from legislators. Only the French have a similar arrangement. Other democratic systems choose their executive leader—and cabinet—from the winning party (or parties) in the parliament. Thus, in most systems the executive and legislative branches are fused, or joined together, rather than separating the powers as our system does.

2.   The United States has a two-house (bicameral) legislature that has extensive powers to check and challenge the executive. Most other democratic systems have a one-house (unicameral) legislature, which usually has little independent power to challenge executive policy. For example, the extensive powers of our Congress to shape and reshape the federal budget are sharply limited in most other democratic legislatures.

3.   The U.S. Supreme Court has the power to declare laws unconstitutional. Such power is unique. Although other supreme courts do exist, as in West Germany, they simply are not such a major force in the constitutional system. Many democracies have no equivalent to the U.S. Supreme Court regarding its capacity to pass on the constitutionality of the nation's laws.

4.   Many American states have the initiative and referendum (discussed in Chapter 8), whereby citizens can directly affect the shaping of legislation. Other democracies, most notably Switzerland, use a national referendum to settle basic questions of law; in the United States this would be comparable to having a national vote about controversial issues like abortion and prayer in the schools. The Swiss believe that the people—not a national court—should have the last word on basic democratic issues. After all, our Constitution does begin with the words "We, the people," not with "We, the Supreme Court" or "We, the Congress . . . or President."

Are other constitutional arrangements better than ours? At this point, let us just note that democracy can and does exist in many forms quite different from our own.

quate instrument for the guidance of our affairs in the twentieth century—especially in the sphere of foreign policy. The domestic sphere, after all, is a sphere of law, enforced by the government (what some of the eighteenth-century philosophers who inspired the Constitution called a "civil state"), whereas the international sphere is a sphere of lawlessness (what the philosophers called a "state of nature"). As long as the United States was kept distant from world affairs, there was little tension between the two spheres, but once it became involved conflicts arose. It seemed reasonable, at least, to worry that if a President entered the lawless international arena feeling himself bound by the laws and standards of domestic American political life he would be at an unfair disadvantage, and the nation he governed would wind up a "pitiful, helpless giant," as Richard Nixon put it. When a great power is on the move abroad or is locked in struggle with another great power around the world—this one a power unconstrained by a press, a constitution, rival governmental powers, any assertion of individual rights, or public opinion—should it keep itself shackled by domestic fetters? Isn't this a formula for defeat? Shouldn't we in the United States at the very least acknowledge that while the Constitution still appropriately applies to some areas of our national life there is now in existence an area in which it cannot apply—an area in which the requirements of national security in the nuclear age override its provisions? For example, is the war-declaring power of Congress any longer relevant or workable? Should an arrangement designed for a world of sailing ships and muskets be continued in a world of communications satellites and nuclear-armed ballistic missiles? And what of the separation of powers in general? In our time of incessant fast-paced interaction on many levels with the entire world, shouldn't the conduct of foreign policy be frankly ceded to the executive branch, for isn't it alone capable of marshalling the facts and acting with the necessary dispatch? Shouldn't the rights of the individual, while being preserved as much as possible, yield when they conflict with the survival of the nation as a whole? Shouldn't the Constitution, like political partisanship, stop at the water's edge? Shouldn't we recognize that national security is an aim of government which does not so much come under the Constitution as stand alongside it, at times superseding it? Are we not, at best, in a sort of tragic situation in which the legal requirements of a constitutional republic inevitably collide with the practical requirements of a great power acting in a brutal world?

The history of the postwar period abundantly demonstrates that the questions are at least well founded. On three distinct occasions in those years, people in power have mounted serious challenges to the rule of law and the Constitution in the name of national security. The first challenge was that of Senator Joseph McCarthy, who trampled on the rights of individuals and ran roughshod over the normal, legal procedures of government in a campaign to ferret out Communists who he said were in the government. Before he was censured by the Senate, in 1954, he had managed to intimidate two Administrations and to strike fear into the whole country—a fear that persists today in politicians' dread of being found "soft" on Communism. The second challenge was the constitutional crisis that was born of the Vietnam War and culminated in the Watergate affair, in which

(among many other things that happened) two former Attorney Generals were sentenced to jail and a President was forced to resign under threat of impeachment. The crisis began in the early nineteen-sixties, when President Kennedy surreptitiously permitted American "advisers" to engage in combat; it continued with President Johnson's expansion of the American presence into a full-scale fighting force; and it came to its conclusion with President Nixon's grandiose claims of almost unlimited executive power and immunity from the law as he was tracked down by law-enforcement agencies and Congress. Throughout this crisis, three Presidents justified their circumvention of Congress and the law by invoking the overriding needs of national security. The third challenge, of course, is the nameless present one of a secret, runaway foreign policy in regard to Iran and Nicaragua which appears to violate the executive's own professed policies as well as those of Congress.

Each of the three postwar political crises might seem at first glance to confirm the tragic view that conflicts between our constitutional system and our role as a great power are inevitable. When one takes a second look, however, another feature of these crises meets the eye: a self-defeating quality is present in each. If there are occasions when individual liberties must yield to the needs of national security, McCarthy's hunt for Communists in the government was not among them; he never found one Communist. Nor does the Vietnam War, in retrospect, look like a great triumph for the national-security interests of the United States; it looks like an unqualified disaster, just one of whose almost immeasurable dire effects was the Watergate crisis. If we are supposed to believe that in matters of war and peace Presidents make wiser decisions than Congress, then someone will have to bring forward something other than the Vietnam War to demonstrate the point. The historical verdicts on our attempts to ransom hostages with arms sales to Iran and to illegally fund the Contras are not in yet, but these endeavors do not have the smell of success about them, either. The point, of course, is not that if the efforts had succeeded they would have been justified. It is that every time the constitutional system has been challenged in the name of national security the policy has failed even in its own terms. In view of this record, it appears that the Constitution isn't as outmoded as we may have feared. If it had been observed faithfully, the venerable document would have saved us from the worst political mistakes in our postwar national life.

The Constitutional Convention, 1787. Did the men we now refer to as our Founding Fathers expect that they would be honored for their efforts two hundred years later? They knew that only some political arrangements stood the test of time—and that however necessary their efforts in Philadelphia were, they were unquestionably experimental. *(The Bettmann Archive)*

SOME TRUTHS ARE NOT SELF-EVIDENT

Howard Zinn

This year [1987] Americans are talking about the Constitution but asking the wrong questions, such as, Could the Founding Fathers have done better? That concern is pointless, 200 years after the fact. Or, Does the Constitution provide the framework for a just and democratic society today? That question is also misplaced, because the Constitution, whatever its language and however interpreted by the Supreme Court, does not determine the degree of justice, liberty or democracy in our society.

The proper question, I believe, is not how good a document is or was the Constitution but, What effect does it have on the quality of our lives? And the answer to that, it seems to me, is, Very little. The Constitution makes promises it cannot by itself keep, and therefore deludes us into complacency about the rights we have. It is conspicuously silent on certain

SOURCE: *The Nation*, Aug. 1 and 8, 1987, pp. 87–88, The Nation Company, Inc. © 1987.

other rights that all human beings deserve. And it pretends to set limits on governmental powers, when in fact those limits are easily ignored.

I am not arguing that the Constitution has no importance; words have moral power and principles can be useful even when ambiguous. But, like other historic documents, the Constitution is of minor importance compared with the actions that citizens take, especially when those actions are joined in social movements. Such movements have worked, historically, to secure the rights our human sensibilities tell us are self-evidently ours, whether or not those rights are "granted" by the Constitution.

Let me illustrate my point with five issues of liberty and justice:

§ First is the matter of racial equality. When slavery was abolished, it was not by constitutional fiat but by the joining of military necessity with the moral force of a great antislavery movement, acting outside the Constitution and often against the law. The Thirteenth, Fourteenth and Fifteenth Amendments wrote into the Constitution rights that extralegal action had already won. But the Fourteenth and Fifteenth

Amendments were ignored for almost a hundred years. The right to equal protection of the law and the right to vote, even the Supreme Court decision in *Brown* v. *Board of Education* in 1954 underlining the meaning of the equal protection clause, did not become operative until blacks, in the fifteen years following the Montgomery bus boycott, shook up the nation by tumultuous actions inside and outside the law.

The Constitution played a helpful but marginal role in all that. Black people, in the political context of the 1960s, would have demanded equality whether or not the Constitution called for it, just as the antislavery movement demanded abolition even in the absence of constitutional support.

§ What about the most vaunted of constitutional rights, free speech? Historically, the Supreme Court has given the right to free speech only shaky support, seesawing erratically by sometimes affirming and sometimes overriding restrictions. Whatever a distant Court decided, the real right of citizens to free expression has been determined by the immediate power of the local police on the street, by the employer in the workplace and by the financial limits on the ability to use the mass media.

The existence of a First Amendment has been inspirational but its protection elusive. Its reality has depended on the willingness of citizens, whether labor organizers, socialists or Jehovah's Witnesses, to insist on their right to speak and write. Liberties have not been given; they have been taken. And whether in the future we have a right to say what we want, or air what we say, will be determined not by the existence of the First Amendment or the latest Supreme Court decision but by whether we are courageous enough to speak up at the risk of being jailed or fired, organized enough to defend our speech against official interference and can command resources enough to get our ideas before a reasonably large public.

§ What of economic justice? The Constitution is silent on the right to earn a moderate income, silent on the rights to medical care and decent housing as legitimate claims of every human being from infancy to old age. Whatever degree of economic justice has been attained in this country (impressive compared with others, shameful compared with our resources) cannot be attributed to something in the Constitution. It is the result of the concerted action of laborers and farmers over the centuries, using strikes, boycotts and minor rebellions of all sorts, to get redress of grievances directly from employers and indirectly from legislators. In the future, as in the past, the Constitution will sleep as citizens battle over the dis-

tribution of the nation's wealth, and will be awakened only to mark the score.

§ On sexual equality the Constitution is also silent. What women have achieved thus far is the result of their own determination, in the feminist upsurge of the nineteenth and early twentieth centuries, and the more recent women's liberation movement. Women have accomplished this outside the Constitution, by raising female and male consciousness and inducing courts and legislators to recognize what the Constitution ignores.

§ Finally, in an age in which war approaches genocide, the irrelevance of the Constitution is especially striking. Long, ravaging conflicts in Korea and Vietnam were waged without following Constitutional procedures, and if there is nuclear exchange, the decision to launch U.S. missiles will be made, as it was in those cases, by the President and a few advisers. The public will be shut out of the process and deliberately kept uninformed by an intricate web of secrecy and deceit. The current Iran/*contra* scandal hearings before Congressional select committees should be understood as exposing not an aberration but a steady state of foreign policy.

It was not constitutional checks and balances but an aroused populace that prodded Lyndon Johnson and then Richard Nixon into deciding to extricate the United States from Vietnam. In the immediate future, our lives will depend not on the existence of the Constitution but on the power of an aroused citizenry demanding that we not go to war, and on Americans refusing, as did so many G.I.s and civilians in the Vietnam era, to cooperate in the conduct of a war.

The Constitution, like the Bible, has some good words. It is also, like the Bible, easily manipulated, distorted, ignored and used to make us feel comfortable and protected. But we risk the loss of our lives and liberties if we depend on a mere document to defend them. A constitution is a fine adornment for a democratic society, but it is no substitute for the energy, boldness and concerted action of the citizens.

THE "NEW SCIENCE OF POLITICS"
AND THE OLD ART OF GOVERNMENT

Sen. Daniel Patrick Moynihan

. . . In the past two centuries, there has been a great transformation in the problematic aspects of government. Consider the bill of particulars in the Decla-

SOURCE: Reprinted with permission of the author from *The Public Interest*, No. 86 (Winter 1987), pp. 22–35. © 1987 by National Affairs, Inc.

ration of Independence. We learn that, in his zeal to oppress the people, the Tyrant George III

> has called together Legislative Bodies at Places un- usual, uncomfortable, and distant from the De- pository of their public Records, for the sole Pur- pose of fatiguing them into Compliance with his Measures.

These are not trivial matters, but, always excepting the threat of religious persecution, they seem some- how innocent given what the twentieth century has learned of tyranny. It is hard not to see the American Revolution and the Constitution that followed as the convergence of two sets of events, the one principally economic, the other mainly intellectual. The colonies had matured to the point where they did not want to be colonies any longer, which is to say plantations set down here to produce profits over there, with all the restrictions and bother of a tolerant but even so pervasive mercantilism and a tedious aristocracy. In the meantime, political thought and economic change had made monarchy seem an outmoded form of gov- ernment. This was hardly a view unknown in Lon- don, but the chance for a big change occurred in Philadelphia.

Can we agree, then, that the great object of the constitutional arrangements we thereupon put in place was that the government should leave the citi- zen alone? Thus the thundering prohibitions of the Bill of Rights: "Congress shall make no law"; "No soldiers shall"; "no Warrant shall. . . ." Fair enough. That was the problem then. *The problem now is that citizens won't leave government alone.* They now plun- der the State as the State was once thought to plunder them. What happened? Many things. Start with Mr. Jefferson's purchase of Louisiana. Of a sudden the national government was *rich.* In land. A century later a central banking system made it rich in credit. In the meantime, interest groups learned the tactical advantage of moving an issue upwards in the federal system, a process described by Schattschneider. And then railroads and especially the airlines made the continent one *place.* And much more. The checks and balances of an early age seem less effective. Are we approaching this newer question with anything like the clarity and method with which the Founders ap- proached the earlier one? I would answer no. . . .

As for the readiness of national governments to spend money, there is no great mystery. It is in the nature of modern society to expand the range of de- sirable collective goods. With his own resources Franklin could afford to purchase most of the essen- tial scientific instruments of his age, and to keep them at home. We, by contrast, must own cloud chambers and space shuttles in common. And hospitals and hospices. We are not a mean people in such matters. But what do we encounter in the Reagan years? The demand for collective goods greatly exceeded the supply of money to pay for them. Whereupon we borrowed a trillion dollars from the Japanese and gave a party.

There is, moreover, an imperative which accom- panies the advancement of knowledge in modern so- ciety. What do we do, for example, when we *know* how to keep people alive but it costs money? Let them die? I have been long enough in government to have known a time when issues of health hardly intruded on the budget-making process. Antibiotics had arrived, but the cost of running hospitals went mainly to clean linen. Budget examiners never had to choose how many persons with kidney failure they would let live in the next fiscal year. Now they do. It is no discredit to society that it errs on the side of the patient. This will continue. . . .

Which brings us back to virtue. It may be I exag- gerate the crisis of the 1980s, but I think not. I believe it is now revealed that the constitutional arrange- ments of 1787 are not necessarily self-correcting, need not return to stability; that opposing appetites do not cancel each other out, that the "defect of better mo- tives" can be a defect indeed. . . .

It comes to this. The psychological realism of the Founders predicted much and served us well in a time of a small and distant national government. It is not clear that this is still the case. Something extra is required in an age when the costs of wholly self- interested behavior can be so great because govern- ment is so large.

DOES THE SEPARATION OF POWERS STILL WORK?

James Q. Wilson

If one is asked to explain why the American govern- ment acts as it does with respect to almost any policy issue, the chances are probably eight in ten that the right answer is the separation of powers. The exist- ence of three separate institutions with independent constitutional standing and, in two cases, distinct electoral constituencies is what distinguishes Amer- ican government from parliamentary democracies. The separation of powers is the source of the enor- mous influence that Congress exercises over both the

---

SOURCE: *The Public Interest*, Winter 1987, pp. 36–52.

broad outlines and minute details of public policy, an influence that has led Daniel Patrick Moynihan to remark that the United States is the only major government with a legislative branch and that leads many European observers to doubt that this country is really governed at all. The separation of powers is also at the root of the courts' authority to declare presidential and congressional acts unconstitutional and thus is a major cause of one kind of judicial activism.

If one is asked what is wrong with American government, the odds are great—maybe not eight in ten, but better than one in two—that the reply will refer to some aspect of our politics that can be explained by the separation of powers: "The president cannot negotiate for the United States on delicate foreign policy matters." "Congress meddles in the work of bureaucratic agencies." "There are too many government leaks to the press." "The Pentagon is not under strong, unified management." "There are too many patronage (i.e., political) appointees in government agencies." "There are too few policy-oriented (i.e., political) appointees in government agencies."

If one makes a list of the most frequently proposed alterations in our constitutional arrangements, the odds are high that these proposals will call for a reduction in the separation of powers: "Let the president put some members of Congress in his cabinet." "Have the president and members of Congress who are from the president's party run as a team." "Allow the president to dissolve Congress." "Allow Congress to call for a special presidential election." "Curb the power of judicial review."

There have always been two distinct, though often intertwined, strands in the case against the separation of powers. One is the liberal case: The federal government should play a large and active role in human affairs by supplying services, reducing economic inequality, and catering to the demands of those who find themselves at a disadvantage in the marketplace. During most of this century, presidents have been more sensitive to the urban and industrial constituencies who make these demands than has Congress. Therefore, the powers of the president should be enlarged and those of Congress (or those parts of Congress that are "obstructionist") should be reduced. . . .

The other case is the rationalist one. Whether policies are liberal or conservative, they should be made decisively, efficiently, and on the basis of comprehensive principles. The public interest was not well served by simply adding up individual preferences into a "patchwork" or "crazy quilt" of inconsistent programs administered in "wasteful" ways by "duplicative" agencies. The public interest was better served by having a unitary view of what was good for the nation "as a whole." Only a single official could design and propose an internally consistent set of policies based on some overriding principle. In our system that person is the president. . . .

But of course the Framers of the Constitution were not trying to create a government that would discern national goals and serve them efficiently and with dispatch; they were trying to create a limited government that would serve only those goals that could survive a process of consultation and bargaining designed to prevent the mischief of factions and the tyranny of passionate majorities or ambitious politicians. . . .

It is not difficult, of course, to produce a litany of difficulties facing the nation: a large budget and trade deficit, the threat of nuclear war, a complex array of international commitments, an economy painfully adjusting to new kinds of international competition, the cancer of crime and drug abuse, and so on. But it is not clear that these "new realities" are fundamentally different from the kinds of problems faced by Washington's first administration and it is certainly far from clear that they constitute a case for constitutional change.

Today, the case for constitutional change is being made to a nation prosperous and at peace whose political institutions enjoy unquestioned legitimacy. Decision making is as contentious and protracted now as it was two hundred years ago, but under circumstances that are far more conducive to success and popular support that once was the case. In 1986, one can only be amused to reread the 1974 essay by Charles Hardin on why our government was then in crisis and why only major "constitutional surgery" could correct it. Watergate, the supposedly "imperial presidency," and popular distrust of government were the crisis; the cure required these changes: electing the president and Congress for coterminous four-year terms, abolishing the office of vice president, allowing Congress to remove a president by a vote of no confidence, giving the president an automatic majority in the House of Representatives, and so on. Of course, the "crisis" ended without any of these "cures." Watergate was handled by the normal constitutional procedures—congressional investigations, criminal trials, and the prospect of impeachment—and the presidency and the president are once again in high repute.

GLOSSARY TERMS

Seven Years' War

Articles of Confederation

Shays's Rebellion

unicameral

bicameral

Virginia Plan

New Jersey Plan

Connecticut Compromise

electoral college

The Federalist Papers

separation of powers

checks and balances

Federalists

Antifederalists

Bill of Rights

amendment

NOTES

[1]James Kirby Martin, *In the Course of Human Events* (Arlington Heights, Ill.: AHM Publishing, 1979), pp. 9–11.

[2]George B. Tindall, *America: A Narrative History* (New York: Norton, 1984), pp. 209–210.

[3]*Ibid.*, pp. 262–263, and Charles Warren, *The Making of the Constitution* (New York: Barnes and Noble, 1967), pp. 55–60.

[4]Robert Dahl, *A Preface to Democratic Theory* (Chicago: University of Chicago Press, 1956), p. 146.

[5]See Daniel H. Pollitt and Frank Thompson, "Could a Convention Become a Runaway?" *Christianity and Crisis*, Apr. 16, 1979.

[6]See George Bancroft, *History of the United States*, R. B. Nye, ed. (Chicago: University of Chicago Press, 1966).

[7]See John Fiske, *The Critical Period of American History, 1783–1789* (Boston: Houghton Mifflin, 1888).

[8]Charles Beard, *An Economic Interpretation of the Constitution* (New York: Macmillan, 1913).

SELECTED READINGS

THE AMERICAN REVOLUTION

For various **perspectives** on the American Revolution, see S. M. Lipset, *The First New Nation: The United States in Historical and Comparative Perspective* (New York: Norton, 1979). Ellen Chase, *Beginnings of the American Revolution, Volume III* (Port Washington, N.Y.: Kennikat Press, 1970); James Kirby Martin, *In the Course of Human Events* (Arlington Heights, Ill.: AHM Publishing, 1979); and Neil R. Stout, *The Perfect Crisis: The Beginning of the Revolutionary War* (New York: NYU Press, 1976).

THE REVOLUTIONARY WAR

Good basic works on **Thomas Paine** include Howard Fast, ed., *The Selected Works of Tom Paine and Citizen Tom Paine* (New York: Modern Library, 1945); Eric Foner, *Tom Paine and The American Revolution* (New York: Oxford University Press, 1976); N. F. Adkins, ed., *Common Sense and Other Political Writings* (Indianapolis: Bobbs-Merrill, 1953); and Henry Collins, ed., *The Rights of Man* (Harmondsworth, England: Penguin, 1969).

For more extensive discussions on the effects of the Revolutionary War on American **social and political development,** see Charles Royster, *A Revolutionary People at War: The Continental Army and American Character, 1775–1783* (Chapel Hill, N.C.: University of North Carolina Press, 1980); and J. Franklin Jameson, *The American Revolution Considered as a Social Movement* (Boston: Beacon Press, 1963).

THE CONSTITUTIONAL CONVENTION

There is no shortage of **commentaries** on the Constitutional Convention. See particularly Vernon L. Parrington, *Main Currents in American Political Thought*, vol. 6 (New York: Harcourt, 1927); Garry Wills, *Inventing America* (Garden City, N.Y.: Doubleday, 1978), chap. 27; and David G. Smith, *The Convention and the Constitution: The Political Ideas of the Founding Fathers* (Washington, D.C.: University Press of America, 1987).

The best discussion of the **political issues** involved in the writing of the Constitution is still James Madison's *Notes of the Debates in the Federal Convention of 1787*, Adrienne Koch, ed. (Athens, Ohio: Ohio University Press, 1966). The philosophical underpinnings of the Constitution can be found in Alexander Hamilton, John Jay, and James Madison, *The Federalist Papers* (Cambridge, Mass.: Belnap Press, 1966); and Paul Conklin, *Self-Evident Truths* (Bloomington, Ind.: Indiana University Press, 1974).

On the particular contributions of **James Madison,** see Saul Padover, ed., *The Complete Madison* (New York: Harper & Row, 1953); Frank Donovan, *Mr. Madison's Constitution* (New York: Dodd, Mead, 1965); Irving Brant, *James Madison and American Nationalism* (Princeton, N.J.: Van Nostrand, 1968); and Robert Rutland, *James Madison: The Founding Father* (New York: Macmillan, 1987).

THE CONSTITUTION

There has been a host of new writing on the **Constitution** connected with the two-hundredth anniversary of its creation. For a sample, see John J. Sexton and Nat Brandt, *How Free Are We? What the Constitution Says We Can and Cannot Do* (New York: M Evans, 1986); Richard B. Morris, *Witnesses at the Creation: Hamilton, Madison, Jay and the Constitution* (New York: NAL, 1986); Elizabeth P. McCaughey, ed., *Government by Choice: Inventing the United States Constitution* (New York: Basic Books, 1987); Walter Berns, *Taking the Constitution Seriously* (New York: Simon & Schuster, 1987); and James Collier and Christopher Collier: *Decision in Philadelphia; the Constitutional Convention of 1787* (New York: Random House, 1986).

3

AMERICAN FEDERALISM

Can Democracy Be Divided Fifty Ways?

© David S. Strickler/Monkmeyer

CHAPTER OUTLINE

Federalism: An Overview
The Evolution of Federalism
Responsibilities of the States
Tensions in the Federal System
Federal Intervention
When Intervention Fails

On January 1, 1988, residents of various states encountered a series of new state laws and regulations that promised to have far-reaching ramifications. For example, Wisconsin and Arizona passed laws that allowed law enforcement authorities to seize a driver's license on the spot if they suspected drunkenness. Louisiana and Illinois began requiring couples to be tested for Acquired Immune Deficiency Syndrome (AIDS) before marriage licenses are issued (in Illinois, both parties must be informed of the test results and counseled on how the disease is spread). In Oregon, larger companies must provide up to three months of unpaid leave to new parents. This is just a small sampling. The reality of American federalism is that laws differ dramatically from one state to another.

Two hundred years after the founding of our political system, the states retain power to regulate numerous functions, and they often choose to experiment with sharply different approaches. Some observers believe the national (federal) government has gained too much power at the expense of the states, while others assert that our system is too decentralized and more functions should be regulated by the federal government.

This chapter examines the workings of American federalism, the controversies surrounding it, various attempts to rectify its shortcomings, and the impact of federalism on democracy.

Federalism: An Overview

Every American holds dual citizenship of a kind: as a citizen of the United States and as a citizen of a particular state. This duality stems from our **federal system,** in which power is shared by different national and regional levels of government. In a federal arrangement each level of government forms an integral part of the constitutionally established political system. Each level has a direct impact on the people and *by right* each exercises authority that (at least theoretically) cannot be taken away from it by the other. The relationship between states and cities thus is not a federal one, for cities are chartered by the state and do not enjoy a legally independent status.[1]

This dual citizenship has many important consequences, most of which we take entirely for granted. In many states, citizens must pay state income tax as well as federal income tax. And because there are fifty separate state jurisdictions, whenever citizens move from one state to another, they must register to vote in the new state, get a new driver's license, learn different traffic regulations, and so on. Some states make it more difficult than others to get married or divorced. Certain crimes, such as driving while intoxicated, carry rather lenient penalties in some states and severe penalties in others.

From the beginning of our political history the federal system has made for tension between the states and the national government. The major domestic crisis in U.S. history, the Civil War (or the War Between the States, as many Southerners prefer to call it), erupted when several states attempted to secede from the Union. Moreover, the racial issues underlying the secession crisis have resurfaced recurrently in U.S. history, often in struggles pitting state against nation. In the 1960s, for example, the federal government had to intervene forcefully in Southern states to protect and extend the civil rights and voting rights of black citizens.

Other nations have suffered similar crises, and many have federal arrangements similar to ours: Canada has provincial governments; Australia, West Germany, and India have state governments. Some federal systems allow the regional governments greater responsibility and latitude for action than do others. Whatever the particular arrangements, however, all federal systems must cope with one key problem: coordinating the actions of the two levels.

The opposite of a federal system in political structure is a **unitary system,** in which the national government's authority is more or less uniformly enforced throughout the country. Under a unitary system no government at the regional level can hold independent power. Even so, administrative subdivisions usually are required for the efficient discharge of political activities. Although these local units are not self-governing, they often have considerable autonomy, and political power may be decentralized to a certain extent. Modern examples of unitary systems include the governments of Great Britain, France, and Sweden. (See **Figure 3–1** for a graphic comparison of unitary and federal systems.)

FIGURE 3–1
Comparison of Unitary and Federal Systems
UNITARY SYSTEM

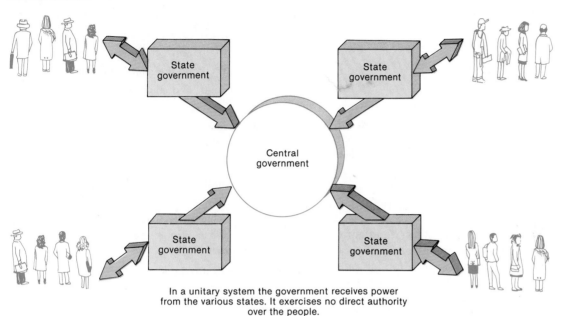

In a unitary system the government receives power
from the various states. It exercises no direct authority
over the people.

FEDERAL SYSTEM

Under federalism both the national government and
state governments receive power from the people,
and both exercise authority over them.

Before addressing the current status of our federal system, let us examine the legal mechanisms on which the system is based, particularly as they relate to division of powers, limitations on government actions, and interstate obligations.[2]

Division of Powers

The Constitution enumerates the political powers to be exercised by the national and state levels of government, respectively (see **Table 3–1**). The national government possesses inherent powers, delegated powers, and concurrent powers. The states exercise concurrent and reserved powers, while they are prohibited from engaging in certain specific activities.

Inherent powers refer to those that are integral to national sovereignty. The most significant inherent power is the power to conduct foreign policy—to declare and wage war, to make treaties, and to maintain diplomatic relations. Inherent powers cannot be possessed *both* by states and by the national government.

Delegated powers—those the Constitution specifically assigns to the jurisdiction of the national government—range from the power to regulate interstate commerce; to the power to coin money; and the power to carry out the many functions assigned to each branch of government, such as Congress's powers to legislate for the general welfare, punish violators of federal laws, and raise taxes, or the executive's power to appoint ambassadors.

These delegated powers carry certain implications. For example, if the national government is granted the power to coin money and maintain a currency, does that not imply that the national government also has the power to create a national bank to carry out these delegated functions? In the early days of our government, Alexander Hamilton, along with others of a "nationalist" orientation, argued for such implied powers, whereas Thomas Jefferson and others of a more "republican" (or state-oriented) bent supported a narrower interpretation of delegated powers. In an 1819 ruling in the case of *McCulloch* v. *Maryland,* the Supreme Court upheld the federal government's right to create a national bank, legitimizing the concept of **implied powers.**[3]

TABLE 3–1
The Federal Division of Powers

Major powers of the federal government

To tax for federal purposes

To borrow on the nation's credit

To regulate foreign and interstate commerce

To provide currency and coinage

To conduct foreign relations and make treaties

To provide an army and a navy

To establish and maintain a postal service

To protect patents and copyrights

To regulate weights and measures

To admit new states

To "make all laws which shall be necessary and proper" for the execution of all powers vested in the U.S. government

Major powers of the states

To tax for state purposes

To borrow on the state's credit

To regulate trade within the state

To make and enforce civil and criminal law

To maintain police forces

To furnish public education

To control local government

To regulate charities

To establish voting and election laws

To exercise all "powers not delegated to the United States by the Constitution, nor prohibited by it to the States," except for those "reserved to . . . the people"

SOURCE: Nicholas Henry, *Governing at the Grassroots* (Englewood Cliffs, N.J.: Prentice-Hall, 1984), p. 233.

This concept has played a major role in the gradual expansion of the powers of the federal government. Many activities of the federal government that now seem fundamental—such as the regulation of key aspects of economic life—are not spelled out anywhere in the Constitution. This is hardly surprising: The Founders could never have anticipated the complexities and problems of modern industrial life. So the Constitution has expanded to meet changing national imperatives,

Limits on Government Power

The Constitution imposes specific limitations on government power, including prohibitions against bills of attainder and ex post facto laws.

Bill of Attainder Any legislative act that singles out a specific individual or group for punishment. Perhaps the most prominent recent controversy involving such bills was that over the papers of former president Richard Nixon. In 1974, Nixon claimed, in effect, that he was the victim of a bill of attainder after Congress passed legislation instructing the General Services Administration to preserve and eventually make public those of his papers that had historic value. Given that other presidents had been permitted to decide which of their papers would be published, Nixon contended that he had been singled out for special treatment. The Supreme Court eventually rejected that view, arguing that Nixon was a "legitimate class of one," particularly because he was the only president ever to have resigned his office.* The disposition of his papers, therefore, was a special situation that Congress could reasonably act upon.

Ex Post Facto Law Any law that designates as criminal an act that was not a crime when it was committed, that increases penalties for a crime after it has been committed, or that retroactively alters the conditions required to prove a crime was committed. The constitutional prohibition against ex post facto laws does not extend to civil law (as opposed to criminal) and does not prohibit retroactive laws that benefit, rather than harm, the accused.

Richard M. Nixon v. *General Services Administration* (1977)

and the doctrine of implied powers has proved invaluable in extending the Constitution's reach.

Concurrent powers—those that can be exercised by both national and state governments—encompass the powers to raise taxes, to charter corporations, to borrow money, and to exercise the right of eminent domain (the right to appropriate private property for public use).

The Tenth Amendment to the Constitution speaks specifically of **reserved powers:** "The powers not delegated to the United States by the Constitution, nor prohibited by it to the States, are reserved to the States respectively, or to the people." In several instances early in this century, the courts invoked the Tenth Amendment to place limits on federal power, a topic we explore later in this chapter.

The Constitution forbids the states to exercise certain powers, including the powers to make war, to make treaties with foreign governments, to maintain armies and navies, and to coin money.

At the same time, the national government is bound by the Constitution to keep import duties uniform throughout the nation, to respect the territorial integrity of the states, and to ensure that each state is appropriately represented in the House and has two senators.

Limitations on Government Actions

The framers of the Constitution erected powerful legal barriers to arbitrary or tyrannical actions by the government. Thus, Article I of the Constitution sets certain limits on the actions of the states, which are forbidden, among other things, to grant titles of nobility and pass bills of attainder or ex post facto laws. Similar restrictions were applied to the national government in Amendments One through Ten, which comprise the **Bill of Rights.** Subsequent amendments added further restrictions. Under Amendments Fifteen and Nineteen, the states are forbidden to limit voting rights on the basis of race or sex, respectively. The Fourteenth Amendment requires that no state shall abridge the privileges and immunities of citizens of the United States, that states must observe **"due process of law"**—a guarantee of fair legal procedure—and that each person is entitled to **"equal protection of the laws"**—a guarantee that each individual is treated equally under the law.

Interstate Obligations

Article IV requires that states grant **"full faith and credit"** to the acts of other states, return fugitives fleeing from criminal proceedings in other states, and grant all "privileges and immunities" to citizens of other states. Under the "full faith and credit" provision, the most far-reaching of these requirements, every state must accept as valid the legal proceedings and records of other states, including mortgages, contracts, and birth certificates. As interpreted by the Supreme Court, this provision does not include the obligation to enforce the *criminal* laws of another state; a person wanted for a crime in one state must be extradited to that state for trial. In general, however, state civil laws must be enforced by all other states. Thus, whenever a person leaves one state to avoid complying with a contract made there, the state to which he flees normally must enforce that contract in a court of law.

The "full faith and credit" provision has not been uniformly followed by the states or enforced by the courts, however. In particular, the requirement that states extradite fugitives to other states has often been ignored, with the acquiescence of the Supreme Court. In several famous cases, state governors have refused to extradite fugitives on the grounds that prison conditions were unsafe or that a fair trial could not be obtained in the state seeking the fugitive's return. A major roadblock to extradition was lifted with recent legislation making it a federal crime to cross state lines to avoid prosecution. As a result, extradition has become more common.

Among the most significant "privileges and immunities" that the states must extend to all U.S. citizens are the right to vote and the right to travel freely. Until relatively recently, many states sought to circumvent this constitutional provision by attaching lengthy residency requirements to the right to vote, even in national elections. The Supreme Court largely ended this practice by ruling that a state must demonstrate the legitimacy of requirements. The right to travel across state lines has generally been accepted by the states. The only significant exception to this rule occurred when thousands of migrants fleeing the Dust Bowl conditions of the Midwest in the 1930s were prevented from entering California under a state law excluding indigent immigrants. In *Edwards* v. *California* (1941), the Supreme Court struck down the California law as an unconstitutional barrier to interstate commerce.[4]

Statehood and the Alternatives

The Constitution grants Congress the right to admit new states but does not establish any fixed procedures for admission. More than half the present states were once "territories" governed by congressional appointees. One by one, these territories petitioned Congress for statehood, and each eventually was the beneficiary of a congressional **enabling act** allowing its citizens to draft a state constitution. Next came congressional and presidential approval of the draft state constitution, and after any differences had been ironed out, admission to the Union. Sometimes additional requirements have to be fulfilled: The citizens of Hawaii and Alaska, for example, were required to approve admission to statehood at special elections. Once admitted, a state stands in complete legal equality with all other states; none has unique privileges or obligations.

In addition to states, the United States comprises one district, one commonwealth, and several territories. The District of Columbia, the seat of our national government, was specified in the Constitution as a *district* granted to the national government by the states of Maryland and Virginia. This arrangement ensured that the national government would not be dependent on the government of any particular state in which it might be located. Despite intense resistance from some members of Congress, in 1961 Washingtonians

The Northwest Ordinance of 1787

The Northwest Ordinance of 1787 has been called the most far-reaching piece of legislation ever enacted in the United States. In mandating that new states were to be created in the area north of the Ohio River, the ordinance stipulated that the new states would enjoy the same legal status as already-existing states and that slavery would be excluded in this area. By decreeing that newly settled territories would be incorporated into the Union as full-fledged states, the ordinance defused the threat of rivalry between the older states, many of which had sought to expand into the Northwest territories. It also precluded any move toward colonial subordination of newly settled areas to established states. The system of "elastic federalism" instituted by the Northwest Ordinance, under which statehood was to be granted to those who actually settled and developed new territories, offered perhaps the most sensible method for opening the continent and expanding the Union.

This 1783 map shows the geographical divisions of that time, including the American states, Florida, Canada, Quebec, and Nova Scotia. The land that would be covered by the Northwest Ordinance is situated northwest of the Ohio River. (*The Bettmann Archive*)

were given the right to participate in presidential elections through the Twenty-third Amendment. (Southern segregationists and conservatives had sought to exclude from the franchise Washington's predominantly black population, which votes heavily liberal and Democratic.) Home rule by a local mayor and city council was also granted. But the District of Columbia remains without U.S. representatives and senators.

Puerto Rico, which is not a state, enjoys the unique status of *commonwealth*. Puerto Rican citizens can freely emigrate to the United States, and more than one million have done so. While relatively well off compared with most Caribbean people, Puerto Ricans earn, on average, only about half what citizens of our poorest state earn. They receive many welfare benefits, including Social Security, food stamps, and Medicare, but they pay no U.S. taxes. Puerto Ricans serve in the U.S. armed forces, but they are not represented in Congress, nor can they vote in presidential elections. Puerto Rico was taken from Spain by the United States in 1898, and it voted to accept commonwealth status in 1950.

U.S. *territories* include the U.S. Virgin Islands, Samoa, Guam, and, until 1978, the Canal Zone. The "Zone," in which the Panama Canal is located, was ceded to Panama in 1978 by treaty. Highly controversial in the United States, the treaty was viewed by some Americans as a giveaway of American rights. In fact, the United States acquired the Canal Zone by fomenting a 1903 rebellion against the government of Colombia that led to the secession of the state of Panama. As

Senator S. I. Hayakawa of California put it at one point, the Canal Zone was ours because, "We stole it fair and square."

The Evolution of Federalism

Abraham Lincoln once asserted that "the Union is older than any of the states, and, in fact, it created them as states." President Ronald Reagan took precisely the opposite view, that "the federal government did not create the states; the states created the federal government." These divergent views of federalism have been in conflict since the founding of the nation. Let us now examine (1) three crises that decisively changed the shape of U.S. federalism; (2) how the courts have influenced our federal system; and (3) drives by the executive branch to remake federalism—the so-called "new federalisms."

Three Crises of State and Nation

THE CIVIL WAR   The crisis with the greatest impact on federalism culminated in the Civil War. In the verbal and ideological battle preceding the war, the renowned South Carolina politician John

C. Calhoun raised basic questions about exactly what "nationhood" meant in the United States. "The very idea of an *American People*, as constituting a single community, is a mere chimera," he argued. "Such a community never for a single moment existed—neither before nor since the Declaration of Independence."[5] For Calhoun, as for Ronald Reagan, the states created the nation: Each state was a sovereign community that voluntarily entered into a compact with the other states to form the national society. A more or less logical deduction from this view was that the states, having agreed to form the union, could also dissolve it.

Calhoun's concept of federalism was vigorously opposed by Daniel Webster, the eloquent senator from Massachusetts. Webster, whom Lincoln would echo, argued that the United States was created not by a compact between the states, but "by the people of the United States in the aggregate." The Constitution, he said, was "the people's Constitution, the people's government, made for the people, made by the people, and answerable to the people." He concluded this argument with the famous line, "Liberty and union, one and inseparable, now and forever."[6]

Webster not only defended a union based directly on the people, he also pointed out that many

The ruins of Richmond and the Union army preparing for battle at Fredericksburg. The Civil War was extraordinarily costly on all sides, taking a heavy toll in lives and leaving a wide trail of destruction. The issues that provoked it were only partially resolved and continued to haunt our national life for a hundred years, as did memories of the war itself. The war did, however, settle one basic matter; there would be only one nation on American soil. The experiment in secession was over. *(Library of Congress)*

John Calhoun of South Carolina eloquently spoke for a state-centered federal system based on the concept that any large subgroup could veto efforts to force it to change. In protecting the slave states, Calhoun raised issues that still draw interest. *(New York Public Library)*

Daniel Webster of Massachusetts, one of the greatest orators of his day and a staunch defender of a strong federal government. He feared that states' rights would become too powerful; indeed, the strain between nation and states could be resolved only by the Civil War. *(New York Public Library)*

common interests of U.S. society as a whole could not be handled by the states. For Webster, as for Alexander Hamilton, national action was absolutely necessary to secure many worthwhile goals that the individual states were not likely to pursue. Only the national government, Webster contended, had the power and the mandate to address the problems of land use, waterway development, and transportation—all increasingly important as the United States grew into an industrial society.

The North's triumph in the Civil War not only resulted in the abolition of slavery and the permanent demise of the concept of secession, but it also led to a major expansion of the powers of the federal government. During and after the war, federal involvement in banking, transportation,

higher education, and land management broadened considerably, as Webster and Lincoln had argued it must.

INDUSTRIAL EXPANSION The second major crisis of federalism grew out of the vast expansion of industry throughout the nation in the second half of the nineteenth century. With the emergence of giant corporations whose interests stretched across state lines, state governments found it nearly impossible to regulate commerce and industry. Monopolistic and predatory business practices, such as price fixing, flourished despite widespread agitation by farmers, workers, and consumers for legislation restricting the power of business. Action by the federal government, principally in the administrations of Theodore Roosevelt (1901–1909) and Woodrow Wilson (1913–1921), was necessary to bring the disruptive forces of industrial power under a modest degree of social control. Congress established new regulations for the conduct of trade, encouraging competition and limiting monopolistic practices, and passed a series of statutes regulating the banking, food and drug, meat packing, and other industries. The Justice Department, with the acquiescence of the Supreme Court, vigorously enforced antitrust laws. Throughout this era (roughly, 1890–1916), then, all branches of the federal government became involved to an unprecedented degree in the regulation of business.

THE GREAT DEPRESSION   The third crisis of federalism developed out of the Great Depression of the 1930s, when the magnitude of the national economic collapse far exceeded the remedial powers of the states. With millions unemployed, local and state welfare efforts were stretched beyond the breaking point. In his 1933 inaugural address, President Franklin D. Roosevelt argued that since the crisis was national, the solutions also had to be national. He called for extensive planning to be carried out by the federal government. Roosevelt's New Deal inaugurated a new phase of federalism. The earliest New Deal efforts consisted of emergency steps toward national planning for economic recovery. However, as the New Deal took shape, federal efforts were extended into new areas, some previously within the province of the states—including welfare and income-maintenance programs, jobs programs, the regulation of wages and prices, and a host of other functions.

Table 3–2 reveals changing public attitudes toward federalism in recent years.

TABLE 3–2
Public Attitudes toward Federalism

	1978	1982	1984	1986
"Which of these statements comes closest to your view about government power?"				
The federal government has too much power	38%	38%	35%	28%
The federal government is using about the right amount of power	18	18	25	24
The federal government should use its power more vigorously	36	30	34	41
Don't know	8	14	6	7

	Federal	*States*
"Should there be one national policy set by the federal government or should the 50 states make their own rules?"		
In controlling pollution	49%	46%
In setting penalties for murder	62	34
On the issue of registration and voting	64	31
In selecting textbooks in public schools	35	61
In setting minimum wages	51	45
In establishing safety standards in factories	65	31
In setting highway speed limits	42	56

SOURCES: Advisory Commission on Intergovernmental Relations, *Changing Public Attitudes on Government and Taxes*, Washington: 1986; and *New York Times*, May 26, 1987, p. 10.

Federal-State Relations after *McCulloch* v. *Maryland*

1824—Gibbons v. *Ogden.* Supreme Court says Congress has broad power to regulate "commercial intercourse"; strikes down New York law granting steamboat monopoly to a private company operating between New York and New Jersey.

1870—U.S. v. *DeWitt.* Supreme Court strikes down federal law prohibiting intrastate sale of certain inflammable petroleum products; says Congress cannot regulate "internal trade" of a state.

1887—Congress creates the Interstate Commerce Commission to regulate railroads.

1895—Sugar Trust Case. Supreme Court says Congress does not have power to regulate manufacturing even if products later enter interstate commerce. Manufacturing is held subject to state regulation.

1914—Shreveport Rate Case. Supreme Court upholds federal regulation of intrastate rail rates because of their effect on interstate commerce.

1918—Hammer v. *Dagenhart.* Supreme Court strikes down federal child labor law on the ground that it invades an area reserved for state regulation.

1937—National Labor Relations Board v. *Jones &* Laughlin *Steel Corp.* Supreme Court says Congress can regulate labor relations at a big steel plant because a work stoppage would have "a most serious effect upon interstate commerce."

1942—Wickard v. *Filburn.* Supreme Court says Congress may control a farmer's production of wheat for home consumption because the cumulative effect of such production by many farmers would influence national supply and price of wheat.

1964—Congress invokes "commerce power" in passing Civil Rights Act; forbids discrimination in public accommodations.

1976—National League of Cities v. *Usery.* Supreme Court says Congress lacks power to regulate wages and hours of key state and local government employees; emphasizes "state sovereignty."

1985—Garcia v. *San Antonio Transit Authority.* Supreme Court overrules 1976 decision; holds that federal wage and hour laws apply to state and local governments.

SOURCES: Domestic Policy Council's Working Group on Federalism; Supreme Court decisions.

The Role of the Courts

The federal courts, and particularly the Supreme Court, have played a crucial role in resolving disputes between the federal government and the states; many key decisions have shaped the evolution of the U.S. federal system.[7] Historically, the Supreme Court's view of federalism has undergone major shifts. In early U.S. history, the Court promoted the growth of national power. After the Civil War, it frequently championed the rights of the states—a pattern that continued until the 1930s. Since then, the Court has favored expanded Federal powers, particularly in the area of commerce. Here we examine (1) a landmark case expanding federal power; (2) the doctrine of dual federalism, which restricted federal power; and (3) efforts to extend the Bill of Rights to the states.

MCCULLOCH V. MARYLAND In the case of *McCulloch* v. *Maryland* (1819), the Supreme Court had to choose between two different interpretations of the Constitution. The focus of contention in the case was the Bank of the United States, an institution established by Congress in 1816 to control the issuance of currency. When the state of Maryland levied a tax against the Baltimore branch of the bank, James McCulloch, a cashier, refused to pay the tax. McCulloch's lawyer, Daniel Webster, argued that a state could not tax a bank that had been established by Congress; Maryland's position was that the states had the constitutional right to levy taxes on any institutions within their borders.

In a historic decision, Chief Justice John Marshall agreed with the proponents of states' rights that the Constitution divided sovereignty between the states and the national government. But, he went on, "the government of the Union, though limited in its powers, is supreme within its sphere of action." Although Congress's power to charter a bank was not specifically stated in the Constitution, Marshall argued, such a power could be inferred from the **"necessary and proper"** clause of Article I, which charged Congress "to make all laws which shall be necessary and proper" for executing its powers. The Chief Justice concluded that Congress had the right to legislate with a "vast mass of incidental powers which must be involved in the Constitution, if that instrument be not a splendid bauble." In other words, Congress could exercise a wide range of powers *implied* in the Constitution. It followed that no state could use its concurrent powers (the right to tax, for example) to hinder the national government's execution of its duties.

The decision in *McCulloch* represented a momentous victory for the national government. Marshall advocated a broad interpretation of the Constitution (going beyond those powers explicitly spelled out in the Constitution). Any other approach, he believed, would unwisely restrict the operations of the national government and thus make the problems of governing a growing nation even more difficult.

THE ERA OF DUAL FEDERALISM   After the Civil War, as the United States rapidly moved toward industrialization, the courts formulated a complex doctrine of dual federalism: Clearly separate spheres of regulation were charted for federal and state laws. Advocates of dual federalism argued, for example, that *intra*state commerce could be separated from *inter*state commerce, and that the former fell under the jurisdiction of state law and the latter was the province of federal law. In practice, such distinctions proved difficult to maintain.

A railroad might cross the boundaries of many states and yet be chartered in one particular state. Manufactured goods could be produced in one state and marketed in another.

Under the reign of dual federalism, the Supreme Court on numerous occasions invoked the reserved powers clause of the Tenth Amendment to restrict federal power. In 1871 it held that the salaries of state officials could not be taxed by the national government. In a highly significant commerce case decided in 1918, the Court struck down congressional legislation that had prohibited the interstate transport of goods produced by child labor, arguing that the power to regulate child labor was reserved to the states. And in 1935, the Court again cited the Tenth Amendment in declaring unconstitutional the National Industrial Recovery Act, a crucial piece of New Deal legislation. This decision, however, proved to be among the last of its kind. From 1937 to the present day, the Court has consistently upheld far-reaching federal ventures into social welfare, labor relations, and commerce regulation. At present, there are no clear constitutional limits on the federal power to legislate in the areas of commerce and the general welfare. It has become increasingly difficult to invoke the Tenth Amendment or the doctrine of dual federalism to limit the scope of the national government's powers.

NATIONALIZING THE BILL OF RIGHTS   The courts have also played a key role in applying the Bill of Rights (the first ten amendments) to the states. In *Barron* v. *Baltimore* (1833), the Supreme Court ruled that the restrictions on government power contained in the Bill of Rights could be applied solely to actions of the national government.[8] Only in this century did the Supreme Court gradually "nationalize" its interpretation of the protections found in the Bill of Rights, applying most of its provisions to state governments as well. This is a complex story, to which we will return in Chapter 4.

"New Federalisms"

Changes in the federal system have become commonplace in recent decades.[9] **Table 3–3** reveals

TABLE 3–3
Federal, State, and Local Expenditures (Percent)

Year	Federal*	State†	Local†
1902	35	6	59
1927	31	13	56
1936	50	14	36
1944	91	3	7
1950	60	16	24
1960	60	15	25
1970	56	17	27
1980	55	18	27
1983	58	17	25

*Figures include social security and trust fund expenditures.
†State payments to local governments are shown as local government expenditures; federal grants-in-aid shown as federal expenditures.
SOURCE: *Statistical Abstract of the United States, 1985–1986*, p. 262.

massive shifts in how expenditures—and therefore responsibilities—were allocated in American government since the turn of the century. Both state and federal roles, in terms of expenditures, have grown, while local spending has declined proportionately.

Since 1933, there have been four distinct efforts by American presidents to alter the federal system. Let us look at each one to assess its key elements and its impact.

FDR'S NEW DEAL The first such "new federalism" was President Franklin D. Roosevelt's New Deal, under which the balance of power tilted toward Washington in an effort to deal with serious problems of national scope. Programs initiated in the New Deal period were often referred to as products of cooperative federalism, in which the national government worked directly with local as well as state governments. The key element in cooperative federalism was federal funding for programs administered by state and local governments, including Aid to Families with Dependent Children, construction projects (hospitals, highways, airports, and so on), public health programs, and unemployment compensation.

JOHNSON'S GREAT SOCIETY The second "new federalism" of modern times emerged in President

Lyndon Johnson's Great Society program of the 1960s. Johnson called his program "creative federalism." This translated into a new and greatly increased level of federal intervention in community affairs. In developing more than two hundred new social and economic programs, President Johnson and his supporters in Congress triggered a vast increase in federal involvement in the day-to-day affairs of U.S. citizens. These programs had a strong urban emphasis; in fact, federal funds often went directly to cities, bypassing state governments entirely. Great Society legislation also channeled large amounts of aid to the disadvantaged. Federal money flowed into such previously sacrosanct preserves of state and local authority as education and law enforcement. Between 1960 and 1970, federal aid to the states increased from $7 billion to $24 billion, and the percentage of federal funds going to urban areas increased from 55 percent to 70 percent of the total.

NIXON'S REVENUE SHARING The Johnsonian concept of federalism was at least partially discarded during the administration of President Richard Nixon. The Nixon administration advocated federal financial assistance for the states but urged that the policy-making and administrative functions of the federal government be reduced. To this end, federal grants to the states were restructured in two principal ways: through the introduction of **revenue sharing** programs, under which a certain portion of federal revenues was disbursed among the states; and through the consolidation of many federal funding programs into block grants, which gave states and localities greater flexibility in putting the funds to use. Under the State and Local Assistance Act of 1972, state and local governments received $5 to $6 billion a year for five years in large noncategorical grants, to use as they saw fit. One-third of the funds was earmarked for the states and two-thirds for local governments, apportioned according to a formula that took into account population, per capita income, and other factors.

Revenue sharing set the tone for intergovernmental relations in the 1970s, and it was enthusiastically supported by most state and local authorities. The concept also drew criticism, however.

Many observers charged that under revenue sharing, less money found its way to poorer citizens and poorer communities, while more money wound up in well-to-do suburbs. Overall, revenue sharing suffered from the excessively complex system of local governments in the United States. Of the eighty thousand or so local governments of various sorts in the United States, a quarter do not even employ one full-time employee, and half of these virtually inactive local entities received revenue-sharing funds. As a consequence, money was often distributed in futile, foolish, and wasteful ways.

For these and other reasons, federal efforts to provide direct aid to cities and localities through revenue sharing were not as beneficial as had been expected. With more aid coming from Washington, many states simply allowed the federal government to supply what state legislatures had once furnished. As a result, local governments as well as the states themselves became increasingly dependent on federal aid. In many cases cities received more from Washington than they raised in taxes. Many feared that federal controls would follow this aid, impinging on state and local functions such as education, transportation, and welfare. Government, they argued, was getting away from the people. Critics continued to maintain that revenue sharing involved too little federal control.

REAGAN'S NEW FEDERALISM Responding to these concerns, President Ronald Reagan's administration devised the so-called New Federalism program, the fourth significant development in federal-state relations over the past fifty years. The Reagan strategy was based on three key elements: devolution, decrementalism, and deregulation. *Devolution* involved an increased delegation of authority to state and local governments. Under *decrementalism*, federal aid was cut from $95 billion in 1981 (accounting for 25 percent of state and local expenditures) to $88 billion in 1982 (22 percent of such expenditures). *Deregulation* involved efforts to reduce federal regulation of business and social activities. The centerpiece of the New Federalism was to be a significant reordering of programs between state and federal levels, under which the federal government was to assume responsibility for certain state and local programs (such as Med-

icaid) and the states were to assume responsibility for certain predominantly federal programs (such as Aid to Families with Dependent Children). In addition, several dozen federal aid programs were to be turned back to the states.

The proposal had one major appeal to the states: It allowed for increased state control over many major programs. At the same time, however, many states and localities saw no way to finance these programs at the funding levels established by the federal government. As a result, the New Federalism proposals garnered mixed reviews, and significant opposition in Congress, as well as at the state and local levels, prevented much of the New Federalism program from being enacted.

Nonetheless, in President Reagan's first term there was a clear shift in federal-state relationships. Most important, federal budget cuts in the early 1980s put considerable financial pressure on state and local governments. In most cases, states were able to replace the lost federal money and maintain social programs at levels higher than had been generally anticipated. The one program that suffered most was the extension of welfare benefits to the working poor. After a Reagan administration initiative removed the working poor from welfare rolls, most states did nothing to restore them.[10]

Yet quite a few states actually increased their support of environmental, educational, and health programs cut back at the national level. Further-

TABLE 3–4
Federal Grants-in-Aid, 1960–1987

Year	Total grants (billions)	Grants as percent of:	
		State, local receipts	Federal outlays
1960	$ 7.0	16.8%	7.6%
1965	10.9	17.7	9.2
1970	24.0	22.9	12.3
1975	49.8	29.1	15.0
1980	91.5	31.7	15.5
1985	105.9	23.0	11.2
1987 (est.)	99.1	19.5	10.0

SOURCE: *Statistical Abstract of the United States, 1985–1986*, p. 90.

TABLE 3–5
Consolidation of Federal Aid Programs through Block Grants

New block grants, 1982	Old categorical grants consolidated, 1981
Preventive health care and health services	Home health, rodent control, emergency medical services, fluoridation, rape crisis, hypertension control, health incentive, health education
Alcohol, drug abuse, and mental health services	Community Health Centers Act, Mental Health System Act, two from each: comprehensive alcohol abuse and alcoholism prevention, drug abuse prevention
Social services	Title XX of the Social Security Act
Maternal and child health	Maternal and child health grants, supplemental security income for children, lead poisoning prevention, genetic disease, sudden infant death, hemophilia screening, adolescent health services
Home energy assistance	Low-income energy assistance
Community services	Various programs of Economic Opportunity Act of 1984 including: senior opportunities and services, community food and nutrition; energy conservation and training
Community development	Small cities community development program (cities under 50,000 population); 701 planning grant; neighborhood self-help development; territories program
Primary health care	Community health centers; primary care research and demonstration grants
Education	Thirty-seven elementary and secondary school categorical programs (such as desegregation aid; National Teachers Corps; metric education; consumer education; education of the handicapped, migrants, the deprived, neglected or delinquent children, and gifted children)

SOURCE: Thomas R. Dye, *Politics in States and Communities*, 6th ed. © 1988, table 3–4, p. 74. Reprinted by permission of Prentice-Hall, Inc., Englewood Cliffs, N.J.

more, many local governments joined civil rights groups in defending the very quotas and affirmative action programs the Reagan administration was attacking.

In addition, revenue-sharing programs were retained only for counties and municipalities; the states themselves were dropped. And in 1985, the Reagan administration made further efforts to eliminate the revenue-sharing program altogether as an economy measure, a move sharply resisted by many local officials. Clearly, the administration had won part of its battle to reverse the patterns of federal-state relationships. But the human and social costs of these adjustments have been high. Shifting taxes from federal to state and local levels has resulted in greater economic inequality.

Table 3–4 offers a clear picture of federal-state-local financial relations over the last three decades.

During the 1960s and 1970s, the federal government supplied state and local governments with an increasing proportion of their annual revenues; these outlays also grew into an ever-greater share of the federal budget. As a consequence, federal aid to states and localities played a larger role in shaping programs at the state and local levels. With the election of the Reagan administration, the picture changed dramatically. States were left to raise more of their own revenues. The federal contribution to state and local governments dropped from 31.7 percent of revenues in 1980 to an estimated 19.5 percent in 1987. **Table 3–5** spells out how federally funded programs were consolidated into block grants in the 1980s.

Responsibilities of the States

Most of the nation's public business is conducted on the state and local levels; there most political conflicts are settled and most public policy decisions are made and carried out (see **Table 3–6**). States and localities handle most of the workaday business of government—schooling, policing, licensing. And the states allow for experiment, innovation, and local adaptation. For example, individual states were the first to eliminate the death penalty, provide old age pensions, and regulate railroads. States also pioneered in developing the income tax, child labor laws, and the vote for women and eighteen-year-olds. State governments can occasionally respond more swiftly than the federal government to popular sentiment—through processes such as the **initiative** (whereby citizens can put a proposal on the ballot) or the **referendum** (whereby citizens can vote on a piece of legislation through the ballot).

State and local governments carry significant responsibilities for public policy especially in the areas of education, transportation, health and welfare, criminal justice, the environment, civil rights, and taxation. We turn now to these issues.

Education

States and localities have substantial latitude when it comes to education: They supply most of the funding for public schools, determine the content of school curricula, set teacher qualifications, and decide how education funds should be spent. Higher education also is principally a state responsibility. Federal funds account for less than 10 percent of all education expenditures.

TABLE 3–6
Federal and State-Local Shares of Expenditures by Policy Areas, 1927–1983 (Percent)

	1927		1938		1970		1980		1983	
	Federal*	State and local	Federal*	State and local	Federal*	State and local	Federal*	State and local	Federal*	State and local
National defense	100	0	100	0	100	0	100	0	100	0
Space research	100	0	100	0	100	0	100	0	100	0
Postal service	100	0	100	0	100	0	100	0	100	0
Education	1	99	6	94	15	85	15	85	13	87
Highways	1	99	23	77	23	77	23	77	20	80
Welfare	6	94	13	87	41	59	52	48	50	50
Health and hospitals	18	82	19	81	34	66	31	69	27	73
Natural resources	31	69	81	19	77	23	85	15	77	23
Housing and urban renewal	—	—	—	—	56	44	67	33	65	35

*Federal grants-in-aid are shown as federal expenditures.
SOURCE: *Statistical Abstract of the United States, 1985–1986*, p. 264.

A pleasant-looking elementary school class, with movable desks, an integrated student group, and a rather good-spirited teacher. Education is one of the major functions of state and local governments. Without federal intervention, we should note, this integrated class might never have come about. *(Michal Heron/Woodfin Camp & Associates)*

Transportation

Highway location, construction policies, funding for highway projects, waterways, airports, railroads, and shipping, gasoline and motor vehicle taxation, and regulation of traffic—these are among the many responsibilities of state and local governments in the area of transportation. Expenditures for transportation compose the second largest item in most state budgets. Although the federal government supplies about 30 percent of funding for transportation and plays a substantial role in the construction and maintenance of the interstate highway network and all major airports, the states and localities carry the primary burden.

Health and Welfare

The states administer the largest programs in the fields of health and welfare—Aid to Families with Dependent Children (AFDC), Medicaid, food stamps, and unemployment compensation. Despite the heavy impact of federal funding in these areas, state governments generally decide for each program how much is to be spent, the rules of eligibility, and the method of administration.

States and localities also maintain facilities for people who cannot care for themselves, such as orphans, the elderly, and those who are mentally or physically ill.

Criminal Justice

Although the federal government does have some important criminal justice responsibilities, state and local governments are charged with protecting public safety. State and local governments employ more than 250,000 police officers, who bear the brunt of law enforcement in the United States. Criminal prosecution and maintenance of courts are largely state and local matters. States and counties maintain extensive jail facilities; more than 90 percent of all convicts are incarcerated in nonfederal prisons.

Other Responsibilities

Protection of the *physical environment* has become an increasingly important government responsibility at all levels, but most environmental matters are handled by states and localities. Maintenance

Criminal justice, including the maintenance of prisons, is a state and local function—and an expensive one. In recent years the American criminal justice system has come under strong criticism; overcrowded conditions and crime *in* prisons have made many dubious about the possibilities for rehabilitation in such an environment. *(David Powers/Stock, Boston)*

of streets and parks, zoning regulations, provision of basic public utilities, rubbish collection, sewage and water systems, the monitoring of air and water pollution—all these tasks must be handled by state and local governments, with some help from the federal government.

Civil rights matters also fall largely within the jurisdiction of the states. The enforcement of both state and federal civil rights laws—especially in the areas of employment, schools, and housing—is generally handled by states and communities. Experience has shown how complicated and frustrating it can be to try to make civil rights meaningful over the nation when local and state governments pit themselves against federal power.

Finally, states and localities are responsible for many forms of *taxation*—sales taxes, property assessments, state income taxes. In raising hundreds of billions of dollars in taxes every year, they must decide who will bear the tax burden, how much that burden will be, and how the funds should be spent. It should be noted that the much-heralded "tax revolt" of the late 1970s began in California as a protest against state and local government tax policies.

Tensions in the Federal System

The politics and structure of the American federal system have changed over the years. Population has shifted, economic and technological advances have been made, investment patterns have favored different areas at different times, and public works have deteriorated. All these factors have shaped the current federal system. Yet in evolving to its present form, the system has sometimes developed inequities, inconsistencies, and inefficiencies. Let us now examine (1) the regional rivalries that create tension in the federal system; (2) the types of issues that strain federal arrangements; and (3) one key issue—the infrastructure—that challenges the federal system's capacity to respond to pressing public concerns.

Regional Rivalries

Under a federal system, the federal government can shift resources from wealthier to poorer areas; specific states can be earmarked to receive more federal funds than they contribute in tax dollars. During the Depression, the South, which was par-

State Taxes: The Burden Varies

In 1987, nine states had no individual income taxes on wages: Connecticut, Florida, Nevada, New Hampshire, South Dakota, Tennessee, Texas, Washington, and Wyoming. Four states had no corporate income taxes: Nevada, Texas, Washington, and Wyoming. And five states had no general sales taxes: Alaska, Delaware, Montana, New Hampshire, and Oregon.

In 1984, the heaviest state tax burden (as a percent of personal income) fell on residents of Alaska, Wyoming, New Mexico, Montana, New York, and Minnesota. Residents of Texas, Florida, Missouri, New Hampshire, and Connecticut paid the lowest percentage of their personal income as state taxes.

ticularly impoverished, received an economic boost in the form of increased federal spending. Today, the Southern states, along with the other so-called Sun Belt states in the Southwest and West, still get back more than they contribute. Meanwhile, states in the so-called Frost Belt, the industrial Northeast and Midwest, generally pay out more to the federal government than they receive.[11]

In recent years, Frost Belt mayors and governors have complained loudly about this inequity in federal disbursements, and have called for increased federal assistance to their region. Once an area starts to depend on government assistance, however, it is difficult for either the president or the Congress to cut those funds. Any politician running for office in a state threatened with a significant reduction in federal funding would be hard pressed not to denounce it.

Tensions between the Sun Belt and the Frost Belt have emerged in the political arena as well. Since World War II, the Sun Belt's rate of population growth has considerably exceeded that of the Frost Belt. From 1950 to 1975, Frost Belt population grew by 32 percent, whereas the Sun Belt increase was 60 percent. **Figure 3–2** (page 104) shows more recent directions of movement. As a result of this large population shift, the Sun Belt states gained a substantial number of seats in the House in 1982 and in the Electoral College in 1984.

This trend could have important implications for U.S. political life. Sun Belt voters generally have a more conservative political outlook, so liberal federal legislation and liberal presidential candidates may encounter increasing difficulties. A large question mark, however, hangs over these calculations—California, a Sun Belt state that has been growing especially fast. Although its citizens spearheaded nationwide efforts to cut state and local taxes in the late 1970s and early 1980s, California by no means ranks as a clearly conservative state. In fact, it has been an innovator in environmental and energy legislation, and its large and growing Chicano and Asian-American populations will have a growing—and possibly liberal—impact on national politics.

Economic pressures have also strained interstate relations. As the states compete with one another for industry, they commonly grant special tax breaks to corporations, attempt to keep union activity low, reduce corporate income taxes, and alter state economic policies to suit large businesses. States now take pride in enticing industries away from neighboring states, even when those neighboring states desperately need the jobs and tax revenues. As an example, in recent years New York and New Jersey have engaged in a fierce competition for area businesses, with New Jersey luring numerous "back-office" operations from Wall Street and even pursuing such glamour corporations as NBC. The balance sheet weighs in New Jersey's favor—the Garden State offers lower

FIGURE 3–2   **Americans on the Move, 1980–1985**

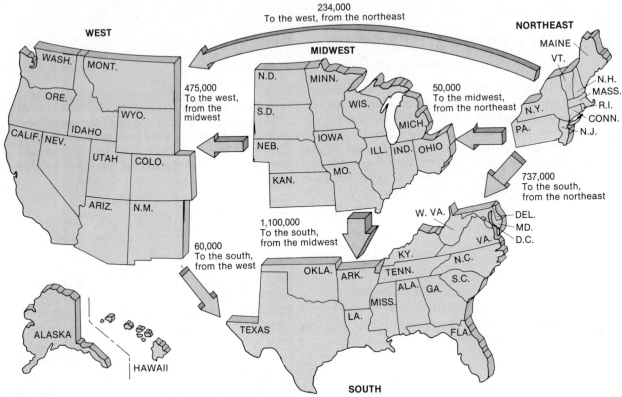

SOURCE: Thomas R. Dye, *Politics in States and Communities*, 6th ed., © 1988, figure 1–3, p. 12.
Reprinted by permission of Prentice-Hall, Inc., Englewood Cliffs, N.J.

taxes, fewer union restrictions, and lower utility costs—while New York City boasts the unparalleled prestige of a world capital.

These destructive state-versus-state rivalries could be remedied by national action—establishing a uniform federal tax rate for corporations, national health coverage, uniform levels of workers' compensation, and a uniform policy on trade unions. However, at this point, no consensus has emerged to press for such wide-ranging federal action, and the only beneficiaries of the intense interstate competition are the corporations, which win huge concessions from states and cities.

Issues That Strain Federalism

Individual states are ill-equipped politically to address many of the most pressing issues in Amer-

ican life. For example, pollution problems in heavily urban areas—including groundwater contamination by toxic chemicals—differ significantly from pollution concerns in the Great Lakes and major river systems. The problems faced by Detroit have much more in common with those of Boston, Houston, and Atlanta than they do with issues significant in northern Michigan. So how can state governments dominated by rural, small town, and suburban votes be expected to respond vigorously to big-city problems like street crime, industrial unemployment, welfare, and housing?

Then, too, cities often experience jurisdictional problems of their own. Most metropolitan areas contain dozens or even hundreds of separate government jurisdictions, and power is often fragmented among many different boards and authorities.

By the early days of 1988, many big-city mayors

Infrastructure: A new overpass in San Diego, California, and the rusting support beams of the Williamsburg Bridge in New York City. Some states and localities are far more burdened with transportation maintenance and construction costs than are others. If the federal government cuts its funding and the states and localities do not have the funds to repair old systems or initiate new ones, who will bear the responsibility? *(Robert Burroughs/Black Star; AP/Wide World Photos)*

were determined to place urban problems at center stage during the 1988 presidential campaign. Meeting in Las Vegas, the mayors sought to counteract what they called the Reagan administration's abandonment of the cities. One Reagan administration domestic policy advisor stated flatly, "It's our view that cities are not mentioned in the Constitution." The administration wanted to strengthen the role of the states, but many mayors believed this was being done at the expense of the cities.[12]

It is instructive to note that the basic government structures of today are the same as those that existed when the Constitution was written: states, counties, and municipalities. But the boundaries and political divisions we have inherited are not necessarily the most useful at present. Perhaps a new federal arrangement, with the United States divided into regions and enlarged metropolitan areas, would serve us better—or, at least, more efficiently—in the twenty-first century.

Infrastructure—Whose Problem?

Infrastructure became the catchword of the late twentieth century. The infrastructure encompasses the entire system of public works that are integral to the smooth functioning of an industrial society: bridges, highways, sewage treatment plants, streets, water systems, port facilities, and so on. Deterioration of these public works threatens the normal operation of economic and social life.

More than a decade ago, U.S. Department of Transportation officials estimated that 45 percent of the nation's bridges were structurally deficient or obsolete, including 126,000 that were seriously unsafe; that more than eight thousand miles of interstate highway were crumbling, and two-thirds of other major roads were in need of repair; and that about 25 percent of bus and subway systems needed replacement. In addition, hundreds of cities need new water and sewage systems. The

COMPARATIVE PERSPECTIVE

Federalism in West Germany

West German political life was reorganized after World War II under the Basic Law, promulgated in 1949. Put together by representatives of the three occupying powers (the United States, France, and Great Britain) and various German leaders, the Basic Law was supposed to be a temporary arrangement providing a constitutional framework that would last until the two portions of Germany, divided after the war, were reunited. The experiences of the Nazi period made the occupying authorities suspicious of centralized power in the new German state, and so the Basic Law provided for a federal system. The Federal Republic of Germany, or West Germany, is currently the only major European state that has such a federal system.

The Federal Republic is organized into ten constituent states (*Länder*). The spheres of authority of the states and the federal government are set out explicitly in the Basic Law. The most important powers of the *Länder* pertain to education, law enforcement, and cultural affairs. The two levels of government jointly exercise some powers, including those having to do with transportation, energy development, and criminal justice. In most cases, the administration of federal legislation is left to the states; the federal government plays a supervisory role, rather than a directly administrative one. As a result, the Federal Republic has a relatively small central bureaucracy.

A unique feature of the West German federal arrangement is the role of the states in selecting the Federal Council, the upper house of the parliament. The forty-one seats in the Federal Council are allocated to the states on the basis of population, and each state delegation in the Federal Council casts its votes as a unit based on instructions received from its state legislature. The powers of the Federal Council are considerable. All drafts of national legislation, for example, must go first to the Federal Council for approval, and about half the bills passed by the popularly elected lower house must be approved by the Council. All executive ordinances must gain majority support in the Council. As a result, the German Federal Council is one of the most important upper chambers in any democratic government, rivaling (though not equaling) the U.S. Senate in power and prestige.

The German states also participate in the selection of the president of the Federal Republic and in the selection of judges for the Federal courts. On the other hand, the states' activities are limited by certain provisions of the Basic Law. The protections of human and civil rights set out in the Basic Law also apply to each *Länder*. The death penalty, for example, is outlawed in the Basic Law and cannot be employed by any of the states.

As in the United States, there has been a gradual trend toward greater centralization of decision making at the national level. Overall, however, the *Länder* have remained a very significant force in West German political life.

deteriorating infrastructure has become an urgent political priority, and numerous politicians have called for action to remedy the situation. Yet throughout the 1980s local bond issues for new public works went down to defeat more often than not, and most proposals to raise taxes met with fierce resistance.

In the past, state and local governments have funded about 75 percent of infrastructure costs, but these governments are facing great difficulties in raising additional revenues. It appears that only a national approach to the problem can generate the resources necessary to deal with it. Some observers have called on the federal government to make a first-ever inventory of needed public works projects. Others have argued for the establishment of a national capital budget ranging up to $100 billion a year. To cope with infrastructure decay, a federal solution—using national resources to establish priorities and raise needed money—may be the only viable response.

Federal Intervention

On several occasions the federal government has concluded that some or many states were failing to serve democratic principles or protect citizens' health and welfare. In such cases the national government has intervened (however reluctantly) to set state governments on a more democratic or appropriate path. We now consider three examples of federal intervention, involving (1) reapportionment of legislative seats, (2) voting rights, and (3) raising the drinking age.

Reapportionment

In 1900, three-fifths of the population of the United States lived in rural areas; by 1960 over two-thirds of Americans lived in cities or suburbs. State legislatures, however, did not change to reflect this trend toward urbanization. In 1962, for example, the 24 inhabitants of Stratton, Vermont, enjoyed the same level of representation in the state's house of representatives as the entire city of Burlington, with a population of 35,531. At the same time, Los Angeles County's 6,038,771 residents received the same state senate representation as the 14,196 inhabitants of three northern California counties. Such disparities left urban dwellers throughout the country in a far weaker political position than rural constituents.

In *Reynolds* v. *Sims* (1964), the Supreme Court ruled that state legislative districts must be apportioned strictly according to population. In the words of Chief Justice Earl Warren, "Legislators represent people, not trees or acres."[13] Basic to a representative form of government, the opinion continued, was the citizen's right to cast a vote that counts in full. Accordingly, any substantial disparity in the population of legislative districts

would have the same effect as allotting a different number of votes to different individuals. This principle of "one man, one vote" was later extended by the Court to cover both houses of state legislatures.[14]

Political scientists still argue over the political consequences of the widespread **reapportionment** of legislative districts that followed the Court's rulings. Some contend that well-apportioned states are scarcely distinguishable in policy making from malapportioned ones. Perhaps reapportionment has simply shifted power from rural anti-city interests to suburban anti-city interests. In the late 1960s, for example, the New York State legislature declined to provide significant help to the New York City subway system, which carries 2 million riders a day, but did underwrite the losses of the Long Island Railroad, which carries 100,000 suburban commuters daily. Perhaps, too, the effects of reapportionment have been more subtle and less dramatic than its proponents had expected.

The Voting Rights Act

In the early 1960s, when civil rights groups launched an all-out effort to register black voters in the South, they ran up against state election laws intended to impede and restrict the registration of blacks. In 1965 the Reverend Martin Luther King, Jr., led a dramatic march on the Alabama state capitol, in Montgomery, to challenge these laws. Television captured scenes of Alabama state police attacking marchers who tried to cross one of the city's bridges. Such scenes stunned the country and propelled efforts to pass the Voting Rights Act of 1965. Under this landmark legislation, federal officials were empowered to register voters and to suspend literacy tests in areas where less than 50 percent of the voting-age population was registered for, or had voted in, the 1964 national election. Under this formula the act applied initially to six Southern states (Alabama, Georgia, Louisiana, Mississippi, South Carolina, Virginia); Alaska; thirty-four counties in North Carolina; and one county each in Maine, Arizona, and Idaho.

The Voting Rights Act, which has been extremely effective, clearly demonstrated that national intervention into matters once handled by

August 6, 1965. One hundred years after the Civil War, President Lyndon Johnson signs the bill that, once effectively enforced, would finally provide adequate protections for black voters. The consequences of the Voting Rights Act were dramatic: Black registration increased tremendously. *(UPI/Bettmann Newsphotos)*

the states could rectify serious and persistent deprivation of democratic rights. Two years after passage of the act, black registration in the South had increased by more than 1,280,000. The percentage of blacks in the South registered to vote jumped

from 33 percent in 1964 to 59 percent in 1972. And by 1980, more than 1,800 blacks held public office in the South (see **Table 3–7**).[15]

The act was renewed in 1970 and again in 1975, and its provisions were extended to bar discrimination against Hispanic-Americans, American Indians, and other minorities. In addition, certain states and counties with substantial non-English-speaking minorities were required to supply bilingual election materials.

In 1982, President Reagan recommended that the Voting Rights Act not be renewed for a third time. He maintained that the act discriminated against the South and placed a stranglehold on state and local government. In the end, however, proponents of extending the act won the day, and even gained the support of the Reagan administration. The provision requiring bilingual ballots and election materials was extended for ten years, and a controversial section requiring Justice Department preclearance of all election law changes was extended for twenty-five years.

The Drinking Age

Each state has its own laws regulating the age when men and women are permitted to drink alcoholic beverages. But now the Congress, through its budgetary powers, has sharply influenced those state laws. Because of this congressional pressure, the nation now has, with only a few ex-

TABLE 3–7
Black Elected Officials in Key States Covered by the Voting Rights Act

State	1968 Number	(Percent)	1980 Number	(Percent)
Alabama	24	(0.6)	238	(5.7)
Georgia	21	(0.3)	249	(3.7)
Louisiana	37	(0.8)	363	(7.7)
Mississippi	29	(0.6)	387	(7.3)
North Carolina	10	(0.2)	247	(4.7)
South Carolina	11	(0.4)	238	(7.4)
Virginia	24	(0.7)	91	(3.0)

SOURCE: Joint Center for Political Studies.

The freedom to drink! Though not protected explicitly by the Bill of Rights, some—especially under 21—view it as essential in the "pursuit of happiness." Should public safety on highways be more important than the liberty of younger citizens to have access to alcohol? For the moment, the nation has decided to rank safety higher. *(Arthur Grace/Stock, Boston)*

ceptions, a uniform drinking age—21. The story of how this came about illustrates an emerging new direction for contemporary federalism.

In the early 1970s many states lowered the drinking age to 18. But within a decade, a movement developed to raise the drinking age again. Fueling this drive was an increasing concern about the effects of drunk driving among teenagers. By 1984 roughly half the states had raised the drinking age to 21, while others set it at 19 or 20. Mothers Against Drunk Drivers (MADD), a powerful grass-roots organization, together with other public-interest groups, pressured state legislatures, arguing that drunk driving was the leading cause of death among teenagers. Indeed, national statistics showed that teens *were* more likely to be involved in drunk-driving accidents. Opponents of federal intervention maintained, however, that teenagers suffered no more casualties than drivers aged 21 to 25.

Congress was called on to act. Some members of Congress asserted that national regulation of the drinking age violated the principle of federalism because this was a matter traditionally under state jurisdiction. But the congressional legislation that finally emerged did not create a uniform drinking age directly. Instead, it required that 10 percent of federal highway funds be withheld from any state that failed to raise the drinking age to 21. States could choose to ignore this rule and thereby forfeit some of their highway money.

Advocates of this novel approach contended that, as with the 55-mile-an-hour speed limit, this issue turned on a compelling national interest in health and safety. Therefore, Congress could legitimately draw on the power of the purse to apply leverage to state governments. Opponents called this federal blackmail. President Reagan expressed reservations early on, but in 1984 he signed the bill into law. Within a few years, almost all the states had complied. Thus, while efforts to raise the drinking age began in the states themselves, Congress acted only after the idea gained considerable momentum.

When Intervention Fails

The Constitution strikes a delicate balance between the federal government and the states, a balance that sometimes skews power disproportionately to the states. A key example of the power of the states under U.S. federalism is the amending process, as the following example—on the ratification fight for the Equal Rights Amendment—illustrates.

In 1972 both houses of Congress passed the Equal Rights Amendment by votes considerably larger than the two-thirds required for a constitutional amendment. Most national political leaders of both parties, including President Nixon (and later Presidents Ford and Carter), endorsed the

FIGURE 3–3
The ERA Ratification Battle

Voted for the ERA

Voted against the ERA

Voted to rescind: Idaho, Kentucky, Nebraska, South Dakota, Tennessee

amendment, which read simply: "Equal rights under law shall not be denied or abridged by the United States or by any State on account of sex."

As with any amendment, approval by three-fourths of state legislatures (or state constitutional ratifying conventions) was necessary to add it to the Constitution. That amounts to thirty-eight of the fifty states. At first, passage seemed assured: Within a few years, twenty-five states had ratified. But by the mid-1970s an anti-ERA movement showed growing strength. Opponents argued that the ERA would deny women many important legal protections, would weaken the traditional family, and would prompt undue intrusion by federal courts into local communities. Scare tactics—call-

ing to mind unisex bathrooms and women on the front lines in wartime—began to have political impact. Meanwhile, ERA supporters argued that an explicit, all-encompassing, constitutional guarantee of equal rights for women would eliminate the need to fight battle after battle in different policy areas. The ERA struggle took on a highly charged symbolic significance.

State approval of the amendment stalled at thirty-five. Then ERA supporters appealed to Congress for more time to win its ratification—beyond the seven-year period originally granted. In the meantime, five states that had passed the ERA voted to rescind approval. Both these developments carried intriguing political implications.

Could a state rescind its approval? The Constitution is silent on that point. Could Congress legitimately extend the time limit? Opponents argued that the rules were being changed in the middle of the game. Nonetheless, Congress did vote for a three-year extension, until 1982. Close battles ensued in several states—including Illinois, Florida, and North Carolina—but the necessary three-fourths approval was never obtained (see **Figure 3–3**).

The ERA ratification battle, like the battle to ratify the Constitution itself, demonstrates the key role of the states in basic political change. It is interesting to note that the U.S. public has shown substantial approval of the ERA for two decades. A survey in 1980 found that 72 percent of respondents supported its passage, including 70 percent of females and 75 percent of males.[16] Does this imply that the amending process is sometimes undemocratic?

Conclusions

It is one of the happy accidents of the federal system that a single courageous state may . . . serve as a laboratory and try novel social and economic experiments without risk to the rest of the country. *Associate Justice Louis Brandeis*

The states are prisoners of their own freedom. *Barney Frank, Massachusetts state legislator, 1979*[17]

Half of all Americans now live in states other than the ones in which they were born. Twenty percent of the country's population moves every year. Problems no longer come cut to state-size shapes—if they ever did. As we have noted, major cities often face issues of national scope, and many environmental, health, energy, and economic problems cannot be confined within convenient state boundaries. Given these facts, does it make sense to remain tied to the concept of state government?

Those who argue for the continued significance of the states can draw on traditional arguments for decentralization. States and localities still do much of the workaday business of government—schooling, policing, licensing. And, as Justice Brandeis noted, the states do provide many different arenas for experiment, innovation, and local adaptation.

Elimination of the death penalty, provision for old age pensions, regulation of railroads, and decriminalization of marijuana were all first accomplished at the state level, and states pioneered in developing the income tax, child labor laws, and the vote for women and eighteen-year-olds. States also keep government closer to the people and give room for popular participation in policy making—through processes like the initiative and referendum. Yet we must also question the worth of providing fifty separate jurisdictions with fifty kinds of marriage and divorce laws, criminal courts, prison systems, alcoholic beverage controls, tax systems, educational and welfare arrangements, and so on. Is this an indication of a healthy localism or of a confusing lack of national standards?

In toting up the balance sheet of democracy in relation to U.S. federalism, we must note that the denial of basic rights to black citizens was probably made easier by the division of powers between the state and national governments. It can be argued, of course, that had the nation not been divided into states, a form of national segregation may have resulted. In such a case, however, a clear confrontation with the reality of racism might have come earlier, and the issues been resolved more thoroughly in a democratic direction. On balance, federalism sheltered racism and blocked solutions to racial problems.

Another negative aspect of our federal system was the long-standing malapportionment of state legislative districts. In this instance, too, democracy was damaged, and that damage clearly grew out of the politics that federal arrangements made possible.

A third negative factor has been the common tendency of many states to neglect minorities, the poor, and other relatively powerless groups. Even more than the federal government, state governments are vulnerable to domination by well-organized and financially powerful groups.

The major question that we cannot answer is what U.S. political life would be like in the absence of the current federal system. What would a unitary United States look like, or a United States divided along regional lines—say, into five or six major areas? What would we lose if we dismantled the existing states? More to the point of this book, what would democracy gain or lose? It is hard to escape the conclusion that democracy would lose rather little.

GLOSSARY TERMS

federal system

unitary system

inherent powers

delegated powers

McCulloch v. *Maryland*

implied powers

concurrent powers

reserved powers

Bill of Rights

due process of law

equal protection of the laws

full faith and credit

enabling act

necessary and proper [clause]

revenue sharing

initiative

referendum

reapportionment

NOTES

[1]For an overview of federalism see William Riker, *Federalism* (Boston: Little, Brown, 1964); and Ivo D. Duchacek, *Comparative Federalism: The Territorial Dimension of Politics* (University Press of America, 1987).

[2]For discussion of the legal issues involved in the distribution of power under federalism, see William B. Lockhard, Yale Komisar, and Jesse H. Choper, *The American Constitution* (St. Paul, Minn.: West, 1975), part II.

[3]4 Wheaton 316.

[4]314 U.S. 160 (1941).

[5]Quoted in Samuel H. Beer, "The Idea of the Nation," *New Republic* (July 1982), pp. 19–26.

[6]*Ibid.*

[7]See Alfred H. Kelly and Winfred A. Harbison, *The American Constitution: Its Origin and Development*, 6th ed. (New York: Norton, 1982).

[8]7 Peters 243 (1833).

[9]For discussion of the changing federal-state bargain, see Daniel J. Elazar, "The Shaping of Intergovernmental Relations in the Twentieth Century," *Annals of the Academy of Political and Social Science* (May 1965), pp. 11–22; and *The American Partnership* (University of Chicago Press, 1962); also see Deil S. Wright, *Understanding Intergovernmental Relations*, 2nd ed. (Monterey, Calif.: Brooks/Cole, 1982).

[10]John Herbers, "State Finance Aid Programs Reduced by U.S., Study Finds," *New York Times*, June 10, 1984.

[11]On the shifting geography of federalism, see Kirkpatrick Sale, *Power Shift* (New York: Vintage, 1976); and Thomas R. Dye, *Politics in States and Communities*, 6th ed. (Englewood Cliffs, N.J.: Prentice-Hall, 1988), chaps. 1, 3.

[12]*New York Times*, Dec. 14, 1987, p. 12.

[13]377 U.S. 533.

[14]See Robert B. McKay, *Reapportionment: The Law and Politics of Equal Representation* (New York: Twentieth Century Fund, 1965).

[15]Howard Ball and Dale Krane, *Compromised Compliance: Implementation of the 1965 Voting Rights Act* (Westport, Conn.: Greenwood, 1982).

[16]J. R. Kluegel and E. R. Smith, *Beliefs about Inequality* (New York: Aldine, 1986), pp. 218, 222.

[17]Both quotes cited in Barney Frank, "Sorry, States," *New Republic*, Dec. 29, 1979.

SELECTED READINGS

FEDERALISM: AN OVERVIEW

The constitutional argument that states were and still should be primarily responsible for the **protection of individual rights** in the federal system is examined (and rejected) in Michael Kent Curtis, *No State Shall Abridge: The Fourteenth Amendment and the Bill of Rights* (Durham, N.C.: Duke University Press, 1986). Compare that argument with Raoul Berger, *Federalism: The Founders' Design* (Norman, Okla.: University of Oklahoma Press, 1987).

Among the more provocative discussions of **federalism** are William Riker, *Federalism* (Boston: Little, Brown, 1964); Ivo D. Duchacek, *Comparative Federalism: The Territorial Dimension of Politics* (University Press of America, 1987); and Valerie Earle, ed., *Federalism: Infinite Variety in Theory and Practice* (Itasca, Ill.: F. E. Peacock, 1968).

THE EVOLUTION OF FEDERALISM

A description of the **recent evolution** of the federal system can be found in Lawrence E. Gelfand and Robert J. Neymeyer, *Changing Patterns in American Federal-State Relations during the 1950s, the 1960s, and the 1970s* (Iowa City: University of Iowa Press, 1985); Ann Bowman and Richard C. Kearny, *The Resurgence of the States* (Englewood Cliffs, N.J.: Prentice-Hall, 1986); and Lewis G. Bender and James A. Stever, eds., *Administering the New Federalism* (Boulder: Westview, 1986).

For general **overviews,** see Samuel H. Beer, "The Idea of the Nation," *New Republic,* July 1982, pp. 19–26; and Daniel J. Elazar, *The American Partnership: Intergovernmental Cooperation in the Nineteenth-Century United States* (Chicago: University of Chicago Press, 1962). For further discussion of the **Supreme Court's role** in the evolution of federalism, see Alfred H. Kelly and Winfred A. Harbison, *The American Constitution: Its Origins and Development,* 6th ed. (New York: Norton, 1982).

The **development** of federalism is described in Daniel J. Elazar, "The Shaping of Intergovernmental Relations in the Twentieth Century," *Annals of the Academy of Political and Social Science* (May 1965), pp. 11–22; and Deil S. Wright, *Understanding Intergovernmental Relations,* 2nd ed. (Monterey, Calif.: Brooks/Cole, 1982).

For a discussion of **recent federal programs,** see James A. Duffy, *Domestic Affairs* (New York: Simon & Schuster, 1978), chap. 10; Richard P. Nathan et al., *Revenue Sharing: The Second Round* (Washington: Brookings Institution, 1977); and John L. Palmer and Isabell V. Sawhill, eds., *The Reagan Experiment: An Assessment of America's Changing Domestic Priorities* (Cambridge, Mass.: Ballinger, 1984).

RESPONSIBILITIES OF THE STATES

For discussions of the states and state-level **policy making** from various points of view, see Ira Sharkansky, *The Maligned States: Policy Accomplishments, Problems, and Opportunities,* 2nd ed. (New York: McGraw-Hill, 1977); Terry Sanford, *Storm over the States* (New York: McGraw-Hill, 1967); and Thomas R. Dye, *Politics, Economics and the Public* (Chicago: Rand McNally, 1966).

TENSIONS IN THE FEDERAL SYSTEM

On the **geographic shift** of political power in the United States, see Kirkpatrick Sale, *Power Shift* (New York: Vintage, 1976); Thomas R. Dye, *Politics in States and Communities,* 6th ed. (Englewood Cliffs, N.J.: Prentice-Hall, 1988), chap. 1. On **cities and infrastructure,** see Roscoe C. Martin, *The Cities and the Federal System* (New York: Atherton, 1965). A wide range of issues is covered in Jeffrey R. Henig, *Public Policy and Federalism: Issues in State and Local Politics* (New York: St. Martin's, 1985).

For case study materials in **municipal government** within a federal system, see Edward T. Jennings et al., ed., *From Nation to States: The Small Cities Community Development Block Grant Program* (Albany, N.Y.: SUNY Press, 1986); and R. Allen Hays, *The Federal Government and Urban Housing* (Albany, N.Y.: SUNY Press, 1985).

FEDERAL INTERVENTION

For discussions of **reapportionment,** see Robert B. McKay, *Reapportionment: The Law and Politics of Equal Representation* (New York: Twentieth Century Fund, 1965); and Gordon E. Baker, *The Reapportionment Revolution* (New York: Random House, 1966).

An enormous amount has been written about **voting rights** in the United States. For a good introduction, see the record of the voting rights hearings before Subcommittee No. 5 of the Committee on the Judiciary, House of Representatives, 89th Congress, 1st session, on H.R. 6400 (Washington: U.S. Government Printing Office, 1965). Also see Howard Ball and Dale Krane, *Compromised Compliance: Implementation of the 1965 Voting Rights Act* (Westport, Conn.: Greenwood Press, 1982).

4

THE EVOLUTION OF RIGHTS AND LIBERTIES

Democracy with a Human Face

CHAPTER OUTLINE

***The Bill of Rights and Constitutional
    Protections***
Civil Rights
Basic Social Rights
Government Repression

August 1968. "Socialism with a human face" comes to an end, as Warsaw Pact tanks roll into Prague. A more liberal society, with free debate and discussion, was apparently not to be tolerated by the Soviet Union. *(P.P./Magnum)*

In 1968 a reform movement surged through the Communist Party of Czechoslovakia. The reformers, including several leaders of the party, wanted to "liberalize" political life in that country. They envisioned a socialist society free from official repression, in which dissent was possible, people with differing ideas could exchange opinions openly, individuals were protected against arbitrary arrest, and the basic civil liberties of citizens were honored by the authorities. The Czech reformers called their movement "socialism with a human face," to signify the shift from an oppressive to a humane form of socialist society. In August 1968, however, the liberalization movement was crushed by Soviet and other Warsaw Pact troops, with whose backing a totalitarian regime was reinstalled.

For the Czech reformers, socialism alone was far from enough: Only if socialism were humanized through respect for individual and group rights would a just society be established. The same holds true for democracy. For the democratic creed to reach its full potential, majority rule alone is not sufficient; it must be accompanied by adequate provisions for individual liberties and rights. Without such protections, democracy can degenerate into yet another system of oppression and exploitation, despite the noble intentions embodied in the concept of majority rule.

The theory behind **civil liberties** and **civil rights** is simple enough: Civil liberties are designed to protect citizens from the abuses of government; civil rights guarantee that all citizens receive equal treatment under the law regardless of race, gender, national origin, or religion. Yet while these concepts sound straightforward, they have been exceedingly difficult to implement. In the eighteenth century, at the time the Constitution and the Bill of Rights were written, there was a conception of fundamental rights and liberties based on the ideals of classical liberalism. This conception encompassed freedom of speech and freedom of religion, protection against the arbitrary exercise of government power, and protection of property rights. Other rights and liberties were not fully accepted, however. The right to vote—the most basic democratic right—was not acknowledged to apply to women or blacks. And the concept of equal treatment under the law was only in its infancy at the end of the eighteenth century.

The realities of twentieth-century life have altered our conceptions of rights and liberties. Eighteenth-century ideas of individual rights now are widely viewed as basic but insufficient. Modern societies must face not only the problem of arbitrary and unrepresentative government, as the American revolutionaries did, but also the complex problems posed by industrial civilization. Accordingly, the rights and liberties of a twentieth-century citizen are generally acknowledged to include the right to form trade unions, the right to a reasonably safe and healthy environment, the right to an education, and so on. The classical liberal view of basic rights and liberties had to be broadened considerably to cover contemporary social, political, and economic realities.

Nevertheless, this chapter opens with an examination of eighteenth-century rights and liberties, because even these long-accepted concepts remain highly controversial in application. Throughout U.S. history, disputes have raged over the interpretation of such basic democratic concepts as free speech and freedom of religion. After examining those disputes, we turn to the struggle for equal protection of the law for all. Finally, we consider rights and liberties unique to the twentieth century, as well as government repression of liberties.

If the United States has fallen short of the mark in granting liberties and rights for all, it is to our credit that we have fought over them and incorporated them to a substantial degree in our political life. The Czechs would envy us at least for this.

The Bill of Rights and Constitutional Protections

What we call the **Bill of Rights** was not included in the original Constitution. As noted in Chapter 2, the first ten amendments were added in 1791 to mollify the Antifederalists, who agreed to back the Constitution only after assurances that a specific list of liberties would be appended to the new document following ratification.

At the time they were drafted, the protections included in the Bill of Rights were considered sufficient to ensure the opportunity for a decent life for each citizen; to guard against arbitrary government interference; and to protect dissent. The rights most central to the preservation of democratic politics are those listed in the First and Fifth Amendments.

First Amendment. Freedom of speech, press, and assembly; the right to petition for a redress of griev-

ances; freedom of religion, along with prohibition of an "establishment of religion."*

Fifth Amendment: Protection from loss of life, liberty, and property without due process of law.

Other significant protections in the Bill of Rights include:

Fourth Amendment: Prohibition of unreasonable searches and seizures.

Fifth Amendment: Protection from being tried twice for the same crime and from being forced to testify against oneself.

Sixth Amendment: Rights to a speedy trial, to counsel, to confront hostile witnesses, and to know the charges against oneself.

Seventh Amendment: Right to a jury trial.

Eighth Amendment: Prohibition of excessive bail and fines and of cruel and unusual punishments.

The Third Amendment deals with an issue of little importance today—the quartering of soldiers in private homes. Until very recently, the Second Amendment's guarantee of the right to bear arms for the purpose of maintaining a militia seemed equally irrelevant to modern life; gun control opponents, however, now cite it as a constitutional bar to government regulation of gun ownership. The Ninth and Tenth Amendments offer vague cautions that the enumeration of rights and powers in the Constitution does not disparage or deny other rights held by the people or the states.

U.S. legal history is replete with controversies over the interpretation of these rights. Does free speech mean citizens may criticize the government in time of war? Or advocate resistance to the draft? Does the right to assemble mean groups may gather to advocate violence against other groups? Does prohibition of an "establishment" of religion mean that even nonsectarian prayers in schools are unconstitutional? Does free exercise of religion mean that polygamy is permissible if one's religion sanctions it? Just when does a search become "un-

---

*As we will see later in this chapter, the phrase "establishment of religion" has been subject to many interpretations. Some have argued that it prohibits only an official state religion; others have maintained that it excludes all favoritism toward any religion, or even toward religion in general.

reasonable"? Is the death penalty a form of "cruel and unusual punishment"?

The issues raised by these questions have formed the constitutional backdrop for significant struggles over the meaning of civil liberties and rights in U.S. political history. Of course, many of the issues we confront today in attempting to give meaning to democratic ideals are rather different from those faced by the framers of the Constitution. The framers did not have to take into account such central elements of modern-day life as the mass media, a powerful and activist government, mass public education, and huge corporations. We can see in the Bill of Rights both issues fundamental to democratic politics at any time and place and issues that reflect more precisely the time and place in which the document originated.

At various times in U.S. history, arguments have raged over one or another of these issues. We now examine (1) how federalism has influenced civil liberties; (2) evolving notions of freedom of speech; (3) issues surrounding freedom of religion; (4) due process and the rights of the accused; and (5) abortion and the emerging doctrine of personal privacy.

Federalism and Civil Liberties

For much of U.S. history the protections spelled out in the Bill of Rights were not applied to state governments. As noted in Chapter 3, the Supreme Court held in *Barron* v. *Baltimore* (1833) that the Bill of Rights was meant to apply solely to the national government. According to the Court, the Bill of Rights placed no restrictions on the actions of state and local governments, which were free to develop their own policies on civil liberties.

This view remained largely unchallenged until the ratification, following the Civil War, of the Thirteenth, Fourteenth, and Fifteenth Amendments, which abolished slavery and extended the rights of citizenship (including the vote) to former slaves. The **Fourteenth Amendment,** in particular, raised the question of state versus federal responsibility for the enforcement of civil rights and liberties. That amendment states, in part, that "no State shall make or enforce any law which shall

abridge the privileges or immunities of citizens of the United States." If the "privileges and immunities" on which the states were forbidden to encroach were interpreted as those mentioned in the Bill of Rights, then the amendment could form the basis for a unitary national civil liberties policy— one applicable to every state.

But advocates of a national civil liberties policy suffered a severe setback when the Supreme Court, in the *Slaughterhouse Cases* of 1873,[1] ruled that the Fourteenth Amendment's "privileges and immunities" clause did not extend responsibility for enforcing the Bill of Rights to the states. The Court held that national citizenship must be distinguished from state citizenship.

The Court maintained this stance until the turn of the century, when it began to apply national standards to state actions under two other clauses of the Fourteenth Amendment: the **due process clause,** which stipulates that no state may deprive a person of life, liberty, or property without due process of law; and the **equal protection clause,** which mandates that no state may deny any person equal protection of the laws. In *Gitlow* v. *New York* (1925), the Supreme Court argued that "freedom of speech and of the press, which are protected by the First Amendment from abridgement by Congress, are among the fundamental personal rights and liberties protected by the due process clause of the Fourteenth Amendment from impairment by the states."[2] Note that the Court did not automatically apply the entire Bill of Rights to the states; rather, it designated certain freedoms guaranteed in the **First Amendment** as so fundamental that they must be universally protected.

Following the *Gitlow* decision, the Supreme Court gradually shifted direction, stipulating more and more provisions of the Bill of Rights that the states were prohibited from violating. Some modern-day justices—most notably Hugo Black and William O. Douglas—have argued that the entire Bill of Rights should pertain to the states—the doctrine that was specifically rejected in the *Slaughterhouse Cases.* Although this view has never been explicitly accepted by a majority of the Court, over the years the justices have applied almost the entire Bill of Rights to the states by means of the Fourteenth Amendment's due process and equal

Case-by-Case Incorporation of Bill of Rights Provisions into the Fourteenth Amendment

Provision	Amendment	Year	Case
"Public use" and "just compensation" conditions in the taking of private property by government	V	1896 and 1897	*Missouri Pacific Railway Co.* v. *Nebraska*; *Chicago, Burlington & Quincy Railway Co.* v. *Chicago*
Freedom of speech	I	1927	*Fiske* v. *Kansas; Gitlow* v. *New York; Gilbert* v. *Minnesota*
Freedom of the press	I	1931	*Near* v. *Minnesota*
Fair trial and right to counsel in capital cases	VI	1932	*Powell* v. *Alabama*
Freedom of religion	I	1934	*Hamilton* v. *Regents of Univ. of California*
Freedom of assembly and, by implication, freedom to petition for redress of grievances	I	1937	*DeJonge* v. *Oregon*
Free exercise of religious belief	I	1940	*Cantwell* v. *Connecticut*
Separation of church and state; prohibition of the establishment of religion	I	1947	*Everson* v. *Board of Education*
Right to public trial	VI	1948	*In re Oliver*
Right against unreasonable searches and seizures	IV	1949	*Wolf* v. *Colorado*
Freedom of association	I	1958	*NAACP* v. *Alabama*
Exclusionary rule as concomitant of unreasonable searches and seizures	IV	1961	*Mapp* v. *Ohio*
Right against cruel and unusual punishments	VIII	1962	*Robinson* v. *California*
Right to counsel in all felony cases	VI	1963	*Gideon* v. *Wainwright*
Right against self-incrimination	V	1964	*Malloy* v. *Hogan; Murphy* v. *Waterfront Commission*
Right to confront witnesses	VI	1965	*Pointer* v. *Texas*
Right to privacy	Various	1965	*Griswold* v. *Connecticut*
Right to impartial jury	VI	1966	*Parker* v. *Gladden*
Right to speedy trial	VI	1967	*Klopfer* v. *North Carolina*
Right to compulsory process for obtaining witnesses	VI	1967	*Washington* v. *Texas*
Right to jury trial in cases of serious crime	VI	1968	*Duncan* v. *Louisiana*
Right against double jeopardy	V	1969	*Benton* v. *Maryland*
Right to counsel in all criminal cases entailing a jail term	VI	1972	*Argersinger* v. *Hamlin*

SOURCE: H. W. Chase and C. Ducat, *1980 Supplement to Constitutional Interpretation: Cases, Essays, Materials* (St. Paul: West Publishing Co., 1980), pp. 888–890.

protection clauses. As a result, proponents of a uniform, national civil liberties policy have achieved incrementally what they were unable to achieve in one blow.

This excursion into constitutional law illustrates a significant national policy choice. According to some, certain liberties are so basic to democratic life that they must be safeguarded throughout the country. Others contend that in a large, complex nation standards and policies should be developed at the local level. For example, should the laws banning "pornography" in New York City apply

Two sides of an argument expressed vividly and publicly. This is one of the things free speech is all about: forming opinions, organizing them, putting them forward—and being able to do so without fear. *(AP/Wide World Photos)*

the same standards as laws in rural Arkansas? Or should "pornography" mean one thing in New York and something else in an area with radically different social mores? As a polity, we have moved steadily in the first of these directions over the past half-century.

Freedom of Speech

In the classical liberal credo, freedom of speech (and the press) is considered essential if humankind is to advance intellectually; the competition of ideas is seen as a necessary condition of progress.[3] According to this rationale, even if an unpopular view turns out to be entirely incorrect, it should still be tolerated because the challenge of the false view forces the holders of truth to examine their position and to flex their intellectual muscles.

Political philosopher Alexander Meiklejohn defended freedom of speech from a different perspective: Free speech, according to Meiklejohn, becomes necessary once people have decided to govern themselves. Free speech, in this view, is mandated by a prior commitment to self-government.[4] For the people to decide how government

should function, they need free access to information so they can make intelligent, informed choices. As a logical corollary to this premise, a distinction can be drawn between political speech (speech that is related to self-government) and nonpolitical speech, and only the former must be protected absolutely. Thus, Meiklejohn could argue, quite consistently, that free speech for political radicals must be protected, whereas slander and libel may be outlawed.

Especially in this century, the Supreme Court has largely followed Meiklejohn's approach. Acknowledging that the basic justification for free speech is its contribution to self-government, the Court has repeatedly ruled that public policy requires greater freedom of expression on political than on other matters. We now consider (1) Supreme Court rulings on the limits of dissent; (2) cases involving the controversial Smith Act, which outlawed advocating the violent overthrow of the government; (3) contemporary trends in freedom of speech; and (4) the Court's view of symbolic speech and "fighting words."

SETTING LIMITS ON DISSENT After the Sedition Act of 1798, Congress made no attempt to regulate free speech until the passage of the Espionage Act of 1917 and the Sedition Act of 1918. Both acts were designed to curb criticism of the government during World War I. In a significant series of cases in the postwar period, the Supreme Court passed on the constitutionality of these acts in rulings that have largely shaped the legal debate on free speech matters to the present day. Through all three cases examined below, we can trace a gradual evolution of the Court's approach to setting limits on dissent. We should also note how profoundly the political and social atmosphere of the times influenced these cases, which involved extremely controversial political speech.[5]

The three cases—*Schenck* v. *United States* (1919), *Abrams* v. *United States* (1919), and *Gitlow* v. *New York* (1925)—all bear striking similarities.

> *Schenck* v. *United States*. In 1917 Charles T. Schenck, a Socialist Party official, mailed out one hundred and fifty thousand leaflets urging eligible young men to resist the draft. The leaflets described conscription as despotism and urged citizens to defend their rights against the interests of Wall Street. Schenck was convicted under the Espionage Act.

> *Abrams* v. *United States*. In 1919, Jacob Abrams and five associates, all Russian immigrants, distributed leaflets (by throwing them out of a factory window in New York) criticizing U.S. involvement on the side of anti-Bolshevik forces in the Soviet Union. The leaflets branded President Woodrow Wilson a hypocrite and a tool of Wall Street and called on workers to join a general strike. In 1919, four of the defendants were convicted under the Sedition Act and sentenced to twenty years in prison.

> *Gitlow* v. *New York*. In 1925, Benjamin Gitlow, a radical socialist, was convicted under New York State's Criminal Anarchy Act of 1902 of advocating the violent overthrow of the government. The main evidence against him was a theoretical piece he had written titled *Left Wing Manifesto*.

In none of the cases was evidence presented that the pamphlets, leaflets, or theoretical writings had any noticeable effect on the conduct of those who read them. Accordingly, the issue in each case came down to this: Could the government limit freedom of expression because of *possible* interference with a government function, or because it found specific views threatening? How far, in other words, did freedom of speech extend?

In *Schenck* the Court unanimously upheld Schenck's conviction. Justice Oliver Wendell Holmes, in expressing the Court's view, attempted to define the free speech issues involved:

> We admit that in many places and in ordinary times the defendants in saying all that was said in the circular would have been within their constitutional rights. But the character of every act depends upon the circumstances in which it is done. The most stringent protection of free speech would not protect a man in falsely shouting fire in a theatre and causing a panic. It does not even protect a man from an injunction against uttering words that may have all the effect of force. The question in every case is whether the words used are used in such circumstances and are of such a nature as to create a clear and present danger that they will bring about the substantive evils that Congress has a right to prevent.[6]

Critics of this famous opinion have argued that although the government may have had the right to prevent obstruction of the draft, Schenck's pamphlet simply did not represent the **"clear and present danger"** alluded to by Holmes.

The convictions of Jacob Abrams and his associates were also upheld by the Court. In this case, however, Justice Holmes and Louis Brandeis dissented, arguing that

> the best test of truth is the power of thought to get itself accepted in the competition of the market. . . . That at any rate is the theory of our Constitution. It is an experiment, as all life is an experiment . . . we should be eternally vigilant against attempts to check the expressions of opinions that we loathe and believe to be fraught with danger, unless they so imminently threaten immediate interference with the lawful and pressing purposes of the law that an immediate check is required to save the country.[7]

To the Court majority, however, the convictions were justified on the grounds that the activities involved had a "dangerous or bad tendency"—that they were meant to instigate riot or revolution. These two positions set the parameters for subsequent debate on the limits of speech and opinion.

The Alien and Sedition Acts of 1798

The French Revolution stirred intense debate in the new United States. Thomas Jefferson and others of similar views, known as Jeffersonian Republicans, welcomed the revolutionary developments in France. The more conservative Federalists, however, generally decried what they viewed as the increasingly destructive and radical direction the revolution seemed to be taking. Feelings ran so high that when Jefferson went to Philadelphia in March 1797 to take the oath of office as vice-president, he noted that "men who have been intimate all their lives, cross the streets to avoid meeting, and turn their heads another way, lest they should be obliged to touch their hats." This deep-seated fear of the radicalism of the French revolutionaries led to the new republic's first brush with political repression.

In 1798, the Federalist-dominated Congress passed the Naturalization Act and the Alien and Sedition Acts, which were ostensibly aimed at protecting the nation from the alleged threat from France. In reality, however, the acts were directed as much at the Republican opposition as at any supposed foreign danger. The Naturalization Act increased the period of residence required to gain U.S. citizenship from five to fourteen years, and the Alien Act and the Alien Enemies Act gave the president the power to expel foreigners by executive decree. Far more controversial was the Sedition Act, which made it a criminal offense to speak or write against Congress or the president with the "intent to defame" or bring either into contempt. Such vague legislation practically invited abuse. Not surprisingly, every person charged under the act was a Republican or Republican sympathizer, including many newspaper editors; every judge and almost every juror in these cases was a Federalist. Of the twenty-five persons prosecuted under the Sedition Act, ten were convicted and punished with heavy fines or jail sentences.

Despite the Sedition Act, criticism of the government continued, and the election of 1800 put Jefferson into the White House. All four acts were allowed to expire in 1800 and 1801.

In *Gitlow*, Holmes and Brandeis again dissented from the Court's majority ruling. Their minority opinion sets out the implications of their views even more fully:

Every idea is an incitement. It offers itself for belief and if believed it is acted on. . . . If in the long run the beliefs expressed in proletarian dictatorship are destined to be accepted by the dominant forces of the community, the only meaning of free speech is that they should be given their chance and have their way.[8]

A majority of justices upheld Gitlow's conviction. But, as we have seen, the Court did take the important step of acknowledging that the Fourteenth Amendment applied to the freedoms of speech and press in the states.

Not until the 1930s did a majority of the Court begin to accept the Holmes-Brandeis view. In several cases decided in that decade, the right of communists to express their views was upheld by the Court on the ground that their activities did not include plans for action, but simply the articulation of opinions.

THE SMITH ACT CASES   In 1940, Congress passed the Smith Act, which made it a crime to knowingly advocate or teach, or to organize or knowingly become a member of a group that advocated the violent overthrow of any unit of the U.S. government. The Smith Act, like most other sedition and criminal anarchy statutes, focused more on speech than on acts against the government.

In 1949, indictments were brought under the act against eleven leaders of the U.S. Communist

Party. They were charged not with committing overt acts against the government, or even with planning such acts, but rather with teaching the duty and necessity of revolution from Marxist texts. All eleven were convicted, and the Supreme Court in 1951 upheld the convictions in *Dennis et al.* v. *United States.* Writing for the Court majority, Chief Justice Fred M. Vinson argued:

> If the government is aware that a group aiming at its overthrow is attempting to indoctrinate its members and to commit them to a course whereby they will strike when the leaders feel the circumstances permit, action by the Government is required. . . . The damage which such attempts create both physically and politically to a nation makes it impossible to measure the validity in terms of the probability of success, or the immediacy of a successful attempt. . . . We must therefore reject the contention that success or probability of success is the criterion.[9]

From this perspective, it made no difference whether there was any evidence of contemplated or planned-for future action: If people merely disseminated the idea of revolution, the government was justified in prosecuting them.

Commenting on this position in a dissenting opinion, Justice William O. Douglas wrote:

> If this were a case where those who claimed protection under the First Amendment were teaching the techniques of sabotage, the assassination of the President . . . the planting of bombs, the art of street warfare . . . I would have no doubts. . . . The case was argued as if those were the facts. That is easy and it has popular appeal, for the activities of Communists in plotting and scheming against the free world are common knowledge. But the fact is that no such evidence was introduced at the trial. . . . What petitioners did was organize to teach and themselves teach the Marxist-Leninist doctrine contained in four books. . . . The opinion of the Court does not outlaw those texts. . . . But if the books themselves are not outlawed. . . . by what reasoning does their use in a classroom become a crime? The crime then depends not on what is taught, but on who the teacher is. . . . Once we start down that road we enter territory dangerous to the liberties of every citizen.[10]

Six years later, in *Yates* v. *United States* (1957), the Court shifted its ground by returning to the "clear and present danger" test.[11] By a 6–1 vote, the Court overturned the convictions under the Smith Act of five second-rank leaders of the U.S. Communist Party and ordered that the nine other party officials involved in the case be remanded for new trials. (None was ever retried.) The Court majority in *Yates* argued that conviction under the Smith Act required proof not just that defendants had advocated a belief in revolution in the abstract, but that they had advocated action to bring about revolution. The *Yates* decision effectively nullified the Smith Act.

CONTEMPORARY TRENDS Since *Yates* the Court has not deviated noticeably from the "clear and present danger" standard in comparable cases—most notably, the so-called Pentagon Papers case in 1971. According to that 6–3 Supreme Court ruling, the Pentagon Papers—classified documents on the U.S. involvement in Vietnam—could be published by the *New York Times* and the *Washington Post* under the protection of the First Amendment. During the Vietnam War, several convictions for draft card burning, flag desecration, and similar activities were upheld by the Court, but there were no free speech convictions on the order of *Schenck* or *Abrams.*

In recent decades the Court has established three basic tests of the constitutionality of laws and regulations designed to limit free expression. Under the concept of "strict scrutiny," the government must prove a compelling interest in its restriction of speech. Also, under the doctrine of "overbreadth," statutes that purport to limit expression must be narrowly and specifically drawn. Finally, the Court has paid careful attention to the "chilling effect" of statutes. This means that a law may be held unconstitutional if its mere existence "chills," or impairs, the exercise of First Amendment rights. In *Shelton* v. *Tucker* (1960), for example, the Court cited the "chilling effect" in invalidating an Arkansas statute that had required every schoolteacher to file an annual report of all organizations to which he or she belonged or contributed money.[12]

SYMBOLIC SPEECH AND "FIGHTING WORDS" Often, political or social views are expressed through symbolic gestures, such as picketing, the

A Chicago suburb, September 1966. While blacks protested segregated housing, some whites focused on issues of their own. Though these protesters seem relaxed here, when do words ignite illegal action, and what limits should the law set on free speech?
(Benedict J. Fernandez)

wearing of armbands, or the carrying of signs or placards, rather than in reasoned political speech. Sometimes people express themselves in particularly heated or intense ways—cursing, screaming, haranguing. Or they may utter "fighting words," or carry on symbolic activities in schools, public buildings, or other centers of public activity. Such intense and/or symbolic expressions of views have raised numerous and complicated First Amendment issues.

Over the years, the Supreme Court has applied First Amendment protections to various forms of symbolic speech and heated expression of views and denied those protections to others. In *Amal-* *gamated Food Employees Local 590* v. *Logan Valley Plaza, Inc.* (1968), for example, the Court held that the "speech" aspect of picketing is fully protected under the First Amendment, but that the conduct of picketers is not. "Because of this intermingling of protected and unprotected elements," the Court decided, "picketing can be subject to controls that would not be constitutionally permissible in the case of pure speech."[13]

Another limitation on symbolic speech came in *United States* v. *O'Brien* (1968), in which the Court held that the burning of draft cards as a symbolic protest was not a constitutionally protected form of free speech.[14] The justices could not accept the principle that an "apparently limitless variety of conduct can be labeled 'speech' whenever the person engaging in the conduct intends thereby to express an idea."[15]

In *Tinker* v. *Des Moines Independent Community School District* (1969), however, the Court upheld the right of students to make a symbolic protest against the Vietnam War by wearing black armbands to school. Such a practice, the justices found, represented a legitimate form of free speech and so was protected under the First Amendment, except for cases in which it would cause serious disruption of school activities.[16]

As for "fighting words," the Court has shown considerable tolerance toward what might seem to be potentially disruptive forms of expression. In 1942, in *Chaplinsky* v. *New Hampshire*, the Court did uphold the right of the state to punish the utterance of "fighting words."[17] In 1972, in contrast, it refused to permit application of a "fighting words" statute against a black man who shouted, "White son of a bitch, I'll kill you," at a white police officer (*Gooding* v. *Wilson*).[18]

More recently, the Court upheld the right of a Nazi group to hold a rally and display the Nazi emblem in a heavily Jewish Chicago suburb (*National Socialist Party* v. *Skokie*, 1977), noting that "anticipation of a hostile audience could not justify . . . prior restraint."[19] In addressing the issue of the "angry audience," the Court generally has ruled that assemblies and parades can be halted by police if a risk of imminent violence has been clearly demonstrated. However, the justices have also made it clear that the police must protect those participating in a rally or meeting, if at all possible.

COMPARATIVE PERSPECTIVE

Political Extremism in Australia and West Germany

The question of how to define and deal with extremist or politically unacceptable political groups has troubled many democratic countries, especially in the decade following World War II. In the United States, as we have seen, groups that advocated the violent overthrow of the government were outlawed under the Smith Act. We will now examine how two other democratic societies dealt with this issue.

In Australia, the government pushed through a bill in 1950 outlawing the Australian Communist Party (ACP). The year is significant: War had just broken out in Korea, and Australian troops were involved in the fighting there. The ACP and several labor unions took the new legislation to the Australian High Court for review. The court found that the political situation in Australia was not perilous enough to warrant such a serious infringement of civil liberties.

By contrast, in the post–World War II Federal Republic of Germany (West Germany), the Basic Law (the equivalent of a constitution) of the Federal Republic prohibited the formation of antidemocratic political groups. This prohibition was intended principally to forestall the revival of the Nazi Party or any similar organization. In 1949, however, a right-wing political group launched the Socialist Reich Party (SRP), whose views were close to those of the Nazis. In 1951 the West German government petitioned the Constitutional Court (equivalent, roughly, to the U.S. Supreme Court) to declare the SRP unconstitutional under the Basic Law. The court, noting the party's similarities to Nazism, its anti-Semitism, and its recruiting of leaders who had been active Nazis, banned the SRP.

At roughly the same time, the West German government also moved against the German Communist Party (KPD). With the KPD, however, the case for political extremism was less clearcut, and the political situation more complicated. German communists had fought bitterly against the Nazis both before and during World War II, and to banish them from postwar political life seemed incongruous to many. Then, too, neighboring East Germany, with which the Federal Republic had tense relations, was committed to a communist ideology. For these reasons, the Constitutional Court delayed issuing a ruling for more than four years, in the hope that the matter would be resolved in some other way. When the decision was finally handed down in 1956, the court found that communist doctrine was not compatible with a democratic political process. Thus the KPD, like the SRP, was banned.

Freedom of Religion

The very first issue addressed in the First Amendment is the relationship between government and religion—as sensitive an issue today as it was in the eighteenth century. Under the First Amendment, Congress is commanded to make no law "respecting an establishment of religion" (the **establishment clause**) or "prohibiting the free exercise" of religion (the **free exercise clause**). On the most basic level, both clauses are clear: Congress may not establish a state religion or prohibit particular religions. These prohibitions were certainly relevant to the forms of religious intolerance and the official state religions found abundantly in eighteenth-century Europe and America. Throughout the nineteenth century, few controversies developed between the national government and religious groups. In the twentieth century, however, many such controversies have arisen—some very subtle and difficult to resolve. Let us now probe (1) the ramifications of the es-

School prayer. No one can prevent students from contemplating their own thoughts, but the Supreme Court has made it clear that *organized* efforts by the government to encourage religious observance in public schools are unconstitutional. *(Bryce Flynn/ Stock, Boston)*

tablishment clause; (2) how the free exercise of religion has been interpreted; and (3) the price of dissent from religious norms.

ESTABLISHMENT OF RELIGION   Was it the intention of the framers of the Bill of Rights merely to prevent the establishment of a national church, such as the Church of England, or to prohibit *any* acts of government that would support certain religions, or even religion in general? Authorities who have taken the latter view have spoken of the need for a "wall of separation" between church and state, to keep government entirely out of matters associated with religion. Most recent church-state controversies have revolved around the many ways that government and religion do, or could, interact.

The best known of these debates centers on prayer in public schools. In a series of decisions in the early 1960s, a divided Supreme Court banned even nonsectarian prayers from public schools. In *Engel* v. *Vitale* (1962), for example, the Court majority declared unconstitutional the saying of a nondenominational prayer written by the New York State Board of Regents for use in state public

schools.[20] The Court later outlawed Bible reading in public schools, even in those that permitted children to be excused if their parents objected. Because such practices aided religion in general, the Court argued, they could not be permitted under the establishment clause. As an alternative, the Court pointed out that religion could be *studied* in an academic context.

These rulings met with immediate and intense opposition. Many school districts simply refused to comply with the Supreme Court guidelines. In addition, proponents of school prayer began working toward passage of a constitutional amendment permitting some religious practices in public schools. According to advocates of the proposed amendment, the Bill of Rights was not intended to prohibit all religious exercises in schools, or *any* government involvement with religion.

In June 1985 the Supreme Court struck down, by a 6–3 vote, an Alabama law that permitted a one-minute period of silent meditation or prayer in public schools. In *Wallace* v. *Jaffree*, the Court affirmed its earlier rulings that "government must pursue a course of complete neutrality toward religion," but indicated at the same time that "moment of silence" laws could be held constitutional as long as they did not have as their primary intention the fostering of religious activity in the classroom. The Alabama law, the majority argued, had intended to characterize prayer "as a favored practice."[21] At the time of the ruling, varying versions of the "moment of silence" law existed in twenty-five states.

Another long-running establishment clause controversy concerns public aid to private schools, most of which are church-affiliated. Generally, the Court has taken the position that the state can assist private-school students or support particular private-school programs that are not related to religion, but that it cannot provide funding for religious instruction. Thus, whereas the Court has upheld tax aid to parents to offset the costs of busing to private schools and the costs of nonreligious textbooks and other study aids, it has not permitted the use of public funds for teachers' salaries, tuition aid, or maintenance and repair of school facilities.

One other sensitive subject has been the tax-exempt status of religious institutions. Many observers consider the tax-exempt status of church property to be a violation of the constitutionally mandated separation of church and state. The Court ruled on this matter in *Walz* v. *Tax Commission of the City of New York* (1970).[22] Chief Justice Burger argued for the Court majority in this case that tax exemption was constitutional and represents "neither the advancement nor the inhibition of religion." He distinguished tax exemption, an indirect economic subsidy, from direct subsidies, which violate the establishment clause.

Church-affiliated schools and colleges may not, however, keep their tax exemptions while violating federal civil rights legislation, as the Court's ruling in *Bob Jones University* v. *United States* (1983) made clear.[23]

FREE EXERCISE OF RELIGION The right to the free exercise of religion has been consistently upheld by the Supreme Court. As Justice Samuel F. Miller wrote in an 1872 case (*Watson* v. *Jones*) involving a dispute within the Presbyterian church, "In this country the full and free right to entertain any religious doctrine which does not violate the laws of morality and property, and which does not in-

fringe personal rights, is conceded to all."[24] Note how many possible conflicts are contained within those qualifying phrases, however. Many of the legal conflicts associated with the free exercise clause have hinged on differing interpretations of the "laws of morality."

In *Reynolds* v. *United States* (1878) for example, the Supreme Court upheld a federal law prohibiting polygamy in U.S. territories.[25] The law had been challenged by the Mormon church, which encouraged its followers to practice polygamy. In upholding the statute, the Court distinguished between religious *beliefs*, which enjoy the full protection of the Constitution, and *actions* based on those beliefs, which can be regulated by government. To allow a person to engage in illegal behavior because of religious beliefs, the Court noted in *Reynolds*, "would be to make the professed doctrines of religious beliefs superior to the law of the land." But exactly *why* polygamy should be illegal, the Court did not make clear. It could be argued that this was a case of the majority deciding what "appropriate morality" should be.

Following *Reynolds*, very few free exercise questions were addressed by the Supreme Court until the early 1940s, when several cases involving the Jehovah's Witnesses reached the Court. At issue in *Minersville School District* v. *Gobitis* (1940) was the expulsion from school of two Jehovah's Witnesses children who had refused to participate in the mandatory salute to the flag and recitation of the Pledge of Allegiance, on the grounds that such an oath violated their religious beliefs and constituted idolatry.[26] The Supreme Court upheld the expulsions, rejecting the contention that the free exercise clause had been violated. Justice Felix Frankfurter, writing for the majority, noted the importance of symbols in American life and argued that "the flag is a symbol of our national unity, transcending all internal differences, however large, within the framework of the Constitution." There was only one dissenter on the Court.

Then, remarkably, the Court reversed itself only three years later, in *West Virginia State Board of Education* v. *Barnette* (1943).[27] Three new members had joined the Court in the intervening years, and in *Barnette* three other justices admitted that they had been wrong in *Gobitis*. In upholding the right of Jehovah's Witnesses to decline to swear an oath,

Marion, N.C., 1988: Matthew and Duffy Strode preach the Gospel (as they understand it) outside their school. But they were supposed to be inside the school, in class. After several suspensions, the boys were permitted to be educated at home. *(AP/Wide World Photos)*

Justice Robert H. Jackson, writing for the majority, stated, "If there is any fixed star in our constitutional constellation, it is that no official, high or petty, can prescribe what shall be orthodox in politics, nationalism, religion, or other matters of opinion or force citizens to confess by word or act their faith therein."

The Supreme Court has also affirmed the right to object to military service on religious grounds. In *United States* v. *Seeger* (1965), the Court extended this concept to cover "sincere and meaningful" religious beliefs that may not be related to a Supreme Being.[28] Five years later, in *Welsh* v. *United States*, the justices upheld the rights of a conscientious objector whose refusal to serve in the armed forces

was based on "considerations of public policy."[29] However, the Court has consistently refused to sanction so-called selective objection to military service—objection based on opposition to a particular war, as opposed to all wars.

THE PRICE OF DISSENT   Oftentimes, those who choose to dissent from the norm face vehement opposition. The pressure on those who dissent from established religious norms can be especially fierce in small communities. Consider the following examples:

Lawyer Valerie White objected to a cross displayed at Christmas on the courthouse lawn in Morrisville, Vermont. The cross had been erected in 1958 in memory of a local sports star who had been killed in a mill accident. Town trustees refused to remove the cross, and eventually the American Civil Liberties Union took the case to federal court, where it has remained undecided. But local townspeople were not amused by Valerie White's actions. A man giving out bumper stickers that read, "Leave Our Cross Alone," argued that White "wants her way and, in her mind, I don't think the majority rules. In a small close-knit town like this, I don't see how she will survive six months." White found that she was hissed as she took the stand at a hearing about the cross, and two assistant county judges refused to speak to her. In White's view, "The concept of allowing majorities to dictate religion is bad history. . . . Doesn't anybody remember the Spanish Inquisition, the Holocaust, even the Irish troubles now? The Huguenots were burned at the stake in France. Most people just don't think about those things."

In a similar case in Littleton, New Hampshire, Donald Bacher objected when a lighted cross was placed on a hill owned by the town. The reaction was swift and startling. A local radio call-in show got 140 calls, all attacking him. His family received threats and was urged to leave town. His daughter overheard classmates calling her father a "crazy person." Bacher, who won the battle, explained that it was something of a thrill to be involved in a good fight. His family, however, was considerably less than pleased.

In 1977 in Ferrisburg, Vermont, the school board decided to ban certain books and restrict access to others in the high school library. The student council opposed the action and sought support from teachers and others. Beth Phillips, the school librarian, signed on as a plaintiff in a court case the students planned to initiate. Phillips was new to the community and, as she put it, "an easy target." She was attacked in church by local clergy, and petitions were circulated demanding that she be dismissed. The case was eventually resolved in favor of the school board, and Phillips left the town. "It took me several years to heal," she said. "Parts of me have never healed. I have anger inside me I have never let go of. I just hope I never have to face something like this again."[30]

The Rights of the Accused

The rights of those accused of crime have always posed difficult issues for democratic societies. There are the inevitable tensions between the need to protect the accused, on the one hand, and to prosecute the guilty, on the other; particularly in times of social strain and tension, the balance seems to tip in the direction of increased police powers. Another complicating factor in U.S. society has been the disproportionate presence in the ranks of defendants of members of minority groups and the poor.

Under Chief Justice Earl Warren, the Supreme Court in the 1960s introduced radical changes into the process by which criminal suspects are apprehended and guilt or innocence is determined. Overall, the Warren Court attempted to tighten the requirements for establishing legal guilt, principally by placing constraints on the kinds of evidence that could be introduced and the procedures that could be followed in criminal courts. The touchstone of the Court's approach to defining the rights of the accused was the Fifth Amendment's injunction that no person "be deprived of life, liberty or property, without due process of law." In comparison with its predecessors (as well as its successors), the Warren Court took a decidedly expansive view of the meaning of **"due process."**

The Court significantly broadened the accused's right to counsel, which is guaranteed in the Sixth Amendment. In a series of cases, the justices ruled that the accused has the right to be represented by an attorney during interrogation by police, at lineups, during preliminary hearings, at trial, and during the appeals process. Moreover, in the land-mark case of *Gideon* v. *Wainwright* (1963), the Court held that if a defendant could not afford to hire an attorney, the state must provide one.[31] Only if representation by an attorney were guaranteed even to the most indigent defendant, the Court reasoned, would the rights of that defendant be adequately protected.

The second basic principle advanced by the Warren Court—*exclusion* of "tainted" evidence—meant that if, in obtaining evidence against a defendant, law enforcement officers violated the defendant's constitutional rights (by conducting unauthorized searches or improper interrogations, for example), that evidence must be excluded from the trial. In this way, no defendant could be convicted on the basis of illegally obtained evidence. The exclusionary rule was also designed to regulate the conduct of police officers. If evidence obtained in illegal searches and seizures or interrogations could not be used in court, then, presumably, law enforcement officers would be less likely to engage in such practices.

In a further effort to curb police abuses of the rights of suspects, the Court in **Miranda v. Arizona** (1963) dictated guidelines to be followed by police in the interrogation of suspects.[32] All persons arrested, the Court declared, must be informed of their right to remain silent and their right to legal representation during questioning, and must be warned that anything they say may be used against them in court.

To their proponents, the Warren Court's decisions on due process went to the very heart of civil liberties doctrine—the need to protect the dignity and humanity of citizens. The Court argued that certain police and prosecutorial procedures simply violated the basic human rights that citizens ought to enjoy. Another defense of the Court's approach is the argument that the best way to avoid the conviction of an innocent person is to establish strict procedural rules governing arrest, interrogation, and trial. Finally, some of the procedural protections set up by the Court, such as the principle of exclusion, were designed to prevent too much intrusion by police in the lives of citizens. Random searches, dragnet arrests, and threatening interrogations of suspects may be useful tools in catching lawbreakers, but they cannot be justified in a society of limited government.

Ernesto Miranda's trial for rape and kidnapping led the Supreme Court to enunciate explicit protections of the rights of the accused—including the right to a lawyer and the right to remain silent. Miranda was later stabbed to death in a fight in a bar. *(AP/Wide World Photos)*

The Warren Court's decisions on due process continue to spark controversy. As we noted in Chapter 1, U.S. society remains divided between the drive for efficient apprehension and punishment of those who break laws and the desire for restrictions on the powers of the state in its dealings with individuals.

In the 1960s, public opinion held that the Warren Court had gone too far in protecting criminals at the expense of law-abiding citizens. The election of President Richard Nixon in 1968 ushered in a gradual retreat from the positions taken by the Warren Court. In his appointments to the Court, President Nixon selected justices who favored efficient law enforcement, and by the mid-1970s the

Court's approach to due process rights had changed significantly. Under Chief Justice Warren Burger the Court, for example, narrowed the application of the "Miranda rules." The Burger Court did not explicitly overrule *Miranda*, but it whittled away at the breadth of the Warren Court decisions in that and other due process areas.

In recent years, the Court has vacillated in its approach to the basic Miranda rules, sometimes upholding them, sometimes amending them, often in closely split votes. The Reagan administration, led by Attorney General Edwin Meese, sought to severely curtail these protections. A 1987 Justice Department staff report stated: "The interesting question is not whether *Miranda* should go, but how we should facilitate its demise and what we should replace it with." The report went on to state that "Overturning *Miranda* would . . . be among the most important achievements of this administration. . . ."

To a minor extent, the Court acquiesced. For example, in *Colorado* v. *Spring* (1987), it held that police need not inform a suspect of the crimes about which he may be questioned in order for him to waive his constitutional right to remain silent. Police, in other words, need not specifically list all crimes that may come up in the questioning. The Court also upheld an oral confession given by a suspect who was told of his rights, and who refused to make a written statement. In a highly controversial case, with the Court divided 5–4, the majority found that a police officer conducted a reasonable search when he reached into a car to move papers on the dashboard covering the vehicle identification number and saw a gun protruding from under the driver's seat. The driver was then charged with illegal weapons possession (*New York* v. *Class*, 1986).

By contrast, the Court ruled unanimously that a suspect's decision to remain silent under questioning could not later be used against him as proof of his sanity at the time of arrest. The majority stated that the Miranda warnings "contained an implicit promise, rooted in the Constitution, that silence will carry no penalty" (*Wainwright* v. *Greenfield*, 1986).

A split (5–4) Court also found in *Maine* v. *Moulton* (1985) that once a suspect invokes the right to counsel, the police must not question that suspect without counsel being present. This also excludes the use of an undercover informant to try to solicit information.

Overall, the Court has still shown no inclination either to overrule *Miranda* outright or even to make significant inroads into the protections it provides.

Abortion

In recent decades the Supreme Court has elaborated a doctrine of "personal privacy" in cases involving contraception and abortion. In 1965 the Court voided a Connecticut law forbidding the issuance of birth control information, on the ground that the law violated the rights of marital privacy. The Court majority spoke of "zones of privacy" and cited the Ninth Amendment, which states that rights not spelled out in the Bill of Rights are retained by the people. Justice Hugo Black, in dissenting, argued that the Court was creating a new right—one that was not to be found anywhere in the Constitution.

Eight years later, in a momentous decision on abortion handed down in *Roe* v. *Wade,* the Court majority noted that "the Constitution does not explicitly mention any right of privacy . . . [but] the Court has recognized that a right of personal privacy . . . does exist under the Constitution."[33] The Court ruled that during the first trimester (three months) of pregnancy, the decision to choose an abortion was a private matter between a woman and her physician. In the second trimester, states could impose restrictions to protect the mother's health; while in the third trimester, states could ban abortions altogether in recognition of the status of the developing fetus.

Roe v. *Wade* (1973) touched off a decade of intense controversy. Some hailed the decision as a decisive step forward for civil liberties and the rights of women. Others regarded the decision as fundamentally immoral—a license for fetal murder. Opponents argued that the Court's ruling failed to take into account the unborn child's "right to life."

The Court has faced a variety of challenges to the *Roe* decision. In 1974, for example, almost immediately after *Roe*, Missouri passed a law requir-

Norma McCorvey, the woman whose desire to have an abortion led to the Supreme Court's *Roe v. Wade* **decision.** *(AP/Wide World Photos)*

ing a husband's consent to his wife's decision to have an abortion. Two years later, in the case of *Planned Parenthood of Missouri* v. *Danforth,* the Court invalidated this statute, arguing that a husband was entitled to influence but not to a veto over his wife's decision. In that same case, the Court invalidated strict rules that parental consent be obtained when a minor was seeking an abortion. Several other cases involving minors and parental consent have also come before the Court. Today, states can require parental consent or notification for minors seeking abortions as long as certain exceptions are permitted: Minors must be allowed to demonstrate their maturity or to testify as to why parental involvement is not appropriate in their case. One-third of states now require parental notification or consent.

In 1986, in the case of *Thornburgh* v. *American College of Obstetricians and Gynecologists,* the Court (voting 5–4) struck down a Pennsylvania law de-

TABLE 4–1
Views on Abortion

Proposed amendment to:	Favor	Oppose	Don't know
Make all abortions illegal	28%	63%	9%
Allow abortions only to save life of mother	43	48	9

Changes in long-term trends

	Percent agreeing in:						
Abortion should be legal if	1972	1974	1976	1978	1980	1982	1984
1. there is a strong chance of serious defect in baby	79	85	84	82	83	85	80
2. a woman is married and doesn't want any more children	40	47	46	40	47	48	43
3. a woman's health is endangered by the pregnancy	87	92	91	91	90	92	90
4. the family cannot afford more children	49	55	53	47	52	52	46
5. a woman becomes pregnant as a result of rape	79	87	84	83	83	87	80
6. a woman becomes pregnant and does not wish to marry	44	50	50	41	48	49	44

SOURCE: Based on CBS/*New York Times* poll (Sept. 30–Oct. 5, 1984) and on polls conducted by National Opinion Research Center.

signed to discourage women from choosing abortions. The law set out detailed instructions specifying how a woman must give her "informed consent," and it also spelled out a series of procedures that doctors were obliged to follow. The ruling was a strong reaffirmation of the *Roe* decision, but it was decided by the narrowest of margins.

Foes of abortion have taken two basic tacks in attempting to reverse or dilute the *Roe* decision. Some antiabortion advocates have sought passage of a constitutional amendment giving the states and the federal government concurrent powers to enact a "Human Life" bill. In other words, either government could pass a bill defining life as beginning at conception and thereby providing constitutional protections for the unborn fetus. In the *Roe* decision, Justice Harry Blackmun had stated that the question of when life begins was one that the Court could not then resolve.

Antiabortion forces have also supported restric-tions on the use of federal funds for abortions. Such restrictions, commonly called the Hyde amendments (after their chief sponsor, Republican Representative Henry Hyde of Illinois) have been passed by Congress in every year beginning with 1976, and were upheld as constitutional by the Supreme Court in 1980. The Hyde restrictions primarily affected poor women. As federally financed abortions dropped from 295,000 in 1976 to 2,400 in 1979, many private abortion clinics dropped fees for women who could not afford to pay.

In recent years, antiabortion activists have energetically picketed abortion clinics; a few of the clinics were attacked or firebombed. It seems unlikely, however, that antiabortion forces will be able to turn back the clock. Given the absence of a strong moral consensus in U.S. society on this issue (see **Table 4–1**), any effort to ban abortion would likely suffer a fate similar to that of Prohibition in the 1920s. The social costs would be very high if abortion were driven underground.

Civil Rights

A citizen's civil rights are, in effect, guarantees that he or she will be treated *fairly and equally* by government and by those segments of society that must meet the same standards. Among the most basic civil rights are the right to vote, the right to equal employment opportunities, the right to equal education, and the right to equal treatment in housing and in public accommodations. In this section, we now examine the most basic civil rights: (1) the right to vote; (2) fundamental elements of racial equality, including education equality; (3) affirmative action; and (4) equal rights for women.

The Right to Vote

The right to vote, also known as the franchise, is the most fundamental of all civil rights in a democracy. Those to whom it is denied are effectively excluded from the most essential element of the democratic process—the chance to register one's political views and to help shape the mandate of popular sentiment. The overwhelming importance of the right to vote can be seen most vividly in societies such as contemporary South Africa, in which more than three-fourths of the population is denied any real electoral voice. If black South Africans could express their views democratically, the current government, which supports white supremacy, would undoubtedly be quickly voted out of office.

In the case of South Africa, as in many similar cases, the exclusion of specific groups from the electoral process is part of a larger picture of deprivation of civil rights. Attainment of the right to vote may not in itself provide a total solution to the deprived circumstances of such groups, but it is a necessary step toward the righting of political wrongs.

In recounting the history of the right to vote in the United States, we see a gradual, and often bitterly contested, broadening of the franchise. At the time the Constitution was ratified, all states except Vermont still imposed property or tax-paying qualifications on the franchise. Only in Vermont was there universal *man*hood suffrage—the democratic ideal of the day. Women were not seriously considered as potential voters—and the same applied to slaves. By the 1820s, most states had dropped property qualifications for voting, and after 1817 universal male suffrage was a prerequisite for admission to the Union. At that point, the United States enjoyed far more democratic suffrage than any other nation.

Extension of the franchise to black ex-slaves was mandated by the Fifteenth Amendment (1870) but not fully secured until the passage of the Voting Rights Act of 1965. As described in the Introduction, women had an even longer struggle to gain suffrage. Not until ratification of the Nineteenth Amendment, in 1920, did *all* adult citizens of the United States win the right to vote. Eighteen-year-olds were accorded the right to vote in federal elections in 1970, and that right was extended to state elections through the Twenty-sixth Amendment, ratified in 1971.

Blacks and Equal Rights

The Declaration of Independence proclaims that "all Men are created equal, that they are endowed by their Creator with certain inalienable Rights, that among these are Life, Liberty, and the Pursuit of Happiness." This revolutionary statement is constantly cited as proof of the fundamental American commitment to equal opportunity. And yet it was written by a slaveowner (Thomas Jefferson) and adopted by a Continental Congress that refused to take action against the slave trade.

When Africans first arrived at Jamestown, Virginia, in the early 1600s, slavery was almost unknown in English society. Initially, blacks were treated as indentured servants who could earn their freedom. However, this approach eventually yielded to an entrenched system of slavery as the need for cheap labor grew and the belief took hold that "savages" of another race were not entitled to the same protections accorded white people. Judges began to recognize sales and wills specifying complete servitude. Intermarriage between whites and blacks, which had been allowed, was forbidden in many colonies. Step by step, the debasement and dehumanization of blacks were crystallized in law, and the law deepened and

Highlights of Civil Rights Progress

Thirteenth Amendment (1865):
Prohibited slavery.

Fourteenth Amendment (1868):
Guaranteed equal protection of the laws.

Fifteenth Amendment (1870):
Extended the right to vote to blacks.

Creation of the Civil Rights Commission (1957).

Civil Rights Act (1964):
Prohibited discrimination in public accommodations on grounds of race, color, religion, or national origin.

Prohibited discrimination in hiring, firing, and pay levels in firms employing twenty-five or more.

Attorney general given the power to bring suits to enforce school desegregation.

Mandated that federal money could be withheld from any project in which discrimination was found.

Voting Rights Act (1965):
Mandated that where discrimination had been found, or where less than 50 percent of eligible voters were registered, the Civil Service Commission could appoint registrars who could require registration of all eligible voters in federal, state, and local elections. Suspended the use of literacy tests.

Housing Act (1968):
Prohibited discrimination in the sale or rental of much housing.

Education Amendments (1972):
Prohibited schools that receive federal aid from discriminating on the basis of sex.

Rehabilitation Act (1973):
Prohibited discrimination against the handicapped.

Institutionalized Persons Act (1980):
Permitted the federal government to bring suit on behalf of inmates of prisons and mental hospitals who are being denied their civil rights.

The Civil Rights Restoration Act (1988):
Restored the principle (temporarily disrupted by the Supreme Court in the *Grove City College* case) that educational institutions which accept federal funds must avoid discrimination in *all* programs—not just those receiving funds.

---

strengthened prejudice. Finally, the institution of slavery created a web of powerful economic interests that were dependent on it. It took a bloody Civil War to force a change in this situation.

Abolition of slavery and full equality for ex-slaves were the primary goals of the Radical Republicans, who dominated Congress in the late 1860s. By 1876, only eleven years after the end of the Civil War, the Constitution had been permanently altered by the addition of the Thirteenth, Fourteenth, and Fifteenth Amendments, which outlawed slavery, made equal protection of the laws a fundamental legal principle, and guaranteed voting rights for ex-slaves. Southern states had to ratify the amendments in order to be readmitted to the Union. During this period, the broad protections of the new constitutional provisions were supported by eleven major civil rights acts passed by Congress.

This monumental civil rights achievement, however, did not outlast the immediate postwar period. By the 1880s, most of the post–Civil War civil rights laws had been rendered inoperative by Court interpretations and by the unwillingness of either the Congress or the executive to enforce them. It required several generations of constant struggle to alter the patterns of legal segregation established in the late nineteenth and early twen-

It took Federal troops dispatched by President Dwight D. Eisenhower to ensure the integration of the schools in Little Rock, Arkansas, in 1957. The Little Rock crisis was one of many as school desegregation was met with intense resistance. *(UPI/Bettmann Newsphotos)*

tieth centuries. One of the key battlegrounds in this struggle was public education, which we now explore in detail.

SCHOOL DESEGREGATION In *Plessy* v. *Ferguson* (1896), the Supreme Court sanctioned as constitutional the establishment of "separate but equal" facilities for whites and blacks. The pernicious effects of this doctrine were especially evident in the creation throughout the South of rigidly separate and decidedly unequal school systems for blacks and whites. After years of determined litigation spearheaded by lawyers for the National Association for the Advancement of Colored People (NAACP), the Supreme Court in the 1930s began to recognize that segregation in education denied blacks basic civil rights. A first step in this direction came in the case of *Missouri ex rel. Gaines* v. *Canada* (1938). Lloyd Gaines, a citizen of Missouri and a black graduate of Lincoln University, had applied for admission to the all-white law school of the University of Missouri. Rather than admit Gaines to the state law school, Missouri offered to pay his tuition at any other law school that would admit blacks. Gaines refused to accept this compromise and took his case to court. The Supreme Court held that Gaines was "entitled to be admitted to the law school of the state university in the ab-

sence of other and proper provision for his legal training within the state."[34]

The Court went beyond the *Gaines* decision in *Sweatt* v. *Painter* (1950), in which the justices rejected Texas's contention that its new law school for blacks provided the same educational opportunities as those at the University of Texas.[35] In this decision, the Court argued that by segregating black students from whites, the state was denying blacks the interactions essential to a successful law career. This came close to saying that such segregated education could never in fact be "equal."

The decisions handed down in *Gaines* and *Sweatt* permitted the NAACP to challenge the whole structure of educational segregation. After the Supreme Court accepted school segregation cases for review in 1952, the U.S. Justice Department entered the fray on the side of those arguing that segregated schools were unconstitutional. Then, in 1954, after a long delay and extremely careful consideration, the Supreme Court unanimously ruled that segregated schools were unconstitutional in ***Brown* v. *Board of Education of Topeka*.**[36]

The *Brown* case signaled a decisive change in the U.S. legal system's approach to the issue of segregation. In the decades following *Plessy*, the Supreme Court had applied increasingly strict standards to the "separate but equal" doctrine but had not questioned the constitutionality of segregation itself. Blacks were granted relief not because they were segregated, but because they were denied equality within a segregated system. In the series of cases from which the landmark *Brown* decision derived, however, the facts showed that in all the school districts involved, "the Negro and white schools . . . have been equalized, or are being equalized." In *Brown,* therefore, the Court chose to face the issue of school segregation itself.

The substance of the Court's unanimous ruling in *Brown* was that segregated education *in itself* deprives black children of equal educational opportunities. In a famous footnote to the *Brown* opinion, the Court cited psychological evidence that black children suffered from a loss of self-esteem and viewed *being* black as inferior to being white. This sense of inferiority, the Court argued, interfered with the black child's motivation to learn and retarded his or her educational and mental development.

Despite the historic *Brown* v. *Board of Education* decision (1954), which called for the desegregation of public schools, only about one in every hundred black children in the South attended a desegregated school a decade later. (See **Figure 4–1**, page 136, for one example of Southern attitudes at that time.) During most of that period, the president and Congress could not decide how to implement desegregation, leaving the matter to the courts. Using the appealing rhetorical banner of "freedom of choice," the courts developed a legal doctrine that put the full burden of desegregation on black families. Thus, black families could challenge the racial status quo only by choosing to enroll their children in predominantly white schools, entering into long and difficult litigation, and accepting all the risks their actions entailed. This system clearly inhibited desegregation.

Finally, at the urging of President Lyndon Johnson, Congress passed the **Civil Rights Act of 1964,** which gave the attorney general the power to file desegregation lawsuits and prohibited federal aid to school districts that remained segregated. For the first time, the government placed the full force of the federal bureaucracy behind desegregation. The Department of Health, Education and Welfare (HEW), now broken into two cabinet depart-

ments—Education, and Health and Human Services—was charged with creating a single set of national standards and setting up a procedure for forcing school districts to desegregate *before* they received any federal assistance. School districts that refused to comply would not only lose needed funds, but would also face the threat of litigation by the Justice Department or by civil rights groups.

President Johnson and his ranking officials committed themselves to enforcing the law. During the first year of enforcement, more school districts were desegregated than during the entire preceding decade. All but a handful of Southern school districts agreed to implement desegregation plans. In the Deep South, where absolute resistance had been the rule, freedom-of-choice plans with token integration became the norm.

The Supreme Court lent the desegregation movement moral force in 1968 in Virginia, in the case of *Green* v. *School Board of New Kent County.*[37] Local authorities, the Court held, must "take whatever steps might be necessary to convert to a unitary system in which racial discrimination would be eliminated root and branch." Unless freedom of choice led to comprehensive integration in a particular community, it was not constitutionally acceptable.

The courts, HEW, and the Justice Department had finally begun to work together. HEW handled most of the massive administrative and political problems involved in desegregation. The courts upheld HEW standards and moved to settle unresolved issues in school desegregation law. The Justice Department threatened districts tempted to defy HEW and prompted the courts to develop new legal principles, which took hold rapidly in the South.

DE FACTO/DE JURE While the schools of the South were undergoing a period of drastic change, however, schools in the rest of the nation were becoming more segregated than ever. In the North people maintained that segregation in their schools was different from that found in the South—it was not imposed by state or local officials, but rather was the unplanned result of having children attend neighborhood schools where intense housing segregation was the rule. North-

FIGURE 4–1 **This letter from 1954 illustrates the intensity of Southern resistance to the Supreme Court's school desegregation rulings.**

Athens College
ATHENS, ALABAMA
DEAN-REGISTRAR OFFICE

FOUNDED 1842

June 2, 1954

Herbert L.Wright
Youth Secretary, NAACP
20 W.40th Street,
New York 18, N.Y.

Dear Sir:

    We thank you for the list of negro teachers who aspire to teach in white colleges. The same is being returned to you with our compliments.
    You are most presumptious in believing that so soon after the Supreme Court ruling, that private white colleges are ready to hire "nigger" teachers. We will probably never hire any of them. Your northern "Yankee" friends will employ them. Not us.
    Don't insult us any more with such expectations.

        Yours truly

        F. S. Ward
        F.S.Ward, Registrar

SOURCE: "Just Schools," *Southern Exposure,* May 1979, p. 28.

erners distinguished their *de facto* ("in fact") segregation from the Southern variety of *de jure* ("under law") segregation.

Because the constitutional guarantee of equal protection of the laws applies only to officially imposed segregation, it seemed that nothing much could be done about *de facto* segregation. For a decade and a half the courts accepted this distinction and required virtually no significant urban desegregation outside the South.

In the case of *Swann* v. *Charlotte-Mecklenburg Board of Education* (1971),[38] the Court finally faced

Hostile reactions to busing occurred in many parts of the country in the mid-1970s, and antibusing sentiment was especially strong in Boston. In this frightening and ironic photo, a demonstrator uses the American flag to stab a black businessman in Boston's City Hall Plaza. The wielder of the flagpole, a 17-year-old, pleaded guilty to assault and battery with a dangerous weapon. *(Stanley J. Forman, Pulitzer Prize 1977—Title: "Soiling of Old Glory")*

the important question of urban segregation. The school board of Charlotte, North Carolina, attempted to justify segregation as an innocent by-product of a racially neutral neighborhood-school policy. In rejecting this argument, the Court declared that if there had *once been* official school segregation, school authorities had an obligation to use whatever means were necessary, including busing, to achieve integration.

Once the neighborhood-school argument fell in the South, the doctrine was rapidly and successfully attacked in Northern cities. Civil rights lawyers found that the history of segregation in Northern districts almost always entailed some official involvement in racial separation, through such factors as zoning and school site decisions, real estate deals, residential covenants, and so on. Federal judges across the country took the Court's strong action in *Swann* as a mandate for rapid, comprehensive desegregation, and soon began handing down decisions requiring extensive transportation of pupils in a number of Northern cities.

Busing Local reaction to school busing orders was intense. Angry protesters filling television screens were as likely to speak in the accents of Michigan, Boston, or Southern California as Loui-

siana or Texas. As political criticism grew, President Richard Nixon announced in August 1971 that HEW and the Justice Department would do everything possible to curtail busing and that officials who disobeyed this directive would be summarily dismissed. The Nixon administration then took the extraordinary step of formally asking that its own desegregation proposals be *disregarded* by the courts. Coming just weeks before schools opened, the president's new position provoked further confusion and resistance.

Opposition to school busing by a majority of Americans intensified when several federal district courts ordered that students be transferred across city-suburban lines, if necessary, to achieve integration. The judges felt compelled to prescribe this remedy because the schools in several of the nation's largest cities—including New York, Chicago, Detroit, Atlanta, Baltimore, Cleveland, Houston, and Richmond—already had such large enrollments of minorities that integration *within* the cities' school systems seemed impossible. Adding to this problem was the growing tendency of white families to move from cities to suburbs to avoid forced busing—a phenomenon known as white flight. These families were vehemently opposed to busing their children back into city schools.

Antibusing sentiment had a profound effect on Congress. With racial issues, unlike many other matters, legislators' votes tend to reflect their constituents' attitudes. Race is such an emotional issue in U.S. society that when public attitudes are mobilized at the local level, members of Congress often feel that their political survival depends on going along with the dominant mood.[39] When asked about "busing of Negro and white schoolchildren from one school district to another" in a 1971 Gallup poll, 82 percent of the respondents opposed it or had no opinion, whereas only 18 percent supported it. Surveys taken among educators showed that three-fourths of school superintendents and teachers were opposed to busing. (See **Table 4–2** for an overview of more recent attitudes.)

The busing controversy raised basic questions about government's ability to sustain civil rights law in the face of a hostile majority. The historical evidence strongly suggests that when the hostile majority remains actively opposed and the issue continues to dominate politics, the courts tend to pull back. Restraints on judicial action can come from within the court system, from new members appointed to the courts, from judicial acceptance of some form of congressional restriction, or from a constitutional amendment.

As the 1970s drew to a close, the Supreme Court, in a series of decisions, made it clear that in general it would not mandate integration between city and suburbs. Thus, one of the obvious remedies for heavily segregated urban school systems seemed to pass out of political reach. At the

TABLE 4–2
Public Attitudes on Busing and Integrated Schools, 1981

	Integrated schools		
	All white parents	South	Rest of U.S.
Object to sending children to schools where:			
A few children are black	5%	5%	5%
One-half are black	23	27	22
More than one-half are black	55	66	51
No objections	45	34	49

	Busing for better racial balance		
	Favor	Oppose	No opinion
NATIONAL	22%	72%	6%
Whites	17	78	5
Blacks	60	30	10
East	23	69	8
Midwest	18	76	6
South	25	71	4
West	24	70	6
College education	21	75	4
High school	22	72	6
Grade school	27	65	8
Under 30 years	31	62	7
30–49 years	21	75	4
50 and older	18	76	6

SOURCE: Gallup poll, January 1981. In January 1981, a Gallup poll found Americans overwhelmingly opposed to busing in order to achieve racial balance. Of interest, white parents did not object to integrated schools as long as half or fewer of the students were black.

same time, however, the prospects for legislative or constitutional action to limit or prevent school busing also diminished considerably. Efforts to pass such legislation failed in the House in 1979.

During the 1980s, school desegregation remained on the back burner, lacking strong leadership from the federal government. New initiatives to eliminate *de facto* segregation have been launched at the local level, including the concept of "magnet schools." Under this approach, a school district puts extra resources into special programs (in the arts, for example, or the physical and biological sciences) at particular schools to create a "magnet," so that parents will want to send their children to that school. If successful, these magnet schools can achieve desegregation even though neighborhoods within the district remain sharply segregated. However, such programs have experienced only limited success. And, of course, magnet schools do not help break down segregation between urban and suburban school districts. Furthermore, special programs are expensive, and they are especially vulnerable when local school districts become financially strapped. In the end, desegregation efforts will succeed only if coaxed along by federal officials or by determined groups of local citizens who make an extra effort to advance toward this goal.

Affirmative Action and Black Progress

Exactly what does *equality* mean? That the door of opportunity be opened for all through the removal of legal barriers? Or that those who actually pass through that door represent a true racial and ethnic cross-section of the population? Simply that more blacks, for example, enter the middle class, or become corporate executives and government officials? Or that blacks as a group achieve real economic parity with whites?

In exploring these questions, we look first at the *Bakke* case, which involved many of the basic issues raised by **affirmative action**—the attempt to remedy current disparities or past discrimination by favoring minorities in particular programs. We then examine black progress in political, economic, and social matters—an issue far more complicated than it may at first appear.

Allan Bakke, whose charge of reverse discrimination was upheld by the Supreme Court in 1978, allowing him to be admitted to medical school. The Court proved so divided about quotas and affirmative action, however, that no clear guidelines emerged. *(AP/Wide World Photos)*

THE BAKKE CASE At age 31, Allan Paul Bakke became interested in pursuing a career in medicine and very determinedly set out to receive training as a physician. In his initial attempts to gain admission to medical school, he was rejected by both the University of Southern California and Northwestern University—Northwestern chiefly because of his age. The following year, he sought entry into eleven medical schools, none of which admitted him. One of these schools was the University of California at Davis, which had a special-admissions program for students who were well-qualified for medical school but who would not have been admitted through the regular competitive admissions procedures. Almost all special-admissions applicants were minority students. Of the one hundred places at the Davis Medical School, sixteen were reserved for special admissions. When Bakke applied yet again, and again was turned down despite scoring higher than some minority applicants who were accepted, he went to court. In a lawsuit filed in state courts, he charged that he had been the victim of discrimination, in that the affirmative action program of the Davis Medical School had unfairly reduced the number of places available for more qualified students. Bakke's main purpose in bringing the suit was not so much to challenge racial "quotas" (as he put it) in general, as to get himself into medical school.

When the California Supreme Court upheld Bakke's position, the state appealed the case to the U.S. Supreme Court. The case involved a serious conflict between two apparently worthy goals: affirmative action to aid disadvantaged groups, and equal treatment for all, regardless of race, ethnicity, or gender. At the same time, law and medical schools were facing mounting pressure to admit minorities: In 1970, only 1 percent of American lawyers and only 2 percent of doctors and 6 percent of medical students were black.

The political atmosphere surrounding the *Bakke* case was notably charged as well. The public was growing increasingly disenchanted with affirmative action programs, on the ground that they led to reverse discrimination. For example, many employers had been required to hire and promote more women and minority group members as a condition for doing business with government agencies. To avoid losing business, employers gave preference in hiring and promotion to applicants on the basis of race and gender—making it correspondingly more difficult for white males, who sometimes raised the claim of reverse discrimination. (See **Table 4–3** for an overview of current attitudes toward affirmative action.)

The Supreme Court decision in *Regents of the University of California* v. *Bakke*, handed down in the spring of 1978, was marked by a notable lack of unanimity.[40] The Court ruled, 5–4, that Bakke should be admitted to the Davis Medical School. But the Court *really* divided 4–1–4. One block of four justices took the position that the Civil Rights Act of 1964 prohibits racial quotas like those used

**TABLE 4–3
Affirmative Action Attitudes**

	White Percentage	Black Percentage
Affirmative action programs that help blacks and other minorities to get ahead should be supported		
Strongly agree	6	26
Agree	70	70
Disagree	21	4
Strongly disagree	3	0
Colleges and universities should set aside a certain number of positions to admit qualified blacks and other minorities		
Strongly agree	5	10
Agree	55	74
Disagree	30	13
Strongly disagree	5	3
Employers should set aside a certain number of places to hire qualified blacks and other minorities		
Strongly agree	3	16
Agree	48	57
Disagree	40	24
Strongly disagree	9	3
Do you personally feel that such preferential treatment (for blacks) is/would be:		
Fair	35	42
Unfair	65	58

SOURCE: J. R. Kluegel and E. R. Smith, *Beliefs about Inequality* (Hawthorne, N.Y.: Aldine, de Gruyter, 1986), pp. 202–203.

by the Davis Medical School. The other group of four argued that the Davis program was constitutionally valid. The swing vote belonged to Justice Lewis F. Powell, Jr. Powell sided with the first group on one set of issues and with the other group on another set. The end result was that whereas the Davis special-admissions program was struck down and Bakke ordered admitted, the use of race as a factor in admissions procedures was deemed acceptable so long as there were no "quotas" and the objectives of the "race-conscious" admissions procedures were "reasonable"—such as ensuring a diverse student body. Powell's "solution" had a certain appeal—it banned quotas while allowing continued preferential admissions under the banner of "student diversity." Yet it was not at all clear what standards, if any, applied to this notion of diversity. Such a vague concept could be used to establish informal quotas of any sort.

Bakke turned out not to be the landmark case many had expected. Because no firm majority emerged on the Court, there was no transformation of legal doctrine comparable to that achieved in the *Brown* decision in 1954. Given only limited guidance, lower courts later handed down contradictory decisions. One U.S. circuit court of appeals approved a plan requiring that blacks comprise 50 percent of those promoted to sergeant in Detroit's police force. Another appeals court, however, declared illegal a plan requiring specific minority representation on two student government boards at a state university. Further, the admissions plan at one law school was struck down, even though it contained no quotas, whereas a minority hiring program that did set quotas was approved.

SINCE BAKKE   In *Fullilove* v. *Klutznick* (1980), the Supreme Court clarified matters a bit.[41] Here the Court upheld federal regulations stipulating that 10 percent of federal public-works contracts be set aside for companies controlled by minority group members. But the Court limited its ruling to *Congress's* powers, leaving educational institutions, government agencies, and the states without definitive guidance on affirmative action issues.

In a ruling that reversed earlier decisions supporting affirmative action arrangements in employment, the Supreme Court found in *Memphis Fire Department* v. *Stotts* (1984) that a court could not order an employer to protect the jobs of recently hired black employees at the expense of whites who had greater seniority.[42] In the majority opinion, Justice Byron White stated that the policy of the Civil Rights Act of 1964 was "to provide make-whole relief only to those who have been actual victims of illegal discrimination." The question is whether an *entire group* is entitled to affirmative action to remedy discrimination without any one member having to prove that he or she was actually discriminated against.

The importance of seniority was reaffirmed by another sharply divided Court in 1986 in *Wygant* v. *Jackson Board of Education* (page 946). In this case, the Court ruled that laying off more senior white teachers violated the constitutional principle of equal protection. But the Court did agree that carefully constructed affirmative action programs were indeed constitutional. In two other recent cases a majority of the Court upheld particular racially based affirmative action programs. One involved voluntary pacts, between unions and public employers, providing for minority hiring preferences. In the other case, the Court ruled that a judge may order agencies to temporarily impose quotas if there is a history of "egregious" racial bias.

The Supreme Court has accorded affirmative action for women a lower priority than racially based affirmative action. Racial policies receive the "strict scrutiny" of the Court, while gender-based policies are reviewed under a less exacting standard. It wasn't until 1987 that the Court specifically upheld an affirmative action program's move to redress gender-based discrimination. In 1979, Diane Joyce was named the road dispatcher for the Santa Clara County (California) Transportation Agency. Paul Johnson was not given the job, even though he received a higher interview score than Joyce. In giving Joyce the job, the agency director took a variety of factors into account, including qualifications, test scores, and affirmative action considerations. No woman had ever held one of the agency's "skilled craft worker" jobs. Justice Brennan, writing for the Court, upheld the agency's actions, finding that "No persons are automatically excluded from consideration; *all* are able to have their qualifications weighed against those of other applicants." The decision clarified the status of affirmative action programs. According to the ruling, a carefully constructed affirmative action program is not unconstitutional when gender or race is taken into account as one of a variety of factors in making hiring or promotion decisions, when affirmative action considerations don't wholly override considerations of seniority, and when a history of discrimination or a clear pattern of current disparity exists. But the Court's willingness to accept affirmative action programs does not guarantee that such programs will be created or that guidelines will be vigorously enforced. Those actions largely depend on other players in the political system.

TABLE 4–4
The Supreme Court and Affirmative Action

Case	Defendants	Issue	Judicial findings of prior discrimination	Basis of challenge	Decision	Vote
Regents of the University of California v. *Bakke* (1978)	State medical school	Voluntary admissions quotas for blacks	No	Title VI of the 1964 Civil Rights Act	Quota impermissible; some consideration of race permissible	5–4 / 5–4
United Steelworkers of America v. *Weber* (1979)	Labor union and private employer	Voluntary quota for blacks in training program	No	Title VII of 1964 Civil Rights Act	Quota permissible	5–2
Fullilove v. *Klutznick* (1980)	Congress and secretary of commerce	Set-aside of federal funds for minority firm contracts	No	Constitution: equal protection, due process guarantees	Set-aside permissible	6–3
Firefighters Local Union #1784 v. *Stotts* (1984)	Public employer (city fire department)	Court order overriding seniority rights in layoffs to preserve jobs of blacks	No, but consent decree entered to settle charges of bias	Title VII of 1964 Civil Rights Act	Order not permissible	6–3
Wygant v. *Jackson Board of Education* (1986)	Public employer (school board)	Voluntary agreement to modify seniority rule for layoffs to preserve jobs of blacks	No	Constitution: equal protection	Seniority modification for layoffs not permissible	5–4

Overall, in its affirmative action decisions between 1978 and 1986, the Court struck down as many plans as it approved (see **Table 4–4**). Among the factors influencing the Court's rulings were a record of past discrimination, the identity of the employer involved, and the extent to which affirmative action would injure individuals.[43]

BLACK PROGRESS   The day after the *Bakke* decision was handed down, a Harvard admissions officer sent the following letter to the *New York Times*:

To the Editor:

It is strange that on the day of the famous Bakke decision ABC televised a frightening documentary, "Youth Terror: A View from Behind the Gun," about the millions of bitter and hopelessly lost members of minorities in the urban centers of this country.

If that documentary accurately reflects the existence of these young people (I have no reason to think it does not), then debating the correctness of the Supreme Court's Bakke decision is like arguing over sun-deck chairs on the *Titanic*.

From this sobering perspective, we will consider black progress over the past thirty years.

Obviously, much has changed. There are no more legally segregated restaurants, motels, drinking fountains, bathrooms, schools, armies. Instead of arguing about whether a black can be admitted

TABLE 4–4 (*continued*)

Case	Defendants	Issue	Judicial findings of prior discrimination	Basis of challenge	Decision	Vote
Local #28 of the Sheet Metal Workers' International Association v. *Equal Employment Opportunity Commission* (1986)	Labor union	Court-ordered quota for admitting blacks to union	Yes	Title VII of the 1964 Civil Rights Act; Constitution: equal protection, due process guarantees	Quota permissible	5–4
Local #93, International Association of Firefighters, AFL-CIO v. *Cleveland* (1986)	Public employer (city fire department)	Consent decree providing for promotions quota for blacks	Yes	Title VII of 1964 Civil Rights Act	Promotions quota permissible	6–3
United States v. *Paradise* (pending)	Public employer (state department of public safety)	Court-ordered promotions quota for blacks	Yes	Constitution: equal protection	Promotions quota permissible	5–4
Johnson v. *Santa Clara County Transportation Agency* (pending)	Public employer (county transportation agency)	Voluntary plan to promote women	No	Title VII of 1964 Civil Rights Act	Plan permissible	6–3

SOURCE: *Congressional Weekly Reports*, Nov. 15, 1986, p. 2899.

to an all-white law school, we're now arguing about *Bakke*. Systematic attempts to keep blacks from the voting booth are a thing of the past. Indeed, blacks are voting in ever-greater numbers, and more and more black officials are being elected. Recognizing political reality, a new crop of Southern governors has buried hard-line segregationist styles. On the economic level, poverty has been diminished, and increasing numbers of blacks are entering the middle class, as opportunities have grown.

Yet much has not changed. The black ghettos remain in Harlem, Bedford-Stuyvesant, Watts. A great disparity still exists between black and white income levels. And the death and infant-mortality rates remain higher among blacks, as do crime and unemployment rates. (Chapter 18 takes a closer look at contemporary aspects of black progress.)

THE REAGAN RECORD The Reagan administration did not place assistance to blacks and other minorities high on its political agenda. Besides cutting many programs designed to assist blacks in particular, the administration showed considerable reluctance to endorse the extension of the Voting Rights Act and initially supported tax exemptions for segregated schools. President Reagan also opposed quotas, affirmative action programs of many kinds, and court-ordered busing arrangements.

In a highly inflammatory political move, the president fired three members of the Civil Rights Commission, the federal government's civil rights watchdog, and replaced them with appointees who did not favor race-based formulas to correct past discrimination.[44] One of the new Reagan appointees, John Bunzel, stated that

> it is a crude oversimplification . . . to suggest that racism and discrimination are the root cause of why certain minority groups fall below the average in income and occupation. To accept this premise is to overlook better-than-average achievements of other minorities that have suffered discrimination. Differences among ethnic groups are complex and deeply anchored. This is why doubling the Equal Employment Opportunity Commission's resources or mandating preferential employment and promotion according to some race-based formula will not really help minorities at the low end of the ladder.

In defense of its positions, the administration argued that quotas constituted a denial of equal protection, both for minorities and for women; that its "free-market" economic programs would do more for the poor than social programs could accomplish; and that mandatory busing should no longer be required where past discrimination had been corrected.

Women and Equal Rights

The battle for female suffrage culminated on August 18, 1920, when Tennessee became the thirty-sixth state to ratify the Nineteenth Amendment, granting women the right to vote. The magnitude of this achievement—after so many years of struggle—was captured in the following statement by Carrie Chapman Catt, president of the National American Woman Suffrage Association:

> [Getting] the word "male" . . . out of the Constitution cost women of the country 52 years of pauseless campaign. . . . During that time they were forced to conduct 56 campaigns to get Legislatures to submit suffrage amendments to voters; 47 campaigns to get state conventions to write woman suffrage into state constitutions; 277 campaigns to get state party conventions to include woman suffrage planks; 30 campaigns to get presidential party conventions to adopt

The full text of the proposed Equal Rights Amendment, unfurled in a dramatic, if familiar, context. Seated is Isola Dubik, a former suffragette and a campaigner for women's rights. *(Bettye Lane/Photo Researchers)*

woman suffrage planks in party platforms; and 19 campaigns with 19 successive Congresses.[45]

Following approval of the Nineteenth Amendment, women made substantial inroads in political and economic life. The League of Women Voters was formed in 1919. At the same time, women's lobbying groups were organized, women's branches of various professional associations sprang up, and the number of women appointed to positions of responsibility in government increased steadily. Nonetheless, women were still excluded from juries and from public office in many states. In addition, many state and federal laws discriminating against women in regard to property ownership and other matters remained in force.

During the 1940s and 1950s, organized political

activity on behalf of women's political and social rights dropped to a low point, although extensive social changes, such as the growing presence of women in the work force, heralded political developments to come. The 1960s and early 1970s marked a watershed in feminist activity and legislative attempts to secure full equality for women. The Equal Pay Act of 1963 required equal pay for equal work for the first time. Title VII of the Civil Rights Act of 1964 banned discrimination in employment on the basis of sex. Through this measure, women gained significant legal protection in the work place, but it stirred up considerable controversy concerning just how far equality of the sexes should go. Also, many states began to eliminate or revise statutes that discriminated both for and against women in matters such as divorce and family law.

However, the step-by-step process of altering laws and customs to achieve equality for women struck many activists as too cumbersome and slow. In the mid-1970s, the women's movement came to focus on the proposed **Equal Rights Amendment** to the Constitution as a way of providing equality in one stroke. After a long political struggle, the amendment was finally defeated—a story detailed in Chapter 3.

Basic Social Rights

Eighteenth-century liberals primarily conceived of rights and liberties as protections against the encroachments of government. It was the arbitrariness of government—its tendency to intrude into the lives of citizens, to become tyrannical—that most concerned the framers of the Constitution.

But in the late nineteenth century, the view of government as tyrant began to make way for a more benign attitude. As rapid industrialization swept through the country, reformers pressed for an activist government—one committed to guaranteeing citizens' rights to health, safety, education, and human services in an increasingly mechanized and dehumanizing industrial society. This radical shift was prompted by the Industrial Revolution.

From a relatively small, agrarian society, the United States had been transformed into a boom-ing industrial society powered by a modern capitalist economy and characterized by rapid urbanization and increasing mechanization of transport and industry. Out of these developments arose a series of complex social problems that involved such fundamental issues as the right to basic security in regard to health and safety. Reformers sought to have government intervene to ensure decent housing for all, to limit the hours employees worked in factories, to protect workers from unsafe working conditions, to provide public health services to counteract serious illnesses, to guarantee that all citizens received a basic education, and so on. Unlike eighteenth-century liberals, then, the social activists of the late nineteenth century envisioned an activist government—one that involved itself in the day-to-day affairs of its citizens. In their view, such a government was essential for a just society.

In Part IV, which deals with contemporary issues of public policy, we will look at recent controversies over government intervention to protect the general welfare. Here, the new concepts of basic social rights are illustrated through two important examples of government action—(1) the creation of the federal Food and Drug Administration and (2) government's role in the drive to form trade unions and to institute collective bargaining.

Pure Food and Drugs

In his novel *The Jungle*, published in 1906, Upton Sinclair drew a graphic sketch of the conditions at the Chicago stockyards. Sinclair had spent seven weeks observing meat-packing workers on the job and studying the meat inspection laws. He wrote *The Jungle* to expose the abominable conditions of the factory workers, but the novel sparked greater public concern over unsanitary ingredients in food and drugs. The following passage from Sinclair's novel demonstrates why the public reacted with such outrage:

There would come all the way back from Europe old sausage that had been rejected, and that was moldy and white—and it would be dosed with borax and

Poultry inspector, circa 1930. At the time, legal provisions to ensure safe food and drugs were still somewhat new. *(National Archives)*

glycerine and dumped into hoppers, and made over again for home consumption. There would be meat that had tumbled out on the floor, in the dirt and sawdust, where the workers had trampled and spit uncounted billions of consumption [tubercular] germs. There would be meat stored in great piles in rooms; and the water from leaky roofs would drop over it, and thousands of rats would race about on it. It was too dark in those storage places to see well, but a man could run his hand over these piles of meat and sweep off handfuls of the dried dung of rats. These rats were nuisances and the packers would put poisoned bread out for them—they would die, and then rats, bread, and meat would go into the hoppers together. . . . The meat would be shoveled into carts, and the man who did the shoveling would not trouble to lift out a rat even if he saw one—there were things that went into the sausage in comparison with which a poisoned rat was a tidbit.[46]

Sinclair's revelations, combined with the efforts of others who had revealed the widespread use of dangerous substances in food and drugs, led to the passage of the Pure Food and Drug Act and the Meat Inspection Act of 1906, under which federal authorities were empowered to ban some forms of adulteration of food and drugs and to stop the use of hazardous preservatives. Over the next two decades, additional legislation broadened the scope of government concern. A 1912 law banned false health claims for patent medicines; a 1913 law required package labels to include the quantity of various contents; a 1919 law required net-weight labels on packaged meat.

Not until 1927, however, did Congress create an agency to enforce this legislation. The Food, Drug and Insecticide Administration (which became the Food and Drug Administration in 1931) recognized that technological changes and various court decisions had largely outdated the 1906 law under which it operated. Yet another scandal was required before the agency gained adequate regulatory powers. When a new "wonder drug," elixir sulfanilamide, was marketed without prior safety testing, it caused the deaths of more than one hundred people. Under the existing law, the FDA had been powerless to prevent the drug from reaching the market—it was empowered to take action against a drug only after it had been demonstrated to cause death or illness. Public outrage over the FDA's inability to stop the marketing of elixir sulfanilamide prompted passage of the Food, Drug and Cosmetic Act of 1938, which specified that drugs be tested prior to distribution, set tolerance levels for toxic substances, provided for factory inspection, strengthened truth-in-labeling provisions of previous laws, and extended health coverage to cosmetics.

Even this strengthening of the health and safety laws did not guarantee that all food, drugs, and other consumer products reaching the market were safe, but it did signal a clear recognition of government's responsibility to ensure the safety of food and drugs. The basic right involved here—one that remains highly controversial in specific applications—is the right to safe, noninjurious products.

The Ludlow Massacre of 1913

Attempts to unionize the coal and mineral miners of Colorado began in the 1890s. Concerted unionizing efforts early in the twentieth century led to the arrest of union organizers and the firing of union sympathizers. The mines were subsequently worked by nonunion laborers, most of whom were recent immigrants from Europe or Mexico. For a time, these workers proved relatively docile, despite the wretched conditions found in the mining camps, where disease was rampant, sanitation poor, and alcoholism common. Water for drinking and washing flowed directly from the mines, without prior treatment. Miners were paid only in scrip, or company money, which could be used only in company-owned stores. Many conditions in the camps violated state law, but because the mining companies exerted great influence over Colorado politics, the state did not intervene to improve conditions.

Eventually the workers organized, and in September 1912 they called for a forty-hour work week, an eight-hour work day, union recognition, and various other work-related improvements. When the mining companies refused to budge on the unionization issue, the workers went on strike. Both miners and employers expected the strike to be serious and violent. The workers had stockpiled weapons, in the well-founded belief that the companies would resort to violence to break the strike. The companies brought in detectives and deputy sheriffs to protect their property. Finally, the governor called out the state militia. A six-month stalemate ensued, and the companies began to import strikebreakers.

On April 19, 1913, in circumstances that are still disputed, a confrontation between state militia and strikers led to violence. A strikers' camp in Ludlow was burned and thirty-three people were killed, including eleven women and children. After this "Ludlow massacre," the strikers prepared for open warfare, and the governor called on President Woodrow Wilson to send federal troops. Ten days later, the U.S. Army occupied the area and calm was restored. The union failed to gain recognition.

The Ludlow massacre was one of the more dramatic examples of labor-management violence in U.S. history.

Trade Unions and Collective Bargaining

Although the rights of workers to organize and to bargain with management are not thought of as fundamental human rights, they are indispensable to the successful functioning of an industrial society. More important, they are closely connected with the meaning of democracy in modern times. Without the opportunity to form trade unions, workers often have little defense against exploitation by management. In the absence of an effective workers' organization, working conditions and pay can largely be dictated by management—a situation resembling tyranny far more than democracy. The right to form a union, then, is one of the basic democratic rights required for a decent life in a modern society.

The history of the union movement in the United States has been punctuated by many episodes of violence. For decades, government forces were brought to bear against workers who attempted to form unions. Until 1842, the courts typically held that union activity *per se* was illegal. After that date, courts were more willing to grant unions the right to exist but generally refused to recognize a union's right to strike or to compel employers to bargain collectively. Beginning in the 1880s, court orders against union activities were widely used to break strikes, and state militia, National Guard, and regular army forces often intervened in labor disputes on the side of employers.

The first piece of federal legislation to provide some protection for labor was the Clayton Act of 1914, which prohibited the issuance of injunctions (court orders) against strikes, boycotts, and picketing except to prevent "irreparable damage." The courts, however, remained generally hostile to unions, and Congress was slow to act on behalf of unions. The Great Depression forced political leaders to recognize that fundamental changes were necessary in the economic life of the nation.

Two pieces of legislation, in particular, signaled government acceptance of unions as a permanent and legitimate force in U.S. society. The Norris-LaGuardia Act of 1932 prohibited the enforcement of "yellow dog" contracts in federal courts. Such contracts, which had been used widely to prevent unionization, required that employees sign a pledge not to join a union as a condition of employment. The Norris-LaGuardia Act also prohibited the federal courts from issuing injunctions against strikes. In effect, then, the act neutralized the role of the federal courts in labor disputes.

The Wagner Act, passed in 1935, went further. Under this measure, workers were guaranteed the right to form unions and to bargain with management. The Wagner Act also created the National Labor Relations Board (NLRB), which was empowered to investigate unfair labor practices by employers and to issue cease-and-desist orders enforceable through the federal courts. Not only did this act effectively end violent labor strife in the United States by firmly establishing the right to collective bargaining, but it also helped create an atmosphere in which unions were more likely to develop. And between 1935 and 1947, union membership increased from 4 million to 15.5 million.

After World War II, federal legislators adopted a more critical stance toward unions. The Taft-Hartley Act of 1947, for example, regulated union activities and prohibited strikes by federal employees. Under Section 14B of the act, states were empowered to pass "right to work" laws, which require that union membership not be a *condition* of employment. Such provisions were adopted by twenty states, despite vigorous opposition by organized labor. The Landrum-Griffin Act of 1959 then mandated more democratic practices *within* unions and established a union membership "bill of rights."

Today, debates continue over union power and management practices. Many observers charge that unions have become too powerful and often obstruct more than facilitate labor relations. Others point out that the United States is one of the least unionized nations in the industrialized democratic world and that many U.S. workers still suffer from a lack of basic protections. For our purposes, the preceding discussion illustrates that political recognition and protection for basic trade union rights came only after a series of painful, costly battles that reflected the social class divisions in U.S. society, in which the many own little property and the few control most of it. The issue of the effects on democratic life of an extremely unequal distribution of property is one we will examine closely in Chapter 5.

Government Repression

Our national history has shown an admirable commitment to defending civil liberties and rights, but the drive to undermine them has run equally strong. Attempts by the federal government to prosecute and harass opponents date back to the Alien and Sedition Acts of the John Adams administration, as we saw earlier in this chapter. As a rule, the tempo of repression quickens when some in government perceive threats to established patterns of social and political life. As a result, throughout U.S. history, groups advocating radical change or appearing to question established norms have often been the targets of government repression.

In the early years of this century, for example, a concerted campaign of prosecutions was directed against the Industrial Workers of the World (IWW), a militant industrial union. Many of its leaders were eventually imprisoned. Then, in the aftermath of World War I and the Russian Revolution, a near-hysterical fear of communism swept the country. During this "red scare," the press relentlessly portrayed anarchists and radicals as serious threats to law and order and to the government itself. In January 1920, about four thousand alleged radicals were arrested. Many were deported and many others imprisoned. Most were held without benefit of legal assistance and some were even prevented from contacting their families.

A teacher at Kent State University honors the memory of four students killed by National Guard troops in May 1970. Nine others were wounded when the Guard was called to campus to contain intense demonstrations against the Vietnam War. This clash between the forces of order and the right to protest had lethal consequences, which many believe could have been avoided. *(AP/ Wide World Photos)*

At the state level, five socialists were deprived of their seats in the New York state legislature. State legislatures passed statutes requiring loyalty oaths for teachers, and measures were drafted to keep the Socialist Party off the ballot.

This pattern of antiradical activity combined with repression or subversion of civil rights was repeated in the 1950s. Tensions raised by the Cold War with the Soviet Union (plus the hot war in Korea) led to restrictions on free speech similar to those imposed by the Smith Act. Loyalty oaths again proliferated. Congress was also active in attempting to ferret out the "disloyal." The House Un-American Activities Committee, in particular, relentlessly hunted communists—past or present —and communist sympathizers in all walks of American life. Many people lost jobs, careers, friends, and self-respect during these investigations. As states copied the national model, many state un-American activities committees sprang up.

Civil rights and antiwar activities in the 1960s led to another outburst of repressive activities. Presidents Lyndon Johnson and Richard Nixon, believing that the antiwar movement and the New Left posed a serious threat to American society, apparently felt that drastic action was needed to

stop disruptions. The federal government's intelligence-gathering and investigatory agencies kept close track of many activists such as Dr. Martin Luther King, Jr. Informers infiltrated groups considered radical, regardless of whether those groups had broken laws or taken part in violence. Illegal break-ins and wiretaps by law enforcement officials were used to monitor such organizations.

The states also joined in the antiradical campaign. Julian Bond, the first black elected to the Georgia state legislature in one hundred years, was denied his seat because of his association with the Student Non-Violent Coordinating Committee, which had outspokenly opposed the Vietnam War. In this case, however, the federal courts stepped in to uphold Bond's rights to the legislative seat.

To some observers, these outbreaks of government repression represented justifiable responses to real threats to the social order. If groups seek to violently alter society or to subvert institutions, it is argued, repression is called for—although in this view "repression" usually is called *"maintaining order."* It is true that at times the threats have been real, and at other times it has been difficult to decide whether threats were real or not. Were anarchists sending bombs through the mail in 1919?

The Harassment of Martin Luther King, Jr.

For more than six years, from 1962 to 1968, the Federal Bureau of Investigation engaged in daily surveillance of civil rights leader Martin Luther King, Jr. Though not publicly revealed until after King's death in 1968, the FBI's campaign against him did much private damage to King's reputation and brought serious emotional turmoil to him and his closest relatives.

The FBI's pursuit of King began six years after he first became a national figure, during the Montgomery, Alabama bus boycott of 1955–1956. In early 1962 the FBI learned that one of King's closest political advisers was a white New York attorney, Stanley D. Levison, who had come to the Bureau's attention a decade earlier when he was playing a crucial role in the U.S. Communist Party. Wiretaps were placed on Levison's telephones and microphones covertly installed in his office, but no evidence of sinister connections or plotting was forthcoming. Nevertheless, FBI Director J. Edgar Hoover sent grim warnings about the Levison-King friendship to President John F. Kennedy and his brother Robert, the attorney general. The Kennedy brothers finally approved Hoover's request that FBI wiretaps be placed on King's home and office phones in Atlanta.

The new electronic surveillance transformed the FBI's interest in King almost overnight. Concern about Levison quickly was replaced by an obsession that King's private life was unacceptable for such a prominent minister and public leader. Agents were assigned to tail King as he traveled from city to city and hotel room to hotel room, and transcribed accounts of his most private moments were sent out to the White House and to dozens of federal agencies. Bureau operatives attempted to interest the news media in the personal material about King, and one FBI executive mailed an anonymous threatening letter to King—enclosing an embarrassing tape and warning of imminent exposure—just days after the black leader had been awarded the 1964 Nobel Peace Prize for his pioneering civil rights efforts. Much to the FBI's disappointment, its efforts to smear or destroy King publicly went for naught; reporter after reporter rebuffed the Bureau's approaches on the grounds that King's private life was not news.

Frustrated but not dissuaded, the FBI kept up its close watch on King's activities, becoming particularly agitated when he strongly denounced the Vietnam War policies of President Lyndon Johnson and advocated a massive but nonviolent "Poor People's Campaign" directed at the nation's capitol. Thorough and painstaking congressional investigations have shown no FBI complicity in King's 1968 assassination. The full record of the Bureau's activities against King, however, reveals that millions of dollars were spent on one of the most appalling violations of personal privacy and civil liberties in U.S. government history.

Was the U.S. Communist Party trying to subvert the government in the 1930s and 1940s? Did antiwar radicals plan to destroy property and disrupt public order during the Democratic Convention in 1968? Were black radicals of the 1960s talking revolution and violence?

The scant elements of truth in these allegations persuaded political leaders and much of the rest of the population that drastic steps had to be taken. Yet *repression*, not just maintaining order, carried the day in each case. Authorities ignored civil liberties, used excessive force, and intimidated people with any sympathies for the targets of repression.

In searching for reasons why government has sometimes resorted to repressive tactics, some authorities contend that government repression is directed against the perceived enemies of private property and the capitalist enterprise. Still others cite a decidedly lukewarm commitment to civil liberties among U.S. political elites. According to this view, many at the top levels of our political establishment are concerned more with maintaining their own power than with respect for the Bill of Rights.

Of course, political elites alone cannot be blamed for repression; it also has a popular base. As we will see in Chapter 6, tolerance for dissent has had a long struggle to become established in the United States. Even reasonable people often disagree about what should be tolerated. For example, should groups preaching racial or religious hatred be permitted to exercise First Amendment rights? Should groups that do not respect civil liberties be entitled to those liberties? Such questions defy simple answers. Yet our constitutional protections play a key role in shoring up defenses against repression.

Conclusions

Looking back over U.S. history, we can take pride in this country's increasing recognition of civil rights and liberties. Thirty-five years ago, for example, basic civil rights were denied to many black citizens, and the civil liberties of all citizens were being threatened amid an outburst of anticommunist hysteria. In most ways, we are far better off today. But it has been a slow, costly, often painful process.

We must also acknowledge that neglect, repression, or erosion of liberties and rights have also marked our history.

Finally, we must recognize the need to reassess rights and liberties as politics and society change. Twentieth-century democrats cannot view civil and social rights in the manner of eighteenth-century liberals. New conceptions of rights and liberties, however, inevitably spark new controversies and disputes.

Overall, the United States of the late twentieth century is a freer country than it has been before—a nation more attentive to the democratic rights of its citizens. However, some U.S. citizens still suffer deprivation of their rights—out of neglect, harassment, or the inability to put those rights and liberties to use. When this happens, true democrats believe that their own rights and liberties have lost some of their meaning.

GLOSSARY TERMS

civil liberties
civil rights
Bill of Rights
Fourteenth Amendment
due process clause
equal protection clause
First Amendment
"clear and present danger"
establishment clause
free exercise clause
due process
Miranda **v.** *Arizona*
Plessy **v.** *Ferguson*
Brown **v.** *Board of Education of Topeka*
Civil Rights Act of 1964
affirmative action

NOTES

[1]16 Wallace 36.

[2]268 U.S. 652.

[3]J. S. Mill, *On Liberty* (New York: Crofts, 1947); and John Milton, *Aeropagitica*, John Hales, ed. (London: Oxford, 1961).

[4]Alexander Meiklejohn, *Free Speech in Relation to Self-Government* (New York: Harper & Row, 1948); and *Political Freedom* (New York: Oxford, 1965).

[5]H. Pollack and A. B. Smith, *Civil Liberties and Civil Rights in the United States* (St. Paul, Minn.: West, 1978).

[6]249 U.S. 47.

[7]250 U.S. 616.

[8]268 U.S. 652.

[9]341 U.S. 494.

[10]341 U.S. 494.

[11]354 U.S. 298.

[12]364 U.S. 479.

[13]391 U.S. 308.

[14]391 U.S. 367.

[15]391 U.S. 367.

[16]393 U.S. 503.

[17]315 U.S. 568.

[18]405 U.S. 518.

[19]432 U.S. 43.

[20]370 U.S. 421.

[21]472 U.S. 38.

[22]397 U.S. 664.

[23]461 U.S. 574.

[24]13 Wall 679.

[25]98 U.S. 145.

[26]310 U.S. 586.

[27]319 U.S. 624.

[28]380 U.S. 163.

[29]398 U.S. 333.

[30]*New York Times,* Dec. 6, 1987, p. 32.

[31]372 U.S. 335.

[32]384 U.S. 436.

[33]410 U.S. 113.

[34]305 U.S. 337.

[35]339 U.S. 629.

[36]347 U.S. 483.

[37]391 U.S. 430.

[38]402 U.S. 1.

[39]Warren E. Miller and Donald E. Stokes, "Constituency Influence in Congress," *American Political Science Review* 57 (March 1963): 45–56.

[40]438 U.S. 265.

[41]448 U.S. 448.

[42]82 U.S. 229. For a discussion of the implications of the Memphis case, see "Seniority vs. Minorities—Impact of Court Ruling," *U.S. News and World Report,* June 25, 1984, pp. 22–23; and F. Barbash and K. Sawyer, "A New Era of 'Race Neutrality' in Hiring?" *Washington Post,* National Weekly Edition, June 25, 1984.

[43]*Congressional Weekly Reports,* Nov. 15, 1986, p. 2898.

[44]John H. Bunzel, "Promoting Rights," *New York Times,* Sept. 20, 1983.

[45]As quoted in Jarol B. Manheim, *Déjà Vu* (New York: St. Martin's, 1976), pp. 147–148.

[46]Upton Sinclair, *The Jungle* (New York: Viking, 1946), p. 135.

SELECTED READINGS

The Bill of Rights and Constitutional Protections

The **history of constitutional rights** is chronicled in Martin Shapiro, *Freedom of Speech: The Supreme Court and Judicial Review* (Englewood Cliffs, N.J.: Prentice-Hall, 1966); Henry J. Abraham, *Freedom and the Court: Civil Rights and Liberties in the United States,* 4th ed. (New York: Oxford, 1982); S. E. Morison, H. S. Commager, and W. E. Leuchtenburg, *A Concise History of the American Republic,* 2nd ed. (New York: Oxford, 1983); and Leonard W. Levy, *Legacy of Suppression: Freedom of Speech and Press in Early American History* (Cambridge, Mass.: Harvard University Press, 1960).

For a critical **assessment of liberal ideas of freedom,** consult Christian Bay, *The Structure of Freedom* (Stanford, Calif.: Stanford University Press, 1970). Discussions of these issues from various political perspectives can be found in Crawford B. Macpherson, *The Political Theory of Possessive Individualism: Hobbes to Locke* (London: Oxford, 1962); Isaiah Berlin, *Two Concepts of Liberty* (London: Oxford, 1958); Frithjof Bergmann, *On Being Free* (South Bend, Ind.: University of Notre Dame Press, 1979); and Erich Fromm, *Escape from Freedom* (New York: Avon, 1971).

The **liberal view of freedom of speech** is presented in John Stuart Mill's nineteenth-century classic *On Liberty* (New York: Crofts, 1947). Alexander Meiklejohn's ideas on the subject are set forth in his *Free Speech in Relation to Self-Government* (New York: Harper & Row, 1948) and *Political Freedom: The Constitutional Powers of the People* (Greenwood, 1979).

On the **Alien and Sedition Acts,** see Morison et al., *A Concise History of the American Republic;* and Levy, *Legacy of Suppression.* Much of the discussion of post–World War I cases involving political speech is drawn from A. B. Smith, *Civil Liberties and Civil Rights in the United States* (St. Paul, Minn.: West, 1978); and Richard Polenberg, *Fighting Faiths: The Abrams Case, the Supreme Court, and Free Speech* (New York: Viking, 1987).

For discussions of the **Smith Act cases,** see Samuel Krislov, *The Supreme Court and Political Freedom* (New York: Free Press, 1968); Abraham, *Freedom and the Court;* and L. J. Barker and T. W. Barker, Jr., *Civil Liberties and the Constitution: Cases and Commentaries,* 5th ed. (Englewood Cliffs, N.J.: Prentice-Hall, 1986), chap. 3.

On **symbolic speech** and limits on expression, see Joel B. Grossman and Richard S. Wells, *Constitutional Law* *and Judicial Policy Making,* 2nd ed. (New York: Longman, 1984), chap. 5; Thomas Emerson, *A General Theory of the First Amendment* (New York: Vintage, 1967).

On **religion and the First Amendment,** see Leo Pfeffer, *Church, State and Freedom* (Boston: Beacon, 1967); Frank J. Sorauf, *The Wall of Separation: The Constitutional Politics of Church and State* (Princeton, N.J.: Princeton University Press, 1976); K. M. Dolbeare and P. E. Hammond, *The School Prayer Decisions: From Court Policy to Local Practice* (Chicago: University of Chicago Press, 1971).

For various treatments of **due process rights,** see Anthony Lewis, *Gideon's Trumpet* (New York: Random House, 1964); Neal A. Milner, *The Court and Local Law Enforcement: The Impact of Miranda* (Beverly Hills, Calif.: Sage, 1971).

A good basic text on the **contemporary legal system** is Ralph Rossum and Alan Tarr, *American Constitutional Law,* 2nd ed. (New York: St. Martin's, 1986).

CIVIL RIGHTS

On the **right to vote,** see especially Kirk H. Porter, *A History of Suffrage in the United States* (Chicago: University of Chicago Press, 1918); and Winthrop Jordan, *White Over Black: American Attitudes Toward the Negro* (New York: Norton, 1977).

The politics of **racial segregation** has spawned a vast literature. For introductions to it, see R. W. Logan, *Betrayal of the Negro* (New York: Collier, 1965); Idus A. Newby, *Development of Segregationist Thought* (Homewood, Ill.: Dorsey, 1968); and C. Vann Woodward, *Reconstruction and Reaction* (Boston: Little, Brown, 1966).

On **school desegregation,** see J. W. Peltason, *Fifty-Eight Lonely Men: Southern Federal Judges and School Desegregation* (Urbana, Ill.: University of Illinois Press, 1971); Clement E. Vose, *Caucasians Only: The Supreme Court, the NAACP and the Restrictive Covenant Cases* (Berkeley, Calif.: University of California Press, 1959); Jennifer L. Hochschild, *The New American Dilemma: Liberal Democracy and School Desegregation* (New Haven, Conn.: Yale University Press, 1984); Raymond Wolters, *The Burden of Brown: Thirty Years of School Desegregation* (Knoxville: University of Tennessee Press, 1978); Tony Freyer, *The Little Rock Crisis: A Constitutional Interpretation* (Westport, Conn.: Greenwood, 1984).

On a variety of **civil rights issues,** consider Richard Kluger, *Simple Justice* (New York: Vintage, 1977); J. H. Wilkinson, *From Brown to Bakke* (New York: Oxford, 1979); James Coleman, *Equality of Educational Opportunity* (Washington, D.C.: U.S. Government Printing Office, 1966); J. Dreyfuss and C. Lawrence, *The Bakke Case* (New York: Harcourt, 1979); Thomas Sowell, *Civil Rights: Rhetoric or Reality?* (New York: Morrow, 1983); Jo Freeman, *The Politics of Woman's Liberation* (New York: Longman, 1975); Janet K. Boles, *The Politics of the Equal Rights Amendment* (New York: Longman, 1979); and Lois G. Forer, *Money and Justice* (New York: Norton, 1984).

BASIC SOCIAL RIGHTS

For introductions to **social-rights issues,** see Peter Temin, *Taking Your Medicine—Drug Regulation in the United States* (Cambridge, Mass.: Harvard University Press, 1980); and John Mendeloff, *Regulating Safety: An Economic and Political Analysis of Occupational Safety and Health Policy* (Cambridge, Mass.: MIT Press, 1979).

On the **FDA** and its problematic relationship to the industries it regulates, see Upton Sinclair, *The Jungle* (New York: Viking, 1946); and Melvin J. Hinich and Richard Staelin, *Consumer Protection Legislation and the Food Industry* (New York: Pergamon, 1980).

For various perspectives on the genesis and evolution of the U.S. **labor movement,** see Stanley Aronowitz, *The Shaping of American Working Class Consciousness* (New York: McGraw-Hill, 1973); Thomas R. Brooks, *Toil and Trouble: A History of American Labor* (New York: Dell, 1986).

On the **Ludlow massacre,** see George S. McGovern and Leonard F. Guttridge, *The Great Coalfield War* (Boston: Houghton Mifflin, 1972); and James C. Dick, *Violence and Oppression* (Athens, Ga.: University of Georgia Press, 1979).

GOVERNMENT REPRESSION

For a **general survey** of government repression of liberties, see Robert J. Goldstein, *Political Repression in Modern America: 1870 to the Present* (New York: Schenkman, 1978); and *Political Repression and Political Development in Modern Europe* (New York: Barnes and Noble, 1983).

On the "**red scare,**" see Harold M. Hyman, *To Try Men's Souls: Loyalty Tests in American History* (Berkeley, Calif.: University of California Press, 1960). Other sources on repression of liberties include S. M. Lipset and E. Raab, "Epilogue: The 1970s," in *The Politics of Unreason: Right Wing Extremism in America,* 2nd ed. (Chicago: University of Chicago Press, 1978); John Roche, *Courts and Rights* (New York: Random House, 1977); Herbert Mitgang, *Dangerous Dossiers* (Chicago: Guild, 1988).

5

THE AMERICAN POLITICAL ECONOMY

Inequality and Democratic Politics

CHAPTER OUTLINE

Capitalism and Socialism
The U.S. Political Economy
Public Policy and the Political Economy

© Barbara Alper/Stock, Boston

Economic issues dominate modern societies, provoking controversy and deep political rifts. In speaking of economics, we refer not only to such specific matters as the day-to-day management of inflation or the regulation of farm prices. Economics, in the larger sense, also encompasses such far-reaching issues as the distribution of wealth and income in society, the ownership of property, and the range of government power. All these economic issues and questions are affected by the actions of government—and government, in turn, is shaped by the economic structure of the larger society. This is what is meant by the **political economy** of a society. We can learn a great deal about what a government accomplishes, and fails to accomplish, by looking at its economic organization.

In this chapter, we first examine the ongoing debate over how a modern economy *should* be structured, and the implications of that debate for democratic politics. We then focus on how the U.S. economy is structured. Finally, we explore the connections between U.S. social and economic structures and the ways in which U.S. government policy is made.

Capitalism and Socialism

One hundred years ago, as industrial capitalism was rapidly developing everywhere in the Western world, defenders and opponents of this economic system predicted an intense struggle over its future. Capitalism and socialism were seen as the great alternatives. Socialists believed their system held out the prospect of genuine economic equality combined with democratic politics. Capitalists contended that only their system would protect individual freedom and promote economic growth and high productivity. Compromise between the two alternatives seemed elusive.[1]

By comparing the theories of socialism and capitalism, we can clarify the debate about the "just society" that has preoccupied Western political thinkers since the eighteenth century. We must recognize, however, that in the United States socialism has not played a prominent role, at least in comparison to Western Europe. In this country, the debate over the political economy has been carried on not so much between socialists and capitalists as between the more liberal reformers of capitalism and the more conservative defenders of it. Generally, U.S. liberals have sought to amend, humanize, or improve the capitalist system, rather than to substitute socialism for it. In this section, we spotlight (1) capitalism as it evolved; (2) the theory of socialism; and (3) contemporary mixed systems that incorporate elements of both.

Capitalism

The essential elements of a **capitalist** system are private ownership of the means of production and a competitive market system, driven by the profit motive, through which wealth and resources are distributed. The major capital goods in such a society—factories, machines, land, and money—are owned by individuals or groups who have the right to use this property for private gain. What goods are produced, what they cost, and who will receive them are determined by the competitive operations of the marketplace according to the costs of supply and the demands of consumers.[2]

According to eighteenth-century proponents of capitalism, the ideal capitalist society would be made up of many small enterprises competing for a portion of the market. Government would play a decidedly minor role in this society, handling various public functions, such as building and maintaining roads; conducting foreign policy and providing for the national defense; and enforcing the law. In this liberal-capitalist concept of minimum government, espoused by many founders and early leaders of the United States, government was seen as the chief threat to freedom. According to this view, freedom to do business as one pleased was linked with freedom of conscience and freedom of speech. The ideal government functioned as a "night watchman"—a guardian of the existing distribution of property.

In the early nineteenth century, it was widely believed that **laissez faire** (unregulated) capitalism would liberate society from the tyrannies of political oppression, bureaucratic control, and stifling traditions. Capitalism, many held, would create a new world of immense wealth, a far more efficient and productive economy—without any conscious

Coal miners, circa 1908. Child labor was an everyday fact of early capitalism, and one that required government action to correct. These young coal miners worked fourteen-hour days and received little or no schooling. Not until the second decade of the twentieth century was child labor curtailed in the United States. *(The Bettmann Archive)*

direction from government. In attempting to profit as much as possible, each person would create wealth, and this would benefit the whole society.[3] Selfishness, in other words, would serve social ends. In this ideal capitalistic world, individuals would be judged on their merits—the value of their skills in the marketplace—not on such noneconomic criteria as social status, color, gender, or religion.

On its own terms, capitalism succeeded almost immediately. The new economic system, which was enormously productive, revolutionized the production and distribution of goods, stimulated worldwide trade, and broke down ancient and often oppressive traditions and social barriers. For many, the economic freedom of capitalism and the political freedom of democracy formed a perfect partnership.

Yet from the first, the capitalist system prompted strong criticism. Its more conservative critics viewed capitalism as inimical to communal ties and social bonds. Nineteenth-century conservatives also were unhappy with capitalism's antigovernment stance. Government was needed, these conservatives argued, to protect the weak (such as children who worked fourteen-hour days in mines and factories) and to limit the ferocity of competition. There were some values, these critics argued, more important than profit.[4]

More radical opponents of capitalism challenged the system's essential premises. They charged that capitalism extolled the value of equality, but the system actually created inequality. Under nineteenth-century capitalism, wealth was distributed very unequally, and it seemed likely to remain that way. Capitalism not only exploited the workers, but it was also highly inefficient, radicals argued. Cycles of inflation and depression caused great suffering and wasted vast resources.

Radicals also charged that capitalism made real democracy difficult to achieve. As long as wealth was distributed so unequally, the few who were rich would wield excessive political power while the many who were poor would exercise too little. Then, too, in a capitalist economy decisions affecting the lives of millions were made by a handful of powerful capitalists who controlled the means of production; this arrangement was inherently undemocratic. For these reasons, most radicals called for some form of collective ownership of the means of production to democratize economic decision making.

The TVA: An Experiment in Socialism

In the early 1930s, 98 percent of the farms in the Tennessee River valley had no electricity, and the few that did paid exorbitant rates to private power companies. The entire area, although rich in natural resources, was steeped in a chronic state of poverty. Water power was being wasted, forests were being destroyed by improper cutting and management, thousands of acres of farmland were being abandoned, and much industry had left the area. With this as a backdrop, Senator George Norris of Nebraska, a Republican, sponsored legislation calling for the creation of a publicly owned Tennessee Valley Authority (TVA) to provide cheap electrical power to residents of the economically deprived Tennessee River valley.

However, in 1931 President Herbert Hoover vetoed Norris's proposed TVA program. To Hoover, state involvement in the economy amounted to "socialism," and therefore was totally abhorrent.

But Norris persisted, and with the backing of President Franklin D. Roosevelt, the TVA was established by Congress in May 1933. The enterprise was gigantic in scope, involving the generation of power, the development of natural resources, and a significant amount of economic planning for an area three-fourths the size of England. It also represented the first essentially socialist project entered into by the U.S. government.

The TVA was an outstanding success by most estimates. Twenty-five dams were built, extensive flood control projects carried out, nitrate production established, thousands of miles of electric transmission lines built, and huge amounts of power sold at low rates to local communities.

The TVA is still in existence, and has even continued to grow. In recent years it has come under attack by conservatives, who have argued that government should sell off the TVA to private enterprise. The authority has also been the target of sharp criticism by environmentalists, both for the monumental pollution caused by its coal-fired generating plants and for its plans to construct an enormous nuclear power plant. After the TVA installed equipment that cut pollution by 50 percent and shelved the nuclear plant, however, environmental groups tempered much of their criticism.

Certainly, questions can be raised about the direction the Tennessee Valley Authority will take in years to come. As S. David Freeman, retired chairman of its board of directors, said in 1984, "My greatest worry is that the TVA will go back to sleep. That's really the natural state of a fifty-year-old bureaucracy. But our mission ought to be activist. We should be the one developing ideas for the electric car; for hammering out practical answers to acid rain. The TVA ought not to be, as President Carter once said, just another utility."*

---

*William E. Schmidt, "The TVA Has Come to a Bend in the River," *The New York Times,* May 20, 1984, Section E, p. 5.

Socialism

While the elements of capitalism are fairly clearcut, there is less agreement on the meaning of **socialism.** Most socialists, however, would argue that private ownership of the means of production should be replaced by some form of social ownership; that the market system should be replaced by some sort of planned economy; and that the distribution of wealth should be considerably more equal than it is under capitalism.[5]

Some early socialists—including the most famous, Karl Marx and Friedrich Engels—predicted that capitalism would inevitably collapse under the weight of its internal problems and that socialism would automatically take its place. Others favored gradual reform, a slow transition from capitalism to socialism through parliamentary processes. Almost all traditional socialists, however, counted on using the vast productive apparatus created by capitalism to achieve a more just social order. In theory, socialism would work in a more rational, planned fashion than capitalism, avoiding the problems of economic boom and bust. Socialism would also promote a more just social order, since wealth would be distributed more equally and large concentrations of wealth abolished. In addition, the system would foster a more compassionate and community-minded society, actively concerned about those who were not economically productive. Socialism would encourage individuals to pursue values more worthy than profit and would neutralize the crass commercialism of capitalism.

Critics of socialism predicted disaster.[6] How could any planner manage the complexities of a modern economy? they asked. Government planning, critics argued, would only produce great inefficiency and concentrate power in the hands of government bureaucracy. Overall, the growth of government power under socialism would threaten democracy and freedom itself. And socialism, in attempting to bring life's uncertainties under control and provide security for all, would merely stultify human creativity.

Mixed Systems

The apocalyptic and utopian forecasts of the early proponents of capitalism and socialism fell very wide of the mark. Rather than evolve into strictly socialist or capitalist societies, the Western industrial democracies adopted a mix of capitalist and socialist elements. The exact mix of elements differs from one society to another: The United States, for example, is more capitalist in orientation; Great Britain and Sweden, more socialist.

These mixed systems developed in fits and starts, often spurred by efforts to deal with the crises of capitalism. In many countries, socialist-type reforms, backed by growing trade union movements and socialist political groups, began gathering momentum in the late nineteenth and early twentieth centuries. The first steps toward what we now call the **welfare state** were taken then, including systematic government aid to the poor and the unemployed, public housing, and government provision of old age pensions. As government took a more and more active role in regulating the economic marketplace, new government agencies were created to protect consumers and workers. Some measures were also designed to break up large concentrations of industrial power, and a few tentative efforts were made to protect the environment.

The Great Depression of the 1930s represented a watershed in the evolution of mixed economies. In grappling with widespread unemployment and social dislocations, governments intervened in the market and created new social programs. This trend toward increasing government intervention firmly took hold during World War II, when governments were forced to do extensive economic and social planning. The Western democracies emerged from the war with new capabilities for dealing with modern economic life.

In the post–World War II period, proponents of socialism gained ground in Western Europe. In Great Britain and Scandinavia, socialist parties held the reins of government in the immediate postwar era, and in West Germany, France, the Netherlands, and other countries they became political forces to be reckoned with. The Labour Party of Great Britain nationalized (that is, placed under government ownership) the failing coal mining industry, as well as the steel industry, road transport, and other major industries. The British also created a system of socialized medicine and greatly increased the reach of the welfare state.

Generally speaking, socialist parties in power proved more moderate than many had expected.[7] In Scandinavia, for example, few industries were nationalized. Instead, Scandinavian socialists concentrated on keeping employment and economic growth high while extending the scope of government benefits. The goal was still equality, socialists argued; the exact means didn't matter that much. In addition, the results of nationalization were often disappointing. In Britain, most workers found their lives little changed by the shift from private to government ownership.

At the same time, capitalism also prospered. The new mixed economies allowed for extensive government stimulation of economic growth—and growth there was. When no serious depression oc-

Irony seems the precise word for this juxtaposition of reality and the world of advertising. Flood victims in Louisville, Kentucky, wait in line for assistance in 1937. America was still mired in the Great Depression, but that doesn't seem to have affected the family in the car. Our beliefs count for a lot. If we *believe* that America is the finest country on earth, that, in itself, creates an important political reality. *(Margaret Bourke-White, Life Magazine © 1937 Time Inc.)*

curred after World War II, many experts argued that the boom-and-bust cycle characteristic of unregulated capitalist economies had been banished permanently, thanks largely to government stimulation of the economy.[8]

The **mixed economies** of most Western democracies today can be characterized as follows:

Private ownership of the means of production is predominant, although the government's role in the economy is substantial (see **Figure 5–1,** page 160).

Government regulation of economic life has become an accepted state of affairs. Through taxation and spending, regulation of interest rates, and other means, the government seeks to maintain high levels of employment and economic growth and to keep inflation under control.

The government regulates many important details of economic life, including working conditions, environmental conditions, and matters affecting health and safety.

The government is deeply involved in promoting the welfare of the citizenry. Basic welfare state programs include old age insurance, aid to the poor, health insurance or socialized medicine, and other provisions for groups such as unemployed young people, the handicapped, and students.

Cooperation between government and business is widespread. The government provides aid to failing industries, special tax breaks to businesses, and subsidies to various groups (such as farmers), and enters into joint private-public ventures (such as exploration for oil). The relationship between government and business is sometimes cooperative and sometimes antagonistic.

Considerable inequality in the distribution of wealth and income persists, even where socialists have held power for long periods. Generally, however, wealth is not so unequally distributed as it was fifty years ago.

Encompassing such diverse elements, this type of political economy defies easy labels. Some observers call it neo-capitalism—a name that highlights its continuity with capitalism of the past. Others consider it conservative socialism—a paradoxical term that emphasizes how much has changed, both in economic life and in the way socialists now think about economic problems.

FIGURE 5–1
The Government's Share of the Economy

Who owns how much?

Privately owned: Private

Publicly owned: 25% | 50% | 75% | All or nearly all

	Postal Service	Tele-communi-cations	Elec-tricity	Gas	Oil Output	Coal	Railroads	Airlines	Autos	Steel	Ship-building	Government spending (percent of gross domestic product) 1975	1982
Australia	All	All	All	All	Private	Private	All	75%	Private	Private	†	24.0	32.0
Austria	All	All	All	All	All	All	All	All	All	All	†	32.1	40.2
Belgium	All	All	25%	25%	†	Private	All	All	Private	50%	Private	30.7	43.2
Britain	All	All	All	All	25%	All	All	75%	50%	75%	All	34.2	44.4
Canada	All	25%	All	Private	Private	Private	75%	75%	Private	Private	Private	29.4	40.0
France	All	All	All	All	†	All	All	75%	50%	75%	Private	36.3	40.3
Italy	All	All	75%	All	†	†	All	All	25%	75%	75%	32.4	41.9
Japan	All	All	Private	Private	†	Private	75%	25%	Private	Private	Private	19.0	23.4
Netherlands	All	All	75%	75%	†	†	All	75%	50%	25%	Private	34.4	51.2
Sweden	All	All	50%	All	†	†	All	50%	Private	75%	75%	32.7	40.4
United States	All	Private	25%	Private	Private	Private	25%	Private	Private	Private	Private	29.5	34.0
West Germany	All	All	75%	50%	25%	50%	All	All	25%	Private	25%	33.6	42.1

†Not applicable or negligible production. *Including Conrail.
Shading indicates countries where government spending grew most rapidly.
SOURCES: *The Economist* and the Organization for Economic Cooperation and Development.

The U.S. Political Economy

In one sense, the United States enjoys an embarrassment of riches: Americans comprise only 5 percent of the world's population and yet generate 30 percent of all the goods and services produced annually in the world. The U.S. **gross national product** (the value of all goods and services produced) is more than $2 trillion a year—an amount equal to the combined GNP of all the nations of Western Europe, plus Japan and Canada. Americans also use about 40 percent of the world's output of raw materials and produce an approximately equal amount of the world's waste products and pollution.

The United States has dominated international economic life since the end of World War II. Beginning in the early 1970s, however, that dominance began to wane. A number of factors figured in the U.S. economic downturn, including the

Vietnam War, energy shortages and oil price increases, the effects of recession followed by huge government budget deficits, and the growing economic power of other nations. No longer is the United States the world leader in **per capita income** (GNP divided by population). Latest figures show that both Denmark and West Germany have passed the United States (see **Table 5–1**).

The United States has also experienced significant new economic problems as a competitor in the international economic arena. America's trade deficit skyrocketed in the 1980s (see **Figure 5–2**), while the value of the dollar on international financial exchanges began to drop rapidly. Many questioned whether America could maintain its pre-eminent economic position. The Reagan administration recruited Japan and West Germany, key U.S. trading partners and competitors, to help shore up the shaky American dollar. The unexpected, sudden crash of the U.S. stock market in October of 1987, which had worldwide repercus-

TABLE 5–1
Per Capita Incomes of Selected Nations

Nation	Year	Income
Denmark	1980	$12,956
West Germany	1982	11,142
United States	1982	11,107
France	1980	8,980
United Kingdom	1979	7,216
Italy	1980	6,914

SOURCE: *World Almanac* (New York: NEA, 1984).

FIGURE 5–2
America's Trade Deficit

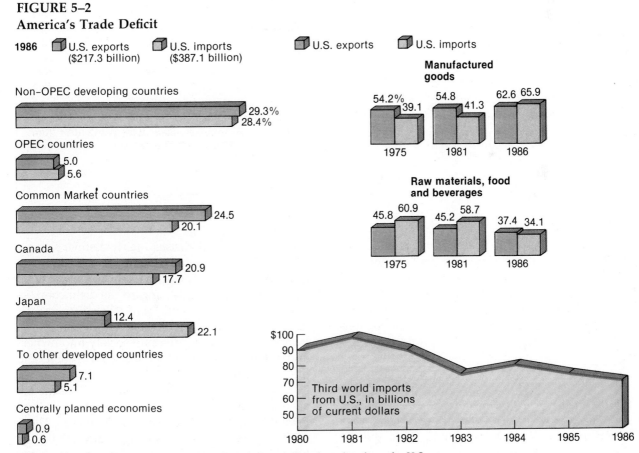

SOURCE: *The New York Times,* Jan. 17, 1988, Section 4, p. 4. Based on data from the U.S. Department of Commerce and the International Monetary Fund.

COMPARATIVE PERSPECTIVE

Income Distribution in Selected Nations

Income distribution is more unequal in the United States than in many other industrial democracies, as well as in some less industrialized ones. The following table compares the share of total income received by the poorest 20 percent to that received by the wealthiest 20 percent in selected nations. In the United States, that ratio is 10 to 1.

Ratio of Income, Top 20% to Bottom 20% of Population

Finland	4/1	Tanzania	8/1
Denmark	5/1	France	9/1
Japan	5/1	United States	10/1
Netherlands	5/1	Malaysia	16/1
Sweden	5/1	Turkey	16/1
United Kingdom	5/1	Venezuela	18/1
Bangladesh	6/1	Mexico	20/1
West Germany	6/1	Peru	32/1
Norway	6/1	Brazil	33/1
Sri Lanka	6/1		
Yugoslavia	6/1		
India	7/1		
Indonesia	7/1		
Spain	7/1		
South Korea	8/1		

SOURCE: Lester R. Brown, "Reshaping Economic Policies," in Lester R. Brown, et al., *State of the World, 1984* (New York: Norton, 1984), p. 202. The data are for the latest year available.

sions, also suggested that deeper instabilities may lie at the core of the American and the international economy.

We now examine three key issues affecting the U.S. political economy: (1) the distribution of income; (2) the distribution of wealth and ownership; and (3) poverty in the world's richest country.

Distribution of Income

Americans do not share equally in either the nation's affluence or its economic problems; our society includes many gradations of wealth and poverty. Traditionally, sociologists view societies as divided into **social classes**—fairly distinct groups, differentiated by occupation or income, that usually have different life-styles and may clash politically.[9] Some sociologists regard the distinction between white-collar and blue-collar jobs as the fundamental division in society. Others emphasize property ownership, dividing society into owners and nonowners. Yet other focus on income and life-style criteria.

Most Americans classify themselves on the basis of annual income, the amount of money brought into the household in a given year. Those with annual incomes ranging from $15,000 to $80,000 commonly think of themselves as being "middle class." But such a broad category includes people with radically different life-styles, political

TABLE 5–2
Incomes of U.S. Families before Taxes, 1929–1985

Sector of population	1929	1941	1950	1960	1970	1980	1985
Lowest fifth	3.8%	4.1%	4.5%	4.8%	5.4%	4.1%	4.9%
Second fifth	8.7	9.5	12.0	12.2	12.2	10.2	10.9
Third fifth	13.8	15.3	17.4	17.6	17.6	16.8	16.9
Fourth fifth	19.3	22.3	23.4	24.0	23.8	24.8	24.2
Highest fifth	54.4	48.8	42.7	41.3	40.9	44.2	43.5
Top 5% of highest fifth	—	—	17.3	15.9	15.6	16.5	16.7

SOURCE: *Statistical Abstract of the United States, 1980*; U.S. Census Bureau, *Current Population Reports*, series P-23, No. 126, August 1983; and series P-60, No. 154, March 1986.

views, occupations, incomes, and degrees of wealth.

A truer picture of the nation's economic classes can be obtained by dividing the population into fifths, according to income levels, and determining the percentage of the nation's total income each fifth of the population receives. As **Table 5–2** shows, in 1985 the poorest fifth of the U.S. population received less than 5 percent of the national income, while the richest fifth received close to 45 percent. Moreover, the second-poorest fifth received about 10 percent of all income, whereas the next-to-the-richest fifth received just under 25 percent.

Merely reciting such dry statistics, however, tells us little about how the poorest 20 percent of the population lives or about the political consequences of unequal income distribution. Fortu-

TABLE 5–3
Perceived Fairness of the Income Received by Persons in Different Types of Occupations

Occupation	Income received is considered:			
	Too little	About the right amount	Too much	Don't know
Government officials	4	24	67	4
Middle-level managers in business	18	58	8	16
Skilled blue-collar workers	8	47	42	3
Owners of small business	40	49	4	8
Lower level white-collar workers	62	33	2	4
Landlords	5	39	49	8
Owners and executives of large corporations	1	23	71	5
Unionized factory workers	14	53	28	5
Professional athletes	3	18	77	2
Teachers in elementary and high schools	62	31	5	2
Medical doctors	2	27	69	1
Stockholders of large corporations	4	34	47	15
Nonunionized factory workers	61	28	2	9
Movie stars and top entertainers	1	18	78	4
Teachers in colleges and universities	53	34	7	—

SOURCE: J. R. Kluegel and E. R. Smith, *Beliefs about Inequality* (Hawthorne, N.Y.: Aldine, de Gruyter, 1986), p. 120.

Our political system provides for one person/one vote, but our economic system leads to a world in which some command far more resources than others. An egalitarian democrat would ask, How much inequality can democracy tolerate and still remain meaningful? *(Eugene Richards/Magnum)*

nately, the U.S. government has attempted to describe the economic situation of families at various income levels, including those above as well as below the so-called poverty line. Above the poverty line (in the mid-1980s, about $12,000 for an urban family of four), the Bureau of Labor Statistics differentiates among low-budget, medium-budget, and high-budget levels. On the basis of these rough income categories, the U.S. population could be divided as follows:

Above the high budget	15%
Between medium and high	30%
Between low and medium	25%
Between poverty line and low	15%
Below poverty line	15%

Table 5–3 (page 163) shows how Americans view the income disparities among various occupations. Americans consider athletes, doctors, entertainers, owners and executives of large companies, and government officials particularly overpaid. Cited most often as underpaid are lower-level white-collar workers, teachers, and non-unionized factory workers.

Upward movement from blue-collar to white-collar occupations is common in the United States, just as it is in other industrial countries. What distinguishes U.S. social mobility is the degree of movement from the bottom to the top—from the working class to the ranks of owners or managers. One out of every ten sons of American fathers employed in manual occupations rises to an elite professional or managerial position, as opposed to only one out of thirty in Sweden, one out of forty-five in Great Britain, and one out of one hundred in Denmark.[10] The Horatio Alger, rags-to-riches story has the distinct ring of truth in the United States, and such success stories reinforce American faith in individualism.

Distribution of Wealth and Ownership

Wealth is the monetary value of what an individual or a household owns, adjusted for indebtedness. Ordinarily, wealth is divided between durable goods (for example, houses, cars, appliances) and financial assets (including stocks, bonds, savings, life insurance).

Wealth is distributed far less equally in the United States than is income. In 1962, for example, the poorest fifth of the population had a zero share of all wealth (because of net indebtedness), the second fifth has 3 percent, the third fifth 5 percent, the fourth fifth 16 percent, and the top fifth 77 percent. Moreover, the wealthiest 5 percent of the population holds 53 percent of all wealth, and the

TABLE 5–4
Inequality of Family Income
(Median Income in Constant 1985 Dollars)

	White families	*Black families*	*Hispanic families*
1950	15,395	8,352	N/A
1965	24,722	13,614	N/A
1980	28,596	16,546	19,212
1985	29,152	16,786	19,027

SOURCE: *Statistical Abstract of the United States, 1987* (Washington: GPO), p. 145.

wealthiest 1 percent holds somewhere between 20 and 33 percent.

For a more dramatic view of the uneven distribution of wealth in the United States, we can divide the total net wealth (holdings minus debts) possessed by each income group by the number of people in that group. For example, if a group of one hundred people owned a total of $10,000 in stock, each hypothetically would be worth $100. Applying this method to the income categories described above, we find that those in the bottom 20 percent are worth $0 each; those in the next 20 percent, approximately $6,000 each; those in the third 20 percent, $10,000 each; those in the fourth 20 percent, $32,000 each; those in the top 5 percent, $200,000 each; and those in the top 1 percent, $800,000 each.

Some of these inequalities break down along racial and ethnic lines as well. As we can see in **Table 5–4,** black family income was 54 percent of white income in 1950, 55 percent in 1965 and 57.5 percent in 1985—not a shift of major dimensions overall. Hispanic income was 65 percent of white income in 1985. What these statistics do not show is that certain black and Hispanic families have significantly improved their income position relative to whites, while many others have not. It is also notable that general income growth has slowed, a trend that began in the 1970s and continued through the 1980s.

Such facts of economic life not only imply radical differences in life-style among Americans—they also have direct and profound political and social consequences. Economics can translate into political power through contributions, advertising, and various sources of influence and assistance.

Great concentrations of wealth also place in the hands of a few decision-making power in economic matters that affect the lives of the multitude—factories can be closed or opened, investments shifted, new products marketed or not developed. Democracy in the political arena, then, faces what is primarily an oligarchy in the economic sphere.

Today the U.S. economy is largely a *corporate* economy. Although vast numbers of small businesses are still in operation, most manufacturing is done by a fairly small number of large corporations.

An ever-increasing concentration of industrial power has marked the American economy in recent decades. In 1955 the five hundred largest corporations controlled 65 percent of all manufacturing and mining assets in the country. By 1965, that figure had increased to 73 percent. By 1977, it had hit 80 percent. This development raises serious questions about the nature of the U.S. economy: How much competition can there be when it is almost impossible to challenge the leading companies in an industry? As fewer and fewer companies dominate the market, don't collusion and price fixing become more and more likely? Has the well-being of huge corporations become tied up with our national well-being? Can we allow major companies to fail economically, when that will mean hundreds of thousands out of work?

Of course, the U.S. economy is by no means entirely "corporatized," and corporations are not the only groups that wield political clout. As politics has penetrated every area of economic life, individuals with common economic interests have formed pressure groups to gain political influence.

Ivan Boesky, hugely successful Wall Street broker, who was convicted of stock market manipulations and sent to prison. Boesky became, in the mid-1980s, a symbol of how far greed could go in violating the "legitimate" rules of the game. But Boesky himself had claimed that greed was good, and many agreed with him. Among the many questions that arise about capitalism are: How much greed is good? And what are the dangers when too many people become too greedy? *(UPI/Bettmann Newsphotos)*

Doctors, teachers, blue-collar workers, sellers of insurance—all are politically organized. This is inevitable in an economy in which political and economic factors are interwoven so thoroughly. If an industry, a corporation, or some sector of the economy fails to become organized in a politically effective way, it may well find itself vulnerable to political forces outside its control.

Poverty

Any assessment of the distribution of wealth in the United States must address the question of poverty. How many suffer severe deprivation in U.S. society? And perhaps more important, what progress is being made toward reducing their number? The issue is not a simple one. Most of us do not interact with the poor, who populate the margins of our society—the ghettos, barrios, migrant farm worker camps, and Indian reservations. Also subject to dispute are who make up "the poor," and how prevalent poverty is. Let us now turn to these two issues.

DEFINITIONS The federal government's definition of poverty is based on calculations made by Mollie Orshansky for the Social Security Administration in the early 1960s.[11] At the core of her computations was an estimate of the dollar equivalent of the minimum amount of nutrition needed for a person to survive. She then multiplied this economy food budget by three, to reflect the findings of a series of studies in 1955 that low-income families spent two-thirds of their budgets on nonfood essentials such as clothing, shelter, and fuel. The figure then arrived at became the basis for establishing poverty lines for various groups of people—those in urban or rural areas, families of four or single individuals, and so on. A person whose income fell below the poverty line of his or her group was counted as "poor."

As **Table 5–5** demonstrates, progress toward the eradication of poverty has been disappointing over the last two decades: Much headway was made between 1960 and 1972, no improvement was noticeable in 1972–1976, and a dramatic *rise* in poverty was recorded in 1976–1982. And if one takes issue with the government's statistical definition of poverty, the picture becomes even less encouraging. By the government's own admission, the nutrition provided by the economy food budget is only *minimally* adequate: It's designed for "emergency or temporary" periods, not for the long term.

TABLE 5–5
Poverty in America, 1960–1984

	Persons below poverty level		Average poverty line for nonfarm family of four*	Median income of all families
	Number (millions)	Percent of total population		
1960	39.9	22.2%	$ 3,022	$ 5,620
1966	28.5	14.7	3,317	7,532
1972	24.5	11.9	4,275	11,116
1976	25.0	11.8	5,815	14,958
1982	34.4	15.0	9,862	21,023
1984	32.4	13.6	10,989	24,458

*Dollar equivalent of minimal nutrition intake is tied to the consumer price index, and thus increases with inflation.

SOURCE: Adapted from *Statistical Abstract of the United States, 1982–1983, 1986* (Washington: GPO, 1984, 1987).

DISTRIBUTION   Although more than 60 percent of all poor people are white, a disproportionate 28 percent of all blacks are poor (blacks make up 11 percent of the population). Also, households headed by females make up 34 percent of the poor. Social attitudes and policies sharply affect who will become and remain poor; poverty is largely a product of generations of discrimination, sexism, exploitation, and neglect. Being born into a poor family places heavy burdens on even the most enterprising of people—the fight for a good education, a decent job, and other opportunities is steeply uphill.

Government policies have had a marked effect on the distribution of poverty. Over the past twenty-five years, the percentage of elderly people who are poor has declined sharply, largely because of higher Social Security payments. In comparison with the late 1960s, the poor today are more likely to be young, black, and female.

Americans believe in opportunities for all, but we all know that some begin with far better opportunities than others. The early environment shapes our capacities and motivations, perhaps indelibly. *(Barbara Rios/Photo Researchers)*

TABLE 5–6
Poverty Population by Selected Characteristics, 1986

Characteristic	Percentage below poverty line
Total population	13.6
white	8.6
black	28.0
Hispanic	24.7
Households headed by females	34.0
white	27.4
black	50.5
Children under 15	19.8
white	15.3
black	42.7
Hispanic	37.1
Persons over 65 years of age	12.4
white	10.7
black	31.0
Hispanic	22.5
Single individuals over 65	
males	19.6
females	26.8

SOURCE: *Statistical Abstract of the United States, 1986* (Washington: GPO, 1987).

TABLE 5–7
Reasons for Poverty, 1969 and 1980

Percentage of respondents saying "very important" or "important"	1969	1980
Lack of thrift and good money management	90	94
Lack of effort by the poor	91	92
Lack of ability and talent	88	88
Failure of society to provide good schools	64	75
Loose morals and drunkenness	72	74
Sickness and physical handicaps	85	84
Low wages in some industries	79	87
Failure of business to provide enough jobs	67	74
Prejudice and discrimination against blacks	73	75
Being taken advantage of by rich people	51	55
Just bad luck	36	44

SOURCE: J. R. Kluegel and E. R. Smith, *Beliefs About Inequality* (Hawthorne, N.Y.: Aldine, de Gruyter, 1986), p. 79. Adapted by the author.

In addition, poverty is far from randomly distributed in the American population (see **Table 5–6**). Blacks and Hispanics are more likely to be poor than are whites (though in terms of sheer numbers, more of the poor are white). Households headed by females, regardless of race, are more likely to be poor, as are children of all races. The single highest incidence of poverty is among households headed by black females, of whom more than half are categorized as poor. Those over 65 are somewhat less poor than the general population, a trend that is probably attributable to some degree to increases in Social Security payments. Single individuals over 65, however, whether male or female, are poorer than the population as a whole.

Interestingly, Americans' attitudes about the causes of poverty have remained quite stable over the last several decades (see **Table 5–7**). Americans tend to believe that poverty emanates largely from factors within the individual; society or the economy, then, is not to blame. On the other hand, most people do recognize that structural conditions in the society do play some role. A similar pattern emerges in explanations about why people are rich: The three factors listed as most important are personal drive and risk-taking, hard work, and inheritance. By contrast, luck, dishonesty, exploitation, and "pull" are all ranked considerably lower, as is talent. (See **Figure 5–3** for a look at how the economy and government policy affect the poor.)

Public Policy and the Political Economy

Heading into the twenty-first century, the industrial democracies face two new sets of problems. For one, the successful methods of economic man-

FIGURE 5–3
The Government, the Economy, and the Poor

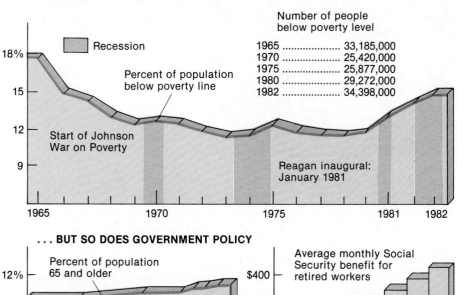

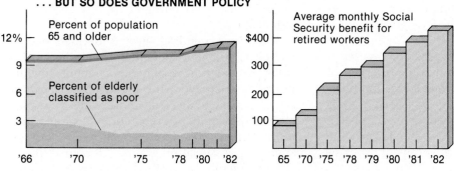

SOURCE: *The New York Times*, May 29 and Aug. 7, 1983; chart from *Newsweek*, Jan. 17, 1983.

agement that Western democratic governments pioneered in the 1930s and expanded in the 1950s no longer seem able to respond fully to the complex economic problems of today. For another, energy/environment issues—problems of declining energy sources, depletion of land and forest, population pressures, environmental pollution that affects air and oceans—have added new dimensions to the economic equation, especially in a changing international economic system. Neither conservatives nor liberals (nor, in Europe, democratic socialists) have offered very persuasive solutions to these deep-rooted problems. With this in mind, we now turn to (1) the ramifications of government spending, taxation, and regulation; and (2) government's impact on inequality.

Government Spending, Taxation, and Regulation

The U.S. government has always affected our economic life. Yet until relatively recently, the government's spending, taxation, and regulatory policies were only marginally significant in terms of the overall economy. In 1929, federal spending represented only 9.8 percent of the U.S. gross national product. Outlays to combat the Depression of the 1930s pushed government spending to 19 percent of the GNP. During World War II government expenditures rose dramatically; to finance military production, the government spent 41 percent of the GNP in both 1943 and 1944. When peace came, government outlays temporarily

The economy and public policy are intertwined, and politics is the means of establishing priorities. Will the expenditures be for school lunches or space programs, for missiles or margarine? *(NASA)*

dropped back to prewar levels, only to rise again in the Cold War era, to 23 percent of the GNP. By the late 1980s, federal spending accounted for between 20 and 25 percent of the U.S. gross national product.

When the government disposes of a quarter of a nation's GNP, it is obvious that the priorities of government spending have great social and political ramifications. Here the basic issues are: (1) How large should the overall budget be? (2) Is the national debt a problem? (3) Who should carry the tax burden? (4) How should government expenditures be allocated?

On the first two issues, modern-day liberals and conservatives generally take opposing views. Liberals tend to favor an involved and active government, and they frequently argue that government spending is too low. Conservatives, by contrast, usually consider government spending as a major social issue in itself, campaigning vigorously for budget cuts. In addition, conservatives often call for a balanced budget—that is, one in which the outflow of funds is roughly matched by government revenues from taxes and other sources. Liberals tend to argue that deficit spending stimulates economic growth. These positions are not written in stone, of course: Liberals as well as conservatives have opposed bloated budget deficits, and it was the conservative administration of President Ronald Reagan that amassed the largest government debt in U.S. history.

The question of who should carry the tax burden is even more controversial. Should individuals

pay most of it, or should corporations? How can we strike a proper balance between the two? The majority of the tax burden currently falls on individuals.

Whatever spending level is decided on, and whoever ultimately foots the tax bill, there will always be differences of opinion about spending priorities. Here, too, the broad political patterns are fairly easy to discern. Conservatives have long emphasized military preparedness as a top priority, whereas liberals have called for increased spending on social programs. (Of course, the full political picture is sketched with shadings—many liberals, for example, are strong proponents of defense spending.)

These differences in political priorities—voiced by social groups from which lawmakers draw support—form the backdrop for the battles fought over the size and composition of the federal budget each year. The president's priorities also determine the terrain on which the budget battles will be fought. President Lyndon Johnson's Great Society programs helped shape the federal budget of the mid-1960s, as his commitment to the Vietnam War shaped those of the late 1960s. In the early 1980s, President Reagan's budget increases in military spending (combined with tax cuts) caused the largest deficits in U.S. history.

Since the 1950s, defense spending as a percentage of GNP has alternately risen and fallen. Government expenditures on defense declined from 9.5 percent of GNP in 1968 to 5.1 percent in fiscal 1979, only to rise (and then fall again) under the

People of differing political views usually differ on economic priorities as well. Whereas conservatives have typically emphasized national defense spending, liberals have championed social programs. *(Mimi Forsyth/Monkmeyer)*

Reagan administration. As a rule, U.S. outlays on defense exceed those of other Western democracies, because of the heavier defense burden the United States carries.

Federal government spending on social programs has increased significantly since 1965. Currently, expenditures for social programs comprise well more than half of all federal expenditures; they also account for more than 70 percent of recent growth in the national budget.[12]

Despite increases in social welfare spending, the U.S. government still spends significantly less than its European counterparts on public welfare. Our income tax levels are also significantly lower, and they have increased less over the past thirty years. As **Table 5–8** shows, tax revenues have increased as a percentage of gross domestic product (GDP) in all of the industrial democracies listed. In some cases, this increase has been spectacular, as in Sweden, where tax revenues doubled in per-

TABLE 5–8
Tax Revenues as a Percentage of Gross Domestic Product, 1955–1984

	1955	1965	1980	1984	1955–1984 Percentage increase
Great Britain	29.8	30.8	35.3	38.5	8.7
France	32.9	31.6	42.5	45.5	12.6
Netherlands	26.3	35.5	45.8	45.5	19.2
Sweden	25.5	35.6	49.4	50.5	25.0
United States	24.6	26.5	30.4	29.0	4.4
West Germany	30.8	31.6	38.0	37.7	6.9

SOURCES: *Revenue Statistics of OECD Countries, 1965–1980* (Paris: OECD, 1984); *Statistical Abstract of the United States* (Washington: GPO, 1987).

centage. This means that in all these nations, government disposed of a larger portion of national income. However, this trend may now be on the wane. As an interesting sidenote, the United States clearly ranks lowest in tax revenues. Most Americans are probably unaware that their taxes are, overall, lower than taxes in most other industrialized democratic nations.

Not surprisingly, the European welfare states have gone further than the United States toward eliminating poverty, deprivation, and neglect. In Norway, for example, where the pretax distribution of income is similar to ours, government policy has virtually ended poverty. The Norwegians allot more of their total GNP for use by the government, and a greater percentage of government expenditures goes into **transfer payments** (money paid to individuals through social programs). The Norwegian tax structure is also highly progressive (that is, the higher one's income, the higher the rate of taxation).

This example illustrates that even in a predominantly capitalist society (like Norway), the government can go to great lengths to combat economic deprivation. It also reflects profound differences in Norwegian and American attitudes toward what government should do, and for whom.

But while the U.S. government may not accord the highest priority to alleviating deprivation, it does perform many essential social welfare functions. As noted in our discussion of the mixed economy, the government regulates the trade cycle; provides social welfare benefits to individuals, without which many more people would fall below the poverty line; and oversees a wide-ranging system of economic regulation designed, in many respects, to protect individuals.

Government and Inequality

Should government actively promote economic equality? Some argue that government has no business interfering with the distribution of income and wealth in society. Others maintain that the redistribution of income is a legitimate government activity, designed to increase equality and assist those in greatest financial need.[13]

In fact, governments do become deeply enmeshed in economic activity, and their rules and programs do benefit and protect various groups. The question is: How much should government do, and for whom? American conservatives contend that since the New Deal, government programs have distorted the workings of the marketplace and sapped individual incentive. Government has tried to produce too much equality, they claim, and has muddled the job. Liberal and socialist critics, on the other hand, point out that most reforms undertaken to promote greater equality have been necessitated by the failings of capitalism, and have not fundamentally changed U.S. economic patterns.

Both sides can cite evidence to support their views. Since the 1930s, government-administered social programs clearly have led to a certain amount of redistribution of income (not wealth). Similarly, government regulatory activities in the areas of health and safety have helped to protect workers and consumers from serious hazards, and civil rights legislation has helped to improve the economic lot of women and minorities. Still, much government activity has undeniably been designed to bolster big business interests and keep capitalism running as smoothly as possible. Efforts to promote positive social change, critics charge, have had no effect on the majority of the disadvantaged.

Studies have shown that, contrary to popular notions, the federal income tax does not redistribute much income. Although the income tax does take proportionately more from wealthier taxpayers, its overall effect is limited. According to the Congressional Joint Committee on Taxation, in 1977 the wealthiest 25 percent of taxpayers took home 55.5 percent of all income and after taxes still held onto 53.2 percent of it. At the same time, the poorest 25 percent of taxpayers received just 4.6 percent of income, and after taxes their share rose to only 5.2 percent.

In the United States, the only substantial redistribution of income by the government is achieved through transfer payments. The income of the poorest sector of the U.S. population rises significantly because of these payments; such noncash assistance as food stamps and public housing provide additional boosts.

The growth of the welfare state also led to new social conflicts. Should disadvantaged groups be given preference in hiring policies? Which programs deserve priority in the federal budget—those dealing with the elderly, unemployed youth, cities, or environmental matters? In many ways, economic competition, once more or less confined to the marketplace, has now been partly redirected into the political arena.

Critics of the U.S. political economy pose another troubling question: How just are current arrangements in the U.S. political economy? Many critics charge that our system merely facilitates each interest group's attempts to bring pressure on the political process to gain special benefits or to protect its position. And even if every organized group enjoys some degree of access, the best organized and the most persistent usually win the greatest benefits.[14]

Overall, then, government has earned a mixed record in promoting equality. Our national governments have shifted emphasis from one administration to another. The social programs of Lyndon Johnson's "War on Poverty," for example, significantly improved the lot of the poor, while the policies of the Reagan administration appear to have increased poverty and inequality.

Conclusions

The successes of mixed economies leave many important issues unresolved.[15] From the capitalist standpoint, Western societies have moved too far to the left. From the socialist perspective, the core problems of capitalism remain, though their edges have been softened somewhat by limited government intervention. The issues confronting U.S. social and economic life today are skirmishes in a long-running battle over what sort of economy and society is a healthy and just one. In the United States, the struggle unfolds not so much between capitalists and socialists as between liberals and conservatives. American liberals take a considerably more moderate view than European democratic socialists, while American conservatives usually adopt positions somewhat to the right of European conservatives.

In light of democratic theory, two key issues stand out: (1) How much economic equality is necessary to make democracy workable and reasonably just, and what are the implications for the quality of democratic life? (2) Does a government-owned economy spell trouble for political freedoms, as some conservatives argue, or can it produce a more equitable social system than we now have?

Orthodox apologists for capitalism often argue that democracy is incompatible with government ownership of large segments of the economy.[16] Only private ownership, they contend, confers the economic freedom that makes political freedom meaningful. Critics of this position maintain that pure, unregulated capitalism in itself threatens democracy, since it creates so much inequality and so many serious economic problems.

GLOSSARY TERMS

political economy

capitalist

laissez faire

socialism

welfare state

mixed economies

gross national product

per capita income

social classes

wealth

transfer payments

NOTES

[1]For a provocative discussion of this period and the ideological alternatives, see Karl Polanyi, *The Great Transformation* (Boston: Beacon Press, 1957); Adam Smith, *The Wealth of Nations* (New York: Modern Library, 1937); and George Lichtheim, *A Short History of Socialism* (New York: Praeger, 1971).

[2]Joseph Schumpeter, *Capitalism, Socialism and Democracy*, 3rd ed. (New York: Harper & Row, 1950); David

Ricardo, *Principles of Political Economy and Taxation* (New York: Dutton, 1962); John Maynard Keynes, *The General Theory of Employment, Interest, and Money* (New York: Harcourt Brace Jovanovich, 1965).

[3]An early expression of this novel concept can be found in Bernard Mandeville, *The Fable of the Bees,* published in 1714.

[4]These views can be found in the works of the poet Samuel Taylor Coleridge as well as in the writings of Thomas B. Macaulay, a British historian, essayist, and statesman; and the British Prime Minister Benjamin Disraeli.

[5]For two thoughtful discussions on socialism, see George Lichtheim, "What Socialism Is and Is Not," *New York Review of Books,* April 9, 1970; and Robert L. Heilbroner, "Socialism and the Future," *Commentary,* December 1961, pp. 35–45.

[6]See, for example, the apocalyptic fears of one conservative in Friedrich Hayek, *The Road to Serfdom* (Chicago: University of Chicago Press, 1944).

[7]For an example of this moderation, see C. A. R. Crosland, *The Future of Socialism* (New York: Macmillan, 1957).

[8]A good discussion of this argument can be found in Andrew Schonfield, *Modern Capitalism* (New York: Oxford University Press, 1965).

[9]For some thought-provoking examples, see Peter Blau and Otis Dudley Duncan, *The American Occupational Structure* (New York: Wiley, 1967); and Stephen J. Rose, *Social Stratification in the United States* (Baltimore: Social Graphics, 1979).

[10]Blau and Duncan, *American Occupational Structure.*

[11]Mollie Orshansky, "Counting the Poor," *Social Security Bulletin,* 25 (1963), pp. 2–21.

[12]Reported by Robert D. Reischauer, deputy director of the Congressional Budget Office in a talk at Duke University, 1979.

[13]See the discussion in Irving Kristol, *Two Cheers for Capitalism* (New York: Basic Books, 1978); and Michael Harrington, *Decade of Decision* (New York: Simon & Schuster, 1980).

[14]Grant McConnell, *Private Power and American Democracy* (New York: Random House, 1970).

[15]A useful, iconoclastic discussion of these issues can be found in Paul Goodman, *People or Personnel: Decentralizing and the Mixed System* (New York: Random House, 1965).

[16]Milton Friedman, *Capitalism and Freedom* (Chicago: University of Chicago Press, 1964).

SELECTED READINGS

CAPITALISM AND SOCIALISM

On **capitalism** see John Kenneth Galbraith, *American Capitalism* (Boston: Houghton Mifflin, 1956); Edward S. Mason, ed., *The Corporation in Modern Society* (Atheneum, 1966); Thomas S. Ashton, *The Industrial Revolution, 1760–1830,* revised ed. (New York: Oxford University Press, 1964); Beth Mintz and Michael Schwartz, *The Power Structure of American Business* (Chicago: University of Chicago Press, 1985).

Among the more readable and provocative presentations of **socialist ideas** are Michael Harrington, *Socialism* (New York: Bantam Books, 1973); George Lichtheim, *A Short History of Socialism* (New York: Praeger, 1971); and Ross Terrill, *R. H. Tawney and His Times: Socialism as Fellowship* (Cambridge, Mass.: Harvard University Press, 1973).

For accounts of the **new "mixed system"** from various points of view, see Daniel Bell, *The End of Ideology* (New York: The Free Press, 1965) and *The Coming of Post-Industrial Society: A Venture in Social Forecasting* (New York: Basic Books, 1976); Andrew Shonfield, *Modern Capitalism;* Robert L. Heilbroner, *Between Capitalism and Socialism* (New York: Random House, 1970); Herbert Marcuse, *One-Dimensional Man* (Boston: Beacon Press, 1966); and M. D. Hancock and G. Sjoberg, eds., *Politics in the Post-Welfare State: Responses to the New Individualism* (New York: Columbia University Press, 1972).

For analyses of the **problems of the mixed economy,** see Seymour Melman, *The Permanent War Economy* (New York: Simon & Schuster, 1976); Leo Srole, *Mental Life in the Metropolis* (New York: McGraw-Hill, 1975); Anne Ehrlich, Paul Ehrlich, and William Holdren, *Ecoscience* (San Francisco: W. H. Freeman, 1977); and Irving Howe, ed., *Beyond the Welfare State* (New York: Schocken, 1982).

THE U.S. POLITICAL ECONOMY

For a general discussion of the field of **political economy,** see Charles E. Lindblom, *Politics and Markets: The World's Political-Economic Systems* (New York: Basic Books, 1977); and Ralph Miliband, *The State in Capitalist Society: An Analysis of the Western System of Power* (New York: Basic Books, 1978).

On **poverty,** see Bradley R. Schiller, *The Economics of Poverty and Discrimination,* 3rd ed. (Englewood Cliffs, N.J.: Prentice-Hall, 1976); Harrell Rodgers, *Poverty and Plenty* (Reading, Mass.: Addison-Wesley, 1979); and Nick Kotz, *Let Them Eat Promises: The Politics of Hunger in America* (Englewood Cliffs, N.J.: Prentice-Hall, 1969).

PUBLIC POLICY AND THE POLITICAL ECONOMY

For discussions of **various ways politics and economics are interrelated,** see Robert Heilbroner, *Between Capitalism and Socialism* (New York: Random House, 1970); A. J. Heidenheimer, H. Heclo, and C. T. Adams, *Comparative Public Policy: The Politics of Social Choice in Europe and America,* 2nd ed. (New York: St. Martin's Press, 1983); and H. L. Wilensky, *The Welfare State and Equality* (Berkeley, Calif.: University of California Press, 1975).

POLITICS

6 *PUBLIC SENTIMENT AND ELECTORAL TRENDS*

7 *POLITICAL PARTIES*

8 *CAMPAIGNS, MONEY, AND THE MEDIA*

9 *INTEREST-GROUP POLITICS*

10 *MASS POLITICS AND PROTEST*

6

PUBLIC SENTIMENT AND ELECTORAL TRENDS

Majority Rule in Practice

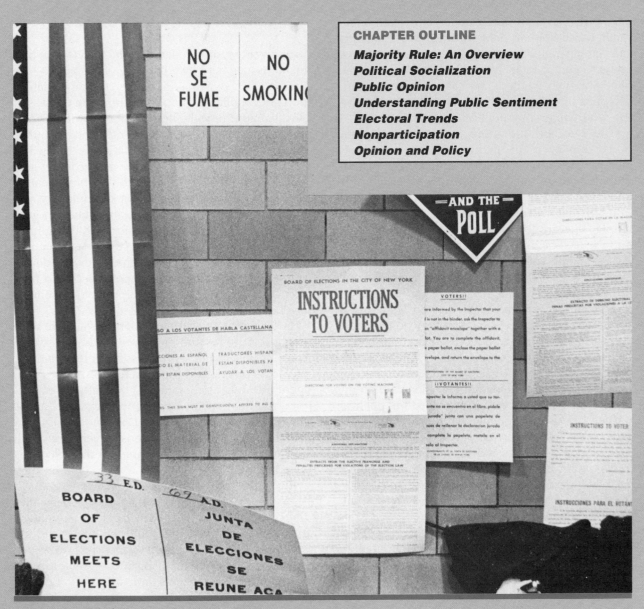

CHAPTER OUTLINE

Majority Rule: An Overview
Political Socialization
Public Opinion
Understanding Public Sentiment
Electoral Trends
Nonparticipation
Opinion and Policy

Michael Kagen/Monkmeyer

The underlying premise of democratic political life is that elections actually matter—that the hoopla of campaigns, the political competition, the media blitz, the primaries, the vote, and the different political parties fundamentally influence the course of society. But do they?

In one sense, they certainly do. Throughout modern history, struggles to win the right to vote and to create real political competition have helped citizens of many countries gain control of government. And in many countries without elections (or without honest elections), citizens can neither register their views on public policy nor retain or remove those holding political office. Governments can be changed by other means—revolutions, coups d'état, politically directed strikes, and the like. But such methods are costly and uncertain. Elections offer a regular, and safe, means of choosing who will occupy political offices.

The question has more complicated implications, however. In many countries, elections change very little: The same individuals or individuals holding the same views are reelected over and over, and they maintain the political status quo. In many Latin American countries, for example, one group of oligarchs succeeds another, and the well-being of the public at large is ignored. As a slogan written on a wall in Ecuador once stated: "One hundred years of elections—one hundred years of misery."

Elections, then, are not magic. They make meaningful change possible, but they do not guarantee it. Under what conditions do elections reflect true majority sentiment and have a significant impact on political processes? Among the key elements underlying meaningful elections are an informed and involved citizenry; competing political parties offering programs that differ from each other, that will be carried out to a significant degree, and that actually address major social issues; and political campaigning that helps raise public knowledge and clarify issues, rather than disguising or clouding them. Such, in any case, is the democratic ideal.

In Part II, we probe the political workings of our government—how majority sentiment influences electoral trends; the impact of political parties; political campaigns in a media-wise world; how in-terest-group politics affects democracy; and the politics of protest. Through various political processes, citizens can voice their views, promote particular public policies, and add a healthy diversity to U.S. political life. However, democracies must also guard against threats from political excesses—influence-peddling, triumphs of campaign razzle-dazzle over substance, patterns of political compromise that skirt the public interest.

Majority Rule: An Overview

In analyzing **majority sentiment**—the view on particular issues held by a majority of the public—we first explore two major topics: political socialization and public opinion. Examining the process of socialization reveals how political attitudes are shaped in this country; exploring trends in public opinion reveals what those attitudes actually are. While probing these areas, we will encounter several significant issues related to American democracy. At the broadest level, for example, we will be asking whether the American public can generally be characterized as an informed, thoughtful, and democratic group. We will also examine whether American political values are truly democratic. Do we endorse freedom of speech and freedom of the press? Do we support a reasonable level of tolerance for unpopular views?

After a look at (1) how Americans acquire their political attitudes and information and (2) the specifics of measuring and assessing public opinion, we next consider (3) the structure of public sentiment in the United States; (4) the patterns of electoral competition; (5) what nonparticipation means for American democracy; and (6) how public opinion influences policy decisions. Overall, we will address two key questions: Are American elections meaningful? and How close do we come to satisfying the democratic ideal?

As a logical starting point, let us now delve into the complex of factors that shapes us as political and social beings—principally, the family and the school system. Through these agencies, we are socialized—inculcated with distinctly American social and political values and attitudes. Because much of the imprint of early socialization is retained throughout life, an interest in the workings of democracy naturally leads us back to the shaping of the values of the child.

Political Socialization

The words have a heavy ring, but their meaning is not that difficult to comprehend. **Political socialization** refers to the processes through which an individual acquires the political attitudes and behavior common to a particular culture. Every culture must socialize its members—indoctrinate them into its language, customs, mores, and institutions. By the time children are just a few years of age, they have been stamped by the formative forces of society.

But which values are inculcated and whose interests do these values serve? Socialization can serve exploitative purposes: American blacks and women, for example, were long socialized to believe in their own inferiority. It is easier for most Americans to acknowledge that this phenomenon takes place in other societies—such as the Soviet Union or Cuba—than to admit that it occurs in the United States as well. It would serve us well to remember, however, that socialization is a two-edged sword in all societies, including our own.

Most Americans take substantial pride in their country and look favorably on its capitalistic economic system. These attitudes, which are inculcated early on, usually form a deeply rooted base of diffuse support[1] for the political and economic structures of U.S. society. A base of *diffuse support* is a set of favorable attitudes toward political and social structures, institutions, and processes that stands firm regardless of day-to-day events. For most citizens, that is, temporary discontent with the government of the day or with the government's approach to specific problems leaves untouched a reservoir of good will and tolerance toward government institutions. Drawing on this deeply rooted support, the United States has weathered many crises over the last thirty years with relatively little change in its fundamental political structures and practices.

Hand on heart, **Michael Dukakis** pledges allegiance to the flag—a simple act that became an issue in the 1988 campaign, when George Bush questioned his opponent's patriotism. Americans are socialized to respect the nation and its symbols; for some, the rituals are an acid test of national allegiance. *(AP/Wide World Photos)*

Diffuse support can be distinguished from *specific support*, which refers to approval of particular policies and practices and is therefore more likely to be withdrawn when an unpopular policy is implemented. From the standpoint of democratic politics, the issue is not whether most of us have positive feelings about the main institutions of U.S. society—that seems to be the case in all reasonably stable societies. Rather, the key issue is how diffuse support and specific support are balanced at any given time. If diffuse support is carried too far, or prevents citizens from appreciating current realities, it hinders critical inquiry and cripples political debate. Citizens must strike a balance between admiring a system's merits and critically assessing its flaws and deficiencies. We now turn to three critical phases in the socialization process: (1) childhood; (2) experiences in school; and (3) college and its influence on political attitudes and outlooks.

COMPARATIVE PERSPECTIVE

National Pride and Military Service

The two questions in the tables below were asked in 1982 by Eurobarometre, a European opinion poll. The survey included samples from the United States and Japan as well as various Western European nations.

Americans, according to this survey, expressed considerably more national pride than did Europeans. A substantial majority of Europeans did express positive feelings toward their nations, but not to the degree that Americans did. The survey revealed greater American self-love, and a European tendency toward self-criticism or a sense of disillusion, probably in some measure because two world wars were fought on European soil in this century.

Americans were also far more willing to say that they would fight for their country. Only the British came close to the American score of 71 percent; the overall European average was only 43 percent "yes" answers. In some nations—most notably Japan, West Germany, and Italy—the balance tilted heavily in the "no" direction.

SOURCE: Stichting European Value Systems Study Group, Tilburg, Netherlands.

How proud are you to be a (citizen of a particular country)?

	U.S.	Europe	Great Britain	Ireland	West Germany	France	Italy	Spain	Japan
Very proud	80%	38%	55%	66%	21%	33%	41%	49%	30%
Quite proud	16	38	31	25	38	43	39	34	32
Not very proud	2	12	8	5	18	8	11	8	28
Not at all proud	1	7	3	1	11	9	6	4	3
Don't know	2	6	3	3	12	7	2	5	7

Of course, we all hope that there will not be another war, but if it were to come to that, would you be willing to fight for your country?

	U.S.	Europe	Great Britain	Ireland	West Germany	France	Italy	Spain	Japan
Yes	71%	43%	62%	49%	35%	42%	28%	53%	22%
No	20	40	27	31	41	46	57	27	40
Don't know	9	17	11	20	24	12	15	20	38

Childhood

Although much remains to be learned about how children acquire their views of society and politics, we do know that both family and school play key roles in socialization, and that socialization is both a direct and an indirect process. In **direct socialization** children are deliberately taught specific political views, values, and behaviors. **Indirect socialization** involves attitudes and behavior patterns that are acquired through emulation. For example, children may learn through direct socialization that the Constitution guarantees all Americans equal rights. Through indirect socialization, however, they may gain a sense that some are "more equal than others," as they grasp cues subtly conveyed by adults.

Most children recognize the political community—the nation and the symbols associated with it, like the flag—before they have any inkling about the workings of politics itself. By the age of six or seven, children come to realize that they are "Americans," to associate themselves with the American flag, to believe that theirs is a "free" country, and to develop a sense of national loyalty.

Young children believe the national government consists mainly of the president and his "helpers." Similarly, they identify local government principally with the mayor or other local executive and, perhaps, the neighborhood police officer. To children, then, authority is highly personalized and idealized. "Government" appears to consist of a series of individuals performing executive functions; legislatures and courts have no significant place in a child's political consciousness.

According to studies conducted in the late 1950s and early 1960s, American grade school pupils tend to view the president as a "benevolent leader," or a "superfriend"—well intentioned, helpful, hard-working, honest, and invariably correct in decisions and actions. Why such a benign and favorable image of the president? For one thing, children tend to transfer feelings from parents (especially fathers) to others in authority; thus, presidents and other authority figures are viewed as children wish to view their parents. Also, parents, teachers, and other adults often deliberately advance the "benevolent leader" image. Even adults who are critical of the president in the company of other adults may screen out negative references and introduce children to politics in a positive light.[2]

When these findings about socialization were first published about thirty years ago, they were thought to apply to all American children. Later investigators, however, discovered that they applied principally to middle-class white children. Studies of poor white children in Appalachia and Mexican-American children in the Southwest found almost antithetical feelings (see **Table 6–1**,

"I pledge allegiance to the flag. . . ." How many times have we each repeated the lines of the Pledge? Do such patriotic rituals of loyalty have any effect on impressionable minds? The evidence seems to be that they do. Democracy demands loyalty to majority decisions, but it also demands that there be a limit to loyalty. Can that also be taught? (*Chuck Fishman/Contact Press*)

page 184). These children were far less likely to see the president as more honest, harder-working, or more knowledgeable than most people—or even as a good person.

These later findings highlight a phenomenon that students of politics have noted in other areas—that social class and ethnicity make for significant differences in attitudes and behavior. Generally, middle-class children are more aware of partisan differences, show a greater sense of political efficacy (a belief that political action will be worthwhile), and are more likely to want to participate in politics than are lower-class children.

During the Watergate scandal of the early 1970s, researchers set out to contrast the responses of grade school students to the questions that had been put to such students in 1962.[3] The survey results were revealing. Whereas 58 percent of fourth-graders surveyed in 1962 rated the presi-

TABLE 6–1
Views of the President among Three Groups of U.S. Children (1968)

Question	Response	Mexican-American children	Appalachian children	Suburban Chicago children
1. How hard does the president work compared with most [people]?	Harder	49%	35%	77%
	As hard	27	24	21
	Less hard	24	41	3
2. How honest is the president compared with most [people]?	More honest	*	23%	57%
	As honest	*	50	42
	Less honest	*	27	1
3. How knowledgeable is the president compared to most men?	Knows more	41%	45%	82%
	Knows about the same	42	33	16
	Knows less	17	22	2
4. What kind of person is the president?	Best in the world	11%	6%	11%
	A good person	63	68	82
	Not a good person	26	26	8

*Data not reported.
SOURCE: Appalachian and Chicago data reported in Dean Jaros, Herbert Hirsch, and Frederic J. Fleron, Jr., "The Malevolent Leader: Political Socialization in an American Sub-Culture," *American Political Science Review* 62 (1968):568. The Mexican-American data are reported in Herbert Hirsch and Armand Gutiarrez, "The Socialization of Political Aggression and Political Affect: A Subcultural Analysis," an unpublished paper.

dent as "my favorite" or "almost my favorite" person, only 7 percent of those surveyed in 1973 did so. The fourth-graders of 1973 were also able to distinguish between negative feelings toward the current occupant of the office, Richard Nixon, and the office of the presidency itself—a distinction that had been considered beyond the grasp of such young children. Despite the Watergate scandal, the children generally retained positive feelings about the presidency, while showing an openness to negative evaluations of the current president.

Political partisanship is also transmitted to children rather early. One study found that by age nine, 60 percent of children were expressing partisan loyalties.[4] Often, political loyalties, like religious affiliations, are inculcated through the child's unconscious identification with parental preferences. Loyalties acquired early in life are subject to later reexamination, however—sociali-

zation does not end at adolescence. Moreover, there is some evidence that young people often—perhaps as much as half the time—do not follow the political leads of their parents. Many declare themselves to be "Independents," thus moving some distance away from the political party preference of their parents (see **Table 6–2**). When the parents do not agree on party affiliation, it is even more likely that the children will strike out on their own.

Families influence not only specific political attitudes or behaviors, but also general emotional orientations—tolerance, generosity, fear of being different, confidence in oneself—that may shape later political responses. Psychological studies have shown that children who grow up in authoritarian households are more likely to take on authoritarian attitudes and to display prejudice and hostility toward those who challenge authority.[5]

TABLE 6–2
Party Identification of Parents and Children

	Parents		
Children	Democrat	Independent	Republican
Democrat	66%	29%	13%
Independent	27	53	36
Republican	7	17	51
	100%	99%	100%

SOURCE: Bruce A. Campbell, *The American Electorate* (New York: Holt, Rinehart and Winston, 1979), p. 112.

Likewise, liberal attitudes and behavior are usually acquired in the family. Of course, many "authoritarian" or conservative families produce liberal children, and vice versa.

The Role of the School

Although socialization begins in the family, the school also plays a major role in the process. Certainly, American schools have the "melting pot" process. Through education in public schools, various economic, ethnic, and religious groups have come to share a common socialization experience. In this sense, schools potentially can teach tolerance and respect for differences—values essential to democratic life. It is not known, however, how successfully schools perform this function.

Schools also inculcate certain basic cultural values. The textbooks used in elementary schools, for example, usually present preferred cultural norms. *McGuffey Readers*, the nineteenth-century American reading texts, expounded the values of self-reliance, hard work, thrift, free enterprise, and individualism, overlaid with nationalism and religiosity. Through such materials, U.S. public schools indoctrinated and reinforced predominantly middle-class values. Considering the powerful role textbooks play in the socialization of children, it is not surprising that many controversies have arisen over their contents. In recent decades, blacks, native Americans, women, and others have protested alleged biases in school texts. Textbooks also have been the focus of debates over the teaching of evolution, as opposed to biblical views

of creation, sex education, and a long list of other topics. A 7–2 decision by the Supreme Court in 1987 struck down a Louisiana law that forbade the teaching of evolution without concomitant instruction in "creation science." In recent years we have seen extensive efforts at book censorship, in both classrooms and school libraries, and parents' groups have organized to gain the right to exercise veto power over school materials. In 1985, a Maryland parents' coalition listed thirty-two topics they wished to have subject to parental approval, including nuclear war, religion, abortion, and euthanasia.

Education took center stage politically throughout the 1980s, as members of the Reagan administration led an attack on the failures of schooling in the United States. Secretary of Education William Bennett, for example, argued that American schools were not providing students with the kind of rich cultural background young people needed to become knowledgeable citizens. In addition, several critiques of U.S. education reached the best-seller lists.[6] A growing consensus held that our teenagers simply were not learning what they needed to know in history, geography, literature, and other areas. A 1986 study found that less than half of all U.S. high school students could place the U.S. Civil War within an appropriate 50-year time period![7] Such startling findings, coupled with complaints about teachers' salaries and qualifications, promised to ensure a prominent place for education on the national political agenda well into the future.

While the Reagan administration had come to Washington with plans to dismantle the then newly created federal Department of Education, by 1988 views had changed. As Secretary Bennett put it: "Republicans and conservatives have come to realize that the federal role in education is here to stay. . . . They also recognize that it is silly to concede the education issue to the Democrats."[8]

Despite the considerable attention being paid to education, no consensus has emerged about how to address its shortcomings. In fact, political leaders and the public at large cannot even agree on precise goals for education: Are schools supposed to make sure students (1) learn specific facts and information; (2) learn to think for themselves; (3) acquire certain values; (4) score high on standardized tests; (5) gain training for future employment—or a combination of all these?[9]

In instilling cultural values, schools traditionally emphasize nationalistic rituals—saluting the flag, reciting the Pledge of Allegiance, and singing patriotic songs. Children also are taught early on to respect leading figures in U.S. history, particularly the Founders and various presidents. Many children even seem to view the Pledge of Allegiance as a prayer; in the United States, nationalism and religion often are mutually reinforcing.

Finally, socialization in schools proceeds indirectly, by example. Children learn in school to compete on an individual basis with other students. They learn much about the need to comply with authority (and, sometimes, the need to suppress dissent), and about how and why majorities rule on some matters. Like parents, teachers also serve as role models. Are teachers willing to discuss controversial issues? Do they emphasize the virtues of U.S. political life while deemphasizing its problems? How teachers approach such matters can help shape the child's growing awareness of how politics works.

Systematic critiques have challenged the way U.S. public schools teach students about politics. A committee of the American Political Science Association has suggested that U.S. schools typically fail to convey a realistic picture of our political life, to transmit knowledge of behavior and processes instead of just formal institutional arrangements, and to develop critical and judgmental abilities in students. Generally speaking, the panel charged, the schools fail to give students a sense of what civil liberties are about, or what role dissent plays in a democratic society.[10]

During adolescence, most young people attempt to establish a personal identity by experimenting with new approaches and challenging the status quo. Sometimes adolescents venture into the political arena as part of these identity-seeking explorations. As one noted expert points out, many adolescents begin to acquire not just political views (often closely related to the views of their peers) but also *ideologies*—more comprehensive political viewpoints that may put them in conflict with the adults in their world.[11] Politically based adolescent rebellion has been a rarity in the United

States, although in the 1960s and early 1970s the radicalism of college students had a marked effect on U.S. politics. This brings us to the final segment in our discussion of political socialization—the effects of higher education.

College and Politics

Until 1964, Republican presidential candidates were usually favored on U.S. college campuses. This political choice reflected the social backgrounds of most college students: Adolescents from poorer families, who were less likely to be Republicans, were also less likely to find themselves on college campuses. Even if a college education tends to exert a liberalizing effect on students of all political persuasions (an argument

Student activism, 1968: A dramatic sit-in at Columbia University. Some viewed campus unrest as courageous rebellion; others saw it as reckless vandalism of our social institutions. (*Bonnie Freer/Photo Researchers*)

Student activism, 1988: Students from Gallaudet University in Washington protest the appointment of a non-hearing-impaired president at the world's only liberal arts institution for deaf students. On this, and several other points, they prevailed. (© *Rick Reinhard*)

advanced by many scholars), U.S. college campuses historically were not scenes of intense political involvement. All that changed in the 1960s.

In February 1960, four black undergraduates at North Carolina Agricultural and Technical State University in Greensboro, N.C., staged the first "sit-in" protest, refusing to leave the whites-only section of a store lunch counter. Four years later, students at the University of California sat in at an administration building to protest college policies limiting student political activities. From that point on, political protests—prompted by the Vietnam War, the drive for civil rights, and other cultural and social issues—pervaded college campuses.

Student activism sparked bitter debate in the 1960s and early 1970s. Some observers considered activist students as humane, conscientious, and committed—individuals who had the courage to act on widely shared ideals. Others saw them as irrational rebels acting out their own troubled emotional lives in the arenas of campus and national politics. Critics of the protest movement called college campuses breeding grounds for political radicalism. By the end of the 1960s, there was widespread speculation that some universities might be torn apart by sustained protest.

But in the 1970s, student activism diminished as the economy worsened and the Vietnam War wound down. By the mid-1970s disillusionment with politics replaced the earlier activism. Student values also changed; young people were becoming more conservative and pragmatic. In the 1984 election, a majority of college students voted for Republican candidate Ronald Reagan. **Figure 6–1**, page 188, shows how college freshmen from 1970 to 1986 characterized their political views.

Student values shifted significantly between the 1960s and the 1980s as well. In the 1960s, a large majority of college students ranked "developing a meaningful philosophy of life" high on their list of future objectives, while students in the 1980s stressed making money as a key future goal (see **Figure 6–2**). In keeping with this shift, business school enrollments have skyrocketed: By 1987, 25 percent of entering freshmen said they intended to major in business; in 1966, the figure was approximately 13 percent. On the other hand, freshmen in 1987 held decidedly liberal views on a variety of social issues, ranging from consumer protection to environmental concerns and disarmament. However, liberal attitudes showed some decline on two issues: sanctioning homosexual relations and legalizing marijuana. Despite these large-scale shifts in values and career choices, student activism resurfaced in a limited way in the 1980s, as students in some parts of the country protested investments in South Africa by U.S. colleges and corporations, CIA recruiting on campus, and the Reagan administration's policies on Central America.

Public Opinion

Public opinion—the voice of the majority—is one of the basic ingredients in the complex recipe for democracy. For a truly comprehensive under-

FIGURE 6–1
How College Freshmen Characterize Their Political Views

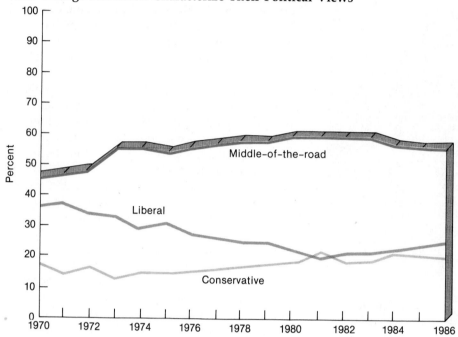

Note: " Liberal" = Far Left + Liberal; "Conservative" = Far Right + Conservative.
SOURCES: *Public Opinion*, April/May 1985, p. 39; and University of California at Los Angeles
Graduate School of Education Survey, 1986.

standing of U.S. political life, we need to know not only how politically informed and democratically inclined Americans are, but also how public opinion affects policy making and what that means for democratic life. In this section we focus on (1) how public opinion is gauged; (2) public opinion and its affects on democracy; and (3) political efficacy and alienation—when people feel their voice is either heard or ignored by political decision makers.

Gauging Public Opinion

Polls of public opinion have become a fixture of national political life. In the 1980s, close to 150 separate polling organizations were operating in the United States. But what is involved in gauging public opinion? What limitations and problems make polling less than totally accurate?

In a democratic polity, the study of public opinion is particularly significant because political life is based on a government responsive to public sentiment. Only since the end of World War II, however, have systematic efforts been made to gauge that sentiment. Contemporary studies of public opinion use *surveys*, in which responses to set questions are elicited from a sample of the population. Survey research is based on two assumptions: that a fairly small sample of people can accurately represent the views of a much larger population, and that the answers people give to survey questions are at least reasonably truthful.

The first problem faced by the survey researcher is to define an appropriate *sample* of opinion. The larger the sample selected, the more likely it is to reflect the opinions of the population as a whole.

A key criterion governing sample selection is *randomness*. Ideally, every individual in the population should have an equal chance of being selected. In practical terms, this is difficult to accom-

FIGURE 6–2
Freshman Goals: Spiritual vs. Financial (Percent of freshmen who identified each goal as "essential" or "very important")

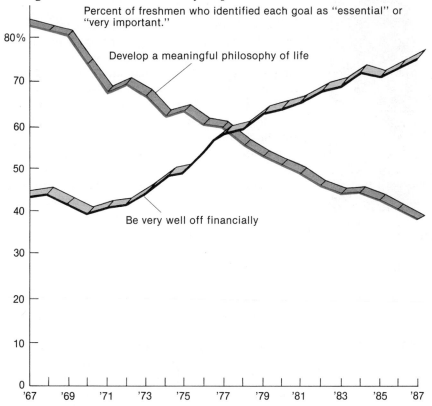

SOURCE: *The Higher Education Research Institute*, University of California, Los Angeles.

plish, since there is no master list of each individual in the United States—and even if there were, the cost of following up on each person randomly selected would be prohibitive. Instead, survey researchers use *cluster sampling*, which involves the selection of a number of geographic units (clusters) within which individuals are sampled. Departures from cluster sampling can lead a surveyor astray. Interviewing people at subway stations or on street corners, for example, can make for highly selective samples and unrepresentative results, as can attempting to judge public sentiment on the basis of letters to the editor or on the number of people who come out to work for a candidate at precinct meetings.

How accurate is public opinion polling? Since the 1950s, the major polls have generally provided accurate predictions of who will win presidential

elections, even in the very close elections of 1960, 1968, and 1976. During the 1980 presidential primaries, in contrast, the polls frequently erred in predicting the victor, because many voters remained undecided until the last minute and because many states allowed crossover voting (that is, they permitted registrants of one party to vote in the other party's primary).

A poll's accuracy as a gauge of public sentiment also depends in large part on the kinds of questions that are asked. For example, an interviewer who asks only if people approve or disapprove of the president's performance will get one set of results, one who asks respondents to rate the president on a "feeling thermometer"—soliciting how strongly they feel about presidential performance—will get another, and one who attempts to determine people's views on a specific set of

It has become common practice for the broadcast media to conduct exit polls and to compete in making early predictions of election results. But do early predictions lower the significance of voting for those whose polls close later in the day because of time-zone differences? *(Bobbie Kingsley/Photo Researchers)*

presidential actions will get yet another. All these results may or may not match up.

Polls present additional problems as well. For one thing, they can "create," rather than reflect, public opinion, usually by fostering the mistaken impression that the public knows or cares more than it really does about particular public issues. Moreover, poll findings don't usually measure to any meaningful extent the depth or sensitivity of public opinion. Polls can also turn people off: Asking people their views has become such a commonplace matter that many people don't believe surveyors care much how they *really* feel. On the other hand, more probing, open-ended questions might reveal that many of the respondents who routinely answer "don't know" or "no opinion" care very much about political issues but cannot easily articulate their views.

Then, too, most sample surveys tend to include few members of various minorities, such as Jews, blacks, or Hispanics. As a result, polls often tell us little about the differences of opinion *within* such groups. While black and white opinion is often compared on specific issues, it is much rarer to see a comparison of blacks with other blacks: There

simply aren't enough blacks in a typical sample to allow for any dependable generalizations. Nuances and conflicts within such groups, therefore, are given short shrift.

Finally, polls can intimidate policy makers, who may shy away from taking necessary action to address difficult social and political problems, for fear of going against public opinion. Poll results can also affect the outcomes of elections: On the one hand, supporters may not bother to go out and vote for a candidate who is far behind in the polls; on the other, supporters of a candiate who looks like a sure winner may not bother voting because the outcome seems so certain.

Whatever their inherent problems, however, polls do help us estimate public sentiment more accurately than was possible before. In the material that follows, we refer often to survey results.

Public Opinion and Democracy

Because public opinion plays so crucial a role in democratic politics, a viable democracy requires a politically informed public. Let us now examine (1) the level of public knowledge in the United States and (2) what this means for democratic norms.

POLITICAL KNOWLEDGE   Those who study the political attitudes and knowledge of Americans characterize the public as roughly divided into four groups: chronic know-nothings, the general public, the attentive public, and the opinion and policy makers.[12] Estimates vary on the sizes of these groups. For example, one analyst estimates the chronic know-nothings at 20 percent of the public, whereas another puts the size of this group at only 4 percent. The size of the general public is also hard to gauge; it seems to vary according to the issue involved. Unlike the know-nothings who never become informed or involved, the general public has some information and can sometimes be stirred to political action. At the next highest level of political involvement is the attentive public, sometimes estimated as 15–20 percent of the population. The attentive public seeks information, develops opinions, and can have a significant impact on policy making. Clearly, the size of the

Not a soap opera, but another kind of afternoon drama. Television brought the Watergate hearings into the living rooms of America. Here John Dean repeats his warning of a "cancer on the presidency," watched by an unusual but spellbound audience. *(Mark Haven)*

attentive public grows as a particular issue develops and becomes dramatized. Most Americans were only vaguely aware of Watergate, Vietnam, Nicaragua, or Lebanon when they first came to public attention. As time went on, however, more and more citizens became attentive to those matters—and that concern had an effect on policy makers. Beyond the attentive public are those who most shape opinions and policies. This group primarily consists of leaders in politics and the media.

Exactly how much does the public at large know about politics? The answer is sobering: Most people know a few fundamentals but not much else. According to one survey, for example, a large majority can name the vice-president and the governor of their state, but only a slim majority of the American people know how many senators represent each state, and just over one-third can name their congressional district's representative. When it comes to foreign affairs, the picture is just as bleak: Even after years of discussion and policy debate, only slightly more than half of us knew which side the U.S. government was backing in Nicaragua. (See **Table 6–3.**)

One can draw either optimistic or pessimistic conclusions from the data in Table 6–3. Other polls have revealed that upwards of 20 percent of the American people believe the Supreme Court is part of Congress and that as few as 1 percent know

TABLE 6–3
Assessing the U.S. Public's Political Knowledge

Question	Percentage knowing correct answer
Name the current vice-president.	79
How many senators represent each state?	52
How many years does a representative serve in Congress?	30
Name the current secretary of state.	34
Which party has the most members in the House?	69
Name one senator from your state.	59
Is the government of China communist?	63
Which side is the United States backing in Nicaragua—the government or the rebels?	54
Name the governor of this state.	78
Name this district's representative in Congress.	37

SOURCE: NORC General Social Surveys, 1978, 1987; ABC/Washington Post Survey, August 1987.

what congressional committees their representatives serve on or what their representatives' areas of expertise are.[13]

This level of political ignorance apparently is not affected by instruction in civics. One poll of fourteen- and seventeen-year-olds found that one out of every two respondents in both groups believed that the president appoints members of Congress; that one of every eight seventeen-year-olds thought the president did not have to obey the laws; and that half of the fourteen-year-olds believed that starting a new political party was illegal.[14] There were similar findings of ignorance among high school students in the 1980s.

A widely held truism of political science is that the older—and further away from school—people get, the more knowledgeable they become about politics. Underlying this observation is the assumption that with age, people are more motivated to participate in politics and thus to learn about it. Yet adults generally do not fare much better than teenagers in surveys of political knowledge, even though today much more information is available than ever before.

Perhaps even worse, much of the public remains uninformed about pressing public issues of the day. More people seem to have a better idea of what they think the government ought to be doing than of what it is doing. From a democratic point of view this is not a totally dismal state of affairs; after all, it is encouraging that people are willing to say what they want from government. But it is unsettling to find that so many base their opinions on little more than personal preferences. This leaves the democratic process vulnerable to catchwords, slogans, and simplistic formulas that may become the common coin of public discourse. In addition, a largely ignorant public may respond only to the very broad contours of policy alternatives and leaders may try to shape public sentiment by playing on prejudice, shallow emotional rhetoric, and the like. The more such demagogic practices prevail, the worse for democracy.

As we have seen, the level of public information, a basic element in the democratic equation, falls short of what it should be in U.S. society. To a certain extent, this degrades the integrity of the democratic process.

DEMOCRATIC NORMS Democracy also demands popular tolerance and support for democratic norms. This breaks down into two key measures: the level of acceptance of democratic politics and the level of tolerance for dissenting views.

Americans emphatically support the basic rules of democratic politics. According to most surveys, more than 90 percent of the public would agree with the following statements:

> Democracy is the best form of government.
> Public officials should be chosen by majority vote.
> Minorities should be free to criticize majority decisions.
> Every citizen should have an equal chance to influence government policy.

However, these are very abstract statements. As more specific elements are introduced into survey questions, the democratic consensus begins to crack. On questions pertaining to demonstrations and protest, undemocratic responses often outnumber democratic responses. Whenever any hint of political extremism appears in a question—such as demonstrations or protests—support for democratic values declines considerably.

How much tolerance is there for unpopular ideas? In 1954, when civil liberties were greatly threatened by anticommunist hysteria, Samuel Stouffer conducted a study of political tolerance in the United States. He discovered that the level of support for the political rights of those with controversial views was low indeed. Stouffer constructed his survey questions around three types of people: an admitted communist, a person who opposes churches and religion, and a person who favors government ownership of railroads and big industries. (In the second and third cases, the words "atheist" and "socialist" were *not* used.) The subjects of the survey were asked if they would allow any of these three types of people to make a speech or teach at a university, and if they would oppose removing from the public library books written by such persons. In 1954, the "tolerant" response totals on these issues were quite low, as **Table 6–4** shows. Only 6 percent said they would allow a communist to teach, only 37 percent indicated that they would allow an atheist to make

TABLE 6–4
Percentages Supporting Freedom of Expression in Specific Situations

	Percent tolerant			
	1954	*1977*	*1982*	*1987*
Allow speech by:				
Atheist	37	62	65	70
Socialist	59	—	—	—
Communist	27	56	58	61
Racist	—	59	61	62
Militarist	—	51	61	58
Homosexual	—	62	68	70
Oppose removing from library books written by:				
Atheist	35	59	63	67
Socialist	53	—	—	—
Communist	27	55	59	59
Racist	—	61	63	65
Militarist	—	55	—	60
Homosexual	—	55	58	59
Allow to teach in college:				
Atheist	12	39	47	49
Socialist	33	—	—	—
Communist	6	39	46	49
Racist	—	41	44	45
Militarist	—	34	—	41
Homosexual	—	49	57	59

SOURCE: Michael Corbett, *Political Tolerance in America* (New York: Longman, 1982), p. 36; and NORC General Social Survey, 1987 (courtesy of the Institute for Social Science Research, University of North Carolina, Chapel Hill).

a speech, and a bare majority opposed removing socialist books from the library.

It is encouraging to note that public attitudes on these same questions have grown considerably more tolerant in the period since Stouffer's study. A 1977 study found that in every category tolerance had increased, often by a great deal. According to one estimate, there was a 25 percent increase in tolerance in the United States from the mid-1950s to the mid-1970s. Part of this increase in tolerance has been attributed to an increase in the overall educational level of populations (see **Table 6–5**, page 194), and part to changing socialization patterns in family and school.

By 1987, 70 percent of Americans said that an atheist or a homosexual should be allowed to make a speech, with somewhat lower support for speeches by communists, militarists, and racists. Although this represents a major shift in the direction of greater tolerance, it is sobering to note that 30 percent or more still oppose the right of various controversial groups even to give a speech. When we consider allowing people with such controversial views to teach in a college, public support drops considerably lower: Less than 50 percent are willing to allow an atheist, communist, racist, or militarist to teach. Despite significant change, then, there remains a latent reservoir of support for intolerance, perhaps based more on fear and ignorance than on accurate knowledge of

TABLE 6–5
Tolerance and Level of Education

Belief	Grade school graduate	High school graduate	College graduate
Allow atheist to speak	30%	68%	82%
Allow atheist to teach in college	18	39	61
Allow atheist's book to remain in libraries	32	63	81
Allow racist to speak	44	61	73
Allow racist to teach in college	37	38	55
Allow racist's book to remain in libraries	15	39	45
Allow homosexual to speak	34	70	81
Allow homosexual to teach in college	21	55	71
Allow homosexual's book to remain in libraries	26	61	76

SOURCE: NORC General Social Survey, 1977. Reprinted from R. S. Erikson, N. Luttbeg, and K. L. Tedin, *American Public Opinion* (New York: Wiley, 1980), p. 89.

the issues involved. This troubling conclusion is supported by the findings of a 1987 survey that asked Americans whether a group that wished to protest a policy of the government should be permitted to undertake various sorts of actions: to organize, to publish a pamphlet, to hold a meeting, and to hold a protest march. A startling 25 percent of the public believed the group should not be permitted to publish a pamphlet or hold a march.

Attitudes toward minorities have also undergone significant changes over the past fifty years. In the early 1940s, for example, antiblack feeling was dominant among the white population of the United States. Over 80 percent of whites favored confining blacks to separate sections of towns; almost 70 percent favored separate restaurants; a similar percentage supported segregated schools; and approximately half favored segregation in public transportation and the armed forces. Since that time, racial attitudes have grown much more tolerant. By the mid-1970s, only 9 percent of Americans supported segregation, while 39 percent favored desegregation and 49 percent favored something "in-between."[15]

Similarly, in 1936–1937 only 31 percent of Americans said they would vote for a woman candidate for president, while in 1986 about 86 percent indicated a willingness to support a woman presidential candidate. Over the same time span, willingness to vote for a Jewish candidate rose from 46 to 88 percent. And between 1958 and 1987, the percentage of Americans willing to vote for a black for president rose from 38 percent to 87 percent.[16]

Overall, Americans have indicated only lukewarm support for laws and activities through which racial integration can be achieved. According to many observers, there has been a substantial change in American attitudes toward minorities, but a substantial amount of prejudice remains.

Efficacy and Alienation

Americans display a strong sense of **political efficacy**. This means they not only are willing to participate in politics, but also believe that such participation can be effective—that their actions will make a difference. Surveys comparing political attitudes in various democratic countries have shown that Americans, to a much greater extent than citizens of other democracies, believe that common citizens should be active in the community, that common citizens can do something about unjust national regulations, and that citizens can successfully challenge harmful local regula-

New issues and new activists spring up constantly in our political system. Americans believe that taking action can make a difference, and they are likely to get themselves organized and try to influence others—as these AIDS activists are doing. *(UPI/Bettmann Newsphotos)*

tions. Such survey results give the impression that the United States is a nation of avid political participants who have a strong sense of their ability to set the political process right, to shape it and make it respond.

Unfortunately, political reality is far more complicated. **Alienation** from government has grown sharply in recent decades. The social upheavals of the 1960s and early 1970s—involving civil rights, the Vietnam War, and the Watergate scandals—as well as the growing ranks of homeless people and AIDS (acquired immune deficiency syndrome) patients in the 1980s, have all contributed to a far-reaching loss of faith in government.

Alienation from political life has three major components: feelings of distrust, meaninglessness, and powerlessness. *Distrust* means people lack faith that the government will or can govern effectively; alternatively, they may believe that government is run by and for a few big interests, rather than for the benefit of all people. *Meaninglessness* grows out of a sense that the existing political choices are irrelevant, that it makes no difference who is in power, and that personal goals are unrelated to party politics. *Powerlessness* involves feelings of political impotence—that one is

ignored, or that the group one identifies with is not taken into account in political decision making.

All three dimensions of alienation increased sharply over the last thirty years, according to most surveys. A 1983 study, for example, found that there had been a significant erosion in confidence in almost every major institution, ranging from Congress to the church. Yet through the 1980s, people began to express slightly more trust in government. This trend appeared among both Republicans and Democrats, as well as among both men and women. Whites in general showed an increased trust in government, and although distrust remained high among blacks, it did not rise noticeably from earlier levels. One possible explanation for this decrease in feelings of alienation is that many who wanted to see the government doing less in general were gratified by the policies of the Reagan administration. Another contributing factor was the improved economic picture in the 1980s (though the 1987 stock market crash sent shock waves through many sectors of American society). Yet the drop-off in alienation was slight in comparison with the increase in such feelings over the previous two decades. It should be noted, however, that Americans showed considerably more confidence in our institutions overall than most Europeans. A 1987 study found, for example, that Americans were much less likely to say they lacked any confidence in the church, labor unions, business, the police, and the judicial system, compared with citizens in France, Britain, and West Germany.

How significant a factor is alienation in political life? It probably fueled the growth in antigovernment sentiment over the past thirty years. It may also have played a role in generating political apathy, which remains a deep-seated problem in U.S. politics. Alienation also leads to violence and antisocial behavior, triggered when political frustration boils over and members of the alienated group have little faith that their grievances will receive a fair hearing. At the same time, however, most Americans think highly of the nation, and continue to voice satisfaction with life as a whole.

Understanding Public Sentiment

How structured is the political thinking of most Americans? It seems safe to say that the average American does not espouse an **ideology**—a highly structured system of ideas applied to political and social issues in a coherent manner. The intense political combat of highly ideological parties, a staple of certain European polities, has largely been absent in the United States. We have something closer to a politics of the center—a politics of pragmatism and moderation. Let us now probe the subtleties of this politics of pragmatism by examining (1) liberalism and conservatism in broad outline; (2) contemporary trends in U.S. politics; (3) liberal and conservative views on specific issues; (4) the emerging post-materialist dimension in U.S. politics; and (5) some key influences on public sentiment.

Liberalism and Conservatism

Liberal and **conservative** have been the most common labels in U.S. politics since at least the 1930s. Yet they defy simple definition because each has several dimensions. For example, there are economic conservatives (favoring a balanced federal budget), foreign policy conservatives (promoting a hard line in dealings with the Soviet Union), law-and-order conservatives (advocating the death penalty), and cultural conservatives (opposing changes in the traditional roles of men and women). Similar categories could also be applied to liberals. Is it likely that an individual will express consistently conservative or liberal views across so many dimensions? Some investigators argue that a common core of attitudes differentiates liberals from conservatives. One often-proposed distinction is that conservatives generally resist change, while liberals generally accept or support change. Still, the applicability of this formula often depends on just what is being changed.

In examining U.S. politics, we will first of all find out where people place themselves, overall, along the liberal/conservative spectrum, and then trace national changes along that spectrum as the public mood has shifted. We will also look at more specific dimensions of liberalism/conservatism, such as economic issues, foreign policy matters, and such social issues as abortion.

Contemporary Trends in U.S. Politics

A casual survey of U.S. politics over the past twenty-five years might register two drastic shifts in popular sentiment: a shift toward liberalism during the 1960s and a counter-shift in the direction of conservatism in the late 1970s and the 1980s. On closer examination, however, the evidence for shifts in popular views is far more elusive than might be expected. Over the period from 1964 to 1983, in fact, there was surprisingly little change in the percentages of the Americans who viewed themselves as conservative or liberal (see **Table 6–6**). Self-professed liberals composed 18 percent of the population in 1983, as opposed to 23 percent in 1964; for conservatives, the figures were 36 percent in 1983 and 39 percent in 1964. Such figures do not reflect startling shifts in political philosophy. More noteworthy, in view of the relatively nonideological nature of U.S. politics, is that even during these two decades of intense social conflict and rapid change, a significant percentage of Americans did not see themselves as either liberal or conservative. Since 1972, middle-

TABLE 6–6
Self-Professed Political Perspectives of Americans, 1964–1987

	1964	*1968*	*1972*	*1978*	*1981*	*1983*	*1987*
Conservative	39%	37%	32%	32%	33%	36%	31%
Middle-of-road	38	31	35	41	45	40	37
Liberal	23	17	22	18	17	18	28
Radical	—	2	2	1	—	—	—
Not sure	—	13	9	8	5	6	4

SOURCES: Louis Harris surveys of June 26, 1967, February 20, 1978, and June 6, 1983; and NORC General Social Survey, 1987.

of-the-roaders have outnumbered adherents of either liberalism or conservatism. Interestingly, during the 1980s, the number of liberals increased sharply, while other identifications declined. By 1987, there were almost as many people saying they were liberals as there were conservatives.

One question raised by these data is just how meaningful self-identification by the public actually is. Often, people who identify themselves as, say, conservative, are at a loss to explain what that term means. We might also ask whether being a liberal or a conservative in 1964 meant the same thing as being a liberal or a conservative in 1983—or 1987. The connotations and nuances of these terms may have changed considerably in the intervening period.

Less problematic than self-identification surveys are polls in which Americans identify those issues they believe distinguish a liberal from a conservative. About two-thirds of the country, for example, consistently characterizes "beefing up national defense," "abolishing welfare," "cutting federal income taxes," and "giving corporations a better tax break" as conservative views. Just as consistently, most people identify "supporting women's rights," "increasing spending to clean up air and water pollution," and "helping minorities move faster toward equality" as liberal positions.

Liberal and Conservative Views on Specific Issues

By taking a closer look at specific issues, we can discern more clearly the pattern of liberal and con-

servative views among the public. We now delve into the liberal and conservative positions on three key matters: (1) social issues; (2) economic issues; and (3) foreign policy.

SOCIAL ISSUES Many of the most significant social issues of the last two decades involve aspects of sexuality—abortion, the ERA, gay rights, and sexual morality itself. The public has generally leaned toward liberalism in the areas of women's rights and abortion. In 1974, when the ERA first surfaced as a significant issue, 78 percent of the population supported it. After considerable controversy, prompted by conservatives, the level of support for the ERA declined to 64 percent in 1978 and 61 percent in 1982. On the abortion issue, a solid majority opposes a constitutional amendment banning all abortions, as well as a legislative ban on federal abortion funding.[17] (Despite public opposition, Congress passed the Hyde Amendments—named for their chief sponsor, Representative Henry Hyde of Illinois—banning federal funding for abortions. The amendments were subsequently upheld by the U.S. Supreme Court.) As for gay rights, the public has remained almost evenly divided between those opposing the legalization of homosexual relations between consenting adults and those supporting legalization. But a vast majority of Americans (77 percent) believed sexual relations between persons of the same sex was "always wrong" in 1987.

Neither liberalism nor conservatism holds sway convincingly on matters of law and order. Public support for capital punishment rose to 72 percent in 1984, from 38 percent in 1965; and 81 percent of

The subway vigilante. For a brief period in 1985, Bernhard Goetz occupied the national spotlight. Threatened by four black teenagers on a New York subway, Goetz (who had been mugged previously) pulled a gun and shot each one. The case raised ambiguous issues for liberals and conservatives alike: Was Goetz defending his rights or taking the law into his own hands? (*Stephen Ferry/Gamma-Liaison*)

the public felt the courts were too lenient on criminals in 1984, as compared with 49 percent in 1967.[18] But in 1982, almost two-thirds of the nation supported a law requiring the registration of handguns, and 45 percent backed a ban on handguns altogether.[19]

Of all social issues, the one on which the public has rallied most firmly behind a conservative position is school prayer. Even well into the 1980s, three-quarters of those polled favored a constitutional amendment to permit prayer in public schools. Support was strongest among those over age fifty and those living in the South and Midwest, but in no region or age group did support fall below 60 percent.[20]

ECONOMIC ISSUES   New Deal–style economic programs remain popular with most Americans, a ma-

jority of whom continue to support efforts to aid the poor, to help improve housing in urban areas, and to provide assistance to people in their old age. For more than thirty years, most of the population has favored some national role in health protection. And since the Great Depression, most people have believed that the government ought to guarantee jobs for people who are unemployed. Generally, then, public opinion has remained solidly committed to the liberal **welfare state** programs that originated in the 1930s.[21]

Public attitudes toward business, meanwhile, have been remarkably ambivalent. On the liberal side, a large majority lacks confidence in those running major companies and supports the idea of consumer representatives on the boards of corporations. Yet Americans consistently and overwhelmingly express faith in the capitalist system.

In analyzing public sentiments toward business, many experts conclude that antagonism to corporations stems from a deep-rooted American distrust of bigness *per se*, and the concentration of power that goes with it. Interestingly, support for business is notably weak not only among blue-collar workers—where this view might be expected to prevail—but also among high-status, well-educated professional people to whom business values are unappealing.

Doubts about big business do not necessarily translate into support for organized labor, however. A 1984 survey showed that the public had far more favorable views toward both environmental and women's political action committees than toward such groups operating on behalf of either business or labor.[22] Americans, then, take a skeptical attitude toward both big business and organized labor, but strongly support the capitalist system as a whole.

FOREIGN POLICY   Until recently the liberal/conservative dichotomy was more difficult to define in the foreign policy arena than in others. Most major foreign policy initiatives were supported by both political parties, and the range of debate about alternatives was limited. Beginning with the Vietnam War years, however, that picture changed drastically, as debate over foreign policy matters intensified.

On the whole, conservatives favor a buildup of

U.S. armed forces, while liberals support arms agreements and other negotiations with the Soviet Union. Conservatives also tend to be more **interventionist,** especially in military terms; liberals generally argue for other means of engagement—or, sometimes, for nonintervention. Such differences could be seen vividly in the 1980s debate over the Reagan administration's policies on Central America.

William Adams suggests that in the area of foreign policy, the public is far more likely to agree with the **human-rights** position of liberals than with the interventionist arguments of conservatives.[23] He argues that most Americans, at least in the abstract, support a foreign policy that emphasizes human rights and looks to negotiated settlements. At the same time, he notes that the public can easily shift to an interventionist stance under certain circumstances. Americans, Adams contends, want a strong defense and do not want to be threatened or intimidated.

Some of these same tensions are reflected in public attitudes toward defense spending and relations with the Soviet Union. From the late 1960s to 1976, public opinion opposed heavy defense spending and favored cuts. Then the trend shifted, as the public became convinced that our international status was weak and that the Soviet Union was engaging in a military buildup. As a result, most of the public supported the U.S. defense buildup of the early 1980s. By 1984, public opinion shifted yet again. A Harris poll published in 1984, for example, found that a large majority of the public preferred cuts in defense spending to cuts in Social Security, Medicare, aid to education, veterans' benefits, or federal health programs.[24]

Table 6–7 traces the pattern of changes in public opinion on a variety of issues between 1973 and 1987. On many issues, public opinion shifted in one direction from 1973 to 1980 and then swung back in the other direction between 1980 and 1987. This trend can be seen most clearly in attitudes toward defense spending. In 1973, when U.S. involvement in Vietnam was halted, only 11 percent felt we were spending too little on defense. By 1980, 56 percent agreed spending was too low. But by 1987, the strength of public opinion was back to the 1973 level. The extreme swings in this case were due to Reagan's emphasis on defense issues

TABLE 6–7
Public Opinion about Government Spending, 1973–1987

Program	Percentage saying current spending is "too little"		
	1973	1980	1987
Defense	11	56	15
Welfare	20	13	21
Protecting the environment	61	48	64
Improving health	60	55	67
Dealing with drug addiction	65	59	65
Halting the rising crime rate	64	69	67
Improving education	49	53	61
Improving conditions for blacks	32	24	34
Foreign aid	4	5	7
Solving big city problems	48	40	38

SOURCE: NORC General Social Survey, 1987.

in the 1980 campaign and the subsequent major military buildup his administration engaged in.

But the same pattern shows up, if less sharply, on other issues such as welfare, environmental protection, health, drug rehabilitation, and improving conditions for blacks. In all these cases, public opinion favored a decline in support for more spending between 1973 and 1980, and then swung back in the previous direction by 1987. With this in mind, many observers noted a significant conservative shift in public opinion in the late 1970s. But that shift seemed to have abated by the late 1980s. In analyzing this pattern, some authorities believe the economic downturn in the late 1970s—when interest rates, for example, hit an all-time high of 21 percent—accounted for the conservative shift.

As an aside, public opinion on educational spending does not fit the pattern, nor do attitudes on big city problems. Support for more spending on education has risen consistently throughout the period, while support for urban spending has declined. By 1987, the only areas in which a large portion of the public felt that "too much" was being spent were defense, foreign aid, and welfare.

In the area of nuclear weapons, American attitudes have remained relatively fixed since the first

Soviet General Secretary Mikhail Gorbachev gets a laugh from President Ronald Reagan by indicating that they have to sign only one more copy of the Intermediate-range Nuclear Forces (INF) Treaty. An unusually personable and astute Soviet leader, Gorbachev successfully courted public opinion in both America and Europe—at least during his first years in power. *(Reuters/Bettmann Newsphotos)*

atomic bomb was dropped in 1945.[25] Most Americans favor curtailing the arms race, even while fearing that the Soviets cannot be trusted. A 1983 study showed that a vast majority (79 percent) supported the idea of a **nuclear freeze,** in which both the United States and the Soviet Union would cease producing new nuclear weapons, though 80 percent believed the Soviets would probably cheat on such an agreement. At the same time, more than half (55 percent in 1981) believe the United States should have military superiority over the Soviet Union (and very few, a scant 4 percent, believe we don't need to be as strong).[26]

Between 1978 and 1987, attitudes toward the Soviet Union also shifted dramatically. In 1978, 53 percent of the public favored a tougher stand toward the Soviets, and only 30 percent favored reducing tensions. By 1984, however, 55 percent favored reducing tensions and 26 percent said that we should be tougher.[27] And by 1987, a substantial majority of Americans reacted favorably to Soviet General Secretary Gorbachev's visit to the United States and the signing of the Intermediate Nuclear Forces (INF) Treaty.

The emergence of Gorbachev as leader of the Soviet Union and subsequent shifts in U.S.–Soviet relations had significant effects on U.S. public opinion. After Gorbachev's trip to Washington and the signing of the INF Treaty in December 1987, a 55-to-40-percent majority of Americans believed the Soviet Union had grown more trustworthy. (In West Germany, 73 percent believed the Soviet Union was more trustworthy than before.) Seventy-three percent of Americans contended that the Senate should approve the INF Treaty, and 76 percent thought the United States and the Soviet Union should sign a strategic arms reduction treaty in 1988. Reagan's approval rating on foreign affairs went up sharply due to the 1987 summit—from 55 percent approval to 74 percent. At the same time, most Americans approved of the Reagan administration's Strategic Defense Initiative (SDI, or "Star Wars" proposal). Sixty-one percent felt the plan strengthened U.S. security, while 29 percent believed it threatened security. Publics in other Western countries, however, were not as favorably inclined. British public opinion, for example, was almost evenly split: 38 percent believed SDI would promote Western security; 36 percent maintained that it would threaten security.

THE OVERALL PICTURE   One of the most difficult aspects of public opinion analysis is judging how long a trend will last. Was the conservatism of the 1970s and 1980s a temporary trend, or will it grow and deepen into the 1990s? Can the antiabortion movement succeed, or is it a last-ditch, rear-guard action doomed to failure? Pollsters have often been

Rallying around the President

In examining American politics, we can discern an odd and disturbing trend during times of international crisis. During a crisis public opinion tends to rally behind the president regardless of the wisdom of the policies pursued. In one observer's view, this reaction stems partly from a patriotic impulse and partly from fear of the unknown. The president becomes a rallying point for national unity.

From the standpoint of democratic theory, this pattern poses some troubling problems. If the public tends to back the president almost instinctively, then criticism will be blunted and the president will be able to count on support even when it is unwarranted. Excessive and uncritical patriotism could prove dangerous to a democratic society, and to the rest of the world.

If we look at the pattern more closely, we find that in forty cases of international crisis since the end of World War II, the public has rallied around the president about three-fourths of the time. Some of these instances of public support were triggered by American military action; others were peace initiatives. Some embroiled us more deeply in war, while others were aimed at extricating troops from a military engagement. The largest increases in support for the president were prompted by the announcement of the Truman Doctrine in 1947, extending U.S. support to Greece and Turkey; the Cuban missile crisis of 1962; the signing of the Vietnam peace agreement in 1973; and military action by President Ford in 1975 when the merchant ship Mayaguez was seized by the Cambodian navy.

But not every crisis has bolstered support for the president. Among the instances where support plunged were the Tet offensive in Vietnam in 1968, when the United States experienced serious military setbacks; the stepped-up bombing of Vietnam at Christmas 1972; and the decision by President Carter to defer a decision on building the neutron bomb.

The president, then, cannot count on an outpouring of public support under *all* circumstances. Indeed, the public is likely to grow impatient and demand results during protracted international crisis. The Iranian hostage crisis, which lasted 444 days from 1979 through 1981, is a case in point.

In most international crises, especially in the early stages, the president retains almost total control of important information and remains the focus of public attention. Most potential opposition is silenced because opponents do not have "all the facts," or out of a certain deference to presidential leadership. After a time, however, more information becomes available and opposition to the president *may* begin to form. Any emerging opposition may also influence the news media. Thus, a key factor in maintaining public support is whether the president can deflect serious criticism by members of the political elite and the media.

As an interesting aside, this phenomenon of "rallying around the flag" is certainly not unique to the United States. When British Prime Minister Margaret Thatcher dispatched British forces to battle the Argentines in the Falkland Islands in 1982, public support for her leadership soared. Since the battle for the Falklands was brief and very successful, Thatcher benefited considerably from this boost in public support, which was sustained through the next election in 1983.

---

wrong in their predictions about such developments.

Overall, the American public exhibits a dynamic mix of liberalism and conservatism. Some studies show that between one-half and two-thirds of Americans adopt conservative views but often are willing to vote liberal and tend to agree with many specific liberal policies. Also, the conservative ethic of individualism remains strong, even as the welfare state and big government enjoy considerable popular support. In U.S. politics, conservative individualism, populist appeals to the common man, and a distrust of "bigness" often coexist in a confusing mélange. This very odd mix forms the common ideological underpinning of our nation.

An Emerging Post-Materialist Dimension

Beginning in the 1960s an intriguing **post-materialist** dimension has emerged in U.S. political life. Post-materialists, who tend to be younger voters, are placing quality-of-life issues—rather than materialistic concerns, like economic development and prosperity—high on the political agenda. Their political priorities range from environmental protection to the quality of community life, opportunities for political and social participation, women's rights, and problems of war and peace. This post-materialist outlook is primarily seen among those who were surrounded in their formative years by relative economic and physical security, and in nations characterized by a good deal of economic equality. The post-materialist drive propelled the rise of the Green Party in West Germany, and has spawned comparable political groups and movements in other democratic nations.

However, we cannot yet determine just how significant or enduring this new dimension will prove. For example, in the 1980s, many younger people in Western nations shifted back sharply to a more materialistic approach. The so-called **yuppies** (young urban professionals) combined some post-materialist attitudes with a determined effort to acquire material things. And while some post-materialists may espouse liberal or radical beliefs, others may adopt conservative, or even reactionary, outlooks. As people come to emphasize the quality of life over more material interests, for example, they may embrace fundamentalist religious doctrines or certain traditionalist views such as opposition to women's rights. So it is not automatically clear where the new post-materialist process will lead.[28]

Influences on Public Sentiment

In analyzing public opinion, comparisons among different segments of the population are especially useful. Key factors include education, age, gender, religion, and region. Some of the resulting conclusions are elementary—for example, that poor people tend to support the political party that promises the most assistance. Yet even this simple generalization must be qualified. Sometimes race or religion might matter more than poverty in choosing a political party. Other questions are harder to peg: Are women more liberal than men when it comes to divorce? Are younger people more likely than elderly people to support the death penalty?

We will now look at three of the factors that significantly affect people's attitudes: (1) class, (2) education, and (3) gender. By delving into these factors, we can discover some of the driving forces behind American public opinion.

CLASS   One of the most enduring divisions in modern politics springs from inequalities in the distribution of wealth and status. Most European political conflict has revolved around such class politics—with workers aligned against the middle class, and labor and socialist parties against the bourgeois parties. We can see such patterns clearly in England, West Germany, France, Italy, and Scandinavia. Even though Americans are much less class conscious than Western Europeans, these divisions still play a significant role in U.S. politics. People's occupations are clearly related to their views on many economic questions, and these, in turn, are related to their political party preference.

Comparing lower-status and higher-status people (in terms of income, education, and occupation) over a range of issues, we discover that, in general, lower-status people express more liberal views on economic questions, while higher-status people take a more liberal stand on civil rights and liberties. On foreign policy, the situation grows more complicated. Higher-status people are more likely to favor internationalist approaches, whereas lower-status people usually support more isolationist policies.

How do such realities affect U.S. politics? We can draw one clear conclusion: that the economic liberalism of the poorer sectors of the population generally translates into support for the Democrats and for trade unions. But qualifications remain. For example, the greater conservatism of less-ed-

An art auction is one way to raise political funds, but not everyone can afford the sort of contribution expected here. Although Americans do not usually like to think in terms of social class, the values, habits, and politics of groups do differ, sometimes markedly. This is not to say that all "upper class" people think alike, however; within any income or status group, there are often important differences. (© *Arlene Collins/ Monkmeyer*)

ucated people on civil rights and liberties, as well as on some foreign policy questions, can lead to political anomalies. For example, Ronald Reagan, a conservative Republican, forged a successful political strategy by appealing to the blue-collar, white, ethnic voters' patriotism and moral values.

As we can see in **Figure 6–3,** income plays a key role in the way people vote. Support for the Demo-

cratic Party increases steadily as we go down the income scale—a pattern that has persisted in American politics since at least the New Deal period. On the right side of the figure—relating income to voter turnout—we clearly see that those with higher incomes are far more likely to vote. Going down the income scale, voter turnout drops off steadily.

FIGURE 6–3
Party Preference and Voter Turnout by Income (1984 Presidential Election)

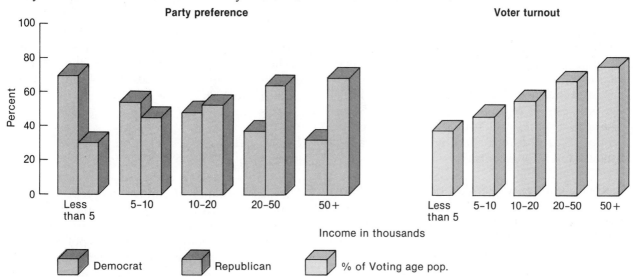

SOURCES: Party preference from ABC News exit poll; turnout from Census Bureau data.

EDUCATION   One fascinating development in recent years has been the widening ideological split between better-educated and less-well-educated Americans. Some argue that the disparity in educational levels now constitutes the fundamental split in U.S. society; education, they say, is the new basis for defining one's social class.[29] We have blue-collar conservatives on the one side and the new professionals on the other. The new professionals tend to favor more liberal positions on a host of social issues; take a more permissive approach in their personal behavior and values; and cast a more critical eye on the political leadership, especially when it comes to foreign and defense policies. The working class, on the other hand, has acquired a real stake in the system and defends it staunchly, taking a somewhat more conservative stance socially while maintaining its traditional economic liberalism.

It is hard to say, from the perspective of the 1980s, whether education will continue to exert so much political significance. In the mid-1980s, the yuppies emerged on the political scene. First seen as a political force during the 1984 presidential campaign, these young, urban professionals (ranging in age from twenty-five to forty) are educated, affluent, and often attuned to political matters. As a group, they are hard to categorize politically. Disillusioned by Vietnam and Watergate, they espouse liberal views on such issues as rights for women and minorites, environmental regulation, and abortion. However, the yuppies also display some distinctly conservative outlooks: They tend to oppose government intervention in the marketplace, for instance. Characterized as selfish and career-oriented, yuppies are also considered to be antiparty, for they seem to identify neither with labor and the New Deal nor with Republican business interests or religious fundamentalists. Some observers even consider the whole concept of "yuppies" as a distinct social group to be rather dubious and impressionistic.

GENDER   On the whole, American women have been characterized as more "puritanical" and more "tender-minded" than men on most issues. On social measures women take a somewhat more conservative position than men. Men are more likely to favor easier divorces, legalized abortion, and premarital sexual relations.[30]

As for the "tender-minded" label, women tend to favor gun control, while they are less supportive of capital punishment than men are. In recent years, women have shown less faith in the economic system than men have.

By the 1980s, talk of a "gender gap" became common political parlance as certain differences grew more marked. Ronald Reagan's presidency underscored these differences. For example, women tended to see Reagan's economic policies as "unfair" and his foreign policies as "risky," whereas men were more likely to characterize the president as "forceful."[31] This gender gap proved significant in the 1984 presidential election, when the Democrats, to their chagrin, discovered a powerful new minority group: white males. Of this group, two-thirds voted for President Reagan, while the women's vote was far more evenly divided.[32] Throughout the 1980s, there was also a marked decline in the percentage of men who identified themselves as Democrats, with no decline among women. In generalizing about sex differences, of course, we may be, and probably are, overlooking important differences *within* the women's group. Shadings one way or another certainly appear among various age groups, or those with differing levels of education or occupational status.

Electoral Trends

After looking at the structure of political sentiment among Americans, we now turn to how political attitudes affect the electoral process. Here we will probe (1) the social bases of voting patterns; (2) the decline of ideology in the 1950s; (3) the reemergence of ideology in the 1960s; and (4) the elections of 1984 and 1986.

Social Bases of Voting Patterns

The basic outlines of contemporary U.S. politics were established in the 1930s, when a significant realignment of the electorate took place. A **realignment** is a major, long-term change in political party allegiance among the electorate, reflecting a shift in the coalitions that support each party. During the Great Depression there was a massive repu-

Ethnicity, religion, and race all surface in this 1988 photo of New York Mayor Ed Koch, presidential candidate Jesse Jackson, and New York Governor Mario Cuomo (looking on, behind Koch). Although Jewish and black groups have often cooperated and have supported similar candidates, tensions arose during the Democratic Party primaries when Koch sharply criticized Jackson. Once Michael Dukakis was nominated, it became important for the party to at least cover over (if not entirely heal) the rift. The two men met in Governor Cuomo's office for several hours before emerging for the press. *(Chester Higgins, Jr./ New York Times Pictures)*

diation of the Republican Party, whose policies were widely blamed for the economic crisis. The beneficiary of this realignment was the Democratic Party of President Franklin D. Roosevelt, who forged a majority coalition primarily made up of Northern blue-collar workers (many with ethnic and immigrant backgrounds) and Southern voters of all classes (a holdover from the South's affiliation with the Democrats since the Civil War). Generally speaking, any understanding of the workings of U.S. politics from the 1930s to the present must be based on this fundamental realignment—even though some observers contend that Roosevelt's New Deal coalition has begun to come apart.

In a study of the presidential election of 1940, Paul Lazarsfeld and colleagues analyzed voting patterns through the use of an "index of political predisposition."[33] This index, based on key elements of the New Deal coalition, was made up of three factors: socioeconomic status, religion, and place of residence (urban or rural). The authors found that a high socioeconomic status, affiliation with Protestantism, and a rural residence tended to lead to a Republican vote. Democrats tended to be poorer, more urban, and Catholic.

Let us examine how these and other demographic characteristics relate to voting behavior in the United States.

Religion. Both Catholics and Jews are much more likely to vote Democratic. The preference can be traced to the patterns of emigration to the United States. Most Catholic and Jewish immigrants—Irish, Russians, Italians, Poles, and others—settled in cities already dominated by Democratic Party political machines. During the waves of immigration of the nineteenth and early twentieth centuries, many within the Republican Party held strong nativist, antiforeign views, which also drove the newcomers toward the Democrats. Catholics, and Jews as well, frequently saw themselves as economic and social underdogs in this country, and in the New Deal period, both groups strongly identified with Roosevelt's policies. For Jews, this identification was solidified during World War II. In contrast, Protestants (outside the South) have been the most strongly Republican of the three major religious groups, partially because of the heavier representation of Protestants in the business classes in small-town America and (until recent decades) among the wealthier, and hence, the better educated.

Social class. Struggles between haves and have-nots have always been a factor in U.S. politics. At least as far back as Andrew Jackson and the election of 1828, the Democratic Party has proclaimed itself the party of the "common man." On the whole, however, the effects of class struggle on U.S. politics have been muted. Yet they were evident in the 1930s, when the Republicans, thanks to Herbert Hoover and the

Depression, became solidly established as the party of big business and the middle classes. The working class voted for the Democrats by at least 10 percent more than the middle class in every national election between 1952 and 1972. In the presidential elections of 1972, 1980, and 1984, however, the Republicans cut into the Democrats' percentage of the working-class vote. Polls in the early phases of the 1988 campaign, however, revealed that the working-class vote was returning, at a rate of about 70 percent, to the Democratic Party.

Race. Until the New Deal, most blacks voted Republican. This preference was rooted in an attachment to the party of Lincoln and an antipathy toward Southern Democrats who disenfranchised blacks around the turn of the century. Black loyalty to the GOP began failing in the New Deal period, as many blacks came to support New Deal economic programs. Blacks moved closer to the Democrats in the 1940s, when the party began to take some steps on the civil rights front. Since the election of 1952, at least 60 percent of black voters have cast their ballots for the Democratic presidential candidate. The election of 1964 represented another turning point for the black vote, as over 80 percent of the black electorate chose Democrat Lyndon Johnson over Republican Barry Goldwater. The black vote has remained overwhelmingly Democratic since then. In the 1980s, blacks gained substantial influence in U.S. politics, principally through heavy voter registration drives. Between 1980 and 1983, over 1 million new black voters were added to the registration lists. In the 1986 senatorial elections, heavy black support led to the election of several Democrats in the South, reflecting the increased clout and organizational capacity of blacks in that region. Building on that clout, the 1988 presidential campaign of Jesse Jackson galvanized black voters, who embraced Jackson's candidacy with fervor. Many observers characterized the Jackson campaign as a barrier-breaking venture—not only for blacks but also for the American political process.

We could consider other demographic factors— age, region, and level of education, for example— but the general picture should be clear. At least since the political realignment of the 1930s, particular groups have remained more or less attached to each party. This sketch gives us only the broad outlines of modern U.S. political life, however. Many people don't fit neatly into the traditional categories used to analyze voter preferences. For example, what sort of voting pattern could be expected from a middle-class Catholic, or from a working-class Protestant living in an urban area? When various demographic factors are mixed, prediction and understanding of voting behavior become more difficult. Then, too, as the issues and even the social bases of political life change over time, voting patterns can be transformed. This happened, for example, as a college education, once reserved almost exclusively for the upper middle class and the upper class, became available to a wider spectrum of Americans; as hundreds of thousands of Southern blacks moved North; and as the New Deal and the Depression faded in the minds of many voters. Finally, there is some question whether voters understand their political preferences in terms of ideology at all. In other words, do people approach political issues from a coherent and consistent perspective that helps them make sense of the political spectrum in terms of liberal or conservative ideals? We turn to this matter next.

The 1950s—Ideology in Decline

The liberal/conservative continuum that has characterized U.S. politics since the nation's founding faded in importance in the 1950s—a time of placid social arrangements and respect for the status quo. Political scientists in the 1950s, dissatisfied with the sketchiness of earlier studies on why people vote as they do, began to seek more refined answers.[34] What they found was startling and discouraging. When investigators tried to tap the ideological dimension of people's thinking—to see if voters viewed elections in terms of liberalism versus conservatism—they discovered that very few Americans exhibited a consistent political outlook. In studying the 1956 national elections, for example, researchers at the Michigan Survey Research Center classified only 3 percent of the voters as "clear ideologues" and only 13 percent as "near ideologues." The researchers did find that the underlying social bases of U.S politics had remained intact, in that a large percentage of the electorate seemed to vote on the basis of group benefits promised by different candidates—"Candidate X will help the working people," for example.

Eisenhower pledged to go to Korea if elected, and go he did. Ike's image as a victorious World War II commander helped him win the 1952 election, a triumph at least in part of personality over party allegiance. *(Black Star)*

In the 1950s, voters usually decided whom to vote for on the basis of party affiliation, personality characteristics of the candidates, or specific issues. Issue voters weighed which party would respond better to unemployment, the Korean War, or some other issue. Personality-oriented voters stressed the honesty, leadership abilities, or experience of a particular candidate. Party loyalists picked the party they felt would better serve them as individuals and the country as a whole. During this period, party identification was still very high in the United States—about 75 percent of the public claimed party affiliation. In fact, party affiliation was one of the best predictors of how people would vote in the 1950s. During that decade, over 90 percent of the voters stuck with their party of choice in congressional elections. Of course, millions of Democrats also voted for Republican presidential candidate Dwight Eisenhower, chiefly based on his personality and his standing as a war hero.

The 1960s—the Reemergence of Ideology

The U.S political scene underwent a radical change in the 1960s. Two students of voting behavior summed up this transformation as follows:

> The year 1956 was the middle of the Eisenhower Era; the Korean War and the McCarthy hearings were in the past, and in a very real sense, not much was happening politically. . . . Politics was indeed, as Robert Dahl described it at the time, merely a sideshow in the circus of life.
>
> The first big change in this picture occurred in 1960 with the advent of a deliberately activist administration, a new focus on the problems of race and poverty and, perhaps most important, a Kennedy-inspired conviction, on the part of many citizens, that involvement in politics could actually bring about desired changes. . . .
>
> The tremendous media focus on Kennedy's assassination brought politics even more to the forefront

of national life. . . . The 1964 election, and the impetus it provided to citizens to structure their political beliefs into a coherent liberal/conservative ideology, was not merely a transient phenomenon. Americans were bombarded with one social and political crisis after another in the middle and late 1960s . . . by the late 1960s the positive involvement of the early and mid-60s had turned decidedly sour. The war lingered on, the Great Society programs appeared to have failed, and it seemed as if the government was incapable of dealing with new problems such as crime, pollution and inflation. The cynicism which arose from government's failure to deal with the society's problems by no means decreased the salience of politics—the feeling that what happens in Washington affects one's life—but, we believe, did cause many people to withdraw from politics in frustration.

The important point is that the pattern of attitudes found among Americans in the 1950s was a transient phenomenon and not an inevitable characteristic of mass politics.[35]

Between 1964 and 1972, ideology, which seemed to have disappeared as a significant political factor in the 1950s, came back with a vengeance. An issue-oriented politics reemerged in the United States; the tendency of the 1950s electorate to embrace unstructured jumbles of beliefs gave way to clearly ideological political thinking. People who held liberal views on one issue, such as the Vietnam War, were more likely to express liberal beliefs on other issues. The same held true for conservatives. The political spectrum grew more polarized and clearer, partly because many Americans increasingly came to feel that politics had an influence on their personal lives.

Candidate personality remained an important political factor through the 1960s, but the salience of issues increased sharply. At the same time, party affiliation diminished in significance. In 1972, only 21 percent of those surveyed mentioned party as an important element in evaluating the presidential candidates.[36] Again and again, party proved to be of secondary importance in presidential politics. In 1964, millions of Republicans defected to Johnson; in 1972, millions of Democrats defected to Nixon.

As the number of people who identified with either major political party declined, the percentage of independent voters grew. By the late 1970s,

an estimated 35–40 percent of Americans characterized themselves as political independents. Younger voters were particularly inclined to reject party affiliation, and the lowering of the voting age to eighteen, starting in 1972, increased the ranks of independents substantially. The youth vote, however, was not the only source of new independents. Many former party members, disillusioned with the events of the 1960s and early 1970s, rejected old affiliation. Partisanship in general weakened, except among those who considered themselves "strong Republicans." Solid evidence for this trend was seen in the rising popularity of split-ticket voting. From the 1950s to the late 1970s, the percentage of voters who voted a straight party line in both presidential and congressional elections dropped precipitously.

The 1976 election marked a return to more traditional voting patterns. Jimmy Carter recreated the New Deal coalition, drawing support from the South, the blue-collar vote, and blacks. (Carter actually lost the election among whites alone.) In 1976, Carter attracted 80 percent of registered Democrats, whereas Gerald Ford won the support of more than 90 percent of all Republicans.

The Democratic defeat in the 1980 election revealed the fragility of Carter's revived New Deal coalition. (Some additional factors also eroded support for Carter's reelection, among them the protracted Iranian hostage crisis and a stubborn economic downturn.) With Reagan's victory came renewed assertions that a Republican majority was taking shape and that a major political realignment was under way. Some observers traced the origins of this realignment back to the 1950s, pointing to the two Eisenhower victories as signs of developments to come. And yet the shape of U.S. partisan politics was anything but clearcut, as recent elections demonstrate.

The Elections of 1984 and 1986

In 1984, Reagan won a victory of substantial proportions. Underlying this victory were a number of crucial factors: the economic recovery, popular support for Reagan as a leader, brilliant use of the media by the Republicans during the campaign,

As the sixties drew to a close, ideology again became an important factor in American political life. People took strong stands on issues and felt that politics had direct effects on their lives. *(© Jim Anderson/Stock, Boston)*

the Democrats' failure to mount a telling attack on the administration, and the growing conservative trend among American voters.

Economic factors had perhaps the greatest bearing on the election. In the 1982 off-year elections, the Democrats made substantial gains that many observers attributed to the recession then in progress. In 1984, however, 60 percent of voters stated that they were "better off" than they had been in 1980, and Reagan captured the votes of this group by a 6–1 margin.[37] Among those who said they were "worse off" in 1984, the margin was 4–1 for Democratic candidate Walter Mondale. With the exception of Jewish voters, all the groups among which Mondale did best were those facing economic hardship—the poor, blacks, union members, and families that had been hit by unemployment. This observation alone could explain the outcome of the elections.

Apart from economic factors, Reagan's victory could be attributed to his strong appeal to white males, who made up 42 percent of the electorate— an electoral bloc second only to white females in size.[38] Reagan captured 66 percent of the white male vote, carrying a majority of white males even among the poorest sectors of the population. The president also outpolled Mondale among women, but by a considerably narrower margin.

The male vote for Reagan was linked to positive perceptions of him as a leader. Among white males, he was widely viewed as a "man's man," a leader who would "stick to his guns," and who was "tough enough" to deal with international problems.[39] Mondale, in contrast, was viewed as cautious.

Some observers interpreted the 1984 election as evidence of a dealignment rather than a realignment. Pointing out that Americans today often switch parties to match their preference in presidential candidates, these commentators argue that party identification no longer means much to U.S. voters. In this view, the American electorate has continued to become more volatile, but has yet to settle decisively into a new voting pattern.[40]

Yet another view holds that the apparent loosening of party ties is in fact part of a new realignment. According to this interpretation, the Republicans are gaining numerous new supporters, perhaps enough to become the new majority party. But public perception of their performance as a governing party will be crucial to their future. Advocates of this view contend that Ronald Reagan's first term gave the GOP cause a considerable boost because a majority of the public endorsed his leadership and gave him credit for the economic recovery.[41]

Classifying Presidential Elections

Political scientists have devised a classification system for elections based on two major dimensions of voting results: how well the majority party does, and the degree of change (if any) in the voter coalition that has supported the majority. In a *maintaining election,* the majority party retains its strength and enjoys the same pattern of support as in the previous election. In a *converting election,* the majority remains a majority but its supporting coalition shows serious signs of change. In a *deviating election,* the basic majority coalition remains intact but short-term factors lead to a victory for the minority party; in such a case, the deviation is not considered likely to last. In a *realigning election,* not only does the former minority party win, but basic changes also take place in voter affiliations and a new majority is created.

Throughout U.S. political history, maintaining elections have been by far the most common. In recent years, however, examples of all four election types have cropped up. The great realigning election of the New Deal occurred in 1932. In the elections of 1936 through 1948, the New Deal coalition maintained its strength. The Republican victories of 1952 and 1956 are considered deviating elections; although the Republican candidate won, the basic pattern of electoral loyalties apparently did not change. Both the 1960 and the 1964 elections were of the converting type. The Democrats, still a majority, won both, but new patterns of voter attachment seemed to be in evidence. Some experts argue that 1964 should be considered a realigning election, in that new coalitions were established: conservative Republicans and liberal Democrats. In retrospect, however, the new coalition that seemed within reach of the Democrats after 1964 never crystallized, and since then, party loyalties have grown less, rather than more, intense. The Nixon victories of 1968 and 1972 are considered deviating, as is Ronald Reagan's 1980 triumph. Carter's 1976 win represented the only maintaining election among the last nine.

Beginning with the 1952 election, then, the patterns of party loyalty established definitively in 1952 have been changing. But in what direction? This question has stumped political analysts for more than a decade. The results of the 1984 election led to speculation that there may no longer be a pattern to deviate from. Perhaps the 1984 election should be characterized as "pre-aligning"; the old Democratic majority disappeared, but no new, durable voting pattern emerged. Or perhaps it represented a "dealigning" election—one that reflected merely the continued breakdown of old political loyalties.

The election of 1986, however, amounted to a sharp rebuff for the Reagan administration. The president himself campaigned vigorously in an effort to keep the Senate in Republican hands. His efforts failed, however, and the Democrats regained control of both houses. In effect, the election made clear that no large-scale Republican realignment had yet taken place. Democrats saw in the results the hope that the public was beginning to turn against Reagan's policies and that 1988 might be a Democratic year.

Nonparticipation

Nonparticipation in the political process is the most serious problem facing U.S. democracy. This is reflected in the following figures:

From 1970 to 1980, more than 15 million Americans who were eligible to vote, including many regular voters, stopped voting altogether.

Between 1960 and 1980, the percentage of eligible voters who actually cast ballots in presidential elec-

The theme of Ronald Reagan's second presidential bid was a renewed and stronger America. Here the man is somewhat dwarfed by a gigantic U.S. flag, but in politics, as in dreams, symbols count. *(AP/Wide World Photos)*

tions decreased sharply, from 64 percent to 52.6 percent; and in 1984, there was only a marginal increase in turnout, to 53.1 percent. A similar trend has been evident in local, state, and congressional elections—and at a substantially lower level of participation than in presidential elections.

Nearly 75 million eligible Americans failed to cast ballots in the 1980 presidential election; nearly 100 million did not vote in the congressional elections in 1974.

Fewer than 27 percent of Ronald Reagan's fellow citizens voted for him for president in 1980. Governor Brendan Byrne of New Jersey received a "mandate" of less than 15 percent of the eligible vote in his successful 1977 reelection bid. Mayor Ed Koch was the choice of less than 12 percent of New York City's eligible voters in 1981. Senator Henry Jackson won the 1976 New York presidential primary by garnering less than 6 percent of the potential vote.

American voting levels rank the lowest of all democratic nations, as shown in **Table 6–8**. American voting has been declining since 1960, and even then had reached just the 60 percent level (see **Table 6–9**). From a democratic perspective, there is reason for concern when so many citizens take so little interest in their society's political life. We now examine (1) barriers to voting and (2) who votes.

Barriers to Voting

The consistently low voter turnouts in U.S. elections can be partially attributed to the law and to elements of the election system that make it difficult, or even impossible, for some people to vote. For example, residency requirements have sometimes restricted voting. Until a decade or so ago, most states made eligibility to vote contingent on residence in the state for at least a year and in a specific county and precinct for several months. Because Americans move so often, as many as five million voters may have been barred from recent presidential elections on these grounds. Supreme Court decisions in 1970 and 1972 reduced residency requirements for national, state, and local elections.

The registration process itself has often created a barrier to voting. In a number of European countries, a voter can register merely by showing up at the polling place on election day. By contrast, in many parts of the United States voters must register well before election day. Some states even require voters to reregister if they have failed to vote for two successive years.

Registration requirements were cited by 31 percent of nonvoters in one poll taken in 1984.[42] Obviously, then, other factors are at work here. One

COMPARATIVE PERSPECTIVE

Fewer Voters, but More Voting

Although the United States lags far behind other Western nations in the proportion of its citizens who vote in national elections, it is far ahead of any other Western nation in the *number of votes* cast by one voter in a given four-year period.

The first reason for this phenomenon is federalism. Americans may vote in at least four jurisdictions—federal, state, county, and municipal elections. This four-layer system of government is not usually found in Europe.

The second reason is the separation of powers. Americans are unique in that they are able to vote for both legislative representatives and executive leaders at all levels—from city council members and mayors to members of Congress and president. In a parliamentary system, individuals vote only for legislative representatives.

A third reason is the long ballot. When Americans vote, they may vote for many executive offices, from dog-catcher or coroner to governor and president. By comparison, parliamentary regimes often are not set up so that citizens may vote for lesser executive offices. France is unique in Western Europe in having a powerful, directly elected president. Countries with figurehead presidents (such as Italy) often still choose the president indirectly or without a contest (as in Ireland), and only a few by popular election (for example, Finland and Austria). America is also distinctive in that some of its judges, and in some cases, police commissioners or sheriffs, are subject to direct election.

Fourth, the United States has many special purpose jurisdictions—school boards, sewer districts, and the like—that are directly elected. In Europe, such bodies almost invariably are appointed by the central government, or do not exist at all.

Fifth, many Americans are able to enact or repudiate legislation through referenda on legislation and on some taxes affecting current or capital expenditure. The principle of the referendum is not unique to America; in Switzerland, for example, national referenda are pivotal. But state and local governments in the United States use the autonomy of federalism to hold more such ballots collectively in a given year than does the whole of Europe put together. The recall of elected officeholders is another distinctive American institution, but, on the whole, it has been rarely used.

Sixth, primary elections in the United States allow registered electors the right to cast a ballot and choose among a party's potential candidates. In continental Europe, the mechanics of proportional representation allow centralized decision making by party committees that determine the party's candidates. Voters have a limited opportunity to alter party endorsements. Primaries at multiple levels of government in America can double many of the opportunities to vote described above. In those states where a runoff election is prescribed when no candidate secures half the vote in the first primary contest, an individual's opportunity to vote can be trebled.

Such contrasting voting opportunities might first lead an American to ask: Why do Europeans have so few occasions to vote? The answers are several: the heritage of aristocratic rather than populist decision making; the belief in the efficacy and impartiality of civil servants as executive agents of government; and reliance on parties to organize and direct government through parliamentary institutions. A European who inquired about the advantages and disadvantages of the American system of multiple voting would first of all be met with answers emphasizing the principle of direct determination of issues by citizens (such as bond issues or school tax referenda) and the superiority of decision making by elected representatives. A European might wonder whether something was not lost by reducing the standing of experts and civil servants, and by the disintegration of parties.

Adapted from Richard Rose, "Citizen Participation in the Presidential Process," *Society,* November/December 1978, pp. 43–48.

TABLE 6–8
Ranking of Countries by Voter Turnout

*Vote as a percentage of voting-age population
(most recent national election)*

Italy	94.0%
Austria	89.3
Belgium	88.7
Sweden	86.8
Portugal	85.9
Greece	84.9
Netherlands	84.7
Australia	83.1
Denmark	82.1
Norway	81.8
West Germany	81.1
New Zealand	78.5
France	78.0
Great Britain	76.0
Japan	74.4
Spain	73.0
Canada	67.4
Finland	63.0
Ireland	62.3
United States	52.6
Switzerland	39.4

SOURCES: D. Glass, P. Squire, and R. Wolfinger, "Voter Turnout: An International Comparison," *Public Opinion,* December/January 1984. The figures for the United States are from the *Statistical Abstract of the United States, 1982–1983.* The data for all other countries for the number of voters and the number of persons registered are from *The International Almanac of Electoral History,* 2nd ed., by Thomas T. Mackie and Richard Rose. The voting-age population was derived from the countries' year books. It was occasionally necessary to extrapolate the present age breakdown on the basis of the last census.

TABLE 6–9
Turnout in Presidential and Congressional Elections, 1920–1984

	Office	
Year	President	U.S. representative
1920	43.5%	40.8%
1922	—	32.1
1924	43.9	40.6
1926	—	29.8
1928	51.9	47.8
1930	—	33.7
1932	52.4	49.7
1934	—	41.4
1936	56.9	53.5
1938	—	44.0
1940	58.9	55.4
1942	—	32.5
1944	56.0	52.7
1946	—	37.1
1948	51.1	48.1
1950	—	41.1
1952	61.6	57.6
1954	—	41.7
1956	59.3	55.9
1958	—	43.0
1960	62.8	58.5
1962	—	45.4
1964	61.9	57.8
1966	—	45.4
1968	60.9	55.1
1970	—	43.5
1972	55.5	51.1
1974	—	36.3
1976	54.3	49.6
1978	—	37.9
1980	52.6	47.4
1982	—	48.5
1984	52.9	—

SOURCES: Data for 1920–1980 from U.S. Bureau of the Census, *Statistical Abstract of the United States, 1982–1983* (Washington: GPO, 1983). Data for 1982 from U.S. Bureau of the Census, "Voting and Registration in the Election of November 1982," *Current Population Reports,* series P-20, No. 383 (Washington: GPO, 1983).

major deterrent to voting can be an overwhelming superiority on the part of one political party. In such **one-party districts** or states, supporters of the excluded party tend to feel that voting is useless, and supporters of the dominant party may come to believe that voting is unnecessary.

Who Votes?

Not all groups or classes of Americans are equally likely to vote (see **Table 6–10**, page 214). In general, the socially disadvantaged are less likely to vote, and the socially advantaged more likely to show up at the polls regularly. The following factors influence voting habits:

Who's most likely to vote? Affluent, highly educated white males aged thirty-five to fifty-five, and especially if they are Republicans. (© *Michael Hayman/Photo Researchers*)

1. *Income.* The more money a person makes, the more likely he or she is to vote.

2. *Education.* The higher a person's level of education, the more likely he or she is to vote.

3. *Age.* People between the ages of thirty-five and fifty-five are considerably more likely to vote than are younger or older persons. In general, people do not develop regular voting habits until they have established themselves in life. The falloff in voting among the elderly may be due to physical infirmity.

4. *Gender.* Men are more likely to vote than women. In recent elections, however, the voting gap between men and women has been disappearing.

5. *Race.* Whites are more likely to vote than nonwhites. In the past, large differences in turnout between the races stemmed from discrimination against black voters. The difference that remains can be ascribed primarily to education and income differences between whites and nonwhites. Minority voter turnout rises greatly when a member of a minority group is running for office.

6. *Party.* Because Republican voters are more likely to be college-educated and to earn high incomes, Republicans are more likely to vote than are Democrats.

7. *Partisanship.* Persons who identify themselves either as Republicans or Democrats are more likely to vote than those who call themselves independents.

It is hardly surprising that those groups most likely to vote—the educated, the well-to-do, the middle-aged, whites, and Republicans—are much more likely to believe in their ability to influence government. One reason for such confidence is that by producing much higher voter turnouts,

these groups do indeed have an impact on elections far out of proportion to their actual numbers. A rich person's vote does not count for any more than a poor person's—except if the rich person votes and the poor person does not.

TABLE 6–10
Voting Turnout by Characteristics, 1968–1980

	1968	1972	1976	1980
Male	69.8%	64.1%	59.6%	59.1%
Female	66.0	62.0	58.8	59.4
Age				
18–20	—	48.3	38.0	35.7
21–24	51.0	50.7	45.6	43.1
25–34	62.5	59.7	55.4	54.6
35–44	70.8	66.3	63.3	64.4
45–64	74.9	70.8	68.7	69.3
65 and over	65.8	63.5	62.2	65.1
Education				
8 years or less	54.5	47.4	44.1	42.6
9–11	61.3	52.0	47.2	45.6
12	72.5	65.4	59.4	58.9
More than 12	81.2	78.8	73.5	73.2
Race				
White	69.1	64.5	60.9	60.9
Black	57.6	52.1	48.7	50.9
Hispanic	N.A.	37.4	31.8	29.9

SOURCE: U.S. Department of Commerce, Bureau of the Census, *Statistical Abstract of the United States, 1982–1983* (Washington: GPO, 1983), p. 493.

TABLE 6–11
Civic Culture: Perceptions in Five Democracies

	United States	Great Britain	West Germany	Italy	Mexico
Percent believing the ordinary person should be active in the community	51	39	22	10	26
Percent who say they can do something about an unjust national regulation	75	62	38	28	38
Percent who say they can do something about an unjust local regulation	77	78	62	51	52
Percent reporting that they regularly or occasionally discuss politics	76	70	60	32	38
Percent saying they would likely have success if they tried to change a harmful local regulation	52	36	32	22	37
Percent who say they have attempted to influence local government	28	15	14	9	6
Percent saying they would likely have success if they tried to change a harmful national regulation	41	25	13	11	29
Percent who follow accounts of political and government affairs regularly	27	23	34	11	15

SOURCES: Gabriel A. Almond and Sidney Verba, *The Civic Culture*, pp. 89, 116, 169, and 185; and the *Inter-University Consortium for Political Research Codebook: The Five Nation Study* (Ann Arbor: ICPR, 1968), pp. 29 and 83.

Another hotly disputed question is whether voters and nonvoters differ very much in their political preferences. Some observers argue that even if American turnout were 100 percent, the results of elections would usually be about the same. Others maintain, however, that increased turnout would either aid the Democrats or threaten the system itself, because of the influx of poorly informed and easily manipulated new voters.

While voting is perhaps the most obvious way people participate in politics, it is far from the only way. **Table 6–11** probes how people in several countries feel about other efforts to participate in politics. Americans, despite a low level of voter turnout, express relatively high levels of optimism about their ability to influence government at various levels.

Opinion and Policy

How does public opinion influence government policy making? In examining this question, several patterns emerge. For example, when public opinion clearly supports programs already in existence, such as Social Security, politicians find it very difficult to make changes in them. Such programs usually have wide impact, touching almost everyone to some degree. Popular rebellion forms another recognizable pattern—when public opinion demands action (or the electorate takes action itself, through a referendum, for instance). In recent years, popular rebellions have broken out over taxation and environmental issues. Policy makers who ignore broad-based discontent often do so at peril to their careers.

A more complex situation arises when an influential or well-organized minority seizes an issue and propels it to political prominence. Abortion, for example, has stirred such intense feelings among some groups that no other issue matters to them. Examples abound of well-organized minorities and poorly organized majorities in U.S. politics. Usually this occurs because the well-organized have more clearly defined and intensely felt interests at stake. For instance, although the majority of the population supports gun control legislation, those who oppose it are so committed to their cause that they have effectively blocked such legislation for years. The medical profession has successfully postponed action on national health insurance time and again. In the same way, small numbers who will benefit greatly from particular tax loopholes press their case on tax reform with great insistence, though the recent success of the more comprehensive tax reform indicates that this pattern need not always prevail.

A somewhat different pattern emerges when public sentiment and legal edicts conflict. When the courts ordered busing to achieve integration in the public schools, for example, most of the public and much of the political elite opposed those rulings. Efforts to overturn those policies through legislation or constitutional amendment largely failed, but the lack of public and elite support for such policies significantly limited their implementation: Enforcement agencies were deprived of adequate funding; protesting parents kept children out of school, or moved from urban areas where integration has been required; and at every level of government, from local school boards to the federal administrative apparatus, attempts to slow down implementation of busing were made.

Generally, however, public opposition usually makes itself felt somewhere in the process of turning policies into realities.

In many areas, public opinion is neither well-formed nor well-organized, even though people may have strongly held views on specific issues. When this is the case—as it often is in matters of foreign policy, for instance—politicians have considerable leeway in policy making. A good example was the Reagan administration's support for the Nicaraguan resistance. The administration was able to keep some level of aid going to the contras throughout most of the 1980s, despite substantial opposition in Congress and a distinct lack of support from the public at large. Here, the president's own commitments were crucial.

A study of the connections between public opinion and policy shifts in the United States between 1935 and the early 1980s demonstrated that policy is definitely affected when public opinion shifts are sufficiently large.[43] The researchers studied hundreds of national opinion polls and 357 federal, state, and local issues on which public opinion showed a "significant" shift—defined as a change of at least 6 percent. In 153 of these cases (43 percent of the total), government action followed major shifts of opinion fairly quickly. For example, the Civil Rights Act of 1964 was passed after a 12 percent shift of public opinion in favor of greater support for equal rights for black Americans. Not surprisingly, the larger the shift in opinion, the greater the likelihood that policy will shift in the same direction. When the opinion shift was 20 percent or greater, the researchers found, policy shifted 90 percent of the time.

This study illustrates that public opinion does influence policy decisions. It does not tell us, however, what factors cause shifts in public opinion. A whole range of factors come into play here, including mass movements, organized protests, the quality of leadership, media attention, and the general readiness of the public to respond to a particular issue.

Conclusions

Majority rule stands at the core of democratic politics. Through political socialization, children are inculcated with essential democratic beliefs—that ours is a free counry, that majority rule serves as the basis of democracy, that individual citizens can make a difference in the political system. These beliefs—and the values of voting and civic participation—are taught and reinforced both at home and at school. In college, young people may adopt political views at odds with those of their parents in an attempt to forge their own political identities.

In theory, democracy is guided by majority rule; in practice, majority sentiment is identified through public opinion polls. Yet while many hold a deep-rooted belief in their power as individuals to influence the political system, alienation from government—expressed through nonvoting or other forms of nonparticipation—has been a persistent problem in U.S. politics.

Some observers of the U.S. political scene find nothing alarming about the sizable number of American citizens who do not even bother to vote. They note that U.S. politics has remained remarkably stable, that our constitutional system has endured many tests. In recent times, they point out, one president was assassinated, and another resigned from office—and neither of these events, which could have been catastrophic, shook the foundations of U.S. political life. This speaks volumes about the basic stability of our political system. Yet others see trouble for democracy when so many take so little interest in the workings of their society's political system.

Whether or not majorities participate, how much influence does majority sentiment exert on U.S. politics? On this question, we must take a cautious view. As we have seen, public sentiment in the United States is not structured along ideological lines. In general, the major shifts in U.S. electoral politics are clearly related to shifts in public sentiment. The New Deal enjoyed strong majority support, much of which remains to this day. Other shifts in law and political practice, such as those dealing with women's rights, tolerance, and racial equality, also reflect—and, in turn, influence—the views of emerging majorities. Yet some majority sentiments have not become law: stricter gun control has not been enacted, national health insurance has not been created, the federal budget has not been balanced. When majority sentiment does not hold sway, a powerful and well-orga-nized interest group or coalition of groups is usually at work.

You may have noticed a missing link in our discussion. One can discuss the meaningfulness of majority sentiment, or the importance of participation, only so long before noting the crucial significance of political parties—the institutions that connect mass sentiment to public policy. We will address that dimension of the electoral process in the next chapter.

GLOSSARY TERMS

majority sentiment

political socialization

direct socialization

indirect socialization

public opinion

political efficacy

alienation

ideology

liberal

conservative

welfare state

interventionist

human rights

nuclear freeze

post-materialist

yuppies

realignment

one-party districts

NOTES

[1]The term *diffuse support* is taken from David Easton, *A Systems Analysis of Political Life* (New York: Wiley, 1965), chap. 17.

[2]Fred I. Greenstein, "The Benevolent Leader: Children's Image of Political Authority," *American Political Science Review* 54, 1960, pp. 943–945.

[3]F. C. Arterton, "The Impact of Watergate on Children's Attitudes Toward Political Authority," *Political Science Quarterly* 89, 1974, pp. 269–288.

[4]Fred I. Greenstein, *Children and Politics* (New Haven, Conn.: Yale University Press, 1965).

[5]T. W. Adorno et al., *The Authoritarian Personality* (New York: Harper, 1950).

[6]See, for example, Allan Bloom, *The Closing of the American Mind* (New York: Simon & Schuster, 1987); and E. D. Hirsch, Jr., *Cultural Literacy* (Boston: Houghton Mifflin, 1987).

[7]Diane Ravitch and Chester E. Finn, Jr., *What Do Your 17-Year-Olds Know?* (New York: Harper & Row, 1987).

[8]*The New York Times*, Jan. 27, 1988, p. 14.

[9]Deborah Meier and Florence Miller, "The Book of Lists," *The Nation*, Jan. 9, 1988, pp. 25–27.

[10]Bernard Hennessey, *Public Opinion* (Belmont, Calif: Wadsworth, 1970), chaps. 13 and 14.

[11]Erik Erikson, *Childhood and Society* (New York: Norton, 1963).

[12]Much of the material in this section was adapted from Alan D. Monroe, *Public Opinion in America* (New York: Harper & Row, 1975).

[13]R. S. Erikson and N. R. Luttbeg, *American Public Opinion: Its Origins, Content, and Impact* (New York: Wiley, 1973), chap. 2.

[14]Erikson and Luttbeg, chap. 2.

[15]Andrew M. Greeley and Paul R. Sheatsley, "Attitudes toward Racial Integration," in Lee Rainwater, ed., *Social Problems and Public Policy: Inequality and Justice* (Chicago: Aldine, 1974), p. 242.

[16]Michael Corbett, *Political Tolerance in America* (New York: Longman, 1982), p. 50.

[17]*Gallup Report*, no. 206, November 1982.

[18]Harris polls of May 24, 1982, and Feb. 10, 1983. It is interesting to note that two-thirds of the respondents did not think that the death penalty was fairly applied. *The Washington Post*, national weekly ed., Feb. 11, 1985, p. 38.

[19]*Gallup Report*, no. 206, November 1982.

[20]*Ibid.*

[21]*Ibid.*

[22]Harris survey, May 31, 1984.

[23]See William C. Adams, "Why the Right Gets It Wrong in Foreign Policy," *Public Opinion*, August/September 1983, pp. 12–15.

[24]Harris survey, Jan. 26, 1984.

[25]Everett Carll Ladd, "The Freeze Framework," *Public Opinion*, August/September 1982.

[26]*Public Opinion*, August/September 1983, p. 30.

[27]Harris survey, April 1, 1984.

[28]Ronald Inglehart and Scott Flanagan, "Value Change in Industrial Societies," *American Political Science Review*, December 1987, pp. 1289–1319.

[29]Everett Carll Ladd, "The New Lines Are Drawn: Class and Ideology in America," *Public Opinion*, July/August 1978.

[30]R. S. Erikson, N. Luttbeg, and K. L. Tedin, *American Public Opinion* (New York: Wiley, 1980), p. 187.

[31]*The New York Times*, Sept. 30, 1984, p. 14 and Oct. 21, 1984, p. 15.

[32]Dan Bolz, "Democrats Discover a Power Bloc: White Males," *The Washington Post*, national weekly ed., Dec. 24, 1984, p. 15.

[33]Paul Lazarsfeld et al., *The People's Choice* (New York: Columbia University Press, 1948).

[34]See Philip Converse, "The Nature of Belief Systems in Mass Publics," in David Apter, ed., *Ideology and Discontent* (New York: The Free Press, 1964), pp. 238–245; and Angus Campbell et al., *The American Voter* (New York: Wiley, 1960).

[35]N. H. Nie and K. Anderson, "Mass Belief Systems Revisited: Political Change and Attitude Structure," in N. G. Niemi and H. F. Wiesberg, eds., *Controversies in American Voting Behavior* (San Francisco: W. H. Freeman, 1976), pp. 94–137.

[36]Paul Allen Beck, "The Dealignment Era in America," in R. J. Dalton, S. C. Flanagan, and P. A. Beck, eds., *Electoral Changes in Advanced Industrial Democracies: Realignment or Dealignment?* (Princeton, N.J.: Princeton University Press, 1984), pp. 242–246.

[37]Hedrick Smith, "The Economy: Still the Key for Reagan," *The New York Times*, Nov. 7, 1984.

[38]Dan Bolz, "Democrats Discover a Power Bloc: White Males," *The Washington Post*, national weekly ed., Dec. 24, 1984, p. 15.

[39]*Ibid.*, pp. 1 and 14.

[40]Seymour Martin Lipset, "The Elections, the Economy and Public Opinion: 1984," *Political Science*, Winter 1985, pp. 34–38.

[41]Everett Carll Ladd, "As the Realignment Turns: A Drama in Many Acts," *Public Opinion*, December/January 1985, pp. 6–7.

[42]Gallup poll, Dec. 9, 1984.

[43]Benjamin I. Page and R. Y. Shapiro, "Effects of Public Opinion on Policy," *American Political Science Review* 77, 1983, pp. 175–190.

SELECTED READINGS

POLITICAL SOCIALIZATION

Among the **classic introductions** to the issues involved in political socialization are R. D. Hess and J. V. Torney, *The Development of Political Attitudes in Children* (Chicago: Aldine, 1967); Bruno Bettelheim, *Children of the Dream* (New York: Avon, 1970); Fred I. Greenstein, *Children and Politics* (New Haven, Conn.: Yale University Press, 1965); and Erik H. Erikson, *Childhood and Society*, 35th anniversary ed. (New York: Norton, 1986).

For stimulating discussions of **political attitudes,** see Kenneth Keniston, *Young Radicals* (New York: Harcourt, Brace and World, 1968); Samuel A. Stouffer, *Communism, Conformity and Civil Liberties* (New York: Doubleday, 1955); Michael Corbett, *Political Tolerance in America* (New York: Longman, 1982); and John E. Mueller, *War, Presidents and Public Opinion* (New York: Univ. Press of America, 1985).

For more specialized studies of particular aspects of **political psychology and public opinion** and their interaction with political action, see Murray Edelman, *Politics as Symbolic Action: Mass Arousal and Quiescence* (New York: Academic Press, 1971); Irving Janis, *Groupthink* (Boston: Houghton Mifflin, 1982); Sara Evans, *Personal Politics: The Roots of Women's Liberation in the Civil Rights Movement and the New Left* (New York: Random House, 1980); Stanley Milgram, *Obedience to Authority* (New York: Harper & Row, 1975); Erich Fromm, *Escape from Freedom* (New York: Avon, 1971); and Nevitt Sanford and Craig Comstock, *Sanctions for Evil: Sources of Social Destructiveness* (Boston: Beacon Press, 1971).

PUBLIC OPINION

Attitudes toward **democratic norms** are treated in James W. Prothro and C. W. Grigg, "Fundamental Principles of Democracy: Bases of Agreement and Disagreement," *Journal of Politics* 22 (Spring 1960):276–294; and Herbert McClosky, "Consensus and Ideology in American Politics," *American Political Science Review* 58 (June 1964): 361–383. See also R. S. Erikson, N. Luttbeg, and K. L. Tedin, *American Public Opinion: Its Origins, Content, and Impact*, 2nd ed. (New York: Macmillan, 1980); Corbett, *Political Tolerance in America*; J. L. Sullivan, J. Piereson, and G. E. Marcus, *Political Tolerance and American Democracy* (Chicago: University of Chicago Press, 1982); David Lawrence, "Procedural Norms and Tolerance: A Reassessment," *American Political Science Review* 70 (1976):80–100; and Stouffer, *Communism, Conformity and Civil Liberties.*

On **alienation,** see Robert S. Gilmour and Robert B. Lamb, *Political Alienation in Contemporary America* (New York: St. Martin's Press, 1975). There is an extensive literature on alienation as an idea and a phenomenon. See, for example, Daniel Bell, "Two Roads from Marx," in his *The End of Ideology* (New York: The Free Press, 1962); Joel D. Aberbach, "Alienation and Political Behavior," *American Political Science Review* 63 (1969):86–99; William Gamson, *Power and Discontent* (Homewood, Ill.: Dorsey Press, 1968); James S. House and William M. Mason, "Political Alienation in America, 1952–1968," *American Sociological Review* 40 (1975):123–147; Murray Levin, *The Alienated Voter* (New York: Holt, Rinehart and Winston, 1960); and Lewis Lipsitz, "The Grievances of the Poor," in P. Green and S. Levinson, eds., *Power and Community* (New York: Pantheon, 1970).

For **general discussions of public opinion** in the United States, see Richard F. Hamilton, *Class and Politics in the United States* (New York: Wiley, 1972); S. M. Lipset, *Political Man: The Social Bases of Politics* (Baltimore: Johns Hopkins Univ. Press, 1981); Robert E. Lane, *Political Ideology: Why the American Common Man Believes What He Does* (New York: The Free Press, 1962); and Studs Terkel, *Working* (New York: Avon, 1983).

On the **meaningfulness of elections,** consult Herbert Asher, *Presidential Elections and American Politics: Voters, Candidates and Campaigns Since 1952* (Homewood, Ill.: Dorsey Press, 1984); R. G. Niemi and H. F. Weisberg, eds., *Controversies in American Voting Behavior*, 2nd ed. (Washington: Congressional Quarterly Press, 1984); Paul Abramson et al., *Change and Continuity in the 1980 Elections* (Washington, D.C.: Congressional Quarterly Press, 1986); and Bernard R. Berelson et al., *Voting: A Study of Opinion Formation in a Presidential Campaign* (Chicago: Univ. of Chicago Press, 1986).

On **political participation,** see Everett C. Ladd, Jr., *Where Have All the Voters Gone?: The Fracturing of America's Political Parties*, 2nd ed. (New York: Norton, 1982); L. W. Milbrath and M. L. Goel, *Political Participation: How and Why Do People Get Involved in Politics?* (New York: Univ. Press of America, 1982); Dirsten Amundsen, *A New Look at the Silenced Majority: Women and American Democracy* (Englewood Cliffs, N.J.: Prentice-Hall, 1977); and Carole Pateman, *Participation and Democratic Theory* (New York: Cambridge University Press, 1970).

UNDERSTANDING PUBLIC SENTIMENT

On the general topic of **ideology,** see David Apter, ed., *Ideology and Discontent* (London: Free Press of Glencoe, 1964); William F. Stone, *The Psychology of Politics* (New

York: The Free Press, 1974), explores liberalism and conservatism from a psychological perspective.

For the substance of **American political attitudes,** see the discussion in Robert Shogun, "The Upright Stuff: Our Values and Our Politics," *Public Opinion,* December/January, 1984.

ELECTORAL TRENDS

The **classic studies of voting** in the United States are Berelson et al., *Voting;* Paul F. Lazarsfeld et al., *The People's Choice: How the Voter Makes Up His Mind in a Presidential Campaign* (New York: Columbia University Press, 1948); Angus Campbell et al., *The American Voter* (New York: Wiley, 1960); and Angus Campbell et al., *The Voter Decides* (New York: Harper & Row, 1954; reprinted 1972 by Greenwood Press).

For a discussion of **some recent trends,** see Theodore H. White, "New Powers, New Politics," *The New York Times Magazine,* February 5, 1984.

For an examination of **the "responsible voter" contro-** versy, see Asher, *Presidential Elections and American Politics,* especially chap. 4; and Bruce A. Campbell, *The American Electorate* (New York: Holt, Rinehart and Winston, 1979). See also Philip E. Converse, "The Nature of Belief Systems in Mass Publics," in Apter, ed., *Ideology and Discontent.*

NONPARTICIPATION

For **overviews** of this subject, see Sidney Verba and Norman Nie, *Participation in America: Political Democracy and Social Equality* (New York: Harper & Row, 1972); Verba and Nie, "Political Participation," in F. I. Greenstein and N. W. Polsby, eds., *Handbook of Political Science* (Reading, Mass.: Addison-Wesley, 1975); and Milbrath and Goel, *Political Participation.*

For **two different views on the subject of participation,** see George F. Will, "In Defense of Nonvoting," *Newsweek,* October 10, 1983; and Pateman, *Participation and Democratic Theory.*

On the question of the **meaningfulness of elections,** see Stanley Kelley, Jr., *Interpreting Elections* (Princeton, N.J.: Princeton University Press, 1983).

7

POLITICAL PARTIES
Do They Offer a Choice?

New York Times/Alan S. Weiner

CHAPTER OUTLINE

Characteristics of Political Parties
The U.S. Party System
Current Issues

olitical parties are generally given short shrift in the classic works on democratic theory, which concentrate on rights, equalities, liberties, and elections. And to many of the Founders of the United States, parties represented a potential threat to decent politics—selfish groups that would seek to exploit government to serve their own interests. James Madison warned of the dangers of "factions" that would use public power to further their own goals. George Washington shuddered at the thought of one faction alternately dominating another—a prospect he characterized as "a frightful despotism."

Even so, U.S. political parties began to develop early on. The beginnings of party disputes were apparent in the controversy over ratification of the Constitution. After George Washington left office, political disputes erupted during the administration of the second president, John Adams. Out of these disputes grew the new republic's first political parties, the Federalists and the Democratic-Republicans.

Why did political parties develop so quickly and so naturally even among people who distrusted the very idea of party? With two hundred years of hindsight, we can see that political parties are necessary components of the democratic process. In fact, our perception of democratic politics has shifted 180 degrees from that of the Founders: They could not bear the thought of a political life that included parties, while we cannot imagine politics without them.

Why are parties vital to the democratic process? How effectively do contemporary U.S. parties fulfill their roles in democratic politics? With these two questions in mind, we will explore (1) the characteristics of political parties; (2) the U.S. two-party system; and (3) current issues involving American political parties.

Characteristics of Political Parties

Numerous attempts have been made to define the notion of political parties. Edmund Burke, the great English statesman of the late eighteenth century, declared that a **political party** was "a body of men united, for promoting by their joint endeavors the national interest upon some particular principle in which they are all agreed." Burke thus focused on the *ideological* basis of a political organization—on what a party stood for. In his time, Burke saw various groups coalescing within the British governing structure. He realized that to combat groups that he and like-minded people opposed, it was necessary to attract and organize followers and allies who were willing to fight for certain principles.

Another way to look at political parties was offered by political scientist Leon Epstein in the 1960s. He defined a political party as "any group, however loosely organized, seeking to elect government office-holders under a given label."[1] This definition spotlights the major *activity* of political parties—the contesting of elections. In this view, a common label and the nomination of candidates for office make for a political party.

Yet a third way to view political parties places the emphasis on *organization*. According to French social scientist Maurice Duverger, writing in the 1950s, parties can best be characterized as structured groups. "A party," he wrote, "is a community with a particular structure."[2] As political parties have evolved in modern times, Duverger pointed out, they have developed particular structural characteristics, and methods of organization become a crucial element in the concept of party. Some parties are loosely organized; others have tightly disciplined arrangements. Every party, however, is organized to engage in political competition.

All three of these factors—ideology, activity, and organization—figure significantly in any discussion of parties, and we will touch on all of them in this chapter. A summary description of a political party, developed by contemporary political scientist Hugh LeBlanc, encompasses all three: "An organized effort to win elective office in order to gain political power and control the policies of government."[3]

Let us now consider (1) three facets of political parties; (2) the functions of political parties; and (3) two-party and multiparty systems.

Three Facets of Political Parties

Most political parties have three distinct dimensions: (1) a formal organization, with distinctive internal politics; (2) an active role in the electorate,

FIGURE 7–1
The Three-Part Political Party

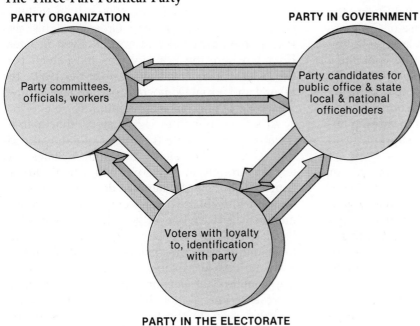

PARTY ORGANIZATION

Party committees, officials, workers

PARTY IN GOVERNMENT

Party candidates for public office & state local & national officeholders

Voters with loyalty to, identification with party

PARTY IN THE ELECTORATE

SOURCE: Frank Sorauf and Paul Allen Beck, *Party Politics in America,* 6th ed. (Glenview, Ill.: Scott, Foresman, 1988), p. 10.

organizing electoral support; and (3) a visible place in the government, with officeholders on every level (see **Figure 7–1**).

As a formal organization, a party conducts business outside of government. The formal party structure includes the national organization and its leadership, various local organizations, and numerous professionals and activists who are heavily involved in party life.

As part of the electorate, a party relies on long-term voter allegiance to its views. Citizens identify with particular parties, building for those parties a solid base of political support at election time. As we will see, party loyalties in the United States have grown significantly weaker in recent times, and candidates now often establish personal organizations that function outside the party structure.

The party-in-the-government encompasses the many officeholders at all levels, who run under the party flag, and the numerous officeholders who are appointed by elected officials. Collectively, these elected officials and appointees are responsible for policy making.

The three aspects of party overlap, of course. Some party professionals may hold office, and strong party-identifiers may work for the party organization. The strength of parties is difficult to determine; they function in so many different ways. Generally, however, U.S. parties are considered to be among the weakest political parties in modern democracies—that is, they are very loosely organized and relatively undisciplined. Many European political parties have millions of formally enrolled members, whereas U.S. parties usually depend on cadres of full-time staffers.

Functions of Political Parties

Parties provide key links between citizens and government. First, they help select candidates for office and mobilize the electorate. As parties come to stand for certain policies, voters link themselves with those policies. And some voters simply identify strongly with a party label. In these ways, political parties simplify the often complex choices facing voters.

Parties also organize the government: They are responsible for the functioning of the legislative and executive branches. In the United States, the party with a majority in either house of Congress organizes that house along partisan lines, selecting a majority leader and structuring the committee assignments in its favor. Likewise, the newly elected president generally makes appointments along party lines. Sometimes, of course, presidents deliberately cross party lines in making appointments to widen their base of support, or to demonstrate fairmindedness.

Finally, parties provide for "responsibility"—or accountability—in government. In modern democratic societies, the governing political party generally is held responsible for the conduct of government. Its candidates run on the party record, and voters can pass judgment on the way government is conducted by choosing to reelect those in office or to turn them out.

This overview of the functions of political parties in a democracy leaves many questions unanswered. What if party labels lose their meaning and voters no longer pay much attention to them? What if control of government is so fragmented that no clear lines of responsibility emerge? And what if there are too many political parties—or too few? As the chapter proceeds, we will address all these issues.

Two-Party and Multiparty Systems

"The best system is to have one party govern and the other party watch," asserted Thomas Reed, Speaker of the House, in 1880. The United States, with its two-party system, fits into this category. Most European democracies, however, have multiparty systems: West Germany, for example, has two major parties and two minor ones, while Italy has eight parties (see **Table 7–1**).

The U.S. political system has become almost exclusively a two-party system. In recent decades, third parties have had a very difficult time gaining any seats in Congress or state legislatures. In other democracies with predominantly two-party systems, such as West Germany, Great Britain, and Canada, third or even fourth parties are often able to gain some seats in the national legislature and

may play significant political roles. In West Germany, for example, the small Free Democratic Party for years played a decisive role in coalition governments, while the new Green Party has also had a significant political impact. Even in Great Britain, where the Conservative and Labour parties have alternated in office since the 1930s, the Liberal and Social Democratic parties have at times been able to attract a sizable minority vote.

At several points in U.S. history, third parties have helped to shape the course of national politics. Overall, however, the United States has tended strongly in a two-party direction. Our reliance on the **single-member district** accounts in large part for this two-party emphasis. In a single-member district whoever gets the most votes in a legislative district represents that district, so votes for a minor party are usually wasted. Countries with multiparty systems, in contrast, commonly use a method of election known as **proportional representation.** Under this system, each party is awarded seats in the legislature in more or less direct proportion to its percentage of the popular vote. Since votes are not wasted in a proportional system, minor parties have an incentive to compete.

As our two-party system evolved, strong ties of party identification have been established between the voters and the two major parties: People have come to think of elections in strictly two-party terms. Moreover, electoral laws place minor parties at a distinct disadvantage—for example, new parties must petition to get on the ballot in most states. And since the two major parties are composed of many factions and interests, new groups usually can make their presence felt *within* an established party, rather than in a new political group. In multiparty systems, by contrast, governing coalitions are worked out among parties when no one party wins a clear electoral majority.

In addition, the way the chief political leader, the president, is selected in the United States lends further support to the two-party arrangement. In many other democratic nations, the executive leader is chosen by the party (or parties, in a coalition government) that controls the parliament, whereas we hold an entirely separate election for president. The national attention focused on this office makes presidential elections the most dramatic political events in the United States. The two

TABLE 7–1
The Political Spectrum in Several Democratic Nations

Country	Radical left	Communism	Democratic socialism	Liberalism	Christian democracy	Conservatism	Reactionary right
Great Britain			Labour Party Social Democratic Party	Liberal Party		Conservative Party	
France		French Communist Party (PCF)	Socialist Party	Radical Party	Democratic Center	Independent Republicans (RI), Gaullists (UDR)	National Front
West Germany		German Communist Party (DKP)	Social Democratic Party (SPD) Greens	Free Democratic Party (FDP)	Christian Democratic Union (CDU)	Christian Social Union (CSU)	National Democratic Party (NPD)
Italy	Proletarian Democracy (DP)	Italian Communist Party (PCI)	Italian Socialist Party (PSI) Social Democratic Party (PSDI)	Republican Party (PRI)	Christian Democratic Party (DC)	Liberal Party (PLI)	Italian Social Movement (MSI)
United States*				Democratic Party		Republican Party	

*Note that the United States is one of the few democratic countries with only two political parties, although there are some nations (Britain and West Germany, for example) where two parties predominate.
SOURCE: Adapted from David M. Wood, *Power and Policy in Western European Democracies*, 3rd ed. (New York: Wiley, 1986), p.78.

TABLE 7–2
Ideological Awareness among Citizens of Several Democracies

	Actively use ideological thinking	Recognize/ understand left vs. right	Aware of nation's left/right placement
West Germany	34%	56%	92%
Netherlands	36	48	90
Great Britain	21	23	82
France	*	*	81
Switzerland	9	39	79
Austria	19	39	75
Italy	55	54	74
United States	21	34	67

*Data were not available.
SOURCE: Adapted from Russell J. Dalton, *Citizen Politics in Western Democracies* (Chatham, N.J.: Chatham House, 1988), p. 25.

COMPARATIVE PERSPECTIVE

Why Margaret Thatcher Won a "Majority" in 1987

In 1987, Margaret Thatcher and her Conservative Party won 42.3 percent of the votes cast in the British national elections. Her rivals, the Labour Party and the Liberal–Social Democratic coalition, won 30.8 and 22.6 percent, respectively. It might appear from these figures that the Conservatives would not be able to rule alone but would have to form a coalition with one of the other parties in parliament to gain a majority. But that was not the case. Having won slightly more than 42 percent of the vote, the Conservatives nonetheless gained 58 percent of the seats in the House of Commons. Labour, with slightly more than 30 percent of the ballots cast, wound up with 35 percent of the seats. The Liberal–Social Democratic coalition fared the worst of all. With almost 23 percent of the vote, it ended up with a mere 3 percent of the seats in the House.

Why did this happen? The answer is that the British do not have a proportional system of representation like West Germany or many other democratic nations. Instead, the British elect members of parliament in single-member districts, as we do in the United States. Thus, if a party's support is spread thinly throughout the country, the vote may not translate into a proportional number of seats in the House of Commons. This was the dilemma of the Liberal–Social Democratic coalition. Although it gained nearly a quarter of the total vote, its voters were spread throughout British society and were not concentrated in sufficient numbers to gain a majority or plurality on a district-by-district basis. Although Labour gained some seats, it was the Conservatives who benefited most, because their support was strategically located in the heavily populated and prosperous southern tier of England. In this portion of the country, they gained a majority or plurality in a large number of districts, despite winning only a minority of the vote nationwide. Thus, a Conservative government was elected with a large parliamentary majority, while being supported by only some four out of ten Britons.

established parties, with their party loyalists, organizations, and patterns of identification, have a nearly insurmountable advantage in the presidential race.

Finally, most political observers credit the overall moderate nature of American public opinion for pushing us toward two middle-of-the-road political parties. As we noted in Chapter 1, U.S. political culture draws heavily on a liberal heritage. Both the extreme left and the extreme right have been notably weak in U.S. political life, allowing little room for political success outside the mainstream.

As we can see in **Table 7–2** (page 225), Americans hold less ideological views than Europeans. Americans use left/right ideological thinking (left column) less than the West Germans, the Italians, or the Dutch, but about as much as the British and

more than the Swiss. We rank next to the lowest (above Britain) in terms of recognizing or understanding the meaning of the left/right dimension (center column). Finally, the United States' placement on the left/right spectrum (right column) stands at the lowest point of all the nations compared, meaning that American attitudes are, overall, the most conservative. These findings indicate that deeply rooted patterns in U.S. politics still shape current attitudes.

The U.S. Party System

Over the years the U.S. party system has undergone several basic shifts. Let us now look at how it has evolved and how its evolution has affected

Andrew Jackson is pictured here in 1829, on the way to his presidential inaugural in Washington. It was during the Jackson era that the idea of a mass-membership political party began to take hold in the United States. Jackson's party, the Democrats, appealed most strongly to those on the expanding western frontier. *(Artist: Howard Pyle/The Bettmann Archive)*

democratic politics in the United States. We turn specifically to (1) the origins of contemporary parties; (2) the reforms of 1896; (3) the New Deal coalition; (4) developments since the New Deal; (5) dilemmas and contributions of third parties; (6) party organization; (7) party reforms after 1968; and (8) how significantly the parties differ from one another.

Origins of Contemporary Parties

In his farewell address, delivered in 1797, President George Washington called on the nation to be wary of the "baneful effects of the spirit of party." This warning resulted from events during his administration that, much to his dismay, clearly signaled the emergence of political party divisions in the new nation.

Two factions had been developing during Washington's eight years in office. Members of one faction, called the **Federalists,** were led by Secretary of the Treasury Alexander Hamilton (and by George Washington himself, despite his disdain for parties in principle). The Federalists were generally wealthy and of high social position. Members of the second group, the so-called **Democratic-Republicans,** were led by Thomas Jefferson and James Madison. Jefferson's party, a coalition of small farmers, small property owners, and local political leaders in the Southern and Mid-Atlantic states, soon came to dominate U.S. politics. By the mid-1820s, the Federalists had ceased to exist as a political force.

With the election of Andrew Jackson to the presidency in 1828, the party of Jefferson and Madison, renamed the **Democratic Party,** was transformed into a mass membership organization and became the dominant force in U.S. political life. Presidents Jackson and Martin Van Buren reorganized their party to accommodate the new states admitted to the Union and to gain support among those who became eligible to vote as economic qualifications limiting suffrage were eased.

Between 1828 and 1856, the Jacksonian Democrats faced opposition mainly from the **Whig Party.** The Democrats drew their primary political support from the frontier, among farmers in the Western states; the Whigs, in contrast, appealed more to New Englanders and especially to those with business interests. Although the Democrats won the presidency and a majority in the House of Representatives in most of those elections, the Whigs attracted a substantial following, electing both William Henry Harrison and Zachary Taylor to the presidency. The Whig-Democratic rivalry

FIGURE 7–2
The Five Major U.S. Political Parties Since 1789

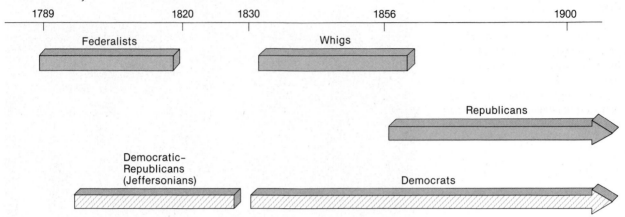

NOTE: Since the founding of the republic, only five parties achieved significant enough strength to compete nationally. A number of third parties enjoyed modest successes for relatively short periods (see **Table 7–3**, page 232).

extended beyond the national level to state and local politics.

Both parties were deeply divided by the slavery issue. The Democrats became dominated at that time by their Southern wing, which controlled Congress. In the 1850s, the Whigs disappeared altogether, many of them merging into the newly formed **Republican Party.** In 1860, the Democratic Party broke into Northern and Southern factions that fielded separate presidential candidates, and the Republican presidential nominee, Abraham Lincoln, won election to the White House. The Republicans, originally a small, radical party formed chiefly to oppose the further extension of slavery, quickly forged a coalition of Northern industrialists, merchants, workers, farmers, and freed slaves.

Although the Democratic Party survived the Civil War, the Republican, or GOP (Grand Old Party), coalition won every presidential election for the next five decades except for those of 1884 and 1892. During this time, the Republican base of support slowly shifted to business people and middle-class white Protestants, while the Democrats began to attract the urban, Catholic immigrants and to erode Republican support among workers. (See **Figure 7–2** and **Table 7–3** for illustrations of the development of major and minor U.S. political parties.)

The System of 1896

Events of the 1890s shaped U.S. politics for generations to come. At that time, socialist parties were gaining political clout in Europe, and the United States seemed ripe for a parallel development. The **Populist Party,** which had arisen in the South and West in the 1880s, demanded many socialist-sounding measures, and a growing trade union movement was pressing its political agenda as well. Workers and Populists together might have forged a new party of the left, or precipitated a decisive shift to the left in the Democratic Party. But while the Democratic candidate in 1896, William Jennings Bryan, voiced populist views, he steered clear of the labor movement and big-city ethnic populations. Thus Bryan failed to put together an electoral coalition that might have realigned the U.S. party system along left/right political lines. William McKinley's victory in the presidential election of 1896 reinstated Republican dominance, which was reinforced by political reforms instituted in 1896.

Prior to 1896, Americans took an intensely partisan view of politics. Electoral contests were waged as full-scale battles, in which each party drummed up partisan enthusiasm through torchlight parades, elaborate campaigns, far-reaching party organization, and extensive patronage. Elections turned on party preference more than on individual candidates. Partisan competition was keen and voter turnout high.

The reforms of 1896 changed political life dramatically. Supporters of the "system of '96," as these reforms came to be known, succeeded in passing new registration laws, in reforming the civil service, in creating direct primaries (whereby voters, rather than party leaders, chose nominees), and in establishing split-ticket balloting. Civil service reforms, in particular, denied parties the patronage that helped build loyal followings. By these means, reformers hoped to introduce a calmer, less partisan atmosphere in U.S. political life. But new registration complexities kept many from voting in the first place—a highly significant factor in view of the growing number of foreign-born potential voters. Turnout declined, the parties lost much of their vitality, and the era of modern, candidate-centered politics began. Walter Dean Burnham estimated that after 1896, fully 50 percent of potential U.S. voters remained outside the political process, alienated from parties and politics, and that only about one-third remained firmly attached to the usual electoral systems. The

functional result of the system of '96, Burnham stated, "was the conversion of a fairly democratic regime into a rather broadly based oligarchy."[4]

Many experts disagree with this highly critical assessment of the contraction of the active electorate at the turn of the century, but there is no doubt that a major depoliticization took place at that time. Burnham felt that the system of '96 left a permanent hole in the American political universe, one that in Europe was filled by Labor and Social Democratic parties. The large-scale politicization of the poor and the working class that might have taken place in the United States in the 1890s, in other words, simply did not occur.

The New Deal Coalition

Between 1896 and 1932, only the victories of Woodrow Wilson in 1912 and 1916 interrupted the Republican lock on the presidential office. And Wilson's election in 1912 was made possible by a split among the Republicans that led to Theodore Roosevelt's candidacy on the third-party Bull Moose ticket.

The beginning of the New Deal: Franklin Roosevelt addresses the 1932 Democratic Convention. FDR's massive victories in the elections of 1932 and 1936 transformed the shape of party competition. The New Deal coalition was to dominate our politics for at least three decades, and its influence remains even today. *(UPI/ Bettmann Newsphotos)*

The Republican Party drew its principal support in this period from a coalition of middle-class Protestant and native-stock Americans (those whose ancestors came here before the twentieth century, mostly from Britain and Germany). Democratic strength was centered in the South. The border states also leaned toward the Democrats, and pockets of Democratic strength—among immigrant voters and the industrial working class—dotted the larger cities of the Northeast. Overall, the distribution of voter support was decisively in favor of the Republicans.

The collapse of the economy in 1929 and the onset of the Great Depression gave the Democrats a strategic opening. In retrospect it seems odd that during the Depression no third party mounted a serious challenge to the dominance of the two major parties. In any case, Franklin Roosevelt won an overwhelming majority in the 1932 election. As we noted in the last chapter, Roosevelt's landslide victory ushered in a new era in U.S. politics, one that still shapes the American political landscape to this day.

The coalition that brought the Democrats to power in 1932 and reelected Roosevelt three times was not entirely new. Some elements of the pre-1932 Democratic strength were still present—the solid South and working-class, Catholic voters. But new groups of voters were largely responsible for the strength of the New Deal coalition. The black population, long loyal to the party of Lincoln, now began to switch to the Democrats in large numbers, attracted by the Roosevelt administration's tentative attack on discriminatory practices and by federal programs for the hungry and the jobless. Labor, heavily concentrated in major cities, also joined the coalition. The experience of the Depression and the economic appeal of New Deal programs redirected U.S. politics along the lines of social class. For the first time since 1896, class factors exerted a decisive influence on election outcomes. The Democrats attracted heavy working-class support and repoliticized many voters who had lost interest in politics, thus overcoming some of the heritage of the system of '96. Still, even during the Depression, class consciousness and voting patterns based on class interests never dominated politics in America as they did in other democratic nations.

Since the New Deal

Since the 1930s, the U.S. political party system has evolved greatly; both parties have undergone considerable change without altering their basic identities. The Democrats, for example, have gradually lost their once-solid hold on the South. This process began abruptly in 1948, when the so-called Dixiecrats (Southern Democrats who opposed integration) broke from the party after a civil rights plank was passed at the Democrats' national convention. By the elections of 1976 and 1980, Democrat Jimmy Carter, himself a Southerner, failed to win the support of a majority of voters in the Southern states. Clearly, a portion of the New Deal coalition had shaken loose.

At an ideological level, the shift of some Southerners away from the Democratic Party reflected the party's increasingly liberal bent. More conservative Southerners moved toward the Republicans—a step in line with their true ideological stance. Some Southern politicians, like South Carolina Senator Strom Thurmond, actually changed their partisan identities, proclaiming themselves Republicans and running successfully on the Republican ticket. On the other hand, Southern blacks remained firmly committed to the Democrats.

A set of social issues that, at times, eclipsed economic questions also helped undermine and reshape the New Deal coalition. In the presidential election of 1952, the issues were communism, corruption, and Korea. In the 1960s, public attention focused on violence in the streets, corruption in high office, and the breakdown of traditional values among youth. In 1968 and 1972, Richard Nixon campaigned on a "law and order" platform, focusing on dissenters, crime, and riots in the cities. In 1984, such issues as abortion and school prayer held center stage. These social issues contributed significantly to the gradual disintegration of the New Deal coalition by prompting many white, ethnic, working-class groups, once strongly affiliated with the Democrats, to throw their support behind Republican candidates, especially in presidential contests.

Both parties have also undergone internal conflicts. Among the Republicans, the long-term struggle for control between the more liberal

Northeastern and Western party members and the more conservative Sunbelt group seemed to be decided in 1980 in favor of the conservative Sunbelt Republicans, but conflicts on specific issues remain. As for the Democrats, in the 1960s sharp splits began to appear between the more liberal, affluent, and better-educated McGovern-Kennedy wing of the party and various conservative factions. These rifts continue to this day.

Between the end of World War II and the late 1980s, then, the U.S. party system has been in a process of gradual transition. But transition to what? On this matter, the experts offer varying predictions. Scenarios for the future shape of our party system range across a broad spectrum—including the prediction that the party system is in such deep trouble that it is likely to disintegrate in the years ahead.

Dilemmas and Contributions of Third Parties

Third parties have an unenviable position in the United States, partly because of the many legal and financial barriers they face. While the two major parties are guaranteed columns on the ballot in all states, third parties must go through elaborate, time-consuming, expensive processes to obtain official recognition.

As for financing, the major parties receive millions of dollars through the federal election laws.

One of our first third parties, the Know-Nothings, is satirized in this 1856 cartoon. Anti-foreign sentiment was the party's dominant policy, an issue that was to arise again and again later in the country's history. *(The Bettmann Archive)*

The greatest third-party vote-getter in U.S. history, George Wallace. Despite his power and his plans, he was unable in the 1968 election to prevent any candidate from getting a majority of electoral votes. *(UPI/ Bettmann Newsphotos)*

TABLE 7–3
Third Parties at the Polls, 1832–1968

Election year	Third party
1832	**Anti-Masonic Party (7 electoral votes)** The Anti-Masons, as their name suggests, were opposed to the secret organization known as the Masons, whom they believed wielded undue political influence.
1856	**American Party ("Know-Nothings") (8 electoral votes)** The American Party's major plank was opposition to open immigration.
1892	**People's Party ("Populists") (22 electoral votes)** The People's Party grew out of agrarian protests against the power of big business and the banks.
1912	**Progressive Party ("Bull Moose") (88 electoral votes)** Founded by dissident Republicans, the Bull Moose Party was anti-monopoly, pro-conservation, and for expanded suffrage. Its standard bearer in 1912 was Theodore Roosevelt, who was seeking a third term as president.
1924	**Progressive Party (13 electoral votes)** A philosophical continuation of the progressive movement, the party of 1924 ran Senator Robert La Follette as its presidential candidate.
1948	**States Rights Democratic ("Dixiecrats") (39 electoral votes)** The Dixiecrats were segregationist Southerners who broke from the Democratic Party after the 1948 convention because of the main party's pro–civil rights plank. Strom Thurmond of South Carolina was their presidential candidate.
1968	**American Independent Party (46 electoral votes)** Less of a party than a movement centering on the presidential candidacy of George C. Wallace, segregationist Governor of Alabama.

SOURCE: Adapted from Frank Sorauf and Paul Allen Beck, *Party Politics in America*, 6th ed. (Glenview, Ill.: Scott, Foresman, 1988), pp. 50–51.

Third-party candidates, however, receive no public funds unless they obtain at least 5 percent of the popular vote. In 1980, for example, John Anderson barely reached this threshold, saving himself from years of struggle to pay off campaign debts.

In U.S. history, only once has a third party (the Republicans) replaced one of the major parties (the Whigs)—and that was more than 130 years ago, during the crisis that led to the Civil War. But while third parties have had to struggle to play a significant role in the political process, several have made valuable contributions to U.S. political life.

With the major parties generally staking out the middle ground—thereby merely offering shifts in emphasis on most major issues—third parties often provide an outlet for protest politics focused on "extreme" solutions to controversial issues (see **Table 7–3**). For example, a third party (the Abolitionists) helped to force the issue of slavery onto center stage in U.S. political life, and another one (the Socialist Party) was moderately successful in raising important questions about industrial capitalism in the late nineteenth and early twentieth centuries. Third parties have also pointed the way toward procedural reforms. A third party (the Anti-Masons in 1831) held the first national nominating convention. And a third party was the first to advocate women's suffrage and to call for a wide range of electoral reforms (the Progressives).

Party Organization

When Will Rogers quipped, "I belong to no organized political party—I am a Democrat," he was poking fun at his own party, but what he said could be applied to either of the major U.S. parties. They are organized in only the loosest sense on the national level, where one might expect them to be most coherent. State party organizations range from those that are highly active to the virtually moribund. Local party organizations tend to be the most tightly structured. At all three levels, U.S. political parties have undergone significant changes in recent decades. This is in sharp contrast to the highly disciplined and centralized parties common in Europe.

Richard Daley, elected mayor of Chicago six times, was an astute politician to some, a manipulative machine boss to others. The last of the urban political bosses, Daley's efficient vote-getting organizations were able to turn out the faithful time after time. Political machines helped meet the needs of many who otherwise were alienated from the political process; on the other hand, they fostered corruption, narrow-mindedness, and a wide variety of shady political practices. *(UPI/Bettmann Newsphotos)*

LOCAL PARTIES The most notorious—and frequently, the most successful—form of political organization in the United States has been the local **political machine,** a coterie of party professionals who get out the vote and provide constituent services. The most successful of these machines, based on "boss" rule and strong standards of loyalty, reached from the mayor's office through the precincts down to the ward and block levels. Most arose in Eastern and Midwestern cities after the Civil War, and a few retained power through the 1960s.

The machines were successful partly because they served important political and social functions. They helped integrate newly arrived immigrant groups into U.S. politics. And in return for votes, rank-and-file members of the machines provided aid to needy families, supplied city jobs, and gave neglected groups recognition they could not find elsewhere.

For years, reformers at both the federal and state levels tried to curtail the power of political machines. The introduction of civil service was intended to limit boss rule by reducing the number of patronage appointments. Sometimes, nonpartisan elections limited the influence of machine-controlled voting.

The power and influence of the urban political machine declined slowly. Even before their de-

mise, however, machines represented only one facet of local politics. Local political life in the United States has always been a highly varied affair, ranging from minimally organized and contested elections to highly partisan and sharply fought campaigns for city councils, county governing bodies, even school boards. One of the distinguishing features of U.S. politics is the large number of local officials who are elected, rather than appointed.

Local politics has often served as the springboard for people who want to become politically involved. Jimmy Carter, for example, launched his political career by winning election to the Plains, Georgia, Board of Education. Many studies have focused on the increasing number of "amateurs" who enter local politics and then make their way onto the national political scene. Such "purists," as they are often called, see politics as the realm of ideas and principles; the old machine-oriented professionals were far more interested in maintaining party organization and winning elections.[5]

STATE PARTIES Heading the state party organization is the state committee, ranging from a few dozen to several hundred members. Typically, the county is the basic unit of representation. Members of the state committees are chosen in a variety

COMPARATIVE PERSPECTIVE

The Disciplined Parties of Great Britain

Unlike the American Congress, where members often vote against a majority of their own party and oppose party leaders, members of the British parliament rarely vote against their party on issues of any significance. British political parties are highly "disciplined" organizations; that is, the system provides for effective means of keeping legislators in line. In practice, this means that members of parliament who oppose party leaders in any consistent way cannot expect to be endorsed by the national party when they run for reelection. Because the national party in Britain has a powerful say over nominations, outspoken opponents who vote against their own party, can expect to be denied the chance to run again. In the United States, by contrast, nominations are controlled at the state and local level; the national party has little say over who runs for office under the party flag.

The British system produces consistent voting patterns in the House of Commons, where party discipline is enforced by the structure of roles and by informal norms and sanctions. Members are expected to attend party meetings in the House and, if possible, to join party committees addressing various policy areas. MPs are also expected to attend important debates and support the party's position; failing to attend to party chores may close off paths to advancement for the offending member.

Responsibility for enforcing discipline rests with the whips. Each party leader in the House of Commons chooses his or her own chief whip, who then appoints assistant, or junior, whips. The whips' authority is real, even though their methods are mostly informal. They use persuasion, if they must, to enforce party discipline. One of the best arguments a majority whip can use is that a vote against the government could help to bring the government down. Whips seldom have to resort to appeals, however. By dispensing favors and accommodating individual MPs, the whips seek to instill reflexive party loyalty in MPs.

Expulsion is an extreme measure, reserved for those who have abandoned basic party principles not only in parliament but also in public speeches and activities.

Party loyalty and discipline are mirrored in parliamentary voting. In practice, this means that if the party in power has a solid majority, the opposition has virtually no chance of influencing government policy. It must wait until the next election to try to gain power.

---

of ways, including primaries, caucuses, and selection by state convention delegates.

Whatever their theoretical powers, few state committees have any say over state party issues. Usually, the committee meets a few times a year and leaves day-to-day business to the party chairperson, normally the key figure in party matters. In most states, the state party chairperson is closely associated with the governor or other high-ranking state officials. As state politics has grown more competitive—and expensive—in recent decades, the chairpersons, and state parties in general, have widened the scope of their functions: They draw on opinion poll data, develop issues for future campaigns, engage in more fund-raising activities, and offer more professional services to candidates. And at almost all levels of politics, the pervasive influence of television—both through political news coverage and political advertisements—has focused voter attention on candidate personality, significantly diminishing the role of state parties in grooming and selecting candidates for political office.

NATIONAL PARTIES   Originally, the sole function of the national party was to nominate a presidential candidate, who was selected by party leaders in Congress. By the 1830s, however, national conventions had become the accepted means of selecting the party's presidential hopeful. Each state was allowed to decide how to choose its delegates to the convention. The adoption of the national convention system, in turn, made it necessary to create an ongoing organization that would make arrangements for the convention and coordinate the campaign. This function was performed by the **national committee,** created by the Democrats in 1848 and adopted by the Republicans eight years later. In both parties, each state elected a single member to the national committee until the 1920s, when a committee*woman* was added for each state.

For over a century the national committees served only as links from one convention to the next. They did not effectively centralize party control; power still remained primarily in the hands of the state chairpersons. Only a few national chairpersons had a strong enough influence over party affairs to exercise significant control over the nominating process.

Not until after the tumultuous 1948 convention did the Democratic Party take steps to curb the overwhelming influence of state parties in the national convention process. At the 1948 convention, several state delegations were allowed to participate even though they were pledged to support the so-called Dixiecrat ticket rather than the Democratic ticket. This capitulation by the national party to Dixiecrat delegations set off a struggle to nationalize party rules. Finally, in 1956 the convention resolved that state parties selecting national convention delegates had to "assure" that the official Democratic Party nominee would appear under the party label on the state ballot. (In the 1948 election, Dixiecrat candidate Strom Thurmond, not Democratic candidate Harry Truman, had been listed as the "Democratic" candidate in four states.) In the 1960s, the Democrats moved further toward national control of state delegations by stipulating that state delegations be selected on a

In New Hampshire, workers for Kansas Senator Bob Dole handle the typical work of a primary—getting out mailings, calling voters, maintaining an office. It all builds to a climax at the party conventions. *(Paul Conklin/Monkmeyer)*

nondiscriminatory basis. Then, after the strife-ridden 1968 Chicago convention, extensive new rules governing delegate selection were instituted. (These are covered in the next section.)

Despite these moves toward nationalization of party rules, the Democratic Party, like the Republican Party, has remained highly decentralized. Formalizing party membership—through requirements that members pay dues and carry party cards—has never taken a high priority. As another indication of the freewheeling approach of U.S. political parties, neither major party requires candidates to adhere to a clearly drawn set of party principles.

The Republican Party has pursued nationalization in its own way. Under a series of dynamic national chairpersons, the GOP has expanded the operations of is national office substantially. Beginning in the mid-1960s, the GOP national or-

TABLE 7–4
Activity of Party Committees through June of Election Year, 1979–1988

	1979–80	*1981–82*	*1983–84*	*1985–86*	*1987–88*
Democrats					
Receipts	$15,612,003	$20,602,218	$59,744,323	$37,660,958	$59,842,462
Disbursements	13,650,197	23,628,111	52,074,330	35,885,668	48,204,299
Cash-on-hand	2,297,346	1,673,519	9,853,937	3,509,430	12,483,507
Contributions	303,304	732,352	743,252	871,044	888,732
Coord. expend.*	163,779	426,904	493,397	760,963	1,401,973
Republicans					
Receipts	$102,841,562	$160,653,283	$207,594,464	$189,836,741	$166,193,953
Disbursements	80,080,893	133,327,864	170,942,834	162,312,643	135,551,679
Cash-on-hand	17,214,915	33,751,840	44,595,311	32,384,269	33,762,354
Contributions	1,482,167	2,681,143	2,180,471	1,699,125	1,224,673
Coord. expend.*	288,870	832,330	1,074,184	1,746,393	415,541

*Coordinated Expenditures are made only in general or special elections.

SOURCE: Federal Election Commission, "FEC Releases 18-month Party Spending Figures for 1987–88 Election Cycle," press release, Aug. 29, 1988, pp. 2–3.

ganization mounted extensive direct-mail fund-raising campaigns. Enough money was raised for the GOP to build its own national headquarters in 1971—the first ever owned by either party. Through the 1970s, the GOP also established a highly complex network of services and activities—recruiting and training candidates for state and local races on an unprecedented scale; handling opinion polling, research, media production, and data processing; offering financial assistance to candidates; establishing advisory councils to craft long-term policies; and publishing a party monthly, numerous brochures, and a semiacademic journal. Somewhat belatedly, the Democrats have undertaken similar fund-raising and service efforts, but they still lag behind.

As we can see in **Table 7–4,** Republicans have been far more successful than Democrats in their fund-raising efforts. In general, this has given Republican candidates an edge in financing and campaign services—including polling, direct mail, and candidate training—provided by the party's national committee. Nonetheless, money does not always translate into electoral success, as the Republicans discovered in the 1986 off-year elections, when they sustained significant losses in House and Senate races.

Both national party organizations, then, have evolved and taken on new functions. Neither, however, serves as an overall coordinator or arbiter of party policy. Instead, both follow a course of partial nationalization through party reform, political services, and campaign strategy, reflecting the decentralized nature of U.S. politics.

Party Reforms after 1968

A watershed year in many respects, 1968 marked a turning point for the presidential nominating process. We now turn to (1) the origins and impact of the dramatic Democratic reforms; (2) the more subtle Republican reforms; and (3) the overall effects of all these reforms.

DEMOCRATIC REFORMS   Political events in 1968 prompted moves to reform the Democratic Party's nominating process. Prior to the 1968 convention, President Lyndon Johnson chose not to seek renomination. Senators Robert Kennedy and Eugene McCarthy then waged a highly visible and intense battle for the presidential nomination in states that had primaries. Meanwhile, Vice-President Hubert Humphrey, fearful that widespread opposition to

Text continues following the color essay.

For many Americans the 1988 presidential election reaffirmed the strength of democracy. Just as Ronald Reagan's two elections had quieted any fears that no one any longer could be elected to, or serve out, two full terms, the election demonstrated that our fractured, nonrational two-party system could get us by. Not everyone was pleased with the results, of course, and almost everybody could offer some criticism of the system. Those looking for dramatic changes— either a great leap forward or a fundamental return to lost values—were, as always, confounded by the incremental nature of routine American politics.

In many ways the 1988 election was unremarkable, which in itself was comforting to some. We seem to need—or at least to get—opposing candidates who are enough alike that, whatever happens on election day, inauguration day retains a benign aspect. We celebrate elections because the stakes are not too high. One could sleep through election day (many do) and not have to worry much about the nature of the world one day later.

This need for a choice, but not too much choice, is an important factor in the two centuries of stability that the American political structure has enjoyed; no doubt it also contributes to the persistence of social inequities. But we are

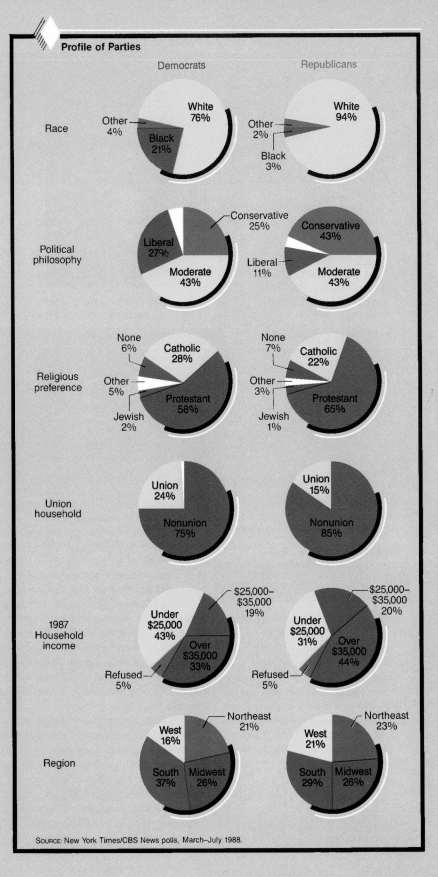

Profile of Parties

Democrats | Republicans

Race
- Democrats: White 76%, Black 21%, Other 4%
- Republicans: White 94%, Black 3%, Other 2%

Political philosophy
- Democrats: Liberal 27%, Moderate 43%, Conservative 25%
- Republicans: Liberal 11%, Moderate 43%, Conservative 43%

Religious preference
- Democrats: None 6%, Catholic 28%, Other 5%, Jewish 2%, Protestant 58%
- Republicans: None 7%, Catholic 22%, Other 3%, Jewish 1%, Protestant 65%

Union household
- Democrats: Union 24%, Nonunion 75%
- Republicans: Union 15%, Nonunion 85%

1987 Household income
- Democrats: Under $25,000 43%, $25,000–$35,000 19%, Over $35,000 33%, Refused 5%
- Republicans: Under $25,000 31%, $25,000–$35,000 20%, Over $35,000 44%, Refused 5%

Region
- Democrats: Northeast 21%, West 16%, South 37%, Midwest 26%
- Republicans: Northeast 23%, West 21%, South 29%, Midwest 26%

Source: New York Times/CBS News polls, March–July 1988.

and avoided divisive attacks. As the primary process wore on, Dukakis gradually emerged as the frontrunner. Although Jackson and Gore each won several states in the Super Tuesday primary in March, Dukakis extended his northeastern base by winning Texas and Florida. In the end, only Dukakis and Jesse Jackson were on their feet. (Jackson's strength and rhetoric were such that some feared he would split the party at the convention, but, instead, he and Dukakis settled their differences amicably, and Jackson faded from the scene.)

The Republican contest was similar. It started with six contenders: General Alexander Haig, former Secretary of State in the Reagan administration; Pierre du Pont, former Governor of Delaware; Representative Jack Kemp of New York; Pat Robertson, television evangelist; Kansas Senator Robert Dole; and Vice-President Bush. Although Dole got a fast start in Iowa, Bush proved more appealing to Republican voters, and his well-organized campaign weathered early setbacks. No one was able to challenge his string of successes, and the other candidates withdrew quickly. Bush entered the convention assured of the nomination.

Money
Money can't guarantee electoral success, but it certainly helps (and its absence may prove fatal). Supporters of the early Iowa caucuses and New Hampshire primary claim that "retail" politics (small-scale, person-to-person campaigning) is a good antidote to the need for large sums of money early in the primary season, but the 1988 election demonstrated otherwise. Although Richard Gephardt and Robert Dole both won their party's Iowa contest, George Bush and Michael Dukakis each managed to raise significantly more money than their rivals and used it to coast past defeats in particular contests. The one real advantage of an early win—the possibility of turning it into exposure and cash—can be nullified by a well-heeled opponent.

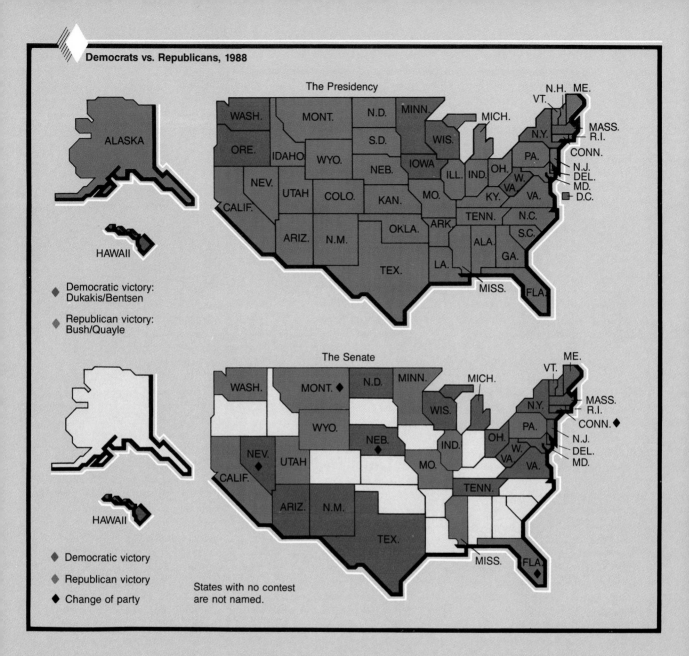

Democrats vs. Republicans, 1988

The Presidency

Democratic victory: Dukakis/Bentsen

Republican victory: Bush/Quayle

The Senate

Democratic victory

Republican victory

Change of party

States with no contest are not named.

Voters

Jesse Jackson's influence at the 1988 Democratic national convention was based partly on his efforts since the 1984 campaign to register large numbers of new voters. In most democracies such a strategy would be impossible; registration is either automatic or simply part of voting. But U.S. registration procedures vary from state to state and nearly always present obstacles to participation—one reason for extremely low voter turnout in American elections. Another factor is that we hold presidential elections on working days, and election day is not necessarily a holiday in all states. Finally, some have argued since at least Barry Goldwater's successful campaign for the Republican nomination in 1964 that large numbers of disaffected citizens could be lured into voting *only* if their choice were between candidates with significantly different ideologies. But the elections of 1964, 1972, and 1984 all had clear ideological distinctions, and they did not generate unusually large turnouts. In 1988 the turnout was 50 percent, the lowest since 1924, but only a few points lower than the four previous elections.

The Electoral College

Because the Electoral College (see Chapter 8) distributes electoral votes all-or-nothing by state, population shifts among states significantly affect presidential elections. Recently, for example, the populations of Sunbelt states have grown more quickly than those of northeastern states. Because the number of electoral votes has shifted with the population, presidential candidates are under pressure to spend more time and money in states that count, especially in a few large southern and western states. The importance of those regions to the Democrats in 1988 was seen in their selection of Atlanta, Georgia, for the national convention, and of Texan Lloyd Bentsen for vice-presidential candidate; the Republicans also convened in the South, in New Orleans, but—given George Bush's strength in that region—the selection of Indiana Senator Dan Quayle as running mate could be made more for ideological balance than for electoral considerations.

The campaign itself reflected the reality of the Electoral College system. As Dukakis fell behind in the popular vote, his campaign strategists focused on states with large electoral votes: California, New York, Texas, and the key states of the Midwest. With Bush having a lock on the South and most of the West, Dukakis's managers hoped to put together a narrow electoral majority by winning all the big states. The plan, of course, failed. Of the five states with the largest electoral counts, Dukakis carried only New York. The 1988 election further demonstrated the pattern of the previous two elections: On the presidential level, Republicans enjoy a solid electoral base in the South and most of the West. For the Democrats, the problem for the future is to find the right candidate and set of issues to penetrate that base.

The 1988 Election and Democracy

Typically enough, many voters were less than thrilled with the process or candidates they faced in the fall, for only half the eligible electorate turned out. Besides this evidence of discontent, the conduct of the campaign itself raised concerns about our democratic process. The Bush campaign's use of negative TV ads drew much attention and criticism, but the success of the ads probably means that we haven't seen the end of negative campaigns. Mudslinging through the

media and the "packaging" of candidates will become even more systematic. Among the suggested remedies to offset such trends are having a greater number of informal debates; giving free radio and television time to presidential candidates; expanding political commercials to at least two or three minutes long; making voter registration more convenient; and establishing a national holiday for elections. Other democracies do such things, and their electorates turn out in impressive numbers.

Another issue that got attention in 1988 is the way vice-presidential candidates are selected. Many doubted that George Bush's choice, Senator Dan Quayle of Indiana, had either the experience or the competence to handle the presidency, if necessary, and there were allegations that family influence had furthered Quayle's career. His performance in a vice-presidential debate against Lloyd Bentsen only increased apprehension about his abilities, and for most of the campaign Quayle's profile was kept low by Bush's managers. Dukakis did make an issue of Bush's selection of running mate, but beyond the campaign rhetoric Quayle's candidacy raises questions: Should the selection of vice-presidents be left to the presidential nominee alone, or should party councils or conventions play a larger role? Given the power of the presidency today, should we be so nonchalant in selecting the person who will be "only a heartbeat away"?

Despite its shortcomings, the 1988 electoral process satisfied some. As Professor Michael Robinson of Georgetown University put it: "We have a centrist political process, and the American people chose two well-educated, decent, responsible men with long histories of public service. I would also argue that this was even a commendable Presidential election year. In the first six months, a black man ran for the Presidency and none of his opponents made that an

D. GOLDBERG/SYGMA

issue...." Going further, however, satisfaction depends in part on how much we expect of democracy, on how close we think we can come to a politics based on reasoned debate and clear public understanding. Satisfaction also depends on the qualities of leadership that result—over the next four years, it depends on George Bush.

Snappy "sound bites," shallow symbolism, telegenic personas—these now infect not only our electoral process but the way we are governed as well. The "managed" presidency, like the "packaged" campaign, makes elected leaders turn to pollsters for advice about what the public will "buy." But leaders often must advocate policies that the public is slow to accept, and they also must prepare and motivate the public for thoughtful, critical scrutiny of issues. Thomas Jefferson summed it up long ago:

Cherish...the spirit of our people and keep alive their attention. Do not be too severe upon their errors, but reclaim them by enlightening them. If once they become inattentive to the public affairs, you and I, and Congress and assemblies, judges and governors, shall all become wolves.

Tyranny, Jefferson believed, prospered on ignorance and superstition. A democratic education—by inculcating skepticism and independence of mind—best protects our politics, our government, and our democracy.

Police stand guard at the scene of the 1972 Democratic convention. Despite fears of violence, there was no repetition of the deep and extensive clashes that marked the 1968 convention in Chicago. *(Bettye Lane/Photo Researchers)*

the Vietnam War among rank-and-file Democrats might hurt his candidacy, avoided most presidential primaries. Instead, Humphrey quietly marshalled support among party regulars in states that did not hold primaries. At that time, 60 percent of the delegates to the Democratic National Convention were selected by state conventions or state committees rather than through primaries. And even in states that held primaries, the delegates selected by popular vote often were not bound to a particular candidate. Humphrey's strategy worked: With little fanfare he garnered enough party support to win the nomination. This outraged many Democrats, largely because they suspected that Humphrey would have lost the nomination in the primary battles.

At the 1968 Democratic convention in Chicago—one of the political low points of the 1960s—control of the proceedings was very tight, and some delegates accused the party bosses of police-style tactics. In the streets of Chicago, protesters of many sorts roamed or paraded through the city, sometimes taunting police, sometimes set upon and beaten by police with little or no provocation. The protesters sought the passage of an anti–Vietnam War plank and a more open convention, as did many inside the convention hall. At the deepest level, the legitimacy of the entire U.S. political process was called into question. More specifically, many Democrats became convinced that reform of the nominating process was absolutely essential.

After the 1968 election, National Party Chairman Fred Harris appointed a reform commission headed by Senator George McGovern of South Dakota and later chaired by Representative Donald Fraser of Minnesota. The McGovern-Fraser Commission introduced several ambitious reforms, the most significant of which were the following:

A requirement that each state delegation take steps to assure that blacks, women, and those under thirty would be represented in "reasonable" relationship to the state's population.

The development of written rules governing each state's method of choosing delegates.

Abolition of the *unit rule,* under which state delegations had been allowed to vote as a unit for one candidate. Henceforth, each delegate's vote would be recorded.

Prohibition of proxy voting in delegate selection (to prevent control by a few power brokers).

Reform of the apportionment of delegate slots given to each state.

A limit on the number of delegates (10 percent) selected by party committees.

These reforms significantly reduced the power of Democratic Party leaders to control or even influence the process of delegate selection. Here was the backlash of the insurgent Democrats against the "boss-controlled" convention of 1968. Even suggesting such reforms shocked many political observers; when the party carried them out, it stunned political experts even more.

George McGovern's nomination as the party's 1972 candidate for president signaled a triumph for the reformers. McGovern supporters took an active role in presidential primaries and, with the aid of the rule changes, wrested control of the convention from party professionals. The nomination was achieved at a heavy price to the party, however. Many regular Democrats, most notably labor union leaders, failed to support the party's nominee. After McGovern's decisive defeat in the general election, it appeared that a thorough reform of the reforms might take place. Instead, over the next decade and a half, a series of gradual changes were made in the delegate selection processes. The McGovern-Fraser reforms were modified, but not totally rolled back.

The Democrats' "Fairness Commission" made some small shifts in rules between 1984 and 1988. After protests in 1984 from candidates Gary Hart and Jesse Jackson, who charged that their delegate totals did not fairly represent the popular vote they won, the commission lowered the threshold needed to qualify for delegates from 20 percent to 15 percent of the vote in a primary. Also, the commission increased the number of "superdelegates" from 568 to nearly 650. These superdelegates—all members of the Democratic National Committee, all Democratic governors, and 80 percent of the Democratic members of the House and Senate—

strengthen the role of party and public officials in selecting the nominee. In 1988 other changes were instituted in the process of choosing the presidential nominee as well; the most prominent was the Super Tuesday primary. We turn to these reforms and related issues in Chapter 8.

REPUBLICAN REFORMS   The GOP never experienced the intense pressures for reform that buffeted the Democratic Party. There was no Republican analogue to the traumatic 1968 Democratic convention; no strong minority groups demanded change; and no overriding liberal ideology pressed for it. Moreover, the Republican Party had dropped the unit rule in the mid-nineteenth century. After 1968, GOP party leaders warned against "McGovernizing" the party—weakening the party's role in the presidential nominating process. Nonetheless, they instituted a more open delegate selection process at the local level. Positive action to end discrimination was discussed, but plans to require action on the issue were pointedly dropped, and the 1976 convention refused to endorse any procedures designed to assure compliance. A party committee in 1981 did recommend that

political parties should (themselves) determine how their nominees are chosen; state party organizations should have the authority to adjust the delegate selection process to fit their local political traditions; national, time zone or regional primaries should not be imposed; and changes in party rules which require state legislative action should be drafted in a manner which would permit rather than require a party to adopt the change.[6]

Such recommendations were unlikely to disturb any sectors of the party—a striking contrast to the conflicts among Democrats.

EFFECTS OF THE REFORMS   The reforms of the nominating process in both parties sharply increased the number of presidential primaries. Opening up party caucus meetings, meanwhile, led to an influx of new people at the local level. Both these shifts reduced the power of party professionals to control the nominating process. Candidates no longer needed to line up the sup-

Reforms of the nominating process reduced the power of political parties and made it possible for relatively unknown candidates to build support. Here, candidate Jimmy Carter shapes his image by addressing a group of handicapped people during his 1980 campaign for the presidency. *(David Burnett/Contact Press)*

port of party leaders and officeholders. This was clearly a gain for democratic principles because the reforms encouraged more widespread popular participation and closed off the kind of "back-room" control that had characterized past conventions. The reforms also led to more wide-ranging representation of women, blacks, and younger party members at both national conventions (see **Table 7–5**).

In both 1972 and 1976, the Democrats nominated candidates who would have stood little chance under the prereform system. The successes of George McGovern and Jimmy Carter demonstrated that committed political unknowns could

TABLE 7–5
Blacks, Women, and Young Delegates to National Conventions, 1964–1988

	Democratic delegates (percentage)			Republican delegates (percentage)		
	Blacks	*Women*	*Under 30*	*Blacks*	*Women*	*Under 30*
1964	2	13	*	1	18	*
1968	6	13	4	2	17	1
1972	15	40	22	3	32	7
1976	11	33	15	3	31	7
1980	15	49	11	3	29	5
1984	18	50	8	4	44	4
1988	21	52	4	3	37	4

*Figures not available.
SOURCE: David Price, *Bringing Back the Parties* (Washington, D.C.: Congressional Quarterly Press, 1984), p. 192 (for data to 1984); *New York Times*, Aug. 14, 1988, p. L32 (for 1988 data).

seize control of the nominating process, that good showings in the early primaries could propel even an unknown candidate to political prominence, and that the new system placed a premium on the shrewd use of mass media and on the personality and ideas of particular candidates. In both races, the Democratic candidate was picked by the voters, rather than by party professionals. In addition, the enlarged primary system has opened the door to vigorous campaigns by candidates who would otherwise find it difficult to gain a national forum for their views, such as Pat Robertson and Jesse Jackson.

Who are better equipped to judge a person's presidential caliber—the voters or the party professionals? That is difficult to answer. In primary contests, the turnouts are generally far lower than those in general elections, and the better-educated, wealthier, and more issue-oriented voters turn out.[7] Party professionals can no longer ignore new issues and new blood, but they also face increased difficulty in forging a united party.

Many supporters of the enlarged primary process and more open conventions admit that the new system is flawed and that further reforms are necessary. Most maintain, however, that there is no going back to the days of the politician-controlled nominating convention. As one student of the subject put it: "We wouldn't have primaries if the old system had worked. The party machines collapsed in the late 1950s and early 1960s when the electorate changed totally."[8]

Overall, the reforms have created a more competitive and open nominating process. But do they consistently produce candidates competent to govern the nation? And how significantly has this more open process eroded the power of our already weak political parties? We will return to this issue shortly.

Do the Political Parties Differ?

To some observers, the Republicans and the Democrats are like two sides of the same well-worn coin: They may differ, but only on the surface. Others argue that Republicans and Democrats offer the electorate clear choices on many issues. Which view comes closest to the truth?

One way to approach this question is to look at the promises made by each party in election years and to assess how much these promises have differed. Studies of platform pledges over the past forty-five years show that Democrats and Republicans hold different images of themselves and tend to make different promises to the citizens.[9] Republicans typically place greater emphasis on national defense and on how the government is run, whereas Democrats give greater weight to labor and welfare matters. However, the parties tend to overlap in many areas, particularly foreign policy.

Party differences carry over into Congress as well. Typically, the parties divide on many of the issues addressed in their platforms.

Can we say, then, that Democrats and Republicans differ enough to offer voters a meaningful choice? We know that the parties do differ in some respects, but that they also overlap considerably. And on some important issues both parties fail to present any real alternatives. For example, neither the Democrats nor the Republicans have presented clear alternatives on energy issues or the infrastructure, and many other party positions are confused and even contradictory.

Some observers argue that both U.S. parties lean toward the center, fudging their disagreements to appeal to the widest range of voters. Party leaders moderate their views so they do not leave the voters behind. The crushing defeats suffered by Goldwater (a staunchly conservative Republican) and McGovern (a decidedly liberal Democrat) in 1964 and 1972, respectively, have often been explained in these terms: The candidates voiced views either further to the right or the left than those held by the vast majority of the electorate.

To sum up, research has shown what common sense indicates: The major parties do differ on many issues and their pledges do make a difference, but parties also ignore some important issues, fudge others, and often fail to convince the public that the choices they offer are truly meaningful. This confusing picture of U.S. political life emerges from the internal disarray and lack of overall cohesion of both major parties. We must remember, however, that each party has more liberal and more conservative wings, and that coalitions across party lines have been quite common in Congress. Were U.S. parties more closely disciplined, it would be far easier to see and to judge the relationships among party pledges, party differences, and the outcomes of government action. We will look shortly at the issue of party responsibility and the failure of U.S. parties in this regard.

Current Issues

In this final section we consider the current state of the U.S. party system. We examine, in particular, three related topics: (1) the disaffiliation of voters from the major parties; (2) the prospects for significant shifts in the party system; and (3) the issues of party responsibility and party reform.

The Decline of Parties

Most political scientists agree that the major U.S. political parties are in decline. Some of the signs are obvious. For example, fewer people identified themselves as Democrats in 1987 (42 percent) than did so in 1937 (50 percent). Those identifying themselves as Republicans declined from a high of 39 percent in 1944 to a low of 24 percent in 1980, before increasing to 30 percent in 1987. Meanwhile, those who identify themselves as independents increased from 16 percent in 1937 to 28 percent in 1987. Among younger voters, the trend toward independent status has been marked. Of all voters under thirty in 1984, 45 percent called themselves independents, and only 16 percent considered themselves "strong" partisans. It also seems clear that younger voters who identify themselves as independents do not tend to shift toward one of the parties in later years.[10]

As another sign of party erosion, both Democrats and Republicans, in increasing numbers, have broken ranks, voting for candidates of the opposite party. Over the past thirty-five years, large numbers of Democrats, for example, have voted for Republican candidates. The same is true for Republican-identifiers. The trend toward ticket-splitting and general defection from party la-

bels is as widespread among older as among younger voters.

In addition, voters' perceptions of the parties have grown increasingly negative, indicating a progressive deterioration of party allegiance in the United States. Between 45 and 55 percent of the nation believes that there are no important differences between the parties, and see parties as more and more irrelevant to the nation's and the individual voter's primary concerns.[11] Voters focus increasingly on candidates and issues regardless of party. No longer do voters use party labels as the primary measure of a domestic issue's merit ("The Democrats support welfare, so I do, too") or a presidential candidate's fitness for office ("I always vote for the Republican nominee for president"). Other signs of party decline include the rise of single-issue groups (such as the Right-to-Life movement), the loss of party cohesion in voting in Congress, and candidates' decreasing emphasis on party labels in election and reelection efforts. Some political observers also contend that the rise of television campaigning and the more effective organization of interest groups have undermined the role of parties. We will consider these factors in Chapters 8 and 9.

The decline of the parties is, of course, linked to the growth of political alienation and mistrust, and the decline in voter participation noted in Chapter 6. Taken together, these elements indicate a growing crisis in the U.S. polity that might lead to a basic realignment of voter preferences.

Many reforms have been suggested that might strengthen American political parties. For example, one student of the subject suggests two distinct sets of changes—one to be initiated by the parties themselves, the other requiring assistance from the government.[12] Among the most far-reaching party-initiated reform proposals are the following:

Building stronger grass-roots party organizations by creating mobile party offices and more daily contact with citizens

Providing services to party members such as discount credit cards, insurance, cut-rate legal services, and the like—paralleling services offered by labor unions

Expanding fund-raising activities for and services to

COMPARATIVE PERSPECTIVE

A New Party in West Germany

When an electorate becomes extremely frustrated with the dominant political parties and their policy positions—or lack of positions—one solution is to form a new party. One of the most dramatic new parties to be formed in a democracy in recent years is the Green Party in West Germany. Their policies stress new issues such as environmental degradation and the need for alternative life-styles. They call for sharp reductions in nuclear armaments and want West Germany to leave NATO. The Greens have drawn supporters from all groups and age levels in German society, but their core activists are younger, unconventional people who look back to the 1960s, when grass-roots action had startling effects on political life. Not all Greens, however, agree on a common agenda.

Begun in 1980, the party's membership by 1983 was estimated at 1.5 to 2 million people. Although they captured only 1.5 percent of the vote in the 1980 national elections, far short of 5 percent necessary to gain representation in the national parliament, the Greens won 5.3 percent of the vote in a state election later that year and entered the state parliament. That victory was followed by showings of 5 percent or better in four other state elections, with the Greens in some cases replacing the Free Democrats as the third parliamentary party. In the March 1983 national election, the Greens captured 5.6 percent of the vote and entered the 496-member lower house of the federal parliament (the Bundestag) with 27 seats.

Ironically, political success created a range of new troubles for the Greens. Gaining 8.3 percent of the national vote in 1987, the Greens won 44 seats in the Bundestag. The Greens were also influencing the other German parties, making them increasingly sensitive to environmental concerns. But with their stronger political position came a new set of problems and opportunities that badly split the party. Radical purists consider the Greens as fundamentally opposed to the existing social and political system and want the party to serve as a moral conscience in the Bundestag. Realists, on the other hand, favor compromise—making deals and entering into coalitions with other parties and groups. In the realists' view, for example, demanding that West Germany abandon NATO is not sensible at the moment, although it can be a long-term goal. One Green who served as a minister for environment in a Social Democratic state government pointed out: "I don't just want to complain that the rivers are dirty, I want to clean them up." But in contrast, others argue that "The opposition would lose its teeth if it became too legal." Despite these serious internal rifts, the Green movement has not come apart, clearly aware that if it does, all its goals will be less likely to be achieved.

SOURCE: Serge Schmemann, "For Germany's Greens Movement: Conventional Success Breeds a Schism," *The New York Times,* Oct. 11, 1987, p. 8.

political campaigns, plus recruiting more candidates and volunteers

Making party institutional advertising (ads emphasizing the party label itself and its meaning) a permanent component of campaigns, and airing them during noncampaign periods as well

Increasing party input in policy formulation by empaneling policy commissions when the party is out of power

Proposed government-assisted reforms would include:

Establishing larger federal tax credits for party contributions—up to 100 percent for small contributions

Channeling money from public financing through the parties, allowing some of it to be used for party building

Requiring all TV and radio stations to make available free air time for major state and national parties

Raising the current limits on parties' contributions to, and coordinated expenses on behalf of, federal nominees

Permitting parties to spend unlimited amounts on volunteer-oriented activities that benefit candidates

Creating a straight-party voting mechanism in every state, discouraging split-ticket voting

Reducing the number of nonpartisan elections

Consolidating elections to strengthen the effects of popular national candidates

Leaving nominating methods to the parties—holding more caucuses and preprimary endorsing conventions—thus reducing the significance of presidential primaries

Taken together, this package of reforms would place parties far closer to the center of our electoral process and help to undo the effects of the party-weakening developments of the last twenty-five years. Yet no one knows whether the nation as a whole or the parties themselves are sufficiently committed to making these reforms a reality or whether Americans overall favor stronger political parties.

Realignment: Who Has the Majority?

Ronald Reagan's first presidential victory in 1980 and his landslide reelection in 1984 led many to speculate that a political realignment of major proportions had finally occurred. The breakdown of the New Deal majority had been predicted for decades, and evidence had been pouring in since the 1950s that FDR's unique coalition of "urban ethnics, Southern Protestants, dirt farmers, Jewish intellectuals, illiterate coal miners, poor blacks and virulent racists"[13] had come apart at the seams. Democrats were told that their party had lost its

vision, that its old constituencies had moved on, that it had become identified as the party of special interests, that it had run out of ideas—particularly ideas about how to get the U.S. economy on track once again. Congressman Tim Wirth of Colorado, one of a group of younger Democrats loosely known as "neoliberals," offered this troubled assessment: "Our problem is that we do not have a single bumper-sticker solution. We're working through some pretty complicated notions."[14] Others had a simpler explanation for the 1984 presidential debacle: "A winning party has to have a vision and a message . . . Mondale's message is Hubert Humphrey."[15] This reference to the heyday of Democratic liberalism implied that Mondale's campaign appeal was largely outdated.

Meanwhile, it was equally unclear how much of a realignment was taking place in the Republican Party. Four Republican presidential victories in five outings between 1968 and 1984 added up to an impressive showing, but Republicans also failed in three strong tries—1980, 1982, and 1984—to come close to gaining a majority in the House of Representatives. Democrats held their own in many state races and made a substantial comeback in the Senate in 1986. Some commentators attributed the size of the 1984 Republican landslide to astute management of television by a uniquely telegenic candidate. Others saw the GOP successes in 1980 and 1984 merely as personal triumphs for Ronald Reagan. Finally, there were doubts that a Republican Party dominated by its conservative wing could ever constitute an effective national majority. As political observer Kevin Phillips put it: "The Republicans' economic sobriety and commitment to national defense must somehow be . . . broadened and infused with a sense of the common man."[16]

In the 1988 presidential campaign, both the Democrats and Republicans rejected candidates from the extreme wings of their parties and settled on nominees who seemed intent on appealing to the "middle" ground of voters. The Democrats nominated Governor Michael S. Dukakis of Massachusetts, who, although considered a Northeastern liberal in his earlier career, selected a conservative senator from Texas (Lloyd M. Bentsen) as his running mate and stressed broadly defined,

The Democratic Ticket, 1988: Governor Michael Dukakis of Massachusetts and Senator Lloyd Bentsen of Texas. Dukakis emerged the winner from among a large and evenly matched field of contenders. His organization's superior ability to raise money played a key role in his success, as did his solid capacities as a debater. The selection of Bentsen as running mate was a gesture in the direction of more conservative Democrats and also an effort to pick up votes in the South, particularly in Texas. *(UPI/Bettmann Newsphotos)*

nonideological issues, such as "competence" and ethics. The Republicans chose Vice-President George Bush as their standard bearer. A self-proclaimed Reagan conservative, Bush faced the difficult task of not alienating the Republican right while at the same time moving toward the center in order to attract votes from groups not ordinarily sympathetic to his candidacy (blacks and women, for example). His running-mate choice was also a conservative senator, J. Danforth Quayle of Indiana.

With both parties seeking to broaden their bases, and thus to harmonize constituencies that were often at loggerheads, the historic paradox was once again evident: the broader the party's base, the less clearly defined the issues; the greater the urge to blur differences within the party, the more the danger of overlapping with the opposing party on specific issues. With this dynamic in place, elections tend to revolve more around public perceptions of the candidates' personalities than around specifically defined issues.

Party Responsibility and Party Reform

Do the two major parties perform the way "responsible" parties should in a democratic society? To many observers, the answer is a resounding no. In 1950, a committee of the American Political Science Association published a document, titled "Toward a More Responsible Two-Party System," in which the authors outlined how U.S. parties could become more disciplined and programmatic.[17] In criticizing the existing parties of that period (and such criticisms would apply equally as well today), the authors found a number of key deficiencies in the organization and approach of U.S. parties: They did not offer citizens fundamentally distinct policy choices; they were too weak organizationally to carry through their programs; they were not united on any basic principles; they failed to reflect the opinions of the electorate sufficiently. The committee advocated reorganizing the party system along British lines, whereby each party would be highly disciplined,

The Republican Ticket, 1988: Vice-President George Bush and Senator Dan Quayle of Indiana. Bush was expected to face tough competition in the primaries, but his victory was surprisingly easy. From a large field of early competitors, no one really emerged to challenge the Vice-President. His selection of Dan Quayle as running mate was a major surprise, since the Senator was not well-known; but Bush saw Quayle's youth as an advantage. Many questioned Bush's judgment as Quayle proved a liability during the presidential campaign. *(UPI/ Bettmann Newsphotos)*

with strong leadership and a large mass membership.

The report did not meet with instant approval. Many political scientists maintained that a weakly organized, somewhat irresponsible pattern of governing had, overall, been a good thing for the United States. Precisely because U.S. parties had not been radically different, or grounded in ideological principles, this argument runs, they had helped to keep the political temperature low; to create an atmosphere of compromise and conciliation, rather than one of distrust and fierce ideological battling; to ensure elections that are not highly disruptive in the United States; and to maintain considerable continuity as well as a certain measure of change.

Although some of the points made by advocates of "nonresponsible" parties clearly make sense, we should also note that democratic theory requires parties that *approach* the "responsible party" model. No one wishes to see parties divide on every issue and fight every battle to the finish. But

if party lines are heavily blurred, if lines of responsibility are not clear, the electorate will find it impossible to figure out what parties stand for—if anything.

Perhaps the key to our problems in responsible policy making lies in the complexity of our federalist system, which pits the federal legislative and executive branches against each other and splits regional policy making into fifty separate jurisdictions. Here political parties could play a pivotal role, reaching across these jurisdictional lines to create at least minimally coherent policy. Unfortunately, they frequently fail at this task, and when they do, citizens are left bewildered, and policy making itself becomes fragmented and even contradictory. Despite the increasing talk about party realignment, it appears that in the near future, our party system will remain largely "nonresponsible."

Interestingly, the eight years of the Reagan administration did provide a taste of what "responsible" politics might look like. The firmly conservative approach of the Reagan program represented a marked change from past policies in many areas. Moreover, although Reagan did not carry through on many of his major campaign promises, he did achieve what many considered a mini-revolution in U.S. politics. What would have happened if Reagan's victories in 1980 and 1984 had been accompanied by similar victories in the House and Senate? Had that taken place, we would have seen the fuller development of the Reagan program, and that administration would have had the full responsibility for its actions and their consequences.

Conclusions

The experience of the last two centuries has demonstrated that political parties are an essential part of the democratic process, rather than an intrusion into it. Parties provide alternative candidates and policies. They help shape voter preferences and educate the electorate. They serve as the key organizational link between the citizenry and the operation of government. It is hard to imagine democratic electoral politics without them.

The American party system has been remarkably stable for over a hundred years. The two major parties now holding sway dominate the political scene and deflect third-party challenges. Our political process makes it difficult for third-parties to gain a permanent foothold, though several third parties have influenced national policy and had an impact on elections in the past.

By comparison with European political parties, American parties are relatively decentralized and undisciplined. Our party organizations are built around the fifty states; the national leadership and organization remain fairly weak. Oftentimes, therefore, national party leaders have not been able to count on uniform support throughout the party.

Since 1968, the parties have been engaged in a process of change and reform. Extensive reforms have been made in the presidential nominating process—reforms some believe have weakened the parties while making them more democratic. Many factors—including the unparalleled impact of the mass media and the rise of better-organized interest groups—have diminished the significance of party attachments. Signs abound that the parties are in decline, yet many observers predict major realignments of political preferences in America. But to date, the envisioned realignment has not materialized.

GLOSSARY TERMS

political party
single-member district
proportional representation
Federalists
Democratic-Republicans
Democratic Party
Whig Party
Republican Party
Populist Party
political machine
national committee

NOTES

[1]Leon Epstein, *Political Parties in Western Democracies* (New York: Praeger, 1967), p. 9.

[2]Maurice Duverger, *Political Parties* (New York: Wiley, 1954), pp. xiii–xv.

[3]Hugh L. LeBlanc, *American Political Parties* (New York: St. Martin's Press, 1982), p. 3.

[4]W. D. Burnham, "The Changing Shape of the American Political Universe," *American Political Science Review* (1965):27.

[5]See James Q. Wilson, *The Amateur Democrat: Club Politics in Three Cities* (Chicago: University of Chicago Press, 1962); and Aaron Wildavsky, "The Goldwater Phenomenon: Purists, Politicians and the Two-Party System," in his *Revolt Against the Masses* (New York: Basic Books, 1971).

[6]Quoted in David E. Price, *Bringing Back the Parties* (Washington, D.C.: Congressional Quarterly, Inc. 1984), p. 159.

[7]See LeBlanc, *American Political Parties*, chap. 7.

[8]Richard Wade, quoted in *The New York Times*, April 12, 1984, p. 15.

[9]See LeBlanc, *American Political Parties*, chap. 10; Gerald R. Pomper, *Elections in America: Control and Influence in Democratic Politics* (New York: Dodd, Mead, 1968); and Anthony King, "What Do Polls Decide?" in D. Butter, H. R. Penniman, and A. Ranney, eds., *Democracy at the Polls* (Washington, D.C.: AEI, 1981), pp. 293–324.

[10]Price, *Bringing Back the Parties*, p. 51.

[11]Price, p. 17.

[12]Larry J. Sabato, *The Party's Just Begun* (Glenview, Ill.: Scott, Foresman & Co., 1988), chaps. 6 and 7.

[13]*Newsweek*, July 16, 1984, p. 15.

[14]*Ibid.*, p. 16.

[15]*Ibid.*

[16]*The New York Times*, April 19, 1984, p. 25.

[17]Committee on Political Parties, "Toward a More Responsible Two-Party System," *American Political Science Review*, September 1950, supplement.

SELECTED READINGS

For **perspectives on political parties,** see Maurice Duverger, *Political Parties: Their Organization and Activity in the Modern State*, 3rd rev. ed. (New York: Methuen, 1964); Richard Hofstadter, *The Idea of a Party System: The Rise of Legitimate Opposition in the United States* (Berkeley, Calif.: University of California Press, 1969); Wilfred E. Binkley, *American Political Parties* (New York: Knopf, 1965); and Frank Smallwood, *The Other Candidates: Third Parties in Presidential Elections* (Hanover, N.H.: University Press of New England, 1983).

On **party reform and our changing party system,** consult David E. Price, *Bringing Back the Parties* (Washington, D.C.: Congressional Quarterly Press, 1984); Gerald M. Pomper, *Elections in America* (New York: Dodd, Mead, 1968); W. N. Chambers and W. D. Burnham, eds., *The American Parties*, rev. 2nd ed. (New York: Oxford University Press, 1975); and James L. Sundquist, *Dynamics of the Party System: Alignment and Realignment of Political Parties in the United States*, rev. ed. (Washington, D.C.: Brookings, 1983).

THE ROLE OF PARTIES IN DEMOCRACIES

The **antiparty sentiments of the Founders** are explored in Richard Hofstadter, *The Idea of a Party System* (Berkeley, Calif.: University of California Press, 1969).

The **role of parties in democratic societies** is probed in Maurice Duverger, *Political Parties*; E. E. Schattschneider, *The Struggle for Party Government* (College Park, Md.: University of Maryland Press, 1948); and Leon D. Epstein, *Political Parties in Western Democracies* (New York: Praeger, 1967).

8

CAMPAIGNS, MONEY, AND THE MEDIA

Packaging Politics

CHAPTER OUTLINE

Campaigning: Beyond the Razzle-Dazzle
Political Campaigns
Campaign Financing
Politics and the Media
Media and Campaigns

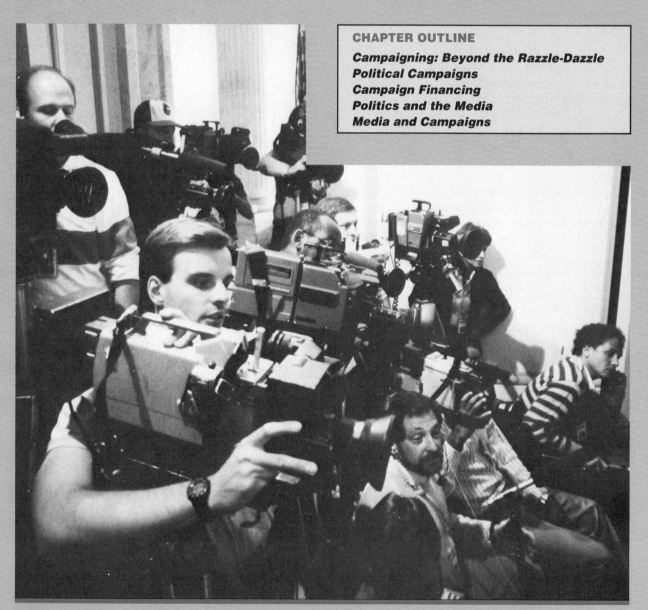

Dennis Brack/Black Star

Campaigning: Beyond the Razzle-Dazzle

Sex, drugs, money, alleged deception. The contest for the American presidency in 1988, although a deadly serious affair, provided a colorful spectacle even by the standards of the nation that gave birth to P. T. Barnum, Evel Knievel, and Michael Jackson. For the first time in twenty years, both party nominations were up for grabs. Yet the protracted accounts of human frailty played out in this campaign sounded more like the stuff of daytime drama than the process for choosing the leader of a superpower.

The preprimary favorite for the Democratic nomination, Gary Hart, challenged reporters to follow him around to see for themselves that there was no substance to the rumors of his sexual dalliances. Unfortunately for Hart, the *Miami Herald* took up the challenge and found what it (and others) reckoned was clear evidence of monkey business. Hart's campaign was suspended. (Much later he returned to the campaign trail with the slogan, "Let the People Decide." When they did, providing supportive crowds but paltry primary tallies, the campaign was suspended again.)

Conventional wisdom was confounded more than it was confirmed in the nomination struggle. There were preachers in both parties (Jesse Jackson and Pat Robertson) who ran surprisingly effective campaigns. Many complained that the Iowa caucuses (the earliest of the contests for convention delegates) had far too much influence on the selection process. But a win in Iowa did *not* propel Richard Gephardt into a sustainable lead, nor did a loss there mark the end of George Bush's campaign. Jesse Jackson's oratorical style distinguished him as the most animated and colorful in the crowded field of Democrats, and by many accounts, the most effective in reaching a live audience. Jackson came to be known for his use of rhyme and alliteration, delivered with the cadence and passion of a country preacher. But Jackson's real triumph was in demonstrating that a black candidate—even a poetic one—could be taken seriously by blacks, whites, and even party power brokers. The season's odd couple were Jackson and Bert Lance, the burly Georgia wheeler-dealer who had been Jimmy Carter's budget director and who became a major Jackson advisor. Jackson wasn't the only accomplished orator in the crowd. Joe Biden was considered an effective speaker, too, until it came to light that he was *borrowing* his speeches—and even childhood experiences—without crediting their source (one came from British Labour Leader Neil Kinnock). Public confessions became the order of the day. Two candidates (Bruce Babbitt and Al Gore, Jr.) admitted to having smoked marijuana a long time ago, and Michael Dukakis's wife, Kitty, revealed she had overcome a dependence on prescription medication. Dukakis's campaign manager, Jim Sasso, confessed that he'd had a hand in releasing the videotape that convincingly demonstrated Biden's plagiaristic tendencies. That cost Sasso his job (he later rejoined the campaign), but it gave Susan Estrich an opportunity to become the first woman to manage a major national campaign.

While all this was going on, a staccato counterpoint was playing in the background. All the Democratic candidates' stock rose and fell as popular New York Governor Mario Cuomo denied—with varying shades of conviction—that he could be drafted as a presidential candidate. When evangelist Jimmy Swaggart's alleged sins with a prostitute hit the front pages, the Robertson campaign suggested that Bush supporters may have leaked that story just to embarrass former evangelist Robertson. Then former presidential press spokesman Larry Speakes, in a published account of his time in the Reagan White House, revealed that he had fabricated statements allegedly made by Reagan when the Great Communicator himself was less than quotable. That was followed by White House Chief of Staff Donald Regan's book, which alleged that Nancy Reagan dictated the president's schedule on the basis of astrological advice from a friend in San Francisco. None of these "kiss-and-tell" accounts of life in the Reagan White House helped George Bush, whose hopes in the campaign were tied to the popularity of Reagan himself.

All these headline-grabbing events happened well before the party nominating conventions, which, in spite of early predictions of a "brokered" Democratic convention (one in which no candidate comes in with enough delegates to win the nomination), turned out to be relatively routine affairs. But in the end, the 1988 campaign for the presi-

Jesse Jackson's enthusiastic supporters challenged the Democratic convention to address an activist social and foreign policy agenda. *(Paul Conklin/Monkmeyer)*

dency was not much different from campaigns of the past.

The American public thrives on spectacle and may actually encourage it. But the gossip and glitzy entertainment merely form the flashy exterior of campaigns in the United States. Just below the surface lies a stratum of candidate-generated, controlled events—the photo opportunities, the TV spots, the stump speeches, promises, slogans, and proposals. And digging deeper, below the manufactured campaign images, we find campaign strategy and the institutionalized processes of election in this country. Here, at the level of events involving institutions and processes, we discern the substance underlying the images and the drama that make political campaigns such compelling enterprises. This is the subject of much of this chapter. We will also look more generally at the role of the media in American politics. These are complicated subjects. We will approach them

with an eye toward how campaigning and media contribute to or detract from democratic hopes. Do campaigns enlighten? Do they help the nation identify and elect capable leaders? Or do they simply package candidates and sell them like commercial products? Do voters hear critical and constructive commentary in the news media? Or do the media distort and play up the superficial at the expense of the substantial? We consider these issues in the following sequence: (1) political campaigns; (2) campaign financing; (3) politics and the media; and (4) the media's impact on and coverage of campaigns.

Political Campaigns

In a democracy, the electorate makes choices—that is what elections are all about. How do the "choices," as represented by opposing candidates, get onto the ballot? In the United States, it is through an often long and tedious process that involves gaining recognition, receiving the endorsement of a party, obtaining funds from supporters, and seeking approval by the voters. Together, these activities make up a political campaign.

A campaign can serve democracy well in several ways: by providing a forum for new political leadership; by disseminating information to potential voters; by mobilizing the electorate, and thus ensuring that the electoral process reflects popular consent. Sometimes, of course, campaigns do not fulfill all, or any, of these functions. The political leaders presented to the electorate may not be qualified to deal with the pressing problems of the day. Issues may not be clarified; worse, they may be obscured. Finally, when a campaign does not reach many potential voters, the legitimacy of the electoral process may be undermined. We now examine (1) nonpresidential campaigns; (2) presidential campaigns; and (3) the electoral college.

Nonpresidential Campaigns

Dividing power among states in a federal system, and then further allotting state power to various local governments, makes it difficult to generalize about political campaigns in the United States. Procedures vary considerably from one jurisdiction to another. In certain states—California, for instance—some elections (city, county, school board, and even some statewide offices) are officially nonpartisan. Candidates run for office without official party ties or backing. Where election laws do allow for party participation, some means must be used to choose a party's candidates to compete in the general election. Sometimes that choice is made by party leaders; more often, the choice is made by ordinary voters in a **primary election**. In a primary, potential candidates vie for nomination as the party's designated candidate in the general election. Primaries may be wide open affairs or virtual shoo-ins, depending on the circumstances. If a particularly popular **incumbent** (the person currently in the office) is seeking renomination, he or she may go unchallenged in the primary. In congressional races, incumbents run unopposed in primaries more than half the time. Where one party is so dominant that it is unlikely that the other party could win, the primary election assumes greater importance than the general election that follows.

Primaries can follow one of three formats, determined at the state level. In a **closed primary**, only voters registered in a particular party may vote in the party's primary. In an **open primary**, voters can choose at the polling place which party primary they wish to vote in, regardless of their registration. A **blanket primary** is one where voters can choose either party's primary for different offices—for example, the Democratic primary for senator and the Republican primary for governor. Most states use a closed primary, in part to discourage **cross-over primary voting**. If your candidate is unopposed or has the nomination locked up, you might choose to vote in the other party's primary for a weak candidate, who could be beaten more easily in the general election. That might advance party interests but it would distort the search for the strongest person to fill the office.

In the general election campaign, candidates must raise funds, make use of the media, meet voters, gain support from prominent groups and individuals, activate the party faithful, and mobilize campaign workers. In the larger campaigns, armies of professionals work behind the scenes to formulate campaign strategy. Such professionals—including pollsters, computer experts, and media strategists—have become almost indispensable to campaigns for major offices. Small, or even nonexistent, campaign staffs are still common in congressional campaigns—particularly those in which an incumbent faces no substantial opposition. Yet more and more political observers see a cause for concern in the increasing expense involved in contemporary campaigns at all levels. Driven in part by the professionalization of campaigning itself, and in part by other factors (like the skyrocketing cost of TV ads), daunting sums of money can be spent to secure even state and local offices. We will consider the issue of campaign financing later in this chapter.

It might seem to be letting the tail wag the dog, but it is important to think about the time in office between elections—the **interelection stage**—as part of the election process as well. Once elected, a representative or senator must continue to attend to the political situation in the home district or state. Ties with important groups, individuals, and the party itself must be maintained. Congressional representatives usually try hard to serve constituents to build up a reservoir of good will for the future. They generally make every effort to bring as much federal money as possible into their districts. In this connection, conservatives usually do not differ much from liberals. The chance to confer benefits on constituents, along with the higher name-recognition that comes with incumbency, can be of great help to a candidate seeking reelection. Incumbency also has its disadvantages, however. An incumbent may offend some constituents by particular votes or actions, or may suffer from association with an unpopular administration. Nevertheless, in most circumstances incumbency is one of the strongest advantages that can be brought into an election. In Congress, for example, the electoral advantages of incumbency are very strong, as we will see in Chapter 11. That assures continuity of leadership, but does it work against the responsiveness that should characterize democracy? When a member of the House of Representatives runs unopposed time after time, we must count on mechanisms other than elections for registering voter choices on policy issues that matter.

The Republican candidates, 1988: Al Haig, George Bush, Pete du Pont, Jack Kemp, Bob Dole, and Pat Robertson. *(UPI/Bettmann Newsphotos)*

Presidential Campaigns

Although all political races have certain elements in common—stumping for votes, seeking media exposure, fund-raising, taking the pulse of the electorate—the intensity and importance of these activities varies from race to race. In presidential campaigns, *everything* counts. These are the most intense, most expensive, most drawn-out political campaigns in any modern democracy. Let us now examine some of the major events in a presidential race: (1) preconvention moves; (2) the national nominating conventions; and (3) the general election campaign.

PRECONVENTION ACTIVITY   Considering the significance of the presidency in U.S. politics, it is not surprising that some politicans spend years generating the level of support needed to gain the nomination of a major party. For those seeking the office of president, years of public appearances, lectures, and wooing of state and local party leaders usually precede the formal opening of the contest.

Since George McGovern's successful four-year campaign to gain the Democratic nomination in 1972, most candidates engage in campaign-style activities for at least two and often four years prior to the election. The 1988 election was no exception

in this regard. Some observed that George Bush had been preparing for this election throughout the eight years he served as Reagan's vice-president. While Michael Dukakis didn't start a concerted effort to capture the Democratic nomination until he had won reelection as governor of Massachusetts in 1986, the morning after the 1986 gubernatorial election, his campaign manager handed him a long memorandum on the presidential race. Several other candidates in both parties had begun undeclared bids for their party's 1988 nomination in 1984. And following the 1988 contest, the posturing for 1992 had begun even before the new president was sworn in.

As we saw in the preceding chapter, until relatively recently presidential nominees generally were selected by powerful party leaders at or before party conventions. But in recent decades, the process of choosing presidential nominees has become much more open, depending heavily on primaries and caucuses involving ordinary voters. The current jury-rigged means of selecting party nominees—a confusing array of party primaries and caucuses in individual states—satisfies no one entirely. Even though the national parties have been asserting more control over candidate selection, our federal system encourages a fragmented process. And circumstances have been changing so rapidly that many candidates find themselves

The Democratic candidates, 1988: Dick Gephardt, Mike Dukakis, Joe Biden, Al Gore, Jesse Jackson, Paul Simon, and Bruce Babbitt (not shown: Gary Hart).
(UPI/Bettmann Newsphotos)

in the position of army generals—always preparing for the *last* war, and not ready for tomorrow's battle. This has been particularly true in the case of the Democrats, for whom party reform has been much more pressing—and more extensive. But, as we saw in Chapter 7, reforms have significantly changed the process of selecting a presidential candidate in both parties.

For Jimmy Carter's successful campaign for the 1976 Democratic nomination, the Georgia governor needed to demonstrate that he was indeed a national candidate to be taken seriously. That meant spending a lot of time on the early contests (the Iowa caucuses and the New Hampshire primary), where surprising wins could be turned into increased backing for later contests. Walter Mondale, as the former vice-president, campaigned in 1984 as broadly as possible, in an attempt to demonstrate that he was the inevitable nominee. Still, a surprisingly strong showing by Gary Hart in Iowa, coupled with a Hart win in New Hampshire, nearly derailed the Mondale express. Again the early contests took center stage in the primary campaign.

After 1984, a group of mostly Southern Democrats, concerned about the poor Democratic showing in presidential contests (one win in the previous five elections) and about what they saw as a "liberal bias" in the selection process, came up with a plan to give the South a greater voice in the nominating process. In an attempt to counteract this liberal bias and choose a more "electable" candidate, several Southern states decided to hold their primaries on the same day early in the nomination process. The masterminds behind this megaprimary believed that a contest with a large number of delegates to be gained on a single day in a single region would focus more attention on the South as well as promote the candidacies of more moderate and conservative presidential hopefuls (who, it was assumed, would do better in the conservative region). So Super Tuesday was born, as fourteen Southern and border states held primaries on the same day early in March 1988. As we will see, however, conservative candidates did not benefit from the Super Tuesday megaprimary.

The Republicans, partly because of the character of the Republican Party, and largely due to presidential electoral success, did not tinker with party rules the way the Democrats did. Successful preconvention strategies have been wide-ranging, while becoming more sensitive to primary results. But because Republican Party rules have not tilted toward the grass roots to the same extent as the Democrats', the GOP's nominee selection process has been less volatile. Since 1976, when Ronald Reagan and incumbent-by-appointment President Gerald Ford battled for the nomination all the way to the convention floor, the Republican contest has been marked by the presence of a clear front-runner as the candidate to beat. In 1980 that was Ronald Reagan; in 1988, George Bush. Considering the importance of raising lots of money and the tendency of campaign contributions to flow to the front-runner, it shouldn't be surprising that these candidates were successful in gaining the Republican nomination.

As in 1984, a series of televised debates in 1988 gave candidates seeking the party nominations a chance to voice their views on a range of issues. While such debates may work against less skilled users of the media (Bruce Babbitt, for instance, blamed his poor showing at the polls in part on his initial inability to sit still for TV cameras), they counterbalance the plethora of stage-managed photo opportunities and TV spot advertisements.

Many preseason predictions about the 1988 nomination races were confounded by events. The importance of early contests in Iowa and New Hampshire diminished in 1988. Missouri Congressman Richard Gephardt did very well in Iowa and poorly after that. George Bush did poorly in Iowa and well later. Super Tuesday may have focused more attention on the South, but in neither party did it advance conservative candidates. In the Republican Party, conservative evangelist Pat Robertson prayed for a Super Tuesday boost that did not come. Tennessee Senator Al Gore, Jr., touting himself as both a Southerner and a moderate/conservative alternative to the other Democrats, didn't fare well enough on Super Tuesday to gain the momentum he needed to survive later contests. Ironically, Jesse Jackson, the most liberal of the Democratic candidates, did very well on Super Tuesday, as did Michael Dukakis (hardly a conservative), and moderate Republican George Bush.

Still, conventional wisdom did hold true on several counts. The best financed campaigns on each side—those of Dukakis and Bush—weathered the long haul successfully. (Jesse Jackson's campaign did surprisingly well with few monetary resources early on in the process—aided by the newsworthiness of a strong black candidacy and Jackson's own telegenic style.) The traditional understanding that it is difficult to run from the House

of Representatives or from a small state was borne out in the failures of Gephardt and former Governors Babbitt of Arizona and Pierre duPont of Delaware. And finally, the expectation that a brokered convention was unlikely in an age of media-based mass campaigns was substantiated as well: Even with a crowded field in both parties, the nominations of Bush and Dukakis were assured well before the conventions. In the Democratic race, where speculation about a brokered convention was hottest, Dukakis was counted the almost-certain winner earlier in the season than any Democrat since Lyndon Johnson's nomination in 1964.

What can be said about the nominee selection process of 1988? It generated two fairly dull but competent candidates, neither from the extreme wing of his party. It was a lengthy, expensive process, media-oriented but not without some attention to issues. It involved a variety of individual contests, requiring different appeals (from the personal-contact campaigns in Iowa farmhouses to the large-scale, media-market campaigns on Super Tuesday). A large number of preconvention debates among candidates did offer a more complete airing of issue positions than in previous presidential elections.

The final word about the nominee selection process in 1988 is that, structurally at least, things won't be much different in 1992. Dissatisfaction with the process of selecting candidates was muted by the emergence of two very mainstream, "safe" standard bearers. At their 1988 convention, the Democrats adopted rules for the 1992 contest that differ only slightly from the ones used in 1988. The new rules tie the distribution of each state's delegates more closely to the results of the state's primary or caucuses, and they modestly reduce the number of "superdelegates" to the national convention. Major reform proposals (which could be imposed on the parties by Congress)—including regional primaries or a national primary—seem unlikely to be implemented before the makeshift machinery is cranked up again. Nevertheless, the fragmented nature of the process as it is currently structured provides an open invitation to reform. Given the American political system, that invitation will only be acted upon when we are con-

Dan Quayle was a Senator from Indiana when George Bush tapped him to be the vice-presidential nominee. The selection of running mates is driven by electoral concerns, not by issues, and candidates for the vice-presidency are supposed to be different from the presidential nominee. Quayle was from the Midwest and was younger and more conservative than Bush, who hailed from the Northeast and from Texas. Quayle's youthful good looks successfully balanced Bush's settled, mature image. *(AP/Wide World Photos)*

fronted with some major electoral scandal or crisis. In the meantime, we seem content to be entertained by the spectacle.

NATIONAL CONVENTIONS The national political conventions retain some of the flavor of the past. Mass demonstrations, marches, music, and behind-the-scenes negotiations take place now as always, complete with exhausted delegates and smoke-filled rooms. And while national conventions remain significant undertakings for both major political parties, today the identity of the nominee is generally known in advance.

At every national convention held between 1956 and 1988, one ballot sufficed to select the nominee. In 1924, by contrast, the Democrats took a record 103 ballots to nominate John W. Davis. Yet some drama still surrounds convention maneuvering. Even though the delegate count is now much better defined, because of primary voting, it is still unclear at times whether a candidate has all the votes needed for nomination. Reagan and Presi-

dent Gerald Ford were almost tied going into the 1976 Republican convention, and both made every effort to woo the small number of uncommitted delegates. Even when a candidate is more or less assured of the party's nomination, there are other tasks that command attention. The candidate must attempt to exert control over critical convention committees—in particular, the one charged with drafting the party's platform. Candidates who have been very successful in primaries and caucuses, but who have not gathered enough support to win the nomination, often try to shape the party platform to reflect their own agendas—especially when these are different from the priorities of the nominee. It is more than awkward for a presidential candidate to run on a platform that is strikingly at odds with the candidate's own views.

The chief remaining source of excitement at convention time is the selection of the vice-presidential nominee. This process occasionally involves some of the anxiety, bargaining, and high drama of old-style convention politics. The Republican

VALUE OF THE DOLLAR

1967-1979

$1.00
90
80

$.45

Lloyd Bentsen, a Senator from Texas, was an asset to the Democratic ticket not despite, but because of, stark differences on some issues with presidential nominee Michael Dukakis. Bentsen, an eloquent, conservative Southerner, nicely balanced the image of Dukakis, an intense, moderate New Englander. There is little recent evidence that vice-presidential candidates can add more than marginal support to a ticket, but the possible addition of a single large state like Texas can justify a nod. *(AP/Wide World Photos)*

convention of 1980, for example, was enlivened by ultimately fruitless backroom negotiations to name former President Ford as Reagan's vice-presidential running mate.

Generally speaking, vice-presidents are selected to balance the ticket geographically or ethnically and/or to pacify another wing of the party. In 1960, Democratic presidential nominee John Kennedy chose Senator Lyndon Johnson of Texas, his chief opponent for the nomination, to attract Southern votes in the election. Reagan's choice of George Bush in 1980 was made partly as a gesture toward more moderate Republicans and partly because Bush's foreign policy experience filled a gap in Reagan's background. In 1984, Mondale selected Geraldine Ferraro, the first female vice-presidential candidate of a major party in U.S. history, in hopes of appealing to women's rights proponents. And in 1988, the liberal Northeasterner Michael Dukakis chose a conservative Texan, Senator Lloyd Bentsen, to provide balance to his ticket.

THE RUN FOR GENERAL ELECTION In the eight weeks between Labor Day (the first Monday in September) and Election Day (the first Tuesday in November), the candidates and their staffs work ceaselessly to woo voters. During this period, candidates must not only seek to convince voters to vote for them, but also broaden their appeal to diverse segments of the electorate and touch base with a variety of special interests.

The candidates work hand in hand with paid political consultants to devise an overall campaign strategy and create a desirable image. Public opinion samples tell consultants what areas of the country the candidate should concentrate on and which issues he or she should emphasize in specific regions. The consultants schedule public appearances, stage "news events" (such as walking tours, rallies, and hospital visits), and make certain that advance work is done properly before a candidate arrives at a destination. Most important, they coordinate a political advertising campaign that culminates in a media blitz the last two weeks of the campaign. (Image-making through the media will be discussed at length later in the chapter.) The candidate, meanwhile, follows a grueling schedule, flying from one part of the country to the other for daily rounds of speech making, interviewing, and working the crowds.

In view of the exhausting and drawn-out campaign process, many critics wonder whether the present system offers the most sensible way of selecting a president. Does this system attract the best people to political life? Many observers contend that the most statesmanlike public figures, the potential Jeffersons and Lincolns, are driven away from political life by the intensity and cost of the contemporary campaign process. Why should anyone be expected to spend two or three years running and preparing to run for office? To do so may well imply an uncommon measure of devotion to public service, or it may merely reflect an all-consuming ambition. Have we, in other words, turned campaigns into huge circuses that favor candidates who are good at performing, but not necessarily at governing?

If so, how can we address these shortcomings? The primary process could be shortened, to reduce the cost and strain of campaigning. Power could be restored to the political parties; this would help attract better people into politics by making politics more of a long-term career. Most important, perhaps, the role of financing in political campaigns could be diminished—a subject we will address a little later.

Richard Joslyn, in an effort to judge how closely U.S. campaigns and elections corresponded to the concerns of the electorate, advanced four alternative models of how popular consent works[1]: (1) the "prospective policy choice" approach, (2) the "retrospective policy satisfaction" approach, (3) the "selection of a benevolent leader" approach, and (4) the "election-as-ritual" approach. In the first of these models, citizens choose candidates on the basis of what they anticipate *future* policies will be. In the second, electoral choices are based on satisfaction with *past* policies. In the third, voters select a reassuring personality as leader. In the fourth, elections serve principally to reinforce deeply held cultural myths.

The model that best fits contemporary U.S. elections is the second, the "retrospective policy satisfaction" approach. It is far easier for the common citizen to assess with some knowledge what has been going on in the world than what directions policy will take. Each presidential election essentially answers one key question: Do you want four more years of this? Although administrations may cover up past policy failures, events frequently confound the pleasing pictures administrations try to cultivate of their policy successes. Voters do, in fact, "punish" administrations when economic conditions take a turn for the worse or foreign policy problems get out of hand.[2]

The Electoral College

The American method of electing a president flies in the face of our modern understanding of de-

mocracy. Why should the president, our national leader, be selected by a group of "electors" chosen on a state-by-state basis, rather than directly by a majority of the voters in a straight popular vote? Here is the simple answer: This is how the framers of the American Constitution arranged it. The original 1787 version of the **electoral college** grew out of a series of compromises struck at the Constitutional Convention. As we have already seen, the framers were wary of direct majority rule. The electoral college, then, filtered the choice of the voters in selecting the national leader.

Originally, the electoral college worked like this: Electors were chosen by each state, with the number of electoral votes equal to the total number of a state's representatives and senators. Each state chose electors in its own way. If no candidate received a majority of electoral votes, the decision was thrown into the House of Representatives, where each state would cast a single vote.

Over the years, the system has undergone extensive reforms. Now all electors are chosen by the popular vote in each state, with the popular vote winner receiving all of that state's electoral votes (except in Maine, where the vote is apportioned by congressional districts). Yet the post of elector remains. Generally, a state's electors are chosen by the state party in party conventions. After the election, in December, the electors assemble and forward their votes to Washington and an official election winner is declared. In recent years some electors have voted for a candidate other than the electoral winner in their home states. In 1976, an elector from Washington state cast his vote for Ronald Reagan rather than Gerald Ford—perhaps a prophetic choice, but certainly not a democratic one.

Critics of the electoral college base their opposition on solid grounds. For one, electoral votes and popular votes may not coincide. Three times in U.S. history—in 1824, 1876, and 1888—the majority vote-getter did not win in the electoral college and America elected a president with a minority of votes. This outcome could easily have occurred several other times in more recent history. A second argument holds that the electoral college promotes an unwarranted emphasis on the larger states that have more electoral votes. In turn, this sways candidates to appeal to critical

COMPARATIVE PERSPECTIVE

The Election Game in Great Britain

In contrast to the various elections Americans hold for president, senator, and representative, Great Britain has only one type of national election—that of the individual member of Parliament. All MPs are elected at the same time, and the government is then formed by the party with the most seats in the House of Commons. The campaigns for these elections are very short—just a matter of weeks from the time a prime minister calls an election (which he or she may do any time within five years of taking office).

Although only one kind of *election* exists at the national level, British *campaigns* are of two distinct types. An official (and therefore legally regulated) local campaign takes place in each of the nation's parliamentary districts. An unofficial (and almost completely unregulated) national campaign is directed by national party leaders and conducted mainly through the mass media. Laws regulating campaign finance apply only to the local campaigns, but there are no legal limits on contributions to or expenditures by national campaigns. Despite this lack of restrictions, party expenditures in the national campaign seem small by American standards: in 1983, for instance, the total reported spending was $10.3 million. The prime reason for the relatively low level of campaign spending is that parties may not spend money on television and radio advertising. Instead, free air-time is provided for all parties, each of which controls the format and content of its broadcasts. The number of broadcasts allowed is based roughly on the relative electoral strength of the parties. Each party-controlled broadcast runs ten minutes and usually focuses on the party rather than on individual candidates.

But party-controlled broadcasts tell only part of the story. Elections, after all, are news. Covering the campaign as news, broadcasters produce interview programs, "man-in-the-street" surveys, and so on, and provide extensive coverage of individual party leaders. In addition, the centralized nature of British politics is reflected in the relatively large number of national newspapers—including the *Guardian* and the London *Times*—that take partisan positions on their editorial pages.

swing groups in those large states. The shifting of 1 percent of the vote in a state like California, Texas, Illinois, or New York, may have much more far-reaching implications under the electoral college system than the shift of 1 percent in Nebraska or New Hampshire.

Several reforms have been proposed, but none has attracted sufficient support to be added to the Constitution. The most minimal change would *require* electors to cast a ballot for the popular vote winner in their state. A more complicated proposal would divide a state's electoral votes in direct proportion to the popular vote in that state—rather than the current winner-take-all system. Finally, some critics favor abolishing the electoral college altogether, and electing the president directly by popular vote. What objections are raised to this obviously democratic arrangement? Some analysts argue that the current system has worked well overall, and that a national vote would undermine the federal system and create even more distance between voters and candidates. In addition, a very close election in the popular vote (Kennedy's in 1960, for example) can be validated by a more substantial electoral-vote margin. Many strategically placed groups, including urban minorities such as Jews and blacks, also fear that direct election might limit their influence, which is greater under the current system. Jimmy Carter proposed a popular-election amendment in 1977, but the amendment failed to obtain the necessary two-thirds majority in the Senate. So, in the absence of a major electoral crisis, the current electoral college system is likely to remain the somewhat awkward and potentially troublesome method of electing our national leader.

Campaign Financing

The cost of winning and holding office has skyrocketed in recent years (see **Table 8–1**). In 1956, candidates for public office in the United States spent $155 million. By 1984, that figure had soared to an incredible $1.75 *billion*.[3] Spending on races for twenty-seven seats in the U.S. Senate in 1986 amounted to over $211 million. The average winner in a U.S. Senate campaign in 1976 spent $609,000; by 1986 the average winner spent $3.1 million. Over the same decade, spending by winners of U.S. House of Representatives seats rose from an average of $87,200 to $355,000. Candidates for the California legislature in 1986 spent $60 million altogether. (Compare these figures with the $10.3 million spent on the entire British general

election of 1983. Great Britain's population is more than double that of California.[4]) Much of this rise in spending came from the increased use of television and radio advertising, public opinion polling, and computers, as well as from the need for ever-larger campaign organizations.

High campaign spending levels pose problems for democracy on several levels. First, they represent allocation of America's resources which could be directed to other projects. In addition, when elections require large sums of money, election results may reflect the distribution of wealth more than wisdom. And because officeholders must spend large amounts of time seeking contributions to retain their offices, other matters—which perhaps should take precedence—must be shunted aside.

Financial outlays cannot guarantee victory in an election. No amount of campaign spending could get a Republican elected in some heavily Democratic districts or a Democrat elected in traditional Republican strongholds. Nor could the most lavish expenditures ensure victory for an outspoken opponent of farm subsidies in a rural Iowa district, or a committed segregationist in a black ghetto. In

George Bush's 1988 presidential campaign seemed to float on a sea of American flags. Was there a legitimate political message in this ostentatious patriotism? Clearly, many voters responded positively to it. Although few sitting vice-presidents have been able to run successful presidential campaigns, Bush used his position in the Reagan administration to advantage in 1988. *(AP/Wide World Photos)*

TABLE 8–1
Costs of Presidential General Election Campaigns, 1860–1988

	Republicans		Democrats	
1860	$100,000	Lincoln*	$50,000	Douglas
1864	125,000	Lincoln*	50,000	McClellan
1868	150,000	Grant*	75,000	Seymour
1872	250,000	Grant*	50,000	Greeley
1876	950,000	Hayes*	900,000	Tilden
1880	1,100,000	Garfield*	335,000	Hancock
1884	1,300,000	Blaine	1,400,000	Cleveland*
1888	1,350,000	Harrison*	855,000	Cleveland
1892	1,700,000	Harrison	2,350,000	Cleveland*
1896	3,350,000	McKinley*	675,000	Bryan
1900	3,000,000	McKinley*	425,000	Bryan
1904	2,096,000	T. Roosevelt*	700,000	Parker
1908	1,655,518	Taft*	629,341	Bryan
1912	1,071,549	Taft	1,134,848	Wilson*
1916	2,441,565	Hughes	2,284,590	Wilson*
1920	5,417,501	Harding*	1,470,371	Cox
1924	4,020,478	Coolidge*	1,108,836	Davis
1928	6,256,111	Hoover*	5,342,350	Smith
1932	2,900,052	Hoover	2,245,975	F. Roosevelt*
1936	8,892,972	Landon	5,194,741	F. Roosevelt*
1940	3,451,310	Willkie	2,783,654	F. Roosevelt*
1944	2,828,652	Dewey	2,169,077	F. Roosevelt*
1948	2,127,296	Dewey	2,736,334	Truman*
1952	6,608,623	Eisenhower*	5,032,926	Stevenson
1956	7,778,702	Eisenhower*	5,106,651	Stevenson
1960	10,128,000	Nixon	9,797,000	Kennedy*
1964	16,026,000	Goldwater	8,757,000	Johnson*
1968	25,402,000	Nixon*	11,594,000	Humphrey
1972	61,400,000	Nixon*	30,000,000	McGovern
1976†	21,786,641	Ford	21,800,000	Carter*
1980§	29,188,188	Reagan*	29,352,767	Carter
1984	40,400,000	Reagan*	40,400,000	Mondale
1988	46,100,000	Bush*	46,100,000	Dukakis

*Winner.

†The first year public funding was used for presidential elections. The Republican National Committee spent an additional $1.4 million on Ford's campaign. The Democratic National Committee spent an additional $2.8 million on Carter's campaign.

§In 1980 the Republican National Committee spent an additional $4.5 million on Reagan's campaign. The Democratic National Committee spent an additional $4 million on Carter's campaign.

SOURCE: Herbert E. Alexander, *Financing Politics*, 3rd ed. (Washington, D.C.: Congressional Quarterly Press, 1984), p. 7. These figures do *not* include large sums spent on behalf of candidates by unaffiliated organizations.

the sixteen most competitive U.S. Senate races in 1986, the Republican candidates raised an average of $3.81 million—a million dollars apiece more than the $2.8 million average of the Democratic candidates. The Republicans lost eleven of those sixteen seats.[5] Moreover, some campaign resources cannot be bought. Scholars, artists, entertainment figures, and the like usually do not hire themselves out to campaigns; however, if a particular candidate captures their imagination, they may volunteer their time and efforts. Sometimes a candidate can come up with a stratagem that garners free media attention. Jesse Jackson mastered the art of winning free media attention during the early primaries of 1988. He had a relatively small budget for his campaign through Super Tuesday, yet gained more votes-per-dollar-spent than any of the other major candidates.

Having more money than your opponent cannot guarantee victory, yet not having enough money will certainly contribute to defeat. "Enough," as one student of elections writes, "is defined by the distribution of other resources and influences in the campaign."[6] These resources and influences run the gamut from how much name recognition one candidate has relative to the other, to incumbency and the characteristics of the district. Most members of Congress find, however, that factors concerning the competition cannot be calculated until relatively close to the campaign itself, while substantial fund-raising must start much earlier. Thus, because campaigns cannot accurately determine how much money will be enough, they work toward raising more than enough. And, as a former member of Congress confided, it is important to soak up contributions in part so that they won't be out there for some potential competitor to grab. These facts of political life are well known to political consultants, one of whom once said, "Money—get it early, get as much as you can."[7]

Who spends the most money? Republicans are usually far better financed than Democrats at all levels of government. Compare the levels of disbursements in Table 8–1. In every year, the Republican National Committee spent substantially more than its Democratic counterpart. The Republican Senatorial Election Committee outspent the Democratic committee by a factor of nearly ten to one. The annual budgets of state political parties reveal the same disproportion. In a survey taken in 1984, 73 percent of the Republican state parties responding reported budgets over $500,000. Only 37 percent of the Democratic state parties had budgets that large.[8]

Much of the money raised by the parties and candidates comes from various interest groups. Business and conservative groups, which generally support Republican candidates, tend to outspend labor and liberal groups, which traditionally support Democrats. Lately, the contributions of such groups have been limited by campaign finance reform laws, as we will see in the following section. We now turn to (1) campaign financing reform efforts; (2) the consequences of reform; and (3) further reforms.

Reform Efforts

The financing of political campaigns—particularly presidential campaigns—has long been a sore point in U.S. politics. In 1962, President John F. Kennedy's Commission on Campaign Costs concluded that the taint of "shoddiness" had to be removed from political campaign finance and that the requirements of the Federal Corrupt Practices Act of 1925 were outdated and useless. It was not until 1971, however, that Congress took any substantial steps to remedy the situation. The Federal Election Campaign Act (FECA), passed that year, limited media spending by candidates in federal elections, required detailed reporting of contributions, and provided for a voluntary $1 checkoff on individual income tax forms to help pay for presidential elections. To avert a threatened veto by President Nixon, Congress stipulated that the act would apply only after the 1972 elections. Ironically, financing irregularities in the 1972 presidential election, culminating in the Watergate scandal, forced Nixon to resign from office and finally triggered large-scale efforts to reform campaign financing.

The 1974 off-year congressional elections swept into office a new wave of representatives and senators bent on changing the way campaigns were conducted. This "Watergate class" was instrumental in passing the far-reaching Federal Election Campaign Act of 1974, which set sharp spending and contribution limits on federal campaigns, beefed up requirements for financial disclosure, and established a scheme for public financing of presidential primaries and presidential general elections. The Federal Election Commission was created to enforce these new rules.

In 1976 the Supreme Court upheld Congress's power to set limits on individual and group contributions made directly to campaigns, but it declared unconstitutional the FECA's $1,000 limit on contributions of individuals not clearly connected

Shown here with Jesse Jackson, Jimmy Carter, and Lloyd Bentsen, in 1988 Michael Dukakis attempted to win back the "Reagan Democrats" and reunite the New Deal coalition, last successfully invoked by Lyndon Johnson in 1964. The pattern of support for Dukakis demonstrated that a lot of water had gone over the dam since LBJ defeated Barry Goldwater twenty-four years earlier. *(Paul Conklin/Monkmeyer)*

with candidates. The Court also voided limits on candidates' expenditures of their own money and on the overall spending in a campaign, unless a candidate voluntarily accepted public funding.[9]

The FECA was amended in 1976 and 1979. It maintained limits on contributions by individuals ($1,000 per election to a federal candidate) and by **political action committees**—organizations formed to channel funds to selected candidates and to work for particular political goals—($5,000 per election to a federal candidate). It also set restrictions on expenditures. Presidential candidates who accepted public financing were limited to $10 million for the campaign for nomination and $20 million for the general election (to be adjusted for inflation). In addition, expenditures by national parties for presidential nominees were restricted, as were expenditures by both state and national parties for Senate and House candidates. Finally, the act provided for public financing of presidential campaigns for all candidates who raised at least $5,000 in each of twenty states. Significantly, public financing of presidential elections has gained widespread acceptance, reflected in a small way by the millions of taxpayers who designate $1 of their federal tax payment for the presidential campaign fund each year.

Early in 1985, the Supreme Court further curtailed the impact of campaign spending limits. In *Federal Election Commission* v. *NCPAC* (National Conservative Political Action Committee), the Court declared unconstitutional the limits on spending by political action committees on behalf of presidential candidates in general elections. Writing for the seven-person majority, Justice William Rehnquist argued that limiting such expenditures is "much like allowing a speaker in a public hall to express his views while denying him the use of an amplifying system."[10]

The case involved NCPAC, a group that had spent $5.5 million on behalf of Ronald Reagan in 1984. One other group, the Fund for a Conservative Majority, spent $2.5 million, and total independent spending for Reagan was $15.3 million. By contrast, independent spending on behalf of Walter Mondale's campaign that year amounted to only $621,000.

In dissent, Justice Byron White argued that the Court had "transformed a coherent regulatory scheme into a nonsensical loophole-ridden patchwork."[11] While many agree with Justice White, no clear consensus has yet emerged on how campaign laws should be revised.

The Consequences of Reform

In many ways, the presidential campaigns of 1976, 1980, and 1984 conformed to congressional intentions. In 1976, for example, 60 percent of campaign

TABLE 8–2
The Ten Largest PACs: Receipts and Disbursements, January 1987–June 1988

Top ten money raisers (receipts)

1.	Democratic Republican Independent Voter Education Committee	$6,852,409
2.	Realtors Political Action Committee	4,841,363
3.	American Medical Association Political Action Committee	4,759,178
4.	Auto Dealers and Drivers for Free Trade PAC	4,154,821
5.	National Congressional Club	3,194,451
6.	American Citizens for Political Action	2,891,244
7.	National Education Association Political Action Committee	2,822,836
8.	Campaign America	2,798,201
9.	League of Conservation Voters	2,642,558
10.	National Security Political Action Committee	2,636,676

Top ten contributors (disbursements)

1.	Democratic Republican Independent Voter Education Committee	$4,041,306
2.	Campaign America	3,295,280
3.	National Congressional Club	3,186,321
4.	American Citizens for Political Action	2,888,123
5.	American Medical Association Political Action Committee	2,856,907
6.	Realtors Political Action Committee	2,684,349
7.	National Security Political Action Committee	2,634,593
8.	League of Conservation Voters	2,570,452
9.	National Conservative Political Action Committee	2,127,446
10.	American Telephone & Telegraph Company PAC	2,046,357

SOURCE: Federal Election Commission, "FEC Releases 18-month PAC Figures for the 1987–88 Election Cycle," press release, Sept. 8, 1988, pp. 6–7.

expenditures were publicly financed, and private funding declined to 50 percent of its previous level. Overall, all three campaigns appear to have been relatively free of financial trickery. But the reforms have also had other, unintended consequences. Perhaps most significant has been a dramatic increase in the number and activities of political action committees. In 1974, there were 608 PACs; by 1988, there were 4,578 (see **Table 8–2** and **Table 8–3**).

Under the new campaign finance laws, restrictions were placed on the amount of money PACs

TABLE 8–3
Summary of PAC Activity, 1979–1988

Jan.–June	Number of PACs	Receipts	Disbursements	Contributions to candidates	Cash on hand
1987–88	4,578	$266,684,124	$215,488,371	$94,924,312	$119,311,823
1985–86	4,421	254,311,230	205,133,765	78,497,202	102,776,627
1983–84	4,243	195,513,802	148,256,938	56,967,307	78,819,005
1981–82	3,479	137,205,474	103,872,530	38,024,563	54,739,689
1979–80	2,571	85,339,184	61,440,336	24,954,991	38,872,996

SOURCE: Federal Election Commission, "FEC Releases 18-month PAC Figures for the 1987–1988 Election Cycle," press release, Sept. 8, 1988, p. 3.

could contribute to an individual's campaign, but there were no restrictions on money spent independently. In other words, PACs were allowed to make unlimited expenditures on a candidate's behalf or in support of certain policy views, so long as those expenditures were not directly coordinated with the candidate's campaign. In practice, such a fine line between direct and indirect financing is often difficult to draw.

Despite these restrictions, PAC contributions to individual candidates have remained substantial. Between 1972 and 1984, the percentage of all House of Representatives' campaign funding coming from PACs rose from 19 percent to 37 percent. PAC contributions to Senate races rose by more than 200 percent between 1976 and 1984, discounting the effects of inflation. PAC contributions to House races in 1984 reached $104 million, a 25 percent increase over 1982. It should be noted that the role of PAC money varied greatly in different campaigns. For example, one senator raised almost 75 percent of his campaign funds from PACs, whereas others received less than 10 percent from that source.[12]

Top PAC contributors to 1984 congressional races included the National Association of Realtors ($2.6 million), the American Medical Association ($2 million), the National Education Association ($1.9 million), the Seafarers Union ($1.4 million), and the National Automobile Dealers Association ($1 million). Interestingly, 73 percent of all these contributions went to incumbents, and often to incumbents with little or no opposition. The goal is clearly to maximize access and influence with key members of Congress.

The disproportionate PAC funding of incumbents (as safe bets) means that it becomes even harder for challengers to mount serious campaigns—at a time when one observer noted that if you wanted to design a Congress to maximize the changes for reelection, you couldn't do better than Congress as it is (see Chapter 11). There are more PACs connected with corporations than any other type, but the largest growth rate is among those labeled "nonconnected" by the Federal Election Commission—including such ideologically oriented groups as NCPAC.

For many representatives and senators, PACs come in particularly handy when large campaign debts must be paid off. One long-time senator noted that the problem of financing congressional campaigns "virtually forces members of Congress to go around hat in hand, begging for money from Washington-based special interests, political action committees whose sole purpose for existing is to seek a *quid pro quo*."[13] Other observers argue that PACs do not exert excessive influence, if only because there are so many in existence that their efforts tend to cancel one another out. Even if this is true, however, the increasing political role of PACs does raise some legitimate concerns.

For example, consider the heavy spending by PACs on efforts to defeat specific representatives and senators. In recent elections, conservative PACs, like NCPAC, have targeted various liberal candidates, spending large sums in attempts to defeat them. Ideological targeting of this kind contributes to the decline of political parties by supplanting the parties' fund-raising and support functions. It may also jeopardize democratic principles by helping to elect candidates whose views represent only a small—but well-financed—segment of the electorate. (For further discussion of PACs, see Chapters 9 and 11.)

Further Reforms

To many observers, the reforms of the 1970s were too limited in scope. With the weakening of the major parties, the proliferation of PACs, and the increasing importance of the mass media in political campaigns, a drive for more radical reforms has gained momentum. Several far-reaching reform measures have been proposed:

Limitations on the costs of political advertising on television, or the granting of free TV time to candidates.

Curbs on the independent spending of PACs, especially funds used to discredit candidates. (There is some question about whether such restrictions might not violate First Amendment protections—a position taken by the Supreme Court in 1976.)

Checks on the unrestricted use of personal wealth by individual candidates.

Provision for public financing of congressional as well as presidential election campaigns.

The last recommendation has been proposed in Congress several times but has not been passed by both houses. One of the difficulties of campaign financing reform is that any proposal will affect different candidates differently. Some critics argue that public financing would assist incumbents, who already enjoy many advantages. Others take the opposite view—that it would unfairly aid challengers. Because many Republican members of Congress perceive Democratic proposals as disguised means to enhance Democratic electoral prospects at the expense of Republicans, partisan splits frequently develop over campaign financing legislation. The extended filibuster of February 1987 that resulted in Senator Bob Packwood's being arrested in his office and carried onto the floor of the Senate feet first was a Republican attempt (successful) to defeat a campaign financing bill. Barring another major financing scandal, the chances of Congress agreeing on further meaningful reform are exceedingly slim.

Politics and the Media

Traditionally, the press has been considered an important check on government power. Ideally the press should act as a watchdog, subjecting government officials and government policies to careful scrutiny. Without disciplined parties in the United States, the press must often play the role of "loyal opposition," analyzing government proposals and suggesting clear alternatives as well. These key roles for the press assume paramount importance during periods of executive dominance (most of the twentieth century in the United States). While legislatures tend to foster open discussion and regularly give rise to internal debate, executives often do not exhibit these democratic traits.

How well the press fulfills its roles as watchdog and loyal opposition to the presidency has varied considerably in recent years. Several factors account for this. First, presidents tend to shy away from direct contact with the press and rely increasingly on spokespersons whose comments are frequently "off the record." Presidential press conferences, when these are arranged, provide little opportunity for sustained dialogue on any topic. During the Reagan administration, for instance, presidential press conferences were extremely rare occurrences.

Second, presidents now sidestep the press, reaching the people directly via television ad-

President John F. Kennedy on television in the early 1960s. Electronic media allowed politics to find its way daily into virtually all American homes. Although large numbers of citizens remained ignorant of the basics of political life, the influence of media in shaping political attitudes in recent decades is undisputed. *(National Archives)*

Foreign Media

Citizens of the United States receive information from a vast number of commercial, privately owned media sources. In many European countries, however, important segments of the media are government-owned and -operated.

In West Germany, for example, each German state has responsibility for broadcasting within its territory, although state networks are tied into the national network for prime time viewing. Each state provides only two television channels and three radio stations, a selection much more limited than that available in most larger American markets. West Germany also has enacted strict regulations governing advertising on government-owned stations; commercials may not be shown after 8 P.M. and are limited to a combined total of twenty minutes during the day.

The situation is very different in Italy and France. In France, the main government television station receives most of its income from advertising, and private radio supported by advertising is allowed. Although French TV was until recently entirely under government control, the country now has three commercial, privately owned stations. In Italy, the government still has a monopoly over broadcast television, but the privately owned media have grown dramatically since 1976, when Italian courts decided that the government could not prohibit private parties from operating FM radio stations or cable television networks.

In addition to the resources their own governments devote to domestically produced broadcasting, European programmers have access to the programs produced by the other national networks. The European Broadcasting Union (EBU) serves to coordinate exchanges of broadcasting between its member countries and between Western Europe and the Soviet bloc countries, who are linked through a net called the International Radio and Television Organization (OIRT).

In addition to the exchange of programs between stations in different countries, the emergence of satellite television technology has encouraged the development of programming designed for the entire European market. Rupert Murdoch, the Australian-born publishing magnate who owns many media properties in the United States and Europe, has created a network called "Sky Channel," which broadcasts via satellites to homes all over Europe. With the growth in both satellite and cable television systems, programming has also shifted from more "serious" cultural and educational offerings to "fun TV" that features game shows, films, soap operas, and other entertainment. The growth of this kind of television has led to an increase in American television imports to Europe, with 20 percent of the programming on some channels coming from the United States.

Although European countries still have fewer broadcasting media than the United States, they boast a far greater number of newspapers and popular periodicals, many of which are owned by political parties, and which act as those parties' political voices. Newspaper readership is higher in most European countries than in the United States, and the number of small-circulation papers is also higher. Paris, for example, has eight different daily newspapers.

Europe's best and most influential newspapers are concentrated in the largest cities. Like *The New York Times* and *The Washington Post* in the United States, *The Times* of London and Paris' *Le Monde* exercise an influence out of proportion to their circulation. Other influential European newspapers include the *Frankfurter Allgemeine Zeitung* (West Germany), the *Neue Züricher Zeitung* and the *Journal de Genéve* (Switzerland), and *Corriere della Sera* and *Il Tempo* (Italy). Another important paper that circulates throughout Europe is the English-language *International Herald Tribune*, which is published by a group of newspapers including *The New York Times* and *The Washington Post*.

SOURCE: Eva Etzioni-Halvey, *National Broadcasting Under Siege: A Comparative Study of Australia, Britain, Israel, and West Germany* (New York: St. Martin's Press, 1987).

dresses. President Reagan was at his best under these controlled circumstances, and used them to great advantage.

Third, from time to time government officials—from presidents on down—attack the credibility or fairness of the press. A memorable confrontation occurred between Vice-President Bush and CBS-News anchor Dan Rather during the 1988 presidential primary campaign. For more than ten minutes on live, national TV, Rather and Bush yelled at each other. Rather complained that Bush would not answer his questions about the vice-president's role in the Iran-contra affair. Bush argued that Rather had "ambushed" him unfairly, simply to create a scene. There is no solid evidence about the extent to which attacks by government officials actually undermine public confidence in the news media, but such attacks do sometimes arouse considerable apprehension among reporters about freedom of the press—especially among broadcast journalists whose medium is subject to federal licensing and thus is potentially vulnerable to retaliation by the executive branch of government.

The Watergate scandal reinforced public acceptance of the press as a watchdog over government activity. While *The Washington Post* was the only major news source to pay any attention to the Watergate scandal when it first unfolded in 1972 and 1973, the national press eventually gave the scandal wide exposure. By contrast, when the Iran-contra affair became public in 1986 and 1987, the Reagan administration's covert activities in that undertaking were instantly the lead story in all major news sources—print and broadcast.

Let us now consider (1) how news is gathered and (2) how the news media frame the issues of political debate.

Gathering the News

The American news media enjoy an unusual degree of freedom in exploring political issues. In some other democratic countries, such as Great Britain or France, public discussion of sensitive political issues can run up against serious legal obstacles. The freedom of the American news media was significantly enhanced in the 1970s by the **Freedom of Information Act**, through which com-

mon citizens (including reporters) can obtain information that the government might otherwise prefer to keep secret (exceptions are made, of course, to protect individual privacy and national security).

Despite press freedom and legal protections, reporters must still investigate and explore to develop good stories. How do they gather their information? A surprising amount of information reported in the press comes directly from government sources. One survey of newspapers found that 78 percent of political news came from "known" sources—meaning information that was released by the government itself. The president and the cabinet alone accounted for 40 percent of all political news. Of course, such sources are under considerable pressure to create and communicate newsworthy material. And they have their own reasons for doing so, which may or may not coincide with the public interest.

Sometimes the press is deliberately manipulated by government officials. On occasion, and for a variety of reasons, officials inside the government "leak" information to the press. The 1971 publication of the **Pentagon Papers**—classified documents on the U.S. involvement in Vietnam—was an example of a massive leak motivated by opposition to government policy. Stories in 1987 about a replacement for President Reagan's chief of staff, Donald Regan, were leaked (by Nancy Reagan herself, according to Regan's account) as a tactic to force him out of that position. Sometimes overt government actions are taken to keep news from reaching the public, as when the Reagan administration prohibited reporters from going to Grenada with U.S. troops in 1983, or when the Israeli government excluded reporters from the occupied territories during the Palestinian uprisings of 1987–1988.

Framing the Issues

How deeply do most reporters probe in researching for their stories? As David Halberstam points out in his book, *The Best and the Brightest*, many reporters were easily taken in by the offical version of events in Vietnam during much of the time that American troops were fighting there. This reflects a general lack of understanding and insight. In many cases reporters do not have enough background or firsthand knowledge to challenge official judgments.

The American press is sometimes criticized for being too easy on the president. This charge was voiced frequently in the early days of the Reagan administration, but was heard less often in the latter half of the second Reagan term. Presidential interviews and off-the-record "inside source" information are often used by the White House to reward sympathetic treatment by members of the press. (And as Larry Speakes, the former Reagan spokesman, writes in his 1988 book *Speaking Out*, he devised his own form of retribution against members of the Washington press corps who wrote or broadcast stories unfavorable to the administration: They had to phone three times before he accepted their calls.) With this in mind, we must recognize that there will always be tension for reporters between trying to secure solid information and avoiding "cronyism."

In the past, newspapers sometimes fabricated news, rather than merely conveying it. At the turn of the century, for example, William Randolph Hearst used his chain of newspapers to arouse American public opinion in favor of involvement in what became the Spanish-American War. During the 1950s, many newspapers carried banner headlines reporting spectacular (and utterly unsubstantiated) charges of communist subversion in the American government, issued regularly by Senator Joseph McCarthy and others. Was this responsible journalism? By watching and reporting on the Iranian hostage situation in 1978–1980, the media have been accused of playing into the hands of the terrorists and raising the stakes for the American government. But here we see a clear example of the interaction between politics and the media. The extensive media coverage of the hostage crisis dovetailed with President Jimmy Carter's decision to make the hostage situation a priority for his administration. Eventually the Carter presidency became a hostage to the hostage crisis.

Important questions remain. Can the press maintain its independence and still gather the information citizens of a democracy need? Will reporters dig below the surface to unearth difficult stories? And will editors give their reporters the time and resources to reach sound conclusions about important issues? Can government officials afford to be open and honest enough to keep in touch with the people through the press?

Media and Campaigns

That the mass media (television, radio, newspapers) play a significant role in U.S. political campaigns is obvious. We now consider four aspects of the media's role in elections: (1) the growing political importance of the mass media; (2) the use of the media for candidate image-making; (3) how televised political debates educate the public about the candidates and the issues; and (4) the overall news coverage of elections—the so-called "horse races." We then try to assess the relationship between the media and politics in terms of democratic theory.

The Media's Impact on Elections

In democratic elections, candidates and parties always try to communicate with potential voters. Since at least the 1950s, however, the manner in which politicians communicate with the electorate has undergone a fundamental change: The mass media, and especially television, now play the most significant role in that communication process. The new-found potency of the mass media to reshape the political landscape was first apparent in the first of the Kennedy-Nixon televised debates in 1960. Many analysts call that single event the decisive factor in Kennedy's victory.

The remarkable emergence onto the national scene of the unknown Jimmy Carter in 1976, and the little-known Michael Dukakis in 1988, was possible only because of extensive media coverage of their campaigns. On the other hand, media attention given to Gary Hart and Joe Biden when they allegedly strayed from acceptable behavior in the 1988 presidential race prompted crises in their campaigns. Compounding the bad press Biden and Hart received for their plagiarism and philandering, respectively, was each candidate's response to the crisis while under the intense scrutiny of the press. Eventually, they were forced to withdraw from the race.

The elevated position of TV broadcast booths, hovering over the heads of conventioneers, reflects the importance of media coverage to campaigns. Increasingly, conventions are staged more for the television cameras than for the delegates. The important decisions (Did the candidate look presidential? Was the candidate in control?) are made in the booths, not on the floor. Author Robert Stone described being in the Superdome for the 1988 Republican convention as "a little like being on a movie set or behind the scenes at a television studio." *(Rick Friedman/Black Star)*

These examples illustrate that the media can sometimes make or break a candidate—enhancing a campaign or undermining it. Undeniably, the media have become a singularly powerful force in virtually all major U.S. elections.

How did this happen? Some of the reasons are obvious. Americans spend almost half their leisure time watching TV, listening to the radio, or reading newspapers and magazines. This adds up to seven hours a day of media exposure, with television accounting for 75 percent of the total.[14] Also, because television reaches millions, no candidate can afford to ignore it. Through the media, candidates create images that can decisively influence elections.

Other reasons for the media's growing importance are more subtle. As more and more U.S. voters disaffiliate from the two major parties, for example, candidates increasingly seek to target specific audiences with media messages. Then, too, the enhanced importance of primaries has made the nominating process more visible—and thus more newsworthy. Media organizations, for their part, have also been changing. The major broadcasting networks—CBS, NBC, ABC, and CNN—now cover campaigns in great detail, and even commission their own public opinion polls.

Media involvement in political campaigns has been aided by several Supreme Court decisions as well. In 1957 the Court ruled that broadcasters could not be held responsible for the content of political spot ads, and thereby opened the airways to such ads. Two years later, the justices relaxed "equal time" requirements for news coverage of candidates. Before that ruling, a network that covered a news event involving one candidate was obligated to provide equal time for coverage of opposing candidates. Then, in 1976, the Court also relaxed the equal time requirements for political debates, freeing broadcasters from the necessity of including minor party candidates in a debate.[15] Finally, in 1987 the Federal Communications Commission (FCC) abolished the **Fairness Doctrine,** which guaranteed equal air-time to present opposing views. This gave broadcasters even more freedom.*

*Originally established by the FCC as a rule for broadcasters, the Fairness Doctrine required broadcasters to provide "equal time" for the presentation of opposing viewpoints. Networks complained that the rule discouraged the presentation of controversial issues altogether. Supporters charged that abolishing the rule would curb the expression of minority viewpoints. Congress's attempt to make the Fairness Doctrine law was vetoed successfully by President Reagan prior to the FCC action in 1987.

The Scripting of the President

Because presidents are now constantly under the watchful eye of the media, presidential advisors must be sure that every move is carefully orchestrated. The following excerpt is from a script prepared for President Ronald Reagan on February 25, 1988:

Time: 11:30 A.M. (20 minutes)

Location: Cabinet Room

Purpose: To brief CEOs of major corporations on the administration's budget initiatives and ask for their support. Also to discuss the INF Treaty and ask for their support.

Background: Support from the business community is important for success on the administration's budget initiatives and the INF Treaty. . . .

Sequence of Events

11:30 A.M. You enter Cabinet Room, are introduced by Senator Howard Baker, and deliver remarks. At the conclusion of your remarks you open the meeting to discussion.

11:47 A.M. Rebecca Range will signal the end of the official portion of the meeting.

You move to the end of the Cabinet Room (under President Coolidge's picture) for handshake photos with the participants.

11:50 A.M. You depart.

Talking Points

—Let me start by saying thanks to all of you for coming today. This is certainly a much friendlier group than I faced at the press conference last night.

—I know you've already heard from Colin Powell on the INF Treaty and from Jim Miller on the budget package, but I would like to make a few remarks on both of these.

—First, on the INF Treaty, I'd like to repeat how important I believe this treaty is.

—It really represents a turning point in history. To actually reduce—not simply limit—the buildup of nuclear weapons.

—And to do that with the most stringent verification procedures in the history of arms control. Procedures that I believe will help pave the way to continued reductions in nuclear arms.

—It is a historic treaty, and I do hope I can count on your support to see that it is accepted by the Senate.

—Secondly, the budget. I'm sure Jim has given you the details, but I would like to make one thing clear.

—As you know, I did agree with congressional leaders on the Bipartisan Budget Agreement last November.

—It isn't a perfect agreement, but it is a good first step. The two-year agreement will reduce the deficit by a total of $76 billion. . . .

—Under the agreement we will balance the budget by 1994—but only if Congress shows some discipline, avoids unnecessary pork and program expansions, and fixes the budget process.

—They are now promising to deliver all thirteen appropriation bills on a timely basis instead of wrapping them all into one and dropping them on my desk at the last minute.

—God bless you all.

SOURCE: *Harper's,* May 1988, pp. 17–18.

Known for misstatements and bloopers, President Reagan held few press conferences. But no matter how skillful the answers, much is determined by the questions posed and by the editing of the story that airs. Like most presidents, Reagan preferred to give major addresses that would be broadcast unedited. *(UPI/Bettmann Newsphotos)*

Because of the media's growing impact on political life, heightened tension has characterized some encounters between candidates and the media. Candidates and their organizations (which usually include sophisticated media specialists) seek to use the media to advance their own perspectives. On the other hand, journalists have to decide which candidates to cover, what activities are newsworthy, and how to treat the "themes" of a campaign. In covering the candidates, the media almost invariably create images that can have important consequences. In the 1988 primary season, for instance, the news media seemed ready to leap on any evidence of the reemergence of the old political hatchetman in Senator Bob Dole. With a few nasty remarks following his New Hampshire loss to George Bush, Dole was perceived to be in trouble. The tensions between media and candidate are summed up as follows:

> [T]he needs of the media and the objectives of candidates differ. The candidates strive to flood television and the press with selective information conducive to their election. Reporters and editors want news—defined as conflict, controversy, duplicity,

scandal. They probe for candidates' weaknesses, deceptions, closeted skeletons. Candidates and their aides try to impose their definitions of what is important in an election on the media. They assert the primacy of the issues which favor them. . . . The media varyingly accept, ignore, or reject these attempts while seeking stories of their own devising.[16]

But how do the media affect public opinion? Are citizens' political perceptions altered by what they read in the papers and see on TV? Is their belief in the electoral process reinforced, legitimizing the way the system works, or are elections a disillusioning experience? We address these issues next.

Image-Making

Public opinion pollsters and professional political consultants now hold key positions in modern campaigns, often usurping the advisory roles previously filled by party officials. They bring to a campaign the expertise and savvy to use the media and other tools of modern campaigning. Among the services they provide are:

> advertising campaigns for radio, television and newspapers, including layout, timing and the actual placing of advertisements; public relations and press services, including the organization of public meetings, preparation and distribution of press releases and statements and detailed travel arrangements for the candidate; research and presentation of issues, including preparation of position papers, speechwriting and arranging for consultations between candidates and outside experts in appropriate areas of public policy; fund-raising solicitations, both by mail and through testimonial dinners and other public events; public opinion sampling to test voter awareness of the candidate, voter response to the campaign and voter attitudes on major issues; technical assistance on radio and television production, including the hiring of cameramen and recording studios for political films and broadcasts; campaign budgeting assistance designed to put campaign funds to the best possible use; use of data processing techniques to plan campaign strategy based on computer evaluations of thousands of bits of information; mobilization of support through traditional precinct-level organizations, door-to-door campaigns and telephone solicitation of votes.[17]

Consultants devise strategies to present a candidate to the media in the best light. These strategies are based on public perceptions of the candidate's strengths and weaknesses. Fundamentally, modern campaign strategists seek to alter or strengthen images of their candidate. To do so they contrive positive and highly appealing images of their candidates and contrary images of the opposing candidates, and they attempt to persuade the public of the truth of such images. These efforts can both educate and inform, but at their core is image-making—a process closer to the marketing of products than to public debate and education.

This kind of political image-making is nothing new, however; it is certainly not unique to the age of mass media. In 1840, the Whigs won a presidential campaign by successfully portraying William Henry Harrison as a man of the people and a successful general. In a campaign legendary for its hoopla and lack of content, the Whigs promised "Tippecanoe and Tyler Too," referring to the Battle of Tippecanoe, an insignificant skirmish with the Indians in 1811, and vice-presidential candidate John Tyler. Other candidates also cultivated specific images, from Teddy Roosevelt the "rough-rider" to Abe Lincoln the honest "rail-splitter." In each of these cases, as in modern media campaigns, the key issue is to what degree pure image-making takes over from a more reasoned and thoughtful assessment of the candidate's character and stands on the issues.

The first presidential candidate to hire an advertising agency was Dwight D. Eisenhower in 1952. His Democratic opponent, Adlai Stevenson, considered advertising beneath the dignity of the political process. Since that time, few politicians competing for major electoral offices have done without media advertising strategies.

In television advertising, the most money is spent on **spot ads,** which usually run thirty seconds or less. The vast majority of spots are candidate-oriented: They ask the electorate to judge the candidate as a person, not as the representative of a party or the champion of a political philosophy. When spots do address political issues, they generally do so in a vague way, only loosely connecting the candidate to a particular position. In 75 percent of all spot ads there is no mention of a political party. Only 20 percent contain enough specific information about a candidate's position on an issue to allow the audience to draw inferences about the candidate's future behavior (see **Table 8–4.**) As for the format and effectiveness of such political spots, the following guidelines are generally accepted by experts in the field[18]:

Commercials can help to make a candidate known—to enhance name recognition.

Commercials can polish a candidate's image considerably, shifting voter perceptions even of a highly visible incumbent.

TABLE 8–4
Content of 156 Televised Political Ads

Partisanship	
Overt	9.6%
Marginal	15.4
Nonpartisan	71.2
Bipartisan, cross-partisan	3.8
	100.0

Issue position	
Specific	19.9%
Vague	37.8
Salience only	19.2
None	42.3
	119.2*

Candidate qualities	
Yes	47.4%
No	52.6
	100.0

Groups	
Yes	39.7%
No	60.3
	100.0

*This category sums to more than 100 percent because more than one type of policy appeal may appear in each ad.

SOURCE: Adapted from Richard A. Joslyn, "The Content of Political Spot Ads," *Journalism Quarterly* 57 (Spring 1980):95. Reprinted by permission. Ads were chosen from a variety of campaign situations over a number of years. The sample is not representative, but the data are suggestive.

An unsuccessful 1988 senatorial candidate poses with one of his TV spots (aimed at incumbent Senator Pat Moynihan). Political commercials usually present either a positive image of the candidate or a negative picture of the opponent, as in this case. Thirty-second spots were never designed to convey specific positions or to probe complex questions. Still, we ought to demand more of political advertising; after all, *we managed to say something in this brief space.* (*Neal Boenzi/New York Times Pictures*)

It is best to pretest ads before selected audiences, to weed out those that do not produce the intended effect.

Negative ads run the risk that voters and the press might label a candidate—or the campaign—as unfair.

Ads cannot blot out reality: They cannot make defeat look like victory, or entirely alter the public's perception of a candidate's character.

What effect do political ads have on citizen awareness? They can alter, to a modest degree, how the audience views a candidate's character and positions on particular issues, and they can sharpen perceived differences between candidates on the issues. Recent research indicates that political ads may contain more issue content than TV news coverage. This may not mean much, however, since TV news, as we will see, frequently ignores issues. Moreover, issues are always presented with a partisan flavor in political ads. A thirty-second spot accusing one's opponent of favoring "baby murder" (a euphemism for abortion) ostensibly deals with an issue, but it does little to advance our political understanding. The real danger of political advertising, then, is that it may befuddle or misinform more often than it enlightens the electorate.

Televised Presidential Debates

Presidential debates are not required by law. In fact, they have been the exception, rather than the rule, since 1960, when Vice-President Richard Nixon surprised observers by giving his challenger, John Kennedy, the chance to appear with him on national television on an equal footing. Kennedy took advantage of the opportunity by demonstrating a mental quickness and command of facts that Nixon could not match, especially in the first of their debates. And because harsh TV lighting made Kennedy look fresh and Nixon haggard, millions of television viewers came away with a more favorable impression of the younger challenger. Analysts generally agree that the debates gave Kennedy a crucial boost toward victory in the election.

Thereafter, front-runners in presidential campaigns were understandably reluctant to give their opponents a chance to shine on national television. The next series of TV debates did not take place until 1976, when challenger Jimmy Carter faced President Gerald Ford. Ford was not the traditional incumbent, having been appointed to the office of president rather than winning it on his own. By general agreement, the challenger

The first presidential "debate" in 1988: George Bush and Michael Dukakis trade canned jabs and flat jokes. Neither candidate made a serious error in their first appearance, and they cannot be held responsible for the disappointing show that events like this have become. Campaigns today demand extravagant claims tied down by few specifics, and the '88 campaign expressed that logic. *(AP/Wide World Photos)*

(Carter) again came away with the prize, although by only a slim margin. Through the debates, Carter was able to establish himself as a legitimate leader, holding his own with the president.

In 1980 the presidential debates were complicated by the presence of a third-party candidate, John Anderson. Carter, the incumbent, refused to debate with both Anderson and Republican candidate Ronald Reagan, on the grounds that he would be facing two Republicans (both had run in the Republican primaries). While this stand may have been based on genuine conviction, it seems more likely that Carter calculated that such a three-cornered debate could only enhance the status of the challengers, as previous debates had done. Reagan, however, did agree to debate Anderson, and that debate helped propel Reagan's candidacy. As election day neared, a one-shot debate between Reagan and Carter was finally arranged. Neither camp was truly anxious to hold the debate at that point, but both were ensnared by previous statements they had made claiming their willingness to debate. Carter was judged to be the loser by a decisive margin.

In 1984, President Reagan, despite holding a wide lead in the polls, agreed to confront challenger Walter Mondale in two debates. The first debate was a near-disaster for the president, who

was off his usual form and gave the impression of being confused and slow-thinking. As a result, many viewers felt that Reagan's age was starting to show. Reagan improved considerably in the second debate, seeming more confident, optimistic, and relaxed. When Mondale was unable to score another clear victory in the second debate, there was a sense that the election, then two weeks away, had been decided.

In 1988, there were no presidential *debates;* instead, there were three "debates." (The quotation marks were used almost universally by commentators, academics, and nonprofessional observers of the political process, in recognition that the campaign-controlled media appearances of the candidates were not genuine debates.) Less lively even than ordinary press conferences, the three "debates" did little to clarify issue positions or even to provide viewers much sense of the candidates as people. Overprepared, and wanting above all to avoid a big mistake, the candidates shared ninety minutes of pitching short bits of their campaign stump speeches, always with an eye out for an opportunity to unleash a "devastating" one-liner that might dominate subsequent news accounts. There were no great gaffes or stirring successes for any candidate. As far as press coverage goes, the single most memorable moment in the

The Lincoln-Douglas Debates

Perhaps the most impressive political debates in American history were held during the 1858 Illinois senatorial campaign. The debates pitted one of the nation's most prominent politicians, Stephen A. Douglas, against a rising Illinois Republican who had served two years in the House of Representatives and had two years earlier unsuccessfully sought the Republican vice-presidential nomination—Abraham Lincoln.

By general agreement, conditions at the start of the campaign favored Douglas, by far the better-known candidate. Douglas's plan was to solidify his support in Illinois as his base for a run for the presidency in 1860. In an effort to offset Douglas's well-established reputation, Lincoln challenged him to a series of debates. Douglas reluctantly accepted. Seven three-hour debates were held. In each, the first speaker opened with a one-hour presentation, the other was allowed ninety minutes to reply, and the first had the final thirty minutes.

The debates attracted considerable attention. Large audiences assembled, coming by train and wagon. Newspapers across the country covered the debates, sometimes publishing entire speeches. The contrast between the two candidates was striking: Douglas, less than five feet tall, a shrewd and ingenious debater; Lincoln, tall and awkward, master of the clear moral statement.

The core question of the debates was slavery, a matter that had almost reached a boiling point in the United States.

Douglas had established a reputation as a pragmatist on the issue, maintaining that the question should be resolved by popular sovereignty, with each state deciding whether to be slave or free. He seemed to accept unquestioningly the conviction of most whites that blacks were inherently inferior and accused Lincoln of being a radical for advocating racial equality. In response, Lincoln admitted there was "A physical difference between the white and black races. . . . " but nonetheless favored the containment of slavery within its existing borders and looked toward its gradual extinction. He accused Douglas of being indifferent to the moral dimensions of slavery. "That is the issue which will continue in this country when these poor tongues of Judge Douglas and myself shall be silent. It is the eternal struggle between these two principles—right and wrong—throughout the world."

Douglas spent $80,000 on the campaign, Lincoln $1,000. In the popular vote to elect the state legislature Lincoln's forces won, 126,084 to 121,940. But because Douglas's backers controlled more seats, Lincoln failed to be elected to the Senate. The larger moral and political victory belonged to Lincoln, however, who had established himself as a future national leader able to frame the debate on slavery during the coming crisis.

SOURCES: A. L. Boulton, ed., *The Lincoln and Douglas Debates* (New York: Henry Holt, 1905); Don E. Fehrenbacher, *Prelude to Greatness* (Palo Alto, Calif.: Stanford University Press, 1962); Harry V. Jaffa, *Crisis of the House Divided* (Garden City, N.Y.: Doubleday, 1959).

three events came when Lloyd Bentsen looked Dan Quayle in the eye to tell him, "Senator, you're no Jack Kennedy." This line well captures the flavor and tone of the 1988 "debates." Fully canned, skillfully delivered, and intended to play on questions about Quayle's competence, Bentsen's line addressed no policy, made no commitment, and provided new information to no one. *Real* debates

are something else, but they may be incompatible with mass-produced, packaged campaigns we now witness.

Is there a future for presidential debates? On the positive side, they attract huge audiences, stimulate interest in the election, and give voters a chance to see the candidates side by side. Presidential debates also help citizens learn more about the policy positions of the candidates, especially since many of the most *un*informed citizens are attracted to the debates. As two political observers noted in reference to the 1976 debates, "Watching the debates increased the level of manifest information that all citizens had . . . those individuals who watched the debaters exhibited a heightened political awareness at exactly the time when political information is crucial."[19]

On the negative side, debates tend to emphasize the superficial; rarely do debates offer an indepth discussion of issues. One political scientist characterizes debates as "the political version of the Indianapolis Speedway. What we're all there for . . . is to see somebody crack up in flames."[20] All too often, gaffes, hesitations, sweat on the upper lip, trivial errors, and the like overshadow the crucial discussion of issues and positions. The media usually focus more on the "winner" in each debate, than on what was said or not said.

As currently organized, then, TV debates leave much to be desired. Improvements that have been suggested include having the candidates question each other, increasing the number of debates (a strategy adopted in the 1988 presidential primary campaigns with limited success), or combining these and other alternatives. Debates *can* be meaningful and informative. The more loosely organized debates among the Democratic Party primary candidates in 1984 and both parties' candidates in 1988, for example, proved to be less tense, more exploratory, and far more interesting than the presidential ones have been.

Media and "Horse Races"

Jimmy Carter made a telling remark in his 1976 campaign for president: "The only presidents I know who emphasized the issues were Presidents Dewey, Goldwater, and McGovern." Of course, none of these men won election, perhaps because they *were* more concerned with issues than image. The nature of the mass media works against issue-oriented candidates: It takes much time (in broadcasting) or space (in the print media) to explore issues, and time and space are at a premium in the media. Hence the disproportionate emphasis in

the media on a candidate's personality, campaign strategy, and relative standing against rivals. These are features of the political "horse race"—an inherently more colorful and exciting media subject than discussion of the issues. In a study conducted in 1975 and 1976, Thomas Patterson found that network news programs devoted 24 percent of their presidential campaign coverage to issue-related matters and 62 percent to the "horse race."[21] Studies of the 1984 and 1988 nominating process produced similar findings. Newspaper and television coverage of campaigns do not differ significantly in this respect.

Then, too, the candidates themselves often play down issues. In part, this may be due to the centrist thrust of U.S. politics, which encourages the blurring of differences. Some candidates, calculating that an emphasis on issues will cost them votes, turn to personality factors and campaign hoopla to divert the public's attention. Others become personality candidates reluctantly, realizing that the media do not deal well with issues and that personality and television seem made for each other. Of course, issues are not entirely neglected, but in the extraordinarily lengthy U.S. presidential campaigns, they are usually eclipsed by other matters.

The public's perception of the candidates' positions on the issues apparently corresponds to how much emphasis the candidates themselves place on issues during the campaign process.[22] Significantly, those exposed to network news do not learn any more about candidates' positions on issues than do those who do not watch the news. Citizens who read newspapers, however, are somewhat better informed on issues than are nonreaders. Daily television, accordingly, seems to do little to inform the electorate about the positions of candidates.[23] On occasion, television can make a very powerful contribution to general public awareness through coverage of important events such as the nominating conventions.

Beyond the hoopla and the horse race, beyond the commentaries and the daily coverage, concerned citizens must read between the lines and listen for the underlying nuances to fathom the candidates' positions on issues, determine which candidate's approach to governing comes closest to their own, and assess whether the candidates can offer the type of leadership the country needs. The news media play a pivotal role in helping citizens reach these conclusions, yet all too often, news professionals find the campaign glitz—and higher ratings—much more appealing than pithy analyses that elucidate important differences between candidates' approaches, views, and positions on specific issues. The American news media have an obligation to inform the electorate about more than the horse race. On that score, however, they only win mixed ratings.

Conclusions

In many ways, U.S. politics makes for an exciting spectator sport. Candidates appear and disappear; contests drag on for months, even years; great amounts of cash are raised and spent; television keeps an eye on the progress of the "horse race." But what do citizens gain from the extraordinary spectacle of political campaigning and from the media coverage of political life? Certainly less than they could.

From a democratic perspective, political campaigning in the United States has several serious shortcomings. Money plays far too substantial a role in the electoral process—and will continue to do so in the absence of fundamental reforms. Also, much of the campaign process drains meaning out of elections rather than instilling in the electorate a clear sense of the issues involved. Compared with most other democratic nations, the American way of selecting and electing candidates is very open, very long, and very complicated.

The media could enhance the democratic process considerably by striving for greater depth, placing more of an emphasis on issues than on aspects of the "horse race," and seeking to educate rather than merely to entertain. If the media did a thorough job of fact-gathering and presented stories dramatically enough, presidential candidates would be forced to explain and defend their views on issues of concern to the electorate. And the public itself has an obligation to learn more about political life, to understand issues more clearly,

and to demand more of both the media and the campaign process.

Most citizens have a sufficiently good idea of what is happening in political life to make reasoned retrospective judgments on an administration and its policies. On the other hand, public ignorance abounds, much of it cultivated by candidates and not dispelled by the media. On balance, however, we can assert that while our democratic electoral processes—and the media's role in campaigns—are less than satisfactory, they are not disastrously flawed.

SUPPLEMENT: A CONSUMING INTEREST IN THE NEWS

Most of us are entirely dependent on professional news-gathering agencies for our information about important events. The conventional wisdom is that Americans get most of their news from television, as opposed to newspapers, magazines, radio, and other sources. Surveys indicate that people *think* they get most of their information from TV. But there is good reason to doubt the accuracy of this belief. Only a small proportion of American families watch the TV evening news as much as four or five times a week. Yet over one-third of adults read news magazines—*Time, Newsweek,* or *U.S. News and World Report*—and even more read daily newspapers regularly. In fact, most Americans get their political information from a variety of sources. Think about your own patterns of "information gathering." You probably depend on print sources (newspapers and magazines) as well as broadcast sources (radio and TV). News also may come to you third-hand, as told to you by someone who has gotten it from one of these sources.

An important part of keeping up with the world is the ability to gather news critically—deciding for yourself, to the extent possible, what the news is and what it means. The following guidelines may help you think about that process and increase your own skills as a consumer of news.

1. *Remember that news gathering is an active process that necessarily involves political choices.*

Choices need to be made by even the largest news organizations—about *where* to send reporters to look for news, about *what* news, of all that is gathered, to include in print or to broadcast, and about *how* to present the news that is finally chosen for presentation. All these choices can have an impact on the news as it appears. One task of a critical consumer is to be aware of the choices that have been made by news organizations. It's a mistake to think of your newspaper or news broadcast simply as the concentrated output of a neutral funnel aimed at the world at large. In your own consumption of news from the media, try to imagine what choices have shaped the news that reaches you. Why is one story on the front page and another on page twenty-six? What kinds of stories appear most frequently? Global issues? Local stories? Celebrity trivia?

2. *Don't depend exclusively on a single news medium.*

No matter how good a professional news-gathering agency is, it can't do everything. Despite a climate of press freedom in the United States, the available sources of news often are limited for most people. At the turn of the century most cities were served by competing daily newspapers. By the 1980s, however, the vast majority of cities served by a daily newspaper had no competing daily to offer an alternative to readers. Another limitation has been the development of "pack journalism," in which competing news organizations tend to emphasize the same stories in the same fashions (which explains the instances of nearly identical cover stories on *Time* and *Newsweek*). Nevertheless, you are not totally without options. Gather your news from a variety of media, relying on general sources (most newspapers, news magazines, and broadcast news) and specialized sources in areas of particular concern. Vary your consumption patterns. Try different networks, newspapers, and news magazines. Compare accounts of the same events. Don't simply become a receptacle for all (but only) the news that happens to come your way. Evaluate the kind and quality of news you're getting, then take steps to improve your news supply.

3. *Think about the sources of news and the motives of newsmakers.*

A large proportion of the news that gets reported comes from "official" sources, that is to say, from some part of the government itself. Often, highly visible persons will provide news with the stipulation that they not be identified as the source, resulting in news from "a high State Department official" or a "well-placed member of the administration." A "leak"—an unofficial report of government activity—may represent some disagreement within the government; a "trial balloon" may be a way for the government to try out a new idea or policy that can be disclaimed later if it proves to be un-

popular. Newsmakers have their own political agendas and will use the news to advance them. Try to figure out why the newsmaker wanted to make that event or bit of information into news.

4. *Read more than the headlines.*

Headlines are meant to capture your attention and are designed to fit into a very small space. Headlines are often composed by someone other than the person writing the story. The result is that headlines can sometimes be misleading, not by design, but by circumstance. The same event may appear quite different to two different observers. Compare the following headlines:

On August 29, 1987:

> **Crime Down in Denver** (*The Denver Post*)
>
> **Number of Serious Crimes Up This Month in Denver** (*Rocky Mountain News*)

On September 2, 1987:

> **Street Protests Banned in Moscow** (*San Francisco Chronicle*)
>
> **Moscow Council OKs Street Demonstrations** (*Sacramento Bee*)

Headlines provide a quick impression, but a good news story should give you enough information to make sound judgments. Read the whole story. Better yet, compare two good news stories from different sources, and you'll be closer to being able to make your own judgments.

5. *A picture can reorient a thousand words.*

Don't look only at pictures in print media or television. Compare the visual presentation to the written or verbal one. This rule is particularly important for television news, which attempts to provide a visual component to every news story, even if the news has no strong visual aspect. When an actual shot is unavailable, news organizations will sometimes use "file footage" or "file photos," or even create "artist's renderings," to fill in the visual side of a story. But wherever the picture comes from, it will have an impact on the way you interpret the words, whether the news is about the performance of the economy or the progress of arms talks or corruption in government. Be aware of the power of pictures, and actively compare them with the verbal message.

About media bias

Most news organizations attempt a nonpartisan, politically balanced presentation of the news, in the spirit of objectivity that has been a strong tradition in most segments of American journalism. The question of how biased the media are is a difficult one to answer. Charges that reporters in the establishment press and the broadcast media are generally liberal in outlook have been around a long time. Charges that publishers, on the other hand, are conservative have been around just as long. Franklin D. Roosevelt would frequently express his frustration at what he perceived to be conservative opposition to the New Deal by referring in conversations with reporters to "what you fellows are told to write" against the administration. A few years ago, conservative Senator Jesse Helms announced a plan—ultimately unsuccessful—to *buy* CBS in order to change it from its errant, liberal ways. In the early 1970s, the Nixon administration made much hay with attacks on its opponents in the "liberal press." The liberal image of the press was associated with its alleged identification with social causes. The assumption that reporters didn't favor people with money was based on an assumption that reporters didn't have any themselves. News reporters favored the underdogs, it was assumed, because their own status was not much higher. Of course, on the other side, the left has for a long time charged newspaper owners with an antileftist bias that reflects their own "secure" financial status.

Generalizations about such diverse groups as news people and news organizations have never been sound. Some of the assumptions which underlie those generalizations may have changed since midcentury, anyway, in a process that one participant calls the "greening" of the news business.* Many news organizations are now highly profitable businesses, and a substantial number of individuals in the news media—not just the superstars—have incomes among the top 5 percent in the country. So the reasons for reporters' identification with the poor underdog may be disappearing. As more and more media organizations become divisions of corporate conglomerates, the bias of the media may be simply to play it safe in order to keep earnings up.

The best reaction to the possibility of media bias is simply to become a critical consumer. Go ahead: Be skeptical! Using the guidelines above, and others of your own, judge for yourself what the implicit political leanings of your news sources are. You'll probably discover that news reporters, editorial-page writers, and publishers are nearly as varied as the American people. In the process, you'll also become a much better-informed participant in our democracy.

GLOSSARY TERMS

primary election

incumbent

closed primary

open primary

blanket primary

cross-over primary voting

interelection stage

electoral college

political action committees

Freedom of Information Act

Pentagon Papers

Fairness Doctrine

spot ads

NOTES

[1]Richard Joslyn, *Mass Media and Elections* (Reading, Mass.: Addison-Wesley, 1984), pp. 273–296.

[2]See, for example, Benjamin I. Page, *Choices and Echoes in Presidential Elections* (Chicago: University of Chicago Press, 1978), pp. 223–227.

[3]L. Sandy Maisel, *Parties and Elections in the United States* (New York: Random House, 1987), p. 235.

[4]Randall Rothenberg, "The Boom in Political Consulting," *New York Times*, May 24, 1987, Section 3, p. 1.

[5]Thomas B. Edsall, "GOP's Cash Advantage Failed to Assure Victory in Close Senate Contests," quoted in Frank J. Sorauf, *Money in American Elections* (Glenview, Ill.: Scott, Foresman, 1988), p. 300.

[6]Sorauf, *op. cit.*, p. 301.

[7]Quoted in Ruth K. Scott and Ronald Hrebenar, *Parties in Crisis* (New York: Wiley, 1979), p. 9.

[8]Maisel, *op. cit.*, p. 261.

[9]On the constitutional dimensions of campaign financing reforms, see Albert Cover, "The Constitutionality of Campaign Expenditure Ceilings," *Public Studies Journal* 2 (Summer 1974): 267–273.

---

*Richard Harwood, "Money and Journalism," *The Washington Post National Weekly Edition*, May 23–28, 1988, p. 28.

[10]*New York Times*, Mar. 19, 1985, p. 1.

[11]*Ibid.*

[12]*New York Times*, Jan. 6, 1985, p. 13.

[13]Senator Thomas Eagleton, as quoted in *New York Times*, Feb. 3, 1983, p. B6.

[14]Doris A. Graber, *Mass Media and American Politics* (Washington, D.C.: Congressional Quarterly Press, 1984), chap. 1; and Joslyn, *op. cit.*, chap. 1.

[15]Joslyn, *op. cit.*, Introduction.

[16]David L. Paletz and Robert M. Entman, *Media, Power, Politics* (New York: Free Press, 1981), pp. 32–33.

[17]*Congressional Quarterly Weekly Report*, Apr. 5, 1968, as quoted in Richard Joslyn, *Mass Media*, p. 33. Reprinted by permission of Congressional Quarterly, Inc.

[18]Edwin Diamond and Stephen Bates, "The Political Pitch," *Psychology Today*, Nov. 1984, pp. 22–32.

[19]Arthur H. Miller and Michael MacKuen, "Learning About the Candidates: The 1976 Presidential Debates," *Public Opinion Quarterly* 43 (Fall 1979): 344.

[20]Nelson Polsby, as quoted in *Time*, Oct. 29, 1984, p. 31.

[21]As reported in the *Washington Post*, Dec. 5, 1976.

[22]Joslyn, *op. cit.*, chap. 6.

[23]*Ibid.*, pp. 178–183.

SELECTED READINGS

Theodore H. White started a tradition of observer-behind-the-scenes accounts of **presidential election campaigns** with his book, *The Making of the President, 1960*. That book, and each of the subsequent books White wrote covering elections through 1980, provides fast-paced, engaging reading about the American national election process and the importance of personalities in it. Every election now spawns a set of election accounts on the White model, and 1988 should be no exception. These accounts are usually heavily journalistic in approach and, although they provide a good first introduction to the problems of elections, they can be supplemented by the more academically oriented items that follow:

POLITICAL CAMPAIGNS

For an interesting discussion of **campaign styles and strategies**, see E. N. Goldenberg and M. W. Traugott, *Campaigning for Congress* (Washington, D.C.: Congres-

sional Quarterly Press, 1984). Two stimulating treatments of U.S. presidential campaigns are Thomas Ferguson and Joel Rogers, *The Hidden Election: Politics and Economics in the 1980 Presidential Election* (New York: Pantheon, 1982); and Lewis Chester et al., *An American Melodrama: The Presidential Campaign of 1968* (New York: Viking, 1969).

Several textbook-style treatments of **American political campaigns** are available, including L. Sandy Maisel, *Parties and Elections in America* (New York: Random House, 1987); Stephen J. Wayne, *The Road to the White House*, 3rd ed. (New York: St. Martin's, 1988); Stephen Hess, *The Presidential Campaign*, 3rd ed. (Washington, D.C.: Brookings, 1988); and Stephen Salmore, *Candidates, Parties and Campaigns* (Washington, D.C.: Congressional Quarterly Press, 1988). A. James Reichley, *Elections American Style* (Washington D.C.: Brookings, 1987), provides a good collection of short essays on this subject.

CAMPAIGN FINANCING

For current information on **campaign costs**, consult Herbert E. Alexander, *Financing Politics, Money, Elections and Political Reform*, 3rd ed. (Washington, D.C.: Congressional Quarterly Press, 1984). See also George Thayer, *Who Shakes the Money Tree?* (New York: Simon and Schuster, 1973); Robert Agranoff, "The New Style of Campaigning: The Decline of Party and the Rise of Candidate Centered Technology," in Robert Agranoff, ed., *The New Style in Election Campaigns* (Boston: Holbrook, 1972), pp. 31–33, and Frank J. Sorauf, *Money in American Elections* (Glenview Ill.: Scott, Foresman & Co., 1988).

THE ROLE OF THE MEDIA

A critical account of the development of **political advertising** can be found in Malcolm MacDougall, "The Barkers of Snake Oil Politics," *Politics Today*, January-February 1980, p. 35. See also Joe McGinness, *The Selling of the President, 1968* (New York: Trident, 1969). More general treatments are Robert Agranoff's *The Management of Election Campaigns* (Boston: Holbrook, 1976); and Doris A. Graber, *Mass Media and American Politics*, 2nd ed. (Washington, D.C.: Congressional Quarterly Press, 1984). The **mindset of consultants** is explored in David Lee Rosenbloom, *The Election Mess: Professional Campaign Managers and American Democracy* (New York: Quadrangle, 1973).

Discussions of **debates** can be found in Arthur H. Miller and Michael MacKuen, "Informing the Electorate: A National Study," in Sidney Kraus, ed., *The Great Debates:*

Background, Perspectives, Effect (Bloomington, Ind.: Indiana University Press, 1979), pp. 209–270; and Austin Ranney, ed., *The Past and Future of Presidential Debates* (Washington, D.C.: American Enterprise Institute, 1979).

For general treatments of the **influence of media** see: David Paletz and Robert Entman, *Media, Power, Politics* (New York: Free Press, 1982); Todd Gitlin, *The Whole World Is Watching: Mass Media in the Making and Unmaking of the New Left* (Berkeley, Calif.: University of California Press, 1980); David Halberstam, *The Powers That Be* (New York: Knopf, 1979); Edward Epstein, *News from Nowhere: Television and the News* (New York: Random House, 1974); Doris A. Graber, *Processing the News*, 2nd ed. (New York: Longman, 1988); Herbert Gans, *Deciding What's News: A Study of CBS Evening News, NBC Nightly News, Newsweek and Time* (New York: Random House, 1980); M. B. MacKuen and S. L. Coombs, *More Than News: Media Power in Public Affairs* (Beverly Hills, Calif.: Sage, 1981), and W. Lance Bennett, *News: The Politics of Illusion*, 2nd ed. (New York: Longman, 1988).

9

INTEREST-GROUP POLITICS

Democracy to the Highest Bidder?

CHAPTER OUTLINE

Interest-Group Dynamics
Major Interest Groups
How Lobbying Works
Regulation and the Public Interest

David Jennings/New York Times Pictures

In December 1987, Michael Deaver was found guilty of perjury. Deaver, a former top White House aide, had been charged with lying to a grand jury and to a House investigating subcommittee looking into his lobbying activities. Deaver claimed he was innocent, citing alcoholism as the reason he couldn't recall specific events. Because he was a close friend of President Ronald Reagan and had been deputy chief of staff in the Reagan White House until 1985, Deaver's trial drew considerable attention. The presidential appointments secretary and the mastermind behind the president's brilliant media strategies, he had the choicest White House office, with a door opening directly into the Oval Office.[1]

In 1985, complaining of "burnout," Deaver left the White House and started a consulting firm. With his close connections to the White House, he had little trouble attracting important clients; soon he had accounts paying millions of dollars. Deaver wasted no time approaching his government contacts on his clients' behalf. For TWA, he made one phone call to then–Transportation Secretary Elizabeth Dole. The call failed to gain the desired result, but it cost TWA $250,000. The Canadian government hired Deaver specifically to influence—and even frame—the U.S. debate on acid rain, a key concern north of the border. Under oath, the former White House aide said he could not recall or simply denied twenty lobbying contacts with the White House on behalf of the government of South Korea, Philip Morris, Inc., Boeing, Rockwell International, and others.

Deaver was not alone. Lyn Nofziger, the former White House political director, was convicted of violating a law that prohibits senior government officials from lobbying their former colleagues for at least a year after leaving office. Charges and suspicions swirled around other Reagan administration officials as well. Most dramatic were the allegations directed at Attorney General Edwin Meese 3d in early 1988, alleging that he, too, wielded influence—while in office—on behalf of various private interests. Meese denied the charges and at first refused to resign, despite mounting pressure from Congress and public interest organizations. (A special prosecutor later issued a report that raised questions about Meese's ethical standards but did not recommend criminal prosecution. Meese resigned in August 1988.)

If we turn back the clock a few years to the late 1970s and early 1980s, we find that similar charges were raging around members of Congress. In the infamous Abscam cases, FBI agents, posing as representatives of wealthy Arabs, sought—and sometimes received—favors from congressional representatives in return for bribes. Although the FBI's methods were widely criticized, the Abscam operation reinforced a commonly held image of how politics works. To many Americans, this series of influence-peddling scandals meant that political life at the highest levels was riddled with corruption; powerful groups purchased influence and traded on the contacts of highly placed officials to win favored treatment.

Does corruption underlie all efforts to organize and seek political influence? If so, we are in deep trouble, because individuals and groups of various stripes work to influence the political process at all levels. Let us now turn to two different examples of interest-group lobbying.

Over decades of legal struggle, lawyers for the National Association for the Advancement of Colored People (NAACP) argued for equal treatment under the law for black Americans. The NAACP maintained that the segregated conditions imposed on blacks in many states denied them the equal protection of the laws. Finally, in the landmark *Brown* v. *Board of Education* school desegregation case of 1954, NAACP lawyers achieved what they had sought—a clear reversal of the 1896 Supreme Court ruling that separate facilities could be equal. As slowly as litigation proceeded in the federal courts, it had been American blacks' most powerful tool to force change in the status quo. Gradually the system of segregation crumbled under the legal pressure brought to bear by the NAACP representing black interests.

Let us consider another case. Recently, local landlords in a small American city, seeing an opportunity to make a substantial profit, sought permission from the town board to convert their apartment complexes into condominiums—a move that has become increasingly common in major cities. In this case, tenants in the apartment complexes organized and protested to the board that they needed the apartments, that they could not afford to buy condominiums, and that the owners were interested only in a quick profit, not in the long-term good of the community. The landlords argued that the property was theirs and that condominiums were an entirely proper use for the apartments. Keeping up the pressure, the tenants organized neighborhood protests, continually appeared at board meetings, and met informally with board members. Eventually, the board rejected the owners' request.

If we surveyed the American political process overall, we would find a vast proliferation of groups seeking to influence politics in various ways. As in any democratic nation, these range from highly organized and well-financed groups to various ad hoc coalitions that spring up in response to particular problems and later disappear.

We can draw a number of conclusions from these cases, including the following:

> Influence-seeking is an everyday part of our political process.

Michael Deaver and wife arrive at court to hear him sentenced for perjury: three years' suspended sentence and probation; a fine of $100,000; and 1,500 hours of community service. His attorneys appealed the conviction. *(AP/Wide World Photos)*

Interest groups come in all shapes and sizes, and their interests are as varied as their makeup.

Influence can be exercised at many political access points in many different ways, ranging from lawsuits and campaign contributions to personal conversations.

There are winners and losers in these battles, and while the public interest may actually be at stake, oftentimes the vast majority of the public knows little about how these battles are either fought or resolved.

The system of influence-seeking is open to corruption, but it has other problems as well.

These fairly straightforward observations lead to a series of more difficult questions. In interest-group lobbying, whose interests are represented most effectively? Which groups get the lion's share of the benefits that the political process has to offer, and why? How do these groups make themselves felt in the political process? Is this complicated system of pressure-group politics democratic? fair? reasonable? We will now take up these questions as we explore (1) the dynamics of interest groups; (2) the major interest groups; (3) how lobbying works; and (4) regulation, representation, and the public interest.

Interest-Group Dynamics

Democratic politics lends itself naturally to group activity. People in all democratic societies tend to coalesce around shared interests and ideas. Concerns about wage scales or job security might lead a person to join a union or other work-related association. The same person might also contribute to an environmental group, because of worries about pollution of a nearby recreational lake. This citizen might also take an interest in better town recreational facilities, and hence attend town meetings or sign petitions. Finally, our hypothetical American might join a synagogue or church, and thereby affirm his or her religious identity—representing a *potential* interest that might be activated under certain circumstances. In U.S. society, such interests spring naturally from the country's economic, religious, regional, ethnic, and racial diversity.

Traditionally, the United States has been characterized as a nation of joiners. Foreigners often marvel at this aspect of American life. In the early 1800s, Alexis de Tocqueville remarked:

> The Americans make associations to give entertainments, to found seminaries, to build inns, to construct churches, to diffuse books, to send missionaries to the antipodes; in this manner they found hospitals, prisons and schools. If it is proposed to inculcate some truth or to foster some feeling by the encouragement of a great example, they form a society. Wherever at the head of some new undertaking you see the government in France, or a man of rank in England, in the United States you will be sure to find an association.[2]

This observation remains pertinent today. According to public opinion polls, about 40 percent of Americans are active in at least one organization, and 40 percent of those are affiliated with more than one group. Group membership is closely related to social class and education, however. Better-educated, middle-class people are much more likely to be joiners, which means their views usually are better represented in the political process.[3]

Organizations that direct their efforts toward political influence are called **interest groups.** While this term has fewer negative connotations than *pressure group,* a term popular in the past, interest groups can effectively pressure legislators, bureaucrats, and public officials. We now examine (1) the various functions of interest groups and (2) problems for democracy inherent in interest-group politics.

Some interest groups arise spontaneously to deal with specific situations. They often have little organization and do not continue in existence for long. Here is a rally of New York City tenants, whose interests are clear. *(Jim Anderson/Black Star)*

Functions of Interest Groups

Interest groups coalesce for various reasons. Some groups serve mainly *symbolic* functions: Ethnic, religious, or racial associations, for example, generally seek to bolster their members' sense of group identity. Such groups may also seek to affirm the symbolic significance of their members' identity in relation to the rest of society. In lobbying to make the Reverend Martin Luther King, Jr.'s, birthday a national holiday, black groups were making such a symbolic statement.

Economic functions naturally loom large in the aims of many interest groups. Often, interest groups promote the economic well-being of whole classes of people or sets of institutions, such as doctors or hospitals. Trade unions and business associations work almost exclusively to further the economic interests of their members.

Groups may also pursue a whole range of noneconomic policy goals. Such goals range from building a monument to Vietnam War dead or ending the use of the stars-and-bars Confederate flag to the preservation of historic sites. Some groups focus on more *ideological* concerns. This category includes, among others, People for the

American Way (liberal causes), Americans for Constitutional Action (conservative causes), and Common Cause (the cause of honest, open government). Because particular issues and overall ideologies tend to blend together, groups seeking specific economic benefits and those pursuing ideological goals often find themselves working toward common ends.

Finally, groups may serve *informational* functions, disseminating information on matters of interest to members. The environmental group Friends of the Earth, for example, publishes a magazine that keeps members up-to-date on environmental issues and related public policy questions.

Problems with Interest Groups

While interest groups certainly deserve a place in the political arena, the proliferation of such groups has created serious problems in democratic life. As far back as the Constitutional Convention, James Madison warned of the deleterious effects of "factions" on the political process; in his eyes, factions represented potentially dangerous social elements that by nature would oppose the public interest. In Madison's view, the only way to counteract the dangers of faction, was to pit factions against one another, so that no majority faction could tyrannize the larger society. This image of counterbalancing factions reflects a commonly held view of the U.S. political process: Because each group is counterbalanced by other groups, no one interest group possesses enough power to enforce its views on a wide range of issues.

It would be comforting to think that the network of interest groups is so well balanced that the "public interest" (however that is defined) is ultimately served. Unfortunately, this is often not the case. The system is heavily biased in favor of those who have the resources that matter most— money, organizational clout, and political and social legitimacy—skewing power disproportionately. The effectiveness of interest groups, in other words, is not determined by the size of their memberships or the intellectual or social merit of their goals.

The interest-group system also fosters the de-

cidedly undemocratic notion that some are more equal than others: Throughout U.S. history many potential interests have lacked effective representation. When the U.S. Constitution was drafted, for example, women, blacks, and those with little property were shut out of the political process. Groups lacking effective representation must battle—often violently and at considerable cost—to break into the system of group politics. The barriers facing these groups can be daunting: They must overcome the psychological barrier of being ignored or scorned by the rest of society; they may also need to overcome legal hurdles, such as those that confronted blacks and women in their decades-long battles for equal rights; and new groups, especially, may lack the resources of more experienced and better-financed groups.

Ironically, causes with almost universal appeal—such as drives to promote clean air and safe consumer goods—are often the most difficult to organize. Some observers argue that broadly shared interests rarely capture the imagination of prospective supporters, and organizational success therefore eludes them. For potential members of groups dedicated to such causes, it may be hard to see how joining the group will make much of a difference; that is, the payoffs for joining an interest group dealing with diffuse public issues usually are exceeded by the costs of joining and acquiring information. Nonetheless, such groups do exist and often prosper, as demonstrated by government and environmental organizations.

Narrowly focused interest groups, in contrast, can count on staunch support because those directly affected by a specific public policy have a strong incentive to organize. Suppose, for example, that regulations allowing competition in the sale of eyeglasses were proposed. Consumers might benefit from such regulations, but most of them would have only a vague idea of how those regulations would affect them. Opticians, however, surely would organize to lobby *against* regulations that would, in effect, force them to lower prices. Here we see a chronic problem of interest-group politics: Widely shared interests that affect many people slightly are less likely to prompt an organized response than are narrowly shared interests that affect a few people more deeply.

A related problem stems from the subtlety of

most interest-group activity: The process of influence-seeking is often hidden from public scrutiny. Interest-group lobbying frequently resembles subtle osmosis much more than pressurized arm-twisting. Critics decry this cozy arrangement, charging that it circumvents the open, public debate so crucial to the exercise of democracy.

Major Interest Groups

In U.S. politics, several key interests exert a disproportionate measure of influence on decision making at all levels. We now examine how and why the following groups gained such prominence in the American political arena: (1) business; (2) labor; (3) the defense lobby; (4) public interest groups; and (5) single-issue groups.

Business

The interests of people in business cover a wide spectrum. An executive of a large corporation who comes to Washington to lobby for restrictions on Japanese imports has little in common with a local florist who needs a small business loan. Small businesses seek protection against larger rivals. Businesses in depressed areas lobby for govern-

ment aid, whereas those that prosper generally oppose such assistance. Import policies often spark business rivalry. Accordingly, the business community does not always speak with one voice, and splits within that community often lead to political conflict. In fact, several major pieces of business legislation, such as the Interstate Commerce Act and the Sherman Antitrust Act, originated in the efforts of smaller companies to protect themselves against larger competitors.

Nevertheless, a certain degree of unity does mark the business community. Generally, business interests oppose tax increases, support restrictions on the power of organized labor, press for cuts in government regulation of business, favor protection against foreign competition, and encourage government to create a favorable climate in which business and investment can grow.

Major business organizations include the Chamber of Commerce, with a membership of 200,000 businesses and individuals and 4,000 associations and a budget of $63 million in 1985; the National Association of Manufacturers (NAM), representing the interests of "big business"; and the Business Roundtable, which represents 190 large companies through the lobbying efforts of high-level business executives.

Specific industries are represented by a host of other groups, such as the Associated Milk Produc-

The connections between interest groups and legislators sometimes become quite relaxed—even silly and odd. Here Congressman Bill Emerson and Senator William Cohen model shoes made in their states. Legislators have to be concerned about local interests, or their constituents may take offense. (© *Art Stein/Photo Researchers*)

COMPARATIVE PERSPECTIVE

British Trade Unions

Organized labor plays a far more important political role in Great Britain than in the United States. In a sense, the British Labour Party is a creature of organized labor—the political voice of a long-active and still powerful social and economic institution. In the last decade, trade unions represented nearly 50 percent of the British working population—more than double the percentage of union membership found in the United States. The Labour Party outside Parliament is organized as a federation of trade unions and individual dues-paying members. The party is almost wholly dependent on trade unions for its routine income.

Trade union involvement with the Labour Party goes far beyond interest-group lobbying and American-style endorsements and campaign activity. Through the National Executive Committee of the Labour Party, trade unions shape party policy. At the annual NEC conference, each union commands a voting strength equal to its total number of members, who contribute part of their union dues to the party.

Most British trade unions are members of the Trades Union Congress (TUC) which represents the interests of member unions. During the ten-

ure of the 1974–1979 Labour governments, leading members of the TUC and the government kept in close contact through monthly meetings and regular private meetings at the prime minister's residence.

Until early 1979, the Labour Party's ability to get along with trade unions was its chief electoral advantage over the Conservatives. But in 1979, Labour lost that edge when it failed to prevent or mitigate the effects of a wave of industrial strikes. A more decisive blow to the power of trade unions occurred, however, in May 1979, with the election of a Conservative government headed by Prime Minister Margaret Thatcher. Her free-market economic policies and unyieldingly hard line against union pressure—demonstrated most dramatically in the long coal miners' strike of 1986—effectively reduced the power of trade unions as a voice in British economic policy making. Thatcher's overwhelming reelection in 1983 and 1987 further crippled the once-powerful role unions had played and led to a reexamination by the Labour Party of its fundamental relationship to the trade union movement.

ers, the National Cotton Council, and the American Meat Institute.

Because government programs affect so many businesses, business interests engage in many forms of influence-seeking. They attempt to shape public opinion through advertising. They lobby extensively in Washington, D.C., and the various state capitals (in fact, the political action committees representing the oil-and-gas lobby alone outspent the entire Democratic Party in 1980). They litigate to delay and defeat regulatory legislation. They seek the appointments to top administration positions of those favorable to business. They fund campaigns and support candidates. We will ex-

amine several of these strategies later in this chapter.

Labor

Most American workers do not belong to labor unions. At their peak, in the 1950s, unions claimed almost 25 percent of the work force. That figure has now declined to below 20 percent. American unions do wield political clout, but they are weaker than those in any other advanced industrial democratic nation.

For most of U.S. history, only a very small sector of the economy was organized in unions. Until the Great Depression and the pro-labor New Deal of the 1930s, only the skilled crafts, such as carpentry and other building trades, and railroad workers were organized to any significant extent. The Congress of Industrial Organizations, which organized industrial workers in auto, steel, and other major industries, spearheaded the rapid expansion of unionization in the 1930s. After a period of intense rivalry, the CIO and the much older American Federation of Labor merged in 1955 to form the AFL-CIO. Despite the importance of several large individual unions, the AFL-CIO remains labor's paramount organization and the source of most of its politically directed activity.

The AFL-CIO attempts to influence national politics on a whole array of domestic issues—social welfare, employment, job training, minimum wages, child labor, occupational health and safety, consumer protection, the tax code. Individual unions often lobby separately for their own agendas. Sometimes labor and business find themselves on the same side of an issue, as when both try to get government help to improve the competitive position of an industry.

Since the end of World War II, labor has also played a major role in shaping U.S. foreign policy. The AFL-CIO has frequently given aid to anticommunist organizations in other societies, sometimes with help from the Central Intelligence Agency. Many unions supported the Vietnam War, and in the 1972 presidential election found themselves at odds on this issue with the hierarchy of the Democratic Party, with which labor had long been affiliated.

Labor's overriding political strategy has been to work within the Democratic Party. Few unions overtly support Republican candidates, although both Richard Nixon and Ronald Reagan were endorsed by some segments of organized labor. The AFL-CIO's Committee on Political Education (COPE) amounted to one of the nation's most powerful political action committees long before such organizations began to proliferate in the 1970s. COPE provides indirect funds and services for Democratic candidates, by mailing campaign literature, making phone calls, getting out the vote, and so on.

As for lobbying, the AFL-CIO carries the most clout among labor interest groups. Its 106 affiliated unions, representing everyone from teachers and plumbers to meat cutters and garment workers,

Trade unions are among the most important blocs of organized interests in industrialized democracies. In recent decades, American unions have exerted much of their influence through the Democratic party. But U.S. unions have never had the clout of unions in other democracies, since most of the American work force is not unionized. *(Olivier Rebbot/Woodfin Camp & Associates)*

enlist some 14 million dues-paying members; counting the families involved, the organization actually represents close to 50 million Americans. The AFL-CIO also supports 300 lobbyists who work on behalf of 50 member unions, along with hundreds of local pressure groups in all states and congressional districts. On issues considered crucial to all of labor, such as minimum wage legislation, leaders mobilize the entire organization. On other issues, only particular affiliates take an interest. Sometimes portions of the organization clash with one another on goals or strategies; at other times, the leadership and the rank-and-file find themselves at odds.

Other active union lobbies include those fielded by the United Mine Workers, the United Auto Workers, and the Teamsters. Overall, though, labor's record since World War II has not been impressive on issues closely related to its immediate interests. For the most part, organized labor has been fighting a defensive battle since 1950.

The Defense Lobby

Defense is very big business. The Pentagon is the biggest single purchaser of goods and services in the nation. Defense spending creates as many as thirty-five thousand jobs for every $1 billion spent—and the defense budget reached almost $300 billion in 1987. The peaks and valleys of defense spending can boost the fortunes of or wreak havoc on particular sectors of the economy, especially in highly defense-dependent areas such as Southern California, Texas, and Connecticut. In California, one job in ten is defense-related.

Nationwide, more than 30 percent of mathematicians, 25 percent of physicists, 47 percent of aeronautical engineers, and 11 percent of computer programmers work in the **military-industrial complex**—the highly interdependent network of military establishment and industries producing military material, which together exert a powerful influence on foreign and economic policy. Many defense contractors work exclusively for the Department of Defense, staking their very survival on continued defense spending. The number of top defense contractors, however, is rather small. In the 1980s, ten companies received more than 30

percent of all large defense contracts and almost 50 percent of all research and development contracts given out by the Defense Department.

Defense contractors often use high-powered advertising and public relations techniques to lobby within the government for new contracts. Under the current system, as Senator William Proxmire, a Wisconsin Democrat, put it, "Contractors get generous allotments from the government to produce weapons systems. But rather than using all of it for production of these weapons systems, they siphon some of it off to lobby for even more money. . . . There is enough favoritism and behind-the-scenes influence on large defense contracts without the added insult of having the taxpayer pay for the bill."[4] The Rockwell Corporation, for example, produced and made one hundred prints of the film *The Threat—What Can One Do?* which dealt with the need to build the B-1 bomber. The film was then shown to the public and members of Congress. Rockwell maintained that this project represented merely a public relations effort, and therefore was a deductible business expense. Government tax auditors took a different view: They considered the film part of an extensive lobbying effort to get the government to build the B-1—and to guarantee that Rockwell got the contract.

Often, weapons systems are kept alive not because of their military value, but because they contribute to the financial health of the area of the country in which they are located or produced. Senator Carl Levin, a Michigan Democrat, described the situation this way: "I think the pressures on Congress from the [military-industrial] complex are great and often successful when they shouldn't be. . . . Part of the problem is that we have a democratic government and every member of Congress is going to try and get as much for his district or state as he can. That's the price we pay for democratic government."[5]

The defense lobby has strong allies, then, both among members of Congress, who want defense contracts in their districts, and Department of Defense bureaucrats, who want to strengthen weapons systems. This kind of alliance is known as an *iron triangle* (see **Figure 9–1**). Typically, it involves (1) a set of interest groups, (2) a portion of the federal bureaucracy, and (3) a congressional com-

Interest-Group Politics **291**

Like other manufacturers, those who make military goods also steadily promote their products. Here, General Dynamics displays a model of one of its jets at an Air Force arms bazaar. Pentagon procurement has come under intense criticism in recent years. Many argue that the relationship between government officials and military manufacturers is far too cozy. *(© Rick Reinhard)*

mittee or some members of a committee. The three sides of this triangle reinforce one another in a strong, protective framework of mutual influence. In addition, people move from one part of the triangle to another, strengthening its influence. Frequently, Defense Department employees subsequently find jobs within the defense industry. The traffic goes the other way as well—from industry into government employment. According to political scientist Gordon Adams, "Once molded, the triangle sets with the rigidity of iron. The three participants exert strenuous efforts to keep isolated and protected from outside points of view."

In the iron triangle, Adams continues, those outside the government (the defense contractors) are "so close to government that they not only carry out military policy, but often create it."[6]

The iron triangle effect operates in other sectors of government as well. **Figure 9–2** spells out some of the subtleties undergirding the strength of interest-group politics in agriculture. Often, many interest groups monitor the same issues without coordinating their efforts, and lobbyists find multiple points of access in the executive and congressional branches. The iron triangle, then, comes to look more like a complex *network* of interactions.

FIGURE 9–1
The Traditional Iron Triangle in Defense

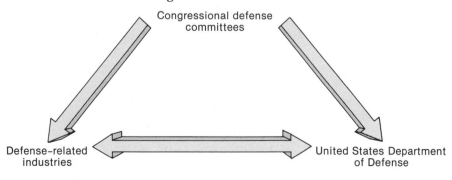

Congressional defense committees

Defense-related industries

United States Department of Defense

FIGURE 9–2
Interest-Group Politics and Agriculture

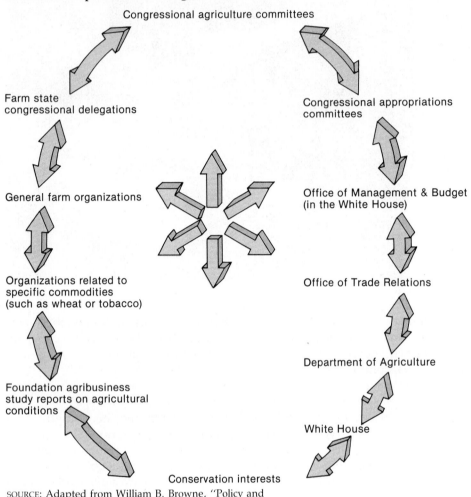

SOURCE: Adapted from William B. Browne, "Policy and Interests: Instability and Change in a Classic Issue Subsystem," in Ciglar and Loomis, eds., *Interest Group Politics,* 2nd ed. (Washington, D.C.: Congressional Quarterly Press, 1986), pp. 183–201.

Public Interest Groups

The rise of public interest lobbies has been one of the most significant developments in recent U.S. political history. One student of the subject defines **public interest groups** as organizations that seek "a collective good, the achievement of which will not selectively and materially benefit the membership or activists of the organization."[7]

Common Cause and the Ralph Nader consumer protection and investigative organizations are the

most prominent of the general-purpose public interest lobbies. **Common Cause,** founded in 1970 by former Health, Education, and Welfare Secretary John Gardner, attracted one hundred thousand members in its first six months of existence. In the 1980s, its membership stood at about two hundred and forty thousand, down from three hundred thousand during the Watergate days of 1974. Common Cause has both a paid staff and a volunteer force working out of its Washington office. It frequently focuses on procedural issues, such as open-hearings requirements in Congress, because it believes that better procedures will yield more honest policy making. Common Cause also supports public campaign financing and reform of the lobbying disclosure laws.

Ralph Nader's career as a consumer activist and the strong network of public interest organizations he helped to create constitute an extraordinary story in recent U.S. political life. Nader started his career as a champion of the ordinary citizen by taking on some of the biggest targets in U.S. industry—beginning in the mid-1960s with General Motors, whose Corvair he attacked as "unsafe at any speed." In Nader's battle with GM, the consumer activist won a decisive victory: Congressional passage of the Motor Vehicle Safety Act of 1966 marked this signal achievement. But that was just the beginning. Nader's efforts have spawned at least fifteen public interest groups, focused on consumer issues, environmental concerns, health, science, regulatory reform, energy, and other matters.

In the 1960s alone, fourteen major pieces of consumer legislation passed Congress with the help of public interest group lobbying. These bills dealt with auto safety, credit bureaus, drugs, flammable fabrics, interstate land sales, natural gas pipeline safety, postal fraud, poultry inspection, product safety, toy safety, truth in lending, truth in packaging, and meat wholesaling.

Not all consumer group efforts, however, have been so successful. The Food and Drug Administration, for example, has been widely criticized for its allegedly cozy relationship with the industries it regulates. Drives to reform the FDA have had only limited success, and battles continue over issues such as adequate testing of food additives. The Consumer Product Safety Commission (CPSC), created in 1972, has also come under fire for its lax enforcement of product safety regulations. In addition, the CPSC has been hampered in its work by two major setbacks: a series of budget reductions and an erosion of its powers.

Despite these reverses, public interest groups have achieved notable success in U.S. political life. By tapping the resilient capacity for middle-class activism and youthful idealism in the country, they pinpoint weaknesses and problems in politics and social life—particularly problems created by

Citizen Nader: Starting out as a lone individual fighting many established economic and political interests, Ralph Nader has been a significant presence on the U.S. political scene for twenty-five years. *(UPI/Bettmann Newsphotos)*

entrenched powers in the economy, Congress, and the government bureaucracy. Public interest organizations also disseminate information vital to consumers. Had Ralph Nader not researched the Corvair and published a book warning of its design flaws, very few Americans would have realized how unsafe its design was. Public interest organizations have repeatedly revealed—and thereby shaken up—long-standing relationships among industry interest groups, regulatory agencies, and Congress.

The David-and-Goliath struggles waged by public interest organizations pit groups whose finances, organizational clout, and recognized legitimacy pale beside those of their adversaries. In addition, since public interest groups are often critical of the political process itself, they tend to provoke the antagonism of key political players whose support they need in the long run. Yet, they carry a few large rocks in their slingshot: They draw support from a deep well of public idealism; they tap the widespread discontent many alienated Americans feel with the political process; and, unlike most other interest groups, they are not looking out for number one.

In recent years, some public interest activists have joined the political establishment. Cities, states, and the federal government have set up consumer protection agencies, for example, and many former activists now make and enforce policy. As Carol Tucker Foreman, former president of the Consumer Federation of America, stated: "You score your points now by negotiation, by data, not by marching around the White House." Some in business have also become more attentive to the rights of the consumer; most major corporations now respond to consumer complaints through their own consumer affairs departments. The nature of the issues has changed as well. As Stuart M. Statlee of the U.S. Consumer Product Safety Committee said, "the problems that remain are much more esoteric, much more complicated . . . and in some ways much more costly."[8]

The Reverend Jerry Falwell, leader of the Moral Majority, greets candidate Ronald Reagan in 1980. Conservative groups offered Reagan fervent support, but many were disappointed with his efforts to enact a conservative social agenda. *(UPI/Bettmann Newsphotos)*

Single-Issue Groups

A **single-issue group** is a well-organized and intensely active organization that focuses exclusively on one issue or set of issues. Among the best known of these groups are the pro- and antiabortion organizations, the **Moral Majority** (a church-based organization interested in moral/religious issues as well as certain foreign policy questions), environmental and consumer groups, and the gun lobby. These groups consider their focus of concern as paramount; for some, support for or opposition to individual legislators rides on lawmakers' views on a single issue. Such groups have enjoyed a measure of success in state and national politics, and they have proliferated. However, political observers are growing increasingly worried about fragmentation and intractability in U.S. pol-

itics: Compromise, which stands at the core of democratic politics, becomes elusive in the face of intense, narrow, and well-organized interests.

Moral intensity and a single-issue orientation are nothing new to U.S. politics. But until recently single-issue groups had been diminishing in intensity and political clout. In the New Deal and the post–World War II period, single-issue economic groups were essentially neutralized, as each won a "piece of the pie" through subsidies, tax breaks, favorable legislation, and the like. And moral issues seemed to disappear from political life as Americans apparently grew more tolerant and as older moral concerns, like Prohibition, faded into memory. A bipartisan consensus on foreign policy also muted discontent.

These patterns began to break down in the 1960s, as new and intensely felt moral and social issues emerged. People discovered that through concerted action—marching, picketing, signing petitions, and participating in political campaigns—they could make a difference. The single-issue groups of the 1970s put these lessons to work. Let us look more closely at four of these groups: (1) the antiabortion lobby; (2) the gun lobby; (3) environmental groups; and (4) the pro-Israeli lobby.

THE ANTIABORTION LOBBY Antiabortion groups are considered among the most successful of all single-issue interest groups. They first achieved prominence after the Supreme Court, in *Roe* v. *Wade* (1973), struck down many state laws restricting abortion. Since then, antiabortion organizations have played substantial roles in certain senatorial and congressional races. Many observers credit them with the defeat of several liberal legislators, although some question just how decisively they influenced the outcome of those contests.

High-pitched emotion and occasional violence have characterized antiabortion actions. For example, at the National Right to Life Convention in 1979, speakers compared abortions to the genocidal Nazi extermination of the Jews. In the 1980s, several abortion clinics were firebombed, allegedly by antiabortionists.

Besides working to defeat pro-abortion legislators, antiabortion groups lobbied for legislation prohibiting the use of federal Medicaid funds for abortions except in a few limited circumstances. Finally, antiabortion activists have spearheaded the campaign for a constitutional amendment banning abortions. Such an amendment has passed several state legislatures and has been introduced in the House and Senate more than sixty separate times.

THE GUN LOBBY An overwhelming majority of Americans favor more restrictive regulation of handguns. The political clout and financial resources of the gun lobby, however, have thwarted all gun control efforts at the national level. The National Rifle Association (NRA)—a loose union of hunters, indoor shooting sportsmen, firearms and ammunition manufacturers, conservationists, and sporting goods merchants—stands at the core of that lobby. With the aid of sophisticated computer and direct-mail techniques, the NRA mobilizes its membership around gun control issues. In

addition to lobbying Congress directly, the NRA effectively campaigns for or against selected senators and representatives.

NRA supporters are committed, well organized, persistent, and well financed. As a recent example, the organization launched a highly graphic and emotional ad campaign arguing that guns are needed for self-defense. One ad showed a high-heeled shoe with the heel ripped off. The headline read: "He's followed you for two weeks. He'll rape you in two minutes."

By contrast, their opponents, although comprising a numerical majority, are not well organized and lack the money and intensity of the pro-gun forces. Still, there are signs that the once seemingly invincible power of the NRA may be waning. Newer organizations such as Handgun Control have been developing organizational clout that sometimes matches the NRA's. In 1987 and 1988, Handgun Control took out a series of full-page ads in such newspapers as *The New York Times* to counter the NRA message. Some of these ads recalled the attempted assassination of President Reagan in 1981, in which his press secretary, James Brady, was shot and partially paralyzed. Brady's wife Sarah, who has become an active advocate for gun control, lent her support to the ads.

Support for gun control legislation remains high in the country as a whole, and particularly among younger Americans. Gun control proposals have been placed on the ballot in various states and localities, and municipalities, such as San Francisco, and one state, Maryland, have banned the sale of certain handguns altogether.

ENVIRONMENTAL GROUPS Concern about environmental issues such as land use, national parks, and wildlife protection originated in the nineteenth century. Early in the twentieth century, President Theodore Roosevelt brought such issues to the forefront of national politics. In many ways, however, environmental activism ebbed for more than half a century thereafter. Amid the rising affluence of post–World War II U.S. society, few Americans considered the hidden and not-so-hidden costs of creating a complex, industrial society.

Only over the past two decades have environmental issues moved to the front burner of national politics. Environmental interest groups now

COMPARATIVE PERSPECTIVE

Guns and Public Policy

Alone among the Western democracies, the United States allows a vast number of guns to circulate in society. According to one estimate, Americans currently possess 200 *million* guns of all descriptions, of which 60 million are handguns.

In contrast, Western European nations impose tough standards for gun ownership. To obtain a gun in West Germany, individuals must undergo physical and mental tests and prove they have a need to protect themselves. Permission to own a handgun is seldom granted in Great Britain, and rifle ownership is carefully regulated. The penalty for carrying a gun illegally is six months in jail; those found guilty of using a gun in a crime are sentenced to fourteen years' imprisonment. Most British police officers do not carry guns, although they can be specially authorized to use them in certain circumstances.

There is no organization in Europe comparable to the National Rifle Association (NRA), the most powerful and vociferous lobby against any form of gun control. What nurtured the NRA's development in the United States? American defenders of the gun base their arguments on the Second Amendment to the Constitution, which guarantees citizens the right to bear arms (although in the view of most experts, this provision was intended to apply not to individuals, but to state militias). The individualistic American tradition has also been an important factor. The right to own a gun has become associated, for some, with personal autonomy, freedom, and a certain macho mystique. Advocates of a more permissible gun ownership policy also argue that guns are needed for self-defense.

Why all the fuss about gun control? Those advocating stiffer regulations point to the statistics. According to one estimate, approximately 200 homicides were committed in self-defense with handguns in 1986, compared with 12,000 handgun suicides, 1,000 accidental deaths, and roughly 9,000 homicides—of which many were crimes of passion that might not have occurred except for the presence of a handgun.* Indisputably, more Americans die of gunshot wounds than do citizens of countries where tough gun-control laws are in place. Most proposals for gun control call for the banning of certain handguns and establishing a waiting period for a gun to be purchased so that dealers can check the background of the purchaser. Some draw an analogy between gun ownership and car ownership, seeking mandatory insurance for gun owners, registration with the state, testing, and a tax on guns.

*The New Republic, Feb. 22, 1988, p. 9.

address many complicated and deeply felt issues—from local air and water pollution questions to toxic waste disposal, the preservation of wildlife and wilderness, and worker health and safety matters. More traditional groups like the Sierra Club have expanded the range of their concerns, while many new organizations have sprung up, including the Friends of the Earth, Environmental Action, Greenpeace, and the Environmental Defense Fund. Their tactics range from court action to referendum drives and civil disobedience, as well as more conventional lobbying activities.

Like other interest groups, some environmental organizations have singled out legislators and executive appointees for political attack. James Watt, Ronald Reagan's first secretary of the interior, drew the ire of environmentalists by supporting commercial development of nationally owned lands. Environmental groups have also taken strong stands on local and state issues, including

Environmental issues have jumped to the top of the political agenda, partly because of efforts by groups like Greenpeace. Here, the group joins a flotilla of boats sailing in New York harbor to protest ocean pollution. *(Keith Meyers/New York Times Pictures)*

nuclear power, bottle return laws, shipment of radioactive wastes, pollution standards, and the like.

PRO-ISRAELI INTERESTS We often think that foreign policy falls outside the realm of interest groups. After all, during foreign policy crises, urgent decisions are made by the president and presidential advisors, while public ignorance and even apathy hold sway. With this in mind, we might conclude that interest groups simply do not play an important role in the foreign policy arena. But this picture, though accurate up to a point, has sizable gaps.[9] In fact, interest groups attempt to influence foreign policy all the time.

One of the most prominent and effective single-issue foreign policy organizations is the pro-Israeli lobby. Sixty pro-Israeli groups spent $3.8 million in the 1985–1986 Congressional elections, helping to elect certain legislators and to defeat others. Compare this with the $2.7 million spent by the realtors' political action committee (PAC), and the $2.1 million spent by the doctors' PAC. Several PACs lobby for Israel, but the best known is the American Israel Public Affairs Committee (Aipac). Aipac has developed an almost legendary reputation. Aipac lobbyists are described by members of Congress as "professionals in every sense of the word." Even opponents in Congress admit that Aipac is "without question the most effective lobby,"[10] sometimes even intimidating in its thoroughness. What makes Aipac so effective? The lobby gets high marks for presenting a simple, coherent message; providing clear rewards and penalties to its friends and enemies in Congress; supplying timely and reliable information; and, perhaps most important, building on an already strong base of support for Israel in Congress and among the American public.[11] Although Aipac has only six registered lobbyists, its fifty-five thousand members are urged to become citizen-lobbyists on issues of particular concern. One other key factor in Aipac's success has been the cohesiveness of the American Jewish community in its support for Israel. There were signs, however, that the Palestinian uprisings in the occupied territories in 1988 might have created some serious divisions among American Jews—a development that might, in turn, reduce Aipac's future effectiveness.[12]

How Lobbying Works

The major resources available to interest groups are money, the clout that comes with membership size, organizational skills, leadership skills, expertise, knowledge of the political process, motivational commitment, and the intangible but highly significant factor of prestige, or legitimacy. How are these resources used by groups that seek to influence policy making?

Money can buy a great deal. It translates into a vast array of potential weapons in the influence-gaining process—campaign contributions, media exposure, the ability to procure the talents of able people. Wealthy organizations can afford to employ large lobbying staffs and offer substantial lecture fees to legislators as a means of winning influence.

Size can also translate into power. The AFL-CIO, for example, has organizations in every congressional district. Farm groups wield considerable political clout in certain districts. Even business has become aware of the potential of grass-roots activism. One Chamber of Commerce lobbyist noted that "lately we've grown aware of the potential impact of the grass-roots membership we have. The Chamber has business proprietors and executives in every congressional district, and we can use them to open a lot of doors for us that were closed before."[13]

Membership unity also matters. Unless a group's members are united around and deeply concerned about an issue, lobbying efforts may fail to make much of an impression. One House member, speaking of agricultural interest groups, put it this way: "If they can't get their own members together, they aren't going to start lobbying."[14]

Lobbyists can parlay political reputation and prestige into influence as well. By developing a solid reputation for honesty and expertise, lobbyists can win the trust—and support—of legislators. Such a reputation is especially important, of course, for lobbyists with little else to offer by way of political power. A group's overall prestige can also make a difference. For example, because the Business Roundtable is made up of the chief executive officers of the country's largest corporations, it is considered one of the premier business groups.

One lobbyist summarized the whole matter of group resources and efforts to obtain influence as follows:

> Different kinds of assets can be effective, but the individual has to, to some extent, decide what are his assets and then use them to the maximum. That is,

if you have a special asset that you can develop arguments, you can do research and develop tight information that is useful and reliable to senators and congressmen. Then you use that to the maximum. If your asset is sitting around the Congressional Hotel, in the Democratic Club, drinking cocktails and just hitting issues lightly but maximizing your contacts with senators and congressmen, then you use that to the maximum. . . . On the other hand, . . . being a source of reliable information to congressmen . . . tends to work better and be a more effective tactic if you are a small group or if you're working for a group that doesn't put large amounts of money into campaigns, one that has good contacts with a minimum number of senators and congressmen. . . . The tactics have to vary with the kind of organization.[15]

Let us now consider (1) overall lobbying strategies; (2) influence-seeking through the courts; (3) insider and outsider strategies; and (4) new dimensions in lobbying.

Overall Strategies

Strategies to gain influence take many different forms. Some groups concentrate their efforts on the legislative process, others on grass-roots organizing, others on the executive branch and such regulatory agencies as the Federal Trade Commission or the Securities and Exchange Commission. Still other groups focus on the courts. Overall, however, most lobbyists seek to influence Congress, either directly (by lobbying for or against legislation) or indirectly (by campaigning for or against congressional candidates).

Lobbying groups adopt two general strategies: (1) monitoring political activity and (2) initiating or opposing government action. Simply keeping track of government activity is a major task in itself. As a representative of one business group put it:

> It's impossible to follow everything. . . . Just the *Congressional Record* and the *Federal Register* take all day to read. We have one person who follows the *Record*, the *Register*, CQ [*Congressional Quarterly*] and things like that, and I'll spend a lot of time on the Hill, talking to members and staff about what's going on. I learn more from gossip and idle chatter about what might happen than from anything else.[16]

A Theorem on Special Interests

A theorem developed by Representative [Fortney H.] Stark was proved true by a line of tax-bill lobbyists that stretched from the door of the Ways and Means Committee room thirty-six meters, twenty-one centimeters down the hall. This was precisely the length predicted by the Stark Theorem. Two working days later, a line of lobbyists waiting to observe the Medicare mark-up [bill consideration] stretched (as Stark had predicted) only fifteen meters, thirty-seven centimeters.

Stark's theorem is as follows:

$$L = \frac{P}{I}\,(AF^2 \times DF)$$
$$- \; 93 \, (AFDC + SSI + \text{food stamps})$$

Basically, Stark postulated that the Length of a Line of Lobbyists (*L*) equals the Population of the nation (*P*) divided by the number of Individuals impacted (*I*), multiplied by the Arcaneness Factor squared (*AF²*), times the Dullness Factor (*DF*), minus 93 times the number of references to poor people.

In other words, the fewer the number of tax-payers affected, and the duller and more arcane the subject, the longer the line of lobbyists.

This was borne out by the small group of lobbyists covering the Medicare hearing (which affects 26,758,000 people) compared with the standing-room-only group listening to the debates on coal royalties, nuclear power plant decommissioning, and certain corporate taxes.

Said Stark, "The Arcaneness Factor was the hardest to postulate. The figure I've developed is obtained by counting the number of 'subparagraphs' in the law being amended after excluding the first ninety lines; adding two lines for each 'except that'; adding 4.2 lines for each 'provided that'; and adding sixteen lines for each Greek alphabet symbol used."

The Dullness Factor is simply the number of crossword puzzles being worked on in the hearing room in any sixty-minute period.

A final element in the Stark Theorem factors in the lack of interest among lobbyists in poor-people issues. Every mention of AFDC, SSI, or food stamps is multiplied by 93 and then subtracted from the total.

SOURCE: A press release issued by California Representative Fortney H. (Pete) Stark, reprinted in *Harper's* magazine, December 1984, p. 15.

When it comes to initiating or opposing government action, a group must know what it wants and have *points of access*. According to one lobbyist, "You have to have lines into the right committee and the right subcommittee. I always make sure I have a friend on the subcommittee, someone who will look after my interests, who will introduce and push bills or amendments for me. If you don't have a friend on the inside, then you're really on the outside looking in."[17]

We now examine (1) lobbying in Congress; (2) lobbying in the executive branch; and (3) intragovernmental lobbying.

LOBBYING IN CONGRESS   How do lobbyists attempt to influence legislators? They can provide information that bears on important policy decisions, and they can help plan political strategies. Lobbyists can also supply innovative ideas and approaches, especially when the lobbying organizations have special expertise in important political areas such as health or welfare policy. And, of course, groups can offer campaign support or threaten opposition.

Lobbying groups can also try to influence the internal structure of Congress itself. During the 1950s and 1960s, for example, oil lobbyists succeeded in barring from membership on the House Ways and Means Committee representatives who did not favor the large oil depletion allowance enjoyed by the industry. Having sympathetic members on key committees is crucial to a lobbyist's long-term success.

Finally, lobbyists and legislators often have close personal relationships. Much interaction between them takes place informally—at parties, vacations, lunches, country clubs, and so on. Such friendships spring naturally from the shared attitudes and backgrounds of many lobbyists and legislators. In addition, former legislators often become lobbyists and maintain ties with ex-colleagues.

LOBBYING IN THE EXECUTIVE BRANCH Lobbying is not confined to Congress; executive branch lobbyists also play a significant political role in shaping proposals before they are sent to Congress. Labor groups, business leaders, consumer representatives—all seek meetings with the president. Executive branch lobbying also focuses on foreign policy questions—Jewish leaders may work to influence policy toward Israel, or black leaders may lobby for particular policies toward South Africa. Frequently, interest groups and the White House work together.

Just as members of Congress often have close relationships with lobbyists, many executive branch agencies maintain close ties with those they oversee and serve. The Department of Commerce has links with the business community, the Agriculture Department looks toward the interests of farmers, the Veterans Administration presses for veterans' concerns, and so on. Relations between executive agencies and interest groups are frequently cordial. The groups usually seek to perpetuate their friendships by influencing the choice of political appointees to the top positions in these executive hierarchies.

The independent regulatory commissions are also prime targets of lobbyists. Rules made by bodies such as the Federal Communications Commission and the Interstate Commerce Commission have a substantial impact on many of the day-to-day operations of major industries. With that in mind, interest groups often go to great lengths to set forth their views before these agencies. Here, too, relationships between the regulator and the regulated may be cozy.

INTRAGOVERNMENTAL LOBBYING Lobbying also goes on within the executive branch itself, as well as between the White House and Congress—a phenomenon known as intragovernmental lobbying. The administration of President Dwight Eisenhower was the first to establish a congressional

Issues connected with the treatment of war veterans periodically surface, and the Veterans Administration itself has sometimes been the focus. Although the VA often lobbied inside the executive branch, it was criticized for avoiding controversial issues such as the effects of Agent Orange on Vietnam veterans, and the cause of veterans who were exposed to radiation during atomic testing. It remains to be seen whether a cabinet-level department will be more responsive to veterans' concerns than the VA has been.
(© Bobbie Kingsley/Photo Researchers)

liaison office in the White House to lobby Congress. Today, many executive branch agencies maintain special congressional liaison staffs: Each cabinet department has such an office, as do most regulatory agencies and many federal bureaus. Typically, agency lobbyists coordinate their activities with White House lobbying efforts.

Influence-Seeking through the Courts

Besides influencing legislation, interest groups may pursue specific goals through the courts. An interest group may mount a legal challenge to a new regulation; various industries have challenged regulations promulgated by the Environmental Protection Agency or the Occupational Safety and Health Administration. Less frequently, an interest group's strategy will turn on such legal efforts. Because courts in the United States have the power of judicial review—the power to strike down a law as unconstitutional—as well as the authority to set certain policies by issuing wide-ranging rulings, the judiciary exerts a decisive influence over public policy. Interest groups can therefore seek change through the courts when other avenues are blocked. As we have seen, the NAACP's long struggle to win equal protection under the law for blacks focused principally on the courts; to this end, the NAACP established a special Legal Defense and Educational Fund in 1939. Ralph Nader created the Public Citizen Litigation Group to represent consumer interests in the courts, and groups opposed to the death penalty have concentrated on the legal arena as well.

Groups sometimes attempt to exercise influence by joining in a lawsuit brought by others. Organizations also sponsor research that might affect court decisions and attempt to shape the selection and confirmation of judges. (See the discussion of Robert Bork's nomination to the U.S. Supreme Court, in Chapter 11.) The shift in decision-making patterns from the more liberal Supreme Court under Chief Justice Earl Warren to the more conservative Court under Chief Justices Warren Burger and William Rehnquist shows how dramatically court appointments can change the tenor of the judicial system.

Recently, some interest groups have taken a new tack—trying to influence the judicial process by making contributions to judges' political campaigns in states where judges are elected. Not long ago, races for judgeships were considered minor political affairs, drawing few contributions and little interest. But that has changed. Now that all sides recognize the importance of the judiciary in shaping public policy, judicial races take center stage. In 1986, for example, a candidate for chief justice in Ohio spent $1.7 million, with labor unions contributing $350,000 to his campaign. In Texas that same year, individual lawyers and law firms spent more than $718,000 in a state supreme court race. But so far, California has set the record, with $11.4 million spent in the election campaigns of three supreme court justices.[18] As one student of the subject put it: "There's a new era. Judicial campaigns have become, and in many places will become, noisier, nastier and costlier."[19]

Many see serious ethical issues at stake here. For example, many of the states that hold elections for certain judgeships do not require the campaigns to keep accurate financial records. In addition, sizable contributions often come from lawyers, raising obvious questions about the buying of influence. And the bulging campaign war chests of judges often finance thirty-second television commercials, where complex issues like the death penalty are given simplistic treatment.

Is this new interest-group tactic compromising the integrity of the judiciary? This concern has prompted some observers to call for developing national standards governing the financing of judicial elections, and establishing state and local watchdog committees to set and monitor those standards.

Insider and Outsider Strategies

Most lobbyists attempt to influence government policy either as "insiders" or "outsiders." Insider methods revolve around direct connections between interest groups and the major political players involved—legislators, bureaucrats, or other members of the executive branch. Outsider strategies build on connections between legislators and their home districts.

INSIDER STRATEGIES   Insider strategies rely on social relationships, friendships, and the political needs of legislators; these elements often come into play while the political process slowly grinds toward a decision. Interest groups that use insider strategies generally try to lighten a legislator's workload by supplying pertinent information, writing speeches, or answering opponents' criticisms. According to one student of the subject, "The corporate representative is often effective because he is a specialist, trading in information about an industry that may be crucial to the wording and effect of a given piece of legislation. 'Every industry has its little quirks,' explained one liberal Democrat. . . . 'Even if you are against them . . . you need their lobbyist to help you get your head on straight.' "[20] This observation illustrates the powerful role of expertise and specialized knowledge possessed by trusted lobbyists. As legislation becomes increasingly intricate and regulation more wide-ranging, the insider's knowledge becomes more and more vital to lawmaking. Hence, interest groups possessing knowledge that lawmakers need often gain considerable political leverage.

Insider lobbyists also try to exert influence by pointing out what effects a particular piece of legislation will have on a lawmaker's home district—that it will hurt a certain local hospital, create three thousand more jobs, reduce federal funds now allocated to the area, and so forth. Groups sometimes supply speech-making materials to overworked legislators and their staffs. As a Senate aide noted: "My boss demands a speech and a statement for the *Congressional Record* for every bill we introduce or co-sponsor. . . . I can't do it all myself. The better lobbyists, when they have a proposal they are pushing, bring it to me along with a couple of speeches, a *Record* insert, and a fact sheet. They know their clout is tripled that way."[21]

The most subtle insider tactic involves cultivating social relationships with legislators. In this way, business contacts and friendships develop between lawmakers and lobbyists. Oftentimes, these relationships take root at the myriad social gatherings held in the nation's capital. Speaking of such gatherings, one Senate aide declared:

They're damned important, especially with the new congressmen. The new man arrives in town with his wife. They're both a little awed. And what happens? All of a sudden, they are invited to a little dinner

The intimacy that often develops between lobbyists and legislators can, on occasion, lead to ruin. Here, Representative Mario Biaggi of New York announces his resignation from Congress following conviction on racketeering charges in 1988. Biaggi maintained his innocence but was among several sentenced to prison terms in connection with the Wedtech scandal. (*AP/Wide World Photos*)

party given by the Washington vice president for a billion-dollar corporation. They're impressed, but there's more to it than that.

Let's say the congressman is a liberal. He's suspicious of big business. What does he find? The big shot is a darned nice guy. He doesn't have horns and a tail. He charms the wife and he's deferential to the congressman. They go away feeling a little differently. Maybe it doesn't affect the way he votes, at least not right away. But it's a softening process.[22]

OUTSIDER STRATEGIES   Outsider methods of lobbying mobilize grass-roots sentiments to influence legislators. Lobbyists choose outsider strategies for a variety of reasons: They may represent the most effective way to influence policy making; they may offer the only alternatives after insider strategies have failed; or they may form one facet in a long-term effort to influence the direction of public opinion. In the last case, the outsider strategy may not be linked to a particular piece of legislation, or to any specific outcome.

A number of grass-roots outsider efforts have achieved a measure of prominence and success in recent years. The Chamber of Commerce has generated opposition among businesspeople to labor legislation. In 1983 the American Bankers Association led a highly successful lobbying blitz in which banks encouraged their customers to send letters and postcards to legislators urging the repeal of a withholding tax on interest payments. Thirteen million pieces of mail arrived, and the measure was repealed. A less successful outsider effort was mounted in 1988 by a network of conservative churches. They opposed the Civil Rights Restoration Act, arguing that it would require churches to hire homosexuals, AIDS patients, and drug users. Despite a large volume of mail, the campaign backfired. Many in Congress resented the extremist tone of the campaign, which some labeled "hysterical." The act was sustained by Congress over the president's veto.

Grass-roots lobbying has grown enormously in recent years, as single-issue campaigns and organizations (promoting gun control, abortion, or antitax measures, for example) have broadened their appeals. Moreover, many corporations, taking a longer-range view of political influence, now work to gain public support for their interests

through **advocacy advertising.** Advocacy advertising takes the form of well-reasoned essays, appearing in the prominent news media, designed to build a favorable corporate image and to boost public support for the corporation, its products, and its goals. As much as one-third of all corporate advertising is now devoted to advocacy ads, according to recent estimates. Mobil Oil, for example, uses ads in the news media to offer its views on energy and regulatory issues.

Other outsider strategies seek to influence the

Advocacy advertising from Philip Morris U.S.A.

More than 24 million of this country's smokers will travel this summer. Make room, America!

America's smokers travel by land, by air, by sea. They travel far and wide. During the summer, resort hotels alone will welcome 5 million smokers and their families. More than 7.5 million will travel the U.S.A. More than 2 million will head overseas. And 5 million will take to the air. Spring, summer, winter and fall, smokers keep the travel industry of America occupied.

The American Smoker— an economic force.

Presented by Philip Morris Magazine in the interest of America's 55.8 million smokers.
Source: The Roper Organization.

general tone of public discourse. A number of corporations contribute to conservative think tanks—centers of research and problem-solving—which produce scholarly and popular materials on a range of public issues. Such intellectual leadership helps shape the issue-agenda of politics, framing the debate on key issues and even circumscribing the arena in which interest-group activity takes place.

The New Lobbying

Since the early 1970s, the absolute volume of interest-group endeavors has increased dramatically. The number of lobbyists registered in Washington, D.C., has almost doubled, to fifteen thousand, in recent years (and that figure does not include thousands of unregistered lobbyists). Lobbies now spend an estimated two billion dollars to influence public policy; about half of that is spent on government lobbying, and the other half goes toward influencing public opinion.

Five hundred corporations now operate their own lobbies, as opposed to only one hundred in the mid-1970s. Why this substantial increase? The growth of lobbying parallels the growing size and complexity of the federal government. The government now regulates an enormous number of areas affecting a wide array of groups. Many seemingly trivial rules or requirements have important ramifications for towns or companies, making the stakes high for the contending interests.

Lobbyists themselves have gained greater sophistication and expertise as well, recognizing more and more how government does or could affect their interests. Most lobbyists now offer guidance and advice to those in government who create the new rules and make the expenditures, as well as informing lawmakers about the possible impact of their work.

Finally, fundamental changes in the power structure in Congress in recent years have given outside influences greater access to legislators. Many members of Congress, especially Democrats, have won election without the benefit of close party ties. As party organizations have declined in power, the nonideological politics of specific issues has replaced party politics to a great extent. For example, business-oriented political action committees support many of the new Democratic members of Congress, who in turn oppose many of the party leadership's pro-labor policies.

Regulation and the Public Interest

Concern about the excesses of lobbying date back to the 1830s, when the term *lobbyist* was first coined. Scandals or alleged scandals were common in the pre–Civil War period. In the 1850s, Washington was a wide-open city "filled with a variety of gambling houses whose proprietors worked closely with the lobbyists. When a representative or a senator was unlucky enough to fall into debt, as he frequently did, the managers of the gambling halls had him where he would do them the most good."[23] Lobbying scandals continued through the late nineteenth and early twentieth centuries. Not until 1946, however, was legislation regulating lobbying activities actually passed. We now explore (1) efforts to regulate lobbying and (2) the symbiotic relationship between government and interest groups.

Regulatory Efforts

The Federal Regulation of Lobbying Act, part of the Legislative Reorganization Act of 1946, required that persons paid to influence Congress (1) be registered, (2) disclose the source and use of all compensation over $500, and (3) state their general legislative objectives in a report to Congress. The measure, then, did not actually restrict lobbying at all: It simply required disclosure, on the theory that publicly available knowledge would create a healthier political climate.

Since its passage, the law has been criticized on legal and constitutional grounds, and critics have deemed it both ineffective and ambiguous. Contentions that it violates the First Amendment protections of free speech and the right to petition were rejected by the Supreme Court in 1954, but the justices interpreted the act very narrowly. In creating the act, Congress showed its ambivalence toward interest-group activity. After all, relations between legislators and lobbyists are often mutually beneficial, and Congress has traditionally been uneasy about taking action that would require closer policing of its members.

The 1946 act suffers from some obvious weaknesses. The disclosure rules apply only to lobbying aimed directly at Congress; executive branch, grass-roots, and other forms of lobbying are not addressed. Interest groups are given considerable latitude in interpreting how much of their money is spent on lobbying, and only those groups that declare their "principal purpose" to be direct contact with legislators are covered. Then, too, the act does not specify exactly what constitutes a lobbying effort. Finally, because the law designates no clear enforcement agency, the law has been rarely enforced.

To demonstrate the gross inadequacies of federal regulation in this area, let us now look at a specific lobbying case. The lobbying drive to defeat President Jimmy Carter's 1977 energy package was nothing short of fierce. American Gas Association Vice-President Nick Laird called it one of the most comprehensive efforts he had ever witnessed. Of the millions of dollars spent on this campaign, very little was reported under the federal lobbying act. Total oil industry expenditures in the first nine months of 1977 were only reported as $639,329, and the gas industry reported only $507,047. One registered lobbyist for an oil company, Standard Oil of Indiana, reported spending $2.94 from July to September—a period of intense lobbying efforts. Other groups also claimed extremely small expenditures.

New and tougher regulations for lobbying have been proposed in almost every recent session of Congress, only to be defeated for lack of a consensus. Among the key questions regulators must address are: Who should have to register? What sorts of lobbying should be covered? Should all contributions to lobbies be made public? Should the overall expenditures of lobbies be limited? and How much regulation is constitutional? Some states, most notably California, have passed tough regulatory legislation. On the federal level, however, interest-group lobbying remains intense, well organized, well funded, and largely beyond the reach of government regulation or control.

Government and Interest Groups

We have already noted that the interests of lobbies frequently coincide with those of both executive agencies and members of Congress. Thus, for example, tobacco growers and manufacturers may find steady allies on the agriculture committees in both houses and in the Department of Agriculture. Such close relationships, like those between regulated industries and regulatory commissions, lead critics to ask who is looking out for the public interest in such situations. Too often, the answer is "no one."

Public interest lobbies have attacked this policy-making process, calling for greater independence on the part of government agencies and more open and publicly reported lobbying. Although various political observers may define the "public interest" in myriad ways, it is easy to see what clearly is *not* in the public interest: policy making that ignores important affected interests; policy making carried on out of public view by small, well-organized groups seeking benefits for themselves; policy making that loses sight of the more permanent and deeper values we supposedly share as a society, such as honesty, equality, and fairness.

Let us consider two specific examples where the public interest might take a back seat to personal concerns. First, is it in the public interest for an expert on the payroll of a private company to serve the government without compensation for an extended period and then return to his private post? He may well have knowledge that is otherwise unavailable to the government, and he may be scrupulously honest—yet he knows that his public service is temporary and that his future lies with the company he will return to. And what if a high government official finds herself in charge of regulating matters that affect a major corporation? She knows that, as a government official, she is likely to be replaced when a new administration is voted into office, yet she is acquiring valuable knowledge in the course of government service that she is understandably reluctant to see go to waste. The thought of a subsequent career with the corporation under her jurisdiction may well affect her decisions in office. These cases illustrate that while particular individuals may not compromise their public trust, a serious problem of persistent and insidious bias exists nonetheless. There may be no conspiracy—or even corruption, in the common sense of that term—but the public interest may well suffer.

An admiral in charge of procuring great quantities of steel retires and joins a steel company; a general leaves the armed services to head a corporation with important military contracts; a civil aviation administrator resigns to become head of a major airline—such moves have become commonplace. A 1984 study found that more than half of Washington lobbyists had experience within the government, mostly at the federal level (see **Table 9–1**).

In an attempt to curb this disturbing trend, Congress passed an ethics law under which former government officials are permanently prohibited from representing those interests they regulated as civil servants. But "representing interests" is a vague term, and the law permits "business contacts" between former civil servants and their agencies after one year. In addition, the ethics law does not deal with the past connections of regulators. One expert, writing in 1982, underscored the consequences of this omission with the following list:

1. More than 100 government officials who decide what drugs can be sold and what chemicals can be added to food once worked for drug or chemical companies.

2. More than 300 top-level regulatory officials are now making the rules for sale of stocks and bonds to the public by their former employers—including brokerage firms and stock exchanges.

3. Common Cause has found that 429 or 65% of top level officials of the Nuclear Regulatory Commission have come from private enterprises, all holding licenses, permits, or contracts from NRC.[24]

Such extensive overlaps between regulators and those they regulate are almost certain to produce a subtle yet important bias in the policy-making process.

Conclusions

Since the 1960s, interest groups in general, and the increasingly numerous single-issue groups in particular, have grown more skillful and influential. At the same time, Congress has become more vulnerable to interest-group pressure. As the power and effectiveness of political parties has ebbed, interest groups have stepped into the political vacuum. While these developments might have bolstered public interest groups, by the 1980s, narrowly focused interest-group politics was gaining a strong foothold, increasingly fragmenting U.S. political life.

Single-issue groups may coalesce under ideologically based umbrella organizations, such as the New Right. Such groups may also play constructive political roles by spotlighting grievances and dramatizing neglected public issues or by counteracting the influence of more powerful but often less visible interest groups. Overall, however, the fragmentation of politics makes compromise difficult and sidesteps the "public interest."

The pervasiveness of business influence also poses a serious problem for U.S. politics, as corporate political action organizations have grown

TABLE 9–1
Previous Government Experience of Lobbyists

Federal government	45.0%
Congressional	16.9
Executive/Commission	22.0
Other (includes field offices, consulting positions, and miscellaneous others)	6.1
State and local	9.4
Total with government experience	54.4%

SOURCE: Robert H. Salisbury, "Washington Lobbyists: A Collective Portrait," in Allan J. Cigler and Burdett A. Loomis, eds., *Interest Group Politics*, 2nd ed. (Washington, D.C.: Congressional Quarterly Press, 1986), p. 153.

dramatically in recent years. Business lobbyists direct their attention to the federal agencies whose regulations affect business life, while corporations mount extensive grass-roots lobbying campaigns, organized by well-financed computer-based operations.

At one time, organized labor matched the lobbying efforts of business groups, but those days are long past. And today public interest lobbyists spend less than one-thousandth of the amount spent by business interests. Especially in recent years, big business has effectively vetoed any legislation it deems sufficiently threatening.

Although many groups exert influence on policy making, money, persistence, organizational capacities, intensity, and legitimacy determine the *degree* of influence various groups exercise. Theoretically the system is open to all interest groups. On a practical level, however, only certain groups have substantial input. The direction of decision making is heavily biased toward those who can wield political clout.

Do interest groups, then, enhance democracy or throw a roadblock in the democratic process? While we might like to believe that in the clash of interest-group politics every group's message is accorded equal time, most would agree that the unequal distribution of power and influence in our pluralistic system places certain groups at a decided disadvantage. Consider migrant farm workers or young, unemployed black people—these groups would certainly scoff at the notion that their voice—even raised collectively—carries equal weight with that of multinational corporations or other influential business interests.

The weakness of pluralism lies in its tacit approval of the status quo—reflecting and helping to sustain the undemocratic distribution of power and influence in U.S. political, social, and economic life. This situation is exacerbated when the major political parties do not make the issues sufficiently visible—leaving room for quiet, behind-the-scenes maneuvering by more powerful interests—and when a large segment of the population, disproportionately poor and poorly informed, remains on the sidelines of the political process.

Besides the problem of excluded or relatively powerless groups, what about the public interest?

In the battles for group influence, the long-term public interest sometimes falls by the wayside. Are agricultural policies that help to destroy the family farm far sighted? Were oil subsidies that contributed to domestic shortages of the 1970s in the national interest? If welfare policy discourages people from finding work, if the gun lobby keeps millions of new pistols circulating—are those policies desirable in the long run?

Some observers regard the rough-and-tumble politics of the interest-group network as the price for open, democratic politics. Robert Samuelson, for example, argues that

> the prejudice against special interests strikes at the heart of the democratic process. One person's special interest is another's crusade. The function of politics is not only to govern in the general interest and to reconcile differences among specific interests; it is also to provide outlets for political and social tensions. . . . No one, of course, should pretend the resulting system is problem-free. . . . The growth of government authority and political activism has led to severe tensions. . . . This is the ongoing drama of government, but it should not be mislabeled. The system is struggling, but it is not corrupt.[25]

But Samuelson also recognizes serious difficulties with interest-group activities: "On the one hand, government faces paralysis: a collision of competing interests so severe that nothing happens. . . . On the other hand, there looms the sort of pervasive contradictions that compels government to act in ways that are ultimately self-defeating."[26] These are sobering reflections on the state of the U.S. polity.

GLOSSARY TERMS

interest groups

military-industrial complex

public interest groups

Common Cause

Ralph Nader

single-issue group

Moral Majority

advocacy advertising

NOTES

[1]*New York Times,* Dec. 20, 1987, Section E, p. 4.

[2]Alexis de Tocqueville, *Democracy in America* (Garden City, N.Y.: Doubleday, 1969), p. 485.

[3]S. Verba and N. H. Nie, *Participation in America* (New York: Harper & Row, 1972).

[4]Quoted in *In Common,* August 1981, p. 27.

[5]Quoted in Rorie Tempest, "U.S. Defense Establishment Wields a Pervasive Power," *Los Angeles Times,* July 10, 1983, p. 3.

[6]Quoted in *In Common,* August 1981, p. 7.

[7]Jeffrey Berry, *Lobbying for the People* (Princeton, N.J.: Princeton University Press, 1977), p. 7.

[8]*New York Times,* Apr. 13, 1985, p. 18.

[9]Eric M. Uslaner, "One Nation, Many Voices: Interest Groups in Foreign Policy Making," in Allan J. Cigler and Burdett A. Loomis, eds., *Interest Group Politics* (Washington, D.C.: Congressional Quarterly Press, 1983), pp. 236–257.

[10]Robert Pear and Richard L. Berke, "Pro-Israel Group Exerts Quiet Might," *New York Times,* July 7, 1987, p. 7.

[11]*Ibid.*

[12]For a critical assessment of the pro-Israeli lobby's influence, see Edward Tivnan, *The Lobby: Jewish Political Power and American Foreign Policy* (New York: Simon & Schuster, 1987).

[13]Quoted in Norman J. Orenstein and Shirley Elder, *Interest Groups, Lobbying and Policymaking* (Washington, D.C.: Congressional Quarterly Press, 1978), p. 73.

[14]*Ibid.,* p. 75.

[15]*Ibid.,* p. 79.

[16]*Ibid.,* p. 56.

[17]*Ibid.,* pp. 57–58.

[18]Sheila Kaplan, "Justice for Sale," *Common Cause,* May/June 1987, pp. 29–32.

[19]*Ibid.,* p. 30.

[20]Orenstein and Elder, *Interest Groups, Lobbying and Policymaking,* p. 84.

[21]*Ibid.,* p. 85.

[22]*Ibid.,* p. 86.

[23]*Ibid.,* p. 97.

[24]Charles Dunn, *American Democracy Debated,* 2nd ed. (Glenview, Ill.: Scott Foresman, 1982).

[25]R. J. Samuelson, "The Campaign Reform Failure," *New Republic,* Sept. 5, 1983, pp. 35–36.

[26]*Ibid.*

SELECTED READINGS

For basic coverage of **what interest groups are and how they function,** consult Norman J. Orenstein and Shirley Elder, *Interest Groups, Lobbying and Policymaking* (Washington, D.C.: Congressional Quarterly Press, 1978); and Allan J. Cigler and Burdett A. Loomis, eds., *Interest Group Politics* (Washington, D.C.: Congressional Quarterly Press, 1983).

For **critical assessments of interest-group politics,** see Theodore Lowi, *The End of Liberalism* (New York: Norton, 1969); Michael Parenti, *Democracy for the Few,* 5th ed. (New York: St. Martin's, 1988); and B. M. Russett, *What Price Vigilance* (New Haven, Conn.: Yale University Press, 1970).

On **public interest lobbies** and the general issue of the public interest, see Jeffrey M. Berry, *Lobbying for the People* (Princeton, N.J.: Princeton University Press, 1977); Robert P. Holsworth, *Public Interest Liberalism and the Crisis of Affluence* (Cambridge, Mass.: Schenkman, 1980); C. J. Friedrich, ed., *The Public Interest* (New York: Atherton, 1962); Richard Flathman, *The Public Interest* (New York: Wiley, 1966); and Andrew S. McFarland, *Common Cause: Lobbying in the Public Interest* (Chatham, N.J.: Chatham House, 1984).

10

MASS POLITICS AND PROTEST

A Threat? Or a Necessity?

CHAPTER OUTLINE

Extraordinary Politics
Protest and Disobedience
How Protest Works
Protest through the Ballot

UPI/Bettmann Newsphotos

On February 1, 1960, four black students from the North Carolina Agricultural & Technical University entered Woolworth's in downtown Greensboro, North Carolina. Violating the norms of the segregated society of that day, the four seated themselves at the lunch counter and asked for cups of coffee. The waitress, following Southern segregationist tradition, refused them service. But the four did not leave. They remained on their stools until the day ended. It was the first sit-in of the 1960s.[1]

The Greensboro sit-in proved contagious. The next day, twenty students joined the original four. By the end of the week, thousands of A&T students and other blacks had violated segregation norms in downtown Greensboro. Some of these protestors were attacked by Ku Klux Klan members and other indignant whites. A few demonstrators were arrested, but all remained nonviolent. With tensions increasing, Woolworth's closed its doors at the end of the week. But the sit-in movement spread, and within a month sit-ins had taken place in more than fifty cities in nine states.

It was a tactic—and an objective—whose time had come. Yet no one had planned the sit-ins. The four students who initiated the sit-in at Woolworth's had decided on that method of protest quite casually. Their action ultimately represented only a small part of a far larger movement involving race relations in the South and, in many ways, the rest of the nation as well. The walls of segregation were about to come tumbling down, but not without the commitment and concerted efforts of tens of thousands and the sympathetic support of millions.

In April 1963 a series of demonstrations and sit-ins took place in Birmingham, Alabama, led by the Reverend Martin Luther King, Jr. While black demonstrators remained largely nonviolent, city police used police dogs, fire hoses, and clubs to control them. National television showed scenes of dogs, fangs bared, leaping at black people and other blacks being pinned against storefronts by powerful streams of water. President John Kennedy was said to have been sickened by the picture of the police dog attack.[2] Later that year, King led the March on Washington for Jobs and Freedom, at which he made his famous "I Have a Dream"

speech. Momentum had gathered for racial change, and the following year, Congress enacted legislation prohibiting segregation in public places.

These events—sit-ins, marches, nonviolent protest campaigns—were not the stuff of ordinary politics. They were extraordinary, unsettling, challenging. They involved dimensions of personal commitment, mass organization and arousal, and conflict that lay outside the day-to-day agenda of political life.

In this chapter we take up some of the issues raised by **extraordinary politics**—the politics of protest and mass involvement. This form of protest can spring from deeply held principles, with protestors pressing for progress toward social justice. Yet protestors can sometimes resort to violence and intimidation as tactics, creating a politics of repression. Do mass politics and protest enlarge democratic options, and help fulfill the promise of democracy? Or do they threaten the civil order and respect for law required in a democracy? In this chapter, we explore (1) the nature and sources of mass protest, as well as government's response to it; (2) how protest and civil disobedience affect democracy; (3) how protest works; and (4) protest expressed through the ballot.

Extraordinary Politics

Extraordinary politics amounts to strategies or actions that heat up the political atmosphere beyond its normal level—that seriously raise the stakes in political struggles. Of course, ordinary political actions in one political system can seem extraordinary in another. A protestor carrying a sign reading "Down with the Government" would raise few eyebrows in Lafayette Park, across the street from the White House, but a similar protestor would prompt a vigorous response in Red Square in Moscow, where the police would surely orchestrate his rapid disappearance. Still, even in a society in which such activity is protected, public protest represents a step toward extraordinary political action.

Extraordinary politics can take a violent or a nonviolent form. It can involve the concerted actions of millions of individuals or the solitary protest of one dedicated person. The most extreme

The simplicity of the sit-in tactic made it easy to practice in many situations, although sit-ins often brought real danger to the participants, who were sometimes beaten, harassed, and arrested. These blacks sit at a lunch counter in Charlotte, N.C., in the early 1960s, shortly after the initial sit-ins in Greensboro. *(Bruce Roberts/ Photo Researchers)*

form of extraordinary politics is violent revolution. Even democracies have justified resorting to violence (the American Revolution is a case in point) by arguing that nothing less would have altered an intolerable political situation. Any comprehensive survey of world politics over the last two hundred years would reveal that instances of extraordinary politics have been common in virtually all nations.[3]

Protestors and protest movements can draw on many tactics. We saw in Chapter 2 the variety of tactics employed by the American colonists in protests against the British government: They refused to pay certain taxes; they held demonstrations; they intimidated government officials and vandalized property; they banded together in secret and semisecret organizations; they armed themselves; and in the end, they made war. New protest tactics are forever being invented.

Between the normal political activities—voting, giving money, lobbying, debating, organizing

campaigns—and the extreme politics of revolution, violence, and intimidation, lies an extensive repertoire of extraordinary political actions and tactics, including marches, sit-ins, and various acts of civil disobedience.

A democratic political process is designed to allow the preferences of citizens to be expressed through nonviolent political means and established political channels on a regular basis. Yet, democratic practices are never perfect—and even if they were, issues that could not be addressed within the context of ordinary politics might arise. The avenues of change may be blocked, or particularly pressing and significant issues may come to the fore. Under such conditions, people are likely, sooner or later, to resort to extraordinary politics. In doing so, they raise the political ante and take risks—both for themselves and for the polity as a whole. In U.S. history, several key issues sparked significant protest movements, including the antislavery movement, the drive for women's suf-

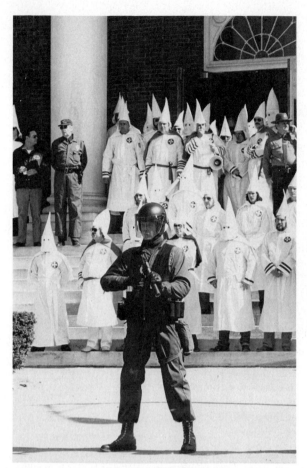

The Ku Klux Klan has often threatened the basic rights of others, particularly of blacks. But the Klan itself has enemies who object to its racist messages. In this ironic photo, police ensure the rights of klansmen to assemble and speak freely. *(© Susan Lapides/ Design Conceptions)*

frage, the Ku Klux Klan, the Prohibition movement, the antiwar movements of World War I and the Vietnam War, the civil rights movement, the environmental movement, the nuclear freeze movement, the gay rights movement, and the anti-abortion movement.[4]

It may come as a shock to find the civil rights movement and the Ku Klux Klan placed in the same category. While democratic theory does distinguish between violent and nonviolent movements and those promoting democratic or non-democratic goals, we must recognize that extraordinary politics can be used by forces of any

political or social persuasion; it can be employed to help prevent change as well as to make change possible; and it can be used by the powerful as well as by the weak, although we usually consider it a strategy of the weak. And as we will see, government itself sometimes resorts to extraordinary politics in dealing with politically sensitive or explosive situations. We now delve into (1) the nature and sources of mass protest and (2) government response to extraordinary politics.

The Whys of Protest

Protests develop in democratic states for various reasons—usually out of some deep sense of frustration with the status quo. Vital issues may be at stake and people may feel compelled to take extraordinary action (as in the case of nuclear freeze advocates or contemporary antiabortion demonstrators). Protestors may view governments as unresponsive to moral issues or involved in immoral actions (as did those who opposed slavery or the Vietnam War). Protestors may seek to arouse the conscience of their fellow citizens (the driving force behind the civil rights movement), or they may simply be making a moral statement (as conscientious objectors do). Finally, protest activities may be directed against the private, rather than the public, sector. Civil rights demonstrators sat in at a Woolworth's store in Greensboro, not at a city office. Auto workers staged dramatic sit-ins at General Motors plants during the 1930s, protesting the company's refusal to recognize their union. Antiabortion demonstrators today gather outside private abortion clinics. In all these examples, protestors felt compelled either to resist a perceived evil or to dramatize a commitment.

Protest may take the form of a chaotic riot rather than a concerted political movement. In the "long, hot summers" of the 1960s, for example, rioting erupted in the black ghettos of many U.S. cities, coupled with widespread looting and arson. At first glance, these violent episodes seem to have contributed little to the struggle for civil rights; however, riots often have important political consequences and they almost invariably represent a form of social assertion, even if a self-destructive one.[5] As Emerson once said, "Sometimes a scream is better than a thesis."

It was not long ago that the right to form a trade union and strike was bitterly contested, and workers often employed protest tactics against their employers. Here, police in Pontiac, Michigan, struggle to haul away automobile workers who formed a picket line to protest the use of nonstrikers in their plant. The year was 1939. *(AP/Wide World Photos)*

One of the most widely argued theories of protest and rebellion (not confined to democratic political contexts) holds that most political protest grows out of a sense of *relative deprivation*: that is, the feeling that one's group is being deprived of the life chances enjoyed by other groups in the society.[6] The precise form that deprivation-caused protest takes depends on how intensely people feel about their deprivation, their views on resorting to protest, how much force is likely to be used against them, how many allies they have, and numerous others factors. Nonetheless, the concept of relative deprivation serves as a useful starting point for exploring the origins of certain forms of protest. Interestingly, people often do not feel deprived until they have entertained *increased* expectations of a better life in the future. Many revolutions have broken out after people who had experienced some improvement in their situation subsequently lapsed into worsened circumstances.

If one group fears that it is losing power or influence, this can also trigger a move toward extraordinary politics. Threatened groups sometimes reach far beyond the usual range of political action to embrace genuinely violent measures. After the Civil War, for example, Southern whites who felt threatened by the new social order founded the Ku Klux Klan and attempted, through violence and intimidation, to prevent blacks and their white sympathizers from gaining or maintaining political control in the South.

Extraordinary Politics and Government Action

Protestors do not have a monopoly on extraordinary political activities. Governments, too, often resort to force, intimidation, coercion, and other unconventional tactics to control or keep track of citizens.

The United States has a long and controversial history of the use of government force in social conflicts. For many years government force was employed to protect the property rights of businesses in labor disputes. In more recent years, the National Guard shootings at Kent State in 1970 left four students dead and others injured. Although some people maintain that the troops were protecting themselves from students protesting

The Invisible Empire

The Ku Klux Klan, born in December 1865, was dedicated to using violence and terror to ensure the social and political subordination of blacks in the South. It flourished in the late 1860s, then ceased to exist as an organized group and lay dormant for close to fifty years. Two developments, however, set the stage for a resurgence of Klan activity.

First, between 1878 and 1914 about 23 million people emigrated to the United States; they were not always welcomed by the sons and daughters of earlier immigrants. Second, World War I left many Americans leery of change. To them, modernity signaled the waning of church influence, a breakdown of parental control over children, and the decline of customs and traditions. Distrustful of aliens and threatened by economic dislocation and rapid social change, some Americans developed a siege mentality, which prompted the rebirth of the Klan.

In 1915 the Klan was reconstituted as the Invisible Empire of the Ku Klux Klan, whose stated purpose was to defend the country against "aliens, idlers, strike leaders and immoral women." In 1920, membership stood at only a few thousand, but then Klan founders reorganized the Invisible Empire. The new pitch was "pro-American," and anyone perceived as a threat to "American" interests was considered anti-American. The Klan of 1920 was like a chameleon: anti-Japanese on the West Coast, anti-Mexican in the Southwest, anti-Catholic in the Midwest, anti-black in the South, anti–foreign-born in the big cities, and anti-Jewish on the East Coast. By appealing to people's fears of change, it built a substantial following. As the list of Klan enemies grew to include "bootleggers, dope, graft, nightclubs, violations of the Sabbath, sex and scandalous behavior," by 1921 membership swelled to about one hundred thousand.

In 1922 the Klan helped elect governors in Georgia, Alabama, California, and Oregon. Texas sent a Klansman to the Senate, and Klan campaigns helped unseat two Jewish members of Congress. By 1924, nationwide membership was estimated at two to three million. In August 1925, forty thousand Klan members marched down Pennsylvania Avenue and on to the Washington Monument.

After peaking at four to five million in the mid-1920s, Klan membership declined precipitously. Klan violence finally backfired, and scandals involving Klan leadership eroded the organization's base of support. A march in 1926 attracted only half the previous number of participants. Klan-controlled candidates were routed at the polls that fall, and in 1928 the Democratic Party nominated Al Smith, a Catholic, as its presidential candidate. By 1930, membership had fallen to a few hundred thousand. It was not until the civil rights struggles of the 1950s and 1960s that a much-reduced Klan was revived yet again.

against the Vietnam War, others argue that the shootings were not necessary.[7]

The government has resorted to other forms of extraordinary political activity as well. In 1919, government agents conducted a nationwide mass arrest of political and labor agitators and deported hundreds of aliens. Similarly, at the outbreak of World War II, thousands of Japanese-Americans were rounded up and interned (see Chapter 1). And in more recent times, both the FBI and the CIA have engaged in illegal or questionable practices such as infiltrating political groups, wiretapping, bugging, and harassing individuals or organizations suspected of subversive activities.

Government force has also been employed for more positive goals. In the 1950s and 1960s, for example, federal or state forces protected black students seeking to integrate schools and protest marchers in dangerous situations.

In the ideal democratic society, all government officials would recognize the legitimacy of dissent and respect the rights of dissenters. They would

An act of civil disobedience may exact a steep price. On September 1, 1987, to protest U.S. intervention in Central America, demonstrators lined the railroad tracks outside the Concord (California) Naval Weapons Station. Authorities had been notified that three demonstrators would sit on the tracks, but for unknown reasons the train was unable to stop in time. Brian Willson's right foot was severed, and surgeons had to amputate his left leg to save his life. He did survive and a year later returned to the site with his wife, Holley Rauen (to the right in this picture), to renew his opposition to Contra aid. *(© 1987, The Oakland Tribune/Marie Felde; AP/Wide World Photos)*

be able to tolerate criticism of their own policies—even serious, sustained criticism—without feeling the urge to repress dissent. In the real world, however, even democratic leaders sometimes resort to extreme measures to curb dissent. The tapes of Oval Office conversations during the Nixon administration reveal a sense of government under siege by dissenters. President Lyndon Johnson, in a move to brand protestors as traitors, claimed that the protest movement against the Vietnam War was aided by North Vietnam. More recently, President Ronald Reagan charged that the Soviet secret police were masterminding the peace movement in the United States and Western Europe.

In dealing with dissent or with alleged threats to national security, the government must carefully judge the amount of force called for in particular situations. Government authorities may simply lose patience and unleash far more force than is warranted. Or they may ignore the rights and dignity of the targets of government force.

Of course, dissenters, too, may interfere with the rights and well-being of various segments of society. During the Vietnam War era, supporters of the war often were not even permitted to state their views on college campuses. And in 1983 United Nations Ambassador Jeane Kirkpatrick was prevented from giving a speech at the University of California at Berkeley by protesting students who shouted her down. Such actions raise basic questions about the limits of protest and the meaning of the **First Amendment** guarantee of freedom of speech.[8]

Protest and Disobedience

When the normal channels of political expression are closed, citizens with intense grievances must find other ways to express their discontent—through mass demonstrations, sporadic violence, even organized warfare. To the Nicaraguan citizens who, through popular protest and armed insurrection, overthrew the dictatorship of Anastasio Somoza in 1979, such extraordinary political activities offered the only realistic means of toppling a tyrant.[9] Similarly, the strikes that paralyzed Poland in the summer and fall of 1980, leading to the departure of Polish leader Edward Gierek, sprang from a citizenry that was forbidden to organize an opposition political party or to engage in open political activity against the government.[10]

Extraordinary politics is easier to understand when democratic forms are lacking. What else can people do when they cannot express themselves freely, when there is no First Amendment, when

TABLE 10–1
Extraordinary Politics in Four Democracies

| | United States | | Great Britain | | West Germany | | France |
	1974	1981	1974	1981	1974	1981	1981
Sign petitions	58%	61%	22%	63%	30%	46%	44%
Participate in lawful demonstration	11	12	6	10	9	14	26
Join in boycott	14	14	5	7	4	7	11
Participate in unofficial strike	2	3	5	7	1	2	10
Occupy building	2	2	1	2	—	1	7
Damage property	1	1	1	2	—	1	1
Personal violence	1	2	—	1	—	1	1

SOURCES: 1974 Political Action Study; 1981 European Values Survey; 1981 CARA Values Survey.

there are no competing political parties or honest elections? Yet many forms of extraordinary politics also take place under more or less democratic regimes. (For a comparison of citizen participation in extraordinary politics in four democracies, see **Table 10–1.**) Here we will explore two complicated issues: (1) why citizens of democracies sometimes feel compelled to engage in extraordinary political activities and (2) when and how such activities can be justified.

Law and Disobedience

The concept of civil disobedience dates back a long way. The ancient Greeks recognized a higher law that prevailed over human law. Christian theologians have long argued over the meaning of Jesus's statement that one should "render unto Caesar that which is Caesar's, and unto God that which is God's." What if the demands of conscience ("render unto God") conflict with the demands of the government ("render unto Caesar")?[11] What if moral justice conflicts with societal laws? In the view of some theologians, a higher law, as expressed in Christian teachings, can *compel* disobedience to human laws in some circumstances. Thus, many pacifists argue that their consciences forbid them to kill, even if the state requires military service.[12]

Perhaps the most eloquent and influential advocate of disobedience in American history was Henry David Thoreau (1817–1862). In the 1840s, as a protest against both the Mexican-American War and the institution of slavery, Thoreau refused to pay a portion of his local taxes. For this action, he was arrested and jailed. He defended his position in a brief essay titled "On the Duty of Civil Disobedience," in which he referred to "a government in which the majority rule in all cases cannot be based on justice." He went on: "I think that we should be men first, and subjects afterward. It is not desirable to cultivate a respect for the law, so much as for the right." And finally: "There will never be a really free and enlightened State, until the State comes to recognize the individual as a higher and independent power."[13]

Thoreau's writings had an enormous impact on modern political and social history. Particularly influenced by Thoreau's defense of civil disobedience were Mohandas Gandhi, India's renowned advocate of nonviolent disobedience to unjust laws, and the Reverend Martin Luther King, Jr., the U.S. civil rights activist. We now examine in detail the issues raised by two pointed cases of civil disobedience: (1) King's civil rights campaign in Birmingham, Alabama, and (2) the Vietnam War protests.

LETTER FROM BIRMINGHAM JAIL   In 1963, Dr. King led a major civil rights campaign in Birmingham, Alabama. The campaign involved protest marches

Gandhi: The Essence of Nonviolence

Mohandas K. Gandhi (1869–1948), widely regarded as one of the premier political innovators of the twentieth century, pioneered the use of nonviolent direct-action campaigns for political and social justice. Educated as a lawyer in England, Gandhi returned briefly to his native India and then moved to South Africa, where he mobilized the Indian population to combat racial discrimination. After returning to India in1915, he led nonviolent campaigns to gain independence from British rule and to rectify injustices in Indian society.

Gandhi coined the term *satyagraha,* or "truth-force," to describe the essence of a nonviolent mass campaign. Those who follow *satyagraha,* Gandhi wrote, believe that it is better to suffer than inflict suffering on others; that one's opponents are also human and therefore can be persuaded; that nonviolence is a truth-seeking instrument through which a political situation can be opened up; that deep-rooted injustice must be confronted; and that in many cases organized nonviolence offers the only real alternative to violence. In Gandhi's view, a *satyagrahi* (follower of *satyagraha*) must be more than simply a passive sufferer—he or she must confront evil with an intense, disciplined conviction. Yet, Gandhi also believed that even a sincere *satyagrahi* could be mistaken, which made nonviolence toward others all the more important.*

Gandhi felt that a well-thought-out nonviolent campaign should involve two stages.[†] In preparing for mass action, the campaigners should launch an educational effort to make people aware of the issues involved. Next should come the action phase of the campaign, in which *satyagrahis* commit carefully considered acts of civil disobedience. Communication with opponents should be maintained during this phase; campaigners must be ready to negotiate at all times, as long as basic principles are not sacrificed. Gandhi's own mass campaigns ranged in duration from seven weeks to sixteen months.

Not all of Gandhi's campaigns were entirely successful or entirely nonviolent. But cumulatively they demonstrated the power of organized nonviolence as a method of social struggle. Not only were they crucial in India's evolution toward independence, but they also had a profound impact on the civil rights movement in the United States.

---

*Mohandas K. Gandhi, *An Autobiography* (Boston: Beacon Press, 1971).
[†]Joan V. Bondurant, *Conquest of Violence* (Berkeley, Calif.: University of California Press, 1969).

and deliberate, nonviolent confrontations with city authorities in an effort to break the hold of segregation. Large numbers of protestors were jailed, including King himself. Eight Alabama clergymen published a letter raising questions about King's decision to confront the law rather than negotiate. In a letter written from the Birmingham city jail, King attempted to respond to these questions.[14] Although this letter does not address all the issues involved in civil disobedience, it does offer some compelling arguments for deliberate disobedience of unjust laws.

Excerpts from Dr. King's letter appear as a supplement at the end of this chapter, so that you can consider his position in some detail. Stated briefly, King argues that one can judge whether a law is unjust, and thus may be disobeyed, by means of four criteria: (1) it degrades human personality, (2) it binds one group but not another, (3) it is enacted by an unrepresentative authority, or (4) it is unjustly applied. In King's view, the first three of these criteria applied to Birmingham's segregation ordinances and the fourth applied to otherwise valid laws, such as the need for proper parade per-

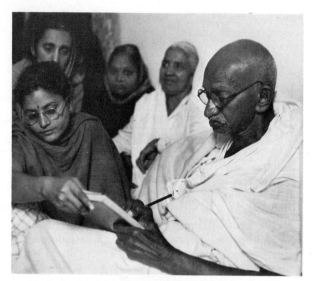

One of the most influential political thinkers and activists of the twentieth century, Mohandas Gandhi led a nonviolent movement to protest British rule of his native India. More than anyone, he elaborated the ideas and tactics of nonviolent protest. *(Henri Cartier-Bresson/Magnum)*

mits, that were being unfairly applied to civil rights protestors.

How valid are these criteria? Although they leave room for interpretation, they do serve as reasonable guidelines. The clearest and most easily applicable is the second—that a law should apply equally to all. When majorities make rules that discriminate against minorities, as was the case with segregation statutes, this flagrantly violates democratic norms. Of course, there are also sensible laws that apply to one group and not others, such as those that deny children access to pornography or alcohol. Such laws, however, are based on *reasonable* criteria; they are not arbitrary.

Considering the third criterion (unrepresentative authority), we often recognize when an unrepresentative authority violates democratic norms—particularly when the political process has been deliberately and systematically skewed against one group. Much more problematic is determining instances of degradation of human personality. Different people would certainly apply such a general principle in different ways. Yet most would agree that segregation degraded

blacks through the systematic imposition of discriminatory laws and practices.

Dr. King's case for direct action against laws perpetuating segregation was, in a way, an easy one to make—although we should remember that it was highly controversial at the time and that King was charged with fomenting anarchy and worse. If we turn to the issues posed by the Vietnam War, however, matters grow more complicated.

VIETNAM AND ILLEGITIMATE AUTHORITY   There has been domestic opposition to most American wars. Abraham Lincoln, as a young congressman, opposed the Mexican War in 1848. During the Civil

As opposition to American involvement in Vietnam mounted, even some veterans of previous wars—not usually expected to protest military activity—took to the streets. *(© Benedict J. Fernandez)*

War, draft riots were common, and opposition to the war was widespread. Many voices were raised against U.S. involvement in World War I and, as we saw in Chapter 4, important civil liberties cases developed out of that dissent. And although World War II was a highly popular war, many conscientious objectors refused to serve in the armed forces. The Vietnam War, however, although supported at first by the American people, eventually became highly unpopular.

In attempting to end the Vietnam War and to change our foreign policy, opponents of U.S. involvement tried many tactics. Individuals refused to serve in the armed forces; some publicly burned their draft cards. Others committed acts of civil disobedience such as blocking the entrances to military facilities with their bodies and sitting in against military recruiters on campuses. In most of these cases the protestors were practicing classic forms of civil disobedience.[15] As the war continued and disenchantment grew more intense, however, radical segments of the antiwar movement advocated an escalation in acts of protest. These radicals envisioned thousands of protestors blocking all the buildings of the federal government, sitting in day after day at the White House, perhaps even bringing to a halt the machinery of government. Some argued that such large-scale protests should be recognized as a legal right.

There was an obvious problem with such proposals: What if those who did not favor antiwar policies reacted by doing their own "coercing"? Activities of this nature actually did take place, most notably when construction workers attacked student antiwar demonstrators in New York City in 1971. Once the Pandora's box of coercion is opened, things can quickly get out of hand. How should we judge protest activities, then? By the motives or goals of those who commit them? Or on the basis of how much harm·they inflict on society?

Civil Disobedience: A Compromise

Even in a perfect democracy, all the problems of making just, sensible, humane public policy would not disappear. And present-day democracies are far from perfect. Political representatives in democracies can and do act cruelly, unjustly, foolishly. Democratic processes do give citizens relatively effective means by which to change or influence public policies. But these means are limited: Elections occur only occasionally; public opinion may be easily swayed; leaders may deceive, or lack judgment or political courage. As a result, citizens may face difficult moral choices.

In forging an effective strategy of civil disobedience, democratic protestors straddle the line between law and justice. Classic **civil disobedience** (that espoused by Thoreau, Gandhi, and King) involves a public act committed to arouse the conscience of the society by a person who is fully willing to accept the punishment prescribed by law. Such persons must be morally serious. They must not act secretly, or use violence to intimidate or harm. In expressing protest or violating laws, they maintain a respect for others and for the law itself. This strategy offers a sensible compromise—one that does not threaten democracy, and that enriches our sense of how individual conscience and social norms interact.[16] According to one student of the subject,

> What society needs is a struggle sufficiently equal to compel a process of public reasoning, which is its best protection against error. To prohibit freedom of speech, to forbid strikes and boycotts, and to punish civil disobedience by death would enable governments to overwhelm protest without having to reason. At the other extreme, not only to permit free speech, strikes and boycotts but also to legalize civil disobedience and disruption . . . would enable the dissenting minority to dictate to the majority. . . . A more equal and fruitful balance might be obtained by permitting boycotts but forbidding disruption and penalizing civil disobedience, but only moderately.[17]

How Protest Works

Effective protest involves more than simply voicing objections to policies or conditions. Many subtle and complex concepts are at work in protest activity. Let us now consider (1) the process of consciousness-raising; (2) activating others; (3) the contexts for effective protest; and (4) the limitations of protest tactics.

Consciousness-Raising

The first and most difficult step in galvanizing a protest movement involves shaping the consciousness of the protestor. The protestor—the person who is willing to make the commitment, to take the step of publicly declaring a grievance—stands at the core of all protest. A movement's leaders must make the victims of an unjust social system recognize the injustices perpetrated against them or the needless suffering they endure. For example, when numerous residents of Love Canal in upstate New York began developing serious illnesses, an active consciousness-raising program was launched by one concerned neighborhood homemaker to make her neighbors recognize that those illnesses were caused by toxic chemicals contaminating area waterways and groundwater. Once that hurdle was overcome, protest activities could be successful. Because inner change must precede public action, leaders must promote a new consciousness and a new sense of courage.

Activating Others

Once a new mass consciousness begins to develop, the protest group must forge alliances with other groups in society. The civil rights movement in the United States, for example, needed significant nonblack support to topple the pillars of segregation. To that end, civil rights leaders sought to activate third parties, to find help both within and outside government institutions. This can be difficult. It is usually accomplished by appeals, by threats, or by a combination of the two.

In making appeals, protestors call attention to the injustice, suffering, or deprivation they face so outside groups or individuals will be moved to help them. The extent to which appeals generate public concern, which in turn activates government officials, depends on several factors: the actual degree of suffering; whether, or to what extent the public acknowledges this suffering and regards it as unjust; whether the protesting group is regarded as worthy of social concern; and whether the public believes that the system has the resources to address these concerns.

If appeals fail, threats can be used. The threat of disruption—of making it more difficult for society to carry on its business—is a staple of democratic protest. Gandhi astutely combined appeals and threats in his nonviolent campaigns. He knew that when the streets are filled with demonstrators, the jails filled with protestors, and the court dockets jammed with cases, business as usual grinds to a halt. Governments are then more willing to listen to protestors' grievances.

Threats can also take more sinister forms: For example, protesting groups can threaten or carry out acts of violence. Such tactics, however, often backfire, toughening the resolve of opponents, and creating antagonism instead of support.

Contexts for Effective Protest

Protest is most effective when it takes place in a favorable context. Protestors have a better chance of success when other, more powerful groups in society embrace protest objectives or when protest tactics coincide with the objectives of influential politicians or public officials. Antiabortion demonstrators were likely to get a favorable hearing during the Reagan administration, for example.

Protest tactics sometimes force a government to recognize that the protestors deserve to be heard in the political process. But once they gain such a hearing, protestors must rely on influence of a more mundane kind. So although protest activities may place issues on the public agenda, help provide a protest group with higher standing in public controversies, or enhance the group's organizational development, protest by itself is not enough to accomplish policy objectives. In fact, it is a somewhat precarious tool on which to rely, as we will see in the next section.

Limitations of Protest Tactics

Effective protest usually lies uneasily on the borderline between legitimacy and illegitimacy. Performing this delicate balancing act, protest demonstrations often run the risk of alienating potentially sympathetic groups and arousing opposing groups to action. As a matter of strategy,

Cesar Chavez, organizer of migrant farm workers, in a moment of repose during one of his hunger strikes. Following the example of Gandhi, Chavez used the fast to dramatize the movement's grievances. Such tactics, however, take their toll on the leader, who must confront his own uncertainties and the possibility of failure. *(Gene Daniels/Black Star)*

leaders must anticipate whether the costs of a given protest tactic will outweigh its benefits (rarely an easy calculation). Decisions involving protest strategy become especially critical once a protest group has begun to gain success, for the wrong choice may jeopardize alliances forged with other groups.

A reluctance to alienate supporters and sympathizers may account in part for the tendencies of protest groups to become more cautious and restrained as they grow in power and status. Protest groups with relatively little power, by contrast, have little to lose. Such groups, however, may lack the resources to organize protest campaigns. In addition, protest success depends on gaining media coverage, which also helps leaders to reach, win over, and mobilize outside groups. Without publicity, protest tactics may be meaningless. The most successful protest leaders in recent years have raised the ability to gain publicity to an art form.

As we saw in Chapter 8, the news media not only report the news—they can also shape it in significant ways. Protest leaders design tactics based on what editors consider newsworthy. Tactics often escalate in severity or militance because what is news one day will be old hat the following week. Forceful communication dramatizes the goals of a protest movement. Consider the powerful symbolism of the Boston Tea Party or the March on Washington in 1963.

Today many activists, particularly in antinuclear groups, are questioning the continued usefulness of civil disobedience. Despite more than 15,000 arrests in the United States and Canada in 1983 for antinuclear civil disobedience, and 3,200 arrests in 1986, many feel that the news media pay little attention to the movement and that public awareness of the issues is not growing. This illustrates one of the dilemmas faced by protest groups: Sincerity of commitment and a willingness to raise basic issues through protest may not be enough to shift public consciousness and build public support. Some argue that issues of nuclear war are too complex and subtle for civil disobedience to succeed. Unlike the civil rights movement, no clearcut connection can be drawn between deliberate violation of an unjust law and the solution demonstrators seek—in the case of the civil rights protests, the repeal of that law. Antinuclear groups like Ground Zero, Plowshares, and others have demonstrated at missile testing sites and submarine bases; they have even attempted to destroy the missiles themselves. But civil disobedience has become far more commonplace than it was twenty-five years ago, and its political impact is consequently diminished. On the other hand, activists argue that even without gaining substantial media coverage they are slowly building resistance to nuclear weapons and their possible use. They also maintain that their acts of civil disobedience grow out of fundamental values they cannot fail to honor.[18]

Protestors may also run up against intense opposition that thwarts the effectiveness of their actions. The targets of protest may command significant resources to limit or undermine protest strategies. For example, established interests may use one or more of the following retaliatory measures:

Delaying tactics—appointing a commission or relegating a problem to study, for instance.

Tokenism—conceding a tiny fraction of what is desired while giving the impression that a significant concession has been made.

Discreditation—attempting to damage a group's credibility or legitimacy in the public arena.

Suppression—using police power against protestors.

Thus, even though protest is one of the few resources available to relatively powerless groups, its potential for success is often highly limited.

Protest through the Ballot

One form of mass participation that has become increasingly prominent in U.S. state politics in recent years stands between protest and normal electoral politics. This is a form of **direct legislation**—bypassing the established legislative mechanisms—specifically, the initiative and the referendum.[19] An **initiative** allows citizens to present a measure directly to voters, circumventing the legislature. A **referendum** is a direct popular vote that allows the electorate to approve or reject a law or policy. Referenda and initiatives are not necessarily forms of protest; often they deal with decidedly uncontroversial issues—a 1978 referendum in Oregon, for example, dealt with allowing lab technicians to fit false teeth. Sometimes, however, they articulate positions on deeply felt issues—nuclear power plants, the death penalty, property taxes, gun control, the manufacture of nuclear weapons.

Referenda in this nation date back to the American Revolution, when several states submitted their new constitutions to citizens for approval. The use of the initiative did not develop until the end of the nineteenth century. Today, in twenty-three states, voters can propose laws or constitutional amendments through a statewide initiative. In every state except Delaware, citizens have veto power over all constitutional amendments passed by the legislature. Also, many cities, counties, and municipalities have initiative and/or referendum power at the local level. Citizens vote on ten to fifteen thousand local referenda a year, dealing with local bonds, tax rate changes, and school financing, as well as such controversial issues as the fluoridation of local water supplies.

Voters in Oregon put the initiative to extensive use at the beginning of the twentieth century, rapidly passing a series of reforms that provided for the direct election of U.S. senators, the establishment of the country's first presidential primary, the abolition of the poll tax, and suffrage for women. For a time, initiative and referendum became known as the "Oregon system."

Use of "I & R" declined in the 1920s, but there was a surge of popular legislation in the 1930s, as people sought solutions to the economic problems of the Great Depression. Voters passed measures to protect the family farm, to provide pensions for the elderly, and Nebraskans cut costs by eliminating one house of their state legislature. The next major swing toward use of I & R began in the 1970s, spearheaded in California. The developments there culminated in the passage, in 1978, of Proposition 13, which had a drastic impact on property tax rates and the financing of local government. Massachusetts also passed a tax-cutting initiative. But overall, voters have rejected sixteen

COMPARATIVE PERSPECTIVE

The Referendum in Switzerland

In Switzerland, final decisions about law and constitutional issues are left firmly in the hands of the people: They do not rest with a national supreme court, or with the people's legislative representatives. Based on their own democratic traditions, dating back to the Middle Ages, the Swiss incorporated the popular referendum in their constitution in 1848. At first, the referendum could only be used to pass on constitutional amendments proposed by parliament. It was later expanded so the people could propose constitutional amendments, as well as holding referenda on legislative bills.

How does this work in practice? If fifty thousand signatures are gathered, voters can hold a referendum on any legislative bill. With one hundred thousand signatures, voters can submit a constitutional amendment, which is first debated in parliament and then voted on by the public. There is no limit to the sort of issue that can be proposed as a constitutional amendment in this manner. For example, in recent years a constitutional amendment was passed requiring a system of hiking trails throughout the nation.

When it was first introduced, many expected that the referendum would chiefly allow for new initiatives to arise directly from popular sentiments. This has sometimes happened, but more often the effect has been to delay passage of legislation that would otherwise have been enacted by parliament. For example, because of repeated defeats in referenda, Swiss women did not obtain the right to vote until 1971. The Swiss parliament would have agreed to women's suffrage decades earlier. A similar situation delayed laws exempting conscientious objectors from military service.

Sometimes the referendum has tyrannized weak minorities. Some anti-Semitic rules were approved early in the twentieth century, prohibiting Jews from slaughtering animals in a manner required by their religious code. On the other hand, efforts to penalize minorities, such as foreign workers living in Switzerland, have failed. Sometimes referenda have been used merely to educate the public about particular issues; approval was beside the point.

One can raise many questions about the dangers and strengths of the Swiss arrangement. Turnout is often low for referenda, ranging from 30 to 50 percent, and propaganda campaigns can be intense. In the Swiss system we see the danger of delaying useful changes and of failing to respect the rights of less powerful groups. However, the referendum has increased the legitimacy of political decisions: Responsibility shifts from courts, politicians, and bureaucrats directly to the people, who must then accept the praise or the blame for the outcomes.

SOURCE: Jurg Steiner, *European Democracies* (New York: Longman, 1986), Chapters 8 and 9.

out of nineteen tax-cutting state initiatives since 1978.

Between 1970 and 1982, state initiatives rose 600 percent. The I & R process gained new meaning in the early 1980s when the nuclear freeze movement launched a nationwide campaign to bring the freeze issue before voters and stimulate discussion on the issue of nuclear weapons. Freeze organizers managed to place a referendum calling for a nu-

clear freeze on the ballot in ten states and thirty-nine cities and counties. One advocate called it the most "effective technique for citizen education and motivation and for making policy changes. . . . " Although citizens' votes on the freeze had no binding effect nationally, they did influence the tone and direction of debate on the issue to some extent.

Oddly enough, political leaders as different in

One of the more famous initiatives in recent U.S. history, Proposition 13, to cut property taxes in California, takes a resounding lead on election night. *(AP/Wide World Photos)*

their views as Ronald Reagan and Ralph Nader are both strong advocates of I & R. As Nader put it: "We have to exercise that democratic muscle . . . without it, democracy isn't an accountable mechanism. The legislative option . . . has shown again and again that it is very subject to being bought . . . or rented."[20]

The United States is one of the few democratic countries that does not have a national referendum or other form of direct national legislation. A proposal submitted in the Senate in 1977 that would have created a national initiative failed to pass.

Some question whether this kind of direct legislation generally leads to liberal or to conservative outcomes. In a number of states, initiatives and referenda have created laws concerning political honesty, consumer protection, nuclear waste disposal, and nonreturnable cans and bottles—all liberal measures that might not have passed state legislatures because of powerful interest-group lobbying. A study of initiatives and referenda between 1945 and 1984 that ranked the measures on a liberal/conservative continuum concluded that the split was close to fifty/fifty.[21]

In recent years, initiative and referendum campaigns have become highly organized and often very expensive. Millions were spent in 1987, for example, in an effort to persuade Washington, D.C. citizens not to pass a referendum requiring a deposit on bottles. The campaign worked. Media campaigns have come to be used extensively in initiative and referendum drives, complete with carefully engineered images, slogans, and brief TV spots.

Does direct legislation promote or sabotage democracy? Among its proponents, the Progressives in the early days of this century argued that "the cure for the ills of democracy is more democracy." They maintained that the initiative and referendum would bring government closer to the people; allow issues to be raised and debated publicly, rather than being suppressed by politicians; provide an accurate gauge of public sentiment; and revive interest in political life. Overall, the increased involvement of the citizens through referenda and initiatives, the Progressives argued, would serve the public interest rather than that of political parties, officeholders, and other politicians. Direct democracy would help clarify public purposes and create a more informed and mature public opinion.

On the other side many doubt the ability of common citizens to understand, let alone decide, complex questions of public policy. Moreover, there is the threat that temporary or passionate majorities may coalesce, enacting laws that may be ill-considered or discriminatory. The delays and compromises required to pass bills in a legislature often protect minority rights. Another danger is that more direct democracy may weaken government institutions and the process of representation in general. Citizens may come to respect legislatures and politicians less than they do now, and potential candidates may be less inclined to seek office if their powers can be undermined by direct legislation. While some observers insist that direct legislation is used only when politicians fail to respond to popular needs, others argue that it is difficult to prevent well-organized (and perhaps undemocratic) interests from using initiatives and referenda regardless of how elected officials conduct themselves.

Conclusions

If we could devise a system so perfect that government officials never made wrong decisions, then we could forget about protest tactics and stick to politics as usual. Of course, such a political process is nowhere to be found. In real democratic politics, some needs are ignored, others deliberately neglected. As society changes, some groups and individuals find their values threatened, their status undermined, their expectations dashed.

"A little rebellion now and then is a good thing, and as necessary in the political world as storms are in the physical," declared Thomas Jefferson, in a particularly revolutionary mood. Protest is useful to a democratic society. For those whose consciences are offended by particular actions or policies, it provides a way of expressing discontent or voicing disagreement. Protest also signals that some of our fellow citizens actively oppose particular government policies. It can educate us about the problems others face. It can arouse the lethargic conscience of the majority. Protest, when successful, helps to focus our attention on matters that otherwise might be ignored.

On the other hand, protest and extraordinary politics can be a nuisance—or worse, a serious danger to life, liberty, and democratic processes. Protest can be animated by a spirit alien to democracy, or carried out so basic democratic values are put in jeopardy. When the Ku Klux Klan sought to stop blacks from exercising basic political rights—when vigilantism was rampant and intimidation a common occurrence—extraordinary politics posed a serious threat to the democratic process.

Deciding whether protest is justified is no simple task. We can assert, however, that when protest is used as a tool of the weak, when it is carried out in a spirit of moral seriousness, and when its goals are compatible with democratic values (as in the case of the civil rights movement of the 1950s and 1960s), then it enriches our political life.

SUPPLEMENT: FROM MARTIN LUTHER KING'S LETTER FROM BIRMINGHAM JAIL

My Dear Fellow Clergymen:

While confined here in the Birmingham city jail, I came across your recent statement calling my present activities "unwise and untimely." Seldom do I pause to answer criticism of my work and ideas. If I sought to answer all the criticisms that cross my desk, my secretaries would have little time for anything other than such correspondence in the course of the day, and I would have no time for constructive work. But since I feel that you are men of genuine good will and that your criticisms are sincerely set forth, I want to try to answer your statement in what I hope will be patient and reasonable terms.

*   *   *

You deplore the demonstrations taking place in Birmingham. But your statement, I am sorry to say, fails to express a similar concern for the conditions that brought about the demonstrations. I am sure that none of you would want to rest content with the superficial kind of social analysis that deals merely with effects and does not grapple with underlying causes. It is unfortunate that demonstrations are taking place in Birmingham, but it is even more unfortunate that the city's white power structure left the Negro community with no alternative.

In any nonviolent campaign there are four basic steps: collection of the facts to determine whether injustices exist; negotiation; self-purification; and direct action. We have gone through all these steps in Birmingham. There can be no gainsaying the fact that racial injustice engulfs this community. Birmingham is probably the most thoroughly segregated city in the United States. Its ugly record of brutality is widely known. Negroes have experienced grossly

unjust treatment in courts. There have been more unsolved bombings of Negro homes and churches in Birmingham than in any other city in the nation. These are the hard, brutal facts of the case. On the basis of these conditions, Negro leaders sought to negotiate with the city fathers. But the latter consistently refused to engage in good-faith negotiation.

*   *   *

You may well ask, "Why direct action? Why sit-ins, marches, and so forth? Isn't negotiation a better path?" You are quite right in calling for negotiation. Indeed, this is the very purpose of direct action. Nonviolent direct action seeks to create such a crisis and foster such a tension that a community which has constantly refused to negotiate is forced to confront the issue. It seeks so to dramatize the issue that it can no longer be ignored. My citing the creation of tension as part of the work of the nonviolent-resister may sound rather shocking. But I must confess that I am not afraid of the word "tension." I have earnestly opposed violent tension, but there is a type of constructive, nonviolent tension which is necessary for growth. Just as Socrates felt that it was necessary to create a tension in the mind so that individuals

Marches were a major dramatic element in the civil rights movement of the 1960s. When Martin Luther King, Jr., led protesters against segregation, their march served as a symbolic affirmation of unity and was a courageous public declaration of their grievances. *(Bruce Davidson/Magnum)*

could rise from the bondage of myths and half-truths to the unfettered realm of creative analysis and objective appraisal, so must we see the need for non-violent gadflies to create the kind of tension in society that will help men rise from the dark depths of prejudice and racism to the majestic heights of understanding and brotherhood.

The purpose of our direct-action program is to create a situation so crisis-packed that it will inevitably open the door to negotiation. I therefore concur with you in your call for negotiation. Too long has our beloved Southland been bogged down in a tragic effort to live in monologue rather than dialogue. . . .

We know through painful experience that freedom is never voluntarily given by the oppressor; it must be demanded by the oppressed. Frankly, I have yet to engage in a direct-action campaign that was "well timed" in the view of those who have not suffered unduly from the disease of segregation. For years now I have heard the word "Wait!" It rings in the ear of every Negro with piercing familiarity. This "Wait" has almost always meant "Never." We must come to see, with one of our distinguished jurists, that "justice too long delayed is justice denied."

*　　　*　　　*

You express a great deal of anxiety over our willingness to break laws. This is certainly a legitimate concern. Since we so diligently urge people to obey the Supreme Court's decision of 1954 outlawing segregation in the public schools, at first glance it may seem rather paradoxical for us consciously to break laws. One may well ask: "How can you advocate breaking some laws and obeying others?" The answer lies in the fact that there are two types of laws: just and unjust. I would be the first to advocate obeying just laws. One has not only a legal but a moral responsibility to obey just laws. Conversely, one has a moral responsibility to disobey unjust laws. I would agree with St. Augustine that "an unjust law is no law at all."

Now, what is the difference between the two? How does one determine whether a law is just or unjust? A just law is a manmade code that squares with the moral law or the law of God. An unjust law is a code that is out of harmony with the moral law. To put it in the terms of St. Thomas Aquinas: An unjust law is a human law that is not rooted in eternal law and natural law. Any law that uplifts human personality is just. Any law that degrades human personality is unjust. All segregation statutes are unjust because segregation distorts the soul and damages the personality. It gives the segregator a false sense of superiority and the segregated a false sense of inferiority. . . .

Let us consider a more concrete example of just and unjust laws. An unjust law is a code that a numerical or power majority group compels a minority group to obey but does not make binding on itself. This is *difference* made legal. By the same token, a just law is a code that a majority compels a minority to follow and that it is willing to follow itself. This is *sameness* made legal.

Let me give another explanation. A law is unjust if it is inflicted on a minority that, as a result of being denied the right to vote, had no part in enacting or devising the law. Who can say that the legislature of Alabama which set up that state's segregation laws was democratically elected? Throughout Alabama all sorts of devious methods are used to prevent Negroes from becoming registered voters, and there are some counties in which, even though Negroes constitute a majority of the population, not a single Negro is registered. Can any law enacted under such circumstances be considered democratically structured?

Sometimes a law is just on its face and unjust in its application. For instance, I have been arrested on a charge of parading without a permit for a parade. Now, there is nothing wrong in having an ordinance which requires a permit for a parade. But such an ordinance becomes unjust when it is used to maintain segregation and to deny citizens the First Amendment privilege of peaceful assembly and protest.

I hope you are able to see the distinction I am trying to point out. In no sense do I advocate evading or defying the law, as would the rabid segregationist. That would lead to anarchy. One who breaks an unjust law must do so openly, lovingly, and with a willingness to accept the penalty. I submit that an individual who breaks a law that conscience tells him is unjust, and who willingly accepts the penalty of imprisonment in order to arouse the conscience of the community over its injustice, is in reality expressing the highest respect for law.

*　　　*　　　*

Oppressed people cannot remain oppressed forever. The yearning for freedom eventually manifests itself, and that is what has happened to the American Negro. Something within has reminded him of his birthright of freedom, and something without has reminded him that it can be gained. Consciously or unconsciously, he has been caught up by the *Zeitgeist*, and with his black brothers of Africa and his brown and yellow brothers of Asia, South America, and the Caribbean, the United States Negro is moving with a sense of great urgency toward the promised land of racial justice. If one recognizes this vital urge that has engulfed the Negro community, one should readily understand why public demonstrations are taking place. The Negro has many pent-up resentments and latent frustrations, and he must release them. So let him march; let him make prayer pilgrimages to the city hall; let him go on freedom rides—and try to understand why he must do so. If his repressed emotions are not released in nonviolent ways, they will seek expression through violence; this is not a threat but a fact of history. So I have not said to my people, "Get rid of your discontent." Rather, I have tried to say that this normal and healthy discontent can be channeled into the creative outlet of nonviolent direct action. And now this approach is being termed extremist.

* * *

Before closing I feel impelled to mention one other point in your statement that has troubled me profoundly. You warmly commended the Birmingham police force for keeping "order" and "preventing violence." I doubt that you would have so warmly commended the police force if you had seen its dogs sinking their teeth into unarmed, nonviolent Negroes. I doubt that you would so quickly commend the policemen if you were to observe their ugly and inhumane treatment of Negroes here in the city jail; if you were to watch them push and curse old Negro women and young Negro girls; if you were to see them slap and kick old Negro men and young boys; if you were to observe them, as they did on two occasions, refuse to give us food because we wanted to sing our grace together. I cannot join you in your praise of the Birmingham police department.

* * *

I hope this letter finds you strong in the faith. I also hope that circumstances will soon make it possible for me to meet each of you, not as an integrationist or a civil-rights leader but as a fellow clergyman and a Christian brother. Let us all hope that the dark clouds of racial prejudice will soon pass away and the deep fog of misunderstanding will be lifted from our fear-drenched communities, and in some not too distant tomorrow the radiant stars of love and brotherhood will shine over our great nation with all their scintillating beauty.

Yours for the cause of Peace and Brotherhood,

MARTIN LUTHER KING, JR.

GLOSSARY TERMS

extraordinary politics
First Amendment
civil disobedience
direct legislation
initiative
referendum

NOTES

[1] For a detailed description of this incident, see Milton Viorst, *Fire in the Streets* (New York: Simon & Schuster, 1979), chap. 3

[2] Frederich F. Siegel, *Troubled Journey: From Pearl Harbor to Reagan* (New York: Hill & Wang, 1984), pp. 148–149.

[3] A detailed analysis of civil strife and protest in many nations appears in Ted R. Gurr, "A Comparative Study of Civil Strife," pp. 572–626, and Raymond Tanter, "International War and Domestic Turmoil: Some Contemporary Evidence," pp. 550–569, both in Ted R. Gurr and Hugh D. Graham, eds., *The History of Violence in America* (New York: Praeger, 1969).

[4] See Alec Barbrook and Christine Bolt, *Power and Protest in American Life* (New York: St Martin's, 1980), chap. 9, for a discussion of what isues prompt protest and how group power is exercised in U.S. politics.

[5] David O. Sears and John B. McConahay, *The Politics of Violence: The New Urban Politics and the Watts Riots* (Boston: Houghton Mifflin, 1973).

[6] Ted R. Gurr, *Why Men Rebel* (Princeton: Princeton University Press, 1970), chaps. 2, 10.

[7] James Michener, *Kent State: What Happened and Why* (New York: Random House, 1971).

[8] See John Bunzel, *Anti-politics in America* (Westport, Conn.: Greenwood Press, 1979); Robert Paul Wolff, Barrington Moore, Jr., and Herbert Marcuse, *A Critique of Pure Tolerance* (Boston: Beacon Press, 1965).

[9] Eduardo Crawley, *Dictators Never Die: Nicaragua and the Somoza Dynasty* (New York: St. Martin's, 1979).

[10] Neal Ascherson, *The Polish August* (New York: Penguin, 1982).

[11] One fascinating discussion of this issue can be found in Oscar Jaszi and John D. Lewis, *Against the Tyrant* (Glencoe, Ill.: Free Press, 1957).

[12]See A. J. Muste, "Of Holy Disobedience," in Hugh Adam Bedau, *Civil Disobedience: Theory and Practice* (New York: Pegasus, 1969), pp. 127–134.

[13]Henry David Thoreau, *Walden and Civil Disobedience* (New York: Signet, 1961), p. 223.

[14]For a thoughtful commentary on King's letter, see Curtis Crawford, ed., *Civil Disobedience: A Casebook* (New York: Crowell, 1973), pp. 226–229.

[15]David Dellinger, *More Power Than We Knew* (Garden City, N.Y.: Anchor Press, 1975).

[16]See Elliot Zashin, *Civil Disobedience and Democracy* (New York: Free Press, 1972), chaps. V–IX.

[17]Crawford, *Civil Disobedience: A Casebook,* p. 241.

[18]Mel Friedman, "Acts of Conscience," *Nuclear Times,* January/February 1988, pp. 22ff.

[19]Much of the information in this section is derived from David Butler and Austin Ranney, ed., *Referendums: A Comparative Study of Practice and Theory* (Washington, D.C.: American Enterprise Institute, 1978).

[20]David D. Schmidt, "Government by the People," *Public Citizen,* June 1986, pp. 12ff.

[21]Austin Ranney, "Referendums and Initiatives, 1984," *Public Opinion,* December/January 1985, pp. 15–17.

SELECTED READINGS

For broad-based accounts of **mass politics and protest,** see David J. Garrow, *Protest at Selma* (New Haven, Conn.: Yale University Press, 1978); Arnold Rice, *The Ku Klux Klan in American Politics* (New York: Haskell House, 1972); Robert Jay Lifton, *Revolutionary Immortality: Mao Tse-tung and the Chinese Cultural Revolution* (New York: Norton, 1976); Irwin Unger, *The Movement: A History of the American New Left, 1959–1972* (New York: Dodd, Mead, 1975); Lawrence Weschler, *Solidarity: Poland in the Season of its Passion* (New York: Simon & Schuster, 1982).

For **more personal accounts** of involvement in protest politics, see Robert Coles, *Children of Crisis: A Study of Courage and Fear* (New York: Dell, 1967); Sara Evans, *Personal Politics* (New York: Knopf, 1979); Kenneth Keniston, *Young Radicals* (New York: HBJ, 1968); William H. Grier and Price M. Cobbs, *Black Rage* (New York: Bantam, 1969); Alice Wexler, *Emma Goldman* (New York: Pantheon, 1984).

On the **moral issues** involved in disobedience and protest, see Michael Walzer, *Obligations* (Cambridge, Mass.: Harvard University Press, 1970); John Rawls, *A Theory of Justice* (Cambridge, Mass.: Harvard University Press, 1972), pp. 363–391; Walter Stein, ed., *Nuclear Weapons and Christian Conscience* (London: Merlin Press, 1965); J. Roland Pennock and John W. Chapman, eds., *Nomos XII: Political and Legal Obligation* (New York: Atherton Press, 1970).

PART **III**

INSTITUTIONS

11 *THE CONGRESS*

12 *THE AMERICAN PRESIDENCY*

13 *THE BUREAUCRACY*

14 *THE FEDERAL JUDICIARY*

THE CONGRESS

The Heart of Democracy?

CHAPTER OUTLINE

Congress: An Overview
The Structure of Congress
Members of Congress
Tradition and Reform
Congress and the President

AP/Wide World Photos

The act of legislating has long been considered the heart of the democratic political process. Early democratic theorists enshrined "the people" as the ultimate arbiters, the makers of law, who would both limit and extend their own freedom through the legislative acts of their representatives. Lawmaking would be a dignified and solemn process in which representatives of the people would gather to debate the issues of the day, develop policy for the entire society, compromise differences, and resolve disputes. Democratic politics would remain viable so long as the people were effectively and honestly represented and their representatives were intelligent and committed enough to create workable and democratic laws.

The descent from the lofty realm of democratic theory to the real world of democratic practice, however, is a steep one. A pungent old saying sums it up this way: "There are two things one should never watch being made: sausage and legislation." At the risk of our appetite for democracy, two questions must be asked in looking at the real world of democratic practices: How well do the structure, functioning, and membership of our own national legislature, the Congress, serve the representative tasks we've assigned it? and How many of those representative tasks have been or should be taken over by the president and the executive branch? While Congress sometimes dazzles us by seizing the initiative in the absence of executive leadership, a close look at the legislative process may disillusion us, or worse. We will have to acknowledge how tawdry, imperfect, deceptive, confused, and occasionally corrupt this process can be.

In Part III we take a hard, realistic look at the primary institutions of the U.S. democratic process—the Congress, the presidency, the bureaucracy, and the federal judiciary. We will explore how each has evolved, how effectively they work, how responsive they are to the general public, and how they interact—sometimes uneasily—with one another.

In probing the workings of our national legislature, several key questions will be addressed: Is Congress organized so it can carry out its responsibilities effectively, honestly, democratically? Are the many varied interests in our society, including the public interest, effectively represented? Are our legislators generally honest and competent?

Congress: An Overview

Unlike most national legislatures, the U.S. Congress is an independent legislative body that does not merely pass laws, but also initiates and creates them. Congress decides how revenues are to be raised and spent, regulates commerce among the states and with other nations, and has the power to declare war. More generally, the Constitution gives Congress the power "to make Laws which shall be necessary and proper for carrying into execution the foregoing powers, and all other powers vested by this constitution in the government . . . or in any department or officer thereof."[1] This innocuous-sounding statement, which has come to be known as the "elastic clause," has provided the basis for a vast expansion of congressional power. To do what is "necessary and proper" gives Congress a great deal of latitude in deciding when and how to legislate.

These tasks add up to a heavy legislative burden, and one that has become more onerous as the world has grown increasingly complex and societal interests more diverse and polarized. Does Congress consistently play a creative, constructive role in democratic life? Or does it more often fail to fashion workable policy, to resolve differences sensibly—even to stand for democratic principles?

To answer these questions, we must examine the workings of Congress. But as a first step, we need to establish what is meant by the term *representation*. As many a member of Congress has discovered, that is no simple task.

The Nature of Representation

Two classic views define how legislators should represent their constituents. One group of political theorists argues that *representation* should be taken literally—that legislators should vote the way the majority of those who elected them would vote. This position is known as the *delegate theory*. Adherents of the opposing view, called the *trustee theory*, maintain that representatives have a respon-

If you are used to seeing the Capitol as a timeless Washington fixture, and used to thinking of Congress as an unchanging institution, look again. Each has changed many times over the last two centuries; each is much larger and far more complex than originally planned. *(The Bettmann Archive)*

sibility to vote their own convictions and to educate and lead their constituents. Constituents who don't like the results can vote the representative out at the next election. In practice, most members of Congress operate at various times under each of these theories, along with a third one—that of the *politico*, whose actions are determined to some degree by the need to compromise and make deals in the legislature itself.

As an added complication for representative government, none of the members of Congress represents the whole of the country. Each of the 535 national legislators represents a specific segment of the nation, and the interests of that segment often conflict with the interests of the nation as a whole. To illustrate this fundamental problem, consider the issue of defense spending. Were defense spending to be cut, many states and districts would lose local defense installations that employ thousands of local inhabitants and pump millions

of dollars into local economies. Although the national interest might best be served by cutting back on defense, that interest is likely to pale in the face of local or regional economic needs. Of course, legislators often do look toward the larger interest, but they tend to be sharply constrained by regional concerns and constituent needs.

Next we probe the diverse functions of Congress. From there we proceed to (1) the structure of Congress; (2) the members of Congress; (3) congressional traditions and congressional reform; and (4) the uneasy interaction between Congress and the president.

Functions of Congress

Congress is more than a machine designed to crank out laws in a mechanical fashion year after year. Among other key functions, it (1) serves as a forum to air public policy issues; (2) crafts and shapes legislative proposals; (3) helps to develop and oversee a national budget; (4) oversees the administration of the laws it enacts; and (5) initiates investigations when called for. The Senate has the added function of accepting or rejecting numerous executive and judicial appointments made by the president. Each of these functions deserves close examination.

A PUBLIC POLICY FORUM   How are policy issues aired in Congress? While debates on the House or Senate floor occasionally serve this purpose, most policy issues are thrashed out in committee and subcommittee hearings, in which legislators go over, often in considerable detail, the particulars of public policy.[2] As a prime example of the degree of public interest that can be generated by congressional hearings, consider the Iran-contra hearings conducted in the summer of 1987, which captured the nation's attention and even became the subject of T-shirts and bumper stickers ("Ollie for President" and "By golly, I'm for Ollie!"). With Lieutenant Colonel Oliver North's televised testimony in July, the telegenic Marine briefly held star status as a new kind of folk hero. In many ways reminiscent of the Senate Watergate hearings fourteen years earlier, the Iran-contra hearings did raise the visibility of foreign policy and separation-of-power issues for a segment of the nation that would not ordinarily pay attention to such matters.

Legislators may also use the media or the lecture circuit to address contemporary issues. Senators, in particular, often speak before national audiences to voice their policy positions. Communication travels the other way, too: Interest groups come to Washington to make their voices heard in the corridors of Congress.

MAKING LAWS Congress contributes to the shaping of laws in many way. Sometimes Congress initiates legislation, rather than waiting for direction from the president. At other times a president picks up ideas originally voiced by members of Congress. Another crucial element of law-shaping is the detailed consideration of proposed legislation. This process usually takes place in the committee and subcommittee hearings and in committee meetings, where legislation is "marked up"— that is, prepared for final consideration. In these discussions, lawmakers delve into the implications of legislative proposals, resolve conflicts, and fine-tune the wording of proposed legislation.

CREATING A BUDGET Congress also is responsible for legislating a budget. For some time now, the budget process has been a chaotic one. Reforms instituted in the 1970s and 1980s have not solved the problem of finding a role for Congress in generating a budget for a large, administrative government. The budget process will be addressed more fully at the end of this chapter.

OVERSEEING GOVERNMENT PROGRAMS Through the *oversight* function, Congress follows up on the implementation of programs that have already been approved. Until relatively recently, Congress usually performed this task in a somewhat haphazard way. Then, public concern over excessive taxes and government waste enhanced the political appeal of the oversight function. Methods of oversight range from routine audits and reporting requirements for agencies to more assertive legislative investigations, congressional vetoes, and even impeachment proceedings (by which Congress can remove certain officials from office).

AN INVESTIGATIVE ROLE In recent years, Congress has moved toward a balanced, serious, and consistent evaluation of federal agencies and programs, principally through studies focused on efficiency and effectiveness in reaching program goals and through investigations. Congressional investigations—focusing on federal programs as well as various controversial aspects of political life—can be wide-ranging and highly publicized affairs. Recent Congressional hearings have explored such matters as immigration, the Central Intelligence Agency's covert role in Central America, the Federal Bureau of Investigation's surveillance of domestic political activity, and (in the wake of insider-trading scandals and the stock market crash of October 1987) the operation of the financial markets.

ADVICE AND CONSENT: A SENATORIAL PREROGATIVE The duty of providing *advice and consent* on presidential appointments is solely a Senate function. Some delegates to the Constitutional Convention of 1787 favored a system whereby the Senate would make all cabinet appointments; others maintained that such appointments should be the prerogative of the president. Under the compromise incorporated in the Constitution, "The President shall nominate, and by and with the Advice and Consent of the Senate shall appoint Ambassadors, other public Ministers and Consuls, Judges of the Supreme Court, and all other Officers of the United States." Although only eight cabinet nominees have been rejected by the Senate since 1789 (the latest in 1959), the nominations of hundreds of appointees to cabinet and other offices have been withdrawn when it became clear that they would not gain approval. Many other appointees have had to face tough questioning in Senate committee rooms. Confirmation hearings give the party out of power a chance to retaliate against the "ins," by bringing up potentially damaging issues for the governing administration. They also give legislators a chance to elicit from appointees specific policy positions.

Although most confirmation hearings are mundane affairs, some have been marked by dramatic confrontations. Nominations to the Supreme Court, always highly visible, are often routine matters when they reach the Senate. President

Judge Robert Bork's nomination to the Supreme Court in 1987 was not confirmed by the Senate. Over the entire history of the Court about one nomination in five has been rejected. Each rejection is controversial, raising again questions about the proper role of the Senate in judicial selection. The hearings on Bork's nomination were long and rancorous. *(AP/Wide World Photos)*

Reagan's 1987 nomination of Robert H. Bork proved to be a notable exception. A range of groups opposed Bork's nomination because of his stand on civil rights and women's issues, and his philosophy of narrow constitutional interpretation (he refused to acknowledge the right to privacy, for example, because no such right was specifically spelled out in the Constitution). Reagan would not withdraw Bork's nomination, even after it became clear that supporters could not marshall enough favorable votes in the Senate to confirm. The battle was waged through the Senate Judiciary Committee and onto the floor of the Senate. After Bork's defeat, Reagan's nomination of Douglas H. Ginsburg raised questions about Ginsburg's "judicial temperament." After admitting to using marijuana on several occasions in the past, Ginsburg withdrew his name from consideration. Reagan's next nominee to fill this slot on the Court, Anthony M. Kennedy, sailed through Senate confirmation hearings with little difficulty, gaining unanimous votes both in the committee and in the Senate as a whole.

The Structure of Congress

Democratic legislatures can be either **unicameral** (consisting of a single house) or, like the U.S. Congress, **bicameral** (consisting of two houses). In bi-cameral legislatures, all laws must run the legislative gauntlet twice—in the case of the U.S. Congress, through the larger House of Representatives and the smaller Senate. The political complexities arising from this situation constitute one facet of the **"checks and balances"** system created by the framers of the Constitution: Each house of Congress was meant to "check" the actions of the other. The framers also stipulated that one house be elected on the basis of population and the other be made up of two members from each state. At the time the Constitution was written, it was thought that the House, directly elected every two years by the people, would serve as a populist forum. Senators, on the other hand, were to be selected by state legislatures, and only one-third of the Senate body would be chosen every two years. Senators were to be at least thirty years old (House members could be twenty-five) and to have been citizens for at least nine years (as opposed to seven years for House members). Thus, it was thought, shielded from popular pressures, senators would serve as the elder statesmen, checking the more populist impulses of the House.[3]

In 1913 the lofty political status of senators was altered by the Seventeenth Amendment, which required that they be popularly elected. Today, senators are subject to many of the same political pressures faced by House members. Often called the

TABLE 11–1
Major Differences between the House and Senate

House	Senate
Larger (435 members)	Smaller (100 members)
Shorter term of office (two years)	Longer term of office (six years)
Less flexible rules	More flexible rules
Narrower constituency	Broader, more varied constituencies
Policy specialists	Policy generalists
Less press and media coverage	More press and media coverage
Power less evenly distributed	Power more evenly distributed
Less prestige	More prestige
More expeditious in floor debate	Less expeditious in floor debate
Less reliance on staffs	More reliance on staffs
Initiates all money bills	Confirms Supreme Court justices, ambassadors, and heads of executive departments
	Confirms treaties

SOURCE: Walter J. Oleszek, *Congressional Procedures and the Policy Process* (Washington, D.C.: Congressional Quarterly Press, 1978), p. 24.

most exclusive club in the world, the Senate is still structured to confer substantial political advantages. The 100 senators serve six-year terms—a lengthy time in office that, in theory at least, allows them to exercise more independence from the immediate concerns of their constituents. Prominent senators can capture wide public attention, counterbalancing to some degree the attention focused on the president. By contrast, the 435 members of the House, who serve two-year terms and usually represent smaller constituencies, rarely gain national recognition; a House member must always keep one eye cocked to constituents' needs and reelection concerns. (**Table 11–1** summarizes some of the major differences between the two houses.)

Congress has developed certain structural or organizational traits in response to its size, workload, and political environment. We look now at the most important of these traits: (1) *hierarchy* of leadership; (2) *specialization* of function; and (3) *routinization* of procedure—in particular, how a bill becomes law.

The Hierarchy of Congress

Party leaders orchestrate the efforts of various congressional work groups to produce coherent legislative results.[4] In attempting to influence the legislative course of events, party leaders have several resources at their disposal. In many cases, they can use parliamentary rules for partisan ends. For example, party leaders—especially those of the majority party—may delay scheduling a controversial bill until they gather enough votes for passage. Another leadership resource involves control or influence over many of the tangible rewards available to individual members, such as choice committee assignments. Party leaders also control many psychological rewards; they can often influence the attitude of House colleagues toward a member, with isolation the possible fate of the maverick. Finally, by dominating the legislature's internal communications process, party leaders monopolize vital information: knowledge of the upcoming schedule, the substance of bills, and the intentions of other members of Congress or the

The British Parliament

The British Parliament, often referred to as "the mother of parliaments" because of its long tradition and wide influence, is made up of the House of Commons and the House of Lords. The functions of the latter are largely ceremonial or advisory; for most purposes, the House of Commons is the equivalent of the U.S. Congress.

In some ways, the House of Commons may seem to be a very weak legislative body. The Cabinet (made up of members of Parliament chosen by the governing party or coalition) initiates virtually all legislation. Party control is very tight, so the majority party rarely fails to win a vote when the chips are down. Members of Parliament (MPs) generally follow party instructions, for failure to support the government in a crucial vote could end an MP's political career. The committee system in the House of Commons is also quite weak. There are few standing committees, none of which have anything like the powers and resources enjoyed by congressional committees.

Debate in the House of Commons is informal. Members speak from their own places, rather than from a podium, and are not permitted to read their speeches. Filibustering is impossible, since all debate must be "germane" to the bill under consideration. Budgets are submitted by the Cabinet, and MPs are permitted only to propose decreases, which then serve as the basis of debate. In general, the opposition parties in the House of Commons have no effective way to obstruct Cabinet policy. For example, the opposition Labour Party has been able to do little to stop Prime Minister Margaret Thatcher's policies of *privatizing* the public sector (selling off government agencies to become private enterprises).

By contrast, the U.S. Congress can have a very important influence in such situations, especially through the use of its powers of appropriation.

A unique and significant tradition in the House of Commons is the Question Period, during which Cabinet ministers must answer, on the floor of the Commons, written questions previously submitted to them by MPs. If an MP is not satisfied with the response, he or she can raise further questions orally. Such questioning sometimes develops into a full-fledged debate on important aspects of policy. The Prime Minister also must submit to such questioning. The U.S. president, in contrast, cannot be questioned directly by Congress, and such questioning of cabinet members as does occur takes place in committee hearings.

One of the most interesting contrasts between the British and U.S. political systems is the official recognition of the opposition's role in the British parliamentary system. The opposition in Britain is an organized countergovernment within Parliament that stands ready to take power. Thus, all national political leaders come up through Parliament and have had considerable experience.

The British House of Lords is a seemingly anachronistic institution. Early in the eighteenth century, the Lords was the dominant house of Parliament and was made up of the hereditary aristocracy. Over time, the House of Commons stripped it of various powers until today it has very little role in legislating. The current House of Lords consists of 809 hereditary peerages, 300 life peerages, 26 bishops, 9 law lords, and a few archbishops. Reforms in 1958 admitted women to the body for the first time and established the life (as opposed to hereditary) peerages. Theoretically, the House of Lords has the power to hold bills up for a year, but this power is almost never employed. In general, it does some amending of legislation and conducts unhurried and sometimes useful debate. It also functions as the supreme court of Great Britain.

Two powerful representatives of the "old Congress"—Sam Rayburn, Speaker of the House, gets a birthday greeting from Senate Majority Leader Lyndon Johnson in 1956. Rayburn's advice to members: "To get along, you have to go along." Both men were extremely skillful players of Capitol politics; each wielded more centralized control over legislation in their respective chambers than is possible today.
(UPI/Bettmann Newsphotos)

president. As we will see, the powers wielded by party leaders tend to be greater in the House than in the Senate. We now consider these varying powers.

LEADERSHIP IN THE HOUSE   The **Speaker of the House,** its presiding officer, is the most influential person on Capitol Hill. Although he (there has never been a female Speaker) is chosen by the members of his own party, his authority extends over the entire House. The Speaker regulates the flow of legislation by recognizing members on the floor (that is, granting them the right to speak), breaking tie votes, and referring bills to committees. The Speaker's unwritten powers depend on his personality and skills. He may influence the assignment of members to committees, influence the activities of the various committee leaders, or take the lead in scheduling legislation for floor consideration.

Despite the potential for power vested in the position of Speaker, the House of Representatives has had only a sporadic history of strong leadership. The few powerful Speakers of the nineteenth and early twentieth centuries included Henry Clay, Thomas ("Czar") Reed, and Joseph ("Uncle Joe") Cannon. When Cannon pushed the Speaker's powers beyond limits acceptable to the membership, the House voted in 1910 to strip the office of some of its formal powers. Today the Speaker's resources are more personal and informal. In this century, only one Speaker has converted these informal resources into real power—Sam Rayburn, a Texas Democrat, who wielded the Speaker's gavel for all but two years from 1940 to 1961.

The Speaker is aided by the **majority leader,** the chief floor spokesman for his party and the person charged with mobilizing party voting strength. The majority leader, in turn, is assisted by the majority **whip,** who notifies members of pending business, polls them on their voting intentions, and works to make sure they are present to vote on key issues. The **minority leader** (who is the opposition party's candidate for Speaker) and minority whip perform similar tasks, although they have fewer rewards to dispense among their colleagues.

LEADERSHIP IN THE SENATE   In the Senate, strong leadership has been much more the exception than the rule. Not until the end of the nineteenth century did coherent leadership patterns appear, and even then Senate leaders were no match for the powerful Speakers presiding on the other side of the Capitol building.

The presiding officer of the Senate has almost no formal power. The vice-president, the constitutionally mandated presiding officer, rarely attends sessions. The **president pro tempore** of the Senate is merely an honorific title bestowed on the senior majority-party senator; usually, the Senate is presided over day to day by freshman senators who take turns. The most important Senate leader is the majority leader, who helps to steer the party's legislative program through the upper house. The majority leader schedules legislation and influences many of the rewards available to senators, such as committee assignments, travel allowances, and office space. In this century, majority leaders have varied widely in effectiveness.

The opposition party elects the minority leader, who looks after the interests of his or her party members and those of the president, if the chief executive belongs to the same party. Both floor leaders are assisted by whips, who operate much as House whips do, although with noticeably looser reins on the troops.

Legislative Committees

A maxim on Capitol Hill holds that "You can't write a bill on the floor." Complex measures simply cannot be worked out by a large body of legislators. By relying on specialized work groups, or committees, Congress can simultaneously consider a variety of matters, and individual legislators can concentrate on a manageable range of problems.

Committees are the key policy-making bodies in Congress. Of the thousands of bills introduced into Congress each year, only a few are seriously considered by the committees—and only those few have a chance to be enacted into law. As President Woodrow Wilson once observed, "Congress in session is Congress on display, but Congress in committee is Congress at work."

Legislative specialization in Congress has increased as the congressional workload has grown more burdensome and diverse. The Legislative Reorganization Act of 1946 consolidated and reduced the number of standing (permanent) committees (see **Table 11–2**) but did nothing to halt the proliferation of subcommittees and other work groups including special and select committees (see **Table 11–3**).

TABLE 11–2
Standing Committees of the 100th Congress (1987–1988)

Committee	Number of members	Number of subcommittees
House—Standing		
Agriculture	43	8
Appropriations	57	13
Armed Services	48	7
Banking	46	8
Budget	35	9
District of Columbia	12	3
Education and Labor	34	8
Energy and Commerce	42	6
Foreign Affairs	45	8
Government Operations	39	7
House Administration	19	6
Interior	41	6

Continued

TABLE 11–2
Standing Committees of the 100th Congress (1987–1988) (*Cont.*)

Committee	Number of members	Number of subcommittees
Judiciary	35	7
Merchant Marine	42	6
Post Office	22	7
Public Works	52	7
Rules	13	2
Science and Technology	45	7
Small Business	44	6
Standards of Official Conduct	12	none
Veterans' Affairs	34	5
Ways and Means	36	6
Senate—Standing		
Agriculture	18	6
Appropriations	29	13
Armed Services	20	6
Banking, Housing, and Urban Affairs	8	4
Budget	24	none
Commerce, Science, and Transportation	20	8
Energy and Natural Resources	19	5
Environment and Public Works	16	5
Finance	20	7
Foreign Relations	20	7
Governmental Affairs	14	5
Judiciary	14	6
Labor and Human Resources	16	6
Rules and Administration	16	none
Small Business	18	6
Veterans' Affairs	11	none
Joint		
Economic	20	8
Library	10	–
Printing	10	–
Taxation	10	–

Outside the congressional hierarchy, the effective influence of members of Congress is based primarily on committee assignments and positions. In committee, members can give detailed consideration to bills, cultivate close relationships with interest groups and executive agencies af-

TABLE 11–3
Select and Special Committees of the 100th Congress (1987–1988)

Committee	Number of members	Number of subcommittees
House—Select Committees		
Aging	65	4
Children, Youth, and Families	30	3
Iran	15	–
Hunger	26	2
Intelligence	15	3
Narcotics	25	–
Senate—Select Committees		
Iran-contra	11	–
Ethics	6	–
Indian Affairs	8	–
Intelligence	15	–
Senate—Special Committees		
Aging	19	–

NOTE: Select and special committees are given mandates to study and report findings to the whole chamber but cannot report legislation.

fected by legislation, and develop expertise in particular areas. Such expertise is often deferred to by other members, who may not feel they have the specialized knowledge necessary to challenge committee judgments.[5] (For an example of the range of issues considered by a typical congressional committee, see **Figure 11–1.**) We now consider (1) the implications of committee assignments; (2) the proliferation of subcommittees; and (3) the consequences of structural fragmentation.

COMMITTEE ASSIGNMENTS Committee assignments are made by the political parties in each house. For the Democrats, the Steering Committee nominates committee members; for the Republicans, the Committee on Committees serves this purpose. Each party caucus (made up of all members of the party in each house) then ratifies the selections. Assignments hinge on several factors: the prestige of a committee, the goals of particular legislators, the seniority of legislators, and whether a committee has in the past deliberately

drawn members from particular states or regions. Although party leaders exercise some influence on all assignments, they generally concentrate on the most prestigious committees—Rules, Appropriations, and Ways and Means in the House; Appropriations, Finance, and Foreign Relations in the Senate. To be appointed to such committees, members must usually demonstrate "responsibility"—the ability to cooperate and accommodate different viewpoints. The most important factors in committee assignments, however, are a member's own desires and whether the assignment will help his or her reelection. As a result, like-minded legislators usually end up on the same committees, as do members who come from constituencies with similar interests, such as urban areas or farm states.[6]

Obviously, members of Congress want to serve on committees that deal with areas of personal or political interest. The problem with this arrangement is clear, however: A committee made up of such members may pay more attention to the spe-

FIGURE 11–1
Jurisdiction of a House Committee,
100th Congress (1987–1988)

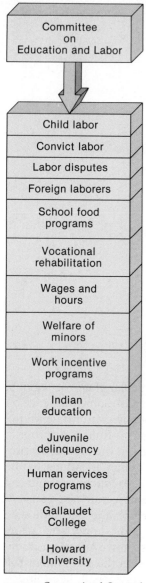

SOURCE: *Congressional Quarterly Weekly,* May 2, 1987, pp. 40–41.

ally is named chairman. This practice, known as **seniority rule,** once was invariably followed. Today, however, party caucuses can and do pass over the senior member at times to install a more junior member as chair.

Committees such as Budget and Appropriations have been particularly popular in recent years, partly because federal spending is such a central issue. Assignments on the House Commerce Committee are also highly sought after by freshman members who campaigned against excessive federal regulation. Some committees are perennially unpopular: House and Senate ethics panels, the District of Columbia Committee, and, lately, the House Judiciary Committee. In the absence of applicants, party leaders must twist some arms to fill vacancies on these committees.

SUBCOMMITTEES Over the past fifty years a definite trend toward "subcommittee government" has emerged. Subcommittees of the standing committees have increasingly taken over the basic responsibility for detailed legislative work, including hearings, debates, and the writing of bills.[7] The sheer number of subcommittees has increased as well. The House had 83 in the Eighty-Fourth Congress and 140 in the Hundredth Congress. A major committee (such as the Senate or House Appropriations Committee) may have as many as 13 subcommittees. The growth of subcommittee government has enhanced the effectiveness of lobbying and single-issue groups. By targeting the relatively few legislators sitting on a subcommittee, lobbies can sharply focus their concerns, often at the expense of other groups—or the public interest.

Numerous attempts have been made to restructure the congressional committee system, to streamline it and to abolish certain committees. All such efforts have failed in the House. Whenever the specter of abolishing a committee or subcommittee is raised, members of Congress with a stake in that committee, as well as key interest groups, organize to oppose it. Some movement toward reform has been made in the Senate. Senators are now permitted to hold no more than eleven committee and subcommittee assignments, instead of the previous limit of eighteen. Conscientious fulfillment of eleven assignments, however, still means spreading oneself rather thin.

cial interests of each local representative than to the overall public interest.

Once assigned to a committee, legislators generally have a right to stay there for as long as they serve in Congress. The majority-party member who has served on the committee the longest usu-

CONSEQUENCES OF STRUCTURAL FRAGMENTATION
As we have seen, Congress has a highly decentralized and fragmented decision-making structure; most of the legislative work is handled by specialized committees and subcommittees. From a democratic point of view, this structure has both positive and negative consequences. On the positive side, the process of specialization helps members focus their energies and talents on particular areas of policy, and thereby develop the expertise that many consider the finest benefit of a legislative career. Decentralization and specialization also help Congress to process the overwhelming volume of information and legislative business that it must deal with.

But specialization also has many drawbacks. Because policy making in Congress is highly fragmented, there is often little coherence in the way the legislature conducts its affairs. Also, since committees usually operate in a highly independent fashion, each committee tends to develop a protectionist attitude toward its own area of jurisdiction. Frequently, legislators of a certain ideological persuasion, or those from a particular geographic area or representing a specific constituency, predominate on a particular committee—those from farm states on agriculture committees, for example. And like-minded members often wind up with a highly partisan view, supporting policies that aid their particular interests. In addition, they develop close relationships with interest groups and agencies in the executive branch that work along similar lines. Congress thus tends to serve many small constituencies, rather than adopting the larger view—the good of the whole nation, or the public interest. Finally, it is often the practice in Congress for one committee to defer to another; this results in a kind of mutual admiration society in which each special area gains some measure of what it wants. Although this process may be useful in building congressional majorities, it often serves only the many special interests involved.

Former Texas Representative Bob Eckhardt called the committee structure of Congress the chief strength and weakness in the congressional system. One political scientist views the matter more somberly: "Congress has proven increasingly incapable of creating an internal structure that could produce decisive, innovative, independent, and authoritative policy decisions on major policy issues."[8] Yet, it would not be fair to blame structural idiosyncracies alone for Congress's difficulties in forming and implementing coherent policy. The variety and fragmenting nature of influences on particular members of Congress, and the constitutional system of separation of powers and checks and balances also contribute to Congress's difficulties. These aspects of the legislative process will be covered later in this chapter, after a look at how a bill becomes a law.

How a Bill Becomes a Law

Procedures in Congress follow a rigid, prescribed routine, especially when it comes to how a bill becomes a law. As **Figure 11–2** shows, passage of a bill is the final step in a laborious process that involves several specified stages in both the House and the Senate.

Nothing is assured once a bill enters the labyrinth of committee perusal and floor debate; at any stage along the way a proposal can be killed or simply left to die a natural death. In fact, the vast majority of proposals never make it out of committee. Those that do are often so loaded with controversial amendments (or **riders**) that legislators refuse to pass them or the president to sign them. Let us now look at each step of the process of passing a bill, to see where these pitfalls lie.

ORIGINATION   Legislation can originate in any of several ways. Some proposals arise from pressing national problems, as the New Deal legislation of the 1930s did from the Great Depression. Others originate in local problems or constituency demands, such as flood control or the building of a harbor. Still other proposals represent efforts to amend or renew existing legislation.

Bills can originate within either Congress or the administration. When the administration initiates legislation, proposals are prepared, or drafted, either by particular government agencies or by administration officials. When Congress takes the initiative, bills are usually drafted by congressional staff members or by experts placed at the disposal of members of Congress.

FIGURE 11–2
How a Bill Becomes Law

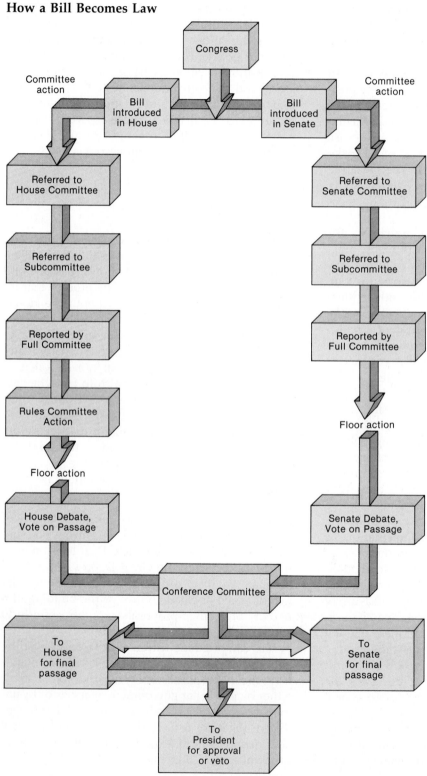

The Rider: A Key Part of the Legislative Process

Legislators often seek to gain attention for pet proposals by attaching them as riders (nongermane amendments) to important pieces of legislation.* Once a rider has been attached to a bill, it is often difficult to separate it from the main legislation, and the rider may gain approval as part of a larger package. This process occurs most frequently with appropriations bills.

In February 1984, for example, President Reagan made a noncontroversial proposal to provide $90 million in emergency food aid to drought-stricken nations in Africa. The House appropriations subcommittee on agriculture approved the request. Then the full committee raised the amount to $150 million, added to the bill a proposal for $200 million in energy assistance to low-income Americans, and sent the package to the House floor. The full House approved the measure. In the Senate, the African aid measure was diverted by the chairman of the appropriations subcommittee on foreign relations, who wanted to attach a rider appropriating $93 million in military aid for El Salvador. The full Senate committee then added to the measure the $200 million in energy assistance contained in the House bill and tacked on a further $21 million for insurgents fighting the government of Nicaragua.

At this point, the main sponsors of the original African aid bill, fearing it would go down to defeat amid battles over Central American policy, shrewdly proposed creating a separate bill that would include $80 million in African aid plus the $200 million in low-income energy assistance. It passed both House and Senate and was signed by the president. Meanwhile, the original bill became laden with even more riders, including money for nutrition programs, summer youth employment, drug interceptor aircraft, various dams, and construction of the proposed Cumberland Gap tunnel. House leaders reacted angrily: "We sent the Senate a $90 million piece of legislation to feed the poor in Africa and it ends up as $1.3 billion."†

This example is extreme, but it illustrates how riders can affect the legislative process. In many cases, proposals have been killed or derailed by being loaded with so many additions that they ultimately became unacceptable to their sponsors. It is easy to see why many observers criticize the rider system as an unreasonable obstruction to the legislative process.

---

*Theoretically, only the Senate can add nongermane amendments to a bill; but by twisting the rules, House members can also vote on riders.

†Martin Tolchin, "Hitching a Ride on Capitol Hill," *The New York Times,* May 2, 1984.

About one-third of all bills that are passed are private bills, dealing with the grievances or needs of particular citizens. The other two-thirds are public bills—those affecting the general public.

INTRODUCTION A proposal is introduced into each house by a member who supports it. In the House, the member simply hands the bill over to the clerk; in the Senate, a member must announce the proposal formally on the Senate floor. Although most bills are introduced simultaneously, or nearly so, in the two houses, a bill may undergo consecutive consideration—first passing through one house, then being considered in the other.

COMMITTEE CONSIDERATION After the proposal is given an official number, the Speaker (for the House) and the president pro tempore (in the Senate) refer it to the appropriate standing committees. Because most of the substantive work on legislation is done in committee, this stage often is crucial in the lawmaking process. Once assigned to a standing committee, most bills are then referred to a specialized subcommittee for detailed discussion. The subcommittees hold hearings, at which interested individuals or groups can voice their views on the proposed legislation. The bill is also referred to committee staff members, who seek expert opinion on its likely effects and costs.

Next, in what is known as the "mark up," the subcommittee goes over the bill in detail—often rewriting it on the basis of what the hearings have revealed and what the subcommittee members believe will be acceptable to members of the larger committee. Finally, the marked-up bill goes back to the larger committee with a favorable or unfavorable recommendation. If the committee votes to approve the bill, it goes to the full chamber for consideration. Bills that are not approved in committee are killed.

FLOOR DEBATE Scheduling a bill for consideration by the full chamber is a fairly simple process in the Senate, where the majority leader is in charge. A majority of the Senate can vote to consider a bill on the floor, or the majority party's Policy Committee can schedule floor action after consultation with the minority leader. In the House, the bill must be listed on a particular "calendar" (according to what type of bill it is—private or public, revenue or nonrevenue, controversial or noncontroversial), which determines when the bill will reach the floor. Most bills must also pass through the House Rules Committee, which decides how the bill will be debated—for example, whether or not it can be amended. Once the rules of debate are established, floor consideration is set by the Speaker.

FLOOR ACTION Every bill that reaches the floor must be considered and voted on by each house. In the House of Representatives, each member is allowed one hour of debate (unless the Rules Committee has decided otherwise). In debates over amendments to a bill, members are allowed only five minutes of speaking time apiece. In the Senate, debate is not limited or subject to specified rules. The smaller size of the Senate permits the luxury of prolonged debate, although in a **filibuster**—the attempt to talk a bill to death—this privilege can be taken to extremes.

After the debate, a vote is taken on the bill. Ordinarily, each house passes its own version of a bill. Those versions may differ in the amounts of money allocated to a particular program, certain specifics of the legislation, or the riders that have been tacked on. When the bills differ, House and Senate leaders appoint a conference committee to work out a version acceptable to both houses. The five to ten members of the conference committee generally include several members of the relevant standing committees, plus other interested members. The version hammered out in conference must then be voted on by each house exactly as it is written; no further amendments are permitted.

PRESIDENTIAL CONSIDERATION A bill approved by both houses is sent to the president, who may consider it for up to ten days. If the president signs the bill, it becomes law. If the chief executive vetoes (rejects) the bill, it is returned to each house with a message explaining the reasons for the veto. To override a veto, each house must repass the bill by a two-thirds majority; otherwise, the bill is killed for that session of Congress. If Congress adjourns within the ten-day period allotted for presidential consideration of a bill, the president can exercise what is known as a **pocket veto**: that is, the chief executive kills the bill by refusing to sign it (by "pocketing" it). If the president does not sign the bill within the ten days *and* Congress is in session, the bill automatically becomes law.

IMPLEMENTATION Once a bill becomes law, the executive branch must put that law into effect. This may mean, for example, issuing new rules in accordance with the bill, or establishing a new government agency or independent commission. Implementation may also require allocating funds to a particular project, or giving the go-ahead for a study. In implementing a bill, the executive branch must interpret the intentions of Congress, and if Congress does not agree with that interpretation, it may pass further laws to clarify its intentions.

REACTION Responses to legislation can range from widespread approval to intense opposition. Supporters may anxiously await implementation and hope that Congress's purposes will be effectively carried through. Opponents may challenge the new law in the courts, a strategy designed to delay implementation. If implementation does not proceed smoothly, Congress may take new initiatives to clarify or amend the bill. At this point, the legislative cycle begins again.

Members of Congress engage in a variety of tasks, but the gestures and forms they use are reassuringly familiar. Senator Nancy Kassebaum here leads a U.S. election-observer team to El Salvador in 1982. Such trips offer visible signs of U.S. support for certain regimes, principles, or programs—and they sometimes are used to show a difference of opinion between the legislative and executive branches. *(UPI/Bettmann Newsphotos)*

Members of Congress

The 535 men and women who represent us in Congress have heavy responsibilities and, some would say, an almost impossible task—enacting and overseeing the basic rules by which Americans live and the programs that help to sustain U.S. society.

Would-be legislators face a tough struggle to gain expertise, to master the arts of legislating, and to learn how and when to compromise, to reconcile various interests, to withstand pressure. But do they have enough time to acquaint themselves with (much less master) the components of complex legislation? Can our lawmakers vote their clear convictions and still win reelection? Does Congress work in a creative and constructive fashion, or does it merely rubber-stamp the wishes of powerful interests? In short, do our representatives represent only some of the people some of the time?

Before addressing more complex questions, we must first examine the types of people who represent us in Congress—(1) their personal characteristics; (2) their professional concerns; (3) the influences they face in voting; and (4) congressional ethics.

Personal Characteristics

The typical member of Congress is a well-educated, affluent, fifty-year-old white male, Protestant in religion and a businessman or lawyer by profession. Of course, many representatives do not fit this prototypical profile, and a few differ on almost every count. Yet the average carries considerable weight. The Hundredth Congress (1987–1988) included only twenty-three blacks, fourteen Hispanics, and twenty-five women (including two in the Senate)—about 4.3 percent, 2.6 percent, and 4.7 percent, respectively, of the total membership. These percentages do not approach those of blacks, Hispanics, and women in the U.S. population. Even more severely underrepresented are blue-collar workers, union members, teachers, housewives, and the like. **Table 11–4** profiles the Hundredth Congress.

In financial terms, our representatives are considerably better off than the average citizen. Although most legislators live largely off their $89,500 annual salary, most receive additional income from investments, legal fees, lecture fees, real estate, partnerships, or businesses. There are about twenty-five millionaires in Congress. Also,

TABLE 11–4
Profile of the 100th Congress (1987–1988)

	House	Senate
Party		
Democrats	258	55
Republicans	177	45
Average Age		
99th Congress	49.4	54.2
100th Congress	50.7	54.4
Sex		
Men	412	98
Women	23	2
Religion		
Protestants	258	66
Roman Catholics	123	19
Jews	29	8
Others	25	7
Profession*		
Actor/entertainer	1	0
Aeronautics	3	2
Agriculture	20	5
Business/banking	142	28
Clergy	2	1
Education	38	12
Engineering	4	1
Journalism	20	8
Labor officials	2	0
Law	184	62
Law enforcement	7	0
Medicine	3	1
Military	0	1
Professional sports	5	1
Public service/politics	94	20

*Because some members have more than one occupation, totals are higher than total membership.
SOURCE: *Congressional Quarterly Weekly*, Nov. 8, 1986, p. 2862.

many members obtain committee assignments that create substantial opportunities for conflicts of interest. When members retain financial interests in areas they deal with as legislators, decision making is, at the least, not disinterested.

Professional Concerns

The individual legislator has two principal tasks: to legislate and to provide constituent service. Simply keeping up with these tasks taxes the average member's resources of time, energy, and intellect. But another time-consuming task goes with the job—running for reelection. Campaigning and fund-raising are particularly onerous burdens for House members, who must run every two years; senators, with six-year terms, don't have to invest the same amount of time and energy in reelection efforts. We now probe how our lawmakers handle (1) the business of legislating; (2) constituent concerns; and (3) the drive for reelection.

LEGISLATING   Most legislators devote a considerable amount of time to the complicated work of lawmaking. As we noted earlier, forging a bill into a law requires legislators to attend numerous committee and subcommittee meetings. They must also be present when important debates take place on the floor of Congress. Proper consideration of a bill also requires a great deal of study: Representatives must make time to read, think, consult with others, and sometimes research important issues. Because familiarity with a particular issue or set of issues builds respect among colleagues and raises the member's stature overall, many legislators work to develop expertise in key areas.

SERVING CONSTITUENTS   Another large block of time in a representative's day is devoted to handling constituents' concerns: answering mail, helping to solve constituents' problems, writing and delivering speeches aimed at constituents, disseminating information by newsletter or press release, meeting with constituents. Much of this work involves so-called casework tasks, which arise when individual citizens ask for help in coping with government bureaucracy. For example, the representative's staff might investigate alleged errors in Social Security or veterans' payments to constituents.

Legislators also provide services to interest groups. For instance, they may be called on to supply pertinent economic and technical data to a group of computer manufacturers, to introduce a

Representative Tony Coelho joins homeless advocate Mitch Snyder for a television interview after a winter night on a Capitol Hill steam grate as part of the "Grate American Sleep Out." Publicity events like this can focus public attention on policy issues. Ironically, for many it may be easier to empathize with the Congressman's temporary discomfort than with the long-term conditions he seeks to publicize. *(AP/Wide World Photos)*

bill on behalf of an environmental group, or to work against a bill opposed by the building industry. In some cases, finally, a legislator may seek to gain specific benefits for his or her whole state or district—by obtaining federal highway money for highway construction, for example, or by steering a defense contract to a home-district firm.

REELECTION CONCERNS Constituency service is not altogether altruistic; much of it is motivated by the desire to get reelected. For members of the House, in particular, reelection is a constant preoccupation. One study found that, on average, House members return to their home districts thirty-five times a year. Some members even complain that they seem to spend more time running through airports and in the air, between Washington and their home states, than they do handling the nation's business. Most trips are made by newer members looking to consolidate a political base. Members who don't make frequent trips to their home states may earn a reputation for being out of touch with constituents, making the legislator more vulnerable to be challenged successfully. When the population of a district changes,

or redistricting occurs, a member must work particularly hard to reestablish strong local ties.

Senators enjoy a more relaxed reelection schedule (every six years), but Senate races tend to be more competitive than House races. From 1976 to 1986, well over 90 percent of all House members up for reelection retained their seats. In the Senate, on the other hand, the reelection success of incumbents over the same period fluctuated between 55 and 93 percent (see **Table 11–5**).[9] In 1986 a record-high 98 percent of House members who ran again were successful, while only 75 percent of their Senate colleagues were reelected.

House districts, then, have become less and less "marginal"—that is, less closely contested—over the years.[10] Several factors account for this change. As party-oriented voting has declined for congressional seats, incumbency has become more significant. Incumbents become known at least by name to a significant number of voters. Anyone challenging an incumbent must therefore overcome the invisibility factor, which is far more serious in House than in Senate races. Ironically, a challenger often finds it easier to raise funds for the more expensive Senate races, which usually feature ex-

TABLE 11–5
The Advantage of Incumbency in Reelection

	Total number of incumbents, general elections			Percentage of incumbents winning
	Running	*Winning*	*Losing*	
1976				
House	381	368	13	96.6
Senate	25	16	9	64.0
1978				
House	378	359	19	95.0
Senate	22	15	7	68.1
1980				
House	398	361	31	90.7
Senate	29	16	9	55.2
1982				
House	393	354	29	90.0
Senate	30	28	2	93.3
1984				
House	408	396	16	96.1
Senate	29	26	3	89.7
1986				
House	391	385	6	98.5
Senate	28	21	7	75.0

SOURCE: *Congressional Quarterly Weekly,* Nov. 10, 1984; and Nov. 8, 1986.

tensive TV coverage. Senators face greater competition, principally because their constituencies are larger and more diverse and because it is usually harder to please a state than a district. Moreover, senators tend to focus more on national concerns than their counterparts in the House, and senators gain greater public visibility when they take stands on controversial issues. Finally, the greater prestige of a Senate seat brings out better-financed and better-organized opposition.

Of course, incumbency still confers advantages. Both House and Senate members, for example, are given substantial financial allowances: for the average House member, about $450,000 a year for staff and office expenses; for senators, anywhere from $700,000 to $1.5 million, depending on the popu-

lation of the state represented. Also, incumbents can use government facilities for making tapes and films, and they have free mailing privileges for publications distributed to constituents. Finally, congressional computer services aid incumbents in directing their mail to specialized groups. According to one estimate, every House incumbent has a $500,000 advantage over any challenger, based on the various perquisites of office. Not surprisingly, legislators tend to draw heavily on these privileges in election years.

The disproportionate amount of time and energy now required of a member of Congress simply to stay in office clearly has a negative impact on the legislative process. Preoccupied with reelection, members must direct their energies toward particular constituencies. Those elected now owe little to their party, and consequently, party leaders in Congress exert less influence on members. Working for reelection also cuts into the time available to learn about and ponder the substantive issues of public policy. As Representative John Hiler said in a 1988 interview, "When you run and get elected, you think you're going to be working on the very large problems of the world. . . . It turns out you work on a lot of things very close to home."[11]

Influences on Voting Patterns

What influences a legislator's vote in Congress? If Congress were like practically any other democratic legislature, the answer would be easy: party discipline. But as we have already seen, U.S. political parties are relatively undisciplined organizations. Party identification still exerts a significant influence on the way a legislator votes, but so do ideological commitments (especially along liberal/conservative lines), informal groups in Congress, constituent desires, and interest-group pressures. We now examine the influence of (1) political parties; (2) ideology; (3) issue and identity groupings; and (4) other factors on congressional voting patterns.

PARTY Over the years, party identification has been one of the more clearcut factors in congressional voting. As we might expect in a legislature

Base-Building: One Way to Stay in Office

Consider the case of Representative Bruce Morrison, first elected to the House in 1982 from Connecticut's Third District. A narrow victor over his Republican opponent, Morrison knew he had to stay closely in touch with the needs and demands of various individuals and groups back home. When Congress recessed in the summer of 1983, Morrison headed home to engage in base-building—making sure he was firmly in touch with what people were saying back in the district.

Here is what Morrison's schedule looked like on a typical day back in the district:

Attended a meeting with the Wallingford Chamber of Commerce, which was seeking federal funds for sewers.

Met with a group that delivers free food in the New Haven area. Through the congressman's efforts they had been able to obtain a small portion of a $4.6 billion federal allocation for areas hard hit by recession. They were worried about getting more money after the allocation ran out.

Attended a dedication ceremony marking the rehabilitation of a group of Victorian townhouses, a task partly financed by federal funds. Through his presence, Morrison claimed some of the credit.

Toured an abandoned church that local doctors were converting into medical offices. Since the building was a historic landmark, the conversion required the permission of the U.S. Department of the Interior. Morrison decided he would try to help the doctors get the permits they needed.

Went to a local nursing home that was seeking better bus service in its neighborhood. Bureaucratic complications had thus far prevented the Department of Transportation from helping with federal funds. Received at his local office a group, including two men in wheelchairs, who advised him on problems of the handicapped.

Attended a cocktail party to raise money for a local landmark, the Schubert Theatre.

Morrison understood that his reelection prospects hinged on many small efforts in the district. Like many legislators, he had financial problems. His campaign debts in 1984, in which he was narrowly reelected, ran between $80,000 and $90,000. Fund-raising issues therefore occupied much of the staff's time, and sometimes took priority. As one staff member said, no matter how busy the congressman is, "check-presentation ceremonies always get scheduled immediately."

SOURCE: Steven B. Roberts, "A Freshman Tends to the Task of 'Base-Building,' " *The New York Times*, August 18, 1983. The author also acknowledges the help of Representative Morrison's office staff, and particularly Barbara Geller.

---

containing only two parties, many issues are fought out along party lines. But we also know that American parties are anything but unified. Party allegiance, therefore, only partially explains why legislators vote as they do. Over the last decade, voting along party lines has increased for the Democrats (the average Democrat in 1977 voted with the party majority 67 percent of the time, but in 1986, 78 percent of the time). Over the same period, voting along party lines stayed about the same for the Republicans (the average Republican voted with the party majority 70 percent of the time in 1977 and 71 percent of the time in 1986).

Regional differences are significant: Southern Democrats tend to vote less frequently along party lines than their Northern counterparts (57 percent to 78 percent, respectively, in the Senate in 1986). Republicans show a similar pattern, though not as pronounced: In 1986 the average Northern Republican senator voted with the party majority 74 percent of the time, while the average Southern Republican senator voted with the party majority 85 percent of the time. Because American parties do not have disciplined ideological standards, an individual party member may adhere to or deviate from the party majority consistently. Senator Don Riegle of Michigan, a Democrat, voted with his party 97 percent of the time in 1986, while his fellow Democrat, Russell Long of Louisiana, voted *against* the Democratic majority 67 percent of the time. A similar diversity exists among Republicans.[12]

Predictably, party voting has been strongest on organizational issues, such as those voted on at the opening of a session. Party members almost invariably vote for their party's candidates for the chairmanships of committees and for leadership positions. Members also tend to follow the party line if the president and/or party leaders give a particular policy or issue high priority. For the most part, however, members of Congress understand that pleasing one's constituents, rather than one's party, is most important at election time. Thus, party loyalty often takes a back seat to loyalty to the legislator's district or state.

IDEOLOGY Deviations from party voting can be explained in part by ideology. The House Boll Weevils, for example, an informal group of Southern Democrats, provided strong cross-party support for the major Republican initiatives of the early Reagan years. What bound these members as a group to the Republican minority and distinguished them from their Democratic House colleagues was a sense that government ought to be smaller and that taxes ought to be lower. Ronald Reagan received crucial support along these ideological lines during his first year in office. Although the Democrats held a clear majority in the House of Representatives in 1981, the Reagan administration enjoyed a success rate of 82.4 percent on key votes.

In contrast to the Boll Weevils, a different ideological orientation led to the formation of the Gypsy Moths, a group of Northern Republicans who by "natural inclination" opposed the Republican president on his early legislative agenda. When ideology does not follow party lines, it may act like a veto on legislative proposals rather than

a support for new initiatives. Beginning in the late 1930s, for example, a coalition of conservative Democrats (mainly Southerners) and Republicans banded together to defeat many liberal initiatives in the areas of civil rights, social welfare, civil liberties, and foreign policy.

In the 1980s, a conservative coalition attempted—largely unsuccessfully at the national level—to gain legislative victories on issues like school prayer, abortion, and a balanced budget. This conservative agenda was more successfully advanced in many state legislatures during the 1980s.

ISSUE AND IDENTITY GROUPINGS Congress has also spawned informal groups organized around particular interests and identities that influence members' voting patterns. These caucuses, which tend to be bipartisan, focus on specific interest areas. There is a Black Caucus, a Hispanic Caucus, a Rural Caucus, a Sun Belt Caucus, a Mushroom Caucus, and a Textile Caucus, among many others. One representative noted: "There's a caucus for just about everything around here and I guess it doesn't hurt. You know, they teach kids in school that this is the United States. But in reality, it is a group of regions and caucuses. It's not the UNITED States."[13]

The extent of the caucuses' influence is hard to gauge. About half of them have paid staff. Some operate more on a symbolic than a practical level, while others try to educate and supply information. A few, such as the Steel Caucus, occasionally demonstrate political clout on issues that concern them most. Overall, the rapid growth of caucuses in the 1970s revealed the strong tendency in Congress to generate single-interest groups, reinforcing the particularism that has always strongly characterized our national legislature.

OTHER INFLUENCES Constituency interests and outside interest groups are not simply "other" influences on members of Congress—their impact on voting patterns often is crucial. Constituency preferences figure prominently in legislators' decisions about how to vote on particular bills. Lawmakers' consideration of these preferences, after all, can sometimes make the difference between victory and defeat at reelection time. Interest

Members of the congressional Black Caucus being briefed by presidential candidate Jesse Jackson. (Standing from left: Representatives George Crockett, D-Mich., and Mickey Leland, D-Texas; District of Columbia Delegate Walter Fauntroy, and Representative William Clay, D-Mo. Seated from left: Representatives Julian Dixon, D-Calif., and William Gray, D-Penn; Jackson; and Representative Mervyn Dymally, D-Calif.) Caucuses in Congress differ greatly in their membership and goals, but they generally focus attention on a particular set of interests. *(AP/Wide World Photos)*

groups also carry clout because of the potency of their political action committees. These subjects, however, have been addressed in detail elsewhere in this chapter and in Chapter 9.

Congressional Ethics

Congress has never enjoyed a reputation for scrupulous ethical behavior. Perhaps the low point in congressional morals was reached in the 1880s and 1890s, when railroads and other big corporations paid cash to advance their interests in Congress.[14] In this century, after several decades of what seemed a clean slate, several members of the Ninety-Fourth and Ninety-Fifth Congresses (1975–1978) were convicted and imprisoned on charges ranging from accepting bribes to taking kickbacks from employees, conspiring to extort money, committing perjury, and violating assorted morals statutes. Thirteen representatives and two senators were caught between 1976 and 1978 alone. In early 1980 came the spectacular Abscam scandal in which FBI agents posing as Arab businessmen caught several representatives and one senator taking bribes in exchange for legislative favors.

Both the House and the Senate rewrote their codes of conduct in 1977, and in 1978 passed the Ethics in Government Act, which required members of Congress, judges, and top executive officials to file financial disclosure reports. The difficulty with enforcing congressional codes of conduct, however, is that each chamber must police itself. The House Committee on Standards of Official Conduct and the Senate Select Committee on Ethics are responsible for monitoring and responding to ethics violations within each chamber. Critics charge that neither committee has been as aggressive as it should be, and that even when one of these committees discovers violations, its response has been remarkably restrained. In 1986 the House committee concluded that Dan Daniel of Virginia was guilty of violating House rules in accepting plane rides from military contractors while charging the government for automobile expenses on those same trips. The same year the committee concluded that Representative James Weaver of Oregon had borrowed money from his campaign fund to speculate in commodities, a violation of House rules. In spite of these findings, the committee recommended that the House of Representatives take no action against either Daniel or Weaver. In February 1988 the committee did

Voices from the U.S. Congress

Looking out from the inside, representatives and senators have a unique perspective on our legislative process. Here, speaking anonymously, some of them voice their views on the system's shortcomings.

The job is tremendously wearing. The pressures are just enormous. . . . What it takes to get the job done is eighty hours a week. That's just not compatible with how much time I'd like to spend with my family. I just wanted to get to know my kids before it was too late.

Yes, government is getting bigger, but what's eating this place alive is the growth of one-issue groups. . . . Neither side listens to the other. Consensus can't be achieved. . . . Moses couldn't lead the country today.

The most disappointing part of being in Congress is the financial pressure. . . . I'm not as good in

my job as I could be because I'm always worried about money. Every minute I waste on campaign fund-raising is a minute I should be using for the taxpayers.

The Senate is a great place. But the Senate is a place, right now, that reminds me of a huge giant lumbermill, with all the high technology and the biggest saws in the world, which is making toothpicks. Here in the Senate, we've kind of turned ourselves into a toothpick factory.

You've got the ABA (American Bankers Association) that can't get their act together. Then you've got the insurance agents that don't give a damn about the whole thing as long as you protect their little bailiwick. Throw in the Realtors, and you go through all these groups, looking out for their own bailiwick. As long as they get their own piece of the bill, it's fine; but if they don't, kill the whole thing.

recommend the expulsion from the House of Representatives of Mario Biaggi, a New York Democrat, but only after he had been convicted in a federal District Court of accepting an illegal gratuity and obstructing justice. Julian Dixon, chair of the House ethics committee, commented: "I think the committee does a good job of, one, being nonpartisan and, two, investigating facts, evaluating facts, and taking appropriate action. But is the committee on a constant search for improprieties by members of Congress? The answer is no. I think the members of Congress have a right to feel the committee is not on a witch hunt." Warren Rudman, vice-chair of the Senate Select Committee on Ethics, said, "We're not supposed to be the national nanny down here. We're supposed to look for true breaches of ethics by people who have stretched the law for their personal advantage."[15]

Some observers argue that punishment should be left to the voters, while others maintain that Congress should genuinely apply to its own mem-

bers the strict standards it sets for judges and members of the executive branch.

Conflicts of interest pose an even more subtle and more critical problem from the standpoint of congressional ethics today. Should a senator accept a lecture fee from a prominent lobbying group? Should a legislator accept campaign contributions from corporations and then push legislation that aids them? Members of committees often have financial interests in the very areas covered by their committees, such as real estate and banking. Should they divest themselves of these interests before taking part in votes that would affect their holdings?

Both the House and Senate have rules governing conflicts of interest, but in general individual members are free to decide for themselves when a conflict exists. In 1977 the Senate killed, by an overwhelming vote, a proposal to prohibit senators from aiding in the passage of legislation that would serve to help their own financial interests.

Given the variety and complexity of legislative matters confronting Congress, members ordinarily must specialize and thus may be identified with particular interests. Representative Claude Pepper, D-Fla., has come to be identified with the interests of the elderly. Chairing the powerful House Rules Committee well into his eighties, Pepper is a vigorous example of his special constituency, and he has used his considerable clout to protect and advance programs for the elderly. *(UPI/Bettmann Newsphotos)*

As Congress carries out its business, the lack of real strictures on accepting lecture fees from lobbying organizations, and the lack of constraints on formulating legislation that might yield personal benefits suggest that the *appearance* of impropriety is likely, impropriety itself far from impossible. Neither will help Congress improve its reputation.

Tradition and Reform

Throughout the middle years of this century, Congress was popularly characterized by the stereotype of an aging Southern senator, a gentleman who had served for many years as a powerful committee chairman.[16] He came from a state with little partisan competition and thus attained seniority by being reelected term after term. He usually determined unilaterally how committee business would be conducted. This powerful senator would vote conservative on most matters; on some, perhaps, he would follow the party line. Above all, he took a decidedly conservative view of the workings of Congress itself—its rules, procedures, traditions, and unspoken understandings. The Congress typified by this stereotypical figure drew the ire of liberals for years. Many liberals argued that

marshalling support for significant social change was all but impossible in a Congress dominated by such stodgy conservatives.

From a liberal standpoint several institutional features added to this formula for political stalemate. For many years, conservative senators seeking to delay or kill liberal legislation raised filibustering to a high art. In the other chamber, the powerful House Rules Committee, which determines when a bill reaches the floor for debate—and under what conditions—gave its chairmen the arbitrary power to block legislation. In both houses of Congress, a strong tradition of deference toward senior colleagues reinforced the structural bias favoring the status quo. In addition, much of the hands-on legislative work—building consensus, striking compromises, making deals to win support for legislation—was not subject to public scrutiny, giving entrenched power brokers a relatively free hand.

What a curious spectacle this Congress presented: a supposedly democratic legislature ruled by officeholders who were not elected in a democratic fashion and who usually shaped and passed legislation not by open, responsible policy debate, but by unwritten rules and behind-the-scenes dealing. This one-sided portrait does not fairly rep-

The Filibuster: The Senate's Sacred Cow

The English word *filibuster* is ultimately derived from the Dutch *Vrjibuiter* ("freebooter"—a term once commonly used to describe pirates), by way of the Spanish *filibustero*. In legislative parlance, a *filibuster* is an attempt to talk a bill to death. If unlimited debate is permitted on a bill, a few legislators can theoretically thwart the majority and stop the legislative process by talking nonstop until the bill's proponents agree to kill it. The actual practice of filibustering began in the House but was quickly put to an end there through passage of a variety of measures designed to curtail debate. In the Senate, however, filibustering became a revered right. Senator Strom Thurmond of South Carolina holds the record for the longest speech—24 hours and 18 minutes of nonstop talk in an effort to stop the Civil Rights Act of 1957.

In 1917 the Senate adopted a *cloture* rule, which stipulated that debate on any specific measure could be curtailed provided that two-thirds of the senators present and voting agreed to do so. This rule was revised in 1975 to require a three-fifths vote of the whole Senate, or sixty votes. Under the current rule, one hundred hours of debate is allowed after cloture is invoked. Generally, filibusters are most effective at the close of a congressional session, when members are in a hurry to wind up pressing legislative business. A bill that is effectively killed by a filibuster has to be put through the entire legislative process again in the next session of Congress.

Lowered cloture requirements have not killed the filibuster. There were eighty filibusters in the Senate between 1968 and the end of 1987, compared to only sixty-two filibusters from 1841 to 1968.* Many of these were carried out within normal working hours. But on February 23–25, 1988, the Senate was treated for the first time in a decade to a full-fledged, around-the-clock filibuster. The object of the filibuster was campaign spending legislation, opposed by the Republicans. The week-long filibuster turned into an all-night affair when Senate Majority Leader Robert Byrd declared, "There is no point in continuing the casual, gentlemanly, good guy filibuster."† It was time to break out the mattresses. As it turned out, Majority Leader Byrd meant business, trying eight times to win a cloture vote and even invoking a rarely used Senate rule that allows for the arrest of senators to bring them to the floor of the Senate for a vote. Senator Bob Packwood of Oregon (a Republican opposed to the bill) was arrested in his office and carried into the Senate chamber feet first.§

Is the filibuster a useful mechanism? In some cases a modest filibuster can provide public information or give senators a chance to learn more about an important question. But filibustering for days on end (often by reading out of the Washington, D.C., telephone directory) to prevent action on important legislative matters seems a self-indulgent way of conducting government in the twentieth century.**

---

*From the Congressional Research Service, quoted in *The New York Times*, Dec. 21, 1987, p. 12.

†Irvin Molotsky, "Senate Begins Filibuster on Campaign Spending," *The New York Times*, Feb. 24, 1988, p. 15.

§*Congressional Quarterly Weekly*, Feb. 27, 1988, pp. 485–487.

**Lawrence C. Dodd, "Congress, The Constitution and the Crisis of Legitimation," in Lawrence C. Dodd and Bruce I. Oppenheimer, eds., *Congress Reconsidered*, 2nd ed. (Washington, D.C.: Congressional Quarterly Press, 1981), pp. 156–185.

resent the full spectrum of Congress's operations. Yet the problems and practices it depicts were real, and they troubled all who cared about democratic politics in the United States, including many members of Congress.

In the 1960s and 1970s reforms were undertaken in congressional rules and structures. In the House of Representatives, the selection of committee chairs became more democratic and the power of the chairs was reduced. Committee meetings were opened more regularly to public scrutiny. The House Ways and Means Committee was reformed and its influence drastically curtailed. These reforms had significant ramifications. By the 1980s the House had become a far more egalitarian body, in which junior members played significant roles. House subcommittees, endowed with greater freedom of action, began delving into new and more controversial areas, such as CIA and FBI invasions of privacy and political rights, and the National Aeronautics and Space Administration (NASA) management of the Space Shuttle program. In the Senate, filibusters were curtailed somewhat by reducing the size of the majority needed to shut off debate (now three-fifths instead of two-thirds). New senators could participate more fully in meaningful legislative work, and they could even hold positions of leadership. Phil Gramm of Texas was a freshman senator in 1985 when Congress passed his Gramm-Rudman-Hollings antideficit bill—in the short run, one of the most significant pieces of legislation to come out of that session. The freshman senators of 1987, in their first year in the Senate, played a critical part in the defeat of Robert H. Bork's nomination to the Supreme Court.

Despite these changes, many traditions of the old Congress survive in some form. In the Senate, especially, the old, informal rules of the game still govern most interaction. When Barbara Mikulski, once described as "a stocky, 4-foot-11, rough-edged East Baltimore politician . . . [with] 'the heft of a stevedore and a voice to match,' " joined the Hundredth Congress in 1987 as the junior senator from Maryland, observers familiar with her street-fighter style expected fireworks on the Senate floor. It is a tribute to her political skill—but, more important, to the transcendent power of Senate tradition—that there were none. "She understands it's still an all-boys club, and she's going to be a player," said Senator Dennis DeConcini of Arizona. "She already is."[17]

Seniority remains the rule, deference to older members is still expected, and the filibuster stands to this day as a potent obstructionist tactic. Most observers wuld agree, however, that liberal-sponsored reforms have made the operations of Congress more democratic. With a sharp reduction in the prerogatives of committee chairs, power has become highly decentralized in some respects.

Many more participants can now affect the outcome of legislative battles, as illustrated by the prominence of junior members of both Houses in recent battles over deficit reduction, tax reform, and welfare policy.

Decentralization of power in Congress has also fragmented policy making. But has this change resulted in *better* policy making? Although presidential legislative initiatives now receive greater scrutiny and are less likely to be rubber-stamped, it has become more difficult for House members to take initiatives for the public good, and easier for interest groups to influence public policy. From the hands of party hierarchies and committee chairs, much of the real power in Congress has now passed into the hands of those who can exert the most pressure—through direct or indirect lobbying at all stages of the legislative process.

Increasing levels of partisan voting in the last years of the Reagan presidency mitigate such generalizations to some degree. President Reagan found it harder and harder to persuade a Democratic-controlled Congress to approve sweeping legislation—the hallmark of his first term in office. Yet, this negatively activated partisanship does not signal an end to legislative stalemate. The institutional and social forces within Congress and within the parties, which work against a coherent legislative program, have not been dampened. The legislative process is, indeed, opening up. Yet the possibility remains that the stereotyped committee chair's autocratic control has been replaced not by democratic control, but by no coherent control at all.

Congress and the President

Perhaps the most striking difference between the U.S. Congress and other democratic legislatures is the adversary relationship between the U.S. legislative and executive branches. The two branches both supplement and check each other, as part of the system of checks and balances and **separation of powers** deliberately built into the Constitution. As we have seen, this system was designed to prevent any one institution or group from accumulating too much power. Because the president and the Congress are elected separately and have different constituencies, the president may or may

In the chamber of the House of Representatives, President Reagan delivers the annual State of the Union address before the assembled members of Congress, Justices of the Supreme Court, members of the Cabinet, the Joint Chiefs of Staff, and foreign ambassadors. The momentary formal appearance of unity of such occasions quickly gives way to the push and shove of political battling that characterize our system of separation of powers. *(Art Stein/Photo Researchers)*

not belong to the party that commands a majority in either house of Congress. As a result, presidents frequently have to deal with a hostile majority in at least one house.

Contrast this with the simplified system of a **parliamentary democracy**, in which executive and legislature are one and the same. Elections are held for the parliament, and whichever party wins a majority organizes the government. Rather than a separation of powers between the different branches, a parliamentary system incorporates a fusion of power. And because parliaments usually maintain strong party discipline, the majority party normally is able to pass its basic program.

Of course, parliamentary systems also can be plagued by complications, such as the absence of a clear majority in a multiparty system. And it is true that presidents and congresses have often worked together harmoniously despite party differences. Nevertheless, the U.S. system of government practically invites muddled lines of legislative responsibility. When legislation is passed or defeated, it may be difficult to sort out which party and which branch is responsible for what results.

One observer described the situation as follows:

> A president . . . may have a coherent program to present to Congress. But each House can add to each of his bills, or take things out of them, or reject them outright, and what emerges from the tussle may bear little or no resemblance to what the president wanted. So when an election comes, the president, the senator, the representative, reproached with not having carried out his promises, can always say, "Don't blame me!" . . . It ends up that nobody . . . can be held responsible for anything done or not done. Everybody concerned can legitimately and honestly say it was not his fault.[18]

Despite its status as one of the democratic world's most independent and powerful legislatures, Congress has found its powers gradually diminished in relation to those of the executive branch. Twentieth-century politics, which emphasizes crisis management and organizational sophistication, promoted this trend. The presidency, with its centralized lines of authority and its greater flexibility, has captured center stage whenever national action was called for, sparking and guiding national policy. Congress now largely reacts to presidential initiatives.

This raises one of the most difficult questions about our government: How is the representative function to be divided among separate branches of government? A glance at the Constitution reveals that the framers counted heavily on Congress to express the wishes of the people. Article I, the legislative article, is by far the longest and most complex. It provides for the most direct ties between ordinary citizens and the federal government.

But many people identify the federal government with the president, not the Congress. Presidents are glamorous, highly visible individuals, loved by the media. Turnout in presidential elections is always higher than in congressional elections. In an important sense, the president is best able to present certain choices to the people, and thus to *re*present their choices within the government. Where does that leave Congress? The problem is particularly acute in our fast-paced, increasingly complex society. Consider, for instance, the following concerns: How can Congress—a largely decentralized, open body—handle matters requiring secrecy? What role can Congress play in matters of urgent national security that require swift, decisive action? And how can Congress develop a national budget of enormous scope and sophistication, not unduly burdened with **pork barrel projects**—appropriations for political patronage—for the home district or state? All these questions reflect the difficulties of sharing power. These thorny issues are addressed next as we take up (1) the legislative veto; (2) Congress and secrets; (3) Congress and the War Powers Act; and (4) Congress and the budget.

The Legislative Veto

A senior White House official recently said, "Congress does only two things well—nothing and overreact."[19] With today's vast, complex, administrative government, the legislature's responsibility is difficult to define. Executive power tends to expand with the expansion of administrators and complex regulations. This shifts the distribution of shared power. One major tool devised by Congress early in the twentieth century to retain some control under these circumstances is the legislative veto—a technique by which Congress delegates authority to the president and at the same time retains enough authority to interfere with the way that presidential power is used. The first use of the legislative veto was in 1932, when Congress gave the president the power to reorganize the executive branch with the understanding that if Congress didn't like any of the changes, it could "veto" them by expressing its displeasure in a resolution. This procedure reflected the increasing intricacies of modern government and the inability of Congress to deal with many such complexities directly.[20]

Through the legislative veto, congressional subcommittees could and often did dictate to executive branch agencies exactly how they wanted particular rules applied. Although the legislative veto was used for more than half a century and appeared in almost two thousand legislative provisions, in 1983 the Supreme Court declared that the legislative veto violated the separation of powers. In the Court's view, the veto circumvented the full legislative machinery, requiring bicameral legislative consideration and subsequent presidential review. Without these procedural safeguards, the Court thought Congress might act too quickly, and unwisely. While this ruling may keep the Congress from overreacting through the legislative veto, it runs the risk of allowing Congress to engage its other skill—doing nothing at all. In fact, Congress seems to be doing just that—nothing—to try to clear up the problems left by this Supreme Court ruling. Of forty-three major laws directly affected, only nine have been amended to conform to the Court's decision.[21]

Congress and Secrets

An ongoing problem for Congress involves overseeing in areas that require secrecy. The institution's size and structure make it difficult for Congress to keep a secret. The reforms covered earlier in this chapter—increasing the democratic and open tendencies in the national legislature—only exacerbate the problem. Thus, the executive branch generally, and the intelligence services particularly, find it easier and safer to keep members of Congress in the dark. This poses a troublesome problem for a democratic government.

Large legislative bodies like Congress are not good at keeping secrets. Although this may broadly serve democratic government by ensuring that policy will be debated, it also may encourage some to keep even Congress in the dark. One recent example of renegade executive action was the Iron-contra affair. Here Oliver North, a central player in the affair, is sworn in at congressional hearings in July 1987. *(AP/Wide World Photos)*

In the Iran-contra affair, which began to unravel in late 1986, members of the Reagan administration sought to make arms-for-hostages deals with Iran while the president publicly, categorically rejected such a policy. Members of the executive branch admitted to and defended misleading the Congress in these matters. Oliver North was applauded when he said that if he had to choose between "lies and lives" he would rather protect agents in the field and deceive Congress. The controversy and outrage surrounding this affair highlight a fundamental principle of democratic theory: A government may find it necessary to keep *strategies* or *tactics* secret from its people, but if it wants to remain a democracy, it cannot maintain secret *policies*. Whatever the means of representation, the people must be able to ratify—and sometimes reject—the policy choices that are made in their name. Of course, implementation of publicly chosen goals may require secrecy under certain circumstances. The design of military hardware and the specifics of military movements or our precise bargaining positions in direct negotiations may properly be kept from public discussion. But the general questions about what a government should and should not be doing must be matters of open debate. Even in areas where secrecy is justifiable in a democracy, secrets should not be kept from the responsible *representatives* of the people.

The actions undertaken in the Iran-contra affair violated this principle on two levels: First, the administration pursued a secret policy, in direct opposition to the government's publicly held position; and second, the actual policy was kept secret from the people's representatives in Congress as well as from the public at large. By way of explanation, the administration maintained that the true nature of the negotiations was not made clear to the president, either. There are no simple answers here. When is a strategy broad enough or distinctive enough to require public consideration?

Following the revelations of the Iran-contra hearings, the White House announced a "philosophy" of secret operations meant to reassure Congress that such operations would not get out of control. Secret operations should be used as a "last resort," should be used only in support of existing policies, and should be of limited duration. But Congress must still make sure the White House is living by its philosophy. And the executive will continue to fear that some information that should properly be kept secret will be exposed if given to Congress. Accordingly, making and keeping secrets will remain a matter for debate and interbranch conflict.

Congress and the War Powers Act

The Vietnam War demonstrated definitively that modern armed conflicts have outgrown eighteenth-century notions about declaring war; these were the basis of the framers' distribution of war-making power between the Congress and the president. The entire Vietnam War was conducted without a declaration of war by Congress. As the Vietnam War wore on, many in Congress realized that they had allowed the president too much freedom in shaping foreign policy. Presidents Johnson and Nixon both had hidden important developments from Congress. While Johnson usually tried to finesse (or, in some cases, deceive) Congress, Nixon confronted Congress with direct challenges to its power. He forbid administration representatives from testifying before congressional committees, and he refused to heed Congress's call to halt the bombings in Indochina.

Congress reponded with the **War Powers Act** in 1973, which it passed over Nixon's veto. This act requires the president to consult with Congress before sending U.S. troops into combat.[22] The act states, in part: "The President in every possible instance shall consult with Congress before introducing United States armed forces into hostilities or into situations where imminent involvement in hostilities is clearly indicated by the circumstances." In addition, it requires that in the absence of a declaration of war, the president must report to Congress within forty-eight hours after troops are sent (in cases where it is not possible to "consult" beforehand). If Congress does not approve the involvement within sixty days, troops must be withdrawn. The history of the War Powers Act epitomizes the difficulty of two branches sharing power in responding to threats to the national security. The executive tendency is to leave Congress out of the decision-making loop by failing to consult prior to taking action and by refusing to acknowledge conditions under which the

War Powers Act should be invoked. The legislative response to this exclusion is often cautious to the point of being timid, as no member of Congress wishes to be seen as an obstacle to the president's vigorous defense of the national security.

President Ford "reported" to Congress on four occasions, the most prominent of which was the 1975 rescue operation of the U.S. sailors from the *Mayaguez*, which had been seized by Cambodians off the Cambodian coast. Many remarked at the time of the rescue (in which many more died than were saved) that the president should have "consulted" with Congress beforehand rather than "reporting" afterward.

In April 1980 President Carter's attempted rescue operation of American hostages in Iran presented a similar situation. The attempt was aborted when some helicopters broke down and collided, but Carter also had failed to consult Congress in advance. Did he violate the spirit or letter of the War Powers Act?

In 1982 Ronald Reagan sent U.S. forces into Lebanon in a peace-keeping effort after Israel had invaded that country. Reagan thereafter obtained permission from Congress to keep the troops there for eighteen months. They were withdrawn considerably earlier, however, after the peace-keeping efforts failed and several hundred Americans were killed when terrorists bombed the U.S. Embassy in Beirut. Nonetheless, in consulting with congres-

President Reagan committed U.S. troops to a peacekeeping force in Lebanon in 1982 and later obtained congressional approval to keep the troops there for eighteen months. Having the executive seek such approval marked the first success of the War Powers Act. On October 23, 1983, a terrorist bomb killed 241 U.S. marines and sailors at the Beirut International Airport—which, along with the general failure of the peacekeeping force, led to withdrawal before the eighteen-month limit. *(Franklin/Sygma)*

sional leaders to obtain support for the mission Reagan had acknowledged the significance of the War Powers Act. It was the first real success of the resolution, actually placing limits on the size and scope of a U.S. mission.

In 1983 the Supreme Court declared a portion of the act unconstitutional when it argued that Congress did not have the authority to order withdrawal of forces before sixty days. The main force of the act remained in place, however.

In 1987, in response to the Iran-Iraq war and its threatened disruption of shipping in the Persian Gulf, President Reagan sent a substantial naval force to patrol the gulf and to escort Kuwaiti oil tankers that flew the U.S. flag under a "reflagging agreement." Although there were open hostilities in the gulf, and even direct attacks on ships flying the U.S. flag (including the *U.S.S. Stark,* a naval destroyer), the White House claimed it was not necessary to invoke the War Powers Act. A suit brought by 110 members of Congress challenging that position was dismissed in December 1987 by a U.S. District Court judge. This failure to marshal the support of the judicial branch in opposing the president underscores Congress's difficulty in securing a significant role in the foreign policy arena.

Prompted by the notable lack of success of the War Powers Act, Senate leaders in 1988 spearheaded a drive to reshape the act. Under the proposal, a "consultative" group of eighteen congressional leaders would confer with the president at the outbreak of a foreign policy crisis. This group could then invoke the War Powers Act by introducing legislation in Congress that would either authorize deployment of military troops or order American forces withdrawn. The proposed measure would also prohibit the use of federal funds for any action that violated the War Powers Act.

Speaking about the impact of the present act, Senator George J. Mitchell, a Maine Democrat, said, "We (in Congress) have rarely reached a consensus but we have often conveyed the appearance of a divided country, and in doing so, we have undermined the positive role that Congress can and should play in crucial national policy decisions."[23]

Skirmishes between the president and Congress over foreign policy often cause considerable con-

fusion for foreign governments. They do not understand how the constitutional separation of powers works, or that presidential power in foreign affairs is not unlimited. Whom are they to negotiate with—Congress or the president? The world was treated to a clear example of this confusion in 1987 when Speaker of the House Jim Wright, seriously at odds with the White House over Central American policy, met with Nicaraguan President Daniel Ortega in an attempt to further the Central American peace process. In the view of some analysts, Congress approaches foreign policy as if it were another aspect of lawmaking, and thus tends "to place a straitjacket of legislation around the manifold complexity of our relations with other nations."[24]

Despite the validity of some of these criticisms, Congress has actually accomplished a great deal through its newly aggressive stance on foreign policy. Admirers of the new Congress point out that it has helped to make future Vietnams less likely, reversed the trend toward unchecked presidential power in foreign affairs, shifted the pattern of American commitments abroad in constructive ways, and broadened the base of foreign policy making.[25]

Congress and the Budget

Traditionally, the budget process in Congress involved a "war between the parts and the whole." The president's budget was divided up among a large number of committees, each of which dealt with one facet of it. Because little attention was paid to how the various parts affected the whole, Congress, unlike the president, had no overview of the budget. Much of the time congressional committees simply deferred to executive judgment on authorizations and appropriations of funds for programs. That part of the budget subject to congressional consideration usually amounted to less than half of total federal expenditures; the remainder was not subject to annual authorizations. As a result, the executive had a relatively free hand. Moreover, presidents sometimes made their own decisions on how much to spend, unilaterally impounding funds authorized for programs they disapproved of.

Text continues following the color essay.

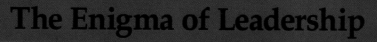

The Enigma of Leadership

What Is *the Right Stuff for Democracy?*

Americans traditionally disparage politicians, and the scorn that we heap on them as a class blurs our criteria for choosing leaders. By an odd logic that has echoes in the Constitution itself, we tend to assume that anyone who seeks political office probably should not be trusted with it. So how should we fill our highest-level jobs in government? Which aspects of leadership should we emphasize in screening candidates?

The German sociologist Max Weber (1864–1920) identified three types of legitimate leadership: *traditional/patriarchal leadership,* whereby the leader is chosen and obeyed simply because "that's how it's always been"; *rational/legal leadership,* based on particular qualifications and training and sanctioned by law; and *charismatic leadership,* for which the only explanation is that the leader has "that certain something" which persuades others to follow.

After two centuries of democratic government it would be nice to think that we choose our leaders rationally. We often do consider qualifications and experience, but not always, and not always strictly. In fact, our selection of leaders reveals a variety of criteria, not all of which are genuinely rational, and we seem to use different models of leadership for each of the three branches of federal government.

Senator and Mrs. John F. Kennedy, 1960   UPI/BETTMANN NEWSPHOTOS

Congressional Leadership
The model for choosing members of Congress is becoming increasingly traditional, particularly in the House, where incumbency almost guarantees reelection. The advantages of incumbency include seniority, high visibility, and larger contributions from political action committees. Indeed, PAC financial support is determined less by a candidate's ideology or competence or party affiliation than simply by incumbency. PACs that want a friendly ear in Congress know that the incumbent is the safest bet. From 1983 to 1988 they gave *fourteen times as much* to incumbents as to challengers; candidates for open seats, with no incumbent, received about the same as challengers.[1] Furthermore, as incumbents become more secure, they appeal even more to contributors.

Within each house of Congress, the traditional model and means of allotting power—seniority—is still important, but less so than in the past. Although committee chairpersons still control the legislative process, power is generally much less centralized today than it was during the 1950s, under House Speaker Sam Rayburn and Senate Majority Leader Lyndon Johnson. Forty years ago it was unthinkable to mount an open challenge to congressional leadership, such as Rep. Newt Gingrich did in 1988 by calling for an Ethics Committee probe into Speaker Jim Wright.

Associate Justice Thurgood Marshall, 1987

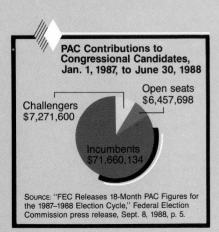

Rep. Claude Pepper, Rep. Thomas (Tip)
O'Neill, and Sen. Jennings Randolph, 1985

Judicial Leadership

The model for judicial leadership seems to be so rational that it sounds naive even to ask why a judge needs to be a lawyer. Today the "cult of the robe" (as legal realists like to refer to the extreme deference granted to judges) is fully served by the priesthood at the bar—by lawyers. Since the 1930s, all federal judges have had formal training as lawyers, but some state court systems elect rather than appoint judges, and so a few nonlawyers have made their way to the bench.

PAC Contributions to Congressional Candidates, Jan. 1, 1987, to June 30, 1988

Open seats
$6,457,698

Challengers
$7,271,600

Incumbents
$71,660,134

Source: "FEC Releases 18-Month PAC Figures for the 1987–1988 Election Cycle," Federal Election Commission press release, Sept. 8, 1988, p. 5.

While many lower state courts and magistrates' offices are staffed by nonlawyers, their numbers are dwindling.

Just how "rational" *is* this model of choosing judicial leaders? Think for a minute about the tasks of a Supreme Court Justice. Yes, many technical, legally complex questions come before the Court, just as many issues confronting presidents are intricate and technical. Yet, although we are comfortable with the notion that a president can consult advisors in deciding policy issues, we dismiss the idea that, with adequate advice and trained counsel, a nonlawyer might decide the political and social issues before the Court. And though we are transfixed by the requirement that judges be lawyers, we do not acknowledge a need for them to have special training, other than what all lawyers receive. (In Great Britain, training for judges differs from training for barristers, who argue before the bench, which differs in turn from training for solicitors, who handle legal matters outside of courtrooms.)

Since federal judicial appointments implicitly recognize the policy functions of judges by demanding proper "political" credentials, why not then admit that nonlawyers might function perfectly well as judges? The question is more than theoretical. Although applicants to law school are increasingly diverse, some observers have argued that the process which sifts successful graduates from the rest of society has significant social and cultural biases. By making a law degree prerequisite to judicial posts, we reproduce such biases in our courts. Yet the issue of proper training for judges is not simple, and no single approach can be suitable for all the different tasks and roles in our judicial system. Perhaps training in business and economics ought to be required in some courts; in others, broad political experience may be the best criterion. In any case, to be rational in selecting judicial leadership, we ought to give the matter of appropriate standards more attention than we do.

Presidential Leadership

No model seems to dominate our selection of presidents, although history shows a shifting of attention from candidates' backgrounds, to their experience, to their personalities.

What *backgrounds* have we found suitable for presidents? Starting with Washington (and including at least Jackson, William Henry Harrison, Taylor, Grant, Teddy Roosevelt, and Eisenhower), being a military hero has been one means of attaining the presidency, especially during the nineteenth century. In this century, except for Ike after World War II, glorious battlefield experience has not been the primary route to battle on the western end of Pennsylvania Avenue. Still, some sort of wartime military experience has always been useful on one's political résumé and could be claimed by Pierce, Buchanan, Hayes, Garfield, Benjamin Harrison, McKinley, Truman, Kennedy, Nixon, Carter, Reagan, and Bush.

Although political leaders in colonial America often came from the ranks of the clergy, the ministry has not been a steppingstone to the president's bully pulpit. Reflect, though, on two recent developments: the rise of the evangelical right (Pat Robertson's 1988 presidential bid was taken seriously enough that he beat George Bush in the Iowa caucuses) and the viability of black presidential candidates (as represented by Jesse Jackson's campaigns in 1984 and 1988). Black Protestant churches have long provided political leadership, and the gradual breakdown of barriers to black participation in national politics enhances their contributions to democracy.

Legal training has long been a favored route to political office, and the presidency reflects this. In this century McKinley, Taft, Wilson, Coolidge, Franklin Roosevelt, Nixon, and Ford had law degrees. Taft was a genuine legal scholar; after serving as president he taught constitutional law at Yale and then became the only president also to serve as Chief Justice of the United States. Teddy Roosevelt and Lyndon Johnson also studied law briefly before going on to other things. Even so, in this century there have been more presidents without legal training than with, and the nature of the office is such that *experience* may be more important than formal education.

Serving as governor is a reasonable executive training ground for presidents—including McKinley (Ohio); both Roosevelts (New York); Taft (the Philippines and Cuba); Wilson (New Jersey); Coolidge (Massachusetts); Carter (Georgia); and Reagan (California). Legislative experience in Congress was had by McKinley, Harding, Truman, Kennedy, Johnson, Nixon, Ford, and Bush, but it provided direct access to the presidency only for Harding and Kennedy. (Truman, Johnson, and Ford went from Congress to the vice-presidency and then, by succession, to the presidency.) No one has come to the presidency directly from a judicial post, and in this century only Hoover came to it from the bureaucracy (he was Secretary of Commerce in the two administrations preceding his election).

The growing importance of primaries has made experience in a particular career less a prerequisite for the presidency, and candidates today enter national politics from any career that gives them access to funds and media exposure. Ronald Reagan emphasized his personality and an upbeat picture of America to move from a career in entertainment to governor of our most populous state and then to president. Campaigns increasingly promote image, personality, and vision as criteria for choosing our leaders—an approach that appeals to voters who have little time for, or interest in, studying issues.

General Dwight David Eisenhower announcing his resignation as Army Chief of Staff

Gov. Leroy Collins, Sen. John F. Kennedy, Sen. Lyndon Johnson, and Rep. Sam Rayburn at 1960 Democratic convention

P. GRIDLEY/FPG INTERNATIONAL

Thus *character* has assumed central importance, and we seem to have accepted Weber's category of charisma as a legitimate qualification. But note the odd, postmodernist twist: We judge candidates by how they manipulate their public personas. Skillful "spin control" (the ability to turn damaging news to beneficial ends) is taken to reflect, or perhaps even to *be*, the substance of leadership.

James David Barber, in a careful study of presidential character, contends that to judge the potential performance of a president we should

look to character first. . . .Character is the force, the motive power, around which the person gathers his view of the world and from which his style receives its impetus. The issues will change, the character of the President will last.[2]

What sort of character do Americans want in leaders? Karl Lamb has made the interesting suggestion that the Mall in Washington, D.C., provides an architectural equivalent for our divergent desires:

They are found at opposite ends of the Mall in Washington. Follow the image of one in the reflecting pools, and it will lead you to the other. You have to visit both to know what the presidential office has meant to America.

The Washington Monument is a single shaft, its design inspired by the obelisks built in ancient Egypt and dedicated to the sun god. It stands there, rising 555 feet into the sky of the city that takes its name from the man it commemorates, George Washington, Father of his country. Austere, forbidding, essentially male, it commemorates in stark simplicity the act of foundation, the birth of the nation. . . .

The Lincoln Memorial is entirely different. It is a temple; the inspiration is Greek, not Egyptian. Inside is the massive statue of the saddened, brooding Lincoln. The atmosphere is reverent. On the walls are engraved the immortal words, the Gettysburg Address and the Second Inaugural. Compared to Washington's shaft, the values commemorated in Lincoln's temple are feminine, and its massive enclosure enfolds the visitor in pensive solemnity. What Washington founded, Lincoln strove to preserve. . . .[3]

What these two monuments reflect best is that the advantages of certain leadership characteristics change as time and circumstances change. At any one time the public may even maintain contradictory expectations, wanting both Washington and Lincoln in the same person.

In any case, if a democracy does not always have a clear definition of leadership, at least it should be engaged in some *debate* about the nature of leadership. That task belongs to students and teachers—and all citizens—alike.

[1]"FEC Releases 15-Month PAC Figures," Federal Election Commission press release, June 2, 1988, p. 2.
[2]James David Barber, *The Presidential Character*, 2nd ed. (Englewood Cliffs, N.J.: Prentice-Hall, 1977), pp. 445–446.
[3]Karl Lamb, *The People Maybe*, 3rd ed. (North Scituate, Mass.: Duxbury Press, 1978), pp. 198–199.

JOHN SCOWEN/FPG INTERNATIONAL

FPG INTERNATIONAL

The history of the Senate is, to a degree, a history of distinctive personalities like Senator William Proxmire of Wisconsin, who retired at the end of the 100th Congress in 1988. Proxmire was best known for his Golden Fleece Awards, given to individuals and agencies for "fleecing" the public via extravagant or inappropriate expenditures. Here he displays a discount store catalog and suggests that the General Services Administration (which buys supplies for the federal government) could do better in its pages than has been done through negotiation with suppliers. *(AP/Wide World Photos)*

In the early 1970s, many legislators felt it was time to reassert Congress's authority as an institution. The Congressional Budget and Impoundment Control Act of 1974, which embodied most sought-after reforms, had several key purposes: (1) to provide Congress with much more information; (2) to streamline committee work on the budget; and (3) to give Congress the power to confront such presidential tactics as impounding federal funds. To these ends, the act established a budget committee in each house and a Congressional Budget Office to provide information and technical assistance. Congressional committees now drafted two budget resolutions annually for Congress's approval: one to set overall spending and tax goals early in the budget planning process, and another to set binding figures before the fiscal year began (July 1). Then, in a step known as *reconciliation,* the House and Senate would agree on a set of matching proposals for each portion of the federal budget.[26] The act also prohibited presidential impoundment of funds appropriated by Congress.

The reformed budget system did not resolve the institutional and partisan pressures at the heart of the budget-making process, however. Conservatives wanted to use the system to place a ceiling on expenditures, but have not been able to get that ceiling as low as they wished. Liberals, who wanted to use the process to set new priorities, sought open debate about the overall emphasis in each new budget. But these debates have fallen short of liberals' expectations.

According to less ideological members of Congress, the budget reforms have given members a clearer way of thinking about the budget. Among the improvements cited are earlier planning, better coordination among various committees, more careful scrutiny of certain spending programs previously left out of budget discussions, and wider dissemination of information to legislators about the consequences of their decisions.

Another gain, in the view of reform proponents, was the creation of the **Congressional Budget Office** (CBO), whose professional staff aids Congress in dealing with budget issues. The CBO, which acts as a counterweight to the expertise of the executive branch's Office of Management and Budget (OMB), reports to Congress on the economic consequences of both proposed and enacted legislation; develops a yearly report on alternative budget options; and provides expert advice for the congressional committees considering specific fiscal issues. In fact, the CBO is widely thought to be both more accurate in its assessments and more politically neutral than the increasingly politicized OMB.

Despite positive steps taken to reform the budget process, one central issue stands as a nearly insurmountable obstacle: The process requires the sharing of power by two branches of government with strikingly different political agendas. During the 1980s the national government was simply incapable of producing a budget in a timely fashion. Continuing budget resolutions (short-term, stopgap measures designed merely to keep the government from running out of money until a budget could be approved) became the norm. Instead of an orderly series of appropriations bills, Congress created omnibus spending measures of such enormous size and complexity that no observer could have much faith in the quality of the review process.

In 1987, one week before Christmas (and three months *after* the start of Fiscal Year 1988), Congress passed two enormous spending bills for Fiscal Year 1988: One was two thousand pages long and covered $600 billion in expenditures. The other was a comparatively short, one-thousand-page companion bill for revenue and irregular programs like Medicare. What member of Congress could possibly grasp the intricacies and subtleties of such massive bills in a short time? Large, last-minute appropriations bills also present an irresistible opportunity to allot funds for pork barrel projects and other pet legislative items that might not survive more careful scrutiny. The FY88 bill, for example, included $8 million inserted by a senator from Hawaii for a religious school in France; a $10 million government purchase of sunflower oil arranged by a senator from North Dakota (a sunflower producing state); and the cancellation of the ceiling on honey price-support payments to any one producer, allowing up to $6 million to be paid by the federal government to fifteen big honey producers (arranged by a pair of senators from Montana and Arkansas).[27] Each of these expenditures might be a worthy addition to sound government policy. But when confronted with two thousand pages of items like these, seeking passage from a Congress that is trying to adjourn for the holidays, who could make a reasoned judgment?

Another factor, not wholly unrelated to the sharing of power between branches, makes the budget process even less manageable. Starting in 1983 the federal government began to post very large annual budget deficits. This reduced the already-scarce negotiating room for Congress and the president, because overall expenditures had to be reduced while certain "fixed" costs (like **enti-**

tlement programs—those to which certain groups are automatically entitled, like Social Security for the elderly—and interest on the debt) were going up. Congress responded in 1985 with an antideficit law that came to be known as **Gramm-Rudman-Hollings** (the names of its Senate sponsors). This measure set 1993 as a target for a balanced budget and specified interim deficit reductions for each year. Automatic, across-the-board spending reductions would be imposed if agreement could not be reached otherwise. The Supreme Court ruled that the specific mechanism for enforcing automatic spending cuts was unconstitutional because—you guessed it—it violated the separation-of-powers doctrine. But the yearly targets were still in place, making budget-writing an almost impossible task.

In October of 1987 the stock market crash sent shock waves throughout the government, creating a sense of mounting crisis. With the crash as a backdrop, a series of hastily arranged budget negotiations between the White House and Congress generated a signed agreement between the two branches, outlining the general provisions of budgets for the next two years. The nature of these negotiations and the agreement that was reached show clearly that sharing power on matters like budget-writing is a continuing challenge. In American democracy, the three branches of government are engaged in a continuous process of defining themselves and their roles in representing the American people. Nothing demonstrates that process more clearly than recent efforts to create a federal budget.

Conclusions

How should we evaluate the Congress from a democratic standpoint? First, we must acknowledge that the U.S. national legislature is unique because the U.S. political process is unique. Unlike parliamentary systems, in which the executive and legislative branches are fused, our system sets these branches at odds. On the one hand, this situation creates unique opportunities for legislative action and power; on the other, it leads to severe and often insoluble problems involving legislative coordination and responsible policy making. In its role as critic, gadfly, and check on the initiatives of the executive, Congress has shown some improvement in recent decades. That is a definite plus. Regardless of what one thinks of particular presidential policies, it is heartening to see informed and searching debate on those policies on the legislative side. Also on the positive side, Congress has reformed some of the procedures that centralized power too greatly in the hands of an unrepresentative few. Today's Congress may seem at times like a Tower of Babel, but most find this preferable to an institution devoted to whispering in the corridors.

On the negative side, it seems unlikely that under current conditions, Congress will ever be able to engage in coherent policy making. Political analysts fault both the internal structure of Congress and, even more important, our party system, which does not provide the discipline necessary to keep members attuned to national needs as well as local constituency interests.

There are solutions available for some of Congress's current dilemmas. For instance, increasing the internal coherence of policy making in Congress may be possible by reducing the immediate, external influences that fragment the process so severely now. Public financing of congressional elections might diminish the power of well-oiled interests that use money to purchase legislative access. Also, a strict rule that legislators not serve on committees that could enhance their own financial or personal interests would lessen the likelihood of conflicts of interest. Congress has been strangely lax in not moving in this direction.

Overall, Congress cuts an interesting, exasperating, occasionally commanding presence in U.S. politics. Newly assertive, our national legislature has been challenging presidential authority in the foreign policy arena, while deadlocking on many tasks where it traditionally exercises considerable latitude, for example, in the budget process.

GLOSSARY TERMS

unicameral
bicameral
checks and balances
Speaker of the House
majority leader
whip
minority leader
president pro tempore
seniority rule
riders
filibuster
pocket veto
separation of powers
parliamentary democracy
pork barrel projects
War Powers Act
Congressional Budget Office
entitlement programs
Gramm-Rudman-Hollings

NOTES

[1] Detailed descriptions of these functions can be found in Malcolm E. Jewell and Samuel C. Patterson, *The Legislative Process in the United States,* 3rd ed. (New York: Random House, 1977); and Randall B. Ripley, *Congress: Process and Policy,* 3rd ed. (New York: Norton, 1983).

[2] For a detailed discussion, see Jewell and Patterson, *op. cit.;* Gary Orfield, *Congressional Power: Congress and Social Change* (New York: Harcourt Brace Jovanovich, 1975); and, particularly, Richard Fenno, *Congressmen in Committees* (Boston: Little, Brown, 1973).

[3] For a detailed treatment of congressional structures and procedures, see Lewis A. Froman, Jr., *The Congressional Process: Strategies, Rules and Procedures* (Boston: Little, Brown, 1967).

[4] For a debate about the effectiveness of party leadership, see Ripley, *op. cit.,* chap. 6.

[5] On specialization, see David E. Price, "Congressional Committees in the Policy Process," in Lawrence C. Dodd and Bruce I. Oppenheimer, eds., *Congress Reconsidered,* 2nd ed. (Washington, D.C.: Congressional Quarterly Press, 1981), pp. 156–185.

[6] Ripley, *op. cit.,* pp. 168–174.

[7] See Ripley, *op. cit.,* chap. 5; and L. C. Dodd and B. I. Oppenheimer, "The House in Transition: Change and Consolidation," in Dodd and Oppenheimer, *op. cit.,* pp. 31–61.

[8] Lawrence C. Dodd, "Congress, the Constitution and the Crisis of Legitimation," in Dodd and Oppenheimer, *op. cit.,* p. 414.

[9]See Albert D. Cover, "One Good Term Deserves Another: The Advantage of Incumbency in Congressional Elections," *American Journal of Political Science*, Aug. 1977, vol. 21, no. 3, pp. 523–541.

[10]Morris Fiorina, "The Incumbency Factor," *Public Opinion*, Sept./Oct. 1978.

[11]Fred Barnes, "The Unbearable Lightness of Being a Congressman," *The New Republic*, Feb. 15, 1988, p. 19.

[12]*1986 Congressional Quarterly Almanac*, p. 31C.

[13]Quoted in Roger M. Davidson and Walter J. Oleszek, *Congress and Its Members* (Washington, D.C.: Congressional Quarterly Press, 1981).

[14]For a discussion of this era, see Norman J. Ornstein and Shirley Elder, *Interest Groups, Lobbying and Policy-Making* (Washington, D.C.: Congressional Quarterly Press, 1978), chap. 4.

[15]Quoted in Jacqueline Calmes, "Ethics Committees: Shield or Sword?" *Congressional Quarterly Weekly*, Apr. 4, 1987, p. 592.

[16]Much of the material in this section is drawn from Norman J. Ornstein, "The Democrats Reform Power in the House of Representatives, 1969–75," in Allan P. Sindler, ed., *America in the Seventies* (Boston: Little, Brown, 1977); and Thomas B. Edsall, "Political Reform—Social Retreat," *Dissent*, Summer 1979, vol. 26, pp. 261–265.

[17]Eric Pianin, "The Debut of Senator Mikulski," *The Washington Post National Weekly Edition*, vol. 4, no. 36, July 6, 1987, p. 6.

[18]Quoted in "TRB," *The New Republic*, May 3, 1980, p. 3.

[19]Steven E. Roberts, "The Mood in Congress Is Bold and Bitter," *New York Times*, June 2, 1987, p. 14.

[20]Steven R. Weisman, "Impact of the Decision," *New York Times*, June 24, 1983; and John Herbers, "Government Poised for Grand Realignment," *New York Times*, June 26, 1983.

[21]*1986 Congressional Quarterly Almanac*, pp. 50–51.

[22]For a good discussion of the War Powers Act, see Cecil V. Crabb, Jr., and Pat M. Holt, *Invitation to Struggle: Congress, the President, and Foreign Policy* (Washington, D.C.: Congressional Quarterly Press, 1980), especially chap. 5.

[23]Tom Baden, "Senate Leaders Push for Revamp of 'Unworkable' War Powers Act" (Newhouse News Service), *The Star-Ledger*, May 20, 1988, p. 6; and Susan F. Rasky, "Senators Seeking to Overhaul War Powers Resolution," *New York Times*, May 20, 1988, p. A3.

[24]Crabb and Holt, *op. cit.*, p. 205.

[25]*Ibid.*

[26]The budget committees have received considerable attention. See James H. Duffy, *Domestic Affairs* (New York: Simon & Schuster, 1978); Randall B. Ripley, *op. cit.*; and Joel Havemann, *Congress and the Budget* (Bloomington, Ind.: University of Indiana Press, 1978).

[27]"New Session, Old Odor" (editorial), *New York Times*, Jan. 26, 1988, p. 6.

SELECTED READINGS

For **general overviews of Congress**, see Richard Bolling, *House Out of Order* (New York: Dutton, 1965); Morris P. Fiorina, *Congress: Keystone of the Washington Establishment* (New Haven, Conn.: Yale University Press, 1977); Donald R. Matthews, *U.S. Senators and Their World* (New York: Vintage, 1960); David R. Mayhew, *Congress: The Electoral Connection* (New Haven, Conn.: Yale University Press, 1974); Walter J. Oleszek, *Congressional Procedures and the Policy Process*, 2nd ed. (Washington, D.C.: Congressional Quarterly Press, 1984).

On **more specific aspects of Congress**, consult Lawrence C. Dodd and Bruce I. Oppenheimer, *Congress Reconsidered*, 3rd ed. (Washington, D.C.: Congressional Quarterly Press, 1985); Richard F. Fenno, Jr., *Home Style: House Members in Their Districts* (Boston: Little, Brown, 1978); John A. Ferejohn, *Pork Barrel Politics: Rivers and Harbors Legislation, 1947–1968* (Stanford, Calif.: Stanford University Press, 1974); Cecil V. Crabb, Jr., and Pat M. Holt, *Invitation to Struggle: Congress, the President, and Foreign Policy*, 2nd ed. (Washington, D.C.: Congressional Quarterly Press, 1984); William R. Shaffer, *Party and Ideology in the United States Congress* (Lanham, Md.: University Press of America, 1980).

For an **insider's look at Congress**, see Stephen Hess, *The Ultimate Insiders: U.S. Senators in the National Media* (Washington D.C.: Brookings Institution, 1986); Glenn N. Parker, *Homeward Bound: Explaining Changes in Congressional Behavior* (Pittsburgh: University of Pittsburgh Press, 1986); Gerald C. Wright, Jr., *et al.*, eds., *Congress and Policy Change* (New York: Agathon, 1986); Douglas C. Waller, *Congress and the Nuclear Freeze: An Inside Look at the Politics of a Mass Movement* (Amherst: University of Massachusetts Press, 1987). For an interesting recent historical account of a prominent U.S. Senator from Nevada, see Betty Glad, *Key Pittman: The Tragedy of a Senate Insider* (New York: Columbia University Press, 1986).

12

THE AMERICAN PRESIDENT

Unique, Necessary, and Dangerous

CHAPTER OUTLINE

The Unique President
The Necessary President
The Dangerous President
Transition of Power

UPI/Bettmann Newsphotos

The framers of the Constitution were faced with a dilemma when it came to setting up the executive branch. The political situation under the Articles of Confederation, which had essentially done away with a central executive authority, had clearly been disastrous. Yet few Americans wanted to return to the days of monarchy. Some delegates to the Constitutional Convention suggested a Council of States—a plural executive that would administer the departments. At the other extreme, some delegates called for a disguised monarchy, in which the president would have monarchial prerogatives but would not be a hereditary ruler. Another option, which the delegates finally settled on, was to establish an effective executive branch whose powers would be limited by checks and balances.

In defining the presidency, the framers needed to accommodate disparate wishes and visions. Political leaders try to reach consensus on different positions as much as possible and to defer choices that cannot be made under current circumstances. Like so many other elements of the Constitution, the provisions of Article II—the Executive Article—reflect a series of compromises, trade-offs, and deferred choices. A majority of delegates clearly favored a strengthened executive. But how strong? What powers would this office have? And what checks would there be on those powers?

The delegates enumerated certain powers—such as the powers to direct all military operations, to grant reprieves and pardons, to see that laws are faithfully executed, to appoint federal officers—but they were also careful to balance executive power with powers granted to the other branches. The ultimate check on the president was **impeachment,** a procedure by which Congress could remove the chief executive from office. In this two-step process, first the House must vote on whether to impeach (to bring charges against) a president, and then the Senate must try the case.

On many matters relating to the executive, the Constitution remained silent. Out of those silences came some epic battles between presidents and other elements in our political system. For the most part, presidents have been able to expand the power of the office through interpretation of the Constitution. In certain cases, presidents have sought to combine powers: Presidents Woodrow Wilson and Franklin Roosevelt, for example, combined "executive power" with the powers of "commander-in-chief" to control mobilization of the domestic economy during wartime. Some presidents have claimed **inherent powers,** which provide latitude for actions, in the international arena, not specifically spelled out in the Constitution. Among these is the power to grant diplomatic recognition to foreign governments. President William Howard Taft spoke of **delegated powers**, by which he meant powers that were *implied* in the Constitution.

The presidency today—the current product of what the framers concocted and what chief executives over the years have refined and elaborated on—is an office that (1) has a *unique* history, (2) is *necessary* as a source of focus and initiative within our political system, and (3) is *dangerous* because any powerful executive can become a threat to democratic politics. These three characteristics of the presidency will serve as the focal points for this chapter. Toward the end of the chapter, we will also explore the transition of power in American democracy.

The Unique President

The presidency of the United States is unique, in part, because of its dynamic character: The responsibilities of the office were not well defined at its inception, setting in motion a perpetual competition for power with the other branches of the national government. The presidency has been shaped by presidents, Congresses, and the Supreme Court. The presidency is also what the *current* president, Congress, and Supreme Court (influenced by a lot of other actors) make of it. Every new occupant of the White House can have a significant influence—for good or ill—on the office itself.

In most democratic countries, executive leadership is divided between a symbolic president or monarch and the political leader who actually runs the government—usually the prime minister or premier. In Great Britain, for example, the monarch functions as a symbolic (but powerless) head of state, while the prime minister is the functioning head of government. The prime minister is the

Since the Constitution says little about the presidency, the office is defined by tradition, its support agencies, and whoever holds it. George Bush came to the Oval Office with experience as Vice-President, Director of the CIA, ambassador, and member of Congress. *(AP/Wide World Photos)*

leader of the party (or coalition of parties) that holds a majority in Parliament. Typically, the prime minister has been involved in political life and in party affairs for many years. Few prime ministers are newcomers to party politics or to the national political scene.

The U.S. president, in contrast, serves as both actual political leader *and* symbol of the nation. The president also runs for office separately: He does not become national leader by being selected as head of the majority party or coalition, but must win on his own in our only genuinely national election. (We refer to the president as ''he,'' using the masculine pronoun, for stylistic simplicity. A woman, of course, could certainly occupy the of-

fice of chief executive—or vice-president—as well.) On occasion, presidents have emerged from outside the major parties altogether, as war hero Dwight D. Eisenhower did in 1952, or from the periphery of the national political scene, as Jimmy Carter did in 1976. With the increasing importance of primaries and the impact of the news media on the presidential nominating process, the presidential race has been opened to contenders who enjoy scant national recognition at the start. Accordingly, a president may come to office with little, if any, national political experience and few or no connections with other major political figures, even within his own party.

The unique political position of the U.S. president also stems from the peculiar strengths and weaknesses of the office. Because the U.S. government is based on a **separation of powers**—with power divided among the three branches—the president often must take an antagonistic stance in relation to both Congress and the federal judiciary. And because of the relatively undisciplined nature of U.S. political parties, the president, unlike most European prime ministers, can rarely count on solid support even from his own party members.

Compensations abound, however, for these structural weaknesses in the presidency. The president towers over all other figures in U.S. politics. As the head of state as well as the political leader, he can position himself above the struggles of party. In addition, the average citizen's psychological investment in the president runs very high.[1] Presidents can rally the nation and command support as no other political figure can. Let us now consider (1) how presidents press against the limits of their power and (2) the paradoxes of the office.

Pressing Against the Limits of Power

Because of the ambiguity in the nature and range of presidential powers and responsibilities, all presidents from time to time feel the need to press against the limits of their power—either to protect it from encroachment from other political forces or to enhance it to achieve certain policy goals. One student of presidential power argues that presi-

COMPARATIVE PERSPECTIVE

The Head of State in West Germany

Only one other democracy has a presidential system somewhat similar to ours—France under the Fifth Republic, which dates from 1958. In other democracies, there is a prime minister or premier, who is head of government, and a separate head of state. The latter may be either a monarch or a civilian, usually known as the president. (Switzerland, the exception, has neither a monarch nor a civilian head of state—showing, as one writer put it, that "a country can survive without any head of state."*

The civilian head of state in the Federal Republic of Germany (West Germany) is the president, who is elected by a special assembly of the federal parliament and deputies from the state parliaments. Since the office was established in 1949, all of its occupants have been leading politicians whose elective political careers had progressed to the point that they no longer had any chance of becoming the actual head of the government (called the chancellor). The president serves for a five-year term and may be reelected once. He must sign all legislation, decrees, and letters of appointment and dismissal—and does not have a choice in doing so.[†]

The West German president has more power than a symbolic monarch, but this power stems largely from personal prestige and respect. He can exercise a certain amount of influence on basic political questions, but very little on day-to-day politics. Thus, he exercises some degree of political leadership, but must avoid becoming excessively political. As one student of the subject put it: "He must earn his prestige through his public statements, which should be neither trivial, abstract nor too concretely political."[§]

It is not entirely clear exactly how far a West German president might be able to push his powers to intervene in affairs of state or to influence public opinion. Thus far, the rule has been that a chancellor backed by a solid majority in parliament need not pay much attention to a president's views.

---

*Jurg Steiner, *European Democracies* (New York: Longman, 1986), p. 161.
[†]Lewis J. Edinger, *Politics in West Europe* (Boston: Little, Brown, 1977), p. 19.
[§]Jurg Steiner, *European Democracies*, p. 164.

---

dents who push their powers to the limit exemplify "prerogative government," which strongly resembles monarchy.[2] Typically in such cases, presidential decisions are made without congressional consultation or collaboration, and often in secret. Events are managed by the White House rather than by the appropriate executive departments. The president justifies decisions on constitutional grounds—either citing enumerated powers or powers claimed or created by his interpretation of the Constitution. When his expansive interpretation is challenged, he appeals directly to the public for support asserting that his actions were prompted by "national security" concerns or the "national interest." Prerogative presidents usually refuse to tailor their actions to party requirements or to majority sentiment in Congress.

The prerogative style has enjoyed only limited success. One expert in the field catalogued three possible outcomes of the exercise of **prerogative powers** by the president: (1) *frontlash*, (2) *backlash*, and (3) *overshoot-and-collapse*.[3] In the case of frontlash, the president wins: The courts and Congress acquiesce in his exercise of power, and he capitalizes on this acquiescence to extend the range of his—and the presidency's—influence. In the backlash effect, the president keeps the crisis under control but his interpretation of his powers is challenged by the other branches; this may result in the erosion of his and his successors' powers. When overshoot-and-collapse occurs, a constitutional crisis develops over the president's use of power, and he is censured or impeached. Let us now consider each of these outcomes at close range.

FRONTLASH Two historical cases illustrate the frontlash effect. In the early 1790s, George Washington decided that the country should remain neutral in the war between Great Britain and France, even though the United States and France were allied by treaty. He issued a proclamation of neutrality and refused to engage the British in naval warfare, as the French had requested. His actions sparked a major constitutional debate over whether the president had the authority to declare the nation neutral. His defenders claimed such powers were inherent in the Constitution, and those who disagreed did not have the votes to defeat Washington in Congress. Shortly thereafter, Congress actually passed neutrality legislation, and Washington went on to assert other new powers—the power to recognize foreign governments, to break off relations with other nations, and to negotiate foreign agreements by the executive alone.

In the second frontlash case, the president and Congress switched roles. After World War II broke out in Europe, President Franklin Roosevelt wanted to help Great Britain in its desperate struggle against Germany, while Congress seemed determined to preserve strict neutrality. Roosevelt therefore engineered a highly controversial military aid deal with Great Britain by using an **executive agreement,** an arrangement between a president and a foreign nation not subject to Senate approval. Under this agreement, known as Lend-Lease, the United States "loaned" Britain fifty old destroyers in return for the lease of several bases in the Caribbean. Roosevelt's critics claimed that transfer violated the 1940 Neutrality Act, but Roosevelt argued it was an inherent power of the chief executive to dispose of military materiel.

Congress, which had been fully informed about the deal, acquiesced. The frontlash effect then took over, and Roosevelt quickly signed a series of war-related executive agreements with other countries. Congress's reluctance to act in the period before the Japanese attack on Pearl Harbor set a pattern of executive initiative that persisted through the 1970s.

BACKLASH Two modern cases spotlight the backlash effect: President Harry Truman's attempted takeover of strike-bound steel mills, and President Ronald Reagan's reinterpretation of a law prohibiting gender discrimination in educational institutions. In 1950, during the Korean War, President Harry Truman ordered the Army to take over the nation's steel mills, which had been idled during a strike. When the steel companies took the matter to court, Truman argued that constitutional and statutory powers gave him the authority to intervene to preserve the national welfare. There were many precedents for Truman's actions, and the Supreme Court had not ruled against a president's use of prerogative powers since 1866. But Truman misjudged both the temper of the country (public opinion opposed him, 43 percent to 35 percent) and the disposition of the Supreme Court. A majority of the Court held that Congress had already mandated an appropriate government response to strike situations in the Taft-Hartley Act; Truman had chosen not to impose Taft-Hartley sanctions in this case. The majority argued that Truman had taken the power of commander-in-chief and had "turned inward, not because of rebellion, but because of a lawful economic struggle between industry and labor."[4] Truman's defeat limited how future presidents could deal with labor disputes. After this episode, presidents could not seize factories, even citing national security considerations, unless backed up by special legislation from Congress.

Often political power consists of having one's own interpretation of law chosen over a conflicting one. A second backlash case deals with the interpretation of a 1972 law barring gender discrimination by educational institutions. In 1984, the Reagan administration argued before the Supreme Court for a new interpretation of this federal law

Perhaps the largest part of presidential power is the power to persuade, and occupants of the Oval Office frequently press against their limits. When they successfully exceed their limits and extend the presidency, the result is *frontlash*. President Franklin Roosevelt provided several examples, including his decisive commitment (by executive agreement, not treaty or statute) of U.S. military resources to Great Britain early in World War II.
(The Bettmann Archive)

in the case of *Grove City* v. *Bell*,[5] suggesting that the law was program-specific in prohibiting discrimination. Under the Reagan administration's interpretation, if a college or university received federal funds for a specific program—the athletic program, for instance—the federal law forbade discrimination *in that program* but not in other programs in the institution. The earlier interpretation of the law held that if an institution accepted federal funds for any of its programs—including federally guaranteed student loans—it was prohibited from gender discrimination in all of them. Depending on one's point of view, the Reagan interpretation would mean much less federal meddling—or much less federal protection against gender discrimination—in higher education. The administration's position prevailed in *Grove City*, setting the stage for four years of legislative attempts to reverse the administration's interpretation. In 1988, Congress passed the **Civil Rights Restoration Act,** which not only reversed the interpretation in *Grove City*, but also *expanded* the coverage of the 1972 law and three others to include gender, age, handicap, and racial discrimination at

noneducational institutions as well as educational institutions. President Reagan vetoed the bill, but the House and Senate overrode the veto. Thus an initial victory in an important area of public policy was turned into a major defeat.

OVERSHOOT-AND-COLLAPSE   History records two famous instances of overshoot-and-collapse: President Richard Nixon's handling of Watergate, and President Andrew Johnson's approach to Reconstruction. Since the Watergate affair will be examined later in this chapter, we will focus on the Andrew Johnson case here. In this example, as in Watergate, a president attempted to subvert the law and the basic rules of the political game, destroying his administration in the process.

Soon after inheriting the presidency in 1865 following the assassination of Abraham Lincoln, Johnson became embroiled in a fierce struggle with Congress over Reconstruction—the political restructuring of the recently defeated South. Johnson was more conciliatory toward the entrenched, white Southern establishment than the majority in Congress, which consistently overrode presiden-

When a president's reach exceeds his grasp, the result can be *backlash,* which limits future presidential prerogatives. When President Harry Truman seized the nation's steel mills during the Korean War, the result was public outcry and a Supreme Court decision against such action, making future seizures of this sort much less likely. Traditionally (perhaps unwisely) we identify our strongest presidents as those who successfully extended the power of the presidency. *(AP/Wide World Photos)*

tial vetoes of Reconstruction legislation. Matters came to a head when Congress passed the Tenure of Office Act, a measure designed to keep Secretary of War Edwin Stanton, a Johnson opponent, in office. Johnson challenged the constitutionality of the act and fired Stanton. The House then voted to impeach Johnson. Although Johnson's impeachment focused on the Stanton issue, articles of impeachment could have been brought against him on many other grounds, including encouraging violations of law and obstructing Reconstruction.

Johnson survived the Senate trial by a single vote, and Stanton was removed from office. But in the process, the presidency suffered a heavy blow. Congress gained a significant measure of control over executive departments, and for the rest of the nineteenth century, the presidency was greatly weakened. During this period, widespread public sentiment favored a move toward parliamentary government, with the president serving merely as a ceremonial figure. Around the turn of the century, the nation's successive chief executives began rebuilding the power and prestige of the pres-

idency, seizing on foreign policy issues to recapture center stage.

Paradoxes of the Office

The electorate's expectations of the U.S. presidency are not only ambiguous—they are often contradictory.[6] Americans generally want a "good person" in the White House—someone honest and trustworthy. Yet they also like tough, forceful, perhaps even ruthless presidents. They admire leaders who can lift the White House above the grubby day-to-day infighting of political life—leaders who can lead *all* the people. Yet the job of president requires preeminently political skills—coalition-building, manipulation, partisan dealings. Most Americans want a president who can pull us together, yet one who can also put forward a forceful national agenda, creating a sense of priorities. Finally, we look for a chief executive who will both act as a referee in the political conflict of group interest and take part in that process of interest-group conflict, using his powers to serve the public interest.

More than a quarter-century after his assassination, John Kennedy remains for many a clear example of the vigorous leadership needed in the White House. His continued popularity is based not on legislative or foreign policy success but on his ability to provide a sense of purpose and to set national priorities during nearly three years in office. *(UPI/Bettmann Newsphotos)*

Winning the office of president—making it through the primaries, the conventions, and the general election—requires ambition, flexibility, and great skill at image-making and public relations. But excessive emphasis on these same skills can spell disaster once in office. Some political analysts argue that winning a presidential election requires an *electoral coalition*—a majority of voters, strategically located across the country—whereas actually running the government requires a *governing coalition*, which is something else entirely. As one student of the subject puts it: "What counts then [once in office] is to mobilize support from the leaders of the key institutions in society and government. . . . This coalition must include key people in Congress, the executive branch, and the private sector 'establishment.' "[7]

No president can fully satisfy popular expectations. Nonetheless, high expectations prompt our chief executives to develop programs and "go to the people" to validate their proposals. Thus, the "necessary president"—the priority-setter and manager of government—has appeared on the scene.

The Necessary President

The president was a "necessary" component of the changes the framers introduced in the Constitution of 1787. But in the twentieth century, the need for a strong president has become compelling. Because of the general fragmentation of power in our political processes, the lack of discipline in U.S. political parties, the size and complexity of the federal government and its agenda, and the profound issues the nation faces, almost no political figure other than the president can draw together the threads of national policy and provide a minimum of politically coherent leadership. The president can create national priorities, articulate national needs, and rally national energies. If the president is unwilling or unable to carry out these functions, they will be carried out, if at all, in a fragmented, haphazard fashion, which is likely to favor private concerns over public ones, and short-term, narrow-range solutions over long-term, broad-range solutions.

Of course, presidents, too, are captives of the times in which they come to power—victims of the pressures of the moment. And many presidents have not seized the organizing initiatives available to them. Still, for our political system to work properly, the president must organize power, gather ideas and put them to use, and cope well with crisis.

Presidential campaigns resound with promises. Once in the White House, however, the president must transform those promises into workable policies or programs. This requires the energies and expertise of hundreds of individuals now charged with directing the thousands of individuals who work for or with the federal government. One key test of presidential leadership revolves around organizing the Executive Office and the cabinet to project leadership—to the rest of the executive branch, the other branches of the federal government, and the country and world at large.

To organize the executive branch and project leadership, the president needs (1) information, (2) advice, and (3) action. When it comes to information, presidents have impressive data-gathering networks. Ironically, a more serious problem comes from having too much information, or, more precisely, knowing how to sift and sort and present needed information to the president. The president cannot deal with all the news and information directly; he must rely on an institutional process to manage the flow of information.

A similar problem arises with advice. The president needs two types of advice: political advice (Is there enough support in Congress to pass a tax reform bill? Will Congress and the public accept a tax increase?) and technical advice (How will a tax cut affect inflation? How will the Soviet Union react if the United States invades Panama?). Both brands of advice call for predictions, whose accuracy frequently is hard to gauge. To confound matters further, the two modes often run parallel: Technical advice—for example, raising taxes to lower inflation—may generate unpleasant political fallout. Therefore, a president cannot simply separate the staff into "political" and "technical" divisions. In addition, as with information, there will always be more advice available than any president could possibly consider. So, again, the president must work out some institutional arrangement to sort, sift, and organize advice.

The president's need for action has two basic components. On one level, there are *operational* needs: Speeches must be written, trips planned, strategy outlined with congressional allies, and so on. On the *policy-making* level, subtlety and complexity shadow each decision. Because the various executive agencies and departments—that is, the federal bureaucracy—do not automatically respond to presidential dictates and desires, a president must plant the stamp of his administration on the operations of the federal government. The president must have confidence that when orders are given actions follow. And the chief executive must be assured that *only* the orders that come from the president—and not from others—carry the presidential imprimatur. All this is complicated enough in matters of open public policy, considering the range and variety of matters that command presidential attention. In matters requiring secrecy, the difficulties multiply exponentially. For example, in 1962 President Kennedy was astonished to discover that the United States still had missile bases in Turkey, even though he had ordered the Defense Department to arrange for their removal more than a year before. And in the Iran-contra affair President Reagan was reduced to saying he was anxious to read the Congressional Committees' reports to find out what happened because he knew nothing of the diversion of funds to the contras by members of his own administration. Presidential instructions must be carried out by a coterie of assistants whose primary loyalty is to the president. The loyalty of close assistants in and of itself, however, does not ensure the smooth functioning of the presidency.

In recent years presidents have confronted a dilemma: How can they structure their immediate organizational environment to optimize the gathering of vital information and advice and to take necessary action? One school of thought holds that presidents, like the government itself, should operate within open, nonhierarchical structures, following a "spokes of the wheel" model. In this view, leaders in the executive branch should play an important role in the discussion and formulation of policy, and each should have direct access to the president. Limiting access to the president, through a chief of staff at the top of a rigid hier-

Ronald Reagan: Revolutionary President?

In his acceptance speech at the 1980 Republican national convention, Ronald Reagan shocked some of the delegates by concluding with a lengthy quotation from the man many conservatives consider their archenemy, Franklin Delano Roosevelt. Reagan quoted a statement FDR made during the 1932 campaign, promising to cut government and balance budgets, policies that were very much a part of Reagan's agenda in the 1980s. Reagan, who professed enthusiasm for some of FDR's policies even after he himself had turned conservative, was well aware that Roosevelt was unable to cut government and balance budgets.

In Reagan's first term, however, many observers drew a comparison with FDR. Reagan, it was said, was accomplishing the most massive shift of government priorities since the New Deal. He was reconstructing the American political agenda by deemphasizing the role of government and reemphasizing the private sector; pulling the nation out of economic troubles; and establishing an enduring new majority coalition for the years to come. Also, like FDR, Reagan seemed to have a certain magic, a capacity to communicate that reached the common person.

How true were these comparisons? Was Ronald Reagan a new FDR, fifty years later? In some respects, obviously, the comparison did *not* hold. Roosevelt took office in 1933 in the midst of the gravest economic crisis in American history, one that threatened the very existence of democratic institutions. No doubt, there were also economic problems inherited by the new president in 1981, but they were of quite a different order; economic stagnation, recession, high inflation—intricate and troubling issues, but not problems that threatened to undermine political institutions.

On the other hand, like FDR, Reagan was able, from the start, to wrest control of the political agenda from his opponents. Following through on conservative promises, Reagan marshalled an impressive legislative program, especially in his first two years in the White House: Extensive tax cuts were passed; defense spending was rapidly increased; heavy cuts were made in various social programs and in discretionary spending. On the other hand, the national debt increased vastly.

Apart from the matter of programmatic substance, there is also a question of style. Reagan became known as "the great communicator." His success in gaining a positive public reaction was likened to FDR's shrewd use of the media, as in his famous fireside chats. No doubt, Reagan did seem to lead a charmed life. Like Roosevelt, he also narrowly escaped a would-be assassin's bullet. Reagan, to a degree, modeled his style on FDR's—confident, cheerful, theatrical, larger than life.

Reagan's popularity defied conventional wisdom. Many who did not see eye-to-eye with the president nonetheless said they liked and trusted him. He seemed to have touched a sympathetic nerve in America. His frequent mistakes, insensitivities, and exaggerations did not affect the popular perception of him. The precise nature of his unusual popular appeal proved hard to pin down, however. Some credit his simple and optimistic approach to things. Others cite his ultra-patriotism and hard-line macho manner. Still others argue that Reagan's popularity was quite brittle and that any significant policy failure, especially domestic economic setbacks, would reduce his appeal. Certainly, the Iran-contra affair tarnished the Reagan image appreciably. But whatever long-term judgments are made about the Reagan presidency, we must note the remarkable short-term turnaround in thinking about the presidency that this president wrought. The office that Reagan assumed in 1981 was reckoned by many to be unworkably demanding—beyond normal human capacities. The American public had taken an almost perverse delight in the parade of failed and one-term administrations that preceded the Reagan presidency. Yet Reagan demonstrated that a president, in spite of human limitations, could hold an administration together for two terms and have a significant impact on national politics.

ample, Richard Nixon's heavy reliance on a hierarchical model (H. R. Haldeman was the most important among a small group of aides that came to be known as "the palace guard") came to be strongly linked in the public's mind with the collapse of the Nixon presidency in the Watergate affair (more on this later in the chapter). This disastrous example made presidents shy away from anything that resembled Nixon's model. Both presidents who served in the immediate wake of Watergate (Ford and Carter) disavowed the hierarchical model. Each tried initially to operate without any chief of staff at all.

On the other hand, recent experience illustrates the high cost of operating in close touch with strong centrifugal forces pulling in many directions. "Cabinet government" becomes unwieldy government by committee. To be effective, according to a second model, a president must be protected from a host of demands that distract his attention. Eisenhower, relying on his experience in the military, set up a clearcut hierarchy in the White House. Ronald Reagan also drew on a hierarchical model. Alexander Haig, Nixon's last chief of staff and Reagan's first secretary of state, felt he was denied access to Reagan by a White House staff that had too much anonymous, unscrutinized power. He wrote of his experience:

> But to me the White House was as mysterious as a ghost ship; you heard the creak of the rigging and the groan of the timbers and sometimes even glimpsed the crew on the deck. But which of the crew was at the helm? Was it Meese, was it Baker, was it someone else? It was impossible to know for sure.[8]

While each new president must make choices about how to structure the top echelon of the executive branch, no president starts with a blank slate. Institutional structures have a remarkable resiliency, resisting change or elimination; each president inherits a structure that must be molded to suit new leadership styles and goals. Thus, we now consider the chief executive's two prime sources of information, advice, and action: (1) the Executive Office and (2) the cabinet—which together comprise "the administration." We then cast an eye on (3) the rest of the bureaucracy and (4) the president's relations with Congress.

President Richard Nixon relied on Chief of Staff Bob Haldeman to screen information. This strict hierarchical model was discredited after the Watergate scandal, but George Bush affirmed the importance of the position by naming his Chief of Staff, John Sununu, shortly after the election. *(Owen/Black Star)*

archy, makes a president both inaccessible and out of touch, according to this model, and public policy suffers because of it. This open model gained strong support through two examples—one positive and one negative. Franklin Roosevelt, the first president with a large-scale Executive Office, operated as his own chief of staff, gathering information from a web of associations rather than a strict hierarchy. FDR's success in managing the executive branch and in changing the course of politics gave a tremendous boost to the open model of presidential administration. As a negative ex-

FIGURE 12–1
Executive Office of the President

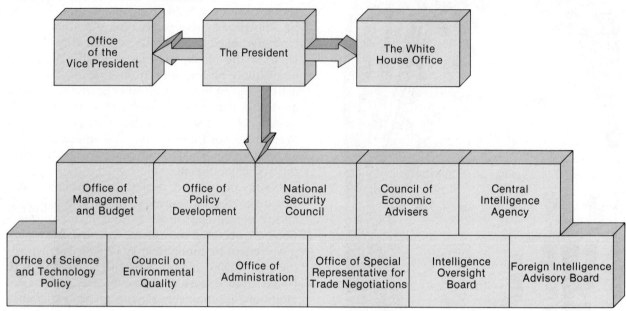

The Executive Office

To deal with the Depression, Franklin Roosevelt had to expand the scope of government activity drastically; in doing so, he established the preeminence of the president as the national policy maker. In 1937, Roosevelt appointed a committee to come up with recommendations on administrative management. The committee's recommendations were tersely summed up in one sentence: "The President needs help." In response, Congress established the **Executive Office of the President,** which represented an important departure from the earlier scheme whereby presidents discharged their duties with the aid of a personal secretary and a handful of clerks. The president has direct control over the various components of the Executive Office (see **Figure 12–1**), the most important of which are examined here.

Closest to the president is the White House Office, which consists of the president's top personal aides. The titles and corresponding duties change from president to president, but whatever their titles, these assistants are a president's most trusted associates. They are responsible only to the president, who can hire and fire them at will.

The White House Office both advises and acts for the president in the areas of national security, the economy, urban affairs, and other domestic policy matters. Some assistants serve as liaisons with Congress and lobby for the president's legislative programs. Others write speeches, handle press relations, plan trips, work with state and local political leaders, and take care of the ceremonial and social aspects of the office. The key aide in the White House Office is the president's chief of staff, who schedules the president's appointments and filters the information that reaches the Oval Office. In general, the chief of staff has instant access to the chief executive and works closely with him.

The largest of the Executive Office components is the **Office of Management and Budget** (OMB), formerly known as the Bureau of Budget.

The OMB has two main functions: to prepare the federal budget and to clear all legislation submitted to Congress by agencies of the executive branch. The OMB also provides the president with summaries and analyses of the budgetary implications of legislation enacted by Congress. As with all agencies in the Executive Office, the impact the OMB has on policy making depends on both the president and the OMB director. For example, President Reagan gave David Stockman, the administration's first OMB director, a major role in policy making, but Stockman's successor, James Miller, had far less influence in the Reagan administration.

The **National Security Council** (NSC) was created by the National Security Act of 1947 to coordinate domestic, diplomatic, and military policies in matters of national security. Invariably, the president, the vice-president, the secretary of state, the secretary of defense, and the director of the CIA sit on the council. The president may also include in NSC meetings other officials whose knowledge he considers relevant to defense planning or in whom he has particular confidence. Thus, President Kennedy included his brother Robert, then the attorney general, in NSC meetings, although the Justice Department is not normally involved in defense planning.

The NSC has its own staff, which prepares detailed analyses and policy options. Once small, this staff grew to over two hundred under President Nixon's special assistant for national security, Henry Kissinger, and has remained at that level. Kissinger, a particularly strong national security advisor, drew national security policy making firmly into the White House, thereby circumventing normal bureaucratic channels of decision making in the State Department and Defense Department. The Reagan administration, which sought to circumvent normal channels to maintain secrecy and "deniability" (the claim that a high government official simply did not know about something on the margins—or beyond the limits—of acceptability) used the NSC's shield of secrecy to carry out covert operations.

Envisioned as a domestic counterpart to the NSC, the **Domestic Council** was created by President Nixon in 1970 to formulate and coordinate the president's domestic policy. President Carter dismantled the Domestic Council and created the Policy Staff, which shared domestic policy making with the OMB. President Reagan created the Office of Policy Development to coordinate all domestic policy recommendations, but in practice, the office did not do much coordinating and was overshadowed by a cabinet council also created by the Reagan administration. The fate of the Do-

mestic Council and its successors illustrates how agencies within the Executive Office compete with agencies represented in the cabinet.

The Cabinet

There is no mention of the cabinet in the Constitution. Since George Washington first gathered his principal government officers together in council, presidents have drawn on the "cabinet" for political advice, for guidance on policy and programs, and for a variety of other reasons. But chief executives differ in how extensively they call on the cabinet. Andrew Jackson did not even convene his cabinet for two years, while James Polk held 350 cabinet meetings.

Today the **cabinet** consists of the thirteen heads of the major administrative departments—Justice, State, Treasury, Defense, Interior, Agriculture, Commerce, Labor, Health and Human Services (HHS), Education, Housing and Urban Development (HUD), Energy, and Transportation—plus others as designated by the president. President Reagan's cabinet originally included the counselor to the president, the directors of the OMB and the CIA, the U.S. trade representative, and the U.S. representative to the United Nations. Each member is subject to Senate approval. In 1988 Congress voted to upgrade the Veterans Administration to a cabinet-level Department of Veterans Affairs.

As an institution, the cabinet is difficult for the president to manage, in part, because it embodies a set of delicate political balances.[9] The cabinet reflects balances between competing interests—business (Commerce) and labor (Labor), rural (Agriculture) and urban (Housing and Urban Development), diplomacy (State) and military interests (Defense). In addition, fiscal restraint (OMB) is balanced against spending (all departments). "Presidential" departments (State, Defense, Treasury, Justice) face off against "congressional" departments (Agriculture, HHS, HUD). Presidents tamper with these precarious balances at their own risk, as President Johnson discovered when he proposed merging Commerce and Labor, and as President Reagan found when he tried to abolish Education and Energy.

Executive patterns vary considerably from one president to another. Ronald Reagan's disengaged management style left considerable power in the hands of top political appointees. Shown here are several of the most influential members of Reagan's management team: Donald Regan (Treasury Secretary and White House Chief of Staff); Caspar Weinberger (Defense Secretary); Vice-President George Bush; George Shultz (Secretary of State); and John Poindexter (National Security Adviser). *(UPI/ Bettmann Newsphotos)*

But because the cabinet as a whole makes for an unwieldy policy-making body, several proposals have been advanced to reshape it. President Nixon's push to create a Super-Cabinet by merging positions fell victim to the storm of Watergate. One scholar has proposed an Executive Cabinet, in which positions would be assigned different hierarchical statuses. President Reagan implemented a more modest reform by creating Cabinet Councils—at first seven of them but then only two (the Economic Policy Council and the Domestic Policy Council). These Councils were designed to coordinate policy formulation both among departments, and between departments and Executive Office agencies. Although they did not assume the power and responsibility of senior presidential staffs, these councils made for a successful reform, playing a role in every stage of White House policy making during the Reagan years.

In addition to the institutional challenge of the cabinet, presidents confront a challenge in dealing with cabinet members individually. The typical cabinet is rife with political tensions. Often, cabinet secretaries are appointed for political reasons— to appease particular segments of the party or to disarm rivals or critics—yet presidents also demand loyalty and competence from appointees.

The question of divided loyalties poses another problem as well: The president invariably expects his appointees to be responsive first of all to directives from him; yet, just as inevitably, cabinet members must also respond to the needs and interests of their departmental constituencies if they are to be effective department managers. Presidents then complain that cabinet members are becoming too independent and are being run *by* the bureaucracy, rather than the other way around. Finally, presidents and cabinet members frequently clash, particularly as national and international crises take up more and more of the president's time and his personal contacts with most cabinet members diminish. He loses touch, and they do as well. If a cabinet member is not part of the president's inner circle, tensions are bound to arise.

Some Washington observers note that cabinet secretaries rely heavily on the many assistants who serve under them. While the secretaries deal with the headline issues, the real management of programs often is handled by the so-called subcabinet—undersecretaries, assistant secretaries, general counsels, and their staffs. Because these little-known officials exert a profound influence on key policy decisions, finding trustworthy and competent people for these positions can be crucial to the success or failure of major administrative programs.

The Rest of the Bureaucracy

Most presidents experience more frustration than success when they push to make the federal bureaucracy responsive to their own priorities. A president has only a few years to impress his views on the departments, but the federal bureaucracy encompasses an array of institutions—each with its own routines, priorities, practices—that remain as elected administrations come and go. Segments of the bureaucracy have well-established connections with Congress and interest groups, and have no interest in seeing their programs gutted, curtailed, or radically changed by an incoming administration. According to a former cabinet secretary:

> The longer one examines the awesome burdens and limited resources of those who help the president from within his immediate circle, the more skeptical one becomes of a strategy for overseeing government by "running" it from 1600 Pennsylvania Avenue. The semiheroic, semihopeless posture has been captured many times in several administrations: dedicated men, of great intelligence and energy, working selflessly through weekends and holidays to master an endlessly increasing array of detail on complex subjects beyond their understanding on which decisions must be made "here" because a resolution elsewhere is not to be trusted. . . . Yet, in the end, the effort to help the president in making government work has not succeeded.[10]

For many members of White House staffs, conflict within the executive branch poses the single most significant problem in contemporary government. Some report more intense and serious conflict between the president and the bureaucracy than between the president and the Congress. Although a few staffers believe that bureaucratic noncooperation stems from conspiracies and malevolent designs against the president, the more thoughtful recognize that to some exent, conflicts are inevitable. Bureaucrats have many constitu-

ents, whereas White House staffers have only one person to please. And many career bureaucrats find White House staffers to be arrogant and bossy—interfering in matters they know little about and politicizing issues needlessly.

Relations with Congress

In Chapter 11 we saw that Congress and the president frequently maintain an adversarial relationship. Although Congress has powerful constitutional tools on its side—control of the purse strings, approval of presidential appointments and treaties, and the veto override—the president can use a wide array of tactics in dealing with Congress. These stratagems can be divided roughly into six categories: (1) wooing, (2) lobbying, (3) exchange of favors, (4) hardball tactics, (5) going to the people, and (6) the veto. Before examining them more closely, we should note that today, presidents have less trouble with entrenched committee chairs, and more with independent-minded legislators. Instead of making deals with a few powerful members of Congress, then, contemporary presidents must persuade and compromise with numerous less powerful ones.

WOOING If a president does not enjoy firm support within his party (consider, for example, Jimmy Carter), or if that party does not have majorities in Congress, the president often must woo members of the opposition. Republican presidents Nixon, Ford, and Reagan, faced with Democratic majorities in one or both houses of Congress, used wooing tactics to build on the conservative coalition that already existed in Congress (see Chapter 11).

LOBBYING The legislative liaison branch of the White House staff is charged with getting the president's point of view across to Congress. Liaison staffers work closely with congressional committees, consult and negotiate with legislators on critical points, and above all, try to convey a firm sense of the president's personal commitment to particular policies and programs. If these staffers do not convince Congress that the president is

As a political scientist before becoming president, Woodrow Wilson had written about the symbolic role of presidential leadership. In the White House, Wilson used the ceremonial aspects of the presidency, sometimes successfully (as in the U.S. entry into World War I) and sometimes less so (as in seeking support for the League of Nations). Here Wilson tosses out the first baseball of the 1916 season—a presidential action universally applauded. *(Culver Pictures)*

committed to a certain program, White House lobbying for that program will be useless.

Support for the president's policies is also cultivated through contacts with interest groups, state and local party officials, and public officials, as well as by wining and dining important members of Congress. These efforts may not directly change votes, but they can help to keep relations cordial between the administration and Congress.

EXCHANGE OF FAVORS   In exchanging favors with members of Congress, the president holds a trump card—patronage. Up to five hundred federal district judges, U.S. attorneys, and federal marshals, as well as numerous executive branch officials, are presidential appointees. Presidents often use these positions as bargaining chips in negotiations with opposition-party legislators. President Truman, for example, promised congressional Republicans that they could name the staff of the Marshall Plan (the U.S. program to assist Europe after World War II) if they supported the program in the first place. A president may also seek to placate a wing of his own party by exchanging favors, as President Kennedy did when he refrained from issuing an executive order ending racial discrimination in federally assisted housing, and made other gestures designed to placate Southern Democrats.

Such exchanges can backfire, however, especially if members of Congress feel they are being pressured to trade votes directly for favors. As a result, exchanges are often quite subtle. President Johnson, for example, declared unequivocally that he would not trade patronage for votes in any direct exchange. But a stubborn unwillingness to trade can also spell trouble, as President Carter discovered when, early in his term, he cut 19 water projects from the budget and called for reviews of another 320. Protests burst from Congress, which rarely faced such blatant presidential interference in its pork-barrel traditions. Eventually, Carter decided not to review 307 projects and to restore funding to 3 of those he had originally dropped from the budget.

HARDBALL TACTICS   When all else fails, a president can resort to outright threats—usually, that federal projects will be eliminated or reduced in the state or district represented by an uncooperative legislator. President Johnson took such actions against Vietnam War opponents, and President Nixon threatened to do so against legislators who were leaning toward opposing his Supreme Court nominees. Nixon also threatened to order IRS audits of particular senators' taxes. In 1985, President Reagan indicated he would have "more time" to

The Presidential Pen, the Congressional Eraser

President Reagan liked to warn Congress that his "veto pen" was ready whenever Congress was considering legislation he opposed, but the record shows that he vetoed far fewer bills than many of his predecessors did. Grover Cleveland, for example, vetoed hundreds of private pension bills passed by Congress. Other presidents (Andrew Johnson, Truman, and Eisenhower are examples) faced Congresses that either were controlled by the opposing party during periods of their presidencies or were sufficiently assertive in their own right to generate legislation opposed by the president. Following is a list of the presidents who cast the most vetoes and those most overridden by Congress. To "erase" the president's veto, Congress requires a two-thirds majority in both houses. These figures demonstrate the difficulty Congress has always had in overriding a presidential veto. Franklin Roosevelt cast 635 vetoes but was overridden only 9 times, reflecting not only the difficulty Congress has in garnering a two-thirds majority on any issue but also the power of the presidency to determine the legislative agenda. SOURCE: Adapted from the *New York Times*, Mar. 23, 1988, p. 12.

Most Vetoes Cast		*Most Vetoes Overridden*	
F. D. Roosevelt (in office 12 years)	635	A. Johnson (in office 4 years)	15
Cleveland (in office 8 years)	584	Ford (in office 2½ years)	12
Truman (in office 7½ years)	250	Truman (in office 7½ years)	11
Eisenhower (in office 8 years)	181	F. D. Roosevelt (in office 12 years)	9
Grant (in office 8 years)	93	Reagan (in office 8 years)	9
T. Roosevelt (in office 7½ years)	82	Cleveland (in office 8 years)	7
Ford (in office 2½ years)	66	Wilson (in office 8 years)	6
Reagan (in office 8 years)	64	Nixon (in office 5½ years)	5

campaign for the reelection of Republican senators who voted for his MX missile program. When this strong-arm approach appeared to be backfiring, Reagan quickly backed away publicly from that position. But he gained the votes he needed.

GOING TO THE PEOPLE The president has one unparalleled advantage in dealing with a recalcitrant Congress: He can focus national attention on selected issues. The president can command a larger audience than an individual legislator, a group of legislators, or even the entire opposition party. Through a major address, a president can raise issues on the national agenda in a fashion that is initially difficult to oppose. Such an address can provoke an immediate surge in support, giving presidents more flexibility in bargaining with Congress and other political players. A recent study concluded that the success of presidential speech-making in building support among various groups does not depend on a president's personal style or oratorical ability: Ford and Carter (neither noted for oratorical skill) were as successful at altering group opinions as the "great communicator," Ronald Reagan.[11] However, too many presidential appearances can lead to diminishing audiences, so this tactic must be used with care. Ronald Reagan's Saturday morning radio addresses, for example, drew very little attention as they became a weekly routine. And at times, even the television networks constrain the president's ability to go directly to the people. Early in 1988, for instance, when President Reagan urged the networks to broadcast live a speech he was making to urge continued support for the contras in Nicaragua, only CNN agreed to cover the speech live; ABC, CBS, and NBC turned down the president's request for live coverage. In the judgment of news executives at those three networks, the news value of the proposed speech to the nation was negligible because the president had covered the same ground numerous times before.

Televised news conferences offer presidents a forum to appeal to the public as well, although the risk of committing a blooper is great in this relatively uncontrolled setting. President Reagan's unwillingness to hold frequent news conferences gave rise to the unseemly and slightly comical practice of reporters shouting questions at him whenever he appeared in public. Presidents can also give off-the-record news briefings and interviews to get their views across. If the president can create a sense of national crisis when he goes to the people, the likely increase in presidential popularity can be used to political advantage.

THE VETO The veto power gives the president considerable leverage with Congress. Knowing a veto is likely, Congress may modify a bill to meet presidential objections; after a veto, it may pass legislation altered to meet presidential demands. Presidential vetoes are rarely overridden—only 4 percent suffer such a fate. Yet a few vetoes of extremely important matters have been overridden—for example, President Nixon's veto of the **War Powers Act,** a measure guaranteeing Congress a voice whenever U.S. military forces are sent into action, and President Reagan's veto of the Civil Rights Restoration Act of 1988 (covered earlier in this chapter).

Presidents cannot veto every measure Congress passes. They cannot veto constitutional amendments, or bills relating to the internal organization of either house. Also, battles frequently break out within the executive branch over whether particular bills should be vetoed. Typically, conflict erupts between cabinet members and White House staffers or OMB officials.

The Dangerous President

Throughout U.S. history, presidents have used the wide latitude available to them in foreign policy making and their position as symbolic leader to foment crises, go to war, or harass opponents. In the early days of the Republic, Presidents John Adams, Thomas Jefferson, and Andrew Jackson were accused of abusing the powers of the office. Then, during the Civil War, President Lincoln stretched the powers of the office considerably. In this century, Franklin Roosevelt, John Kennedy, Lyndon Johnson, Richard Nixon, and Ronald Reagan have all been charged with abuses of power.

Not every accusation is justified, of course; partisanship often plays a role here. For many years, beginning in the 1930s, conservative Republicans attacked the growing power of the presidency, largely out of dislike for particular policies or particular incumbents. Those who attacked the power of the president, who saw it as a threat to the constitutional system, often were the same people who railed against an activist government—who preferred to see society remain as it was. During this period, liberals championed the strong presidency because of its potential for making needed changes and responding to urgent national concerns.

In the 1960s, this pattern of debate shifted, as liberals voiced concern about excessive presidential power and many conservatives found themselves backing the president. The Vietnam War, more than any other factor, accounted for this shift. Liberals came to oppose the war, and the mounting—and, in their view, dangerous—growth of presidential power associated with it. Conservatives, on the other hand, tended to support Presidents Johnson and Nixon in their conduct of the war. A similar pattern of conservative endorsement of an activist president emerged in the 1980s, as President Reagan curtailed administrative support for domestic programs he opposed and advanced the Reagan doctrine of covert, low-intensity intervention around the globe.

Partisanship aside, there is real cause for concern that the president's constitutional powers and the additional responsibilities of the modern pres-

Congress Manipulated: The Gulf of Tonkin Resolution

In the summer of 1964, President Lyndon Johnson and his advisors were planning to escalate U.S. involvement in the fighting in Vietnam. In early August, North Vietnamese ships allegedly fired on a U.S. destroyer in the Gulf of Tonkin, in what the administration characterized as an unprovoked incident that had taken place in international waters. The next day another incident took place, this one involving two American destroyers; it has never been made clear what (if anything) happened in this incident. President Johnson and his advisors seized on these incidents to press Congress to authorize the president to take any action necessary to deal with North Vietnamese aggression. That way the administration would not have to go through the lengthy and potentially difficult process of obtaining a formal declaration of war.

The president told congressional leaders that he intended to retaliate against North Vietnamese targets and that he wanted a congressional resolution to back him up. Although he emphasized that he wanted only a "limited resolution," the one that reached the floor of Congress authorized him to "take all necessary measures" to repel "any armed attack" on American troops and to prevent "further aggression" in Vietnam. Johnson asked Senator William Fulbright, an Arkansas Democrat and the chairman of the Senate Foreign Relations Committee, to guide the Gulf of Tonkin Resolution through the Senate. Although Fulbright had been critical of the war, he and Johnson enjoyed cordial relations, so he rushed the Resolution through his committee. His main opposition in the committee was

Senator Wayne Morse of Oregon. Morse warned Fulbright that the resolution would give the president all the authority he needed for carrying on an expanded war in Vietnam. Congress, Morse warned, would never be consulted about the war again.

Morse's reservations about the resolution stemmed, in part, from his awareness of certain falsehoods and distortions in the administration's version of events in the Gulf of Tonkin. (Later, congressional investigators discovered that the destroyers had been engaged in disrupting North Vietnamese radar—with electronic interference.) Morse pleaded with Fulbright to hold open hearings on the resolution. What was the emergency? he inquired. Why the need to rush the resolution through? But Fulbright and Johnson had their way: The resolution passed the Senate with two dissenting votes, and the House without a single dissent.

Thus, the president was given what he claimed was a blank check for conducting the war in Vietnam. But Lyndon Johnson eventually paid a price for his manipulation of Congress. Fulbright, after learning that he had been lied to and that the administration had deliberately misconstrued the evidence about the Tonkin Gulf incidents, became a determined enemy of the Vietnam War and used his power as Foreign Relations Committee chairman to direct a steady stream of serious criticism at the war. The Gulf of Tonkin Resolution triggered a widespread distrust of the executive branch. This distrust culminated in the passage of the War Powers Act of 1973, which limited presidential war-making powers.

---

idency could easily threaten democratic politics. Presidential abuses of power generally fall into three categories: (1) betraying the public trust, when the president and/or his aides deliberately mislead the public or arouse public emotion in a manipulative way; (2) undermining the separation of powers by usurping functions that properly belong to Congress or the courts; and (3) manipulating the political and legal processes.

But particular presidential abuses of power usually encompass some combination of these categories. We now examine three examples of the misuse of presidential power—(1) the Vietnam War; (2) the Watergate affair; and (3) the Iran-contra affair.

The Vietnam War

The Vietnam War was a "presidential" war, fought entirely without a declaration of war from Congress. The war lasted more than a decade, cost this country $165 billion, and claimed fifty-one thousand American lives. Throughout most of the war, Congress more or less passively supported U.S. military involvement, but that support was gained, at least in part, through a series of presidential abuses of power.

According to historian Arthur Schlesinger, we had a taste of the so-called *imperial presidency* under President Johnson and his successor, Richard Nixon.[12] From 1963 to 1974, Schlesinger suggested, presidential power was expanded and abused, and the nation was threatened with a presidential style that ignored reasonable limits on the office.

Schlesinger focused on two aspects of the expansion and use of presidential powers: *war powers* and *the manipulation of secrecy*. In an era of nearly constant crisis, the president's war powers gradually expanded until they came to include prerogatives once associated with monarchs, not elected officials. Both presidents deliberately misled Congress and the public about matters of war and peace. Johnson shrewdly arranged for Congress to pass the Gulf of Tonkin Resolution of 1964, which he claimed gave him virtually a free hand in Vietnam. The information the president gave Congress to justify such sweeping new powers turned out to be at the least misleading and probably deliberately deceptive. Nixon conducted a secret bombing campaign in Cambodia in 1969 and 1970. He then significantly altered the scope and nature of the war—again without consulting Congress or the American people—by ordering an invasion of Cambodia by ground troops in 1970. Every significant expansion of this war was undertaken unilaterally by the president, with Congress entirely excluded or at best given the opportunity to consent meekly after the fact. Even attempts to extricate the United States from the war through international agreements were entirely executive in nature.

Emergency powers also accumulated in the president's hands. From the 1930s to the 1960s, Congress passed approximately five hundred laws granting the president such powers, including the powers to seize property, control production, impose martial law, and restrict travel. These laws were used by President Franklin Roosevelt to justify the internment of Japanese-Americans in 1942, and by President Nixon to justify his cover-up of the bombing of Cambodia.

In response to these and other perceived abuses of presidential power, Congress passed the War Powers Act of 1973, curtailed the president's emergency powers, and imposed some restrictions on future executive agreements (see Chapter 11 for further details). But with increased U.S. involvement as regional conflict heated up in Central America in the 1980s, no one could be sure that the lessons of Vietnam—the danger to democracy posed by presidential abuse of power and congressional acquiescence—had been learned.

The Watergate Affair

On the night of June 17, 1972, five burglars were apprehended in the headquarters of the Democratic National Committee, located in the Watergate complex in Washington, D.C. At first, administration spokesmen dismissed the break-in as a "third-rate burglary." But two reporters for the *Washington Post*, Carl Bernstein and Bob Woodward, traced a connection between the break-in and Nixon's reelection campaign committee (the Committee to Re-Elect the President, or CREEP). Several White House aides in contact with CREEP also had a hand in the bungled burglary. A plan to cover up these connections was put into place: Incriminating documents were destroyed, and the Watergate burglars were offered money for their defense and their families in exchange for their silence. Despite efforts by the Democrats to focus attention on the Watergate affair at that point, the administration's cover-up muted most calls for further investigation prior to the elections of November 1972. Nixon was returned to office in a landslide.

Richard Nixon was the first president to resign, tainted by involvement in the Watergate scandal. Here he bids the White House staff good-bye in August 1974. But public opinion of Nixon mellowed, and he played the role of senior statesman during the 1980s. *(UPI/Bettmann Newsphotos)*

In January 1973, however, the Watergate burglars were convicted and sentenced to jail, and one of the burglars told Judge John Sirica that they had been pressured into pleading guilty. Sirica reopened the case and grand jury hearings were held. A Senate Select Committee on Watergate began an investigation in May 1973. Under pressure from Congress and the press, Nixon appointed a special prosecutor to look into the matter, although he and his aides continued to maintain their innocence.

The Senate hearings soon brought some startling facts to light. It became clear that the Nixon administration had violated most of the rules of U.S. political life. White House personnel and Republican Party members illegally wiretapped political opponents, stole documents, lied to grand juries, and engaged in large-scale falsifications about illegal campaign contributions. As the evidence reached closer to the Oval Office, some of Nixon's aides resigned.

Yet Nixon himself might have been able to weather the Watergate storm had the public not learned that he had installed a taping system that secretly recorded every conversation in the Oval Office. Claiming executive privilege, Nixon refused to release the tapes until the Supreme Court unanimously ordered him to supply copies of the tapes to the court hearing the Watergate burglary case.

The tapes doomed Nixon. Nixon and his aides emerged on the tapes as vindictive schemers bent on settling scores with their enemies and gaining more and more power. With impeachment proceedings imminent, Nixon resigned in August 1974.

Many of the charges against Nixon involved activities that previous presidents had engaged in or condoned. Other chief executives had received illegal campaign contributions, used "dirty tricks" in political campaigns, provided direct or indirect payoffs to those who had helped in election efforts, used government agencies to harass enemies, tried to manage the news, and kept some activities secret from the public and Congress. But Nixon's personal involvement in the cover-up of crimes and the obstruction of justice distinguished him from other presidents. In the final analysis, the sheer number of violations of law and norms, and the range of questionable activities designed to enhance the powers and prerogatives of a president and his cohorts—these were unique to the Nixon administration. Here was a president and a group of advisors who not only tried to skirt the law, but who actually believed that the president (at least *their* president) was above the law.

The Iran-Contra Affair

The Iran-contra affair exemplifies executive abuse of power.[13] Although President Reagan's specific involvement in the affair remains unclear, the pattern of abuse in this episode closely matches the preceding examples. Leaving the matter of personal presidential culpability aside, this event demonstrates the abuse of power carried out by members of the president's administration in the president's name.

The stern, resolute visage of the Ayatollah Khomeini and the tentative look of fear or hope on the face of this Nicaraguan contra are an unlikely pairing—but no less likely than the Iran-contra affair itself, a tangled web of deception and naivete involving inscribed Bibles and key-shaped cakes, misplaced millions, and the outright violation of public trust. (*UPI/Bettmann Newsphotos*)

The Iran-contra affair was an odd pairing of operations in two widely separated parts of the globe. In Iran, the administration's objective was to win the freedom of American hostages held by terrorist groups in Lebanon that were more or less associated with the revolutionary government of Iran. In Nicaragua, the administration sought to support the contra opposition to the Marxist Sandinista government. Two sets of constraints limited administration action. In its dealings with Iran, the administration was bound by an embargo on arms to Iran and a firmly asserted public policy of refusing to bargain with terrorists for the release of hostages. According to official policy, such bargaining would only encourage terrorists to seize more hostages in the long run. In Nicaragua, the administration was constrained by the Boland Amendment, signed into law in October 1984 as part of the 1985 omnibus appropriations bills. The Boland Amendment cut off all federal funds for the contras' military and paramilitary operations, prohibited the American government from soliciting donations for the contras from third-party countries, and barred the CIA and other U.S. government agencies from participating in covert op-

erations in support of the contras. Lieutenant Colonel Oliver L. North, a staff member of the National Security Council, was placed in charge of both operations.

Between June 1984 and the beginning of 1986, North raised $34 million in secret contributions for the contras from other countries and from private sources in the United States. Initially these funds were sent directly by the donors to accounts controlled by the contras. But starting in July 1985, North took control of the funds and, with the support of two national security advisors (and, according to North, the director of the CIA), used those funds to run a covert operation supporting the contras.

In the meantime, the American government learned of the possibility that sales of U.S. arms to Iran (engaged in a stalemated war with Iraq) might lead to the release of American hostages and a new, more friendly relationship with Iran. Weapons sales were arranged through "the Enterprise," a private concern run at North's direction by a retired U.S. Air Force major general. Using good old Yankee ingenuity, the Enterprise managed to charge Iran more for the weapons than it had paid

Democracy can tolerate hardware secrets (like the Stealth bomber), secret plans (like the invasion of Normandy), but not secret policies that contradict public statements, like trading arms for hostages and diverting the "profits" to the contras. *(Claude Urraca/Sygma)*

the U.S. government for them, generating more than $16 million in "spare cash." The two operations were joined when North directed that some of this "profit" be used to support the contras.

These transactions abused executive power on several counts. Most significantly, the administration was conducting a secret foreign policy in direct contradiction to its publicly stated policy. In addition, active efforts were made to deceive Congress about the nature of these operations. The deception even reached within the executive branch itself; North ordered intelligence agencies not to disseminate information on these operations to the secretaries of state and defense. (Both secretaries claimed to have opposed the plan when they learned about it in broad outline.) The NSC used private individuals and the Enterprise to carry out the government's business, deliberately avoiding accountability for these actions in the po-

litical arena. Finally, the NSC itself had been turned from its original mission—to give the president advice on national security matters and foreign policy issues—into a base for covert operations.

The Executive Summary of the Report of the Congressional Committees Investigating the Iran-Contra Affair ended with this quotation from Supreme Court Justice Louis Brandeis: "Our Government is the potent, the omnipresent teacher. For good or ill, it teaches the whole people by its example. Crime is contagious. If the Government becomes a lawbreaker, it breeds contempt for the law, it invites every man to become a law unto himself, it invites anarchy." The *Report* concluded that the Iran-contra affair resulted from a failure to heed this message.

Although we have addressed the specific issues raised by these three examples of executive excesses, we still need to confront a key dilemma: How can we prevent presidential abuses of power when the president holds such a predominant place in U.S. political life? Most Americans do not favor weakening the presidency in any constitutional manner. And most believe the United States needs an activist president who leads the nation vigorously. Those views are reinforced by institutional prerogatives: No other political actor can shape and organize the government in a way comparable to the president. Thus we continue to face the ongoing risk of presidential abuse of power.

Transition of Power

Transitions at the top levels of a political system frequently provoke controversy. In many polities, such changeovers touch off intense struggles for power among individuals and groups seeking to gain political control. When Josef Stalin died in 1953 after ruling the Soviet Union for twenty-five years, the succession crisis lasted several years. Similarly, Mao Zedong's death in 1976 sparked epic political struggles in China.

In democratic nations, by contrast, struggles for leadership are usually settled by legal, constitutional means. As a result, democratic political leaders normally do not resort to illegal means to remain in office following electoral defeat. Yet many

COMPARATIVE PERSPECTIVE

Political Crisis and Transition in France, 1958

During World War II, General Charles de Gaulle was the acknowledged leader of the Free French. After the liberation of France from Nazi occupation, he presided over a provisional government while an assembly wrote a new constitution establishing the Fourth Republic. Disgusted with the weak government he felt had been created, De Gaulle retired to the political sidelines in 1946.

By May 1958, the Fourth Republic had gone through twenty-four governments, and the country was being torn apart over the problem of Algeria—whether to acknowledge the grievances of Algerian rebels opposing French rule or to repress all colonial unrest. The Algerian question proved too much for the successively weaker governments. In 1956, the French Army had stood by while French settlers in Algiers attacked their own premier, socialist Guy Mollet, whom they felt had been too weak in dealing with the rebels. The disaffected military coalesced into a powerful and potentially antidemocratic threat to French political stability.

The twenty-third government of the Fourth Republic fell on April 15, 1958, when the hard-line Algerian lobby withdrew its support. Four tense weeks passed before a new government could be formed. Meanwhile De Gaulle was poised to reclaim political power. As anti-Gaullist politicians scrambled to scrape together enough support to keep him out of power, several prominent military officers planned a coup d'état against the Republic, to be carried out on the orders of the senior military command in Algiers.

What came next has been termed the De Gaulle revolution. Through a process of secret negotiations with members of the government and public pronouncements warning the military to "maintain exemplary behavior," De Gaulle was able to position himself for an official call to establish a new government. Legality was preserved as De Gaulle, like his predecessors, was voted into office by the National Assembly. But his terms for taking the reins of government were stiff: emergency powers and governance by decree, the temporary (six-month) dissolution of the Assembly, and the mandate to draw up a new constitution. France had preserved the form, if not the substance, of institutionalized succession.

SOURCES: Don Cook, *Charles de Gaulle* (New York: Putnam, 1983); and Bernard Ledwidge, *De Gaulle* (New York: St. Martin's Press, 1982).

---

intricacies can develop in the process of transition at the top. What happens when a U.S. president is disabled, dies, or is removed from office? We now consider (1) modes of succession in the United States and (2) the vice-presidency.

Modes of Succession

Under normal conditions, presidents leave office because they choose not to run again or are defeated in an election. Only about one-third of U.S. presidents—thirteen in all—have won a second term in office, and only Franklin Roosevelt served more than two terms. (No president can now duplicate Roosevelt's four-term record: Under the Twenty-second Amendment, ratified in 1951, no person may be elected president more than two times, and a person who has gained the presidency through succession as vice-president is limited to only a single election if he serves more than two years of the unexpired term of the previous president. This means that no one may serve more than ten years as president today.)

Slightly more than 20 percent of U.S. presidents have died in office, including four who were assassinated: Abraham Lincoln (1865), James Garfield (1881), William McKinley (1901), and John Kennedy (1963). Since 1945, moreover, four out of eight presidents have been attacked by assassins—a record among contemporary Western democracies. So far, no president has been removed from office by impeachment, although Andrew Johnson came close and Richard Nixon resigned before an impeachment trial could be held.

The mechanics of presidential succession are not spelled out in the Constitution. When President William Henry Harrison died one month after taking office in 1841, John Tyler, the vice-president, assumed the presidency. That was the first time a president had died in office, and it sparked a political controversy. Should Tyler simply become president, or should he take office temporarily until a new election could be held? Tyler preferred the first alternative, and Congress acquiesced.

The Succession Act of 1886 mandated specific procedures for presidential succession. The act made the secretary of state second in line behind the vice-president, followed by the other members of the cabinet in order of seniority. But this system had two inherent drawbacks: It placed a whole series of unelected officials in line for the presidency, and it allowed a vice-president who inherited the presidency to pick his own successor by choosing the secretary of state.

This pattern of succession was altered in 1947, when the Speaker of the House and the president pro tempore of the Senate were placed next in line after the vice-president. This system did not work either, however, because it placed in the line of succession officials who might not be of the president's party. Finally, the Twenty-fifth Amendment, ratified in 1967, addressed the twin issues of succession and presidential disability. Twice in U.S. history, presidents had become seriously disabled—James Garfield after being shot in 1881, and Woodrow Wilson after a stroke in 1919. Others, such as Dwight Eisenhower, had been temporarily incapacitated by illness. The Twenty-fifth Amendment provided that if the president were unable to carry out his duties, the vice-president would serve as acting president. If the president were to

decline to step down, he could be removed by a two-thirds vote of each house of Congress. In dealing with succession, the amendment specifies that on assuming the presidency, the vice-president must nominate a new vice-president, who must then be confirmed by a majority of both houses of Congress. If no new vice-president is selected and the new president must be replaced, the 1947 arrangements prevail.

Not long after the Twenty-fifth Amendment was ratified, its provisions were put to use. Nixon's vice-president, Spiro Agnew, resigned from office after pleading no contest to bribery charges. Nixon then nominated Gerald Ford to the vice-presidency. Not long thereafter, Nixon resigned the presidency, and Ford became the president. He in turn nominated Nelson Rockefeller as vice-president, and Rockefeller was confirmed by both houses. When he was sworn in as vice-president on December 19, 1974, it marked the first time in U.S. history that neither of the two people holding the highest offices in the nation had been elected to those positions. The procedure worked smoothly, despite the turmoil of Watergate and the novelty of the succession process. The procedures were also engaged in 1985, when Ronald Reagan was briefly unable to serve as president during an operation for colon cancer. George Bush became acting president for that short period.

The Vice-Presidency

The vice-presidency has been the target of scorn and derision throughout U.S. history. According to John Nance Garner, who gave up his position as Speaker of the House to become Franklin Roosevelt's running mate in 1932, the vice-presidency was "not worth a pitcher of warm spit." And when Daniel Webster rejected a nomination for the vice-presidency in 1848, he declared, "I do not choose to be buried until I am really dead."

The vice-president's duties are minimal. Presiding over the Senate and breaking tie votes in the Senate—a rare occurrence—constitute the vice-president's only official functions. Vice-presidents are sometimes given certain responsibilities by the president, such as chairing government commissions or undertaking foreign missions of various

Presidential succession is highly routinized in the United States, whether under traumatic conditions, like the assassination of President Kennedy in 1963, or the calm normalcy of President Bush's succession of Ronald Reagan in 1989. Such a stable transfer of power is a credit to our democracy and the envy of less tranquil political systems. *(Dan McCoy/Black Star)*

sorts. For the most part, however, vice-presidents are hemmed in by the constraints of the position. They cannot openly break with the administration without jeopardizing their own future political careers.

Some observers argue that given its nebulous functions and overall uselessness, the vice-presidency should be done away with and presidential succession handled through a second national election. Others contend that to make the office more meaningful, presidential candidates should select their running mates early and run for nomination as a team. Neither proposal, however, has attracted much political support.

Conclusions

In dealing with the presidency, we tend to reach for extremes. To one generation, presidential leadership holds the key to political soundness, progress, and effective policy making. To another, the presidency is a source of unbridled hubris. To-

day, when the president has his finger on the nuclear trigger, issues of presidential abuse of power become enormously magnified. What sort of person should sit in the White House? How much latitude should we give the occupant of the Oval Office? While presidents sometimes find it necessary to stretch the limits of their power, Congress, the courts, and the electorate may either sanction presidential initiatives or assert their own power to cut the president short.

And how do democracy and the drive for democratic values figure in the scheme of presidential policy making? Clearly, presidents can enhance their historical standing by championing democratic causes. When Lyndon Johnson introduced the Voting Rights Act of 1965, it marked a turning point in U.S. history. Lending the weight and prestige of the presidency to democratic causes can make the difference between progress and stagnation. But presidents can also work against democratic politics, as Richard Nixon did in his conduct of the Vietnam War and the Watergate affair, and as Lyndon Johnson did in deceiving Congress and the American people about his Vietnam policy. In the area of foreign policy, presidents have the most latitude, can do the most damage, and are most likely to play on popular fears. Therefore, it is here that we encounter the most pressing problems for democratic values. Only an informed and vigorous Congress and an attentive public can ensure that presidents do not overreach in foreign affairs.

We expect presidents to lead. But is it possible for presidents to lead without deception and without offering simplistic solutions? The post may be, as Theodore Roosevelt called it, a "bully pulpit" from which to rouse the nation, but by the same token, it can be used to exploit public fears, to play on popular stereotypes, to offer facile solutions to tough problems.

All presidents are confronted with problems and events that the chief executive simply cannot change or wish away. Yet, it is clear that *the person* can make a difference. How would Reagan have reacted to the Bay of Pigs crisis? How would Eisenhower have handled Vietnam? Had he been elected to a second term, would Carter have proposed a tax policy similar to Reagan's?

In our democratic polity, many critical issues and approaches depend on one person and those who surround that person. And today an individual can become president of the United States—a global superpower—without the benefit of experience in any comparable office. Therefore, democrats are compelled to keep a watchful eye on the presidency—and the president.

SUPPLEMENT: U.S. PRESIDENTIAL ELECTIONS, 1789–1988

Candidates (Party)	Popular vote (Percent)	Electoral vote	Candidates (Party)	Popular vote (Percent)	Electoral vote
1789			**1832**		
George Washington		69	Andrew Jackson (D)	55.0	219
John Adams		34	Henry Clay (N-R)	42.4	49
Others		35	William Wirt (A-M)		7
1792			John Floyd (N-R)	2.6	11
George Washington		132	**1836**		
John Adams		77	Martin Van Buren (D)	50.9	170
George Clinton		50	William H. Harrison (W)	36.7	73
Others		5	Hugh L. White (W)	9.7	26
1796			Daniel Webster (W)	2.7	14
John Adams (F)		71	**1840**		
Thomas Jefferson (D-R)		68	William H. Harrison* (W)	53.1	234
Thomas Pinckney (F)		59	(John Tyler, 1841)		
Aaron Burr (D-R)		30	Martin Van Buren (D)	46.9	60
Others		48	**1844**		
1800			James K. Polk (D)	49.6	170
Thomas Jefferson† (D-R)		73	Henry Clay (W)	48.1	105
Aaron Burr (D-R)		73	James G. Birney (L)	2.3	
John Adams (F)		65	**1848**		
Charles C. Pinckney		64	Zachary Taylor* (W)	47.4	163
1804			(Millard Fillmore, 1850)		
Thomas Jefferson (D-R)		162	Lewis Cass (D)	42.5	127
Charles C. Pinckney (F)		14	Martin Van Buren (F-S)	10.1	
1808			**1852**		
James Madison (D-R)		122	Franklin Pierce (D)	50.9	254
Charles C. Pinckney (F)		47	Winfield Scott (W)	44.1	42
George Clinton (I-R)		6	**1856**		
1812			James Buchanan (D)	45.4	174
James Madison (D-R)		122	John C. Fremont (R)	33.0	114
DeWitt Clinton (F)		89	Millard Fillmore (A)	21.6	8
1816			**1860**		
James Monroe (D-R)		183	Abraham Lincoln (R)	39.8	180
Rufus King (F)		34	Stephen A. Douglas (D)	29.5	12
1820			John C. Breckinridge (D)	18.1	72
James Monroe (D-R)		231	John Bell (C-U)	12.6	39
John Quincy Adams (I-R)		1	**1864**		
1824			Abraham Lincoln* (R)	55.0	212
John Quincy Adams† (D-R)	30.5	84	(Andrew Johnson, 1865)		
Andrew Jackson (D-R)	43.1	99	George B. McClellan (D)	45.0	21
Henry Clay (D-R)	13.2	37	**1868**		
William H. Crawford (D-R)	13.1	41	Ulysses S. Grant (R)	52.7	214
1828			Horatio Seymour (D)	47.3	80
Andrew Jackson (D)	56.0	178	**1872**		
John Quincy Adams (N-R)	44.0	83	Ulysses S. Grant (R)	55.6	286
			Horace Greeley (D)	43.9	66

SUPPLEMENT: U.S. PRESIDENTIAL
ELECTIONS, 1789–1988 (*Cont.*)

Candidates (Party)	Popular vote (Percent)	Electoral vote
1876		
Rutherford B. Hayes (R)	48.0	185
Samuel J. Tilden (D)	51.0	184
1880		
James A. Garfield* (R)	48.3	214
(Chester A. Arthur, 1881)		
Winfield S. Hancock (D)	48.2	155
James B. Weaver (G-L)	1.8	
1884		
Grover Cleveland (D)	48.5	219
James G. Blaine (R)	48.2	182
Benjamin F. Butler (G-L)	1.8	
1888		
Benjamin Harrison (R)	47.8	233
Grover Cleveland (D)	48.6	168
1892		
Grover Cleveland (D)	46.0	277
Benjamin Harrison (R)	43.0	145
James R. Weaver (PE)	8.5	22
1896		
William McKinley (R)	50.8	271
William J. Bryan (D ; PO)	46.7	176
1900		
William McKinley* (R)	51.7	292
(Theodore Roosevelt, 1901)		
William J. Bryan (D ; PO)	45.5	155
1904		
Theodore Roosevelt (R)	56.4	336
Alton B. Parker (D)	37.6	140
Eugene V. Debs (S)	3.0	
1908		
William H. Taft (R)	51.6	321
William J. Bryan (D)	43.1	162
Eugene V. Debs (S)	6.0	
1912		
Woodrow Wilson (D)	41.8	435
Theodore Roosevelt (PR)	27.4	88
William H. Taft (R)	23.2	8
Eugene V. Debs (S)	6.0	
1916		
Woodrow Wilson (D)	49.3	277
Charles E. Hughes (R)	46.1	254

Candidates (Party)	Popular vote (Percent)	Electoral vote
1920		
Warren G. Harding* (R)	61.0	404
(Calvin Coolidge, 1923)		
James M. Cox (D)	34.6	127
Eugene V. Debs (S)	3.5	
1924		
Calvin Coolidge (R)	54.1	382
John W. Davis (D)	28.8	136
Robert M. LaFollette (PR)	16.6	13
1928		
Herbert C. Hoover (R)	58.2	444
Alfred E. Smith (D)	40.8	87
1932		
Franklin D. Roosevelt (D)	57.3	472
Herbert C. Hoover (R)	39.6	59
Norman Thomas (S)	2.2	
1936		
Franklin D. Roosevelt (D)	60.7	523
Alfred M. Landon (R)	36.4	8
William Lemke (U)	1.9	
1940		
Franklin D. Roosevelt (D)	54.7	449
Wendell L. Wilkie (R)	44.8	82
1944		
Franklin D. Roosevelt* (D)	52.8	432
(Harry S. Truman, 1945)		
Thomas E. Dewey (R)	44.5	99
1948		
Harry S. Truman (D)	49.5	303
Thomas E. Dewey (R)	45.1	189
J. Strom Thurmond (S-R)	2.4	39
Henry A. Wallace (PR)	2.4	
1952		
Dwight D. Eisenhower (R)	55.2	442
Adlai E. Stevenson (D)	44.5	89
1956		
Dwight D. Eisenhower (R)	57.4	457
Adlai E. Stevenson (D)	42.0	73
1960		
John F. Kennedy* (D)	49.9	303
(Lyndon B. Johnson, 1963)		
Richard M. Nixon (R)	49.6	219
1964		
Lyndon B. Johnson (D)	61.1	486
Barry M. Goldwater (R)	38.5	52

SUPPLEMENT: U.S. PRESIDENTIAL ELECTIONS, 1789–1988 *(Cont.)*

Candidates (Party)	Popular vote (Percent)	Electoral vote
1968		
Richard M. Nixon (R)	43.4	301
Hubert H. Humphrey (D)	42.7	191
George C. Wallace (A-I)	13.5	46
1972		
Richard M. Nixon§ (R) (Gerald R. Ford, 1974)	60.6	520
George S. McGovern (D)	37.5	17
1976		
Jimmy Carter (D)	50.6	297
Gerald R. Ford (R)	48.4	240
1980		
Ronald Reagan (R)	51.0	489
Jimmy Carter (D)	42.3	49
John Anderson (I)	6.6	0
1984		
Ronald Reagan (R)	58.8	525
Walter Mondale (D)	40.6	13
1988		
George Bush (R)	53.4	426
Michael Dukakis (D)	45.6	111

PARTY ABBREVIATIONS: **A** = American; **A-I** = American Independent; **A-M** = Anti-Masonic; **C-U** = Constitutional Union; **D** = Democratic; **D-R** = Democratic-Republican; **F** = Federalist; **F-S** = Free Soil; **G-L** = Greenback-Labor; **I** = Independent; **I-R** = Independent-Republican; **L** = Liberty; **N-R** = National-Republican; **PE** = People's; **PO** = Populist; **PR** = Progressive; **R** = Republican; **S** = Socialist; **S-R** = States' Rights; **U** = Union; **W** = Whig.
†Elected by the House of Representatives.
*Died in office.
§Resigned.

GLOSSARY TERMS

impeachment

inherent powers

delegated powers

separation of powers

prerogative powers

executive agreement

Civil Rights Restoration Act

Executive Office of the President

Office of Management and Budget

National Security Council

Domestic Council

cabinet

War Powers Act

NOTES

[1] Richard Pious provides an interesting discussion of American attitudes toward the presidency in *The American Presidency* (New York: Basic Books, 1979), Introduction and Part 1. Fred Greenstein, who studied reactions to the Kennedy assassination, reported that 43 percent of adults suffered loss of appetite; 48 percent, insomnia; 25 percent, headaches; 68 percent, nervousness and tension; 26 percent, rapid heartbeat; and 17 percent, perspiration. See his "Popular Images of the President," *American Journal of Psychiatry*, 122 (1965). Also on this subject consult B. S. Greenberg and E. B. Parker, *The Kennedy Assassination and the American Public* (Stanford, Calif.: Stanford University Press, 1965).

[2] See Pious, *The American Presidency*, chap. 2.

[3] These examples are derived from Pious, *The American Presidency*, Part II, secs. 2, 3, and 4.

[4] *Sawyer, Petitioner* v. *Youngstown Sheet and Tube Co. et al.* (1952).

[5] *Grove City College* v. *Bell*, 465 U.S. 555 (1984).

[6] The following discussion is derived from Thomas E. Cronin, *The State of the Presidency*, 2nd ed. (Boston: Little, Brown, 1980), chap. 1.

[7] *Ibid.*, pp. 19–22.

[8] Quoted in James P. Pfiffner, "White House Staff Versus the Cabinet: Centripetal and Centrifugal Roles," in *Presidential Studies Quarterly*, vol. xvi, no. 4, Fall 1986, p. 863.

[9] This discussion is drawn from Nolan Argyle and Ryan Barilleaux, "Past Failures and Future Prescriptions for Presidential Management Reform," *Presidential Studies Quarterly*, vol. xvi, no. 4, Fall 1986.

[10] Cronin, *op. cit.*, pp. 228–229.

[11] Lyn Ragsdale, "Presidential Speechmaking and the Public Audience: Individual Presidents and Group Attitudes," *The Journal of Politics*, vol. 49, no. 3, Aug. 1987, p. 732.

[12] See A. M. Schlesinger, Jr., *The Imperial Presidency* (Boston: Houghton Mifflin, 1973).

[13]This account is drawn from Joel Brinkley and Stephen Engelberg, eds., *The Report of the Congressional Committees Investigating the Iran-Contra Affair*, abridged ed. (New York: Times Books/Random House, 1988).

SELECTED READINGS

For various **overviews concerning the presidency**, see Richard Neustadt, *Presidential Power: The Politics of Leadership from FDR to Carter* (New York: Macmillan, 1980); Richard Pious, *The American Presidency* (New York: Basic Books, 1979); Thomas Cronin, *The State of the Presidency*, 2nd ed. (Boston: Little, Brown, 1980); and Arthur M. Schlesinger, Jr., *The Imperial Presidency* (Boston: Houghton Mifflin, 1973).

On the **problems of managing the presidency**, see Emmette S. Redford and Richard T. McCulley, *White House Operations: the Johnson Presidency* (Austin: University of Texas Press, 1986); Colin Campbell, *Managing the Presidency: Carter, Reagan, and the Search for Executive Harmony* (Pittsburgh, Pa.: University of Pittsburgh Press, 1986); Peri E. Arnold, *Making the Managerial Presidency: Comprehensive Reorganization Planning, 1905–1980* (Princeton, N.J.: Princeton University Press, 1986).

On more **specific aspects of the presidency** and the executive branch, see Michael Nelson, ed., *The Presidency and the Political System* (Washington, D.C.: Congressional Quarterly Press, 1984); James David Barber, *Presidential Character* (Englewood Cliffs, N.J.: Prentice-Hall, 1985); James M. Burns, *Roosevelt: The Lion and the Fox* (New York: Harcourt Brace Jovanovich, 1963); David Halberstam, *The Best and the Brightest* (New York: Penguin, 1983); Carl M. Brauer, *Presidential Transitions: Eisenhower Through Reagan* (New York: Oxford University Press, 1986); Cecil V. Crabb, Jr., and Kevin V. Mulcahy *Presidents and Foreign Policy Making: From FDR to Reagan* (Baton Rouge: Louisiana State University Press, 1986); Samuel Kern, *Going Public: New Strategies of Presidential Leadership* (Washington: Congressional Quarterly, 1986); Robert E. Denton, Jr., and Dan F. Hahn, *Presidential Communication: Description and Analysis* (New York: Praeger, 1986); and John Orman, *Comparing Presidential Behavior: Carter, Reagan, and the Macho Presidential Style* (Westport, Conn.: Greenwood, 1987). For an interesting account of a president that also reveals much about contemporary American society, see Gary Wills, *Reagan's America: Innocents at Home* (Garden City, N.Y.: Doubleday, 1987). Finally, for a fuller look at an institution that rarely gets a look at all, see Marie D. Natoli, *American Prince, American Pauper: The Contemporary Vice Presidency in Perspective* (Westport, Conn.: Greenwood, 1985).

13

THE BUREAUCRACY

Servant or Master?

CHAPTER OUTLINE

**The Structure of the National
    Bureaucracy**
Bureaucracy and the Political Process
Bureaucracy Evaluated

Patricia Hollander Gross/Stock, Boston

Certain terms carry connotations that are hard to escape. *Bureaucracy*, for example, inevitably evokes thoughts of endless red tape, inefficiency, and unresponsiveness. To most people, the bureaucracy is that faceless entity responsible for forcing them to fill out tax forms or stand in line at post offices or register for a Selective Service system when there is no draft. But bureaucrats touch people's lives in many other ways as well. The food we eat, the prescription drugs we take, the cars we drive, the sports equipment we play with, even the inflammable Dr. Dentons we wore as children—all these fall under regulations established by the federal bureaucracy.

Here, when we speak of **bureaucracy,** we refer to the millions of full-time career employees who do the day-to-day work of government. The bureaucracy's impact on government policy is immense. Often, bureaucrats must interpret vague and sometimes contradictory directives from Congress or the president. And even though, on the surface, the bureaucracy may appear nonpolitical, bureaucrats often make highly controversial decisions that spark intense political struggle, as this chapter will illustrate. While the bureaucracy sometimes helps carry out policies (at least when those policies are clear), it can also thwart, redirect, and even work in direct opposition to either Congress or the president.

The Constitution only refers in passing to the structure and role of the federal bureaucracy: It recognizes the president's right to demand periodic reports from the head officials in the executive departments. Undoubtedly, the Founders were aware that the administrative apparatus of government would need to remain flexible, to change with the times. But they also failed to anticipate how much the government would grow. To them, executive departments were small operations aiding the president—hardly a major matter in 1792, when the entire federal government consisted of only 780 employees.

For many years the size and structure of the federal government hardly changed at all (except for temporary expansions during wartime). The permanent bureaucracy grew most dramatically during and after the New Deal (the 1930s and early 1940s), when the federal government pioneered many new social programs. Since 1950, the overall growth of federal government employment has been minimal.

Today the federal government has approximately 3 million civilian employees. However, only one-tenth of those work in the Washington, D.C., area. A little more than a third of all federal civilian employees—more than 1 million—work for the Department of Defense, which is the largest single employer in the United States. (The largest private employer, General Motors, employs about 800,000 workers.) About 85 percent of the federal civilian employees are career Civil Service. They are protected by the Civil Service system and their salaries (from $9,339 to $84,157 as of 1988) are set by Congress. Only about one-sixth of the government's civilian employees hold characteristically bureaucratic positions, like clerk or general administrator. It may be hard to reconcile with preconceived notions of bureaucracy, but the government employs hundreds of thousands of special professionals—engineers, architects, scientists. Someone recently counted 2,400 veterinarians who work for the federal government.

Most government employees are white males. In the lower levels of government service, however, blacks are overrepresented. Similarly, although nearly one-third of all federal employees are women, the vast majority of female federal employees occupy such lower-level positions as secretary and typist. In the upper salary ranges, the proportion of women dwindles sharply.

The federal government owns about 438,000 separate buildings, with a total of almost 3 *billion* square feet of floor area (that doesn't count an additional 203 million square feet of space leased by the federal government). The government owns 727 million acres of land and leases an additional 1.8 million acres. For a single month, the federal civilian payroll runs $7.5 *billion*, give or take a few million.

Despite the size of the federal bureaucracy, it has grown at a slower rate than state and local governments collectively. Only about 18 percent of all government employees work for the federal government. Local school districts account for about a quarter of all government employment in the United States. And much of the work of government at all levels is done by so-called **contract bureaucracies**—private firms hired by the government. The Department of Defense, for example, hires firms such as Boeing and General Dynamics to design and build military hardware; the Corps of Engineers contracts with private firms to design and construct dams and hydroelectric projects; and most of the personnel involved in the space program are contract bureaucrats. In this way a great many Americans work for the government indirectly—they are not on the federal payroll and their jobs are not protected by Civil Service regulations.

The government bureaucracy is not a monolith—rather, it encompasses a huge complex of bureaus, agencies, boards, and commissions, created at different times, with different functions and different mandates. Frequently, one segment of the federal bureaucracy will be at odds with another: A jurisdictional dispute may erupt between two agencies, or policies and clienteles may have antithetical objectives. For example, while the Department of Health and Human Services works to discourage smoking, the Department of Agriculture helps farmers grow tobacco more efficiently. Similarly, plans by the Army Corps of Engineers to build a dam may be opposed by the Environmental Protection Agency, on the ground that the dam will adversely affect wildlife. The government has grown so large and complex that simply keeping abreast of what other agencies are doing becomes a monumental task.

Does the concept of bureaucracy accord with democratic ideals? Those who attack bureaucracy claim that through it, big government too often harasses individuals and groups, places too many restrictions on people's actions, and engages in costly and inefficient practices. In this view, bureaucrats have become a power unto themselves, dictating from Washington the way people throughout the country ought to live their lives. In rejoinder, defenders of bureaucracy argue that a modern society could not function without bureaucratic procedures. After all, they say, someone must send out the Social Security checks and make the appropriate rules for eligibility; someone must police mine safety and check on air pollution; and so on. In addition, they maintain that at times government bureaucracy stands as the sole defender of citizens who would otherwise be powerless against discrimination and other violations of in-

This photo was staged to dramatize the argument that government regulatory efforts had gone too far. The boxes represent the additional paperwork that federal rules forced on one major corporation in one year; the long line of people represents the extra employees needed to process the paperwork. *(John Mamares/ Woodfin Camp & Associates)*

dividual rights and threats to health and safety. Rather than abolishing bureaucracy, they conclude, we need to establish a better, more responsive, more efficient bureaucracy. Even if we accept this view, however, we must still answer two fundamental questions: How much bureaucracy is enough? and How well do our current bureaucratic arrangements function?

In this chapter, we will examine three key issues involving the federal bureaucracy: (1) how it is structured; (2) how bureaucrats interact with the political process; and (3) whether the current proposals for reform of the bureaucracy—Civil Service reform, third-party government and privatization, and deregulation—address these concerns adequately.

The Structure of the National Bureaucracy

Bureaucracies tend to be structured according to areas of specialization—one agency handles only law enforcement, another only medical care, and so on. The principle of organization by speciali-

zation is illustrated in the structure of the federal executive branch, as outlined in **Figure 13–1** and **Table 13–1.** But don't be fooled by orderly organization charts: The federal bureaucracy encompasses an almost byzantine array of agencies and divisions, set up over a two-hundred-year history in response to specific political pressures. In the twentieth century, as each succeeding administration brought its own political agenda to the executive branch and confronted the established structures of earlier administrations, most found it easier to add a new agency—defining its mission from scratch—than to change the direction of an already existing one. Thus, inconsistent and overlapping jurisdictions abound. Still, the executive branch frequently attempts to impose order within the bureaucracy. The Environmental Protection Agency, for example, was created by consolidating a group of bodies, each more limited in scope.

FIGURE 13–1
The President and the Cabinet

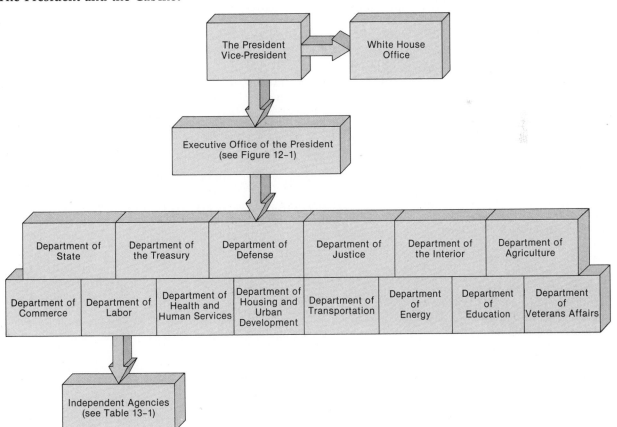

TABLE 13–1
Independent Agencies of the U.S. Government

Agency	Year established
Action	1971
Arms Control and Disarmament Agency	1961
Board for International Broadcasting	1973
Commission of Fine Arts	1910
Commission on Civil Rights	1957
Commodities Futures Trading Commission	1974
Consumer Protection Safety Commission	1972
Environmental Protection Agency	1970
Equal Opportunity Employment Commission	1965
Export-Import Bank of the U.S.	1934
Farm Credit Administration	1916
Federal Communications Commission	1934
Federal Deposit Insurance Corporation	1933
Federal Election Commission	1975
Federal Emergency Management Agency	1979
Federal Home Loan Bank Board	1955
Federal Maritime Commission	1961
Federal Mediation and Conciliation Service	1947
Federal Reserve System	1913
Federal Savings and Loan Insurance Corporation	1934
Federal Trade Commission	1915
General Services Administration	1949
Inter-American Foundation	1969
International Development Cooperation Agency	1979
International Trade Commission	1916
Interstate Commerce Commission	1887
National Aeronautics and Space Administration	1958
National Credit Union Administration	1970
National Foundation on the Arts and Humanities	1965
National Labor Relations Board	1935
National Mediation Board	1934
National Science Foundation	1950
National Transportation Safety Board	1966
Nuclear Regulatory Commission	1974
Office of Personnel Management	1979
Overseas Private Investment Corporation	1971
Postal Rate Commission	1970
Postal Service	1970
Railroad Retirement Board	1935
Securities and Exchange Commission	1934
Small Business Administration	1953
Smithsonian Institution	1846
Tennessee Valley Authority	1933
United States Information Agency	1977

Before we consider the problems inherent in bureaucratic specialization, we must examine the primary components of the bureaucracy—(1) the cabinet departments; (2) the independent executive agencies and government corporations; and (3) the regulatory commissions.

Cabinet Departments

In 1789, there were only three **cabinet departments**—State, War, and Treasury. As new needs arose, new departments were created. In 1849 the Department of the Interior was set up to deal with the government's vast land holdings and with the Native American population. The Department of Agriculture was established in 1862, the Justice Department in 1870, and the Departments of Commerce and of Labor in 1913. The War and the Navy Departments were merged into the Defense Department in 1947. Health, Education and Welfare, created in 1953, was redesignated Health and Human Services in 1979. Housing and Urban Development appeared in 1965, Transportation in 1966, Energy in 1977, Education in 1979, and Veterans Affairs in 1988.

The fourteen cabinet departments make up the bulk of the federal bureaucracy, employing a majority of federal workers. As we saw in Chapter 12, the head of a department is appointed by the president and serves as the department's representative in the president's cabinet. The other top officials in cabinet departments are also appointed

by the president. Many of them have no prior experience in the department, and they rarely remain in office for more than a few years. Just below them, however, are career civil servants who have risen through the ranks and whose experience and skill are vital to the efficient functioning of the departments. These senior civil servants have powers that must be reckoned with when policies are formulated.

Independent Agencies

Independent agencies like the National Aeronautics and Space Administration (NASA), the Environmental Protection Agency (EPA), and the Small Business Administration (SBA), are generally smaller than cabinet departments and tend to have considerably more focused missions. Like cabinet secretaries, the heads of independent agencies serve at the pleasure of the president. These agencies come into being to serve specific functions and are established outside cabinet departments usually to insulate them from partisan or interest-group pressure.

The Selective Service system, for example, was created hastily, prior to World War II, as an entity independent of the War Department (now the Department of Defense) to reassure citizens that the draft was a civilian operation with a limited scope. The Central Intelligence Agency, another independent organization, fused into one organization many competing government intelligence agen-

Former Pennsylvania Governor Richard Thornburgh, to the right of President Reagan, is sworn in as Attorney General by Supreme Court Justice Antonin Scalia. Thornburgh was chosen by Reagan to head the Justice Department in 1988 (after Ed Meese left the job under a cloud) and stayed on as part of President Bush's cabinet. *(AP/Wide World Photos)*

cies. The CIA was not placed under a cabinet department because it was designed to resolve interdepartmental power struggles.

Also included among the independent agencies are government corporations—the Post Office, the Tennessee Valley Authority (TVA), and the Federal Deposit Insurance Corporation. A government corporation, as the name suggests, is intended to operate in a business-like way in its management practices.

Regulatory Commissions

Another type of independent agency is the **regulatory commission.** These agencies regulate certain kinds of activities, particularly in the economic sphere. They perform a quasi-judicial function: They can bring charges, hold hearings, and impose penalties for violations of rules. The Federal Communications Commission, for example, may revoke the licenses of television and radio stations for a number of reasons, including a station's failure to provide sufficient community-service broadcasting. Regulatory commissions are also quasi-legislative bodies: They make, as well as interpret, rules. For example, the Federal Trade Commission imposes a wide variety of regulations on manufacturing and on advertising to protect consumers from unsafe or misrepresented merchandise.

The independent regulatory agencies fall outside the executive branch chain of command "freeing" them, to some extent, from politics. Commission members are appointed by the president to relatively long terms, subject to Senate confirmation. Once in office they are not required to report to the president and may not be removed until the end of their terms, except through impeachment. Unlike cabinet officers and heads of other executive agencies, then, they do not resign when a new president is elected. A new president can only name members to commissions as terms expire or as vacancies occur because of death or resignation. By law, moreover, members of these agencies must be drawn from both major political parties.

In spite of these precautions, the regulatory commissions become deeply immersed in behind-the-scenes politics. Their activities are of intense concern to interest groups, which, over time, often develop close and sometimes cozy relationships with the agencies. Critics point out that some commission members work harder to protect the interests of drug companies, trucking firms, brokerage houses, and other concerns they are supposed to regulate than to protect the interests of the public.

The history of the Interstate Commerce Commission illustrates this point. Originally set up in 1887 to protect consumers against the predatory practices of railroad monopolies, the ICC, by 1920, was almost solely responsive to the railroad interests. In case after case, ICC rulings benefited the railroads. More recently, the ICC has struck a balance between the interests of railroads and those of trucking companies, with consumers running a poor third.

As an additional barrier to effective regulation, these federal commissions typically don't have enough staff members to fulfill their regulatory functions. Hearings to develop new regulations for an industry often pit a handful of Civil Service accountants and lawyers against battalions of highly paid industry lawyers and accountants.[1]

Bureaucracy and the Political Process

Bureaucracies are embedded firmly in the political process. Consider the example of an automobile safety device, developed in Detroit more than twenty years ago, called the air bag. The bag, normally stored beneath a car's windshield, inflates instantaneously on collision impact to cushion occupants in the front seat. In 1971, President Richard Nixon's transportation secretary, John Volpe, issued Safety Standard 208, which required the installation of air bags or safety belts in all new cars. The Nixon White House, however, apparently responding to pressure from the automobile industry, postponed implementation of the standard in 1972. Four years later, in 1976, President Gerald Ford's secretary of transportation rescinded 208.

In 1977, with the Carter administration more favorably inclined to consumer safety, the attempt to get an air bag ruling began again. A revised version of 208, providing automakers with greater time for installation, was promulgated. Either automatic seat belts or air bags would be manda-

British and French Bureaucracies

One of the best-known aspects of the British bureaucracy is the "administrative class," made up of approximately seventy-five hundred senior personnel selected through a civil service system. These top civil servants are closely involved in the formulation of public policy. It is their job to screen important information for the ministers of each department, to provide political advice, and to comment on the wisdom and practicality of various policy proposals. What they do *not* do is "administer" the various departments of the bureaucracy; that task is left to others. British civil servants usually view their jobs as lifetime commitments, not as steppingstones to positions in industry or politics. Most regard themselves as the long-term protectors of the public interest and the upholders of high civil standards. They are sometimes criticized for being too cautious and unimaginative.

France was one of the first European nations to create a modern-style bureaucracy, and the existence of a top administrative class similar to the one in Great Britain has been a distinguishing feature of French bureaucratic organization. At the top of the French administrative hierarchy are several thousand bureaucrats, three to five hundred of whom are highly active in the political decision-making process.

What is most striking about the top French administrators is that they have become almost a hereditary group. The entrance exams for the two schools that train French administrators tend to favor people from upper-class backgrounds. Over the last thirty years, there has only been a very gradual increase in the number of middle-class students admitted, despite various government efforts to open the schools to all talented individuals. Candidates from working class and farming backgrounds are almost never accepted. Of the top seven thousand French civil servants in the most prestigious sectors of the bureaucracy, about 75 percent come from the highest levels of Parisian society.

These administrators have long considered themselves not mere civil servants, but managers for society as a whole and agents of change in the modernization of France. Many top bureaucrats resent French political parties and the French legislature for interfering with plans hatched among the administrative class. A large number of top bureaucrats move into industry if their ambitions are not fulfilled within the bureaucracy. Over 40 percent of the major French business concerns are headed by former bureaucrats.*

When the Socialist government of François Mitterand came to power in 1981, it implemented proposals to decentralize the French bureaucracy. Mitterand's goal was to loosen central bureaucratic control and provide more decision making to local governments in France. It was the first move toward decentralization in a bureaucratic system that had been highly centralized for centuries.

---

*Henry W. Ehrmann, *Politics in France* (Boston: Little, Brown, 1983), pp. 161-174.

tory on new cars in 1984. But in 1981 the Reagan administration took office with a commitment to deregulate. Shortly thereafter, 208 was completely revoked. In response, a coalition of consumer groups filed suit in federal court. Their litigation was upheld in 1982. The administration and the auto companies appealed the ruling to the Supreme Court, which, in 1983, found unanimously against them, saying: "For nearly a decade the automobile industry waged the regulatory equivalent of war against the air bag and lost—the inflatable restraint was proven sufficiently effective."[2]

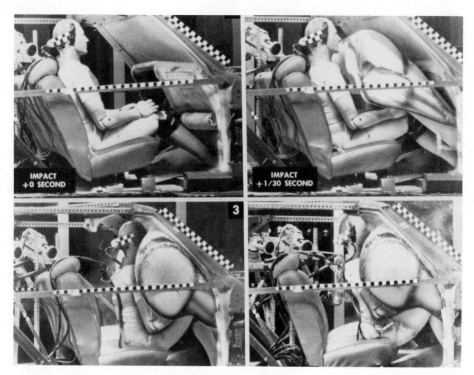

IMPACT +0 SECOND

IMPACT +1/30 SECOND

3

In these 1977 photos from General Motors, an air bag is shown cushioning the impact of a crash. As the text notes, the combination of politics and bureaucratic decision making was less efficient than business competition in bringing air bags to the marketplace.
(UPI/Bettmann Newsphotos)

In late 1983, reacting to the decision, Secretary of Transportation Elizabeth Dole postponed compliance until 1987 and, at the same time, proposed several other alternatives to air bags. Air bags would be required only if a certain number of states failed to pass mandatory seat belt legislation. Many states did pass seat belt laws in the last half of the 1980s, but the laws were difficult to enforce independently and usually carried nominal penalties. Then the 1987 compliance date was, like earlier deadlines, postponed. While the government backpedaled, the market moved forward. European manufacturers began to offer airbags on expensive models. From the mid-1980s on, Ford and GM offered driver-side airbags as an expensive option on a small number of models. In 1988 Chrysler Chairman Lee Iacocca announced that by 1990 all Chrysler Motors Corporation cars built in the United States would have driver-side airbags as standard equipment.

According to statistics, in the 10 years from 1976 to 1985, ninety thousand Americans lost their lives and six hundred fifty thousand were injured in cars that might have been equipped with air bags. While political struggles overwhelmed the processes of bureaucratic decision making, thousands lost their lives.[3] In this case, all three branches of government intervened to change bureaucratic behavior. But where *should* decisions like this one be made? Congress? The courts? Or should bureaucrats look first to their own conception of the public good or the public interest?

Further complicating the issue is the need for accountability in government. It can be argued that presidents should be able to put a stamp on an administration—to make policies in line with their political agendas and to have the bureaucracy carry out those policies. As Charles Peters, a seasoned bureaucrat, observes, "The key to democratic politics is accountability. If you don't deliver the goods, the voters can throw you out."[4] Peters goes on to argue in favor of filling administrative positions with qualified politicians and making administrative decisions on a partisan basis, with re-elections the compelling motive.

However, this approach creates its own problems: Political considerations can lead to short-term planning and the implementation of splashy programs that actually serve the public worse in the long run. In trying to make government *appear* to be running well, partisan bureaucrats might ignore the reasoned judgments of long-range planners.[5]

Apparently, then, a balance must be worked out between the need for unfettered administrative expertise and the need for responsible and responsive political control. To understand the ramifications of this dichotomy, we must analyze how and to what extent the bureaucracy is involved in the political process. As we will see, the bureaucratic apparatus has evolved into a collection of highly specialized subdivisions, sometimes highly insulated (from the public), sometimes essentially self-governing, often backed by subdivisions of Congress and by powerful interest groups.[6] Bureaucratic discretion, expertise, and support systems strengthen the bureaucracy's political position, while the extensive use of contract bureaucrats weakens it to some extent.

We now turn to (1) bureaucratic discretion—the wide latitude extended to the bureaucracy; (2) bureaucratic expertise; and (3) how the bureaucracy mobilizes support for or opposition to specific programmatic and policy initiatives.

Mathilde Krim, an AIDS researcher, represents a major source of bureaucracy's power: expertise. As government's activities become more technical and sophisticated, its general goals and strategies must be implemented by bureaucratic experts. (© *Ira Berger*)

Bureaucratic Discretion

When bureaucracies are called on to implement legislation—whether that involves promulgating specific regulations for cleaner air, work-place safety, fireproofing clothing, or the like—bureaucrats have considerable latitude in applying laws to particular cases. This administrative discretion forms the basis for bureaucratic political participation. For example, according to the Food and Drug Amendments of 1962, new drugs must be effective, as well as safe, to receive approval from the Food and Drug Administration. But Congress left it up to the FDA to determine specific standards of drug effectiveness. Similarly, the Justice Department has the power to decide whether or not to prosecute an antitrust case—a decision that may have far-reaching consequences for the national economy. In these and thousands of other cases, government bureaucrats make policy by applying the broad powers granted them by Congress and the president.

Several factors involved in legislative decision making contribute to bureaucratic discretion. Most fundamentally, the legislature could not possibly establish clear rules covering all contingencies—an exercise for which it has neither the time nor the expertise. Then, too, vague rules or guidelines often reflect legislative conflicts that could not be resolved in Congress and so are handed over to the bureaucracy. In this sense, bureaucratic administration represents an extension of the legislative process, as particular parties work to advance their interests by lobbying in the offices of the bureaucracy. Indeed, administrative lobbying is as important as legislative lobbying in Washington.[7]

In policy-making matters as well, bureaucracies do not remain neutral. They have interests of their own, and they push those interests vigorously in the political arena. Like most participants in the political system, bureaucrats usually claim that the programs they administer serve the public interest and that expansion of those programs would benefit the nation. Some of these claims are cynical, but most are entirely sincere. Believing in the value of and the need for their programs, bureaucrats seek to expand—or at least to protect—those programs by lobbying for favorable legislation and increased appropriations.[8] The EPA, for example, actively lobbied for Superfund monies to help clean up toxic waste sites, while the Department of Agriculture regularly presses for dairy price supports and other farm subsidies.

Bureaucratic Expertise

The power of the bureaucracy also stems from its expertise. Because a bureaucracy is designed to apply specialized competence to an area of policy, bureaucrats frequently have a near-monopoly on expertise in certain political areas. Who, for example, knows more about building a space station, or sending a person to Mars than the experts at the National Aeronautics and Space Administration? When other policy makers accept such claims of expertise, the bureaucracy gains an important political resource. By the same principle, however, when events like the disastrous in-flight explosion of the space shuttle *Challenger* call an agency's expertise into question, other policy makers are much less likely to let agency decisions go unchallenged.

Economist John Kenneth Galbraith points out that technology has become so complex that it would take a formidable genius to command all of the knowledge and skill required to deal with even a few of the ordinary decisions confronting business or government organizations.[9] Responsibility for decision making has therefore passed to groups of specialists. As Galbraith puts it, modern organizations are composed of a "hierarchy of committees." Decisions tend to flow upward from these committees, and the person at the top usually lacks the special knowledge and skills to challenge those decisions.

Galbraith recognizes that because of the technical and organizational complexity of issues facing most business concerns and government agencies, power inevitably passes into the hands of a great many subordinate specialists. He labels this powerful set of specialists "the technostructure." The alternatives they favor ultimately shape public policy, because other political participants presume that these specialists must know what the best alternatives are.

Expertise can be used as a political resource in two principal ways: Experts can hold important advisory positions, particularly in relation to the president; or they can make presentations to Congress concerning complex matters about which most legislators know little. Simply because bureaucrats are more knowledgeable in a particular area, however, does not mean they always get their way. Under the present system, though, they have far greater influence than they would if Congress could turn to an equally knowledgeable alternative source of information.

Mobilization of Support

The bureaucracy also draws political power from its ability to mobilize support among the general public, Congress, and its clientele groups. Government agencies like to demonstrate that they provide useful and beneficial services to the public. These public relations efforts can take the form of public-service television messages, such as the FDA's TV spots on the proper use and storage of hazardous household products, or inexpensive pamphlets, such as the Agriculture Department's extensive series of booklets on cooking, canning, gardening, and other topics. Such efforts, which advertise the agency and enhance its public reputation, fulfill one of the most significant bureaucratic functions: supplying the public with needed information. Sometimes, however, efforts to mobilize public support may cross the line from information dissemination to sheer public relations. The advertising efforts of the Department of Defense, for example, prompted Senator William Proxmire to coin the pejorative term "Pentagon Propaganda Machine." To promote a favorable image of the military, the services aided in the production of "war" movies, gave tours of military installations to prominent citizens, provided speakers for civic groups, and produced an extensive set of advertisements for military life.

Bureaucratic agencies also try to maintain good relationships with interest groups that are directly

One important task of the bureaucracy is to mobilize public support by providing information. In 1988 the Public Health Service of the Department of Health and Human Services sent an eight-page brochure, "Understanding AIDS," to every postal customer in the country. This information about AIDS testing is from that brochure.

Should You Get An AIDS Test?

You have probably heard about the "AIDS Test." The test doesn't actually tell you if you have AIDS. It shows if you have been infected with the virus. It looks for changes in blood that occur after you have been infected.

The Public Health Service recommends you be confidentially counseled and tested if you have had any sexually transmitted disease or shared needles; if you are a man who has had sex with another man; or if you have had sex with a prostitute, male or female. You should be tested if you have had sex with anyone who has done any of these things.

If you are a woman who has been engaging in risky behavior (*see page 3*), and you plan to have a baby or are not using birth control, you should be tested.

Your doctor may advise you to be counseled and tested if you are a hemophiliac, or have received a blood transfusion between 1978 and 1985.

If you test positive, and find you have been infected with the AIDS virus, you must take steps to protect your partner.

People who have always practiced safe behavior (*see page 3*) do not need to be tested.

There's been a great deal in the press about problems with the test. It is very reliable if it is done by a good laboratory and the results are checked by a physician or counselor.

If you have engaged in risky behavior, speak frankly to a doctor who understands the AIDS problem, or to an AIDS counselor.

For more information, call your local public health agency. They're listed in the government section of your phone book. Or, call your local AIDS hotline. If you can't find the number, call 1-800-342-AIDS.

AMERICA RESPONDS TO AIDS

affected by their activities. Such groups are commonly referred to as **clientele groups**. The railroads and trucking companies are clientele groups of the Interstate Commerce Commission, labor unions are the clientele groups of the Labor Department, and so on. As long as these groups benefit from agency programs, they will lobby on the agency's behalf in Congress and the Oval Office. Clientele groups draw much of their strength from their ability to influence Congress. Indeed, as we saw earlier, it is common for a bureaucratic agency, a clientele group, and a congressional subcommittee to be linked in a three-way alliance—the so-called Iron Triangle (covered in Chapter 9). For example, the Pentagon has close ties with large defense contractors, which in turn exert a great deal of influence in Congress.

Bureaucracy Evaluated

"The entrenched bureaucracy" is an easy target for aspiring candidates for public office in the United States. U.S. political life is punctuated regularly by a variety of attacks on the bureaucracy. Although the most recent presidential campaign (1988) was surprisingly muted in these attacks, the three that preceded it placed the federal bureaucracy—and its alleged waste, fraud, and mismanagement—at center stage. Candidates called for radical reductions in government waste and a reorganization of the bureaucratic structure. They were aligning themselves with what appeared to be strong public sentiment against bureaucracy.

In fact, however, most Americans have decidedly mixed attitudes toward bureaucratic institutions. When people are asked by pollsters about actual relationships they have had with various agencies, the report card is generally quite good. But when surveyors inquire about bureaucracy in the abstract, highly negative opinions surface. One study found that whereas 71 percent of respondents reported that their own problems had been handled well, only 30 percent thought government agencies in general respond well to citizens' concerns.[10]

In this section we will examine three clusters of specific charges against the federal bureaucracy—(1) that it is undemocratic because it is unresponsive to political leadership; (2) that there is, on the whole, too much of it and that it is too distant from the people; and (3) that there are too many rules and regulations governing things that are better left alone. We will also consider the national bureaucracy's responses to those charges: Civil Service reform, "third-party government" and privatization, and deregulation, respectively.

Is It Too Unresponsive?

The first cluster of specific complaints charge that the bureaucracy is too unresponsive to political initiatives. Bureaucrats, it is said, are primarily concerned with keeping their own jobs. A new president finds it almost impossible to make significant changes because the bureaucrats frustrate any drive toward innovation or policy change. To understand these charges we must examine the history of the Civil Service.

The first federal job appointments were made by George Washington, who declared that his choices were based entirely on "fitness of character." It soon became apparent, however, that most of those found fit were associated with the emerging Federalist Party, which Washington and Alexander Hamilton headed. When Thomas Jefferson became president in 1801, he set a precedent by dismissing hundreds of Federalists from government jobs and installing his supporters in their places.

Thereafter, under what became known as the **spoils system**, elected officials routinely rewarded friends and supporters with government jobs. The spoils system reached its peak under President Andrew Jackson. After his election in 1828, Jackson dismissed more than one-third of the six hundred upper-level officeholders and from 10 to 20 percent of the ten thousand government officials who occupied lower-level positions.

To some extent, the spoils system made sense. The political parties needed some form of **patron-age** (the power of appointment to government jobs) to reward party workers. During the nineteenth century, the government had little need for trained specialists, so a high turnover in personnel usually did not endanger operating efficiency. Furthermore, any president is entitled to fill key positions with people who share his political philosophy. (There is a difference, it should be noted, between a patronage system that rewards political loyalists regardless of competence and a system of partisan appointments that rewards competent loyalists with key policy-making positions. In practice, however, this distinction is sometimes hard to discern.)

Nevertheless, by the 1870s, obvious abuses of the spoils system had produced a clamor for reform. These demands led to action after President James A. Garfield was assassinated by a disappointed office seeker in 1881. With the support of Garfield's successor, Chester A. Arthur, Congress passed a bill establishing a bipartisan Civil Service Commission to administer competitive examinations and make appointments to office based on merit. Under the **Civil Service system** now in place, the commission sets up formal descriptions of job requirements and classifies civil servants according to job description. Once the various Civil Service positions are described and classified, examinations are given to determine the candidates

The alleged unresponsiveness, inhuman scale, and penchant for paperwork of the federal bureaucracy have made it the butt of many jokes and the object of much ire. Yet the characteristics that we disparage are also the source of benefits, for bureaucracy was designed to deal with vast numbers of cases uniformly and efficiently. The Social Security Administration, shown here, covered more than a hundred million civilian employees in 1986; benefits of more than $176 billion were paid out by the Old Age and Survivors Insurance Trust Fund. *(Dennis Brack/Black Star)*

best suited for the available positions. After taking examinations, candidates are placed on lists, from which agencies select employees.

The federal Civil Service system now places college graduates in most bureaus. Very high levels of educational specialization also mark the federal bureaucracy. Chemists employed by the Department of Agriculture, biologists employed by the National Institutes of Health, safety engineers employed by the Federal Aviation Agency—all these professionals typify the high degree of specialization and education found in modern public service.

Yet this emphasis on expertise, to the exclusion of political factors, has its costs. Most civil servants cannot be removed from their jobs except for gross misconduct, and many promotions are based on seniority rather than on merit. The laudable purpose of these procedures—to insulate the bureaucracy from unwarranted political interference—also protects bureaucrats from demands for high performance. As Peter Drucker points out, "Mediocrity in the Civil Service [may be] a lesser evil than politics [but] a good many people today have come to believe that we need some way of rewarding performance and of penalizing nonperformance, even within the Civil Service."[11]

These and other concerns prompted calls to make the system more responsive to considerations of merit. President Jimmy Carter instituted a number of Civil Service reforms designed to enhance the role of merit in promotions, salary increases, and firings. The Carter administration created a Senior Executive Service (SES) apart from the regular Civil Service. Top managers were given the option of switching to the SES, trading job security for higher pay and rewards for superior performance. Of the first four thousand eligible bureaucrats, all but ten opted to join the SES.

Another of the Carter reforms called for pay raises based on performance, not just longevity, for thousands of middle-level managers and supervisors. The Civil Service system gained greater flexibility in firing and demotion, but safeguards for employees were provided by an appeals process and union arbitration proceedings. In addition, the Civil Service Commission was split into two bodies: the Office of Personnel Management, charged with managing the federal work force;

and the Merit System Protections Board, designed to protect the rights of employees.

The reasoning behind the Carter reforms was twofold: that merit should be rewarded, and that top civil servants should not become too deeply entrenched in their positions and unresponsive to changes in policy.

Have these reforms made the bureaucracy more responsive? In the first few years of operation the new system seemed to have little impact. Of the six thousand senior civil servants who gave up tenured positions in the late 1970s and early 1980s, only one was dropped for poor performance, and very few were shifted from one part of the bureaucracy to another.[12] But a recent study concluded that there was no question that the SES had played a "major role" in Reagan's ability to obtain the cooperation of the career bureaucracy in implementing his policies. On the other hand, a survey of SES careerists found that a "perceived breaking of faith by the larger political system with members of the SES has had a devastating effect on their own perception of the reform," which they came to view as *punitive and political.*" Another study accused the Reagan administration of "blatantly politicizing" the SES.[13] These findings illustrate that responsiveness in the bureaucracy is always subject to trade-offs. We want public servants to do the bidding of the public. Ordinarily that means doing the bidding of elected officials. But we're skeptical enough to assume that sometimes that means *not* doing the bidding of elected officials, whose personal interests may take precedence over the public's. How responsive is responsive enough? That is a question that, like almost all questions in politics, calls for continual reevaluation.

Is There Too Much of It?

The second cluster of specific complaints about our national bureaucracy revolves around how much of it there is. That sometimes means too much government per se, and sometimes too much of *this* government—one that is too far from the people. The notion of a *limited* national government undergirds our Constitution. As we saw in Chapter 3, the national government was granted a small

The Pentagon houses 23,000 employees in offices occupying 3,707,745 square feet. Such massive scale reflects both the sheer size of the federal government and the competition for its resources. Given recent federal budget deficits, opinions differ widely on the proper relative size of defense versus domestic spending. *(AP/Wide World Photos)*

number of powers, while the states were left with the residual, or reserve, powers. Yet the national government has grown enormously in this century. Even though federal employment has been relatively stable for three decades now, federal programs and expenditures continue to grow. A frequently heard complaint is that the federal government grows by an inner logic that has little to do with the nation's needs. In response to these complaints, two strategies for limiting the size of the federal bureaucracy have been attracting increased attention recently: (1) "third-party government" and (2) privatization. We turn to these now.

THIRD-PARTY GOVERNMENT   **Third-party government** refers to federal programs that are farmed out to states, localities, special districts, nonprofit corporations, hospitals, manufacturers, banks, and other groups outside the bureaucracy. In addition, grants-in-aid, loan guarantees, new forms of contracting and procurement, credit insurance, and a host of other programs are handled through nonfederal organizations. Many federal programs, in other words, are no longer run by federal bureaucrats.

The federal government's much-criticized social welfare apparatus, for example, is in reality 50 dif-

ferent programs run separately by the 50 states—or, more precisely, about 3,000 programs run by the nation's counties. State and local officials have the power to decide the eligibility rules for and the duration and exact amounts of assistance given out under these programs. A welfare recipient in Mississippi, for example, receives substantially less money each month than an individual on welfare in New York. Likewise, the U.S. Labor Department distributes billions of dollars for employment and training assistance, but the money is actually spent by 450 "prime sponsors" organized by local politicians and community groups.

Such programs create thorny management problems and make for difficulties in coordination. And because those who operate the programs are not responsible to Congress, which authorizes the programs, little can be done to address even blatant abuses or to make program managers accountable for their actions. In the late 1970s and early 1980s, for example, the federal Comprehensive Employment and Training Act (CETA) program, which was designed to bolster employment opportunities for the chronically unemployed, was found to be riddled with patronage. Local and county officials were placing friends, relatives, and political supporters on the CETA rolls—at federal expense. The federal government, under Ronald Reagan, eventually abolished the program entirely. The "bureaucrats in Washington," then, have far less actual control in many areas than the American public believes.

Third-party government programs do offer some advantages. They allow the federal government to draw on the talents and resources of those outside the government, and they give the government greater flexibility in adapting programs to local needs and circumstances.

PRIVATIZATION The move to **privatization,** an effort to transfer a wide range of public assets and programs to the private sector, dovetailed with President Ronald Reagan's ideological goal of reducing government's role in society and enhancing the role of private enterprise. The administration argued that private industry would do a better, cheaper job than government bureaucracies in providing many services.

In keeping with this philosophy, the administration placed both Conrail, the government-run freight rail system of the Northeast, and Landsat, the government's land-mapping satellite, on the market. It also housed aliens in detention centers that were privately operated; contracted with private firms to run many airport control towers; and used private consumer credit companies to screen applicants for government loans. Finally, the administration identified eleven thousand commercial activities conducted by government that could be carried on by private contractors, including fire protection, landscaping, protective services, laundry and food services, movie-making, medical laboratory work, transportation data processing, and geological surveys.

Privatization can mean that certain services provided by the government would be provided by a private organization, as in the Conrail case with rail shipping. But what services ought to be provided by the government itself? And what services should the government arrange for but not provide? Privatization also encompasses cases in which the government contracts with a private firm to handle work the government previously did for itself, such as hiring private credit companies to screen applications for government loans or housing federal detainees in a privately run de-

tention center. In these cases the questions become even more complex. Are there certain tasks that ought to be handled by the government directly, even at higher cost? If private detention centers can replace federal prisons, what about private dispute-resolution bodies to ease the load of overworked federal courts? The answers are hardly simple or clear.

The Reagan administration's zeal for privatization triggered an ideological debate that echoed basic philosophical differences about the nature and purposes of government. Some critics in Congress charged that the administration's real purpose was to take the government out of social policy matters altogether. Others feared that privatization would rob Congress of effective control over many programs, or that the quality of services would suffer when private firms took over. Finally, some argued that privatization simply could not get the job done in many areas.

Are There Too Many Rules?

The third cluster of complaints about the federal bureaucracy focuses on whether there are too many rules, too many forms to fill out, and too many strictures on activities that should be unrestricted—or at least less restricted. Although these complaints are lodged against all segments of the government, few elements of the bureaucracy spark as much debate as the regulatory agencies.

Federal regulatory agencies affect the health and safety of most individuals, the rules under which most business is carried on, and many other vital matters. Critics of these agencies argue that too much regulating goes on, and that the regulators are far from efficient. It has been asserted that government regulation costs the country $100 billion per year[14]—although it is rarely estimated how much is saved through regulation. Particular regulations are often singled out as the most burdensome, such as the health and safety rules for the work place created and enforced by the Occupational Safety and Health Administration. Of course, the regulatory picture is hardly black and white: Criticisms applicable to one agency may not apply at all to another. We must also recognize

Reduce Speed: Bureaucracy at Work

Why should it take the Environmental Protection Agency years to issue regulations needed to carry out antipollution laws and then many more years before the rules are put into effect? The answer: The bureaucratic rule-making process has been arranged so that all affected parties may continuously challenge regulations at every stage of the approval process. A classic example was the EPA's inability to formulate and then to carry out rules affecting wood preservatives. In 1976, the agency began to investigate the effects on the environment and on health of three chemicals used to preserve wood: creosote, pentachlorophenol, and inorganic arsenic compounds. In 1984, after three extensive studies and hearings about the new rules, EPA promulgated its guidelines limiting use of the preservatives. A year later, however, the guidelines still had not been put into effect, and the products remained on the market. Further challenges to the rules could require years to adjudicate.

Under the law, EPA rules can be challenged by makers or users of the products involved. Challengers are entitled to a first hearing before an administrative judge, after which they may take their case to the courts. Sixty companies challenged the proposed wood-preservative rules.

Some EPA administrators point to this case as an example of how, in the name of fairness, rules can be abused. A representative of a coalition of consumer groups argued that this was a "prime example of how administrative procedures . . . provide an advantage to manufacturers that want to keep their products on the market despite health and safety information that shows a clear danger to the public."

Some call for changes in the law to shorten the administrative process. Others maintain that such rules are necessary to protect the companies whose business is at stake.

SOURCE: Philip Shabecoff, "This Sisyphus Rolls a Wooden Stone," *New York Times*, June 29, 1985, p. 8.

that frequently, those who participate in the regulatory debate are not disinterested observers.

Now we turn to (1) the nature of regulation and (2) several proposed reforms of the regulatory process. In examining these topics, keep in mind two key points: first, that regulation usually costs someone and benefits someone else, and that these costs and benefits must be weighed; and second, that proregulation and antiregulation trends follow cycles, and what is topical at the moment does not necessarily make sense in the long run.

TYPES OF REGULATION   Both critics and proponents of government regulation—particularly its critics—commonly make the mistake of lumping together two different types of regulation.[15] One group of regulatory agencies regulates prices, competition, and entry into various industries. Examples of such agencies are the Interstate Commerce Commission and the Federal Communications Commission. Both were created at the request of the regulated industries, whose principal motive was to discourage competition. Generally, regulatory agencies of this type help the regulated industries maintain artificially high prices and avoid the rigors of competition.

A newer variety of regulatory agency enforces standards of health, safety, and fairness. Agencies of this type include the Environmental Protection Agency (EPA), the Occupational Safety and Health Administration (OSHA), the Consumer Product Safety Commission (CPSC), and the Equal Employment Opportunity Commission (EEOC) (see **Table 13–2**). These regulators usually come under fire for limiting the freedom of business to do as it wishes and adding to the costs of doing business, despite estimates that this second group of regulatory agencies has been responsible for considerably less than half the costs of all regulation.[16]

TABLE 13–2
Regulating Health, Safety, and the Environment

Organization	Regulatory function
Packers and Stockyards Administration, Department of Agriculture	Determines plant conditions and business practices in livestock and processed-meat production to provide healthful meat products
Food and Drug Administration, Department of Health, Education and Welfare	Controls labeling and content of foods and drugs
Agricultural Marketing Service, Department of Agriculture	Determines standards for most farm commodities and also sets minimum prices for milk in some areas
Federal Aviation Administration, Department of Transportation	Operates air-traffic-control systems and sets safety standards for aircraft and airports
Animal and Plant Health Inspection Service, Department of Agriculture	Sets standards for plant safety and inspects and enforces laws relating to meat and poultry
Federal Highway Administration, Department of Transportation	Sets safety regulations for interstate trucking
Federal Railroad Administration, Department of Transportation	Sets safety standards for interstate railroads
National Highway Traffic Safety Administration, Department of Transportation	Sets safety standards for automobiles to reduce highway fatalities
Environmental Protection Agency	Develops environmental standards and approves state abatement plans to curtail industrial pollution
Consumer Product Safety Commission	Sets product safety standards
Mining Enforcement and Safety Administration, Department of the Interior	Sets mine safety standards
Drug Enforcement Administration, Department of Justice	Controls trade in narcotics and drugs
Occupational Safety and Health Administration, Department of Labor	Sets and enforces safety and health regulations to reduce work-related accidents and diseases
Nuclear Regulatory Commission	Licenses construction and operation of civilian nuclear power plants and other uses of nuclear energy

SOURCE: *The Challenge of Regulatory Reform: A Report to the President from the Domestic Council Review Group on Regulatory Reform* (Washington, D.C.: U.S. Government Printing Office).

The problems targeted by the newer agencies affect many facets of citizens' lives. "Urban air had become unhealthy as well as unpleasant to breathe. Rivers were catching fire. Many working people were dying from exposure to chemicals on their jobs. Firms were selling products of whose hazards consumers were ignorant. And the nation faced a legacy of racial and sexual discrimination."[17] Since the establishment of OSHA, the number of accidental work-place deaths has been cut in half, and workers' exposure to harmful substances has been sharply curtailed. Water and air pollution has been reduced, as have pesticide levels in rivers. Racial and sexual discrimination has been diminished.

Of course, the costs of such regulation are usually passed on to consumers, and mistakes, excessive pettiness, and overzealous advocacy have sometimes put regulators on the defensive. But as one observer points out: "Much of the new social regulation benefits more disadvantaged groups in society. To put it somewhat simply—but not, in my view, unfairly—those who argue, say, that OSHA should 'go soft' on its health regulations in order to spare the country the burden of additional costs, are saying that some workers should die so that consumers can pay a few bucks less for the products they purchase and stockholders can make a somewhat higher return on their investments."[18]

DEREGULATION Deregulating aspects of the economy gained popularity during the administration of President Jimmy Carter. The first to be deregulated, at least partially, were the railroad and airline industries, followed by the trucking, interstate bus, and banking sectors. Arguments supporting **deregulation**—the drive to eliminate many regulations currently on the books and to cut back on the power of regulatory agencies—center on the premise that government's heavy hand has been suppressing competition and thereby discouraging both innovation and the provision of better service to customers.

What had been a modest movement during the Carter years became a rush of change under President Ronald Reagan. In his first six weeks in office, Reagan lifted price controls on domestic crude oil, abolished the Council on Wage and Price Stability, prevented implementation of dozens of business regulations promulgated in the last days of the Carter administration, dropped energy efficiency standards for appliances and temperature guidelines for office buildings, and urged curbs on the powers of the Federal Trade Commission, Interstate Commerce Commission, the Securities and Exchange Commission, and the Federal Communications Commission. The effects of deregulation were particularly striking in the automobile industry. The Reagan administration rescinded four major regulations in this area: those mandating the installation of automatic seat belts or air bags, the display of crash test results on window price stickers of new cars, the setting of new standards of window visibility for cars and trucks, and the development of new types of speedome-

These airline passengers stand on the frontier of deregulation. With the abolishment of the Civilian Aeronautics Board in 1984, airlines were left much freer to establish fares and services according to market forces. Have the quality and safety of air travel deteriorated as a result of deregulation, or are frustrating delays at the baggage carousel simply a result of increased traffic? (© *Eric Kroll/Taurus Photos*)

Seven Propositions about Regulation

Economist Lester Thurow spells out seven basic propositions about regulation in his book *The Zero-Sum Society*. His aim is to clarify how regulation works in an industrialized society. Here are the propositions he presents, along with the reasoning behind them:

All economies involve rules and regulations; there is no such thing as an unregulated economy. For example, the right to own property is itself a "rule" that requires protection: that is, disputes over property require regulations and enforcement. Normal economic life is unthinkable without such rules of behavior.

There are many silly government regulations. For example, it is impossible to write universally applicable rules, for exceptional cases will always turn up. Any attempt to apply a rule uniformly in a large and diverse country is sometimes going to look silly.

In many areas, there should be fewer regulations. Many regulations remain in force only because some groups gain from them in terms of income security, while the rest of us pay the cost.

In the United States, regulations almost invariably arise from real problems, rather than from ideology. Among these real problems were occupational health and safety, clean air, and private pension failures. It is not, therefore, very useful to be for or against regulations in the abstract.

There is no "left" versus "right" when it comes to the virtues of regulation versus deregulation. Liberals do not always support regulation, and conservatives do not always oppose it. On some issues, such as tobacco and alcohol, neither has a clear position.

There is no simple correlation between the degree of economic success and the degree of economic regulation. Many successful economies are far more regulated than that of the United States—for example, those of West Germany and Japan. In fact, regulation can aid economic growth.

Regulations lead to regulations. The drafting of regulations to protect one industry may lead to efforts to protect others. If you protect steel from import competition, for example, you may also have to protect autos in the same way.

SOURCE: Lester Thurow, *The Zero-Sum Society: Distribution and the Possibilities for Economic Change* (New York: Basic Books, 1980).

ters and tamper-resistant odometers. General Motors estimated that the rollback on air bag regulations alone saved the corporation $500,000 a day in production costs. GM executives stated that compliance with all the various government regulations would have cost the company $2.2 billion a year. On the other hand, William Nordhaus, a former member of the Council of Economic Advisers, calculated that dropping the air bag requirement cost the nation $4.5 billion between 1982 and 1985, principally in medical expenses, insurance payments, and lost wages due to deaths and injuries.

The clearest institutional example of deregulation was the abolition of the Civil Aeronautics Board (CAB) in 1984. For half a century the CAB had set fares and regulated routes and schedules for the air-travel industry in the United States. When it was abolished, only a few of its responsibilities were transferred to the Federal Aviation Administration—the rest simply fell by the wayside. The results were mixed. Prices continued a well-established trend downward, and the number of passengers flown continued to rise. The development of "hub-and-spoke" route systems meant that many small- and medium-sized cities depended almost exclusively on less convenient, small commuter planes. But the consumers' major concern about airline deregulation has been safety. A former director of the National Highway and

Transportation Safety Board said, "I've felt all along that deregulation has had an adverse effect on safety."[19] Quantitative evidence about air safety itself was far from conclusive: Near-midair collisions increased but actual accidents did not. How does all this add up? How much does inconvenience cost? And how much does deregulation increase the likelihood of an accident?

The Scorecard

What does this evaluation reveal about bureaucracy? More than anything, we discover that the more we delve into the workings of bureaucracy, the more complex the issues become. Critics can justifiably blast bureaucratic conflicts of interest—cozy relationships between regulatory agencies and the industries they regulate, for instance—but keen observers must also recognize the vast number of dedicated, professional government employees who keep critical programs running smoothly in the face of numerous political and institutional obstacles. Of the millions of individuals who work for federal, state, county, and local agencies, the vast majority are honest and hardworking. And while some agencies are overstaffed and wasteful, others are short of staff, underbudgeted, and faced with overwhelming tasks.

Then, too, the well-publicized mistakes made by some agencies should be put into perspective. For example, the often-criticized Social Security Administration may make thousands of errors in its monthly mailings of checks—but those errors represent only a fraction of the millions of checks sent out each month.[20] We also should remember that many bureaucratic agencies are charged with enforcing complex laws and making decisions on who does or does not qualify for benefits on the basis of only slight differences among applicants. These are hardly easy tasks.

Large, complex societies inevitably give rise to bureaucracies. Thus, the question we need to ask here is not whether we want a bureaucracy, but rather, what kind of bureaucracy do we want? What sort of agencies, run in what fashion, and with what mandates from Congress and the people? Is the bureaucracy run humanely and openly, and is it run in the larger interests of the public, rather than the interests of the strategically placed few?

Conclusions

Economist Herbert Kaufman points out that "if there were not such a diversity of interests in our society, if we did not subscribe to such a variety of values, if we were not so intolerant of corruption and insistent on our rights, and if the governmental system were not so responsive, however imperfectly, to so many of these claims on it, we would have a great deal less red tape."[21]

Public bureaucracies spring from the complexity of modern societies. Government agencies often incorporate all the functions of legislatures, executives, and judiciaries: They make rules, enforce them, judge appeals, and adjudicate controversies. How else could we ensure that the disabled receive assistance, or that the Stock Market functions honestly, or that food and drugs are not adulterated? How else could we deal with fraud in businesses, or monitor the environmental impact of new factories, dams, and housing developments? How else could we educate the young and administer social insurance programs fairly? Or even begin to crack down on price fixing and monopolistic practices in business? Without regulation and careful supervision, society would degenerate into a raw competition, which those with the means and the ambition to exploit others would win hands down.

Public bureaucracy, then, has not been thrust on us by a conspirational group of fools or villains—we all contribute to it. And we certainly could not eliminate it, once and for all. The best we can do is to chip away at each individual irritant through the normal processes of politics rather than seeking a blanket solution. As for the magic formulas proposed by some critics of the bureaucracy—wholesale contraction of the federal government, devolution of authority to the states and localities, concentration of authority in administrative "czars" empowered to cut through red tape—on close inspection, each turns out to hold little promise, for they all ignore values treasured by many people.

This is not to argue that because bureaucracy is needed, any sort of bureaucracy will do. From the standpoint of democratic theory, bureaucracies should be highly responsive, sensitive to human needs, and respectful of the rights of the common citizen.

Unfortunately, it is difficult to tote up a balance sheet on the U.S. bureaucracy as a whole in light of democratic theory. Some agencies act in a highly autocratic fashion, some diminish freedom rather than protecting it, some harass citizens and ignore basic rights. By contrast, many agencies do a creditable job of protecting life and limb, helping raise the level of public information, and guaranteeing that democratic rights are protected and that equality and liberty are safeguarded. No sweeping statements, therefore, can be made to characterize the bureaucracy as a whole.

GLOSSARY TERMS

bureaucracy

contract bureaucracies

cabinet departments

regulatory commission

clientele groups

spoils system

patronage

Civil Service system

third-party government

privatization

deregulation

NOTES

[1]Bernard Schwartz, *The Professor and the Commissions* (New York: Knopf, 1959).

[2]*Motor Vehicle Manufacturers Assoc.* v. *State Farm Mutual Automobile Insurance Co.* (1983), 103 SC 2856.

[3]Joan Claybrook *et al.*, *Retreat from Safety* (New York: Pantheon, 1984), pp. 166–185.

[4]Charles Peters, "The Solution: A Rebirth of Patriotism," *Washington Monthly*, Oct. 1978.

[5]Charles Malek, *Washington's Hidden Tragedy: The Failure to Make Government Work* (New York: Free Press, 1978).

[6]Randall B. Ripley and Grace H. Franklin, *Congress, the Bureaucracy and Public Policy* (Homewood, Ill.: Dorsey, 1984), chap. 2.

[7]*Ibid.*, chap. 3.

[8]For a discussion of these problems, see Herbert Kaufman, *Red Tape* (Washington, D.C.: Brookings Institution, 1979).

[9]John K. Galbraith, *The New Industrial State*, 2nd ed. (Boston: Houghton Mifflin, 1971), chaps. 2 and 3.

[10]Richard E. Cohen, "Regulatory Focus: The Cut-Rate Fares Dilemma," *National Journal*, Sept. 3, 1977, p. 1384.

[11]Peter Drucker, *The Age of Discontinuity: Guidelines to Our Changing Society* (New York: Harper & Row, 1969).

[12]Leonard Reed, "Bureaucrats 2, Presidents 0," *Harper's*, Nov. 1982.

[13]Nolan Argyle and Ryan Barilleaux, "Past Failures and Future Prescriptions for Presidential Management Reform," *Presidential Studies Quarterly*, vol. xvi, no. 4, Fall 1986.

[14]Murray Weidenbaum, *The Future of Business Regulation* (New York: AMACCM, 1979); and *Prospects for Reallocating Public Resources* (Washington, D.C.: American Enterprise Institute, 1967).

[15]This discussion draws on Steven Kelman, "Regulation That Works," *New Republic*, Nov. 25, 1978, pp. 16–20.

[16]*Ibid.*

[17]*Ibid.*, p. 17.

[18]*Ibid.*, p. 19.

[19]Quoted in Larry N. Gerston *et al.*, *The Deregulated Society* (Pacific Grove, Calif.: Brooks/Cole, 1988), pp. 232–233.

[20]R. Kahn *et al.*, "Americans Love Their Bureaucrats," *Psychology Today*, June 1975, pp. 66–71.

[21]Herbert Kaufman, *Red Tape*, pp. 58–59.

SELECTED READINGS

For analyses of the **problems of bureaucracy** in a democratic setting, see John P. Burke, *Bureaucratic Responsibility* (Baltimore: Johns Hopkins, 1986); John A. Rohr, *To Run a Constitution: The Legitimacy of the Administrative State* (Lawrence: University Press of Kansas, 1986); Judith E. Gruber, *Controlling Bureaucracies: Dilemmas in Democratic Governance* (Berkeley: University of California

Press, 1987); Dennis D. Riley, *Controlling the Federal Bureaucracy* (Philadelphia: Temple University Press, 1987); Charles T. Goodsell, *The Case for Bureaucracy: A Public Administration Polemic,* 2nd ed. (Chatham, N.J.: Chatham House, 1985).

For a variety of accounts about bureaucratic behavior in **particular policy areas,** see Neal Shover *et al.*, *Enforcement of Negotiation: Constructing a Regulatory Bureaucracy,* which concerns the regulation of surface mining (Albany: SUNY Press, 1986); Charles Noble, *Liberalism at Work: The Rise and Fall of OSHA* (Philadelphia: Temple University Press, 1986); Serge Taylor, *Making Bureaucracies Think: The Environmental Impact Statement Strategy of Administrative Reform* (Stanford, Calif.: Stanford University Press, 1984); Evelyn Brodkin, *The False Promise of Administrative Reform: Implementing Quality Control in Welfare* (Philadelphia: Temple University Press, 1986); and Bernice Rothman Hasin, *Consumers, Commissions, and Congress: Law, Theory, and the Federal Trade Commission* (New Brunswick, N.J.: Transaction Books, 1987).

14

THE FEDERAL JUDICIARY

Nonelected Defenders of Democracy

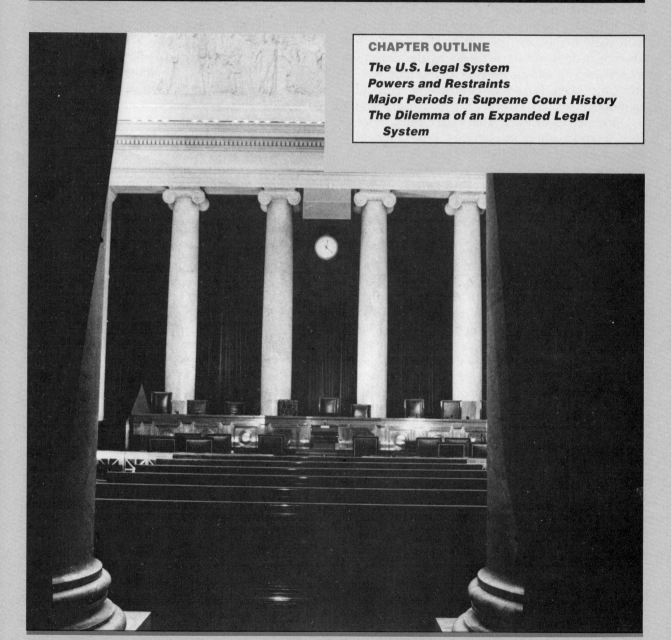

CHAPTER OUTLINE

The U.S. Legal System
Powers and Restraints
Major Periods in Supreme Court History
The Dilemma of an Expanded Legal System

Fred Ward/Black Star

In an ideal world, peopled with committed democrats, there might be little need for a Supreme Court to decide issues involving fundamental democratic rights. Such rights would simply be observed, and the courts would concentrate exclusively on complex and abstruse aspects of litigation. But ours is far from an ideal world. In our society, the Supreme Court, empowered to review the constitutional merits of legislation, ensures that rights are protected, or extended, to conform with basic democratic principles. The Court can (though it does not have to) act as the nation's conscience, upholding its basic democratic commitments, even in the face of hostile or reluctant majorities.

Once such an institution has been created, however, it can largely go its own way. Federal judges are appointed, not elected, to a life tenure, and they are politically accountable to no one. Whatever their individual foibles, preferences, experiences, and limitations, they have the power to reshape society, and their decisions profoundly affect our political life. If these "guardians" do not rule sensibly, if they substitute narrow or short-sighted economic and social philosophies for democratic approaches, society will be at the mercy of a judicial aristocracy.

Because the judiciary was established as a "co-equal" branch of government and given an important part to play in the system of checks and balances, disputes confronting the Supreme Court and other federal courts reflect a complex mix of procedural concerns, policy questions, partisan politics, and issues of personal power. In ruling on these matters, the judiciary is compelled to justify its actions by careful legal reasoning, yet ultimately, the judiciary's success in defending democracy can be measured only by whether specific rulings have a positive impact on political and social life in our country. Two examples demonstrate the profound extent—and the limitations—of the Supreme Court's power to influence U.S. politics and social life.

Consider, first, the Court's role in the New Deal of the 1930s. Sweeping statutes, which substantially expanded federal control over the economy, had been passed to address the unprecedented economic crisis of the Great Depression. Enacted hurriedly, some of the legislation was poorly con-structed and vague. A majority of Supreme Court justices were convinced that extensive government control of the economy ran counter to democracy. In their view, democratic institutions needed to be saved from democratic representatives. Building from this assumption, and capitalizing on the technical weaknesses of the legislation, the Court's majority declared several key statutes unconstitutional.

In the eyes of many, including President Franklin D. Roosevelt, the Court's actions jeopardized the nation's economic recovery and thus its very existence. The Court came under fire for reading into the Constitution its own conservative, anti-government economic principles rather than interpreting the document as a flexible set of guidelines to help the nation deal with changing circumstances. Defenders of the Court argued that it was playing an essential role by curtailing the overextension of federal power. Roosevelt's landslide reelection victory in 1936, and his proposal to enlarge the Court (to allow him to appoint more liberal justices) finally persuaded some justices that certain New Deal legislation was legitimate. The Court changed course and began allowing newly reconstructed New Deal statutes to stand. Since this confrontation, the Court has rarely interfered with legislation concerning the federal government's power to regulate economic life. The grave conflict the Court provoked in the 1930s illustrates its power to oppose majoritarian pressures in the short run. However, the ultimate outcome of this conflict demonstrates one key limitation of the Court's power: The Court has little success in opposing a determined majority over an extended period.

A second example, in which the Court played a different sort of role, was the school desegregation decision of 1954, *Brown* v. *The Board of Education of Topeka.* In that case (discussed in detail in Chapter 4), the Court held that segregated schools were inherently unequal. This decision involved a moral and legal leap for the Court, overturning a precedent that had stood for fifty-eight years, and challenging head on long-established and deeply rooted local customs. Like the Court's rulings on the New Deal legislation, the *Brown* decision sparked intense anger: Critics charged that the ruling was based on the particular philosophy

George Hayes, Thurgood Marshall, and James M. Nabrit, who led the fight against public school segregation in *Brown* v. *Board of Education*. Marshall later became the first black to serve on the high court. *(AP/Wide World Photos)*

of the justices rather than on an unbiased reading of the Constitution. Defenders of the Court argued, however, that segregation itself violated the Constitution, and that the Court had simply marshalled the courage to acknowledge that. It took nearly twenty years after the *Brown* decision for public schools to undertake serious desegregation efforts. In some controversial cases, then, the Court doesn't always achieve its objectives immediately. But the Supreme Court's stand on this case exemplifies how the Court, because of its insulation from pressing political pressures, can take the lead on important moral issues. In *Brown* the Court made a clear appeal to the conscience of the majority, and this ruling helped move the country forward in a critical area where leadership lagged in both the executive and the legislative branches.

Certainly, the Supreme Court can play a powerful role in U.S. politics. The justices' views of

law, morality, and the appropriate role of the Court all contribute to the actions they take. But how much power should the courts—particularly the U.S. Supreme Court—have in shaping our national life? In a democratic society, should nine nonelected individuals play a decisive role in how the polity approaches important national issues? With these questions in mind, we will look carefully at (1) how the national court system works; (2) the powers of and restraints on the courts; (3) major periods in Supreme Court history; and (4) the dilemmas posed by an expanded legal system. Then we will address how the courts do or do not serve democratic principles.

The U.S. Legal System

Every court case begins with a dispute between two or more parties. These parties may be individuals, groups, corporations, or government bodies. Jones may sue Smith to recover damages caused by a traffic accident. Acting under the provisions of a civil rights statute, the U.S. government may sue a state government to stop state officials from discriminating against blacks in the electoral process. The state of Nebraska may charge Adams with burglary and bring him to court to answer the charge. A group of women may attempt to have the abortion law in their state declared unconstitutional.

Unlike legislatures or bureaucracies, most courts do not control their own agendas. Judges cannot decide unilaterally to make policy about abortion, voting rights, or racial discrimination. Rather, they must wait for others to bring matters to them for resolution. In the course of resolving disputes brought before them, judicial institutions must divide their attention between two different tasks. On one hand, the court must resolve an actual dispute between the parties in the case at hand (the so-called "instant case"). At the same time, however, courts in our common law system must consider the broad principles that ought to undergird the resolution of disputes like the one at hand. In the narrower view, the court must determine who wins and who loses this particular case. In the more wide-ranging perspective, the court must establish what the law is and ought to be for all cases like this one.

At the heart of the common law tradition is the principle of *stare decisis*, which demands that current cases be decided in the same manner as past cases ("precedents") have been decided. For centuries, jurists in this tradition maintained that judges merely "discovered" the law through precedent, but took no active part in creating the law. In the twentieth century most students of the law recognize that judges do play an active part in creating law, even as they apply precedent. In most cases precedents are clear enough that reaching a decision simply means applying strict rules of law to familiar circumstances. In some cases, though, no clear precedent fits the circumstances of a particular case. When this occurs, the court must search among precedents for circumstances that are reasonably close to those in the instant case, and extend the line of precedents in this new direction. The instant case then becomes a precedent for the next case like it.

Let us now examine (1) state court systems; (2) the federal court system; (3) the flow of litigation; (4) the judicial decision-making process; and (5) the recruitment of judges.

State Court Systems

The U.S. court system is actually fifty-one separate court systems—one for the federal government and a separate one in each state. As a member of a federal system of government, each state is free to design a court system according to its own needs, but they all follow a common pattern. A case usually enters a state court system in a special jurisdiction court (such as traffic court, small claims court, family or juvenile court), or in a general jurisdiction trial court that handles all serious criminal and civil cases. (A criminal case arises because of an alleged violation of a criminal statute and involves a **prosecutor**—representing the interests of the state—and a **defendant**—the person charged with the crime. A civil case represents a dispute between two parties: the **plaintiff,** who claims to have suffered some harm, and the defendant, who is, allegedly, responsible for the harm.) The vast majority of cases that enter the state court system are resolved in the court of original jurisdiction, where they first are heard. If one of the parties in a case is not satisfied with the outcome at the trial level, however, the case can then be appealed.

A moment of ritual in the American courtroom. The prosecuting attorney approaches the bench, with defendant and defense attorney in the foreground. The bailiff is seated at the far left; to the right, the witness is on the stand, and the court reporter keeps track of the proceedings. Although other democracies may organize things differently, their legal systems have similar basic elements. *(Bill Bachman/Photo Researchers)*

The next tier of courts in most states is a general jurisdiction court of appeals. Appellate courts have little in common with our images of Perry Mason. While trial courts may use **grand juries** (to determine if there is enough evidence to warrant a trial) and **petit juries** (to decide the disputed matter itself), appellate courts rely exclusively on panels of judges. Trial courts ordinarily gather evidence from oral testimony, but appellate courts usually rule on the basis of the trial record plus briefs and oral arguments submitted by the opposing counsel in the case. Most appellate hearings are boring affairs to observe. The judges, having read the written materials, listen to the oral arguments and question the counsel. Then they retire to confer among themselves, vote on a decision, and write one or more **opinions** (legal explanations of the decision).

At the top of the state court system stands the highest state court, usually called the state supreme court. Cases not resolved satisfactorily in the courts of appeals may be appealed to this court, along with a small number of cases that, due to the nature of the dispute involved, start here. Again, a panel of judges—often called justices at this level—read the records of the case from the lower courts, listen to oral arguments, confer, and decide, issuing opinions to explain their decision and the general principles of law on which it rests.

The Federal Court System

The federal court system is also structured like a pyramid, mirroring the pattern just described for state court systems (see **Figure 14–1**). There are specialized federal courts (Tax Court, the Court of International Trade, and the Court of Claims, for example), but the workhorses of the federal system are the **Federal District Courts.** Most cases enter the system through the District Courts, and most are resolved without going further. Each state has at least one district, and large states may have as many as four District Courts. Several judges sit in each district, which may be divided into administrative divisions. Federal District Courts use both grand juries and petit juries. If a criminal defendant or a party to a civil suit loses

in the District Court, an appeal may be made to the next level in the federal system.

At the intermediate level in the federal system are the **U.S. Courts of Appeals,** or **Circuit Courts.** There are twelve circuits, one for the District of Columbia and the rest encompassing several states each. These courts have no original jurisdiction—that is, all cases they consider have been heard previously by a lower court. These appellate judges decide matters while sitting in panels.

The **U.S. Supreme Court** is the highest court in the federal system and the nation. Cases come to the U.S. Supreme Court from lower federal courts *and* from state court systems when a federal question is involved. (A federal case can deal with a federal statute, treaty, or the U.S. Constitution. Federal questions may also arise when the United States is a party to the case, when two states are involved, when a dispute affects citizens of different states, or when official foreign representatives are involved.) The Supreme Court is asked to hear several thousand cases every year, yet the Court is able to hear and decide only a few hundred. That means the Supreme Court has a large measure of control over its own docket; with certain exceptions it can choose which cases it wishes to hear. If it chooses not to hear a case, the lower-court decision is allowed to stand. In deciding which cases to hear, the Court follows the **"rule of four":** If four of the nine justices vote to hear a case, the case is placed on the Court's docket. From that point, briefs are filed by the opposing sides, oral arguments are heard, and a decision is rendered.

The Flow of Litigation

The flow of litigation through the court system is characterized by a winnowing process. Most cases are decided at the level where they are first heard, either because the losers are satisfied with the outcome or because they do not have the resources to mount an appeal. Appeals can drain litigants of both time and money. The typical Supreme Court case wends it way through the court system for two or three years. The legal expenses involved—attorneys' fees for legal research, preparation of briefs, time spent in court—can be considerable.

FIGURE 14–1
The Court System of the United States

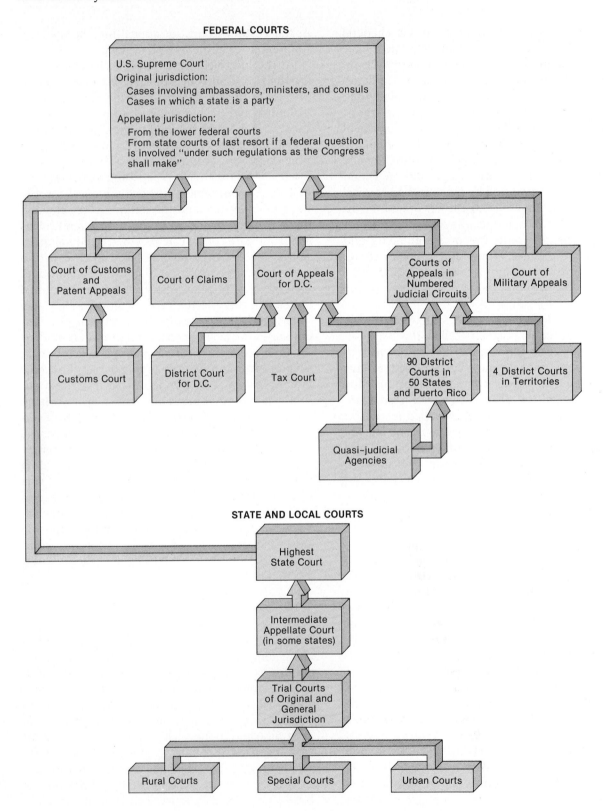

FEDERAL COURTS

U.S. Supreme Court
Original jurisdiction:
　Cases involving ambassadors, ministers, and consuls
　Cases in which a state is a party

Appellate jurisdiction:
　From the lower federal courts
　From state courts of last resort if a federal question
　is involved "under such regulations as the Congress
　shall make"

Court of Customs and Patent Appeals

Court of Claims

Court of Appeals for D.C.

Courts of Appeals in Numbered Judicial Circuits

Court of Military Appeals

Customs Court

District Court for D.C.

Tax Court

90 District Courts in 50 States and Puerto Rico

4 District Courts in Territories

Quasi-judicial Agencies

STATE AND LOCAL COURTS

Highest State Court

Intermediate Appellate Court (in some states)

Trial Courts of Original and General Jurisdiction

Rural Courts

Special Courts

Urban Courts

Winnowing occurs not only because litigants give up or run out of resources, but also because appellate courts refuse to hear many cases. A case that reaches the Supreme Court must be important enough to the litigants to merit a substantial investment of time and money, but the Court must also deem it important enough to merit consideration on a crowded and limited docket. Cases for which a clear line of precedents establishes an appropriate rule of law rarely reach the Supreme Court (unless, as sometimes happens, members of the Court decide to modify or reverse an existing rule). Unlike lower courts, the Supreme Court acts as a policy-review court; it works toward making decisions that have an impact on the entire legal system. Our legal system assumes that justice can be served under ordinary circumstances by a trial and a single chance for review in an appellate court. This is not to suggest that the work of lower courts is purely technical and unimportant. Lower-court decisions dealing with the enforcement of criminal statutes and traffic laws and the application of legal norms in, say, landlord-tenant relations ordinarily have a more direct impact on the daily lives of individual citizens than do decisions handed down by the Supreme Court. However, when it comes to developing and modifying legal norms, involving important areas of social policy, the appellate courts, and especially the Supreme Court, generally hold sway.

The Decision-making Process

Disputes that reach the Supreme Court often reflect basic disagreements about public policy in society at large. The High Court addresses questions concerning broad-based issues—the primacy of home rule versus particular state or federal mandates, whether one corporation's dominance of an industry constitutes an undemocratic antitrust violation, whether a nativity scene on government property amounts to an unconstitutional violation of the separation of church and state. Judges, like other policy makers in our society, have a great deal of latitude in decision making, and the decisions they make can have significant effects on public policy. Thus, we now consider how a judge decides a case.

Judges in our system resolve disputes according to the law. In the United States, we have four sources of law: the Constitution (written by "the people"), statutes (written by a legislature), case law (precedents decided by the courts), and administrative rules and regulations (established by administrative agencies). Sometimes these sources produce conflicting laws; then the legal hierarchy determines which law should prevail, according to the dictates of justice and fairness. Administrative rules and case law ordinarily give way to statute, because the legislature represents the people more directly than judges or administrators. But statutes

The U.S. Supreme Court at the end of the Reagan administration. The Chief Justice always sits in the middle, with Associate Justices alternating outward to his right and left, in descending order of years of service.
Seated: **Thurgood Marshall (appointed by Johnson in 1967); William Brennan (Eisenhower, 1956); Chief Justice William Rehnquist (Associate Justice, Nixon, 1972; Chief Justice, Reagan, 1986); Byron White (Kennedy, 1962); Harry Blackmun (Nixon, 1970).**
Standing: **Antonin Scalia (Reagan, 1986); John Paul Stevens (Ford, 1975); Sandra Day O'Connor (Reagan, 1981); William Kennedy (Reagan, 1988).** *(AP/Wide World Photos)*

in our system must give way to the Constitution, because the Constitution is supposed to reflect principles of "higher law." Federal laws supersede state laws (even state constitutions) because of the primacy of the national government in our federal system.

The process of applying law to particular cases is often far from straightforward. Precedents may conflict, or there may be no appropriate precedent. Statutes and administrative rules may be poorly written or deliberately vague. The challenge of interpreting the broad provisions of the Constitution is especially difficult. The Constitution says, for example, that police may not engage in *unreasonable searches and seizures,* and that no citizen may be deprived of *equal protection of the laws* or **due process** in the implementation of laws. How does a judge assess a statute or the actions of a government official in light of these constitutional guarantees? Does stopping and frisking a suspicious-looking individual constitute an unreasonable search? Does the racial segregation of school children deny blacks equal protection of the laws? Does a law regulating the wages and hours of employees deprive them of due process of law in contracting with employers for their services? Each of these questions prompted considerable debate among jurists both before and after the Supreme Court reached decisions on these issues. Additionally, personal values and characteristics of judges, their interactions with fellow judges, and the limitations placed on them by their positions all influence their decisions and opinions. The judicial decision-making process, then, cannot be reduced to a mechanical process of applying the relevant law to the facts of a case.

Recruitment of Judges

One important influence on judicial decision making is the background of the person appointed to the bench.[1] In the federal judicial system, judges are nominated by the president and confirmed by the Senate. Before making a choice public, the president normally consults with the attorney general and the senators from the state where a proposed nominee lives. The American Bar Association's Committee on the Federal Judiciary then prepares a report on the candidate for the Senate Judiciary Committee, which holds a hearing. Finally, the full Senate votes on the nominee. At every stage in this process, the participants are intensely lobbied by interest groups, as well as by political nominees and their friends and political allies.[2]

A large measure of politics infuses federal judicial appointments, from lobbying in favor of various candidates, to ideological judgments about the decisions a person might make on the bench, campaign or other partisan debts owed or receivable, and consideration of the symbolic effects of a judicial appointment. Moreover, nominees to federal judgeships traditionally participate in political activity themselves. This brings an individual to the attention of those who choose judges and provides an avenue for the personal relationships that lead to appointment to the bench. Political participation by a potential nominee has another significant purpose: to reveal the nominee's attitudes on public policy. Because most presidents seek to appoint men or women whose philosophy of government does not radically differ from their own, they tend to pick nominees whose political views have been made known through participation in public life. (**Table 14–1** lists recent Supreme Court justices in the order of their appointment.)

Once justices are appointed to the Supreme Court, predictions about their future decisions may be unreliable. Serving on the Supreme Court imposes a unique responsibility, and it sometimes elicits surprising responses from justices. Eisenhower came to rue his appointment of Earl Warren, who, in his earlier political career demonstrated a solid conservative record, but as chief justice of the United States adopted a substantially liberal outlook. Nixon appointees voted to strike down abortion laws and uphold busing requirements, policies he did not support. One Nixon appointee, Harry Blackmun, was originally called one of the "Minnesota Twins" because his conservative voting so closely matched the other Minnesotan on the Court, the conservative Warren Burger. As the Court moved to the right, however, Blackmun adjusted his own positions to the left. Ronald Reagan's appointment of William Rehnquist as chief justice resulted in a first-year series

TABLE 14–1
Supreme Court Justices, 1937–1989

Justice	State of residence	Position at appointment*
Black	Alabama	Senator
Reed	Kentucky	Solicitor General
Frankfurter	Massachusetts	Law professor
Douglas	Washington	Chair, Fed. Regulatory Comm.
Murphy	Michigan	Attorney General
Byrnes	South Carolina	Senator
Jackson	New York	Attorney General
Rutledge	Iowa	U.S. Ct. App.
Burton	Ohio	Senator
Vinson[†]	Kentucky	Sec. of Treasury
Clark	Texas	Attorney General
Minton	Indiana	U.S. Ct. App.
Warren[†]	California	Governor
Harlan	New York	U.S. Ct. App.
Brennan	New Jersey	State Sup. Ct.
Whittaker	Missouri	U.S. Ct. App.
Stewart	Ohio	U.S. Ct. App.
White	Colorado	Dep. Atty. General
Goldberg	Illinois	Sec. of Labor
Fortas	Washington, D.C.	Private practice
Marshall	New York	Solicitor General
Burger[†]	Minnesota	U.S. Ct. App.
Blackmun	Minnesota	U.S. Ct. App.
Powell	Virginia	Private practice
Rehnquist[†]	Arizona	Asst. Atty. General
Stevens	Illinois	U.S. Ct. App.
O'Connor	Arizona	State Ct. App.
Scalia	Washington, D.C.	U.S. Ct. App.
Kennedy	California	State Sup. Ct.

*Positions are federal except where noted.
[†]Chief Justice.

of opinions written or assigned by William Brennan, the liberal senior associate justice on the Court. (The chief justice, only when in the majority, can choose who writes the Court's opinion. Rehnquist chose to put himself in the minority rather than compromise to have control over the opinion.) Still, the Court has definitely been molded from time to time by the political orientation of particular presidential appointments. Striking transformations have been wrought in the Court when one president has made several appointments in a short period. Ordinarily a presi-

dent makes an appointment to the Court every few years. This ongoing recruitment process ties the Supreme Court into the broad currents of thought that distinguish the political life of the day.

Powers and Restraints

The U.S. court system has enormous power. Many matters that in other nations are considered outside the realm of legal institutions are treated as legal issues in the United States. To understand the significant policy role played by the courts in this country, we must examine the nature of judicial power, its development, and its limitations. We now spotlight (1) the concept of judicial review; (2) self-imposed restraint on the courts' power; (3) legislative reaction to court rulings; and (4) noncompliance with court decisions.

Judicial Review

The extensive powers of the federal courts are rooted in the concept of **judicial review.** Under this concept, the courts are empowered to review the acts of federal and state legislatures and the actions of members of executive agencies, to determine whether they conform to the provisions of the Constitution and the laws of the land. Thus, for example, state laws dealing with abortion or the appointment of legislatures, congressional legislation focusing on subversive activities, and police activities in investigating criminal suspects may all come under the scrutiny of the federal courts.

Judicial review confers extraordinary power: It enables courts to negate the activities of other branches of government by overturning laws and regulations deemed unconstitutional. Critics argue that judicial review is highly undemocratic, because the judges who exercise it serve for long terms or for life and thus are not accountable to the public in the way elected officials are. From the opposite standpoint, judicial review protects the rights of minorities—a vital function in a democratic society. Only the courts, in this view, have the necessary detachment to restrain the volatile and sometimes repressive will of the majority.

Marbury v. Madison

Thomas Jefferson was elected to the presidency in the fall of 1800. In the period between his election and his inauguration, the lame duck president, John Adams, made a series of appointments to federal judgeships designed to ensure continued Federalist control of the judiciary. One of those appointments, as a justice of the peace, went to William Marbury. When Jefferson was inaugurated, he forbade his secretary of state, James Madison, from giving Marbury his official commission. Marbury thereupon requested that the Supreme Court issue a writ of *mandamus* (an order compelling an official to perform his duties under the law). In his suit, Marbury cited the Judiciary Act of 1789, which gave the Supreme Court original jurisdiction to issue such writs.

In writing the majority opinion for the Court in the case of *Marbury* v. *Madison*, Chief Justice Marshall, a Federalist, neatly sidestepped the central issue of the case and at the same time established the pivotal principle of judicial re-

view. Marshall argued that although Marbury was legally entitled to the commission, the Supreme Court lacked the authority to issue the writ of *mandamus*, because the Judiciary Act of 1789 had unconstitutionally conferred on the Court original jurisdiction to issue writs of *mandamus* to federal officials. As Marshall pointed out, the Constitution explicitly listed those areas in which the Court was to exercise original jurisdiction and left to Congress the power to specify only its appellate jurisdiction. Marshall went on to argue that because the Constitution was the supreme law of the land, binding on judges and all other government officials, Congress could not pass a law that contradicted it: "a law repugnant to the Constitution is void . . . ; courts as well as other departments are bound by that instrument." With this decision, the Supreme Court assumed the sweeping power of judicial review—the power to overturn particular laws the Court deemed unconstitutional.

The concept of judicial review is not explicitly spelled out in the Constitution. The framers of the Constitution, although certainly aware that judicial review was an issue, did not expressly address the question. Lacking a clear constitutional mandate, the courts simply asserted that they had the power of review, and that power gradually became an integral part of the U.S. legal system.

The Supreme Court first asserted the power to declare federal legislation unconstitutional in *Marbury* v. *Madison* (1803).[3] In *Marbury,* the Court declared that a provision of the Judiciary Act of 1789 violated the Constitution and thus was null and void. This ruling had profound implications. Because many of the provisions of the Constitution are vague, applying them in the context of judicial review gives the courts enormous power. Over the following two decades, the Court built slowly on the provisions of *Marbury.* In *McCulloch* v. *Mary-*

land (1819),[4] Chief Justice Marshall cited the supremacy of national law (Article I) in ruling that Maryland's attempt to tax national banks was unconstitutional. And that same year, the justices held that states were prohibited from passing legislation impairing contracts.

Since the mid-nineteenth century, there has been little dispute over whether the Supreme Court has the power of judicial review. Some Courts have been more active than others in exercising this power, however, and debate continues over how far the Court should go in nullifying the actions of other, more democratic institutions.

Self-Restraints on Power

The courts' power of judicial review is circumscribed by a series of self-imposed rules for re-

Principles of great significance are molded from the facts of individual cases. The assignment of 9-year-old Linda Brown to an all-black school in Topeka, Kansas, in 1952, ultimately desegregated our public school system. *(AP/Wide World Photos)*

straint. The most significant of these rules holds that the courts will consider only those cases in which the parties have standing to sue: that is, in which the plaintiff (the party that brings suit) can demonstrate actual injury—loss of money, property, freedom, and so on—from the government law or action in question. Standing rules may be relaxed or tightened depending on the courts' case load burdens and, more important, the likelihood that policy debates that should take place in other arenas will be imposed on the judiciary instead. For example, a taxpayer, in a "taxpayer suit," may wish to challenge any policy approved by Congress and the president that requires the expenditure of federal funds. For a long time the Supreme Court simply refused to hear such suits. The willingness of the Court to loosen standing requirements to some extent in the 1960s was followed by a more restrictive period in the 1970s and 1980s.

Another rule for self-restraint rests on the "political question" doctrine. Although, as we have

already noted, the courts form an integral part of the political process and thus must necessarily make decisions with political implications, the courts routinely shun certain types of political disputes. These include matters that would place the Supreme Court in direct conflict with other branches of government; issues involving foreign relations that might embarrass or compromise the government if a multiplicity of voices spoke for the nation in contradictory ways; and matters that have been assigned by the Constitution to other branches for resolution. For instance, the Court decided *not* to decide which of two governments in Rhode Island was the legitimate government— that was a matter for the president and Congress to work out. The Court refuses to hear cases involving "political questions" that are political rather than legal in nature; these must be resolved elsewhere in the political system. In the end, because the Supreme Court can simply refuse to hear any case it wishes to avoid, these restraints are most effective in preventing cases from entering the federal court system at all.

Because the Supreme Court has effective control over its own agenda, it can inject itself directly in public policy disputes and even set an agenda for the development of law. However, too much direct involvement may undermine the Court's legitimacy in the eyes of other political players and the public at large. As Justice Anthony M. Kennedy said in a speech prior to his nomination to the Supreme Court, "The unrestrained exercise of judicial authority ought to be recognized for what it is: the raw exercise of judicial power. If in fact that is the basis of our decisions, then there is no principled justification for our insulation from the political process."[5] Since the Court's power depends entirely on its perceived legitimacy (as Madison reminded us long ago, the Supreme Court controls neither the sword nor the purse), self-restraint is critical if the Court is to play a major role in shaping public policy. Individual justices, and those who evaluate their work, must recognize when the Court is using its political insulation to substitute the choices of a judicial elite for the choices of the people's representatives, and on the contrary, when the Court is properly resisting the unfair demands of an oppressive majority.

COMPARATIVE PERSPECTIVE

Court Systems in Sweden and Great Britain

The court systems of other democratic countries differ in several fundamental respects from the U.S. system. For example, jury trials, which are common in the United States, are comparatively rare in many European nations. In Sweden, juries are reserved for cases of criminal libel only. Instead of juries, the Swedes employ "lay judges," who are elected by communal assemblies to assist professional judges in their work. Stockholm, for example, has 750 lay judges; together with chief magistrates, they hear evidence and participate in court decisions. Lay judges and magistrates usually concur in their decisions; should they differ, a majority on a panel of lay judges can overrule a magistrate. Lay judges are used in all criminal and almost all civil cases.

Great Britain generally reserves jury trials for more serious crimes. Overall, its judicial system is simpler and smoother in operation than ours, mainly because the British are less concerned with procedural formalities that protect the accused. For instance, the exclusionary rule, which bars the introduction in court of illegally seized evidence, was explicitly rejected in Great Britain in 1979.

The British system of justice also is not as adversarial as ours is. In the courtroom, prosecutor and defense counsel sit together, wearing identical robes. Lawyers steer away from controversial and theatrical tactics and often reach informal agreements outside the courtroom. In fact, British prosecutors are private lawyers who may work for the defense in another case. In the United States, public prosecutors must work only for the government.

Legislative Reaction

An additional limit on the power of the Supreme Court to participate decisively in public policy making is Congress's ability to overrule unpopular court decisions by passing new laws or proposing constitutional amendments. Even when attempts to overturn Court rulings through the legislative process do not succeed, they give the Court important cues that it has gone too far and should reconsider the policy it has been pursuing.

During the 1950s, for example, strong anticommunist sentiment throughout the country triggered a barrage of government activity designed to ward off the alleged communist menace. In a series of decisions handed down in 1957 and 1958, the Court introduced limits on the power of congressional committees to investigate communists, on the use of criminal sanctions against

members of the American Communist Party, and on the power of government agencies to dismiss employees whose loyalty was suspect. In Congress and the newspapers, opposition to these decisions grew, and legislation was introduced to overturn them. In addition, Congress threatened to restrict the Court's ability to hear appeals of lower-court decisions dealing with such matters as loyalty and security. Although none of this proposed legislation passed, the message to the Court was unmistakable.

During the period from 1959 to 1961, the Court handed down a series of decisions that lifted many of the restraints imposed in 1957 and 1958. What had changed was not the Constitution or the factual issues of the cases, but rather the willingness of the Court to intervene in this area. Thus, the congressional and public response prompted the Court to back off a bit in rulings that dealt with the powers of the government to restrict liberty in the name of national security.[6] This averted a constitutional crisis.

More recently, Court decisions outlawing prayer in public schools and government restrictions on abortion have sparked intense legislative reactions. Efforts to overturn the school prayer decisions have failed to produce the constitutional amendment critics have sought, even though President Reagan lent the prestige of his office to the drive. Critics of the abortion decision have had some success in complicating the process of obtaining an abortion in some states and in restricting funding for Medicaid abortions, but not in altering the Court's decision itself. In both these instances, the Court has shown little inclination to shift its position, despite the intensity of legislative and popular reactions. In 1985 the Supreme Court ruled that an Alabama law calling for a moment of silence in public schools at the beginning of the school day, to be used for personal prayer, violated the constitutionally mandated separation of church and state. And in 1986 the Court reaffirmed its stand on abortion in a 5–4 decision overturning the Pennsylvania Abortion Control Act of 1982.

Noncompliance

When citizens refuse to comply with court decisions or other government mandates, public policy makers face an enormous obstacle. Court decisions, in particular, are not self-executing: In order for them to take effect, individuals or agencies outside the court must implement them. Some decisions require relatively simple changes in behavior: Let John Smith out of prison or give him a new trial. Other decisions require major changes by large numbers of people and the significant reallocation of resources if they are to be translated into new public policy.

Local officials and bureaucracies in both the public and the private spheres frequently assert their braking power on policy emanating from the courts. Local school districts, for example, used a series of evasive schemes to thwart the Supreme Court's goal of school desegregation as mandated in *Brown* v. *Board of Education* (1954). And when the Court held in 1963 that reading the Bible as

When emotional issues spark civil disobedience, local law enforcement agencies must defend policies defined by the courts. In this photo, supporters of women's rights felt the need to protect an abortion clinic themselves. (© *Rick Reinhard*)

part of devotional services in public schools violated the First Amendment, compliance with the decision was spotty.[7] Where school prayer was most common, in the East and South, there was less compliance than in the Midwest and West.[8] A similar record of noncompliance followed the Court's 1966 ruling that all police officers were required to inform criminal suspects about their rights (the Miranda warnings) before interrogating them.[9] Nearly ten years later, however, some officers were still interrogating suspects without informing them of their rights or were reading them their rights in tones that implied that they were meaningless.[10]

To overcome official noncompliance requires someone willing to assume the costs of challenging official actions that do not conform to established policy. These costs can be high, in personal as well as economic terms. Imagine the costs to an entire family of challenging a school district's popular silent prayer observance. Or the costs to a person who challenges a chemical plant that employs hundreds of local residents but is polluting the groundwater with toxic chemicals. In addition, complying with the letter of the law sometimes falls far short of the spirit of a particular Court decision. Consider, for example, a police officer who reads a suspect the Miranda warnings in such a way that the suspect knows that invoking these rights will prompt official displeasure and probably some retribution for making the officer's life more difficult. At times even compliance fails to yield the results anticipated by policy makers. Desegregation plans, for instance, merely encouraged white flight and helped create entire school districts segregated along racial lines.

We tend to view instances of noncompliance with Court decisions as signs that something is wrong in the system. But noncompliance can also be viewed as a defining characteristic of the U.S. political system. The court system participates in the political process by deciding cases that sometimes establish broad new policies. At that point, these policies reenter the arena of public affairs; other institutions and groups, and society at large then react to these policies—sometimes through noncompliance—setting the process in motion once again.

Major Periods in Supreme Court History

The Supreme Court's participation in U.S. politics has taken different forms over the last 200 years. During its first 130 years, the Court focused primarily on questions involving the distribution of power within and among governments. The Constitution left unanswered important questions about which powers belonged to each branch of the federal government, as well as which powers the federal government could exercise and which were reserved to the states. John Marshall was the first chief justice to lead the Court to consider the great political questions of the day. Let us now consider (1) the Court's rulings on intergovernmental and intragovernmental distribution of power; (2) concern for individudal rights; (3) the impact of the Warren Court; and (4) the post-Warren era.

Focus on the Distribution of Power

Under Chief Justice Marshall (whose term ran from 1801 to 1835), the Court established the prin-

Perhaps the most important of all Chief Justices, John Marshall, who helped shape the significant power and enduring presence of the Supreme Court as an ultimate arbiter in the American constitutional system. *(UPI/Bettmann Newsphotos)*

ciple of judicial review of both state and federal laws and activities. During this era the Court also advocated a flexible interpretation of the Constitution to serve changing needs, and determined that the national government has implied powers to achieve the ends established in the Constitution. (See the discussion of the *Marbury* and *McCulloch* cases earlier in this chapter.)

Marshall's successor, Chief Justice Roger B. Taney—pronounced "Tawny"—whose term extended from 1836 to 1864, took a greater interest in states' rights than Marshall had. The doctrine of dual federalism, developed during this period, reaffirmed the position of states as sovereign units within the federal system. The most disastrous decision (both for the nation and for the Court) made under Taney was ***Dred Scott* v. *Sanford*.**[11] In this 1857 case involving slavery, a badly split Supreme Court declared the Missouri Compromise, which prohibited slavery in certain territories, unconstitutional on the ground that Congress was thereby depriving citizens of their property (slaves) with-

The Taney Court's attempt to resolve slavery issues after a half-century of executive and legislative failure was folly; its nine separate opinions on *Dred Scott* smashed the Court's legitimacy in the North.
(The Bettmann Archive)

out due process of law. Heavily weighted toward Southern interests and extremely racist in its assumptions, *Dred Scott* threw the Court's legitimacy into question in the North and propelled the nation toward civil war. The Fourteenth Amendment, adopted in 1866, formally overturned the *Dred Scott* decision.

From the end of the Civil War through the close of the nineteenth century, the Court gradually regained power, bolstered by its close identification with conservative business interests that dominated this period. As the century waned, the Court struck down many state and federal laws designed to aid workers, farmers, and others who had been hurt by rapid industrial development and the evolution of the modern corporation. Narrowly interpreting the Fourteenth Amendment, the Court rendered it useless in extending rights to the newly freed blacks. In addition, the Court supported Jim Crow laws (those favoring discrimination and segregation) through decisions like *Plessy* v. *Ferguson* (1896),[12] establishing the "separate but equal" doctrine that was not overturned

until 1954. The Court's conservative, laissez-faire, pro-business stance lasted (with some significant deviations) into the mid-1930s. Then, prompted by the near-crisis brought on by the Court's overturning significant New Deal legislation, the High Court altered its approach, as we saw at the beginning of this chapter.

Concern for Individual Rights

In the three decades following 1937, the Court moved to guarantee civil rights and civil liberties for all. This was largely achieved by extending the protections of the Fourteenth Amendment to encompass the specific protections of the Bill of Rights (see Chapter 4). There were exceptions to this trend, however: The Court upheld the internment of Japanese-Americans during World War II; and under Chief Justice Fred M. Vinson, who served from 1946 to 1953, the Court upheld prosecutions of American Communist Party members.

The Warren Court (1953–1969)

The Warren Court established the most controversial record in modern Supreme Court history. Under Chief Justice Earl Warren, the Court decided issues that struck deep into areas of strongly held beliefs about American life. School desegregation, legislative reapportionment, school prayer, pornography, and the rights of the accused—all these issues were tackled head on by the Warren Court. The Court's rulings frequently sparked vehement public opposition, particularly in the cases of school desegregation, school prayer, and the rights of the accused.

The Warren Court did not upset precedents in every area: It upheld Sunday closing laws, for example, and refused to expand First Amendment protections to those who burned their draft cards. Overall, however, the Court left a legacy of liberalism that often ran counter to majority sentiment.

The far-reaching decisions of the Warren Court reopened the controversy about the role of the Supreme Court, but from a different direction. Whereas the Court had been attacked in the 1930s for its conservatism, the Warren Court was criticized for its excessive liberalism—for making

Chief Justice Earl Warren donning his robe and chatting with Associate Justice William O. Douglas. Warren, a Republican appointed by Eisenhower, surprised observers by leading one of the most liberal and controversial Courts in U.S. history. *(UPI/Bettmann Newsphotos)*

rather than interpreting law. Conservatives called for a return to "strict construction" (literal interpretation) of the Constitution. Supporters of the Court, meanwhile, claimed that the Court's willingness to stretch the Constitution (through "loose construction") made that document useful in the modern era.

The Post-Warren Era

In the last twenty years, without strong leadership and with shifting majorities, the Court—under Chief Justice Warren Burger and most recently under Chief Justice William Rehnquist—has empha-

sized a case-by-case consideration of issues rather than a distinct set of judicial principles. The intense activism of the Warren years has clearly subsided. Liberals criticize the Court for backpedaling on civil liberties and civil rights issues. And yet even its critics acknowledge that the Court has made some highly controversial decisions of a strongly liberal stamp. (**Table 14–2** shows the degree of confidence the Court has enjoyed compared with other branches of the government.) Most notably, during Chief Justice Burger's tenure, the Court established liberalized standards for abortion in 1973,[13] a decision that continues to spark intense controversy. The Court also found against the government in the "Pentagon papers" case (1971), permitting those photocopied government documents to be published by *The New York Times* despite government claims that publication would jeopardize national security.[14] President Richard Nixon's effort to prevent release of his White House tapes was also thwarted by the Burger Court,[15] an action that sealed Nixon's downfall (see Chapter 12).

Nevertheless, the post-Warren courts have shown a considerably conservative bent. The Burger Court, for example, limited school busing as a remedy for segregation[16] and held that the state of Texas did not deny its citizens equal protection of the laws by allowing considerable disparities in the financing of local school districts.[17] In the Texas case, the Court majority held that only if students experienced an "absolute deprivation" would their constitutional rights be violated. In criminal justice matters, the Court majority sharply limited the rights of suspects in the streets, in interrogation rooms, in police lineups, and in

---

TABLE 14–2

Confidence in Supreme Court Compared with Other Branches of Government (Percent)

	1973	*1980*	*1987*
Supreme Court	32	25	37
Executive branch	29	12	19
Congress	24	9	16

SOURCE: NORC General Social Surveys.

the courts. The justices also allowed far greater intrusions on individual rights to privacy, allowing banks to pass checkbook records on to the government and telephone companies to keep track of numbers dialed—without the consent of the bank depositor or dialer. The Rehnquist Court further restricted the right to privacy by ruling in 1988 that law enforcement officers could search a person's trash without a warrant. The Court also restricted the rights of the press and permitted more police intrusions into newsrooms. Most striking, in the area of criminal law the Court made the first exceptions to the exclusionary rule in decades. Under the exclusionary rule, first fashioned in 1914 and greatly expanded by the Warren Court, the authorities were forbidden to use illegally obtained evidence in court. The rule was designed to circumscribe police actions: According to the theory, if police knew they could not use illegally obtained evidence to convict, they would be motivated to obey legal strictures and obtain proper search warrants. In two cases, however, the Burger Court decided that evidence *could* be used in court, even when the warrants obtained were faulty in one respect or another.[18] The Court majority argued that the crucial point was whether police had acted in "good faith" in trying to stay within the requirements of the law. Purely technical issues involving warrants, the Court argued, were not sufficiently important to keep significant evidence out of court. In contrast to many of the Burger Court's conservative decisions, however, were rulings upholding women's rights in a case involving discrimination by the Minnesota Jaycees (an all-male organization) and declaring unconstitutional a federal law barring editorials on public radio and television stations that receive federal funds.[19]

Although we cannot know how history will treat the tenure of William Rehnquist as chief justice, it is clear that in Rehnquist's first years in the center seat, the Court has maintained its recent pattern of case-by-case decisions that cannot be characterized in sweeping generalizations. Regarding the free exercise of religion, for instance, the Court in 1987 ruled in favor of a right to unemployment benefits for a recently converted Seventh Day Adventist who refused to work on the sabbath defined by her new religion (Saturday). But in another case, the Court ruled that prison

Chief Justice Warren Burger's highly readable, generally conservative opinions failed to satisfy those wanting to wipe out the liberal decisions of the Warren Court. *(Yoichi R. Okamoto/Photo Researchers)*

inmates are not entitled to attend religious exercises at a specific time and place if prison security may be jeopardized thereby. However, the Court did overrule an ordinance banning all "First Amendment activities" in the Los Angeles Airport terminal because it violated the right to the free exercise of religion.

In the area of free press, Chief Justice Rehnquist himself wrote the Court's opinion in *Hustler* v. *Falwell* (1987), stressing "the fundamental importance of the free flow of ideas and opinions on matters of public interest." The Court struck down a trial jury's award of $200,000 in damages to television evangelist Jerry Falwell for the emotional distress he suffered after *Hustler* magazine published a risqué cartoon depicting Falwell as drunk and immoral. Yet in another case the Court ruled that school officials could censor a high school newspaper's articles on pregnancy and divorce "so long as their actions are reasonably related to legitimate pedagogical concerns."

The most striking evidence of the Court's divided pattern of decisions can be found in two

Chief Justice William Rehnquist's first two years in the Court's center seat continued the pattern of mixed, case-by-case decision making that has been dominant since Earl Warren's retirement in 1969. The weight of conservative appointments by Reagan—if supplemented by moderate-to-conservative appointments by Bush—seems certain to nudge the Court to the right. *(Abe Frajndlich/ Sygma)*

cases handed down while the Court was not at full strength, awaiting the ultimate arrival of Justice Anthony Kennedy following Justice Lewis Powell's retirement. In these two cases the Court split 4–4, upholding the lower-court decision by default. The first of these cases dealt with a provision of the Cold War era McCarran-Walter Act, under which the government could refuse entry to the United States to an alien who would "engage in activities which would be prejudicial to the public interest." The second case involved a constitutional challenge to an Illinois law that prohibited a doctor from performing an abortion on a minor without first notifying both her parents and then waiting twenty-four hours. In each case the lower court had reached a "liberal" decision—against the exclusion and the notification law. But with the High Court so evenly divided, such outcomes are clearly subject to change.

The Supreme Court's post-Warren record offers an odd array of decisions argued from various positions on the political spectrum. Few observers would deny that since 1969 the Court has gradu-

ally moved in a conservative direction, as conservative presidents from Nixon to Reagan have appointed justices with conservative views. But, paradoxically, "nonactivist" conservative justices are reluctant to sweep away offensive precedents wholesale.

The Dilemma of an Expanded Legal System

In recent decades, Americans have turned more and more to the judiciary to solve their problems. The courts have tackled the complexities of school integration, police behavior, environmental pollution, and standards for assistance to the poor. Many observers believe these new and complicated issues have taxed the traditional resources and procedures of the courts.

Judicial responsibility has grown as government has extended the scope of its responsibilities. Yet much of the increase in judicial activity has taken place independent of Congress and the bureauc-

Judge Garrity: Educator or Judicial Imperialist?

In 1982 the city attorney of Quincy, Massachusetts, filed suit against state and local sewage treatment agencies, charging them with illegally polluting Boston harbor. Judge Paul Garrity of the Massachusetts Superior Court, before whom the case was brought, appointed Professor Charles M. Haar of Harvard Law School, to investigate the problem. One month later, Haar and his technical advisers reported that because treatment plants in the harbor area were drastically inadequate, 12 billion gallons of raw sewage were flowing into the harbor each year.

The report startled many people, since Boston harbor was still commonly used for swimming and other recreational activities. Massachusetts Governor Michael Dukakis proposed that the state legislature create a new state water and sewage authority with powers to deal with the situation, but this proposal stalled in the state house of representatives.

Late in 1984, Judge Garrity, seeing that no political action was forthcoming, issued an order prohibiting almost all new tie-ins to the metropolitan sewer system—a move that threatened to stop all construction in the area. A higher judge set aside the order, but Garrity proceeded with a suit brought against the primary state agency involved. Pressure from public opinion, as well as from business and banking interests, finally pushed the legislature to act, and the new water and sewer authority was approved in December 1984.

Here a judge acted on the best information available to protect the interests of a poorly organized and unfocused majority. Did this constitute judicial imperialism, as some in the legislature charged? Or was the judge acting properly as an educator and a goad to the legislature?

SOURCE: Anthony Lewis, "Why Judges Act," *The New York Times,* Dec. 20, 1984, p. 29.

racy—or even in opposition to their policies. In many cases, the courts have seized the initiative, usurping, according to critics, some of the functions of legislatures.[20] In Alabama, for example, various federal court decisions forced the state to raise annual spending for mental institutions from $14 million to $58 million.

Such actions by the courts encourage lawsuits that seek solutions to widespread problems rather than simply redress of specific grievances. The particular person bringing the suit becomes less important, as the general problem presented grows in significance. Some consider this new tendency distasteful, arguing that too many federal judges believe they have a mandate to act when political institutions fail to. How did this happen?

More than any other factor, the school desegregation decisions propelled the expansion of judicial powers. The massive amount of litigation on that issue turned the courts into a force for social change. Once considered conservative institutions, the courts were now taking the lead when other institutions, supposedly better designed to grapple with change, were reluctant to act. This happened because federal judges, with life-tenure positions, are protected from waves of popular sentiment. Yet the judicial system's insulation from public opinion has both advantages and drawbacks. On the one hand, judges do not have to account for their actions; this is an obviously undemocratic feature of U.S. politics. On the other hand, only judges can defend the liberties of groups that a majority would rather ignore. And on occasion, courts may be better informed and show a clearer comprehension of complex issues than legislatures or other organs of government.[21]

In recent years, political conservatives have sought to limit the powers of the courts. One way to overrule a court decision is to amend the Constitution, but in practice this involves a lengthy, cumbersome, and highly uncertain process. More recently conservatives have attempted to limit the jurisdiction of the Court through congressional legislation, thereby curbing the Court's powers. (Article III of the Constitution gives Congress the power to create lower federal courts and gives the Supreme Court jurisdiction over state and federal appeals "with such exceptions, and under such regulations as the Congress shall make.") Conservatives have also called for popular election of judges and the abolition of life tenure. This conservative attack on the courts has ironic undertones, however, since the courts have traditionally been considered the most conservative of the three branches of government.

Along with growth in the powers and activism of the courts has come an epic expansion of the legal profession. The United States has three times as many lawyers per capita as Great Britain, and twenty times as many as Japan. Laws are multiplying even faster. Each year, legislative bodies at all levels pass hundreds of thousands of new laws, each of which calls for issuing new regulations. At the same time, the legal system remains far from "just." For example, the federal Legal Services Corporation (LSC), which handled 1 million cases a year in the 1970s, met less than 15 percent of the needs for legal services among the poor. LSC had to severely curtail its operations under the Reagan administration, which would have abolished the agency altogether were it not for congressional resistance. The current availability of legal services for poor people remains very low. Middle-class people are also being priced out of the legal market by increasing fees.[22]

Some expansion of law is inevitable in a complex society in which economic competition and exploitation are common and individuals seek to protect their rights. As social customs, habits, and traditions break down in a more fragmented and mobile society, law replaces other means of social control. As long ago as the mid-nineteenth century, however, observers like Alexis de Tocqueville were commenting on the tendency of Americans to take all their controversies to court.

How do we deal with our litigious tendencies? Several remedies have been suggested. One is deregulation: If we could eliminate cumbersome gov-

ernment regulations and replace them with greater competition, it is argued, the number of lawsuits could be sharply diminished. However, deregulation can create its own problems, as we saw in Chapter 13.

Another possible remedy is a move toward dejudicialization—keeping issues out of the courts. There are good reasons for doing so. For example, litigants often face a five-year wait to have a case heard in a federal courtroom, and defendants who cannot afford bail may have to wait up to six months in jail before their cases are dealt with. Despite passage of the Speedy Trial Act of 1975, which requires a trial within 125 days after arrest on most charges, delays still pose the most serious problem for the courts. The speedy trial provisions have also been criticized for not allowing the government sufficient time to prepare a case.

Clogged court calendars could also be eased considerably through passage of no-fault legislation, according to some analysts. No-fault automobile insurance, for example, has cut motor vehicle damage suits by as much as 87 percent in some states. The no-fault concept has also been applied to divorce cases in a number of states.

The concept of dejudicialization could be expanded to include the development of neighborhood justice centers, which would resolve disputes through arbitration and mediation. Such centers, which handle family arguments, minor assaults, and disputes between landlords and tenants, bosses and workers, consumers and stores, already exist in some cities and counties. A Justice Department experiment in Kansas City demonstrated that hearings at such centers commonly take only two hours, and only two weeks elapse before final hearings are held. Eighty-six percent of all cases heard were successfully resolved, with the remainder going into the court system. California has voted to make arbitration mandatory in all civil cases involving less than $15,000.

Some initiatives must come from Congress as well. For example, the Sherman Antitrust Act, which dates back to the last decade of the nineteenth century, is exceedingly difficult to enforce: It takes an average of eight years before a judgment is reached in an antitrust case. Some cases go on indefinitely. Major corporations are difficult to attack in the courts: Exxon, for example, has more lawyers on retainer than the entire Department of Justice has on staff. Only clarification of the Sherman Act by Congress could place less of the burden of proof on the government and thereby make it easier to pursue antitrust violations.

Conclusions

Over the past fifty years, the federal courts on the whole have served important democratic purposes in extending equality, strengthening the protection of rights and liberties, and ruling on issues that other branches of government could not or would not resolve. Lacking a legislative consensus, how could reapportionment, school desegregation, and rights of the accused have been settled in any national fashion? Yet the courts, in addressing these issues, entered that "political thicket" that many legal experts warn against. As a result, the courts have thrust themselves into the center of intense controversy in recent decades.

Policy making by the courts obviously poses problems. In intruding into this area, courts may actively thwart majority rule, or weaken legislation designed to protect basic rights. After the Civil War, for example, an interventionist Court undercut the substance of the Fourteenth Amendment and prevented black Americans from achieving legal equality for decades. The same antidemocratic trend characterized the Court's later conservative rulings to thwart unions, delay child labor legislation, and to strike down key elements of the New Deal program.

Ideally, the courts can exercise power on behalf of those who have little or no political clout. All citizens—whether they are blacks seeking school desegregation, mental patients whose rights need protection, or unionized workers trying to gain recognition—should be able to turn to the courts when the other components of the political process ignore their interests. Often in recent decades such individuals found an advocate in the courts. From the standpoint of democratic politics, this represents an important development.

However, much depends on the political philosophies of the judges, their concern for democratic life, and their willingness to risk controversy. Given the power of courts in our political process, we are perhaps more dependent than we should be on the instincts and opinions of the people who wear the judicial robes.

GLOSSARY TERMS

Brown v. *The Board of Education of Topeka*
prosecutor
defendant
plaintiff
grand juries
petit juries
opinions
Federal District Courts
U.S. Courts of Appeals
Circuit Courts
U.S. Supreme Court
rule of four
due process
judicial review
Marbury v. *Madison*
Dred Scott v. *Sanford*
Plessy v. *Ferguson*

NOTES

[1] Although we are dealing here with the appointment of federal judges, many of the points made are relevant to the appointment or election of state and municipal judges.

[2] See Howard Ball, *Courts and Politics: The Federal Judiciary System* (Englewood Cliffs, N.J.: Prentice-Hall, 1980); and R. K. Burke, *The Path to the Court* (Ann Arbor, Mich.: University Microfilms, 1959).

[3] 1 Cranach 137 (1803).

[4] 4 Wheaton 316 (1819).

[5] Quoted in Carll Everett Ladd, *The Ladd Report #7* (New York: Norton, 1988), p. 27.

[6] Walter Murphy, *Congress and the Court* (Chicago: University of Chicago Press, 1962).

[7] *Abdington School District* v. *Schempp*, 374 U.S. 203.

[8]Frank Sorauf, *The Wall of Separation* (Princeton, N.J.: Princeton University Press, 1976).

[9]*Miranda* v. *Arizona*, 384 U.S. 436 (1966).

[10]M. Wald *et al.*, "Interrogations in New Haven: The Impact of Miranda," *Yale Law Journal,* July 1967.

[11]19 Howard 393 (1857).

[12]163 U.S. 537.

[13]*Roe* v. *Wade,* 410 U.S. 113 (1973).

[14]*New York Times Company* v. *United States,* 403 U.S. 713 (1971).

[15]*United States* v. *Nixon,* 418 U.S. 683 (1974).

[16]*School Board of the City of Richmond* v. *State Board of Education,* 412 U.S. 92 (1973).

[17]*San Antonio Independent School District* v. *Rodriguez,* 411 U.S. 1 (1973).

[18]*United States* v. *Leon,* 82-1771 (1984); *Massachusetts* v. *Sheppard,* 82-963 (1984).

[19]*Roberts* v. *V. S. Jaycees,* 83-724; *FCC* v. *League of Women Voters of California.*

[20]The issues are spelled out comprehensively in Donald Horowitz, *The Courts and Social Policy* (Washington, D.C.: Brookings Institution, 1977). See also Nathan Glazer, "Should Judges Administer Social Services?" *The Public Interest,* Winter 1978. For a fuller discussion, see James Duffy, *Domestic Affairs* (New York: Simon & Schuster, 1978).

[21]Stephen L. Wasby, "Arrogation of Power or Accountability: 'Judicial Imperialism' Revisited," paper delivered before the American Political Science Association, New York City, Sept. 1981.

[22]These matters are debated in Lawrence Tribe, "Too Much Law, Too Little Justice," *Atlantic Monthly,* July 1979.

SELECTED READINGS

For general treatments of **courts and the federal judiciary,** see Alexander Bickel, *The Least Dangerous Branch* (Indianapolis: Bobbs-Merrill, 1962); Henry R. Glick, *Courts, Politics and Justice,* 2nd ed. (New York: McGraw-Hill, 1988); Marvin Comisky *et al., The Judiciary: Selection, Compensation, Ethics, & Discipline* (Westport, Conn.: Greenwood, 1987); Peter G. Fish, *The Politics of Federal Judicial Administration* (Princeton: Princeton University Press, 1973); and Sheldon Goldman and Thomas P. Jahnige, *The Federal Courts as a Political System,* 3rd ed. (New York: Harper & Row, 1985).

For analyses comparing **courts in different countries,** see Martin Shapiro, *Courts: A Comparative and Political Analysis* (Chicago: University of Chicago Press, 1986); Jerold L. Waldman and Kenneth M. Holland, *The Political Role of Law Courts in Modern Democracies* (New York: St. Martin's, 1987); Henry J. Abraham, *The Judicial Process: An Introductory Analysis of Courts in the United States, England, and France,* 5th ed. (New York: Oxford, 1986); and Theodore L. Becker, *Comparative Judicial Politics: The Political Functioning of Courts* (New York: University Press of America, 1987).

Richard Posner, whose name came up several times during the Reagan administration as a potential Supreme Court nominee, writes about the proper role of courts in a democracy in *The Federal Courts: Crisis and Reform* (Cambridge, Mass.: Harvard University Press, 1985). Jerome Frank provides the classic explanation of "legal realism" (which acknowledges that judges *do* make law, within limits) in *Courts on Trial: Myth and Reality in American Justice* (Princeton: Princeton University Press, 1949). Robert Woodward (of Watergate fame) and Scott Armstrong provide a gossipy look behind the scenes of the Supreme Court in *The Brethren* (New York: Simon & Schuster, 1979).

Case studies are an engaging—and particularly appropriate way—to learn about the working of the judiciary. See Richard Kluger, *Simple Justice* (New York: Random House, 1977); and Anthony Lewis, *Gideon's Trumpet* (New York: Random House, 1964). For examinations of current issues surrounding the courts, see Michael Meltsner, *Cruel and Unusual* (New York: Morrow, 1974); Frank Sorauf, *The Wall of Separation* (Princeton: Princeton University Press, 1976). For a look at an example of complex legal theory, see David M. Speak, *Living Law: The Transformation of American Jurisprudence in the Early Twentieth Century* (New York: Garland, 1987).

PART **IV**

PUBLIC POLICY

15 CREATING PUBLIC POLICY

16 MANAGEMENT OF THE ECONOMY

17 THE WELFARE STATE

18 CIVIL LIBERTIES, CIVIL AND
SOCIAL RIGHTS

19 FOREIGN AND DEFENSE POLICY

20 ENERGY AND ENVIRONMENT

CREATING PUBLIC POLICY
Power and Agendas

Dennis Brack/Black Star

CHAPTER OUTLINE
How Issues Reach the Political Agenda
Processing Issues
Policy Formulation and Implementation
Policy Evaluation
Who Rules and Why It Matters

he U.S. government is a powerful force in contemporary society. The government envisioned by most of the Founders—a minimum state protecting rights and performing a limited number of functions—is a thing of the past. While many Americans may still believe that "the government is best which governs least," we are unlikely to see such a government again. And in reality, most Americans expect government to carry out a whole series of tasks, ranging from national defense to education, from regulating the economy to providing for the public welfare. This necessarily means that government will play a highly significant role in our national life.

Today, governments rule over populations that reach into the tens of millions in societies that are enormously complex. Modern governing involves so many highly technical functions that the range of government powers and the complexity of many bureaucratic functions are often difficult to grasp. Over the past two decades, for example, the U.S. government has expended considerable resources to fight a covert war in Central America, educate handicapped children, provide Social Security to tens of millions, issue pamphlets on how to grow alfalfa, design and operate a space shuttle, oversee vast national forests, make rules about the disposal of nuclear wastes, send registrars to protect black voters in the South, mount a massive research effort against AIDS, and spy on alleged domestic dissidents.

In exercising such powers, the government must set public policy priorities, and these priorities are, or should be, the focus of intense public debate. Should government focus on defense or on domestic needs? On the unemployed or on investors in the stock market? On cleaning up pollution or on boosting economic growth? Of course, such alternatives are overly simplistic. Usually policy making involves a compromise among contending priorities—yet even compromises carry priorities of their own.

In studying the complexities of modern government, we often lose sight of the human element. We tend to think of Social Security, for example, in terms of a faceless class of tens of millions of recipients, rather than the particular individuals and families involved. This is one of the hazards of discussing vast institutions: We can easily forget that behind the calculations, policy questions, and arguments, we are really dealing with the lives of individual human beings.

In Part IV we will focus on specific policy areas: economic management, the welfare state, civil and social rights and liberties, foreign and defense policies, and energy and the environment. We will delineate some of the most significant government policies and explore major controversies surrounding them. We will also attempt to judge their success or failure.

Before jumping directly into the arena of public policy, however, we must examine several key areas relating to the study of policy: (1) how issues arise; (2) how issues are "handled" or "processed"; (3) how policy is formulated and implemented; (4) how policy is evaluated; and (5) who rules, and how that affects our democratic processes.

How Issues Reach the Political Agenda

Many political scientists assert that the best guide to what government will do next year is what government does this year. In this view, the work of government most often proceeds by tiny steps, or *increments*.[1] This process builds conservatism into policy making: Budgets go up or down slightly, policies are carried out with greater or lesser vigor—all within a well-established and -understood political framework.

Looking back over the development of the U.S. government's policy-making agenda, we can see that government functions arise to meet social needs and to cope with the requirements of coordination, order, stability, and growth. This growth often occurs piecemeal, step by step, over time.

Sometimes government acquires new functions because of **spillover effects** in economic and social life. A spillover is a side effect, unintended and not included in the calculations of the original decision maker. In the absence of government environmental regulation, for instance, a manufacturer will calculate whether to build another factory by assessing the costs and benefits to the manufacturer without taking into account the very real costs (spillovers) the factory may impose on the

Any study of the policy process must start by recognizing the limits of human foresight and control. Major events—natural, economic, or social—may drastically shift the government's agenda. During the economic chaos of the Great Depression in the early 1930s, the argument for innovative federal action was compelling, given the magnitude of human suffering and the inability of smaller governmental units to respond to it. *(Brown Brothers)*

people and creatures living near it, such as rising health risks, or a reduced quality of life. As another example, when water is polluted by industrial waste and people who drink it get sick, there is usually a call for government intervention. Occasionally, spillovers are caused by the government itself. The building of the interstate highway system in the United States stimulated the growth of suburbs and led to the decline of central cities after World War II. The decline of the cities, in turn, prompted further government action to deal with the new problems of urban areas.

History also reveals several drastic shifts in the government agenda, however. The Great Depression, which created massive unemployment and severe economic dislocations, gave rise to one such shift, in the form of the New Deal. And as we have already noted (see the text's Introduction), new groups occasionally break into the arena of policy making and put their needs on the public agenda. For years, women and blacks struggled for the right to participate in setting the political agenda.

Yet **incremental politics**—policy making in steps, or increments—describes much of the day-to-day business of government. But we must supplement our understanding with a longer view,

taking into account the crises that develop in political life, the emergence of new groups with new demands and needs, and the rise and fall of issues on the policy agenda. Sometimes a serious social problem lies dormant for years without being "officially" recognized. Poverty, for example, had little place on the public agenda in the 1950s, then was rediscovered at the beginning of the 1960s by a new administration. By contrast, prohibiting the sale of alcoholic beverages was *dropped* from the national policy agenda when the Eighteenth Amendment was repealed in 1933. Up to that point, Prohibition had been high on the agenda of national issues for several decades. Sometimes forces outside the political process impose a new issue on the public agenda, as did the AIDS epidemic in the late 1980s, and the significant droughts in the Southeast, a part of the country not familiar with battles over water rights.

How an issue is defined and its priority in relation to other issues stand at the core of political conflict. The candidate who effectively defines the issues in a campaign usually controls that campaign. Thus, liberals and conservatives battle over whether the "real" issue is inflation or unemployment, or whether too much government spending

TABLE 15–1
Percent Who Think Government Should Deal with Problems

Problem area	United States	Great Britain	West Germany
Fighting pollution	56	69	73
Fighting crime	53	56	78
Providing good medical care	42	74	63
Providing good education	47	68	55
Looking after old people	41	58	51
Guaranteeing jobs	34	55	60
Providing adequate housing	25	60	39
Equal rights for minorities	33	24	20
Reducing income inequality	13	25	29
Equal rights for sexes	24	19	27
Number surveyed	(1,719)	(1,483)	(2,307)

SOURCE: Political Action Study.

or too little neglects the needy. To cite another example, consider American competitiveness on world markets. Is this an issue of technology, requiring more investment in research and development? Or is it a matter of unfair trade practices, requiring hard bargaining and perhaps protectionist legislation? Or does it center on the financial markets, which fluctuate based on the size of the American budget deficit? This issue was fought out in the 1988 presidential nominating campaigns. The final definition of the problem will clearly have an impact on the solutions policy makers pursue.

One of the most controversial public issues focuses on government itself and the types of functions it can legitimately take on. For example, some Americans maintain that government can legitimately set limits to fees that doctors or hospitals charge; others believe that violates appropriate limits for government action. In another policy sphere, some believe that school officials, state legislatures, or Congress can legitimately prescribe that prayers be said in public schools. Others contend, however, that prayer in public schools violates constitutional principles and represents wrongful interference by government in the realm of individual conscience. These controversies center not on how government should respond to the issues involved, but on whether government can legitimately act at all. For some Americans, government itself—its size, complexity, and power—

constitutes one of the major public policy issues. (**Table 15–1** gives a comparative perspective of the attitudes of the citizens of three countries concerning problems governments should deal with.)

Processing Issues

Whose agenda becomes *the* agenda of politics? And how are issues dealt with once they become part of the national agenda? We now consider how our political system (1) handles competing agendas and (2) deals with issues.

Competing Agendas

We have been spotlighting the larger agenda of political life—the rough ordering of pressing political problems at a particular time. But there are also specific agendas held by, among others, interest groups, professional politicians, and the bureaucracy. Conflicts among these various agendas flare up both in and out of government, as each struggles to have its own agenda prevail.

The issues that make up these competing agendas take shape in the measures Congress acts on, the proposals made by the president, the activities of the federal bureaucracy, and the principal matters before the courts. Sometimes an issue in one political arena is picked up elsewhere: Abortion,

A bombed abortion clinic—re-minder of the complexity of some policy issues. Since politicians in a democracy often seek compro-mise to satisfy a broad segment of the public, most politicians would rather avoid issues with no ready position in the middle and with passionate opposing blocs. But when competing claims are mutually inconsistent and antago-nistic, government may be forced to provide resolution. *(© Susan Meiselas/Magnum)*

for example, a matter that Congress refused to ad-dress, was finally acted on by the courts. Official agendas also may differ or conflict. Conflicts often generate new issues that must be dealt with. Fre-quently, battles within the executive branch have clear and important effects on the shape of public policy. For example, competition among the army, air force, and navy for shares of the defense budget often results in a higher budget overall and may encourage the development of unnecessary weapons systems.

Dealing with Issues

Once an issue emerges, how is it resolved? Two significant factors come into play here: *who* par-ticipates in dealing with an issue and how much the *scope* of the issue is enlarged, making new pol-icy options available.[2] New groups may seize on an issue that offers an opportunity to make suc-cessful demands for change. For example, the civil rights movement sparked the growth of ethnic consciousness, prompting new groups, such as Hispanics, women, and white ethnics, to make similar demands for attention and equality. The scope of an issue widens as the range of consid-erations being dealt with expands. In addressing

the welfare issue, for example, policy makers might focus narrowly on one problem of the poor, such as adequate housing. Enlarging the scope of this issue might spur decision makers to examine a whole range of related matters—health, employ-ment, even the distribution of wealth. The broader the scope, the wider the range of solutions policy makers consider—and the more complex the issue.

Many issues reach the public agenda without ever being substantially resolved. Some issues are resolved only at a *symbolic* level. A symbolic action aims at reassurance—giving the public the impres-sion that the issue is being handled or resolved.[3] Consider the health warnings on cigarette pack-ages: For years the federal government's action to counter the hazards of smoking did not go much beyond this symbolic act; in fact, tobacco farmers continue to enjoy generous government subsidies. Local governments, less subject to direct pressure from the tobacco industry and more responsive to the pressures of the antismoking lobby, were the first to enact significant smoking restrictions. Only recently has the balance at the federal level been moving away from the tobacco interests and in fa-vor of more than symbolic government action.

Symbolic moves are extremely common in for-eign policy. For years, the U.S. government called officially for the "liberation" of Eastern Europe from the Soviet Union, but never contemplated pressing the issue very far.

Symbolic actions can have real consequences, however. Frequently, symbolic policy making generates public quiescence—people feel reassured and cease to agitate. Commissions established to investigate social problems, such as crime, pornography, or racism, are sometimes designed to buy off activists or at least to buy time for political actors. The recommendations of these commissions, although attended by much publicity, are frequently ignored. In some cases this symbolic demonstration of concern satisfies certain political groups. In other cases, people take the symbols seriously and expect further action to follow.

Issues can also be dealt with by being displaced, deferred, or diverted,[4] rather than being completely resolved. **Displaced issues** are those that flare up and then fade from public view, to be replaced by other issues or fragments of the original issue. The energy crisis of 1973–1974, for example, quickly shot to the top of the public agenda, only to fade within a few years. **Deferred issues,** by contrast, generally return in one form or another. For many years, the civil rights issue was deferred by politicians who sought to avoid deep and potentially violent conflicts.

Diverted issues, finally, are handled by calling for a reevaluation of the problems involved. Sometimes the public focus is shifted from the issue itself to a debate over various government-initiated solutions; this has happened in the area of health policy. At other times, the issue becomes whether government ought to be involved in a particular area at all: Should there be federal action to deal with abortion, pornography, or ghetto unemployment? Also, particular policies spawned by the original issue may replace that issue as the focus of debate. In the policy debate over school desegregation, for instance, the pros and cons of busing took center stage rather than the drive for desegregation itself.

Policy Formulation and Implementation

When policy makers conceptualize problems and discuss alternative positions, ideological factors enter political debate. One group's "solution" constitutes a mere gesture to another. Let us now examine how policy makers (1) develop proposals for action and (2) implement those proposals.

Proposals for Action

As we have already seen, proposals for public policy come from many sources. Interest groups concerned with an issue commonly approach their allies in Congress or the administration with specific proposals. Government bureaucracies in the executive branch may also advance policy proposals; in fact, it is part of their job to do so. Privately financed research institutes, or "think tanks," can also originate new policy ideas. Such institutes can be liberal, conservative, or even radical in orientation. When the Reagan administration took office in 1981, for example, the Heritage Foundation, a conservative think tank, issued a series of policy recommendations to guide the new administration. Individual legislators and legislative committees or groups develop new policy proposals or refine the proposals offered by others. The courts also play a powerful role in the process of policy formulation. Only through court decisions were standards established for school desegregation, legislative reapportionment, and criminal justice procedures, for example. Another—and perhaps the most influential—source of policy proposals is the president, who has increasingly become the focus of government leadership.

The formulation of policy alternatives, however, may or may not lead to new policies. Many items have been on the public agenda for years, even decades, without being resolved; they are "nibbled at" rather than dealt with in any thoroughgoing manner. The chaotic state of health policy in the United States exemplifies this political stalemate or nonresolution. Most often, issues remain unresolved when interest groups marshal enough power to thwart any bold action, or when confusion or conflict stand in the way of decisive policy making. The alternatives may be there, but none can be chosen. Instead, incrementalism continues.[5]

In formulating policy, decision makers must balance what needs to be done with what can real-

To implement policy often requires large amounts of technical information, some of it quite speculative. For example, what will our radioactive-waste dumps look like in 25,000 years? Another difficulty for policymakers these days is the NIMBY phenomenon—more and more citizens are flatly saying, "Not in *My* Backyard!" In our system of separated power and federal decentralization, coherent policy—in this case covering the whole cycle of decisions to create, use, and dispose of toxic materials—may be difficult or impossible to achieve.
(Michael O'Brien/Archive Pictures)

istically be accomplished. To enact any wide-ranging piece of legislation, diverse elements must find it acceptable. Here the law of *anticipated reactions* applies.[6] After assessing the expected reactions, policy formulators shape proposals to fit with what is considered possible. This idea of politics as the "art of the possible" is considered a basic, realistic approach to political life. Yet sometimes it is all too easy to argue that nothing is possible at a particular time in a particular branch of the government. The real "art" in the "art of the possible" lies in sensing how far current arrangements can be modified by determined action. This can be a hard judgment to make—often, only a crisis or large-scale mass action makes possible what was previously beyond the realm of possibility.

Implementation

The subtle process of policy implementation is often overlooked. Most citizens assume that once a bill is passed and a policy adopted, the political battles are over and the problems are solved. But implementation presents difficulties of its own. For example, new policies are often phrased in very vague terms.[7] Just what do phrases like "the public interest or convenience," or "maximum feasible participation," or "fairness" mean? When a policy is implemented, specifics must be attached to such vague terms.

Implementation also requires information. Very often, policy makers simply don't know enough about the conditions in which policies will be carried out. One of the difficulties confronting the Occupational Safety and Health Administration (OSHA), for example, is the huge number of potentially dangerous substances found in workplaces. The difficulty is compounded by the need to establish a *level* of exposure to a particular substance above which health risks are unacceptable. One attempt by OSHA to set a standard for exposure to benzene was overturned by the Supreme Court in 1980. And governments often look foolish when attempting to carry out ill-conceived policies. When the Kennedy administration tried to overthrow the Cuban government of Fidel Castro by launching the Bay of Pigs invasion in 1961, the result was what one observer called "a perfect fiasco."[8] In this case, intelligence estimates were drastically wrong. Inaccurate information can lead to disaster not only in the foreign policy arena, but also in education, housing, welfare, and many other public policy sectors. Oftentimes, government cannot accurately anticipate the effects of its own actions.

Bear in mind as well that political activity continues during the implementation process. Interest groups actively lobby throughout this stage, trying to shape the decisions of the bureaucrats who implement policy. And sometimes administrative agencies resist new policies. It took a federal Circuit Court order in 1987 to force OSHA to establish safety and health rules concerning the availability of drinking water and sanitation facilities for migrant workers. There was never any question about the need for such facilities, and evidence showed that fewer than half the farms in America using eleven or more migrant workers provided drinking water, toilets, and hand-washing facilities for these workers. But pressure from agricultural employers kept the rules from being issued in spite of fourteen years of urging by farmworkers' representatives. When the rule was finally put in place in mid-1987 there was widespread concern that the limited number of planned farm inspections would ensure that the new rule would be widely violated.[9]

Policy Evaluation

In recent years, serious attempts have been made to evaluate the effects of public policies. It is important to know, for example, whether efforts to control water pollution are really having any impact, or whether occupational health and safety measures are achieving the intended results. Evaluation can give policy makers a sense of the successes and failures of policy making, and thereby help in formulating new guidelines. Yet systematic evaluations of public policies are often difficult to make, and frequently they require controversial judgments.

Frequently, policies are carried out haphazardly or, once implemented, grow in an uncontrolled fashion. This further complicates the effort to evaluate them. Even when rigorous methods of assessment are conscientiously applied, values and ideologies can cloud the evaluation. For example, to some observers the Great Society programs of the Johnson administration stand as an obvious and almost predetermined failure, while others regard them as a reasonable success.[10] The facts are not in dispute here, but rather which perspective should be brought to bear in judging them. Objective methods of evaluation are helpful, but they cannot substitute for political judgment, which figures in ethical factors as well.

Much policy evaluation is still completely un-systematic. Such "seat-of-the-pants" judgments, however, often represent the best we can do in the absence of more objective methods.

Who Rules and Why It Matters

One of the central questions of politics (and certainly a crucial one for comprehending policy making) is, Who rules? Which individuals and groups exercise the most power, and why? Obviously, in a democratic system, this is sensitive and important territory. We now examine (1) elitist and pluralist views and (2) the boundaries of policy making.

Elitist and Pluralist Views

Who actually "runs" the United States? Proponents of the elitist point of view argue that a relatively homogeneous group of people—similar in background, life-style, and most of all, political outlook—make the key decisions that shape our political and economic lives.[11] This elite encompasses the top officials in major corporations, key politicians, the upper stratum of the national bureaucracy, and leading military officials. Of course, the argument goes, these people do not agree on everything, nor do they see or talk to each other constantly. Elites, in other words, do not engage in a conspiracy of some sort. But the views and attitudes of this group tend to coincide to a very high degree. According to this school of thought, the American people, as a whole, are largely excluded from effective political decision making. The people can cast their votes, but that is about all they do. The real power rests in the hands of the elites, who have the information needed to address policy questions and who hold the strategic positions in society necessary to carry out their decisions.

The alternative to the elitist view is the more popular pluralist conception of U.S. politics.[12] Adherents of this view argue that no *one* elite group dominates our national life; rather, there are many influential groups, whose degree of influence var-

Who occupies the positions of greatest influence in our system? Whether the pluralists or the elitists seem more persuasive, Americans remain hopeful in part because democratic institutions and processes maintain a certain level of openness. New players and new ideas will improve policy as long as ordinary processes create some open political spaces. (© *Stephen L. Feldman/Photo Researchers*)

IN GOD WE TRUST

ies according to the particular policy area involved. In defense policy, for example, an array of interest groups exercise influence over decision making: major defense contractors, legislators whose districts or states have defense interests, members of the armed forces, and so on. In addition, a few groups hold strong ideological interests in foreign policy and defense decisions, such as Physicians for Social Responsibility, opposing further nuclear buildup, and a group called High Frontier, advocating the development of the Strategic Defense Initiative (Star Wars) program. Turning to health policy, we find a different array of groups competing for influence: associations of health professionals, private insurance agencies, public health groups, and some representatives of health care consumers.

Thus, the pluralists contend, the patterns of interest-group competition vary in different policy areas. According to one version of the pluralist argument, the U.S. political system is characterized not by majority rule, but by *minorities rule*,[13] whereby important groups exert influence in those areas of chief concern to them. In the pluralist view, then, the U.S. political process is basically a highly subdivided arena, each portion of which has different participants and different winners and losers.

Theodore Lowi, a political scientist, coined the term **interest-group liberalism** to describe the pattern of political decision making most commonly

found in recent U.S. politics.[14] In this form of politics, according to Lowi, each participant in every controversy receives something, and thus each has some impact on the decision-making process. As a result, the government rarely says no to any well-organized interest; instead, it gives some reward, some subsidy, some benefit to each interested party. While this pluralistic pattern tends to minimize conflict, such a system avoids any thoroughgoing effort to determine what the public interest is in a policy area.

Who is right—the pluralists or the elitists? Most students of U.S. politics side with the pluralists. Obviously, different groups *do* have power in different areas. Moreover, the patterns of group success and failure do change from time to time. For example, the elderly as a group once exercised little influence in U.S. politics, but they have grown into a significant force that cannot easily be ignored in public policy making.

Yet the elitist position also has merit. Despite the bewildering array of policy arenas and the proliferation of groups with some sort of influence on some aspects of public policy, larger patterns of policy making do tend to take hold over the long term. Examining these long-term patterns, we discover that some groups tend to benefit much more than others, and that certain individuals have disproportionate influence over policy making. In addition, certain issues simply do not make it onto the policy agenda in U.S. politics.

The Boundaries of Policy Making

The boundaries of policy making are clearest in three broad areas. To begin with, there is no real debate over whether the distribution of wealth and economic power in U.S. society is equitable, fair, or democratic. In the United States, a strong consensus holds that the current capitalistic society, which allows for large measures of economic inequality, is a "good" society. As we noted in Chapter 1, the absence of a viable political left in U.S. politics has kept this issue off the political agenda.

A second area in which political consensus sets clear boundaries is foreign policy. For two decades after World War II, many policy options that the United States might have pursued were never even seriously considered. Our anticommunist Cold War policy went virtually unchallenged. With the Vietnam War, however, that foreign policy consensus broke down. For the first time, the range of debate over our future foreign policy began to widen.

The third policy area with rather clear boundaries is represented by the Constitution. The fundamental political structure of the nation has rarely been challenged directly. But as we will see in the following chapters, various aspects of our constitutional form of government have come under fire from time to time.

Conclusions

The elitist/pluralist debate offers us a framework for examining the bewildering arena of policy making. This debate focuses on the larger, long-term patterns of policy making. Is there a "consensus" in some area of policy making? And *if* there is, what sorts of questions are excluded from consideration?[15] In addition, the debate directs us toward a careful look at the participants in various policy areas. Who actually influences policy decisions? How do they exercise their influence? Do some groups find it impossible to be effective?

Often these considerations help us evaluate policy from a democratic perspective. If decisions are made by a few, if large numbers of people are excluded or ignorant, if the public interest plays little

role in decisions, then a democrat has cause for worry.

Democracy does not come easily. In the policy discussions to follow, the reader should consider how well most people grasp the main dimensions of the issues. Are most of us reasonably well informed? Do we *want* to know more? Can we trust that those in authority have a firm grasp on the issues underlying public policy?

It takes more than knowledge, of course, to create a democratic public and to provide an intelligent dialogue in public life. Among policy makers we also hope to find a firm commitment to democratic values, a sense of equality, a good measure of fairness, a willingness to involve the public in policy debate. In reading the policy chapters, ask yourself how "democratic" these debates sound. Are our leaders guided by a clear commitment to a democratic ethic?

GLOSSARY TERMS

- spillover effects
- incremental politics
- displaced issues
- deferred issues
- diverted issues
- interest-group liberalism

NOTES

[1]The term *incrementalism* was popularized by Charles E. Lindblom in *The Intelligence of Democracy* (New York: Free Press, 1965). It has also been widely used in the literature on budgeting.

[2]E. E. Schattschneider, *The Semi-Sovereign People* (New York: Holt, 1975).

[3]Murray Edelman, *Politics as Symbolic Action* (New York: Academic Press, Institute for Research on Poverty Monographs, 1971).

[4]Robert Eyestone, *From Social Issues to Public Policy* (New York: Wiley, 1978).

[5]On the role of leadership in this process, see R. T. Nakamura and Frank Smallwood, *The Politics of Policy Implementation* (New York: St. Martin's, 1980), chap. 4.

[6]See Schattschneider, *op. cit.*, chaps. 2, 3.

7George C. Edwards III, *Implementing Public Policy* (Washington: Congressional Quarterly Press, 1980), chaps. 1, 2.

8Irving L. Janis, *Groupthink* (Boston: Houghton Mifflin, 1982), chap. 2.

9William Glaberson, "Is OSHA Falling Down on the Job?" *New York Times*, Aug. 2, 1987, section 3, p. 1.

10On the negative side, see Peter Steinfels, *The Neoconservatives: The Men Who Are Changing America's Politics* (New York: Simon & Schuster, 1979); on the positive side, see John E. Schwartz, *America's Hidden Success* (New York: Norton, 1983).

11For two perspectives on elitism, see C. Wright Mills, *The Power Elite* (New York: Oxford, 1959); and William Domoff, *Who Rules America Now? A View for the Eighties* (Englewood Cliffs, N.J.: Prentice-Hall, 1983).

12There are many sorts of pluralists. For a look at two very different views, both pluralist, see Robert Dahl, *Who Governs?* (New Haven, Conn.: Yale University Press, 1961); and Grant McConnell, *Private Power and American Democracy* (New York: Random House, 1970).

13The term is from Robert Dahl, *A Preface to Democratic Theory* (Chicago: University of Chicago Press, 1963), chap. 5.

14Theodore S. Lowi, *The End of Liberalism* (New York: Norton, 1979), chap. 3.

15This is one of the views taken by Peter Bachrach and Morton S. Baratz in "Two Faces of Power," *American Political Science Review* 56 (1962).

SELECTED READINGS

BROAD INTRODUCTION

For a good recent introduction to public policy, see Iain McLean, *Public Choice: An Introduction* (New York: Basil Blackwell, 1987); also see Duncan MacRae, Jr., and James A. Wilde, *Policy Analysis for Public Decisions* (North Scituate, Mass.: Duxbury, 1979); M. H. Moore and G. T. Allison, eds., *Public Policy* (Cambridge, Mass.: Harvard University Press, 1979); and Sheldon H. Danziger and Kent E. Portney, eds., *The Distributional Impacts of Public Policies* (New York: St. Martin's, 1988).

Some commentators see policy primarily as the reflection of the **distribution of power.** See, for example, S. N. Eisenstadt, L. Roniger, and A. Seligman, eds., *Center Formation, Protest Movements and Class Structure in Europe and the United States* (New York: New York University Press, 1987), a collection of essays that explain policy generally in terms of the normative beliefs of elites; or see Michael Schwartz, ed., *The Structure of Power in America: The Corporate Elite as a Ruling Class* (New York: Holmes & Meier, 1987). Older, but still worth reading, are Peter Bachrach and M. S. Baratz, *Power and Poverty: Theory and Practice* (New York: Oxford, 1970); and Murray Edelman, *Politics as Symbolic Action: Mass Arousal and Quiescence* (New York: Academic, 1971).

Others treat public policy mostly as a matter of **organizational structure and expertise.** See Bruce E. Seely, *Building the American Highway System: Engineers as Policy Makers* (Philadelphia: Temple University Press, 1987). Jack DeSario and Stuart Langdon, eds., *Citizen Participation in Public Decision Making* (Westport, Conn.: Greenwood, 1987), shows concern that policy has been delegated to technocrats.

Robert A. Dahl's writings have been very influential in this area of scholarship. See *Modern Political Analysis* (Englewood Cliffs, N.J.: Prentice-Hall, 1976); and *Dilemmas of Pluralist Democracy: Autonomy vs. Control* (New Haven, Conn.: Yale University Press, 1982). For a recent defense of Dahl, see Robert J. Waste, *Power and Pluralism in American Cities: Researching the Urban Laboratory* (Westport, Conn.: Greenwood, 1987).

IMPLEMENTATION

The implementation of policy was only belatedly recognized as a **separate subfield** of study. See George C. Edwards III, *Implementing Public Policy* (Washington: Congressional Quarterly Press, 1980); and Robert T. Nakamura and Frank Smallwood, *The Politics of Policy Implementation* (New York: St. Martin's, 1980). Implementation studies are often specific to a particular area of policy, as with these **health policy studies:** Lawrence D. Brown, ed., *Health Policy in Transition: A Decade of Health Politics, Policy, and Law* (Durham, N.C.: Duke University Press, 1987); and Malcolm L. Goggin, *Policy Design and the Politics of Implementation: The Case of Health Care in the American States* (Knoxville: University of Tennessee Press, 1987). Several **specific areas of policy** are examined in Robert D. Holsworth and J. Harry Wray, *American Politics and Everyday Life*, 2nd ed. (New York: Wiley, 1987).

COMPARATIVE PERSPECTIVE

For comparative policy analysis, see S. N. Eisenstadt *et al.*, listed above; or Charles F. Adrian, *Politics and Economic Policy in Western Democracies* (North Scituate, Mass.: Duxbury, 1980); or Meinolf Dierkes, Hans Weiler, and Ariane Berthoin Antal, eds., *Comparative Policy Research: Learning from Experience* (New York: St. Martin's, 1987).

16

MANAGEMENT OF THE ECONOMY

In Whose Interest?

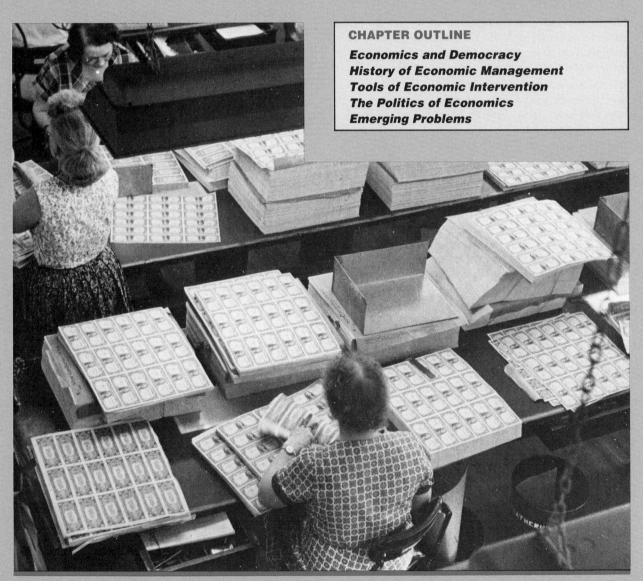

CHAPTER OUTLINE

Economics and Democracy
History of Economic Management
Tools of Economic Intervention
The Politics of Economics
Emerging Problems

Magnum

Economics has often been referred to as "the dismal science."[1] This can actually be taken as a compliment, for most economists like to think of their discipline as a science. The "dismal" part does not please economists, however. One "dismal" aspect of economics is that it deals with scarcity—with alternative ways of allocating resources. It is also filled with numbers and calculations. Economists turn flesh-and-blood human beings and their busy social and commercial lives into dollars and cents, and into abstractions like supply and demand. Economists ascend from the real world of people—sweating and working, haggling in the marketplace—to the airy (but usually arid) realm of inflation and recession, money markets and gold standards.

Economics and Democracy

What does economics have to do with democratic concerns? The answer may well be, *everything*. Economic matters are intricately intertwined with democratic aspirations. Some students of democratic evolution advance the theory that a certain level of economic development is a prerequisite for the establishment and maintenance of a modern democratic society.[2] Historically, they argue, poor and economically primitive societies tend to be authoritarian, intolerant, and politically stagnant. Democratic politics usually evolves only when affluence increases, education is made available to the masses, urbanization helps widen people's horizons, communications improve, and greater sophistication fosters tolerance and a spirit of compromise.

From another perspective, however, economic crises can sometimes precipitate the decline and destruction of democracies. Consider how the catastrophic economic conditions of the 1920s and 1930s helped promote fascist movements in many nations. A drastic economic decline in Germany, for example, set the stage for the Nazis' political successes in the 1930s.

History and theory aside, how do economic matters mesh with issues of democratic life in our society today? We must recognize that all public policy making has economic dimensions. Through the economy, citizens gain rewards and suffer deprivations. Many of the welfare state programs (explored in Chapter 17), for example, were developed in response to specific economic needs. Our civil liberties and civil and social rights (Chapter 18) had economic roots in racism, based on slavery, a form of absolute economic exploitation. In considering foreign and defense policies (Chapter 19), we examine how the U.S. economy interacts with the world economy and other national economies. And in balancing energy and environmental issues (Chapter 20), we run head on into key economic questions that will determine our nation's response to coming crises of energy supply and environmental hazards. In a sense, then, all of Part IV, Public Policy, deals with the economy. But in this chapter we focus specifically on the mechanisms of economic management and the ramifications of economic policy for American democracy by spotlighting (1) how the U.S. economy has been and is being managed; (2) the tools of economic intervention; (3) the politics of economics; and (4) emerging problems in the U.S. political economy.

History of Economic Management

By taking a historical perspective, we can gain important insights into how the U.S. government currently manages the economy. In the course of U.S. history, the government has adopted three major approaches to economic policy: **mercantilism,** which stressed direct government intervention in the economy; **laissez-faire capitalism,** in which government gave business a relatively free hand; and today's **controlled capitalism,** in which government intervenes to some extent to regulate the economy. By no means, then, is government management of the economy a twentieth-century phenomenon; in the broadest sense, management of the economy is as old as the nation itself.[3] Let us now examine four stages in the history of U.S. economic management: (1) mercantilism; (2) laissez-faire and the growth of regulation; (3) controlled capitalism; and (4) our recent past.

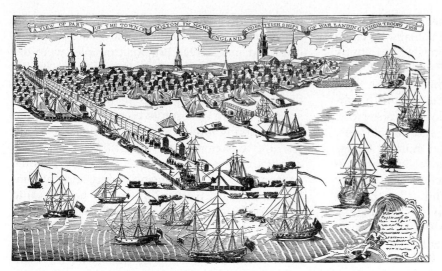

Government control of the economy is at least as old as this print of Boston Harbor. Indeed, mercantilism, a system of economic control through government-chartered corporations, was largely responsible for creating the North American colonies. The British warships depicted here were part of the investment required to keep the outlying economic activities from becoming independent profit centers. *(The Bettmann Archive)*

Mercantilism

The economic theory of mercantilism evolved in seventeenth-century Europe. In practice, mercantilism worked this way: The rulers of nation-states such as England and Holland established government-chartered corporations and encouraged their growth through subsidies, or financial support. The corporations were protected from competition through grants of monopoly status, and their output, production, and distribution were extensively controlled. Colonies were formed overseas to provide raw materials for these government-chartered corporations and markets for exports. In exchange for these privileges, the semipublic corporations gave the government a share of their profits. Mercantilism benefited both government and business, but profits often were made at the expense of the general public, in nation and colony alike.

The American colonies rebelled against the taxation policies and regulations imposed by the British government. In developing their own political economy, however, Americans eventually adopted many of the same mercantilist policies that aided business growth at the expense of farmers, artisans, and laborers.[4] The U.S. government imposed high taxes on imported goods (protective tariffs), gave subsidies to business, and granted monopoly powers to a national bank. Although the Founders disagreed over how extensive government control of economic affairs should be, a general consensus held that the protection and promotion of propertied interests was one of the vital functions of government.

Laissez Faire and the Growth of Regulation

By the mid-nineteenth century, laissez-faire capitalism had replaced mercantilism as the favored economic policy of Western governments. Underlying laissez-faire capitalism was a belief that national wealth would be increased if government restrictions on economic activity were kept to a minimum. In theory, this policy called for the abolition of such mercantilist strategies as government-backed corporate monopolies, detailed regulatory laws, and high protective tariffs. In practice, the laissez-faire movement "democratized" capitalism by throwing open to all comers those sectors of the economy previously restricted to the government-chartered corporations. The new, privately held corporations that emerged under the laissez-faire doctrine wanted to be free of competition from government enterprises and from the detailed regulations imposed on the previously chartered companies. President Andrew Jackson (1829–1837) endorsed the movement and gave it a substantial boost with his successful fight to close down the government-chartered National Bank.

Ironically, however, as the laissez-faire period progressed, competition declined and monopolies returned. The more successful corporations expanded, either buying out their competitors or driving them out of business. In essence, then, the public monopolies of the 1820s were replaced by the private monopolies of the 1880s. This development sparked vehement public protest, particularly from farmers and small business owners, and led to the passage of regulatory legislation. In the 1880s, many states, bowing to the demands of Western farmers and Eastern merchants, imposed restrictions on the rates charged by railroads. Regulatory legislation on the federal level, however, came more slowly because of doubts about its constitutionality. The first federal regulatory commission, the Interstate Commerce Commission, was established in 1887. In 1890, Congress passed the Sherman Antitrust Act, which was designed to prevent monopolies and trusts (the pooling of resources by several companies for the purpose of controlling a market). Only in a few cases, however, was the act vigorously enforced.[5]

Controlled Capitalism

U.S. economic policy changed course again around the turn of the century, as policy makers embraced controlled capitalism, an econmic doctrine that is still evolving today. Rather than dismantling large corporations or allowing them to operate unfettered, the government now creates regulatory agencies (see Chapter 13) to oversee and control their activities. Under controlled capitalism, public interests are protected by these regulatory agencies from blatant abuses by business and corporate interests, while private capital is guaranteed a more stable business environment in which to make profits. In addition, the federal government assumes many of the regulatory activities formerly handled by the states. Federal regulatory agencies multiplied first during the Progressive Era (1900–1917) and again during the New Deal of the 1930s, as the nation tried to cope with the Great Depression. (A depression is a severe economic crisis marked by a downward spiral in which investment, hiring, paychecks, consumption, and savings all plummet at once, leading one

another into further declines. A recession is a milder, shorter version of the same tendency.) The Great Depression, an economic catastrophe, marked a turning point in economic management. As such, it is worth examining in greater detail.

There was no single cause for the Great Depression, which swept over all industrialized nations and lasted for close to a decade. Its onset usually is linked to the collapse of the U.S. stock market in October 1929. But the crash only brought into sharp relief how severely skewed economic life had become. The 1920s saw a vast expansion of credit buying in the United States, plus extensive land and stock speculation. Consumers and investors shared a supreme confidence that the high-rolling days of "the Roaring '20s" would never end. Speculators' "get-rich-quick" schemes and consumers' over-reliance on credit combined with several larger trends to seriously undermine the economy. As the decade progressed, the production of goods increased more rapidly than the incomes required to buy those goods. The distribution of income in the United States also grew increasingly unequal during the 1920s: In 1929, the richest 1 percent of the population received as much income as the poorest 42 percent. These striking economic imbalances propelled the nation into a depression.

Much of American economic life at that time operated on the faith that large profits would continue into the indefinite future. But demand could not keep up with supply. As incomes grew more unequal, demand for goods began to dry up, despite installment buying. The economy then became more and more dependent on a high level of luxury spending and investment by the rich. Any loss of confidence among the wealthy in the continued expansion of the economy could lead to a catastrophic decline in investment and purchases. This is just what happened when the stock market crashed in October 1929. The crash shattered the confidence that had fueled the expansion of the 1920s. After the crash, both consumption and investment spiraled downward in a vicious cycle of declining confidence, and declining investment and income, sending the nation and its leaders reeling.

Never before had the United States experienced an economic crisis of such scope and proportions.

Consternation on Wall street: Black Monday, October 29, 1929. The stock market collapse marked the onset of the Great Depression but was merely one factor among a variety of economic imbalances that had developed during the 1920s, including industrial over-production and marginalized investment. The recent stock market crash, on October 19, 1987, also created consternation, but it was not part of a general economic collapse, partly because of federal regulation of investment. *(UPI/Bettmann Newsphotos)*

Gross investment fell 35 percent from 1929 to 1930, and 35 percent more from 1930 to 1931. In the next year, it fell by 88 percent. From 1929 to 1933, gross national product (the value of all goods and services produced in the nation) dropped by 29 percent, construction declined by 78 percent, and unemployment rose from 3.2 percent to 24.9 percent.[6]

Before the Depression, most Americans rejected the idea that government could or should have a hand in shaping the nation's economic life. The New Deal remedies proposed by President Franklin Roosevelt's administration in the 1930s, however, involved large-scale government intervention in the economy. By reducing taxes, starting new programs, and creating new jobs, Roosevelt and his advisors hoped to infuse new life into the economy. The concept of regulating the business cycle by deficit spending—that is, by allowing the government to spend more money than it takes in—was championed by British economist John Maynard Keynes, whose views on economic policy had an enormous impact after 1930. This philosophy of economics, accordingly, is referred to as **Keynesian economics.**

Although it was once thought that there was no way for government to help end a depression, in-creased government spending in the late 1930s and during World War II did draw the nation out of economic stagnation and bring about a return to high employment levels.

The New Deal experience marked a genuine watershed in U.S. history. Although some observers argued for a reduction in government involvement in and regulation of the economy after World War II, few talked of turning back the clock to the pre–New Deal situation.

The Recent Past

After pulling through the rigors of the Depression and World War II, the United States and the Western European nations entered a new phase of economic development. During the 1950s and much of the 1960s, industrial democracies achieved unprecedented levels of affluence. Economic growth was rapid, but prices remained stable. The capitalist system, previously viewed as predestined to great cycles of boom and bust, was now propelling steady, sustained economic growth. And while the capitalist economies were driven by powerful forces, the system itself was still responsive to government intervention.[7]

The Great Depression, City and Country

Ben Isaacs

Owner of a small business

I was in business for myself, selling clothing on credit, house to house. . . .

All of a sudden, in the afternoon, October, 1929 . . . I was going on my business and I heard the newspaper boys calling, running all around the streets and giving news and news: stock market crashed, stock market crashed. It came out just like lightning. . . .

We lost everything. It was the time I would collect four, five hundred dollars a week. After that, I couldn't collect fifteen, ten dollars a week. I was going around trying to collect enough money to keep my family going. It was impossible. Very few people could pay you. Maybe a dollar if they would feel sorry for you or what.

We tried to struggle along living day by day. Then I couldn't pay the rent. I had a little car, but I couldn't pay no license for it. I left it parked against the court. I sold it for $15 in order to buy some food for the family. I had three little children. . . .

I didn't want to go on relief. Believe me, when I was forced to go to the office of the relief, the tears were running out of my eyes. I couldn't bear myself to take money from anybody for nothing. If it wasn't for those kids—I tell you the truth—many a time it came to my mind to go commit suicide. Than go ask for relief. But somebody has to take care of those kids. . . .

Oscar Heline

A farmer from Iowa

The farmers became desperate. It got so a neighbor wouldn't buy from a neighbor, because the farmer didn't get any of it. It went to the creditors. And it wasn't enough to satisfy them. . . . First, they'd take your farm, then they took your livestock, then your farm machinery. Even your household goods. And they'd move you off.

The farmers were almost united. We had penny auction sales. Some neighbor would bid a penny and give it back to the owner.

Grain was being burned. It was cheaper than coal. Corn was being burned. A county just east of here, they burned corn in their courthouse all winter. '32. '33. You couldn't hardly buy groceries for corn. It couldn't pay the transportation. In South Dakota, the county elevator listed corn as minus three cents. *Minus* three cents a bushel. If you wanted to sell 'em a bushel of corn, you had to bring in three cents. They couldn't afford to handle it. . . .

We had lots of trouble on the highway. People were determined to withhold produce from the market—livestock, cream, butter, eggs, what not. If they would dump the produce, they would force the market to a higher level. The farmers would man the highways, and cream cans were emptied in ditches and eggs dumped out. They burned the trestle bridge, so the trains wouldn't be able to haul grain. Conservatives don't like this kind of rebel attitude and aren't very sympathetic. But something had to be done. . . .

Some of the farmers with teams of horses, sometimes in trucks, tried to get through. He was trying to feed his family, trying to trade a few dozen eggs and a few pounds of cream for some groceries to feed his babies. He was desperate, too. One group tried to sell so they could live and the other group tried to keep you from selling so they could live. . . .

Through a federal program we got a farm loan. A committee of twenty-five of us drafted the first farm legislation of this kind thirty-five years ago. . . . New money was put in the farmers' hands. The Federal Government changed the whole marketing program. . . . People could now see daylight and hope. It was a whole transformation of attitude. You can just imagine. . . . (He weeps.). . . .

SOURCE: Studs Terkel, *Hard Times: An Oral History of the Great Depression* (New York: Pantheon, 1970).

British economist John Maynard Keynes advocated government intervention to smooth out the peaks and valleys of the business cycle. His prescriptions of deficit spending to stimulate the economy and excess taxation to slow it down could not cure the stagflation of the 1970s. *(UPI/Bettmann Newsphotos)*

The so-called age of affluence began to unravel in the late 1960s. Economic fluctuations became more unpredictable and growth more erratic. Throughout the 1970s both unemployment and inflation increased, a combination of economic ills that, according to accepted understanding, would not occur simultaneously. (Inflation occurs when "too much money chases too few goods," driving the price of goods up and, thus, the value of money down.) In fact, each of these conditions (inflation and unemployment) had been seen— and sometimes actively sought—as a solution to the other, since high unemployment decreases consumer demand (fewer paychecks to buy things with). When both appeared in tandem, elected policy makers could not use the traditional remedies to eliminate either one. To decrease unemployment by pumping more money into the economy (by increasing government spending and decreasing taxes) would worsen already high inflation (and further boost interest rates). To decrease inflation by tightening up on money would drive even more people into unemployment. Nei-

ther strategy was politically feasible. By the end of the 1970s, the combination of a stagnant economy and high inflation ("stagflation") presented what many considered an insurmountable problem.

The economic policies of the 1980s constituted an odd array of dramatic and in some ways contradictory initiatives. The Federal Reserve Board's aggressive attempt to reduce the money supply was designed to reduce high levels of inflation. Meanwhile, a dramatic tax reduction, engineered by the Reagan administration, was intended to stimulate business expansion by putting more money back into the hands of consumers and investors. However, the tax reduction was not matched by a reduction in overall government spending, so the federal government had to borrow heavily, competing with the private sector for scarce investment dollars. Early in the 1980s, the United States experienced a sharp economic downturn, followed by a broad and long-term expansion. In October 1987 the stock market crashed, wiping out $500 billion in investments in a single day and shaking the confidence of investors who had expected the economic expansion to continue unabated. As the Reagan presidency ended, inflation was down significantly from the late 1970s. Unemployment, after climbing sharply in the 1982–1983 downturn, was back to about the level Reagan had inherited from Carter. Federal spending as a proportion of the Gross National Product stood almost exactly where it had been at the end of the Carter presidency. Stagflation had disappeared, but new difficulties of equal complexity arose, as we will see later in this chapter.

The United States, along with the Western European democracies, remains a capitalist nation characterized by private control of most of the economy. Yet in every industrial democracy the government now assumes much responsibility for the overall management of economic life. The reasons for this are numerous. For one thing, the public sector has grown so significantly that government itself has become one of the major forces in economic life. In most countries, government is the chief purchaser of goods and services, the largest distributor of income (through income maintenance programs and the jobs it provides), and the largest single borrower of money. Considering these factors, governments can hardly avoid tak-

These stock traders witnessed—
and participated in—the evapora-
tion of *$500 billion* on a single
day, October 19, 1987. On the anniversary of this event in 1988
much was made of the fact that
the crash had not been the first
step toward chaos. Even today,
expressions of relief are more
common than explanations.
(AP/Wide World Photos)

ing a leading role in economic management. Then, too, modern economic theory, as well as political practice, promotes increased government involvement in the economy. The Great Depression convinced many economists and politicians that capitalist economies could not function successfully without government intervention. According to key policy makers, governments could help stimulate employment and growth, and keep prices stable. Finally, governments have become inextricably enmeshed in a set of financial relationships with the private economy—guaranteeing the safety of bank deposits, supporting home loans and payments to farmers, giving tax incentives to certain industries, and bolstering various segments of the economy.

For all these reasons, it would be virtually impossible for any democratic government to detach itself from economic affairs without disastrous consequences. So the real issues today are not whether government should intervene in the economy but rather how government can intervene most effectively, what interventions are most important, and who should gain and lose by this intervention.

Tools of Economic Intervention

In the area of economic management, there is widespread agreement that democratic governments should pursue full employment, stable prices, and steady levels of economic growth. But what is the best means of achieving these economic goals? Here political observers have sharp differences of opinion. Should government spend more or reduce taxes? Expand the money supply or contract it? Worry more about inflation or about recession? About rising prices or rising unemployment? In addressing these difficult and complex questions, democratic governments can draw on several tools of economic management. These fall into the general categories of (1) fiscal policy and (2) monetary policy, which we now examine.

Fiscal Policy

When government decision makers adopt **fiscal policies** they deliberately manipulate elements of the national budget to change the direction of the economy. Since government at all levels accounts for the expenditure of roughly 35 percent of the GNP in the United States, and the federal government alone accounts for more than 20 percent, budgetary manipulations by the government clearly have major economic impacts. Government can alter the budget in two ways: through spending policies and tax policies.

When government spends, it pumps money into, and thereby stimulates, the economy. According to Keynesian economics, there are times when government should *deliberately* spend more than it takes in. This produces a budget deficit in the short run, but by stimulating economic growth this so-called deficit spending eventually yields increased tax revenues, thereby eliminating the deficit. In addition, the theory goes, government spending creates employment opportunities and alleviates a good deal of human suffering. Government, then, can counteract the worst effects of the business cycle by running a deficit when the economy is sluggish and taking in a surplus when the economy is booming. This approach is known as a countercyclical policy.

A deficit can be created through either tax cuts or spending increases. By contrast, surpluses can be created through either tax increases or spending reductions. In practice, however, tinkering with the economy is never so simple. Political considerations play an important part in economic decisions. For example, governments usually avoid raising taxes or cutting back on programs that have substantial political support. Largely as a result, the federal budget has run a surplus in only two of the last twenty-five years. Let us now probe the subtleties of (1) spending policies and (2) the tax system.

SPENDING POLICIES The dictates of fiscal policy demand hard choices. Most basically, governments must set budget priorities. If spending is increased, will that mean more funds for national defense, more for highway construction, more for Social Security, or more for urban revitalization? Oftentimes, all pressing priorities simply cannot be addressed at once. In the late 1960s, President Lyndon Johnson attempted to increase spending on the Vietnam War as well as on domestic programs. In doing so, he overstimulated the economy and paved the way for many of the economic problems of the 1970s. President Ronald Reagan sought to curtail federal expenditures, yet he simultaneously increased spending for defense. These policy decisions forced deep cuts in social programs. Yet fiscal policy does not dictate *where* to expand the budget or to contract it. Such decisions reflect the larger priorities of the administration in office.

In addition, fiscal policy makers must work within substantial constraints. Up to two-thirds of the national budget is fixed by past commitments, such as those to Social Security and pensions, in-

terest on the national debt, and contractual obligations. Because the discretionary portion of the budget is relatively small, then, cutting the budget is a difficult business. In fact, the three largest sources of growth in the federal budget in future years are all fixed costs: interest on the national debt, Social Security, and Medicare.

THE TAX SYSTEM Policy makers also face many difficult decisions in formulating taxation policies. Which taxes should be raised or lowered—the individual income tax, corporate taxes, excise taxes (taxes on commodities)? If taxes are cut, who should receive the chief benefits? If they are raised, how should the burden be spread?

Americans have always been sensitive about taxes. Taxes imposed by the British were resented by American colonists because they had no voice in how much they were taxed, or in how tax revenues were spent. The first American government, under the Articles of Confederation, had no power to tax at all. In the Constitution, Congress was granted the power to "collect taxes, duties, imposts and excises to pay debts and provide for the common defense and general welfare." For over a century, the federal government relied almost exclusively on customs and excise taxes to raise money. An income tax was levied for the first time, briefly, to pay for the Civil War. A second attempt to impose an income tax in 1894 was declared unconstitutional by the Supreme Court. The Sixteenth Amendment, ratified in 1913, established the clear basis for a federal income tax, but during World War I, only about 5.5 million people paid any income tax at all. Tax revenues actually declined in the 1920s and 1930s, and in 1939 only 4 million people—about 4 percent of the population over age fourteen—paid federal income tax. By 1945, 43 million Americans were paying income tax. At the same time, corporate taxes increased and the modern system of withholding income taxes from wages and salaries was established.

During and after World War II, as the federal income tax system grew in size and complexity, it began to reflect another side of tax policy. Taxes can be used for more than simply raising revenue: A tax code can be used to regulate behavior—to

Taxes come in great variety and affect the members of society differently. In general, states depend heavily on sales taxes, as in this supermarket. But a sales tax on necessities is hardest on people with low incomes, since they spend a greater proportion of their income on necessities—and thus on the *taxes* on necessities. (© *Susan Woog Wagner/Photo Researchers*)

encourage certain kinds of activities and discourage others. Through loopholes and "tax incentives," a tax code sometimes masks real government policy by allowing benefits and transfers of wealth indirectly and unobtrusively. What makes the tax system so complex, and genuine tax reform so difficult, is the large number of specific, diverse, and often conflicting interests that are embedded in the structure itself. Tax breaks, of course, do not necessarily thwart the public interest—many allowances built into the federal tax code serve legitimate public interests. Others do not. The Tax Reform Act of 1986 was originally billed as a means of eliminating from the tax code many special treatments and loopholes. In a process that one political scientist compared to cleaning encrusted barnacles off an old ship's hull, many special-interest tax breaks were removed from the tax code. But barnacles grow back. In the two years following the passage of the Tax Reform Act, more than 840 bills were introduced into either the House or the Senate to modify the act, nearly all of which involved reinstating tax breaks of one sort or another.[8]

Today, Americans pay a host of different taxes, including sales tax, property tax, state and federal income taxes, and Social Security tax. Some of these taxes are considered *progressive*—that is, the rate of taxation is related to one's ability to pay. The federal income tax is theoretically a progressive tax, in which progressively higher rates are levied on those with progressively higher incomes. Actual taxes paid, however, are far less progressive than the rates on paper. This stems from specific tax breaks built into the system. Other taxes are *regressive* in effect: They impose a higher-percentage tax on those with lower incomes. A sales tax on food is a regressive tax, because lower-income people are likely to spend a higher percentage of their income on food than are higher-income people. A *proportional* tax draws the same percentage of income from all income groups. In some ways the Social Security tax is a proportional levy; however, because it does not tax income beyond a certain point, wealthier taxpayers actually pay a lower percentage than do poorer ones.

Despite frequent complaints about taxation in the United States, our overall tax rates are considerably lower than those in many other countries. Among the industrial democracies, only Switzerland, Australia, and Japan have lower rates of taxation. As **Table 16–1** shows, most federal tax revenue comes from the individual income tax, followed by payroll taxes (primarily Social Secu-

TABLE 16–1
Source of Federal Tax Revenues,
Selected Fiscal Years

	Percent of total		
Federal tax	*1954**	*1969**	*1988†*
Individual income tax	44	45	43
Corporation income tax	30	20	13
Payroll taxes	11	23	36
Excise taxes	13	8	4
Other	2	4	4

*Secretary of the Treasury, *Annual Report* (Washington, D.C.: U.S. Government Printing Office, 1980), p. 11.
†*Budget of the United States Government,* Fiscal Year 1988 (Washington, D.C.: U.S. Government Printing Office, 1987), pp. 6c–34, 35.

rity). The proportion of tax revenue from corporate income tax is much lower today than it was in 1954.

Monetary Policy

Another major tool of economic management is monetary policy, the regulation of the supply of money in the economy. If the demand for money by borrowers and consumers exceeds the existing supply of money, then interest rates on borrowed money go up. As a result, people take out fewer loans and investment declines. In short, a tight money supply could drastically limit the growth of the economy. Until 1971, all paper money in the United States was redeemable in gold. This "gold standard" put significant limits on how quickly the money supply could expand, since it depended on how much gold was mined or brought in from abroad. In response to the economic problems of the early 1970s, President Richard Nixon removed the United States from the gold standard.

The U.S. money supply is controlled by an independent regulatory agency, the **Federal Reserve System** (the Fed)—in essence, the central bank of the United States. The president appoints the members of the Fed Board but has no direct control over them. The Federal Reserve Board oversees 12 regional Federal Reserve banks and approximately

5,500 member banks in the various states. All nationally chartered banks must belong to the Federal Reserve System, and many state banks voluntarily join. The member banks are required to keep a certain percentage of assets in one of the reserve banks. In addition, member banks may borrow money from the reserve banks to finance lending activities.

The Federal Reserve Board can manipulate the economy in several ways. It can control the amount of money circulating in the economy by raising or lowering the percentage of money that each member bank must keep in reserve rather than loan out or invest. More frequently, the Fed manipulates the economy by raising or lowering the interest rate charged to member banks (the prime rate); member banks, in turn, pass on this charge to customers. Generally, as interest rates drop, the amount of money businesses and individuals borrow increases, and the economy expands. To cool down an overheated economy, the Fed can boost the interest rate, thereby discouraging borrowing and slowing economic growth.

There has been considerable debate over whether the government should rely primarily on fiscal policy or monetary policy in regulating the business cycle. Proponents of monetary policy argue that it is more direct in application, quicker to take effect, and, if handled properly, more effective in stabilizing the economy. As long as presidents cannot directly control monetary policy, however, our chief executives will continue to prefer the fiscal tools.

Many observers decry the Fed's lack of accountability to the larger public through the democratic process. If the Fed is accountable to anyone, it is to the banking community. Yet political factors sometimes influence the Fed's decisions as well. In the past, the Fed has made sudden shifts linked to the political preferences of its directors, and timed to promote the political prospects of a particular administration. As an example, the money supply was expanded to help Richard Nixon avoid a more serious recession before the 1972 presidential election. At times, the Fed has also acted under the assumption that full employment is inflationary—an attitude that some economists label as callous because of the human costs involved in unemployment.

The Federal Reserve Board, by changing banks' reserve requirements and interest rates, can have a major impact on the nation's economy. How should the Federal Reserve advance democratic interests? The Framers of the Constitution expressed their conviction that economic matters could not be entirely responsive to majority opinion. *(Dennis Brack/Black Star)*

Defenders of the current Federal Reserve System contend that bringing it under direct presidential control would signal the intrusion of politics into economic policy making. However, critics of the Fed argue that such a move would give presidents greater freedom of action when economic crises loom.

The Politics of Economics

Unlike a pure science, economics draws practitioners from every point on the political spectrum. There are liberal economists, conservative economists, radical economists, and many shades in between. When people argue economics—when they speculate about why the economy is doing well or badly, or when they argue about exactly what "well" or "badly" means—they are not just talking science or mechanics. Inevitably, they are deeply enmeshed in political debate.

In the real world, economic ideas interact with political realities. Economic theory can be perverted, misused, or skillfully manipulated. Economic ideas can be employed as a form of rhetoric to obscure real problems or twisted to advance political ends. Economic considerations can also be ignored, with either good or bad results. Such in-

teractions between economic theories and the real world of U.S. politics are exemplified in the three cases presented in this section: (1) fiscal policy in the 1960s; (2) Paul Volcker, the Fed, and monetarism; and (3) Reagan and supply-side economics.[9]

Fiscal Policy in the 1960s

One example of an economic policy that succeeded was the tax cut of 1963. But that policy was shaped as much by politics as by economics. The economists who came to Washington with President John Kennedy in 1961 were, without exception, Keynesians: They believed strongly in government intervention to strengthen the economy, and they were convinced that the economy needed to be bolstered through fiscal policy. Administration insiders favored increased spending on social programs to address the problem of poverty, in particular, while stimulating the overall economy. But Congress resisted higher spending, so Kennedy gradually adopted a more politically practical approach—a tax cut.

In his famous 1962 Yale University commencement address, which focused on economic myths, Kennedy attacked the near-sacred concept of a balanced budget and advanced the Keynesian argument that judiciously formulated tax cuts could lead to increased government revenues in the long run. In proposing this course of action, Kennedy was contradicting what his chief economic adviser Walter Heller called America's "Puritan ethic" in the economic sphere: "Balance the budget, stay out of debt, live within your means." Kennedy maintained that a government budget should not be compared with a family budget, in which income should equal expenses. Instead, he argued, the government was more like a major corporation that must borrow for future expansion. As it grows, it pays off the debt, and at all times its total indebtedness is dwarfed by its economic potential.

After Kennedy was assassinated in 1963, President Lyndon Johnson quickly obtained a tax cut from Congress, totaling $14 billion for individuals and corporations. The tax-cutting strategy worked just as the Keynesians had said it would. Economic growth spurted, the gross national product increased, unemployment dipped, and federal revenues rose. In 1965, unemployment hit a post-Depression low of 4 percent.

Johnson also persuaded Congress to increase spending on social programs and spending for the war in Vietnam. But then when the economy began to overheat, he was left with no politically attractive alternatives. At that point, the only way to bring the economy under control, according to Johnson's economic advisors, was either by imposing a tax increase or by cutting government spending. Johnson refused to sanction reductions in spending on either the Vietnam War or his Great Society programs, and he sought to avoid a debate on a tax increase altogether. As a result, within another year, wage and price increases spiraled upward in tandem, and inflation skyrocketed. Johnson finally proposed a tax increase in 1967, but Congress did not pass it until a year later. By then, inflationary pressures had become solidly entrenched.

Paul Volcker, the Fed, and Monetarism

In the summer of 1979, with the economy stagnating, inflation rising, and the country suffering a crisis of confidence, President Jimmy Carter appointed Paul Volcker chairman of the Federal Reserve Board. Volcker, an imposing six-foot-seven-inch cigar smoker, was described as brilliant, strong-willed, and conservative. Volcker was also a monetarist, persuaded that inflation was the most serious threat confronting the economy and that it could be controlled through restrictions on the growth of the money supply. By reducing the supply of money, demand for goods would fall, reducing inflationary pressure, in Volcker's view.

Paul Volcker, Chairman of the Federal Reserve Board from 1979 to 1987, viewed inflation as the chief threat to the economy, and he restricted the money supply to counteract President Reagan's tax cut. Monetary policy (interest rates and money supply) and fiscal policy (taxing and spending) are controlled by different parts of the government, and they sometimes are used in opposing ways. *(UPI/Bettmann Newsphotos)*

The focus of attention would be on M1—the principal aggregate measure of money, including cash and checking accounts. An initial attempt to squeeze M1 during 1980 resulted in a brief recession followed by a short, inadequate recovery that left the country no better off than it had been twelve months earlier. Interest rates, driven up by inflation and by the Fed's restrictive monetary policies, reached painfully high, double-digit levels. The poor state of the economy made for a potent issue in the 1980 presidential election—candidate Ronald Reagan's most successful question was a rhetorical one posed to average voters: "Are you better off now than you were four years ago?" Volcker called the Fed's initial attempt at monetarism "a false start," but was undeterred in his strategy. Reagan's campaign promises of substantial tax reductions merely reinforced Volcker's determination to use monetarist policies to slay the dragon of inflation. Indeed, in the face of such reductions, the Fed would have to squeeze the money supply that much harder to wring inflation out of the economy. This would entail a good deal of economic hardship in the short run. Everyone who needed credit (to run a business or buy a house or a car) would feel the pinch of higher interest rates. Many workers would be laid off and unable to find work. The costs of recession are not all written on ledger sheets: Medical research shows that recessions are accompanied by measurably higher rates of suicide, cardiovascular disease, and cirrhosis of the liver.

With the exception of a slight easing of the money supply in the weeks following Ronald Reagan's inauguration in January 1981, Volcker led the Fed in a sustained campaign to limit the money supply from the time he was appointed until late in 1982. By then the country was in the midst of a severe recession—by some indicators, the worst since the Great Depression. The costs of this economic contraction were not borne equally, however. One study concluded that of the $570 billion loss in output in 1981–1982, 58 percent was absorbed by wage earners, 25 percent by declining corporate profits, and 13 percent by farmers and small businesses.[10] The costs were enormous, but inflation rates subsided to very low levels. The dragon was slain.

Because members of the Federal Reserve Board

are not elected, they are well positioned to make politically unpopular decisions. But deciding when painful tactics are necessary is not a straightforward or simple task. Some observers—and at least one member of the Fed itself—claimed that the Volcker restrictions were too severe and held the economy back longer than necessary. Volcker supporters point to the unresponsively high inflation rates during the 1970s and the low inflation rates through most of the 1980s as proof that the Volcker medicine, though painful, was the right policy. But the actions of the Fed do not take place in a vacuum, so it is difficult to assign all the credit *or* all the blame to that body.

Reagan and Supply-Side Economics

Ronald Reagan became president at a time marked by high rates of inflation and high unemployment. The Keynesian model offered no politically acceptable solutions to this combination of ills. Further, Reagan was committed to three particular policies that did not, in themselves, promise much hope for recovery within a traditional understanding of economic forces. First, Reagan was determined to reduce the size of the federal government's domestic activities, meaning reductions in both expenditures and regulations. Second, he was committed to a substantial *increase* in defense programs and expenditures. Finally, Reagan sought to reduce the tax burden on individuals and businesses. Spending policies that stimulated the economy were not attractive to a president bent on reducing the size of the federal government domestically. Yet to reduce taxes during a time of high inflation and relatively large budget deficits ran counter to beliefs held strongly by many in the country—including many within the president's own Republican Party. From an ideological standpoint, Reagan supported monetary policy, but the early members of the Reagan administration believed that monetary policy was largely beyond their control. What brought together the three policy goals and the hope for economic recovery was **supply-side economics.** This economic theory seemed almost too good to be true—it offered a painless, everybody's-a-winner route to economic recovery. According to supply-

David Stockman, Ronald Reagan's first Budget Director, helped design the 1981 tax cut. His frustration with internal politics in the administration led to a damaging interview in a popular magazine, and Stockman ultimately departed from the executive branch. *(UPI/Bettmann Newsphotos)*

side economics, a large, across-the-board, equal cut in income tax rates would not reduce but rather would raise government revenues (through increased production), thereby reducing rather than increasing the budget deficits.[11]

In supply-side economics, supply, or production, is the crucial element in economic recovery. Supply-side economists argue that tax cuts encourage more people to invest more money, thereby stimulating vital new productive enterprise. Government taxation, according to the supply-siders, discourages investment and removes incentives to better one's financial state. This, in turn, leads to a dropoff in government revenue, since there is less income to tax. The supply-side solution to this problem is to slash taxes, thereby increasing incentives and productivity—and, in the end, increasing government revenues, since there is *more* income to tax. Supply-side theorists also call for eliminating various government regulations, such as environmental requirements, that tend to raise the costs of doing business and, in their view, reduce the amount of money available for investment and growth. In their emphasis on the role of the private sector—particularly wealthy investors and corporations—in stimulating economic recovery, the supply-siders took an opposing view from that of the Keynesians. Keynesians rely on government to stimulate demand and create jobs by putting money in the hands of ordinary citizens through deficit spending, government investment, and public works projects.

The Reagan team knew that the large tax cut in 1981 would not be offset immediately by reductions in spending. Reducing expenditures for domestic programs was difficult at best, and reductions in social spending were countered by increases in defense spending. But the economic expansion envisioned by supply-siders would increase revenues enough to allow for a balanced budget before the midterm elections in 1982, according to supply-side theorists, *if* domestic spending could be reduced sufficiently.

In presenting the supply-side package, the administration emphasized that everyone would suffer—all programs would be subjected to careful scrutiny with an eye toward budget trimming. Powerful interest groups, accustomed to receiving large subsidies, would simply have to reconcile themselves to making do with less. The Reagan team also stressed the urgency of immediate action on the package. Congress must act, they claimed, because the health of the whole economy was at stake. Reagan gave assurances that a "safety net"

Steelworker Bob Jones blames his unemployment on the economic policies of the Reagan administration. Since the middle of this century, every administration has taken credit (and gotten the blame) for the nation's economic health. *(Earl Dotter/Archive Pictures)*

of social programs would be maintained for all truly needy individuals.

How well did supply-side economics work? It is difficult to make a clear assessment on this point because some supply-siders claim that the theory wasn't given a fair chance. The 1981 tax cuts were followed by some modest "revenue enhancement" (a euphemism for tax increases) in 1982 and again in 1984. The Fed's extra-tight monetary policy, imposed during the first two Reagan years, certainly had an impact on economic expansion. The Reagan administration itself complained that Congress stood in the way of needed reductions in federal expenditures.

In addition, economic analysts noted an odd mix of economic results during the Reagan years, further complicating an evaluation of supply-side economics. Most striking was the growth of the

national debt. Fueled by large budget deficits each year (three over $200 billion), the debt more than doubled, reaching $2 trillion. By the end of the Reagan administration the national debt was three times the size of all the deficits of the preceding thirty-nine presidents. In spite of large deficits, inflation did fall dramatically during the recession early in the decade, and stayed low throughout the Reagan years. Unemployment remained relatively high through most of Reagan's tenure but fell gradually in 1987. Economic expansion was broad and sustained from 1984 through 1988; the stock market crash of October 1987, however, did shake confidence in the economy's uninterrupted growth. Federal taxation throughout the period remained relatively stable at around 19 percent of GNP, but taking into account the increase in Social Security taxes during the period, revenues raised for discretionary functions fell significantly.[12] With a larger federal debt, the rising cost of federal interest payments (from around $50 billion in 1980 to over $125 billion in 1987) also reduced the share of expenditures over which the government could exercise direct control. Net domestic savings, which had averaged 7 percent in the 1970s, fell to 1.9 percent by 1987.

The economic expansion was not spread evenly across income levels, either. According to one estimate, people in the bottom 60 percent of the income ladder lost real income during the period, while people in the top 40 percent gained income. The number of children living in poverty increased by one million, from 17.9 percent of all children in 1980 to 19.8 percent.[13]

But in spite of the unevenness of the economic recovery and concerns about the deficits, the economy by several measures was in better shape as Reagan left the Oval Office than when he entered it. But were the improvements due to supply-side economics? Even this question defies easy answers. Paul Volcker at the Federal Reserve Board is credited by some for taming inflation. And traditional Keynesians claim that the expansion of the economy during the 1980s was due to the large deficits themselves, and not the result of stimulating the supply side with tax reductions.

The cases we examined here reveal that economic strategies are chosen, in part, because of the ideological implications they carry. The Reagan administration, for example, adopted supply-side economics in response to specific ideological concerns. And those who oppose extensive government involvement in the economy are less likely to be Keynesians. The cases demonstrate that strictly political considerations often play a pivotal role in economic strategies as well. Tax increases are hard to implement and rarely popular (as President Johnson learned); cutting popular government programs, too, is hard to accomplish. Policy makers, therefore, walk a fine line in managing the economy against a political backdrop.

Emerging Problems

Not long ago, the United States was regarded as the most powerful, productive, and successful world economy. Like all the industrial nations, however, the United States has experienced many economic setbacks in the last two decades. In this section, we consider an array of problems connected to our political economy: (1) tax equity and tax expenditures; (2) federal budget deficits; (3) the transformation of the work force; and (4) the decline in industrial power.

Tax Equity and Tax Expenditures

In analyzing any tax system, one of the primary issues that arises involves equity—that is, how equitably the tax burden is shared. By *equitable*, we generally mean that those who are better able to pay should be taxed more than those less able to pay. In that way, the tax burden does not fall too heavily on the poorer sectors of the community.

In the United States, however, the less well off pay a considerable portion of their income in taxes. This anomaly stems, in part, from the many regressive taxes in the U.S. tax scheme. In addition, the federal income tax structure was always less progressive than it looked on the surface, primarily because of the large numbers of loopholes available to middle- and upper-income taxpayers. A more dignified name for these loopholes is tax expenditures. The term *expenditure* is used because, in effect, the government makes grants of money to various taxpayers through the tax code, rather than through the federal budget. In this sense, the

various loopholes in the tax code actually constitute a hidden form of government spending.

The **Tax Reform Act of 1986** was designed to simplify the tax code and make it more equitable. Overall, reformers sought to make the *rate structure* less progressive by dramatically lowering the highest tax rates and reducing the number of tax brackets. (A tax bracket is a range of income within which a particular rate applies. Since 1988 there are technically only two brackets for the federal income tax: For single individuals with up to $17,850 in taxable income—after exemptions and deductions—the tax rate is 15 percent; taxable income beyond $17,850 is taxed at 28 percent. The cutoff for the brackets changes with different filing statuses.) At the same time the *actual tax structure* would become more progressive because a large number of loopholes would be closed, ensuring that high-income taxpayers would pay taxes at rates closer to the published ones (because more of their income would be considered taxable). An increase in the personal exemption would reduce or eliminate the tax burden for those with low incomes. No more favorable treatment would be afforded capital gains (investment income), increasing the tax liability of persons with substantial investments.

Since the first returns under the new tax law were only filed in 1988, it is difficult to assess the actual impact of the new tax system, but a few observations can be made. First, for individual taxpayers trying to fathom the new tax forms, the goal of simplification was lost almost entirely. The complexity of the new, "simple" 1040 tax return and accompanying schedules was the butt of many jokes and the object of considerable frustration. Even professional tax preparers had trouble understanding the new forms. Frustration did not subside when it was learned that, by the Internal Revenue Service's own estimates, nearly one in five answers to tax questions, provided by IRS employees, was wrong.

A more substantive criticism concerns the premise of the Tax Reform Act itself: Even if all taxpayers paid taxes at precisely the published rates, a two-bracket system is barely progressive. And since the tax code still contains a large number of tax-expenditure items (like mortgage interest deductions for a first *and a second* home), the actual tax paid is less progressive than the published rate. An even more serious threat to equity is posed by various "reforms" that are creeping back into the tax structure. Even before the first returns were filed under the new law, President Reagan was proposing that favorable treatment for capital gains be reinstated in the law. Hundreds of specific bills have been introduced in Congress to reinsert tax breaks for particular groups. The workings of the legislative system make it virtually inevitable that many of these proposals will be signed into law. Such tax expenditures represent a hidden—and undemocratic—dimension of public policy making. **Table 16–2** demonstrates that tax-expenditure items form an enormous welfare program for the nonpoor (not necessarily the rich only). Welfare payments to the poor are highly publicized and frequently investigated. But benefits conferred on the wealthy through the tax system are rarely scrutinized. For example, a person in the high tax bracket who buys an expensive house and makes a substantial mortgage interest payment each month receives a proportionately larger benefit in tax relief than someone who has a lower income and buys a cheaper house. If large checks from the government went out each month to wealthy homeowners, people might begin to ask whether this public policy made sense.

Federal Budget Deficits

Despite its public commitment to a balanced budget and President Reagan's often-proclaimed desire for a balanced budget amendment to the U.S. Constitution, the Reagan administration created the largest federal deficits in U.S. history. The massive Reagan tax cuts caused the giant deficits, which also grew because of increased defense spending and because supply-side economic strategies did not produce the expected revenues. During the first months of the administration in 1981, the Office of Management and Budget (OMB) had predicted a balanced budget by 1984 despite tax reductions. These predictions turned out to be way off the mark.

How serious a problem is the deficit? Some analysts, including many balanced-budget conservatives in the Reagan administration, argued that the

TABLE 16–2
Tax Expenditure Estimates by Budget Function, FY 1988–1992

Expenditure	Dollars (billions)
Corporate research and development expenses	12.2
Interest on state and local bonds	57.0
Rehabilitation of historic structures	8.7
Income on life insurance and annuity savings	26.5
Home mortgage interest (first and second residence)	149.8
Property tax on homes	40.3
Deferral and/or exclusion of capital gains on home sales	48.9
Depreciation on business buildings and equipment	216.5
Reduced rates on first $75,000 of corporate income	27.0
Deductibility of nonmortgage interest	10.7
Deductibility of charitable contributions	61.9
Exclusion of miscellaneous fringe benefits	20.3
Contributions by employers for medical insurance and care	139.2
Pension contributions and earnings	286.9
Individual retirement plans	45.3
Exclusion of untaxed social security benefits	94.8
Exclusion of veteran benefits and GI bill	7.5
Deductibility of state and local property and income taxes	93.5

SOURCE: *Report of the Committee on the Budget,* House of Representatives, Concurrent Resolution on the Budget, FY 1988, 100th Congress, 1st Session, Report No. 100–41 (Washington, D.C.: U.S. Government Printing Office, 1987), pp. 125–130.

deficits were not that important. They stated that the general health of the national economy would sooner or later allow the budget to be balanced.

But many saw dangers in the deficit. David Stockman, a central figure in the early days of Reaganomics and OMB director until he left in 1985, put it this way: "The basic fact is that we are violating badly, even wantonly, the cardinal rule of sound public finance: Governments must extract from the people in taxes what they dispense in benefits, services and protections. . . ."[14] Others considered rising interest rates and economic recession as an inevitable result. There were predictions that the United States would soon have to borrow money from foreign sources to pay interest on the debt owed to foreign sources.

Finally, some contended that the Reagan administration used the deficit situation to turn back the clock and cut deeply into or eliminate completely social programs developed since the 1930s. Because of the huge deficit, the administration argued that social programs would have to be scaled back, while it continued to champion a rising military budget.

The Transformation of the Work Force

Many of the changes in our society and economy over the recent past are reflected in the changing nature and boundaries of the work force. More and more families have two wage earners. (See **Table 16–3** for the increase in the number of women in the work force since 1950.) The number of service industry jobs has grown much more rapidly than those in manufacturing, government, or agriculture; in 1986 13 million more people were employed in service jobs than the total number working in the other three categories (see **Figure 16–1** and **Figure 16–2**).

Despite a strong work ethic in this country, it is possible to work full time, year round, and still be poor. In 1986, a person working full time, all year, for the minimum wage of $3.35, earned only $6,968—only 80 percent of the income needed to lift a family of three above the poverty line. According to the Census Bureau, the number of fully employed working poor increased by 22 percent between 1980 and 1986. Two million adults held full-time jobs year round in 1986 and were still poor. An additional 6.9 million poor people worked either part time or full time part of the

TABLE 16–3
Women in the Labor Force

Year	Percent
Married, with children under age 6	
1950	11.9
1955	16.2
1960	18.6
1965	23.3
1970	30.3
1975	36.6
1980	41.5
1985	53.4
1987	56.8
With children under age 1	
1976	31.0
1978	35.3
1980	38.0
1982	43.9
1983	43.1
1984	46.7
1985	48.4
1986	49.8
1987	50.8

SOURCE: Department of Labor, Bureau of Census.

year. Although the minimum wage has been raised once since 1986, full-time work at minimum wage still offers no guarantee against poverty for many families.

Unemployment figures, kept by the Bureau of Labor Statistics (BLS) in the Department of Labor, cover people who are out of a job but are actively looking for work. But the BLS reports that six million people who say they want work are not even seeking jobs. This includes "discouraged workers" (folks who have given up the job searches because they don't believe they can find work), mothers for whom the costs of day care and the lost welfare benefits simply add up to more than a modest wage, and others (see **Figure 16–3**). Although the numbers are hard to calculate, even more people are "underemployed," working only part time, or full time only part of the year, when they would prefer to be fully employed. The BLS reports that in 1988 there were 5.4 million persons working part time because they could not find full-time

FIGURE 16–1
Profile of the Labor Force (in millions)

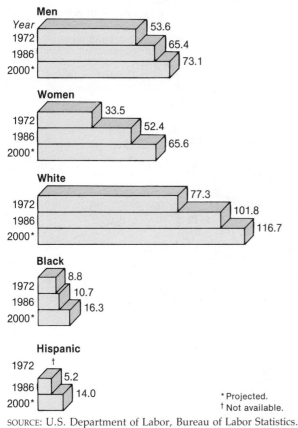

Men

Year	
1972	53.6
1986	65.4
2000*	73.1

Women

1972	33.5
1986	52.4
2000*	65.6

White

1972	77.3
1986	101.8
2000*	116.7

Black

1972	8.8
1986	10.7
2000*	16.3

Hispanic

1972	†
1986	5.2
2000*	14.0

* Projected.
† Not available.

SOURCE: U.S. Department of Labor, Bureau of Labor Statistics.

work. That figure represents a 53 percent increase over 1979. The increasing proportion of jobs in the service sector accounts for some of this underemployment. The manager of the local fast food restaurant, for example, may find it advantageous to hire a large number of part-time employees (whose schedules are flexible and who are not eligible for certain benefits) than a smaller number of full-time workers. The trend toward temporary workers as a cost-cutting measure has even reached the federal government, which in 1988 employed about 300,000 workers on a temporary basis (up from about 80,000 five years earlier).[15]

The Decline in Industrial Power

As far back as the early 1960s, some observant critics of the American economy noted that the generally rosy picture of U.S. economic achievements had a dark underside. Unemployment always seemed to be higher here than in many European nations. In addition, portions of U.S. industry were not being modernized. Finally, pockets of poverty and deprivation were not sharing in the economic resurgence, and much of the infrastructure (roads, water systems, bridges, and the like) was deteriorating.

Not until the 1970s, however, did the full impact of the nation's industrial decline become

The American economy has changed in significant, unanticipated ways. The success of fast-food restaurants and other service establishments puts an increasing proportion of workers in part-time jobs, at low wages and with few benefits. (© *Paul Sequiera/ Photo Researchers*)

FIGURE 16–2
Where the Jobs Are—And Will Be (in millions)

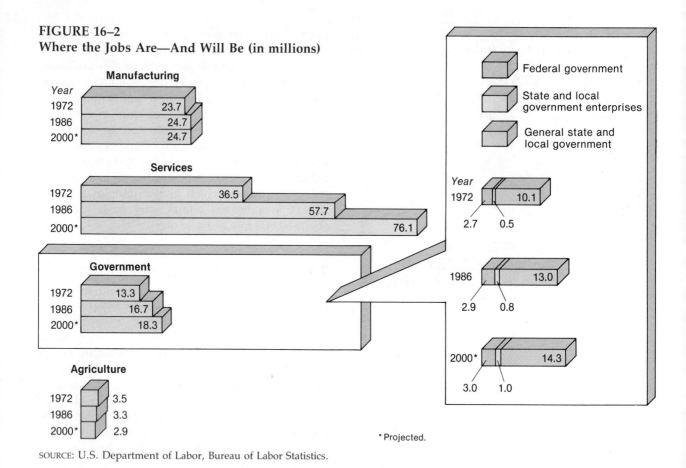

Manufacturing

Year	
1972	23.7
1986	24.7
2000*	24.7

Services

1972	36.5
1986	57.7
2000*	76.1

Government

1972	13.3
1986	16.7
2000*	18.3

Agriculture

1972	3.5
1986	3.3
2000*	2.9

Federal government

State and local government enterprises

General state and local government

Year	
1972	10.1
	2.7 0.5
1986	13.0
	2.9 0.8
2000*	14.3
	3.0 1.0

* Projected.

SOURCE: U.S. Department of Labor, Bureau of Labor Statistics.

The decline of American industrial dominance has stimulated policy debates. The United States has never had the kind of centrally coordinated industrial policy that is found in Western Europe and Japan, but factors like the planned integration of the European Economic Community in 1992 increase the pressure for more systematic economic policy. Would such planning make American more—or less—democratic? (© *Bob Adelman/Magnum*)

FOR LEASE
INDUSTRIAL
PROPERTY
5 ACRES · 20,000 Sq.Ft.Bldg.
681-0754 · Zoned M3 · 521-4257

FIGURE 16–3
Discouraged Workers—Who They Are

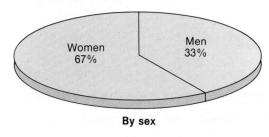

By sex

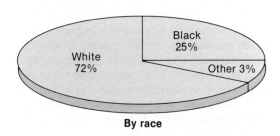

By race

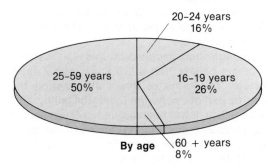

By age

SOURCE: U.S. Department of Labor, Bureau of Labor Statistics. Figures for the months of April-June, 1987.

clear. At that point the United States ceased to be the world leader in many industrial areas. Even in our own nation, consumers disparaged the quality of American products. Japanese and European cars, TVs, and electrical and electronic appliances took over a substantial share of the U.S. market. Some major industries were especially hard hit: Automakers fell on hard times, and the steel industry suffered a steep decline. The industrial heartland of the nation, stretching from Chicago to Boston, became an economically depressed area.

This decline stemmed from several interrelated factors. American industries had failed to inno-

vate. Capital investments had gone to countries where labor was cheaper and profits higher. The U.S. job market was also undergoing profound changes, as more and more of the population moved into service jobs and away from jobs in production industries. And through policies that had protected particular industries (such as steel) against foreign competition, the government had reduced incentives to innovate and compete internationally.

What could be done to revive U.S. industry and stimulate full employment? Most conservatives, including President Reagan and his advisors, argued that market forces would do the job. Government, they asserted, should do what it could to create spirited economic competition, which would, in turn, spark a general economic recovery. More liberal analysts assailed this approach, recommending a mix of market stimulation and closer cooperation among government, business, and labor—paralleling the trend in various European nations. Such cooperation would mean sacrifices from all groups to reestablish the nation's competitive position in the world. Still other critics took the position that nothing short of strong government intervention would cure our economic malaise. According to this view, the only way the United States could regain its economic edge, while providing full employment, would be to rebuild its own society, targeting investment funds for economically hard-hit inner cities, rural counties, and other areas in dire need of help. During the 1988 presidential campaign, candidate Michael Dukakis stressed the need for education and training as the keys to regaining a competitive edge. Democratic primary candidate Richard Gephardt advocated a protectionist trade bill. Should the United States raise barriers against foreign-made goods entering the American market? Those arguing in favor of such barriers assert that Japan, South Korea, and Taiwan, as well as our major European trading partners have enjoyed unimpeded access to our markets while raising outright restrictions or tariff obstacles to U.S. goods in their own domestic markets. Opponents of such legislation charge that trade barriers simply encourage a spiral of escalating trade restrictions that make all countries suffer. They contend that competitiveness thrives in free-market conditions. In

COMPARATIVE PERSPECTIVE

Industrial Policy

Democratic governments employ various forms of *direct* intervention in the economy to promote growth, employment, or economic stability. In many Western European industrial democracies, as well as in Japan, interventionist policies have become standard and highly sophisticated.* Forms of direct intervention include government ownership of portions of the economy; close collaboration between business and government, including fairly detailed planning of economic goals; and cooperation between government and labor to avoid strikes. These instruments of industrial policy are more highly developed in some nations than in others. France, for example, has emphasized close collaboration between business and government, with extensive use of government loans and credit arrangements to help industry achieve agreed-on goals. Both France and Great Britain have nationalized certain major industries, although under the Conservative government of Margaret Thatcher in the 1980s, many nationalized businesses reverted to private ownership. Both the British and the Swedes are notable for clear, long-term relationships between labor and major political parties. In West Germany, the banking system plays an important collaborative role with government in the management of the economy. In all these cases, there has been a focused, long-term effort to link overall economic goals to specific policies

aiding particular industries, though such efforts have not always been successful.

A clear industrial policy has always been lacking in the United States. Except in time of war, the U.S. government has not sought to develop the tools for detailed intervention in particular industries and aspects of the economy. There have been occasional interventions: The government bailout of the failing Lockheed Corporation during the Nixon administration and the guaranteeing of loans for the near-bankrupt Chrysler Corporation during the Ford and Carter administrations are examples. These instances, however, were not part of an overall plan. Rather, they were simply cases in which particular interest groups were able to plead successfully to have their demands met.

Although some people think this is as it should be, others believe that the U.S. economy needs precisely the forms of direct intervention that would be part of a coherent industrial policy. Only such a policy, it has been argued, will provide the help needed by many ailing American industries and by those areas of the nation afflicted by chronically high unemployment.

*See Arnold J. Heidenheimer, Hugh Heclo, and Carolyn T. Adams, *Comparative Public Policy*, 2nd ed. (New York: St. Martin's, 1983), pp. 141–148.

April 1988, Congress passed a trade bill with some protectionist elements, however, the bill did not garner enough votes to override a Reagan veto. As the Reagan administration was drawing to a close, the country was moving toward a consensus favoring a pragmatic, slightly protectionist compromise. Yet whichever strategy, or mix of strategies, eventually is chosen, many sectors of U.S. society will continue to suffer serious problems of economic decline.

Conclusions

According to many students of politics, successful management of the economy, more than any other factor, can determine how history—and the electorate—treats a president. In a reelection campaign, or in historical perspective, the president may stand or fall on whether unemployment has been lowered to a reasonable level, inflation has been controlled, or public confidence in the economy has been restored. Of course, administrations are not moved to pay careful attention to economic management by political considerations or history's judgments alone. They are also influenced by ideological factors—that is, by beliefs about how the economy should be run. President Herbert Hoover believed so strongly in not interfering with the free market that he did not take actions that might at least have softened the brunt of the Great Depression. And President Ronald Reagan was sufficiently committed to the free market to push deregulation and tax reductions as top priority items throughout his administration.

Today every national government comes to power with a specific strategy for economic management as the centerpiece of its political agenda. This holds true not only in the United States, but also in all industrialized nations—and in most other nations as well. Managing economies has become, in one form or another, a key function of government. Even governments professing that the best way to run the economy is to do *less* managing continue to perform many essential functions: regulating interest rates and the money supply, settling rates of taxation, formulating spending policies, maintaining the extensive network of regulation that affects virtually every form of economic activity, and so on.

In short, economic life has become highly politicized. Many of the battles fought in Congress, between Congress and the executive branch, and in many of our election campaigns, now revolve around how the economy should be managed, and in whose interest it should be run. How far should government go in reshaping the workings of the marketplace? Is it legitimate to assist an ailing Chrysler Corporation with special loan arrangements, but not to assist farmers about to lose their land?

And how far should government go in altering the composition of the work force and mending its frayed margins? Is it government's responsibility, for example, to make sure that everyone who wants to work is able to find a job? What part should government play in making sure that people who do work can earn a decent wage?

Consider, as well, how much, if anything, government should do to redistribute income through our tax system. As we have seen, the current tax system is not particularly progressive in impact. Should it be made more so—not just in theory, but in practice? From the standpoint of democratic politics, fairness in taxation should stand as a prime goal of our policy makers. Overall, there is good reason to question the fairness of the U.S. system of taxation. From the perspective of democratic theory, a fair method of taxation would seem essential, since this is the way we go about paying for our government.

Another facet of our economic policy-making machinery—the Federal Reserve Board—is accountable to no one, yet the actions of this set of unelected decision makers have far-reaching implications for both the national economy and individual consumers, homeowners, and businesses. Largely insulated from political pressures, the Fed can pursue politically unpopular actions that elected policy makers could not. Yet in light of democratic politics, this arrangement raises serious concerns. If the Fed decides to tighten the money supply for a prolonged period, as it did in the early 1980s, how much individual hardship will we tolerate as the price of economic stability? Should the Fed, then, be made more responsive to popular pressures, or does the economy benefit from the Fed's independence? At this point, changing the structure of the Federal Reserve Board does not stand high on the political agenda.

A final point, from the perspective of democratic theory, concerns economic planning. Our government does not do very much overall economic planning. Many of us associate the very term *economic planning* with communist governments that manage their entire economies. Various sectors of the economy do benefit from planning, however. The government provides farmers with certain price supports, for example, and plans new weapons systems more than a decade in advance. But as a society we are reluctant to engage in the kind of long-term economic planning that might enable us to cope with the most severe problems of dislocation and deprivation some citizens face. The United States has lived with a considerable level of unemployment for decades. We have also seen central cities deteriorate and whole regions of the nation suffer prolonged economic crisis. Yet our distrust of government and our reverence for private property and the workings of the market make it difficult for us to undertake a serious national effort to address these issues.

GLOSSARY TERMS

mercantilism

laissez-faire capitalism

controlled capitalism

Keynesian economics

fiscal policies

Federal Reserve System

supply-side economics

Tax Reform Act of 1986

NOTES

[1]This term was first used by British writer Thomas Carlyle (1795–1881) to describe his attitude toward economics.

[2]Seymour Martin Lipset, *Political Man* (Garden City, N.Y.: Doubleday, 1960), chap. 2.

[3]W. A. Williams, *The Contours of American History* (Cleveland: World, 1961); and Louis Hartz, *Economic Policy and Democratic Thought* (Cambridge, Mass.: Harvard University Press, 1948).

[4]Richard Hofstadter, *The American Political Tradition* (New York: Knopf, 1948).

[5]Clair Wilcox, *Public Policies Toward Business* (Irwin, Ill.: Homewood, 1971).

[6]Robert S. McElvaine, *The Great Depression* (New York: Times Books, 1984), chaps. 2, 4.

[7]Arnold J. Heidenheimer, Hugh Heclo, and Carolyn T. Adams, *Comparative Public Policy*, 2nd ed. (New York: St. Martin's, 1983), chap. 5.

[8]Anne Swardson, "Tax Reform: One Deduction Forward, Two Deductions Back," *Washington Post National Weekly Edition*, Apr. 25–May 1, 1988, p. 21.

[9]Much information for these cases was derived from Lawrence G. Brewster, *The Public Agenda* (New York: St. Martin's, 1984), chap. 1.

[10]This study was conducted by the Urban Institute and quoted in William Greider, "Annals of Finance: The Price of Money, Part III: The Hardest Choice," *New Yorker*, Nov. 23, 1987, pp. 49–104. Greider's article was a general source for this section on monetarism and the discussion of supply-side economics that follows it.

[11]This discussion is drawn from Herbert Stein (former chairman of the President's Council of Economic Advisors and a conservative economist who coined the term "supply-side economics," though not a supply-sider himself), *Presidential Economics*, rev. ed. (New York: Simon & Schuster, 1985), chap. 7 ("The Reagan Campaign: The Economics of Joy").

[12]Dale Russakoff and Tom Kenworthy, "Studies Suggest Reagan Misdirects Blame for Deficits," *Raleigh News and Observer*, Nov. 8, 1987, section D, p. 1.

[13]Morton Kondracke, "Are You Better Off?" *New Republic*, Mar. 7, 1988, p. 14.

[14]Quoted in Daniel Patrick Moynihan, "Reagan's Inflate-the-Deficit Game," *New York Times*, July 21, 1985, p. E21.

[15]Figures cited here are from Dale Russakoff and Cindy Skrzycki, "Working 9 to 2," *Washington Post National Weekly Edition*, Mar. 21–27, 1988, p. 7; Louis Uchitelle, "America's Army of Non-Workers," *New York Times*, Sept. 27, 1987, section 3, p. 1; and Robert Pear, "Increasingly, Those Who Have Jobs Are Poor, Too," *New York Times*, Dec. 27, 1987, section 4, p. 5.

SELECTED READINGS

For an engaging **history of economics** from Aristotle to Reagan, see John Kenneth Galbraith, *Economics in Perspective: A Critical History* (Boston: Houghton Mifflin, 1987). A widely used and very good standard economics textbook is Paul Samuelson and William Nordhaus, *Economics* (New York: McGraw-Hill, 1985).

On the long-standing debate about **public control of the economy,** see Charles Wolf, *Markets or Government: Choosing between Imperfect Alternatives* (Boston: MIT Press, 1988); Robert Heilbroner, *Between Capitalism and Socialism* (New York: Vintage, 1970); William Simon, *A Time for Truth* (New York: McGraw-Hill, 1978); and Milton Friedman and Rose Friedman, *Free to Choose* (New York: Avon, 1979).

For examinations of the **Reagan era,** see Michael J. Boskin, *Reagan and the Economy: The Successes, Failures and Unfinished Agenda* (San Francisco, Calif.: ICS Press, 1987); John L. Palmer and Isabel V. Sawhill, eds., *The Reagan Experiment: An Examination of Economic and Social Policies under the Reagan Administration* (Washington, D.C.: Urban Institute Press, 1982); and *The Reagan Record: An Assessment of America's Changing Domestic Priorities* (Cambridge, Mass.: Ballinger, 1984).

A **comparative perspective** is available in M. King and D. Fullerton, eds., *The Taxation of Income from Capital: A Comparative Study of the U.S., U.K., Sweden and West Germany* (Chicago: University of Chicago Press, 1984); and Anne Romanis Braun, *Wage Determination and Incomes Policy in Open Economies* (Washington, D.C.: International Monetary Fund, 1986).

Several intriguing studies of the interaction between **politics and economic policy** are available, including William Grieder, *Secrets of the Temple: How the Federal Reserve Runs the Country* (New York: Simon & Schuster, 1988); Donald F. Kettl, *Leadership at the Fed* (New Haven, Conn.: Yale University Press, 1986); Thomas J. Reese, *The Politics of Taxation* (New York: Quorum Books, 1980); Edward R. Tufte, *Political Control of the Economy* (Princeton, N.J.: Princeton University Press, 1978); and Anthony E. Brown, *The Politics of Airline Deregulation* (Knoxville: University of Tennessee Press, 1987).

For **up-to-date information** about the economy, consult *The Economic Report of the President* (Washington, D.C.: Government Printing Office, issued annually), but remember that any president's political agenda will be reflected in this report.

17

THE WELFARE STATE

Benefiting the Poor and the Nonpoor

CHAPTER OUTLINE

The U.S. Welfare State
Income Security Programs
Health Care Programs
Nutrition and Housing Programs
Evaluating the Welfare State

New York Times Pictures

To many people, the term **welfare state** conjures up images of unemployment lines, needy people receiving food stamps, public housing. Such images are accurate, but they tell only part of the story. We tend to forget that many welfare programs serve all Americans and have little or no relationship to *need*. The welfare state offers education and veterans' benefits, as well as medical care for the indigent. The single largest welfare state program, Social Security, provides benefits virtually universal in scope: They go to those with high incomes as well as those living below the poverty line. The welfare state is not usually viewed so comprehensively because most of the controversy surrounding the concept of welfare focuses on programs targeted at the needy, such as Aid to Families with Dependent Children and food stamps. In this chapter we spotlight these controversial aspects of the welfare state. But we must recognize that need-related programs are only *aspects* of the welfare state. Therefore, in addressing this segment of public policy, we will explore the underpinnings of *all* welfare state programs.

The concept of providing for the social welfare is neither new nor, in the main, controversial. Almost all societies offer programs or other forms of help to care for the poor, the elderly, the disabled, and others who need assistance. In Great Britain, welfare programs date back to the poor laws of the Elizabethan period; in the United States, government had a hand in assisting the poor even before the Revolution. The modern welfare state, however, is distinctive in several respects. Today, government, rather than families or private charities, plays the dominant role in helping those who cannot help themselves. Moreover, national, rather than local, governments now direct and fund many welfare programs. Finally, modern welfare states, unlike their predecessors, work to redistribute wealth, by lessening the disparities that arise from social and economic systems.

Fundamentally, the welfare state is designed to ensure a minimum of economic security and a degree of social equality. By the end of World War II, after a century of struggle, most Western societies had arrived at a consensus that individuals should not be allowed to fall below an economic minimum and that opportunities for advancement, principally through the educational system, should be open to all. Beyond this broad agreement, however, lay many areas of controversy, particularly in the United States. To what income level should poor families be supported through public funds—and with what strings attached, if any? How low a level of unemployment can or should society tolerate? What should be done about high levels of youth unemployment among disadvantaged groups? Some of these questions deal with practical concerns. For example, how can we best ensure that poor children receive adequate nutrition? But some involve values or beliefs, such as whether—or how—a society should foster greater equality in income. Oftentimes, these practical and ideological issues are intertwined, and when new welfare reform proposals are debated, strongly held convictions surface, generating heated political controversy.

How do democratic ideals figure in welfare state issues? From a democratic standpoint, the welfare state raises three basic issues: *security* (Do all Americans have the opportunity to live reasonably secure and healthy lives?), *equality* (Do welfare programs promote economic equality among our citizens, especially in helping to raise the standard of living for the poorest members of society?), and the problem of *paternalism* (In administering welfare programs, does the government interfere excessively with individual freedom and democratic rights?).

Making judgments on these matters is neither simple nor straightforward. Numerous programs make up the welfare state; their objectives and methods span a wide range, and their scope of achievement varies along a broad spectrum. To assess how—and how well—our welfare state works, we will (1) provide an overview of the U.S. welfare state; and then probe (2) income security programs; (3) health care programs; and (4) nutrition and housing programs. Finally, we will (5) evaluate the welfare state and its impact on democracy.

The U.S. Welfare State

Efforts to provide security and various welfare protections were undertaken prior to the 1930s, but the origins of the modern welfare state can be found in New Deal legislation of that decade. New Deal reforms laid the foundation for the "positive state"—one in which the government is an active partner in economic and social life. The New Deal was conceived in response to economic and social problems that had always existed in the United States, but these were greatly exacerbated by the Great Depression. With unemployment idling 25 percent of the work force, millions of people living in abject poverty, and state and local governments running out of resources, national action was imperative. Many other industrialized societies took a similar approach.

Some New Deal programs were designed to undo the economic damage of the Depression and to prevent such a catastrophe from occurring again. Yet even without the crisis of the Depression, some social welfare programs would certainly have evolved in this and other democratic nations. As societies grew more complex and families and communities became more fragmented and less closely knit, political systems were forced to assume some of the responsibilities that previously had been carried out by families, communities, and private groups. And despite vocal criticisms of welfarism and socialism, the basic elements of the welfare state—including Social Security, a degree of national responsibility for health care, unemployment insurance, and some forms of aid to the poor—now form an integral part of all industrialized democratic societies.

The centerpiece of New Deal legislation was the Social Security Act of 1935, which established unemployment compensation, aid to dependent children, grants to states for maternal services, old age assistance (including our present-day understanding of "Social Security"), and aid to states for pensions. The act did not set forth uniform national welfare standards for the poor, nor was any provision made for national health coverage. Neither of these shortcomings has been adequately addressed to this day, according to many welfare experts.

The next significant expansion of the welfare state occurred in the 1960s, during the administration of Lyndon Johnson. Under the heading of the Great Society, programs were initiated to help the poor and to provide added security for others in

need. In 1965 alone, Congress passed legislation designed to

Provide medical care for the elderly, the disabled, and the indigent, through Medicare and Medicaid.

Offer aid to public schools and loans to college students.

Supplement rents for poor people.

Establish grants, loans, and training programs for health professionals.

Support development efforts in Appalachia.

Through the Economic Opportunity Act, passed in 1964, Johnson launched his War on Poverty. The act set in motion community action programs, VISTA (a domestic Peace Corps), legal aid programs for the poor, and other services.

The Great Society programs promised more than they could deliver—an end to poverty, racial

It is August, 1964, and President Lyndon B. Johnson has just signed the War on Poverty legislation allocating almost $1 billion to the task. LBJ's "war," by most estimates, was a considerable help to the American poor, but it fell far short of abolishing severe deprivation. *(UPI/Bettmann Newsphotos)*

Appalachian Development: Success or Failure?

When John Kennedy traveled to West Virginia in 1960 to campaign in the Democratic Party primary, he was shocked by the desperate poverty he encountered. These conditions were typical of "Appalachia"—a region that stretches from Mississippi to New York State along the spine of the Appalachian Mountains.

In 1965, Congress established the federally funded Appalachian Regional Commission to address the region's abject poverty. Over the next fifteen years, the commission financed $15 billion in economic development and social welfare programs. Road building, which was expected to attract more industry to the area and help end the isolation of many mountain people, accounted for more than 60 percent of all the commission's funds. The remainder helped subsidize some seven hundred projects in areas ranging from vocational education to community health, child development, sewer and water systems, and regional industrial parks.

Was the effort a success? By some standards, yes. Infant mortality dropped dramatically, and per capita income increased modestly. The percentage of Appalachians living under the poverty line dropped significantly until it approached the national average. Serious problems remain, however. In 1988, after twenty-three years of the ARC help, many counties within the region had unemployment as high as 40 to 50 percent. New industry had little incentive to locate in these

areas. In some pockets of extreme poverty, infant mortality remains high and per capita income barely reaches 70 percent of the national average. Conservative critics argue that many of the big highway projects served no useful purpose and that economic development actually resulted from the revival of the coal industry. Radical critics, by contrast, maintain that antipoverty efforts in Appalachia did not go far enough. Thousands of acres, suitable for new housing, were kept off the market by corporate owners. And coal mining companies continued to hold vast reserves of land that were not included in development efforts—a significant deprivation among a desperately land-poor people.

The Reagan administration attempted to kill the Appalachian Regional Commission in 1981, but succeeded only in cutting its budget in half. For the duration of the administration, funding for the ARC stabilized at this reduced level. An ARC staff person, interviewed in 1988, said, "The problems of the Appalachian region are stubborn and not easily solved. The resources necessary to solve these problems are not in the region itself—that's why the Commission was established in the first place." No timetable exists for completing the Commission's work.

SOURCE: Sandra Sugawara, "Appalachian Sunset," *Washington Post National Weekly Edition*, April 22, 1985, pp. 9–10.

and ethnic equality, equal educational opportunities, a vastly improved welfare system, employment for everyone seeking a job, decent housing for all, a greater sharing of the wealth. According to their critics, however, these programs were overly ambitious, poorly conceived, and ineffectual. Critics also maintain that rather than helping most Americans create a better life for themselves, the Great Society left a legacy of bitterness and disappointed hopes, and gave rise to an overly bureaucratic federal establishment that continues to dissipate our national resources.

Yet without the Great Society's antipoverty programs, a far higher percentage of the nation's citizens would be poor. As we saw in the last chapter, even an expanding economy may create large numbers of working poor because of low wages and the availability of only part-time work. The

Bureau of Labor Statistics estimates that 5.4 million people in the United States are working part time simply because they cannot find full-time work. Because most part-time work does not offer benefits (like medical insurance and pension plans), adding two half-time jobs together does not make a whole. Additionally, families with a single parent (usually a woman) make up a large proportion of poor people in the United States. These single heads of household face a double disadvantage: They often must pay for day care yet the jobs they are likely to secure are low-paying. In 1986, the median income of families headed by a woman with no husband present was less than *half* that of all families and came to only 60 percent of the earnings of families with a male head of household, with no wife present. Even a healthy, expanding economy, then, leaves many of these people behind.

Since the Johnson administration, few new welfare programs have been created. But even with the tightened eligibility requirements and fiscal austerity of the Reagan years, spending on social welfare increased in the 1980s, driven by "indexed" Social Security payments (payments that rise automatically with inflation) and surprisingly large increases in the demand for and cost of medical care under Medicaid and Medicare. As a result, welfare programs of all sorts have come under increased scrutiny. In fact, the system of aid to the needy has been under attack for years, from all points on the political spectrum. Increased levels of mandatory participation and higher tax rates have brought the Social Security system past a period of financial insecurity, but serious questions of fairness still remain. The system, after all, taxes young, low-income working people to give benefits that are not need-based to retirees who may be quite well off. (Of course, wealthier taxpayers also contribute to Social Security, but they pay a proportionately smaller share of their total income.) New challenges have arisen to social welfare in the United States, including the enormous costs of AIDS and the appearance of thousands of homeless people on our streets. In the meantime, poverty, even destitution, remains a serious problem.

In the United States, the term *welfare* is commonly associated with severe deprivation, prolonged unemployment, lack of incentive to succeed—even lack of "moral fiber" on the part of the recipient. Many Americans think of welfare as a handout, a form of public charity. Such programs exist, but they compose only one segment of the welfare state. As used here, the term *welfare state* refers to the whole complex of benefits, protections, forms of insurance, and services that provide security and a measure of equity for most citi-

"Camp LaGuardia," a shelter for the homeless in New York's Catskill Mountains. Although homelessness is often associated with other economically disabling factors, such as unemployment, it is not simply a result of problems like substance abuse and mental illness. Most homelessness is created by the lack of adequate low-cost housing. (© Carrie Boretz/ Archive Pictures)

zens. Under this definition, Social Security is part of the welfare state, and so is Medicare, even though neither of these programs is targeted at the poor. The government also aids many people with housing needs—some through housing built with federal housing grants, others with a subsidy built into the deductibility of home mortgage interest on federal income taxes. All these programs are part of the welfare state as well.

There are three types of welfare state programs: **social insurance programs,** such as Social Security, in which past contributions are related to the benefits received; **public assistance programs,** in which need is the main basis for eligibility; and **tax expenditure items,** in which benefits for particular activities are derived through reductions in tax liability. In the first two categories, benefits are distributed in three ways: through **cash transfers,** such as cash payments for Social Security or the various types of public assistance to the poor; **services,** like education and job training; and **inkind transfers,** such as food stamps or Medicaid, which are designated for particular products or services. Most welfare state programs address either income security, health, nutrition, or housing needs. Each category may encompass several types of programs—some directed at poor people, others targeted for the nonpoor.

Programs aimed at the poor tend to be more controversial than programs created for the overall population or the nonpoor specifically. Most controversial are public assistance programs. Over the last twenty years fierce arguments have raged over welfare payments to mothers in the Aid to Families with Dependent Children (AFDC) program, job training, food stamps, Medicaid, and public housing. All these programs have been criticized as inadequate and poorly organized, as well as excessively generous, destructive of motivation, and wasteful. In contrast, social insurance programs and tax expenditure programs, which are available to nearly everyone, are extremely popular. If we add tax expenditure items—like the deductibility of home mortgage interest, pension funds, and the exclusion of interest on individual retirement accounts—to broad-based social insurance programs, we can see that virtually all households in the United States benefit from one or more government-sponsored social program.

Income Security Programs

Income security programs are straightforward attempts to raise the level of cash available to beneficiaries. Recipients may be designated by status (for example, disabled people), prior participation (as in Social Security), or circumstance (AFDC payments are based on low income). Some of these programs are aimed at poor people (AFDC); others benefit nonpoor individuals (the tax expenditure on the deductibility of pension plan contributions). The total cost of federal income security programs, including tax expenditures, was about $215 billion in 1989.

Social Security

The **Social Security system** has long formed a stable and noncontroversial part of the U.S. welfare state. It encompasses old-age and survivors' insurance (OASI) and disability insurance (DI) programs. The nation's largest income security program, Social Security, will represent about one-fifth of the total federal outlays in 1989, providing benefits to one in every six Americans. A prorated share of each employee's wages is collected for Social Security, and the payments to beneficiaries are prorated in terms of their previous incomes. Benefits are indexed to increase with inflation. About 25 percent of Social Security recipients have incomes below the poverty line; about 30 percent have an outside income, such as private pensions or investments, that exceeds their Social Security income. The average benefit for a retired worker and spouse came to roughly $10,500 in 1988. The 1989 federal outlay for OASI is estimated to be $234.5 billion. Since a portion of Social Security benefits can be excluded from income tax, the tax expenditure associated with Social Security adds $17.5 billion to that figure. Up to one-half of Social Security benefits are subject to tax, for single taxpayers whose incomes exceed $25,000 or married taxpayers whose combined income exceeds $32,000. For many of the approximately forty million people who receive monthly Social Security payments, those checks represent the difference between abject poverty and being able to make do.

Although many senior citizens face financially precarious circumstances, many more enjoy reasonable security because of New Deal and Great Society programs. "Welfare" is not only for poor people; many older Americans of comfortable financial means participate in entitlement programs like Social Security and Medicare. (© *Richard Kalvar/Magnum*)

In recent years, however, several factors have destabilized the Social Security system. Although many people think of Social Security as an enforced savings plan, in which the government takes a worker's money now and gives it back later, the program has always worked as a transfer payment from those currently employed to those currently retired. Such a transfer works well as long as the number of active employees expands more rapidly than the number of current beneficiaries—the situation from the beginning of the program in the 1930s through the 1960s. But in the 1980s, three key factors caused serious strains in the system: the number of post–World War II baby boomers (people born between 1946 and 1956) entering the work force subsided; workers began to retire earlier; and retirees were living longer. As a result, the ratio between current contributors and current beneficiaries became less favorable. Now about ten workers pay into the system for every three recipients drawing money out of the system. By the year 2030, that ratio will be ten workers to *five* recipients. An additional strain was placed on the system when benefits were indexed. During times of high inflation, benefits now rise substantially, and automatically.

By 1982 the Social Security system had to borrow money from Medicare to pay out benefits, making it look more like Social Insecurity. Then in 1983 Congress passed legislation reforming Social Security: Tax rates were increased in a series of

steps; more people were brought into the system as contributors (including federal employees who joined the government in 1984 or later, and all state and local government employees); the cost of living adjustment was delayed and redrawn; and benefits to "double-dippers" (retired military personnel who draw a military pension in addition to Social Security) were reduced. All these reforms were properly calculated to return the Social Security system to actuarial soundness. By 1988 the system was generating large *surpluses*. These would be necessary to fund the baby boomers' retirement several years down the road.

All would now be fine if the Social Security system could stash its cash somewhere and let it accumulate. Unfortunately, the high deficits of the 1980s forced the federal government to borrow from the Social Security trust fund, just as it had borrowed from Medicare earlier in the decade. That prompted some observers to worry that a crunch might still come when the time to reckon the bill arrives several years hence. Will workers then be willing to pay higher Social Security taxes to continue the transfer to a large population of retired baby boomers? Or support higher income taxes to repay the loans made to cover general federal expenses? Pessimists contend that the system will run into trouble down the road. And many people question the basic equitability of the system, both in terms of how it distributes income to the elderly and how it shifts income across the generations. As the ratio of workers to beneficiaries declines, the issue of generational equity will certainly become more significant. But the system has worked relatively well for fifty years, and has engendered such widespread support that, whatever adjustments are necessary, it should continue functioning successfully into the distant future.

AFDC

In contrast to the widespread acceptance and lack of controversy enjoyed by Social Security, **Aid to Families with Dependent Children** (AFDC) is the most controversial welfare state program, and the one most people cite when they speak pejoratively of "welfare." AFDC conjures up images of women having babies solely to receive increased welfare benefits and able-bodied men spending their girl-friends' welfare money on alcohol while they lounge away the daylight hours. AFDC, critics argue, destroys the initiative to work and encourages the breakup of marriages so that the mothers may qualify for benefits.

Aid to Families with Dependent Children, which dates back to the New Deal of the 1930s, provides cash benefits (unusual in programs aimed at the poor) to families with a dependent child or children. Because the program has no na-tional standards, benefits differ from state to state. State governments determine the level of state participation in this largely federal- and state-funded—but locally administered—program. In August 1988 (a typical month for AFDC), there were 10,967,200 AFDC recipients in this country. Maximum benefits for a family of four ranged from $144 in Mississippi to $823 in Alaska. The total allocation of federal and state funds for the month was $1.43 billion.

For many years, AFDC was a noncontroversial program that provided aid mainly to widows and their families not covered by other programs. In the 1960s, however, the number of recipients more than doubled—from 4 to 10 million—and costs quadrupled, to $4 billion. This explosive growth was due primarily to an increasing awareness of the welfare programs among potential recipients, and a lessening of the social stigma traditionally attached to those on welfare.

Other factors contributed to the dramatic increase in AFDC recipients as well: The Supreme Court outlawed rules requiring recipients to be without husbands or any other "man in the house"; state residency requirements were outlawed in 1969; and states raised benefit levels and loosened eligibility requirements so that, by 1970, 81 percent of new applicants were approved, compared with 54 percent in 1953.

These single mothers share a house as one means of coping with the pressures on single-parent families. Imagine the difficulties single parents face in juggling the demands of housing, jobs, child care, and—often—job training or education. What kinds of help should society provide? In America social programs have always tempered community concern with a heavy dose of individualism. *(© Shelley Gazin/ The Image Works)*

Many critics of the welfare system argue that it has created a permanent class of dependent and disadvantaged people, particularly black people. Welfare, in their view, contributes to the disintegration of the black family and provides incentives for teenagers to become pregnant and go on welfare for themselves, thereby gaining independence from their own families. Welfare dependence, critics maintain, can be passed on from one generation to another. When the government becomes the chief supplier of economic well-being, the role of the husband and father is diminished and his place in the family is undermined.

Are such allegations grounded in fact? The evidence is mixed. One large-scale study found that the children of families living on welfare were no more likely to go on welfare themselves than were other people. The charge that welfare programs such as AFDC encourage illegitimate births was also challenged by statistics showing that such births also increased among whites and nonwelfare teenagers. Yet some elements in these criticisms have stuck, if only in popular attitudes about welfare.[1]

Perhaps the most difficult question concerns work motivation. Why should a welfare mother, for example, take a low-paying job when she could make almost as much by not working? Yet if welfare payments are lowered to create greater work incentives, children in poor families will suffer. Is that fair, or wise, policy? The federal government requires all welfare recipients with children over age six to register for work. Many states have created "workfare" programs, which require welfare recipients to take low-paying jobs in order to remain eligible for assistance. To their critics, workfare often fails because welfare recipients view it as punitive—even as a form of slavery. In one successful program, developed in Massachusetts, the recipients were allowed to decide for themselves whether to seek a job, get career counseling or training, or participate at all. Many welfare recipients chose to participate. The program saved the state $100 million over five years, even including expenses paid by the state for day-care and job placement services.[2]

The pressure from state governors for welfare reform intensified in 1987, and in June of 1988 the Senate passed a workfare measure aimed at getting people off the welfare roles and into jobs.

The significant growth in AFDC through the 1960s and into the 1970s was a healthy development in many ways. More of those in need found help, and thus the proportion of Americans living in poverty fell. AFDC benefits have gradually approached the poverty line and, in combination with other assistance programs, such as food stamps, have helped pull many poor families out of poverty. New methods of counting family income tightened eligibility requirements significantly in 1981 and again in 1984. The tighter standards resulted in a large drop in the number of AFDC recipients in 1982, just when poverty rates were at their highest during the recession. There were fewer participants in 1985 than there had been five years earlier, although the number of persons in poverty had increased by 10 percent. From 1985 to the end of the Reagan administration in 1988, the number of AFDC recipients increased slightly. The cost of the program increased faster than the number of participants.

Job Programs

Almost everyone agrees that the best source of income security for poor people is a steady job. Unfortunately, that's as far as consensus reaches. A wide variety of federal programs, put in place over the last two decades, emphasize one of two general approaches—job placement or job training. The Great Society programs of the 1960s simply focused on *placing* people in jobs. One strategy (used, for example, by the Work Incentive Program, aimed at welfare mothers but now discontinued) was to provide federal money to state and local governments to hire poor people to do community service work. But the jobs led nowhere, and when funding for these programs ran out, participants were right back where they started. The Comprehensive Employment and Training Act (CETA), enacted in 1973 to replace several earlier, more diverse programs, tried a different tactic. Here the idea was to encourage certain nongovernment employers to hire people for newly created jobs, providing federal funds for a limited

Text continues following the color essay.

Life in the Margin

Poverty Now

UPI/BETTMANN NEWSPHOTOS

One difficulty of policy making—or, as citizens, of evaluating how well policy is being made—is our tendency to cling to stereotypes. Naturally, we must simplify and organize images of the world to avoid being overwhelmed by its booming, buzzing complexity. Yet we should always be sensitive to the possibility that the world is not quite so simple nor so static as our stereotypical images make it. Ask most kids—or adults—to draw a stick-figure picture of a family, and you'll likely get something straight out of a 1950s or 1960s TV sitcom: a Daddy, a Mommy, and two kids. Daddy may even have a briefcase, and Mommy an apron, to indicate their "traditional" roles as breadwinner and housewife. That may be a reassuring picture, but according to recent estimates it's accurate for only 7 percent of U.S. families—fewer than 1 in 14!

Our ideas about poverty are similarly "reassuring." If we think about it at all, we tend to use images left over from Charles Dickens or Horatio Alger—turn-of-the-century stereotypes barely transformed by contemporary touches. Daily life offers few opportunities to correct these images, since poverty both creates and reinforces its own isolation (a fact Michael Harrington brought home in the title of his 1971 book about poverty: *The Other America*). Toward the end of our own century, poverty in America is not quaint; it is not restricted to a tiny minority of persons, primarily black or Hispanic; and it is not the fate of only the shiftless or lazy or undermotivated.

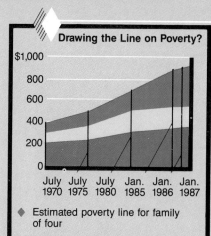

Drawing the Line on Poverty?

$1,000
800
600
400
200
0

July 1970 July 1975 July 1980 Jan. 1985 Jan. 1986 Jan. 1987

◆ Estimated poverty line for family of four

Median monthly income at minimum wage

◆ Estimated maximum monthly welfare benefits

The reality of poverty today is irritatingly mundane and frustratingly resistant to amelioration. It is a web of interrelated circumstances that traps its victims in some combination of inadequate nutrition; deferred or denied health care; substandard or nonexistent housing; a lack of educational and employment opportunities; and, rather than a supportive, encouraging social environment, the presence of various "social pathologies"—self-defeating behaviors ranging from child neglect to gang violence. (Social pathologies are not associated only with poverty, of course, but one factor which supports them is that the nonpoor frequently, and wrongly, perceive the poor as alien, and thus not fully sympathetic persons.) Caught in such a web, many are slowly worn down, and few escape. Today large numbers of Americans move regularly into and out of poverty, as their circumstances shift marginally for better or worse. Stereotypes aside, there are no sharp boundaries to poverty. Its costs to society are incalculable, but immense.

Children and Poverty

By the mid-1980s the U.S. Census Bureau conservatively estimated that

SUPERSTOCK

12½ million children were living in poverty—slightly more than one-fifth of all children in the country. Among kids in families headed by a single woman, more than half—almost 7 million—were living in poverty.

Health statistics provide one of the clearest measures of poverty among children. The 1985 infant mortality rate (the number of deaths per live births) was 11 per 1,000 in the United States, higher than in Finland, Japan, Sweden, France, Denmark, Norway, the Netherlands, Switzerland, Australia, Belgium, Canada, Hong Kong, Singapore, West Germany, East Germany, Ireland, Spain, and the United Kingdom. Most of these American infants die not of rare ailments but simply because their mothers lacked adequate prenatal care; the babies were born too tiny

and too frail to survive. As the Executive Director of a Congressional Commission to Prevent Infant Mortality put it: "Infant mortality is not a medical problem. It is a social problem with medical consequences."[1] Supporting that view is the unequal distribution of infant mortality. The rate for black infants is almost twice the rate for whites (19 per 1,000 compared with 10 per 1,000); in Washington, D.C., the rate averaged 22.1 per 1,000 between 1980 and 1985—twice as high as the nation's rate.

Among women of childbearing age in the United States, 26 percent have no medical insurance to cover maternity. Making matters worse, 18 million children under thirteen have *no* health insurance at all, even though many have working parents.[2] Faced with such facts, in 1979 the

Percent of Population Living in Poverty

1979	1982	1985	1987
11.7 9.7 16.8	15.0 13.4 19.5	14.0 12.5 18.3	13.5 12.0 17.5

◆ Official poverty rate (includes cash benefits as income)
◆ Poverty rate counting food and housing benefits as income
◆ Poverty rate not counting other benefits as income

SOURCES: Public Information Office, Bureau of the Census, U.S. Department of Commerce.

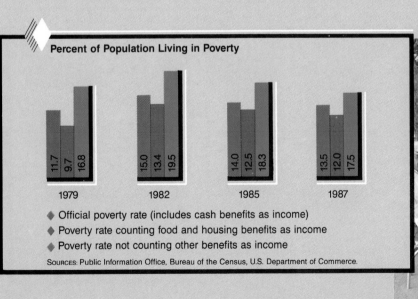

SUPERSTOCK

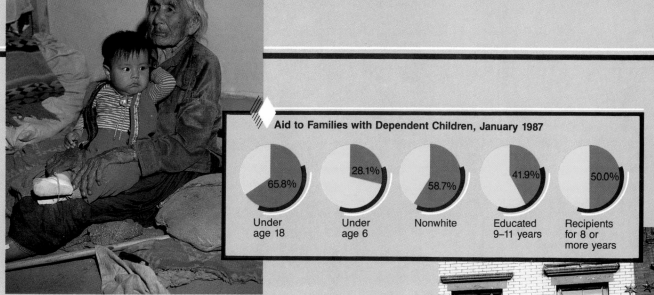

Aid to Families with Dependent Children, January 1987

65.8% Under age 18 | 28.1% Under age 6 | 58.7% Nonwhite | 41.9% Educated 9–11 years | 50.0% Recipients for 8 or more years

federal government set thirteen top-priority goals relating to pregnancy and infant health, but current projections indicate that only three of the goals will be met by 1990. One goal which will not be met is that no more than 10 percent of pregnant women—regardless of county, race, or ethnic group—will go without prenatal care during the first three months of pregnancy. The projection for 1990 is that 23.6 percent of pregnant women *will* go without such care—almost 1 in 4. For pregnant black women, the projected rate is *38.5 percent*.[3] Statistics like these are the clearest indicator of how poverty is regenerated.

Nonurban Poverty

Stereotypes notwithstanding, many poor Americans do *not* live in urban ghettoes. In fact, the rural poverty rate (18.1 percent in 1988) is slightly higher than the urban rate. These nonurban poor persons differ from their urban counterparts in significant ways. Their households often include two parents, with at least one holding a menial job at or near minimum wage, which thus reduces the family's eligibility for government assistance. And since many of them live in small towns or sparsely populated areas, relief offices and job-training programs are hard to find.

The nonurban poor represent 30 percent of the poverty population, but they receive only 20 percent of the money spent on poverty programs. And since 7 out of 8 new jobs created in the United States are in metropolitan areas, they are far from whatever programs and support structures are available. Indeed, although Congress has been responsive to farm interests, including a sizable drought-aid package passed in 1988, most of the rural poor are not family farmers; only 7 percent of them depend on farms for work and sustenance.[4]

The Homeless

The cause of homelessness is a lack of housing.[5]

"Street People" is a reassuring name for homeless persons, because it distances them from us by implying that they have *chosen* the street or, perhaps, that they are different somehow ("mental cases," mostly). Again, the facts contradict the stereotypes. Families with young children are the fastest-growing segment of the homeless population in America, which numbered somewhere between 300,000 and 3,000,000 in 1988. A recent study found that—except for alcohol and drug abuse—the most frequent illnesses among a sample of the homeless population

were trauma (31 percent), upper respiratory disorders (28 percent), limb disorders (19 percent), mental illness (16 percent), skin diseases (15 percent), hypertension (14 percent), and neurological diseases (12 percent).[6]

Given this array of ills, and the relatively small proportion of mental illness in the sample, it is impossible to dismiss homelessness as a psychiatric problem. People turn to the street for a variety of particular reasons specific to each case. Yet two generalizations *can* be made about homelessness: first, that life in the street cannot be a reasonable goal for most persons who end up there and, second, that street life reinforces the conditions of poverty for its inhabitants. In the words of one homeless man: "It's like there isn't any bottom. It's like a black hole sucking you inside."[7]

The Working Poor

Perhaps the most persistent fallacy about poverty in the United States is that escape is simply a matter of finding and keeping a job. In 1988 working a full-time job for one year at minimum wage yielded $6,968—an annual income that was $431 *below* the poverty line for a family head with one dependent, and $4,644 below the line for a family of four. The plight of the working poor is apparent in this conclusion from a 1985 study: "Two million adults—fifty percent more than in 1978—worked full time throughout the year, yet they and their families remained in poverty. Another 7.1 million poor worked either full-time jobs for part of the year or in part-time jobs."[8]

There are at least two major problems with the existence of substantial numbers of working poor persons. First, in a nation attached to the notion of rewarding work, it hardly seems fair to reward full-time work with poverty conditions.

UPI/BETTMANN NEWSPHOTOS

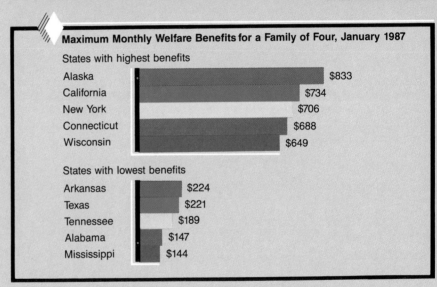

Maximum Monthly Welfare Benefits for a Family of Four, January 1987

States with highest benefits

Alaska	$833
California	$734
New York	$706
Connecticut	$688
Wisconsin	$649

States with lowest benefits

Arkansas	$224
Texas	$221
Tennessee	$189
Alabama	$147
Mississippi	$144

Second, the incentive for getting off the welfare rolls and onto the work rolls must necessarily be small when the effort will not lift oneself or one's family from poverty. The insult on top of these injuries is the social stigma many Americans attach to being poor, on the mistaken assumption that persons in poverty have chosen their own lot and deserve their station.

[1]Kathleen Sylvester, "Infant Mortality: It's as American as Apple Pie," *Governing* (a publication of *Congressional Quarterly*), July 1988, pp. 49, 58.
[2]"Forgotten Patients: 37 Million Americans Don't Have Health-Insurance Protection," *Newsweek*, Aug. 22, 1988, p. 53.
[3]"US Falling Short on Its Infant Health Goals," *New York Times*, July 10, 1988, Sec. 1, p. 13.

[4]John McCormick, "America's Third World," *Newsweek*, Aug. 8, 1988, pp. 20–24.
[5]Jonathan Kozol in *Rachel and Her Children: Homeless Families in America* (New York: Crown, 1988); reviewed by Kai Erickson in "The Chronic Calamity," *The Nation*, Apr. 2, 1988, p. 465.
[6]The Massachusetts Medical Society study, cited by Jonathan Kozol in "Are the Homeless Crazy?" *Harper's*, September 1988, pp. 17–18.
[7]"Richard Lazarus," from Kozol, *Rachel and Her Children*, p. 465.
[8]Sar A. Levitan and Isaac Shapiro, *Working but Poor: America's Contradiction* (Johns Hopkins U Press, 1987); quoted in Julie Kosterlitz and Jonathan Rauch, "Working, but Still Poor," *National Journal*, June 18, 1988, p. 1601. The data are from Kosterlitz and Rauch directly.

SOURCES: Unless otherwise cited, data are from House Committee on Ways and Means; Census Bureau; Congressional Research Service; and Federal Register.

time to pay their salaries, with the expectation that the jobs would then be maintained by the employer after program funding ceased. Again experience showed that these jobs were dead-end positions, which were frequently dropped when CETA funding ended.

The second approach, job *training*, took shape in one of the War on Poverty programs called the Job Corps, aimed at young adults 16 to 21. This program is still in existence. Job Corps enrollees go to Job Corps Training Centers to learn a trade, where they are given spending money, which increases over time, as an incentive to stay in the program. Participants spend an average of 8 to 12 months at a training center. After graduating from the training center, participants receive placement help and job counseling at local offices in their home towns. Another training-oriented program, the Job Training Partnership Act (JTPA), replaced CETA in 1982. Most JTPA participants go through classroom training and then gain help in job placement. Eligibility requirements for JTPA are much stricter than CETA requirements were, substantially reducing the number of participants. Although some on-the-job training is available, most JTPA training takes place in classrooms. To participate, however, a person must have some outside source of income for the period of training— JTPA does not pay wages or living expenses. This excludes many who might benefit from and are anxious to receive such training. Federal outlays for job training and employment dropped significantly during the 1980s, from $10.8 billion in 1979 to an estimated $5.2 billion in 1989.

Other Income Security Programs

We now consider three additional types of income security programs: (1) Supplemental Security Income (SSI); (2) unemployment compensation; and (3) tax expenditures for income security.

SSI In 1974 Congress created the **Supplemental Security Income** (SSI) program to provide added assistance to the aged, blind, and disabled. More like AFDC than Social Security, SSI pays benefits on the basis of need and is federally funded with state supplements. This program nearly doubled the number of people receiving federal income security assistance (other than through Social Security). SSI outlays from the federal government totaled over $12.6 billion and reached about 4.3 million people in 1988. A recent government study estimated that only about half those eligible for certain categories of SSI payments were applying for them. One of the major reasons cited by eligible nonparticipants for not seeking benefits was that they "don't like the idea of accepting what some people might call welfare."[3] In this country there is an unfortunate stigma attached to "welfare" programs (that part of the welfare state aimed primarily at the poor).

UNEMPLOYMENT COMPENSATION Unemployment compensation is a federal program administered by the Labor Department through various state employment agencies. It is predominantly state-funded through a tax on employers that varies from 0.6 percent to 4.6 percent of wages, depending on the state.

Benefits differ from state to state, as do eligibility requirements and the length of time benefits can be received. Most states provide basic coverage for twenty-six weeks, and federal legislation extends coverage for an additional thirteen to twenty-six weeks. The average duration of benefits received is sixteen weeks. The system covers workers who have a history of regular employment and have lost their jobs, but not those who have never held a regular job or who hold jobs not covered by the program, such as domestic work. The federal outlay for unemployment compensation varies with the unemployment rate. It reached $31 billion at the height of the recession in 1983 and subsided to $15.7 billion in 1988. Increasing *under*employment has reduced the number of persons eligible for unemployment compensation. According to the Federal Reserve Bank of San Francisco, the number of people covered by unemployment insurance declined about 25 percent between 1980 and 1988.[4]

TAX EXPENDITURES FOR INCOME SECURITY The federal government also provides income security support through tax expenditure items. The largest single item in this category is the exclusion of employer contributions to pension plans, which amounted to a tax expenditure of $56.1 billion in 1988. Taken together, such tax expenditures totaled close to $95.4 billion for 1988. These benefits are generally regressive; that is, they increase with increased income and are worth more to persons in the high tax bracket.

Health Care Programs

Several aspects of the U.S. health care system are almost universally acknowledged: Many Americans receive excellent health care; American medicine ranks among the most advanced in the world; American health care is among the world's costliest; health care costs are increasing rapidly; many Americans do *not* receive adequate health care; the distribution of care is highly related to the patient's ability to pay; and the system needs reforming. There is no agreement, however, on what sort of reforms should be instituted. Some argue for a national health insurance scheme that would cover major medical expenses for all; others call for government controls on increasing costs; yet others advocate greater government involvement in the distribution and planning of health care.

In the United States, much of the average citizen's health care bill is paid for out of his or her own pocket. This stands in stark contrast to most other democratic, industrialized nations. The U.S. health care system has two major elements: a private health care system, in which costs are paid by consumers or through group insurance plans; and a public system, financed through government programs supplemented by consumer contributions. Those served only by the various publicly supported health services—the poor—are likely to have the lowest levels of health. Having the money to pay for services or buy insurance makes a significant difference in the quality of health care individuals receive.

For the average middle-class American covered by some form of private health insurance, basic health care is essentially guaranteed. Still, many insurance plans do not meet important medical needs. Catastrophic illness may boost costs beyond what insurance covers. Preventive measures

may not be covered by medical insurance. Then, too, millions of Americans have no medical insurance at all; they are constantly at risk. According to one estimate, one American out of six today lacks health insurance coverage from either public or private sources. Eleven million of these uninsured—almost a third of the total—are under age 18.[5]

President Franklin Roosevelt considered adding a national health insurance section to the Social Security Act of 1935, but chose not to because he feared arousing too much political opposition. The issue of a national health care plan has been politically volatile ever since. Most Americans favor some sort of national insurance, but the powerful opposition of the American Medical Association and other interest groups has doomed specific proposals over the years. The one major step toward government responsibility for health care was taken in 1965, when Congress, under the prodding of President Lyndon Johnson, created the Medicare/Medicaid programs. We now examine (1) Medicare and (2) other health care programs.

Medicare

Since its establishment in 1965, **Medicare** has become one of the mainstays of the U.S. welfare state. Medicare provides payments to everyone eligible for Social Security, to those classified as disabled, and to almost anyone who suffers from kidney failure. The program has two parts. Part A covers hospital, nursing home, and home health services for a specified period; it is available to all eligible persons and is financed through a payroll tax of 2.6 percent, split between employer and employee. Part B, which covers doctors' bills, outpatient hospital services, home health services, and certain other costs, is a voluntary program based on monthly premiums. Medicare, like private medical insurance, has limited benefits; that is, recipients must pay a portion of the costs out of their own pockets. Despite these limits, Medicare has come to cover an increasing share of the health care costs of the elderly.

Medicare has expanded rapidly. The steady and sharp increase in Medicare spending since its inception stems from three key factors. First, the es-

COMPARATIVE PERSPECTIVE

A Cure for British Health Care?

All national health systems have their problems. The National Health Service (NHS) of Great Britain, which serves 90 percent of the British population, has recently come under severe criticism. The service offers its users free cradle-to-grave medical and dental care. Established after World War II, the National Health Service has gained widespread acceptance in Britain. It cost about $40 billion in 1988, which was paid out of general revenue funds. Believed to be Europe's largest single employer, the NHS staff of over 1 million includes government-salaried physicians and other health care professionals. In England alone, the NHS contracts for the services of more than 25,000 general practitioners and 14,000 dentists. Although the government's 1988 NHS allocation was three times the size of the allocation in the last Labour government in 1979, most British citizens agree that the service needs more money to continue to function as currently structured. There is considerable difference of opinion, however, over whether the system of national health *should* remain unchanged, or whether it should be fundamentally restructured to allow for much more private-practice medicine in Britain.

In 1988, for the first time, a majority of Britons polled considered the NHS the most urgent problem facing the nation. The well-publicized death of an infant whose heart surgery was postponed five times because of nursing shortages spotlighted the problems. In March of 1988, fifty thousand trade unionists and health care workers demonstrated in London and other cities, advocating higher budget allocations for the NHS. The British government, in spite of a large budget surplus and plans to cut income tax rates, refused to raise the allocation beyond a $2 billion increase promised earlier by Prime Minister Margaret Thatcher. Many maintained that the Thatcher government was intentionally underfunding the NHS to disrupt the delivery of health care and bolster public acceptance of an expanded private health care system. Thatcher launched an "all-options-considered" review of the system. Even its supporters recognize that there are difficulties with the highly centralized structure of NHS. The task is to figure out how best to return the system to health.

SOURCE: Karen DeYoung, "Condition Critical: Britain's National Health Service Is Fighting for Its Life," *Washington Post National Weekly Edition*, March 28–April 3, 1988, pp. 6–7.

tablishment of Medicare prompted millions of people to seek medical care they would otherwise have done without. Second, the size of the elderly population covered by Medicare has been growing: By the year 2000, 13 percent of Americans will be over age sixty-five. Finally, hospital costs have soared, climbing at more than double the inflation rate.

In response to skyrocketing health care costs and a Medicare budget whose growth had exceeded all expectations, a major change was made in 1983, in the formula for allocating reimbursement for Medicare patients. Instead of reimbursing hospitals on a cost-plus basis (which allowed hospitals to set their own fees), the government established fixed-price reimbursement. The fixed-price scheme grouped medical procedures into 468 diagnosis-related groups. Based on this categorization, the hospital was reimbursed according to a predetermined fee, regardless of the actual cost of treatment. The effects of this change were both immediate and far-reaching. Within a year, the average hospital stay covered by Medicare had declined 20 percent and hospital occupancy rates had dropped to the lowest point in twenty years. Medical inflation was cut in half.

But negative effects were also rampant. Hospitals, now forced to economize, sometimes neglected necessary tests. Shortened hospital stays occasionally jeopardized a patient's recovery. Under the old system, hospitals could make internal, hidden transfers of benefits, bringing in a little extra money on Medicare patients to make up for the money lost on indigent patients without insurance. Under the new repayment scheme, such transfers were impossible. In an increasing number of cases, poor patients were turned away from private hospitals and referred to public facilities that became heavily burdened. By 1985, two years after the new payment system was introduced, transfers from private to public hospitals showed startling increases in many cities—up 680 percent, for example, in the Cook County Hospital in Chicago. Many feared that in the effort to economize, the nation was creating a two-tiered medical system, with separate and unequal care for the poor. Nevertheless, the federal outlay for Medicare continues to climb rapidly. For 1989 estimates ranged upwards of $84 billion—up from only $26.5 billion a decade earlier and up from $52.5 billion in 1983, when the new repayment scheme was first instituted.

In spite of spiraling expenditures, Medicare still covers only a fraction of the actual health costs of Medicare participants. The 1988 Catastrophic Health Care Law did begin to close the gap between coverage and actual costs, but it was only a beginning. And millions are not eligible for Medicare benefits at all.

Other Health Care Programs

We now probe (1) Medicaid, (2) nursing home care, and (3) health research, with an eye toward their initial goals, how they are—or are not—reaching those goals, and their overall impact.

MEDICAID **Medicaid,** a state-option program extends medical assistance to the needy. Each state establishes its own eligibility rules and compen-

sation levels. In many states, Medicaid coverage is limited to those receiving public assistance benefits. Other states use broader definitions of the "medically indigent." Medicaid has become the largest federal "in-kind" program: In 1988 the *federal* outlay for Medicaid (not counting state contributions) was $32.7 billion. Although Medicaid was originally intended to provide health care protection for the *non*elderly poor, 40 percent of Medicaid allocations now cover nursing home care, mostly for the elderly. Furthermore, Medicaid now assists only 40 percent of America's poor, and only half of America's poor children. Between 1977 and 1983, the number of Americans living in poverty grew by 10.5 million while the number of Medicaid recipients *declined* by 1.3 million. Between 1983 and 1987 the number of Medicaid recipients increased gradually (1.6 million over five years), while costs increased at a slightly higher rate.[6]

NURSING HOME CARE An editorial in the *New York Times* compared the cost of nursing home care to the San Andreas fault: Each is a disaster waiting to happen. Most people who enter nursing homes are not poor. Most people *in* nursing homes are poor, however, and the nursing home bills are often the reason. About half the $38 billion dollars that Americans spent on nursing home care in 1986 came from Medicaid. In 1988 the average cost of a year's stay in a nursing home was $22,000. By 2018, the estimated cost will more than double. It was the Reagan administration's position that the federal government had no role in providing long-term care to the nonpoor. The catastrophic health-care bill passed in 1988 provides very little coverage for custodial care. Medicare provides for skilled nursing home care only in an approved institution and only after three-days' hospitalization—conditions that apply to a tiny fraction of the persons now in nursing homes.

How is a nonpoor person going to meet the costs of nursing home care? "Medigap" insurance is designed to fill the gap between actual costs and what Medicare pays. But insurance policies to cover the possibility of an extended stay in a nursing home are very expensive, limited in coverage, or simply unavailable. The alternative? Check into a nursing home, become poor, and rely on Medicaid. Politicians tend to stay away from the nurs-

The American health system is often hard to figure out, especially for the elderly. One of the most pressing needs is for adequate nursing home care. A portion of that care is provided by government. This photo shows a resident of a Veterans Administration nursing home in Johnson City, Tennessee. *(Kenneth Murray/ Photo Researchers)*

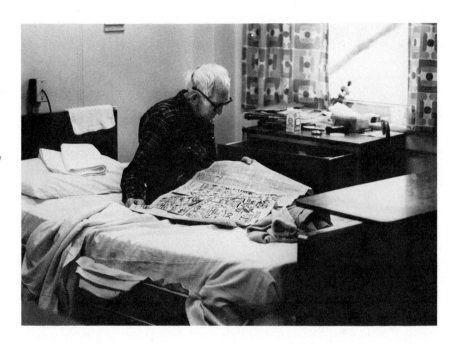

ing home issue because of the enormous potential costs to government of taking on a larger share of the nursing care burden.[7]

HEALTH RESEARCH An important but relatively inconspicuous part of the welfare state involves health research undertaken by or subsidized by the federal government. The advent of AIDS has made federal health research both more visible and more controversial, but federal involvement in health research dates much further back and covers a much broader range than the AIDS crisis suggests. Through the National Institutes of Health (NIH), a group of associated research organizations, and the Centers for Disease Control (CDC), the federal government conducts its own health research. Additionally, through a series of grants to universities and private research organizations, the government supports more health-related research. All together the federal government spent $6.5 billion on health research in 1988. Added to that figure is some significant portion of the $1 billion tax expenditure in health-related charitable contributions.

Health research has never been particularly controversial in the United States, yet the heightened visibility of medical research raises important and clearly debatable public policy issues. As an ex-

ample, in 1988, the NIH decided not to use tissue from aborted fetuses until the practice could be adequately regulated. The allocation of resources for certain kinds of medical research also generates public concern. Some very costly research has resulted in costly procedures that provide great benefits to a very small number of individuals—the development of artificial hearts, for example. And because many of the leading causes of illness and death in the United States are life-style related, perhaps there should be a more vigorous debate about spending large sums treating ills that result from life-style choices that individuals have some control over. In 1987, an estimated 136,000 deaths were caused by lung cancer, and 150,000 new cases of lung cancer were diagnosed. According to the American Cancer Society, smoking is responsible for 83 percent of all lung cancer cases and about 30 percent of all lung cancer deaths. This represents an enormous health care cost. How much of that cost should be borne by the public at large? Smoking is just one example of many. Our society has always wanted to act on the principle that no cost was too great to bear to save a human life, but the limitations of the real world give the lie to this principle. Choices have to be made. In a democracy those choices should be the subject of public discussion.

FIGURE 17–1
Gross Domestic Product Spent on Health Care (percent)

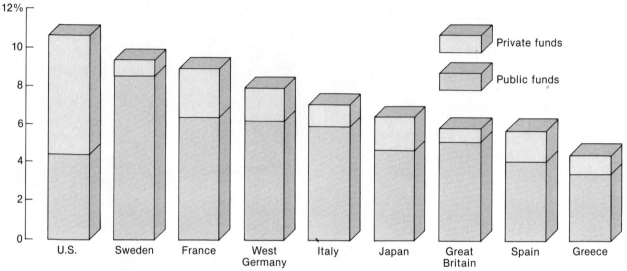

SOURCE: Organization for Economic Cooperation and Development

The United States spends a higher percentage of its gross domestic product on health care than several European countries, and twice as much per capita as Great Britain (see **Figure 17–1** and **Figure 17–2**). But money for health care doesn't translate directly into good health. Several Western European nations and Japan have longer life expectancies and lower infant mortality rates than the United States. Some of the best health care in the world is available in the United States, but medical services here are spotty and are often tied to wealth. As we have seen, many millions of people are significantly underserved.

Nutrition and Housing Programs

Let us now consider the impact of several nutrition and housing programs: (1) food stamps; (2) other nutrition programs; and (3) housing programs.

Food Stamps

In 1967 a group of American doctors traveled to an area where malnutrition had been reported. Their report stated: "Wherever we went and wherever we looked we saw children in significant numbers who were hungry and sick, children for whom hunger is a daily fact of life, and sickness in many forms an inevitability. The children we saw were more than just malnourished. They were hungry, weak, apathetic. Their lives are being shortened. They are visibly and predictably losing their health, their energy, their spirits."[8] Where was this tragedy taking place? In the United States itself, where according to the doctors' report, roughly 10 to 15 million people suffered from hunger or malnutrition.

The **food stamp program,** designed to respond to the problem of hunger in America, actually began as an experiment in 1961. The goal of the food stamp program was to give nutrition-program participants greater choice than was provided by the surplus-commodities program, which passed out a lot of peanut butter and canned chicken that was wasted because recipients didn't like it or want it. From the beginning, the food stamp program has gained important political support from food producers and marketers, who clearly benefit from the increased purchasing power the program generates for their industry exclusively. The linkage between benefits to participants and benefits to producers has always been explicit—food stamp

FIGURE 17–2
Annual Per Capita Expenditure for Health Care (in U.S. Dollars)

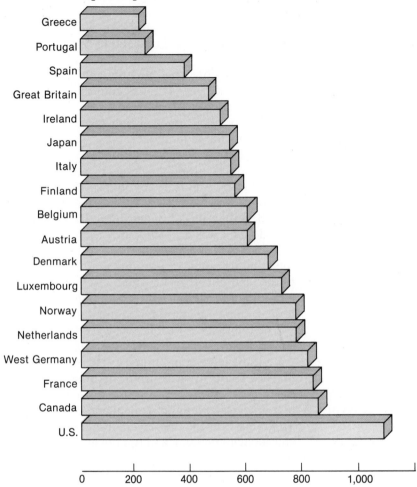

SOURCE: Organization for Economic Cooperation and Development

legislation is paired in the House of Representatives with legislation to help farmers. And the food stamp program is administered at the federal level through the Department of Agriculture and not, as we might expect, through the Department of Health and Human Services.

By 1973, food stamps had become the predominant federal program providing nutritional assistance for the poor. The food stamp program provides food coupons for all recipients of public assistance, as well as those whose income falls below specified levels. Administered jointly by the states and the federal government, it is funded entirely by the federal government. Each month those who qualify receive food coupons redeemable at groceries and supermarkets. Recipients qualify on the basis of need, as determined by income plus other assets. The food stamp program is one of the few government programs open to the working poor; candidates for food stamps, that is, need not be utterly destitute to qualify.

The food stamp program has dramatically reduced hunger and malnutrition in the United States. Because of food stamps, many poor people at least have food to eat. Along with several other nutrition-oriented assistance programs—particularly those providing school breakfasts and lunches—the food stamp program has been one of the bright spots for the poor in recent times.

According to its critics, however, the program grew too fast. Some argue that benefits should be cut back so only "truly poor" families receive assistance. Others claim that fraud is rampant—that benefits go to many nonpoor people. The Reagan administration, convinced that many undeserving people were receiving food stamps, curtailed food stamp eligibility and cut several hundred thousand people from the program in the 1980s. The number of participants in the food stamp program peaked in 1981 (at 22.1 million) and has been declining since then, in spite of a dramatic rise in the number of people living in poverty during the first half of the 1980s and a leveling off in the second half. In 1985 there were 19.1 million participants.

Other Nutrition Programs

The other major federal nutrition programs include the Child Nutrition program, which gives cash subsidies for food to day care centers and schools. The largest component of this program is the National School Lunch program. All together, federal outlays for the Child Nutrition program in 1988 amounted to $4.3 billion. In addition, the federal government sponsors the Temporary Emer-

gency Food Assistance program, providing commodities to people in urgent, short-term need of food, and the Women, Infants, and Children (WIC) program offering nutrition supplements for one segment of the population. Taken together, federal nutrition programs cost about $20.5 billion in 1988—roughly one-third the amount saved by taxpayers that year because contributions to employer-sponsored pension programs were tax deductible, or about one-seventh the total spent on interest for the federal debt.

In spite of the success of food stamps and the school lunch program, hunger has not disappeared from America. A commission created by President Reagan to look into the issue of hunger admitted there was hunger in the nation, but declared that it was not "rampant" or "widespread," as others had maintained. The report sided with the administration in asserting that the states, not the federal government, should design their own antihunger programs with federal money. No uniform national standards, it argued, were needed.

The Physicians' Task Force on Hunger in America, by contrast, reported in 1985 that 20 million Americans were going hungry at least some of the time—a sharp increase from the hunger levels of the late 1970s.[9] This rise in hunger was traced to higher levels of unemployment and cuts in federal programs. Some families went hungry because unemployment benefits had run out and they did not

By 1990 as many as 80 percent of mothers with infants under one year may be working—which makes some form of day care a necessity. To what extent should the government become involved? Are tax breaks for the expenses of day care enough? Or should government and employers actually provide services? *(Randy Piland/ New York Times Pictures)*

Child Care Programs: Sweden v. the United States

The social welfare system of Sweden provides a vast array of services for children and parents. To begin, the nation's compulsory health care system covers all pregnant women and provides contraceptive information, prenatal care and training, and preparation for parenting. Sweden also has an optional parental-leave program. Either parent may choose to stay home with the infant for the first nine months and still draw 90 percent of his or her salary. An additional leave of three months can be taken at a reduced salary, and parents can take up to 60 days leave each year (for each child) in the event of illness.

The Swedish government also provides financial aid to families with a child under 16. In 1985 the allowance was $380 a year for each child, and it increased with third and subsequent children. Single parents are also protected by the system. Child support is required from the absent parent, but, if it is not paid, the government advances the money and assumes responsibility for regaining it. National and municipal governments provide a housing allowance to families that meet a means test (in 1983 approximately one-third of Swedish families received some housing supplement). A network of preschool facilities is sponsored and licensed mainly by the national and regional governments; however, demand for preschool programs exceeds availability.

Child care in the United States is less comprehensive, and the delivery of services is more complicated and scattered. People who are financially able can purchase excellent prenatal and infant care, while those who are not must depend on help from various government programs, charities, and voluntary groups. The WIC (Women, Infants, and Children) federal program has provided assistance to millions of poor women and children, and help is also available through Medicaid at the state level. Cuts in these programs during the 1980s, however, left large numbers without financial help. The United States is the *only* industrialized western nation without a statutory maternity leave or parental benefit. In 1978, federal law declared that pregnancy and childbirth must be treated like any illness or disability and therefore could not jeopardize one's job. However, no federal policy yet exists concerning parental leave for childbirth; parents must negotiate leave time with their employers. While Americans can claim a tax deduction for dependent children, no child allowance program has been enacted. Housing subsidies, too, are far less available than in Sweden; although the mortgage interest deduction in the U.S. tax code is a major subsidy to homeowners, it is not targeted for families with children. Child support is also handled differently than in Sweden. When support is not paid, the aggrieved parent must seek relief in the courts. No provision exists yet for the government to supply missing financial support.

Day care arrangements in the United States are varied. Again, for those who can pay, excellent facilities or caretakers may be found, and, over the years, federal programs have provided some day care facilities. Nonetheless, many parents cannot afford day care and do not qualify for assistance. The Children's Defense Fund estimates that seven million children under age 13 now spend part of each day without any adult caretaker.

These different patterns of provision for children reveal differences in each society's philosophy. Sweden is far more committed to a welfare state approach that is comprehensive and emphasizes equality of services. The American approach illustrates a scattered and less comprehensive adoption of welfare measures. The United States more or less provides for those who are worst off but does not extend protections and programs to the degree found in Sweden. Even with recent congressional proposals for a larger federal role in child care, the U.S. system reflects our ambivalent attitudes about the welfare state.

SOURCES: Ruth Sidel, *Women and Children Last* (New York: Penguin, 1986); UNICEF, *The State of the World's Children* (New York: Oxford, 1987); R. Berfenstam and I. William-Olsson, *Early Child Care in Sweden* (London: Gordon and Breach, 1973); Halbert B. Robinson *et al.*, *Early Child Care in the United States of America* (London: Gordon and Breach, 1973); and Laura Walker, "Early Child Care in Sweden and the United States," unpublished paper, University of North Carolina, Department of Political Science, 1988.

qualify for welfare. This happened because in most states two-parent families did not fall under the usual welfare provisions, which were designed for mothers and children alone. The presence of a husband disqualified needy families. (This was a perverse element in welfare policy that some states did not follow. Congress has been unwilling to impose uniform national standards to remove this aspect of eligibility, which works against a stable family—one of the best long-term solutions to poverty.) In other cases, the hungry were children who were no longer receiving diet supplements and formulas through the WIC (Women, Infants, and Children) program, which reached only 28 percent of those eligible in 1984.[10]

The federal government provides indirect nutrition subsidies to everyone in America through the agricultural income stabilization programs ($20.3 billion in 1988), and tax expenditures on agriculture, which amounted to a whopping $795 million in savings to corporations and individuals in 1988. The benefits of these programs are enjoyed directly by the producers of food, but also, in part, by all of us who eat food produced in the United States.

Public housing has sometimes been a modest success; other times, it has been spectacularly flawed. In this photo, we see tenants working at a low-income housing project in Boston. Overall, spending on low-income housing falls far short of acknowledged needs. *(AP/Wide World Photos)*

Housing Programs

Federal programs to provide housing assistance fall into two large categories: (1) tax expenditures and credit programs to lower the cost of buying housing for the nonpoor and (2) programs to provide public housing or housing supplements for the poor. Both categories also benefit the housing industry—an important segment of the economy. Private purchasers of homes in the United States are eligible for the first set of housing assistance. This comes in the form of tax deductions on the amount paid in interest on a home mortgage and the amount paid in home property taxes. These deductions may be used for a principal residence and a second home. The deductibility of mortgage interest and property tax on owner-occupied homes created a tax expenditure of $43.7 billion dollars in 1988—that's the amount saved by homeowners and given up by the federal government. Additionally, the federal government provides loans through the Federal Housing Administration (FHA) and the Veterans Administration (VA) to qualified purchasers of homes. These loans are offered on more favorable terms than loans from private lenders, thus lowering the cost of borrowing money to buy a home. These housing programs are aimed at a broad spectrum of Americans—everyone able to buy a home.

The second category of federal housing programs is specifically for the poor. Initially, this category was restricted to public housing. Since 1937, the federal government has given funds to local governments to construct or buy inexpensive housing units. Although never glamorous, these housing units were designed to be structurally sound and made available at low rents based on income and family size. While some small-city public housing projects are very successful, high-density public housing in urban areas is frequently marked by high crime rates and vandalism. Public housing has never been favored by private real estate interests like the National Association of Home Builders and the National Association of Real Estate Boards, which would rather not have the federal government compete with the private sector in building and renting apartments. In 1968, Congress launched a set of subsidy and rent supplement programs to help the working poor rent or buy a home from designated nongovernment sources. These programs were revised in 1974, tightening up eligibility requirements for individuals, and requiring higher levels of individual contributions to the total housing costs. Section 8 of the 1974 legislation provides cash supplements to individuals seeking to buy or rent a home. These supplements were intended to stimulate the construction of private-sector, low-cost housing.

Housing programs for poor people suffered some of the most severe cutbacks when social spending was reduced in the 1980s. The number of new housing units built under Section 8 plummeted from nearly 100,000 in 1982 to one-tenth that number in 1987. In 1981, funding for low-income housing projects totaled $30 billion. *All* federal subsidized housing program outlays in 1988 totaled just $7.5 billion.

The cutbacks in federal housing programs during the 1980s were coupled with a large increase in homelessness. The homeless problem rose to crisis proportions during the 1980s, landing on the covers of *Time* and *Newsweek*. Estimates in 1988 of the number of Americans without homes ranged from a conservative 300,000 to over 3 million. Of course, there have always been homeless people in this country, as in all countries. But the sheer numbers and the variety of individuals living on the streets points to a genuine public policy problem. Los Angeles County alone estimates that it has 34,000 homeless persons. Whole families, unable to pay their rent or meet mortgage obligations, live in dilapidated cars or move from one emergency relief shelter to another. (Studies of homeless children indicate that more than 50 percent display signs of clinical depression and lack of significant developmental progress.) Deinstitutionalization—releasing marginally self-sufficient individuals from financially burdened public mental institutions—further swells the ranks of the new street people. In some cities, veterans, most from the Vietnam War, make up close to half of all homeless males. And large numbers of immigrants—some legal, some not—add to the homeless total.

As the 1980s come to an end, governments in the United States at all levels must grapple with the enormity and complexity of the homeless problem. Some actively seek innovative responses to this expensive and burdensome problem in a time of fiscal austerity. Others try to deny the magnitude of the problem. The questions raised by the homeless crisis are those that constantly confront the welfare state: What does a society owe to its members in trouble? and How should that debt be paid?[11]

Evaluating the Welfare State

How we view the welfare system depends to some extent on our individual political philosophy. Conservatives tend to cast a jaundiced eye on government intervention in the marketplace and spending on social programs, while liberals generally support welfare state programs. We now explore (1) the conservative view; (2) the liberal perspective; and (3) how welfare policy reflects political and societal realities.

The Conservative Approach

Conservatives advocate minimal government involvement in the marketplace—even in the labor market. According to many conservatives, government welfare benefits discourage people from seeking employment, thereby undermining market mechanisms that would efficiently deal with unemployment. When benefits are raised too high, the argument goes, incentives to work are reduced, and those who do work become discouraged. In areas such as health care and housing, conservatives also contend that the market should do more and the government less. Private enterprise should be looked to as the primary solution.

Conservative critic Charles Murray denounces the Great Society programs of the 1960s. Like many conservatives, he believes these welfare programs encouraged poverty, rather than combating it: "The first effect of the new [welfare] rules was to make it profitable for the poor to behave in the short term in ways that were destructive in the long term. Their second effect was to mask these long-term losses—to subsidize irretrievable mistakes. We tried to provide more for the poor and produced more poor instead. We tried to remove the barriers to escape from poverty, and inadvertently built a trap."[12]

President Reagan made significant reductions in many federal welfare programs. Reagan assured observers that no cuts would affect the "truly needy"—a term repeated by many members of his administration. The implication was that many who were not "truly needy" were receiving benefits. The problem was determining exactly who the "truly needy" were.

The Reagan administration maintained that the poor would be supported by a basic "safety net" of programs—Social Security, Medicare, veterans' compensation and pensions, Supplemental Security Income, free school lunches, Head Start and summer jobs for youth, and AFDC. However, the three largest safety net programs—Social Security, Medicare, and veterans' benefits—provide benefits for millions who do not live in poverty.

As it turned out, 23 percent of the approximately 25 million Americans with incomes below the poverty line were receiving no benefits from the safety net programs, and 60 percent were getting either nothing or no more than a free school lunch on school days for their children. Ironically, the Reagan cuts, as enacted, hit the working poor the hardest. For example, a typical working mother in New York with two school-age children had her disposable income reduced by 15 percent from $700 to $600 a month, as a result of the cuts.

Reagan administration policies designed to shrink allocations for entitlement and welfare programs generally accomplished their goals. The largest cuts in percentage terms were made in AFDC, food stamps, and Medicare. The only programs that showed an increase in percentage terms over this period were Supplemental Security Income and the nutrition program for women, infants, and children (known as WIC). Both these

programs were increased by Congress contrary to the original proposals of the administration.

The Liberal Critique

The U.S. welfare state has been largely a liberal creation, so liberals tend to be defensive about it. But they have also criticized its inadequacies. Liberals cite three key problems with the welfare system, summarized as *too little, too complicated,* and *too late.*

TOO LITTLE To liberals, the system provides less than it should. Many people fall through the cracks, and millions who are eligible for various welfare benefits never apply. As a result, poverty continues to pose a major problem for U.S. society. Many liberals charge that the absence of a comprehensive national health plan constitutes a critical failing of the welfare state. Although liberals differ on how to address the system's shortcomings, they generally acknowledge the need for more comprehensive health coverage.

TOO COMPLICATED This criticism centers on the absence of a genuinely *national* welfare system. Benefits vary considerably from state to state, often with no reasonable basis for the differences. Under the influence of Daniel Patrick Moynihan (later elected as a Democratic senator from New York State), President Richard Nixon proposed a nationalization of welfare benefits, in 1969, in his Family Assistance Program. Ironically, this initiative was defeated in Congress by a coalition of conservatives who found it too liberal and liberals who found its assistance provisions too stingy.

TOO LATE Many liberals view the current U.S. welfare system as more of a series of Band-Aids than a comprehensive solution to poverty. The various programs, it is argued, patch up the victims of our social and economic systems—those who fail, who fall by the wayside, who can't keep up. But the real problem is that our social and economic systems themselves create so many needy. The proposed solution here is a full-employment economy: With everyone working, the burdens

The best cure for poverty is a good job, which often depends on education or training, affordable child care and transportation, and economic policies aimed at creating jobs and lowering unemployment. Most Americans now expect the government to play an active role. *(UPI/Bettmann Newsphotos)*

and needs of welfare would be sharply reduced, although not eliminated. At the same time, more people would gain needed skills and self-respect. Liberals in Congress have introduced various bills that would provide jobs for the unemployed by making government an employer of last resort. But no such program has ever been acted on. The Comprehensive Employment and Training Act (CETA), which provided a relatively small number of public service jobs for the chronically unemployed, was not the full-scale employment program many had called for, and it has widely been viewed as a failure.

Noting that more and more children have become the victims of poverty, some liberals have

proposed programs specifically for our youngest citizens. By 1985, 40 percent of the poor were children. One in five American children lived in poverty as officially defined—twice the rate for adults. More than half of these poor children lived in female-headed households, where mothers typically were young, unmarried, and uneducated. During the 1980s, black children particularly had lost ground.

Reflections on Policy

The U.S. welfare state has become more humane, more extensive (and more expensive) over the last twenty-five years, yet notable problems remain in both social insurance and public assistance programs. Welfare state programs have made a difference, as **Table 17–1** shows. Poverty has been reduced substantially through government assistance, and the combination of federal taxes and transfer payments has made a significant impact on the overall distribution of income.

By liberal standards, however, the U.S. welfare state still falls short, especially by comparison with most Western European nations. We lack universal health coverage, millions of Americans live in poverty, and hunger continues to sap our human resources. U.S. welfare programs simply have not eliminated real need. Although Americans spend more per capita on health care than the citizens of most other nations, the quality of that care is uneven—better for those with the ability to pay more, worse for those relying on publicly supported medical programs. And we spend considerably less of our national income on welfare state programs overall, compared with most other democratic, industrialized countries.[13]

The reasons for this disparity are obvious. Fundamentally, the forces that created the welfare state in Europe have been far weaker in the United States. Most notably, as we mentioned in Chapter 1, left-wing political parties and trade unions have been less influential here. As a result, most of the major leaps forward in welfare state programs have come only in the face of severe crises or unusual political circumstances. And, as we noted in

TABLE 17–1
Poverty in the 1980s

	Poverty rate	Rate including food stamps and noncash benefits	Rate without government benefits
1979	11.7	9.7	16.8
1982	15.0	13.4	19.5
1985	14.0	12.5	18.3
1987	13.5	12.0	17.5

SOURCE: Public Information Office, Bureau of Census.

Chapter 6, the poor are less likely to vote and become politically involved.

The effectiveness of anti–welfare interest groups has also played a role in weakening the U.S. welfare state. Were the American Medical Association to support national health insurance, for example, changes in the U.S. health industry would happen very quickly.

Yet another factor that works against the welfare state is the generally conservative ethos in U.S. politics when it comes to public assistance. Unlike Europe, here we have no tradition of paternalistic concern for the poor. U.S. political culture, as we pointed out in Chapter 1, emphasizes independence, individualism, and economic success. The values of cooperation, community concern, and charity are supposed to be private, not public, matters. As a result, "welfare" still has a stigma attached to it and the percentage of national wealth devoted to welfare programs is considerably lower in the United States than in almost any European nation.[14]

Moreover, incongruities abound in our system. Whereas elderly millionaires may be entitled to generous pensions and medical care, poor mothers with sick children often go unaided. Programs that serve the large middle-class constituency—Social Security and Medicare—are difficult to touch politically. The largest elements (in dollar terms) of the welfare state—tax expenditure items—are so inconspicuous as to be absent from most discussions of welfare. The vast majority of those who benefit from the welfare state believe in the myth that welfare is for poor people. Programs that are targeted mainly toward the poor—such as food stamps, housing, AFDC, and child nutrition—are far more vulnerable politically because their constituency is smaller, less organized, and generally weaker. In addition, as many studies have shown, programs designed for poor people become poor programs: They stigmatize recipients and are often administered in a demeaning and uncaring way.

Many of these issues are further complicated by racial feelings. Since a larger percentage of blacks than whites are poor (although many more of the poor are white than black), many Americans associate poverty with race. As a result, racial antagonisms interfere with efforts to forge a sounder national policy concerning poverty and deprivation.

The U.S. welfare system is so complicated, the rules so varied, the results so difficult to gauge, that policy makers have trouble effectively coordinating individual programs, much less the system as a whole. Benefit levels for the needy vary considerably from state to state, and many are set below any reasonable standard of assistance. Most students of welfare politics advocate a further nationalization of our system, with less financial responsibility, as well as less power, in the hands of state and local officials.

Conclusions

Americans tend to view themselves as an individualistic people, crediting individual talents and hard work for their successes and blaming personal shortcomings for their failures. But the hard times of the Great Depression demonstrated that poverty and unemployment—the lack of basic security—were not solely personal issues; they were integrally connected with larger social arrangements that no one individual could change. Yet the individualistic ethic persists, intensifying the antigovernment attitudes so common in our nation. Oddly, however, we are quite willing to have government step in to help people during disasters, to bail out major corporations, to aid business through tax loopholes, to keep farmers solvent.

This ambivalence has stood in the way of solving the pressing problems of need in our midst—problems that affect almost all Americans sooner or later. We have taken some steps, but they have been hesitant, inconsistent, and often inefficient.

When it comes to *equality*, the U.S. welfare state does effect a modest redistribution of resources, and government programs do aid most of the vulnerable poor. At the same time, some Americans still fall below a minimally decent standard of living. How can we reconcile the increasing numbers of homeless and hungry people in America with the deeply rooted American belief in equality of opportunity?

Finally, consider the *paternalism* of our welfare state. Various programs demean those receiving benefits, especially when the recipients must continually prove they are poor enough to qualify. Fortunately, the infamous welfare regulations of the past, which often involved extensive surveillance of poor people, have largely been humanized.

Is there a solution to this complex web of problems? One proposed solution to the problems of insecurity and inequality is a national income security policy that would provide a minimum income adjusted to a national level of cost for food, clothing, shelter, transportation, and health care. The costs, however, would be high, especially if an effort were to be made to help the working poor as well as the unemployed or the desperately poor.[14] Such a policy would at least help settle the issue of what level of government should ultimately be responsible for dealing with poverty and need. To a substantial extent, our federal system has confused and tangled the issues of welfare.

With fifty separate jurisdictions, it becomes nearly impossible to implement an effective, uniformly applied national policy.

Another suggestion has been to focus our attention on children and orient many programs around their well-being. Senator Daniel Patrick Moynihan proposed the following child-centered rearrangements for the welfare state:[15]

> Indexing welfare aid for children: All federal entitlement programs, such as aid to veterans and Social Security, have been adjusted (indexed) for inflation, but programs affecting children have not.
>
> Establishing a national benefit standard for child welfare.
>
> Supporting programs with demonstrated success rates, such as Head Start.
>
> Creating programs aimed at preventing teenage pregnancy and abortion.

Another proposal, advocated by the Reagan administration, has been to slash social programs that assist the poor and allow economic factors—the spur of want and fundamental economic insecurity—to encourage people to find work and to help each other. This agenda could be supplemented by programs, such as "workfare," that require welfare recipients to take some sort of employment.

In the end, basic ideological commitments shape the ways we view welfare state issues. Although we may have arrived at a mixed economy that incorporates elements of both capitalism and socialism, the old debates continue between those who take a more egalitarian outlook and those favoring a less egalitarian approach. More egalitarian democrats argue that democracy cannot function well without a substantial degree of social and economic equality. The less egalitarian rejoin that too much equality dulls motivation and requires excessive government interference in the economy and in personal life. Yet out of the heated rhetoric that frequently marks discussions on the U.S. welfare state, we can extract the following facts:

> A substantial government involvement in welfare state policies is here to stay.

The U.S. government does less in this regard than most other governments in industrial democracies.

So far, we have not been able to develop programs that strike a reasonable balance between compassion and regulation.

The distribution of the good things of life remains, even after the activities of the welfare state, highly unequal in U.S. society.

GLOSSARY TERMS

welfare state

social insurance programs

public assistance programs

tax expenditure items

cash transfers

services

in-kind transfers

Social Security system

Aid to Families with Dependent Children

Supplemental Security Income

Medicare

Medicaid

food stamp program

NOTES

[1]John E. Schwarz, *America's Hidden Success* (New York: Norton, 1983), pp. 42–43. See also Cesar Perales, "Myths about Poverty," *New York Times*, Oct. 26, 1983, p. 27.

[2]William Raspberry, "Choosing Work over Welfare," *Washington Post*, July 6, 1984, p. A19.

[3]Martin Tolchin, "Aid Plan Marked by Low Participation Rate," *New York Times*, May 10, 1988, p. 14.

[4]Cited in Louis Uchitelle, "As Jobs Increase, So Does Insecurity," *New York Times*, May 1, 1988, Section 3, p. 1.

[5]A study by the Employee Benefit Research Institute, cited in "A Health Insurance Void," *Raleigh News and Observer*, Nov. 16, 1987, p. 14A.

[6]Rashi Fein, "Toward Adequate Health Care, *Dissent*,
Winter 1988, p. 99; Health Care Financing Administration. The official projections foresee a similar rate of increase in the near future.

[7]Jan M. Rosen, "Your Money: Meeting the Need for Health Care," *New York Times*, Sept. 17, 1988, p. 18; "The Good News about Nursing Homes," *New York Times*, Dec. 13, 1988, p. 22; "Who Can Afford a Nursing Home?"*Consumer Reports*, May 1988, pp. 300–311; Julie Kosterlitz, "The Coming Crisis," *National Journal*, Aug. 6, 1988, pp. 2029–2032.

[8]Citizens' Board of Inquiry into Hunger and Malnutrition in the United States, *Hunger USA* (Washington, D.C., 1972); see also Nick Kotz, *Let Them Eat Promises: The Politics of Hunger in America* (Garden City, N.Y.: Anchor, 1971).

[9]*New York Times*, Feb. 27, 1985, p. 8.

[10]*New York Times*, Mar. 5, 1985, p. 26.

[11]The foregoing section on housing was drawn from James E. Anderson *et al.*, *Public Policy and Politics in America*, 2nd ed. (Monterey, Calif.: Brooks/Cole, 1984), pp. 142–149; Peter Marin, "Helping and Hating the Homeless," *Harper's*, Jan. 1987; Susan J. Smith, "New Thinking about the Homeless: Prevention, Not Cure," *Governing* (a Congressional Quarterly journal), Feb. 1988; "To Help Families, Help Housing," *New York Times* (editorial), Feb. 1, 1988, p. 18; and "The Public Health Challenge of the Housing Crisis," *Nation's Health* (American Public Health Association), May–June 1988.

[12]Quoted in Christopher Jencks, "How Poor Are the Poor?" *New York Review of Books*, May 9, 1985, p. 41.

[13]A. Heidenheimer *et al.*, *Comparative Public Policy* (New York: St. Martin's, 1983), chaps. 3, 4, 7.

[14]*Ibid.*, p. 204.

[15]Such a policy was proposed by Democratic Governor Bruce Babbitt of Arizona. See Nick Kotz, "The Politics of Hunger," *New Republic*, Apr. 30, 1984, pp. 19–20.

[16]*New York Times*, Apr. 9, 1985.

SELECTED READINGS

The historical context of the rise of the welfare state can be found in Neil J. Smelser, *Social Change in the Industrial Revolution* (Chicago: University of Chicago Press, 1959); Karl de Schweinitz, *England's Road to Social Security* (Philadelphia: University of Pennsylvania Press, 1947); Roy LuBove, *The Struggle for Social Security, 1900–1935* (Cambridge, Mass.: Harvard University Press, 1968).

A useful **comparative perspective** on welfare-state issues is well-documented in Peter Flora, ed., *Growth to Limits: The Western European Welfare States Since World War II*, vol 1: Sweden, Norway, Finland, Denmark; vol 2: Germany, United Kingdom, Ireland, Italy (New York: Walter de Gruyter, 1986). This massive work provides strong documentation of the expansion and current status of the welfare state in Western Europe. Although now a bit dated, see Donald Hancock, *Sweden: The Politics of a Post-Industrial Society* (Hinsdale, Ill.: Dryden, 1972), for a good single-nation study.

For **critiques from the left**, see Sar A. Levitan and Isaac Shapiro, *Working but Poor: America's Contradiction* (Baltimore: Johns Hopkins, 1987); Michael Harrington, *The New American Poverty* (New York: Holt, 1984); and Robert Kuttner, *The Economic Illusion: False Choices between Prosperity and Social Justice* (Boston: Houghton Mifflin, 1984).

Examples of **critiques from the right** can be found in Charles Murray, *Losing Ground: American Social Policy, 1950–1980* (New York: Basic Books, 1984); and Stuart M. Butler and Anna Kondratas, *Out of the Poverty Trap: A Conservative Strategy for Welfare Reform* (New York: Free Press, 1987).

Class-based analyses are presented by F. F. Piven and R. Cloward, *The New Class War* (New York: Pantheon, 1982); and William Julius Wilson, *The Truly Disadvantaged: The Inner City, the Underclass, and Public Policy* (Chicago: University of Chicago Press, 1987), a book that has caused a lively discussion of the notion of underclass. For a sociological point of view, see Jay McLeod, *Ain't No Makin' It: Levelled Aspirations in a Low-Income Neighborhood* (Boulder, Colo.: Westview, 1987).

For making a **case study in health programs**, consult Eli Ginzberg, *American Medicine: The Power Shift* (Totowa N.J.: Rowman and Allanheld, 1985); Victor Fuchs, *The Health Economy* (Cambridge, Mass.: Harvard University Press, 1986); U.S. Congress, Office of Technology Assessment, *Life-Sustaining Technologies and the Elderly*, (Washington: GPO, 1987); and Eli Ginzberg, Edith M. David, and Miriam Ostow, *Local Health Policy in Action: The Municipal Health Services Program* (Totowa N.J.: Rowman and Allanheld, 1985).

18

CIVIL LIBERTIES, CIVIL AND SOCIAL RIGHTS

Is Justice Being Done?

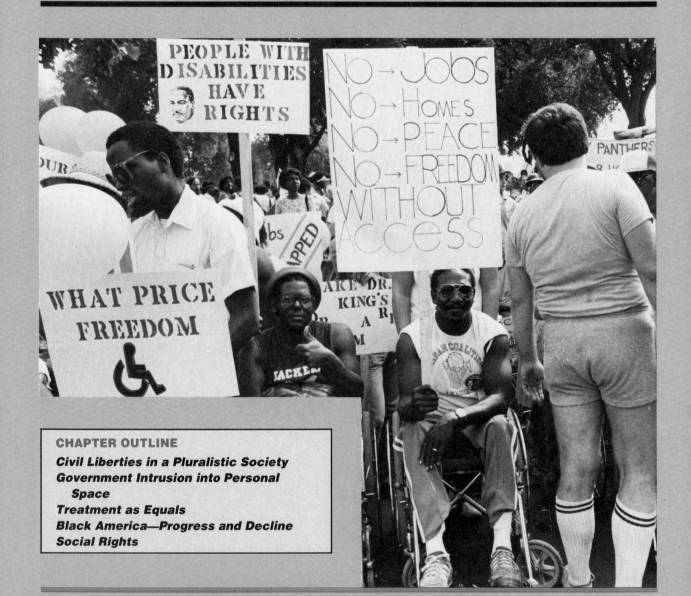

CHAPTER OUTLINE

Civil Liberties in a Pluralistic Society
Government Intrusion into Personal
Space
Treatment as Equals
Black America—Progress and Decline
Social Rights

© Jacques Charlas/Stock, Boston

Democratic rights and liberties are not simply "givens"—things we have always, somehow, had, and can therefore take for granted. In fact, intense struggles over the nature of these rights and liberties have taken place throughout U.S. history. For long periods, basic democratic freedoms were denied to various groups and individuals, who obtained their rights only after sustained and bitter social conflicts. The course of American history has demonstrated that rights and liberties came into being as part of social and political processes involving confrontation, changes in attitudes, efforts at accommodation, and, very often, personal courage.

In our own time, such struggles have continued, although their focus has changed. Because minority or disadvantaged groups for the most part have obtained basic civil rights, a major issue now is to define and implement the idea of equal protection under the law. The evolution of our ideas of what democracy involves has led to such dilemmas as when—or even if—such categories as race and gender may be used legitimately in official policies, and when government may forbid private parties from using such categories. The concept of a "right to privacy" is broadly supported in our society and is reflected by the courts in a series of decisions involving sexual matters (like birth control and abortion) and other concerns. But exactly what this right (which is not mentioned in the Constitution) encompasses still sparks heated debate. The notion of a right to be left alone, tied to the image of some "personal space" into which government should not intrude, at times conflicts with society's need to put certain restrictions on behavior that is deemed harmful to individuals or to society as a whole. Should adults be free to obtain any sort of pornography they wish, or is possession of such material harmful? Under what conditions can society order individuals to submit to intrusive tests (for drug use or for AIDS, for example)? When should the results of such required tests be kept confidential, and when do other individuals in society have a right to know the results?

In the area of social rights, we now accept the basic idea of government responsibility for public health and safety. Yet how much protection do we need? At what cost? In what form? These questions raise thorny and difficult issues.

In this chapter we offer a sampling of current debates over democratic rights and liberties. In examining the controversies, you should ask yourself several questions: Does our politics allow new rights and liberties to evolve? Can the political process cope with the conflicts generated? Can all groups make their views heard? Are important rights and liberties being ignored or inadequately protected?

We begin with a discussion of two current civil liberties issues: gay rights and government policies on the treatment of immigrants. We then turn to the question of government intrusion into private spheres, focusing specifically on how society has attempted to define and deal with obscenity; on domestic surveillance by the FBI; and on mandatory drug testing. Next, we look at the rights of the disabled and at government actions in the area of gender discrimination, two examples of how our society attempts to deal with issues involving the treatment of all people as equals. Finally, through an examination of specific policies and trends in the 1980s, we turn to the issues of black progress—or lack thereof—and social rights.

Civil Liberties in a Pluralistic Society

As we enter the 1990s and prepare for the twenty-first century, advocates of improved civil liberties in our democracy are tackling a set of concerns that, although hardly new, have only recently gained much visibility on the national agenda. Issues revolving around gay rights, for example, and the treatment of immigrants—both striking deeply into life-styles and cultures in America—have proved difficult to resolve. If any issue is perceived to involve alleged core "personal characteristics" of the people involved, an easy solution usually has not been forthcoming. Thus, what is at stake in such matters is often seen as more than the specific issue or agenda being fought over. The success or failure of a measure involving gays or immigrants, for instance, may often be seen as a symbolic affirmation or rejection of a group as a whole and the life-style it is supposed to embrace.

In contemporary U.S. society, most conservatives call for less regulation in the area of business but more regulation of life-style choices. For conservatives, the link between these two tendencies is that a free market (which, according to conservative doctrine, is the bedrock foundation of personal liberty) is only possible when society imposes a certain minimal level of common expectations on individuals, including common moral expectations. Most liberals display opposing tendencies, favoring more regulation of the economy in the name of the public welfare but less regulation in the area of morals—or "personal choice," as they are more likely to call it. The liberal position rests on the notion that individuals acting alone are no match for large-scale economic forces and must rely on the intervention of society to even things up in the marketplace. But in matters of personal choice, individuals should be allowed to make their own way.

From the beginning of the twentieth century, U.S. society moved gradually toward a greater acceptance of more public regulation of economic matters and less conformity in life-style choices and cultural patterns, although in the 1980s this trend became less certain and in some cases seemed to reverse itself. This is not to say that government has sought to interfere in every aspect of business life, or that regulation has always been effective. Compared with the pre–New Deal era, however, economic regulation is extensive. Meanwhile, we have on the whole become more tolerant of moral and cultural diversity in areas such as sexual behavior and the maintenance of cultural heritage against the standardizing tendencies of the so-called melting pot. Yet the vigorous and sometimes nasty tone of debates in the 1980s about moral and cultural values should remind us that these issues are far from settled. Nor has U.S. society in the twentieth century marched serenely or consistently toward greater tolerance. In fact, the gradual increase in tolerance has provoked intense reactions from persons who sense that their own moral and cultural values are under attack. Periods of tolerance have been succeeded by periods of greater demands for conformity. The active, public

debate of these issues is frustrating for those with strongly held positions as well as for those without. But in matters like these, the absence of public debate can mean enforced conformity as often as it means consensus. The debate itself is good for a democracy and a sign of strength.

Gay Rights

The exact number of gays in the United States is not easy to estimate, but current guesses range from 5 to 10 percent of the population. Kinsey's studies in the 1950s also showed that something like half of all Americans have had some homosexual experience in their lives, most in adolescence. Until recently, homosexuality between consenting adults was commonly unlawful in many American communities, reflecting deeply held homophobic attitudes.

Gay rights nonetheless became an issue starting in the 1960s, partly because so many gays publicly proclaimed their homosexuality and began to mobilize and exercise their political and economic power. Gay activism stressed a political agenda aimed at eliminating all statutory manifestations of discrimination, whether in housing, employment, or even the tax laws. The gay rights movement was met with significant and impassioned opposition—based on such groundless fears that homosexuality is "contagious" or that gays might be more likely than heterosexuals to mislead children—and despite the fact that the American Psychoanalytic Association had abandoned its position that homosexuality was a mental illness.

The gay rights movement achieved some successes, especially at the local level, in the 1970s, but during the 1980s antigay rights activists mounted some striking reversals. Antidiscrimination legislation was repealed in Dade County (Miami), Florida, and there were even defeats in liberal communities like Eugene, Oregon, and St. Paul, Minnesota. These events took place, however, in the context of what many believed was a growing acceptance of sexual orientation as a protected right or liberty. One element in the debate was the question of a community's right to enforce the viewpoint of the majority in sexual matters

"When I was in the military
They gave me a medal for killing two men
And a discharge for loving
one"

Leonard Matlovich's discharge from the Air Force for homosexuality became a *cause célèbre* among gay rights activists. Awarded the Purple Heart and the Bronze Star for heroism in the Vietnam War, Matlovich settled out of court and received an honorable discharge and other compensation. He died in 1988 of complications associated with AIDS and was buried in Congressional Cemetery with military honors. *(AP/Wide World Photos)*

ranging from pornography to abortion. It seems unlikely, in any case, that sexual behavior can be effectively discouraged or even controlled by law.

One indication of homophobia in U.S. society was seen in the public discussion of AIDS. Not only was the disease initially misrepresented as a gay disease, but some even characterized it as a form of divine retribution for the "sin" of homosexuality. Initial resistance to public expenditures for AIDS research was based in part on a smug but misguided sense that the disease was not a threat to non-drug-using heterosexuals. The error of that position eventually became clear, but in the short run AIDS almost certainly reinforced intolerance for gay rights, no matter how unreasonably.

An interesting test of gay rights issues occurred in Georgia in the 1980s. Michael Hardwick, a homosexual living in Atlanta, was arrested in 1982 for engaging in oral sex in the privacy of his home with another consenting homosexual. Under Georgia criminal law, the penalty for conviction could have been as much as twenty years in prison. Although the state prosecutor decided not to submit the charge to the grand jury unless there was additional evidence, Hardwick challenged the

Georgia statute in a civil suit in federal court. That suit gave the Supreme Court the chance to weigh in on the issue of gay rights. Although the Georgia sodomy statute applied to *any* oral or anal sex act, and thus could be used against heterosexuals as well as homosexuals, Justice Byron White, writing for a five-person majority, chose to frame the question only in terms of the homosexual issue. The question, for White, was "whether the Federal Constitution confers a fundamental right upon homosexuals to engage in sodomy." The Court's answer was "No." The Circuit Court's decision that the constitutional right to privacy extended to homosexual sodomy was in error. Justice Harry Blackmun wrote in dissent:

> This case is no more about a "fundamental right to engage in homosexual sodomy," as the Court purports to declare, than *Stanley* v. *Georgia* was about a fundamental right to watch obscene movies, or *Katz* v. *United States* was about a fundamental right to place interstate bets from a telephone booth. Rather, this case is about "the most comprehensive of rights and the right most valued by civilized men," namely, "the right to be left alone" *Olmstead* v. *United States* (1928). . . .

This case involves no real interference with the rights of others, for the mere knowledge that other individuals do not adhere to one's value system cannot be a legally cognizable interest, let alone an interest that can justify invading the houses, hearts, and minds of citizens who choose to live their lives differently. . . .

I can only hope . . . that the Court will soon reconsider its analysis and conclude that depriving individuals of their right to choose for themselves how to conduct their intimate relationships poses a far greater threat to the values most deeply rooted in our nation's history than tolerance of nonconformity could ever do.[1]

The sentiments expressed by Justice Blackmun did not convince the Court in 1986, and the reconsideration he hoped for does not seem likely soon.

The Treatment of Immigrants

A nation is defined by its borders in more ways than one. In addition to geographical limits, our borders and the way they are policed provide some measure of the condition of liberty in America. The borders of the United States have become a source of considerable debate in recent years, as illegal immigration and the entry of illegal drugs into the country posed what some characterized as a serious threat to the national security. To understand the problems of the borders, two facts are important: First, the United States has throughout its history restricted immigration; second, immigrants from Mexico and other Central American countries, who in recent years have streamed into the United States, are driven by strong economic incentives for jobs and income that cannot be found in their native countries. Migrant farmworkers, for example, have been an important source of cheap labor for agriculture in the United States.

After years of debate, Congress enacted legislation in 1986 meant to address the problem of illegal immigration. The 1986 **Immigration and Reform Act** took a three-pronged approach: (1) *amnesty*, (2) *enforcement*, and (3) *employer sanctions*. For illegal immigrants who could prove residence in

the country since 1982, amnesty meant legal status in the United States and the possibility of eventual naturalization. The Immigration and Naturalization Service, the federal agency charged with regulating the flow of people into the country, would increase its efforts to reduce the illegal entry of new immigrants. And for the first time, employers who hired illegal immigrants would be subject to penalties.

The threefold approach of the Immigration and Reform Act was related to problems with current policy. Amnesty was difficult for some to secure: After years of evading U.S. officials (contact with INS meant deportation), many illegal immigrants would not approach an agency they did not fully trust; others were unable to produce adequate documentation of their residence in the United States. The time limit on filing for amnesty under the 1986 law expired in May 1988.

Comprehensive patrolling of the U.S.–Mexican border is impossible. Along the southern border there were only 1,550 customs and immigration officers to handle the traffic at points of entry and about 2,900 border patrol agents to cover the area between and around the ports. The sheer numbers of people crossing this vast border were staggering; in 1987 alone 1.1 million were apprehended trying to enter the United States illegally. According to a U.S. Customs representative, to do their jobs customs agents need to know about 400 to 1,000 complex laws involving forty different agencies. "This is really a problem. We've got so many laws on the books [that the agents] have to enforce. Frankly, I don't know how they do it."[2]

Under such conditions of bureaucratic overload, selective enforcement is the only possible response. Yet such limited enforcement poses serious questions of fairness. When border patrol agents enter a Greyhound bus and ask for documentation only from persons who have the dark hair and olive complexion typical of much of the Mexican population, does that constitute a reasonable search, or is it discriminatory harrassment? INS agents have broad discretion to search vehicles on the basis of "reasonable suspicion." The INS argues that agents must rely on well-developed instincts to be effective. Critics charge that such instincts may be grounded in prejudice as

The Immigration and Naturalization Service border patrol seizes a group of suspected "illegals" near the Mexican border. The man being searched was sent back to Mexico the next day. *(Olivier Rebbot/Woodfin Camp & Associates)*

much as practice. The most careful and well-intentioned official behavior is subject to misinterpretation under such circumstances. And not all official behavior is necessarily careful and well-intentioned.

The sanctions against employers of illegal aliens that are part of the 1986 law have provoked controversy since the act was debated in Congress. Such sanctions reinforce ethnic prejudices in employers and in society at large. Critics charge that legal aliens and native-born citizens of Hispanic background bear the burden of suspicion and bureaucratic hassle, while unscrupulous employers continue to evade the law.

The situation at the southern border is exacerbated by illegal drug trafficking and the political unrest in Central America. And nothing has changed the basic economic realities that underlie most Mexicans' desire to enter the United States. Until these larger problems are resolved, the entry of illegal immigrants into the United States will continue to challenge our attempts to do justice.

A telling example of the way in which domestic disputes about foreign policy complicate the treat-

ment of illegal immigrants is seen in how asylum is granted. **Political asylum** is the ancient principle of offering haven to persons fleeing from some other country for political reasons. Asylum became politically controversial during the 1980s as the Reagan administration pursued anti-Marxist policies in El Salvador and Nicaragua. Congressional legislation provided for asylum for political refugees whose lives were in danger in the countries from which they fled. The Reagan administration welcomed Nicaraguan refugees because it supported the contra rebels trying to overthrow the Marxist Nicaraguan government. Thus, Nicaraguans were considered "political" refugees. But Reagan administration policy supported the Salvadoran government and opposed the "illegitimate" (i.e., Marxist) rebels. Salvadorans seeking refuge in the United States were accordingly labeled "economic" refugees and thus were not eligible for asylum. The description of refugees from one country as "political" and those from another as "economic" was based on sympathies for the respective struggles, not on humanitarian ideas of providing a safe haven for refugees.

Freedom to Visit

In 1984, Gabriel García Márquez, a Colombian novelist who had won the Nobel Prize for Literature, sought an unconditional five-year visa from the U.S. State Department in order to participate in a conference in the United States. For many years García Márquez had been denied any type of visa, solely because he had worked for the official Cuban news agency in the 1960s.

Later, he was granted a restricted visa. The department offered him another such visa in 1984, but he declined it "for reasons of principle and personal dignity."

The Colombian author was only one of many visa applicants who have been turned down or permitted only restricted visits by the State Department. Under the McCarren-Walter Immigration Act of 1952, passed at the height of the anticommunist fervor in the United States, visas can be denied to foreigners who are or were affiliated with a communist or procommunist organization, as well as to any others the State Department deems undesirable for reasons of "the public interest."

No other Western democracy imposes visa restrictions on ideological grounds.

Representative Barney Frank (D. Mass) has introduced a bill into Congress that would eliminate the McCarren-Walter Act's exclusionary provisions, which he calls "a hangover from one of the grim periods of American history, the McCarthy period at its worst." Frank claims that these provisions deny human rights and violate American ideals. He is also realistic about the chances for his bill's success. "There's no built-in constituency. By definition, the people to whom this law applies can't vote." That very fact makes our treatment of these issues a good standard by which to judge the fairness of our democracy.

SOURCES: *Harper's,* June 1984, p. 23; *New York Times,* Apr. 24 and July 15, 1984; Barney Frank, interviewed in Linda Greenhouse, "Redefining the Boundaries: Who May Come In," *New York Times,* Apr. 10, 1988, section 4, p. 5.

Government Intrusion into Personal Space

One standard by which civil liberties can be judged is the extent and manner of government intrusion into the "personal space" of citizens and others. It would be easy if we could simply judge governments by the criterion of how *little* they imposed on citizens. But as the issues addressed in this chapter demonstrate, there are times when a proper concern for individual rights and liberty demands some government intervention. Let us now turn to three issues of such government intervention: (1) obscenity; (2) the FBI's domestic surveillance; and (3) mandatory testing for drug use and AIDS.

Obscenity

For decades the Supreme Court has grappled with the complex problem of defining exactly what is "obscene." In case after case, the Court has been called on to decide whether a specific magazine, movie, or book is really obscene. And even were society to agree that obscenity should be censored, there would remain the question, By what (or whose) standards? Yet a deeper issue is whether there actually *is* such a thing as obscenity—and if there is, why it should not simply be viewed as a form of "speech" protected by the First Amendment.

The first significant attempt by a court to define *obscenity* came in the landmark British case of *Hick-*

lin v. *Regina* (1868). The case dealt with an antireligious tract called *The Confessional Unmasked*, which described, among other things, the seduction of women during "confessions." The judge in *Hicklin* sought to define *obscenity* as follows:

> The test of obscenity is this, whether the tendency of the matter charged as obscene is to deprave and corrupt those whose minds are open to such immoral influences, and into whose hands a publication of this sort may fall.

Vague as it was, the *Hicklin* decision became the basic standard for U.S. obscenity cases for almost a century. Under *Hicklin*, even small parts of books or other materials could be taken out of context and declared obscene. In 1934, however, the Supreme Court accepted the argument of the publisher of James Joyce's *Ulysses* that a work should be considered *as a whole*. Finally, in 1957 the Court altogether rejected the *Hicklin* rule in the case of **Roth v. United States**. Although upholding the conviction of Samuel Roth himself, a New York publisher, on the charge of mailing obscene materials, the Court rejected the Hicklin rule as unconstitutional, and proposed a new standard:

> The test is not whether it would arouse sexual desires or sexually impure thoughts in those comprising a particular segment of the community, the young, the immature or the highly prudish. . . . The test in each case is the effect of the book . . . considered as a whole, not upon any particular classes, but upon all those whom it is likely to reach. . . . [Y]ou determine its impact upon the average person in the community.[3]

What, if anything, should the government do to regulate access to pornography? Is this an issue of personal choice? Or does the easy availability of pornography harm society in unacceptable and avoidable ways? *(© Bettye Lane/Photo Researchers)*

In other words, one class of society should not be singled out in judging the effect of the material. What should count, rather, is how the material, taken as a whole, affects the "average person." This rule was loosened further in 1966, when the Court held that obscene material had to offend national standards, not just those of a small community.[4]

What followed was a liberalization of the application of obscenity laws. As more sexually explicit materials became more easily obtainable, public opposition grew. In *Miller* v. *California* (1973) the Court shifted ground again, voting, 5–4, to uphold a group of obscenity convictions.[5] In the majority opinion, Chief Justice Warren E. Burger argued that there *was* such a thing as "obscenity," and that it was *not* protected by the First Amendment. To be considered obscene, the Court declared, a work, taken as a whole, must appeal to "prurient interest" in sex, portray sex offensively, and "lack serious literary, artistic, political or scientific value." For such materials, the Court ruled, local standards should be used as the basis for judgment.

Many people question the entire basis for subjecting obscene materials, however defined, to prosecution and censorship. What is wrong, they ask, with appealing to what the Supreme Court has called prurient interest ("having morbid or lascivious longings")? After all, a majority on the President's Commission on Obscenity and Pornography, appointed by Lyndon Johnson, found there was no connection between exposure to pornography and any sort of crime, sexual or otherwise. If pornography does not demonstrably cause social harm, why should it be subject to legal restraints? Conservatives contend that the widespread availability of obscene materials sooner or later contributes to the destruction of order, civility, and various civic virtues. Is there any evidence supporting such a hypothesis?

Yes, according to an unusual coalition of feminists and conservative and religious groups. Feminist Andrea Dworkin has maintained that "pornography is the theory and rape is the practice," and argued that pornography discriminates against women and hence is a violation of equal protection of the laws. In May 1984, Indianapolis, Indiana, passed an ordinance that declared pornography to be a violation of women's civil rights. According to the ordinance, "Pornography is central in creating and maintaining sex as a basis for discrimination." This statute was later declared unconstitutional by the Supreme Court.

Both sides in the debate take absolutist positions. Some feminists and right-wing crusaders view all pornography as illegitimate, while free speech advocates proclaim a pervasive protection under the First Amendment for virtually all forms of "speech." Both arguments seem somewhat inflated. Certain types of pornography appear, at least to common sense, far more pernicious than others—child pornography, for example, or particularly degrading and brutal forms of pornography.

Some communities have sought to isolate pornographic establishments through zoning laws. This strategy is designed to reduce the amount of pornography available and to keep it out of sight of people who do not wish to come in contact with it. The Supreme Court has upheld the right of communities to take such steps. One advocate of this sort of compromise on the pornography issue has stated her case as follows:

To the extent that pornography is symptomatic of, and helps to further, social disintegration, in which the least powerful (especially children) suffer the most, it becomes an appropriate target for action, regulation, and reproof. But with this proviso: the knowledge that we cannot return to a past in which Americans harmoniously shared one set of moral values. Communities must put pornography "in its place" rather than seek to eradicate it altogether.[6]

The FBI and Domestic Surveillance

The Federal Bureau of Investigation's domestic image goes through cycles of esteem, repudiation, and renewal. The varying degrees of public acceptance of the FBI reflect the tensions, in a democracy, of an agency that combines the powers of a police force and the tools of an intelligence agency. As former FBI Director William Webster said in a 1988 interview, "You cannot have liberty without order, and so you've got two important values—the right to be left alone and the right to be safe and free—and you want them both, and it usually falls on law enforcement to try to achieve safety without sacrifice of liberty."[7] The FBI has not always managed that balance very well. J. Edgar Hoover was the original director and the person responsible for the agency's white-shirt-and-tie professional image. As he became obsessed with the danger to the United States from communism and domestic unrest, the bureau became involved in a series of "cointelpros"—counterintelligence programs. Such programs were of dubious constitutionality and were frequently disruptive and ruinous to the reputations of those under investigation.

With Hoover's death, a series of reform-minded directors stressed the FBI's image of general restraint, propriety, and professionalism. Congress passed legislation, which, among other things, prohibits government agencies from gathering or maintaining information about Americans' exercise of their First Amendment rights unless pursuant to an authorized law enforcement investigation. But the FBI insists that its decision to investigate provides its own authorization, effectively nullifying the legislation as far as the bureau is concerned. During the late 1970s, critics of the FBI advanced a proposal to pass a charter for the

Knowledge is power, and power sometimes breeds fear in those who lack it. Whose fingerprint appears on the FBI screen? Will bureaucracy be run fairly and openly, or will agencies pursue their own political or personal vendettas? *(Frank Muller-May/ Woodfin Camp & Associates)*

bureau, which would prohibit the FBI from investigating and building files on people solely because of their antigovernment views and associations.[8] But nothing ever came of the charter idea. And incidents recur that raise questions about the bureau's ability to stay within the bounds that democracy requires. In 1979 the FBI set up an elaborate sting operation (Abscam) to catch members of Congress taking bribes. Although the operation did result in some convictions, and the end of certain political careers, many observers were concerned about what they perceived to be the bureau's blatant entrapment.

For more than two years, starting in 1983, the FBI engaged in extensive surveillance of members and affiliates of the Committee in Solidarity with the People of El Salvador (Cispes), to determine if that organization funneled arms to leftists in El Salvador or otherwise participated in violent acts. The nature of the investigation, when revealed in 1988, seemed to most observers to have transgressed the bounds of proper government action in a democracy. The tone of documents from the investigation raised images of the bad old days of cointelpros. One agent wrote, "It is imperative to formulate some plan of attack against Cispes and, specifically, against individuals [names deleted]

who defiantly display their contempt for the U.S. government by making speeches and propagandizing their cause while asking for asylum." In Norfolk, Virginia, agents on the Cispes case conducted a "visual inspection" of a bookstore containing "posters and other literature in support of black power and black militancy."[9] As it turns out, the FBI could uncover no evidence of illegal acts by Cispes members, and the investigation was terminated. Several agents were eventually disciplined by the bureau.

In a world where terrorist threats of domestic violence have to be taken seriously, defining bounds for the FBI becomes complicated and ever-changing. Still, limits can and should be maintained to discourage an attack mentality against groups and individuals whose political views do not accord with the bureau's. The task for William Sessions (the director who assumed control of the FBI just before the Cispes story broke) was to polish the FBI's image once more.

Mandatory Testing

As we noted earlier in this text, the "police powers" of a society refer not simply to traffic cops and investigations of theft, but to the general respon-

These Miami police officers volunteered to be tested for drugs, but mandatory routine testing is becoming common. Even "voluntary" tests can be coercive under certain circumstances. Should government protect individuals from routine drug tests, or should it continue its recent practice of testing federal employees in specific high-risk positions? *(UPI/Bettmann Newsphotos)*

sibility of a government to look out for the health, safety, and welfare of its citizens. Even the most avid civil libertarian recognizes that government's police powers sometimes legitimately emcompass the ability to require positive acts from citizens. And even the strongest advocate of government regulation recognizes that governments can go too far in their demands on individuals. One civil liberties issue that evokes extreme judgments and yet defies simple solutions is the matter of **mandatory testing.** Testing programs can have a variety of ends—to protect society from some harm, to protect individuals from some harm, to produce evidence for a criminal trial, or to ensure fairness. Americans have accommodated themselves to certain mandatory tests under specific circumstances—for example, blood tests to detect traditional sexually transmitted diseases as a requirement for marriage licenses, or breath or urine tests to detect alcohol when a person is stopped for driving under the influence. These tests raise few eyebrows now (although that was not always the case). But two public health crises of the 1980s have now made testing one of the hottest of hot potatoes: drug abuse and AIDS.

The drug test issue came to the fore as a result of two well-publicized Amtrak accidents in the 1980s, in which evidence indicated employee drug use. Should the government as an employer require routine drug tests for government workers?

Is the argument for testing more compelling when an employee's use of drugs on the job might endanger the employee or others (consider airline pilots)? If probable cause were used as a standard for imposing tests, what would constitute probable cause to believe that an employee was using drugs? Should the government restrict the ability of private employers to require routine drug tests? Should public educational institutions be permitted to require drug tests of students?

The National Institute of Justice, the research agency of the Justice Department, conducted voluntary, anonymous tests on a sample of two thousand persons arrested between June and November 1987. The tests revealed that 53 to 79 percent of the suspects arrested for serious offenses tested positive for illicit drugs. Edwin Meese, President Reagan's attorney general, cited this evidence in 1988 as he issued a call for uniform testing of all persons arrested in the United States. The tests, Meese suggested, could be used to determine eligibility for pretrial release. In addition, they would provide a useful base of data about the link between drug use and crime. Meese also called for extensive drug testing in the workplace.[10]

Critics of drug testing programs suggest that uniform testing without probable cause violates the Fourth and Fifth Amendents, that the costs of drug testing are high while the benefits are relatively low, that American society is taking a hypocritical attitude toward hard drugs in the face of its relative indifference about the most commonly abused drug of all—alcohol—and that drug problems are symptoms rather than causes. Society would be better served by turning its attention to poverty, the profitability of drug sales, and other social conditions conducive to drug abuse.

AIDS testing as a civil liberties issue has all the complications of drug testing, plus more. Some suggest that AIDS is a public health problem and not a matter of civil liberties at all. Seeing a serious threat to the public health, these persons would force victims and potential victims to take any action that would reduce the threat, including mandatory tests and even quarantine. Most observers, however, see clear civil liberties implications in any public response to AIDS. In addition to the questions about mandatory testing (Should employers be permitted to require an AIDS test? What about health insurers?), how to handle the results of tests is even more problematic. For example, should doctors be free to warn sexual partners of AIDS patients even if the patients object? Should they be required to do so? Should parents or physicians be required to tell school officials that a child has tested positive for AIDS? Should school officials, in turn, be required to or restricted from informing other parents of the test results?

In September 1988, recognizing that the potential for seriously disruptive discrimination is great, the Congress passed the Federal AIDS Policy Act; anonymous testing is permitted in the interest of building a data base, but for the time being there will be no screening of hospital patients or marriage partners.

Treatment as Equals

In considering matters of equality in a democracy, a clear distinction should be drawn between "equal treatment" and "**treatment as equals.**" Ronald Dworkin explains this difference in a story about a parent with two children. One child is desperately ill and will die if not given adequate medication. The other child is only slightly ill and will almost certainly recover even without medicine. If the parent has only one dose of medicine, it would be cruelly wrong to treat the children equally, dividing the single dose of medicine between the

two. Such treatment would likely result in the death of one child. The parent should treat the children *as equals*, meaning with an equal respect for each child's health, even though that means giving one child all the medicine and the other child none.[11] Similarly, democratic governments should treat people as equals even when that sometimes means (as it inevitably will) treating them differently.

Our government has always recognized distinctions that require different treatment of certain citizens. Those differences in treatment have been more or less controversial, depending on the circumstances and the political climate of the time. Some of the policies that treated persons differently in the past have come to be discredited—slavery and segregation of public facilities are obvious painful examples. Some policies that treat different groups differently are maintained currently, as in the Selective Service system (now conducting registration for a draft but not a draft itself), which applies to young men but not to young women. The Supreme Court has recognized the principle of unequal treatment and has thrown its weight behind specific policies that treat groups differently. In 1981, in the case *Michael M.* v. *Superior Court of Sonoma County*, the Supreme Court upheld a California statutory rape law even though the criminal penalties of that law could only apply to males.[12] Justice William Rehnquist concluded that, in this instance, a "criminal sanction imposed solely on males . . . serves to 'equalize' the deterrents" to engage in intercourse. The general principle underlying this ruling is that there are times when treatment as equals requires something other than strictly equal treatment. The fascinating and troubling task is to decide when all persons, given equal respect, should be treated the same, and when they should be treated differently. Among the current controversies in this area are policies concerning the handicapped and those relating to gender.

Rights of the Disabled

By one estimate, there are 37 million people with some form of disability in the United States.[13] This number includes the deaf, the blind, the physically and mentally handicapped, and those with various

Youngsters who have had polio share a meal with someone who understands their condition—the President of the United States, Franklin Roosevelt, who was stricken with the disease in 1921. One of the highest symbolic services politicians can provide is to demystify personal differences—such as physical disabilities in FDR's case, or minority status in the case of Jesse Jackson. *(UPI/Bettmann Newsphotos)*

learning disabilities. Until the 1970s, they were rarely a factor in the minds of those who shape public policy and were more likely to be objects of pity or aversion than active participants in shaping their own fates. But a combination of grassroots activism and federal legislation has moved the **rights of the disabled** to a central point in the public agenda at the national, state, and local levels.

The Rehabilitation Act of 1973 and the Education for All Handicapped Children Act of 1975 were crucial steps along the path to equal rights for the disabled. The 1973 legislation had been vetoed twice by President Nixon (on financial grounds) before it finally was passed. Section 504 of this act requires that handicapped people have equal access to all federally financed programs. Though the legislation had been on the books several years, activists for the disabled argued that it was not being implemented, and in the spring of 1977 they staged a series of sit-ins in the offices of the Department of Health Education and Welfare. Soon thereafter, regulations implementing the act were issued. The 1975 legislation on education ensured disabled children free public education regardless of the severity of their disability. It established new norms, ending separate education and bringing disabled children into the educational mainstream.

But the pace of progress has not been steady or uncomplicated. The Reagan administration, for example, concerned about the budget deficit, has taken far more of a hands-off attitude, with the result that disabled activists have had to fight the erosion of gains made during the 1970s. Much public transportation remains inaccessible to a majority of those with restricted mobility. Lawsuits are often still needed to force local school districts to comply with federal legislation. And more than 65 percent of working-age disabled people are still unemployed.[14]

Sometimes progress brings its own problems. Many parents of deaf children, for example, prefer education in a school where signing is the primary form of communication; as such, mainstreaming their children into the public schools is not considered a gain.[15] The de-institutionalization of the mentally ill, which began in the late 1960s, was regarded at first as a positive step. The idea, however, has in many ways failed on the practical level because large numbers of the mentally ill have added to the homeless population living uncared for in the streets. The local mental health clinics that were supposed to supply services to such people never received the funding and support that was envisioned.

Advocates for the disabled have recently called for the passage of a comprehensive Americans with Disabilities Act, whose purpose would be to rectify the shortcomings of earlier piecemeal legislation. The act would prohibit discrimination against the disabled in employment, housing, education, transportation, and communication. In its way, it woud be as comprehensive as the Civil Rights Act of 1964. It is not clear, however, whether the legislation will be able to garner the support it needs for passage in Congress.

Government Actions on Gender Discrimination

Two of the most important pieces of civil rights legislation of the 1960s were to have great effect on the issue of **gender discrimination**—the Equal Pay Act of 1963, which required that men and women receive equal remuneration for similar jobs; and Title VII of the Civil Rights Act of 1964, which prohibited sexual discrimination in employment and by state and local governments. In 1972 the Title VII provisions were extended to educational institutions under Title IX. The enactment of Title IX led to a steady stream of litigation brought by women—and even, occasionally, men—who felt they had been discriminated against in admissions procedures, financial aid, extracurricular activities, athletics, health services, sex-stereotyped courses, counseling programs, dormitory rules, and other campus regulations.

Two executive orders lent momentum to the drive to reduce discrimination based on gender. A 1967 executive order forbade discrimination in federal employment and required companies with $50,000 or more in federal contracts to submit affirmative action plans for women in addition to such plans for minorities. Another executive order, promulgated in 1969, called for equal opportunities for women throughout the federal government itself and established a program to implement this commitment.

At the same time, the courts began to play a more significant role in redefining "gender discrimination." Until 1971 the courts had largely upheld the government's authority to "classify by gender." Some court decisions prevented women from entering certain professions (such as bartending); other decisions were aimed at "protecting" women (as in certain family issues connected with child custody and alimony). For decades the courts, reflecting the views of society as a whole, found that a woman's place was still in the home.

As legislative and social attitudes changed, however, the courts faced many new problems. From 1974 to 1977 the Supreme Court dealt with more cases related to the rights of men and women

Some positions, such as secretarial work, have become so strongly identified with gender that stereotypes prevent fair access to job opportunities and distort pay scales. Traditional "female" jobs isolate many women in a "pink-collar ghetto" where compensation and job discretion are generally lower than in traditional "male" jobs. The concept of comparable worth is one attempt to redress such injustice.
(© Joel Gordon)

than it had decided in all its previous history. Since that period, gender discrimination cases have constantly been on the Court's agenda. Two significant cases in particular marked new departures.

The first concerned a young man who committed suicide at the age of nineteen. His mother, Sally Reed, applied to be the administrator of his estate; his father applied two weeks later. Both were residents of Idaho, and under Idaho law, "As between persons equally entitled to administer a decedent's estate, males must be preferred to females." The American Civil Liberties Union took the case to the Supreme Court, which unanimously ruled that the drawing of a sex line was inconsistent with the equal protection provisions of the Fourteenth Amendment.[16]

The second case was brought by Charles Moritz, a 63-year-old unmarried man who lived with and took care of his mother. Moritz had hired a nurse to look after his mother during the day. The Internal Revenue Service permitted the partial deduction of such expenses for a daughter who had never been married and was caring for a parent, but did not allow sons to make such deductions. Moritz sued, charging discrimination, and a U.S. Appeals Court overturned the IRS regulation, ruling that the distinction between dutiful sons and dutiful daughters was arbitrary.[17] After the *Moritz* case the U.S. solicitor general informed the Court that its decision called into question hundreds of laws nationwide that contained "gender-based references." The Supreme Court refused to hear the case on appeal.

Although the Court has struck down sex discrimination in a number of other cases involving both men and women, it has not been willing to exclude gender considerations completely. Most important, in a 6–3 decision handed down in 1981, it upheld the all-male draft registration mandated by Congress. The Court majority argued that Congress had carefully studied the inclusion of women and had decided that for reasons of "military flexibility" women should be excluded. The Court minority argued that the all-male provision violated equal protection guarantees in the Constitution. In 1984 the Supreme Court narrowed some of the protections against gender discrimination in education in the *Grove City College* case (examined in detail in Chapter 11), in which it found that the

government could enforce antidiscrimination requirements in federal law only in the *specific* educational "program or activity" receiving federal money, and not in all programs at the university in question. The *Grove City College* decision was later rendered void when Congress passed the Civil Rights Restoration Act of 1988, over President Reagan's veto.

No clear guidelines exist for drawing gender-linked legal lines, in part because the Supreme Court has not been as hard on gender discrimination as on racial discrimination. The Court has argued that certain gender distinctions are legally valid because men and women are not always "similarly situated." In the *Michael M.* case, discussed earlier in this chapter, the Court upheld a California statutory rape law, thus leaving the man but not the woman at risk of criminal prosecution. The Court accepted the state's argument that its law properly addressed a natural asymmetry between the sexes. Gender distinctions were also upheld in a 1974 Court decision (*Kahn* v. *Shevin*, 416 U.S. 351) upholding a Florida statute giving widows but not widowers a $500 property tax exemption, on the assumption that, upon losing a spouse, women as a class suffered economic disadvantages not shared by men. In *Geduldig* v. *Aiello* (417 U.S. 484) in 1974 the Court upheld California's disability insurance program against charges of sexual discrimination because the program did not cover disability resulting from normal pregnancy. The Court said that the state was not obligated to restructure the program. In all cases like those described above, the root consideration is the same: When is it legitimate to treat women as a class differently from men? In sorting out these questions, the Court must cut through the stereotypes and prejudices of the past concerning what gender roles ought to be.

Comparable worth emerged in the 1980s as a gender-related issue. Advocates of the concept of comparable worth argue that a long history of sex-based discrimination created systematic pay inequalities between certain female-dominated jobs and comparable male-dominated jobs. Women were being paid less, in other words, for jobs demanding comparable skills and training. Proponents of comparable worth called for job evaluation studies, to establish equitable pay standards, and the idea caught on. By the mid-1980s several states had adopted comparable-worth standards for state jobs. Predictions of enormous increases in state payrolls and general economic chaos proved to be exaggerated. Although comparable-worth legislation has been advanced in Congress, and court challenges to the status quo have been mounted, the federal government has not yet adopted the concept of comparable worth and seems unlikely to do so any time soon. Critics of the concept worry about the distortion of free-market forces in the official redesignation of whole categories of salaries. The market itself, they argue, has roughly defined the current structure of salaries and should be allowed to continue to do so. Advocates of comparable worth also attribute the current structure of salaries to the market, but argue that the market is hardly neutral, and that this sometimes is not the fairest way to allocate resources.

Throughout the 1980s the Reagan administration opposed comparable-worth legislation. A Reagan-appointee majority in the Civil Rights Committee voted to reject the doctrine in April 1985. The chairman of the committee, Clarence M. Pendelton, Jr., argued that comparable-worth advocates were taking "a disingenuous attempt to restructure our free enterprise system into a state-controlled system under the false guise of fairness.[18]

Black America— Progress and Decline

As we saw in Chapter 4, black Americans have made considerable progress in achieving equal treatment under the law. Yet, despite more than two decades of civil rights legislation, and despite efforts at affirmative action, millions of blacks continue to lag considerably behind whites, particularly in economic status and in prospects for financial improvement. In fact, in many cases the gap between blacks and whites has grown since the late 1960s (see **Figure 18–1**). In 1968 the median family income for blacks was $5,360; for whites it was $8,937. By 1986 that gap had widened considerably: The median family income for blacks was $17,604, but for whites it was $30,809. In 1986, 42.6 percent of white families had incomes over $35,000, but only half that percentage of black families (21.2 percent) had incomes that high. The unemployment rate for nonwhites in 1968 was 6.7 percent; for whites it was 3.2 percent. In 1987 black unemployment was 13 percent, compared with 5.3 percent for whites (see **Figure 18–2**). The unemployment rate for black youths, traditionally extremely high, has continued at around 40 percent and is even higher in certain ghetto areas.

Blacks have also experienced setbacks in education after some promising earlier progress. Since 1976 the number of black high school graduates

FIGURE 18–1
Income Levels of Black and White Families (1986 Dollars)

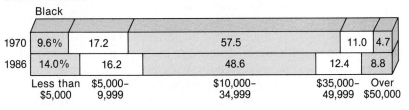

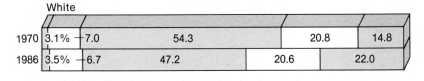

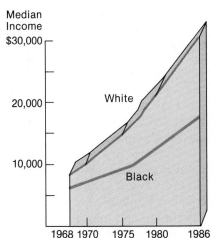

SOURCE: U.S. Census Bureau.

FIGURE 18–2
Unemployment, 1968–1987

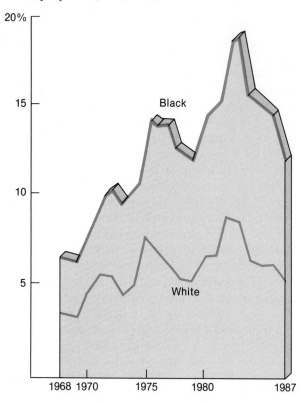

SOURCE: Bureau of Labor Statistics.

starting college declined from 34 to 26 percent. It is also notable that of those who do start college only 42 percent graduate. Some observers predict further declines in the 1990s. Many also believe that life in the inner cities continues to deteriorate as drug use, crime, and other forms of social disintegration persist. (See **Figure 18–3.**)

How are we to account for these inequities? The Kerner Commission Report, issued in 1968 in the wake of widespread urban rioting, argued that white racism was the primary factor limiting blacks' struggle for equality. The report suggested that a change in "white attitude and behavior" toward blacks was the essential element in moving society toward more genuine and thoroughgoing equality in all areas. Many believe that racism is still the primary problem, and that the Reagan administration failed to enforce civil rights laws vigorously and did not continue or expand social pro-

grams important for the poor. On the other hand, others decry the notion that racism and discrimination can adequately explain the persistence of poverty among blacks. According to them, the problem lies within the black community itself. The breakup of the family is often cited as a major destabilizing force, as are the ill-effects of federal welfare programs. Critics argue that some programs themselves contribute to a decline of work incentives and induce attitudes of dependency among recipients.

For other students of the subject, the explanations are more complex. They argue, for example, that the disappearance of well-paid blue-collar jobs in major cities has made it far more difficult for blacks to find reasonable employment. (A Bureau of Labor Statistics report in 1986 showed that black men and women continued to hold a disproportionate percentage of low-paying jobs. See **Table 18–1, page 528.**)

Some observers attempt to combine all these explanations. They believe that a solution to the economic problems of blacks must include self-help within the black community, federal programs that provide the right sort of assistance, a focus on restructuring of inner-city employment opportunities, and a continued effort to combat racism and discrimination. Although the economic standing of some blacks has improved considerably, the persistence of poverty and hopelessness remains a major national issue.

Social Rights

Throughout the twentieth century, as we saw in Chapters 4 and 13, the federal government has played a steadily widening role in protecting citizens against various health and safety hazards. But the Reagan administration deemphasized federal regulation, arguing for increased "voluntary compliance" as opposed to federal enforcement, and dropped or diluted specific standards and procedures designed to impose stricter standards on U.S. industry.[19] Are there basic rights to health and safety that transcend economic considerations? The debate continues to this day, as whole new industries needed to be evaluated for risks.

FIGURE 18–3

'Impoverished aliens in an affluent society'
Martin Luther King Jr., 1966

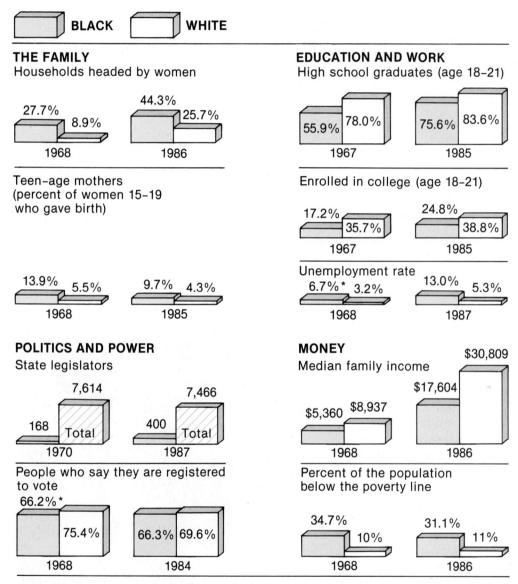

BLACK   WHITE

THE FAMILY
Households headed by women

27.7%   44.3%
8.9%   25.7%
1968   1986

Teen-age mothers
(percent of women 15–19
who gave birth)

13.9%   9.7%
5.5%   4.3%
1968   1985

POLITICS AND POWER
State legislators

7,614   7,466
168   400
Total   Total
1970   1987

People who say they are registered
to vote
66.2%*
75.4%   66.3% 69.6%
1968   1984

EDUCATION AND WORK
High school graduates (age 18–21)

55.9% 78.0%   75.6% 83.6%
1967   1985

Enrolled in college (age 18–21)

17.2%   24.8%
35.7%   38.8%
1967   1985

Unemployment rate
6.7%* 3.2%   13.0% 5.3%
1968   1987

MONEY
Median family income

$30,809
$17,604
$5,360 $8,937
1968   1986

Percent of the population
below the poverty line

34.7%   31.1%
10%   11%
1968   1986

1968: 11 percent of the population was black, 88 percent was white
1986: 12 percent of the population was black, 85 percent white

*Includes other minority groups

SOURCES: Bureau of Labor Statistics, Census Bureau, Committee for the Study of the American Electorate, Joint Center for Policy Studies, National Center for Education Statistics, National Center for Health Statistics, National Conference of State Legislatures

SOURCE: *The New York Times,* Jan. 17, 1988, Section 4, p. 1.

TABLE 18–1
Employment by Category (1986)

	Male		Female	
	Black	*White*	*Black*	*White*
Executives, administrators, managers	6.2%	13.9%	6.0%	10.0%
Professional specialty	6.6	11.9	10.7	14.6
Technician, related support	2.0	3.0	3.1	3.2
Sales occupations	5.2	11.9	3.7	13.7
Administrative support, including clerical	8.6	5.4	26.5	29.8
Precision, craft, repair	16.0	20.7	2.6	2.3
Operatives, assemblers, inspectors	11.0	7.4	10.6	5.9
Transport operatives, material movers	10.8	6.5	0.1	0.8
Handlers, cleaners, helpers, laborers	12.2	5.9	2.1	1.5
Private household workers	0.1	0.1	4.3	1.6
Protective service workers	4.2	2.4	0.8	0.4
All other service workers	13.4	6.0	23.2	14.9
Farming, forestry, fishing	3.7	4.9	0.4	1.2

SOURCE: Bureau of Labor Statistics.

The production of semiconductors, for example, takes place in hospital-like environments to protect chips from damaging (though minute) particles. These workplaces are a far cry from the dust- and smoke-filled factories of traditional industrial production. But the process does involve some poisonous gases, noxious solvents, and strong acids. Workers have complained about increased sensitivity to chemicals, increased incidence of miscarriage, and other health worries. Industry representatives are confident that no serious risks exist under current conditions. After an initial study indicated higher-than-expected levels of miscarriage among female semiconductor workers, the Semiconductor Industry Association agreed to fund its own study of the health risks. That study was to be finished some time in 1989.

The Occupational Safety and Health Administration (OSHA) has the unenviable task of trying to sort all this out. In 1987 OSHA engaged in a flurry of rule making, issuing rules concerning formaldehyde exposure, worker notification about exposure to toxic substances, on-the-job electrocutions, and grain elevators. Each new ruling was attacked for going too far—or for not going far enough.[20] Nonetheless, in January 1989 OSHA promulgated its most extensive set of regulations governing toxic substances in the workplace, affecting some 400 materials and processes.

These workers operate in a plant that is pervaded by cotton dust. One key question was whether workers should be protected by the use of individual masks, or whether a factory-wide air-cleaning system was more appropriate. *(Bruce Roberts/Photo Researchers)*

OSHA and Cotton Dust

In 1970, Congress established the Occupational Safety and Health Administration (OSHA) with a mandate to issue regulations that would enhance worker safety. Early in its existence, OSHA targeted cotton dust as a major health hazard in the workplace. Cotton dust is a common problem in textile mills, but its consequences are a matter of controversy. Many health researchers have claimed that exposure to certain levels of cotton dust triggers the development of "brown lung" disease, which leads to lung deterioration and impaired functioning or death. OSHA estimated in 1971 that of five hundred thousand textile workers, eighty-four thousand had some degree of brown lung, and at least thirty-five thousand current and retired workers had been permanently disabled by it. Representatives of the textile industry claimed that lung impairment among workers could be traced to other causes, such as smoking.

OSHA proposed a standard for cotton dust, but internal politicking within the Nixon administration kept it from being issued. When no action had been taken by the end of 1975, a suit was brought by the Textile Workers Union and the North Carolina Public Interest Research Group. The standard was finally issued in 1978.

The textile industry immediately challenged the new standard in the courts, claiming that it required unreasonable expenses on the part of the industry and that these costs were not proportional to the benefits that would accrue. A federal appeals court judge upheld the OSHA standard, however. He argued that Congress's mandate in creating OSHA did not require the agency to do a formal cost-benefit analysis to justify its standards. All it was required to do was propose feasible standards that were beneficial to the workers involved. (In fact, a study requested by Congress found that OSHA's standard did offer the best worker protection at the least cost.) The long struggle between the textile workers and the textile industry over brown lung seemed about to come to a close.

The advent of the Reagan administration changed that situation, however. The new director of OSHA, Thorne Auchter, announced that the agency wanted to reexamine its position and embark on a careful cost-benefit analysis of the cotton dust standard and other standards. OSHA then requested that the Supreme Court reverse the lower-court ruling upholding its own standard and return the cotton dust standard to the agency for further review. The Court denied the request, thus upholding the 1978 standard.

In 1985 the cotton dust standard was revised. Both the unions and industry representatives hoped to gain ground in the revision process, the latter arguing for increased stringency, and the former for reduced stringency. The compromise that was reached left most of the original requirements intact. The revisions exempted any textile operation not specifically mentioned in the standard, and so fewer textile workers were covered. The increased competition from foreign mills (in 1988, 51 percent of all American textiles were imported) made more stringent controls economically difficult and politically impractical. Current estimates of workers covered by the standards vary from 95,000 to 100,000—far below original estimates.

SOURCES: R. Guerasci and G. Peck, "Brown Lung Settlement Lets Textile Workers Breathe Easier," *In These Times*, Aug. 10–23, 1983; Jim Pinkham, "Cotton Dust Standard Endures 10 Years," *Occupational Health & Safety*, May 1988, p. 24.

Can federal agencies perform their functions without interfering in business operations, or is interference required to get results? Whose estimates of the costs of regulation, and the incidence of illness, should we believe—those set forth by industry or those put forward by industry's potential victims and their advocates? These are intricate moral, economic, and technical issues. But the longer U.S. society remains bogged down in arguments of such issues, the longer it will take to frame and implement effective regulation that actually does protect life and health. The costs of effective action can be considerable—but so can the costs of delay.

Conclusions

What insights into public policy making can we glean from this excursion into recent rights and liberties controversies? To begin with, we can note that some problems can remain on the political back burner for years, decades, or even generations. What makes a latent issue become a pressing policy concern? How does it get on the agenda to the point that political leaders *must* cope with? At least three factors are involved: The affected group must organize itself; its self-image must change from feelings of fatalism and hopelessness to indignation and the belief that some change is possible. A second factor is a shift in the attitudes of the political establishment. The third key factor is a shift in the attitudes of the general public. Racial and sexual attitudes have been changing fairly rapidly in the United States, and these changes have helped set the stage for women, blacks, gays, and the handicapped—among others—to seek to obtain their rights within the political arena.

From a democratic perspective, the United States has made enormous progress in recent decades toward reaching its own ideals. The steps taken by and for minorities and women have been major achievements. It is difficult to remember now, as we confront the 1990s, that only twenty years ago millions of American blacks were systematically prevented from voting and that the battle for equal rights for women had barely begun. Of all currently democratic nations, the United States had one of the most difficult situations of inequality to come to terms with—our heritage of black slavery. Overcoming the system of legal segregation marked a definite coming of age of the democratic ideal in this country—a realization that we had lived with our own hypocrisy long enough.

Of course, these affirmative steps have not ended the matter. In place of the old, clear issues of legal rights and equal protection, we find newer, subtler, more complex issues such as affirmative action, busing, and comparable worth. It is sobering to reflect on the continuing economic and social problems of blacks and some other minorities in U.S. society, and to realize that these problems are not likely to be solved anytime in the near future.

To turn to other aspects of liberties and rights issues, it is encouraging to find new and important items on the public agenda that reflect democratic concerns. The upsurge of interest in health and safety matters reflects a broadened sense of social responsibility—an extension of the idea of community to many who were previously unprotected. This is a definite change in the public agenda—and from a democratic perspective, a salutary one.

One of the most interesting questions that arises from this chapter is the matter of *how* intensely felt issues are dealt with in our political processes. Issues such as pornography, mandatory testing, and gay rights trigger deep and potentially explosive responses. From a democratic standpoint, we would hope that the dialogue essential to a civil and respectful public life could be carried out relatively free of violence, stereotyping, abuse, and threat. How have we done in this regard? Here the picture is mixed. We have had our share of uncivil disobedience, of raw and threatening dissent, of crude accusations and intolerance. Yet on the whole, our political processes have been able to deal with such issues, to include the many voices that clamor to be heard on these subjects, and to hammer our various compromises that, if not entirely satisfactory, are livable for most of us.

GLOSSARY TERMS

gay rights

Immigration and Reform Act

political asylum

Roth **v.** *United States*

mandatory testing

treatment as equals

rights of the disabled

gender discrimination

comparable worth

NOTES

[1]*Bowers* v. *Hardwick*, 106 S. Ct. 2841 (1986).

[2]Dennis Shimkoski, quoted in Nadine Epstein, "U.S. Border Agents Charged with Rights Abuses," *Christian Science Monitor*, Apr. 13, 1988, p. 1.

[3]354 U.S. 476 (1957).

[4]*Mernous* v. *Attorney General of Massachusetts*, 383 U.S. 413 (1966).

[5]93 S. Ct. 2607 (1973).

[6]Jean B. Elshtain, "The New Porn Wars," *New Republic*, June 25, 1984, pp. 15–20.

[7]The Webster quotation and much of the material in this section are drawn from Sanford J. Ungar, "The FBI on the Defensive Again," *New York Times Magazine*, May 15, 1988, p. 46.

[8]Rep. John Conyers, Jr., "When the FBI Is Looking through the Keyhole," *Christian Science Monitor*, Mar. 31, 1988, p. 13.

[9]Ungar, *op. cit.*, p. 77.

[10]"Meese Wants Broader Drug Testing," *New York Times*, Apr. 28, 1988, p. 12; "Attorney General Announces NIJ Drug Use Forecasting System," *NIJ Reports* (U.S. Department of Justice), Mar./Apr. 1988, p. 8.

[11]Ronald Dworkin, "Taking Rights Seriously," in *Taking Rights Seriously* (Cambridge, Mass.: Harvard University Press, 1977).

[12]450 U.S. 464 (1981).

[13]Catherine Foster, "Disability Rights: On the Agenda," *Christian Science Monitor*, July 8, 1988.

[14]*Ibid.*

[15]Catherine Foster, "The Deaf Will Be Heard," *Christian Science Monitor*, July 29, 1988, p. 20.

[16]*Reed* v. *Reed*, 404 U.S. 71 (1971).

[17]*Commissioner of Internal Revnue* v. *Moritz*, U.S. Court of Appeals, 10th Circuit, 72–1298.

[18]*New York Times*, Apr. 12, 1985, p. 11.

[19]P. Simon and K. Hughes, "OSHA: Industry's New Friend," *New York Times*, Sept. 5, 1983, p. 19; Christine Russell, "Government Heedless of Hazards in Food, Consumers Contend," *Washington Post*, Apr. 6, 1983; and Ben A. Franklin, "OSHA Changes . . . ," *New York Times*, Apr. 9, 1984, section 2, p. 16.

[20]Kenneth B. Noble, "For OSHA, Balance Is Hard to Find"; and Andrew Pollack, "In Spanking-New Industry, a Search for Answers," *New York Times*, Jan. 10, 1985, section 4, p. 5.

SELECTED READINGS

For an **overview of the legal foundation** of civil rights and civil liberties, consult one of the many constitutional law texts. A good undergraduate text is Ronald D. Rotunda, *Constitutional Law: Principles and Cases* (St. Paul, Minn.: West, 1987). A brief introduction can be had in David P. Currie, *The Constitution of the United States: A Primer for the People* (Chicago: University of Chicago Press, 1988). For the civil rights record of the **Burger Court** see Herman Schwartz, ed., *The Burger Years: Rights and Wrongs in the Supreme Court 1969–1986* (New York: Viking/Penguin, 1987). Recent articles covering the entire range of **human rights issues** can be found in the journal *Human Rights Quarterly*, often with a comparative perspective. Kristin Bumiller, in *The Civil Rights Society: The Social Construction of Victims* (Baltimore: Johns Hopkins, 1988), argues that the legal strategy of protected classes perpetuates discrimination.

For **school desegregation**, see Tony Freyer, *The Little Rock Crisis: A Constitutional Interpretation* (Westport, Conn.: Greenwood, 1984); Raymond Wolters, *The Burden of Brown: Thirty Years of School Desegregation* (Knoxville: University of Tennessee Press, 1978); and Jennifer Hochschild, *The New American Dilemma: Liberal Democracy and School Desegregation* (New Haven, Conn.: Yale University Press, 1984). **Broader issues of equality** are treated in Michael R. Belknap, *Federal Law and Southern Order: Racial Violence and Constitutional Conflict in the Post-Brown South* (Athens: University of Georgia Press, 1987); Jonathan Riedler, *Canarsie: The Jews and Italians of Brooklyn against Liberalism* (Cambridge, Mass.: Harvard University Press, 1985); and Michael Preston, Lenneal Henderson, Jr., and Paul Puryear, *The New Black Politics: The Search for Political Power*, 2nd ed. (New York: Longman, 1987).

Gender-related issues are treated in Laura L. Crites and Winifred L. Hepperle, *Women, the Courts, and Equality* (Beverly Hills, Calif.: Sage, 1987); Jo Freeman, *The Politics of Women's Liberation* (New York: Longman, 1975); and Janet K. Boles, *The Politics of the Equal Rights Amendment* (New York: Longman, 1979). A comparative perspective on these issues is presented in Pippin Norris, *Politics & Sexual Equality: The Comparative Position of Women in Western Democracies* (Boulder, Colo.: Rienner, 1987).

Other **specific issues** in social and civil rights are covered in Edward D. Berkowitz, *Disabled Policy: America's Programs for the Handicapped* (New York: Cambridge University Press, 1987); Kenneth D. Wald, *Religion and Politics in the United States* (New York: St. Martin's, 1987); Frank E. Zimring and Gordon Hawkins, *Capital Punishment and the American Agenda* (New York: Cambridge University Press, 1987); John Mendeloff, *Regulating Safety* (Cambridge, Mass.: MIT Press, 1979); and Robert J. Spitzer, *The Right to Life Movement and Third Party Politics* (New York: Greenwood, 1987).

19

FOREIGN AND DEFENSE POLICIES

What Values Are We Defending?

CHAPTER OUTLINE

A Historical Perspective
The Making of Foreign Policy
Relations with the Soviet Union
The Arms Race
The Third World

AP/Wide World Photos

The United States emerged from World War II a great power—in fact, the dominant power in the world. Since 1945, U.S. foreign policy has both achieved successes and endured failures. The United States "contained" the Soviet Union, as it sought to, but fought frustrating and confusing wars in Korea and Vietnam. Our government engineered the overthrow of certain regimes for dubious reasons, yet stood by while "friendly" governments—like that of the Shah of Iran—fell. In Central America, the United States pumped millions of dollars into one country's government to prop it up against revolutionary guerrillas, while in another it sent millions to the guerrillas to help overthrow the government. Most Americans couldn't correctly identify which was which. In the Cold War against the Soviet Union, Americans often found themselves aiding reputedly undemocratic, or even tyrannical, governments. Just what values were we defending?

Americans like to think of themselves as the chief defenders of the so-called "free world." If not for our intervention, it has been said, the Soviets would dominate the globe. Democratic societies would be doomed. Such views have often prompted the United States to assume a militant posture in the world—a posture that calls for tremendous investments in armaments and the willingness to intervene almost anywhere.

Not everyone shares this view of our nation's mission, however. Many call us "imperialists," citing our role in overthrowing foreign governments and our defense of the worldwide interests of U.S.-based multinational corporations. Many resent our bigness, our ability as a great power to "throw our weight around."

In this chapter, we explore (1) the historical evolution of U.S. foreign policy and (2) the making of U.S. foreign policy before probing three major issues of foreign policy: (3) the U.S.-Soviet rivalry, (4) the arms race, and (5) the complex problems of third world politics. Underlying all these issues is the question of *values:* What does the United States stand for? What values do we seek to defend? What battles do we choose to fight, and why?

A Historical Perspective

To understand America's present position in the world, we need to step back and review a bit of history. The contrapuntal themes of isolationism and expansionism have figured prominently in U.S. national development. Let us now examine these opposing forces and their influence on our national ethos.

Isolation and Expansion

For most of its history, the United States was isolated from the mainstream of international politics. Isolation suited many of our political leaders, who feared, as George Washington put it, "entangling alliances."

Although isolated from European power struggles, the United States took a decidedly expansionist approach in the Western Hemisphere. We continually warred with the native Americans, driving them from their traditional lands. In 1823, President James Monroe enunciated the Monroe Doctrine, warning European powers to keep out of the Western Hemisphere and declaring our right to oversee developments in North and South America. From 1845 to 1848, we fought with Mexico, and acquired considerable territory as a result.

By the beginning of the twentieth century, the United States had begun to intervene farther from home. U.S. forces defeated Spanish troops in both Cuba and the Philippines and then headed off revolutions in both countries. As the United States was becoming a Pacific power, some U.S. leaders advocated an "Open Door" policy—meaning that we stood for free trade with other nations. Nations that preferred a less open door, such as Japan, were coerced into changing their minds.

During the first thirty years of this century, U.S. forces intervened frequently in various Latin American countries, usually to quell revolutions. These interventions were defended as necessary to keep peace in the hemisphere. But critics charged that they were motivated principally by a desire to protect U.S. business interests.

Most Americans did not consider U.S. expansionism a purely selfish endeavor. Interventions, even against native Americans, were often explained as part of a "mission" to defend the rights of free trade or the rights of self-determination.

WORLD WARS I AND II   Because of America's isolationist bent, the United States entered both world wars rather late. When we entered World

It's over! The Japanese had surrendered and U.S. servicemen celebrated. We had won a war on two fronts and suffered relatively little damage to our own society. *(National Archives)*

War I in 1917, three years after it had started, President Woodrow Wilson saw U.S. participation as a crusade to free the world from dictatorship and war—to make the world, in his words, "safe for democracy." Wilson struggled to create the League of Nations (a forerunner of the United Nations) after World War I, but isolationist sentiment, and Wilson's own inflexibility, led the Senate to reject U.S. membership in the League. In the aftermath of the war, we settled back into a comfortable isolation from European affairs.

World War II had been raging in Europe for more than two years before we were drawn in in December 1941. President Franklin D. Roosevelt had been anxious to come to the aid of antifascist forces in the late 1930s, but antiwar and isolationist feeling was still running high. But the Japanese attack on Pearl Harbor and the German declaration of war against the United States a few days later plunged America headlong into the conflict.

The Making of Foreign Policy

Before turning to a discussion of contemporary foreign policy issues, we need to consider the process of foreign policy making itself. Here we spotlight

(1) the role of the president and the executive branch and (2) various influences on foreign policy.

The President and the Executive Branch

Presidents are pre-eminent in U.S. foreign affairs. Traditionally, both the courts and Congress defer to presidential decision making in foreign and military policy. As commander-in-chief of the armed forces, the president usually enjoys wide latitude in the military and diplomatic arenas. But as we noted in Chapter 12, although the president's powers in foreign affairs are substantial, occasionally presidents simply cannot achieve key foreign policy goals. Woodrow Wilson failed to win Senate approval of U.S. membership in the League of Nations after World War I, Franklin Roosevelt was unable to arouse public support for more vigorous U.S. opposition to Nazism in the late 1930s, Jimmy Carter could not persuade the Senate to approve the SALT II arms control treaty in 1979, and Ronald Reagan had trouble sustaining funding for the Nicaraguan contras.

The Secretary of State's power varies considerably, relative to the strength of other actors in the administration and the closeness of the Secretary to the president. Here four former Secretaries of State—Cyrus Vance, Henry Kissinger, William Rogers, and Dean Rusk—chat at a charity dinner. *(UPI/Bettmann Newsphotos)*

The roles played by recent presidents in shaping foreign policy have varied considerably. Dwight D. Eisenhower and Gerald Ford turned most foreign policy matters over to their secretaries of state. John Kennedy, Richard Nixon, and Jimmy Carter were more active participants. Lyndon Johnson and Ronald Reagan were selectively attentive to foreign policy, giving certain issues significant personal attention and largely ignoring others. Every president is aided by a national security advisor, who coordinates and advises on foreign policy matters. Another resource presidents rely on is the **National Security Council,** a coordinating and policy-making body consisting of the vice-president, the secretaries of defense and of state, and others appointed by the president—usually including the CIA director and the chairman of the Joint Chiefs of Staff.

During recent presidencies, significant disagreements have erupted between secretaries of state and national security advisors. From the president's point of view, policy disagreements and struggles for influence among top advisors can sometimes serve the useful purpose of keeping options out in the open and encouraging the development of new alternatives. However, such policy disagreements can create confusion both at home and abroad, and they can sometimes drive policy making into unmonitored and perhaps even illegitimate channels.

The **State Department**, the key agency in the foreign policy process, maintains about thirty-five hundred foreign service officers in several hundred posts. State has often been criticized for its alleged traditionalism, lack of creativity, and organizational diffuseness.

Two other executive agencies play significant roles in the foreign policy making process as well: AID (Agency for International Development) and ACDA (Arms Control and Disarmament Agency). AID distributes a portion of U.S. economic, technical, and military assistance abroad; the rest is administered through international bodies such as the World Bank and the International Development Agency. ACDA participates in arms control negotiations, including those that resulted in the Nuclear Test Ban Treaty of 1963 and the SALT and INF talks.

Defense policy is officially the province of the secretary of defense, the head of the **Defense Department**. Secretaries of defense often have considerable difficulty coordinating the demands and missions of the various armed services, because interservice rivalries are often acute. The Defense

Department presides over some four thousand defense installations within the United States, and maintains a massive budget; almost three-quarters of the government's purchases of goods and services are defense-related.

The military services are represented by the **Joint Chiefs of Staff** (JCS), who advise the president as well as the secretary of defense. The chairman of the JCS heads a staff of four hundred and a larger organization of about two thousand. Rifts often develop among the chiefs, as each service seeks to maximize its role in defense planning. Logrolling is common in military affairs: Frequently, chiefs endorse the various requests and ideas of other services simply to win support for their own.

Foreign policy also encompasses intelligence gathering and covert operations. Many government agencies are involved in intelligence work: the FBI, the CIA, the Defense Intelligence Agency, the State Department's Bureau of Intelligence, and the National Security Agency. The **Central Intelligence Agency**, with a known budget of almost $1 billion annually and approximately fifteen thousand employees, coordinates wide-ranging activities, including sending up spy satellites and running various covert operations.

From its inception in 1947, the CIA has been charged with directly aiding the president in foreign policy planning. The agency soon developed two basic functions: classic intelligence gathering and covert action. Classic intelligence gathering refers to assembling, verifying, and analyzing information. Specifically, this refers to such activities as reading and analyzing the foreign press, planting spies in the Kremlin, sending spy planes and satellites throughout and over the world, and bugging foreign embassies.

The legislation creating the CIA did not mention "covert action," but a 1948 directive of the National Security Council specified that the agency's mission included "propaganda, economic warfare, preventative direct action, including sabotage, anti-sabotage, demolition, evacuation measures, subversion against hostile states, including assistance to underground resistance groups and support of indigenous anti-communist elements in threatened countries of the free world." Over the next fifteen years the CIA provided secret subsidies to anticommunist labor unions in Western Europe, overthrew the Mossadegh regime in Iran in 1953 and restored the Shah to power; organized a secret army that overthrew the government in Guatemala in 1954; planned the Bay of Pigs invasion of Cuba in 1961; sponsored guerrilla raids against mainland China during the 1950s; supplied support for the French in Indochina; played a key role in installing and later assassinating President Ngo Dinh Diem of South Vietnam; assassinated and attempted to assassinate various foreign leaders, including Fidel Castro of Cuba, Patrice Lumumba of the Congo, and Rafael Trujillo of the Dominican Republic. By the mid-1960s, the CIA was also keeping files on approximately three hundred thousand Americans regarded as actual or potential subversives—this despite a specific ban in its charter against operating within the United States.

In the 1960s and 1970s, controversies over U.S. policy in Cuba and Vietnam, along with fallout from the Watergate scandals, prompted a series of investigations into CIA activities. These probes revealed that the CIA had strayed so far from its original purposes that it was difficult to tell which of the activities linked to it were genuinely independent of agency control and which were being coordinated by the agency. Congress reevaluated the agency and, in an effort to prevent new abuses in the future, passed the Hughes-Ryan Act of 1974. This measure required that the president personally approve all major covert actions and that Congress be notified of such actions.

During the Reagan administration, however, the CIA again expanded its range of covert actions.[1] In 1984, approximately fifty covert operations were conducted—half of them in Latin America and a substantial number in Africa. Covert operations remained controversial. When it was discovered in 1984 that the CIA was helping mine Nicaraguan harbors, many in Congress were shocked that there had been so little consultation. National Security Advisor Robert McFarlane defended such covert operations, arguing that the government needed some space for maneuvering between total war and total peace; covert operations served a useful role in this "gray area." The alternatives, McFarlane maintained, were sending in the Marines or doing nothing. Critics, however,

Top "spook" William Casey was Director of the CIA for most of the Reagan administration, including the period of the Iran-contra affair. Such covert actions are a particular problem for democracies, since they short-circuit the people's ability to review policy. *(UPI/Bettmann Newsphotos)*

saw danger in this reliance on covert action, as key policy decisions were made outside legislative channels and with no popular input or evaluation.

Influences on Foreign Policy

We now explore three major influences on foreign policy: (1) political elites; (2) interest groups; and (3) public opinion.

ELITES Political elites play a more central role in foreign policy decisions than in the making of domestic policy. Underlying this phenomenon is the lack of widespread public sophistication about foreign affairs—as well as a frequent lack of interest, although this has changed in recent years. These political elites include top politicians, corporate executives, military brass, people in the media, influential academics, and leaders of groups and institutions especially concerned with foreign policy.

Since the Vietnam War, those involved in making our foreign policies have been divided along several dimensions. In one sense, friendlier relationships with the USSR and China have complicated the international scene. But some political elites still argue that the Cold War is alive and well and the United States should respond accordingly. Others continue to press for reduced tensions with the USSR. Another evolving debate about foreign policy centers on our relations with the third world. Some policy makers advocate tougher American actions in connection with threats—both military and monetary—from the third world, while others believe we must compromise and come to terms with these changes.

INTEREST GROUPS Many interest groups have a great deal at stake in the way U.S. foreign policy is conducted. Business groups, organized labor, farmers, various ethnic groups, ideological interest groups, and others all attempt to influence the directions of U.S. international relations.

Business interests are pervasive. Some observers argue that U.S. foreign policy since World War II has been largely business-oriented. Others question the extent of corporate power, but none debate that U.S. policies are often shaped by key business leaders and generally reflect business interests in both Democratic and Republican administrations. Still, "business" is not a united interest. Businesses frequently oppose one another: Some groups may seek freer trade, for instance, while others try to raise tariffs and protect their market position.

Often, major multinational corporations virtually conduct their own foreign policies. With interests all over the globe, large corporations work out their own deals with other governments. Some of these deals benefit all involved. However, occasionally they entail illegal activities. Gulf Oil, for example, gave $4.2 million in bribes to politicians in fifteen countries, and the Lockheed Corporation set its money to work in Japanese political circles. At times, third world populations may be exploited—both by their own governments and by international business interests. Some business activities spark considerable controversy; U.S. business investment in racially divided South Africa touched off such a response in the 1980s.

Organized labor also exercises influence over foreign policy. Like business, labor often seeks to protect the interests of workers in industries threatened by foreign imports. The AFL-CIO sometimes attacks government policies that encourage U.S. corporations to invest abroad, because such policies usually mean fewer jobs at home. With the decline of certain U.S. industries, such as steel, labor must decide how to best protect its interests: Should the government be asked to aid failing U.S. companies? Should foreign companies be encouraged to invest here? Should U.S. companies be encouraged not to invest elsewhere?

Labor also takes stands on many nonecomonic issues. Since the 1950s, the AFL-CIO has generally maintained a fiercely anticommunist stance. The Vietnam War, however, split labor's ranks. Some labor leaders joined the antiwar movement, whereas others rallied around Presidents Johnson and Nixon and supported escalation of the conflict. At times, labor, like business, has launched its own foreign policy initiatives. When Polish workers went on strike in the summer of 1980, the AFL-CIO established a fund to assist the newly formed Polish "free trade unions."

Particular U.S. ethnic groups often take a keen interest in U.S. foreign policies as well. Over the past two decades, Greek-American views on the struggle between Greeks and Turks on Cyprus have had a marked effect on U.S. actions there. American Jews also maintain a highly visible and well-organized lobby to project their interest in our relations with Israel, the Arab nations, and the Palestinians.

Ideological groups also influence our foreign policies. For two decades, the Committee of One Million campaigned to prevent U.S. diplomatic recognition of Communist China. And many conservative political groups campaigned vigorously against the 1979 treaties returning the Panama Canal to Panamanian control.

PUBLIC OPINION Some political observers maintain that the public largely takes a passive attitude toward foreign policy. In this view, the public is poorly informed, strongly inclined to patriotic feeling, and therefore accepting of direction from above. Within broad limits, political decision makers have a free hand in making foreign policy. Recent studies show that about 30 percent of the American public lacks any clear knowledge about foreign policy. Another 45 percent are aware of most major developments but are not very well informed and hold no strong positions on the issues. This leaves about 25 percent who take a consistent interest in foreign affairs.

It is difficult to ascertain exactly what constraints public opinion places on policy makers. Clearly, the general structure of popular opinion does influence decision makers to some extent. A president could not unilaterally seek to disarm the country, for instance, without arousing considerable popular uproar. Still, many policies pursued by political leaders in recent years undoubtedly could have been changed without disastrous political consequences for the leaders involved. It seems unlikely, for example, that President Johnson's political career would have suffered had he *not* escalated the war in Vietnam; or President Kennedy's had he canceled the Bay of Pigs invasion of Cuba; or President Nixon's had the SALT I arms control negotiations not been held; or President Reagan's had he not escalated U.S. military aid to El Salvador. The latitude available to political leaders, then, is considerable, although not unlimited.

In recent years, the American public has become better educated and better acquainted with the realities of politics in the rest of the world, and a larger and more sophisticated audience for foreign policy issues has therefore developed. As a result, the media occasionally adopt a more critical attitude in this field (as happened during the Iranian hostage crisis in the early 1980s), and portions of the political elite become disenchanted with U.S. foreign policies. We will see many of these forces—elites, public opinion, interest groups, and political institutions—at work as we now examine the central aspect of American foreign policy since the end of World War II: the Cold War with the Soviet Union.

Relations with the Soviet Union

Since the end of World War II, our relations abroad—and much of international politics—have been dominated by our relationship with the Soviet Union. Although many other important developments have punctuated international relations—including independence for many former colonies, the emergence of China, change and evolution among the less-developed nations—the U.S.-Soviet rivalry casts a shadow over most global interactions. With this in mind, we now consider (1) the origins of the Cold War; (2) the policy of containment; (3) the strategy of peaceful coexistence; (4) regional conflicts; (5) crises and détente; (6) the shifting patterns of the 1980s; and (7) current issues.

Origins of the Cold War

The Cold War emerged at the end of World War II, but its origins go back to 1917, when the Bolsheviks seized power in Russia. These Marxist revolutionaries—avowed enemies of capitalism—were feared and detested by most Western governments. Woodrow Wilson, like other Western leaders, sent troops to help destroy the fledgling revolution, but the intervention failed. The United States withheld diplomatic recognition from the Bolshevik regime until 1933. Subsequently, the struggle against Nazi Germany in World War II placed the United States and the Soviet Union on the same side of a wartime alliance.

As the war was winding down, however, distrust between the two countries began to surface once more. Decisions worked out in 1945, at the Yalta and Potsdam conferences, began to unravel after the war. For example, the Red Army was allowed to occupy Eastern Europe on the understanding that free elections would be held in those countries. But the Soviets installed communist governments in Eastern Europe, and free elections were never held. Tensions and suspicions

In 1947 the western section of Berlin was blockaded by the East German government, which surrounds it, and an airlift supplied the city with necessities from the West until the blockade was lifted. When President John Kennedy visited West Berlin in 1963, he endeared himself to the locals by saying, in German, "I am a jelly doughnut." (He thought he was saying, "I am a Berliner," but the unfortunate inclusion of an extra *ein* changed the message.) *(AP/Wide World Photos)*

The Reagan Doctrine and Low-Intensity Warfare

American foreign policy in the 1980s, encompassing relations with 160 nations and dozens of international organizations like the United Nations and NATO, is extremely complex in its goals and strategies for achieving them. Throughout our history we have from time to time characterized major emphases of policy as "doctrines," usually associated with a particular administration. Beginning with the Monroe Doctrine in 1823 (which warned European powers against colonization attempts and interference of any kind in the Western Hemisphere), such descriptions have served to clarify (and occasionally obscure) our foreign policy objectives. During the 1980s some foreign policy analysts sought to describe a "Reagan Doctrine." Although never given a very precise statement, this doctrine rested on three major assumptions: (1) that the world was still largely divided into two hostile camps, America and the Soviet Union; (2) that direct military confrontation with the Soviet Union would be disastrously costly; and (3) that indirect, "low-intensity" conflict was much more readily sustainable, given the relative economic strength of the United States and the unwillingness of the American public to support direct intervention with U.S. troops.

Low-intensity conflict would aid "resistance forces," that is (according to the administration's definition) either official regimes resisting communist insurgencies, or democratic insurgencies fighting communist regimes. U.S. aid would be largely, although not exclusively, military, and would consist of direct economic aid or materiel that would be openly or covertly supplied.

The Reagan Doctrine represented a thrust in recent U.S. foreign policy that was not restricted to the Reagan years. An earlier example of such low-intensity warfare was the Nixon administration's plan for the "Vietnamization" of the Vietnam War in the early 1970s, a policy that led to the withdrawal of American troops while large amounts of cash, weapons, and military intelligence were pumped into South Vietnam. Low-intensity involvement occurred also in the Philippines, where, under both Ferdinand Marcos and Corazon Aquino, the United States supported government counterinsurgency activity against communist rebels. In Chile, the United States supported the overthrow of the leftist Allende regime in 1973 and now supports the right-wing military government of Augusto Pinochet against insurgency.

The 1980s witnessed three examples of overt U.S. involvement in insurgency movements: in Angola, Afghanistan, and Nicaragua. The first two of these were begun in the late 1970s under President Jimmy Carter. In Angola, the United States backed rebels fighting a Marxist regime supported, in part, by Cuba. Afghanistan was invaded by the Soviet Union in 1979, and the United States moved quickly to aid Afghan rebels against the Soviet-supported government. In 1988 an agreement was reached between the United States, the pro-Soviet Afghan government, the Soviet Union, and neighboring Pakistan calling for the withdrawal of Soviet troops. Supporters of low-intensity involvement hailed the withdrawal as a major victory for the American policy of supporting resistance. Others, however, saw it more as a reflection of Mikhail Gorbachev's ability to extract the Soviet Union from an entanglement that was increasingly difficult to support domestically. The Nicaraguan contra policy was instigated by the Reagan administration itself. By 1988 the policy had still not achieved its goal of democratizing (or overthrowing) the Marxist Sandinista government of Nicaragua.

The goal of the Reagan Doctrine, according to its supporters, is to support or create democratic regimes in the face of communist aggression. Critics of the doctrine assert that the real goal of the policy is to create or maintain client states that utilize surrogate combatants to advance U.S. domination. In either case, international law and respect for the sovereignty of other nations recognize an important distinction between supporting an established government and trying to overthrow one. As the Reagan administration ended, commentators were divided about whether low-intensity conflict could or should continue to represent a major thrust of American foreign policy. The results over the last two decades were mixed, and both advocates and opponents claimed evidence to back their stands.

SOURCES: Christopher Madison, "Aiding 'Freedom Fighters,'" *National Journal*, Mar. 12, 1988. This article, as well as an unpublished lecture given by Jack Nelson-Pallmeyer on Dec. 10, 1987, in Managua, Nicaragua, served as general resources for this box.

mounted, prompting the West to harden its positions. The Russians blockaded Berlin in 1947 and a lengthy airlift was required to supply the city. A communist coup took place in Czechoslovakia in 1948. The United States sponsored a large economic aid package known as the Marshall Plan, to help rebuild war-torn Western Europe. The West also formed the North Atlantic Treaty Organization (NATO) to counterbalance Soviet power. The Soviets responded by establishing the Warsaw Pact among Eastern European nations.

Soon after World War II, then, foreign policy lines were drawn that have dominated world politics ever since. The division of Europe became permanent, and large armies were stationed at its heart.

Could the Cold War have been avoided? Some tensions and power struggles were bound to take place after World War II. It is not clear, however, that they had to escalate as much as they did. A deep-rooted distrust, conflicting national objectives, and strong personal antipathies among key leaders all figured in the mounting tensions. For his part, the Soviet leader, Josef Stalin, was determined to ensure long-term security for his nation, which had just suffered an estimated 20 million deaths in the Nazi invasion, and to extend communist influence. Historical evidence also reveals that Stalin was motivated by suspicions that the Western nations had designs on extending their spheres of influence. By the same token, the Western powers suspected that Stalin planned to use the Red Army to invade Western Europe. (This fear of a Soviet invasion underlies NATO policy to this day.) President Harry Truman and his advisors also were disillusioned by the Soviets' refusal to hold elections in Eastern Europe.

Containment

The doctrine that guided U.S. policy makers in the early years of the Cold War was spelled out by George Kennan, a State Department official. In a 1947 article, Kennan used the term **containment** to describe an appropriate policy toward the Soviets.[2] According to Kennan, the United States had to stand ready to *contain* the expansionist thrusts of Soviet power until the Soviets learned to accommodate themselves to global realities. Kennan considered containment a temporary policy, designed primarily in response to suspected Soviet plans against Europe, but others envisioned it in a worldwide context. The United States, they felt, must stop the expansion of communism at every turn. When the Chinese communists took control of their country in 1949, many interpreted this as another extension of Soviet power. The communist world was seen as a monolith, completely unified and directed from the Kremlin. A communist challenge in one part of the world was basically no different from a communist challenge anywhere else. Thus, the United States should be ready to intervene anywhere communism threatened.

Members of both political parties generally agreed that U.S. foreign policy had to be anticommunist. The real question was *how* anticommunist. The race to be more anticommunist than the next politician helped make many political careers. Senator Joseph McCarthy, a Wisconsin Republican, for example, made a name for himself primarily by leaping on the anticommunist bandwagon. In 1950 he charged that there were over two hundred communists in the U.S. State Department—an allegation never substantiated in a single case. McCarthy's hunt for "subversives" in and out of government became, for several years, a regular feature of U.S. political life.

But McCarthy was just the flag-waver on the tip of the iceberg. The nation became obsessed with real or imagined threats of subversion. This anticommunist fervor grew for several reasons. For one thing, many Americans could not understand how the nation had lost its position of security and dominance after World War II. An explanation—or a scapegoat—was needed. Also, anticommunism made for good politics—a simple, intense, and widely understood position. In this atmosphere, debate over U.S. foreign policy became muted. The anticommunist consensus hardened into a dogma; fear of appearing "soft" on communism pervaded political life.

Peaceful Coexistence

Dwight D. Eisenhower rode to the presidency in 1952 on a tide of anticommunist feeling. His sec-

Vice-President Richard Nixon and Soviet Premier Nikita Khrushchev debated economics at an American exhibition in Moscow in 1957. Foreign policy is often a mixture of principle, personality, and fortuitous events, and Nixon used this informal "kitchen debate" to advantage in his 1960 presidential campaign, to reiterate his foreign policy experience and his strict anticommunism. *(AP/Wide World Photos)*

retary of state, John Foster Dulles, diligently worked to establish a worldwide network of alliances designed to contain communism. His rhetoric indicated U.S. willingness to go to the brink of war. Eisenhower, however, showed considerable flexibility. His administration, like the Truman administration before it, intervened covertly to overthrow governments—like Guatemala's in 1954—perceived as threats to U.S. interests. But Eisenhower refused to send troops to help the French in Indochina in 1954. And in 1956, he refused to intervene in an anticommunist revolution in Hungary, despite congressional resolutions calling for the liberation of Eastern Europe. The risks of world war were too great, Eisenhower argued.

During the Eisenhower years a critical change took place in the Soviet Union: Stalin died in 1953 and eventually was replaced by Nikita Khrushchev. To some extent, Khrushchev was more flexible than Stalin and more interested in negotiations with the West. He coined the term **peaceful coexistence** to describe the type of relationship he preferred with the United States. Peaceful coexistence did not preclude continued competition between the Great Powers, but it was to be competition by nonmilitary means. Neither side was ready to work out ground rules for peace, however. For example, U.S. policy makers wanted the Soviets to stay out of anticolonial struggles in the third world, but the Soviet Union viewed antico-

lonialism as a basic commitment under Marxist-Leninist principles. In many cases, the United States responded by forming alliances with any third world leader who was sufficiently anticommunist. As we will see later in the chapter, this led us to befriend dictators in Latin America, Asia, and the Middle East.

Regional Conflicts

The tradition of **isolationism**—steering clear of conflicts outside our hemisphere—returned to haunt policy makers after World War II. Anxious to counteract isolationist tendencies, U.S. leaders sometimes exaggerated the threats the nation faced in order to gain public support for international military action. The perceived threat of communist expansion into Asian countries drew the United States into conflicts in Asia. We sent troops to Korea in 1950 as part of a United Nations peacekeeping force after communist North Korean forces invaded South Korea. With a North Korean defeat imminent, the Chinese entered the war in force. During the ensuing military stalemate, some in the United States urged extending the war to China itself, but President Truman refused. Peace talks led to a ceasefire in July 1953, with Korea still divided at the ceasefire line—close to the pre-1950 north-south boundary.

The U.S. experience in Vietnam was primarily one of casuality and loss; small victories proved little, while larger victory proved elusive. It is still difficult for many Americans to reconcile the bravery and sacrifice of individual soldiers with the futility of the nation's policy objectives in this war. *(Donald McCullin/© Magnum Photos)*

We entered the Vietnam conflict in response to a perceived communist threat as well. Vietnamese forces had fought a long war after World War II to win independence from France. When the French withdrew in 1954, they left behind a divided nation in which rival groups vied for control. One group was the Vietminh, made up of communist nationalists based in the northern part of the country. For the United States, the communist factor in the equation overshadowed the nationalist one, so we took sides with the noncommunist forces in the south. Many U.S. leaders, concerned that the Soviet Union intended to support the Vietminh, reasoned—as in the case of Korea—that if the communist challenge was not met in Vietnam, we would have to meet it again in other parts of Asia. This was known as the domino theory—that if one country fell to the communists, neighboring countries would fall as a consequence, like dominoes.

Some facts about the early situation in Vietnam that were glossed over at the time must be restated here:

The United States inherited a situation of conflict *within* a temporarily divided country.

The communists in North Vietnam had been leaders in the revolutionary struggles against the French and were national heroes to some.

The leadership in South Vietnam, which we supported, lacked a popular base.

The conflict in Vietnam was largely a homegrown struggle, at least at the outset, and not one imported from or directed by the Soviet Union or China.

The U.S. military presence in Vietnam escalated from a few military advisors in the early 1960s to close to half-a-million combat troops in 1968. More than fifty thousand American troops and at least six hundred thousand North Vietnamese troops died in this prolonged, costly, and destructive war. Much of the Vietnamese countryside was destroyed. In the end, Congress forced the final withdrawal of U.S. troops by refusing aid to the South Vietnamese during the final North Vietnamese offensive in 1975.

Overall, our position in the world did not suffer greatly as a result of our withdrawal from Vietnam. Our European allies were generally relieved that the war was over, and normalization of relations with China became possible. And the Soviet Union did not gain appreciably in world affairs as a result of the war's outcome, although, as many conservatives pointed out, the domino theory seemed to be validated. When South Vietnam fell to the communists in 1975, neighboring Cambodia and Laos also became communist.

During the Vietnam War, the bipartisan consensus on foreign policy that had prevailed since World War II was shaken. A president can no longer expect the virtually unanimous support Lyndon Johnson obtained for the 1964 Tonkin Gulf resolution, which gave him a free hand (temporarily) in Vietnam. Both parties are divided over when, where, how, and if the United States should intervene in foreign conflicts. The debates over Central American policy, discussed later in this chapter, bear out the enduring quality of these new divisions.

What were the lessons of Vietnam? One key point stands out: It is dangerous to make policy by analogy. Some policy makers in the 1950s and 1960s compared the situation in Vietnam to the 1930s, when the Western powers had an opportunity to stand up to Nazi aggression but instead gave in to their demands. In the 1980s, some compared Central America to Vietnam. The roots of any conflict, however, have to be understood in their own terms. In Vietnam, American power proved to be limited. The limits were not only military but moral and political. In the words of two observers of politics, "The U.S. sent its troops into Vietnam to reverse the verdict of a local struggle, which meant, in turn, imposing a ghastly death and suffering upon the Vietnamese. As it turned out, the U.S. could not reverse that verdict finally; it could only delay its culmination."[3]

Crises and Détente

Throughout the 1960s, many serious world crises threatened to turn the Cold War into a hot one. In 1961 the East Germans constructed the Berlin Wall, an attempt to insulate East Germany from the capitalist influence of the Western sector of Berlin and to stem the flow of emigrants to the West. Cuba underwent a revolution in 1959 and the radicals who came to power developed close ties with the Soviet Union. This set the stage for what many consider the low point in modern U.S foreign policy—the Bay of Pigs invasion, a U.S.-sponsored attack on Cuba mounted by Cuban refugees in April 1961. The invaders were routed, but Cuba was the focus of yet another crisis a year later,

when the United States discovered that the Soviet Union had placed offensive nuclear weapons in Cuba. President Kennedy demanded that the missiles be withdrawn and instituted a naval blockade of the island. After some very tense moments, the Soviets backed down. President Kennedy himself estimated the odds of war as "between 2–1 and even money."[4] The Vietnam War provided another obstacle to improved East-West relations, as did the Soviet invasion of Czechoslovakia in 1968.

Despite these crises, the process of easing tensions moved forward, with U.S. presidents and secretaries of state meeting and negotiating with their Soviet counterparts. By the early 1970s, Soviet-U.S. relations seemed to have entered a new stage—one the Soviets called *razriadka* and the West knew as **détente**. Both words connote a form of relaxation, or "unwinding." Ironically, President Richard Nixon, who had built his political career on staunch anticommunism, instigated the rapprochement with the Soviet Union. Nixon also was the first U.S. president to improve relations with Communist China—a move he had once opposed.

Nixon's national security advisor and, later, secretary of state, Henry Kissinger, was highly influential in the détente process. Kissinger argued that certain basic realities had to be recognized in Soviet-U.S. relations:

> that direct confrontation between the Great Powers would only result in mutual suicide;
>
> that the growing split between the Soviet Union and China gave the Soviets an incentive to improve relations with the United States;
>
> that a crusading anticommunism was no longer popular in the nation, and that "limited" wars, such as in Vietnam, were too costly and uncertain; and
>
> that rivalry with the Soviet Union would continue, but at a lower level of tension.

Over a period of years, U.S. and Soviet negotiators hammered out a series of agreements that comprised the heart of détente. The agreements covered issues ranging from the control of nuclear weapons to forms of technical cooperation. Nixon and Soviet leader Leonid Brezhnev signed the

President Nixon's reputation as a strict anticommunist helped defuse criticism of his approaches to the regimes in the Soviet Union and the People's Republic of China. Here he shares a banquet with Chinese Premier Chou En-lai, the architect of China's turn away from strict, anti-Western Maoism. *(UPI/Bettmann Newsphotos)*

SALT I agreements (Strategic Arms Limitation Treaty) in 1972 and also a statement of basic principles agreeing to consult in dangerous situations. Then, in the Helsinki Accords of 1975, East and West endorsed human rights for the citizens of all nations, called for reduced tensions in Central Europe, and pledged increased cooperation in economics, science, and technology. In retrospect, it is clear that Brezhnev never intended to comply with the human rights provisions of this agreement, and Soviet failure to honor the Helsinki Accords occasionally has proved a source of embarrassment for the Soviet leadership.

The Carter administration pursued arms control talks and concluded an agreement, known as SALT II, in 1978. SALT II, however, represented the last stage of the period of détente initiated under Nixon and Kissinger. Senate approval of the treaty, dubious from the outset, was doomed by the Soviet invasion of Afghanistan in December 1979.

The 1980s: A Decade of Shifting Patterns

Jimmy Carter would later say that he learned more about the Soviet Union from its invasion of Afghanistan than he had in all his earlier dealings

with that nation. In January of 1980, calling the invasion an "extremely serious threat to peace," Carter initiated a series of punitive measures against the Soviet Union, including an embargo on the sale of U.S. grain and high technology. Thus, even without a change in administration, the 1980s would have seen a different pattern of U.S.-Soviet relations. With the transition from the Carter to the Reagan administration in 1981, the atmosphere shifted to the right. The Reagan administration returned to a hard-line policy toward the Soviet Union—reminiscent of the harsher anticommunism of the 1950s. This position had substantial public support in the early 1980s. Reagan sharply increased defense spending and strongly supported anticommunist regimes. No one talked of détente any more, and Reagan did not meet with any of the three Soviet leaders who held office in turn during the first Reagan term.

In March 1985 Mikhail Gorbachev became general secretary of the Soviet Communist Party. Realizing that the Soviet economy was in a disastrous condition, he quickly undertook a series of reforms, known popularly by the code words *perestroika* (restructuring of the Soviet economy) and *glasnost* (a new "openness" in the Soviet society).

This desire to improve the Soviet economy and standard of living would require a decrease in military spending, and with this reality in mind, the

Gorbachev regime became more willing to engage the United States in serious arms-reduction negotiations. Concurrently, the Reagan administration, with its own domestic agendas shifting, agreed to bargain with the Soviets. Thus, during the last half of the 1980s, tensions eased somewhat between the United States and the USSR. Summits were held in Geneva; Washington; Reykjavik, Iceland; and Moscow. In 1988, the Soviet Union negotiated a retreat from Afghanistan. The Soviet engagement there had turned into a costly, no-win situation, likened in this country to our involvement in Vietnam. *Détente* was still a forbidden word in Washington, but a spirit of rapprochement was alive again.

Opponents of broad negotiation with the USSR—usually conservatives—argue that while we were negotiating, the Soviets had been making important gains in many military areas. In addition, they claim that the Soviet Union or its proxies—Cuba, Vietnam, and Angola—had gained new influence in Central America, Asia, and Africa.

But some challenge the contention that the Soviets have been extending their sphere of influence around the globe, noting that China has made distinct overtures to the West and that U.S. influence is clearly dominant in the Middle East. Further, upheavals in Poland in 1980 and 1988 showed that the Soviet empire was highly vulnerable even on its doorstep. *Glasnost* was reassuring in two respects: It was a step toward greater freedom within the USSR, and it allowed for a more open discussion of the real domestic problems (low productivity and alcoholism, for example) confronting the Soviet Union. Some observers in the West assumed that such openness would be self-reinforcing, leading to even more openness. Yet despite the *glasnost* movement, the entrenched Soviet leadership retained the power to crack down brutally if reform appeared to threaten its control.

Current Issues

Contemporary U.S. policy makers—and the general public—must decide what policy to pursue vis-à-vis the Soviet Union. Our original goal of containment implied a willingness to learn to live with the Soviets, but not to countenance efforts to expand their influence, particularly by military means. More militant U.S. anticommunists, however, strive to diminish Soviet power, and even to undermine the dominance of the Communist Party in Russia itself. Are we, then, looking to live on a more or less equal footing with communism, or are we seeking to destroy it?

The rulers of the Soviet Union must also decide whether they prefer cooperation or confrontation; that is, whether they will work to undermine Western democracies or live with the West as it is. On both sides, power brokers—some seeking confrontation, others pressing for cooperation—jockey to gain the upper hand in public policy making.

In this superpower standoff, *whose* agenda finally prevails has enormous impact on all of international relations.

Deep inside an air-conditioned underground silo near Wichita, Kansas, a massive Titan II missile—armed and aimed at targets halfway around the world—stands ready for all-out nuclear exchange.
(AP/Wide World Photos)

The two Great Powers have accumulated vast stores of weapons that threaten the lives of hundreds of millions. And the arms race casts a menacing shadow over all international developments.

The Arms Race

Arms races date back millennia, but a *nuclear* arms race is something distinctly new. Some analysts contend that because both sides possess nuclear weapons, we have actually avoided World War III. Had NATO and the Warsaw Pact countries been armed only with conventional weapons, the argument goes, World War III might have occurred long ago, probably in Central Europe. Nevertheless, if nuclear weapons *are* ever unleashed, it could spell the end for the United States, the Soviet Union, and all of Europe, with serious consequences for the rest of life on earth. We now explore (1) nuclear strategy; (2) arms control talks; (3) reduced expectations in a dangerous world; and (4) the costs of the arms race. The gamble of nuclear weapons is enormous.

Nuclear Strategy

The initial rationale for nuclear weapons was simple and straightforward: The United States built atomic bombs out of fear that Nazi Germany would develop them. Once scientists figured out how to build these bombs, however, any nation with the requisite scientific and industrial ability could amass a nuclear arsenal. By the 1950s, both the United States and the Soviet Union had nuclear weapons. The Eisenhower administration devised a nuclear strategy based on "massive retaliation": Were the Soviets to attack us with nuclear weapons, we would retaliate with every nuclear warhead we possessed. This would mean mutual suicide. Accordingly, nuclear weapons came to be viewed solely as a deterrent whose actual use would be irrational.

President Eisenhower, along with most experts of that time, took the view that a relatively small number of bombs on each side would be sufficient

to ensure a "balance of terror." By the late 1950s, however, anxieties about possible Soviet military superiority began to surface in the United States. These concerns took on a sense of tremendous urgency after the Soviets launched the first space satellite in 1957. In 1960, presidential candidate John Kennedy focused on the alleged "missile gap," claiming that the Soviet Union was building a great lead over the United States in intercontinental ballistic missiles (ICBMs) which could reach their targets in a matter of minutes. Once in office, the Kennedy administration embarked on a crash program of missile building, despite the discovery that earlier estimates of Soviet missile superiority had been exaggerated. As a result, the United States pulled ahead—so far ahead, in fact, that the Soviets may have begun to fear that they were in a position of severe military weakness.

At the same time, U.S. strategists were arguing that a new and influential doctrine, called **counterforce,** mandated nuclear superiority in numbers and accuracy. The counterforce concept called for a first-strike capability, so we could destroy the enemy's nuclear weapons—in missile silos, and at submarine and air bases—thus leaving the enemy defenseless. But counterforce logic applied to both sides. Some observers believe that anxiety over the counterforce doctrine prompted Soviet Premier Khrushchev to place missiles in Cuba in 1962 in an attempt to counteract U.S. missile superiority.

To ensure greater security, each side began diversifying its nuclear weapons delivery systems. By the mid-1960s both the United States and the Soviet Union maintained three distinct nuclear delivery systems: long-range ICBMs, submarine-launched ballistic missiles (SLBMs), and long-range bombers. To head off a counterforce first strike, strategists in both camps also turned their attention to possible defenses against incoming missiles. For a time in the late 1960s, both nations experimented with ABMs (antiballistic missiles), which could, theoretically, shoot down incoming missiles before they reached their targets.

Nuclear technology gained a powerful momentum. To counter the perceived threat from ABMs, scientists experimenting with increasing the power of offensive missiles developed the MIRV (multiple independently targeted delivery vehicle). One missile could now be equipped with three or five

Nuclear War: No Place to Hide

A single one-megaton nuclear weapon detonated over a major city would produce the following effects:

A fireball over 1 mile in diameter if the bomb were detonated above ground. A crater 1,000 feet in diameter and 300 feet deep if it were detonated on the ground. Fifty square miles of total destruction by blast and fire; in a 600-square-mile area, all unprotected people would be killed. Close to 500,000 fatalities; total casualties of over 750,000.

In a 1,000-square-mile area—about the size of Rhode Island—all persons looking at the fireball would be permanently blinded. A 4,000-square-mile area—the size of Connecticut—would be blanketed with deadly radioactive contamination.

In a full-scale nuclear war between the United States and the Soviet Union, here would be some of the results:

As many as fifty thousand nuclear weapons would be detonated.

In excess of 100 million Soviet citizens and a comparable number of Americans would be killed outright, and at least another 50 million in each country would die of injuries.

Deadly fallout would blanket large portions of the United States and the Soviet Union; air, water, and land would be contaminated; livestock and crops would suffer enormous destruction.

In both nations, medical facilities would be largely destroyed; little help of any kind would come to the survivors, many of whom would die from starvation and epidemics.

Industry, agriculture, and communications would be destroyed in both countries, which would be unable to recover for an indefinite period. Widespread death and destruction would hit many bystander nations.

Smoke and dust from blast and fire, along with destruction of ozone in the atmosphere, might severely damage the global environment and the biosphere.

SOURCE: Union of Concerned Scientists, 1982.

---

or ten or twenty nuclear weapons, each programmed to hit a different target. Such a large number of warheads would overwhelm any possible missile defense.

At this point, some Soviet and American leaders began to recognize the futility of the arms race. Simply building more and more nuclear weapons of ever-increasing sophistication would not get either side anywhere, they reasoned. Why not slow down the arms race and place limits on the weapons each side could amass? Determined to control the escalating arms race, both countries came to the negotiating table in the **Strategic Arms Limitation Talks** (SALT).

Arms Control Talks

The SALT talks were conducted over a period of roughly ten years. Negotiators tackled complex and often highly specialized issues: One important question, for example, concerned whether a particular Soviet bomber should be considered a long-range or a medium-range weapon. But underlying the talks was one clear premise: that it was in the interests of both nations to limit the arms race, to curtail the momentum of nuclear weapons development. In this area, both superpowers shared a common interest—*survival.* They also stood to save huge amounts of money.

The talks accomplished a good deal. SALT I set overall limits on the number of missiles and bombers each side could deploy. The United States was granted an edge in bombers, the Soviets in land- and sea-based missiles. Both sides agreed not to develop antiballistic missile systems. However, advances in nuclear technology, such as MIRVs, were allowed to continue unchecked. In the end, both nations greatly increased their total number of nuclear warheads during the 1970s.

SALT II came to grips with the MIRV issue by limiting the number and type of warheads as well. Yet newer technological developments, including the virtually undetectable cruise missile and an even more accurate ICBM called the MX missile, made it even more difficult to bring the arms race under control. Technological momentum was outstripping the ponderous process of negotiation. (See **Table 19–1** for an overview of U.S.-Soviet arms control treaties.)

The Reagan administration responded to reported Soviet advantages in nuclear weapons by embarking on a vast arms buildup at all levels. Over its first term in office, the administration proposed about $1.1 *trillion* dollars in defense spending.[5] Congress cut back these proposals somewhat, but military spending still accelerated dramatically until 1987, when massive budget deficits and growing opposition in Congress put a halt to the levels of expansion undertaken from 1981 on.

Taking a new tack in the arms race, the Reagan administration proposed developing the **Strategic Defense Initiative** (SDI)—or "Star Wars"—space-based defenses against missile attack. Experts argued that SDI was not technically feasible, that even if it were it would be prohibitively expensive, and that it would destabilize the arms race. The

---

TABLE 19–1
Basic Elements of the SALT I, SALT II, and INF Treaties

SALT I (1972)

1. Deployment of antiballistic missiles was limited to one site apiece, with strict controls on the number of missiles installed. This headed off an ABM race.

2. The numbers of land-based ICBM and SLBM launchers was frozen for five years at the numbers operational or under construction in 1972. At that time the United States had 1,054 ICBMs and 656 SLBMs; the Soviets had 1,607 ICBMs and 740 SLBMs. The United States were permitted to maintain its advantage in heavy bombers and in total numbers of warheads.

SALT II (1978); (unratified)

1. Each side was limited to a *total* of 2,250 strategic nuclear delivery vehicles of all types, including ICMBs, SLBMs, air-to-surface missiles, and heavy bombers.

2. Sublimits were established for various types of launchers carrying MIRVs—for example, only 820 MIRVed ICBMs were permitted.

3. Bans on various technical developments were imposed, including increases in the number of warheads and the "throwweight" (carrying capacity) of ballistic missiles of all types.

INF (1987; ratified 1988)

This treaty marks the first *reduction* of nuclear arms by the elimination of one "class" of weapons.

1. The treaty allows three years to eliminate all ground-launched missiles with ranges between 1,000 and 5,500 kilometers; eighteen months to eliminate all ground-launched missiles with ranges between 500 and 1,000 kilometers; and specific procedures for weapon destruction are detailed. Guidance systems and warheads may be removed from weapons before destruction.

2. Neither country may manufacture or flight-test missiles with ranges between 500 and 5,500 kilometers.

3. Specific verification procedures are detailed, including an inventory of sites where missiles covered by the treaty were manufactured, repaired, tested, and deployed; allowance for on-site observation of weapons destruction; two teams of resident inspectors; "short notice" inspections, in which the country being inspected has nine hours to transport inspectors to the inspector-chosen site.

The treaty does not cover weapons of other nations, nor does it cover sea-launched and air-launched missiles with comparable ranges.

Source for INF provisions: *Congressional Quarterly Weekly Report,* Jan. 23, 1988, p. 150.

Soviets vigorously opposed the idea, although they, too, were working to develop a similar defensive capability.

Toward the end of the 1980s, we had some reassuring news from the arms control front. The Reagan administration proposed Strategic Arms Reduction Talks (START) to supersede the SALT talks. Rather than simply limiting the further production and deployment of nuclear weapons, the Reagan administration argued publicly for the actual reduction and eventual elimination of nuclear weapons. This represented a significant break from several postwar doctrines favoring some stable pattern of nuclear opposition. European observers worried that if the United States and the Soviet Union managed to elminate nuclear weapons, the United States would be "uncoupled" from the defense of Western Europe (in the face of a generally acknowledged Soviet superiority of conventional forces in Europe). Many considered the SALT proposals as simple posturing on Reagan's part, with no serious commitment to push the project forward. The main obstacle to START was the Star Wars program that Reagan had begun in the United States. Reagan refused to use SDI as a bargaining chip in arms control talks; he contended that because it was a purely defensive system, it thus posed no threat. The Soviets refused

to bargain if SDI were not included in the negotiations. They claimed that even a defensive system could be viewed as a threat if it encouraged the United States to feel free to strike first. The Reykjavik summit came exasperatingly close to a tentative START agreement, but deadlocked on the Star Wars issue.

In 1987 neogotiators for both sides forged an agreement for the scheduled elimination of short- and intermediate-range nuclear weapons. The treaty spelled out specific procedures so each side could verify that the other was adhering to the terms of the treaty. Verification had always been a sticking point in the past, because it meant leaving one's most sensitive security systems open to inspection by the other side. But by the late 1980s, the relatively small size and high mobility of nuclear "delivery systems" (the vehicles that carry the warheads to their targets) made on-site inspections crucial to verification. The 1987 agreement, called the **Intermediate Nuclear Forces (INF) Treaty,** was signed by Gorbachev and Reagan at the Washington summit in December 1987. The Senate hesitated a bit, but eventually ratified the treaty in 1988. We must recognize that the INF treaty did not cover long-range (strategic) nuclear weapons or submarine-based missiles, nor did it address the SDI issue. And INF did not encompass

Soviet leader Mikhail Gorbachev and President Reagan met five times, including an informal meeting that President-elect Bush attended in December 1988. Given the complexity of disarmament issues, trade agreements, and other foreign policy matters, summit meetings are best suited for ceremonial announcements of agreements already negotiated. But they also can shape the relations between leaders and their people. *(UPI/Bettmann Newsphotos)*

nuclear weapons held by Western European nations. In fact, the NATO powers agreed unanimously in the spring of 1988 to modernize their nuclear forces as a deterrent to a Soviet bloc attack with conventional forces. But despite its limited scope, the INF treaty did represent the first time that the two superpowers had agreed to a reduction of in-service nuclear weapons. As such it was a major achievement. The success of the INF negotiations gave new momentum to the START process, and it also encouraged some talk about the reduction of *conventional* forces in Europe. In the West, the Soviet/Warsaw Pact numerical superiority in conventional forces was often *over*stated to add weight to the case for NATO nuclear forces. The INF treaty forced a harder look at the numbers of forces on each side. In December 1988 Mikhail Gorbachev announced a substantial unilateral reduction of Soviet troops in Europe and Asia. Although the Reagan administration called this an important "first step," it maintained that even such reductions would leave an imbalance favoring the Warsaw Pact.

Reagan's supporters place the progress toward arms control in the last two years of the Reagan presidency in the context of Reagan's hard line against the Soviet Union and the large buildup of U.S. military forces through the 1980s. We were, in this view, negotiating from a position of strength. Others credit Gorbachev for taking the initiative on arms control, citing his drive to save an ailing Soviet economy from the huge costs of escalation in the arms race.

Reduced Expectations in a Dangerous World

As the 1980s drew to a close, the huge budget deficits and a changing domestic political climate forced large reductions in planned military expenditures. Between 1987 and 1988 the administration reduced its five-year military spending by $200 billion. From 1981 to 1985, military spending for research and development (adjusted for inflation) grew at least 10 percent a year. In 1988 and 1989, military R & D spending actually decreased by about 1 percent each year. Plans for new weapons systems were dropped or drastically reduced.[6]

The SDI program was definitely flying in a lower orbit as the Reagan years ended. The non-partisan Congressional Office of Technology Assessment (OTA) concluded that the extraordinarily complex computer program necessary to guide the SDI's destruction of thousands of incoming missiles probably cannot "be produced in the foreseeable future" and that "little analysis of any kind" had been done by SDI contractors to eliminate the possibility of effective countermeasures to the SDI system. OTA predicted that an SDI system would probably "suffer a catastrophic failure" the first time it was used. The administration itself shifted from advocating a full-scale system to one that had far more limited capabilities. Privately, senior U.S. officials acknowledged that this shift indicated the administration's recognition that Reagan's dream of an impenetrable shield probably could not be fulfilled. The more modest system, reportedly structured to protect military targets, would likely stop only 30 percent of incoming missiles in a massive Soviet first strike. Doubts about the feasibility of SDI eroded budgetary support for the program. In addition, funding for SDI was dramatically reduced because the armed services saw the Star Wars program as a rival for scarce funds.[7]

Costs

It is difficult to overestimate the cost burden of the arms race. The burden on the U.S. economy is serious; on the Soviet economy, staggering. If defense dollars were diverted for civilian use, that money also could go very far toward solving major social ills in areas like health and education (see **Table 19–2**).

As increased military spending in this country helped push the budget deficit to record high levels, an old complaint gained new currency. In the 1988 election, presidential candidates from both parties favored pressing our NATO allies and Japan to bear a larger share of the cost of Western defense. Naturally, this suggestion provoked an overwhelmingly positive response among American voters. However, data supporting the claim that the United States bears more than its fair share of defense costs are mixed. Military spending per capita, and military spending as a percentage of gross national product are higher in the United States than in Britain, Canada, France, Germany, Italy, or Japan. But contributions to defense cannot

TABLE 19–2
The Costs of Protection—and Some Nonmilitary Alternatives

Weapons	Dollars	Other Options
50 MX "Peacekeepers"	= **$4,540,000,000** =	Year's cost of long-term home care for about 1 million chronically ill children and elderly
Research on Star Wars (*fiscal year 1988*)	= **$3,900,000,000** =	An elementary school education for 1,400,000 children in Latin America
1 aircraft carrier (Nimitz class)	= **$3,900,000,000** =	1 meal a day for 6 months for the 20 million Americans who do not get enough to eat
1 Trident submarine	= **$1,436,000,000** =	5-year program for universal child immunization against six deadly diseases, preventing 1 million deaths a year
2 fighter aircraft (JA 37)	= **$45,000,000** =	Installation in third world of 300,000 hand pumps to give villages access to safe water
1 nuclear weapon test	= **$12,000,000** =	Training of 40,000 community health workers in the Third World
1 twin-engined attack helicopter =	**$11,500,000** =	Insecticide spraying of housing for African population of 8 million

Source: Ruth Leger Sivard, *World Military and Social Expenditures 1987–88* (Washington, D.C.: World Priorities, 1987), p. 35.

be counted by military spending alone. Ninety percent of the ground forces and 80 percent of the aircraft that would be in Europe on the first day of a Warsaw Pact attack would be European—not American or Canadian.[8] More than 58 percent of NATO active troops, and 80 percent of the reserves are not American. Our allies provide 83 percent of the ships and 54 percent of the planes in the NATO forces.[9]

The Third World

The nations of the so-called **third world**—the developing and less-developed countries of Asia, Africa, and Latin America—loom large in discussions of the future of the international system. Most people on earth live under conditions that vary from serious economic privation to absolute poverty. In most of Africa and much of Asia, as well as in substantial portions of Latin America, poverty is endemic. Of course, third world nations vary greatly in wealth, ranging from the oil-rich Arab states of the Middle East to nations suffering extreme deprivation, such as Bangladesh.

U.S. foreign policy toward the third world combines self-interest with humanitarianism, and fear of communism with concern for human rights. We now examine the U.S. response to (1) movements for social change and (2) economic deprivation in the third world.

Movements for Social Change

World War II unleashed anticolonial sentiments in many parts of the third world. Prior to 1950, the British withdrew from the Indian subcontinent, the Dutch from Indonesia. France lingered in Indochina, fighting a losing battle. Most African nations gained independence in the 1950s and 1960s. The whole structure of world power stood on the brink of realignment, with social change inevitable. But who would control the change, who would channel the newly released energies?

Here those guiding U.S. foreign policy face a dilemma. Officially, the United States identifies with popular aspirations for a "better life" and drives for democracy and national independence. But how should we respond to an independence movement inspired or directed by communists, threatening U.S. interests or violating our concept of democratic ideals? Historically, our response oftentimes was to oppose movements for social and political change. Out of fear of communist or other left-wing revolutions, the United States has often supported military or right-wing governments that, to our leaders, looked like a safer alternative. Of course, many of our leaders hope for some choice between these two alternatives, but in reality, moderately progressive, democratic alternatives frequently do not exist. Over the years, the United States has trained and lent significant military aid to many a police state. Through covert CIA operations, we also helped overthrow several left-wing governments, including some that had significant popular support, as did the regime in Chile in 1973.

U.S. policy toward South Africa reflects many of the vexing problems of exercising superpower might in a complex world. *Apartheid* (pronounce it "apart-hate") is an official legal policy of racial segregation and disenfranchisement that began in South Africa in 1948, but as an extension of the country's history, culture, and religion, its roots are centuries old. Eventually, there came to be 317 South African apartheid laws, which, among other things, set strict definitions of races and prohibited marriage or sex between white and nonwhite persons; required segregated public facilities and residential areas; established a different curriculum to educate black schoolchildren into lower status than whites; required blacks to carry an internal passport at all times; reserved certain jobs for specific racial groups; and removed the right to vote from nonwhites. Virtually all civil liberties were eliminated, allowing the white Afrikaner Nationalist Party and government to imprison anyone without a trial; to banish anyone from one part of

the country to another; to forbid anyone to speak in public, write for publication, or travel; to ban any gathering, march, meeting, or demonstration and forbid anyone even to be in a room with more than one other person at a time; to ban any organization; and to enter any premises without a search warrant. As a result of international and internal pressures, the South African government is now ostensibly ending apartheid, but its policies and the ruling Afrikaner National Party clearly remain committed to maintaining control over the black majority.

How should the United States respond to a nation where democratic principles are so obviously subverted? The Reagan administration's policy, called "constructive engagement," allowed economic and diplomatic relations to continue while applying gentle persuasion to change South African domestic policies, on the assumption that direct sanctions would simply harden the Afrikaner nationalists while increasing the economic suffering of South African blacks. An economic boycott against South Africa would have serious negative effects on our own economy as well—which some saw as the real reason for U.S. policy.

By 1986, the failure of South Africa to respond positively to constructive engagement led to efforts in Congress to impose economic sanctions, but these were nominal. Although Jesse Jackson raised South Africa as an issue in his 1984 and 1988 presidential campaigns, and there have been scattered student demonstrations in favor of removing all U.S. investments from South Africa, the 1988 campaigns of Michael Dukakis and George Bush barely mentioned South African policy. The October 1988 municipal elections in South Africa gave significant gains to the Conservative party (a far-right group that advocates strict apartheid), which only makes the ruling Afrikaner Nationalist Party more resistant to change. As this book goes to press, violence is increasing again in South Africa, and few observers are hopeful of peaceful resolution.

The U.S. dilemma in dealing with movements for social change was highlighted by developments in the 1980s in two Central American countries—Nicaragua and El Salvador. We now consider our changing relationship with these two nations.

How should the United States respond to the government of South Africa, where democratic principles are subverted? President Reagan's policy of "constructive engagement" allowed economic and diplomatic activities to continue, rather than risking worse conditions by imposing economic sanctions. *(AP/Wide World Photos)*

NICARAGUA   In Nicaragua, administrations prior to President Carter's had had generally cordial relations with the Somoza family regime since the 1930s, despite widespread repression and corruption associated with the ruling family. When revolutionary efforts began to undermine the regime's stability, the Carter administration did not rush to Somoza's support. Instead, the United States pressured Somoza to give up the presidency, which he refused to do. A popular revolution, led by the Sandinista guerrillas, overthrew Somoza in the summer of 1979. In many ways, U.S. influence in Nicaragua had sunk to its lowest point.[10] By failing to intervene to protect Somoza, we had alienated the military and the right wing, while the leftist revolutionaries remained suspicious of U.S. intentions and hostile toward the United States itself. The United States favored moderate forces in Nicaragua, such as Christian Democratic and Social Democratic political groups, but they were losing ground as conflicts became more and more polarized.

The more conservative Reagan administration then moved back toward policies pursued in the 1950s, when the U.S. government had extended support to right-wing regimes, including many that violated human rights. The Reagan administration supported efforts by groups of guerrilla rebels (contras) to overthrow the Sandinista government in Nicaragua, arguing that the Sandinistas had formed a Marxist government that was suppressing civil liberties and private enterprise in Nicaragua and transporting arms to revolutionaries in El Salvador. Many observers took issue with this assessment, however. Critics of the administration's policy toward the Sandinistas pointed out that various freedoms in Nicaragua had been maintained to some degree, political debate continued on many issues, and while some of Nicaragua's leaders were no doubt hard-line communists, the political situation there was fluid.

In 1984 the Sandinistas held elections, won by Daniel Ortega, the Sandinista candidate. The U.S. government condemned the elections as fraudulent; other observers contended that the elections had been substantially open and that Ortega had real popular support.[11] Was this another case of U.S. unwillingness to live with a leftist revolution, whether entirely Marxist-Leninist or not? Or was the Sandinista government likely to jell into a Cuban mold, regardless of what the U.S. government might do? In either case, was U.S intervention—in support of the Nicaraguan contras—justified?

Congress was of two minds on the Nicaragua question, seeking to limit the administration's attempts to engage the United States directly, and yet afraid of being seen as "soft on communism" in our own backyard. Because of this ambivalence, Congress kept vacillating in its approach to Central American policy. Starting in 1982, a series of amendments restricting aid to the Nicaraguan contras alternated with a series of appropriations to the contras either for military aid or for "humanitarian" aid. Members of the Reagan administra-

The presidents of five Central American nations meet to discuss Esquipulas II (the Arias peace plan). From the left, seated, are Daniel Ortega, Nicaragua; Jose Napoleon Duarte, El Salvador; Vinicio Cerezo, Guatemala; Jose Azcona, Honduras; and Oscar Arias, Costa Rica, who received the Nobel Peace Prize for his efforts. *(AP/Wide World Photos)*

tion, with a charge from the president to help the contras "keep body and soul together," began raising funds privately and from third-party nations to aid the drive to overthrow the government of Nicaragua. These efforts also came to include secretly diverting funds to the contras from the covert sale of arms to Iran (see Chapters 11 and 12). In March 1987, responding in part to revelations about the Iran-contra affair, but also reflecting an apparent majority sentiment in the population, Congress voted to suspend further aid to the contras.

In August 1987, the presidents of the five Central American nations reasserted some control over their own fate and, ignoring a peace proposal offered by the Reagan administration, signed their own peace agreement (called the Arias peace plan, for its primary sponsor, Costa Rican President Oscar Arias, who was awarded the Nobel Peace Prize for his efforts). The Arias plan called for an end to outside intervention, national dialogue within the war-torn countries, amnesty for political crimes, and a broad expansion of civil rights. The Nicaraguan government moved, with mixed results, to comply with the Arias plan. Then in March 1988, the contras and the Nicaraguan government signed a cease-fire agreement and set a schedule for talks to end the fighting permanently. Again, American influence was at low ebb.

EL SALVADOR The Reagan administration also focused attention on events in El Salvador, alleging that an insurgency in that country was being substantially bankrolled by various communist countries, including Cuba and Vietnam. A memorandum issued by the State Department in February 1981 argued that "the insurgency in El Salvador

has been progressively transformed into a textbook case of indirect armed aggression by Communist powers."[12] Critics of this interpretation insisted that the State Department's case was full of factual errors, misleading statements, and ambiguities, and that its conclusion—that the insurgency was inspired by external forces—was far too sweeping. Even the Salvadoran government itself considered the war primarily an internal struggle. Perhaps most important, critics declared, the Reagan administration ignored the many moderate elements connected with the insurgency—democratic leftists who had despaired of bringing change to El Salvador in any other fashion.

By 1985, political analysts saw evidence that a democratic center might be emerging in El Salvador. Jose Napoleon Duarte won several electoral victories, and the Reagan administration hailed Duarte as a distinctly positive alternative to right-wing and left-wing terrorism. As the decade progressed, however, the situation looked much bleaker for El Salvador. In spite of $2.5 billion in U.S. aid and seven years of intense support from the Reagan administration, by 1988 the Salvadoran civil war was intensifying. Under increasing pressure from the old oligarchy and the army and under extremely adverse economic conditions, exacerbated by a major earthquake in the capital city of San Salvador in October 1986, the Duarte government failed to deliver on the reforms it had promised in 1984. Local elections in 1988 revealed strong support for factions on the right that had been closely identified with death squads (gangs of thugs that roamed the countryside terrorizing citizens by committing wanton acts of violence, including murder). Factions on the left boycotted the election and attempted to thwart it with violence.

Text continues following the color essay.

A Race with No Winners

Nuclear Arms and National Security

Arms races are nothing new in human history. Building armies and stockpiling weapons are reflex reactions when societies feel threatened and believe that they may be attacked. Sometimes, of course, nations also have armed with deliberate intentions of attacking other nations, and it is often difficult to distinguish a "defensive" military posture from one that is "offensive." Throughout history a major dilemma of international relations has been that, once arming begins, it can easily escalate into a competition in which each nation seeks the strongest position. An arms race thus gains a momentum of its own.

Until only fifty years ago, weapons—whether clubs, crossbows, or battleships—were designed for actual use in war. But since the creation of nuclear weapons in 1945 the United States and the Soviet Union have led the way in developing and stockpiling weapons of mass destruction that no one hopes to use. The rationale for the buildup in the United States has been the idea of *deterrence*—the belief that, simply by existing, a vast nuclear arsenal will deter any enemy from waging war. Today the superpowers each hold enough destructive force to eliminate the other many times over. By one estimate their combined nuclear arsenals contain the explosive equivalent of three tons of TNT for every person on earth. And yet the arms race continues. To gain a sense of what the race is all about, we need to consider the types, destructive power, and numbers of these incredible weapons; then we will look at the history of the arms race from 1945 to the present.

Types of Nuclear Weapons

Nuclear weapons are classified either as strategic or as tactical, depending on their range and destructive power. *Strategic nuclear weapons* are designed to travel long distances and are the most destructive weapons ever developed. They may be dropped or fired from aircraft; launched from submarines (*SLBMs,*

Missile fired from a Trident submarine

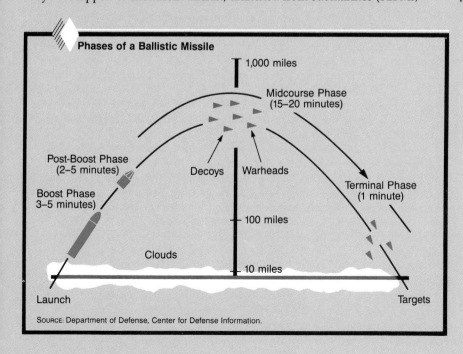

SOURCE: Department of Defense, Center for Defense Information.

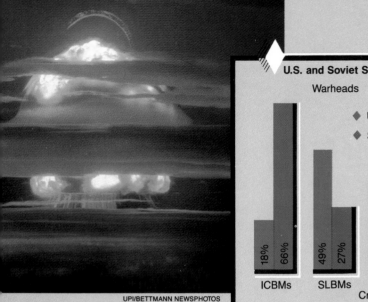

UPI/BETTMANN NEWSPHOTOS

Nuclear test at Pacific Proving Grounds in the Marshall Islands, 1952

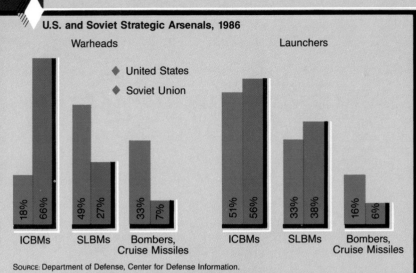

U.S. and Soviet Strategic Arsenals, 1986

Warheads   Launchers

◆ United States
◆ Soviet Union

	ICBMs	SLBMs	Bombers, Cruise Missiles		ICBMs	SLBMs	Bombers, Cruise Missiles
United States	18%	49%	33%		51%	33%	16%
Soviet Union	66%	27%	7%		56%	38%	6%

SOURCE: Department of Defense, Center for Defense Information.

Number of Strategic Weapons, 1945–1986

United States

Soviet Union

12,000
10,000
8,000
6,000
4,000
2,000

1945 1950 1955 1960 1965 1970 1975 1980 1985

SOURCE: Department of Defense, Center for Defense Information.

which stands for submarine-launched ballistic missiles); or launched from sites on or under the ground (*ICBMs,* short for intercontinental ballistic missiles).

These basic strategic nuclear weapons can all be enhanced by the *MIRV* (multiple independently targeted reentry vehicle). When a missile is "MIRVed," it contains and acts as several separate weapons. The Trident II submarine, for example, which the United States deployed in the late 1980s, carries 24 missiles, each of which contains 8 warheads; a single Trident thus can fire missiles targeted to hit 192 different locations. The MIRVing of strategic weapons began in the early 1970s and was a quantum jump in weapons technology.

Tactical nuclear weapons have far less destructive power than the various strategic weapons and are designed for battlefield use. Examples include nuclear artillery shells with ranges of 10 to 15 miles and the Lance missile, which travels 75 miles. Both the United States and the Soviet Union possess tens of thousands of tactical nuclear weapons poised for use along potential battle lines.

A comparison of the superpowers' nuclear arsenals reveals some differences that have affected the arms race. The Soviets depend more heavily on the ICBM delivery system, whereas the United States relies far more on submarine-launched missiles and on bombers and cruise missiles. Because of their mobility, submarines are considered the least vulnerable delivery system, and so—even though some Soviet weapons are more powerful—many experts view the United States as being ahead technologically, a position it has held virtually throughout the nuclear arms race.

Overall, the United States has about 12,000 strategic nuclear weapons, and the Soviet Union has about 10,000. In terms of their destructive power, consider that one atomic bomb dropped on Hiroshima, Japan, in 1945 killed more than 100,000 people with its equivalent force of 20,000 tons of TNT. That first bomb was small and primitive compared with modern weapons. *Each* warhead on a Trident II submarine has the equivalent force of 32 such bombs, and the entire submarine, with its 24 missiles, can devastate the equivalent of 6,144 Hiroshimas.

The Nuclear Arms Race
The first atomic bombs were dropped on Hiroshima and Nagasaki, in 1945, ending the war. At the time the United States was the only nation with an atomic bomb, but by 1949 the Soviets had developed their own. Soon both nations had an even more powerful weapon—the hydrogen, or thermonuclear,

The Proliferation of Nuclear Capabilities

Have nuclear weapons now	May have nuclear weapons now	May soon develop nuclear capability
United States Soviet Union Britain France China India	Canada West Germany Israel Italy Japan Pakistan South Africa Sweden Switzerland	Argentina Australia Austria Belgium Brazil Denmark Iraq South Korea Netherlands Norway Spain Taiwan Egypt Finland Libya Yugoslavia

UPI/BETTMANN NEWSPHOTOS

Soviet ship *Leninsky Komsomol* sailing from Cuba in 1962, followed closely by the USS *Dahlgren*

bomb. Throughout the 1950s H-bombs were tested in the atmosphere, and the earth's winds carried their radioactive particles around the planet. It was not until the early 1960s that the two superpowers agreed to halt above-ground testing. By then, Great Britain, France, and China had also become nuclear powers. Today, as many as fifteen nations may have nuclear capabilities, and a similar number may develop them soon.

As nuclear weapons proliferated in the 1950s, so also did fear, suspicion, and even panic. Despite America's apparent lead in the arms race, no one was absolutely sure of its extent. The Soviets, having suffered devastating losses in World War II, were also deeply suspicious of U.S. motives and were determined to strengthen their nuclear arsenal. In mutual anxiety and ignorance, each side feared the worst from the other. When the Soviets sent the first man into space in 1957, U.S. policy makers were stunned. Almost at once, fear spread that the Soviets were far ahead in developing ballistic missiles, which could be used to deliver nuclear weapons. (Until this point, the only form of delivery had been the long-range bomber.) In the 1960 presidential campaign, Democrat John F. Kennedy blamed the incumbent Republican administration for having allowed a "missile gap" to develop, a charge that later proved to be exaggerated.

Probably the most frightening confrontation of the nuclear arms race was the Cuban missile crisis of October 1962. The United States had discovered through overflights of Cuban territory that the Soviets were installing offensive nuclear weapons on the island, only 90 miles from American shores. In response, President Kennedy imposed a naval quarantine on Cuba to prevent the arrival of more missiles and to pressure the Soviets into withdrawing those already in place. For two weeks the nations seemed on the brink of war, but finally the Soviets backed down and removed the missiles. The crisis gave U.S. policy makers a far more realistic sense of the risks of nuclear war, and similar feelings must have been experienced by the Soviets. Tensions between the two countries eased almost immediately, and the most tangible result was the treaty that ended atmospheric testing, ratified in 1963.

Technological and strategic theorizing, however, continued. In the mid-1960s the United States developed a new approach to nuclear strategy, a doctrine known as *Mutual Assured Destruction (MAD)*. This theory argued that each side needed to maintain only enough missiles to survive a first strike by the other side and still be able to inflict unacceptable damage in a retaliatory attack. But what is "unacceptable" damage? Defense Secretary Robert McNamara suggested that the level might be 50 percent of the population and two-thirds of industrial capacity.

Such an approach had the potential to slow the competitive momentum of the arms race, but translating it into policy proved elusive. Throughout the 1960s the United States appeared to hold its substantial lead in technology and numbers of weapons, but toward the end of the decade a new destabilizing factor emerged: defense against nuclear attack through the use of *antiballistic missiles*, or *ABMs*. These weapons would destroy enemy missiles in the air,

President Carter and Soviet President Brezhnev signing Salt II in 1979

The first step in destroying a Pershing II missile, May 1988   UPI/BETTMANN NEWSPHOTOS

before they reached their targets. Many U.S. policy makers believed that the Soviets were developing an ABM defensive shield, although no one was sure that such a defense was even possible. Meanwhile, the development and stockpiling of offensive weapons continued.

In the 1970s the Nixon administration opened negotiations with the Soviet Union seeking to set some limits on the arms race. The effort culminated in the first major nuclear arms control treaty, known as SALT I (for *Strategic Arms Limitation Talks*), which was ratified by the U.S. Senate in 1972. The administrations of Gerald Ford (1974–1977) and Jimmy Carter (1977–1981) continued negotiations but also continued to develop and improve weapons, including the cruise missile (a small nuclear weapon that can be fired from aircraft or ships and is highly flexible and difficult to detect). The Soviets, on their part, placed multiple warheads on some ICBMs and improved their accuracy. But talks continued, and the second set of SALT negotiations concluded in 1978. Although some thought the SALT II treaty would have strengthened the U.S. position, many in Congress feared a growing Soviet lead in land-based missiles. When the Soviet Union invaded Afghanistan in 1979, the treaty's prospects were damaged further.

SALT II never came to a vote in the U.S. Senate, but for years both sides adhered informally to its limits. The Reagan administration, however, took a far more aggressive stance toward the Soviets, and in a few instances intentionally exceeded the treaty's limitations. Negotiations continued intermittently at lower levels throughout the first Reagan administration (1981–1985), but no treaties emerged, and relations between the two countries remained frosty.

The atmosphere changed after Mikhail Gorbachev became leader of

the Soviet Union in 1985. Wanting to divert more resources to economic development and away from costly military expenditures, Gorbachev met with Reagan in Iceland in 1986, and the two leaders came close to agreeing on a drastic dismantling of nuclear weapons. The chief obstacle seemed to be Reagan's attachment to his *Strategic Defense Initiative (SDI) program*, known widely as "Star Wars," a high-technology space-based shield against incoming nuclear weapons. The Soviets insisted that all such research be abandoned, and when the United States refused, the talks appeared stalled. In fact, they continued at lower levels, and eventually the Soviets dropped their demands about Star Wars. The United States also made some concessions, and greater trust gradually developed. One result was the *Intermediate Nuclear Forces (INF) treaty*, signed in Washington in 1987.

After half a century of nuclear arms, we have spent billions to amass more weapons than we will ever need, but we also have not had to use them. Is there a connection, or are we edging toward the brink? The issues will be debated for years to come, but as we enter the 1990s the arms race between the United States and the Soviet Union at least seems to have slowed down.

Rush-hour protest of nuclear arms testing, Denver, 1987

UPI/BETTMANN NEWSPHOTOS

Government compliance with the Arias peace plan was lax, in part because many of the civil rights violations in El Salvador were carried out by nameless assassins, and the government disavowed any connection with these activities. The U.S. hope that a politically moderate government could be supported by major infusions of outside aid was crashing up against the realities of entrenched power and a mass movement attempting to undermine those in power.

While El Salvador and Nicaragua each present unique political and diplomatic challenges, they illustrate the difficulties of using U.S. resources to combat violence and poverty and to promote progressive governments in Central America. And in a larger perspective, the complexities of our relations with these two Central American countries parallel our ambivalent relations with the third world generally. Our ability—and perhaps even our will—to bolster entrenched privilege has clearly diminished. Yet we still resist the idea that mass political movements may be genuine expressions of popular will, and not simply disguised, Soviet-inspired efforts at domination.[13]

Economics: Rich and Poor

Approximately 1 billion people throughout the world live in desperate poverty—including 750 million in the poorest of conditions. About 10 million die every year of diseases related to malnutrition; half of those are children. Most of the abject poor, who comprise nearly one-fifth of humanity, live in what are referred to as less-developed countries, or LDCs.

The U.S. government has often sounded a strongly humanitarian note in its proclamations about the problems of third world poverty. President Carter, for example, stated that "We cannot have a peaceful and prosperous world if a large part of the world's people are at or near the edge of hunger." The United States is often in the vanguard of relief efforts in emergency situations such as the Ethiopian famine of 1984–1985 and the San Salvador earthquake in 1986. Also, American volunteers and relief agencies play important roles in

such crises, and the Peace Corps helps with development projects in many poor nations.

Clearly, such activities serve our own interests. The poor nations are now among our more important trading partners: The United States sells more of its goods to LDCs than to Europe and the Soviet Union combined. And the developing countries supply us with many critical raw materials and low-cost consumer goods.

There are three types of foreign aid agencies: private agencies, like OXFAM and the Save the Children Fund; government agencies, operating bilaterally (from one country to another), such as the U.S. Aid for International Development (AID) and the Canadian International Development Agency; and agencies formed cooperatively by several governments or international organizations and operating multilaterally. The largest players in foreign aid internationally fall into this last group, including the five multilateral development banks (MDBs): the World Bank, the Inter-American Development Bank, the Asian Development Bank, the African Development Bank, and the Carribean Development Bank. Together, these banks lend about $24 billion a year for development projects, and arrange for an additional $50 billion a year in loans for their projects from other aid agencies, governments, or private lenders. The largest MDB, the World Bank, controls about 70 percent of the money loaned by these MDBs. The World Bank is controlled by the 150 member nations of the bank, according to their share of support for the bank. The United States, which contributes about one-fifth of the bank's assets, has by far the largest vote.[14]

The problem with multilateral development banks as the main source of foreign aid is that loans are not the solution to all the problems of developing countries. In fact, loans become part of the problem when debtor nations must devote large portions of their national economic output to debt service. In addition, development loans tend to exaggerate economic disparities between well-off, partially well-off, and abjectly poor nations.

What would the poor nations like from the rich? They want new terms of trade to aid them in selling their goods and worldwide stabilization of prices for the raw materials they export. The many poor nations that are energy-short have called for

Human Rights Policy

Concern for human rights as an explicit element in U.S. foreign policy distinguished the Carter administration. Addressing the United Nations in 1977, President Carter outlined a commitment to basic human rights that included condemnation of all torture and mistreatment of political prisoners. He also established a State Department office for human rights enforcement, and endowed it with significant powers. During the Carter years, sanctions were imposed on many alleged human rights violators, including Argentina, the Philippines, South Korea, Ethiopia, Zaire, Guinea, Haiti, Brazil, Guatemala, Chile, Paraguay, and Uruguay. U.S. economic aid, loans, and military sales to these nations were sometimes stopped or limited. Carter's human rights policies also increased concern with human rights internationally.

Were Carter's policies successful or sensible? On the plus side, the United States dissociated itself from some very unsavory regimes and exerted moral pressure, in the view of most Americans. In addition, the policy occasionally had concrete results: Some political prisoners were released, and some regimes did show more respect for human rights. Critics made three chief arguments against the policy. They maintained that little attention had been paid to human rights violations in communist countries, such as China and the Soviet Union. Further, they attacked Carter for a lack of consistency and for allegedly making enemies needlessly. Finally, critics took the position that the United States should aid its friends, whether those friends were human rights violators or not.

President Reagan deemphasized human rights in foreign relations, and close relations were resumed with many sanctioned countries. Vice-President George Bush spoke of the "wonderful democracy" of the Philippines under Ferdinand Marcos, a virtual dictator whose massive expropriation of wealth from the Philippines became apparent after the Marcos regime was toppled (see the Introduction). But in certain arenas even the Reagan administration spoke the language of human rights—in talks with the Soviet Union about the "Refusniks" (Soviet Jews who were denied the right to emigrate) and in charges against the Nicaraguan Sandinistas, for example. As the 1980s progressed, the Reagan administration's early emphasis on terrorism as the most important issue in international relations gave way to more explicit concern with issues of human rights. President Reagan even claimed some credit for an improvement in human rights in several countries—Argentina, for example, where civilian rule replaced a military government.

the creation of an energy affiliate of the World Bank that would provide credits to developing nations.

What policies has the U.S. government followed in dealing with the precarious economic conditions of the third world? Since the end of World War II, America has regularly extended economic assistance to poorer nations. But in spite of our generous rhetoric, foreign aid has never been very popular with the American people, many of whom regard it as a kind of international handout. For most of the 1960s and all of the 1970s, foreign aid expenditures declined. By 1980 the United States ranked close to the bottom of all the rich nations in terms of nonmilitary foreign aid as a percentage of GNP.

During much of the 1970s, U.S. foreign aid efforts focused on alleviating poverty and bringing poorer nations into the mainstream of the world economy. The theory underlying this effort was that such aid would help prevent economic failure and social disruption, thereby ensuring more stable politics as well as reducing suffering. U.S. aid in the 1970s was often *multilateral*; that is, it was channeled through international organizations, such as the World Bank and the International

A Peruvian Indian carries a U.S. food aid bundle to a village in the Andes. Despite considerable donations of surplus food, underlying problems of underdevelopment persist. These cannot be remedied by emergency efforts. *(Carl Frank/Photo Researchers)*

Monetary Fund, where it was pooled with contributions from other countries.

In the 1980s, President Reagan, while pushing for increases in foreign aid, also shifted the priorities of that aid. First, a larger percentage of aid was given for security—that is, military—purposes, as opposed to economic development (see **Figure 19–1**). Second, more aid was distributed to fewer nations. The chief recipients in 1986, for example, were Israel, Egypt, the Philippines, El Salvador, Turkey, and Honduras. Third, the aid was more likely to be *bilateral*; that is, given directly to the recipient nation. This gave the U.S. government greater control over how the aid was used. These new policies were defended on the pragmatic grounds that they better served our immediate interests in various world trouble spots. We should also note that U.S. aid programs have given a big boost to U.S. multinational corporations. About 75 percent of total development assistance money is spent on purchases in the United States itself.

Reagan administration policy makers were sounding a domestically popular theme when they called for poor nations to pull themselves up by their bootstraps. Reagan maintained that the magic of the free market would work for third world nations as it had for the United States. Not many LDCs were convinced by this argument, however, particularly because most were at least partially socialist in economic orientation. Yet because of the international economic power wielded by the United States, it would be virtually impossible to revise world economics without U.S. participation.

Why should the United States care about the problems of people in other nations when we have our own problems to deal with? Senator John Danforth, a Missouri Republican, reasons as follows: "The answer, I think, has to do with who we are and how we perceive ourselves as a country. America is more than a place to hang your hat. It does represent a value system most of us believe in very strongly. That value system has to do with

FIGURE 19–1

U.S. Economic and Military Assistance, 1977–1984 (billions of dollars by fiscal year)

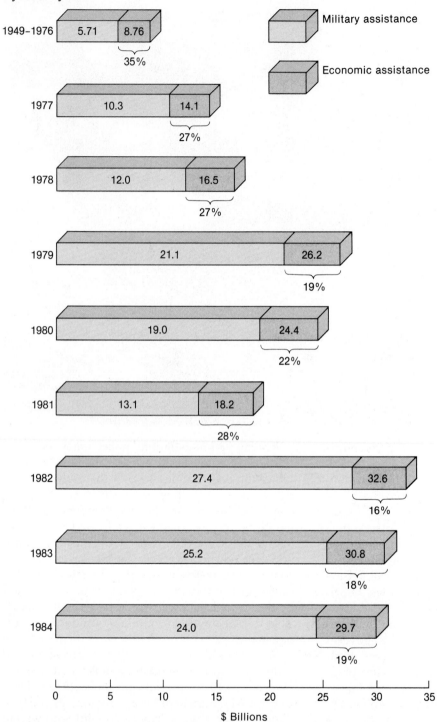

SOURCE: Adapted from *U.S. Overseas Loans and Grants and Assistance from International Organizations*, 1980: 4; *U.S. Overseas Loans and Grants and Assistance from International Organizations*, 1985: 4; and *Foreign Military Sales, Foreign Military Construction Sales and Military Assistance Facts*, 1985: 2ff.

the worth of human beings, whoever they are, wherever they are. We believe that lives are worth saving, that our fellow humans must be fed. But it is not enough to profess this belief. We must act on it."[15]

Conclusions

Democratic concerns are clearly related to U.S. foreign policy objectives, even if those relationships are often controversial. To begin with, most U.S. leaders maintain that the question of democracy stands at the core of our conflict with the Soviet Union: We defend the "free world"; the communists advocate tyranny. This argument sounded persuasive in the early days of the Cold War, but it seems increasingly simplistic of late.

A whole series of issues have come to complicate the relationship between U.S. foreign policy and the defense of democracy:

1. Should the United States seek to destabilize governments whose structure, policies, or ideological orientation our policy makers dislike, even if they have the support of their own people?

2. Should we ally ourselves with dictatorial governments simply because they are anticommunist? Conversely, should we oppose any government that styles itself as communist, Marxist, or radical?

3. Does cooperation between the United States and the Soviet Union help the cause of human rights in the communist world, or is it a naive policy that permits the Soviets to gain global advantages?

4. Since democracy rests on the premise of survival, should we seek superiority over the Soviets in the arms race, hoping that will prevent them from a first strike? Or should we strive to reduce the threat of nuclear war through arms limitation or reduction?

5. What role should the United States play in the development of the poorer nations? How much of our own wealth should we be willing to share? Should the United States support only capitalistic regimes in these nations, or should it assist other types of economic systems? What can we—and should we—do to further democratic development in LDCs?

Some practitioners of U.S. politics once argued that foreign affairs were far less important in deciding elections than were domestic politics. In 1960, for example, the governor of Illinois told his party's presidential nominee, Richard Nixon, that "what is really important is the price of hogs in Chicago." How ironic this remark now strikes us in light of thirty years' additional experience! Foreign policy issues have assumed paramount importance in recent presidential elections, and will continue to do so in the near future.

Since the Vietnam War, a far larger "attentive public" has become involved in foreign policy debates. In addition, the old bipartisan foreign policy consensus has broken down, broadening the range of debate on foreign policy. Conflict among opposing views can lead to paralysis or contradictory actions, but it can also help us clarify our goals as a nation and reassess our policies designed to reach those goals.

Many observers wonder, however, whether it makes sense for a large electorate to actively debate complex foreign policy issues or the kinds of technical questions that arise, for instance, in negotiations related to nuclear weapons. Yet because foreign policy and defense matters affect us all, policy making in this area is too important to be left to a few elected officials and their advisors. Certain issues may require a high level of knowledge and expertise, but many others can be understood and assessed by almost any democratic citizen. And because the stakes are high, citizens must actively voice their views and policy makers have an obligation to gain informed consent from citizens. If leaders believe they can simply do whatever they think best in foreign and defense matters, we will all be less safe—and we will lose an essential element of democracy.

As the political philosopher Michael Walzer once commented on the issue of nuclear weapons strategy: "The day-to-day drift is always toward specialized, secret, technically complex, and esoteric doctrine. But real political leaders, *if they can hear the clamor of their constituents,* can stop the drift. Nuclear deterrence will defend democracy only if it is democratically constrained."[16] This point holds true for all the areas of foreign policy we addressed in this chapter.

GLOSSARY TERMS

National Security Council

State Department

Defense Department

Joint Chiefs of Staff

Central Intelligence Agency

containment

peaceful coexistence

isolationism

détente

counterforce

Strategic Arms Limitation Talks

Strategic Defense Initiative

Intermediate Nuclear Forces (INF) Treaty

third world

NOTES

[1]*U.S. News and World Report*, "Inside the CIA," June 25, 1984.

[2]George F. Kennan, "The Sources of Soviet Conduct," *Foreign Affairs* 25 (July 1947): 566–582.

[3]Irving Howe and Michael Walzer, in *The New Republic*, Apr. 29, 1985.

[4]On the missile crisis, see Robert Kennedy, *Thirteen Days* (New York: New American Library, 1969); and Irving Janis, *Groupthink* (Boston: Houghton Mifflin, 1982), chap. 6.

[5]Mark Rovner, *Defense Dollars and Sense* (Washington, D.C.: Common Cause, 1983), p. 14.

[6]John H. Cushman, Jr., "The Pentagon Is Learning to Live with Less," *New York Times*, Apr. 3, 1988, Section 4, p. 5.

[7]R. Jeffrey Smith, "SDI Comes Down to Earth," *Washington Post*, national weekly edition, Apr. 4–10, 1988, p. 9.

[8]John H. Cushman, Jr., "Splitting the Check for Allied Defense," *New York Times*, May 8, 1988, Section 4, p. 6.

[9]"The False Promise of Burden-Sharing," editorial, *New York Times*, May 1, 1988, Section 4, p. 26.

[10]Richard Millett, "Central American Paralysis," *Foreign Policy*, Summer 1980, pp. 99–117.

[11]John B. Oakes, " 'Fraud' in Nicaragua," *New York Times*, Nov. 15, 1984, p. 31. See also *Report of the Latin American Studies Association Delegation to Observe the Nicaraguan General Election of November 4, 1984.*

[12]U.S. Department of State, *Communist Interference in El Salvador*, Special Report #80 (Washington, D.C.: U.S. Government Printing Office, Feb. 23, 1981).

[13]See Martin Needler, *The Problem of Democracy in Latin America* (Lexington, Mass.: Lexington Books, 1987); Walter LaFeber, *Inevitable Revolutions: The United States in Central America*, expanded ed. (New York: Norton, 1984); and Richard A. Nuccio, *What's Wrong, Who's Right in Central America?* (New York: Facts on File, 1986).

[14]Patricia Adams, "All in the Name of Aid," *Sierra*, Jan./Feb. 1987, pp. 48–49.

[15]John C. Danforth, "Africa: Does Anybody Really Care?" *Washington Post*, national weekly edition, Feb. 13, 1984, p. 29.

[16]Michael Walzer, "Deterrence and Democracy," *The New Republic*, July 2, 1984, p. 21.

SELECTED READINGS

Among **general introductions** to U.S. foreign policy, consider Terry Boswell and Albert Bergesen, eds., *America's Changing Role in the World System* (New York: Praeger, 1987); Seyom Brown, *The Faces of Power: Constancy and Change in the United States Foreign Policy from Truman to Reagan*, 2nd ed. (New York: Columbia University Press, 1983); Gerald Combs, *Brief U.S. Foreign Policy* (New York: Knopf, 1986); Thomas M. Franck and Michael J. Glennon, *United States Foreign Relations Law, Cases, Materials, and Simulations* (St. Paul, Minn.: West, 1987); Henry Kissinger, *American Foreign Policy: A Global View* (Brookfield, Vt.: Gower, 1982); Hans J. Morgenthau, *In Defense of the National Interest: A Critical Examination of American Foreign Policy* (Lanham, Md.: University Press of America, 1983); Henry T. Nash, *American Foreign Policy: A Search for Security*, 3rd ed. (Chicago: Dorsey, 1985). The Reagan era is the focus of Kenneth A. Oye, Robert J. Leiber, and Donald Rothchild, *Eagle Resurgent?* (Boston: Little, Brown, 1987).

Regarding the **Third World,** see Douglas S. Blaufarb, *The Counterinsurgency Era: U.S. Doctrine and Performance 1950 to the Present* (New York: Free Press, 1977); I. William Zartman, ed., *Positive Sum: Improving North–South Relations* (New Brunswick, N.J.: Transaction Books, 1987); Richard E. Feinberg, *The Intemperate Zone: The Third World Challenge to U.S. Foreign Policy* (New York: Norton, 1983); and Steven R. David, *Third World Coups d'Etat and International Security* (Baltimore: Johns Hopkins, 1987).

U.S. relations with **Central America** are covered in Thomas Anderson *Politics in Central America,* rev. ed. (New York: Praeger, 1988); Richard Nuncio, *What's Wrong, Who's Right in Central America?* (New York: Facts on File, 1986); Martin Needler, *The Problem of Democracy in Latin America* (Lexington, Mass.: Heath, 1987); Walter LeFeber, *Inevitable Revolutions* (New York: Norton, 1984); Christopher Dickey, *With the Contras: A Reporter in the Wilds of Nicaragua,* (New York: Simon & Shuster, 1987); Karl Bermann, *Under the Big Stick* (Boston: South End, 1986); and Glen Caudill Dealy, *An Honorable Peace in Central America* (Belmont, Calif.: Wadsworth, 1988).

For a **comparative perspective,** see Andrew Cox and Stephen Kirby, *Congress, Parliament, and Defense: The Impact of Legislative Reform on Defense Accountability in Britain and America* (New York: St. Martin's, 1986); Joel Krieger, *Reagan, Thatcher, and the Politics of Decline* (New York: Oxford University Press, 1986); and, for a British viewpoint, James Piscatori, *Islam in a World of Nation-States* (New York: Cambridge University Press, 1984).

For the **Iran-contra affair,** see *The Tower Commission Report,* with an introduction by R. W. Apple, Jr. (New York: Bantam/Times, 1987); and the *Report of the Congressional Committees Investigating the Iran-Contra Affair,* abr. ed., edited by Joel Brinkley and Stephen Engelberg (New York: Times Books, 1988).

For **warfare, weapons, and strategic concerns,** see Seyom Brown, *The Causes and Prevention of War* (New York: St. Martin's, 1987); Desmond Ball and Jeffrey Richelson, eds., *Strategic Nuclear Targeting* (Ithaca, N.Y.: Cornell University Press, 1986); Joshua M. Epstein, *Strategy and Force Planning: The Case of the Persian Gulf* (Washington, D.C.: Brookings, 1987); Paul Stares, *Space and National Security* (Washington, D.C.: Brookings, 1987); and Wolfram F. Hanreider, *Technology, Strategy, and Arms Control* (Boulder, Colo.: Westview, 1986). Deterrence is covered in Robert Jervis, Robert Ned Lebow, and Janice Gross Stein, *Psychology and Deterrence* (Baltimore: Johns Hopkins, 1985); for treatments of particular systems, see Nick Kotz, *Wild Blue Yonder: Money, Politics and the B-1 Bomber* (New York: Pantheon, 1988); and Daniel Ford, *The Button: The Pentagon's Strategic Command and Control System* (New York: Simon & Shuster, 1985). For an anti-SDI book in the style of a campaign biography, see the Council on Economic Priorities, *Star Wars: The Economic Fallout* (New York: Ballinger, 1988).

20

ENERGY AND ENVIRONMENT

Fulfilling or Polluting the American Dream?

CHAPTER OUTLINE

Environmental Impacts
*The Environment: From Exploitation
  to Protection*
*Environmental Problems and Government
  Responses*
The Politics of Environmental Issues
Energy: Its Sources and Problems

© Burk Uzzle

A host of new terms have entered the common language of American politics over the last twenty years. Political leaders now speak of "acid rain," "radioactive waste," "solar power," "fossil fuels," and "meltdowns." Enormous controversy often surrounds "environmental impact statements." Particular places and organizations—Three Mile Island, OPEC, Bhopal, Greenpeace, Chernobyl—have come to symbolize specific policies—or policy failures. They also signal the emergence of a new set of complex and vital issues. Only in the last two decades have the interrelationships between energy and the environment taken center stage in U.S. society, posing critical challenges for our political processes.

Environmental Impacts

What prompted this sudden concern for the environment? We can isolate two "shocks" and a "realization":

Shock 1: We discovered (and are still discovering) that we have been poisoning and degrading our environment. Environmental degradation takes the form of air pollution, water pollution, the widespread and uncontrolled use of toxic chemicals, and the like.

Shock 2: When the Arab nations placed an embargo on their oil exports in 1973–1974, Americans sharply and suddenly realized that energy was a problem. We could no longer take for granted a continuous, unlimited, and relatively cheap supply of fuel. And even if the Organization of Petroleum Exporting Countries (OPEC) continued producing oil at peak capacity, sooner or later the world supply of fossil fuels would run short.

Realization: Resources are not infinite, and neither is the carrying capacity of the environment. We could use up our resources, pollute our environment, destroy the fertility of the land, kill off other species, and create serious dangers to ourselves. We could, through neglect or even deliberate planning, create vast pollution and resource depletion problems for future generations—who may or may not be able to cope with them.

After these shocks and realization, a whole series of difficult and highly political questions must be answered. How much pollution, if any, can we live with? How much economic growth are we willing to sacrifice for a cleaner environment? Who will bear the costs of needed changes? What role should government play?

To complicate the picture further, U.S. society has failed to reach a national consensus on just how serious these issues are. Many Americans, including many politicians and political activists, do not believe that either environmental or energy problems need to command our attention. Defining the problems themselves, therefore, has provoked considerable controversy.

Many of these issues are also interrelated. For example, solutions to energy problems are likely to have serious consequences for the environment: Coal is a major polluter; nuclear power has safety and waste disposal problems. Whatever course we pursue, we must pay a price: Energy and environmental issues are both tied closely to economic questions.

Energy issues also have important international dimensions. As the nations of OPEC bargain and quarrel among themselves about oil prices and supplies, their decisions—or indecision—reverberate throughout the international economy. The dependence of the United States and its Western allies on oil from the Middle East prompted President Carter to announce that we would take whatever steps were needed to protect oil supplies flowing through the Persian Gulf. Our dependence on foriegn oil also played a role in President Reagan's decision to reflag Kuwaiti oil tankers—placing them under the U.S. flag and under the protection of American military forces—a move that repeatedly exposed the U.S. navy to combat situations in the Persian Gulf in 1988.

In this chapter, we will (1) set out the major issues involving energy and the environment; (2) examine our choices and government policies; (3) explore the politics of environmental issues; and (4) consider the various sources of energy and the problems each one generates. We begin with a look at the distinctly American context of these issues.

The Environment: From Exploitation to Protection

Alexis de Tocqueville, a young Frenchman, visited the United States in the 1830s. He, like many other

One of the major symbols of environmentalism, the giant sequoias of California. Some regarded these trees with a special reverence; others quipped that if you'd seen one redwood you'd see them all. But what if it becomes impossible to see even one?
(Alexander Lowry/Photo Researchers)

foreign observers, was awed by the bountifulness of the American continent, what he called "Fortune's immense booty to the Americans." Many students of U.S. history have noted the wide-ranging impact of this abundance on the national psychology and political culture of the United States. Abundance influences the way we think about (or fail to think about) our political, social, and economic problems. We long ago accepted a philosophy of growth—of "more" and "bigger"—as our national ethos. Ours was a nation of producers and consumers—enjoying the fruits of our good fortune.

In taking maximum advantage of these vast resources, we have radically transformed this land. Unlike native Americans, European settlers were not content to live in harmony with nature, using only a small portion of the environment for their purposes. Instead, the settlers sought to make *the most* of resources, to transform nature and make her serve our needs.

Historically, government has facilitated this process of developing the continent. The U.S. water system and the energy resources related to it, for example, were developed through the federal Bureau of Reclamation and the Army Corps of Engineers. Without a doubt, these agencies did a great deal of good, however, critics decry the large numbers of fish killed in the process, the immense tracts of land that were flooded, and the numerous wildlife habitats essentially destroyed as a result. Government policies also promoted land development, the growth of railroads, and the creation of suburbia, a product of the vast network of superhighways. All these developments had deleterious effects on our environment. They also shaped the ways we use energy today and the amount of energy we use.

In the 1960s, our government's commitment to harnessing the nation's environmental resources gave way to greater environmental concern and energy consciousness. Ever since, frequent battles have erupted within the government between advocates of environmental conservation and those favoring increased economic growth and concomitant energy consumption.

Concern for the environment was not solely a product of the 1960s, however. Its roots extended back into the nineteenth century, when nature lovers and sportsmen sought protection for park areas. In 1872, Yellowstone was designated as the first national park. President Theodore Roosevelt, working with an aide, Gifford Pinchot, expanded the national forest reserves to 190 million acres. Additional conservation measures were passed in the 1960s, including the Wilderness Act (1964), the Land and Water Conservation Act (1965), and the Wild and Scenic Rivers Act (1968).

Pollution had also been a concern for decades. A few cities began treating their sewage in the nineteenth century. But not until 1948 was the first federal water pollution legislation passed by Congress. Air pollution, too, had been on the agenda of U.S. municipalities for years. Cincinnati and Chicago passed smoke control ordinances as far back as 1881. California made efforts to control smog and industrial pollution, and added auto emission controls in the 1960s. The first federal air pollution law took effect in 1955.

By the mid- to late 1960s, environmental con-

Hoover Dam with Lake Mead behind it, and power generators below. Built in the 1930s, the dam (and many others like it) provided immense new sources of power. In addition, they created areas for recreation and were useful in flood control. At the time they were built, there was little attention paid to the question of any negative effect the dams might have on fish or the natural environment. *(Joe Munroe/Photo Researchers)*

cerns had reached the mainstream of politics. Many Americans had decided that *more* was not necessarily *better*, especially if *more* meant polluted air, fish kills, dying lakes, a landscape strewn with unsightly waste, and crowded, sprawling, and unplanned urban and suburban developments. In 1966 the Sierra Club staged a major political battle, running ads that opposed a federal Bureau of Reclamation plan to place a dam on the Colorado River to generate electricity for the City of Los Angeles. (One ad headline read: "SHOULD WE ALSO FLOOD THE SISTINE CHAPEL SO THE TOURISTS CAN GET NEARER THE CEILING?") In May 1970, several environmental groups staged the first Earth Day celebration, designed to heighten public awareness of environmental problems. Later came Sun Day, focusing on solar energy as an alternative to fossil fuels.

Responding to the mounting wave of public concern, Congress passed the National Environmental Policy Act (NEPA) in 1969. Passed overwhelmingly, the act constituted a pledge by the federal government to protect and renew the environment. The next year an executive order by Richard Nixon established the **Environmental Protection Agency** (EPA), designed to coordinate environmental policy. The act also laid the ground-

work for the President's Council on Environmental Quality (CEQ), which reviews federal programs, recommends legislation, and sponsors independent studies. In addition, the NEPA required that **environmental impact statements**—spelling out specific environmental impacts—be prepared whenever proposals for legislation or other major federal actions may significantly affect the quality of the environment.

The EPA assumed control over and consolidated many of the then-fragmented federal environmental programs. For example, it took over water pollution management tasks from the Department of the Interior, air pollution and solid-waste management matters from the Department of Health, Education, and Welfare, and the regulation of pesticides from the Department of Agriculture. Soon the EPA became the government's most massive regulatory agency, overseeing the largest budget and the greatest number of employees.

The NEPA was passed by Congress without much controversy, but once it became law it set off sparks. For many federal agencies, there was no more business as usual: Billions of dollars worth of programs had to be reassessed; thousands of hours were spent considering environ-

TABLE 20–1
Environmental Attitudes (percent)

	United States	Great Britain	West Germany	France
Issue salience				
Environmental protection is an important issue	–	90	93	92
Condition of environment is a large problem	76	81	91	–
Pollution is rising to serious levels	70	79	91	–
Issue position				
Approve of strong environmental measures	–	97	95	96
Environment more important than growth	61	50	64	58
Environment more important than prices	–	57	54	63
Positive opinion of environmental groups	–	75	51	75
Oppose nuclear energy	32	24	36	32

SOURCE: Reprinted from Russell J. Dalton, *Citizen Politics in Western Democracies* (Chatham, N.J.: Chatham House, 1988), p. 109.

mental impacts. The law also spawned considerable litigation. Industry and conservative politicians joined forces to resist the EPA's regulatory requirements.

Today many U.S. citizens give environmental issues a high priority. Protecting the environment has strong majority support, and citizens expect government to take all necessary action in this area, as **Table 20–1** illustrates. Comparing the prominence of environmental issues in Europe and the United States, the table shows that concern for the environment ranks high on both sides of the Atlantic. The picture is somewhat more complicated when environmental issues are pitted against other values like growth and prices. Yet even here, most citizens favor the environment. Interestingly, in all four nations, only 36 percent or less oppose nuclear power, even though this issue has touched off the greatest number of political battles. Few people want to live near nuclear plants, but most feel that nuclear power is necessary.

Let us now look at particular environmental problems and the specific ways government has responded to them. Later, we will take a closer look at the political conflicts involved.

Environmental Problems and Government Responses

The environment comprises an extremely complicated, interconnected net of relationships. Poisons poured into the waters can come back to haunt us through the fish we eat or the tap water we drink. Pollution in the air affects not only our lungs, but also rivers, lakes, and trees. Our living spaces—their construction, dimensions, lighting, and proximity to others—determine the visual and auditory sensations we respond to. The environment also includes other living things—plants, insects, animals, fish—some of which may perish prematurely because of human choices. We are only beginning to understand how we fit in to various ecological systems. Whether those systems operate in a healthy fashion has important consequences for us, and for nature itself.

Today's environmental problems encompass a range of issues: air pollution, water pollution, toxic waste, solid-waste management, natural resource use, coastal ecology, land use, and noise. In this section we will focus on the first three of these issues, which are considered among the most significant.

There's no place like downtown LA if you're a connoisseur of smog. Los Angeles consistently registers the most air pollution among the nation's cities. In this picture City Hall and other buildings just blocks from the camera can barely be seen. *(AP/Wide World Photos)*

Air Pollution

The prime sources of air pollution are factories, cars and trucks, and electric generating plants. Every one of the country's major manufacturers is a major air polluter; on average, U.S. industry produces 300 pounds of air pollution a year for each American citizen. The more than 3,400 plants that generate electricity produce tons of sulfur oxides, nitrogen oxides, and ashes. Nevertheless, vehicles are responsible for the majority of air pollution—about 60 percent of the total.

One of the more subtle environmental hazards created by the combustion of fossil fuels is **acid rain,** a highly acidic form of precipitation. A by-product of industrial pollutants emitted into the air, acid rain poses problems throughout the industrial world. Some rain now falling on the Eastern United States has an acidity roughly equal to that of lemon juice. Although experts disagree about the effects of acid rain, it is known to kill aquatic life and vegetation and to erode stone and steel structures. It may also be introducing dangerous elements into drinking water.

The other effects of air pollution are fairly well documented. For example, in Los Angeles, which is famous for its smog, doctors advise thousands to leave the area every year for their health. The National Academy of Science estimates that fifteen thousand deaths a year and 7 million sick days are traceable to air pollution. According to EPA figures, we spend about $9 billion a year on health costs incurred from air-related ailments, such as lung cancer and emphysema. The EPA also estimates that air pollution causes $8 billion a year in property losses and $7.6 billion annually in destruction of vegetation.[1] Finally, some scientists have linked the release of carbon dioxide and heat into the atmosphere to a "greenhouse effect," which is already leading to a gradual and potentially dangerous increase in the earth's temperature.

In 1963, Congress passed the **Clean Air Act,** establishing national air quality standards; amendments in 1970 put some teeth in the act. Over the years, the EPA has adopted various strategies for achieving cleaner air: imposing standards limiting emissions of pollutants from power plants, for example, and requiring that cars be equipped with emission-control devices and that unleaded fuel be used in most new vehicles.

But the agency has relaxed some of its standards in the face of severe political pressures, as well as disagreements among experts. For example, some

The Ozone Layer

Among the most versatile families of chemicals developed in the last fifty years are chlorofluorocarbons, or CFCs, which also are among the most destructive and potentially devastating of chemicals. CFCs are widely used in refrigeration, air conditioning, the manufacture of plastics and computer chips, as propellants for aerosol cans, and in numerous other products considered vital to contemporary society. Although they enhance our lives, they also have silently been undermining the life-support system of the planet. As they rise through the earth's atmosphere, CFCs change character; through various chemical interactions they destroy the ozone layer, which partially screens ultraviolet rays from reaching the earth's surface. It is now understood that ozone—which at low altitudes is a pollutant—shrouds the planet in a veil that helps prevent skin cancer, cataracts, crop and fish damage, and global warming (the greenhouse effect; see *Figure 20–1*).

The potential dangers of CFCs began to be recognized in 1974, when studies revealed damage to the ozone layer. The National Academy of Science issued a report in 1976, and a month later the Environmental Protection Agency announced a ban on the use of CFCs in aerosol cans, effective in 1978. The EPA recommended a freeze on U.S. production of CFCs in 1980, but the incoming Reagan administration—eager to deregulate and citing a new, more optimistic study—delayed taking action. DuPont, the leading manufacturer of CFCs, stopped looking for substitute chemicals in June 1980. But further studies found clear evidence of ozone depletion in the atmosphere. Above Antarctica, ozone concentrations fell dramatically by the mid-1980s. Finally, an important study documented a 3 percent loss of ozone over Europe and North America. In 1987, fifty-three nations signed a treaty agreeing to cut CFC production in half over the next decade. DuPont then announced plans to phase out CFC production by early in the next century.

By late 1988, however, the ozone issue had grown more serious. Lee Thomas, Director of the EPA, called for a total ban on CFCs and other chemicals (notably, methyl chloroform), and he suggested amending the 1987 treaty to reflect new studies which found that the ozone layer was being destroyed far more quickly than earlier estimates had shown. Thomas was supported by the Alliance for a Responsible CFC Policy, an industry group which acknowledged that the new information dictated the phasing out of CFCs to the maximum extent possible.

David Doniger of the Natural Resources Defense Council sums up the situation: "If we had taken early warnings more seriously and phased out these chemicals in the '70s, there would be no detectable depletion [but] because industry dropped [its search for] substitutes we're stuck."

SOURCES: Philip Shabecoff, "As Ozone Is Depleted, Much of Life Could Go with It," *New York Times,* Mar. 17, 1988, Section 4, p. 28; and Michael Weisskopf, "Operation Ozone," *Washington Post,* national weekly edition, Apr. 18–24, 1988, pp. 8–9.

---

of the EPA's strategies to reduce pollution from automobiles—such as banning cars from high pollution areas, raising tolls on access routes, and imposing parking taxes—have encountered fierce opposition. Congress legislated against some of these strategies explicitly in the Clean Air amendments of 1977, which also postponed until 1987 the date for achieving a satisfactory level of air quality nationwide. Opponents of these and other EPA proposals take issue with the drastic changes they would force in people's habits, such as driving cars in urban areas; the excessive costs, particularly for industries that must install new equipment; and the vast increase in federal interference with local governments and industry they would require. On the other side, environmentalists argue that pres-

FIGURE 20–1
The Greenhouse Effect on Temperatures

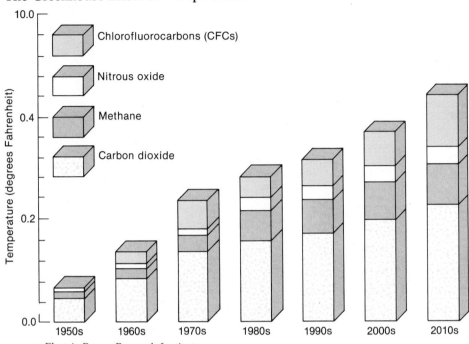

SOURCE: Electric Power Research Institute.

sures on the EPA to delay implementation of clean air standards or to relax them only mean additional long-range health costs for society as a whole.

By some measures, air quality in the United States shows significant improvement. Between 1975 and 1985, particulate matter in the air dropped by 30 percent, sulfur dioxide by 19 percent, carbon monoxide by 19 percent, and volatile organic compounds by 7 percent. Most impressive of all, lead content in the air was reduced a dramatic 86 percent in that decade because lead additives were banned from gasoline. On the other side of the ledger, nitrogen oxides, widely considered one of the prime sources of acid rain, increased 4 percent. Did these achievements signal enough progress? In 1970, the Clean Air Amendments called for a 90 percent reduction in urban carbon monoxide and other pollutants by 1977. But the compliance deadlines were postponed repeatedly. And most cities failed to require strict pollution-reducing measures such as controls on auto and power-plant emissions. At present, sixty areas have too much carbon monoxide and ozone in

their air. An estimated 80 million Americans breathe unhealthy concentrations of ozone, which can cause loss of lung function, chest pain, coughing, and wheezing. Some city officials claim that the act set an unrealistic deadline. For example, some maintain that to meet the standards in Los Angeles (the city with the worst air quality), 80 percent of automobile and industrial emissions would have to be eliminated—a totally unrealistic goal. One proposal would give cities with the poorest air quality an additional fifteen-year extension, while setting specific requirements they would have to meet in the meantime. The conditions in Southern California are by far the nation's worst, and some argue that most cities would soon be in compliance. Others contend that the EPA itself—through a lack of strong leadership—is responsible for many of our failures so far.

In 1988, Congress again debated revision of the Clean Air Act, and considered imposing severe sanctions against urban areas found not to be in compliance. For Congress, the key issues were how strict the act's standards would be, and how

FIGURE 20–2
Acid Rain and Coastal Decline

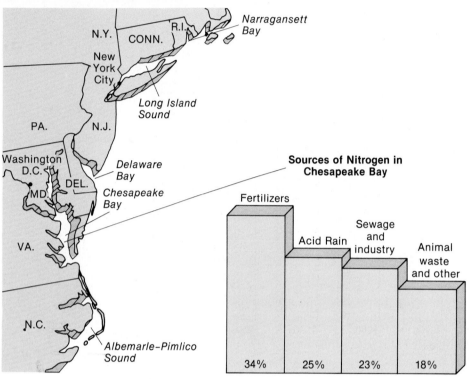

SOURCE: Environmental Defense Fund.

much more time cities would be given to meet antipollution standards when they had not come close to meeting those standards in the preceding eighteen years.[2]

On the issue of acid rain, legislators and administrators have been slow to act as well. Even when faced with powerful pressures to reduce industrial emissions—the major source of acid rain—the Reagan administration refused to act, claiming that more research was necessary. For industries that burn high-sulfur coal, the costs of installing the necessary antipollution equipment would raise utility rates 20 to 50 percent, according to industry figures. The United Mine Workers estimated that as many as eighty thousand mining jobs might be lost if the use of high-sulfur coal were banned. Environmentalists countered that unless steps were taken to lower the acidity of acid rain, many lakes and forests would be killed entirely, and acid rain's highly corrosive effects on buildings and other structures, would cause damage ranging

well into the billions of dollars. A 1988 report linked acid rain to fish kills and the deterioration of coastal fishing conditions in the United States (see **Figure 20–2**). According to the study, acid rain contributes far more nitrogen to the waters of Chesapeake Bay and other Atlantic coastal waters than previously thought. The accumulation of these toxins leads to the growth of algae, which consume oxygen needed by other plants and fish. The acid rain problem also strained relations between the United States and Canada: The Canadians urged U.S. action, arguing that 50 percent of their acid rain originated in the United States.

The first systematic study of toxic chemicals emitted into the air was released in 1985. The study, ordered by Congressman Henry A. Waxman, chairman of the House Subcommittee on Health and the Environment, found hazardous materials at far higher levels in many more locations than had been previously estimated, and concluded that thousands of tons of potentially carcinogenic agents were being released into the air from hundreds of factories. Waxman pointed out that there were no national standards regarding emissions of most of the chemicals involved.[3]

Water Pollution

Many of the nation's rivers, bays, and lakes have become seriously degraded. Industry accounts for approximately 80 percent of the pollutants that deprive water of oxygen. The volume of water used in industrial production is staggering. The steel industry alone uses close to 4 trillion gallons a year, and steel production generates suspended solids, oils, acids, and poisonous gases that mix with the wastewater. Another prime source of water pollution is the waste released by cities into nearby waterways.

Agricultural producers generate over 20 billion tons of waste a year, principally in the form of manure from feed lots. In the Missouri River basin, an area known for cattle production, organic wastes that leach from commercial feed lots into the surrounding water system generate as much pollution as the untreated sewage of 37.5 million people. In addition, agricultural pesticides that find their way into the water supply are respon-

sible for large kills of shellfish, birds, and aquatic animals. Ingested pesticides are also passed up the food chain, further increasing the health risks for animals.

In 1972, Congress passed amendments to the federal Water Pollution Control Act that were aimed at restoring and maintaining the "chemical, physical, and biological integrity of the Nation's waters." The new law set a target date of 1983 for achieving fishable, swimmable waters. Subsequent laws extended these protections to oceans and drinking-water supplies.

The 1972 amendments were designed to control **effluent,** the polluted water released by cities and industries. Engineering standards were set, timetables for cleanups were established, and large federal grants were provided to induce cooperation; in particular, Congress appropriated huge sums for wastewater treatment plants. This cleanup effort proved to be the largest public works program in U.S. history. Between 1970 and 1982, the number of people served by municipal wastewater treatment systems almost doubled, to 150 million. The volume of some pollutants entering waterways largely from industrial sources was drastically reduced—oil and grease by 71 percent, dissolved solids by 52 percent, phosphates by 74 percent, and heavy metals by 78 percent.[4]

Polluted waterways can devastate aquatic life. Many of the nation's prime shellfish and fishing areas have been hard hit, and the delicate balances of coastal wetland ecosystems have been upset. Here, freshwater carp are the victims in a Rhode Island pond. (© *Jack Spratt/The Image Works*)

A 1985 report prepared by the Association of State and Interstate Water Pollution Control Administrators found that, since 1972, 296,000 miles of streams had maintained their water quality, 47,000 miles had improved, and 11,000 were degraded. As for lakes, 10.1 million acres had maintained their quality, 390,000 acres had improved, but 1.6 million acres had become degraded, while an additional 4.1 million acres were of unknown status. Overall, six key pollutants in the water had been reduced 52 percent since 1972. Yet a study of trends in forty-four major cities showed that pollution had increased in 28 percent, decreased in 46 percent, and was unchanged in 26 percent.[5]

The Great Lakes present a special environmental problem. The repository of approximately 20 percent of the world's supply of fresh water, these five lakes once were regarded as an inexhaustible source of high-quality water. By the 1960s, however, Lakes Erie and Ontario had become seriously degraded, and the other three lakes were in trouble as well. Costly efforts to limit polluting discharges into the Great Lakes brought some improvement in water quality in the 1970s and 1980s. Less fortunate have been the many East Coast estuaries and coastal areas currently suffering the most serious pollution problems in the nation. The problem areas run down the coast from New England to Virginia, and include Narragansett Bay, Long Island Sound, Raritan Bay, New York harbor, coastal New Jersey, and Chesapeake Bay.[6] In 1987, the EPA gave New York City permission to dump sludge into the Atlantic Ocean 106 miles off the New Jersey coast. Since then, much of New York's garbage—including medical waste—has been washing up on the Jersey shore, endangering the health of thousands of summer vacationers and year-round residents as well as threatening aquatic life just off the coast. This has created tensions between New York and New Jersey; however, no resolution from the federal government has been forthcoming.

We have had some success in cleaning up our interior waterways. Under the Clean Lakes program, federal money has been used to restore several biologically dead lakes, such as Lake Washington, east of Seattle. In the East, fishermen have returned to the Connecticut and Penobscot rivers.

Moreover, restoring these bodies of water has not left area industries in economic ruins. However, state and local governments have not taken an active enough role in the process, and their lack of commitment has slowed cleanup efforts.

Many sources of water pollution still remain: runoff from farms and construction projects, storm-sewer runoff from urban areas, airborne wastes and wastes disposed of on land that eventually seep into soil and water. All these problems involve serious technical problems and controversial political issues. Money alone will not resolve them. Yet even as surface water quality improves, there has been growing concern about the pollution of ground water supplies—such as underground aquifers—in many parts of the nation.

Toxic Chemicals

The EPA has classified some thirty-five thousand chemicals as either definitely or potentially hazardous to human health, and a growing body of evidence confirms these hazards. Perhaps the best-publicized case involved the Love Canal area in upstate New York. In 1979, toxic chemicals were found to have seeped from a Love Canal landfill site into a nearby residential neighborhood containing twelve hundred homes and a school. As a result of the toxic chemicals in the soil, retention pools, and even many basements, it was claimed that Love Canal residents suffered from abnormally high incidences of cancer, birth defects, and respiratory and neurological problems.[7] On the other hand, the health commissioner of New York State found no clear evidence of health problems, leaving the issue in some controversy.

The EPA estimates that toxic chemicals have been dumped at up to 50,000 sites nationwide, at least 2,500 of which pose serious health hazards. Others place the number far higher. The Office of Technology Assessment in 1985 estimated that there were 10,000 priority waste sites and that costs of cleanup would be closer to $100 billion than the $16–$22 billion the EPA had estimated.[8] Toxic spills became commonplace in America in the 1980s. Of course, the dangers of leaks and spills of toxic chemicals were worldwide. Several

The threat of toxic contaminants near Niagara Falls, New York, forced many families in the Love Canal area to move away. These residents have split their modular home and loaded it onto two trailers in preparation for their move. *(AP/Wide World Photos)*

European nations suffered serious accidents. Perhaps the most terrifying, however, took place in Bhopal, India, in 1984, when a toxic chemical leaked from a Union Carbide plant there, killing 2,500 people and seriously injuring tens of thousands. The Bhopal tragedy made clear just how devastating a large-scale toxic leak could be. Many feared that there would be other tragedies in developing nations where controls and inspection might be less effective. One study estimated that there were thousands of U.S. chemical plants without effective safety equipment in case of a major toxic leak.[9]

There are other aspects to the toxic waste problem. In industry, for example, workers are exposed to toxics during production. We are just beginning to recognize the illnesses and conditions induced by toxic chemicals—lung cancer from asbestos, leukemia from benzene, cancer of the liver from vinyl chloride, sterility from Kepone—because the symptoms of such diseases usually do not show up for years. Some health experts speculate that a substantial percentage of all cancers may be environmentally induced—from exposure at the workplace, from toxic dumps, from chemicals that seep into water supplies, from food additives, radiation, and other sources.

In November 1980, the EPA put into effect new rules designed to prevent the haphazard dumping of toxic chemicals. The rules mandated that hazardous wastes be carried only by government-approved transporters and be disposed of only at approved disposal sites. And some municipalities, like New York City, have banned the transport of all toxic chemicals within city limits because a leak would pose a threat to human health and safety. In addition, companies that use and manufacture dangerous substances were made responsible for disposing of them legally. Violations of the new procedures were punishable by stiff penalties, such as $1 million fines and five-year prison terms. Subsequently, however, the EPA moved slowly on setting guidelines for acceptable disposal techniques. Since proper disposal techniques often are costly, many companies simply find cheap and unsafe methods, such as dumping wastes in the ocean or depositing them in unprotected sites.

Beginning in the 1980s, a **"Superfund"** was established by Congress to assist state and local governments in cleaning up hazardous toxic dumps. Enforcing the tough new rules about future disposal of toxic materials did not prove to be easy, however, despite mandated penalties. Illegal dumping practices were hard to keep track of, much less to stop.

The EPA's approach to the toxic dumping issue took an entirely new turn under the Reagan administration, which moved at a glacial pace on the toxic waste issue. In 1981 and 1982, the EPA allocated less than one-third of the Superfund, and by 1985, only 538 sites were being cleaned up. EPA's budget for enforcing toxic waste control in 1985 was 25 percent below that in 1981, and the agency's director of the Office of Solid Waste admitted that 60 percent of major disposal facilities were not in compliance with new federal laws. The picture

COMPARATIVE PERSPECTIVE

The Europeans Deal with Toxic Wastes

Like the United States, the industrial democracies of Europe began to face the problem of toxic chemicals in the 1970s. Their responses have varied considerably. Denmark was the first country to introduce a centralized system for dealing with waste disposal. The Danish railroads transport toxic chemicals in specially designed cars that are loaded at designated collection points around the country and unloaded at a central treatment plant. That plant either destroys the wastes or recycles and stores them.

Italy, by contrast, has no national plan to deal with toxic waste, and the Italian parliament has passed no legislation pertaining to waste materials. As a result, Italy has been plagued with more and bigger scandals involving toxic materials than any other European country. In a controversial incident in 1976, a plant explosion sent a cloud of highly lethal materials over the surrounding countryside, causing many animal deaths and the evacuation of 500 people.

A West German waste disposal law passed in 1972 closed down 50,000 illegal dump sites and opened up 5,000 new, regulated ones. New factories built in West Germany must show that they have made adequate plans to deal with the waste materials they produce. Although German business executives are relatively happy with the prevailing laws, many German environmentalists regard U.S. toxic waste laws as more comprehensive. They note that German laws exclude many potentially dangerous chemical products and worry that the safe dumping areas in the nation are rapidly being filled up.

Great Britain has, on paper, an effective and comprehensive system for dealing with toxic waste. Responsibility lies mainly with 165 local councils, each of which must draw up a plan and license dumping sites. Although the national legislation was passed in 1976, by the early 1980s only 12 of the local councils had completed their tasks.

SOURCE: *New York Times*, Feb. 20, 1983.

---

improved from 1985 to 1988, with substantially increased Superfund expenditures. Nonetheless, this was only a beginning in the efforts to clean up toxic waste sites, and in a 1986 report the EPA conceded that there were 888 hazardous sites in the continental United States, Alaska, and Hawaii (see **Figure 20–3**).

Another pressing environmental hazard comes from pesticides—toxic chemicals widely used in American agriculture. Under the federal Insecticide, Fungicide, and Rodenticide Act, a number of common pesticides, including DDT, were banned. However, the law permitted the continued sale of chemicals already on the market, many of which were suspected of causing cancer and birth defects. In the roughly fifteen years since the act's

passage, the EPA has banned 32 of 600 pesticide ingredients, while 47 others have been voluntarily removed from the market. But hundreds of other ingredients remain to be evaluated and new ones are introduced every year. This means that before the EPA finishes evaluating them all, we will be well into the next century. We should also note that under current law, if a chemical is banned the federal government must pay the manufacturer for financial losses incurred as a result. With a pesticide program budget of only $60 million a year, this means that banning even one widely used chemical could bankrupt the entire evaluation process. Efforts are now under way to rescind the indemnification provision in the law. Consider, as well, that pesticides banned in the United States

FIGURE 20–3
Hazardous Waste Sites (1986)

SOURCE: Environmental Protection Agency, National Priorities List Fact Book, June 1986.

TABLE 20–2
Responsiveness of States to Environmental Problems

State	Rank*	State	Rank*
Alabama	41	Montana	25
Alaska	41	Nebraska	22
Arizona	34	Nevada	45
Arkansas	48	New Hampshire	10
California	3	New Jersey	3
Colorado	25	New Mexico	40
Connecticut	5	New York	6
Delaware	20	North Carolina	9
Florida	8	North Dakota	32
Georgia	30	Ohio	24
Hawaii	10	Oklahoma	45
Idaho	34	Oregon	6
Illinois	25	Pennsylvania	22
Indiana	29	Rhode Island	14
Iowa	18	South Carolina	37
Kansas	34	South Dakota	30
Kentucky	38	Tennessee	43
Louisiana	43	Texas	45
Maine	15	Utah	25
Maryland	17	Vermont	15
Massachusetts	1	Virginia	18
Michigan	10	Washington	20
Minnesota	10	West Virginia	32
Mississippi	48	Wisconsin	1
Missouri	38	Wyoming	50

*Because of ties, some states have the same rank.
SOURCE: *Fund for Renewable Energy and the Environment.*

can be marketed abroad, and pesticide manufacturers now aggressively market their products to third world nations. Critics argue that the use, overuse, and misuse of dangerous pesticides throughout the third world is poisoning large numbers of people: Estimates range from five hundred thousand to one million people who are affected to some degree each year. A study in Kenya found high concentrations of DDT in mother's milk. A Philippine study found increased death rates among rice farmers using high levels of pesticides. West Germany exports the most pesticides to the third world, but U.S., Swiss, French, Japanese, and Dutch manufacturers ship substantial quantities of pesticides there as well.[10]

In February 1988, the Fund for Renewable Energy and the Environment released its assessment of how well the fifty states were responding to various environmental problems (see **Table 20–2**). States were ranked on six issues: surface water protection (North Carolina first); pesticide contamination (California first); land use planning (Oregon first); indoor pollution, such as no smoking laws (New Jersey first); highway safety (Maryland first); and energy pollution (standards for appliances and other forms of conservation—Massachusetts first). Overall, Wisconsin and Massachusetts ranked as the most progressive. Other issues

might also have been included in the survey, such as air and groundwater pollution and toxic waste problems. It should be noted that the survey focused more on governmental *efforts* than on environmental results.

Advocates of environmental protection throughout the country are expected to benefit from the federal Community Right to Know Act, passed by Congress in 1986 and implemented in 1988. The act requires manufacturers and other businesses that use chemicals to file reports spelling out which chemicals they use and the quantities of each that are emitted into the air, disposed of in water or poured into the ground. These data are made available to local planning boards, state agencies, and the federal EPA.

The Politics of Environmental Issues

Environmental issues tend to be highly technical, yet they stir intense political conflict. Groups struggle to define the issues—and resolve them—in accord with their own views. Let us now examine (1) group strategies and (2) the Reagan record on the environment.

Group Strategies

In many ways, the early environmental movement mirrored the pattern set by the civil rights and peace movements: marches, symbolic protests, and personal commitment. Later, with the creation of federal and state environmental agencies, political action moved into more traditional channels, such as lawsuits, lobbying, education, and campaign activity. In the area of nuclear power, however, 1960s-style activism remained a major tactic. Some of the new environmental laws encouraged citizen activism: Certain NEPA provisions, for example, give citizens standing to sue, a prerequisite for legal action. Frequently, environmental groups differ over priorities and strategies. Some take a "hard line"—insisting on the pure preservation of wilderness areas, for example—whereas others are willing to allow for multiple uses, including recreation and commercial development.

Opposing environmental activists are corporate interests. Business is a major producer, consumer, and polluter. Many businesses are directly affected by the government's decisions on the environment. For example, the lumber industry harvests over one-third of its commercial softwood from federal forests, and tens of millions of federally owned acres are leased for mineral development. Although U.S. business is highly diverse (11 million corporations and three thousand trade associations), the strategies used in combating new environmental standards and attitudes do not vary much from industry to industry.[11] Businesses typically argue that environmental problems are exaggerated, that regulations are too strict and unreasonable, and that these regulations threaten economic growth. When the Oregon legislature passed strict environmental legislation, for example, an Oregon labor lobby argued: "As a result of overzealous, erroneous governmental regulations and actions, that segment which produces jobs and profits has been rendered a serious economic blow."[12] Business interests spend millions of dollars on advertising campaigns to sway the public to their point of view; lobby extensively in Congress and state legislatures; and support political action committees to gain access to candidates.

The Reagan Record on the Environment

Ronald Reagan and his aides strongly favored U.S. economic growth—which, in their view, meant drastically curtailing environmental rules. Shortly after Reagan took office, administration officials moved to delay the imposition of many new environmental standards; fired the entire staff of the President's Council on Environment Quality, whose views were distinctly pro-environment; made deep cuts in outlays for environmental protection (see **Table 20–3**); and dismissed several thousand EPA employees, including attorneys

TABLE 20–3
The Decline in EPA Spending (in millions of dollars)

Year	Air	Drinking water	Water quality	Noise	Pesticides	Radiation	Hazardous waste	Toxic substances	Energy	Management	Total outlays
1980	$277	$69	$363	$12	$68	$12	$78	$59	$137	$160	$1,251
1982	225	65	253	5	50	10	100	66	73	171	1,002
1984	74	24	90	NA	33	7	39	34	5	246	589
1987	85	32	97	NA	38	10	67	40	6	320	749

James G. Watt, Ronald Reagan's highly controversial first Secretary of the Interior, who antagonized environmentalists and others by—among other things—selling and leasing federal lands to mining and timber interests. *(UPI/Bettmann Newsphotos)*

trained in environmental law. Reagan's first secretary of the interior, James Watt, moved to open up coastal areas for oil drilling, proposed the sale of millions of acres of federal land for development, and sought to water down strip-mining laws. In addition, sweeping powers were delegated to the states, which lacked the resources to handle them. Then, in 1983, Reagan appointed as EPA director William Ruckelshaus, a respected figure who had headed the agency under President Nixon. Still, many observers believed it would take years to repair the damage done to environmental programs.

Certain Reagan administration moves made sense. Some strip-mining rules needed to be relaxed, for instance, and some government-owned lands could reasonably be sold. In addition, many agreed that business should have a voice in shaping regulations that affected the economy and were so closely tied to prospects for economic growth. However, rather than striking a balance between environmental and economic concerns, critics charged that the Reagan administration seemed bent on boosting business interests while ignoring environmental hazards.

Reagan's second interior secretary, Donald Hodel, came under fire for opening up new coastal areas for oil exploration, including portions of the Arctic National Wildlife Preserve, as well as parts of the Atlantic coast, which could threaten the renowned Georges Bank fishing ground off New England. Conservationists also criticized how the administration was managing the nation's forests. Some charged that the Reagan administration's drive to exploit public resources made no sense—even from an economic standpoint. Logging in national forests provoked the greatest controversy. Plans unveiled by the U.S. Forest Service in 1988 called for building new roads and clear-cutting timber in many of the nation's national forests. Opponents of the plans argued that logging ruins wildlife habitats and degrades water quality. In addition, in areas like the dry Rocky Mountain forests it takes more than a century for a new tree to grow to a diameter of six inches. Moreover, critics pointed out that the government loses money on its timber leasing because the public pays for all road building and maintenance: An estimated $600 million was lost in 1985, according to the U.S. Office of Management and Budget. The National Park Service has also come under fire for management problems and what many consider a sharp decline in the state of our national parks.[13]

Energy: Its Sources and Problems

Energy issues are complex and they affect us all. Here we must consider a set of highly interrelated factors, and recognize that tampering with one factor in the energy equation may have unexpected consequences elsewhere. In addition, we must rely on numerous conjectures and estimates whose accuracy is often hard to determine. Yet the figures we choose to believe influence our views and the decisions we make. For instance, how much natural gas, coal, or petroleum is currently available for use? Estimates of energy reserves are absolutely vital to any sensible assessment of our energy situation, yet few experts agree on the correct numbers. To address other issues, we must weigh gains against losses. Should we mine more coal, despite the erosion and destruction of the land that will likely result? Should we proceed with nuclear development, despite the safety risks? Many important interests—both organized and unorganized—help shape energy policy: producers, including the major oil companies; trade unions, such as the United Mine Workers or United Auto Workers; consumers; and others. Questions of power—who decides, who benefits, and who pays—invariably arise. Finally, some issues touch on basic questions of values. Should we change our life-styles, for example, to conserve resources for ourselves and others?

The United States has a reputation for being an energy guzzler (see **Table 20–4**). Heavy energy consumption is necessary to turn out the vast quantities of consumer goods available in the United States. Americans use considerably more energy than people in other developed nations: The Swedes, West Germans, and Swiss use only about 60 percent of the energy we do, per person.

TABLE 20–4
Comparative Energy/Output Relationships

Country	Gross National Product per capita (dollars)	Energy consumption per capita (tons of coal equivalent)
United States	11,500	10.4
Britain	9,100	4.9
Canada	10,300	10.1
France	12,300	4.8
Japan	9,400	3.9
Mexico	2,400	1.8
Spain	5,500	3.0
Sweden	14,300	6.3
Venezuela	4,000	3.1
USSR	5,200	6.0
West Germany	13,400	6.4

SOURCE: Stobaugh and Yergin, *Energy Future* (New York: Random House, 1983), p. 181.

Governments at all levels can no longer avoid making energy policy. But what sort of policies will be made? Will they be made by conscious design or by default?

Let us now take a closer look at the U.S. energy situation, (1) outlining the current status of U.S. energy use and production; (2) considering several proposed alternatives and the problems posed by each; and (3) delving into the recent politics of energy.

Energy Production and Consumption

Three nonrenewable fuels account for the vast majority of our energy supply: crude oil, natural gas, and coal. These are **fossil fuels,** created from organic matter (fossils) deep in the earth by a process involving powerful forces of heat and pressure. Coal and natural gas supplies are still abundant in the United States, but about half our supplies of crude oil come from foreign sources. Nuclear power accounted for a little over 1.4 percent of all U.S. energy use in the early 1980s. Nuclear plants produce about 13 percent of our electricity, but electricity accounts for only about 10 percent of overall energy use.

About 37 percent of the energy consumed in the United States goes for heating, air conditioning, lighting, and the like, in residential and commercial establishments. Industry uses about an equal amount, with transport consuming the remaining 25 percent or so. We now spotlight four key sources of energy: (1) oil; (2) natural gas; (3) coal; and (4) nuclear power.

OIL   Oil is the key fuel in international trade and the basis of modern transport. Yet it is highly vulnerable to disruptions of supply, as the 1973–1974 Arab oil embargo demonstrated. Long lines at the gas pump and soaring prices for home heating oil vividly illustrated how these disruptions can affect American consumers.

At the moment, oil is vital, vulnerable, and over the long haul, expensive. The supply of oil is subject to wide fluctuations, however. After the squeeze in oil supplies and sharp increases in oil prices during the 1970s, an oil glut developed in the 1980s as a result of two parallel developments: increases in the supply of oil and conservation

Here comes the oil! We see part of a pipeline carrying oil the 780 miles from Prudhoe Bay to Valdez, in Alaska. The pipeline is made with bends in order to slow the movement of the oil. The Alaskan find was one of the major new U.S. domestic oil discoveries. *(James M. McCann/Photo Researchers)*

measures undertaken in the industrialized countries. These measures included the production of more fuel-efficient vehicles. The oil glut lowered prices and produced significant strains in the OPEC countries. In 1987–1988, for example, Saudi Arabia—one of the world's largest oil producers—experienced a sharp economic recession.

NATURAL GAS   The United States has large supplies of natural gas. Use of this fuel increased steadily after World War II, peaking at 40 percent of all energy consumed in 1971. Natural gas has two clear advantages over other fossil fuels: It burns cleanly and it is easily transported. Gas can be substituted for oil in many situations, and such substitutions have become increasingly common in recent years. Industry currently accounts for the bulk of natural gas usage—about two-thirds.[14]

Just how much natural gas the United States has is a matter of some dispute. In addition, competition for natural gas among domestic users—specifically, households, industries, and utilities—makes this fuel less than ideal as an alternative to other energy sources. At times, shortages of natural gas have forced closings of schools and factories in some parts of the country. Allocation by region and use remains a key concern.

COAL   Through the nineteenth century, coal fueled the vast expansion of industrial economies in Europe and the United States. Oil, cheaper and cleaner, replaced coal as the dominant fuel in industrialized societies in this century, but now many consider coal a vital energy source for our nation's future. The United States is the Saudi Arabia of coal—the repository of an estimated one-third of the total world reserves.[15] Appalachia, the Midwest, and relatively unexploited areas of the West are the prime sources of these reserves. Although coal supplies account for only about 20 percent of current U.S. energy consumption, coal accounts for about 90 percent of our remaining fossil fuel resources. Most coal is consumed by utilities to produce electricity.

Coal poses some serious environmental problems, however. Strip mining of coal often decimates a countryside, while burning coal for energy produces noxious fumes and acid rain. Stricter rules on strip mining have cut back on some of the destructive effects of this mining technique in recent years, and industry has made some headway in filtering fumes from coal-burning plants before they reach the atmosphere. Even so, these concerns militate against any large-scale switch to coal in the near future.

NUCLEAR POWER   In the 1950s, when scientists first discovered peaceful uses for the atom, many expected that energy generated by nuclear power would be so cheap and abundant we would no longer even need electric meters to keep track of its use. By some estimates, nuclear power has turned out to be slightly cheaper than oil or coal in producing electricity—although those estimates have been contested. By the late 1970s, the nuclear power industry itself began to entertain doubts on the cost issue. Despite heavy government subsidies, amounting to tens of billions of dollars, safety and other concerns have upped the costs to the point where nuclear power is no longer considered the cheap energy alternative.

The accidents at the nuclear power plant on Three Mile Island in 1979 and at Chernobyl in the USSR in 1986, underscored many of these issues and generated greater public skepticism about the benefits of nuclear power. Nevertheless, Presidents Carter and Reagan insisted that nuclear plants could be safe and beneficial.

In West Germany, the political opposition to nuclear power has had substantial success in curbing construction of new plants (see **Table 20–5** for a comparative perspective on nuclear power

TABLE 20–5
Major Adjustments to Nuclear Programs (Selected Countries)

Country	Nature of shift	Major reasons for shift
Brazil	Government canceled 6 of 8 planned plants in 1986; delayed 2 others.	Financial problems; foreign debt; new civilian government.
China	8 of 10 planned plants canceled in 5-year plan of 1986.	Foreign exchange requirements.
France	Slowdown from 6 orders in 1980 to 1 each in 1986 and 1987; government still plans 90 percent of electricity from nuclear.	Slowed electricity demand growth; nuclear overcapacity.
Japan	Capacity goals cut in 1984; construction down to 2 plants per year; government remains committed to program.	Slowed electricity demand growth; technical problems.
Mexico	Plans to build 20 plants reduced to 2.	Financial problems; foreign debt.
Sweden	1980 referendum called for phaseout by 2010; 1986 statements affirm course.	Safety and waste concerns, intensified by Chernobyl.
United Kingdom	No plants ordered in 7 years; 5-year delay at proposed Sizewell plant.	Political pressure from environmental and local citizens' groups.
United States	54 plants canceled, no orders; de facto moratorium.	Rising costs; slowed electricity demand growth.
West Germany	Major delays in most plant construction; de facto moratorium on new orders.	Slowed electricity demand growth; political pressure by local groups and parties.

SOURCES: Diplomatic reports and news articles; reprinted from Christopher Flynn, *Reassessing Nuclear Power: The Fallout from Chernobyl,* Worldwatch Paper 75 (Washington, D.C.: Worldwatch Institute), pp. 54–55.

Public concern about the safety of nuclear power plants has been heightened by frightening accidents involving the leakage of radiation. The 1979 accident at the Three Mile Island plant in Harrisburg, Pennsylvania, still looms in people's minds, much as the plant's cooling towers loom over nearby homes. *(© David Wells/ The Image Works)*

around the world). Proposed construction of German nuclear projects has touched off large and sometimes violent protest demonstrations, and several projects have been stopped because of public protests combined with antinuclear legal maneuvers.[16]

Alternative Solutions

Proposed solutions to the country's energy problems focus on (1) increasing the supply of energy and (2) diminishing energy demands through conservation. We now address these issues.

INCREASING THE SUPPLY The nation's remaining oil reserves lie principally in Alaska and offshore along the continental shelf. Eventually, according to some estimates, we may be able to locate upwards of 200 billion barrels—about twice what has been discovered since the 1960s. Much domestic natural gas also remains to be found, although there has been considerable disagreement over just how much.

Increasing domestic production of these two fuels presents two major problems—one technical and one political. From a technical standpoint, no one knows how much oil and natural gas remains to be discovered. Because of this uncertainty, we

cannot count on such supplies in future energy planning. Politically, the government will have to consider providing incentives to find and exploit potential resources. Policy makers must recognize that additional supplies will not be easy to locate and, therefore, exploration will be costly.

What are the possibilities for increasing coal production? Known coal reserves could supply us with fifty years' worth of energy at a rate equal to more than all present energy used each year. However, as we noted earlier, increased use of coal presents serious environmental problems. Coal burning increases air pollution, unless costly antipollution equipment is used. Also, strip mining for coal defaces the land; this has already occurred in much of Appalachia. Strip-mined land can be restored to some degree—but again, only at significant cost.

Nuclear power also has drawbacks, of which ominous safety issues loom the largest. Pronuclear power proponents point out, however, that by taking steps to ensure safety in design and operation, nuclear power can be surprisingly safe. But other problems have surfaced as well: Disposal of nuclear wastes remains a sensitive and unresolved matter, and increasing costs have made nuclear plants less economically attractive. Even proponents of nuclear power believe nuclear energy will play only a minor role in the future—supply-

Scene from a major solar project in New Mexico, 1984. Although there was some experimentation with deployment of large-scale solar devices, the real breakthroughs in terms of solar energy still awaited the extensive investment that nuclear power had once obtained from government and other sources.
(Fred Ward/Black Star)

ing 20–25 percent of electric power and perhaps 10 percent of overall U.S. energy needs.

One attractive alternative boosted by many observers is solar power—a category that includes a variety of renewable energy sources, such as the sun itself, wind, water, and plants. Dependence on solar energy would minimize pollution problems, cut energy costs significantly, and reduce our reliance on foreign sources of fuel. But how practical is solar power? In the Netherlands, wind power has long been used as a source of energy. In other countries, houses are constructed to make use of the sun for passive solar heating. In the United States, solar hot water collectors were widely used in Florida several decades ago. New breakthroughs in the solar area seem possible, even likely. For example, **photovoltaic cells,** which transform sunlight directly into electricity, already exist, although production costs are still too high for common use.

Another solar energy alternative that deserves specific mention is the use of biomass. **Biomass** refers to all organic waste materials, such as animal manure, garbage, rotting plants and trees, and, particularly, crops raised for the purpose of supplying fuel. These materials can either be burned to produce energy or converted into a gas or liquid fuel. Instead of presenting a substantial disposal problem, they can serve as a novel energy source.

The major problem with solar alternatives is a deep-seated unwillingness to shift to radically different ways of creating energy. Since U.S. society now runs largely on fossil fuels, the extent of the necessary changeover would be considerable, and it could not be accomplished overnight. Most solar advocates argue that solar could become the major source of energy by the year 2025, supplying about 25 percent of our energy needs early in the twenty-first century—but only if we turn emphatically in that direction soon. Critics of solar alternatives contend that they are technologically uncertain and unlikely to meet the full energy needs of U.S. society.

CONSERVATION   Another way of dealing with our energy needs is to reduce them. More than half of all energy used in the United States is wasted. Aside from the economic benefits to be gained by reducing such large-scale waste, serious efforts at conservation would buy us precious time as petroleum supplies begin to dwindle. Too often, conservation has been confused with curtailing important energy uses. But as conservationist Denis Hayes points out, there are sharp differences between the two: "Curtailment means giving up automobiles, conservation means trading a 7-mile-per-gallon status symbol for a 40-mile-per-gallon commuter vehicle. Curtailment means a cold house; conservation means a well-insulated house with an efficient heating system."[17]

Hayes maintains that we could save significant amounts of energy in transportation, heating and cooling, the food system, electrical generation, industrial efficiency, waste recovery, recycling, and lighting. Energy-saving measures could include tripling the gasoline mileage of vehicles, decreasing vehicle size, increasing our use of trains and buses, imposing strict standards for building in-

The Tellico Dam: A Triumph of Bad Sense

In June 1979, President Jimmy Carter signed the Energy and Water Development Appropriations Act. Attached to the act was a rider, added at the last moment in a slick parliamentary maneuver, that authorized the Tennessee Valley Authority to complete the controversial Tellico Dam project "notwithstanding the Endangered Species Act or any other law." It was an extraordinary step to take—placing a federal building project beyond the reach of the law. Carter signed "with regret," not wanting to involve himself any further in a battle with those members of Congress for whom the Tellico project had become a personal battle.

The issue at Tellico seemed to be between those who wanted to save the last remaining habitat of a three-inch minnow known as the snail darter and those who wanted to complete a major hydroelectric and flood control dam and not waste the $120 million already spent. Seen in this light, the struggle had a touch of the absurd about it—was it really sensible to stop a vast project for the sake of a few tiny fish?

Yet the reality of the situation differed considerably from the public image of a fish-versus-dam battle. In fact, the Tellico Dam was only a small part of a much larger project involving the creation of a 38,000-acre lake. Few Americans realized that the figure of $120 million usually mentioned was largely spent not on the dam itself, but on road development and acquisition of land, including 22,000 acres that were not to be flooded. Supporters of the dam argued that the dam and the lake it would create were needed for recre-ation and electric power, but it turned out that there were already twenty-four major dams and lakes within sixty miles of Tellico. Many of these had undeveloped shores. Moreover, Tellico would produce only 23 megawatts of electricity within a regional capacity of 27,000 megawatts. Even the TVA was willing to admit in 1978 that the lake to be created when the dam was closed was not necessary, and that the farmland to be flooded exceeded in value the benefits to be obtained from the dam project. In 1977, a General Accounting Office study argued that the dam was uneconomic and that only 1 percent of the claims of future benefits were justified. In addition, archeologists discovered a Cherokee Indian burial site of worldwide significance in the area.

Faced with mounting opposition, Republican Senator Howard Baker, a Tennessean, called for a special cabinet level review committee to consider the project. A unanimous committee found the project unsound on economic, not just ecological, grounds. Baker and his allies, however, wouldn't give up. On June 18, 1979, in a virtually empty House of Representatives, the rider was attached to the appropriations bill—a process that took 43 seconds. It squeezed by the Senate by four votes.

SOURCES: On the Tellico Dam project, see L. J. Carter, "Lessons from the Snail Darter Saga," *Science*, Feb. 23, 1979; "TVA's Bitter Victory," *Newsweek*, Nov. 26, 1979; and "Snail Darter vs. Dam: Pork Barrelers Win," *Science News*, Oct. 6, 1979.

---

sulation, boosting the use of solar power, increasing the efficiency of electrical power generators, and using waste heat from power generation.

With these and other measures, Hayes estimates, we could cut our energy consumption in half without altering our standard of living. Of course, we could not achieve such goals without extensive government involvement and clearly defined public policy.

We must keep in mind, however, about 40 percent of the difference between U.S. and European rates of energy use is rooted in factors that are not easily changed, such as greater distances between cities and industrial specialization. The other 60 percent of our excess energy use arises from various inefficiencies. Historically, because of relatively cheap petroleum and natural gas, Americans have been less than diligent in pursuing fuel economy. Also, politicians are loath to burden the U.S. public with heavier taxes on energy supplies.

The Politics of Energy Issues

For decades, government policies (or the absence of such policies) have affected energy supplies and prices. Our government tends to consider each energy area separately, rather than forging a unified, national energy policy. Coal, for example, was a relatively unregulated energy source until very recently. By contrast, politics has surrounded the production, distribution, and pricing of the prosperous oil and gas industries. In the late 1970s, political battles centered on oil and gas, both of which were eventually "decontrolled"—meaning that complex sets of regulations governing production and pricing were relaxed.

All U.S.-produced oil was effectively decontrolled in 1981, but at the same time the oil companies were assessed a special "windfall profits" tax to reduce the financial bonanza accorded them by decontrol. Politically, decontrol of oil could not have been accomplished without this tax: Congress and the public were outraged over the immense profits oil companies were making at the time. As legislated, the windfall profits tax was expected to lead to increased federal revenues during the 1980s. Congress mandated that these revenues were to be used in the following ways: approximately 25 percent for assistance to lower-income persons, to help them cope with increased energy costs; 60 percent for tax reductions to individuals and businesses; and 15 percent for energy development and mass transit.

The windfall tax issue illustrates some important points about energy policy making. In this case, public opinion forced legislators to tax the industry's windfall profits because oil companies were already making enormously high profits, even before decontrol went into effect. Accordingly, the oil companies, once virtually unchallenged in their own domain, had to yield to coun-

tervailing political forces. The bureaucracy also had a hand in decontrolling oil: The newly created Department of Energy, a staunch advocate of decontrol, lobbied for it extensively within the government. This gave the process an even stronger push.

We now consider the drive for energy independence and its influence on presidential policies.

ENERGY INDEPENDENCE AND PRESIDENTIAL POLICIES   Presidents Nixon and Ford both sought greater U.S. energy independence—which meant lower oil imports. President Carter pressed for conservation measures and solar energy as well as favoring gradual gas decontrol, an increase in the federal gasoline tax, and a heavy tax on gas-guzzling cars. Toward the end of his administration, Carter also sought large-scale financial subsidies for a synthetic fuels (synfuels) program. In the end, he got much of what he wanted: Synfuels, conservation measures, and gas decontrol were approved, even though the gasoline tax was defeated, except for emergency situations, and the gas-guzzler provisions were watered down.

Ronald Reagan came to the presidency determined to increase U.S. production of fossil fuels. He encouraged greater exploration for oil and gas on federal lands, while cutting back drastically on federal expenditures for energy alternatives, such as synthetic fuels and solar energy. During his first term, the United States reduced its dependence on Middle East oil by greatly increasing imports of oil from Mexico and Venezuela.[18] As a result, the Reagan administration came to regard Central America and the Caribbean as increasingly vital to U.S. interests.

Complex in themselves, energy issues also interact with other political concerns: conservation, foreign policy, safety, and the like. In 1987, for example, Congress passed a law setting minimum federal energy efficiency standards for major appliances such as refrigerators, washers, and hot water heaters. Some estimated that the new standards would ensure $28 billion in energy savings by the year 2000, equivalent to the output of twenty-two nuclear power plants. President Reagan had vetoed the bill in 1986, but changed his mind and signed it in 1987. At the same time, after years of debate, speed limits on selected U.S. highways were raised from 55 mph to 65 mph. Speed limits had been lowered in the 1970s in the wake of the Arab oil embargo of 1973–1974. Originally promoted as a conservation measure (because cars running at lower speeds use less gasoline), the 55 mph limit was not debated in those terms in the 1980s. Instead, the debate revolved around safety (the number of lives saved by the lower speed limit) versus convenience. The Reagan administration also moved to reflag Kuwaiti oil tankers in the Persian Gulf, signaling the nation's continued dependence on foreign oil supplies. Then, to boost domestic oil production, the administration advocated oil exploration in the Arctic National Wildlife Refuge in Alaska. Yet many maintained that the quantity of oil beneath the refuge (at most one year's supply for the United States) hardly merited the threat to one of the world's most sensitive and rare ecosystems.

Taken together, these examples illustrate the variety of issues influencing the energy debate, the intricacy of interactions among them, and the sometimes unexpected ramifications of energy policy making. Is a coherent energy policy possible? How should we balance energy needs against other important values? In an age of diminishing resources, future administrations will have to grapple with these issues, navigating a course around explosive political controversies at home and the subtleties of international politics.

Conclusions

Can democratic theory shed light on energy and environmental issues? Three issues command our attention here. First, who decides how energy/environment issues are resolved, and how do they make those decisions? Second, who benefits and who pays for the ways we deal with energy/environment questions? Are some being victimized to make life easier for others? Finally, democratic concerns should make us wonder about the long-term significance of our decisions about energy/environment issues. How will these decisions affect future generations?[19]

Until quite recently, energy/environment decision making had not played a prominent role in the U.S. political process. Before 1973, most key decisions on energy, were made or shaped by the interests most directly involved. Oil interests essentially determined the politics of oil; companies with a strong interest in nuclear power pressed for—and generally obtained—government subsidies for their efforts. In addition, the courts often frustrated citizens' efforts to set limits on degradation of the environment. Air and water pollution and the dumping of toxic wastes had no place on the political agenda.

Now that energy/environment issues *have* reached our political agenda, many experts argue that the intricacies of these issues, like the complex problems involved in foreign policy, are simply too difficult for common citizens to comprehend. In some respects, this argument has merit: Few of us have the time or inclination to probe the problems of waste disposal or to master the alternatives to air pollution. But in general, the public has taken a resolutely pro-environment stance. On energy questions, neither policy makers nor the public at large have reached any coherent consensus on how to grapple with our coming energy dilemmas. It seems likely, however, that once such a consensus emerges, popular sentiment will play a constructive role in shaping future energy and environment policy.

In considering the costs and benefits of energy/environment policy, basic human rights come into play. If air pollution is taking years off our lives, if toxic dumps increase health risks for millions, if carcinogens in the workplace mean that many will die prematurely, then core issues of democratic politics are at stake. The basic guideline for democratic policy making is this: The life and health of some should not be sacrificed for the ease and convenience of others. An aroused public, concerned about environmental hazards, can demand serious, sustained action by the political leadership.

Democratic commitments should also prompt us to consider the long-term effects of current actions. Should we push for the maximum feasible production now, even if that means further polluting the environment? How vigorously should we press for cleanup of the environment in the immediate future, as opposed to leaving the job to the next generation?

Democratic theory can take us only so far, however. It cannot tell us whether a high-energy, high-consumption life-style is preferable to something simpler and more conservation-oriented. It cannot tell us whether the investment in solar options will be worthwhile or not. It cannot tell us how strictly we should enforce laws on toxic dumping. Nevertheless, it does remind us that no one person's life is more important than any other's, and that the profits or comforts of a few are not so important as the well-being of the many.

Finally, we must recognize that Americans have always wanted to "develop" their nation. Historically, we have sought more and better, bigger and richer. Now the complex issues of energy and environment cast a shadow over this hallowed American dream. Americans believe in capitalism—but in this area, capitalistic approaches sometimes fall short of the mark. Capitalism does not force those who should be paying the real costs of doing business to actually pay those costs. Therefore, government has a particularly important role to play in energy/environment issues. But what should that role be? Can we preserve the environment and still generate the energy for an "American" life-style? And if this proves impossible, who will have the political courage to say so?

GLOSSARY TERMS

Environmental Protection Agency

environmental impact statements

acid rain

Clean Air Act

effluent

Superfund

fossil fuels

photovoltaic cells

biomass

NOTES

[1]Council on Environmental Quality, *Environmental Quality* (Washington, D.C.: U.S. Government Printing Office, 1979), chap. 3.

[2]The material on air pollution changes between 1975 and 1985 was drawn from Barry Commoner, "Failure of the Environmental Effort," speech delivered at the Seminar Series of the U.S. Environmental Protection Agency, Jan. 12, 1988; Marla Cone, "L.A. to E.P.A.: Don't Hold Your Breath," *Sierra*, Nov./Dec. 1987, pp. 27–32; and *Newsweek*, Jan. 4, 1988, p. 62.

[3]*New York Times*, Mar. 26, 1985, p. 18.

[4]CEQ, *Environmental Quality, 1983* (Washington, D.C.: U.S. Government Printing Office, 1983), p. 4.

[5]*New York Times*, May 13, 1985.

[6]CEQ, *Environmental Quality, 1983* (Washington, D.C.: U.S. Government Printing Office, 1983), pp. 106–114.

[7]Michael Brown, *Laying Waste: The Poisoning of America by Toxic Chemicals* (New York: Washington Square Press, 1981).

[8]*New York Times*, Mar. 10, 1985, p. 1.

[9]*New York Times*, Aug. 19, 1985.

[10]The material on pesticides is drawn from Philip Shabecoff, "Congress Again Confronts Hazards of Killer Chemicals," *New York Times*, Oct. 11, 1987, Section E, p. 5; and Mort Rosenbaum, "Pesticides Considered Big Threat," *Chapel Hill Newspaper*, Oct. 18, 1987, Section C, p. 1.

[11]Walter A. Rosenbaum, *The Politics of Environmental Concern* (New York: Holt, 1977), pp. 81–87.

[12]*Ibid.*, pp. 83–84.

[13]The foregoing paragraph was drawn from Alston Chase, "How to Save Our National Parks," *The Atlantic*, July 1987; Jim Robbins, "Are Forests Worth More Unspoiled or Developed?" *New York Times*, Apr. 10, 1988, Section E, p. 4; and John B. Oakes, "Hodel Blunders Even as He Plunders Land," *Chapel Hill Newspaper*, May 18, 1987, p. 7.

[14]David Howard Davis, *Energy Politics* (New York: St. Martin's, 1982), chap. 4.

[15]*Ibid.*, chap. 2.

[16]Christopher Flynn, *Reassessing Nuclear Power: The Fallout from Chernobyl*, Worldwatch Paper 75 (Washington, D.C.: Worldwatch Institute, 1987), p. 55.

[17]Denis Hayes, *Rays of Hope* (New York: Norton, 1977).

[18]Leslie H. Gelb, "Oil = X in a Strategic Equation," *New York Times*, Oct. 7, 1983.

[19]These questions were suggested by the insightful work of David Orr. See his articles, "Leviathan, the Open Society and the Crisis of Ecology" (with Stuart Hill), *Western Political Quarterly*, Dec. 1978, pp. 457–469; and "Perspectives on Energy," *Dissent*, Summer 1979, pp. 280–284.

SELECTED READINGS

For a widely read and influential presentation of an "environmental ethic," see E. F. Schumacher, *Small Is Beautiful* (New York: Harper & Row, 1973). A variety of particular perspectives are represented in Garrett Hardin and John Baden, eds., *Managing the Commons* (New York: Freeman, 1977); Barry Commoner, *The Closing Circle* (New York: Knopf, 1971); Wendell Berry, *The Unsettling of America* (San Francisco: Sierra Club, 1977); P. Portney et al., *Current Issues in U.S. Environmental Policy* (Baltimore: Johns Hopkins, 1978); and S. P. Hays, *Beauty, Health and Permanence* (New York: Cambridge University Press, 1987).

For more explicit treatments of the **political implications of environmental policies,** see Walter A. Rosenbaum, *The Politics of Environmental Concern* (New York: Holt, 1977); F. Capra and C. Spretnak, *Green Politics* (New York: Dutton, 1984); and N. Vig and M. Kraft, *Environmental Policy in the 1980s* (Washington, D.C.: Congressional Quarterly Press, 1985). The "Not in My Back Yard" (NIMBY) phenomenon—local residents' resistence to environmentally damaging construction—is explored in Sidney Plotkin, *Keep Out: The Struggle for Land Use Control* (Berkeley: University of California Press, 1987). For an interesting case study of one town's backyard problem, see Anthony F. C. Wallace, *St. Clair: A Nineteenth Century Coal Town's Experience with a Disaster-Prone Industry* (New York: Knopf, 1987).

For a **comparative perspective,** see Cynthia H. Enloe, *The Politics of Pollution in a Comparative Perspective* (New York: McKay, 1975); or Jeffrey Leonard, *Natural Resources and Economic Development in Central America: A Regional Environmental Profile* (New Brunswick, N.J.: Transaction Books, 1987).

On the **energy debate,** see Pietro S. Nivola, *The Politics of Energy Conservation* (Washington, D.C.: Brookings Institution, 1986); D. Kash and R. Rycroft, *U.S. Energy Policy: Crisis and Complacency* (Norman, Okla.: University of Oklahoma Press, 1984); Amory Lovins, *Brittle Power: Energy Strategy for National Security* (Andover, Mass: Brick House, 1982); J. L. Simon and H. Kahn, *The Resourceful Earth* (London: Blackwell, 1984); Daniel F. Ford, *Three Mile Island* (New York: Penguin, 1982); D. H. Davis, *Energy Politics* (New York: St. Martin's, 1982); and Daniel Yergin, *Energy Future* (New York: Random House, 1983). On a controversial issue of the late 1980s (who pays when a nuclear power plant is partially or completely built and then canceled?), see Joseph P. Tomain, *Nuclear Power Transformation* (Bloomington: Indiana University Press, 1987).

ON IMPROVING AMERICAN DEMOCRACY

In one of his famous pithy aphorisms, the young Karl Marx wrote: "The philosophers have only interpreted the world: the task however is to change it." He might also have said "preserve it" (as some environmentalists and antinuclear activists do these days), but such an observation on the part of a 26-year-old would not have impressed anyone except the authoritarian heads of state whom Marx opposed.

Textbooks also only "interpret" the world—and only the best do *that;* many texts hardly even approach the level of analysis required for interpretation. Yet most American government texts conclude with a paean to praise our democratic system and to recommend that readers get out there in the world and *participate* (the magic word). Rather than throwing the usual ritualistic phrases at you, we want, in this last section of the book, to offer specific recommendations for improving democratic life in America. We hope to stimulate your thinking one last time, to give you something to focus on as you finish this text and move on to other concerns.

First, consider the matter of our **electoral system.** For a nation that takes conspicuous, often noisy pride in its democracy, we have strikingly low levels of electoral participation. Political campaigns are increasingly complicated and too expensive, and they emphasize the negative while providing little of substance on which to base informed choices. Elections for the House of Representatives, in which virtually all incumbents running for reelection are successful, seem to have been reduced to mere formalities. The 1988 presidential election set new standards for an unrewarding campaign. A *Newsweek* poll two weeks before the election found that only 20 percent of respondents thought the presidential candidates were "Mostly giving honest views on issues"; 74 percent responded that the candidates were "Saying what they need to in order to get elected"; 66 percent said that "The people running the campaigns seem to have more control than the candidates themselves"; and 60 percent said "The candidates are not discussing issues that are important to me."*

There have been many suggestions for improving our elections. We should make voting easier through automatic registration of high school graduates. We ought to create a national election holiday, to call more attention to the importance of voting and to make it easier for people to do so. The United States is one of the few democratic nations that does *not* make election day a national holiday or hold it on a Sunday, when most people are not working. There is nothing sacred about the first Tuesday after the first Monday in November as the time to hold elections.

As for campaigns, public financing of congressional elections deserves to be tried, and free time should be made available on TV and radio. After

---

*"The Voters: Disgusted, Disappointed and Mistrustful," *Newsweek,* Oct. 31, 1988, p. 19.

all, the media operate on public airwaves, and there is no reason why elections should be a source of profit. Changes like these would limit the cost of congressional campaigns and reduce the enormous advantage that incumbency now offers. We need to level off the playing field on which candidates for Congress compete. These suggestions are hardly revolutionary, but together they *might* raise both the quality and the level of participation in elections. And freeing members of Congress from almost-constant fundraising should allow them to pay more attention to the business of legislation.

Second, we need to take **democratic education** more seriously. As Aristotle taught twenty-five centuries ago, no object of study is more richly various, more comprehensive, or more important than the study of the political system. Yet most American children learn little about such democratic keystones as civil liberties, civil rights, and social rights. Students know very little about the historical struggles of democracy, and so they bring little perspective to issues that affect them today. Some form of "democratic curriculum" should begin in elementary school and continue with increasing complexity through high school and college. We're not talking here about "How a Bill Becomes a Law"—that sort of thing is far too dry to engage young students (or even the not-so-young). Rather, the educational system should convey the living soul of American democracy—its triumphs along with its shortcomings—in real, human terms.

Third, democratic reforms should extend to **remedying the serious deprivations in our midst.** Severe poverty and powerlessness engulf tens of millions in our society. It is one part of the American ethic that such conditions are basically an individual responsibility. This perspective is, in some sense, correct and will always remain so; but a democrat cannot be unconcerned when so many fellow citizens lack the basics of a decent life. More freedom and more security for the least free and the least secure should be a high priority—not as a matter of charity but as a matter of sound democratic policy. A "land of the free" needs to provide expanding opportunities for better housing, health care, and jobs.

Fourth, we should experiment with **increasing democracy in the workplace.** The workplace can be an environment where we practice democratic attitudes rather than attitudes of superiority and subordination. Reformers have discussed such possibilities for a century and a half, but we in America have done little about them. Many factors push us into larger and larger organizations—government among them—in which ordinary workers have little to say about management and the conduct of business. More democratic decisionmaking in the workplace would transform not only the process of work but also the objects of our labor. It's possible to make work more meaningful while strengthening our democratic character at the same time.

Finally, we need to reassess the meaning of democracy as it applies to **the conduct of foreign policy.** The United States often operates as though only *our* version of democracy is appropriate. We have displayed this attitude most clearly in our own hemisphere—for example, in our opposition to the Cuban government of Castro since the early 1960s, the Chilean government of Allende in the early 1970s, and the Sandinista government of Nicaragua since the early 1980s. Generally speaking, American political leaders have equated democracy and capitalism, leaving little room for experimentation with other forms of democratic life that combine political rights with a "leftist" economic system. Yes, it *is* entirely appropriate for us to be concerned about the totalitarian practices of leftist governments, wherever they are; but we also should recognize that such regimes may represent a more democratic choice than the right-wing dictatorships which they sometimes replace. We can attempt to induce leftist governments to become more democratic just as we have attempted to move right-wing regimes toward greater respect for human rights. Such a policy would provide greater flexibility than the one we often pursue, of equating revolution from the left with anti-Americanism. Our usual course may actually create the conditions we fear. But a policy of examining each case on its own merits is not simple, either to think through or to implement.

Very little about democracy is simple, and so government textbooks seem to try to include everything. Yet no textbook really does include *everything*, despite appearances to the contrary. Instead, authors must be highly selective in what they include, and in the process their biases, sensitivities, and judgments are revealed. One interesting question about a text, then, is: What have the authors omitted or neglected? Students often know too little about a subject to answer this question, and so we want to spend a little time mentioning what *isn't* in our book.

What would we include if we had more space? One area that would expand is foreign and defense policy. The important domestic implications of our enormous defense establishment are barely indicated in Chapter 19. Although the world is constantly changing, certain regions represent long-term challenges for U.S. policy—the Middle East, for example, and much of sub-Saharan Africa. In a very shortsighted way, American consciousness of Vietnam and Southeast Asia seems to have stopped short in 1975, with the withdrawal of our troops from Saigon (now Ho Chi Minh City). Although Chapter 19 does have brief sections about El Salvador and Nicaragua, our involvement in those nations is far too complex and extensive to be introduced adequately in so little space. And there are three other important Central American nations, and Mexico, and all of South America, where the United States has been directly involved for most of this century. Nor have we given space to the European Economic Community and its projected creation of a single European economy in 1992.

Another topic not covered, and a good example of how foreign and domestic policies interact, is drugs. How should the various issues be addressed? What can we ask of nations that produce or supply drugs in response to our own demand for them? How can we counter the corrupting influence of drug money on our police and regulatory agencies? What intrusions on personal choice and privacy should we impose to ensure that drug use does not impair public transportation and other services?

There are many subjects that we have had to omit or cover briefly. Among them are certain aspects of the criminal justice system—including the workings of our courts and prisons and the overall questions of why crime occurs and how we ought to deal with it. We did not have much chance to discuss federal investments in education or to what degree the government should finance artistic endeavors. We have barely touched on the problems of government-held information—on the need for privacy, on the one hand, and for secrecy, on the other. Access to information is an essential element in democratic life, and yet it often conflicts with various rationales for secrecy. How are such issues to be resolved?

Larger questions of the world environment could themselves take up an entire text and deserve far more attention than we could give them. Diminishing resources, pollution and the greenhouse effect, endangered species, land erosion, and famine all loom large on the political agenda even now.

Finally, we did not sufficiently discuss either the structures of power or the political philosophies that are current in America. How is power exercised? Which groups tend to have it, and which do not? We gave more than glimpses of answers—especially in Chapters 5 and 9 and in Part IV—but a great deal more needs to be said. In talking of power, it is important to remember that *ideas do matter* in politics (just ask Michael Dukakis, who spent much of his presidential campaign denying that he was a liberal). Since the late 1960s American liberals have been confused and divided, even though liberalism has had many successes. More recently, however, various forms of conservative ideology have become powerful, ranging from the Christian Right of Pat Robertson to the sophisticated neoconservatism of Jeane Kirkpatrick and other intellectuals. Why is liberalism in disarray and conservatism dominant? Does this reflect the value of conservative ideas compared with liberal ones? And what has happened to the streak of radicalism in America? Is the American left politically dead, a mere generation after its tremendous effectiveness in the 1960s? We hope that you will pursue such subjects on your own or in other courses, and we have pointed the way with our bibliographic notes at the ends of chapters.

By now you must have gathered that democracy in the abstract is not our primary concern as authors. Real democracy, and commitment to it, is found not in words but in the actual operation of government, and in the lives of the people it affects. Generally, we Americans have a strong tendency (even missionary zeal) toward self-righteousness and high self-regard. We are better than other nations, we think, and sometimes that brings the feeling that whatever we do, or did, cannot basically be very wrong. We don't like being losers. It was a humiliation to watch the American embassy being taken and hostages held in Iran, a feeling that was echoed on a smaller scale with each hostage taken later in the Middle East. Similarly, we were impatient with the inability of the U.S.-backed contras to make much headway in Nicaragua. Both in the Middle East and in Central America, the hostility expressed against the United States must have sprung from misguided fanatics (Muslim or Marxist, they are equally inexplicable to us). We know we were right. Our inability to act effectively must have come from a failure of American leadership. But such attitudes do not help us get a clear picture of the world, or of ourselves. Instead, they pave the way for deceptions, like those leading to the Iran-contra scandal, and for the misguided patriotism which allowed some employees of the executive branch to believe that our democracy was best served by declaring one policy but carrying out its opposite. The first requirement of a healthy, skeptical patriotism is objectivity: We need to know ourselves and to see the world clearly. This is not easy.

We Americans also like to consider ourselves first in everything, which also presents problems. If the Soviet Union has more land-based missiles than we, does that mean we must catch up and build even more to get ahead? Do such comparisons matter at all? As we saw in Chapter 19, it makes little sense to compare each category of strategic weapons, since the arsenals of the United States and the Soviet Union are quite different. In the end, the apocalyptic meaning of those arsenals is the same. Nonetheless, such logic will not appeal to those who worry that the United States is no longer first in every category. Similarly, we are uncomfortable comparing our recent economic performance with Japan's. We find it hard to believe that our huge deficits may be linked to the unfavorable disparity between Japanese per-

formance and our own; we would rather believe that Japan isn't playing fair. This obsession with being on top can blind us to deeper long-term issues.

America is a very great power in the world. What we do, and what we don't do, influences the lives of many. We can destroy and create, can nurture and cut down, in a way that few nations can. Yet at times we seem impotent and rage inside our boundaries, not knowing whether to seek revenge, to employ all our vast power, or to be patient. Was President Reagan right to bomb Libya in 1986 for its alleged role in terrorist acts, or was that stooping to the level of the terrorists? Should the United States have responded more forcefully in 1983, when the Soviet Union shot down a Korean airliner and killed 269 people, including a U.S. Congressman; or in 1987, when an Iraqi missile in the Persian Gulf struck the USS *Stark* and killed 37 American sailors? There is a long, long list of such painful questions, and as a society we are not sure of the answers.

Yet no nation can withdraw from the world, and so it is important to think about our participation and our ideas of patriotism. We have talked about foreign policy commitments in this book, but what about loyalty? What should patriotism mean? At least three conceptions deserve our thought. One form of patriotism is the sense of gut loyalty—the feelings we have about the flag and other national symbols. This is an unreflective patriotism that says, "My country, right or wrong." A second form is attached to the "meaning" of the nation—to its historic commitments, its heritage, its higher values. This form of patriotism can criticize as well as affirm; it can be expressed in dissent as well as allegiance. A third kind of patriotism arises out of concern for national security and our "vital interests." This sort of patriotism is highly pragmatic and hardnosed and is concerned with assessing the nation's capabilities and the balances of power in the world.

In creating this Second Edition of *American Democracy* we hope to nurture the second form of patriotism—loyalty based on principle and an ethic of thoughtful involvement. If citizens become more skeptical and morally concerned, leaders also are likely to consider the ethical side of their policies more fully. Politics is and always will be about power, but power takes many forms. It can grow out of the barrel of a gun, as Mao Zedong and many others have argued and practiced. Or it can be shaped by the ethical concerns of citizens. If the world is not to end in paroxisms engulfing democracies and tyrannies alike, it may be that citizens who are skeptical patriots will be required to save it from the abyss.

APPENDIXES

A   *THE DECLARATION OF INDEPENDENCE*

B   *THE CONSTITUTION OF THE UNITED STATES*

C   *GLOSSARY OF TERMS*

THE DECLARATION OF INDEPENDENCE

When in the Course of human events, it becomes necessary for one people to dissolve the political bands which have connected them with another, and to assume among the Powers of the earth, the separate and equal station to which the Laws of Nature and of Nature's God entitle them, a decent respect to the opinions of mankind requires that they should declare the causes which impel them to the separation.

We hold these truths to be self-evident, that all men are created equal, that they are endowed by their Creator with certain unalienable Rights, that among these are Life, Liberty and the pursuit of Happiness. That to secure these rights, Governments are instituted among Men, deriving their just powers from the consent of the governed. That whenever any Form of Government becomes destructive of these ends, it is the Right of the People to alter or to abolish it, and to institute new Government, laying its foundation on such principles and organizing its powers in such form, as to them shall seem most likely to effect their Safety and Happiness. Prudence, indeed, will dictate that Governments long established should not be changed for light and transient causes; and accordingly all experience hath shown, that mankind are more disposed to suffer, while evils are sufferable, than to right themselves by abolishing the forms to which they are accustomed. But when a long train of abuses and usurpations, pursuing invariably the same Object evinces a design to reduce them under absolute Despotism, it is their right, it is their duty, to throw off such Government, and to provide new Guards for their future security.—Such has been the patient sufferance of these Colonies; and such is now the necessity which constrains them to alter their former Systems of Government. The history of the present King of Great Britain is a history of repeated injuries and usurpations, all having in direct object the establishment of an absolute Tyranny over these States. To prove this, let Facts be submitted to a candid world.

He has refused his Assent to Laws, the most wholesome and necessary for the public good.

He has forbidden his Governors to pass Laws of immediate and pressing importance, unless suspended in their operation till his Assent should be obtained; and when so suspended, he has utterly neglected to attend to them.

He has refused to pass other Laws for the accommodation of large districts of people, unless those people would relinquish the right of Representation in the Legislature, a right inestimable to them and formidable to tyrants only.

He has called together legislative bodies at places unusual, uncomfortable, and distant from the depository of their public Records, for the sole purpose of fatiguing them into compliance with his measures.

He has dissolved Representative Houses repeatedly for opposing with manly firmness his invasions on the rights of the people.

He has refused for a long time, after such dissolutions, to cause others to be elected; whereby the Legislative Powers, incapable of Annihilation, have returned to the People at large for their exercise; the State remaining in the mean time exposed to all the dangers of invasion from without, and convulsions within.

He has endeavoured to prevent the population of these States; for that purpose obstructing the Laws of Naturalization of Foreigners; refusing to pass others to encourage their migration higher, and raising the conditions of new Appropriations of Lands.

He has obstructed the Administration of Justice, by refusing his Assent to Laws for establishing Judiciary powers.

He has made Judges dependent on his Will alone, for the tenure of their offices, and the amount and payment of their salaries.

He has erected a multitude of New Offices, and sent hither swarms of Officers to harass our People, and eat out their substance.

He has kept among us in times of peace, Standing Armies without the Consent of our legislature.

He has affected to render the Military independent of and superior to the Civil power.

He has combined with others to subject us to a jurisdiction foreign to our constitution, and unacknowledged by our laws; giving his Assent to their acts of pretended Legislation.

For quartering large bodies of armed troops among us:

For protecting them, by a mock Trial, from punishment for any Murders which they should commit on the inhabitants of these States:

For cutting off our Trade with all parts of the world.

For imposing taxes on us without our Consent:

For depriving us in many cases, of the benefits of Trial by Jury:

For transporting us beyond Seas to be tried for pretended offences:

For abolishing the free System of English Laws in a neighbouring Province, establishing therein an Arbitrary government, and enlarging its Boundaries so as to render it at once an example and fit instrument for introducing the same absolute rule into these Colonies.

For taking away our Charters, abolishing our most valuable Laws, and altering fundamentally the Forms of our Governments:

For suspending our own Legislature, and declaring themselves invested with Power to legislate for us in all cases whatsoever.

He has abdicated Government here, by declaring us out of his Protection and waging War against us.

He has plundered our seas, ravaged our Coasts, burnt our towns, and destroyed the lives of our people.

He is at this time transporting large Armies of foreign Mercenaries to compleat the works of death, desolation and tyranny, already begun with circumstances of Cruelty & perfidy scarcely paralleled in the most barbarous ages, and totally unworthy the Head of a civilized nation.

He has constrained our fellow Citizens taken Captive on the high Seas to bear Arms against their Country, to become the executioners of their friends and Brethren, or to fall themselves by their Hands.

He has excited domestic insurrections amongst us, and has endeavoured to bring on the inhabitants of our frontiers, the merciless Indian Savages, whose known rule of warfare, is an undistinguished destruction of all ages, sexes and conditions.

In every stage of these Oppressions We have Petitioned for Redress in the most humble terms: Our repeated Petitions have been answered only by repeated injury. A Prince, whose character is thus marked by every act which may define a Tyrant, is unfit to be the ruler of a free People.

Nor have We been wanting in attention to our British brethren. We have warned them from time to time of attempts by their legislature to extend an unwarrantable jurisdiction over us. We have reminded them of the circumstances of our emigration and settlement here. We have appealed to their native justice and magnanimity, and we have conjured them by the ties of our common kindred to disavow these usurpations, which, would inevitably interrupt our connections and correspondence. They too have been deaf to the voice of justice and of consanguinity. We must, therefore, acquiesce in the necessity, which denounces our Separation, and hold them, as we hold the rest of mankind, Enemies in War, in Peace Friends.

We, therefore, the Representatives of the United States of America, in General Congress, Assembled, appealing to the Supreme Judge of the world for the rectitude of our intentions, do, in the Name, and by Authority of the good People of these Colonies, solemnly publish and declare, That these United Colonies are, and of Right ought to be Free and Independent States; that they are Absolved from all Allegiance to the British Crown, and that all political connection between them and the State of Great Britain, is and ought to be totally dissolved; and that as Free and Independent States, they have full Power to levy War, conclude Peace, contract Alliances, establish Commerce, and to do all other Acts and Things which Independent States may of right do. And for the support of this Declaration, with a firm reliance on the protection of divine Providence, we mutually pledge to each other our Lives, our Fortunes and our sacred Honor.

B

THE CONSTITUTION OF THE UNITED STATES

Outline of the Constitution

Article I	The Legislative Branch	⎫
Article II	The Executive Branch	⎬ The three branches of government
Article III	The Judicial Branch	⎭
Article IV	State and Territories	The other partners in the federal system
Article V	Amendments	A mechanism for changing the Constitution

[Italic type indicates passages that were altered by later amendments, which are specified in the notes.]

We the People of the United States, in Order to form a more perfect Union, establish Justice, insure domestic Tranquility, provide for the common defence, promote the general Welfare, and secure the Blessings of Liberty to ourselves and our Posterity, do ordain and establish this Constitution for the United States of America.[1]

[1]The *Preamble* "walks before" the Constitution and is used to understand the "intention of the Framers." This is a compact among *people*, not *states* (an important distinction when the federal government seeks to limit states' power).

ARTICLE I

Section 1   All legislative Powers herein granted shall be vested in a Congress of the United States, which shall consist of a Senate and House of Representatives.

Section 2   The House of Representatives shall be composed of Members chosen every second Year by the People of the several States, and the Electors in each State shall have the Qualifications requisite for Electors of the most numerous Branch of the State Legislature.[2]

No Person shall be a Representative who shall not have attained to the age of twenty-five Years, and been seven Years a Citizen of

[2]Voting qualifications for national elections are determined by each state, subject to federal limitations (see Amendments 15, 19, 24, 26).

[3]"Other persons" means slaves. The word *slavery* does not appear in the Constitution until Amendment 13, which abolishes it. Also see Amendment 14.

[4]Most representatives now represent more than half a million people. The Detroit area has more people today than the entire country had in 1789. Districts are drawn to have equal populations, but since they cannot cross state lines, variations exist. (The last census gave all of Alaska one district for only 400,000 residents.)

[5]"Impeachment" is only the formal charge of wrongdoing, like an indictment; removal from office is a separate task—the Senate's.

[6]See Amendment 17.

[7]See Amendment 17.

[8]Today the Senate majority leader (as a *party* official, unanticipated here) "leads" the Senate. The Vice-President seldom presides in the Senate, and the position is almost entirely ceremonial.

the United States, and who shall not, when elected, be an Inhabitant of that State in which he shall be chosen.

Representatives and direct Taxes shall be apportioned among the several States which may be included within this Union, according to their respective Numbers, *which shall be determined by adding to the whole Number of free Persons, including those bound to Service for a Term of Years,* and excluding Indians not taxed, *three fifths of all other persons.*[3] The actual Enumeration shall be made within three Years after the first Meeting of the Congress of the United States, and within every subsequent Term of ten Years, in such Manner as they shall by Law direct. The Number of Representatives shall not exceed one for every thirty Thousand, but each State shall have at Least one Representative; and until such enumeration shall be made, the State of New Hampshire shall be entitled to chuse three, Massachusetts eight, Rhode-Island and Providence Plantations one, Connecticut five, New-York six, New Jersey four, Pennsylvania eight, Delaware one, Maryland six, Virginia ten, North Carolina five, South Carolina five, and Georgia three.[4]

When vacancies happen in the Representation from any State, the Executive Authority thereof shall issue Writs of Election to fill such Vacancies.

The House of Representatives shall chuse their Speaker and other Officers; and shall have the sole Power of Impeachment.[5]

Section 3 The Senate of the United States shall be composed of two Senators from each State, *chosen by the Legislature thereof,*[6] for six Years; and each Senator shall have one Vote.

Immediately after they shall be assembled in Consequence of the first Election, they shall be divided as equally as may be into three Classes. The Seats of the Senators of the first Class shall be vacated at the Expiration of the second Year, of the second Class at the Expiration of the fourth Year, and of the third Class at the Expiration of the sixth Year, so that one third may be chosen every second Year; *and if Vacancies happen by Resignation, or otherwise, during the Recess of the Legislature of any State, the Executive thereof may make temporary Appointments until the next Meeting of the Legislature, which shall then fill such Vacancies.*[7]

No Person shall be a Senator who shall not have attained to the Age of thirty Years, and been nine Years a Citizen of the United States, and who shall not, when elected, be an Inhabitant of that State for which he shall be chosen.

The Vice President of the United States shall be President of the Senate, but shall have no Vote, unless they be equally divided.[8]

The Senate shall choose their other Officers, and also a President pro tempore, in the Absence of the Vice President, or when he shall exercise the Office of President of the United States.

The Senate shall have the sole Power to try all Impeachments. When sitting for that Purpose, they shall be on Oath or Affirmation. When the President of the United States is tried, the Chief Justice shall preside: And no Person shall be convicted without the Concurrence of two thirds of the Members present.

Judgment in Cases of Impeachment shall not extend further than to removal from Office, and disqualification to hold and enjoy any Office of honor, Trust or Profit under the United States: but the Party convicted shall nevertheless be liable and subject to Indictment, Trial, Judgment and Punishment, according to Law.[9]

Section 4   The Times, Places and Manner of holding Elections for Senators, and Representatives, shall be prescribed in each State by the Legislature thereof; but the Congress may at any time by Law make or alter such Regulations, except as to the Places of chusing Senators.

The Congress shall assemble at least once in a Year, and such Meeting shall be on the first Monday in December, unless they shall by Law appoint a different Day.[10]

Section 5   Each House shall be the Judge of the Elections, Returns and Qualifications of its own Members, and a Majority of each shall constitute a Quorum to do Business; but a smaller Number may adjourn from day to day, and may be authorized to compel the Attendance of absent Members, in such Manner, and under such Penalties as each House may provide.

Each House may determine the Rules of its Proceedings, punish its Members for disorderly Behavior, and, with the Concurrence of two thirds, expel a Member.[11]

Each House shall keep a Journal of its Proceedings, and from time to time publish the same, excepting such Parts as may in their Judgment require Secrecy; and the Yeas and Nays of the Members of either House on any question shall, at the Desire of one fifth of those Present, be entered on the Journal.

Neither House, during the Session of Congress, shall, without the Consent of the other, adjourn for more than three days, nor to any other Place than that in which the two Houses shall be sitting.

Section 6   The Senators and Representatives shall receive a Compensation for their Services, to be ascertained by Law, and paid out of the Treasury of the United States.[12] They shall in all Cases, except Treason, Felony and Breach of the Peace, be privileged from Arrest during their Attendance at the Session of their respective Houses, and in going and returning from the same; and for any Speech or Debate in either House, they shall not be questioned in any other Place.[13]

No Senator or Representative shall, during the Time for which he was elected, be appointed to any civil Office under the Authority of the United States, which shall have been created, or the Emoluments whereof shall have been increased during such time; and no Person holding any Office under the United States, shall be a Member of either House during his Continuance in Office.[14]

[9]The Watergate special prosecutor decided that Richard Nixon, as a sitting president, could not be indicted (he was termed "an unindicted co-conspirator" by the grand jury); but because he might have been indicted *after* leaving office, Nixon was granted a controversial pardon by his successor, Gerald Ford.

[10]See Amendment 20.

[11]Congress monitors itself. A central assumption of our system is that competing political interests eventually will detect and correct wrongdoing and bad policy. "Eventually" sometimes takes a while.

[12]Regular pay and extensive staff support allow Congress to be "professionalized"—members can devote full time to their legislative tasks. (Increasingly, though, they spend large portions of time raising money for their own elections.)

[13]Immunity from slander and libel charges is extended to speeches on the floor, in committee, or in the *Congressional Record* (which includes vast amounts of text never uttered in either House); the protection does *not* apply to members' newsletters.

[14]Members of Congress cannot simultaneously serve in the executive branch (as they can in parliamentary governments) or in the judiciary. The separation of powers is absolute in terms of personnel. Unfortunately, this separation frees presidents from the often healthy requirement of having to formulate and defend policy in open debate.

[15]Even a *threatened* veto increases the president's ability to persuade Congress on policy issues. But the veto is a blunt, all-or-nothing weapon, which does not allow the removal of particular provisions in a bill. A "line-item" veto would certainly alter this, but would it be an improvement? Does the president already have too much power over legislation? Before deciding, remember that we never know who the *next* president will be.

[16]The "presentment" requirement is one that the Supreme Court, in *INS* v. *Chadha* (462 U.S. 919 [1983]), found missing from the legislative veto; see Chapter 11. Requiring decisions to be shared across branches lets competing interests frame the issues in full, open debate. But it also slows things down and sometimes stymies policymaking altogether (as it has with efforts to create a coherent energy policy).

[17]Section 8 lists the powers of Congress, and thus of the federal government, representing, in positive form, complaints about the weaknesses of the Articles of Confederation. The "firm league of friendship" which the Articles created was replaced by a government that did not need the friendship of the states to carry out its will. Then, as now, the economy and national defense were dominant issues, as most of the following clauses demonstrate.

[18]The "interstate commerce clause" has been used to justify much federal activity in our century. Chief Justice John Marshall pointed out in 1824 (*Gibbons* v. *Ogden*, 9 Wheaton 1) that this clause reads "among" the states—not just between them—allowing the federal government to control commerce *within* states. In *Wickard* v. *Filburn* (317 U.S. 111 [1942]) the Supreme Court agreed that federal interstate commerce power extended even to twelve acres of wheat intended for use on the *same* small Ohio farm where it was grown.

[19]The vast power of the federal judiciary derives from the ability of Congress to establish a complete system of federal courts to implement federal policy.

Section 7   All Bills for raising Revenue shall originate in the House of Representatives; but the Senate may propose or concur with Amendments as on other Bills.

Every Bill which shall have passed the House of Representatives and the Senate, shall, before it become a Law, be presented to the President of the United States; if he approve he shall sign it, but if not he shall return it, with his Objections to that House in which it shall have originated, who shall enter the Objections at large on their Journal, and proceed to reconsider it.[15] If after such Reconsideration two thirds of that House shall agree to pass the Bill, it shall be sent, together with the Objections, to the other House, by which it shall likewise be reconsidered, and if approved by two thirds of that House, it shall become a Law. But in all such Cases the Votes of both Houses shall be determined by Yeas and Nays, and the Names of the Persons voting for and against the Bill shall be entered on the Journal of each House respectively. If any Bill shall not be returned by the President within ten Days (Sundays excepted) after it shall have been presented to him, the Same shall be a Law, in like Manner as if he had signed it, unless Congress by their Adjournment prevent its Return, in which Case it shall not be a Law.

Every Order, Resolution, or Vote to which the Concurrence of the Senate and House of Representatives may be necessary (except on a question of Adjournment) shall be presented to the President of the United States; and before the Same shall take Effect, shall be approved by him, or being disapproved by him, shall be re-passed by two thirds of the Senate and House of Representatives, according to the Rules and Limitations prescribed in the Case of a Bill.[16]

Section 8   The Congress shall have Power to lay and collect Taxes, Duties, Imposts, and Excises, to pay the Debts and provide for the common Defence and general Welfare of the United States;[17] but all Duties, Imposts and Excises shall be uniform throughout the United States;

To borrow Money on the credit of the United States;

To regulate Commerce with foreign Nations, and among the several States, and with the Indian Tribes;[18]

To establish an uniform Rule of Naturalization, and uniform Laws on the subject of Bankruptcies throughout the United States;

To coin Money, regulate the Value thereof, and of foreign Coin, and fix the Standard of Weights and Measures;

To provide for the Punishment of counterfeiting the Securities and Current Coin of the United States;

To establish Post Offices and post Roads;

To promote the Progress of Science and useful Arts, by securing for limited Times to Authors and Inventors the exclusive Right to their respective Writings and Discoveries:

To constitute Tribunals inferior to the Supreme Court;[19]

To define and punish Piracies and Felonies committed on the high Seas and Offences against the Law of Nations;

To declare War,[20] grant letters of Marque, and Reprisal, and make Rules concerning Captures on Land and Water;

To raise and support Armies, but no Appropriation of Money to that Use shall be for a longer Term than two Years;

To provide and maintain a Navy;

To make Rules for the Government and Regulation of the land and naval Forces;[21]

To provide for calling forth the Militia to execute the Laws of the Union, suppress Insurrections and repel Invasions:

To provide for organizing, arming, and disciplining, the Militia, and for governing such Part of them as may be employed in the Service of the United States, reserving to the States respectively, the Appointment of the Officers, and the Authority of training the Militia according to the discipline prescribed by Congress;[22]

To exercise exclusive Legislation in all Cases whatsoever, over such District (not exceeding ten Miles square) as may, by Cession of particular States, and the Acceptance of Congress, become the Seat of the Government of the United States,[23] and to exercise like Authority over all Places purchased by the Consent of the Legislature of the State in which the Same shall be, for the Erection of Forts, Magazines, Arsenals, dock-Yards, and other needful Buildings;—And

To make all Laws which shall be necessary and proper for carrying into Execution the foregoing Powers, and all other Powers vested by this Constitution in the Government of the United States, or in any Department or Officer thereof.[24]

Section 9   The Migration or Importation of such Persons as any of the States now existing shall think proper to admit, shall not be prohibited by the Congress prior to the Year one thousand eight hundred and eight, but a Tax or duty may be imposed on such Importation, not exceeding ten dollars for each Person.[25]

The Privilege of the Writ of Habeas Corpus shall not be suspended, unless when in Cases of Rebellion or Invasion the public Safety may require it.[26]

No Bill of Attainder or ex post facto Law shall be passed.[27]

No Capitation, or other direct, Tax shall be laid, unless in Proportion to the Census or Enumeration herein before directed to be taken.

No Tax or Duty shall be laid on Articles exported from any State.

No Preference shall be given any Regulation of Commerce or Revenue to the Ports of one State over those of another; nor shall Vessels bound to, or from, one State, be obliged to enter, clear, or pay Duties in another.

No Money shall be drawn from the Treasury, but in Consequence of Appropriations made by Law; and a regular Statement

[20]In our era of "troop incursions," "insurgency," and "counterinsurgency," declarations of war appear as relics of an ancient time. No war was declared in Korea or Vietnam, and no declaration of war can outdistance an ICBM. Under modern circumstances is there any way for Congress and the president to share the war power as the Framers intended? (See Chapter 11 on the War Powers Act.)

[21]Active members of the armed forces are subject to the Uniform Code of Military Justice and do *not* enjoy all the constitutional rights of civilians. Presumably, such rights would make military discipline impossible.

[22]In 1957, when Governor Orval Faubus used the Arkansas National Guard to help maintain segregation at Little Rock High School in defiance of a federal court, President Eisenhower called the Guard to national service, thus using the same troops to *integrate* the school.

[23]If one is caught speeding in the District of Columbia, or on an army base, it's a federal offense. Despite common usage, then, a "federal offense" is not necessarily more serious than an offense against state law. Most criminal prosecutions are state matters.

[24]This is the "elastic clause," the basis of the federal government's *implied powers*—as in the power to charter a bank in *McCullough* v. *Maryland* (4 Wheaton 316 [1819]; see Chapter 3).

[25]Section 9 lists what the federal government *cannot* do, including here a shameful provision protecting slavery for the first twenty years of the new government.

[26]*Habeus corpus* is a legal means of having a judge verify grounds for imprisonment, although this clause recognizes exceptions. Courts rarely interfere with military authority during wartime but have overturned military decisions after the conflict (see *Ex parte Milligan*, 4 Wallace 2 [1866]).

[27]Under a *bill of attainder* a legislature functions as a court, convicting and punishing individuals by legislation.

An *ex post facto law* creates criminal liability or increases criminal penalties for actions in the past.

[28]This published "Account of the Receipts and Expenditures of all public Money" does not include the CIA's budget, nor can it practically include large sums of money spent for national security.

[29]Since the Framers were in a restrictive mood, in Section 10 they listed what states cannot do. Similar provisions here and in Section 9—such as the prohibition of bills of attainder and ex post facto laws—mean that *no* government in the United States can engage in these activities.

The "Obligation of Contracts" clause reveals the Framers' fear that debtors, who naturally far outnumber creditors in our system, would prevail on states to wipe out debts through legislation. The Supreme Court had to stretch a bit to get around this clause in saving the Minnesota Mortgage Moratorium Act during the Depression (see *Home Building and Loan Association* v. *Blaisdell,* 290 U.S. 398 [1934]).

[30]The short length of Article II, and its position *after* the legislative article, indicates that the Framers viewed Congress as the focus of government. This century has seen a steady shifting of emphasis to the executive branch in the development of national policy (see Chapters 11 and 12).

[31]The Electoral College may seem anachronistic today, but it does increase the influence of certain groups and state actors who are unwilling to give it up. It also tends to increase the apparent margin of victory for a successful candidate, which, according to some, makes it easier for the new president to govern. Don't look for any change here soon. (See Chapter 12.)

[32]The bizarre circumstances of the election of 1800 demonstrated the weaknesses of the following provisions and caused the Constitution, indirectly, to acknowledge the existence of political parties. Thomas Jefferson and Aaron Burr, running on the same ticket, tied in Electoral College votes, throwing the election into the House of Representatives (which was controlled by the Federalists, whose can-

and Account of the Receipts and Expenditures of all public Money shall be published from time to time.[28]

No title of Nobility shall be granted by the United States: And no Person holding any Office of Profit or Trust under them, shall, without the Consent of the Congress, accept of any present, Emolument, Office, or Title, of any kind whatever, from any King, Prince, or foreign State.

Section 10 No State shall enter into any Treaty, Alliance, or Confederation; grant Letters of Marque and Reprisal; coin Money; emit Bills of Credit; make any Thing but gold and silver Coin a Tender in Payment of Debts; pass any Bill of Attainder, ex post facto Law, or Law impairing the Obligation of Contracts, or Grant any Title of Nobility.[29]

No state shall, without the Consent of the Congress, lay any Imposts or Duties on Imports or Exports, except what may be absolutely necessary for executing its inspection Laws: and the net Produce of all Duties and Imposts, laid by any State on Imports or Exports, shall be for the Use of the Treasury of the United States; and all such Laws be subject to the Revision and Control of the Congress.

No State shall, without the Consent of Congress, lay any Duty of Tonnage, keep Troops, or Ships of War in time of Peace, enter into any Agreement or Compact with another State, or with a foreign Power, or engage in War, unless actually invaded, or in such imminent Danger as will not admit of delay.

ARTICLE II

Section 1 The executive Power shall be vested in a President of the United States of America. He shall hold his Office during the Term of four Years, and, together with the Vice President, chosen for the same Term be elected as follows:[30]

Each State shall appoint, in such Manner as the Legislature thereof may direct, a Number of Electors, equal to the whole Number of Senators and Representatives to which the State may be entitled in the Congress; but no Senator or Representative, or Person holding an Office of Trust or Profit under the United States, shall be appointed an Elector.[31]

The Electors shall meet in their respective States, and vote by Ballot for two Persons, of whom one at least shall not be an Inhabitant of the same State with themselves.[32] And they shall make a List of all Persons voted for, and of the Number of Votes for each; which List they shall sign and certify, and transmit sealed to the Seat of the Government of the United States, directed to the President of the Senate. The President of the Senate shall, in the Presence of the Senate and House of Representatives, open all the Certificates, and the Votes shall then be counted. The Person having the greatest Number of Votes shall be the President, if such Number be a Majority of the whole Number of Electors appointed; and if there be more than one who have such Majority, and have an equal Number of Votes, then the House of Representatives shall immediately chuse by Ballot one of them for President; and if no Person have a Majority, then from the five highest on the List the said House shall in like Manner chuse the President. But in chusing the President, the votes shall be taken by States, the Representation from each State having one Vote; A quorum for this purpose shall consist of a Member or Members from two thirds of the States, and a majority of all the States shall be necessary to a Choice. In every Case, after the Choice of the President, the Person having the Greatest Number of Votes of the Electors shall be the Vice President. But if there should remain two or more who have equal Votes, the Senate shall chuse from them by Ballot the Vice President.[33]

The Congress may determine the Time of chusing the Electors, and the Day on which they shall give their Votes; which Day shall be the same throughout the United States.

No Person except a natural born Citizen, or a Citizen of the United States, at the time of the Adoption of this Constitution, shall be eligible to the Office of President; neither shall any Person be eligible to that Office who shall not have attained to the Age of thirty-five Years, and been fourteen Years a Resident within the United States.

The Case of the Removal of the President from Office, or of his Death, Resignation, or Inability to discharge the Powers and Duties of the said Office, the Same shall devolve on the Vice President, and the Congress may by Law provide for the Case of Removal, Death, Resignation, or Inability, both of the President and Vice President, declaring what Officer shall then act as President, and such Officer shall act accordingly, until the Disability be removed, or a President shall be elected.[34]

The President shall, at stated Times, receive for his Services, a Compensation which shall neither be encreased nor diminished during the Period for which he shall have been elected, and he shall not receive within that Period any other Emolument from the United States, or any of them.

Before he enter on the Execution of his Office, he shall take the following Oath or Affirmation:—"I do solemnly swear (or affirm) that I will faithfully execute the Office of President of the United States, and will to the best of my Ability, preserve, protect, and defend the Constitution of the United States."

Section 2　The President shall be Commander in Chief of the Army and Navy of the United States; and of the Militia of the several States, when called into the actual service of the United States; he may require the Opinion, in writing, of the principal Officer in each of the executive Departments, upon any Subject relating to the Duties of their respective Offices, and he shall have Power to grant Reprieves and Pardons for Offences against the United States, except in Case of Impeachment.[35]

He shall have Power, by and with the Advice and Consent of the Senate, to make Treaties, provided two thirds of the Senators present concur;[36] and he shall nominate, and by and with the

didate, incumbent President John Adams, had lost). Although Burr was originally understood to be the vice-presidential candidate, the tie produced much behind-the-scenes maneuvering in the House. This was resolved only when Alexander Hamilton threw his support behind his old rival, Jefferson. Four years later, Hamilton was killed by Burr in a duel.

The fact that the Constitution does not make political parties a formal part of the governing scheme has had some negative consequences. Southern segregationists for years excluded blacks from political participation by excluding them from "private" party functions (which were the sole avenue to public office). The Supreme Court originally agreed to that logic, but in 1944 ruled that Amendment 15 prohibits a party's primary from being restricted to white persons (see *Smith* v. *Allwright*, 321 U.S. 649 [1944]).

[33]See Amendment 12.

[34]Congress has provided for a line of succession that starts with the Speaker of the House of Representatives and the President Pro Tempore of the Senate before moving to cabinet officers, but Amendment 25 makes the use of this line of succession most unlikely.

[35]Compare this relatively puny list of presidential powers with those reserved for Congress in Article I, Section 8. The enormous influence that presidents can exercise over U.S. policy comes not from this list but from the opportunities that the presidency offers to inspire, goad, and guide the nation.

[36]Presidents also may sign Executive Agreements with other governments—without Senate ratification—and these may have the legal force of treaties.

[37] The president's appointment power is important—especially for judicial appointments—but it is subject to Senate confirmation. Should the Senate refuse to confirm a nominee based on policy differences, or only when the competence of the person is in question? The issue was raised but not resolved by the failed Supreme Court nominations of Abe Fortas, Clement Haynesworth, and Robert Bork.

[38] The annual State of the Union Address lets the president set before Congress and the nation the outlines of the administration's agenda for the year. These addresses rarely rise to inspirational heights, but one memorable moment came in 1988, when Ronald Reagan brandished thousands of pages of a budget resolution passed at the last minute and sent to him for signature. His point—that there must be something wrong with such a budget system—was well taken; unfortunately, no equally memorable solution was found.

[39] What is a "high crime"? The Constitution doesn't say. In the debate about impeaching Supreme Court Justice William O. Douglas, House Minority Leader Gerald Ford claimed that "high crimes" meant whatever the House decided it meant. His perspective no doubt changed when he became vice-president, and then president, upon the resignations of Spiro Agnew and Richard Nixon.

[40] The Constitution establishes only one court—the Supreme Court—on the assumption that, at least initially, state courts would be competent to decide matters of federal law. The first major legislation under this Constitution, the Judiciary Act of 1789, took advantage of the power here (and in Article I, Section 8) to create inferior federal courts. Thus, every state has two separate court systems, one federal and one state. (See Chapter 14.)

[41] In general, federal jurisdiction exists only when certain *laws* or certain *parties* are involved. The provisions here make sense: Broadly, if federal law (Constitution, statute, or treaty) is involved, or if the federal government is a party to the case, or if the parties come from across state boundaries, then the case can be heard by a federal court. Amendment 11 returns to the states only part of the prerogative of sovereign entities not to be taken to court without their own permission.

Advice and Consent of the Senate, shall appoint Ambassadors, and other public Ministers and Consuls, Judges of the supreme Court, and all other Officers of the United States, whose Appointments are not herein otherwise provided for, and which shall be established by Law;[37] but the Congress may by Law vest the Appointment of such inferior Officers, as they think proper, in the President alone, in the Courts of Law, or in the Heads of Departments.

The President shall have Power to fill up all Vacancies that may happen during the Recess of the Senate, by granting Commissions which shall expire at the End of their next Session.

Section 3   He shall from time to time give to the Congress Information of the State of the Union, and recommend to their Consideration such Measures as he shall judge necessary and expedient;[38] he may, on extraordinary Occasions, convene both Houses, or either of them, and in Case of Disagreement between them, with Respect to the Time of Adjournment, he may adjourn them to such Time as he shall think proper; he shall receive Ambassadors and other public Ministers, he shall take Care that the Laws be faithfully executed, and shall Commission all the Officers of the United States.

Section 4   The President, Vice President, and all civil Officers of the United States, shall be removed from Office on Impeachment for, and Conviction of, Treason, Bribery, or other High Crimes and Misdemeanors.[39]

ARTICLE III

Section 1   The judicial Power of the United States, shall be vested in one supreme Court and in such inferior Courts as the Congress may from time to time ordain and establish.[40] The Judges, both of the supreme and inferior Courts, shall hold their Offices during good Behavior, and shall, at stated Times, receive for their Services, a Compensation, which shall not be diminished during their Continuance in Office.

Section 2   The Judicial Power shall extend to all Cases, in Law and Equity, arising under this Constitution, the Laws of the United States, and Treaties made, or which shall be made, under their Authority;—to all Cases affecting Ambassadors, other public Ministers and Consuls;—to all Cases of admiralty and maritime Jurisdiction;—to Controversies to which the United States shall be a Party;—to Controversies between two or more States;—*between a State and Citizens of another State;*—between Citizens of different States;—between Citizens of the same State claiming Lands under Grants of different states, *and between a State, or the Citizens thereof, and foreign States, Citizens, or Subjects.*[41]

In all cases affecting Ambassadors, other public Ministers and Consuls, and those in which a State shall be Party, the supreme

Court shall have original Jurisdiction.[42] In all the other Cases before mentioned, the supreme Court shall have appellate Jurisdiction, both as to Law and Fact, with such Exceptions, and under such Regulations as the Congress shall make.

The Trial of all Crimes, except in Cases of Impeachment, shall be by Jury; and such Trial shall be held in the State where the said Crimes shall have been committed; but when not committed within any State, the Trial shall be at such Place or Places as the Congress may by Law have directed.[43]

Section 3   Treason against the United States, shall consist only in levying War against them, or in adhering to their Enemies, giving them Aid and Comfort. No person shall be convicted of Treason unless on the Testimony of two Witnesses to the same overt Act, or on Confession in open Court.[44]

The Congress shall have Power to declare the Punishment of Treason, but no Attainder of Treason shall work Corruption of Blood, or Forfeiture except during the Life of the Person attainted.[45]

ARTICLE IV

Section 1   Full Faith and Credit shall be given in each State to the public Acts, Records, and judicial Proceedings of every other State. And the Congress may by general Laws prescribe the Manner in which such Acts, Records, and Proceedings shall be proved, and the Effect thereof.

Section 2   The Citizens of each State shall be entitled to all Privileges and Immunities of Citizens in the several states.[46]

A Person charged in any State with Treason, Felony, or other Crime, who shall flee from Justice, and be found in another State, shall on Demand of the executive Authority of the State from which he fled, be delivered up, to be removed to the State having Jurisdiction of the Crime.

No Person held to Service or Labour in one State, under the Laws thereof, escaping into another, shall in Consequence of any Law or Regulation therein, be discharged from such Service or Labour, but shall be delivered up on Claim of the Party to whom such Service or Labour may be due.[47]

Section 3   New States may be admitted by the Congress into this Union; but no new State shall be formed or erected within the Jurisdiction of any other State; nor any State be formed by the Junction of two or more States, or Parts of States, without the Consent of the Legislatures of the States concerned as well as of the Congress.[48]

The Congress shall have Power to dispose of and make all needful Rules and Regulations respecting the Territory or other Property belonging to the United States; and nothing in this Constitution shall be so construed as to Prejudice any claims of the United States, or of any particular State.

[42]As a practical matter, the Supreme Court does *not* exercise its original jurisdiction—it doesn't have time to conduct trials, and so it leaves that to lower federal or state courts.

[43]The right to trial by jury in *civil* (not criminal) cases is guaranteed in Amendment 7.

[44]"Treason" was (and still is, in many places) a convenient charge for governments to use in dispensing with political opponents. The Framers took special care here to define treason and to establish specific legal requirements to prove such a charge.

[45]A *corruption of blood* is, literally, visiting the sins of the fathers upon the sons, or imposing penalties on the children and grandchildren of a wrongdoer—a strategy inconsistent with individual responsibility.

[46]Section 1 of Article IV concerns the relations of states to other states; Section 2 concerns the relations of states to *citizens* of other states. Both sections prescribe a sort of golden rule of fair play. Section 2 does not prevent a state from charging out-of-state tuition in its public universities and colleges, for example, but it would prohibit state courts from giving preferential treatment to state residents.

[47]Another of the constitutional provisions protecting slavery without mentioning it by name. See Amendment 13.

[48]The formation of new states was, for a time, bound up with the issue of slavery. Particularly striking was the case of West Virginia (a mountainous region where slave-based agriculture had never been feasible), which was created from the territory of Virginia at the onset of the Civil War.

[49]What is a "republican form" of government? One that is responsive, but not directly, to the people. But the simplicity of such a definition is often hard to apply (see the Introduction). The "republican guarantee" clause is now considered a nonjusticiable political question: A complaint under it must be addressed to Congress or the president, not to the courts. See *Luther* v. *Borden* (7 Howard 1 [1849]), a case arising from claims of two opposed governments to the rightful rule of Rhode Island.

[50]Although a convention to propose amendments has never been called, the *threat* of it, represented by numerous state petitions calling for one, has several times prompted Congress to propose amendments that otherwise would not have been proposed.

[51]With one exception, the task of ratification has always been given to state legislatures. The repeal of prohibition (see Amendments 18 and 21) was the exception—state legislators were glad to have Congress designate the state convention method for resolving that sticky issue.

[52]The "supremacy clause" explicitly makes federal law superior to state law and constitutions. Like the "elastic clause" (Article I, Section 8), this provision justifies certain federal powers. For example, in *Missouri* v. *Holland* (252 U.S. 416 [1920]), the use of federal power to protect migratory birds was justified on the basis of a treaty with Canada.

[53]The difference between an oath (before God) and an affirmation (before fellow citizens) is significant to certain groups like the Society of Friends (Quakers), whose religious beliefs forbid oaths.

[54]Although this passage forbids religious tests for public office, it was 172 years before the first Catholic president (Kennedy, in 1961) and 127 years before the first Jewish member of the Supreme Court (Brandeis, in 1915).

[55]This article, rather like the starter on your car, has no function after the mechanism is set in motion.

[56]Notice the claim to the unanimous consent of the *states*. Actually, fifty-five men attended the convention; nineteen others were chosen but declined. Thirty-nine signed the final document, including Washington, Hamilton, Madison, and Franklin. Thomas Jefferson and John Adams were both in Europe on diplomatic missions.

Section 4   The United States shall guarantee to every State in this Union a Republican Form of Government, and shall protect each of them against Invasion;[49] and on Application of the Legislature, or of the Executive (when the Legislature cannot be convened) against domestic Violence.

ARTICLE V

The Congress, whenever two thirds of both Houses shall deem it necessary, shall propose Amendments to this Constitution, or, on the Application of the Legislatures of two thirds of the several States, shall call a Convention for proposing Amendments,[50] which, in either Case, shall be valid to all Intents and Purposes, as Part of this Constitution, when ratified by the Legislatures of three fourths of the several States, or by Conventions in three fourths thereof, as the one or the other Mode of Ratification may be proposed by the Congress;[51] Provided that no Amendment which may be made prior to the Year One thousand eight hundred and eight shall in any Manner affect the first and fourth Clauses in the Ninth Section of the first Article; and that no State, without its Consent, shall be deprived of its equal Suffrage in the Senate.

ARTICLE VI

All Debts contracted and Engagements entered into, before the Adoption of this Constitution, shall be as valid against the United States under this Constitution, as under the Confederation.

This Constitution, and the Laws of the United States which shall be made in Pursuance thereof; and all Treaties made, or which shall be made, under the Authority of the United States, shall be the supreme Law of the Land; and the Judges in every State shall be bound thereby, any Thing in the Constitution or Laws of any State to the Contrary notwithstanding.[52]

The Senators and Representatives before mentioned, and the Members of the several State Legislatures, and all executive and judicial Officers, both of the United States and of the several States, shall be bound by Oath or Affirmation, to support this Constitution;[53] but no religious Test shall ever be required as a Qualification to any Office or public Trust under the United States.[54]

ARTICLE VII

The Ratification of the Conventions of nine States, shall be sufficient for the Establishment of this Constitution between the States so ratifying the Same.[55]

Done in Convention by the Unanimous Consent of the States[56] present the Seventeenth Day of September in the Year of our Lord one thousand seven hundred and eighty seven and of the Independence of the United States of America the twelfth. In witness whereof We have hereunto subscribed our Names.

* * *

Articles in addition to, and amendment of, the Constitution of the United States of America, proposed by Congress, and ratified by the several States, pursuant to the fifth Article of the original Constitution.[57]

AMENDMENT 1

Congress shall make no law respecting an establishment of religion, or prohibiting the free exercise thereof; or abridging the freedom of speech, or of the press; or the right of the people peaceably to assemble, and to petition the Government for a redress of grievances.[58]

AMENDMENT 2

A well regulated Militia, being necessary to the security of a free State, the right of the people to keep and bear Arms, shall not be infringed.[59]

AMENDMENT 3

No Soldier shall, in time of peace be quartered in any house, without the consent of the Owner, nor in time of war, but in a manner to be prescribed by law.[60]

AMENDMENT 4

The right of the people to be secure in their persons, houses, papers, and effects, against unreasonable searches and seizures, shall not be violated, and no Warrants shall issue, but upon probable cause, supported by Oath or affirmation, and particularly describing the place to be searched, and the persons or things to be seized.[61]

AMENDMENT 5

No person shall be held to answer for a capital, or otherwise infamous crime, unless on a presentment or indictment of a Grand Jury,[62] except in cases arising in the land or naval forces, or in the Militia, when in actual service in time of War or public danger; nor shall any person be subject for the same offence to be twice put in jeopardy of life or limb;[63] nor shall be compelled in any criminal case to be a witness against himself,[64] nor be deprived of life, liberty, or property, without due process of law;[65] nor shall private property be taken for public use, without just compensation.[66]

[57]The first ten amendments form the federal *Bill of Rights.* These (and two never ratified) were proposed by the first Congress, in 1791. Most of these federal restrictions were later "incorporated" under Amendment 14.

[58]The "expression" rights in the First Amendment are central to our understanding of democracy. Justice Hugo Black often pointed out the absolute language here ("*no* law"), but hard cases require *some* restriction, if only because these protections bump up against each other.

[59]Is our right to bear arms subordinate to states' rights to have militias? The Supreme Court tends to stay away from hotly contested policy matters, as with gun control.

[60]It's been a long time since "Guess who's coming to dinner?" included the possibility of an army regiment.

[61]Notice that we are protected only from *unreasonable* searches and seizures; most searches can be made "reasonable" through warrants secured from a judge or on the basis of "probable cause."

[62]A grand jury protects us from trumped-up charges, since the jury decides whether the prosecutor has enough evidence for a trial.

[63]The "double jeopardy" clause does not prevent a second trial if the first one was faulty (for example, if illegal evidence was admitted) or if the act constituted two separate offenses (assaulting a president in Atlanta, for example, violates both federal law and Georgia law, and can result in two separate prosecutions).

[64]"Taking the Fifth" means refusing to testify against oneself. This provision cannot be used to avoid appearing in a line-up or giving fingerprints. But should it include the right to refuse to give blood, semen, or tissue samples for identification purposes?

[65]"Due process" is a very old concept that has numerous applications. See Amendment 14.

[66]Do land-use restrictions that greatly reduce property's value constitute "taking without just compensation"? That argument was used (unsuccessfully) against the first zoning laws, and more recently against extensive environmental legislation.

[67]"Speedy trial" is not what it *can* be in our system, which encourages delays from both sides. A case may take more than a year to come to trial, be many months in trial, and then take years to exhaust appeals. Partly because of this, most criminal proceedings are resolved before a full trial, often through plea bargaining.

[68]The right to counsel originally meant that a defendant's lawyer could not be excluded from the courtroom; now it means that if a defendant cannot afford a lawyer in a criminal trial, the government must provide one. (See *Gideon* v. *Wainwright*, 372 U.S. 335 [1963].)

[69]This amendment refers to *civil cases*, disputes between two parties in which the court acts as umpire. In *criminal cases* (see Amendment 6) the government prosecutes an individual for violating a criminal statute.

[70]Is capital punishment "cruel and unusual"? A majority of the Supreme Court has never said that it is per se, but the Court has agreed that it is so under certain circumstances. What about executing someone who committed a capital crime while a minor? George J. Stinney, Jr., was *fourteen years old* when he was executed in 1944. As this text was going to press, the Court was trying to decide whether such executions are constitutional.

[71]One reason for not including a bill of rights in the original Constitution was that unlisted rights would be prejudiced. But how much protection does this passage give an unnamed right?

[72]A principle of constitutional interpretation is that every provision must have some legal effect. Is this amendment meant to be a barrier to federal action, or does it simply reflect the nature of the federal system? For arguments, see *National League of Cities* v. *Usery* (426 U.S. 833 [1976]) and *Garcia* v. *San Antonio Metropolitan Transit Authority* (469 U.S. 528 [1985]).

[73]In *Chishom* v. *Georgia* (2 Dallas 419 [1793]) a claim to recover a Revolutionary War debt against Georgia was allowed into a federal court. In response to that case, this amendment partially restores the states' sovereign ability to decide when to be sued.

[74]A reflection of the birth of political parties, this amendment separates the elections of the president and the vice-president in the electoral college. (See Article II, Sec. 1.)

AMENDMENT 6

In all criminal prosecutions, the accused shall enjoy the right to a speedy and public trial,[67] by an impartial jury of the State and district wherein the crime shall have been committed, which district shall have been previously ascertained by law, and to be informed of the nature and cause of the accusation; to be confronted with the witness against him; to have compulsory process for obtaining witness in his favor, and to have the Assistance of Counsel for his defence.[68]

AMENDMENT 7

In Suits at common law, where the value in controversy shall exceed twenty dollars, the right of trial by jury shall be preserved, and no fact tried by a jury, shall be otherwise re-examined in any Court of the United States, than according to the rules of the common law.[69]

AMENDMENT 8

Excessive bail shall not be required, nor excessive fines imposed, nor cruel and unusual punishments inflicted.[70]

AMENDMENT 9

The enumeration in the Constitution, of certain rights, shall not be construed to deny or disparage others retained by the people.[71]

AMENDMENT 10

The powers not delegated to the United States by the Constitution, nor prohibited by it to the States, are reserved to the States respectively, or to the people.[72]

AMENDMENT 11   [January 8, 1798]

The Judicial power of the United States shall not be construed to extend to any suit in law or equity, commenced or prosecuted against one of the United States by Citizens of another State, or by Citizens or Subjects of any Foreign State.[73]

AMENDMENT 12   [September 25, 1804]

The Electors shall meet in their respective states and vote by ballot for President and Vice President, one of whom, at least, shall not be an inhabitant of the same state with themselves[74]; they shall name in their ballots the person voted for as President, and in distinct ballots the person voted for as Vice President, and they shall make distinct lists of all persons voted for as President, and of all persons voted for as Vice President, and of the number of votes for each, which lists they shall sign and certify, and transmit sealed to the seat of the government of the United States, directed to the President of the Senate:—The President of the Senate shall, in the presence of the Senate and House of Representatives, open all the certificates and the votes shall then be counted;—The person having the greatest number of votes for President, shall be the President, if such number be a majority of the whole number of Electors appointed; and if no person have such majority, then from the persons having the highest numbers not exceeding three on the list of those voted for as President, the House of Representatives shall choose immediately, by ballot, the President. But in choosing the President, the votes shall be taken by states, the representation from each state having one vote; a quorum for this purpose shall consist of a member or members from two thirds of the states, and a majority of all the states shall be necessary to a choice. And if the House of Representatives shall not choose a President whenever the right of choice shall devolve upon them, *before the fourth day of March next following,*[75] then the Vice President shall act as President as in the case of the death or other constitutional disability of the President.—The person having the greatest number of votes as Vice President, shall be the Vice President, if such number be a majority of the whole number of Electors appointed, and if no person have a majority, then from the two highest numbers on the list, the Senate shall choose the Vice President; a quorum for the purpose shall consist of two-thirds of the whole number of Senators, and a majority of the whole number shall be necessary to a choice. But no person constitutionally ineligible to the office of President shall be eligible to that of Vice President of the United States.

AMENDMENT 13   [December 18, 1865]

Section 1   Neither slavery nor involuntary servitude, except as a punishment for crime whereof the party shall have been duly convicted, shall exist within the United States, or any place subject to their jurisdiction.[76]

Section 2   Congress shall have power to enforce this article by appropriate legislation.

AMENDMENT 14   [July 28, 1868]

Section 1   All persons born or naturalized in the United States, and subject to the jurisdiction thereof, are citizens of the United States and of the State wherein they reside. No state shall make or enforce any law which shall abridge the privileges or immunities of citizens of the United States; nor shall any state deprive any person of life, liberty, or property, without due process of law; nor deny to any person within its jurisdiction the equal protection of the laws.[77]

[75]See Amendment 20.

[76]Amendments 13, 14, and 15 are the "Civil War amendments," which, combined, attempt to eliminate the institution of slavery and its effects—a process that remains incomplete after 125 years (see Chapters 4 and 18).

[77]Amendment 14 is the most frequently litigated of all amendments, since it is the source of "incorporating" the Bill of Rights as protections against state action. It has three important clauses: (1) "privileges and immunities" (which was gutted by the *Slaughterhouse cases* in 1873 and never recovered); (2) "due process" (an ancient notion applied to actions as diverse as the right of a baker to contract freely for his own labor without regard for maximum-working-hour laws [see *Lochner* v. *New York* 198 U.S. 45 (1905)], and the right to view pornographic material in the privacy of one's home [see *Stanley* v. *Georgia* 394 U.S. 557 (1969)]); and (3) "equal protection," which is the focus for affirmative action and discrimination debates. Notice that "equal protection of the laws" does not mean equal treatment but, rather, treatment *as an equal.* See Chapters 4 and 18.

[78]This section was meant to exclude, with few exceptions, the entire leadership of the Southern states during the Civil War from holding public office. Was Reconstruction a noble but ill-fated attempt to move the nation radically toward a more egalitarian democracy? Or was it simply the victor grinding its heel on the vanquished?

[79]Lincoln had, at one time, advocated compensating former slaveholders for emancipation, but the bitterness of the war and Lincoln's assassination led to this less compromising position.

[80]Although a small, short-term, Court-approved income tax had helped finance the Civil War, when Congress tried to reinstitute it in 1894, the Court found it unconstitutional as a "direct tax" (*Pollock* v. *Farmers' Loan and Trust Co.*, 158 U.S. 601 [1895]). This amendment cleared the way for the one part of the federal government that everyone loves to hate—the Internal Revenue Service.

Section 2   Representatives shall be apportioned among the several States according to their respective numbers, counting the whole number of persons in each State, excluding Indians not taxed. But when the right to vote at any election for the choice of electors for President and Vice President of the United States, Representatives in Congress, the Executive and Judicial officers of a State, or the members of the Legislature thereof, is denied to any of the male inhabitants of such State, being twenty one years of age, and citizens of the United States, or in any way abridged, except for participation in rebellion, or other crime, the basis of representation therein shall be reduced in the proportion which the number of such male citizens shall bear to the whole number of male citizens twenty one years of age in such State.

Section 3   No person shall be a Senator or Representative in Congress, or elector of President and Vice President, or hold any office, civil or military, under the United States, or under any State who having previously taken an oath, as a member of Congress, or as an officer of the United States, or as a member of any State legislature, or as an executive or judicial officer of any State, to support the Constitution of the United States, shall have engaged in insurrection or rebellion against the same, or given aid or comfort to the enemies thereof. But Congress may by a vote of two thirds of each House remove such disability.[78]

Section 4   The validity of the public debt of the United States authorized by law, including debts incurred for payment of pensions and bounties for services in suppressing insurrection or rebellion shall not be questioned. But neither the United States nor any State shall assume or pay any debt or obligation incurred in aid of insurrection or rebellion against the United States, or any claim for the loss or emancipation of any slave; but all such debts, obligations, and claims shall be held illegal and void.[79]

Section 5   The Congress shall have power to enforce, by appropriate legislation, the provisions of this article.

AMENDMENT 15   [March 30, 1870]

Section 1   The right of citizens of the United States to vote shall not be denied or abridged by the United States or by any State on account of race, color, or previous condition of servitude.

Section 2   The Congress shall have power to enforce this article by appropriate legislation.

AMENDMENT 16   [February 25, 1913]

The Congress shall have power to lay and collect taxes on incomes, from whatever source derived, without apportionment among the several States, and without regard to any census or enumeration.[80]

AMENDMENT 17 [May 31, 1913]

The Senate of the United States shall be composed of two Senators from each State, elected by the people thereof, for six years; and each September shall have one vote. The electors in each State shall have the qualifications requisite for electors of the most numerous branch of the State legislatures.[81]

When vacancies happen in the representation of any State in the Senate, the executive authority of such State shall issue writs of election to fill such vacancies: *Provided,* That the legislature of any State may empower the executive thereof to make temporary appointments until the people fill the vacancies by election as the legislature may direct.

This amendment shall not be so construed as to affect the election or term of any Senator chosen before it becomes valid as part of the Constitution.

[81]The Senate, with appointments from state legislatures, had become a club of millionaires. Although this amendment helped democratize American government, the Senate—according to certain calculations—is still a millionaires' club.

AMENDMENT 18 [January 29, 1919]

Section 1 *After one year from the ratification of this article the manufacture, sale, or transportation of intoxicating liquors within, the importation thereof into, or the exportation thereof from the United States and all territory subject to the jurisdiction thereof for beverage purposes is hereby prohibited.*[82]

Section 2 *The Congress and the several States shall have concurrent power to enforce this article by appropriate legislation.*

Section 3 *This article shall be inoperative unless it shall have been ratified as an amendment to the Constitution by the legislatures of the several States, as provided in the Constitution, within seven years from the date of submission hereof to the States by the Congress.*

[82]Should hard drugs be legalized? Serious advocates of such a policy cite the failure of Amendment 18 as evidence that legal attempts to deter consumption fail in their primary goal while encouraging lawlessness and organized crime. The "noble experiment" of Prohibition was ended, after nearly fifteen years, by Amendment 21.

AMENDMENT 19 [August 26, 1920]

The right of citizens of the United States to vote shall not be denied or abridged by the United States or by any State on account of sex.[83]

Congress shall have power to enforce this article by appropriate legislation.

[83]Except for the Bill of Rights, the largest cluster of amendments concerns expanding suffrage (15, 19, 23, 24, and 26) or altering electoral procedures (12, 17, 20, and 22). The central importance of elections to democracy is well reflected in our Constitution.

AMENDMENT 20 [February 6, 1933]

Section 1 The terms of the President and Vice President shall end at noon on the 20th day of January, and the terms of Senators and Representatives at noon on the 3rd day of January, of the years in which such terms would have ended if this article had not been ratified; and the terms of their successors shall then begin.[84]

[84]When the Constitution was written, winter travel was difficult, and the pace of public events was much slower. By the 1930s the long gap between the presidential election early in November and the inauguration late in March seemed to allow too much time for mischief by "lame ducks."

Section 2   The Congress shall assemble at least once in every year, and such meeting shall begin at noon on the 3rd day of January unless they shall by law appoint a different day.

Section 3   If, at the time fixed for the beginning of the term of the President, the President elect shall have died, the Vice President elect shall become President. If a President shall not have been chosen before the time fixed for the beginning of his term, or if the President elect shall have failed to qualify, then the Vice President elect shall act as President until a President shall have qualified; and the Congress may by law provide for the case wherein neither a President elect nor a Vice President elect shall have qualified, declaring who shall then act as President, or the manner in which one who is to act shall be selected, and such person shall act accordingly until a President or Vice President shall have qualified.

Section 4   The Congress may by law provide for the case of the death of any of the persons from whom the House of Representatives may choose a President whenever the right of choice shall have developed upon them, and for the case of the death of any of the persons from whom the Senate may choose a Vice President whenever the right of choice shall have devolved upon them.

Section 5   Sections 1 and 2 shall take effect on the 15th day of October following the ratification of this article.

Section 6   This article shall be inoperative unless it shall have been ratified as an amendment to the Constitution by the legislatures of three fourths of the several States within seven years from the date of its submission.[85]

AMENDMENT 21   [December 5, 1933]

Section 1   The eighteenth article of amendment to the Constitution of the United States is hereby repealed.

Section 2   The transportation or importation into any State, Territory, or possession of the United States for delivery or use therein of intoxicating liquors, in violation of the laws thereof, is hereby prohibited.

Section 3   This article shall be inoperative unless it shall have been ratified as an amendment to the Constitution by conventions in the several States, as provided in the Constitution, within seven years from the date of the submission hereof to the States by the Congress.[86]

AMENDMENT 22   [February 26, 1951]

Section 1   No person shall be elected to the office of the President more than twice, and no person who has held the office of President, or acted as President, for more than two years of a term to which some other person was elected President shall be elected

[85]Provisions like this are a means of keeping the books clear of unratified amendments. The proposed Equal Rights Amendment had such a provision, although the time limit for ratification was extended by Congress (to no avail: The second deadline passed without the votes needed for ratification).

[86]The repealing of Prohibition is the only amendment submitted to conventions in each state for ratification. Elected officials are naturally (and reasonably) wary of passionately debated issues that involve a large bipolar split. To side with either faction is to lose. It is far wiser to ignore such issues, if possible—and to pass them along to someone else, if not.

to the office of President more than once. But this Article shall not apply to any person holding the office of President when this Article was proposed by the Congress, and shall not prevent any person who may be holding the office of President, or acting as President, during the term within which this Article becomes operative from holding the office of President or acting as President during the remainder of such term.[87]

Section 2   This article shall be inoperative unless it shall have been ratified as an amendment to the Constitution by the legislatures of three fourths of the several States within seven years from the date of its submission to the States by the Congress.

AMENDMENT 23   [March 29, 1961]

Section 1   The District constituting the seat of Government of the United States shall appoint in such manner as the Congress may direct:

A number of electors of President and Vice President equal to the whole number of Senators and Representatives in Congress to which the District would be entitled if it were a State, but in no event more than the least populous State; they shall be in addition to those appointed by the States, but they shall be considered, for the purposes of the election of President and Vice President, to be electors appointed by a State; and they shall meet in the District and perform such duties as provided by the twelfth article of amendment.[88]

Section 2   The Congress shall have power to enforce this article by appropriate legislation.

AMENDMENT 24   [January 23, 1964]

Section 1   The rights of citizens of the United States to vote in any primary or other election for President or Vice President, for electors for President or Vice President, or for Senator or Representative in Congress, shall not be denied or abridged by the United States or any state by reason of failure to pay any poll tax or other tax.[89]

Section 2   The Congress shall have power to enforce this article by appropriate legislation.

AMENDMENT 25   [February 10, 1967]

Section 1   In case of the removal of the President from office or of his death or resignation, the Vice President shall become President.

Section 2   Whenever there is a vacancy in the office of the Vice President, the President shall nominate a Vice President who shall take office upon confirmation by a majority vote of both Houses of Congress.[90]

[87]Some see Amendment 22 as a posthumous slap at Franklin Roosevelt, the only president to break the two-term tradition established by Washington (who was ready to retire anyway). Would a single, six-year term be better, allowing presidents to make their mark but eliminating shortsighted first-term policy-making aimed mostly at ensuring reelection? There are valid arguments on both sides of this question, but don't expect much tinkering in this area.

[88]It was odd that, before this amendment, residents of the Capital (the one city absolutely obsessed with the operation of federal government) were unable to vote in presidential elections. Another proposal, not yet ratified, would give the District of Columbia voting representation in Congress as though it were a state.

[89]Strictly speaking, a poll tax is a "capitation" tax—a tax levied on every individual *as* individual. In the South, however, the poll tax was one of several means to deny blacks access to voting polls. This amendment, along with the Civil Rights Act of 1964 and the Voting Rights Act of 1965, has radically transformed electoral politics in the South. (See Chapters 4 and 18.)

[90]This is the only presidential appointment that must be approved by *both* houses of Congress. The nation's two top offices thus become self-regenerating, as evidenced by President Gerald Ford and his vice-president, Nelson Rockefeller. President Nixon chose Ford to be vice-president when Spiro Agnew resigned; Ford then became president when Nixon resigned, and he chose Rockefeller to be vice-president.

[91]Section 3 was used formally only once, when Ronald Reagan underwent surgery.

[92]The provisions in Section 4 regarding a president's disability are untested and fraught with potential difficulties. What if the vice-president and the required number of cabinet officials perceive a disability to exist but the president refuses to agree? Can Congress make a dispassionate, nonpartisan determination of a sitting president's ability to resume power? The dramatic possibilities are infinite.

Section 3   Whenever the President transmits to the President pro tempore of the Senate and the Speaker of the House of Representatives his written declaration that he is unable to discharge the powers and duties of his office, and until he transmits to them a written declaration to the contrary, such powers and duties shall be discharged by the Vice President as Acting President.[91]

Section 4   Whenever the Vice President and a majority of either the principal officers of the executive departments or of such other body as Congress may by law provide, transmit to the President pro tempore of the Senate and the Speaker of the House of Representatives their written declaration that the President is unable to discharge the powers and duties of his office, the Vice President shall immediately assume the powers and duties of the office as Acting President.

Thereafter, when the President transmits to the President pro tempore of the Senate and the Speaker of the House of Representatives his written declaration that no inability exists, he shall resume the powers and duties of his office unless the Vice President and a majority of either the principal officers of the executive department[s] or of such other body as Congress may by law provide, transmit within four days to the President pro tempore of the Senate and the Speaker of the House of Representatives their written declaration that the President is unable to discharge the powers and duties of his office. Thereupon Congress shall decide the issue, assembling within forty-eight hours for that purpose if not in session. If the Congress, within twenty-one days after receipt of the latter written declaration, or, if Congress is not in session, within twenty-one days after Congress is required to assemble, determines by two-thirds vote of both Houses that the President is unable to discharge the powers and duties of his office, the Vice President shall continue to discharge the same as Acting President; otherwise, the President shall resume the powers and duties of his office.[92]

AMENDMENT 26   [June 30, 1971]

[93]When does a child become an adult? The age of majority has many legal definitions. Before this amendment, 18-year-olds could be drafted but could not vote in many states; even after it, in most states they could vote but could not buy alcohol. In several states, persons too young to vote, be drafted, or buy a drink can be executed for a capital crime.

Section 1   The right of citizens of the United States, who are 18 years of age or older, to vote shall not be denied or abridged by the United States or by any state on account of age.[93]

Section 2   The Congress shall have power to enforce this article by appropriate legislation.

GLOSSARY OF TERMS

acid rain A highly acidic form of precipitation caused by the combustion of fossil fuels, which can kill aquatic life and vegetation and may introduce dangerous pollutants into drinking water.

advocacy advertising Corporate advertising in the form of well-reasoned essays in prominent news media, designed to build a favorable corporate image and boost public support for the corporation, its products, and goals.

affirmative action The attempt to remedy past discrimination by favoring minorities or women in hiring in certain federal or federally funded programs.

Aid to Families with Dependent Children (AFDC) A welfare program begun in the 1930s to provide assistance to mothers raising children by themselves; program most commonly thought of as "welfare."

alienation The sense of being an outsider, leading to feelings of powerlessness, futility, or meaninglessness.

amendment Addition to the U.S. Constitution; must be proposed by the Congress and then ratified by at least three quarters of the states.

Antifederalists Those at the 1787 Constitutional Convention who opposed the new Constitution, primarily citizens of rural and poorer areas.

Articles of Confederation The first written constitution, ratified by the thirteen states shortly before the end of the War of Revolution (1781); established a weak national government and left strong powers to the states.

basic rights Fundamental claims that are believed to inhere in individuals as individuals and that government and society should honor, such as the right to equal protection and expression.

bicameral Term referring to a lawmaking body composed of two houses; the system adopted for the U.S. Congress and most state governments.

Bill of Rights The first ten amendments to the U.S. Constitution, which supporters of the document (Federalists) agreed to add in response to criticisms and to ensure the protection of various rights and liberties.

biomass All organic waste materials, such as animal manure, garbage, rotting plants and trees, and, particularly, crops raised for the purpose of supplying fuel.

blanket primary An election in which voters can choose to vote in more than one party's primary for different offices—for example, the Democratic primary for senator and the Republican primary for governor.

Brown v. Board of Education of Topeka The 1954 U.S. Supreme Court ruling that segregated schools were unconstitutional.

bureaucracy The complex, hierarchically arranged organization composed of small subdivisions with specialized functions that carries out the day-to-day work of government.

619

cabinet The fourteen heads of the major federal administrative departments, plus any others specially designated by the president.

cabinet departments The sections of the federal executive branch represented in the cabinet that comprise the bulk of the federal bureaucracy and employ the majority of federal workers.

capitalism An economic system characterized by private ownership of most wealth and based on full freedom to buy and sell, accumulate wealth, and conduct business without government interference.

cash transfers Method of disbursing benefits from welfare-state programs, such as cash payments for Social Security or various types of public assistance to the poor.

Central Intelligence Agency (CIA) The chief intelligence-gathering agency of the U.S. government; also engages in covert action.

checks and balances The political ideal embodied in the separation of powers, whereby each branch of government serves as a limit or check on the powers of the others.

Circuit Courts See U.S. Courts of Appeals.

civil disobedience A public act committed to arouse the conscience of society by a person fully willing to accept the punishment for that action prescribed by law.

civil liberties Basic freedoms embodied in the Bill of Rights designed to protect citizens from the abuses of government.

civil rights Constitutional guarantees that all citizens receive equal treatment under the law, regardless of race, gender, national origin, or religion.

Civil Rights Act of 1964 Legislation passed by Congress prohibiting segregation in public accommodations and discrimination in hiring based on race, religion, color, sex, or national origin.

Civil Rights Restoration Act of 1988 Legislation passed in Congress to expand the mandate of the 1972 law barring gender discrimination in educational institutions to include age, handicap, and race.

Civil Service System A method of filling government posts based on "merit" as determined through competitive examinations overseen by the Civil Service Commission; contrast with the spoils system (q.v.).

Clean Air Act of 1963 Legislation that establishes national air quality standards; amendments added in 1970 strengthened the act considerably.

"clear and present danger" An interpretation of the conflict between free speech and public order elaborated by Justice Oliver Wendell Holmes in the 1920s. The doctrine argues that only speech presenting a "clear and present danger" can be limited, as when someone shouts "fire" in a crowded theater.

clientele groups Interest groups that are directly affected by bureaucratic agencies; for example, labor unions are clientele groups of the Labor Department.

closed primary Election in which only voters registered in a particular party may vote in that party's primary election.

Cold War Global rivalry between the United States and the Soviet Union carried on since the late 1940s that has divided the world into communist and Western spheres of influence.

Common Cause A general-purpose public interest lobby formed in 1970 that frequently focuses on procedural issues in Congress and supports public campaign financing and reform of the laws pertaining to lobbying disclosure.

comparable worth The concept that men and women should be paid according to equitable pay standards, instead of unequal standards based on gender discrimination.

concurrent powers Those powers exercised by both national and state governments, for example, the power to tax.

Congressional Budget Office (CBO) A research arm of Congress formed to aid Congress in dealing with budget issues; serves as a counterweight to the executive branch's Office of Management and Budget (OMB).

Connecticut Compromise Compromise of the Constitutional Convention of 1787 by which Congress would be bicameral: in the Senate each state would have two representatives, and in the House of Representatives the representation would be proportional to population.

conservatives In modern usage, those whose political philosophy stresses the virtues of individualism, unfettered economic activity, and minimal government involvement except in matters of defense.

containment A term coined in 1947 by George Kennan to describe the doctrine of "containing" the expansionist thrust of Soviet power until the Soviets learned to accommodate themselves to global realities.

contract bureaucracies Private firms hired by the government to perform the work of government, for example, defense contractors who build military hardware.

controlled capitalism Contemporary economic policy characterized by limited and specific government intervention in the regulation of the economy.

counterforce An influential doctrine developed in the late 1950s regarding nuclear weapons that argued for the need for a U.S. first-strike capability that would leave the Soviet Union defenseless by destroying its nuclear weapons before they could be deployed against the United States.

cross-over primary voting Voting for a candidate of the opposing party in the primary, especially a weak candidate, in order to advance the electoral chances of a different candidate.

defendant The person charged with a crime in a legal proceeding.

Defense Department The agency of the U.S. government that coordinates the country's military services to carry out the administration's defense policy.

deferred issues Public issues that are likely to return in one form or another if they are not originally dealt with satisfactorily.

delegated powers Those powers that the U.S. Constitution specifically assigns to the jurisdiction of the national government.

democracy A system of government based on majority rule, providing protections for individual rights and liberties, and striving to achieve a significant degree of equality among its citizens.

Democratic Party Dominant force in American political life after the 1828 election of Andrew Jackson as president.

Democratic-Republicans A political party that emerged in the 1820s from the split within the Republican party. A coalition of small farmers, small property owners, and local political leaders in the southern and mid-Atlantic states, it came to dominate American politics and was renamed the Democratic party.

democratic socialist parties Political parties that support socialism within the context of democratic government; examples are the British Labor Party and the French Socialist Party.

deregulation The drive to eliminate many existing government regulations and to reduce the power of regulartory agencies.

détente A phase of improved U.S.–Soviet relations in the early 1970s associated mainly with the Nixon administration.

direct legislation The establishment of a law by methods that bypass established legislative mechanisms; usually involves initiatives and/or referenda (q.v.).

direct socialization The process by which children are deliberately taught specific political views, values, and behaviors.

displaced issues Public issues that flare up and then fade from public view, to be replaced by other issues or fragments of the original issue.

diverted issues Public issues that are handled by calling for a reevaluation of the problems involved.

Domestic Council Body created by President Nixon in 1970 to formulate and coordinate presidential domestic policy.

Dred Scott* v. *Sanford 1857 Supreme Court case that upheld the Missouri Compromise, allowing the extension of slavery in the territories. The Fourteenth Amendment (q.v.) overturned the *Dred Scott* decision.

due process of law Procedural legal guarantees against the arbitrary use of government power, including guarantees of life, liberty, and property for citizens acting within the laws.

effluent The polluted water released by cities and industries. Amendments to the federal Water Pollution Control Act passed in 1972 were designed to control the disposal of effluent by establishing schedules and standards.

egalitarian democracy Rule by the people based on a redistribution of wealth, equalization of educational opportunities, and enforcement of laws protecting individuals from exploitation.

electoral college Electors from the fifty states who formally elect the president and vice-president. Each state's electors are equal to its number of representatives and senators in Congress.

enabling act An act of Congress allowing the citizens of a territory to draft a state constitution as part of the procedure for admission to the Union as a state.

entitlement programs Items in the national budget to which certain groups are automatically "entitled" by law, for example, Social Security for the elderly.

environmental impact statements Federally mandated reports spelling out specific environmental effects; must be prepared whenever proposals for legislation or other federal actions may significantly affect the quality of the environment.

Environmental Protection Agency (EPA) Body created in 1970 as a federal agency to coordinate national policy for issues affecting the environment.

equal protection of the laws The constitutional guarantee that no individual or group can be denied rights and privileges that are granted to others.

Equal Rights Amendment Proposed amendment to the U.S. Constitution, providing equality for women in all areas; defeated in 1982.

establishment clause Portion of the First Amendment to the U.S. Constitution commanding that Congress make no law "respecting an establishment of religion."

executive agreement An arrangement between a president and a foreign nation that, unlike treaties, is not subject to Senate approval.

Executive Office of the President The complex of auxiliary services, including staff support, research, and high-level consultative bodies that provide the president with assistance.

extraordinary politics The politics of protest and mass involvement.

Fairness Doctrine Rule originally established by the Federal Communications Commission to require broadcasters to provide "equal time" for opposing viewpoints; abolished in 1987 after President Reagan vetoed congressional attempts to make it law.

Federal District Courts The lowest level of the federal court system, which uses both grand and petit juries (q.v.) and from which appeals may be made to the next federal level of court.

Federal Reserve System An independent regulatory agency that controls the U.S. money supply. It functions essentially as the central bank of the United States.

federal system A form of government characterized by a constitutional division of power between national and local levels.

The Federalist Papers Essays written by James Madison and Alexander Hamilton in 1787–1788 stressing the need for a strong central government and defending the new Constitution.

Federalists Supporters of the Constitution at the Constitutional Convention of 1787.

filibuster A Senate tradition by which vote on pending legislation may be delayed or killed by a senator's engaging in unlimited speechmaking. A filibuster may be terminated only by a vote of cloture.

First Amendment The amendment to the U.S. Constitution that provides for freedoms of speech, assembly, and press; for the right to petition for the redress of grievances; for the protection of religious freedom; and for the separation of church and state.

fiscal policies Government policies that involve the deliberate manipulation of elements of the national budget to change the direction of the economy.

food stamp program A welfare program designed to give recipients greater purchasing power in the supermarket by making available stamps that have greater redemption value than their cost.

fossil fuels   Nonrenewable energy sources created from organic matter (fossils).

Fourteenth Amendment   Amendment to the U.S. Constitution ratified in 1868 that extended citizenship to the former slaves and provided the basis for a unitary national civil rights policy.

free enterprise   An economic system that proposes that supply and demand be allowed to regulate the marketplace without government interference.

free-exercise clause   Part of the First Amendment to the U.S. Constitution commanding that the Congress make no law "prohibiting the free exercise" of religion.

Freedom of Information Act   Congressional act originally passed in 1966 and amended in 1974 entitling citizens access to government information, including some classified documents.

full faith and credit   A Constitutional provision that each state accept as valid the legal proceedings and records of every other state.

gay rights   Term used to describe those legal remedies being sought by homosexual men and women to eliminate discrimination on the basis of sexual orientation.

gender discrimination   Discrimination on the basis of gender, especially in the area of pay, employment, and availability of such resources as education.

Gramm-Rudman-Hollings   The title of a 1985 congressional antideficit law (named for its Senate sponsors) that set 1993 as a target for a balanced budget and specified interim deficit reductions for each year. The enforcement of automatic spending cuts was ruled unconstitutional by the Supreme Court for violating the separation of powers.

grand juries   Bodies of jurors who determine if there is enough evidence to warrant a trial by petit jury in a specific case.

gross national product   The value of all goods and services produced by a nation.

human rights   Basic rights that are considered to belong to all human beings, for example, the right to decent treatment, to be free from torture, and to have a voice in shaping one's own government.

ideology   A highly structured system of ideas applied to political and social issues in a coherent manner.

Immigration and Reform Act of 1986   Legislation designed to address three issues raised by the increase in illegal immigration into the United States: amnesty for those already in this country; enforcement of immigration laws; and employer sanctions, designed to prevent employers from hiring undocumented illegal immigrants.

impeachment   A legal procedure that empowers Congress to remove the president from office through trial by the U.S. Senate.

implied powers   Those powers not specifically enumerated in the Constitution that are useful to Congress in carrying out its delegated powers.

incremental politics   Policy making in steps, or increments, which describes much of the day-to-day business of government.

incumbent   The person currently holding a particular political office.

indirect socialization   The acquisition of attitudes and behavior patterns through emulation rather than deliberate teaching.

inherent powers   Those powers integral to national sovereignty, for example, the power to wage war.

initiative   Mechanism by which citizens, through petition, can present a measure directly to voters, thus circumventing the legislature.

in-kind transfers   Components of welfare-state programs that supply a specific kind of help as opposed to cash, for example, food stamps, or Medicaid benefits.

interelection stage   Elected officials' time in office between elections.

interest-group liberalism   Pattern of decision making described by Theodore Lowi, in which each participant in a political controversy receives something and therefore has some impact on the decision-making process.

interest groups   Nongovernmental organizations unified by common goals or attitudes that organize and lobby in order to influence policy formulation and implementation.

Intermediate Nuclear Forces (INF) Treaty   Agreement signed by President Reagan and Soviet General Secretary Gorbachev in December 1987 that calls for the scheduled bilateral elimination of short- and intermediate-range nuclear weapons.

interventionist One who argues for involvement in the affairs of other countries, often in military terms, as a tool of foreign policy.

isolationism The policy of keeping the United States separate from, and uninvolved in, affairs outside the Western Hemisphere; a dominant force in U.S. foreign policy from the 1790s until the 1940s.

Joint Chiefs of Staff A committee made up of the heads of each of the armed services, with a chief appointed by the president, which oversees military policy matters and reports to Congress and the president.

judicial review Power of the federal courts to review the acts of federal and state legislatures as well as the actions of executive agencies to determine if they conform to the provisions of the U.S. Constitution.

Keynesian economics Economic practices based on the theories of John Maynard Keynes, who argued that governments could use tax policy and government expenditures, including deficit spending, to stimulate economic recovery and growth.

laissez faire An economic policy that favors nonintervention by government in a nation's economy.

laissez-faire capitalism An economic policy in which government allows business to operate relatively free of regulation.

liberal In modern usage, one who favors strong protections for civil rights and liberties as well as government involvement to remedy economic problems and social injustices.

liberal democracy A form of government in which majority rule is combined with respect for civil liberties and protection of individual rights.

liberalism A political philosophy in which social and political values are based on a belief in government by consent of the governed and in which rights and liberties are guaranteed to all persons.

majoritarian democracy Rule by the people based on preferences of more than 50 percent of voters.

majority leader Chief floor leader for his or her party in the U.S. House of Representatives or Senate and the person charged with mobilizing party support during roll-call votes.

majority rule Decision making by more than 50 percent of the voters.

majority sentiment The view on particular issues held by a majority of the public.

mandatory testing Medical testing mandated by law; an issue in the 1980s with regard to testing individuals for drug use and for AIDS.

Marbury* v. *Madison The 1803 U.S. Supreme Court Case in which the Court set forth for the first time its power to declare acts of Congress unconstitutional.

maximalist view of democracy The opinion that democracy encompasses more than free elections, which are a necessary but not sufficient condition for democratic life.

McCulloch* v. *Maryland The 1819 U.S Supreme Court decision that upheld the federal government's right to create a national bank and thus legitimized the concept of implied powers (q.v.) and the supremacy of the national government.

Medicaid A state-option component of welfare-state programs that provides medical assistance to the needy.

Medicare A component of welfare-state programs that provides partial payments for medical care to everyone eligible for Social Security and those classified as disabled.

mercantilism An economic philosophy developed in the seventeenth century that advocated strong protectionist measures that would strengthen the nation's economy and lead to a favorable balance of trade.

military-industrial complex The highly interdependent network of the military establishment and private industries producing military goods, which together exert a powerful influence on foreign and economic policy.

minimalist view of democracy The opinion that democracy is the best way of avoiding the greater evils inherent in other political forms.

minority leader The leader of the minority party in the U.S. House of Representatives or Senate.

Miranda* v. *Arizona The 1963 U.S. Supreme

Court case dictating guidelines to be followed by police in the interrogation of suspects.

mixed economies An economic system in which private ownership of the means of production is predominant, although government maintains a substantial role; characteristic of most Western democracies.

Moral Majority A church-based organization of fundamentalist Protestants founded in the 1970s with the goal of exerting pressure in the political arena to advance right-wing causes.

national committee A coordinating group at the top levels of both the Democratic and Republican parties that attempts to establish basic party policy and plan national party activity.

National Security Council (NSC) Body created by the National Security Act of 1947 to advise the president and coordinate domestic, diplomatic, and military policies in matters of national security.

natural rights Essential human guarantees, such as freedom, that a government cannot curtail or eliminate arbitrarily and still remain just.

necessary and proper clause A portion of Article I of the U.S. Constitution empowering Congress to pass the laws required for the execution of its powers.

New Deal President Franklin D. Roosevelt's administrative and legislative program of the 1930s that introduced government regulations in the economic sphere and welfare programs in the social sector.

New Jersey Plan A proposal at the Constitutional Convention of 1787 to limit each state to one representative in a unicameral legislature.

nuclear freeze A proposal popular among the left of the United States and Western Europe that the United States and the Soviet Union agree to halt the production, testing, and deployment of nuclear weapons pending further negotiation between the two nations.

Office of Management and Budget (OMB) The largest component in the Executive Office of the President, charged with preparation of the federal budget. It plays a significant role in shaping and overseeing governmental policy making and in choosing its priorities.

oligarchy Rule by a small group.

one-party districts Voting areas characterized by overwhelming superiority on the part of one political party.

open primary Election in which voters are free to vote in any party primary regardless of their party registration.

opinions Legal explanations of a judicial decision, handed down by judges.

parliamentary democracy A form of government in which the legislature (parliament) is the supreme governing body, and from which the executive leadership (the cabinet) is drawn.

patronage The power to appoint specific people or groups to government jobs.

peaceful coexistence Term coined in the 1950s by Soviet Premier Nikita Khrushchev to describe the type of relationship he preferred with the United States, which did not, however, preclude continued competition between the two countries.

Pentagon Papers Classified government documents on the U.S. involvement in Vietnam leaked to and published by the *New York Times* in 1971; the subject of an intense legal battle in which the U.S. Supreme Court upheld the newspaper's right to publish the documents.

petit juries Bodies of jurors called to decide a disputed matter or determine a person's guilt or innocence in a trial court.

photovoltaic cells Devices used in the solar energy industry to transform sunlight directly into electricity; their production costs have thus far been too high to allow widespread use.

plaintiff A person or institution (including government) claiming to have suffered some harm who brings legal action in a civil or criminal court case.

Plessy* v. *Ferguson The 1896 U.S. Supreme Court decision that "separate but equal" treatment of the races was legitimate under the Constitution; it established the legal basis for segregation and was not overturned until 1954.

pocket veto The president's ability to veto a piece of legislation, by failing to sign it within ten days after the adjournment of Congress.

political action committees (PACs)   Organizations formed to channel funds to selected candidates and to work for particular political goals.

political asylum   The ancient principle of a country's offering a haven to those fleeing from another country for political reasons.

political culture   A society's attitudes toward the processes and institutions of politics.

political economy   The complex interrelations between politics and economics, and the study of their mutual effects.

political efficacy   A belief that participation in politics can be effective, usually accompanied by a willingness to participate.

political machine   A coterie of party professionals who get out the vote and provide services to constituents in return for steady support in elections.

political party   A group of people organized on the basis of common political objectives who seek to gain political power.

political socialization   The processes through which an individual acquires the political attitudes and behavior common to a particular culture.

populist   Term applied to a number of political movements in U.S. history that have arisen to defend the interests of the common citizen against institutions perceived as too big and oppressive.

Populist Party   A political party that arose in the South and West in the 1880s that campaigned for many socialist-sounding measures and for increased unionization.

pork-barrel projects   Special-interest bills advanced in Congress by a legislator for the benefit of his or her home district or state.

post-materialist   Term to describe political attitude characterized by greater emphasis on quality-of-life issues than on materialistic concerns such as economic development and prosperity.

prerogative powers   Powers held by some to be inherent in the office of president that allow the president wide latitude in dealing with crises.

president pro tempore   The presiding officer of the U.S. Senate; an honorific title usually bestowed on the senior majority-party senator, who serves as president of the senate in the absence of the vice-president, the constitutionally mandated presiding officer.

primary election   Political contest in which opponents vie for nomination as a party's designated candidate in a general election.

privatization   The effort to transfer a wide variety of public assets and programs to the private sector in an attempt to reduce government's role and enhance private enterprise; especially popular during the Reagan years.

proportional representation   A system under which each party is awarded seats in the legislature in more or less direct proportion to the percentage of the popular votes it receives in an election.

prosecutor   The representative of the interests of the state in criminal legal proceedings brought against a defendant (q.v.).

public assistance programs   Components of welfare-state programs in which need is the main basis for eligibility.

public-interest groups   Organizations that seek to advance causes that will benefit society as a whole and will not necessarily materially benefit the organization or its activists.

public opinion   The patterns of attitudes of citizens on various subjects.

Ralph Nader   Consumer activist whose efforts championed the consumer movement and have spawned public interest groups focused on consumer issues, the environment, health, science, regulatory reform, and energy.

realignment   A major, long-term change in political party allegiance among the electorate.

reapportionment   Alteration of the pattern of representation among different electoral districts in accordance with changes in population in those areas over time.

referendum   Procedure by which citizens can vote on a piece of legislation directly.

regulatory commissions   Agencies that regulate certain kinds of activities, particularly in the economic sphere, and that can perform a quasi-judicial function (bring charges, hold hearings, and impose penalties for violations of rules).

Republican Party   Political party formed in the

1850s primarily to oppose the further extension of slavery; formed from a coalition of northern industrialists, merchants, workers, farmers, and freed slaves.

reserved powers Those powers defined by the Tenth Amendment to the Constitution as "not delegated to the United States by the Constitution, nor prohibited by it to the States respectively, or to the people."

revenue sharing Programs under which a portion of federal revenues is disbursed among the states.

rider A special section added to a piece of legislation, often having little to do with the main content of that legislation.

rights of the disabled Legal remedies being sought on the part of the deaf, blind, physically and mentally handicapped, the learning disabled, and their advocates to end discrimination.

Roth v. *United States* 1957 U.S. Supreme Court ruling that rejected a previous ruling deeming as obscene any *part* of a book or other material that might "deprave and corrupt those whose minds are open to such immoral influences." It substituted the concept of the *whole* work's effect on the "average person."

"rule of four" The U.S. Supreme Court practice of hearing a case if four of the Court's nine justices vote to hear it.

seniority rule The convention of having the longest-serving majority-party member of a congressional committee named as chairperson. Party caucuses now sometimes pass over the senior member and install a junior person as chairman.

separation of powers The distribution of governmental authority among the legislative, executive, and judicial branches to prevent the dominance of one branch.

services Programs provided as part of welfare-state programs, for example, education and job training.

Seven Years' War The conflict from 1756 to 1763 between Great Britain and France for control of Canada and Spain for Florida, won by the British; known in the colonies as the French and Indian War.

Shay's Rebellion Uprising in 1786 by farmers, led by Daniel Shays, to protest mortgage foreclosures in western Massachusetts.

single-issue group A well-organized and intensely active special interest group that focuses exclusively on one issue or set of issues.

single-member district A political area in which the person gaining the most votes in an election represents that district.

social classes Distinct groups, differentiated by occupation or income, that usually have different life-styles and may clash politically.

social insurance programs Components of welfare-state programs in which past contributions are related to the benefits received (for example, Social Security).

Social Security system A self-supporting component of the U.S. welfare state that encompasses old-age and survivors' insurance and disability insurance programs.

socialism A political philosophy advocating the deliberate creation of greater economic equality, public ownership of major means of production, and considerable economic planning by government.

socialist One who favors collective and government ownership of the means of production over individual or private ownership.

Speaker of the House Presiding officer of the U.S. House of Representatives, chosen by the members of the majority party.

spillover effects Unintended side effects that are not included in the original calculations of a policy maker.

spoils system Process by which elected officials reward friends and supporters with government jobs.

spot ads Political advertising on television, usually of short duration; usually candidate-oriented, rather than addressing issues or party loyalty.

State Department Executive agency of the U.S. government responsible for foreign policy; maintains foreign service officers in several hundred posts in this country and overseas.

Strategic Arms Limitation Talks (SALT) U.S.–Soviet negotiations from the late 1960s to late 1970s aimed at limiting the growth of certain nuclear weapons.

Strategic Defense Initiative (SDI) Popularly known as "Star Wars," the proposed space-based defense against Soviet nuclear attack.

Superfund Funding mechanism established by Congress in the 1970s to assist state and local governments in cleaning up hazardous toxic waste dump sites.

Supplemental Security Income (SSI) Program created as part of the welfare state in 1974 to provide added assistance to the aged, blind, and the disabled; pays benefits on the basis of need and is federally funded with state supplements.

supply-side economics The central economic theory of the first Reagan administration, which states that tax cuts will raise government revenues through increased production and thereby reduce rather than increase the budget deficits.

tax expenditure items Components of welfare-state programs in which benefits for particular activities are derived through reductions in tax liability.

Tax Reform Act of 1986 Changes in the tax code designed to simplify it and make it more equitable; lowered the highest tax rates and reduced the number of tax brackets.

third-party government A process by which government functions are carried out by state and local governments and by organizations in the private sector through contracts with the government.

third world The developing and less-developed countries of Asia, Africa, and Latin America.

transfer payments The money paid to individuals by governments through social programs.

treatment as equals The attempt by government to treat all people as equals.

tyranny of the majority The belief that political equality might lead to "mob rule."

unicameral Term describing a lawmaking body composed of only one house.

unitary system A form of government in which the national government's authority is more or less uniformly enforced throughout the country.

U.S. Courts of Appeals Intermediate-level federal courts with no original jurisdiction; they consider cases that originated in a lower level of federal court.

U.S. Supreme Court Highest court in the U.S. federal system and in the nation.

Virginia Plan A plan submitted at the Constitutional Convention of 1787 for a bicameral legislature based on proportional representation.

War Powers Act Legislation passed in 1973 over the veto of President Nixon that requires the president to consult with Congress before sending U.S. troops into combat.

wealth The monetary value of what an individual or household owns, adjusted for indebtedness.

welfare state A set of social policies including pensions, unemployment insurance, health care coverage, and other benefits in which society accepts responsibility for the collective welfare of individuals.

Whig Party Political party formed in 1828 from a fraction of the Republican Party and remnants of the Federalists, which primarily appealed to New Englanders, especially those with business interests.

whip A subleader of either political party in the U.S. House of Representatives who notifies members of pending business, polls them on their voting intentions, and works to make sure they are present to vote on key issues.

yuppies Acronym for young urban professionals, generally believed to espouse post-materialist attitudes combined with a determined effort to acquire material things.

INDEX

Abolitionists, 232
Abortion, 130–31, 197, 216, 435, 450–51
Abrams v. *United States,* 120
Abscam scandal, 283, 355
Accused persons, rights of, 128–30
Acid rain, 283, 569, 572
Activating others, 320
Adams, Carolyn T., 480
Adams, Gordon, 291
Adams, John, 17, 148, 222, 434
Adams, William, 199
Advertising
  advocacy, 303
  political campaigns and, 271–73
Affirmative action, 139–44
  Bakke case, 139–43
  Reagan record, 143–44
  women and, 140, 141
Afghanistan, 541, 546–47
AFL-CIO, 289–90, 298, 539
Age
  voting and, 214
Agencies, bureaucratic, 405–6
Agency for International development (AID), 536
Agnew, Spiro, 393
Agriculture, Department of, 499
AIDS, 411, 449, 497
  mandatory testing for, 513, 511
Aid to Families with De-pendent Children

(AFDC), 97, 98, 100, 485, 489, 491–92, 506
Air pollution, 566, 569–73
Algeria, 392
Alienation, 13–15, 195–96
Alien Enemies Act (1798), 121, 148
Allende, Salvador, 21, 541
Amalgamated Food Employ-ees Local 590 v. *Logan Valley Plaza, Inc.,* 123
American Bankers Associ-ation, 303
American Civil Liberties Union (ACLU), 127
American Federation of Labor, 289
American Gas Associa-tion, 305
American Israel Public Affairs Committee (Aipac), 297
American Party ("Know-Nothings"), 231, 232
American revolution. *See* Revolutionary war
Americans for Constitu-tional Action, 286
Anderson, John, 232, 274–76
Angola, 541
Animal Farm (Orwell), 10
Antiabortion groups, 295, 320
Anticommunism, 48, 78, 192, 542
Antidemocratic attitudes,

12–13
Antifederalists, 72–73, 116
Anti-Masonic Party, 232
Antinuclear movement, 321–22
Antiwar movement, 25–26, 149, 150. *See also* Vietnam war
Apartheid, 554
Appalachian Regional Commission, 487
Aquino, Benigno, 22
Aquino, Corazon, 22, 541
Argentina, 201
Argersinger v. *Hamlin,* 118
Arias, Oscar, 556
Arias peace plan, 556
Arms Control and Disar-mament Agency (ACDA), 536
Arms race, 548–53
  costs of, 552–53
  counterforce and, 548
  INF Treaty and, 550–52
  nuclear strategy and, 548–49
  SDI and, 550–51
  START treaty and, 551, 552
Arthur, Chester A., 412
Articles of Confederation, 61–63, 370, 466
Assassination, 45–46
Auchter, Thorne, 529
Australia, 467
Austria, 225, 226
Automobile industry, 406–9, 418–20

Babbitt, Bruce, 249, 253, 254

Bacher, Donald, 127
Backlash effect, 373–74
Baker, Howard, 585
Baker, James, 3d, 379
Bakke, Allan Paul, 139–40
Bakke case, 139–43
Banks, multilateral devel-opment (MDBs), 557–59
Barron v. *Baltimore,* 96, 117
Basic rights, 5
Beard, Charles, 75–76
Bennett, William, 185
Benton v. *Maryland,* 118
Bentsen, Lloyd M., 243–44, 256, 275
Berfenstam, R., 501
Bernstein, Carl, 388
Bhopal (India), toxic chemical leak in, 575
Biaggi, Mario, 356
Bicameral legislature, 337
Biden, Joe, 249, 253, 268
Bill of Attainder, 89
Bill of Rights, 71, 81, 89. *See also specific amendments*
  abortion and, 130–31
  due process clause, 128–30
  freedom of religion and, 124–28
  nationalizing, 96
  rights of the accused and, 128–30
  state and local govern-ment and, 117–19
  Supreme Court and, 117–18

Bills, legislative, 345–48.
    See also Lawmaking
    process
    riders and, 345, 347
Biomass, 584
Black, Hugo, 117
Blackman, Harry, 131,
    430, 513–14
Blacks, 525–26, 530. *See
    also* Civil rights;
    Desegregation; Ra-
    cial issues; Slavery;
    *and other specific
    topics*
    affirmative action and,
        143–44
    Declaration of Inde-
        pendence and, 132
    Fifteenth Amendment
        and, 117
    health care and, 143
    poverty and, 143
    progress of, 142–43
    public opinion polls
        and, 190
    school desegregation
        and, 134–39
    segregation, 19–21
    unemployment among,
        143
    voting patterns of, 206
    voting rights of, 115,
        132
Blanket primary, 251
Blaustein, Albert, 64
Block grants, 99, 100
Bob Jones University v.
    United States, 126
Boggs, Hale, 46
Boland Amendment, 390
Books, banning of, 127–28
Booth, John Wilkes, 46
Bork, Robert H., 39, 301,
    337, 359
Boston Tea Party, 58, 321
Brady, James, 295
Brady, Sarah, 295
Brandeis, Frank, 111
Brandeis, Louis, 120, 121,
    391
Bremer, Arthur, 46
Brennan, William, 141,
    431

Brezhnev, Leonid, 545–46
Brown lung disease, 529
Brown v. *Board of Educa-
    tion of Topeka*, 80,
    134–35, 141, 283,
    424–25, 435–36
Bryan, William Jennings,
    228
Budget
    Congress and, 336,
        364–66
    entitlement programs
        and, 366
    Office of Management
        and Budget (OMB)
        and, 365, 380–81,
        475
Budget deficit, 170, 366,
    473, 475–76
    Gramm-Rudman-Holl-
        ings Act and, 359,
        366
Bull Moose Party, 229,
    232
Bunzel, John, 144
Bureaucracy, 401–21
    cabinet departments,
        405
    Civil Service system,
        412–13
    contract, 401–2
    deregulation and,
        418–19
    discretion and, 409–10
    evaluation of, 411–20
    expertise and, 410
    independent agencies,
        405–6
    mobilization of support
        and, 410–11
    patronage, 412
    political process and,
        406–11
    privatization and, 415
    regulatory agencies
        and, 406, 415–19
    spoils system, 412
    structure of, 403–6
    third-party government
        and, 414–15
Burger, Warren, 129, 301,
    430, 438, 439, 517
Burke, Edmund, 222

Burnham, Dean, 229
Bush, George, 244, 249,
    252, 254, 256, 267,
    271, 393, 558
Business. *See also* Capital-
    ism
    interest groups and,
        287–88
    public opinion and, 198
Business Roundtable, 287,
    298
Busing, 137–39, 216
Bute, Lord, 57
Byrd, Robert, 358
Byrne, Brendan, 211

Cabinet, 381–83
    departments, 405
Calhoun, John C., 92
California, 103
    Proposition 13, 322, 324
Cambodia, 26, 201, 363,
    388
Campaigns. *See* Political
    campaigns
Canada, 224, 283
Canal Zone, 91–92
Cannon, Joseph, 340
Cantwell v. *Connecticut*,
    118
Capitalism, 5, 23, 34–35,
    155–56. *See also*
    Political economy
    controlled, 459, 461–62
    criticism of, 156
    democracy and, 156
    free enterprise and, 38
    laissez-faire, 155–56,
        459–61
Carter, Jimmy, 157, 230,
    233, 239, 371, 379,
    381, 383–85, 413,
    418, 582–83
    economic issues, 464,
        480
    energy issues, 305, 565,
        585
    foreign affairs, 21, 535,
        536, 541, 546, 555,
        557
    Iranian hostage crisis
        and, 208, 268, 363
    political campaigns,

249, 253, 258,
    273–74, 276
    public opinion, 201
Carter, L. J., 585
Cash transfers, 489
Castro, Fidel, 17, 453
Catastrophic Health Care
    Law (1988), 496
Catholic church, 49
Catt, Carrie Chapman,
    144
Caucuses, congressional,
    354
Centers for Disease Con-
    trol (CDC), 497
Central America, 187,
    315, 336, 364, 586.
    *See also specific
    countries*
    liberation theology in,
        49–50
Central Intelligence
    Agency (CIA), 187,
    336, 405–6, 537
Cermak, Anton, 46
Chamber of Commerce,
    287, 298, 303
Chaplinsky v. *New Hamp-
    shire*, 123
Chavez, Cesar, 321
Checks and balances sys-
    tem, 68–69, 337
Chernobyl nuclear acci-
    dent, 582–83
*Chicago, Burlington &
    Quincy Railway* v.
    Chicago, 118
Child care, 501
Child labor, 147, 156
Child Nutrition program,
    500
Children. *See also* Schools
    Aid to Families with
        Dependent Chil-
        dren (AFDC), 97,
        98, 100, 485, 489,
        491–92, 506
    nutrition programs,
        498–500, 502
    political parties and,
        184–85
    political socialization of,
        182–86

president as viewed by, 183–84

Chile, 21–23, 541

China, 391

Churchill, Winston, 9

Circuit Courts, 427

Cities
federalism and, 104–5
school desegregation and, 137, 138

Citizens, relationship between government and, 15–17

Civil Aeronautic Board (CAB), 419

Civil disobedience, 315–19, 325–28
antinuclear, 321–22

Civil liberties, 115, 511–13, 525–26
of the disabled, 521–23
federalism and, 117–20
gay rights, 512–14
gender discrimination and, 523–25
government intrusion and, 516–21
FBI and domestic surveillance, 518–19
mandatory testing, 519–21
obscenity, 516–18
health and safety hazards and, 526, 528–30
of immigrants, 514–16
right to privacy, 130–31, 511, 513
FBI and domestic surveillance, 518–19
mandatory drug testing and, 519–21
treatment as equals, 521–25

Civil rights, 115, 132–45, 283–97, 310, 312, 325, 530. *See also* Bill of Rights
affirmative action and, 139–44
Bakke case, 139–43

Reagan record, 143–44
Constitution and, 71
Greensboro sit-in, 310
March on Washington (1963), 310, 321
school desegregation and, 134–39
state and local government and, 102
student activism and, 187
voting, 71, 132–33, 144

Civil Rights Act (1957), 358

Civil Rights Act (1964), 95, 133, 135, 140, 141, 216, 523
women and, 145

Civil Rights Commission, 133, 144

Civil Rights Restoration Act (1988), 133, 303, 374, 386, 524

Civil Service system, 401, 412–13

Civil War, U.S., 19, 73, 133
federalism and, 92–93
political parties and, 228

Class. *See* Social class

Clay, Henry, 340

Clayton Act (1914), 147–48

Clean Air Act (1963), 569–71

"Clear and present danger" standard, 120, 122

Cleveland, Grover, 23, 385

Closed primary, 251

Cluster sampling, 189

Coal, 581–82

Coal miners, 147, 156

Cold War, 48, 149, 540, 542

Collazo, Oscar, 46

Collective bargaining, 147–48

College, political socialization and, 186–89

Colonial America. *See also* Revolutionary war
economics and, 460
slavery in, 132–33
society in, 54–55

Colorado v. *Spring*, 129

Commerce, Constitution and, 71

Committee in Solidarity with the People of El Salvador (Cispes), 519

Committees, congressional, 341–45

Committee to Re-Elect the President (CREEP), 388

Common Cause, 292–93, 306

Common Sense (Paine), 59

Commonwealth, 91

Communism, 516. *See also* Anticommunism; Socialism
freedom of speech and, 121–22
repression of, 148–50

Comparable worth, 524–25

Comprehensive Employment and Training Act (CETA), 414–15, 492–93, 505

Current powers, 89

Congress, 68, 82, 334–67. *See also* House of Representatives; Senate
under Articles of Confederation, 62–63
the budget and, 336, 364–66
constituency interests and, 350, 354–55
constitutional amendments and, 73–74
defense spending and, 335
differences between the House and Senate, 337
elections and, 350–53
functions of, 335–37

interest groups and, 350–51, 354–57
intragovernmental lobbying and, 300–1
investigative role, 336
lawmaking in, 334, 336, 345–48
committee consideration, 347
floor action, 348
floor debate, 348
implementation, 348
introduction, 347
origination, 345, 347
presidential consideration, 348
reaction, 348
riders, 345, 347
legislative veto and, 361
lobbying in, 299–300, 302–5
the media and, 336
members of, 349–57
committee assignments, 343–44
ethics, 355–57
influences on voting patterns, 352–55
personal characteristics, 349–50
professional concerns, 350–51
nature of representation and, 334–35
overseeing government programs, 336
pork barrel projects, 361
the president and, 359–64, 383–86
legislative veto, 361
prerogative powers, 372–75
secrecy, 361–64
War Powers Act, 362–64, 386, 387
as public policy forum, 335–36
racial issues and, 138
secrecy and, 361–64
structure of, 337–45
committees, 341–45
fragmentation, 345

hierarchy, 338
Senate majority
 leader, 341
Speaker of the
 House, 340
tradition and reform in,
 357–59
World War II and, 373
Congressional Budget
 and Impoundment
 Control Act (1974),
 365
Congressional Budget Of-
 fice (CBO), 365
Congressional committees
 committee assignments,
 343–44
 subcommittees, 344
Congress of Industrial
 Organizations
 (CIO), 289
Connecticut Compromise,
 65
Conscientious objection,
 127
Consciousness-raising,
 320
Consensus, 32–34
Conservation, 584–86
Conservatism, 38–39, 185
 civil liberties and, 512
 Republican Party and,
 230–31, 243, 244,
 246
 social issues and,
 197–98
 Supreme Court and,
 437–40
 welfare and, 487, 503–4
Consociational democ-
 racy, 18
Constitution, U.S.,
 429–30
 amendments to, 73–74.
 See also Bill of
 Rights; specific
 amendments
 antifederalists and,
 72–73
 Article 1, 96
 Articles of Confedera-
 tion, 61–63
 checks and balances

and, 68–69, 337
chronology of, 70–71
civil rights and, 71
definition of, 64
due process, 429–30
economic justice and,
 80
electoral system and, 71
Equal Rights Amend-
 ment, 109–11
federalists and, 72–73
interpretations of,
 75–76
as model for Japan, 75
national security and,
 76–78
"necessary and proper"
 clause, 96
racial equality and,
 79–80
ratification of, 71–73
regulation of commerce
 and, 71
relevance of, 76–82
separation of powers
 and, 68, 81–82,
 359–60
sexual equality and, 80
voting rights and, 71
Constitutional Conven-
 tion, 63–74, 79
Consultants, political,
 271, 272
Consumer groups, 293
Consumer Product Safety
 Commission
 (CPSC), 293
Containment, 542
Continental Congress,
 First, 58
Contract bureaucracies,
 401–2
Controlled capitalism,
 459, 461–62
Converting election, 210
Cook, Don, 392
Cooper, John Sherman,
 46
Corporate economy, 165
Cotton dust, 529
Council on Environmen-
 tal Quality (CEQ),
 567

Counterforce, 548
Courts of Appeals, U.S.,
 427
Court system. See Legal
 system
Crime. See also Law en-
 forcement; Vio-
 lence
 political assassination,
 45–46
 rights of the accused
 and, 128–30
Criminal Justice. See also
 Legal system
 state and local govern-
 ment and, 101, 102
Cross-over primary vot-
 ing, 251
Cuba, 48, 453, 541, 545
Cuban missile crisis, 201
Culture. See Political culture
Cuomo, Mario, 249
Czechoslovakia, liberali-
 zation movement
 in, 115
Czolgosz, Leon, 46

Dahl, Robert, 69, 207
Danforth, John, 559
Daniel, Dan, 355
Daughters of the Ameri-
 can Revolution, 41
Davis, John W., 255
Day care, 501
Deaver, Michael, 283
Declaration of Independ-
 ence, 58
 blacks and, 132
 slavery and, 66
DeConcini, Dennis, 359
Decrementalism, 98
Defendants, 426
Defense, U.S. Depart-
 ment of, 290, 401,
 402, 405, 536–37
Defense industry, 290–91
Defense policy. See Arms
 race
Defense spending,
 170–71, 290
 Congress and, 335
 public opinion and, 199

Deferred issues, 452
De Gaulle, Charles, 392
DeJonge v. Oregon, 118
Dejudicialization, 442
Delegated powers, 88
Delegate theory of repre-
 sentation, 334
Democracy
 capitalism and, 23,
 34–35, 156
 consociational model
 of, 18
 definition of, 3–8
 economics and, 459
 effectiveness of, 17–19
 egalitarian, 6
 elite and, 17
 extending, 23–26
 ideal vs. real, 7–10
 interest groups and,
 11–12
 liberal, 4–6
 majoritarian, 3–4
 maximalist view of, 10
 minimalist view of, 9
 oligarchy and, 12
 parliamentary, 339, 360
 political culture and, 32
 problems in, 10–17
 failure to exercise
 rights, 12–15
 government-citizen
 relationship, 15–17
 uneven distribution
 of power, 10–12
 restricting, 19–23
 varieties of, 77
Democratic norms, 192–94
Democratic Party, 227–28,
 230–31
 1968 convention, 237
 Dixiecrats, 230, 232, 235
 gender and, 204
 Great Depression and,
 230
 liberalism and, 230,
 231, 243
 McGovern-Fraser Com-
 mission, 237–38
 nominating process
 and, 253–54
 organization, 235, 236
 realignment, 243–44

reforms of, 236–40
Republican Party compared to, 240–41
social issues and, 230
the South and, 230
unions and, 289
Democratic-Republicans, 222, 227, 228
Denmark, 161, 576
Dennis et al. v. *United States,* 122
Depression, economic, 461. *See also* Great Depression
Deregulation, 98, 418–19
Desegregation, 216
of schools, 134–39, 441
Brown v. *Board of Education* case, 80, 134–35, 141, 283, 424–25, 435–36
busing and, 137–39
in cities, 137, 138
de facto vs. de jure, 135–39
Johnson and, 135
Nixon and, 137
Détente, 545–46
Deviating election, 210
Devolution, 98
Dewey, Thomas Edmund, 276
DeYoung, Karen, 495
Diffuse support, 181
Direct legislation, 322–25
Direct socialization, 182
Disability insurance (DI), 489
Disabled, the, 489, 493
rights of, 521–23
Discrimination, 41–44. *See also* Affirmative action; Civil rights; Desegregation; Racial issues
gender-based, 141, 373–74
comparable worth and, 524–25
reverse, 140–41
Displaced issues, 452
Dissent, 192. *See also* Protest

Distribution of income, 162–64
income tax and, 172
Distribution of power, 10–12
Distribution of wealth and ownership, 164–66
District of Columbia (Washington D.C.), 90–91
Distrust, 195
Diverted issues, 452
Dixiecrats, 230, 232, 235
Dixon, Julian, 356
Dole, Bob, 252, 271
Dole, Elizabeth, 283, 408
Domestic Council, 381
Douglas, Stephen A., 275
Douglas, William O., 117, 122
Draft cards, burning, 122, 123
Dred Scott v. *Sanford,* 436–37
Drinking age, 108–9
Drucker, Peter, 413
Drugs, right to pure, 145–46
Drug use, testing for, 511, 519–21
Duarte, Jose Napoleon, 556–57
Due process, 6, 90, 117, 128–30, 429–30
Dukakis, Kitty, 249
Dukakis, Michael S., 243–44, 249, 252–54, 256, 268, 441, 479
Dulles, Allen, 46
Dulles, John Foster, 543
Duncan v. *Louisiana,* 118
Du Pont, Pete, 252, 254
Duverger, Maurice, 222
Dworkin, Andrea, 518
Dworkin, Ronald, 521

Eckhardt, Bob, 345
Economic Interpretation of the Constitution, An (Beard), 75–76
Economic Opportunity

Act (1964), 486–88
Economic power, political power and, 10–11
Economics (economic management; the economy), 459–81. *See also* Capitalism; Political economy; *and specific economic issues*
colonial America and, 460
Constitution and, 80
democracy and, 459
depression, 461
elections of 1984 and 1986 and, 208–9
fiscal policy, 465–74
in 1960s, 469–70
Federal Reserve System, 468–69
monetarism, 470–71
monetary policy, 468–69
spending policy, 466
supply-side economics, 471–74
tax system, 466–68
Volcker, 470–71
history of, 459–65
controlled capitalism, 459, 461–62
laissez-faire capitalism, 459–61
mercantilism, 459, 460
recent, 462, 464–65
industrial power and, 477–80
foreign trade, 479–80
policy, 480
international, U.S. dominance of, 160–61
Keynesian, 462, 465, 469–70, 472–74
liberal vs. conservative view of, 198
politics and, 469–74
recession, 461
stagflation, 464
third world aid and, 557–61

work force and, 476–77
Edinger, Lewis J., 372
Education. *See also* College; Schools
banning of books and, 127–28
church-affiliated schools, 126
desegregation, 134–39
discrimination and, 373–74
political, 185, 190–92
political parties and, 185
public opinion and, 204
Reagan and, 185
social class and, 204
state and local government and, 100, 101
teaching of evolution and, 185
voting and, 214
Education, U.S. Dept. of, 185
Education Amendments (1972), 133
Education for All Handicapped Children Act (1975), 522
Effluent, 573
Egalitarian democracy, 6
Ehrmann, Henry W., 407
Eighteenth Amendment, 449
Eighth Amendment, 116
Eisenhower, Dwight D., 207, 208, 300–1, 371, 379, 385, 393, 430, 536, 542–43
Elderly, the. *See also* Social Security
nursing home care for, 496–97
poverty and, 167
Elections. *See also* Political campaigns; Voting
candidate personality and, 207, 208
Congress and, 350–53
converting, 210
deviating, 210
electoral college and, 257–59

of judges, 301
maintaining, 210
presidential, 396–98
primary, 251
realigning, 210
Electoral college, 257–59
Electoral system
Constitutional Convention and, 65–69
Constitution and, 71
Elites
democracy and, 17
foreign policy and, 538
Elitist view of U.S. politics, 454, 455
El Salvador, 50, 347, 515, 519, 556–57
Enabling act, 90
Energy, 579–89
coal, 581–82
conservation of, 584–86
fossil fuels, 580–82
increasing supply of, 583–84
natural gas, 581
nuclear power, 582–83
oil, 580–81
politics and, 586–87
solar power, 584
Engels, Friedrich, 157
Engel v. Vitale, 125
England. *See* Great Britain
Entitlement programs, 366
Environment, 216, 565–88
acid rain, 283, 569, 572
air pollution, 566, 569–73
Environmental Protection Agency, 567, 568, 578
Friends of the Earth, 286
greenhouse effect, 571
group strategies and, 578
interest groups and, 295–97
Love Canal, 320
NEPA and, 567–68, 578
ozone layer, 570
pesticides, 576–77
regulatory agencies

and, 416–18
state and local government and, 101–2
Superfund, 575
toxic chemicals, 572, 574–77
water pollution, 566, 573–74
Environmental Action, 296
Environmental Defense Fund, 296
Environmental impact statements, 567
Environmental Protection Agency (EPA), 403, 405, 416, 417, 567, 568, 578
Epstein, Leon, 222
Equality, government promotion of, 172–73
Equal Pay Act (1963), 145, 523
Equal protection of the laws, 6, 90, 117, 283
Equal Rights Amendment (ERA), 109–11, 145, 197
Equals, civil liberties and treatment as, 521–25
Espionage Act (1917), 119–20
Estrich, Susan, 249
Ethics, congressional, 355–57
Ethics in Government Act, 355
Europe, 182, 479, 498, 505
gun policy in, 296
ideology in, 225, 226
industrial policy in, 480
media in, 266
multiparty systems in, 224–26
political parties, 228, 229
violence in, 45
voting in, 211–13
welfare states in, 171–72

Everson v. *Board of Education*, 118
Executive agreement, 373
Executive branch. *See also* President, the
bills and, 345
foreign policy and, 535–38
intragovernmental lobbying and, 300–1
lobbying in, 300
Executive Office of the President, 377, 379–81
Expansionism, 534
Ex post facto law, 89
Extraordinary politics, 310–11. *See also* Protest
government and, 313–15

Fairness Doctrine, 269
Falklands War, 201
Falwell, Jerry, 439
Family, political socialization and, 184–85
Far right, the, 41
Fascism, 13, 48
FDA. *See* Food and Drug Administration
Federal AIDS Policy Act (1988), 521
Federal Bureau of Investigation (FBI), domestic surveillance by, 518–19
Federal Communications Commission, 416
Federal court system, 427
Federal District Courts, 427
Federal Election Campaign Act (FECA), 261–62
Federal Election Commission v. *NCPAC*, 262
Federal Housing Administration (FHA), 502
Federal income tax, 172, 466–67
Federalism, 86–113

cities and, 104–5
civil liberties and, 117–20
Civil War and, 92–93
division of powers in, 88–89
dual, 96–97
evolution of, 92–100
federal-state relations and, 95
grants-in-aid, 98–100
Great Depression and, 94
industrial expansion and, 93–94
interstate obligations and, 90
limits on government power and, 89–90
new, 96–100
Great Society, 97
New Deal, 97
Reagan's, 98–100
revenue sharing, 97–98
problems of
cities, 104–5
infrastructure, 105–7
regional rivalries and, 102–4
state and local government and
drinking age, 108–9
Equal Rights Amendment, 109–11
intervention, 107–11
reapportionment, 107
responsibilities, 100–2
voting rights act, 107–8
statehood and other alternatives, 90–92
Supreme Court and, 95–96
unitary system vs., 86
voting and, 211
in West Germany, 106
Federalist Papers, The (Madison, Hamilton and Jay), 67–68
Federalists (Federalist Party), 222, 227, 228, 412

Constitution and, 72–73

French revolution and, 121

Federal Regulation of Lobbying Act (1946), 304–5

Federal Reserve Board, 68, 470–71, 473, 481

Federal Reserve System, 468–69

Federal Trade Commission, 406

Ferraro, Geraldine, 256

Fifteenth Amendment, 79–80, 89–90, 117, 132, 133

Fifth Amendment, 116, 128–30, 520

Fighting words, 122–23

Filibuster, 348, 358, 359

First Amendment, 116, 117, 315, 517. *See also* Freedom of speech
  "clear and present danger" standard, 120, 122
  freedom of religion and, 124–28
    establishment clause, 124–26
    free exercise clause, 126–28
    school prayer, 125–26
  lobbying and, 304
  Supreme Court and, 117

Fiscal policy, 465–70
  in 1960s, 469–70
  Federal Reserve System, 468–69
  monetarism, 470–71
  monetary policy, 468–69
  spending policy, 466
  supply-side economics, 471–74
  tax system, 466–68
  Volcker, 470–71

Fiske v. *Kansas*, 118

Flag, U.S., 126, 183

Food, right to pure, 145–46

Food and Drug Administration (FDA), 146, 293, 409

Food and Drug Amendments (1962), 409

Food stamps, 101, 485, 489, 498–500, 506

Ford, Gerald, 46, 201, 208, 255–56, 273, 363, 379, 383, 385, 393, 406–9, 480, 536, 586

Foreign policy, 535–48. *See also* Arms race
  Central America and, 545
  executive agreement and, 373
  expansionism and, 534
  foreign aid and, 557–61
  historical perspective, 534–35
  human rights and, 199, 546, 558
  influences on, 538–40
  interest groups and, 538–39
  interventionism and, 48, 199
  isolationism and, 534–35
  liberal vs. conservative view of, 198–200
  president and executive branch and, 535–38
  regional conflicts and, 543–47
  religious groups and, 49
  Soviet-American relations, 540, 542–53
    arms race, 548–53
    cold war, 540, 542
    containment, 542
    crises and détente, 545–46
    Cuba and, 545
    current issues in, 547–48
    human rights and, 546, 558

peaceful coexistence, 542–43
    SALT, 535, 536, 549–51
  symbolic actions and, 451–52
  third world and, 553–61
    foreign aid, 557–61

Foreign trade, 479–80

Foreman, Carol Tucker, 294

Fossil fuels, 580–82

Fourteenth Amendment, 19, 20, 79–80, 90, 117, 121, 133, 437, 524
  due process clause, 117
  equal protection clause, 117
  Supreme Court and, 117–18

Fourth Amendment, 116, 520

France, 158, 182, 196, 202, 224, 266, 316, 392, 407, 480
  Revolutionary War and, 60

Franco, Francisco, 48

Frank, Barney, 111, 516

Frankfurter, Felix, 126

Franklin, Benjamin, 63, 64

Fraser, Donald, 237

Freedom of Information Act, 267

Freedom of religion, 124–28
  Supreme Court and, 124–27

Freedom of speech, 80, 116, 119–23
  chilling effect and, 122
  communism and, 121–22
  overbreadth and, 122
  political extremism and, 119–23
  political vs. nonpolitical, 119
  protest and, 315

public opinion and, 192–94
  strict scrutiny and, 122
  Supreme Court and, 119–23
  symbolic speech and fighting words, 122–23

Free enterprise, 38

Freeman, S. David, 157

French and Indian War, 56

French Revolution, 56, 59, 62, 121

Friends of the Earth, 286, 296

Fromme, Lynette, 46

Frontlash effect, 372, 373

Frost Belt states, 103

Fulbright, William, 387

Full faith and credit, 90

Fullilove v. *Klutznick*, 141

Gaines, Lloyd, 134

Galbraith, John Kenneth, 410

Gandhi, Mohandas K., 316–18, 320

Garcia Marquez, Gabriel, 516

Garcia v. *San Antonio Transit Authority*, 95

Gardner, John, 292

Garfield, James A., 46, 393, 412

Garner, John Nance, 393

Garrity, Paul, 441

Gay rights, 197, 512–14

Geduldig v. *Aiello*, 524

Gender
  public opinion and, 204
  voting and, 209, 214

Gender discrimination, 141, 373–74, 523–25
  comparable worth and, 524–25

General Motors (GM), 293

George III, king of England, 57, 81

Gephardt, Richard, 249, 253, 254, 479

Gibbons v. *Ogden*, 95

Gideon v. *Wainwright*, 118, 128
Gierek, Edward, 315
Gilbert v. *Minnesota*, 118
Ginsburg, Douglas H., 39, 337
Gitlow v. *New York*, 117, 118, 120, 121
Goethe, Johann Wolfgang von, 33
Goetz, Bernhard, 198
Goldwater, Barry, 206, 240–41, 276
GOP. *See* Republican Party
Gorbachev, Mikhail, 200, 541, 546–47, 552
Gore, Al, 253
Gore, Al, Jr., 249, 253, 254
Government. *See also specific topics*
  under Articles of Confederation, 62–63
  checks and balances and, 68–69
  citizens' relationship to, 15–17
  colonial, 55–56
  economic equality and, 172–73
  extraordinary politics and, 313–15
  federalism. *See* Federalism
  powers of. *See* Powers
  spending by, 169–72, 466. *See also* Budget; Fiscal policy
  transfer payments, 172
  state and local. *See* State and local government
  third-party, 414–15
Gramm, Phil, 359
Gramm-Rudman-Hollings bill, 359, 366
Grants-in-aid, 98–100
  block grants, 99, 100
Grass-roots lobbying, 303
Grass-roots movements, 35

Great Britain, 158, 182, 196, 201, 202, 296, 316, 370, 407, 480, 498, 576. *See also* Revolutionary War
  campaigns and elections in, 258
  court system, 432, 442
  health care in, 495, 498
  Parliament, 339
  political parties in, 222, 224–26, 234
  trade unions in, 288
Great Depression, 39, 41, 158, 204–5, 322, 345, 449, 461–63, 481, 507. *See also* New Deal
  Democratic Party and, 230
  federalism and, 94
  unions and, 289
Great Lakes, 574
Great Society, 97, 486–87, 492–93, 503–4
Greece, 201
Greenhouse effect, 571
Green Party, 202, 224, 242
Greenpeace, 296, 297
Green v. *School Board of New Kent County*, 135
Grenada, 267
Grenville, George, 57
Grimke, Angelina, 23, 25
Grimke, Sarah, 23
Griswold, Roger, 73
Griswold v. *Connecticut*, 118
Gross national product, 160, 161
Grove City College case, 133, 524
Grove City v. *Bell*, 374
Guatemala, 543
Guerasci, R., 529
Guiteau, Charles, 46
Gulf of Tonkin Resolution, 387, 388, 545
Gun ownership, tradition of, 44–45, 47
Gun control, 116, 216, 295
Gun lobby, 295, 296

Haar, Charles M., 441
Haig, Alexander, 252, 379
Halberstam, David, 267
Haldeman, H. R., 379
Hamilton, Alexander, 63, 66, 67, 93, 227, 412
Hamilton v. *Regents of Univ. of California*, 118
Hammer v. *Dagenhart*, 95
Handicapped, the. *See* Disabled, the
Hardin, Charles, 82
Hardwick, Michael, 513
Harris, Fred, 237
Harrison, William Henry, 227–28, 272, 393
Hart, Gary, 249, 253, 268
Hayes, Denis, 584
Head Start, 504, 507
Health, Education and Welfare, U.S. Department of, 135
Health insurance, national, 216
Health policy (health care), 494–99. *See also* Nutrition programs
  automobile air bags, 406–9
  blacks and, 143
  British, 495, 498
  hazards to health, 526, 528–30
  Medicaid, 98, 100, 488, 489, 496
  Medicare, 488–90, 494–96
  nursing home care, 496–97
  research, 497–98
  regulatory agencies and, 417
  state and local government and, 101
Hearst, William Randolph, 268
Heclo, Hugh, 480
Heidenheimer, Arnold J., 480
Heline, Oscar, 463
Heller, Walter, 470
Helms, Jesse, 38, 279

Helsinki Accords, 546
Heritage Foundation, 452
Hicklin v. *Regina*, 516–17
High Frontier, 455
Hinckley, John, 46
Ho Chi Minh, 48
Hodel, Donald, 579
Holmes, Oliver Wendell, 120
Hoover, Herbert, 157, 205–6, 481
Hoover, J. Edgar, 518
House of Representatives. *See also* Congress
  elections and, 350–53
  House Rules Committee, 348, 357
  lawmaking process, 345–48
  majority leader, 340
  members of, 337–38
  minority leader, 340
  select committees of, 343
  Senate compared to, 337–38
  Speaker of the, 340
  standing committees of, 341–42
  whip, 340
House Rules Committee, 348, 357
Housing, 283–85
Housing Act (1968), 133
Housing programs, 502–3, 506
Human rights, 199, 546, 558
  in Chile, 21
Humphrey, Hubert, 236–37, 243
Hungary, 543
Huntington, Samuel, 17
Hustler v. *Falwell*, 439
Hyde, Henry, 131, 197
Hyde amendments, 131, 197

Iacocca, Lee, 408
Ideology, 196, 206–8, 225, 226
  congressional voting and, 354

Ronald Reagan and, 354
Ignorance, 14–15
Immigrant rights, 514–16
Immigration and Reform Act (1986), 514, 515
Immigration law, 41–43
Imperial presidency, 388
Implied powers, 88
Income
  distribution of, 162–64, 525
  per capita, 161
Income security, tax expenditures for, 493–94
Income tax, federal, 172, 466–67
Incremental politics, 448–50
Incumbents, 251, 351, 352
Indirect socialization, 182
Industrialization
  federalism and, 93–94
  social rights and, 145
Industrial Workers of the World (IWW), 148
Industry, 477–80
  foreign trade and, 479–80
  policy for, 480
Inflation, 464
Infrastructure, 105
Inherent powers, 88
Initiative process, 100, 322
Initiatives and referenda (I & R), 322–25
Inkind transfers, 489
In re Oliver, 118
Institutionalized Persons Act (1980), 133
Insurance, national health, 216
Integration. *See* Desegregation
Interelection stage, 251
Interest-group liberalism, 455
Interest groups, 11–12, 283–97
  AFL-CIO, 298
  antiabortion, 295
  anti-welfare, 506

business, 287–88, 306–7
Chamber of Commerce, 303
Congress and, 350–51, 354–57
defense industry, 290–91
dynamics of, 284–85
environmental, 295–97
foreign policy and, 300, 538–39
functions of, 285–86
gun lobby, 295, 296
iron triangle and, 290–91
labor unions, 288–90
lobbying by, 297–306
  advocacy advertising, 303
  Congress, 299–300, 302–5
  through the courts, 301
  executive branch, 300
  government experience of lobbyists, 305–6
  grass-roots, 303
  insider-outsider strategies, 301–4
  intragovernmental, 300–1
  new, 304–5
  oil and gas lobby, 288, 299–300, 305
  public interest, 307
  regulation of, 304–6
  relationship with lawmakers, 302
  strategies, 298–99
membership unity, 298
money and, 298
oil, 299–300
political action committees (PACs), 262–64,
  corporate, 306–7
problems with, 286–87
pro-Israeli, 297
public, 292–94
reputation and, 298
resources of, 297–98
single-issue groups, 294–97, 306

size of, 298
Intermediate Nuclear Forces (INF) Treaty, 200, 536, 550–52
International economics, U.S. dominance of, 160–61
Interstate Commerce Commission (ICC), 406, 416, 461
Interstate obligations, 90
Interventionism, 48, 199
Iran-contra affair, 17, 80, 267, 335–36, 362, 363, 377, 378, 389–91, 556
Iranian hostage crisis, 208, 268, 363
Iran-Iraq war, 364
Ireland, 182
Iron Triangle, 290–91, 411
Isaacs, Ben, 463
Isolationism, 534–35, 543
Israel, 267
  pro-Israeli interest groups and, 297
Issues. *See* Public policy; *specific issues*
Italy, 182, 202, 224–26, 266, 576

Jackson, Andrew, 205, 227, 381, 412, 460
Jackson, Henry, 211
Jackson, Jesse, 206, 240, 249, 253, 254
Jackson, Robert H., 127
Japan, 75, 161, 182, 442, 467, 479, 480, 498, 552
Japanese-Americans, 42, 44, 314
Jay, John, 67, 76
Jefferson, Thomas, 34, 48, 58, 61, 73, 121, 132, 227, 325, 412, 434
Jeffersonian Republicans, 121
Jehovah's Witnesses, 126–27
Jews, American, 297
Job programs, 492–93

Job Training Partnership ACT (JTPA), 493
John Paul II, Pope, 49
Johnson, Andrew, 374–75, 385, 393
Johnson, Lyndon B., 206, 208, 236, 254, 256, 315, 362–63, 381, 384, 387, 388, 394, 454, 466, 474, 486–88, 518, 536, 545
  Civil Rights Act and, 135
  economics and, 470
  Great Society programs, 97, 486–87, 492–93, 503–4
  school desegregation and, 135
  Voting Rights Act and, 108
Johnson, Paul, 141
Joint Chiefs of Staff, 537
Joslyn, Richard, 257
Joyce, Diane, 141
Judicial review, 431–32
Judiciary. *See also* Legal system; Supreme Court
  lobbying and, 301
  recruitment of judges, 430–31
Jungle, The (Sinclair), 145–46

Kahn v. *Shevin*, 524
Katz v. *United States*, 513
Kaufman, Herbert, 420
Kemp, Jack, 252
Kennan, George, 542
Kennedy, Anthony, 337, 440
Kennedy, Edward, 39
Kennedy, John F., 41, 46, 78, 207–8, 256, 258, 261, 264, 268, 273, 310, 377, 381, 384, 393, 453, 469–70, 487, 536, 545
Kennedy, Robert, 45, 46, 236, 381
Kennedy family, 231
Kent State, 17, 313–14

Kerner Commission Report, 526
Keynes, John Maynard (Keynesian economics), 462, 465, 469–70, 472–74
Khrushchev, Nikita, 543
King, Martin Luther, Jr., 45, 107–8, 285, 310
  letter from Birmingham jail, 316–18, 325–28
Kinnock, Neal, 249
Kirkpatrick, Jeane, 315
Kissinger, Henry, 21, 381, 545
Klopfer v. *North Carolina*, 118
Know-Nothings (American Party), 231, 232
Koch, Ed, 211
Korean War, 373, 543
Ku Klux Klan, 38, 41, 310, 312, 314, 325

Labor unions (trade unions), 288–90
  AFL-CIO, 289–90, 298, 539
  foreign policy and, 539
  picketing, 123
  public opinion and, 198
  right to organize, 147–48
La Follette, Robert, 232
Laird, Nick, 305
Laissez-faire capitalism, 155–56, 459–61
Lance, Bert, 249
Land and Water Conservation Act (1965), 566
Landrum Griffin Act (1959), 148
Laos, 25–26
Latin America, 23
Law enforcement. *See also* Police
  capital punishment and, 197–98
  due process and, 128–30
Lawmaking process, 334, 336, 345–48

committee consideration, 347
  floor action, 348
  floor debate, 348
  implementation, 348
  introduction, 347
  origination, 345, 347
  presidential consideration, 348
  reaction, 348
  riders, 345, 347
Lazarsfeld, Paul, 205
Lebanon, 363–64, 390
LeBlanc, Hugh, 222
Ledwidge, Bernard, 392
Left, the, 40–41
Legal representation, right to, 128
Legal Services Corporation (LSC), 442
Legal system, 424–44. *See also* Supreme Court
  dejudicialization, 442
  due process of law and, 6
  equal protection of the laws and, 6
  expansion of, 440–43
  federal court system, 427
  flow of litigation, 427–29
  Great Britain, 432, 442
  powers and restraints, 431–36
    judicial review, 431–32
    legislative reaction, 434–35
    noncompliance, 435–36
    self-restraints, 432–33
  recruitment of judges, 430–31
  stare decisis and, 426
  state court system, 426–27
Legislation. *See* Bills; Lawmaking process
Legislative Reorganization Act (1946), 304–5, 341

Levin, Carl, 290
Lewis, Anthony, 441
Liberal democracy, 4–6
Liberalism, 34–52, 185, 196–204
  civil liberties and, 512
  college students and, 187–89
  in colonial America, 55–56
  Democratic Party and, 230, 231, 243
  eighteenth-century, 35, 37
  interest-group, 455
  legacy of, 37–38
  the media and, 279
  new, 39–40
  radicalism and, 40–41
  social issues and, 197–98
  Supreme Court and, 437–38
  traditional, 38–39
  values of, 35, 37
  welfare and, 487, 504–5
Liberation theology, 49–50
Lincoln, Abraham, 46, 206, 228, 272, 275, 318, 393
Lobbying, 297–306. *See also* Interest groups
  advocacy advertising, 303
  Congress, 299–300, 302–5
  through the courts, 301
  executive branch, 300
  government experience of lobbyists, 305–6
  grass-roots, 303
  insider-outsider strategies, 301–4
  intragovernmental, 300–1
  new, 304–5
  oil and gas lobby, 288, 299–300, 305
  by president, 383–84
  public interest, 307
  regulation of, 304–6
  relationship with law-

makers, 302
  strategies, 298–99
Local government. *See* State and local government
Local parties, 233
Locke, John, 35
Louis XVI, king of France, 62
Love Canal, 320, 574
Lowi, Theodore, 455
Low-intensity warfare, 541
Ludlow Massacre (1913), 147
Lyon, Matthew, 73

MacArthur, Gen. Douglas, 75
McCarren-Walter Immigration Act (1952), 440, 516
McCarthy, Eugene, 26, 236
McCarthy, Joseph, 78, 268, 542
McCarthyism, 516
McCloy, John J., 46
McCorvey, Norma, 130
McCulloch v. *Maryland*, 88, 95–96, 432, 436
McFarlane, Robert, 537
McGovern, George, 231, 237–40, 252, 276
McGovern-Fraser Commission, 237–38
McGuffey Readers, 185
Mackie, Thomas T., 213*n*
McKinley, William, 46, 228, 393
Madison, Christopher, 541
Madison, James, 61, 63, 67–68, 76, 222, 227, 286
Maine v. *Moulton*, 129–30
Maintaining election, 210
Majoritarian democracy, 3–4
Majority leader, 340
Majority rule, 5, 180–81
Malcolm X, 45
Malloy v. *Hogan*, 118

Mao Zedong, 391
Mapp v. *Ohio*, 118
Marbury v. *Madison*, 432, 434, 436
March on Washington (1963), 310, 321
Marcos, Ferdinand, 22, 48, 541, 558
Marshall, John, 96, 432, 436
Marshall Plan, 542
Marx, Karl, 157
Maximalist view of democracy, 10
Mayaguez incident, 363
Meaninglessness, 195
Meat Inspection Act (1906), 146
Media, the
  bias of, 277–79
  Congress and, 336
  foreign, 266
  framing the issues, 267–68
  Freedom of Information Act and, 267
  gathering the news, 267
  initiative and referendum campaigns and, 324
  liberal image of, 279
  news gathering, 277–78
  political campaigns and, 254, 268–77
    advertising, 271–73
    consultants, 271, 272
    image-making, 271–73
    the issues and, 276–77
    Supreme Court and, 269
    televised debates, 268, 273–76
  politics and, 265–68
  president and, 265, 267, 268, 270
Medicaid, 98, 100, 488, 489
Medicare, 488, 489, 490, 494–96, 504
Meese, Edwin, 3d, 129, 283, 379, 520

Meiklejohn, Alexander, 119
Melting pot, 41, 42
Memphis Fire Department v. *Stotts*, 141
Mercantilism, 459, 460
Mexican-American War, 316, 318
Mexican immigrants, 514–15
Michael M. v. *Superior Court of Sonoma County*, 521, 524
Michel, Robert, 12
Mikulski, Barbara, 359
Military-industrial complex, 290
Military service, 182
  conscientious objection to, 127
Military expenditures. *See* Defense spending
Miller, James, 381
Miller, Samuel F., 126
Miller v. *California*, 517
Minersville School District v. *Gobitis*, 126–27
Minimalist view of democracy, 9
Minorities. *See also* Racial issues; *and specific minorities*
Minority leader of House, 340
Miranda v. *Arizona*, 128–30
Missouri Pacific Railway Co. v. *Nebraska*, 118
Mitchell, George J., 364
Mitterand, François, 407
Mixed economies, 158–60
Mollet, Guy, 392
Mondale, Walter, 39, 209, 243, 253, 256, 262, 274–76
Monetarism, 470–71
Monetary policy, 468–69
Monroe, James, 534
Monroe Doctrine, 534, 541
Moore, Sara Jane, 46
Morality, 39, 49–50
Moral Majority, 294

Moritz, Charles, 524
Mormon church, 126
Morrison, Bruce, 353
Mothers Against Drunk Drivers (MADD), 109
Motor Vehicle Safety Act (1966), 293
Moynihan, Daniel Patrick, 80–82, 507
Multilateral development banks (MDBs), 557–59
Multiparty systems, 224–26
Municipal government. *See* State and local government
Murdoch, Rupert, 266
Murphy v. *Waterfront Commission*, 118
Murray, Charles, 503–4

NAACP v. *Alabama*, 118
Nader, Ralph, 292, 293, 301, 324
Napoleon Bonaparte, 62
National Aeronautics and Space Administration (NASA), 405, 410
National Association for the Advancement of Colored People (NAACP), 134, 283, 301
National Association of Manufacturers (NAM), 287
National committees, 235–36
National conventions, 237–40, 255–56
National Environmental Policy Act (1969), 567–68, 578
National Guard, 313–14
National Institutes of Health (NIH), 497
Nationalism, 182, 186
  religion and, 185

National Labor Relations Board (NLRB), 148
National Labor Relations Board v. *Jones & Laughlin Steel Corp.*, 95
National League of Cities v. *Usery*, 95
National parties, 235–36
National pride, 182
National Rifle Association (NRA), 295, 296
National School Lunch program, 500
National security, Constitution and, 76–78
National Security Council (NSC), 381, 391, 536
National Socialist Party v. *Skokie*, 123
Native Americans, 41, 48
Natural gas, 581
Naturalization Act (1798), 121
Natural rights, 35
Nazi Germany, 12–13, 48
Near v. *Minnesota*, 118
"Necessary and proper" clause of Constitution, 96
Nelson-Pallmeyer, Jack, 541
Netherlands, the, 158, 225, 226
New Deal, 39, 94, 97, 205, 206, 208, 210, 279, 289, 345, 401, 424, 437, 449, 461, 462, 486
New Deal coalition, 229, 243
New federalism, 98–100
New Jersey, 103–4
New Jersey Plan, 64–65
New liberalism, 39–40
Newspapers, 266–68. *See also* Media, the
New York, 107
New York v. *Class*, 129
Nicaragua, 16, 22, 48–50, 216, 315, 386, 390–91, 515, 535, 537, 541, 555–58

Nineteenth Amendment, 89–90, 132, 144
Ninth Amendment, 116, 130
Nixon, Richard M., 208, 210, 230, 261, 268, 273, 279, 289, 315, 363, 381–84, 386, 388, 393, 394, 406, 430, 438, 468, 480, 536, 541, 545–46, 567, 579, 586. *See also* Watergate scandal
  Chile and, 21–22
  revenue sharing programs of, 97–98
  school desegregation and, 137
  Supreme Court and, 129
Nofziger, Lyn, 283
Nonparticipation, 210–15
  barriers to voting, 211, 213
  factors influencing, 213–15
Nonpolitical speech, 119
Nonpresidential campaigns, 250–51
Nonviolent protest, 316, 317
Norris, George, 157
Norris-LaGuardia Act (1932), 148
North, Oliver, 335–36, 362, 390–91
North Atlantic Treaty Organization (NATO), 542
Norway, 172
Nuclear freeze, 200
Nuclear power, 582–83
Nuclear Regulatory Commission (NRC), 306
Nuclear Test Ban Treaty, 536
Nuclear weapons. *See also* Arms race
  neutron bomb, 201
  public opinion and, 199–200
Nursing home care, 496–97

Nutrition programs, 498–500, 502, 506
  food stamps, 101, 485, 489, 498–500, 506

Obscenity, 516–18
Occupational Safety and Health Administration (OSHA), 416–18, 453–54, 528–29
Office of Management and Budget (OMB), 365, 380–81, 475
Office of Policy Development, 381
Oil, 580–81
Oil and gas lobby, 288, 299–300, 305
Old-age survivors' insurance (OASI), 489
Older people. *See* Elderly, the
Oligarchy, 12
Oliver, Andrew, 57
Olmstead v. *United States*, 513
Open primary, 251
Opinion, public. *See* Public opinion
Opinions, state court, 427
Oregon system of initiative and referendum, 322
Organization of Petroleum Exporting Countries (OPEC), 565
Organized labor. *See* Labor unions
Ortega, Daniel, 364, 555
Orwell, George, 10
Oswald, Lee Harvey, 46
Overshoot-and-collapse effect, 374–75
Oversight function of Congress, 336
Ownership, distribution of, 164–66
Ozone layer, 570

Packwood, Bob, 265, 358
PACs. *See* Political action committees

Paine, Thomas, 58, 59
Palestinian uprisings, 297
Panama Canal, 91–92
Parker v. *Gladden,* 118
Parliamentary democracy, 339, 360
Parties, political. *See* Political parties
Paterson, William, 64–65
Patronage, 412
Peaceful coexistence, 542–43
Peck, G., 529
Pentagon Papers, 122, 267, 438
People for the American Way, 285–86
People's Party, 232
Per capita income, 161
Pesticides, 576–77
Peters, Charles, 408
Petit juries, 427
Philippines, 22, 48, 541, 558
Phillips, Beth, 127–28
Phillips, Kevin, 243
Photovoltaic cells, 584
Physicians' Task Force on Hunger in America, 500
Physicians for Social Responsibility, 455
Picketing, 123
Pinchot, Gifford, 566
Pinkham, Jim, 529
Pinochet, Augusto, 22, 541
Plaintiff, 426
Planned Parenthood of Missouri v. *Danforth,* 130
Pledge of Allegiance, 126–27, 183, 185
Plessy v. *Ferguson,* 20, 134–35, 437
Pluralist view of U.S. politics, 454–55
Pocket veto, 348
Pointer v. *Texas,* 118
Poland, 315
Police. *See also* Law enforcement
  rights of the accused and, 128–30

Policy making, public opinion and, 215–16
Policy Staff, 381
Political action committees (PACs), 262–64
  corporate, 306–7
  oil-and-gas lobby, 288, 299–30
  pro-Israeli, 297
Political asylum, 515
Political campaigns, 240–81
  1988, 243–44, 249–50, 252, 274–76
  electoral college, 257–59
  financing, 257, 259–65
  general election, 256–57
  the media and, 254, 268–77
    advertising, 271–73
    consultants, 271, 272
    image-making, 271–73
    the issues and, 276–77
    Supreme Court and, 269
    televised debates, 268, 273–76
  national conventions, 237–40, 255–56
  nonpresidential, 250–51
  PACs and, 262–64
  preconvention activity, 252–55
  primaries, 253–54
  reforming, 256–57
  vice-presidents and, 256
Political consultants, 271, 272
Political culture. *See also* Liberalism
  cohesiveness in, 32–34
  definition of, 32
  democracy and, 32
Political economy, 155–75. *See also* Economics
  capitalism, 155–56
  mixed systems, 158–60
  socialism, 155, 157–58

U.S., 160–73
  budget deficit, 170
  corporate, 165
  defense spending,
    170–71
  distribution of in-
    come, 162–64
  distribution of wealth
    and ownership,
    164–66
  government and in-
    equality, 172–73
  government spend-
    ing, taxation and
    regulation, 169–72
  poverty, 166–68
  public policy, 168–73
  social welfare spend-
    ing, 171–72
  trade deficit, 161
  welfare state, 158
Political efficacy, 194–95
Political extremism
  freedom of speech and,
    119–23
  repression of, 148–50
Political knowledge,
    190–92
  the media and, 277–79
  presidential debates,
    276
Political machine, 233
Political parties, 222–47.
    See also Democratic
    Party; Political
    campaigns; Pri-
    mary elections;
    Republican Party
  since 1930s, 230–31
  Anti-Masonic, 232
  Bull Moose, 229, 232
  characteristics of,
    222–23
  children and, 184–85
  civil war and, 228
  congressional voting
    and, 352–54
  decline of, 241–43
  definition of, 222–23
  differences between,
    240–41
  education and,
    185
  Europe, 228, 229

Federalist, 222, 227,
    228, 412
  functions of, 223–24
  gender and, 204
  in Great Britain, 222,
    224–26, 234
  "Know-Nothings", 231,
    232
  New Deal coalition, 229
  one-party districts and,
    211
  organization of, 232–36
    local parties, 233
    national parties,
      235–36
    state parties, 233–35
  origins of, 227–28
  People's, 232
  Populist, 228, 232
  presidential nominating
    process and,
    236–40
  Progressive, 229, 232,
    324–25
  proportional repre-
    sentation and, 224
  race and, 206
  realignment and,
    204–5, 208, 210,
    243–44
  reform of, 236–46
    Democratic, 236–40
    effects of, 238–40
    Republican, 238
  religion and, 205
  responsibility and,
    244–46
  single-member district
    and, 224
  social class and, 205–6,
    228–29
  States Rights Demo-
    cratic, 232
  system of 1896 and,
    228–30
  third parties, 231–32
  two-party and multi-
    party systems,
    224–26
  voting and, 214
  Whig, 227–28, 272
Political power, economic
    power and, 10–11
Political socialization,

181–87. *See also*
    Public opinion
  childhood, 182–86
  college and, 186–89
  the family and, 184–85
  social class and, 183–84
Political speech, 119
Politico, 335
Politics. *See also specific
    topics*
  in colonial America,
    55–56
  energy and, 586–87
  incremental, 448–50
  the media and, 265–68
  religion and morality
    in, 49–50
Polk, James, 381
Polls, public opinion,
    188–90
  political campaigns
    and, 269, 271
Pollution. *See* Environ-
    ment
Polygamy, 126
Populism, 35
Populist Party, 228
Pork barrel projects, 361
Pornography, 516–18
Post-materialism, 202
Poverty, 166–68. *See also*
    Welfare
  blacks and, 143
  the elderly and, 167
  in Norway, 172
  racial issues and,
    167–68
Powell, Lewis F., Jr., 140,
    440
Powell v. *Alabama*, 118
Powerlessness, 195
Powers
  checks and balances
    and, 68–69, 337
  concurrent, 89
  of corporations, 165–66
  delegated, 88
  distribution of, 10–12
  division of, 88–89
  economic vs. political,
    10–11
  implied, 88
  inherent, 88
  prerogative, 372–73

reserved, 89
  separation of, 68,
    81–82, 359–60, 371
Prayer in schools, 125–26
Prerogative powers,
    372–73
President, the, 370–99.
    See also Executive
    branch; *specific
    topics*
  abuses of power by,
    386–91
    Gulf of Tonkin, 387,
      388
    Iran-contra affair,
      389–91
    Vietnam War, 387,
      388, 394–95
    Watergate, 388–89,
      394
  backlash and, 373–74
  cabinet and, 381–83
  children's view of,
    183–84
  Congress and, 359–64,
    383–86
    legislative veto, 361
    prerogative powers,
      372–75
    secrecy, 361–64
    War Powers Act,
      362–64, 386, 387
  election of, 396–98. *See
    also* Political cam-
    paigns
  executive agreements,
    373
  executive branch or-
    ganization and,
    377, 379–83
  Executive Office of the
    President, 377,
    379–81
  federal bureaucracy
    and, 377, 383
  foreign policy and,
    535–38
  frontlash and, 372, 373
  imperial, 388
  lawmaking process
    and, 348
  limits on power of,
    371–72
  lobbying and, 383–84

the media and, 265, 267, 268, 270
as necessity, 376–79
needs of, 377, 379
operational and policy-making components of, 377, 379
overshoot-and-collapse and, 374–75
paradoxes of, 375–76
power of, 68
prerogative powers and, 372–73
public opinion and, 201
separation of powers, 81–82, 359–60, 371
succession and, 392–93
transition of power, 391–93
uniqueness of, 370–71
veto power, 385, 386
pocket veto, 348
Presidential campaigns. *See* Political campaigns
President pro tempore of the Senate, 341
Press, the. *See* Media, the
Pride, national, 182
Primary elections, 251, 253–54
Privacy, right to, 130–31, 511, 153
FBI and domestic surveillance, 518–19
mandatory drug testing and, 519–21
Privatization, 415
Progressive Era, 461
Progressive Party, 232, 324–25
Progressives, 232
Prohibition, 449
Proportional representation, 224
Prosecutor, 426
Protest (protest movements), 187, 283–329. *See also* Dissent
activating others, 320
antinuclear, 321–22
civil disobedience, 315–19, 325–28

consciousness-raising and, 320
contexts for effective, 320
direct legislation, 322–25
freedom of speech and, 315
initiatives and referenda (I & R), 322–25
limitations of, 320–22
nonviolent, 316, 317
reasons for, 312–13
retaliatory measures, 322
sit-ins, 310, 311
Vietnam War and, 313–15
Protestant church, 49
Protestant Reformation, 34
Proxmire, William, 290
Public assistance programs, 489. *See also* Welfare
Public Citizen Litigation Group, 301
Public interest groups, 292–94
Public opinion, 187–204. *See also* Political socialization; Voting
democratic norms and, 192–94
diffuse support and, 181
education and, 204
efficacy and alienation and, 194–96
foreign policy and, 539–40
freedom of speech and, 192–94
gender and, 204
ideology and, 196
liberal vs. conservative, 196–202
economic issues, 198
foreign policy, 198–200
government spending, 199
overall picture, 200–2

social issues, 197–98
national pride and military service, 182
policy and, 215–16
political knowledge and, 190–92
polls, 188–90, 269, 271
post-materialism and, 202
president and, 201
racial issues and, 194, 216
social class and, 202–3
specific support and, 181
Public policy, 448–57
boundaries of, 456
competing agendas, 450–51
dealing with issues, 451–52
elitist and pluralist views and, 454–55
evaluation of, 454
formulation and implementation of, 452–54
incremental politics and, 448–50
political economy and, 168–73
spillover effects and, 448–49
symbolic actions vs., 451–52
Puerto Rico, 91
Pure Food and Drug Act (1906), 146

Quayle, J. Danforth, 244, 275

Racial issues, 19–21. *See also* Blacks; Civil rights; *specific topics*
Congress and, 138
Constitution and, 79–80
as emotional issues, 138
immigration law, 41–43
income and wealth and, 165
melting pot, 41, 42
poverty and, 167–68

public opinion and, 194, 216
reverse discrimination, 140–41
voting and, 206, 214
Radicalism (radicals), 40–41
repression of, 148–50
Randomness, opinion polls and, 188–89
Rather, Dan, 267
Rauen, Holley, 315
Rayburn, Sam, 340
Reagan, Nancy, 249, 267
Reagan, Ronald, 38, 47, 243–46, 249, 254–56, 269, 274, 289, 315, 320, 324, 347, 363–64, 379, 381, 383–86, 393, 413, 430, 452, 464, 466, 546–47, 550–52, 555–56, 559, 578–79, 582–83
affirmative action and, 143–44
assassination attempt against, 46, 295
budget deficits and, 170, 475–76
bureaucracy and, 412, 414
Chile and, 21–22
civil liberties and, 522, 524
college students and, 187
Congress and, 359
Deaver and, 283
defense spending and, 170–71
discrimination and, 373–74
drinking age and, 109
economics and, 471–74
education and, 185
elections and, 208–11
environment and, 296
federalism and, 92, 98–100
foreign policy and, 535–37
ideology and, 354
immigration law and, 43

industry and, 479–80
Iran-contra affair, 17, 80, 267, 335–36, 362, 363, 377, 378, 389–91, 556
low-intensity warfare and, 541
the media and, 265, 267, 268, 270
Nicaragua and, 216, 515
National Security Council and, 381
public opinion and, 203
religion and, 49–50
Roosevelt and, 378
Soviet Union and, 200
Supreme Court and, 39, 129, 337
taxation and, 475–76
trade deficit and, 161
Voting Rights Act and, 143
welfare and, 487, 488, 500
white males' vote and, 209
women and, 204
Reagan Doctrine, 541
Realigning election, 210
Realignment, 204–5, 208, 210
Reapportionment, 107
Recession, definition of, 461
Reconstruction, 374–75
Reed, Sally, 524
Reed, Thomas, 224, 340
Referendum process, 100, 322
Regan, Donald, 249, 267
Regents of the University of California v. *Bakke,* 139–43
Regional differences, congressional voting and, 353–54
Regional rivalries, 102–4. *See also* Civil War
Regulatory agencies, 406, 415–19
Rehabilitation Act (1973), 133, 522
Rehnquist, William, 262,

301, 430–31, 438, 439, 521
Religion (religious issues). *See also* First Amendment
Central America and, 49–50
in colonial America, 55
freedom of, 124–28
nationalism and, 185
politics and, 49–50
sanctuary movement, 50
taxation and, 126
voting and, 205
Renaissance, 34
Representation, definition of, 334–35
Repression, 148–51
Republican National Committee, 261
Republican Party, 228–32, 232. *See also specific individuals*
campaign spending and, 261–62
conservatives and, 230–31, 243, 244, 246
Democratic Party compared to, 240–41
nationalization of, 235–36
nominating process and, 253–54
realignment and, 243–44
reforms of, 238
Republicans, Jeffersonian, 121
Research, health, 497–98
Reserved powers, 89
Revenue sharing programs, 97–98
Reverse discrimination, 140–41
Revolutionary War, 54–61, 81, 311, 322
France and, 60
imperial authority and, 56–58
military aspects, 58–61
politics and, 55–56

postrevolutionary era, 61–76
socioeconomic environment and, 54–55
Reynolds v. *Sims,* 107
Reynolds v. *United States,* 126
Riders, 345, 347
Right, far, 41
Rights. *See also* Bill of Rights; Civil rights; Social rights
of the accused, 128–30
basic, 5
failure to exercise, 12–15
government intervention to protect, 107–11
government repression of, 148–51
legal representation, 128
natural, 35
of privacy, 130–31
to remain silent, 128
Rights of Man, The (Paine), 59
Right to privacy, 511, 513, 513, 513
FBI and domestic surveillance, 518–19
mandatory testing and, 519–21
Robertson, Pat, 240, 249, 252
Robinson, Halbert B., 501
Robinson v. *California,* 118
Rockefeller, Nelson, 393
Rockwell Corporation, 290
Roe v. *Wade,* 130–31, 295
Rogers, Will, 232
Roosevelt, Franklin, 12, 38, 40, 41, 46, 157, 205, 230, 243, 279, 373, 378–80, 385, 392, 393, 424, 494. *See also* New Deal
Roosevelt, Theodore, 46, 93–94, 229, 232, 272, 295, 395, 566
Roth v. *United States,* 517

Rousseau, Jean-Jacques, 8
Ruckelshaus, William, 579
Rudman, Warren, 356
Russell, Richard, 46

Safety Standard 208, 406–9
SALT (Strategic Arms Limitation Talks), 535, 536, 549–51
Sample of opinion, 188
Samuelson, Robert, 307
Sanctuary movement, 50
Sasso, Jim, 249
Scandinavia, 158, 202. *See also specific countries*
Schenck v. *United States,* 120
Schlesinger, Arthur, 388
Schmidt, William E., 157
Schools. *See also* Education
church-affiliated, 126
desegregation of, 134–39, 441
Brown v. *Board of Education* case, 80, 134–35, 141, 283, 424–25, 435–36
busing and, 137–39
in cities, 137, 138
de facto vs. de jure, 135–39
Johnson and, 135
Nixon and, 137
lunches, 504
political socialization and, 182, 183
prayer in, 125–26, 198, 435
Second Amendment, 116
Secrecy, Congress and, 361–64
Sedition Act (1798), 119, 121, 148
Sedition Act (1918), 120
Segregation, 19–21. *See also* Desegregation
Selective Service system, 405
Self-government, freedom of speech and, 119
Senate, U.S., 68. *See also* Congress

elections and, 350–53
filibuster, 348, 358, 359
House of Representatives compared to, 337–38
lawmaking process, 345–48
leadership in, 340–41
majority leader, 341
members of, 337–38
president pro tempore of, 341
select and special committees of, 343
standing committees of, 342
Supreme Court and, 336–37
Senior citizens. *See* Elderly, the
Senior Executive Service (SES), 413
Separation of powers, 359–60, 371
Constitution and, 81–82
Sessions, William, 519
Seventeenth Amendment, 337
Seventh Amendment, 116
Seven Years' War, 56
Sex discrimination. *See* Gender discrimination
Sexual equality, Constitution and, 80
Shabecoff, Philip, 416, 570
Shays's Rebellion, 63
Shelton v. *Tucker*, 122
Sherman Antitrust Act (1890), 11, 442–43, 461
Shreveport Rate Case, 95
Sidel, Ruth, 501
Sierra Club, 296, 567
Simon, Paul, 253
Sinclair, Upton, 145–46
Single-issue interest groups, 294–97, 306
Single-member district, 224
Sirhan, Sirhan, 46

Sit-ins, 187, 310, 311
Sixteenth Amendment, 466
Sixth Amendment, 116, 128–30
Sixties, the. *See also* Vietnam War
voting in, 207–8
Slaughterhouse Cases, 117
Slavery, 61, 117, 132–33, 275
Constitutional Convention and, 65
Jefferson and, 66
Smith Act, 121–22, 149
Social class, 162
education and, 204
political parties and, 228–29
political socialization and, 183–84
public opinion and, 202–3
voting and, 205–6, 214
Social insurance programs, 489
Socialism, 155, 157–58
TVA and, 157
Social issues
Democratic Party and, 230
liberal vs. conservative view of, 197–98
Socialist parties, European, 228
Socialist Party, 149, 232
Socialization. *See also* Political socialization
direct vs. indirect, 182–83
Social rights, 145–48, 511, 526, 528–30
pure food and drugs, 145–46
trade unions and collective bargaining, 147–48
Social Security, 167, 216, 485, 488, 489, 489–91, 504
tax and, 467–68
Social Security Act (1935), 486

Social welfare. *See also* Welfare
transfer payments and, 172
U.S. spending on, 171–72
Solar power, 584
Somoza, Anastasio, 48, 315
Sons of Liberty, 57
South, the
Democratic Party and, 230
school desegregation and, 135–37
South Africa, 132, 187, 554
South Korea, 479
Soviet-American relations, 540, 542–53
arms race, 548–53
arms control talks, 549–52
costs of, 552–53
INF Treaty, 200, 550–52
nuclear strategy, 548–49
SALT, 535, 536, 549–51
SDI and, 550–51
START treaty and, 551, 552
cold war, 540, 542
containment, 542
crises and détente, 545–46
Cuba and, 545
current issues in, 547–48
human rights and, 546, 558
peaceful coexistence, 542–43
Reagan and, 200
Soviet Union, 391, 541. *See also* Soviet-American relations
Afghanistan, 541, 546–47
Chernobyl nuclear accident, 582–83
invasion of Czechoslo-

vakia (1968), 115
public opinion and, 199, 200
Spain, 48, 182
Speaker of the House, 340
Speakes, Larry, 249, 268
Speaking Out (Speakes), 268
Specific support, 181
Speech, freedom of. *See* Freedom of speech
Speedy Trial Act (1975), 442
Spillover effects, 448–49
Spoils system, 412
Spot ads, political campaigns and, 272–73
Stagflation, 464
Stalin, 543
Stalin, Josef, 391, 542, 543
Stamp Act, (1765), 57–58
Stanley v. *Georgia*, 513
Stanton, Edwin, 375
stare decisis, 426
Stark, Fortney H., 299
Star Wars, 550–51
State and local government. *See also* Federalism
Bill of Rights and, 117–19
civil rights and, 102
court system, 426–27
criminal justice and, 101, 102
education and, 100, 101
environmental issues and, 101–2
federal-state relations and, 95
Frost Belt states, 103
health and welfare and, 101
initiative process and, 100
interstate obligations and, 90
referendum process and, 100
regional rivalries and, 102–4
Sun Belt states, 103

taxation and, 102, 103
transportation and, 101
State Department, 536
Statehood, 90
alternatives to, 90–92
State parties, 233–35
States Rights Democratic
(party), 232
Statlee, Stuart M., 294
Steiner, Jurg, 372
Stevenson, Adlai, 272
Stockman, David, 381
Stock market crash (1929),
461, 463
Stock market crash (1987),
161, 336, 464, 473
Stouffer, Samuel, 192
Strategic Arms Limitation
Talks (SALT), 535,
536, 549–51
Strategic Arms Reduction
Talks (START),
551, 552
Strategic Defense Initia-
tive (SDI, Star
Wars), 200, 455,
550–51
Student activism, 187
Succession Act (1886), 393
Sugar Trust Case, 95
Sun Belt states, 103
Superfund, 575
Supplemental Security
Income (SSI), 493,
504
Supply-side economics,
471–74
Supreme Court, 68, 359,
424–25, 427–30. *See
also specific cases*
abortion and, 130–31,
435
affirmative action and,
140–42
appointments to, 301
Bill of Rights and,
117–18
campaign spending
and, 260–62
civil rights and, 436–37
conservatism and, 437,
438–40
decision-making

process, 429–30
distribution of power
and, 436–37
due process and,
128–30
federalism and, 95–96
First Amendment and,
117
Fourteenth Amend-
ment and, 117–18
freedom of religion
and, 124–27
freedom of speech and,
119–23
gay rights and, 513–14
gender discrimination
and, 523–24
health and safety haz-
ards and, 529
individual rights and,
437
legislative reaction,
434–35
legislative veto and, 361
liberalism and, 437–38
media and campaigns
and, 269
Nixon and, 129
noncompliance and,
435–36
pornography and,
516–18
post-Warren era,
438–40
Reagan and, 39, 129,
337
reapportionment and,
107
rights of the accused
and, 128–30
school desegregation
and, 134–38
school prayer and,
125–26, 435
segregation and, 19–20
self-restraints, 432–33
Senate and, 336–37
Smith Act Cases, 122
teaching of evolution
and, 185
uniqueness of, 77
War Powers Act and,
364

Warren Court, 437–38
Surveillance, domestic,
518–19
Surveys, public opinion,
188–90
Swaggart, Jimmy, 249
Swann v. *Charlotte-Meck-
lenburg Board of Ed-
ucation*, 136–37
Sweatt v. *Painter*, 134
Sweden, 36, 158, 171–72,
432, 480, 501
*Sweden: Prototype of
Modern Society*
(Tomasson), 36
Switzerland, 225, 226,
323, 467
Symbolic speech, 122–23
System of 1896, 228–30

Taft, William Howard,
370
Taft-Hartley Act (1947),
148, 373
Taiwan, 479
Taney, Roger B., 436
Taxation, 169–72, 216
equity and expendi-
tures and, 474–75
fiscal policy and,
466–68
income tax, 172, 466–67
initiatives and, 322–24
religious institutions,
126
Social Security, 467–68
state and local govern-
ment and, 102, 103
supply-side economics
and, 472–74
Tax expenditure items,
489, 493–94
Tax Reform Act (1986),
467, 474
Taylor, Zachary, 227
Television. *See also* Media,
the
political campaigns
and, 269–76
advertising, 271–73
debates, 268, 273–76
Tellico Dam, 585
Temporary Emergency

Food Assistance
program, 500
Tennessee Valley Author-
ity (TVA), 157, 406,
585
Tenth Amendment, 96,
116
Tenure of Office Act, 375
Terkel, Studs, 463
Territories, U.S., 91–92
Testing, mandatory, 511
Thatcher, Margaret, 201,
226, 288, 339, 480,
495
Theology, liberation,
49–50
Third Amendment, 116
Third parties, 231–32
Third-party government,
414–15
Third world, 553–61. *See
also specific countries
and areas*
foreign aid and, 557–61
pesticides imported to,
577
Thirteenth Amendment,
79, 117, 133
Thoreau, Henry David,
316
Thornburgh v. *American
College of Obstetri-
cians and Gynecolo-
gists*, 130–31
Three Mile Island, 582–83
Thurmond, Strom, 230,
232, 235, 358
Thurow, Lester, 419
Tinker v. *Des Moines Inde-
pendent Community
School District*, 123
Tocqueville, Alexis de,
285, 442, 565–66
Tomasson, Richard F., 36
Torresola, Griselio, 46
Toxic chemicals, 572,
574–77
Trade, foreign, 479–80
Trade deficit, 161
Trade unions. *See* Labor
unions
Traditional liberalism,
38–39

Transfer payments, 172
Transportation, state and local government and, 101
Truman, Harry S, 46, 235, 373, 384, 385, 542, 543
Truman Doctrine, 201
Trustee theory of representation, 334–35
Turkey, 201
Twenty-fifth Amendment, 393
Twenty-second Amendment, 392
Twenty-sixth Amendment, 132
Tyler, John, 272, 393

Unemploment, blacks and, 143
Unemployment compensation, 101, 493
Unicameral legislature, 337
Unions. *See* Labor unions
Unitary system of government, 86
U.S. v. *DeWitt*, 95
United States v. *O'Brien*, 123
United States v. *Seeger*, 127

Van Buren, Martin, 227
Veterans Administration (VA), 502
Vice-presidency, 256, 392–94
Vietnam War, 17, 78, 198, 201, 237, 318–19, 362–64, 387, 388, 394–95, 456, 470, 541, 544–45
   burning of draft cards and, 122, 123
   freedom of speech and, 122, 123
   Pentagon Papers, 122, 267
   protest against, 25–26
   student activism and, 187
Vinson, Fred M., 122

Violence, 44–47. *See also* Crime
   in Europe, 45
   in Sweden, 36
Virginia Plan, 64, 65
VISTA, 486–88
Volcker, Paul, 470, 473
Volpe, John, 406–9
Voting, 204–14
   in 1950s, 206–7
   in 1960s, 207–8
   in 1970s, 208
   in 1980s, 208–10
   age and, 214
   blacks and, 115, 214
   congressional, 352–55
   direct legislation, 322–25
   education and, 214
   in Europe, 211–13
   federalism and, 211
   ideology and, 206–8
   initiatives and referenda (I & R), 322–25
   nonparticipation, 210–15
      barriers to voting, 211, 213
      factors influencing, 213–15
      number of votes cast per individual, 211
      one-party districts and, 211
      political parties and, 214
      racial issues and, 214
      registration and, 211, 229
      social bases of, 204–6, 214
      social class and, 214
      turnout, 14, 16
      women and, 23–25, 115, 209, 214
Voting rights, 132–33, 144
   Constitution and, 71
Voting Rights Act (1965), 107–8, 132, 133, 394
   Reagan and, 143

Wagner Act (1935), 148
Wainwright v. *Greenfield*, 129
Walker, Laura, 501
Wallace, George, 45, 46, 231, 232
Wallace v. *Jaffree*, 125–26
Walz v. *Tax Commission of the City of New York*, 126
War. *See also specific wars*
   protest and, 316, 318–19
Warfare, low intensity, 541
War Powers Act (1973), 363, 386, 387
Warren, Earl, 46, 107, 128, 301, 430, 437–38
Warren Commission, 46
Washington, D.C. (District of Columbia), 90–91
Washington, George, 48, 59, 222, 227, 373, 381, 412, 534
Washington Post, The, 267
Washington v. *Texas*, 118
Watergate scandal, 78, 82, 183–84, 261, 267, 374, 388–89, 394
Water pollution, 566, 573–74
Watson v. *Jones*, 126
Watt, James, 296, 579
Waxman, Henry A., 572
Wealth, distribution of, 164–66
Weapons system. *See also* Nuclear weapons
   defense industry and, 290
Weaver, James, 355
Webster, Daniel, 92–93, 96, 393
Webster, William, 518
Welfare (welfare state), 41, 158, 173, 198, 485–509. *See also specific programs*
   Aid to Families with Dependent Chil-

dren (AFDC), 97, 98, 100, 485, 489, 491–92, 506
   Appalachian Regional Commission and, 487
   child care, 501
   child-centered, 507
   conservative criticism of, 487, 503–4
   cuts in, 504
   evaluation of, 487, 503–6
   food stamps, 101, 485, 489, 498–500, 506
   housing programs, 502–3
   income security programs, 489–94
      AFDC, 491–92
      job programs, 492–93
      social security, 489–91
      SSI, 493
      tax expenditures for, 493–94
      unemployment compensation, 493
   interest groups and, 506
   liberal criticism of, 487, 504–5
   Medicaid, 98, 100, 488, 489
   Medicare, 488, 489, 490, 494–96, 504
   nutrition programs, 498–500, 502, 506
   state and local government and, 100
Welsh v. *United States*, 127
West Germany, 158, 161, 182, 196, 200, 202, 224–26, 242, 266, 296, 316, 372, 480, 576, 577, 582–83
   federalism in, 106
   Green Party, 224, 242
West Virginia State Board of Education v. *Barnette*, 126–27
Whig Party, 227–28, 232, 272

Whip, House of Repre-
sentatives, 340
White, Byron, 141, 262,
513
White, Valerie, 127
Wickard v. *Filburn*, 95
Wild and Scenic Rivers
Act (1968), 566
Wilderness Act (1964),
566
William-Olsson, I., 501
Willson, Brian, 315
Wilson, James Q., 81–82
Wilson, Woodrow, 24, 48,
94, 147, 229, 341,
370, 393, 535, 540

Wirth, Tim, 243
Wolfinger, R., 213*n*
Wolf v. *Colorado*, 118
Women, 144–45
affirmative action and,
140, 141
Civil Rights Act and,
145
Equal Pay Act and, 145
Equal Rights Amend-
ment and, 145, 197
in labor force, 476
public opinion and, 204
Reagan and, 204
single heads of house-
holds, 488

voting and, 23–25, 115
Women, Infants, and
Children (WIC),
500, 502, 504
Woodward, Bob, 388
Work force. *See also* Labor
unions
health and safety haz-
ards and, 526,
528–30
job programs, 492–93
transformation of,
476–77
World Bank, 557, 558
World War I, 534–35
World War II, 48, 373,

535
Japanese-Americans
and, 42, 44, 314
Japanese constitution
and, 75
Wright, Jim, 364
Wygant v. *Jackson Board of
Education*, 141

Yates v. *United States*, 122
Yuppies, 202, 204

Zangara, Giuseppe, 46
Zero-Sum Society
(Thurow), 419
Zinn, Howard, 79